# In the Beginning, There Was CHAOS

## Other *For Better or For Worse*® Collections

*Just a Simple Wedding*
*Home Sweat Home*
*Seniors' Discount*
*Teaching ... Is a Learning Experience!*
*She's Turning Into One of Them!*
*Never Wink at a Worried Woman*
*Striking a Chord*
*Reality Check*
*With This Ring*
*Family Business*
*Graduation: A Time for Change*
*The Big 5-0*
*Sunshine & Shadow*
*Middle Age Spread*
*Growing Like a Weed*
*Love Just Screws Everything Up*
*Starting from Scratch*
*"There Goes My Baby!"*
*Things Are Looking Up ...*
*What, Me Pregnant?*
*If This Is a Lecture, How Long Will It Be?*
*Pushing 40*
*It's All Downhill from Here*
*Keep the Home Fries Burning*
*The Last Straw*
*Just One More Hug*
*"It Must Be Nice to Be Little"*
*Is This "One of Those Days," Daddy?*
*I've Got the One–More–Washload Blues ...*

## Retrospectives

*Suddenly Silver: Celebrating 25 Years of For Better or For Worse*®
*All About April: Our Little Girl Grew Up!*
*The Lives Behind the Lines: 20 Years of For Better or For Worse*®
*Remembering Farley: A Tribute to the Life of Our Favourite Cartoon Dog*
*It's the Thought that Counts ... Fifteenth Anniversary Collection*
*A Look Inside ... For Better or For Worse*®*: The 10th Anniversary Collection*

## Treasury

*Something Old, Something New*

## With Andie Parton

*I Love My Grandpa!*
*So You're Going to Be a Grandma!*
*Graduation ... Just the Beginning!*
*Leaving Home*
*Wags and Kisses*

# In the Beginning, There Was CHAOS

*For Better or For Worse*® 2nd Treasury
by Lynn Johnston

Andrews McMeel
Publishing, LLC

Kansas City • Sydney • London

Andrews McMeel Publishing, LLC
an Andrews McMeel Universal company
1130 Walnut Street, Kansas City, Missouri 64106

www.andrewsmcmeel.com

11 12 13 14 15 RR3 10 9 8 7 6 5 4 3 2 1

ISBN: 978-1-4494-0954-8

Library of Congress Control Number: 2011923009

www.FBorFW.com

───── **ATTENTION: SCHOOLS AND BUSINESSES** ─────

Andrews McMeel books are available at quantity discounts with bulk purchase for educational, business, or sales promotional use. For information, please e-mail the Andrews McMeel Publishing Special Sales Department: specialsales@amuniversal.com

# Foreword

Reading through this material really does take me back in time. For the most part, the gags and the story lines in *For Better or For Worse* were fabricated, but the characters were definitely based on our family and the people I knew — sometimes, all too well. The small town of Lynn Lake, Manitoba, was a perfect place to do research. We all seemed to live in each other's back pockets, and if a story wasn't true, I knew it had happened to somebody, somewhere!

Syndication deadlines and other comic art-related stuff kept me busy from nine in the morning (when Aaron was in school and my friend Marian Barnstorf looked after Katie) until noon. Then I was a mom again. After dinner, I could get back to the studio — and, fortunately, I worked fast! Even so, there was a lot to do in a day and there were times when life was chaos!

We owned a small floatplane at the time, and my husband, Rod, would fly into one of the native villages each month to provide dental care to people who were unable to travel to clinics in the south. I knew the sound of our Cessna 185 so well, I could hear him flying overhead and would be able to drive to the airport before he landed.

We made our own fun in Lynn Lake. There were no "city" restaurants. We made dinners for friends, entertained with rented movies, and got involved with events in town. We put on skits, joined the curling club, organized festivals and carnivals, and watched our kids play hockey. In the winter, the sun came up around ten in the morning and set before four in the afternoon. In the summer, it was the reverse: The sun came up at four a.m. and went down again around midnight. Winter temperatures could go down below fifty degrees Celsius making even a short walk to town for milk or a change of scenery dangerous. Outside, we hid in our heavy parkas with hoods covering our faces. We walked with a purpose, and knew folks on the street by the shape, size, and colour of these arctic coats — which puffed white clouds of steam from frosty faces inside. Cars not plugged into block heaters wouldn't start, and at times it was too cold to fly.

Summers came fast. The ice would begin to "candle" around mid-May. June would bring clouds of mosquitoes and black flies, then dry, hot, sunny days would follow until September, when the leaves of the short, sparse deciduous trees would turn yellow and fall. Summers were wonderful. We spent our time at a small cottage on Berge Lake, which was about four miles from home. Here the kids learned to swim, paddle a canoe, and enjoy the clean, untouched wilderness of northern Manitoba. Because the sun went down so late, we put quilts on the windows, but still you could see daylight and hear the sounds of kids playing and neighbours fixing their cars, building things, or socializing outdoors. It was a lifestyle so new to me that I went from loving it to hating it and then loving it again. For our two young children, it was healthy, exciting, and fun. Where else could you travel regularly by floatplane, watch dog teams run, and play baseball at midnight?

I want to tell you about Lynn Lake because it was a world away from the imaginary town the Pattersons lived in. *For Better or For Worse* was about a family living in "Millborough"— a fictional suburb of Toronto. People would ask how autobiographical the comic strip was, and I had to say, "not at all." On the other hand, it was about us, our friends, our families, our memories, and so on. It was life as I saw it, drawn and written from a perspective that was, perhaps, made clearer from a distance. I could look at these characters from space — my space — not clouded by the realities of city living.

In a way, I was lucky to have been sequestered. The publicity that accompanied the strip took me away from my family all too often, and it would have been far too easy to believe the hype. I had a hard enough time separating fantasy from reality as it was! Those first few years were chaos. But they were rich with experiences, accomplishments, adventures, and friends. Some of this you will read here, between the lines. Some is from somewhere I can't explain. All of it is from the heart.

Lynn Johnston

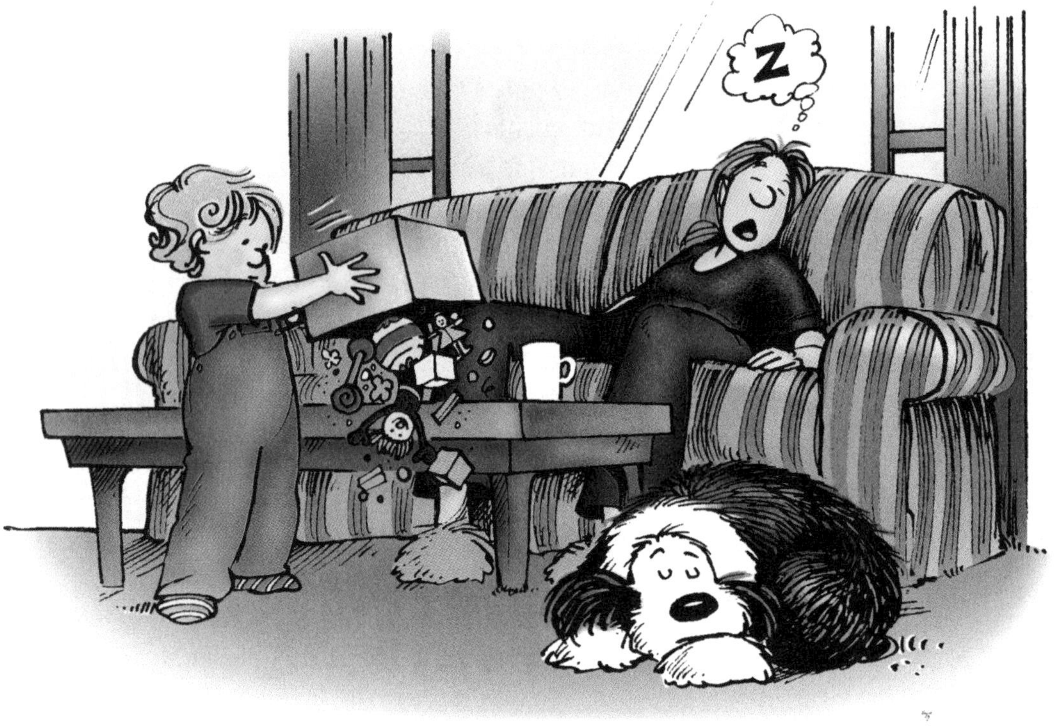
Z

The strips in this treasury include almost everything published between the spring of 1981 and the fall of 1983. At the time, *For Better or For Worse* was running in more than 350 papers ... and I was running in all directions!

A few Sundays were moved forward to the first treasury, and a few new strips have been added here (these are marked with an asterisk).

We've sorted through countless boxes of photos, slides, and newspaper clippings to try and show you where the ideas came from, who inspired the characters, and how the process evolved. This job has been a gift in so many ways ... and the best part of this gift is passing it on.

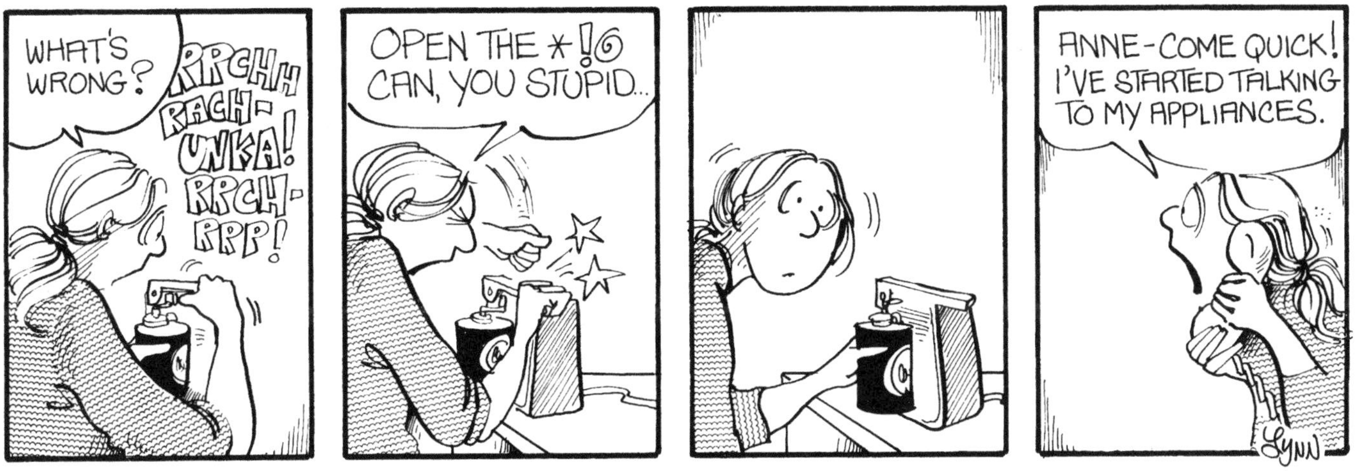
WHAT'S WRONG?
RRCHH RACH-UNKA! RRCH-RPP!
OPEN THE *!@ CAN, YOU STUPID...
ANNE-COME QUICK! I'VE STARTED TALKING TO MY APPLIANCES.
LYNN

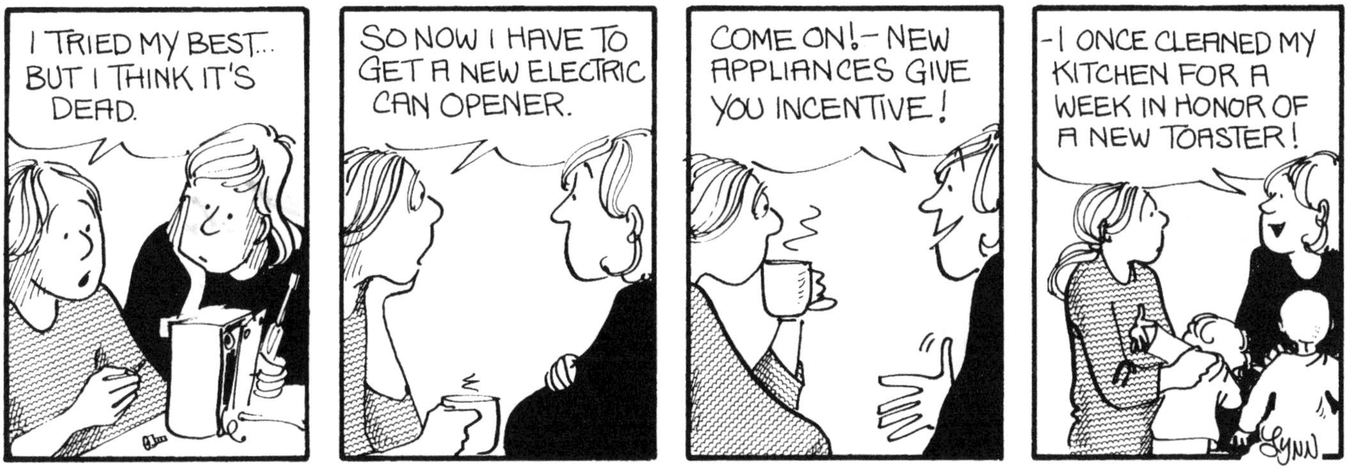
I TRIED MY BEST... BUT I THINK IT'S DEAD.
SO NOW I HAVE TO GET A NEW ELECTRIC CAN OPENER.
COME ON!-NEW APPLIANCES GIVE YOU INCENTIVE!
-I ONCE CLEANED MY KITCHEN FOR A WEEK IN HONOR OF A NEW TOASTER!
LYNN

Getting something new — ANYTHING, can enhance my tolerance for mundane chores. Get a new coat? Clean the closet. Get a new bath mat? Clean the can. I think of it as a reward in advance for doing something I really don't want to do.

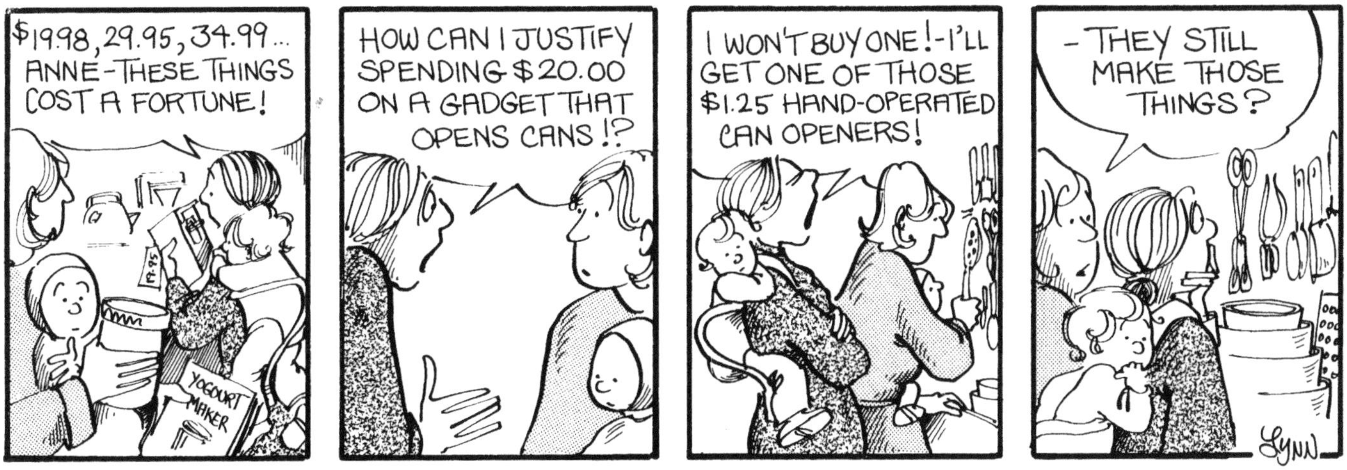
$19.98, 29.95, 34.99... ANNE-THESE THINGS COST A FORTUNE!
YOGOURT MAKER
HOW CAN I JUSTIFY SPENDING $20.00 ON A GADGET THAT OPENS CANS!?
I WON'T BUY ONE!-I'LL GET ONE OF THOSE $1.25 HAND-OPERATED CAN OPENERS!
-THEY STILL MAKE THOSE THINGS?
LYNN

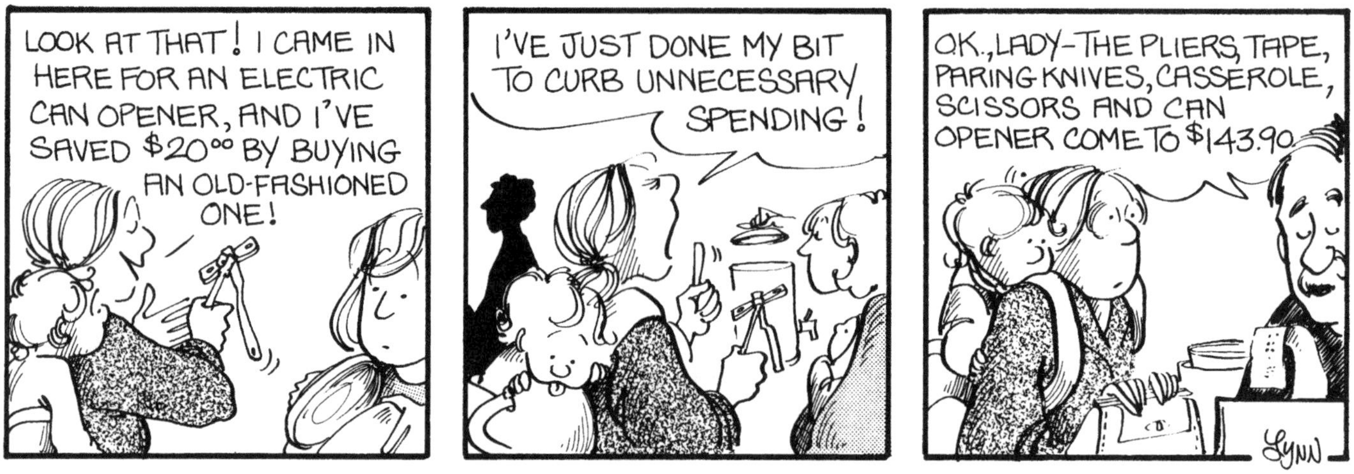
LOOK AT THAT! I CAME IN HERE FOR AN ELECTRIC CAN OPENER, AND I'VE SAVED $20⁰⁰ BY BUYING AN OLD-FASHIONED ONE!
I'VE JUST DONE MY BIT TO CURB UNNECESSARY SPENDING!
O.K., LADY–THE PLIERS, TAPE, PARING KNIVES, CASSEROLE, SCISSORS AND CAN OPENER COME TO $143.90
LYNN

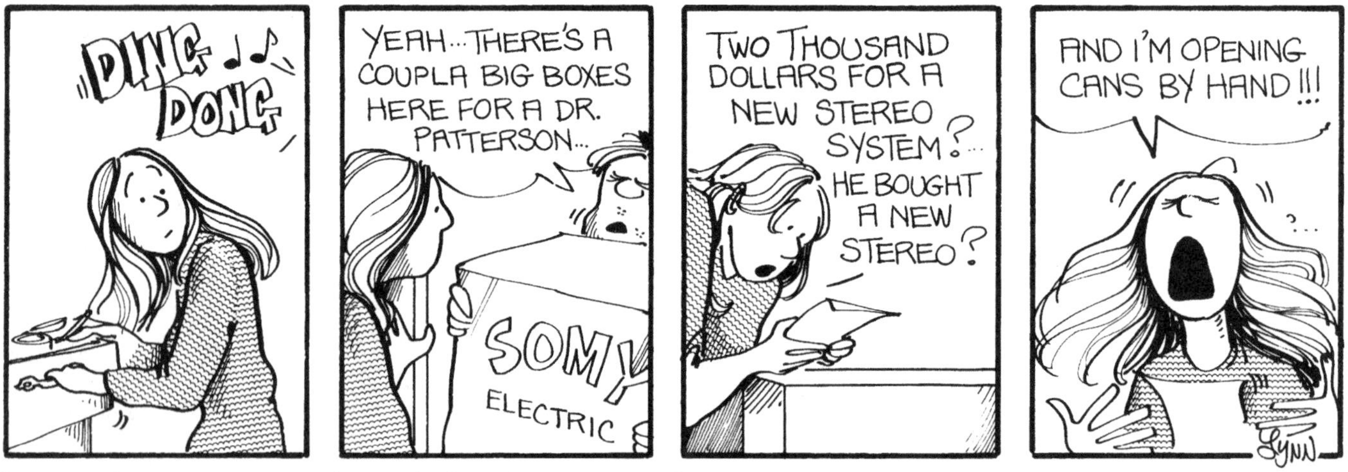
DING DONG
YEAH... THERE'S A COUPLA BIG BOXES HERE FOR A DR. PATTERSON...
SONY
ELECTRIC
TWO THOUSAND DOLLARS FOR A NEW STEREO SYSTEM?...
HE BOUGHT A NEW STEREO?
AND I'M OPENING CANS BY HAND!!!
?...
LYNN

I was earning my own money, but we budgeted just the same. I was used to living close to the wire, so when an expensive stereo arrived, I was miffed beyond measure. When this strip was published, I was accused of airing my grievances in public. I said that I wasn't … oh, but I was!

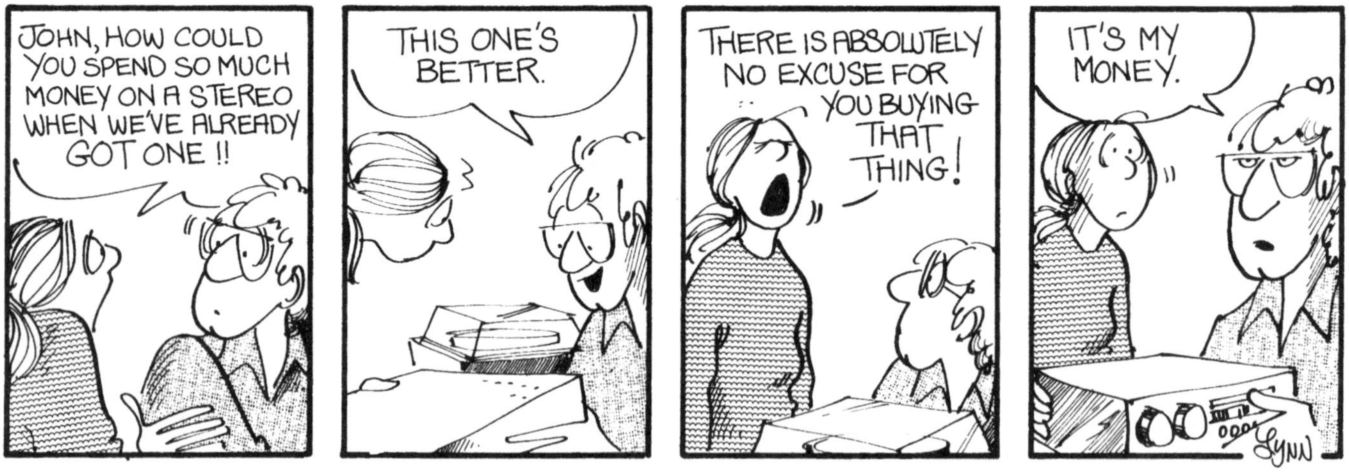
JOHN, HOW COULD YOU SPEND SO MUCH MONEY ON A STEREO WHEN WE'VE ALREADY GOT ONE !!
THIS ONE'S BETTER.
THERE IS ABSOLUTELY NO EXCUSE FOR YOU BUYING THAT THING!
IT'S MY MONEY.
LYNN

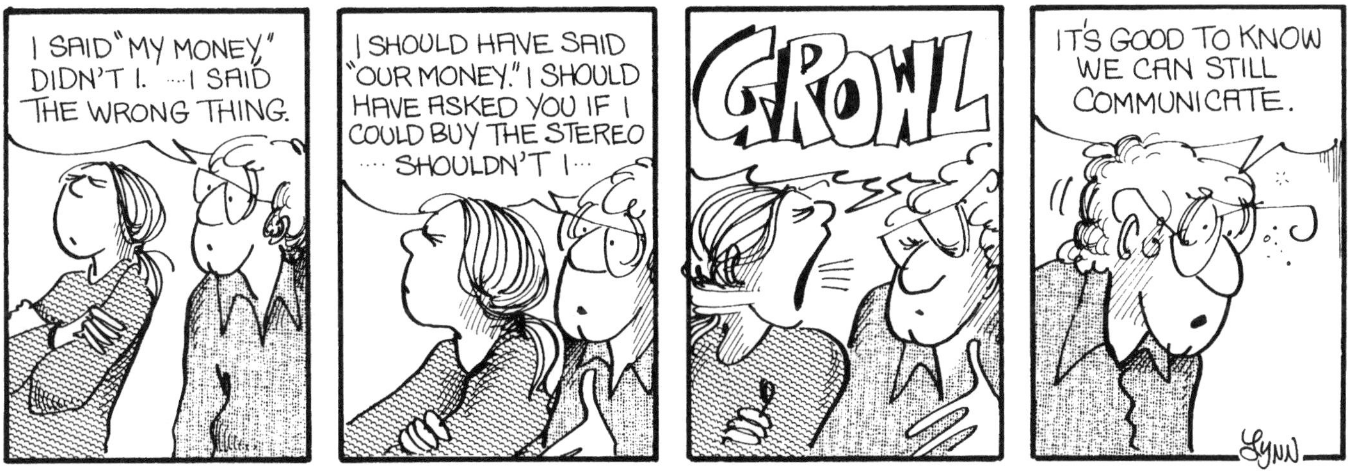
I SAID "MY MONEY," DIDN'T I. ....I SAID THE WRONG THING.
I SHOULD HAVE SAID "OUR MONEY." I SHOULD HAVE ASKED YOU IF I COULD BUY THE STEREO .... SHOULDN'T I...
GROWL
IT'S GOOD TO KNOW WE CAN STILL COMMUNICATE.
LYNN

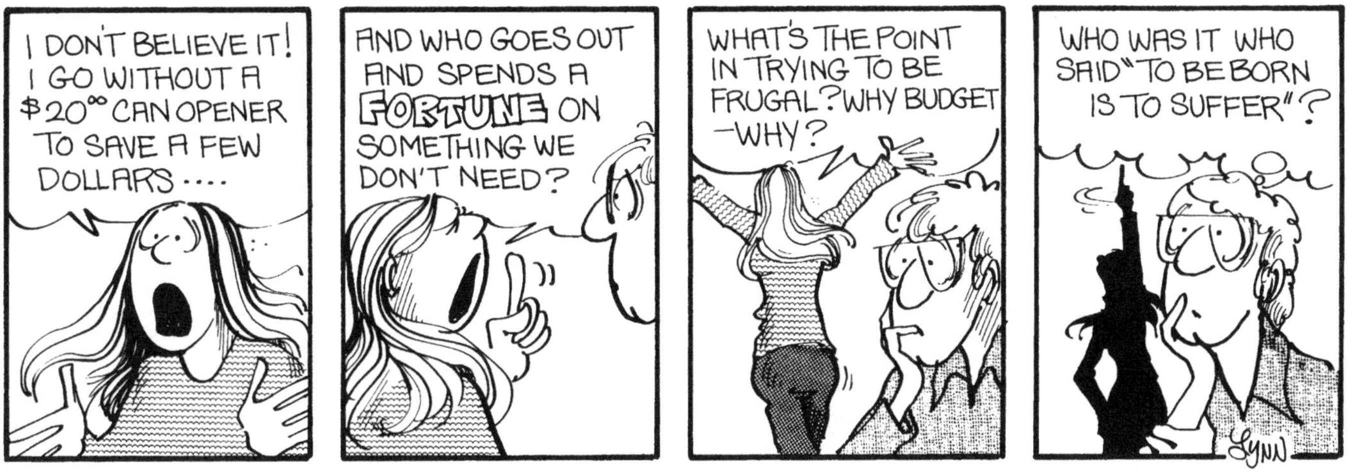
I DON'T BELIEVE IT! I GO WITHOUT A $20.00 CAN OPENER TO SAVE A FEW DOLLARS ....
AND WHO GOES OUT AND SPENDS A FORTUNE ON SOMETHING WE DON'T NEED?
WHAT'S THE POINT IN TRYING TO BE FRUGAL? WHY BUDGET —WHY?
WHO WAS IT WHO SAID "TO BE BORN IS TO SUFFER"?
LYNN

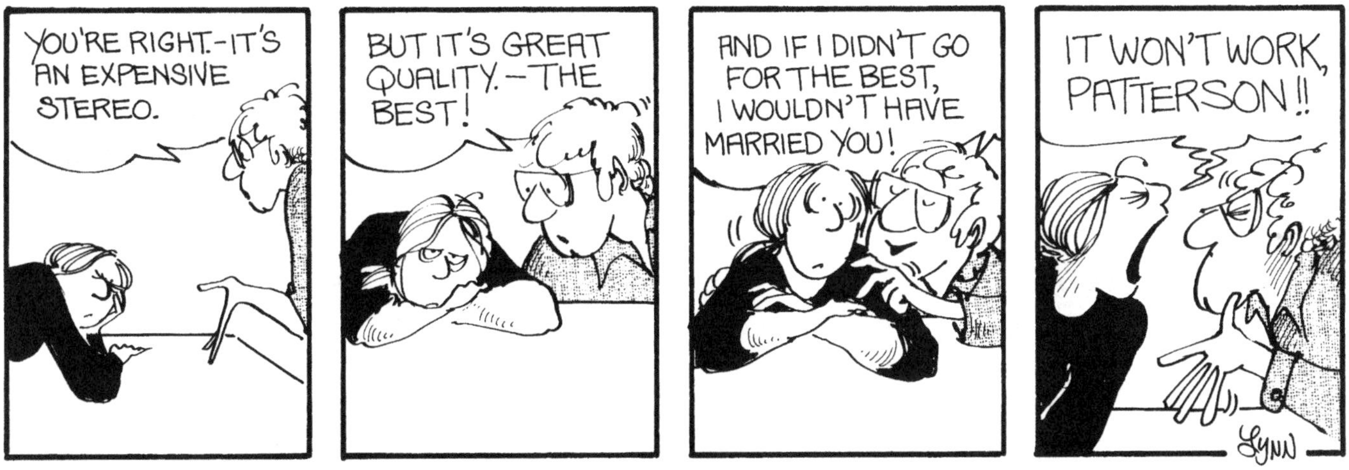
YOU'RE RIGHT.-IT'S AN EXPENSIVE STEREO.
BUT IT'S GREAT QUALITY.—THE BEST!
AND IF I DIDN'T GO FOR THE BEST, I WOULDN'T HAVE MARRIED YOU!
IT WON'T WORK, PATTERSON!!
LYNN

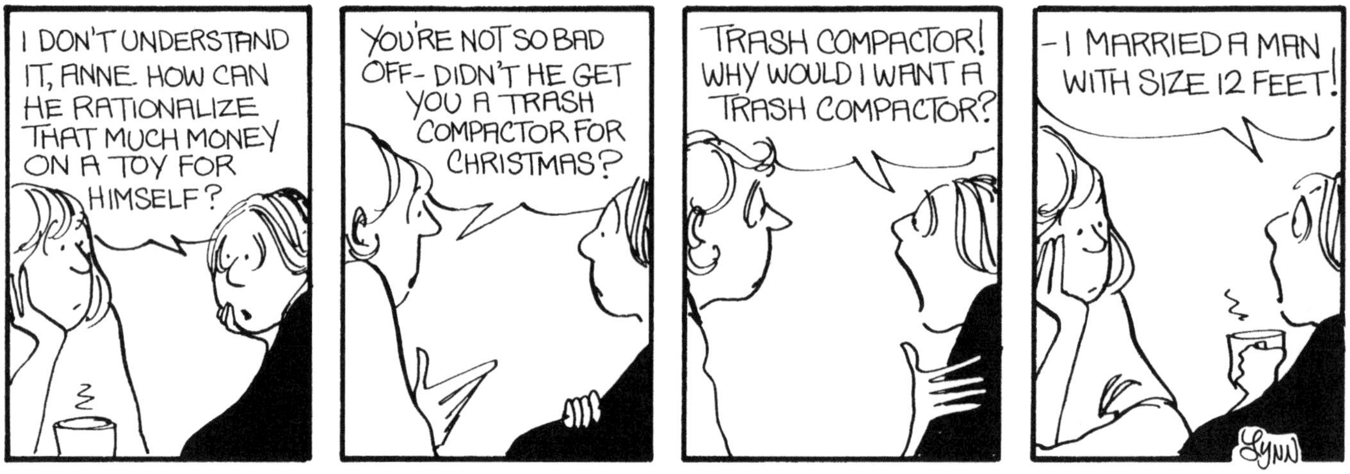
I DON'T UNDERSTAND IT, ANNE. HOW CAN HE RATIONALIZE THAT MUCH MONEY ON A TOY FOR HIMSELF?
YOU'RE NOT SO BAD OFF- DIDN'T HE GET YOU A TRASH COMPACTOR FOR CHRISTMAS?
TRASH COMPACTOR! WHY WOULD I WANT A TRASH COMPACTOR?
-I MARRIED A MAN WITH SIZE 12 FEET!
Lynn

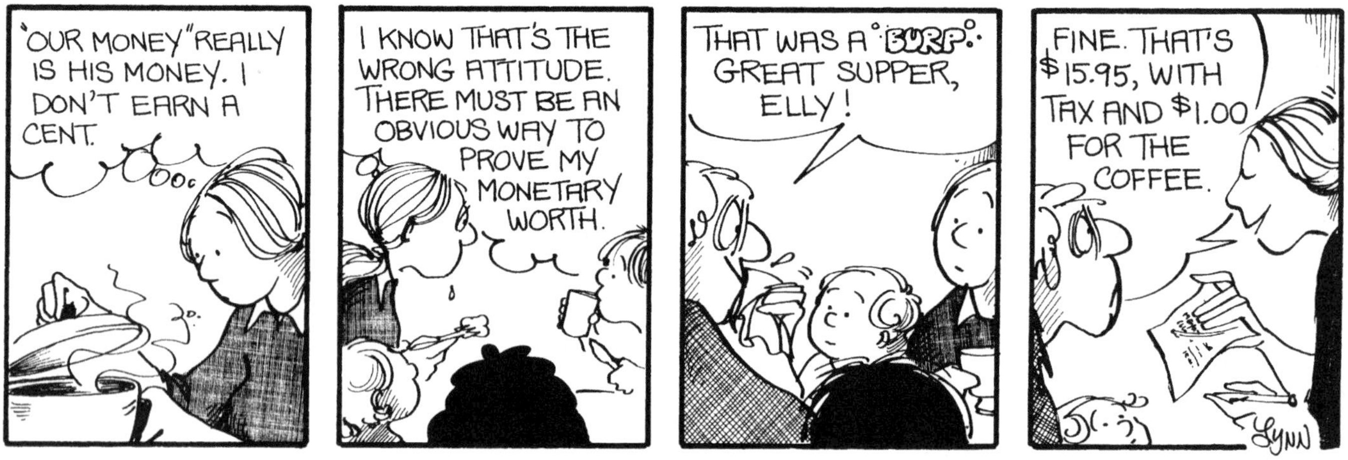
"OUR MONEY" REALLY IS HIS MONEY. I DON'T EARN A CENT.
I KNOW THAT'S THE WRONG ATTITUDE. THERE MUST BE AN OBVIOUS WAY TO PROVE MY MONETARY WORTH.
THAT WAS A BURP GREAT SUPPER, ELLY!
FINE. THAT'S $15.95, WITH TAX AND $1.00 FOR THE COFFEE.
Lynn

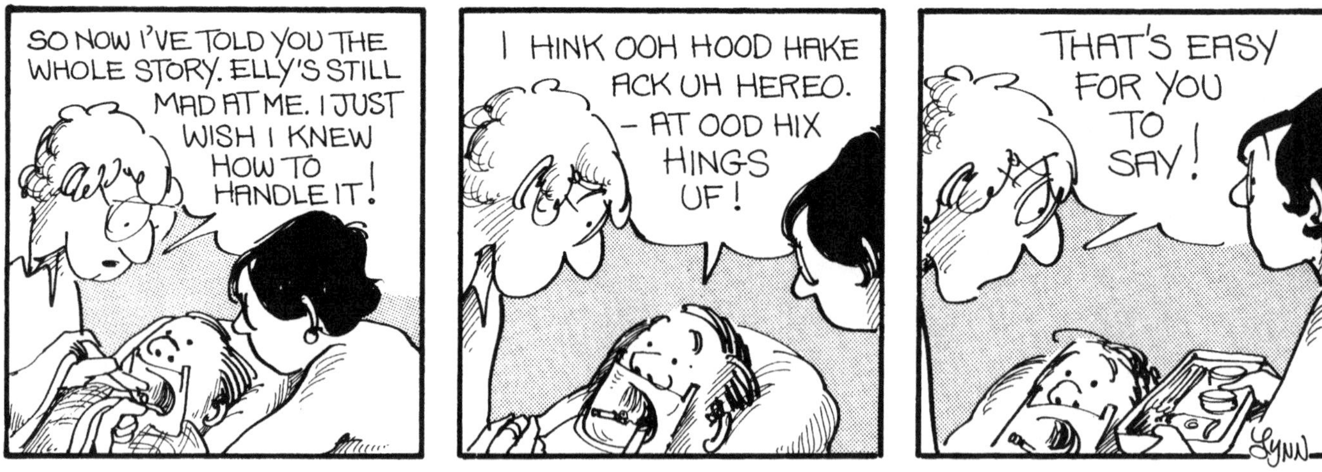
SO NOW I'VE TOLD YOU THE WHOLE STORY. ELLY'S STILL MAD AT ME. I JUST WISH I KNEW HOW TO HANDLE IT!
I HINK OOH HOOD HAKE ACK UH HEREO. - AT OOD HIX HINGS UF!
THAT'S EASY FOR YOU TO SAY!
Lynn

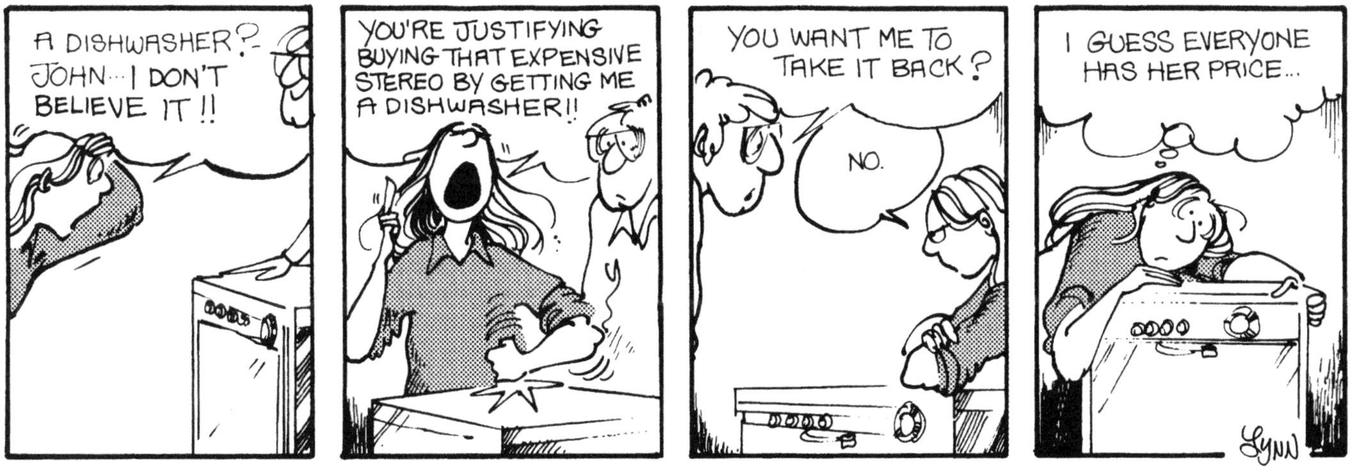
A DISHWASHER?- JOHN... I DON'T BELIEVE IT!!
YOU'RE JUSTIFYING BUYING THAT EXPENSIVE STEREO BY GETTING ME A DISHWASHER!!
YOU WANT ME TO TAKE IT BACK?
NO.
I GUESS EVERYONE HAS HER PRICE...
LYNN

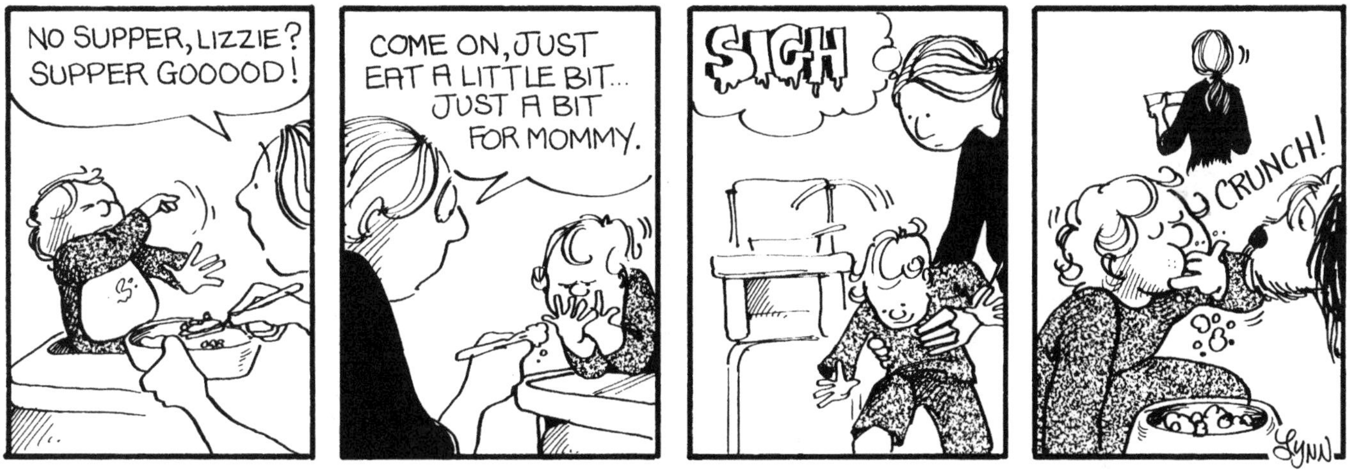
NO SUPPER, LIZZIE? SUPPER GOOOOD!
COME ON, JUST EAT A LITTLE BIT... JUST A BIT FOR MOMMY.
SIGH
CRUNCH!
LYNN

Katie would toss food onto the floor for the fun of watching both the "splatt" and my expression. Fortunately, she enjoyed her own leftovers, and if eating meant sitting under the table, so be it. I readily washed down a lunch space and let her dine. Isn't it amazing how relaxed we are with the "second kid"?!

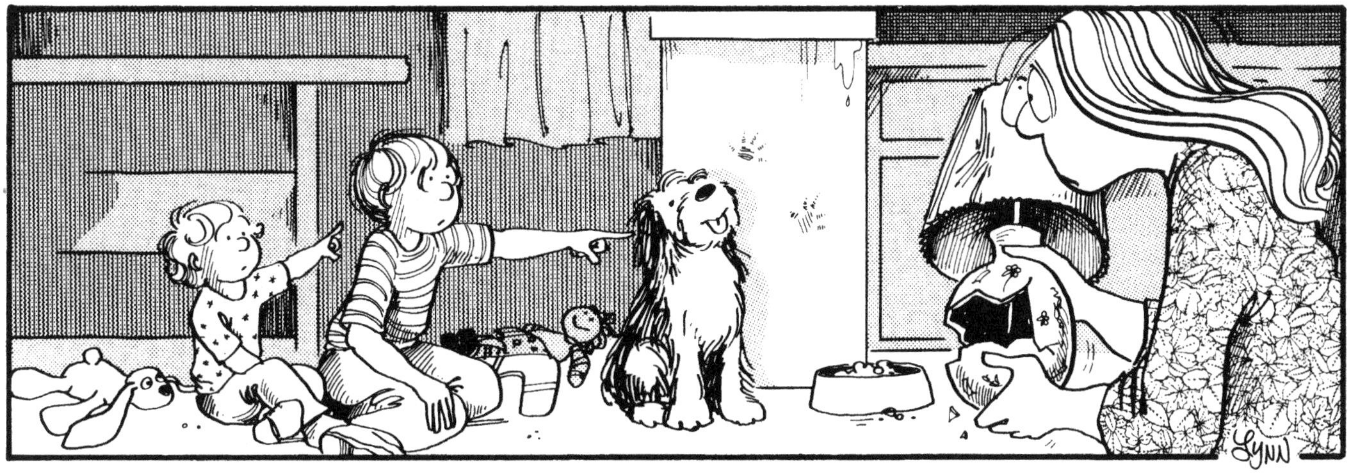
LYNN

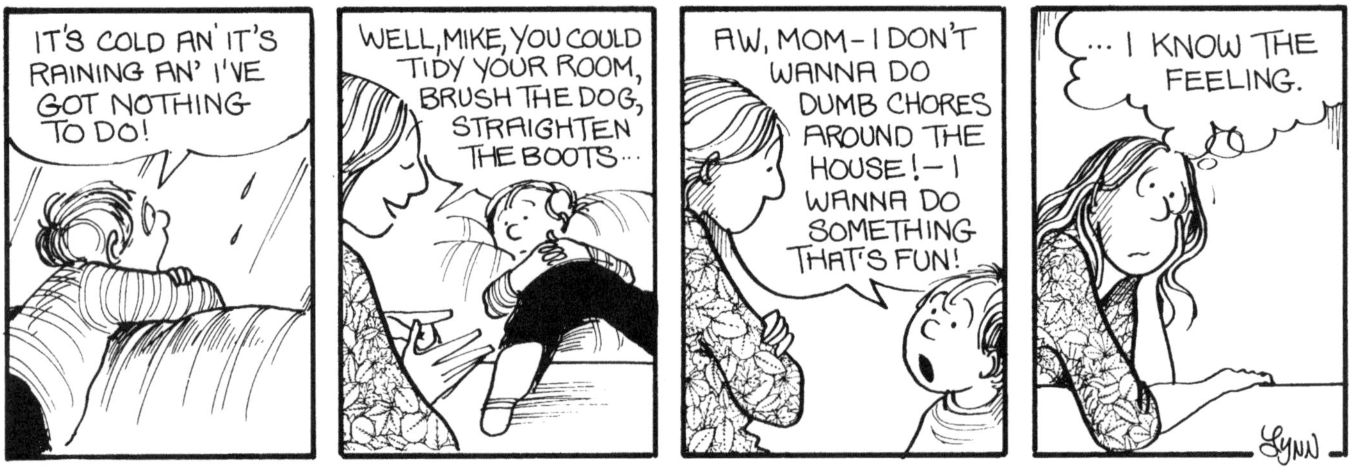
IT'S COLD AN' IT'S RAINING AN' I'VE GOT NOTHING TO DO!
WELL, MIKE, YOU COULD TIDY YOUR ROOM, BRUSH THE DOG, STRAIGHTEN THE BOOTS...
AW, MOM - I DON'T WANNA DO DUMB CHORES AROUND THE HOUSE! - I WANNA DO SOMETHING THAT'S FUN!
... I KNOW THE FEELING.
LYNN

I remember kneeling on the couch in the living room, looking through the window at the rain, and thinking, "There must be more to life than this." My mother would suggest any number of things to do, but the feelings of boredom and confinement weighed heavily. With no wheels, no money, and nowhere to go, I wished I was a grown-up. Meanwhile, my parents were saying, "But, Lindy! These are the best days of your life!"

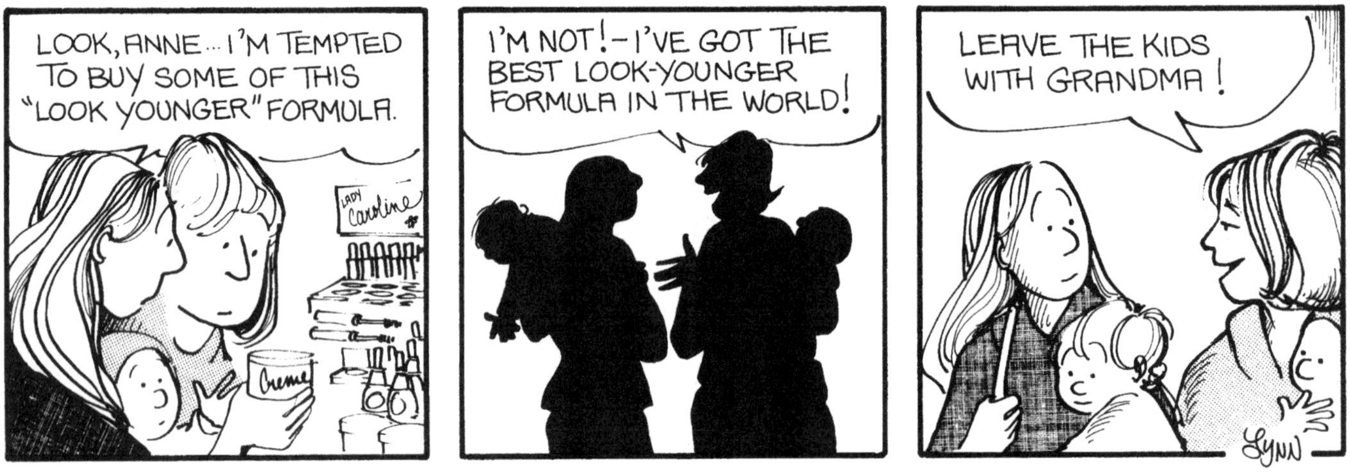
LOOK, ANNE... I'M TEMPTED TO BUY SOME OF THIS "LOOK YOUNGER" FORMULA.
LADY Caroline
Creme
I'M NOT! - I'VE GOT THE BEST LOOK-YOUNGER FORMULA IN THE WORLD!
LEAVE THE KIDS WITH GRANDMA!
LYNN

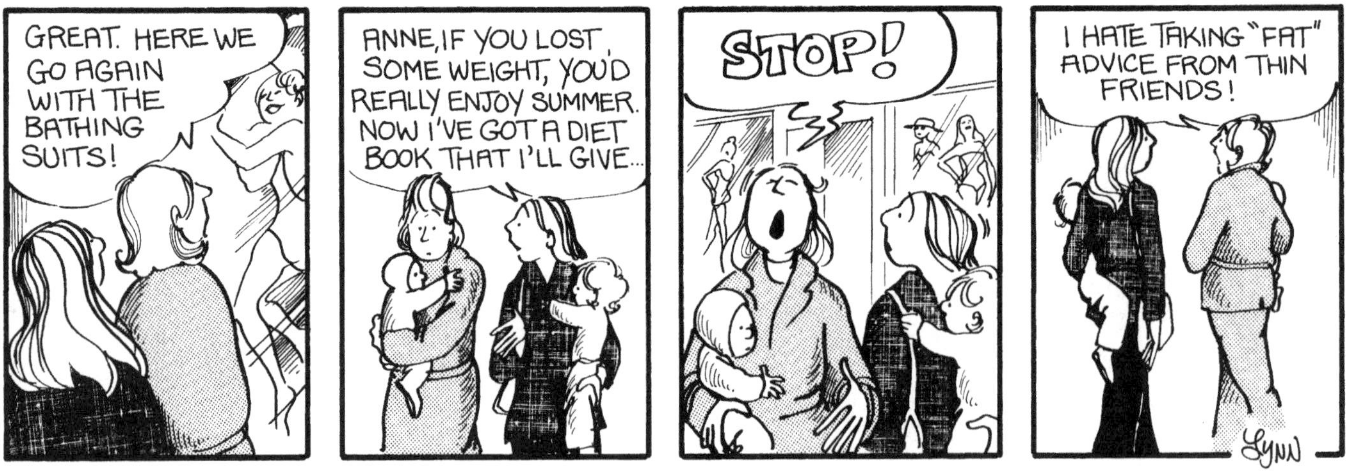
GREAT. HERE WE GO AGAIN WITH THE BATHING SUITS!
ANNE, IF YOU LOST SOME WEIGHT, YOU'D REALLY ENJOY SUMMER. NOW I'VE GOT A DIET BOOK THAT I'LL GIVE...
STOP!
I HATE TAKING "FAT" ADVICE FROM THIN FRIENDS!
LYNN

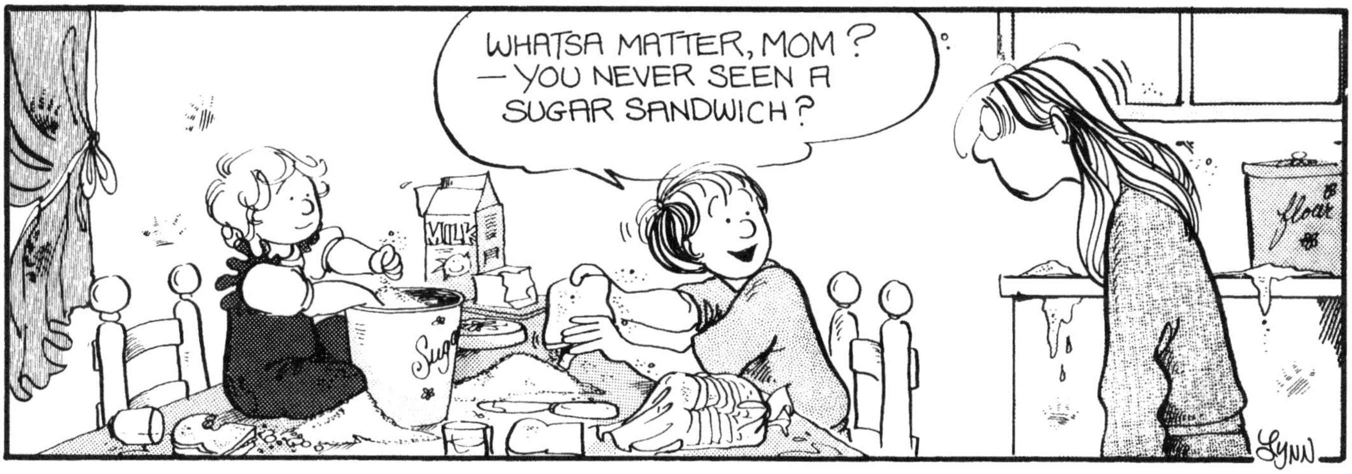
WHATSA MATTER, MOM? — YOU NEVER SEEN A SUGAR SANDWICH?
MILK
Sugar
flour
LYNN

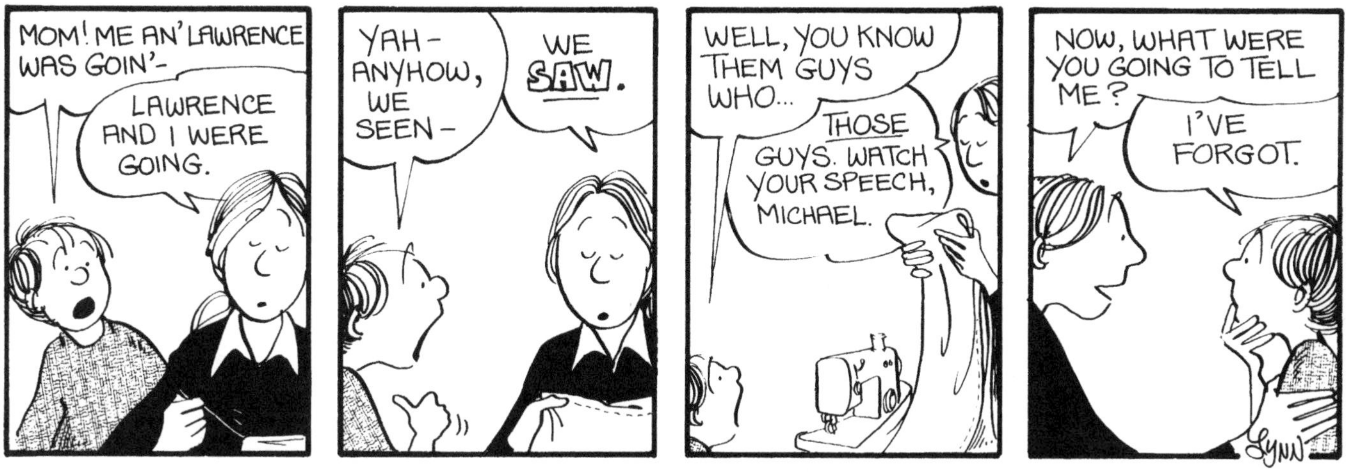
MOM! ME AN' LAWRENCE WAS GOIN'-
LAWRENCE AND I WERE GOING.
YAH - ANYHOW, WE SEEN -
WE SAW.
WELL, YOU KNOW THEM GUYS WHO...
THOSE GUYS. WATCH YOUR SPEECH, MICHAEL.
NOW, WHAT WERE YOU GOING TO TELL ME?
I'VE FORGOT.
LYNN

My parents were determined to teach us the proper way to speak. My mother would say, "If we only have one language, we're going to learn it well." My brother and I were given a thesaurus as soon as we could read. We were encouraged to learn a new word every day, and to know how to use it in a sentence.

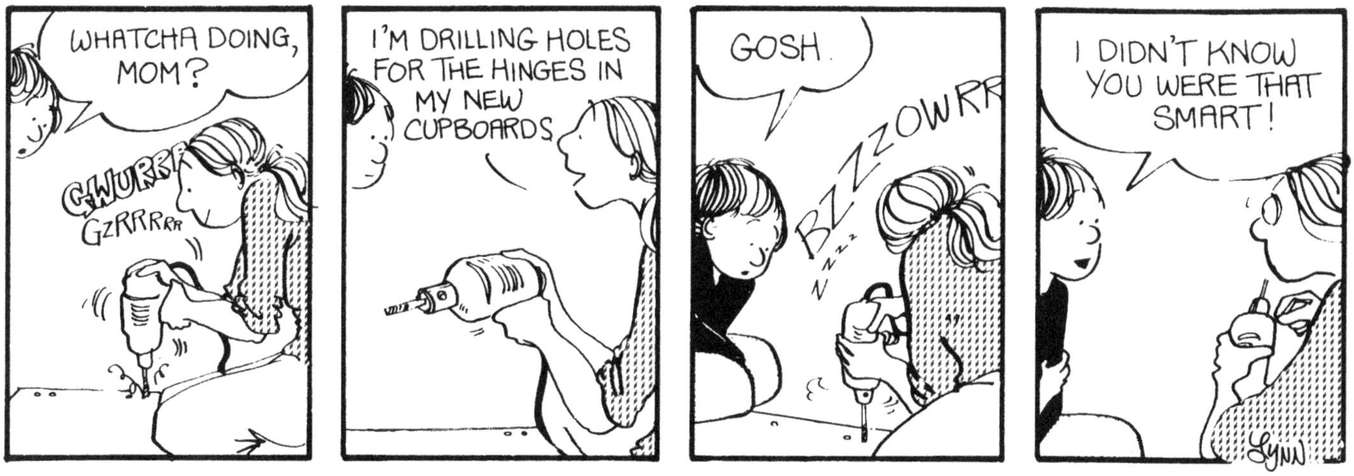
WHATCHA DOING, MOM?
GZRRRRR
I'M DRILLING HOLES FOR THE HINGES IN MY NEW CUPBOARDS
GOSH.
I DIDN'T KNOW YOU WERE THAT SMART!
LYNN

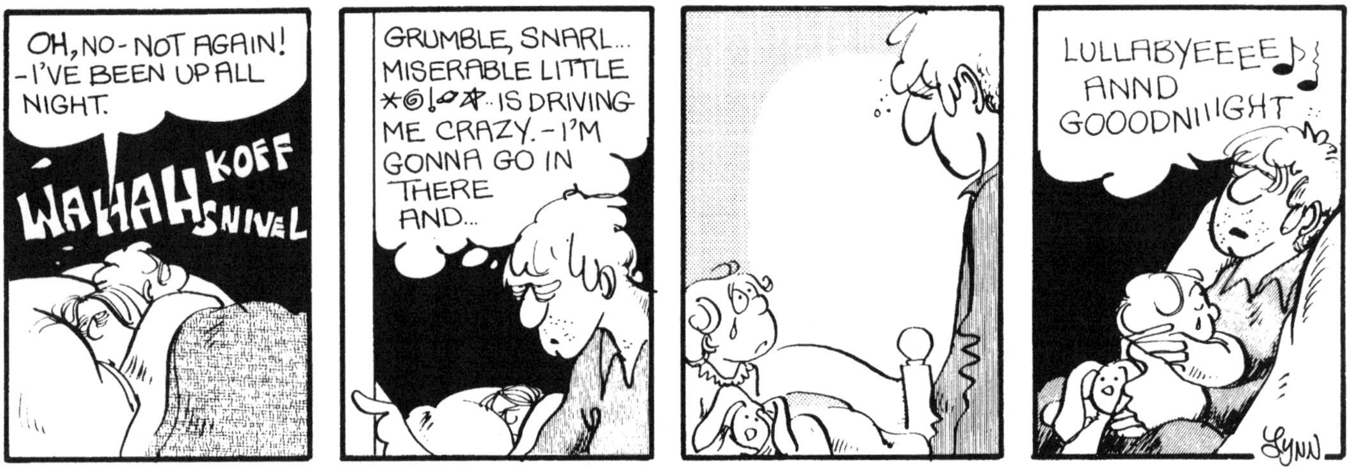
OH, NO - NOT AGAIN! - I'VE BEEN UP ALL NIGHT.
WAHAH KOFF SNIVEL
GRUMBLE, SNARL... MISERABLE LITTLE ... IS DRIVING ME CRAZY. - I'M GONNA GO IN THERE AND...
LULLABYEEEEE ANND GOOODNIIIGHT
LYNN

I didn't panic when the kids were sick, but I was on red alert the whole time. Every scenario, every dangerous possibility crossed my mind. Even with little or no chance of emergency, I was ready for anything. Never have I cared so much for someone else. When it came to the lives of my children, I discovered I was more than willing to sacrifice my own.

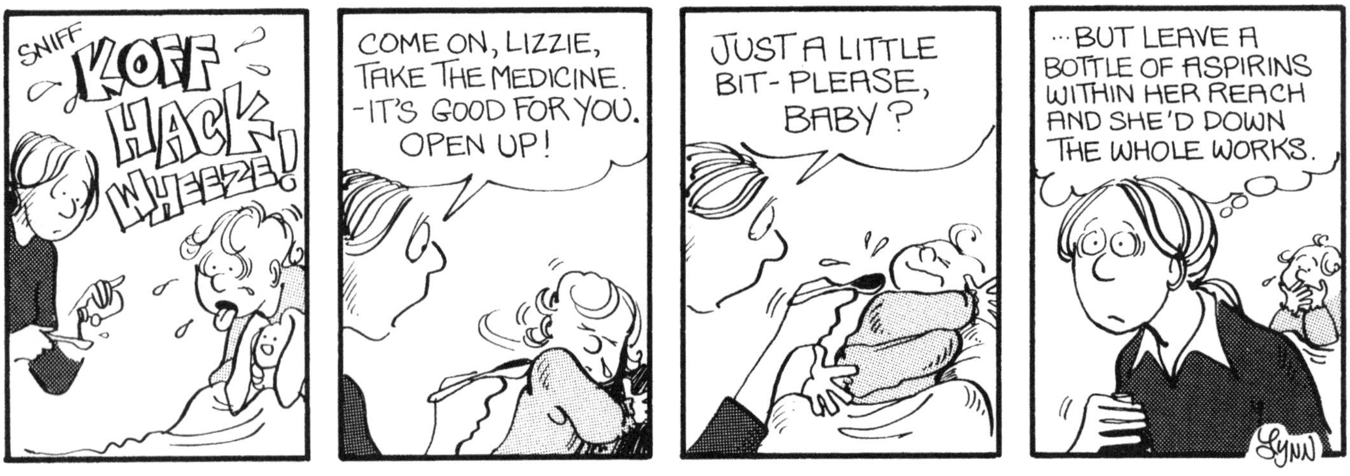
SNIFF
KOFF HACK, WHEEZE!
COME ON, LIZZIE, TAKE THE MEDICINE. - IT'S GOOD FOR YOU. OPEN UP!
JUST A LITTLE BIT - PLEASE, BABY?
... BUT LEAVE A BOTTLE OF ASPIRINS WITHIN HER REACH AND SHE'D DOWN THE WHOLE WORKS.
LYNN

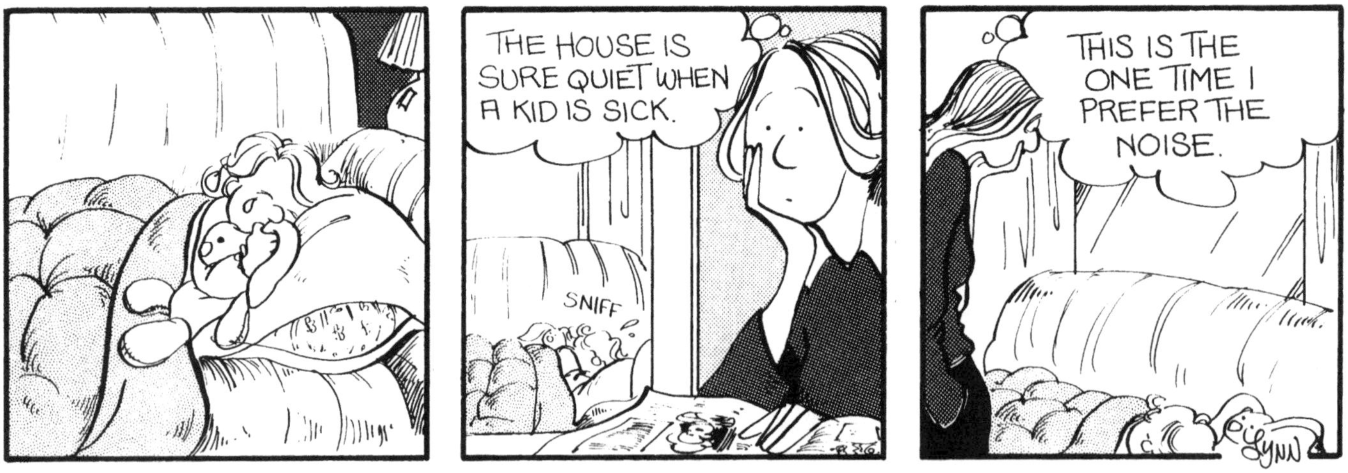
THE HOUSE IS SURE QUIET WHEN A KID IS SICK.
SNIFF
THIS IS THE ONE TIME I PREFER THE NOISE.
LYNN

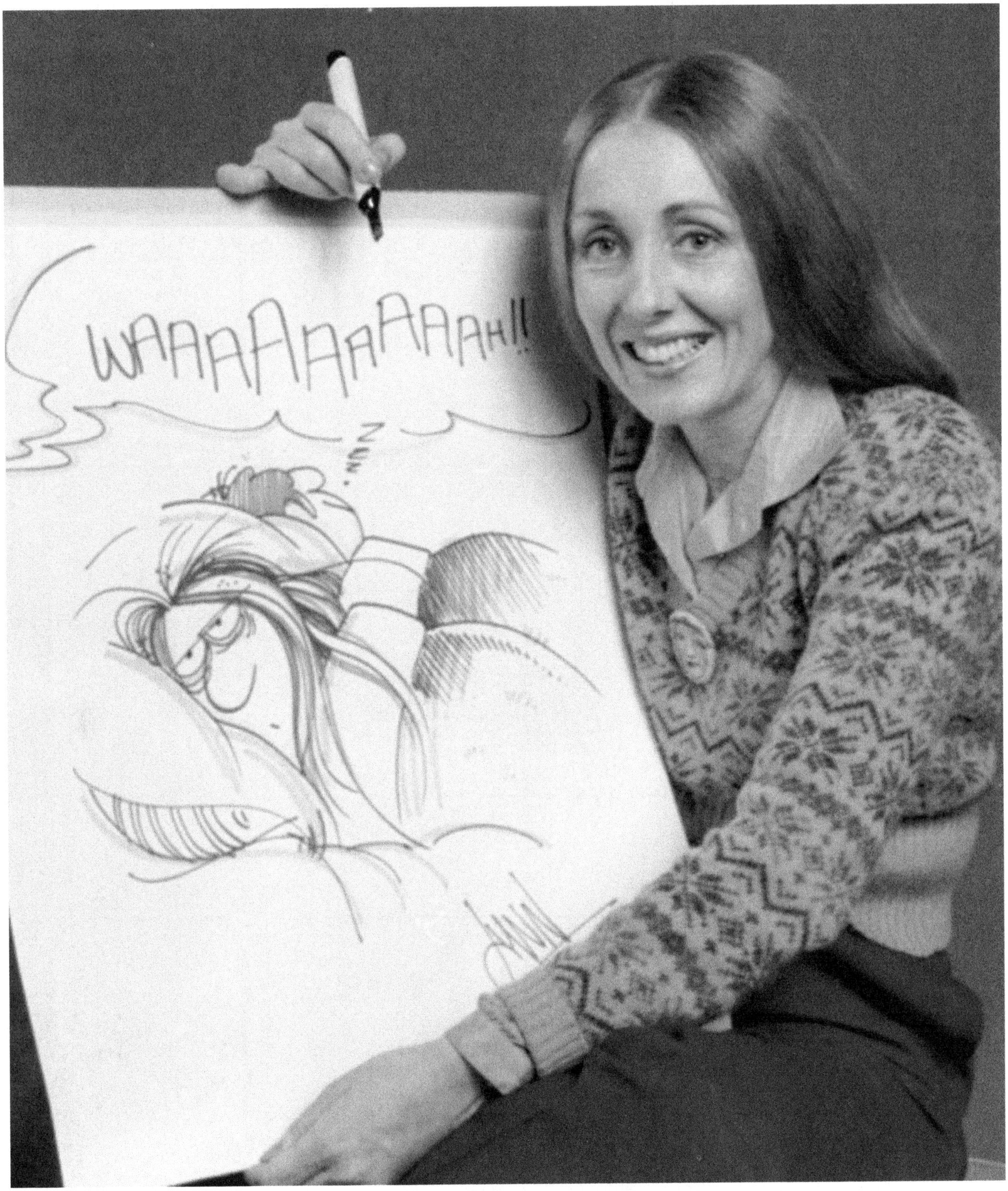
WAAAAAAAAAAH!!

This was a publicity photo taken by the *Hamilton Spectator* for a newspaper article in 1982.
It ties in well with this story line!

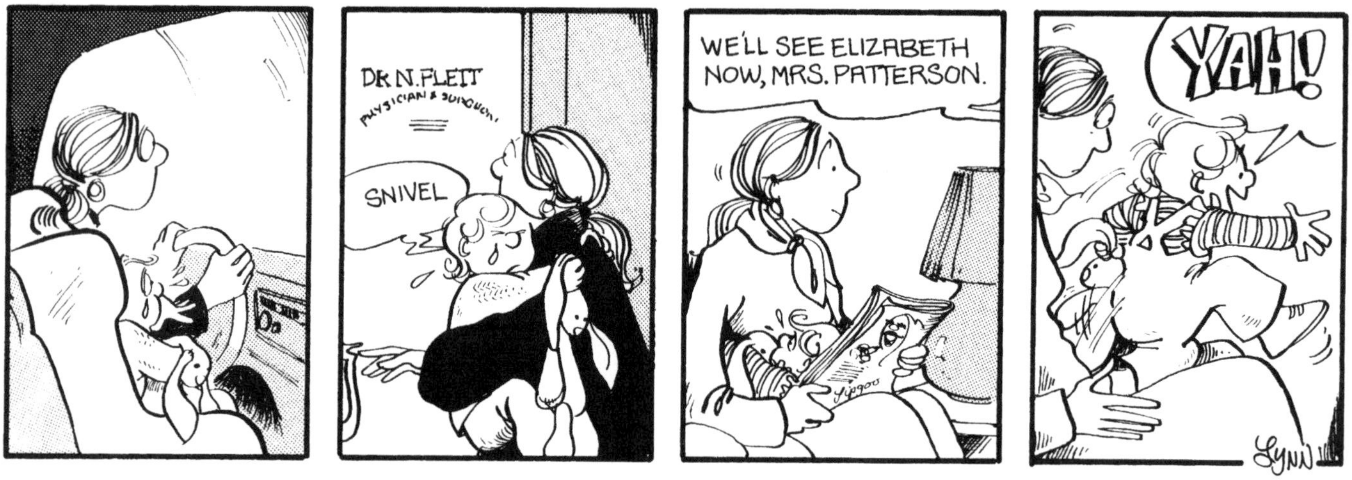
DR N.FLETT
SNIVEL
WE'LL SEE ELIZABETH NOW, MRS. PATTERSON.
YAH!
LYNN

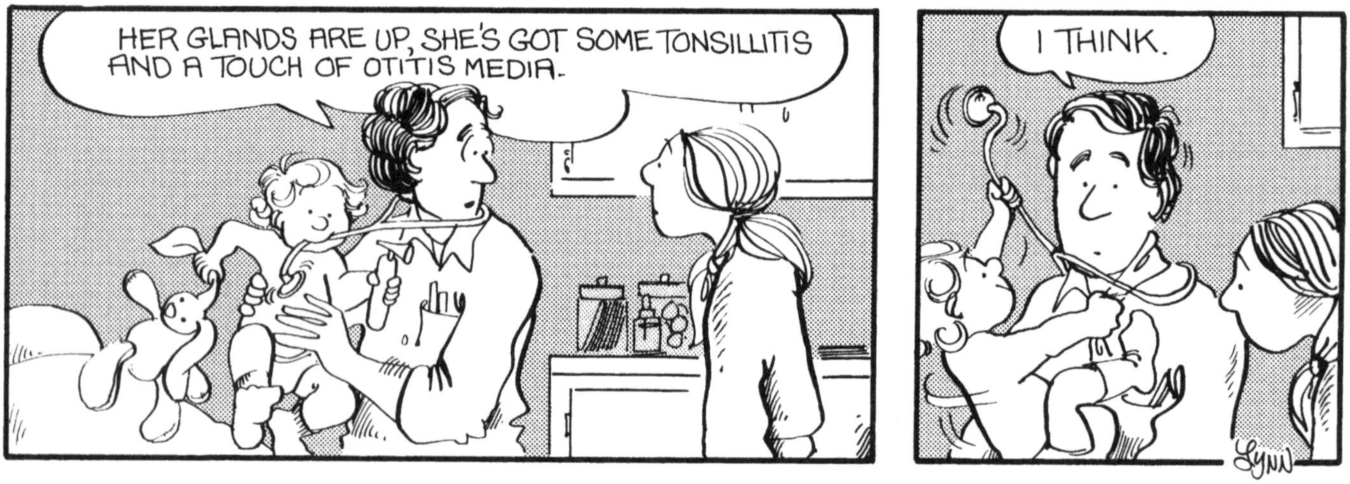
HER GLANDS ARE UP, SHE'S GOT SOME TONSILLITIS AND A TOUCH OF OTITIS MEDIA.
I THINK.
LYNN

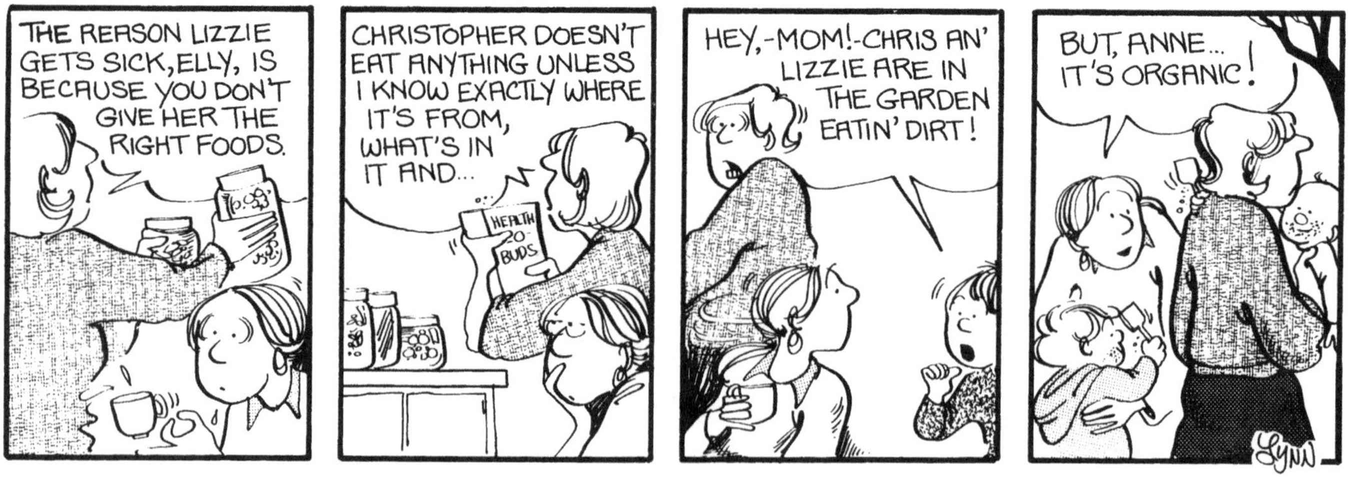
THE REASON LIZZIE GETS SICK, ELLY, IS BECAUSE YOU DON'T GIVE HER THE RIGHT FOODS.
CHRISTOPHER DOESN'T EAT ANYTHING UNLESS I KNOW EXACTLY WHERE IT'S FROM, WHAT'S IN IT AND...
HEALTH-O-BUDS
HEY,-MOM!-CHRIS AN' LIZZIE ARE IN THE GARDEN EATIN' DIRT!
BUT, ANNE... IT'S ORGANIC!
LYNN

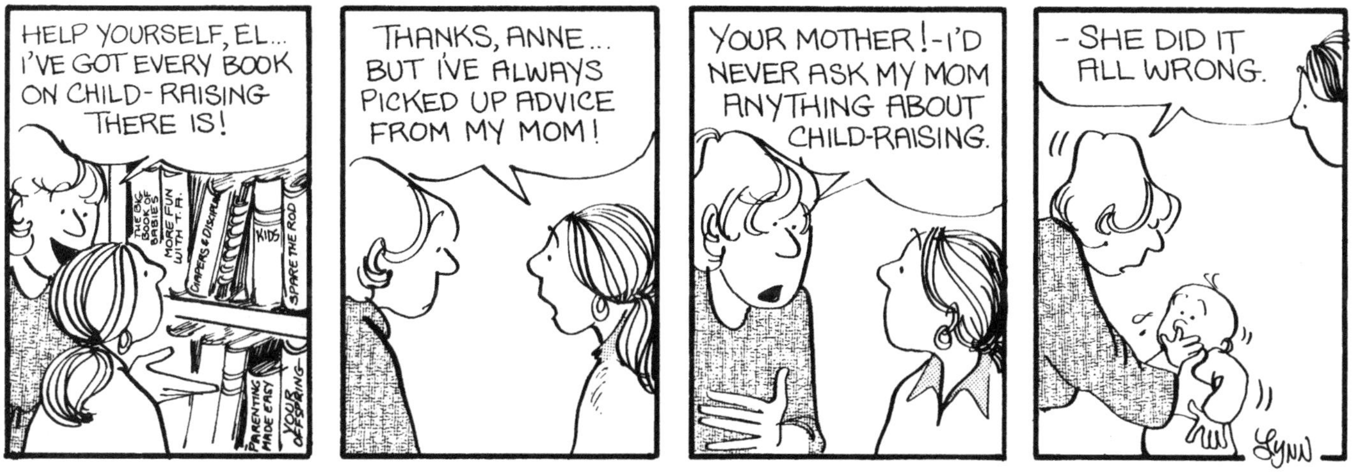
HELP YOURSELF, EL... I'VE GOT EVERY BOOK ON CHILD-RAISING THERE IS!
THE BIG BOOK OF BABIES
MORE FUN WITH T.A.
DIAPERS & DISCIPLINE
KIDS
SPARE THE ROD
PARENTING MADE EASY
YOUR OFFSPRING
THANKS, ANNE... BUT I'VE ALWAYS PICKED UP ADVICE FROM MY MOM!
YOUR MOTHER!-I'D NEVER ASK MY MOM ANYTHING ABOUT CHILD-RAISING.
- SHE DID IT ALL WRONG.
LYNN

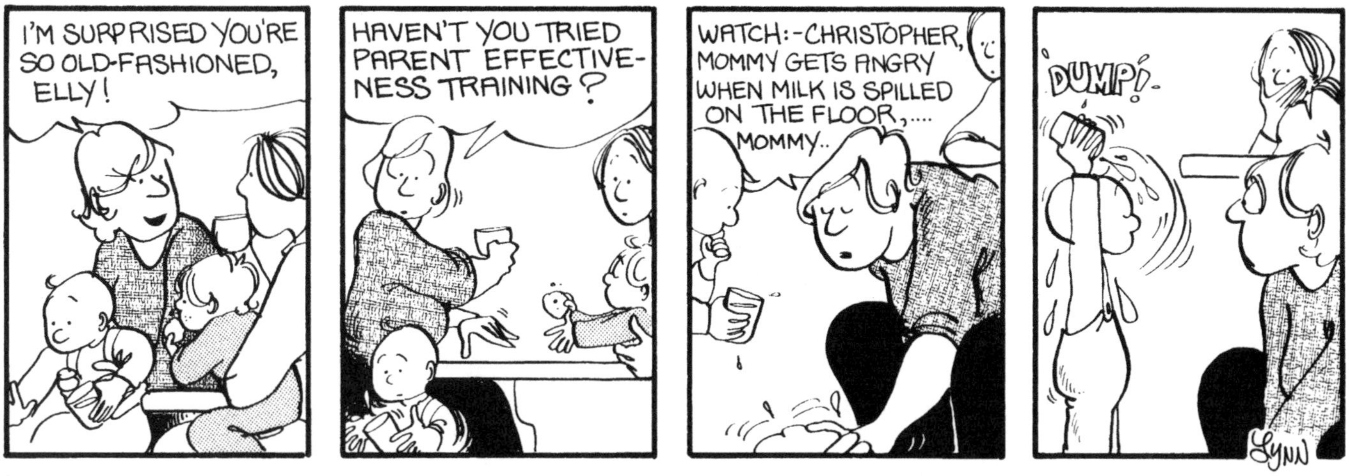
I'M SURPRISED YOU'RE SO OLD-FASHIONED, ELLY!
HAVEN'T YOU TRIED PARENT EFFECTIVE-NESS TRAINING?
WATCH:-CHRISTOPHER, MOMMY GETS ANGRY WHEN MILK IS SPILLED ON THE FLOOR,....
MOMMY..
DUMP!
LYNN

Parenting is such a complex career, and these panels reflected my insecurity. We all have our own spin on the subject, our own rules and strategies. We all ask each other for advice, but in the end our families are unique and whatever works is generally what happens! I used to have all kinds of advice for friends with children until ... I had kids of my own!

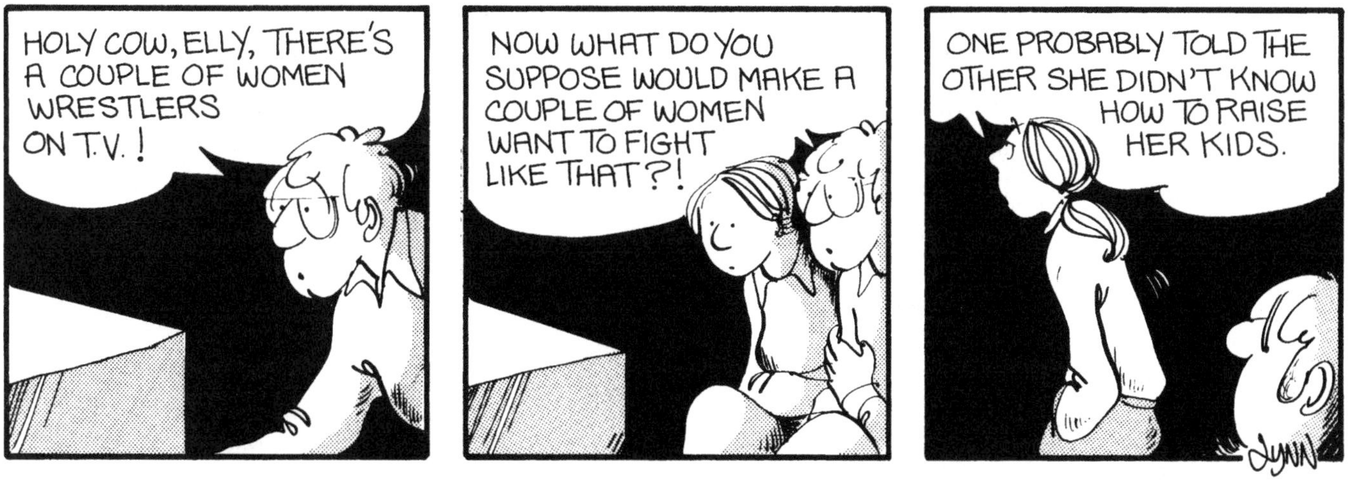
HOLY COW, ELLY, THERE'S A COUPLE OF WOMEN WRESTLERS ON T.V.!
NOW WHAT DO YOU SUPPOSE WOULD MAKE A COUPLE OF WOMEN WANT TO FIGHT LIKE THAT?!
ONE PROBABLY TOLD THE OTHER SHE DIDN'T KNOW HOW TO RAISE HER KIDS.
LYNN

SPECTRUM

# For better or for worse, Lynn loves her job

By EILEEN MORROW
Special to The Spectator

LYNN JOHNSTON could be the envy of the coffee klatsch

Sure, she cooks and cleans, mops and shops, just like the rest of us. She even has a career she pursues every morning from nine to noon.

But, unlike the rest of us, Lynn literally gets to tell the world about it.

In her successful daily comic, For Better or For Worse, she creates a cheerful but realistic rendering of the domestic frustrations, worries and guilts of the '80s housewife. As her alter ego, Elly, she can "talk non-stop to a million people".

Now, the best of her strips has been collected in her newest book, I've Got the One-More-Washload Blues.

Lynn was in Hamilton Saturday to promote the new book and to surprise a few friends she's not seen enough of since she left Dundas four years ago with her husband and two children, for the far reaches of Lynn Lake, Man., 750 miles (450 kilometers) northwest of Winnipeg.

A lot's happened since then, admits the 34-year-old cartoonist.

## Left Mac

When she left Dundas, and a five-year job at McMaster's Medical Centre illustration department, Lynn hadn't signed the $80,000 a year, ten-year contract with Universal Press Syndicate of Kansas, that introduced her comic strip family to what is now 250 daily papers in Canada and the U.S. She wasn't inundated with offers to market her domestic funnies on toys, pillow cases and numerous other household items. She hadn't been asked to animate the strip or to humanize her characters in a daytime television serial.

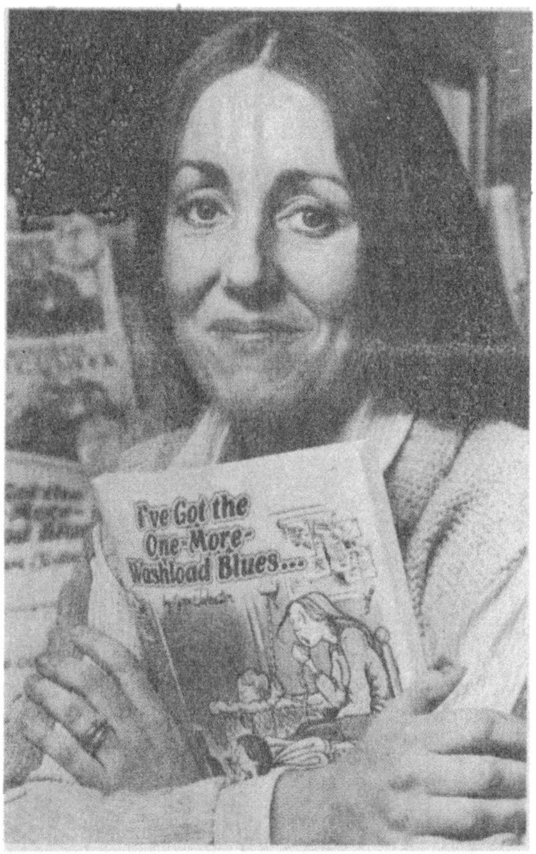
I've Got the
One-More-
Washload Blues...

"Once you become successful with something like this, you become a property," says Lynn. "You no longer exist as a person really. You exist as a machine that grinds out stuff. So once your stuff starts to sell, the word "market" becomes the watchword."

But Lynn has managed to avoid most of the traps that accompany fame. She says being a wife and mother has afforded some protection from the rat race.

"Being female and being a mother means I just don't have the time. And if I did all those things, I wouldn't be able to be a mother. I'd lose everything."

Besides, she says, her family life is essential to the comic. Without it, she admits, she'd have no basis for material.

Although it wasn't planned that way, Lynn says living up north provides a chance to lead the low-profile life she likes.

"I think that because we're up north, we're allowed to be very private and to lead a life very similar to the life that we led in Hamilton. We have our circle of friends, and we go out and shop and we lead a very ordinary life."

Lynn says she enjoys the small town closeness of Lynn Lake.

"It's very busy, very active. There's all kinds of different sorts of people who move up there: very adventurous, bright, intelligent people, and they make their own fun."

With her dentist husband, Rod, she works with the department of Northern Affairs to bring cultural events to the communities around Lynn Lake. And each year she helps to organize the annual Beer and Skits event in town.

Still, she admits, she loves to balance the rural quiet with occasional visits to Toronto and Hamilton, where she says, she feels at home.

"Hamilton is an enormous city to us now. Before, it was a city but it wasn't beyond out ken. Now, it just blows your mind to come and have more than one place where you can buy shoes, and there's more than one size."

Lynn tries to keep the balance in her family life too. She doesn't tour with the children, she says,

• The Spectator, Monday, September 21, 1981

# For better or for worse, Lynn loves her job

because it's a burden they shouldn't be affected by. And while she still uses her family as models for the strip, she carefully keeps some distance between the strip characters and her real-life children, Aaron, 8, and Kate, 4.

The strip children, Michael and Elizabeth, are a year younger than her own, she says, and live in a suburban setting. She hopes the differences will keep Aaron and Kate from identifying too much with the comic.

## Will age

Michael and Elizabeth will age in the funnies as Aaron and Kate grow, but, says Lynn, she anticipates some delicate moments when her real-life kids become teens.

"The teenage years are very, very special, and I'm going to really enjoy working on those, but I'm going to have to have a lot of close contact with my kids during those times and make sure I'm not treading on their toes."

As for herself, Lynn feels she's growing too. And she says, she has a lot of friends in Hamilton to thank for believing in her when she didn't have faith in herself. Friends like her obstetrician, who prompted her to publish the collection of cartoons she gave him during her first difficult pregnancy. The collection became her first book, David, We're Pregnant.

"I didn't have that faith in me," she says. "I've never been able to sell my work. I have a lot more confidence now, of course. And especially since the strip has been out for two years because now, I'm starting to be able to draw much better. I'm getting very comfortable with the characters and I know that I've improved."

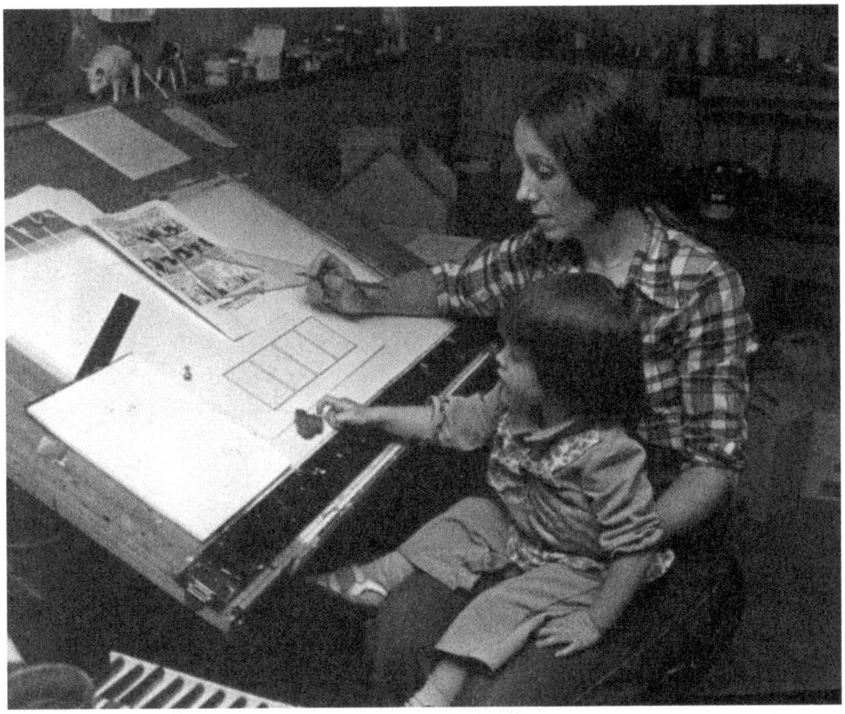

This photo was taken by the National Film Board of Canada when a crew was sent to Lynn Lake to make a documentary about our family. Katie, sitting on my knee, was about two years old.

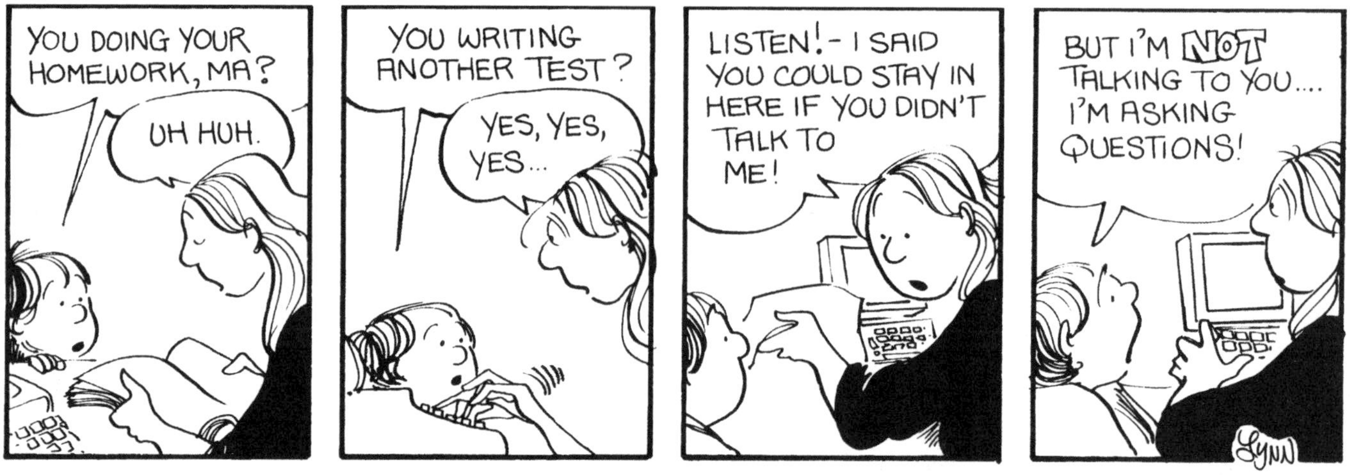
YOU DOING YOUR HOMEWORK, MA?
UH HUH.
YOU WRITING ANOTHER TEST?
YES, YES, YES...
LISTEN! - I SAID YOU COULD STAY IN HERE IF YOU DIDN'T TALK TO ME!
BUT I'M NOT TALKING TO YOU.... I'M ASKING QUESTIONS!
LYNN

Elly grumbled so bitterly about being a housewife that I began to get letters from folks who suggested she go back to school. This was a good idea. Since she had been an English major, it made sense for her to take a course in creative writing. I sent her off to class, not knowing where this would all be leading.

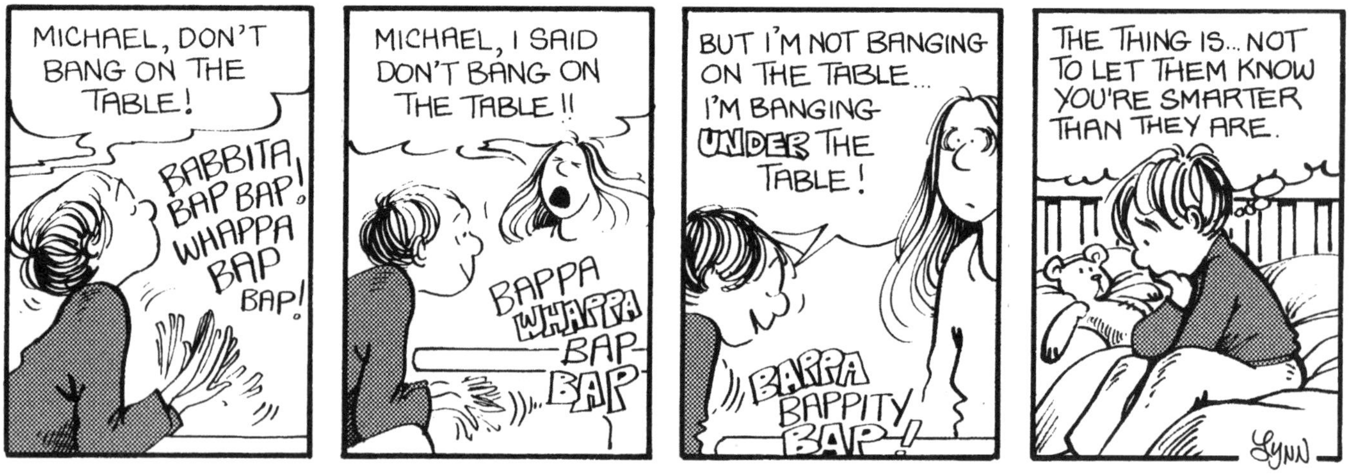
MICHAEL, DON'T BANG ON THE TABLE!
BABBITA BAP BAP! WHAPPA BAP BAP!
MICHAEL, I SAID DON'T BANG ON THE TABLE!!
BAPPA WHAPPA BAP BAP
BUT I'M NOT BANGING ON THE TABLE... I'M BANGING UNDER THE TABLE!
BAPPA BAPPITY BAP!
THE THING IS... NOT TO LET THEM KNOW YOU'RE SMARTER THAN THEY ARE.
LYNN

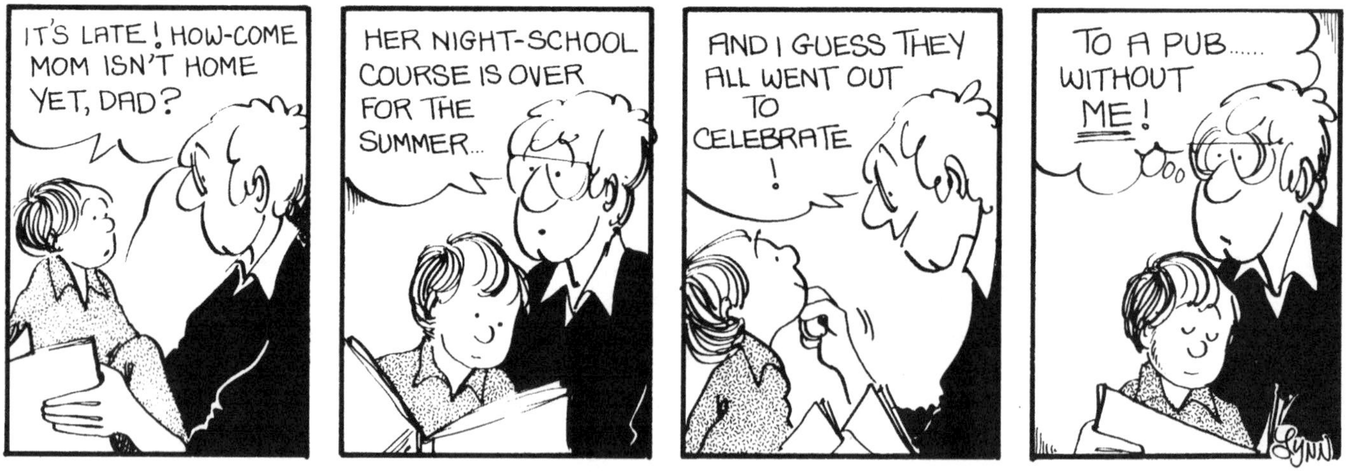
IT'S LATE! HOW-COME MOM ISN'T HOME YET, DAD?
HER NIGHT-SCHOOL COURSE IS OVER FOR THE SUMMER...
AND I GUESS THEY ALL WENT OUT TO CELEBRATE!
TO A PUB...... WITHOUT ME!
LYNN

I wanted Elly to gain some independence, to have a life outside the family, and make a few new friends. Complicating my life by complicating hers was something I did too often perhaps, and I often wrote myself into a corner. Does one develop new characters and new locations ... or stay focused on the family? With only a few seconds a day to tell a story, it was hard to decide, and I often left ideas hanging.

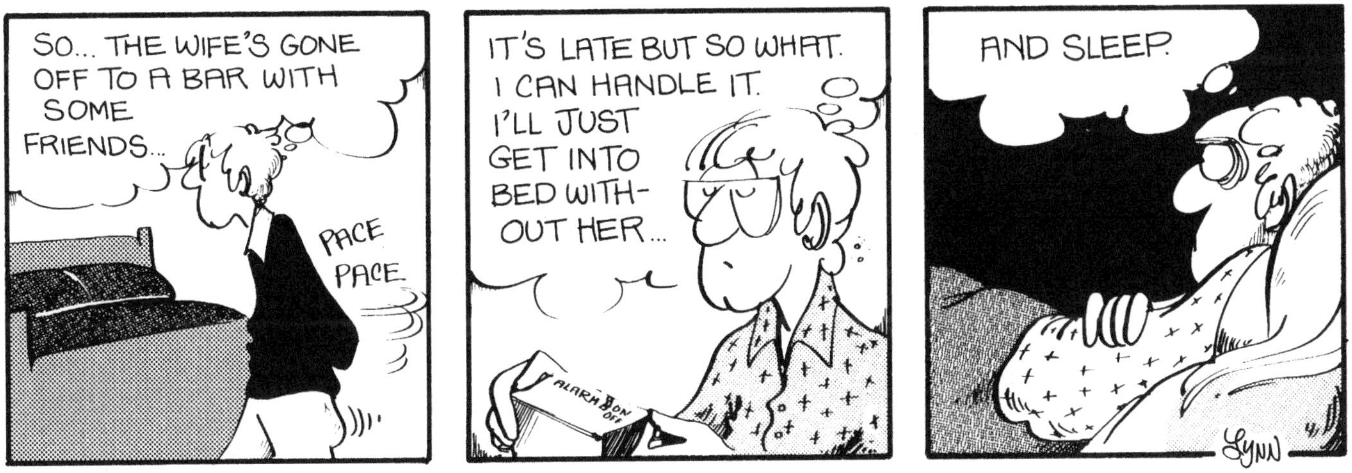
SO... THE WIFE'S GONE OFF TO A BAR WITH SOME FRIENDS...
PACE PACE
IT'S LATE BUT SO WHAT. I CAN HANDLE IT. I'LL JUST GET INTO BED WITH-OUT HER...
AND SLEEP.
LYNN

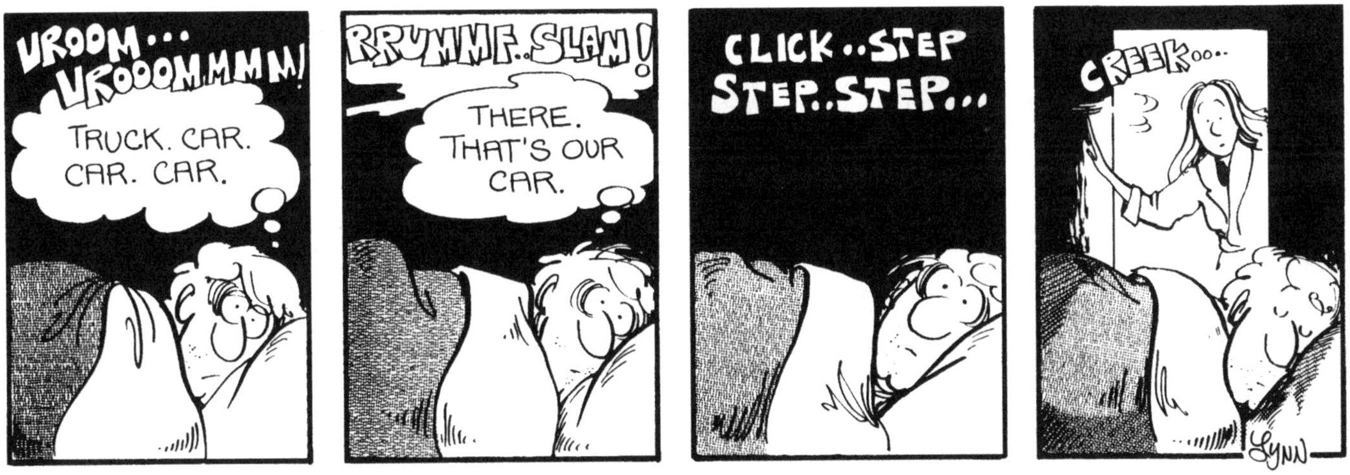
VROOM... VROOOMMMM!
TRUCK. CAR. CAR. CAR.
BRUMMF..SLAM!
THERE. THAT'S OUR CAR.
CLICK..STEP STEP..STEP...
CREEK...
LYNN

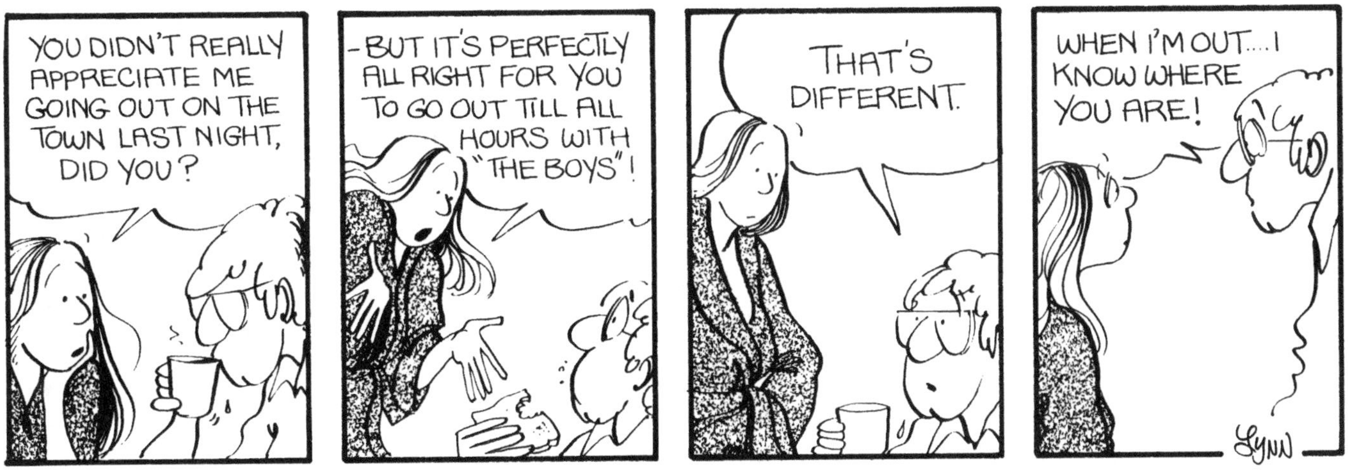
YOU DIDN'T REALLY APPRECIATE ME GOING OUT ON THE TOWN LAST NIGHT, DID YOU?
-BUT IT'S PERFECTLY ALL RIGHT FOR YOU TO GO OUT TILL ALL HOURS WITH "THE BOYS"!
THAT'S DIFFERENT.
WHEN I'M OUT....I KNOW WHERE YOU ARE!
LYNN

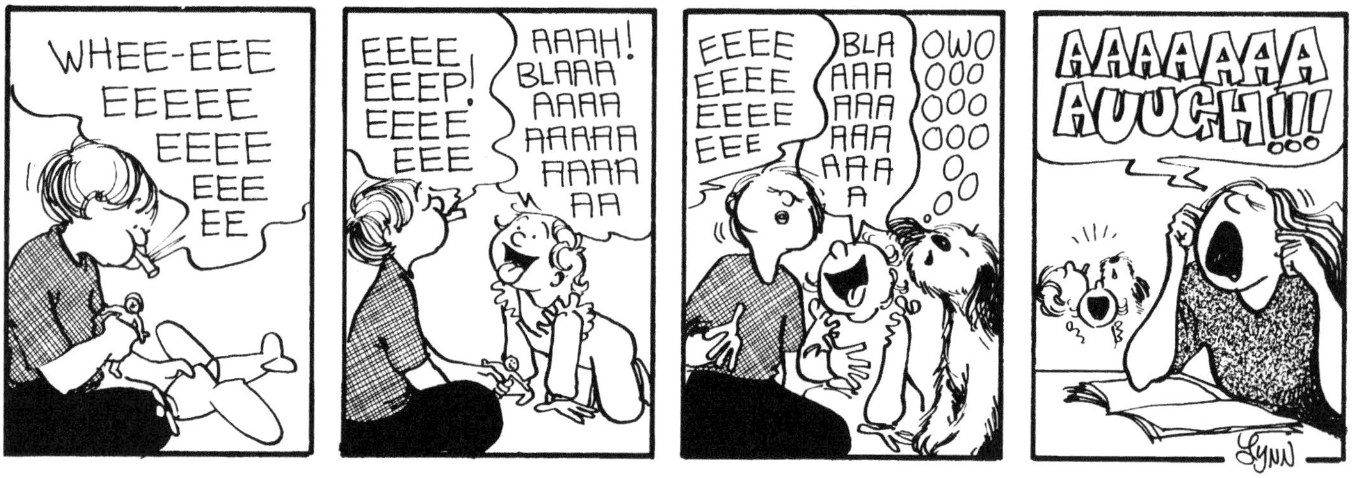
WHEE-EEE EEEEE EEEE EEE EE
EEEE EEEP! EEEE EEE
AAAH! BLAAA AAAA AAAAA AAAA AA
EEEE EEEE EEEE EEE
BLA AAA AAA AAA AAA A
OWO OOO OOO OOO O O O
AAAAAAA AUUGH!!!
LYNN

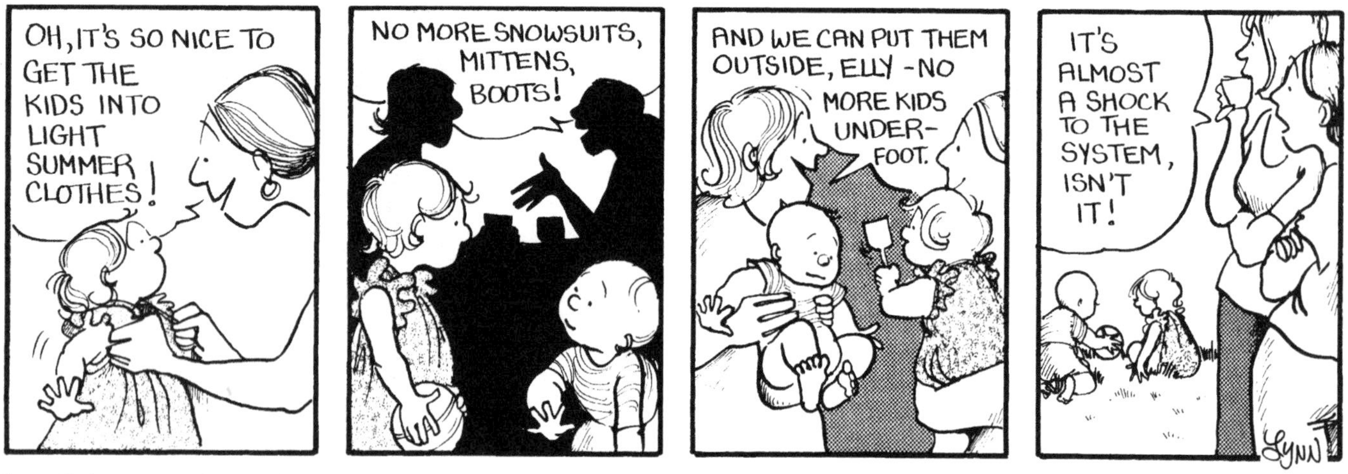
OH, IT'S SO NICE TO GET THE KIDS INTO LIGHT SUMMER CLOTHES!
NO MORE SNOWSUITS, MITTENS, BOOTS!
AND WE CAN PUT THEM OUTSIDE, ELLY - NO MORE KIDS UNDER-FOOT.
IT'S ALMOST A SHOCK TO THE SYSTEM, ISN'T IT!
LYNN

Lynn Lake was so far north that spring didn't arrive much before May. The lakes were still frozen when the buds began to form, and I remember taking the kids to the lake, where they waded in the slushy water in their rubber boots, wearing shorts on the bottom and winter jackets on top.

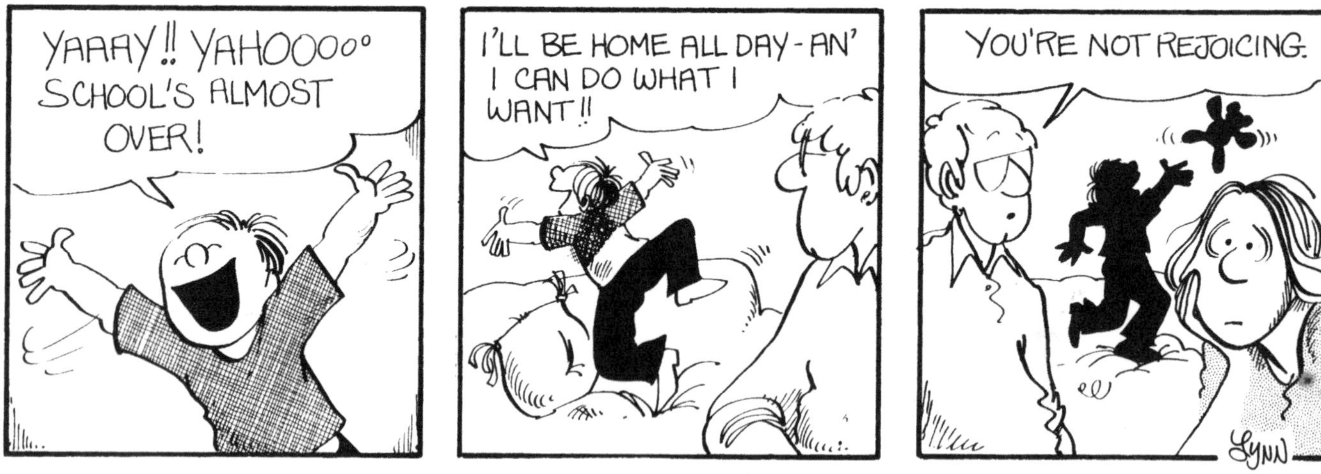
YAAAY!! YAHOOOOo SCHOOL'S ALMOST OVER!
I'LL BE HOME ALL DAY - AN' I CAN DO WHAT I WANT!!
YOU'RE NOT REJOICING.
LYNN

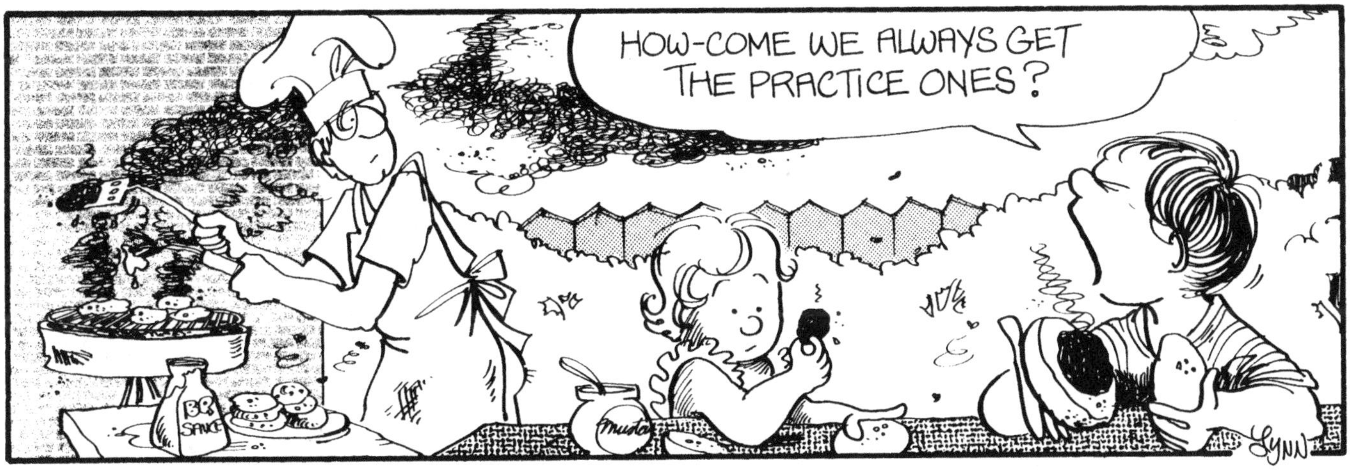
HOW-COME WE ALWAYS GET THE PRACTICE ONES?

As summer progressed, the days lengthened until sunset was around eleven in the evening. People barbecued, washed their cars, and let their kids run wild until midnight.

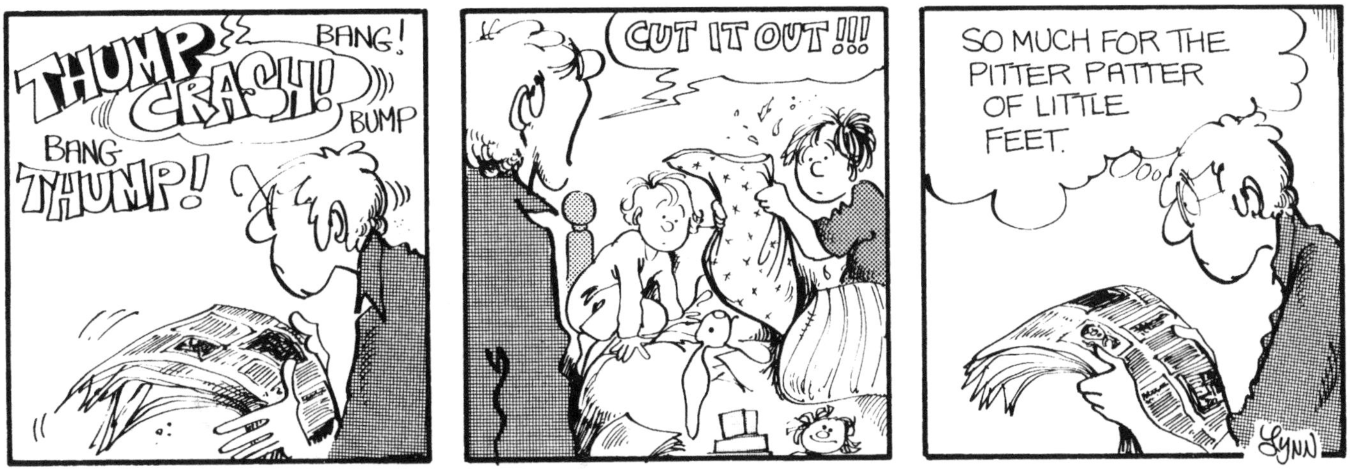
THUMP
CRASH!
BANG!
BUMP
BANG-
THUMP!
CUT IT OUT!!!
SO MUCH FOR THE PITTER PATTER OF LITTLE FEET.

Getting kids to sleep while it was still light outside was a challenge. A pillow fight was a good way to tire them out, but if that didn't work … we used threats.

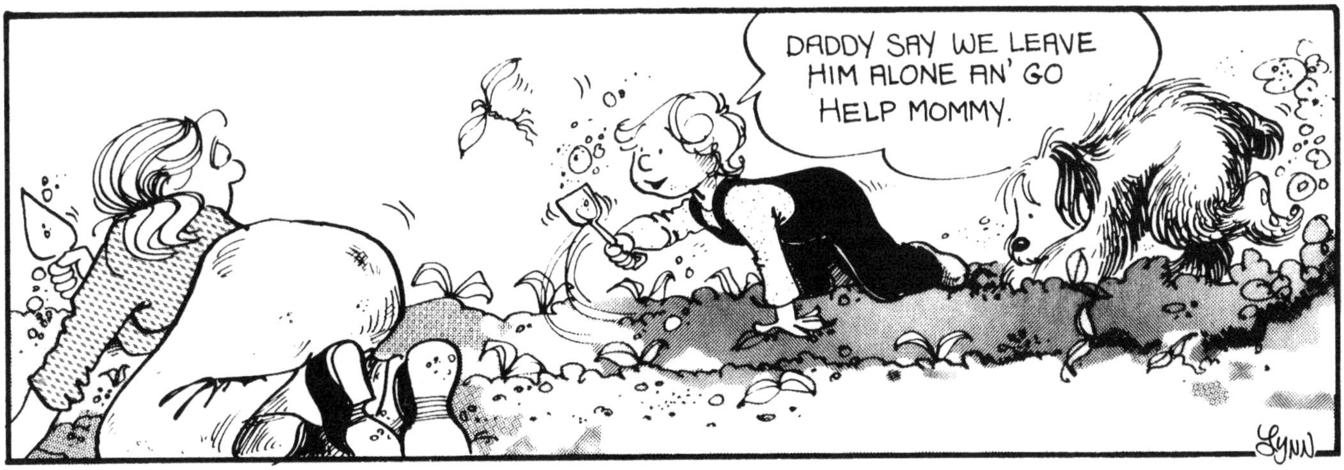
DADDY SAY WE LEAVE HIM ALONE AN' GO HELP MOMMY.

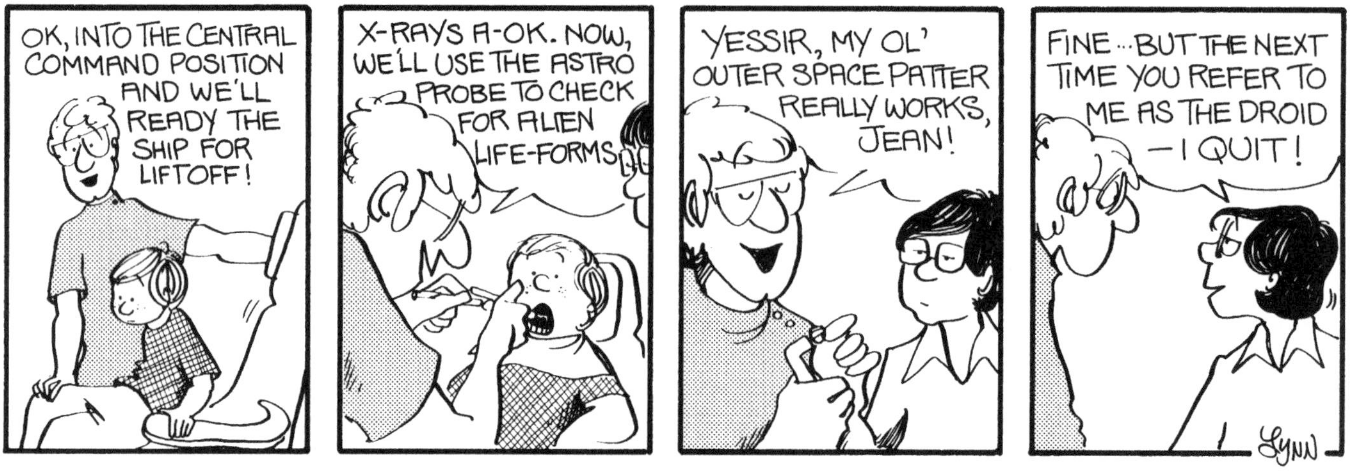
OK, INTO THE CENTRAL COMMAND POSITION AND WE'LL READY THE SHIP FOR LIFTOFF!
X-RAYS A-OK. NOW, WE'LL USE THE ASTRO PROBE TO CHECK FOR ALIEN LIFE-FORMS
YESSIR, MY OL' OUTER SPACE PATTER REALLY WORKS, JEAN!
FINE... BUT THE NEXT TIME YOU REFER TO ME AS THE DROID —I QUIT!
LYNN

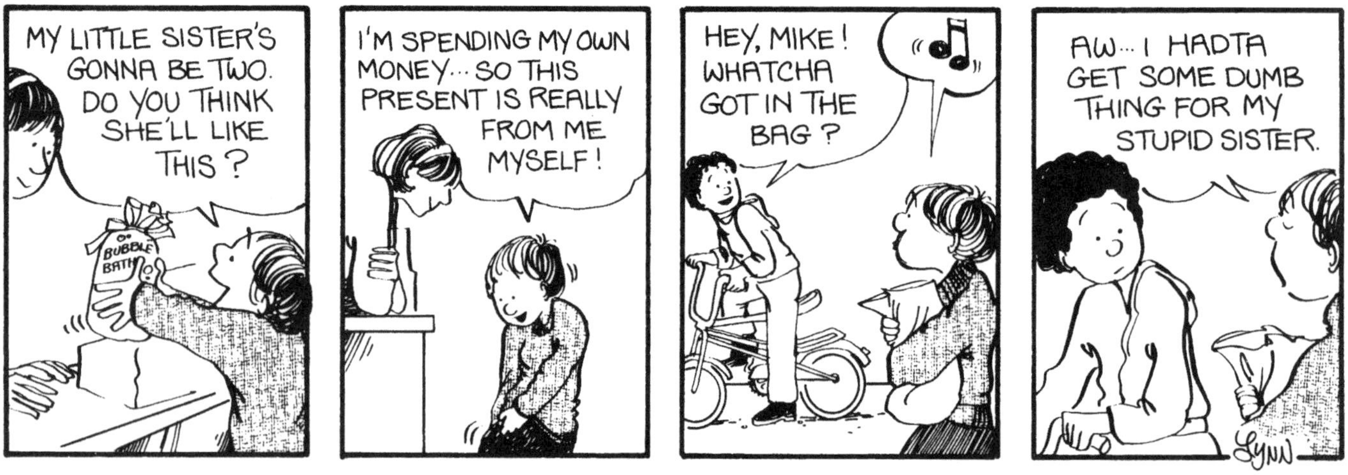
MY LITTLE SISTER'S GONNA BE TWO. DO YOU THINK SHE'LL LIKE THIS?
BUBBLE BATH
I'M SPENDING MY OWN MONEY... SO THIS PRESENT IS REALLY FROM ME MYSELF!
HEY, MIKE! WHATCHA GOT IN THE BAG?
AW... I HADTA GET SOME DUMB THING FOR MY STUPID SISTER.
LYNN

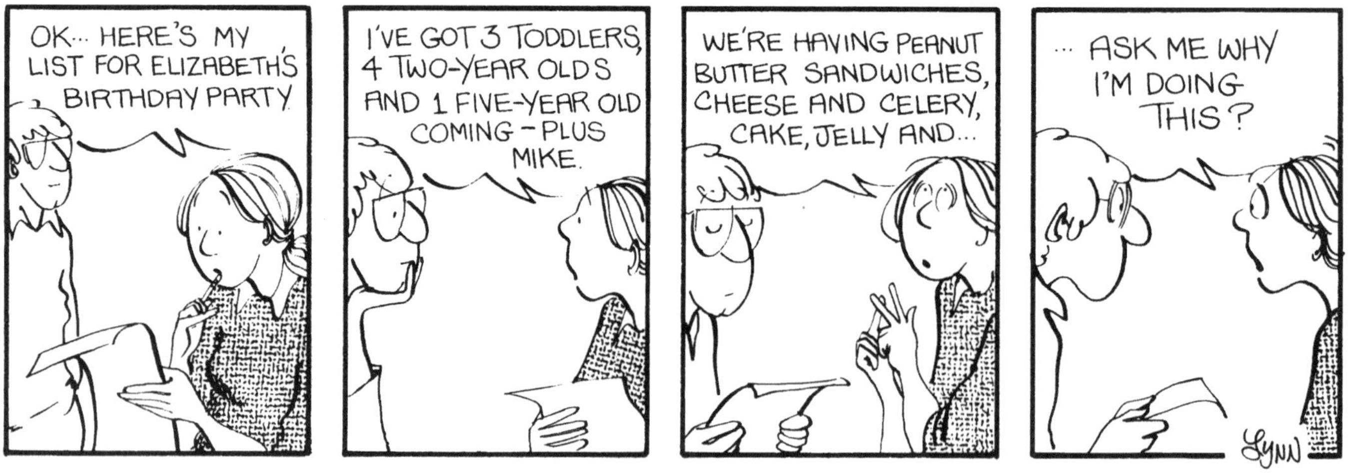
OK... HERE'S MY LIST FOR ELIZABETH'S BIRTHDAY PARTY
I'VE GOT 3 TODDLERS, 4 TWO-YEAR OLDS AND 1 FIVE-YEAR OLD COMING —PLUS MIKE.
WE'RE HAVING PEANUT BUTTER SANDWICHES, CHEESE AND CELERY, CAKE, JELLY AND...
... ASK ME WHY I'M DOING THIS?
LYNN

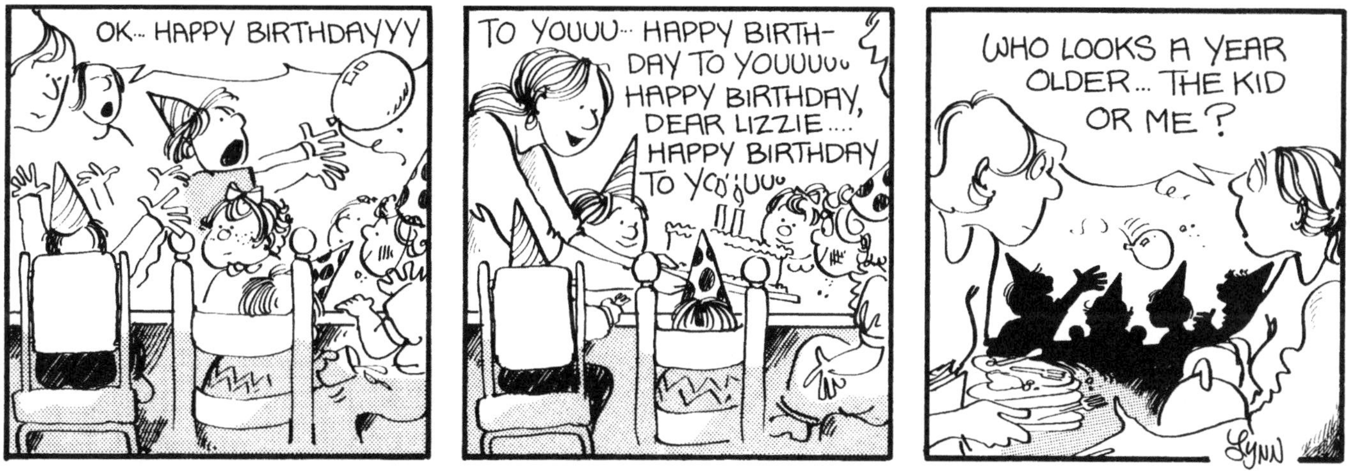
OK... HAPPY BIRTHDAYYY
TO YOUUU... HAPPY BIRTH-DAY TO YOUUUUU HAPPY BIRTHDAY, DEAR LIZZIE.... HAPPY BIRTHDAY TO YOUUU
WHO LOOKS A YEAR OLDER... THE KID OR ME?
LYNN

The rule I established for parties was: You can have as many people over as your age. (This came back to hit me when the kids turned ten and fifteen!) Two friends at a two-year-olds' birthday party was a perfect number — but, we lived in a small town. If you leave one kid out, you're doomed. I cleaned up after Katie's second birthday party for days!

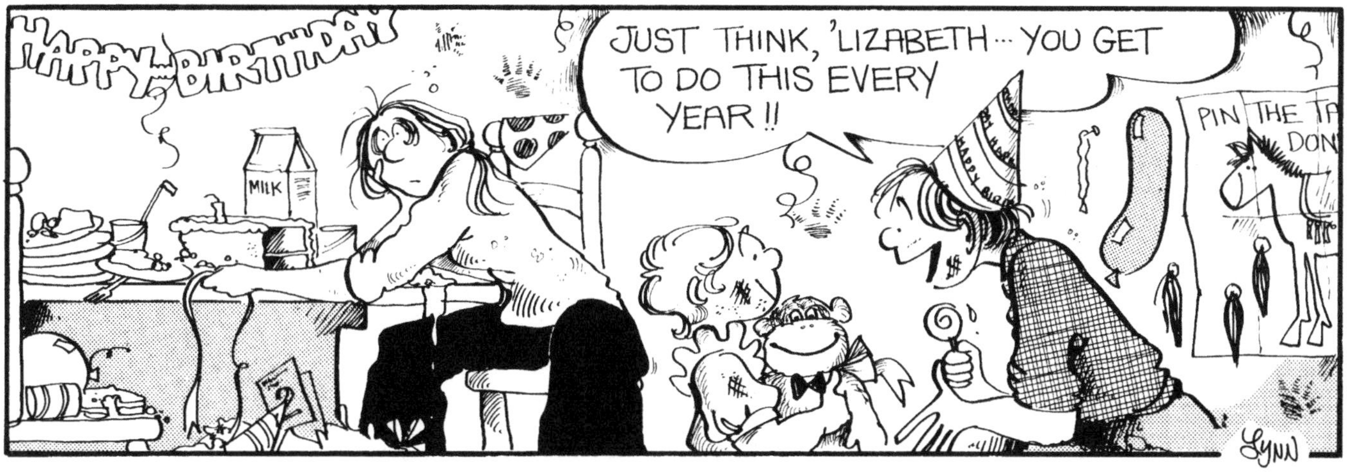
HAPPY BIRTHDAY
MILK
JUST THINK, 'LIZABETH... YOU GET TO DO THIS EVERY YEAR !!
LYNN

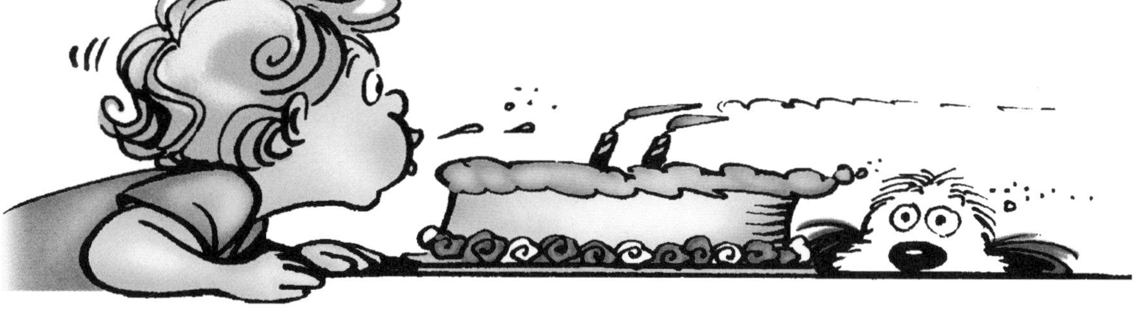

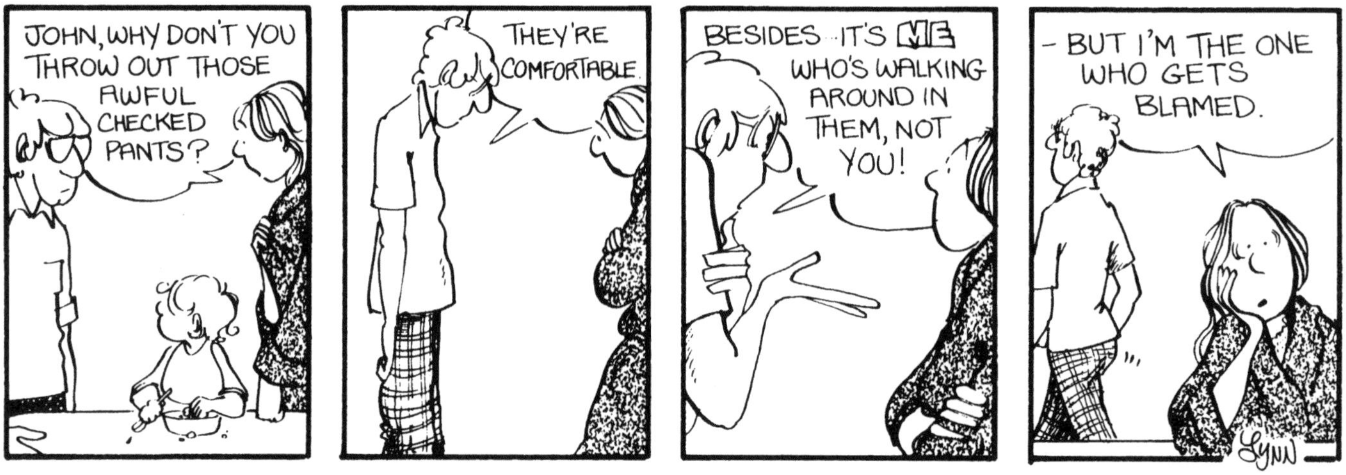
JOHN, WHY DON'T YOU THROW OUT THOSE AWFUL CHECKED PANTS?
THEY'RE COMFORTABLE.
BESIDES... IT'S ME WHO'S WALKING AROUND IN THEM, NOT YOU!
- BUT I'M THE ONE WHO GETS BLAMED.
LYNN

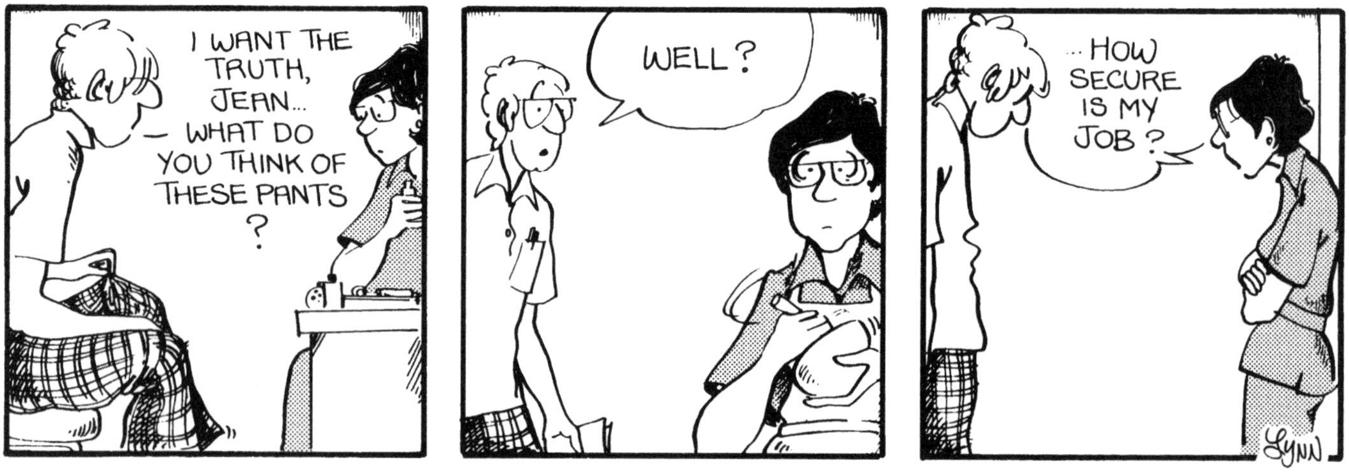
I WANT THE TRUTH, JEAN... — WHAT DO YOU THINK OF THESE PANTS ?
WELL ?
...HOW SECURE IS MY JOB ?
LYNN

These checkered pants were real. They had been worn until the cuffs frayed and the pattern was worn from the knees. When I finally convinced my spouse that he should divest himself of this vestment, the pants disappeared. Twenty years later, I discovered them in a container of fabric saved for costumes — and he wanted to wear them again!

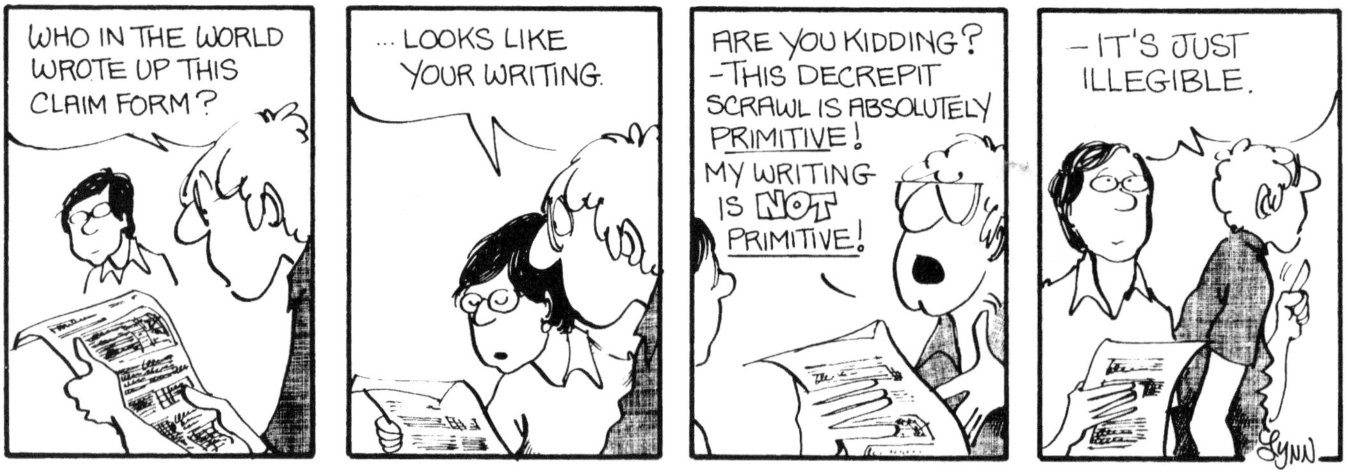
WHO IN THE WORLD WROTE UP THIS CLAIM FORM?
... LOOKS LIKE YOUR WRITING.
ARE YOU KIDDING? -THIS DECREPIT SCRAWL IS ABSOLUTELY PRIMITIVE! MY WRITING IS NOT PRIMITIVE!
- IT'S JUST ILLEGIBLE.
LYNN

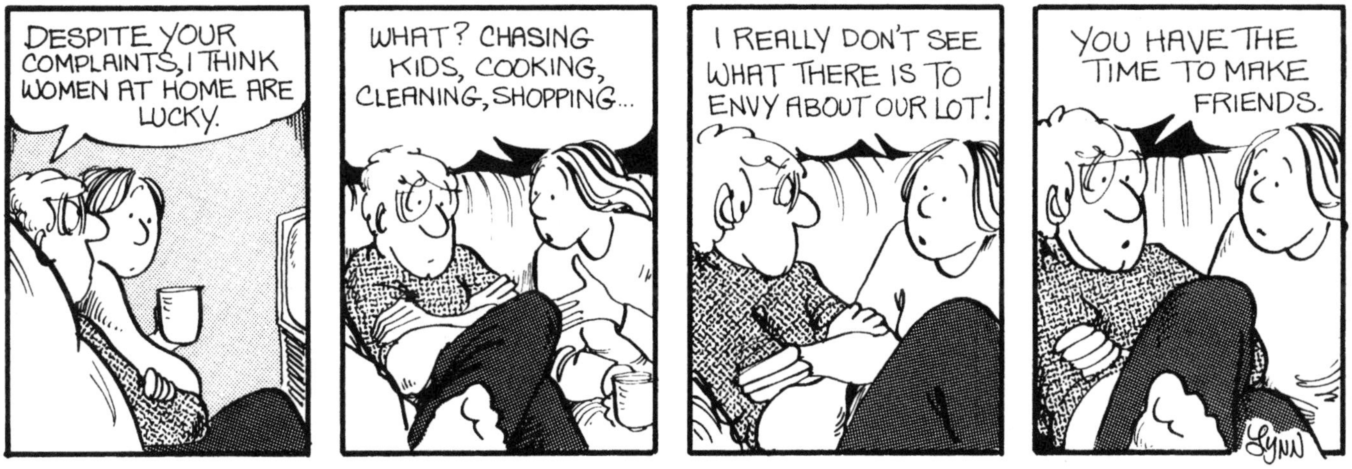
DESPITE YOUR COMPLAINTS, I THINK WOMEN AT HOME ARE LUCKY.
WHAT? CHASING KIDS, COOKING, CLEANING, SHOPPING...
I REALLY DON'T SEE WHAT THERE IS TO ENVY ABOUT OUR LOT!
YOU HAVE THE TIME TO MAKE FRIENDS.
LYNN

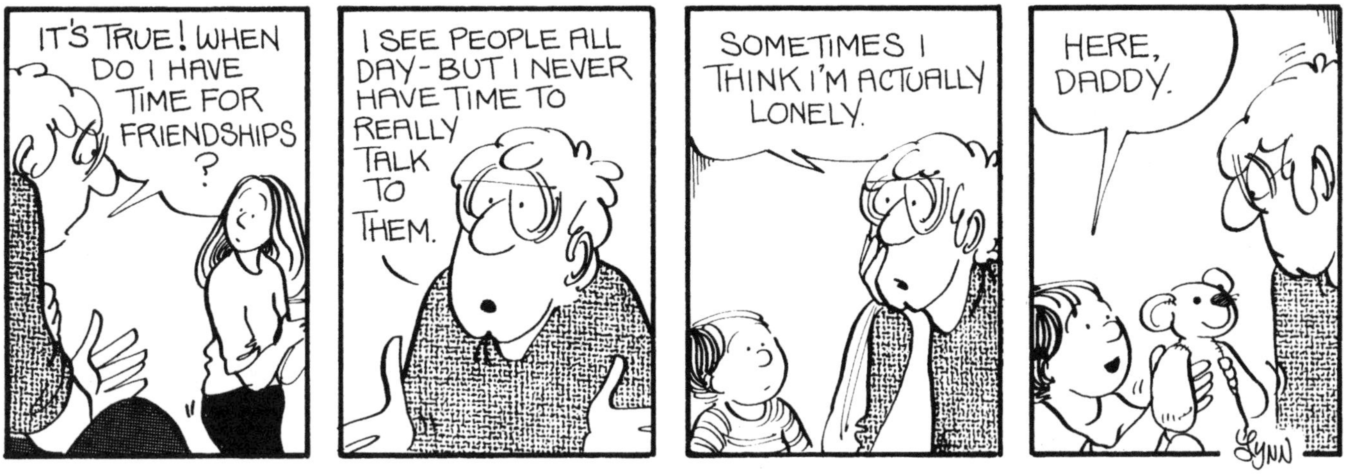
IT'S TRUE! WHEN DO I HAVE TIME FOR FRIENDSHIPS?
I SEE PEOPLE ALL DAY - BUT I NEVER HAVE TIME TO REALLY TALK TO THEM.
SOMETIMES I THINK I'M ACTUALLY LONELY.
HERE, DADDY.
LYNN

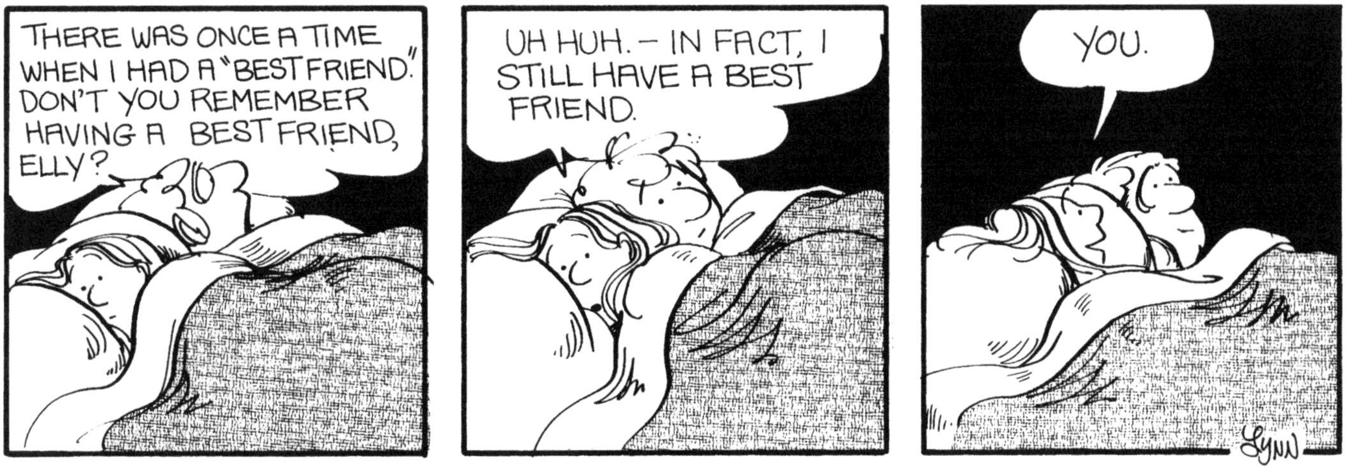
THERE WAS ONCE A TIME WHEN I HAD A "BEST FRIEND." DON'T YOU REMEMBER HAVING A BEST FRIEND, ELLY?
UH HUH. - IN FACT, I STILL HAVE A BEST FRIEND.
YOU.
LYNN

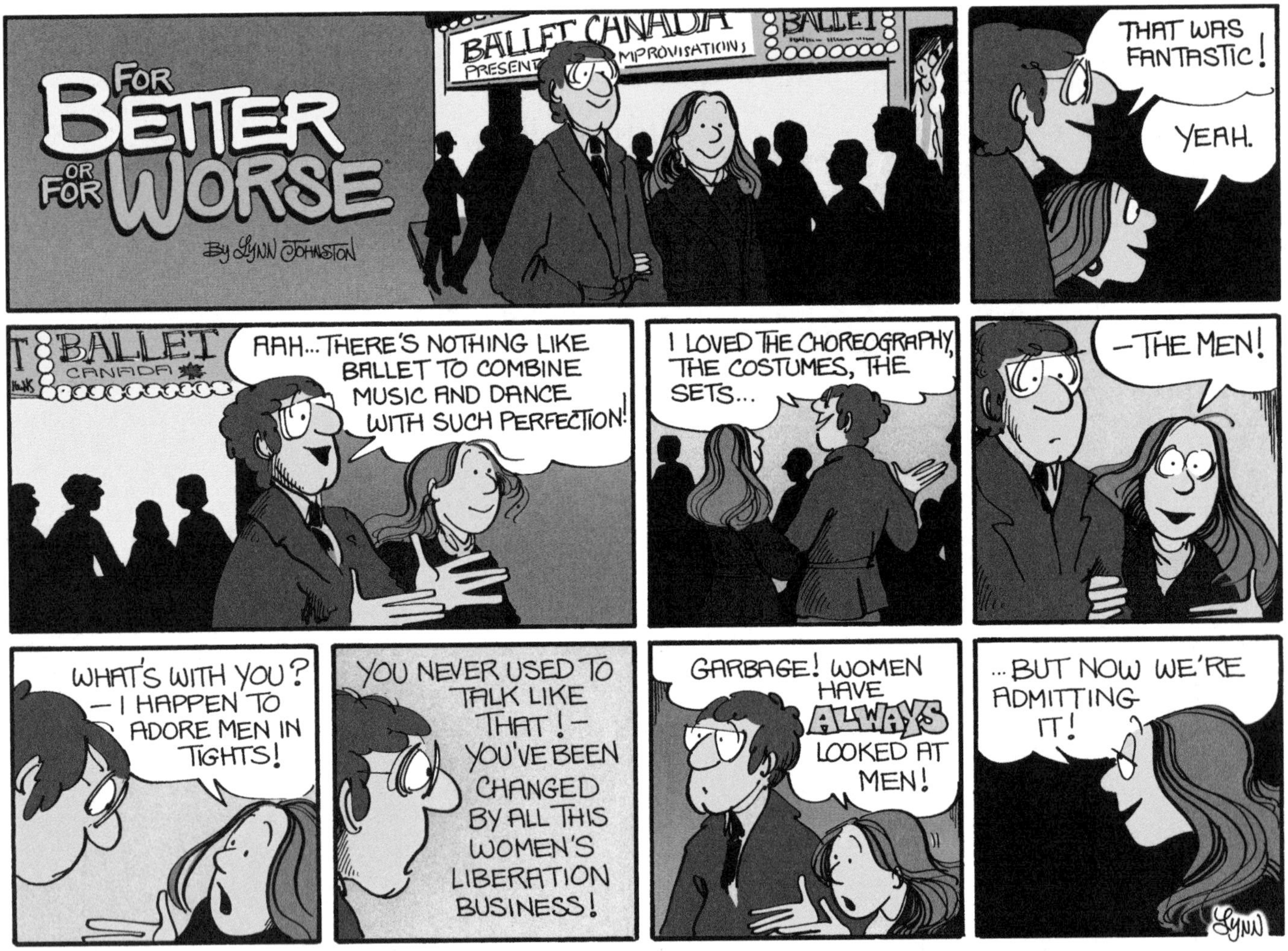
FOR BETTER OR FOR WORSE
BY LYNN JOHNSTON
BALLET CANADA PRESENTS IMPROVISATIONS
BALLET
THAT WAS FANTASTIC!
YEAH.
BALLET CANADA
AAH... THERE'S NOTHING LIKE BALLET TO COMBINE MUSIC AND DANCE WITH SUCH PERFECTION!
I LOVED THE CHOREOGRAPHY, THE COSTUMES, THE SETS...
–THE MEN!
WHAT'S WITH YOU? –I HAPPEN TO ADORE MEN IN TIGHTS!
YOU NEVER USED TO TALK LIKE THAT! –YOU'VE BEEN CHANGED BY ALL THIS WOMEN'S LIBERATION BUSINESS!
GARBAGE! WOMEN HAVE ALWAYS LOOKED AT MEN!
...BUT NOW WE'RE ADMITTING IT!
LYNN

Both my husband and I enjoyed the ballet. He liked to sit farther back in the audience so he could see the whole picture. I liked to sit up front. I guess this goes back to art school when some of our best and most talented models were dancers. These amazing people would often pose in costume, and the positions they chose inspired us all. They could stand unmoving — sometimes on one foot or with an arm extended until their limbs quivered. It was an endurance test as much as it was a static pose with which we could take our time. Their bodies were perfect, their faces were beautiful, and we could see why the painter Degas was so enamored that he drew and painted dancers again and again.

*

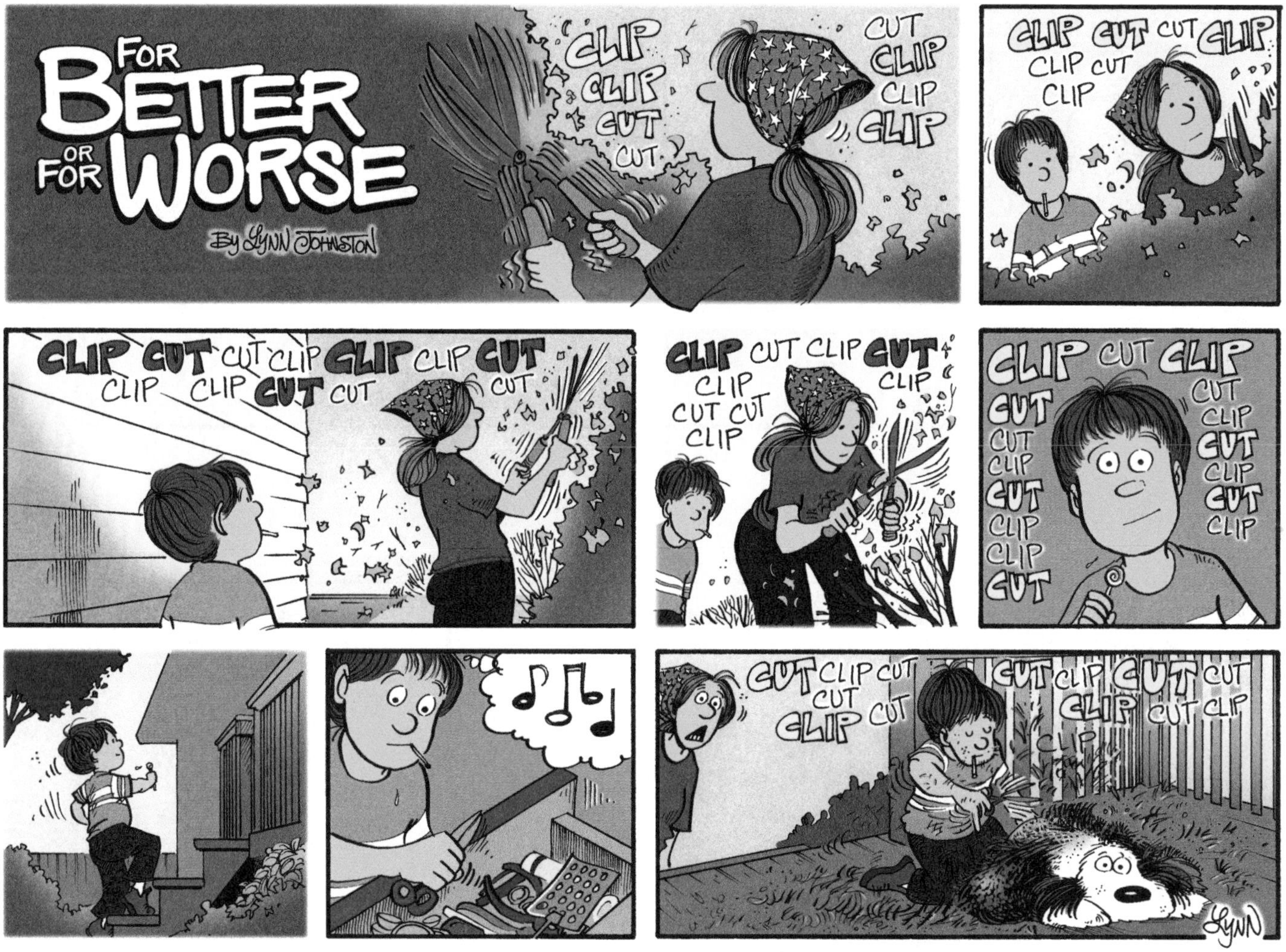
FOR BETTER OR FOR WORSE
By Lynn Johnston
CLIP CLIP CUT CUT
CUT CLIP CLIP CLIP
CLIP CUT CUT CLIP
CLIP CUT
CLIP
CLIP CUT CUT CLIP CLIP CLIP CUT
CLIP CLIP CUT CUT
CUT
CLIP CUT CLIP CUT
CLIP
CUT CUT
CLIP
CLIP CUT CLIP
CUT CUT CLIP CUT CLIP CLIP CUT
CUT CLIP CUT CLIP CUT CLIP
CUT CLIP CUT
CUT
CLIP CUT
CUT CLIP CUT CUT
CLIP CUT CLIP
CLIP
LYNN

One of the things I love to do is sound effects. I also like to draw clutter, chaos, and crud. This scenario nicely covered all the bases!

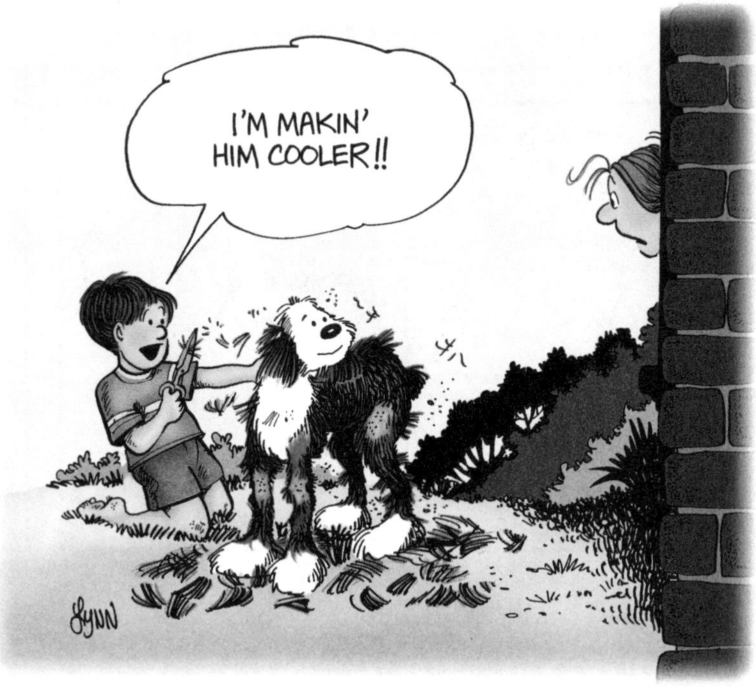
I'M MAKIN' HIM COOLER!!
LYNN

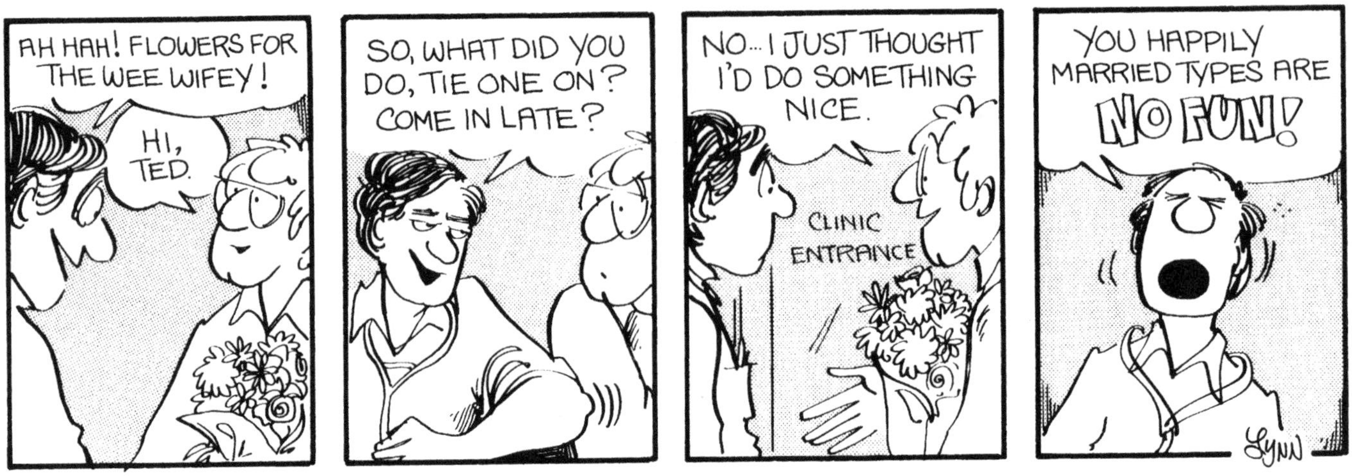
AH HAH! FLOWERS FOR THE WEE WIFEY!
HI, TED.
SO, WHAT DID YOU DO, TIE ONE ON? COME IN LATE?
NO... I JUST THOUGHT I'D DO SOMETHING NICE.
CLINIC ENTRANCE
YOU HAPPILY MARRIED TYPES ARE NO FUN!
Lynn

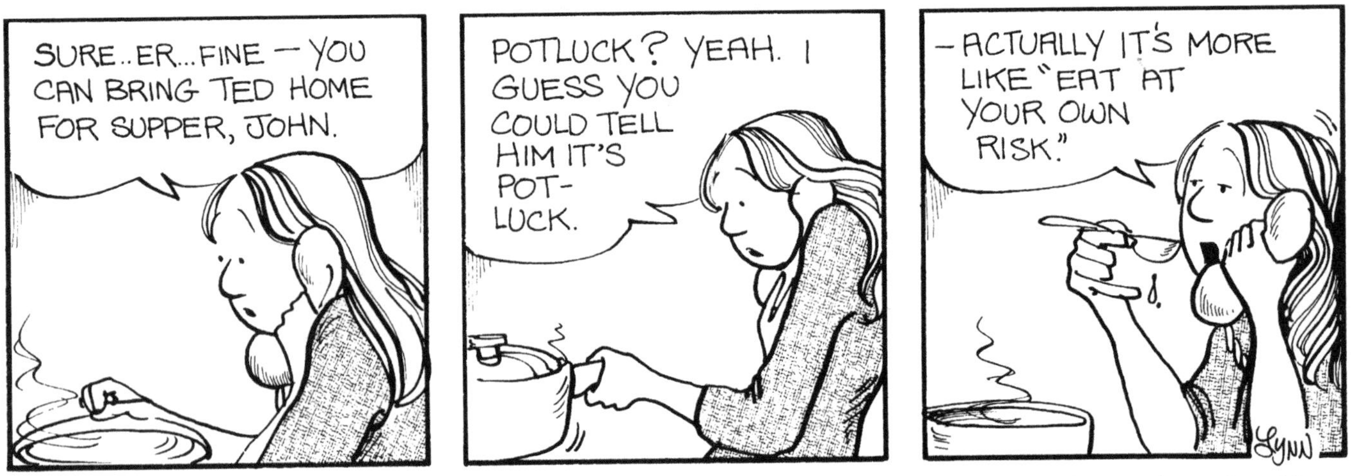
SURE.. ER... FINE — YOU CAN BRING TED HOME FOR SUPPER, JOHN.
POTLUCK? YEAH. I GUESS YOU COULD TELL HIM IT'S POT-LUCK.
– ACTUALLY IT'S MORE LIKE "EAT AT YOUR OWN RISK."
Lynn

I'm a pretty good cook. Still, I was uncomfortable inviting folks for supper because I wanted everything to be perfect. My most successful dinner parties were the ones I gave spontaneously — when I was blindsided by an extra set of chops and had to make do. My mother-in-law had the best advice, however: "A meal tastes best when your guests are a bit drunk and really, really hungry." … It works every time!

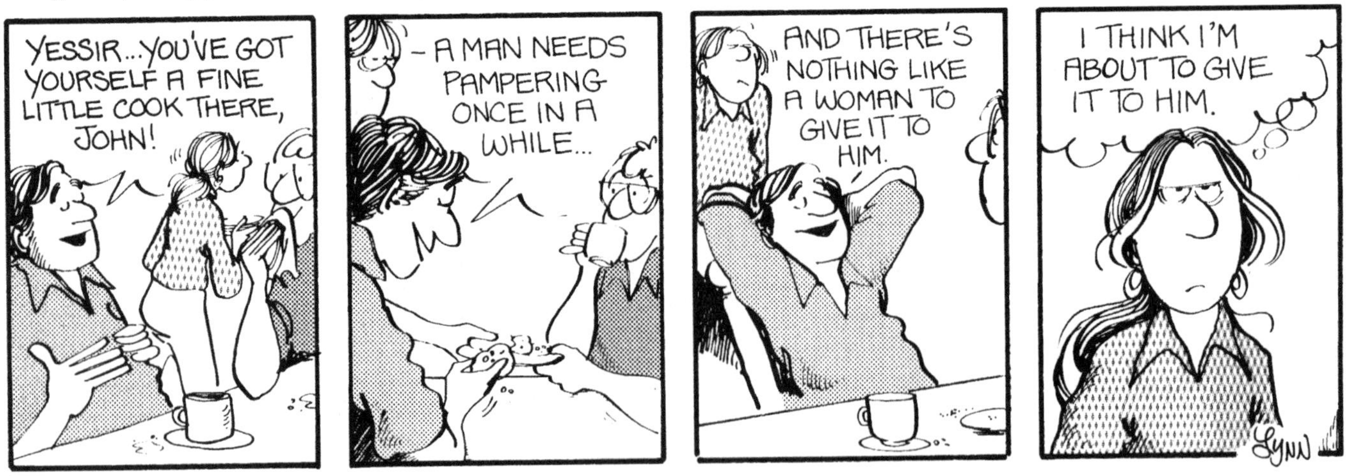
YESSIR... YOU'VE GOT YOURSELF A FINE LITTLE COOK THERE, JOHN!
– A MAN NEEDS PAMPERING ONCE IN A WHILE...
AND THERE'S NOTHING LIKE A WOMAN TO GIVE IT TO HIM.
I THINK I'M ABOUT TO GIVE IT TO HIM.
Lynn

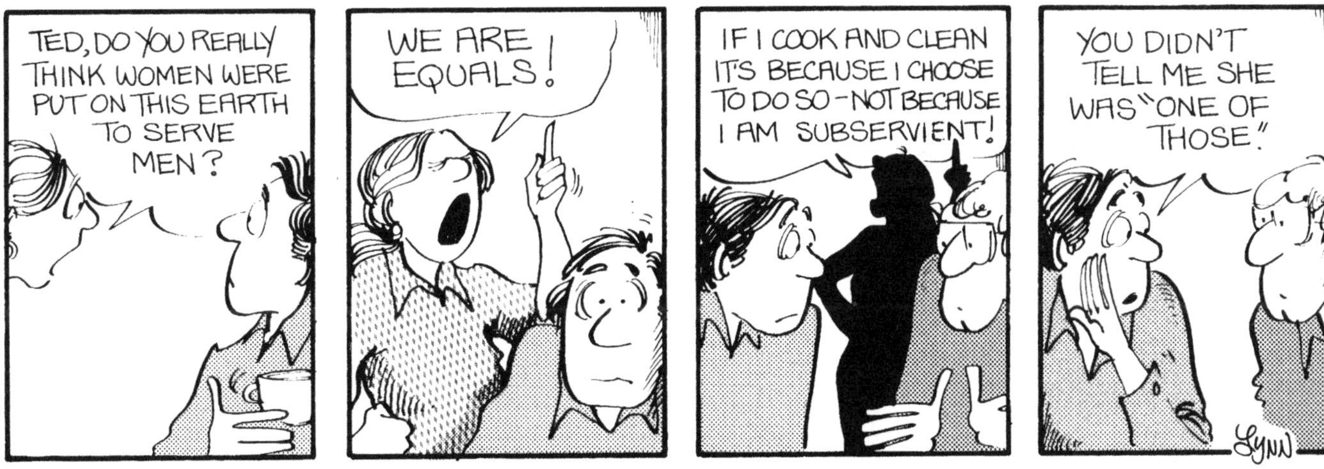
TED, DO YOU REALLY THINK WOMEN WERE PUT ON THIS EARTH TO SERVE MEN?
WE ARE EQUALS!
IF I COOK AND CLEAN IT'S BECAUSE I CHOOSE TO DO SO - NOT BECAUSE I AM SUBSERVIENT!
YOU DIDN'T TELL ME SHE WAS "ONE OF THOSE."
LYNN

Women's liberation was a force to contend with when I was in high school. There were marches and demonstrations. Editorials depicted these activists as right-wing bra burners, determined to wrest the work from the menfolk and upset the status quo. This was all very entertaining, and from my point of view, a bit over the top. Not until I was fighting beaurocracy and warding off wandering hands, myself, did I come to appreciate what the fight was for. … And, sad to say, it's still ongoing!

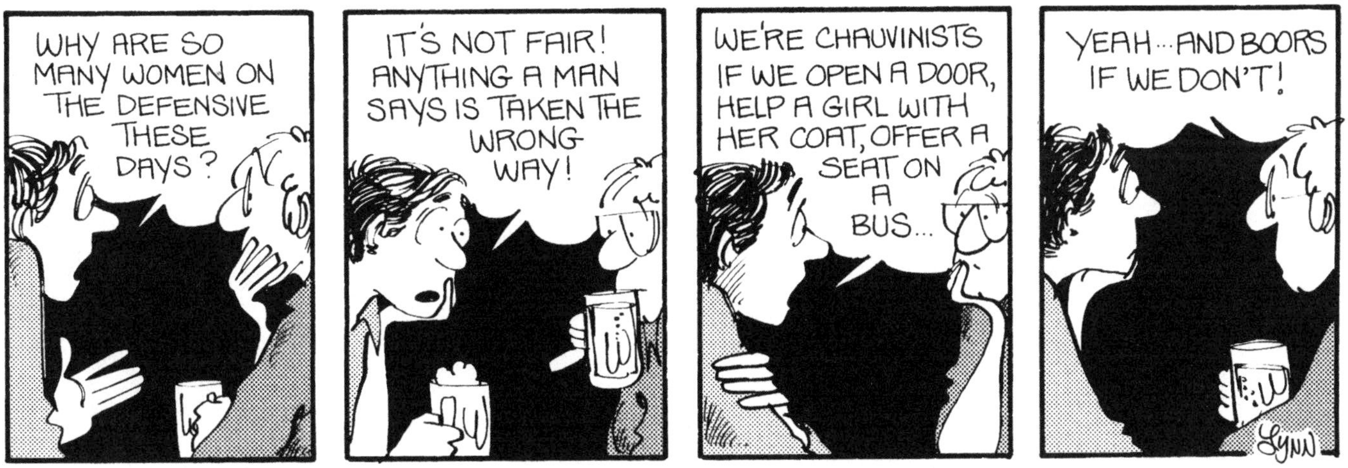
WHY ARE SO MANY WOMEN ON THE DEFENSIVE THESE DAYS?
IT'S NOT FAIR! ANYTHING A MAN SAYS IS TAKEN THE WRONG WAY!
WE'RE CHAUVINISTS IF WE OPEN A DOOR, HELP A GIRL WITH HER COAT, OFFER A SEAT ON A BUS...
YEAH... AND BOORS IF WE DON'T!
LYNN

By the same token, I empathized with men. How can we be equal when one woman is insulted if a man opens a door for her and another is miffed if he doesn't? When this strip was drawn, we were finding solutions, but still waging the war. Perhaps the NEXT generation will find a way to straighten it out.

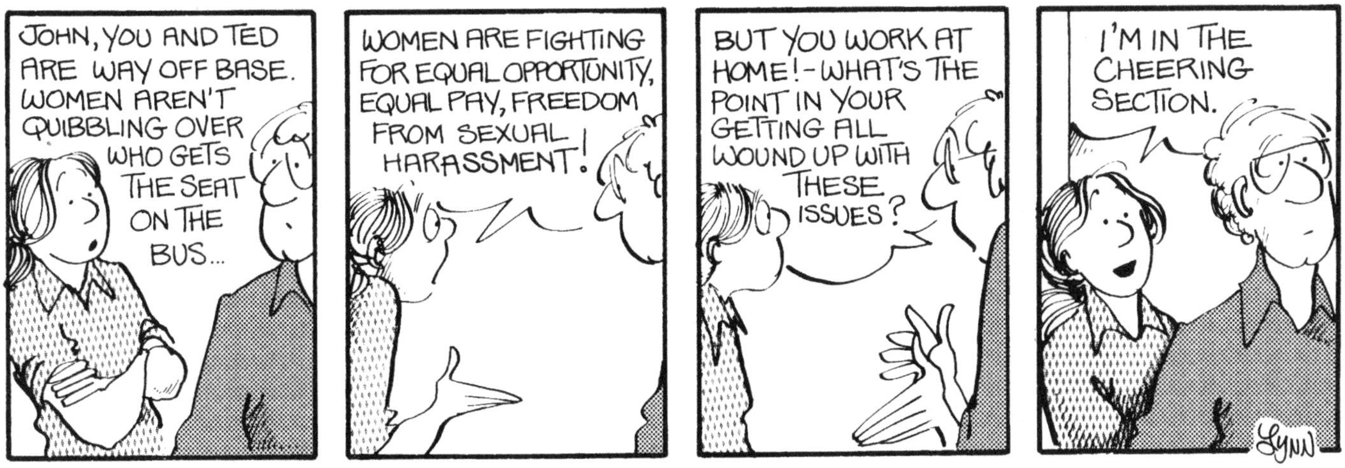
JOHN, YOU AND TED ARE WAY OFF BASE. WOMEN AREN'T QUIBBLING OVER WHO GETS THE SEAT ON THE BUS...
WOMEN ARE FIGHTING FOR EQUAL OPPORTUNITY, EQUAL PAY, FREEDOM FROM SEXUAL HARASSMENT!
BUT YOU WORK AT HOME! - WHAT'S THE POINT IN YOUR GETTING ALL WOUND UP WITH THESE ISSUES?
I'M IN THE CHEERING SECTION.
LYNN

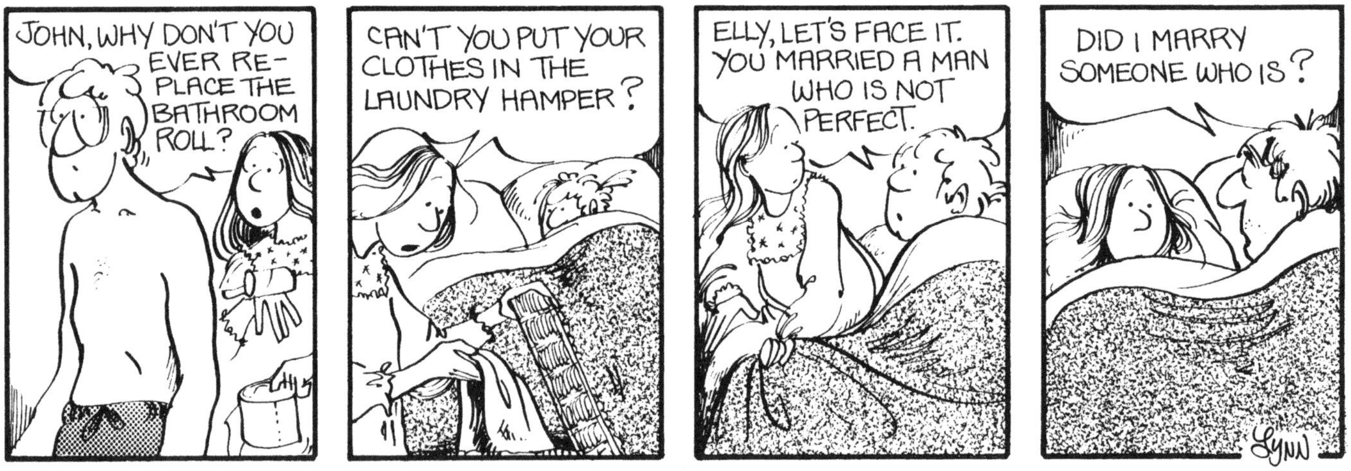
JOHN, WHY DON'T YOU EVER RE-PLACE THE BATHROOM ROLL?
CAN'T YOU PUT YOUR CLOTHES IN THE LAUNDRY HAMPER?
ELLY, LET'S FACE IT. YOU MARRIED A MAN WHO IS NOT PERFECT.
DID I MARRY SOMEONE WHO IS?
Lynn

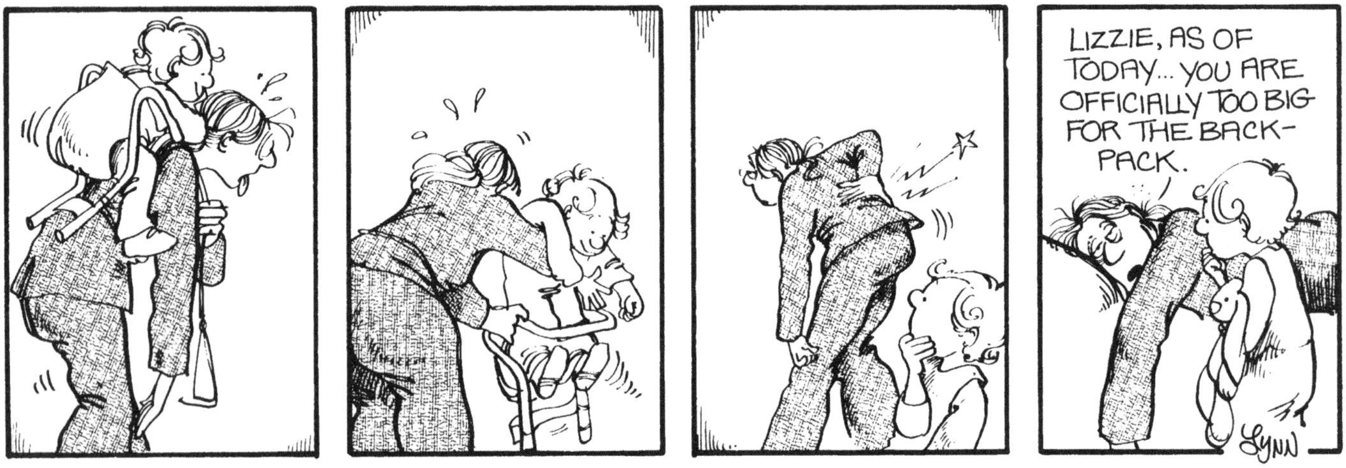
LIZZIE, AS OF TODAY... YOU ARE OFFICIALLY TOO BIG FOR THE BACK-PACK.
Lynn

I had Katie in a carrier like this until she was three. It was easier to schlep her about on my back than try and keep her from running amok. Besides, her brother was a handful, as well, and as soon as I was busy with one, I knew I'd soon be chasing the other. I was in better shape then than at any other time in my life, and today I owe my strong spine to my life as a packhorse!

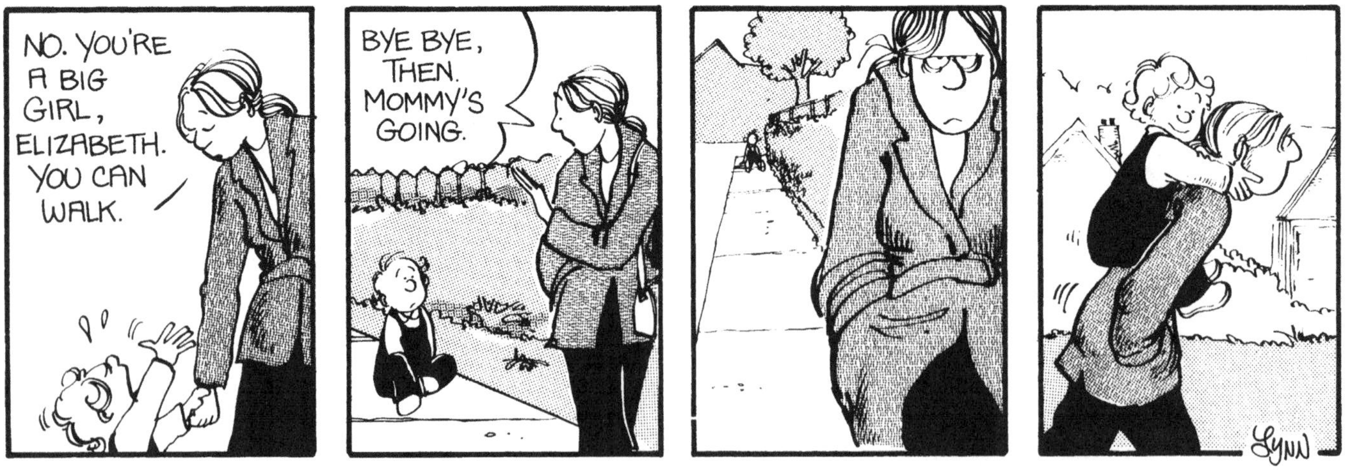
NO. YOU'RE A BIG GIRL, ELIZABETH. YOU CAN WALK.
BYE BYE, THEN. MOMMY'S GOING.
Lynn

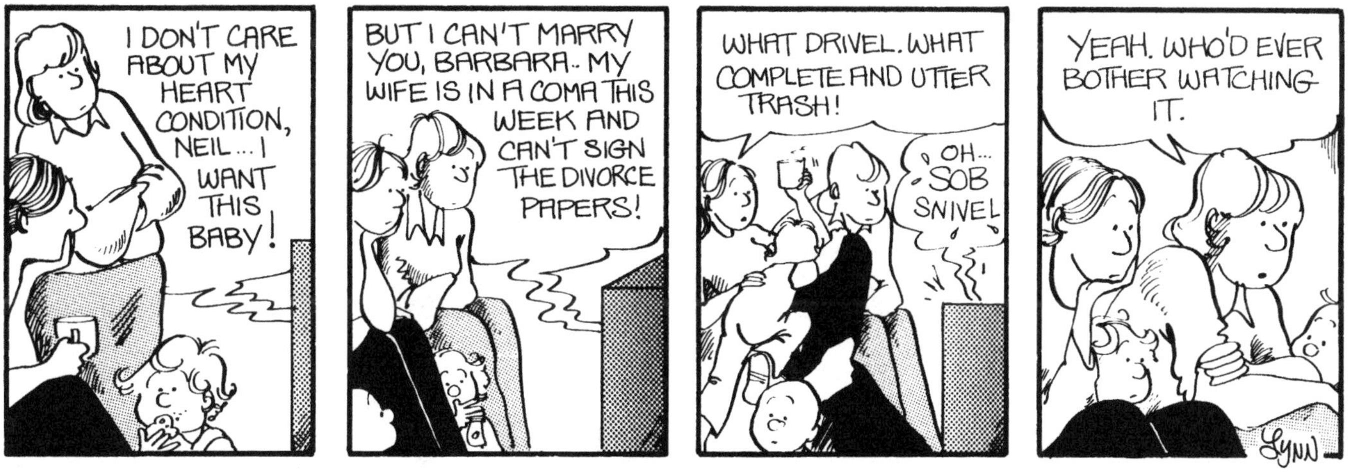
I DON'T CARE ABOUT MY HEART CONDITION, NEIL... I WANT THIS BABY!
BUT I CAN'T MARRY YOU, BARBARA.. MY WIFE IS IN A COMA THIS WEEK AND CAN'T SIGN THE DIVORCE PAPERS!
WHAT DRIVEL. WHAT COMPLETE AND UTTER TRASH!
OH... SOB SNIVEL
YEAH. WHO'D EVER BOTHER WATCHING IT.
Lynn

I didn't have time during the day to watch daytime soaps. With a demanding job, two small kids, and a busy life, TV was something left for weekends and Saturday morning cartoons. For some reason, I created a stereotypical situation, in which few moms can indulge, and I was reminded by readers that if Annie and Elly were to be believable, they would not have extra time to waste!

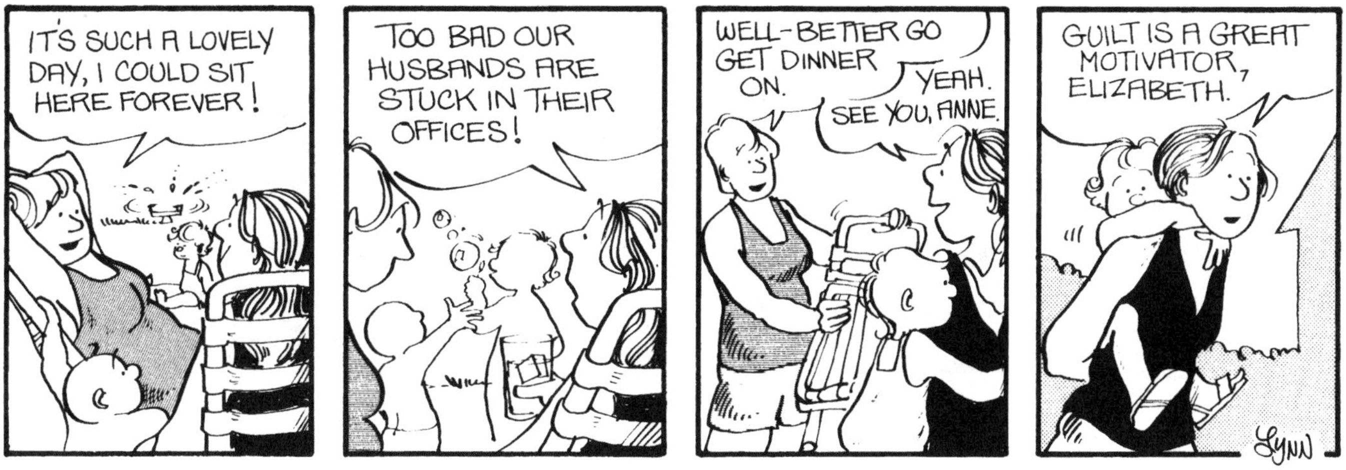
IT'S SUCH A LOVELY DAY, I COULD SIT HERE FOREVER!
TOO BAD OUR HUSBANDS ARE STUCK IN THEIR OFFICES!
WELL-BETTER GO GET DINNER ON.
YEAH. SEE YOU, ANNE.
GUILT IS A GREAT MOTIVATOR, ELIZABETH.
Lynn

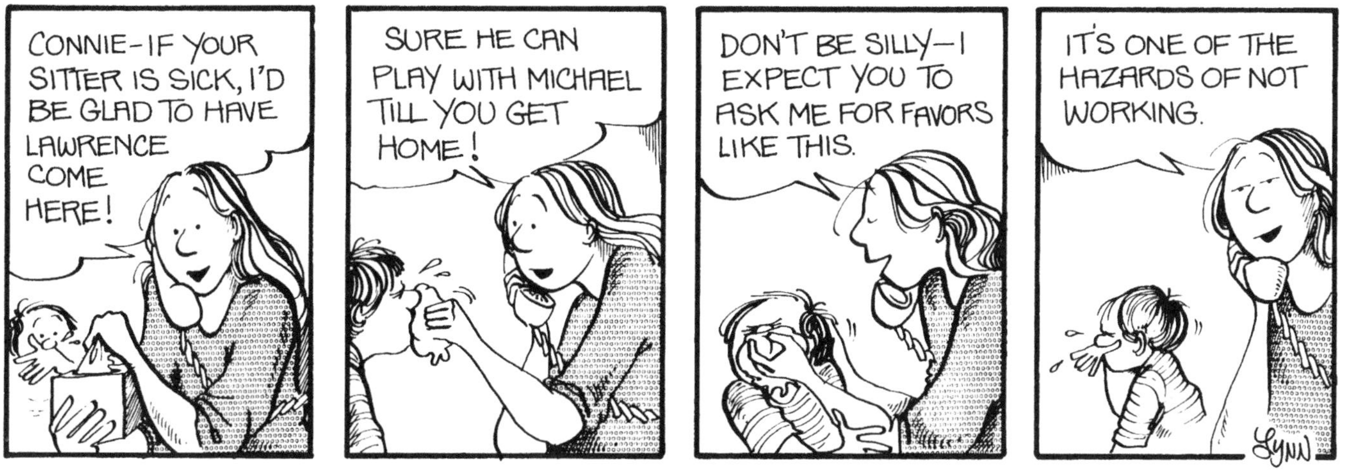
CONNIE-IF YOUR SITTER IS SICK, I'D BE GLAD TO HAVE LAWRENCE COME HERE!
SURE HE CAN PLAY WITH MICHAEL TILL YOU GET HOME!
DON'T BE SILLY—I EXPECT YOU TO ASK ME FOR FAVORS LIKE THIS.
IT'S ONE OF THE HAZARDS OF NOT WORKING.
Lynn

*

FOR BETTER OR FOR WORSE
By LYNN JOHNSTON
GOOD NIGHT, DR. P.!
GOOD NIGHT, JEAN. HAVE A GOOD WEEK END.
WHOA!..WHAT A WEEK!
Dr. J. Patterson DENTIST
AHHH...FRIDAY!!
CLICK!
I CAN ESCAPE FROM THE OFFICE FOR TWO DAYS!
NO PATIENTS, NO STAFF, NO BUSINESS HASSLES...
?!!!! ???
AHHHH...MONDAY!!
CHORE LIST
PAINT PORCH
FIX SANDBOX
FIX shower
FIX FENCE
LYNN


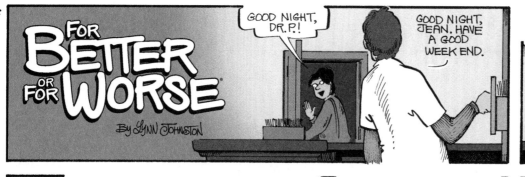

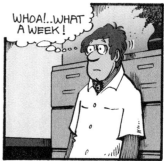

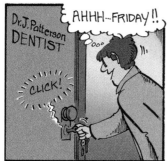

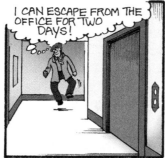

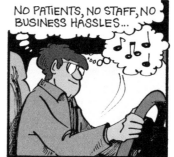

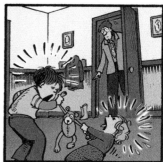

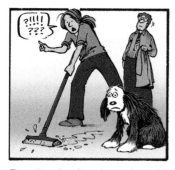

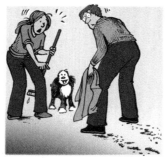

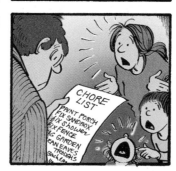

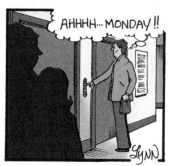

Despite the freedom of working in my studio downstairs, at my own pace, I envied those who left the confines of home to work in an organized space in the company of other adults. I knew that as much as my husband looked forward to Fridays, he was equally pleased when the weekend was over and he could escape to the serenity of the clinic! This strip was done recently, and was another reminder of how fast the time has gone by!

*

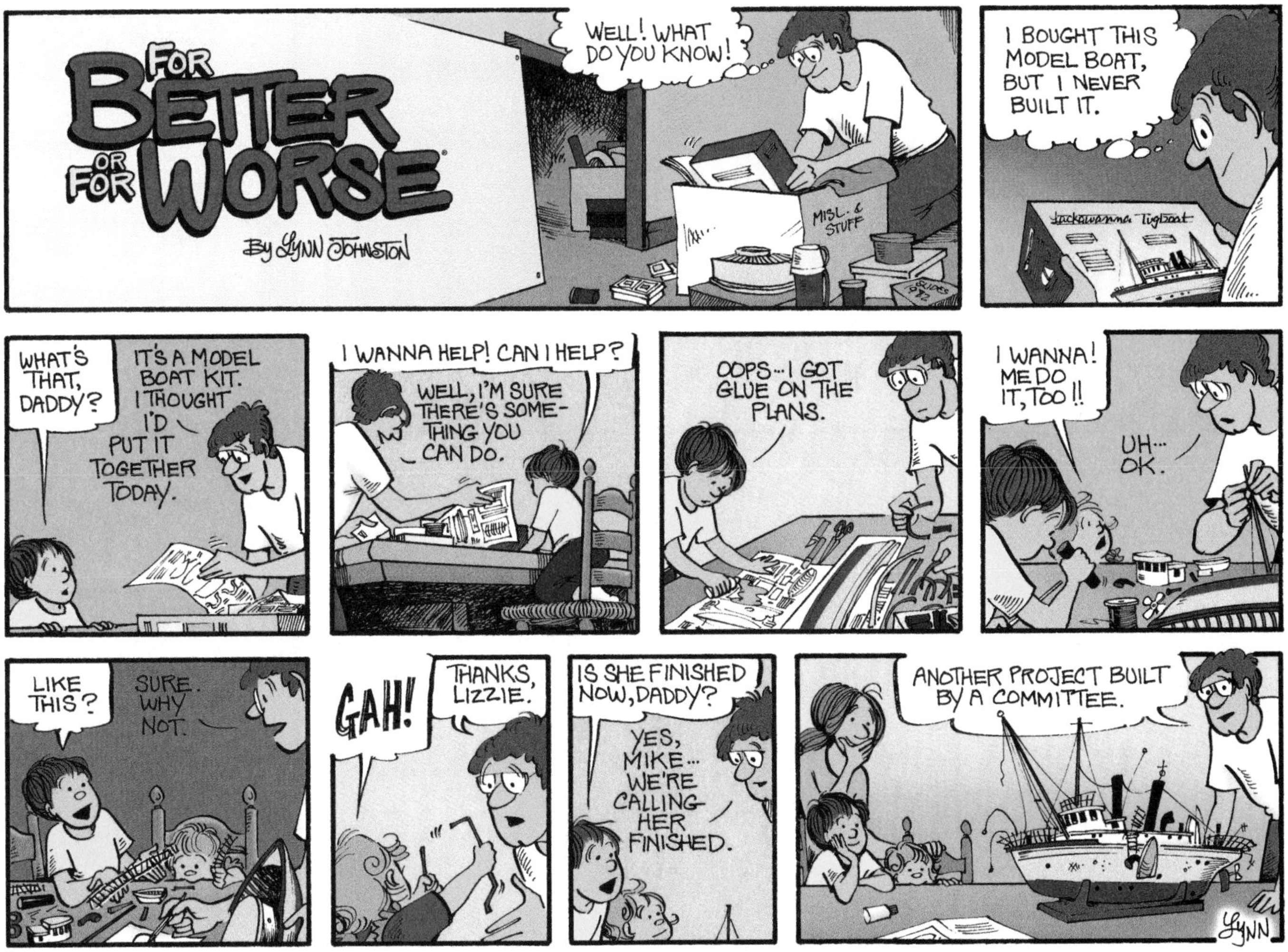
FOR BETTER OR FOR WORSE
By Lynn Johnston
WELL! WHAT DO YOU KNOW!
MISL. & STUFF
I BOUGHT THIS MODEL BOAT, BUT I NEVER BUILT IT.
WHAT'S THAT, DADDY?
IT'S A MODEL BOAT KIT. I THOUGHT I'D PUT IT TOGETHER TODAY.
I WANNA HELP! CAN I HELP?
WELL, I'M SURE THERE'S SOME-THING YOU CAN DO.
OOPS...I GOT GLUE ON THE PLANS.
I WANNA! ME DO IT, TOO!!
UH... OK.
LIKE THIS?
SURE. WHY NOT.
GAH!
THANKS, LIZZIE.
IS SHE FINISHED NOW, DADDY?
YES, MIKE... WE'RE CALLING HER FINISHED.
ANOTHER PROJECT BUILT BY A COMMITTEE.
LYNN

My husband was a model builder to the core. Every vacation meant looking first for an easy model to build; he even built a model plane while we were on our honeymoon. The challenge of putting the thing together was more important than the model itself, and many housekeepers have remembered our visits by the finished models left in our hotel rooms.

In teaching the kids how to build things, we had to abandon the idea that a finished model would actually look like the picture on the box, and some curious creations ensued. Today, Katie is the one with the patience to put stuff together. She learned a lot by watching her dad in his workshop.

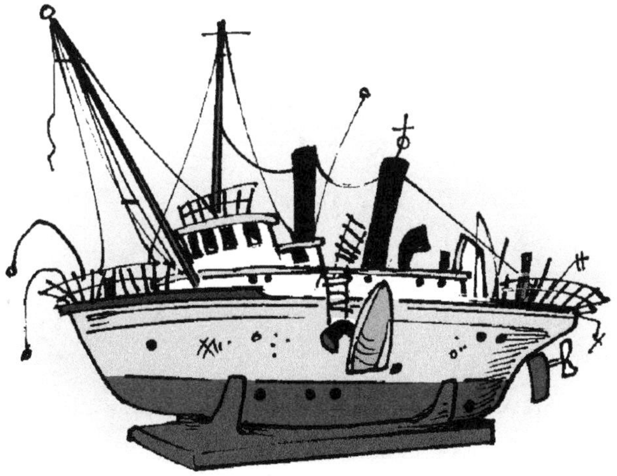

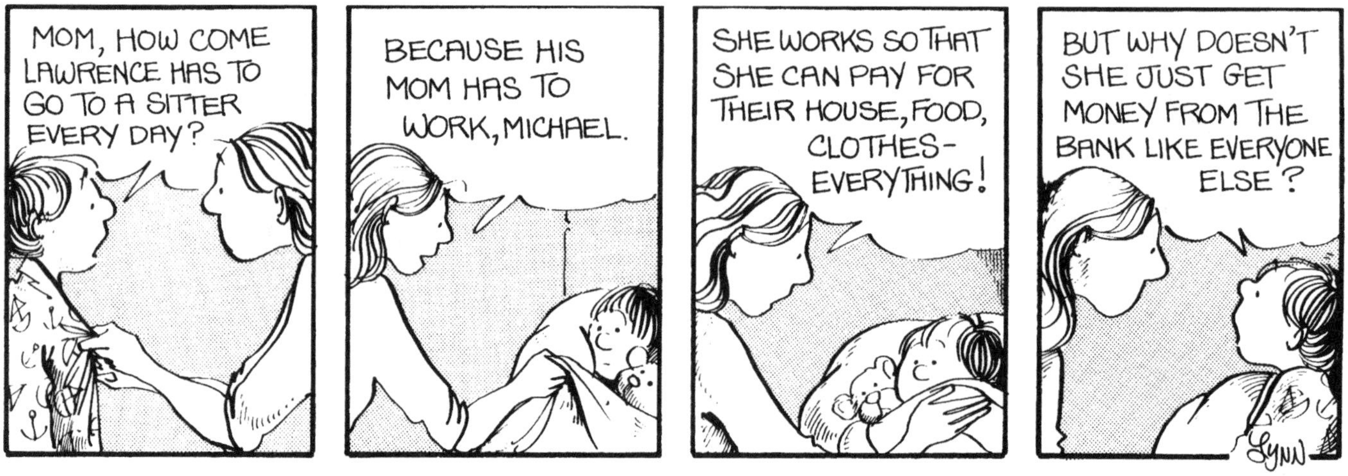
MOM, HOW COME LAWRENCE HAS TO GO TO A SITTER EVERY DAY?
BECAUSE HIS MOM HAS TO WORK, MICHAEL.
SHE WORKS SO THAT SHE CAN PAY FOR THEIR HOUSE, FOOD, CLOTHES- EVERYTHING!
BUT WHY DOESN'T SHE JUST GET MONEY FROM THE BANK LIKE EVERYONE ELSE?
Lynn

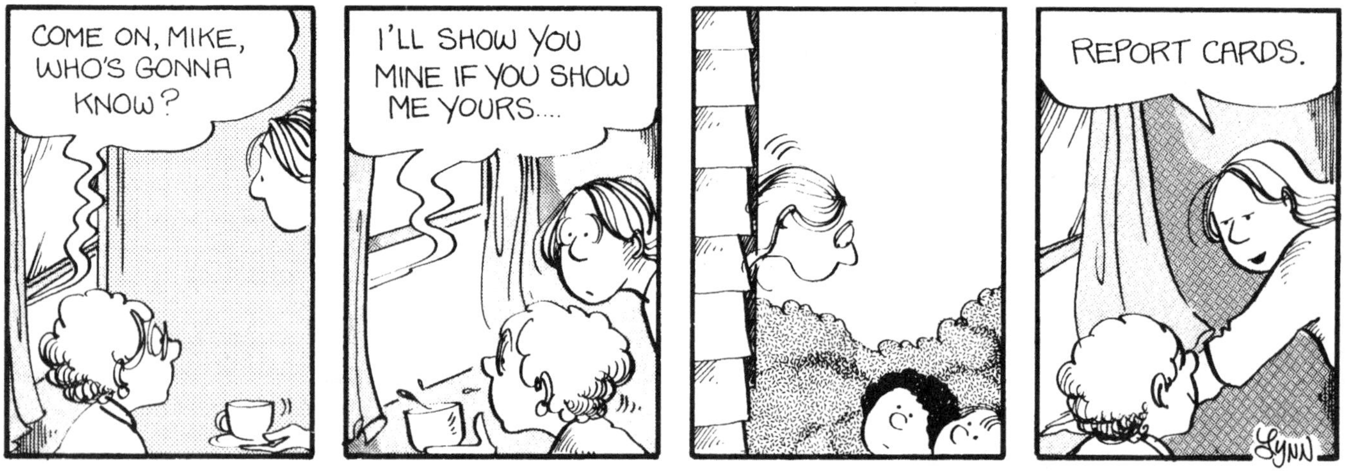
COME ON, MIKE, WHO'S GONNA KNOW?
I'LL SHOW YOU MINE IF YOU SHOW ME YOURS....
REPORT CARDS.
Lynn

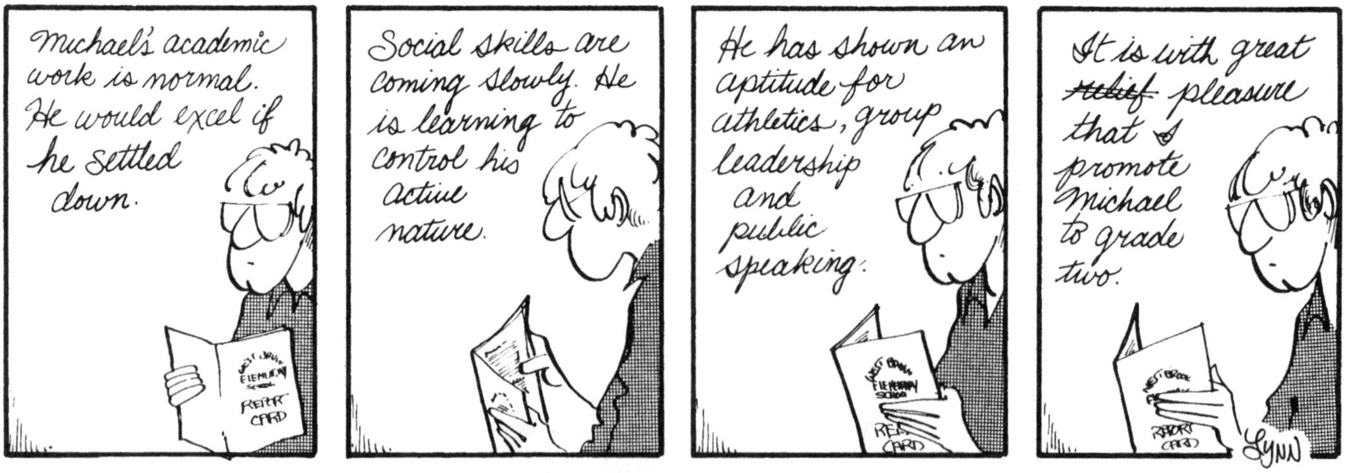
Michael's academic work is normal. He would excel if he settled down.
Social skills are coming slowly. He is learning to control his active nature.
He has shown an aptitude for athletics, group leadership and public speaking.
It is with great ~~relief~~ pleasure that I promote Michael to grade two.
Lynn

This was my report card. These remarks were typical of my teachers, trying to make sense of a kid who would rather fool around and show off than listen. I remember someone saying to me, "We're not laughing at you, we're laughing with you," and I thought, "Nuts! I want you to laugh AT me!!" The moniker "class clown" was not an insult, as far as I was concerned ... it was a compliment!

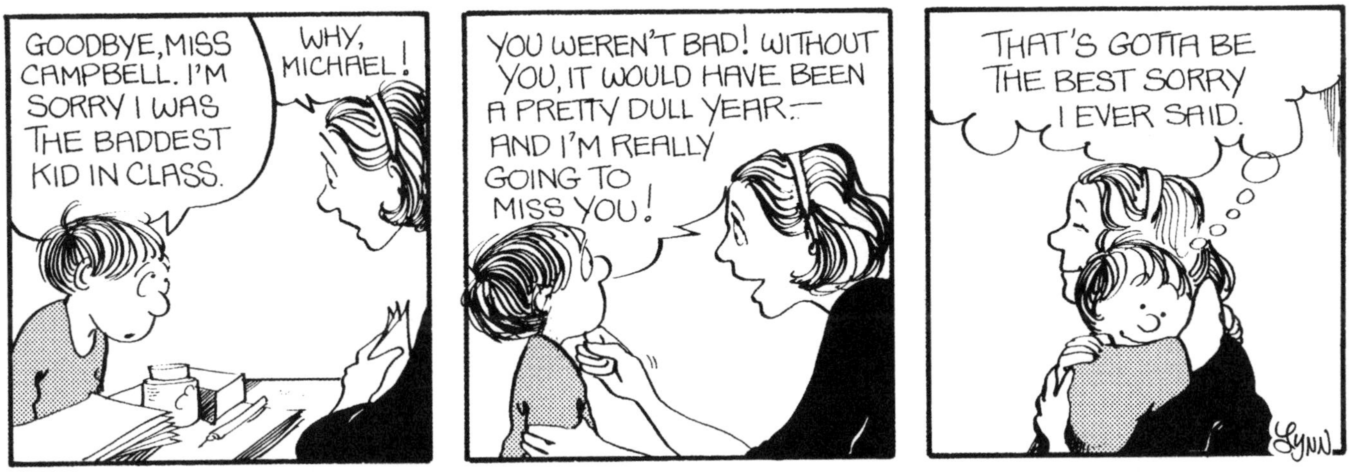
GOODBYE, MISS CAMPBELL. I'M SORRY I WAS THE BADDEST KID IN CLASS.
WHY, MICHAEL!
YOU WEREN'T BAD! WITHOUT YOU, IT WOULD HAVE BEEN A PRETTY DULL YEAR.— AND I'M REALLY GOING TO MISS YOU!
THAT'S GOTTA BE THE BEST SORRY I EVER SAID.
LYNN

Miss Campbell was my second-grade teacher. She was young, strict, and mean (I thought). I tried her patience at every opportunity, and in return, was punished: I was seated alone in the class, sent to the office, excluded from activities, and even sent home. On the last day of school, however, I cried, knowing I wouldn't be seeing her again. It surprised me when she cried and said she'd miss me, too! Maybe it was relief … but I rather think we had a sort of mutual affection!

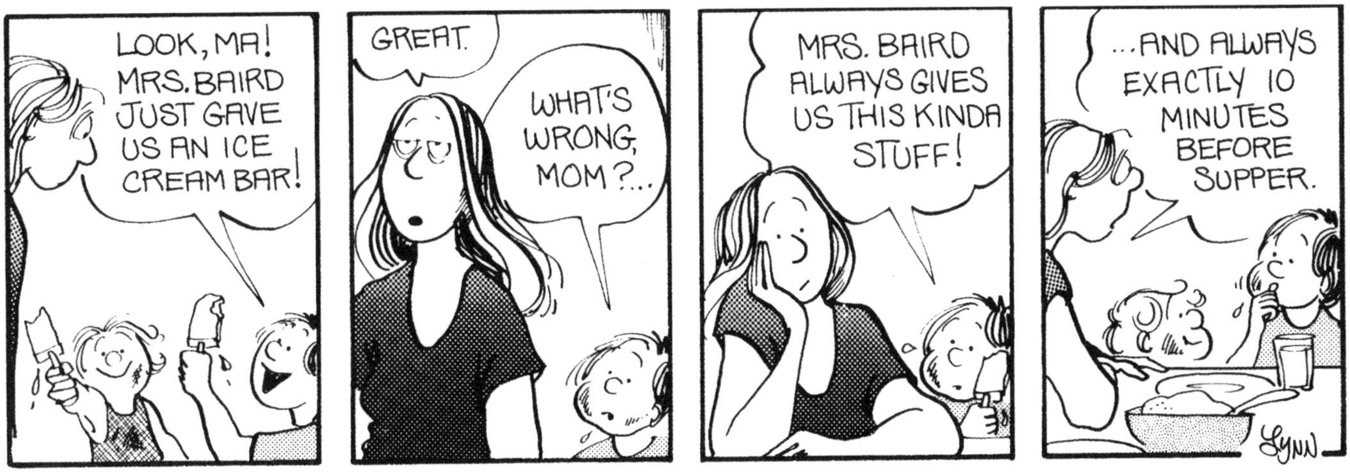
LOOK, MA! MRS. BAIRD JUST GAVE US AN ICE CREAM BAR!
GREAT.
WHAT'S WRONG, MOM?...
MRS. BAIRD ALWAYS GIVES US THIS KINDA STUFF!
...AND ALWAYS EXACTLY 10 MINUTES BEFORE SUPPER.
LYNN

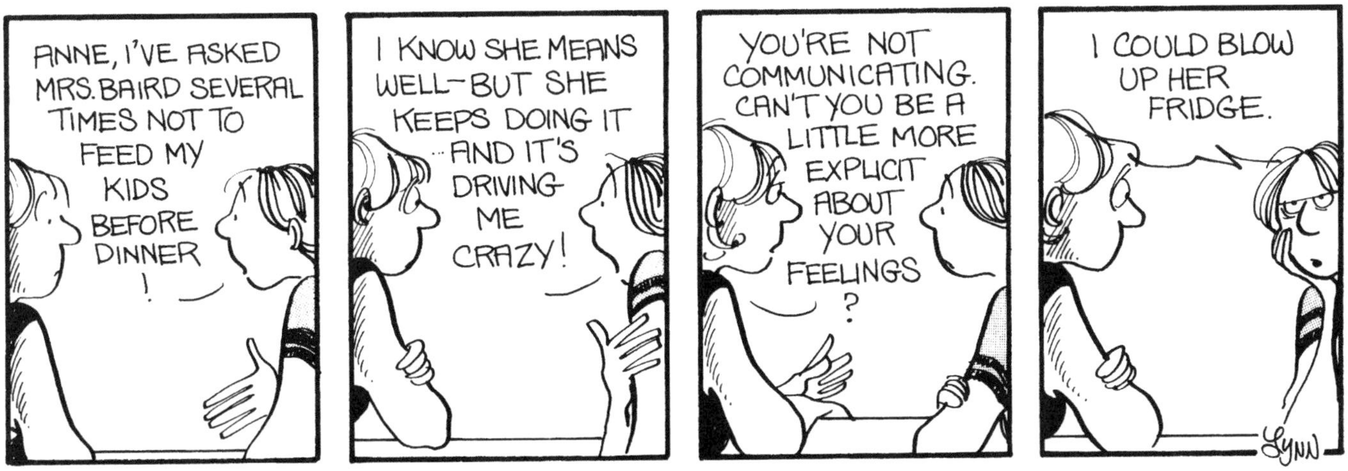
ANNE, I'VE ASKED MRS. BAIRD SEVERAL TIMES NOT TO FEED MY KIDS BEFORE DINNER!
I KNOW SHE MEANS WELL—BUT SHE KEEPS DOING IT ...AND IT'S DRIVING ME CRAZY!
YOU'RE NOT COMMUNICATING. CAN'T YOU BE A LITTLE MORE EXPLICIT ABOUT YOUR FEELINGS?
I COULD BLOW UP HER FRIDGE.
LYNN

*

FOR BETTER OR FOR WORSE
By Lynn Johnston
DIG DIG DIG DIG DIG DIG DIG DIG DIG DIG
WHAT DO YOU THINK?
LOOKIN' GOOD!
DIG DIG DIG DIG DIG DIG DIG DIG DIG DIG
MOM? IS IT POSSIBLE TO DIG THROUGH THE EARTH TO CHINA?
I'M NOT SURE, HONEY. IT'S A LONG WAY!
AND, BEFORE YOU GET THERE, YOU'LL HAVE TO DEAL WITH WATER AND ROCK AND THEN, THERE'S THE HEAT OF THE EARTH'S CORE!
YOU MEAN LIKE, VOLCANOES?
UH-HUH. THE MIDDLE OF THE EARTH IS LIKE A VOLCANO.
WHOA!
SO, IF WE DIG DOWN TO THE MIDDLE... IT WOULD ALL COME UP THROUGH THE HOLE?
SURE WOULD!
WOW. THAT SOUNDS PRETTY DANGEROUS.
YEAH! REALLY DANGER-OUS!!
COME ON!
... WE'D BETTER FILL IT IN!!
LYNN

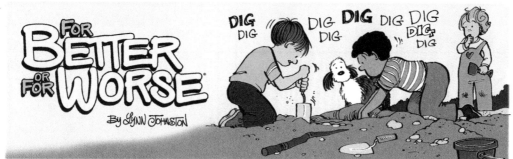

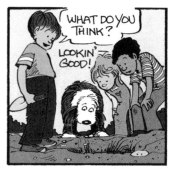

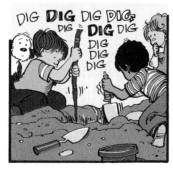

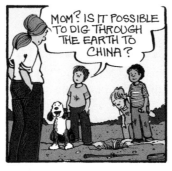

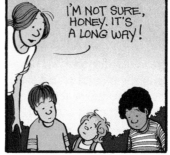

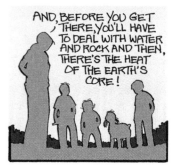

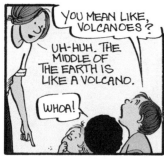

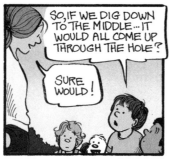

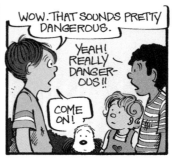

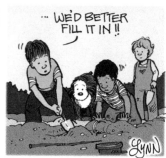

In our childhood home, there was a border of gravel between the sidewalk and the hedge that surrounded the lawn. This is where we built ant traps, played marbles, and dug holes. My dad told me I could dig to China, and so I diligently worked for most of an afternoon trying to get to the other side of the world. I readily bought into the fantasy he described of pagodas and dragons and chopsticks and tea. I was sad to discover he'd been pulling my leg. Later, I had the fun of talking my brother into digging for the same passage. "Kids!" I said to myself. "They'll believe anything!"

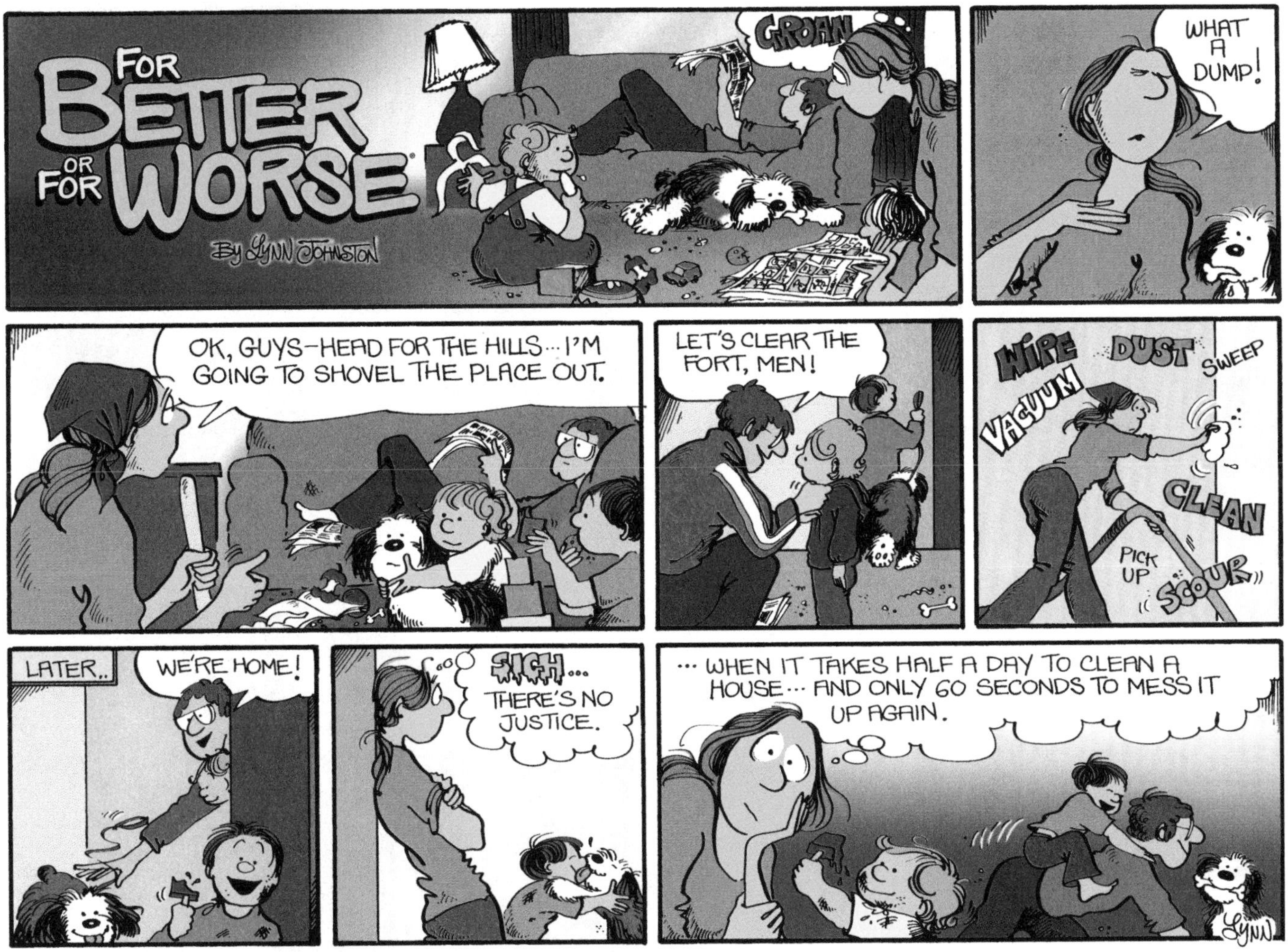
FOR BETTER OR FOR WORSE
BY LYNN JOHNSTON
GROAN
WHAT A DUMP!
OK, GUYS–HEAD FOR THE HILLS... I'M GOING TO SHOVEL THE PLACE OUT.
LET'S CLEAR THE FORT, MEN!
WIPE
DUST
SWEEP
VACUUM
CLEAN
PICK UP
SCOUR
LATER..
WE'RE HOME!
SIGH...
THERE'S NO JUSTICE.
... WHEN IT TAKES HALF A DAY TO CLEAN A HOUSE... AND ONLY 60 SECONDS TO MESS IT UP AGAIN.
LYNN

My mother had her own set of truisms, one of which was: "Put one person in a clean house, and in less than an hour, you'll have garbage." She was right. With four people in our house, it took seconds!

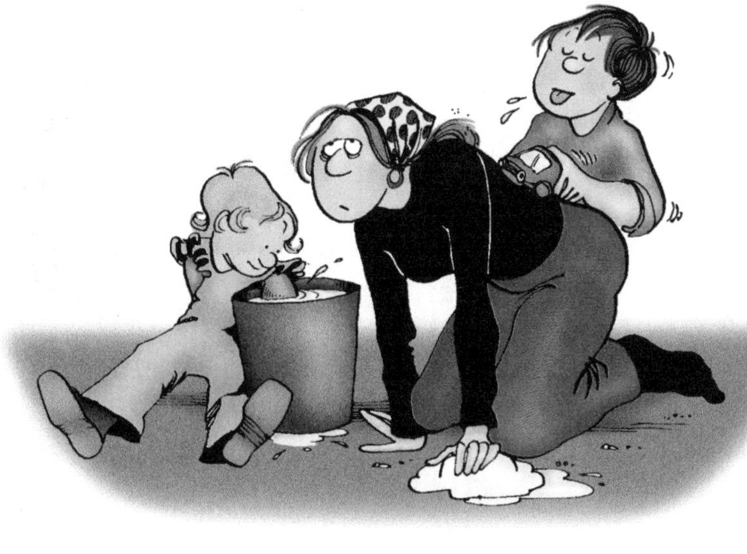

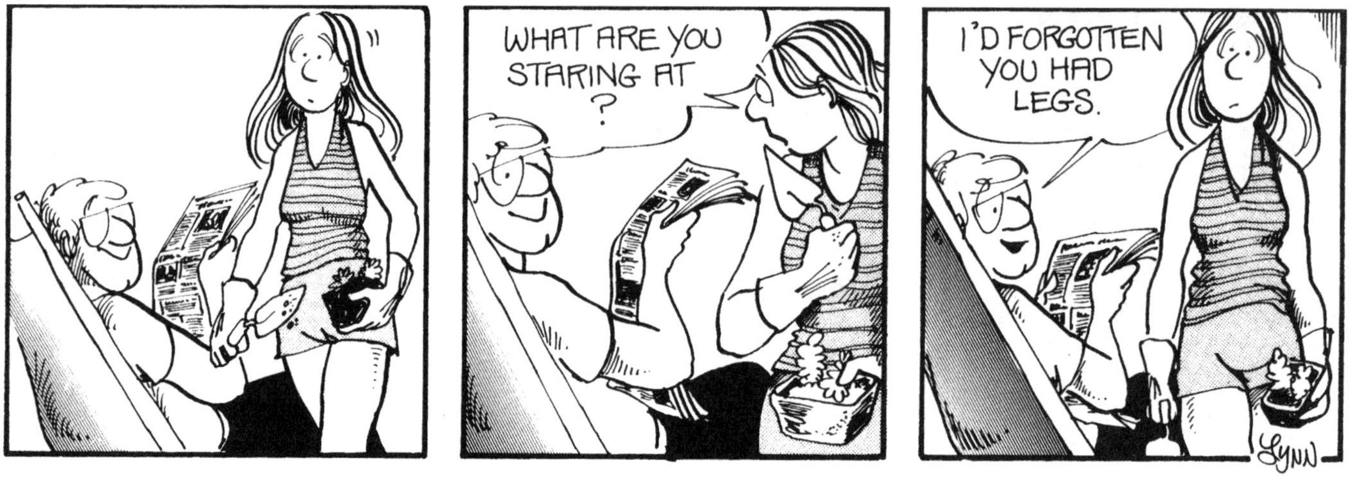
WHAT ARE YOU STARING AT ?
I'D FORGOTTEN YOU HAD LEGS.
LYNN

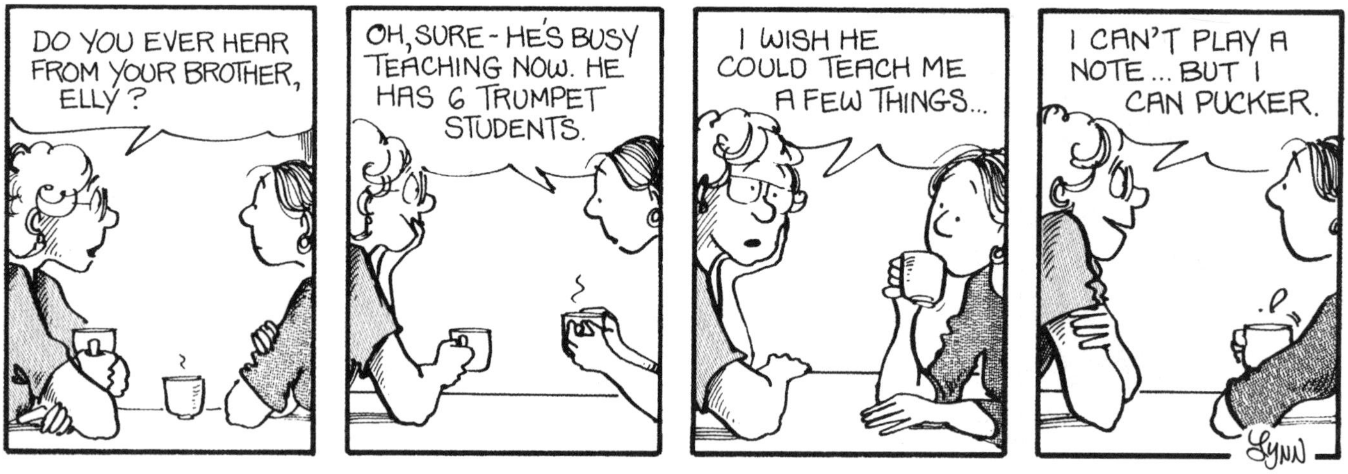
DO YOU EVER HEAR FROM YOUR BROTHER, ELLY ?
OH, SURE - HE'S BUSY TEACHING NOW. HE HAS 6 TRUMPET STUDENTS.
I WISH HE COULD TEACH ME A FEW THINGS...
I CAN'T PLAY A NOTE ... BUT I CAN PUCKER.
LYNN

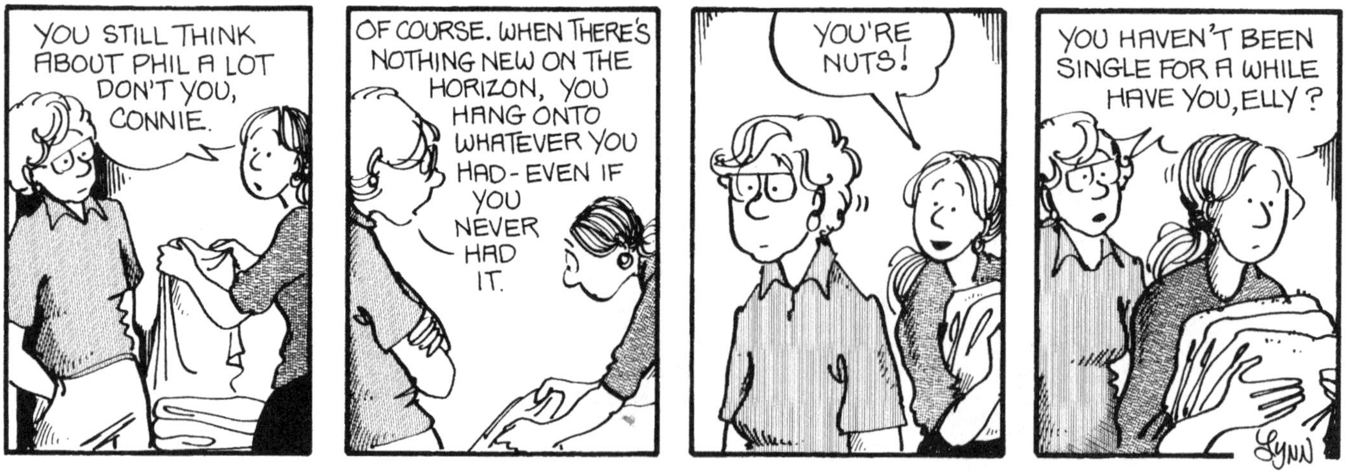
YOU STILL THINK ABOUT PHIL A LOT DON'T YOU, CONNIE.
OF COURSE. WHEN THERE'S NOTHING NEW ON THE HORIZON, YOU HANG ONTO WHATEVER YOU HAD - EVEN IF YOU NEVER HAD IT.
YOU'RE NUTS!
YOU HAVEN'T BEEN SINGLE FOR A WHILE HAVE YOU, ELLY ?
LYNN

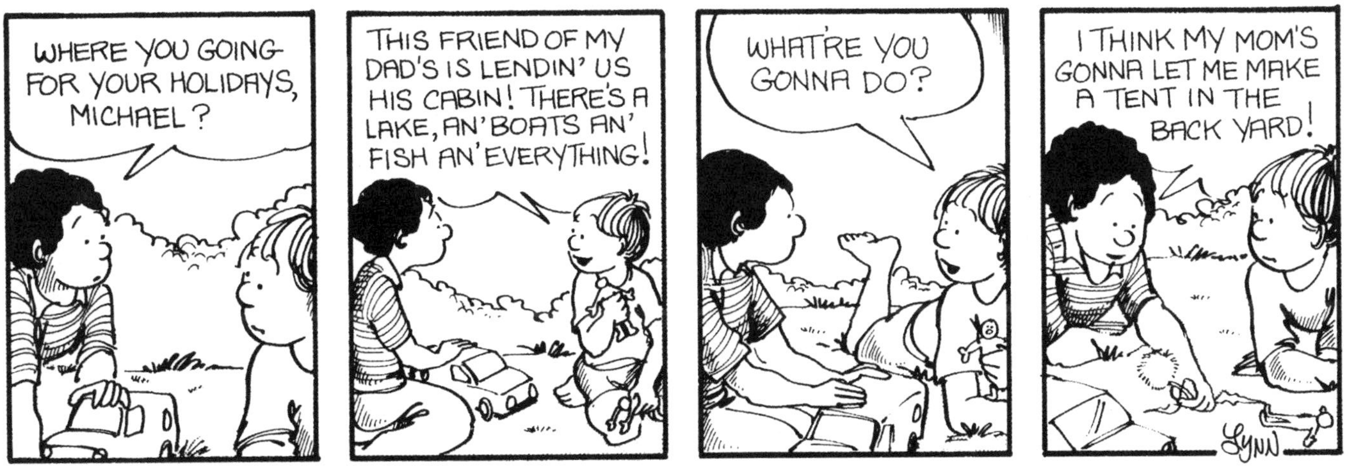
WHERE YOU GOING FOR YOUR HOLIDAYS, MICHAEL?
THIS FRIEND OF MY DAD'S IS LENDIN' US HIS CABIN! THERE'S A LAKE, AN' BOATS AN' FISH AN' EVERYTHING!
WHAT'RE YOU GONNA DO?
I THINK MY MOM'S GONNA LET ME MAKE A TENT IN THE BACK YARD!

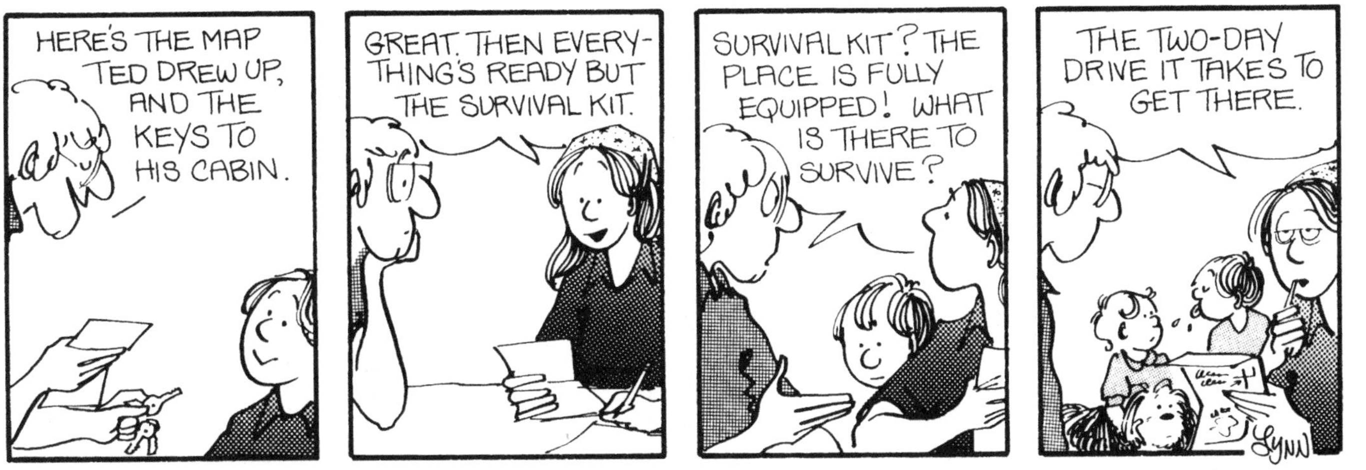
HERE'S THE MAP TED DREW UP, AND THE KEYS TO HIS CABIN.
GREAT. THEN EVERYTHING'S READY BUT THE SURVIVAL KIT.
SURVIVAL KIT? THE PLACE IS FULLY EQUIPPED! WHAT IS THERE TO SURVIVE?
THE TWO-DAY DRIVE IT TAKES TO GET THERE.

Memories of two old wooden cabins were the catalyst for this story: our cabin at Berge Lake, in Manitoba, and the summer camp where I went with my family when I was a kid. It was a small cabin on Bowen Island in British Columbia, where our parents took us for two weeks of every year. My brother and I learned to swim at Rocky Bay. We fished for bass from the bridge into town; dug for clams at low tide; and watched the ferry as it came into the harbour to see if we knew anyone on it.

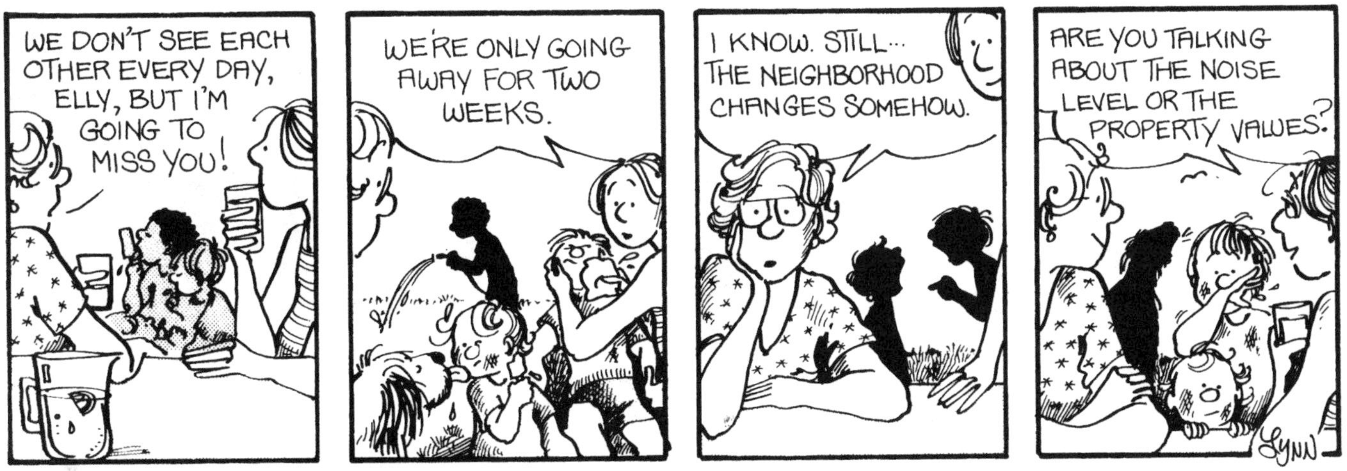
WE DON'T SEE EACH OTHER EVERY DAY, ELLY, BUT I'M GOING TO MISS YOU!
WE'RE ONLY GOING AWAY FOR TWO WEEKS.
I KNOW. STILL... THE NEIGHBORHOOD CHANGES SOMEHOW.
ARE YOU TALKING ABOUT THE NOISE LEVEL OR THE PROPERTY VALUES?

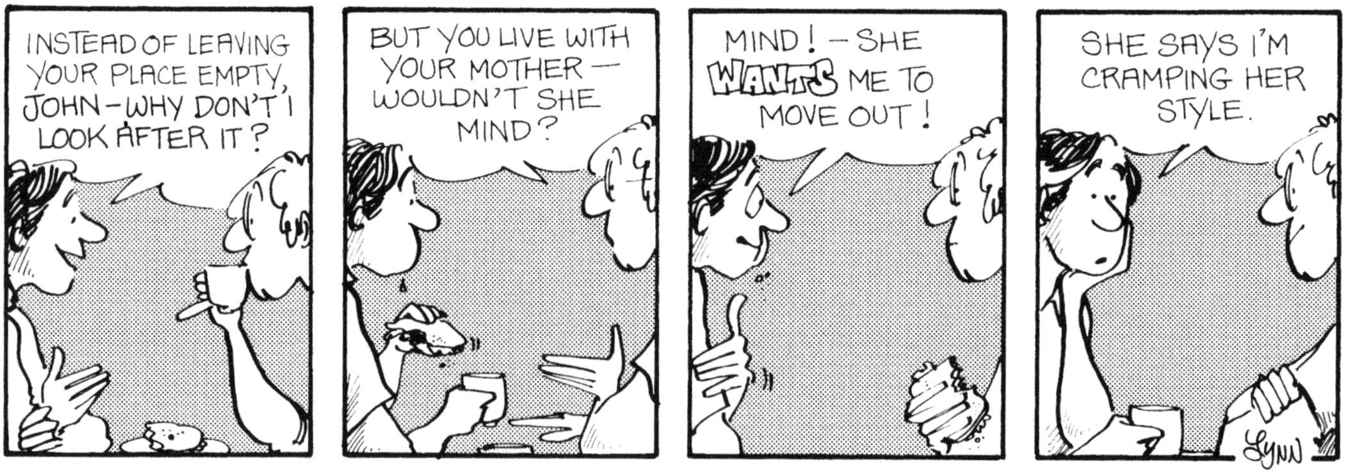
INSTEAD OF LEAVING YOUR PLACE EMPTY, JOHN – WHY DON'T I LOOK AFTER IT?
BUT YOU LIVE WITH YOUR MOTHER – WOULDN'T SHE MIND?
MIND! – SHE WANTS ME TO MOVE OUT!
SHE SAYS I'M CRAMPING HER STYLE.
LYNN

We did not borrow a friend's cabin, and nobody looked after our house while we were gone. This was a fictitious tale that all began with "What if?" What if the Pattersons went on a holiday? What if their cabin was a wreck? What if it was the wrong cabin? This all seemed to tie in with Ted and Connie, and a twisted tale began. Sometimes, imagination really does take over, and the writer is just along for the ride!

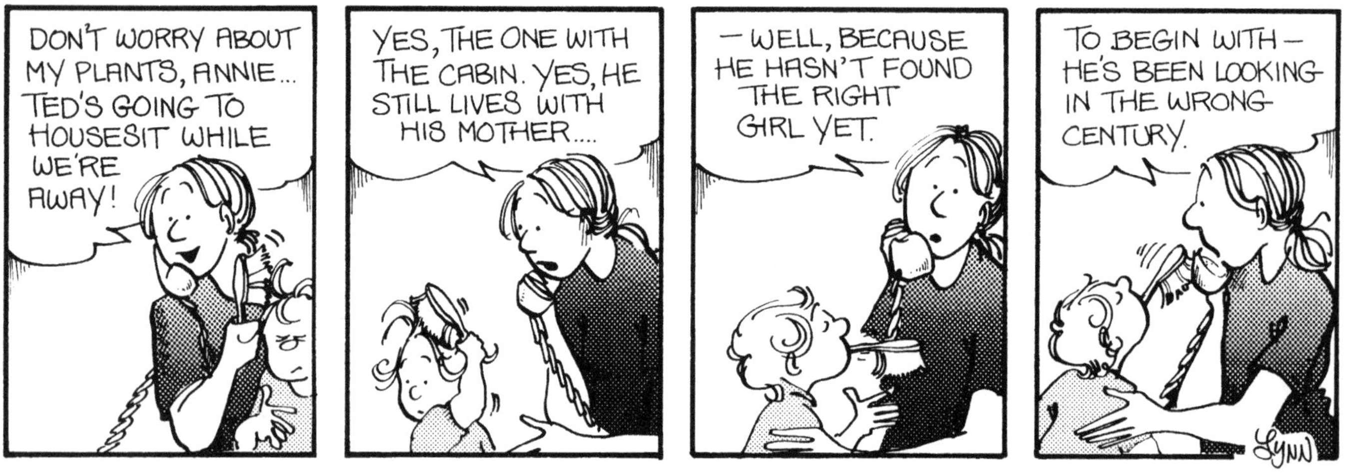
DON'T WORRY ABOUT MY PLANTS, ANNIE... TED'S GOING TO HOUSESIT WHILE WE'RE AWAY!
YES, THE ONE WITH THE CABIN. YES, HE STILL LIVES WITH HIS MOTHER....
– WELL, BECAUSE HE HASN'T FOUND THE RIGHT GIRL YET.
TO BEGIN WITH – HE'S BEEN LOOKING IN THE WRONG CENTURY.
LYNN

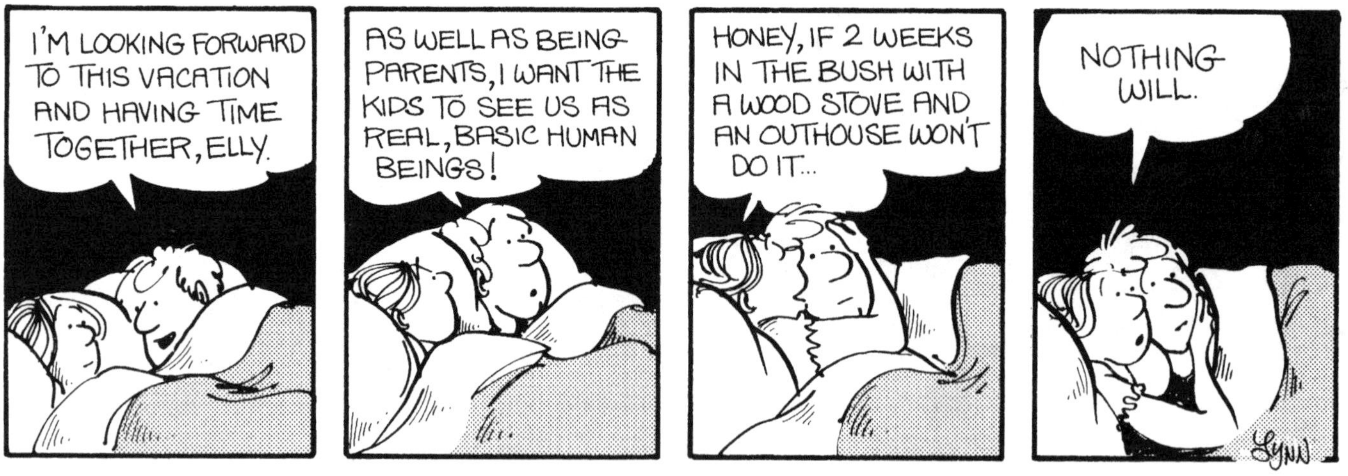
I'M LOOKING FORWARD TO THIS VACATION AND HAVING TIME TOGETHER, ELLY.
AS WELL AS BEING PARENTS, I WANT THE KIDS TO SEE US AS REAL, BASIC HUMAN BEINGS!
HONEY, IF 2 WEEKS IN THE BUSH WITH A WOOD STOVE AND AN OUTHOUSE WON'T DO IT...
NOTHING WILL.
LYNN

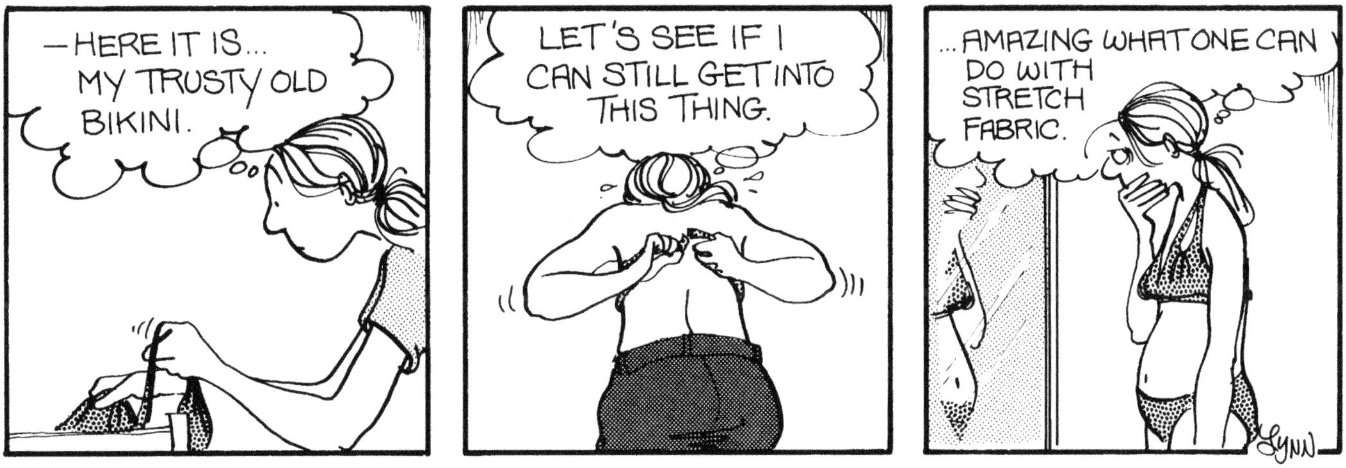

–HERE IT IS... MY TRUSTY OLD BIKINI.
LET'S SEE IF I CAN STILL GET INTO THIS THING.
...AMAZING WHAT ONE CAN DO WITH STRETCH FABRIC.
LYNN


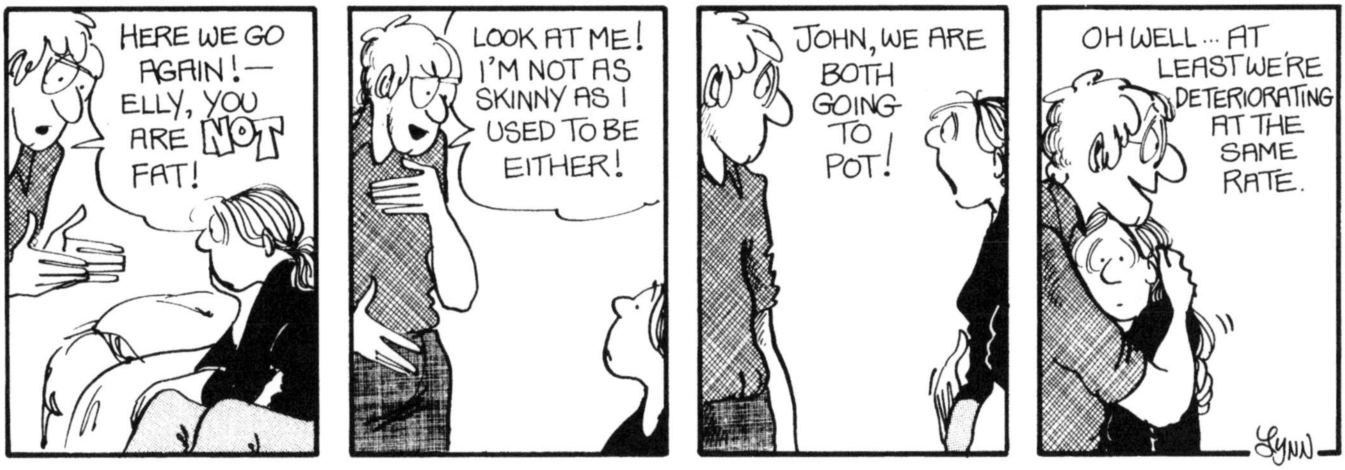

HERE WE GO AGAIN!— ELLY, YOU ARE NOT FAT!
LOOK AT ME! I'M NOT AS SKINNY AS I USED TO BE EITHER!
JOHN, WE ARE BOTH GOING TO POT!
OH WELL... AT LEAST WE'RE DETERIORATING AT THE SAME RATE.
LYNN


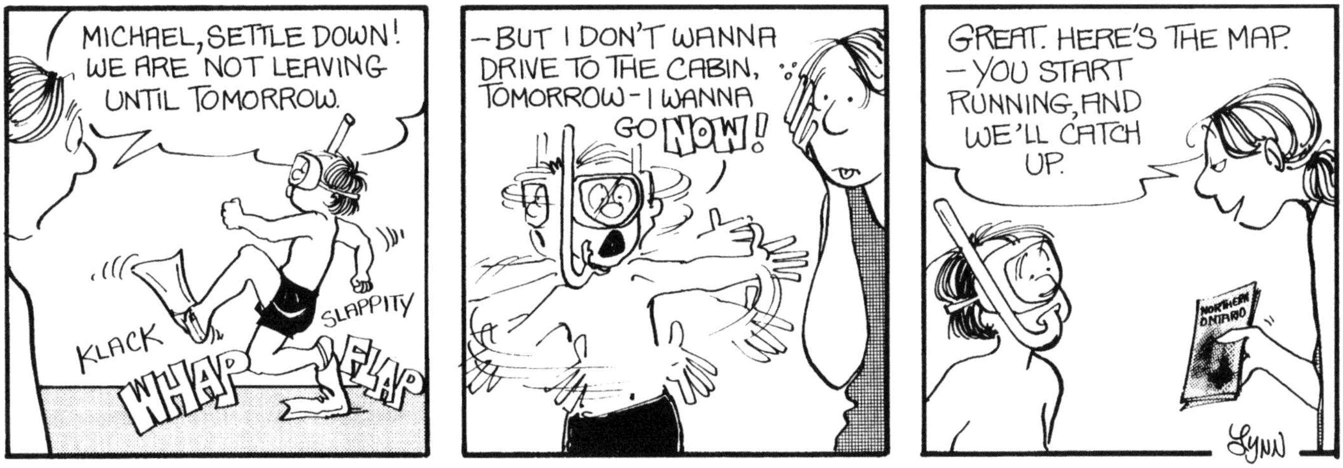

MICHAEL, SETTLE DOWN! WE ARE NOT LEAVING UNTIL TOMORROW.
SLAPPITY
KLACK
WHAP
FLAP
–BUT I DON'T WANNA DRIVE TO THE CABIN, TOMORROW – I WANNA GO NOW!
GREAT. HERE'S THE MAP. –YOU START RUNNING, AND WE'LL CATCH UP.
NORTHERN ONTARIO
LYNN

*

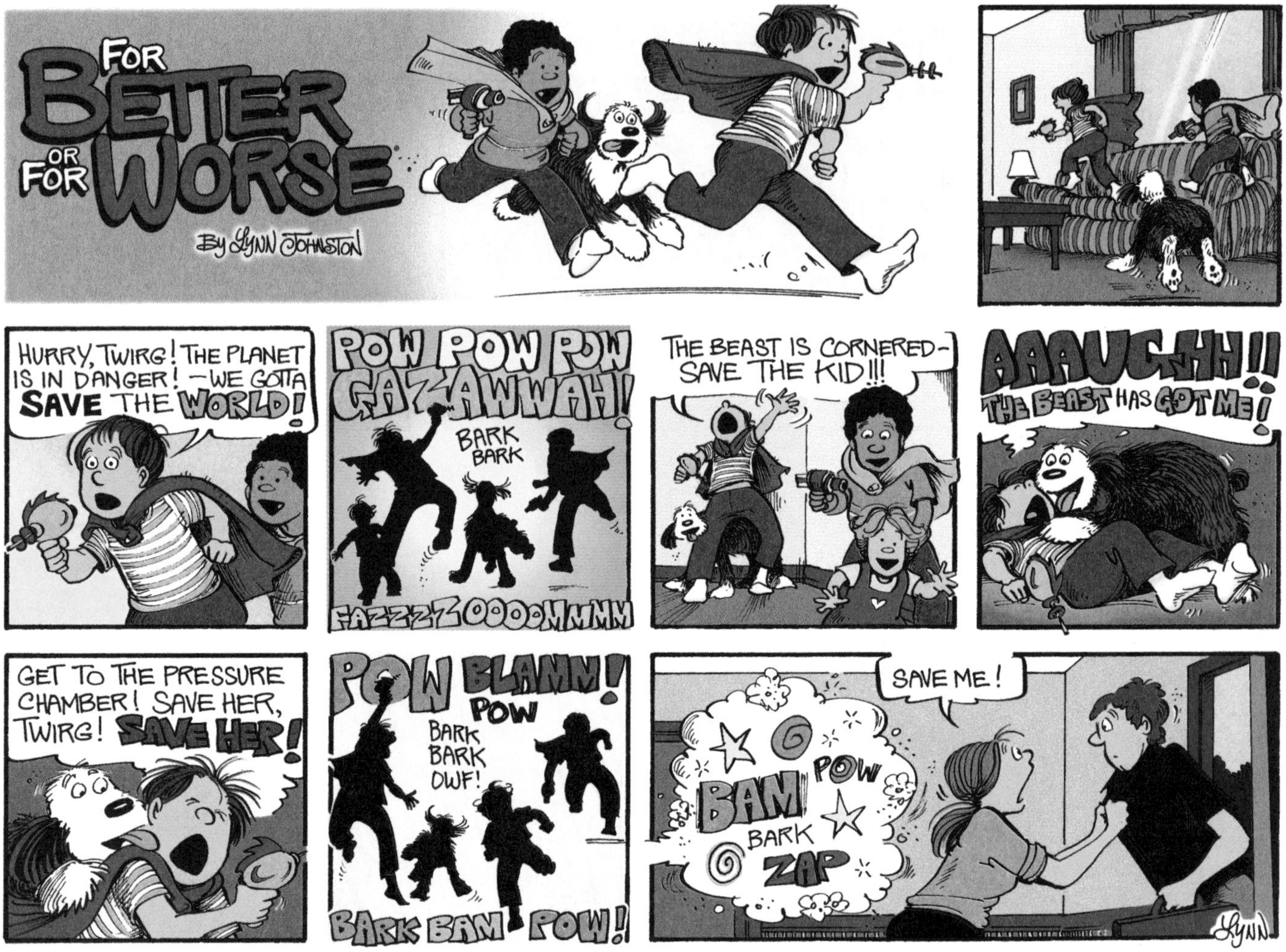

FOR BETTER OR FOR WORSE
BY LYNN JOHNSTON
HURRY, TWIRG! THE PLANET IS IN DANGER! —WE GOTTA SAVE THE WORLD!
POW POW POW POW
GAZAWWAH!
BARK BARK
FAZZZZOOOOMMMM
THE BEAST IS CORNERED— SAVE THE KID!!!
AAAUGHH!!
THE BEAST HAS GOT ME!
GET TO THE PRESSURE CHAMBER! SAVE HER, TWIRG! SAVE HER!
POW BLAMM!
POW
BARK BARK OWF!
BARK BAM POW!
SAVE ME!
BAM POW
BARK
ZAP
LYNN


Here is another Sunday full of sound effects, flying figures, and fun. What's great about doing a strip like this is "being a kid again"; getting into the situation as you write it, and then seeing it clearly as you draw it up. It doesn't take much for me to be this age, or to remember my son yelling "Kowabunga!" with his mouth full of Cheezies. I often enjoyed doing the Sunday page more than I did the dailies.

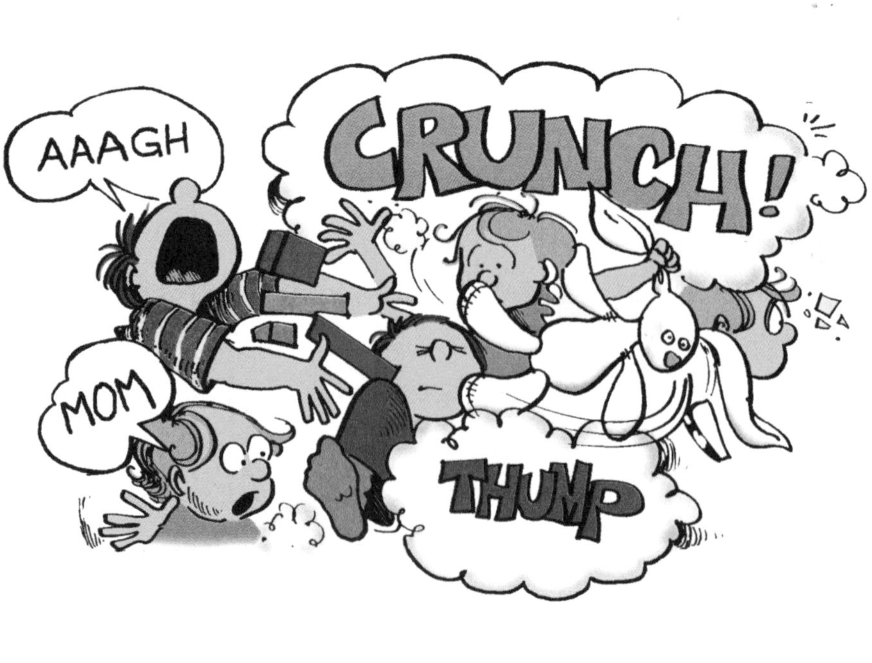

AAAGH
CRUNCH!
MOM
THUMP

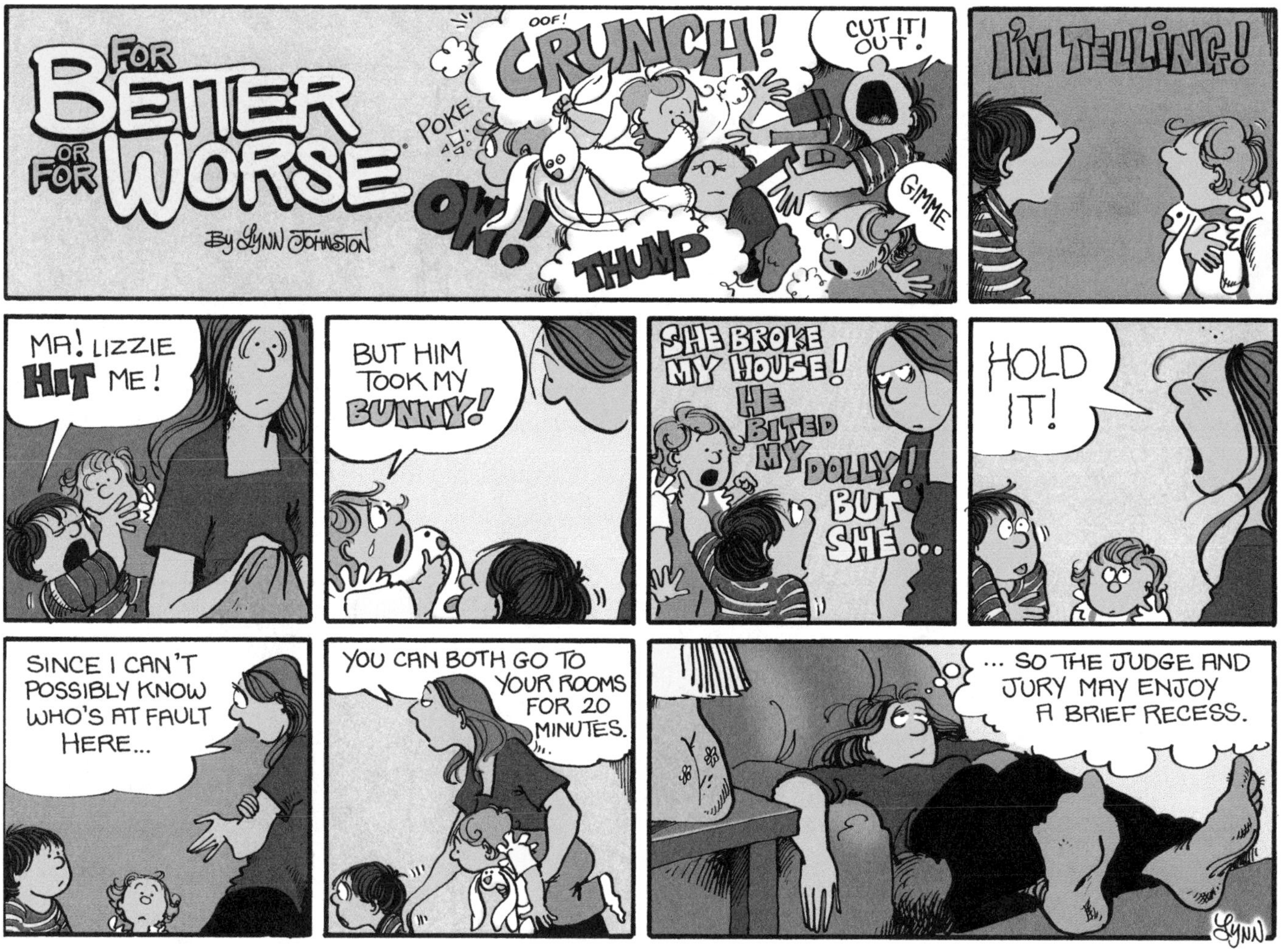
FOR BETTER OR FOR WORSE
By Lynn Johnston
OOF!
CRUNCH!
CUT IT! OUT!
POKE
OW!
THUMP
GIMME
I'M TELLING!
MA! LIZZIE HIT ME!
BUT HIM TOOK MY BUNNY!
SHE BROKE MY HOUSE! HE BITED MY DOLLY! BUT SHE...
HOLD IT!
SINCE I CAN'T POSSIBLY KNOW WHO'S AT FAULT HERE...
YOU CAN BOTH GO TO YOUR ROOMS FOR 20 MINUTES.
... SO THE JUDGE AND JURY MAY ENJOY A BRIEF RECESS.
Lynn

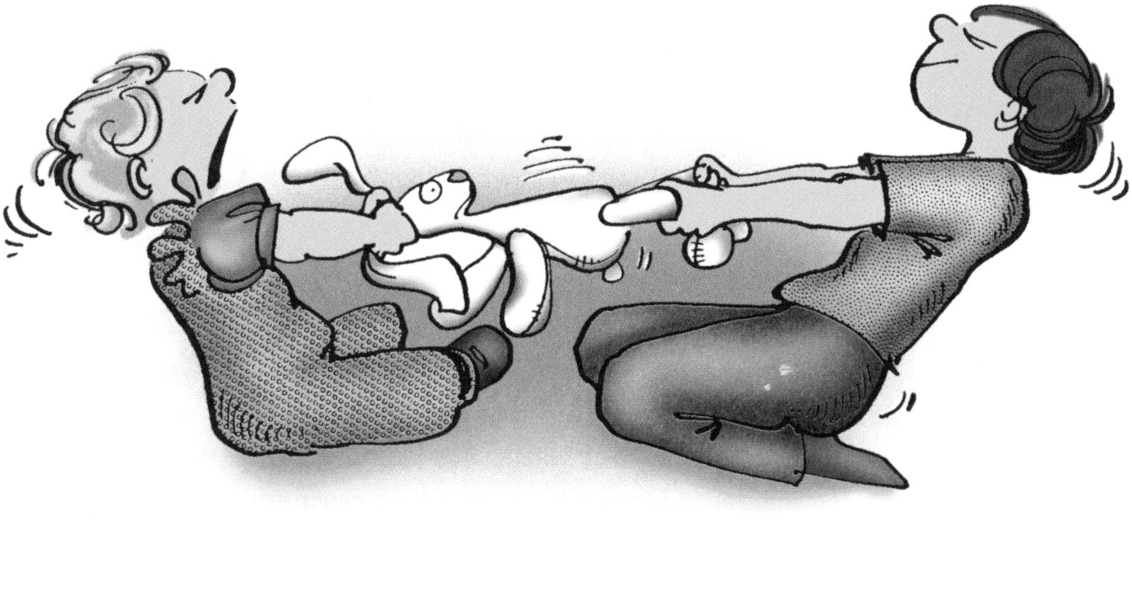

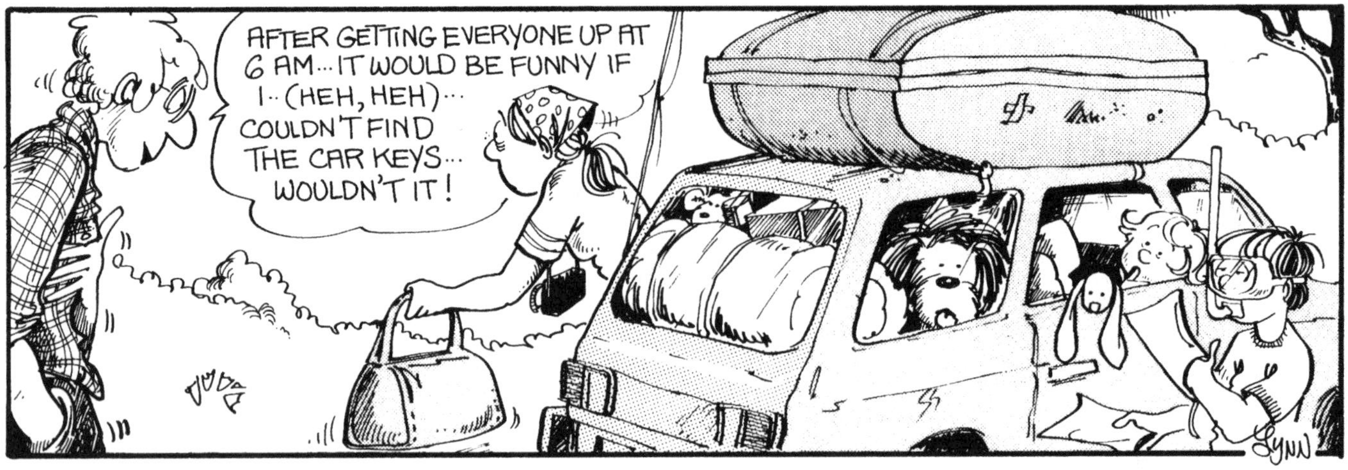
AFTER GETTING EVERYONE UP AT 6 AM... IT WOULD BE FUNNY IF I.. (HEH, HEH)... COULDN'T FIND THE CAR KEYS... WOULDN'T IT!

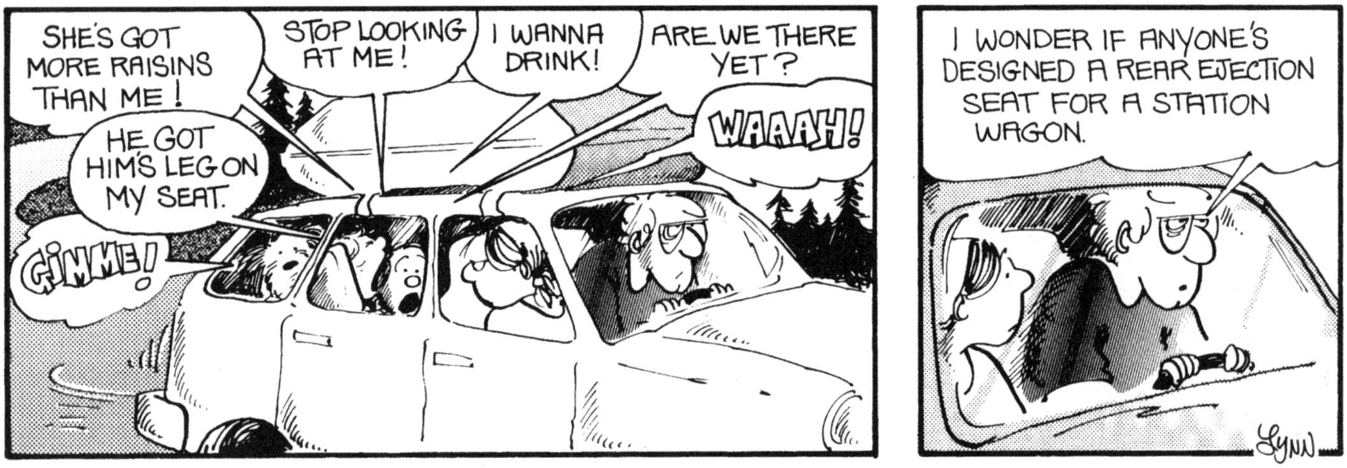
SHE'S GOT MORE RAISINS THAN ME!
STOP LOOKING AT ME!
I WANNA DRINK!
ARE WE THERE YET?
HE GOT HIM'S LEG ON MY SEAT.
WAAAH!
GIMME!
I WONDER IF ANYONE'S DESIGNED A REAR EJECTION SEAT FOR A STATION WAGON.

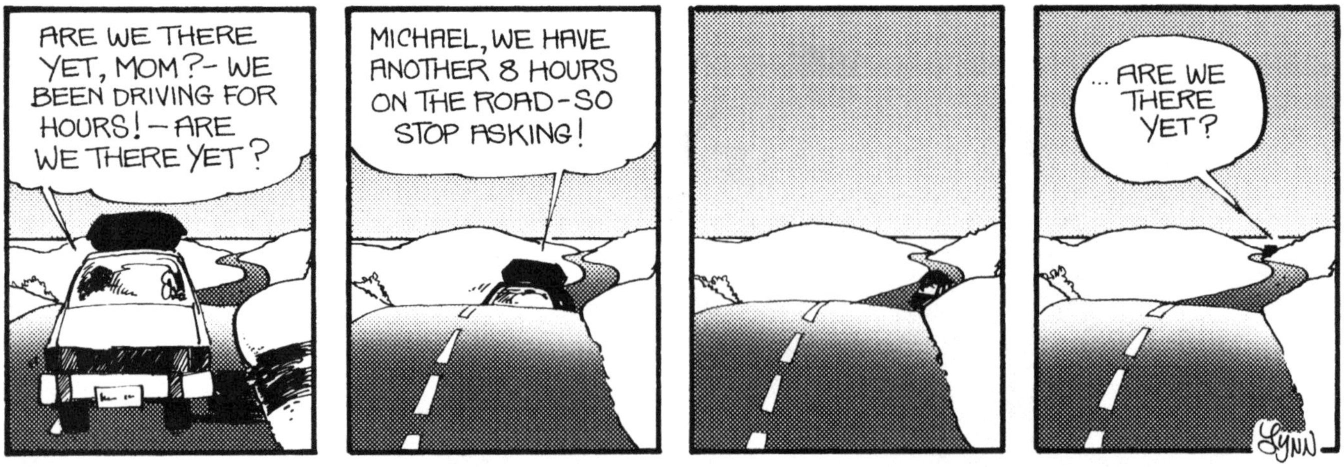
ARE WE THERE YET, MOM?- WE BEEN DRIVING FOR HOURS! -ARE WE THERE YET?
MICHAEL, WE HAVE ANOTHER 8 HOURS ON THE ROAD-SO STOP ASKING!
...ARE WE THERE YET?

This is the lonely dirt road between Thompson and Winnipeg, Manitoba. A three-hour drive made the occasional pit stop necessary, and if you could find a squat spot out of sight, you were golden. There was nothing but scrub brush and tag alders to hide one's hide, so privacy was at a premium. It's not just the family dog who craves a good solid tree now and then!

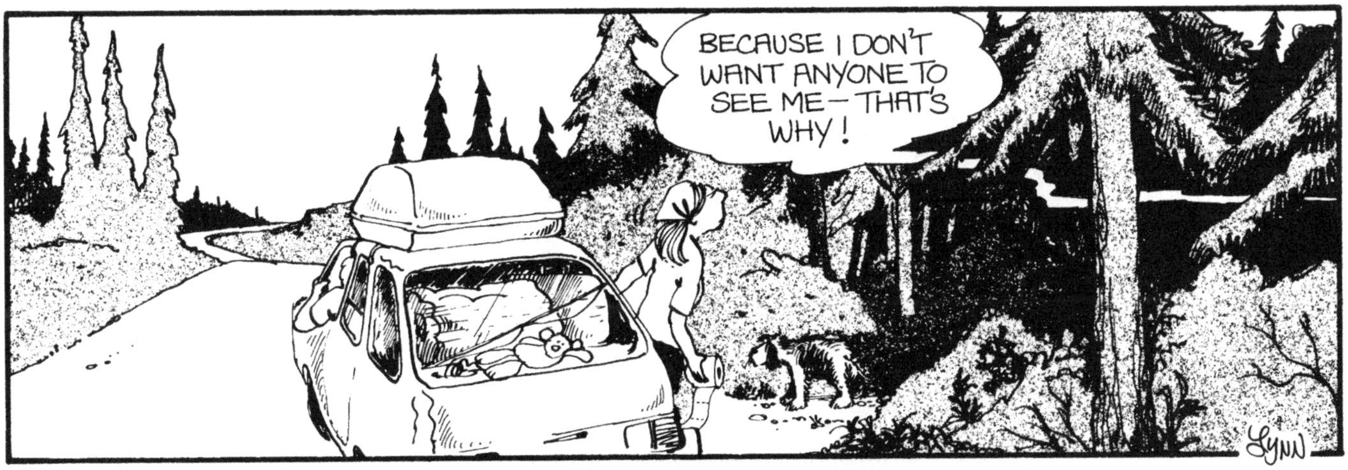
BECAUSE I DON'T WANT ANYONE TO SEE ME — THAT'S WHY!
Lynn

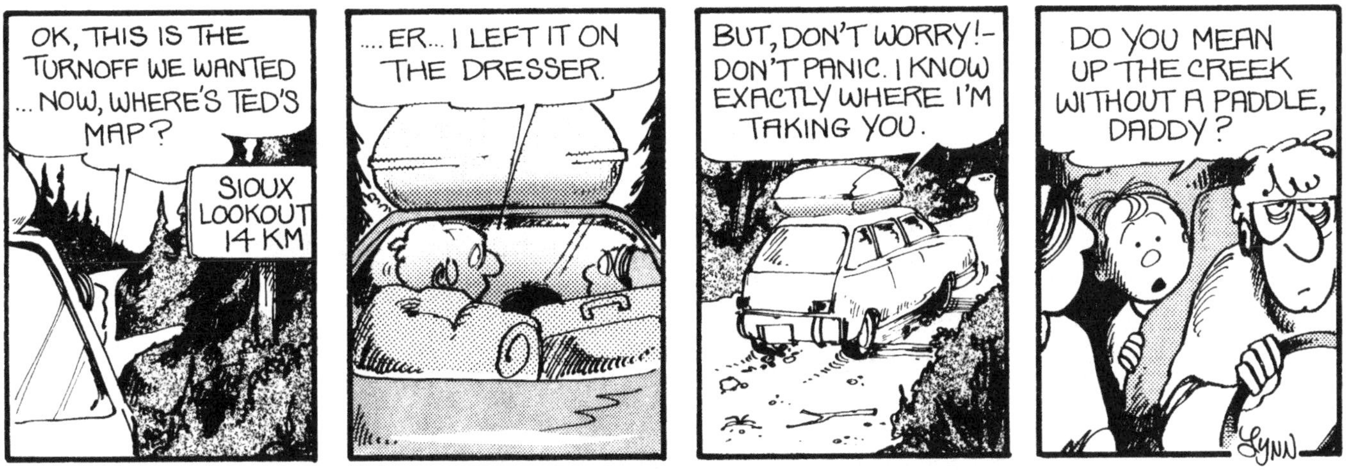
OK, THIS IS THE TURNOFF WE WANTED ... NOW, WHERE'S TED'S MAP?
SIOUX LOOKOUT 14 KM
.... ER... I LEFT IT ON THE DRESSER.
BUT, DON'T WORRY! - DON'T PANIC. I KNOW EXACTLY WHERE I'M TAKING YOU.
DO YOU MEAN UP THE CREEK WITHOUT A PADDLE, DADDY?
Lynn

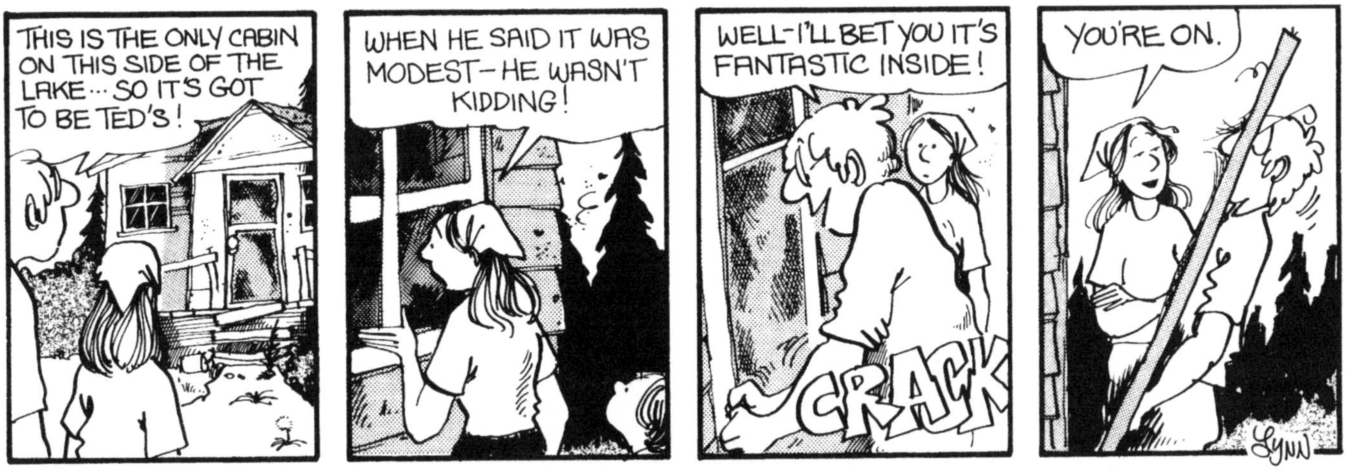
THIS IS THE ONLY CABIN ON THIS SIDE OF THE LAKE... SO IT'S GOT TO BE TED'S!
WHEN HE SAID IT WAS MODEST - HE WASN'T KIDDING!
WELL - I'LL BET YOU IT'S FANTASTIC INSIDE!
CRACK
YOU'RE ON.
Lynn

Our cabin at Berge Lake was the perfect place to stage a comedy. The shack was called a "12 x 20," it had been a miner's shack, and was a work in progress as we replaced everything from window frames to flooring only to find something else was rotting underneath. The great advantage to living in a shack was that nothing mattered. Here, I could watch sand falling off sandals, and I didn't care at all.

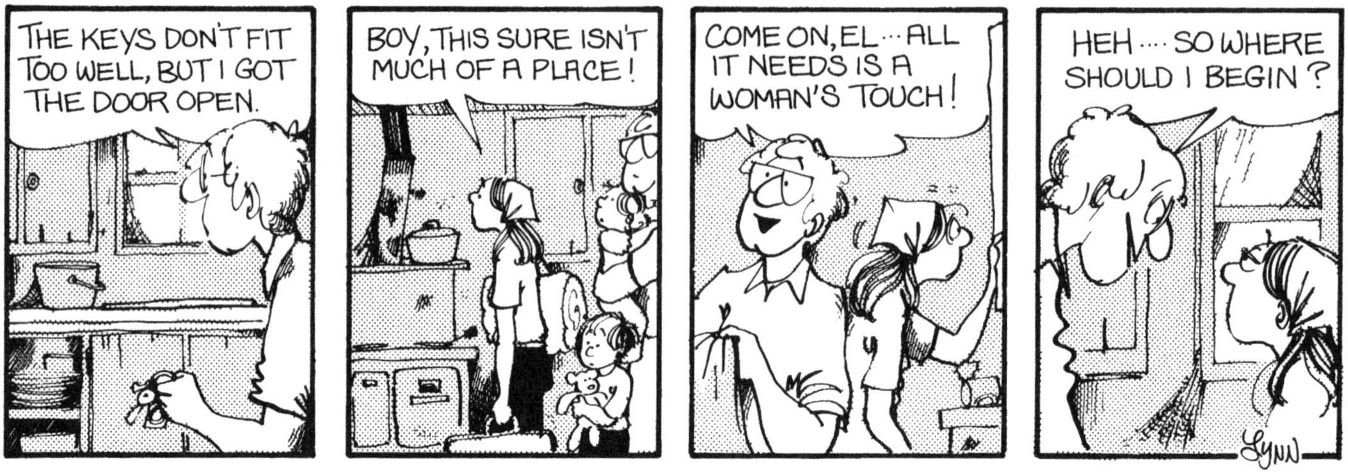
THE KEYS DON'T FIT TOO WELL, BUT I GOT THE DOOR OPEN.
BOY, THIS SURE ISN'T MUCH OF A PLACE!
COME ON, EL... ALL IT NEEDS IS A WOMAN'S TOUCH!
HEH.... SO WHERE SHOULD I BEGIN?
Lynn

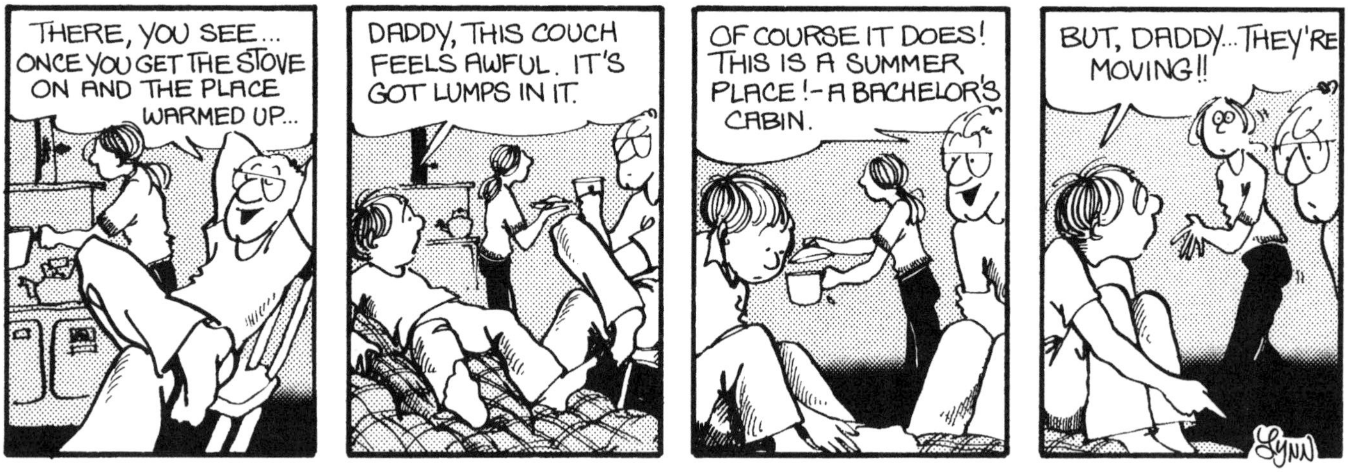
THERE, YOU SEE... ONCE YOU GET THE STOVE ON AND THE PLACE WARMED UP...
DADDY, THIS COUCH FEELS AWFUL. IT'S GOT LUMPS IN IT.
OF COURSE IT DOES! THIS IS A SUMMER PLACE! - A BACHELOR'S CABIN.
BUT, DADDY... THEY'RE MOVING!!
Lynn

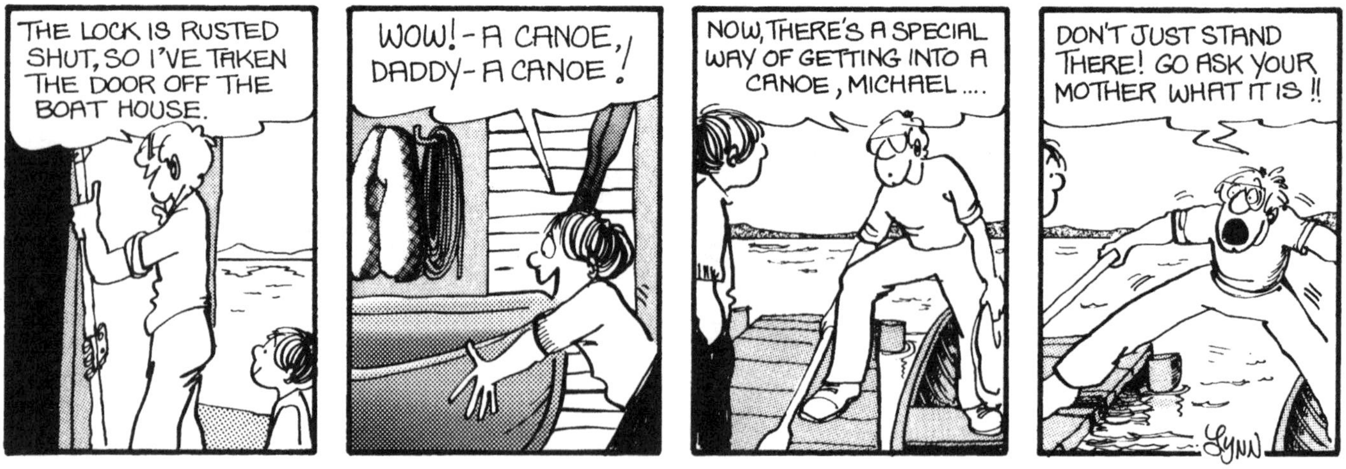
THE LOCK IS RUSTED SHUT, SO I'VE TAKEN THE DOOR OFF THE BOAT HOUSE.
WOW! - A CANOE, DADDY - A CANOE!
NOW, THERE'S A SPECIAL WAY OF GETTING INTO A CANOE, MICHAEL....
DON'T JUST STAND THERE! GO ASK YOUR MOTHER WHAT IT IS!!
Lynn

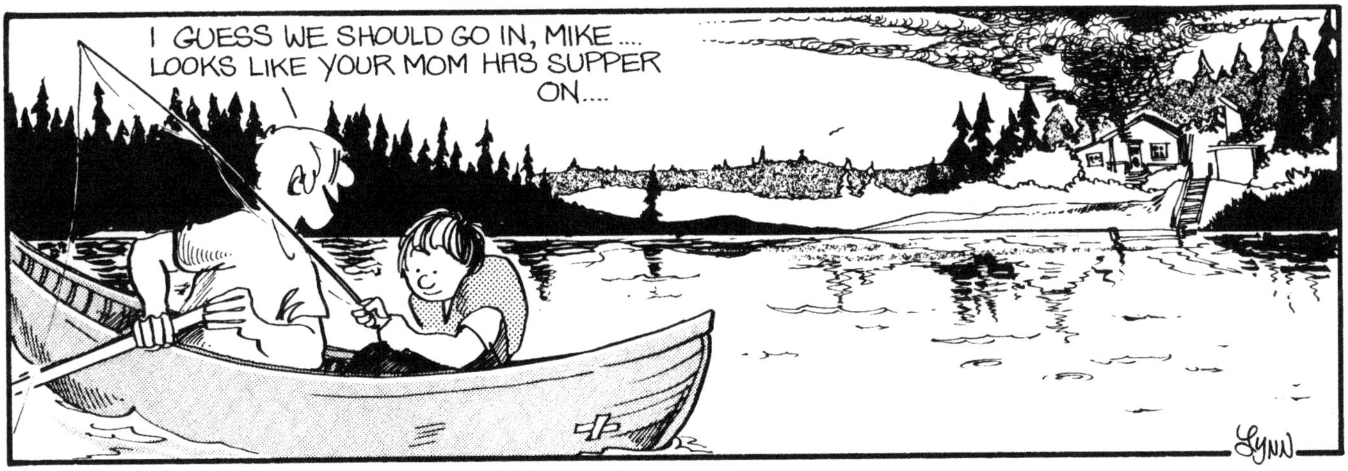
I GUESS WE SHOULD GO IN, MIKE....
LOOKS LIKE YOUR MOM HAS SUPPER ON....
LYNN

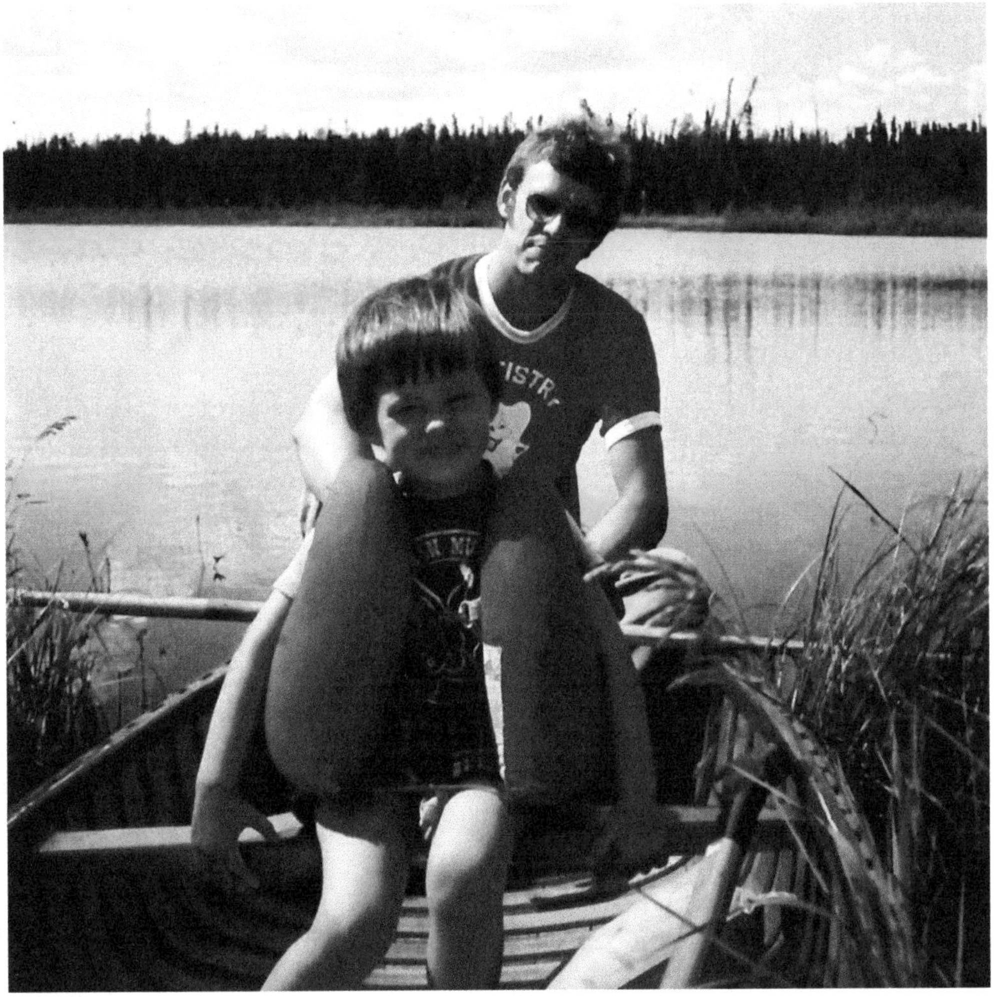

Aaron and Rod canoeing in Manitoba.

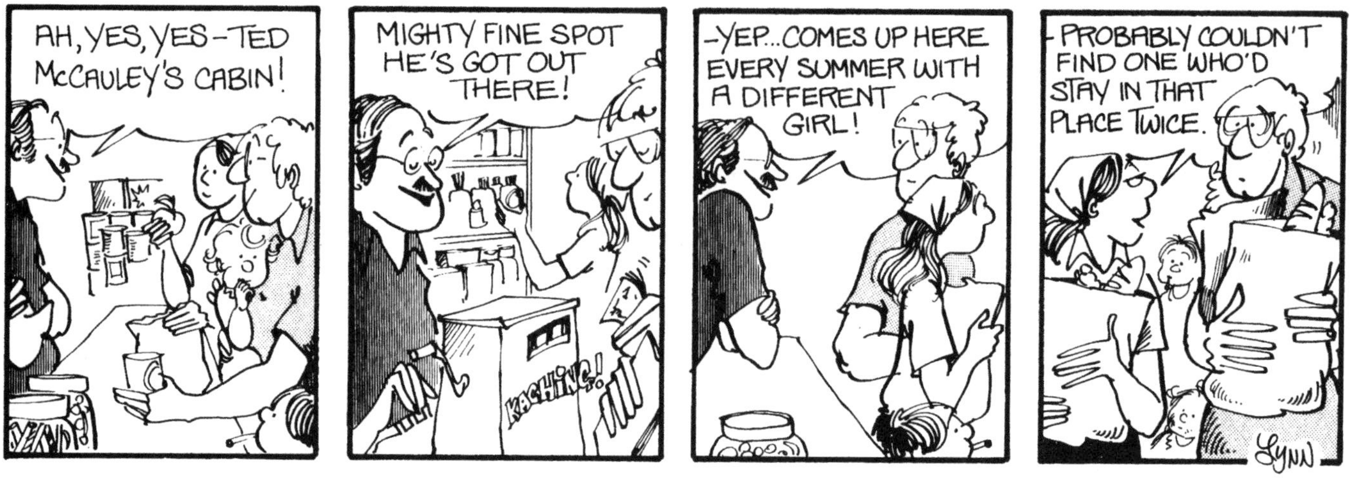
AH, YES, YES–TED McCAULEY'S CABIN!
MIGHTY FINE SPOT HE'S GOT OUT THERE!
KACHING!
–YEP...COMES UP HERE EVERY SUMMER WITH A DIFFERENT GIRL!
–PROBABLY COULDN'T FIND ONE WHO'D STAY IN THAT PLACE TWICE.
LYNN

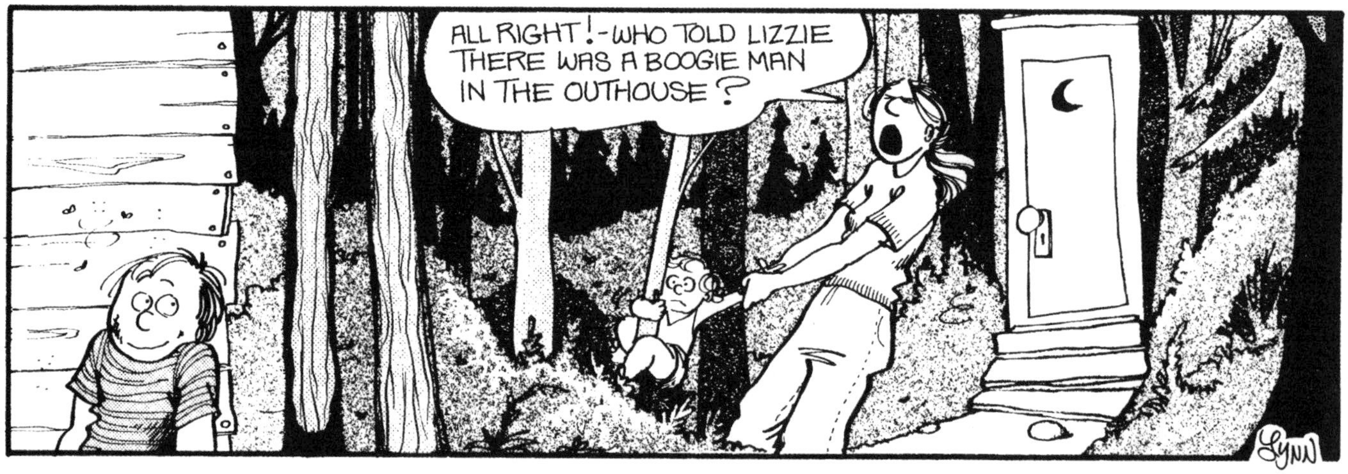
ALL RIGHT!–WHO TOLD LIZZIE THERE WAS A BOOGIE MAN IN THE OUTHOUSE?
LYNN

We had an outhouse at our cabin and, thanks to Aaron, Katie believed there were spooks inside. When we salvaged an electric toilet (dubbed the "wonder-biff") from the town dump, we were thrilled to have indoor facilities, until we discovered why it had been discarded. Apparently, the drying element inside had gone berserk, and had burned the backside of the previous owner. This made for a good laugh. We were cautious using the biff after that and, in the end, the kids were happier using the outhouse.

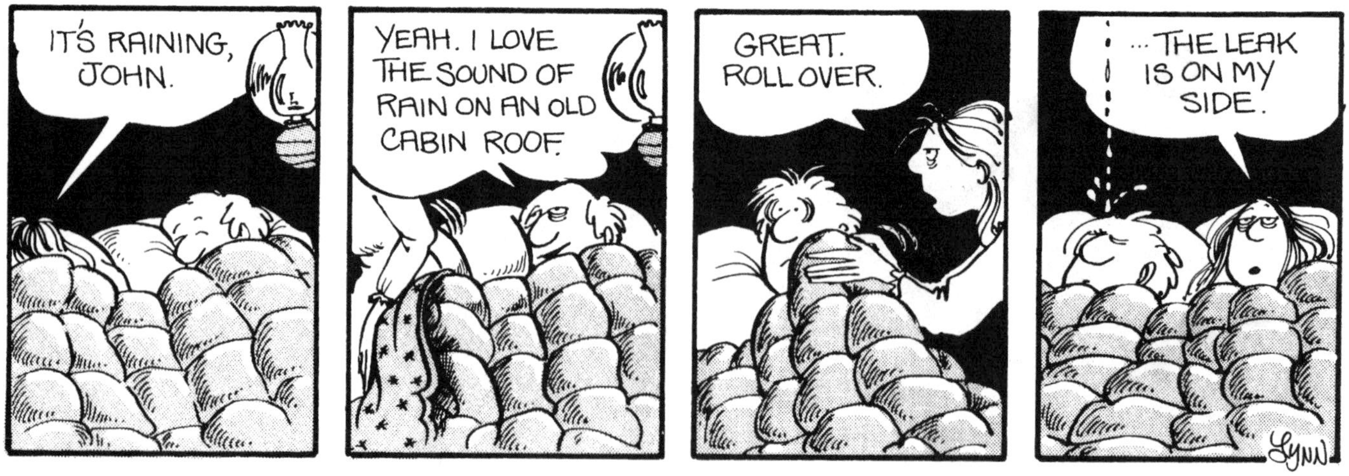
IT'S RAINING, JOHN.
YEAH. I LOVE THE SOUND OF RAIN ON AN OLD CABIN ROOF.
GREAT. ROLL OVER.
...THE LEAK IS ON MY SIDE.
LYNN

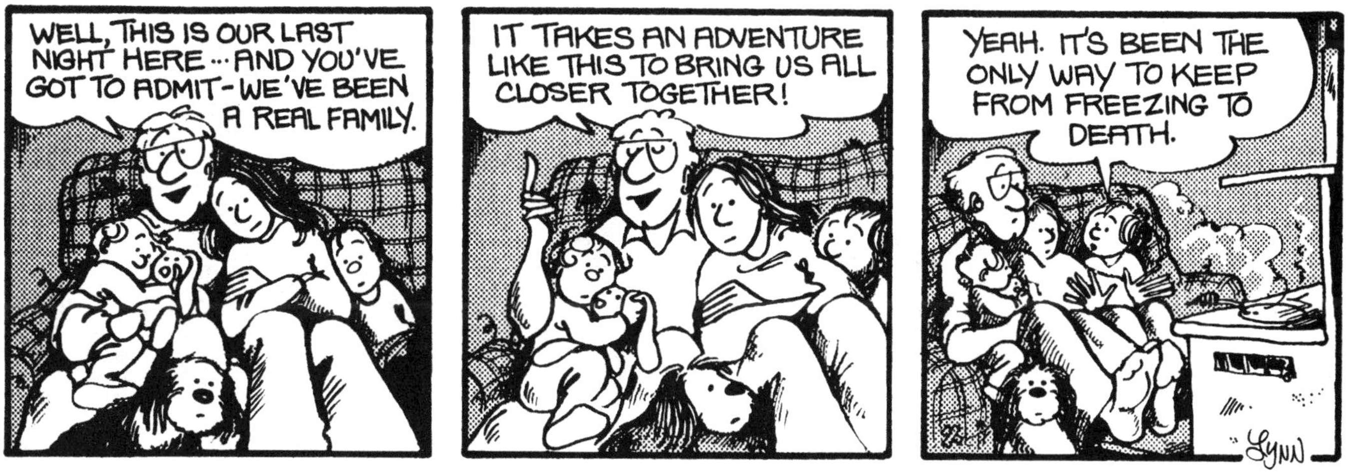
WELL, THIS IS OUR LAST NIGHT HERE... AND YOU'VE GOT TO ADMIT- WE'VE BEEN A REAL FAMILY.
IT TAKES AN ADVENTURE LIKE THIS TO BRING US ALL CLOSER TOGETHER!
YEAH. IT'S BEEN THE ONLY WAY TO KEEP FROM FREEZING TO DEATH.
LYNN

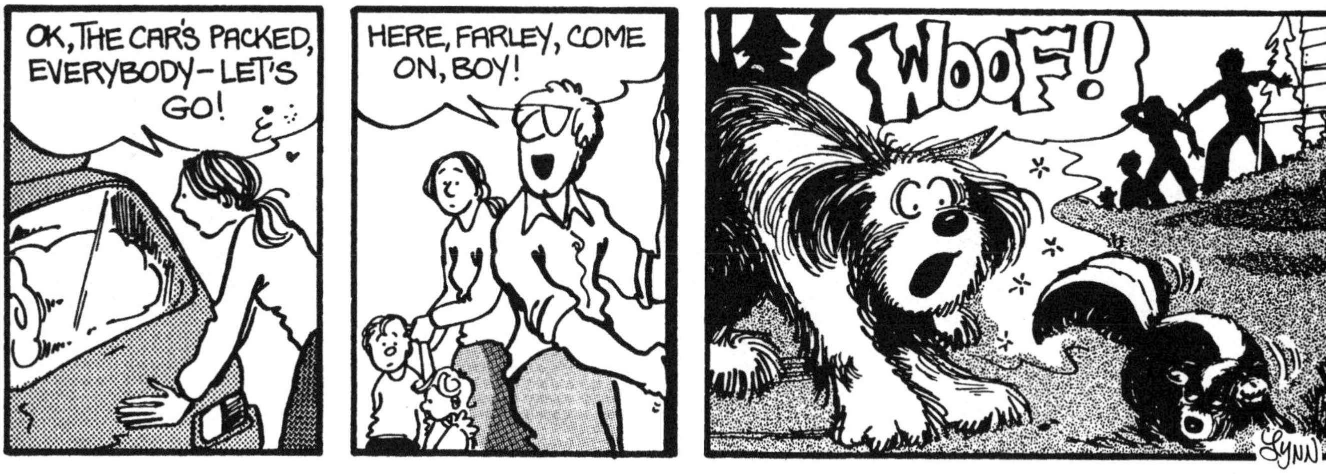
OK, THE CAR'S PACKED, EVERYBODY- LET'S GO!
HERE, FARLEY, COME ON, BOY!
WOOF!
LYNN

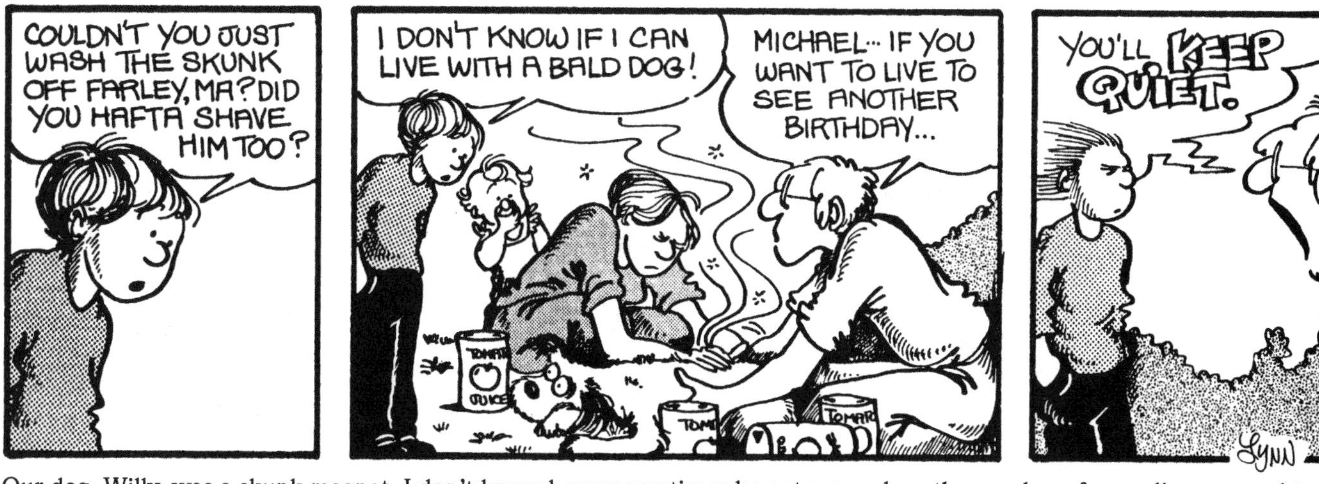
COULDN'T YOU JUST WASH THE SKUNK OFF FARLEY, MA? DID YOU HAFTA SHAVE HIM TOO?
I DON'T KNOW IF I CAN LIVE WITH A BALD DOG!
MICHAEL... IF YOU WANT TO LIVE TO SEE ANOTHER BIRTHDAY...
YOU'LL KEEP QUIET.
LYNN

Our dog, Willy, was a skunk magnet. I don't know how many times he got sprayed, or the number of remedies we used to clean him. I do know that the most efficient remover of "eau de skunk" is to let your dog roll on the lawn all night long. It might not be your number one plan of attack — but it works!

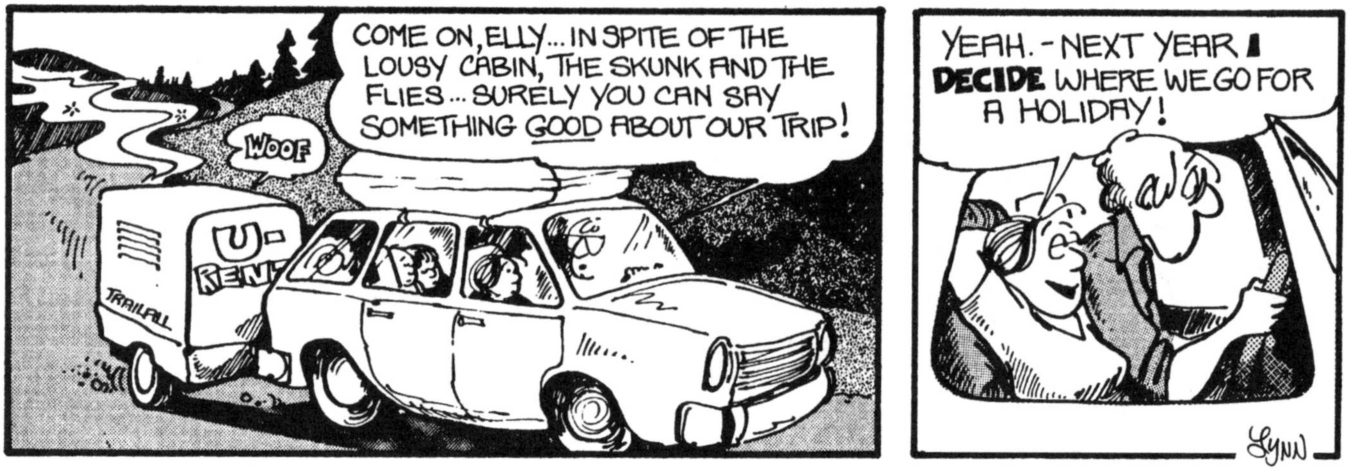
COME ON, ELLY... IN SPITE OF THE LOUSY CABIN, THE SKUNK AND THE FLIES... SURELY YOU CAN SAY SOMETHING GOOD ABOUT OUR TRIP!
WOOF
YEAH. - NEXT YEAR I DECIDE WHERE WE GO FOR A HOLIDAY!

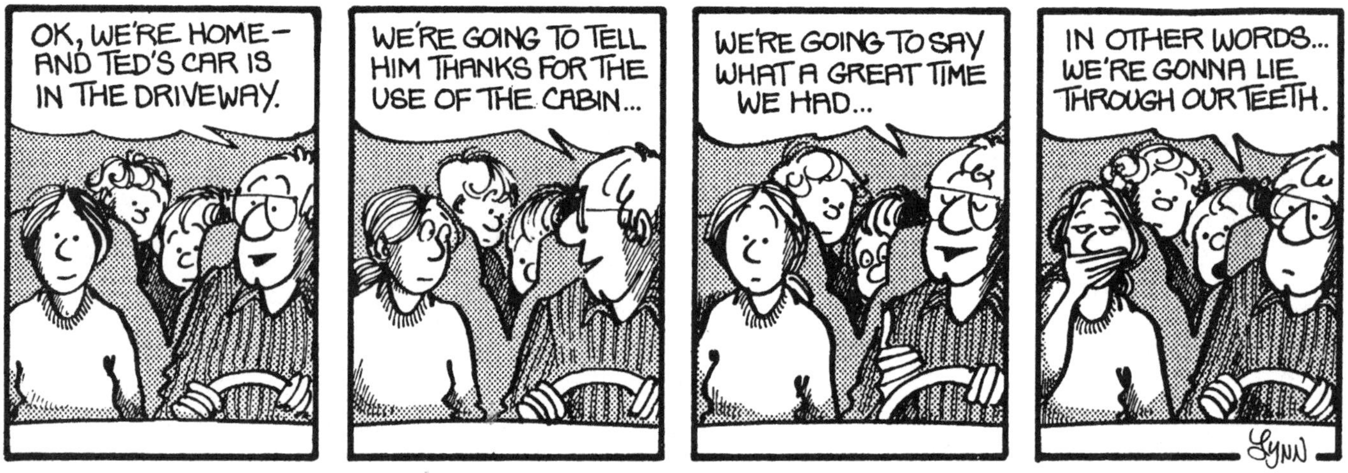
OK, WE'RE HOME - AND TED'S CAR IS IN THE DRIVEWAY.
WE'RE GOING TO TELL HIM THANKS FOR THE USE OF THE CABIN...
WE'RE GOING TO SAY WHAT A GREAT TIME WE HAD...
IN OTHER WORDS... WE'RE GONNA LIE THROUGH OUR TEETH.

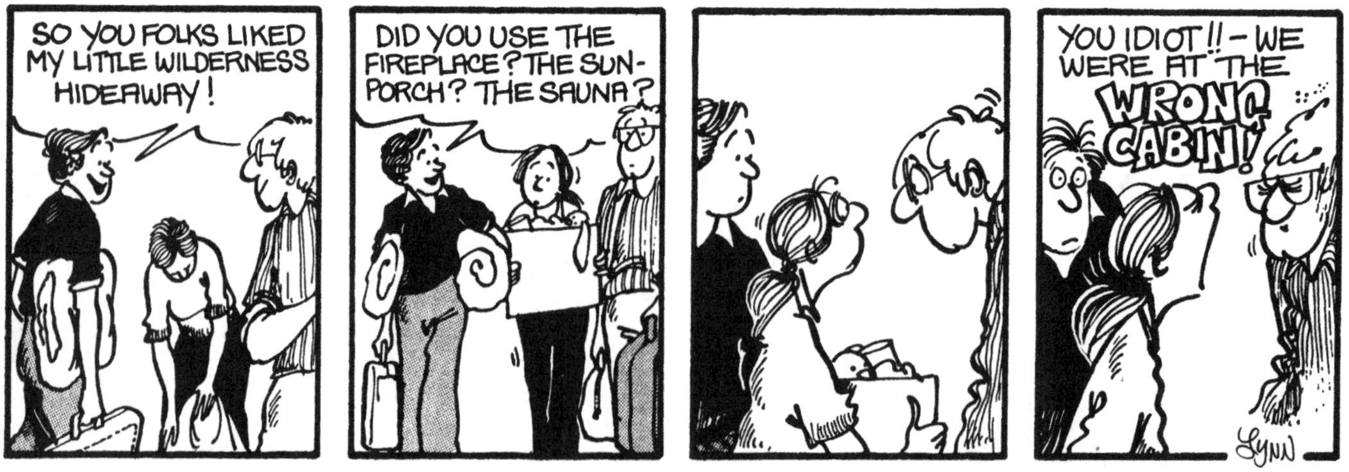
SO YOU FOLKS LIKED MY LITTLE WILDERNESS HIDEAWAY!
DID YOU USE THE FIREPLACE? THE SUN-PORCH? THE SAUNA?
YOU IDIOT!! - WE WERE AT THE WRONG CABIN!

When this story ran, I had a number of letters from people who had been there and done that. Apparently, staying in the wrong holiday home is not uncommon! I was always pleased to see that I was writing and drawing things that didn't happen to us ... but COULD have!

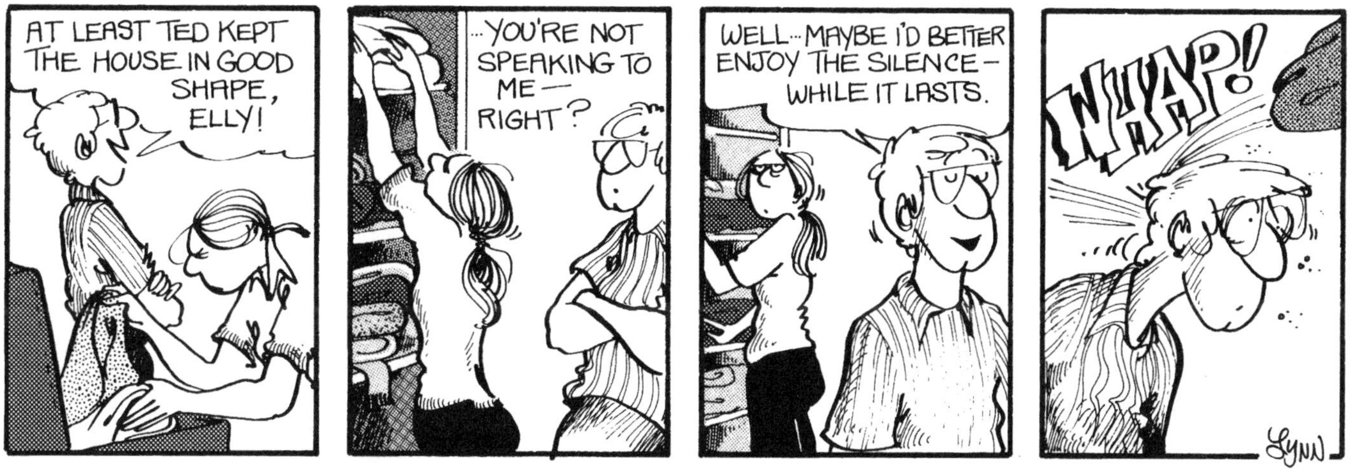
AT LEAST TED KEPT THE HOUSE IN GOOD SHAPE, ELLY!
...YOU'RE NOT SPEAKING TO ME — RIGHT?
WELL... MAYBE I'D BETTER ENJOY THE SILENCE — WHILE IT LASTS.
WHAP!
LYNN

This was probably one of the last "tossed article" punch lines I did. I don't know what else to call it! ... If a cartoon character has the desire to throw something at someone, he does — but it's not a literal attack; it's an imaginary one. There's an unspoken law in comics; like the cloud of depression, which hangs metaphorically over one's head — the thrown object isn't real, it's just symbolic of the mood at the time. I was reprimanded for turning to "violence," and had to convey emotion by other means.

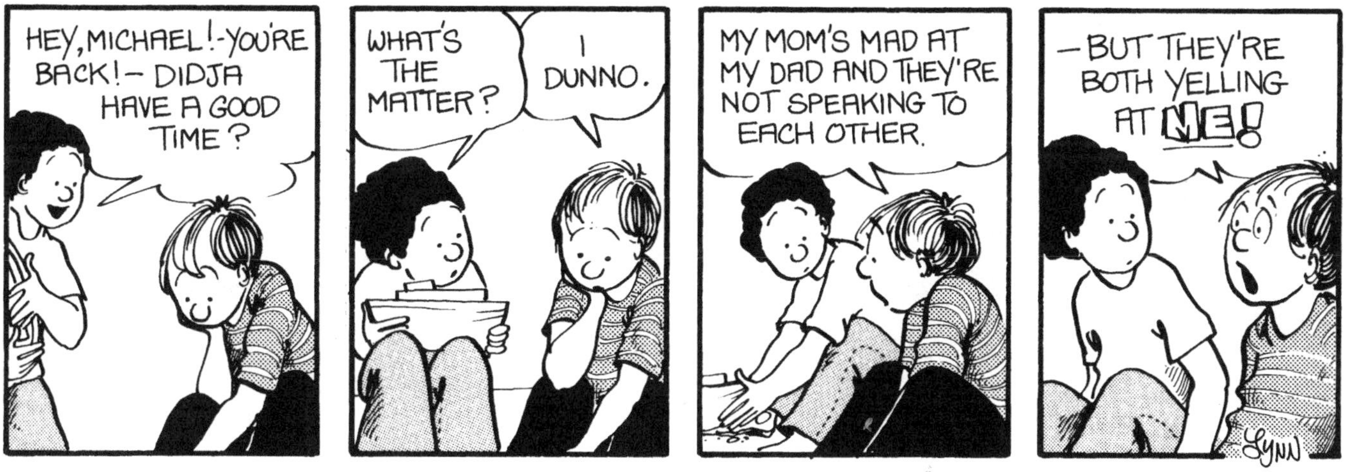
HEY, MICHAEL! - YOU'RE BACK! - DIDJA HAVE A GOOD TIME?
WHAT'S THE MATTER?
I DUNNO.
MY MOM'S MAD AT MY DAD AND THEY'RE NOT SPEAKING TO EACH OTHER.
— BUT THEY'RE BOTH YELLING AT ME!
LYNN

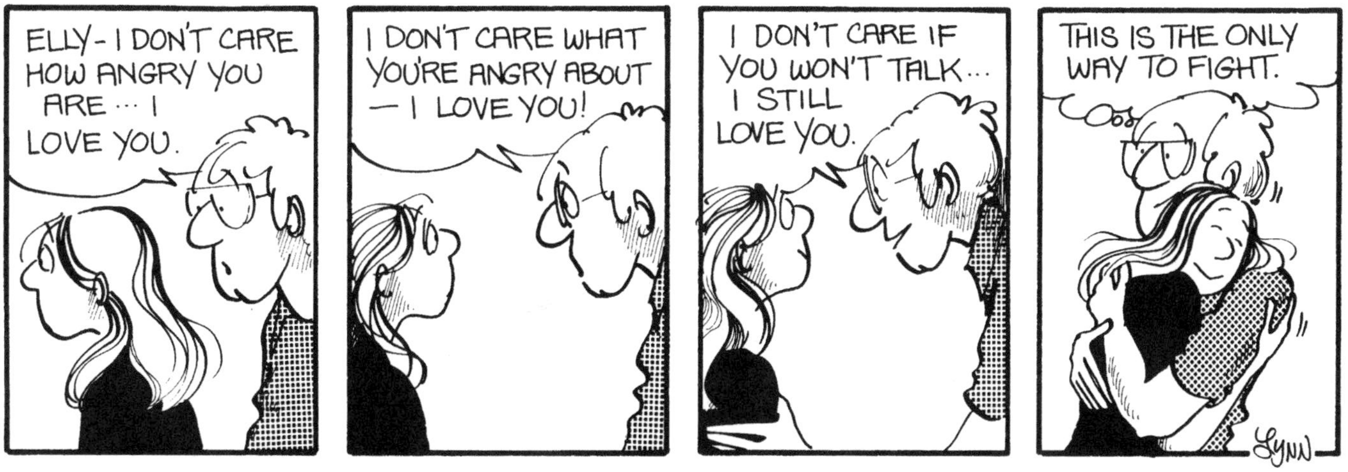
ELLY - I DON'T CARE HOW ANGRY YOU ARE ... I LOVE YOU.
I DON'T CARE WHAT YOU'RE ANGRY ABOUT — I LOVE YOU!
I DON'T CARE IF YOU WON'T TALK... I STILL LOVE YOU.
THIS IS THE ONLY WAY TO FIGHT.
LYNN

*

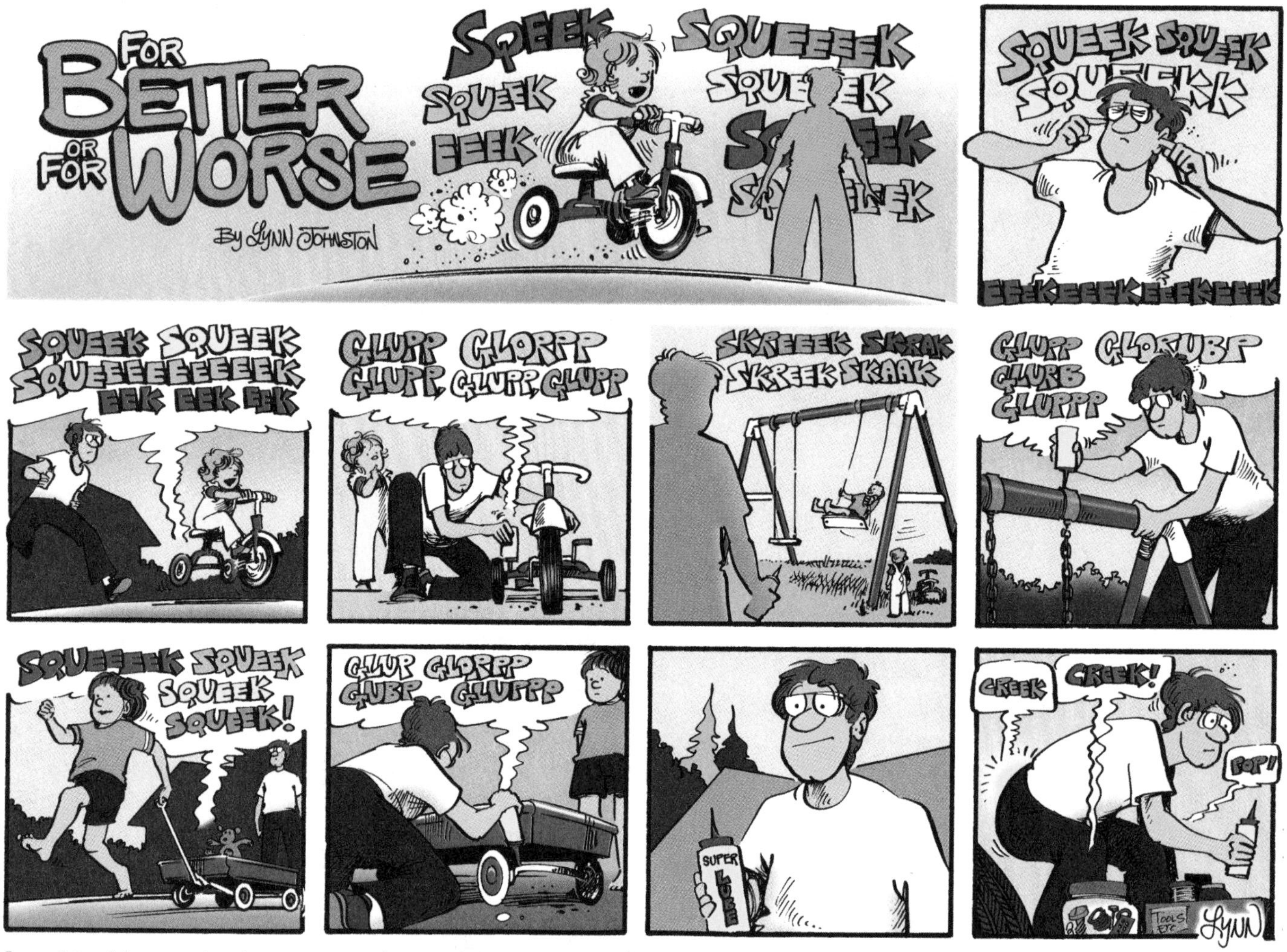

FOR BETTER OR FOR WORSE
BY LYNN JOHNSTON
SPEEK
SQUEEK
EEEK
SQUEEEEK
SQUEEK SQUEEK
SQUEEKK
EEEKEEEKEEEKEEEK
SQUEEK SQUEEK
SQUEEEEEEEEEEK
EEK EEK EEK
GLUPP GLORPP
GLUPP, GLUPP, GLUPP
SKREEEK SKRAK
SKREEK SKAAK
GLUPP GLORUBP
GLURB
GLUPPP
SQUEEEEK SQUEEK
SQUEEK
SQUEEK!
GLUP GLORPP
GLUBP GLUPPP
SUPER LUBE
CREEK
CREEK!
POP!
TOOLS ETC
LYNN


I used to ride my tricycle at top speed up and down Fifth Street in North Vancouver. I'd pump the pedals till my thighs burned, trying to go as fast as the big kids, wishing I could fly. One of the neighours, Mr. Harold Smith, hated the sound of squeaking wheels, and would come bounding out of his house with an oil can. He'd block our way on the sidewalk, then gruffly oil our trikes — often without saying a word. He had once been the principal of a school, and I guess he'd had enough of noise. When the silent-film comedies depicted the villain as "Oil Can Harry," my folks would laugh. We had our own "Oil Can Harry" right there on Fifth Street!

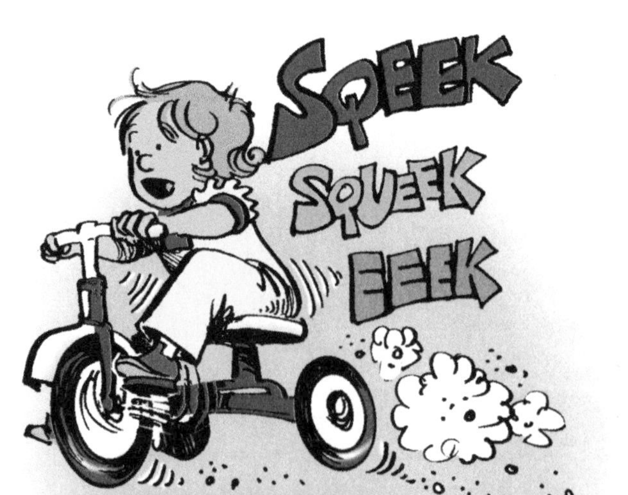

SPEEK
SQUEEK
EEEK

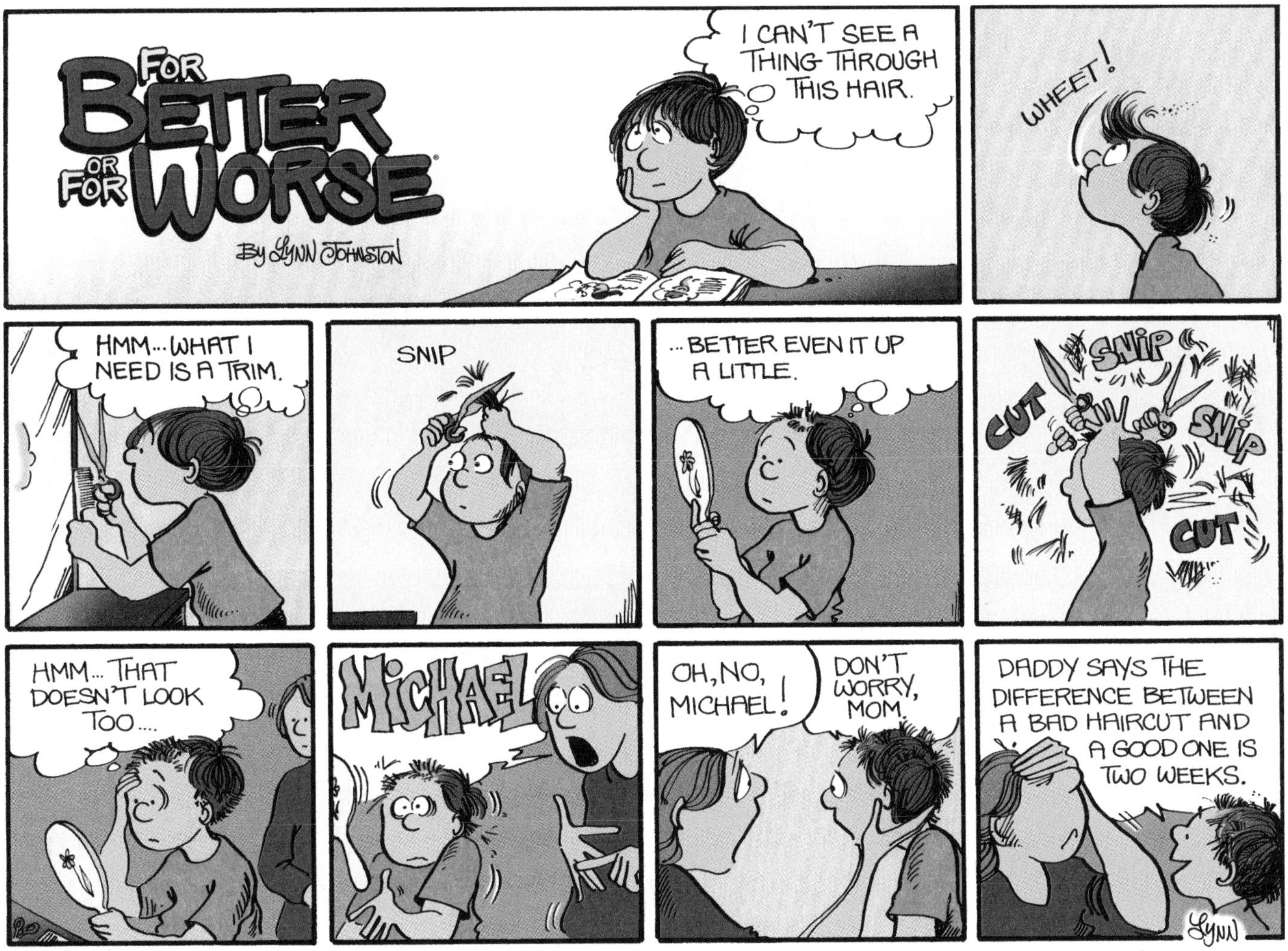
FOR BETTER OR FOR WORSE
BY LYNN JOHNSTON
I CAN'T SEE A THING THROUGH THIS HAIR.
WHEET!
HMM... WHAT I NEED IS A TRIM.
SNIP
... BETTER EVEN IT UP A LITTLE.
CUT
SNIP
SNIP
CUT
HMM... THAT DOESN'T LOOK TOO....
MICHAEL
OH, NO, MICHAEL!
DON'T WORRY, MOM.
DADDY SAYS THE DIFFERENCE BETWEEN A BAD HAIRCUT AND A GOOD ONE IS TWO WEEKS.
LYNN

It was I who cut my bangs off, but Michael was a perfect foil here — and the punch line came from "a day in the life" in our small northern town.

In Lynn Lake, there was one barber, and he loved to chat. The problem was that he would continue to cut your hair for as long as the conversation lasted. I remember my husband coming home with hardly any hair on his head, and I asked why he had talked for so long! The answer was that it had been a good conversation … and a bad haircut only lasts for two weeks.

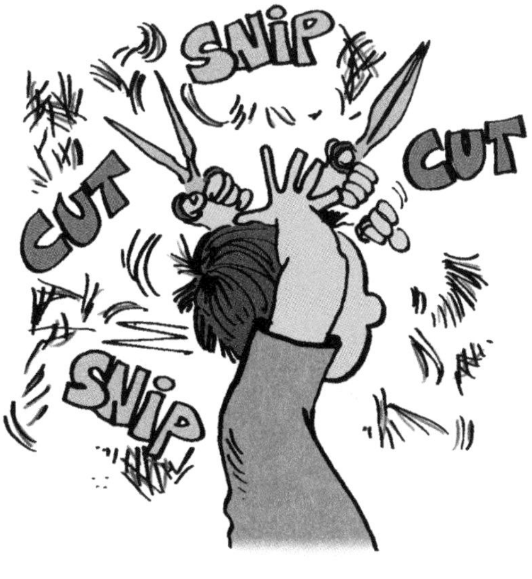
SNIP
CUT
CUT
SNIP

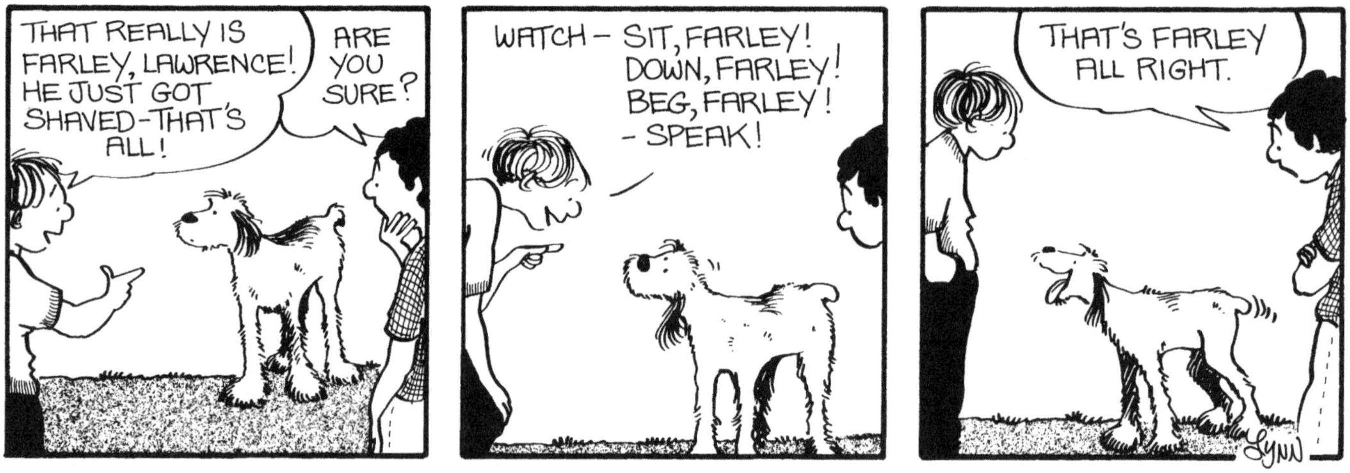
THAT REALLY IS FARLEY, LAWRENCE! HE JUST GOT SHAVED-THAT'S ALL!
ARE YOU SURE?
WATCH - SIT, FARLEY! DOWN, FARLEY! BEG, FARLEY! - SPEAK!
THAT'S FARLEY ALL RIGHT.
LYNN

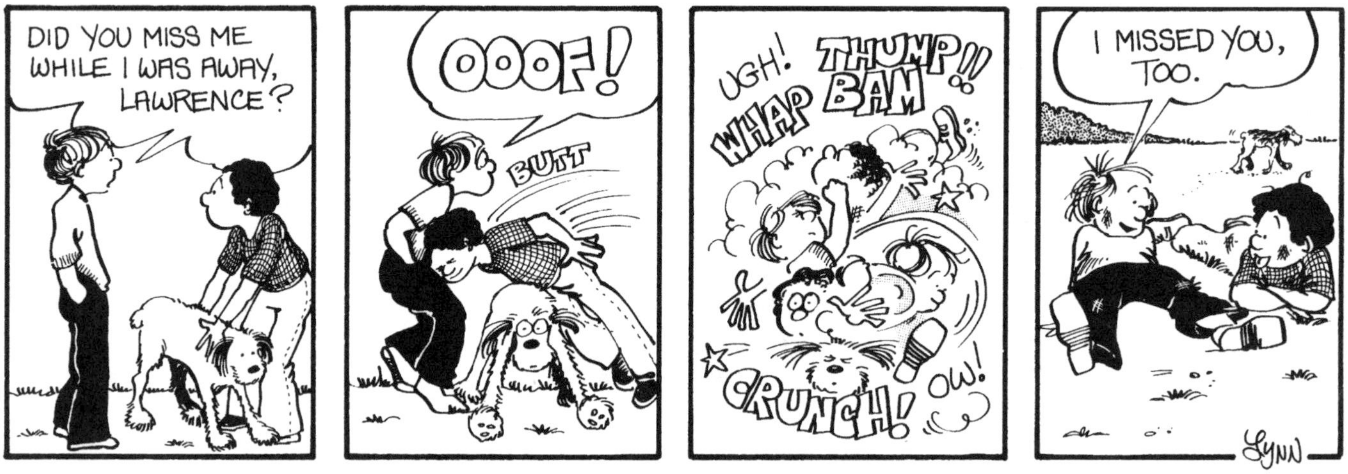
DID YOU MISS ME WHILE I WAS AWAY, LAWRENCE?
OOOF!
BUTT
UGH!
THUMP!!
WHAP
BAM
CRUNCH!
OW!
I MISSED YOU, TOO.
LYNN

I've seen over the years how men and boys express their affection for each other with slaps on the back and warm punches. For children, it's wrestling. Many times I've watched my brother and his friends wrestle in friendship, careful not to let the contest go too far. Aaron, too, pushed and shoved his pals, and it was all in good fun. Call it fighting if you like, guys … but it's really just another kind of hug!

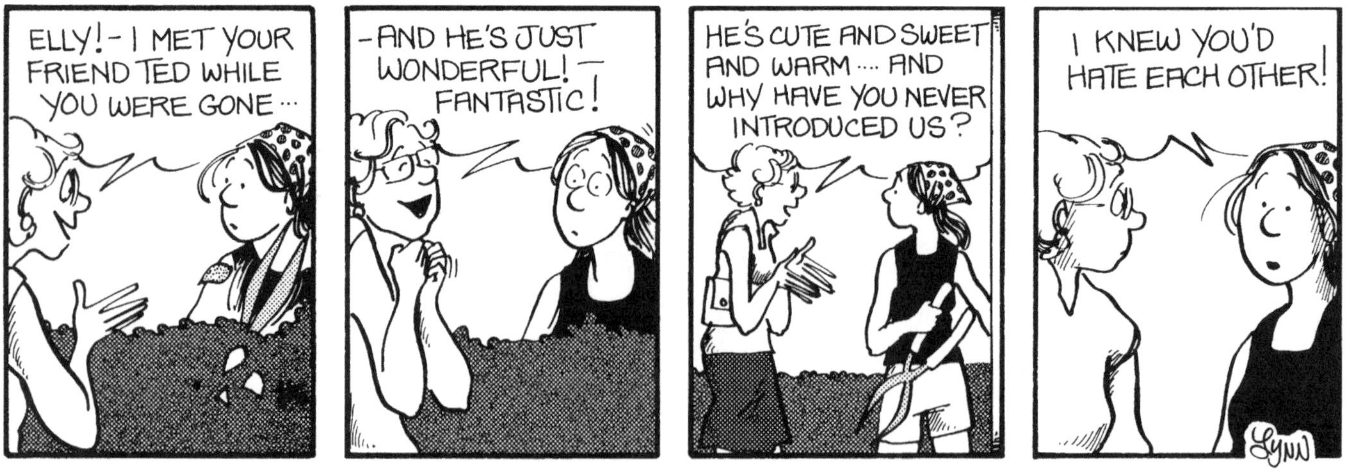
ELLY! - I MET YOUR FRIEND TED WHILE YOU WERE GONE…
- AND HE'S JUST WONDERFUL! - FANTASTIC!
HE'S CUTE AND SWEET AND WARM…. AND WHY HAVE YOU NEVER INTRODUCED US?
I KNEW YOU'D HATE EACH OTHER!
LYNN

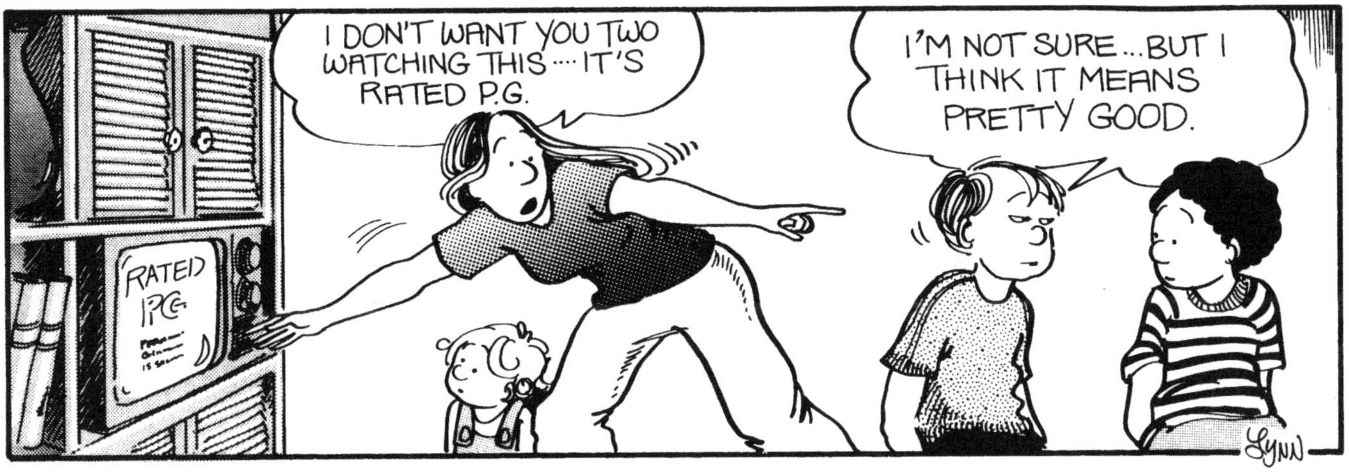
RATED PG
I DON'T WANT YOU TWO WATCHING THIS .... IT'S RATED P.G.
I'M NOT SURE...BUT I THINK IT MEANS PRETTY GOOD.
Lynn

The urge to let kids watch whatever television has to offer is pretty hard to resist — especially when you need time to do other things. Making sure they're not absorbing trash is a constant challenge, and it angered me to see how much garbage there was disguised as entertainment. It's sad to think that the stuff my kids were kept from watching then, is considered tame by the standards of today!

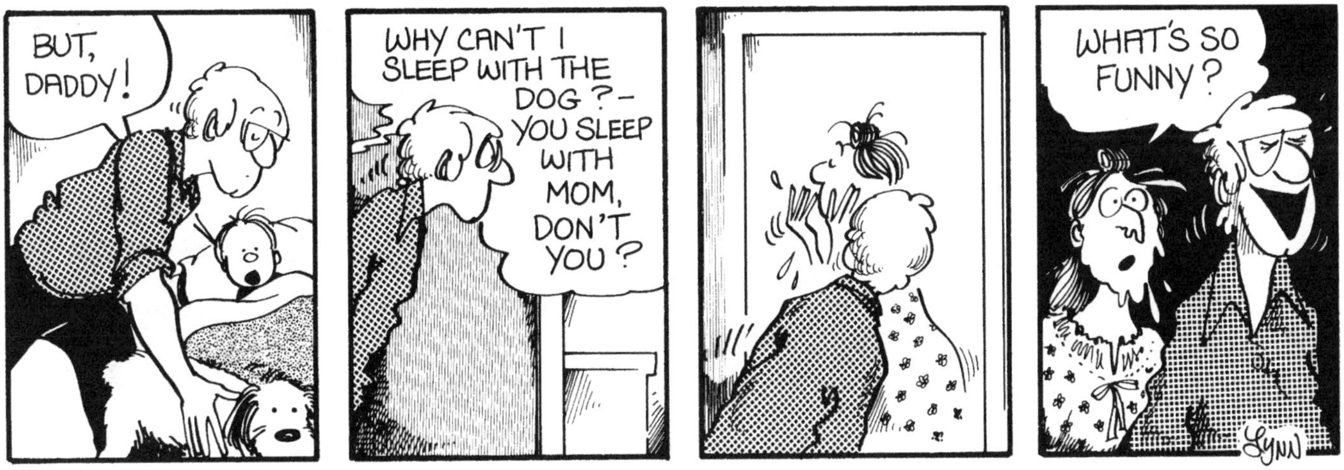
BUT, DADDY!
WHY CAN'T I SLEEP WITH THE DOG?- YOU SLEEP WITH MOM, DON'T YOU?
WHAT'S SO FUNNY?
Lynn

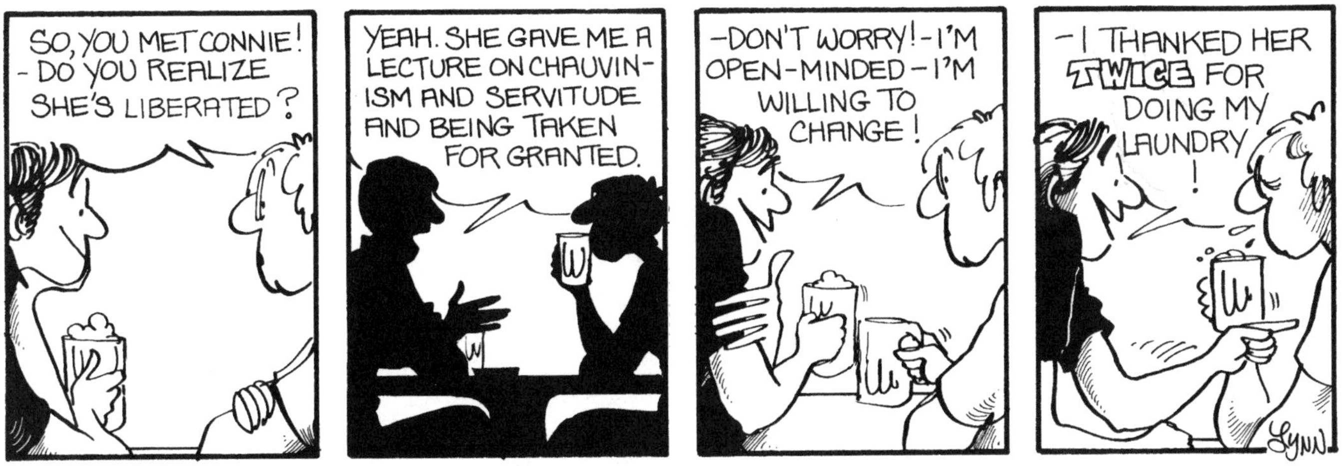
SO, YOU MET CONNIE! - DO YOU REALIZE SHE'S LIBERATED?
YEAH. SHE GAVE ME A LECTURE ON CHAUVIN-ISM AND SERVITUDE AND BEING TAKEN FOR GRANTED.
-DON'T WORRY! - I'M OPEN-MINDED - I'M WILLING TO CHANGE!
- I THANKED HER TWICE FOR DOING MY LAUNDRY!
Lynn

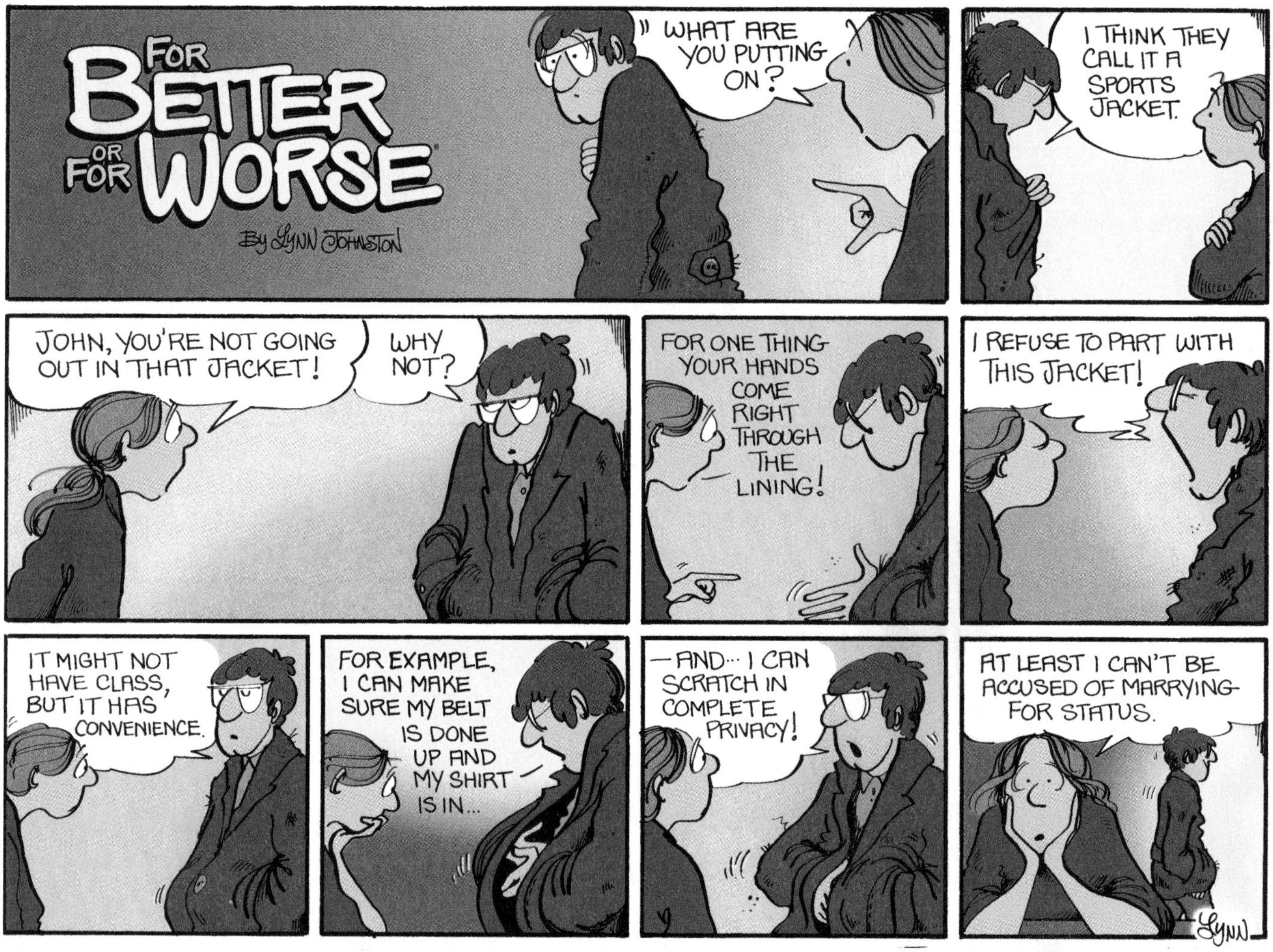
FOR BETTER OR FOR WORSE
BY LYNN JOHNSTON
WHAT ARE YOU PUTTING ON?
I THINK THEY CALL IT A SPORTS JACKET.
JOHN, YOU'RE NOT GOING OUT IN THAT JACKET!
WHY NOT?
FOR ONE THING YOUR HANDS COME RIGHT THROUGH THE LINING!
I REFUSE TO PART WITH THIS JACKET!
IT MIGHT NOT HAVE CLASS, BUT IT HAS CONVENIENCE.
FOR EXAMPLE, I CAN MAKE SURE MY BELT IS DONE UP AND MY SHIRT IS IN...
—AND... I CAN SCRATCH IN COMPLETE PRIVACY!
AT LEAST I CAN'T BE ACCUSED OF MARRYING FOR STATUS.
LYNN

I have done a lot of stage presentations over the years. I tell stories and talk about cartoons while I doodle. One of the illustrations I love to do is Elly wearing a chenille housecoat. She looks like a wreck, with baggy eyes and a head full of old-fashioned plastic hair rollers. I tell the audience that this is what we look like when we are being ourselves — completely at ease in the comfort of our own homes. I can feel an electric hum of solidarity as I explain the difference between the housecoat we wear for company and the one we wear every day. The "good one" is velour and perfect and looks great when you're entertaining a guest at breakfast. The comfortable one is usually chenille. Chenille softens with every washing, and after awhile the pockets wear through. You can then reach down and scratch whatever you need to scratch, and nobody knows what or where you're scratching. I do this with actions — and it always gets a laugh. This Sunday is really my chenille housecoat story, made palatable for a newspaper audience!

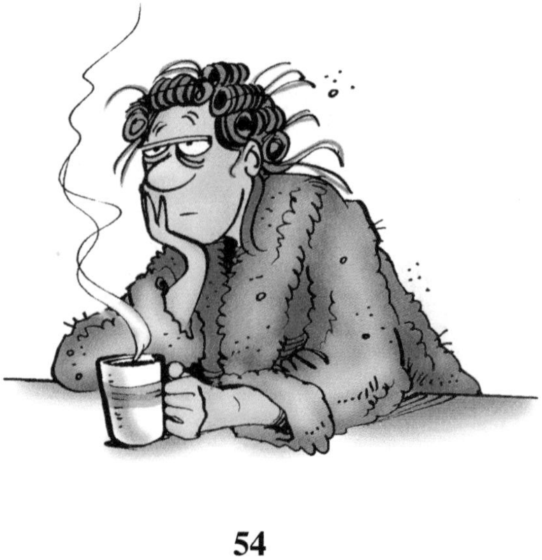

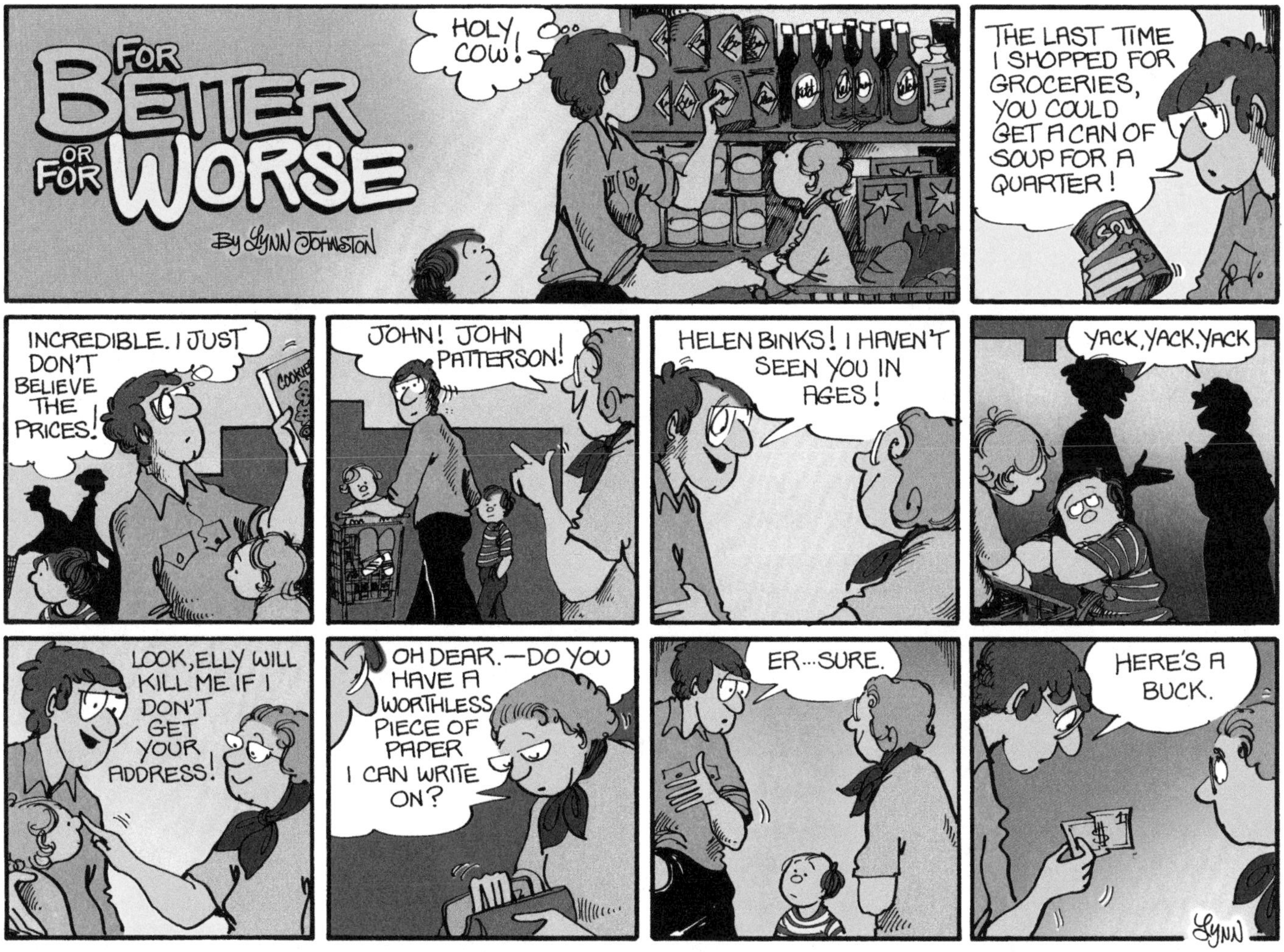
FOR BETTER OR FOR WORSE
BY LYNN JOHNSTON
HOLY COW!
THE LAST TIME I SHOPPED FOR GROCERIES, YOU COULD GET A CAN OF SOUP FOR A QUARTER!
INCREDIBLE. I JUST DON'T BELIEVE THE PRICES!
JOHN! JOHN PATTERSON!
HELEN BINKS! I HAVEN'T SEEN YOU IN AGES!
YACK, YACK, YACK
LOOK, ELLY WILL KILL ME IF I DON'T GET YOUR ADDRESS!
OH DEAR.—DO YOU HAVE A WORTHLESS PIECE OF PAPER I CAN WRITE ON?
ER...SURE.
HERE'S A BUCK.
LYNN

Helen Binks was a dear lady with whom my husband, Rod, lived while he was going to university in Toronto. She rented him a small room in her home, and became like a surrogate mom. After Rod and I were married, his brother, Ralph, rented the same room. He, too, became a part of Helen's life. Both had such fond memories of her that I did this strip, hoping she would see it and know that we were thinking of her.

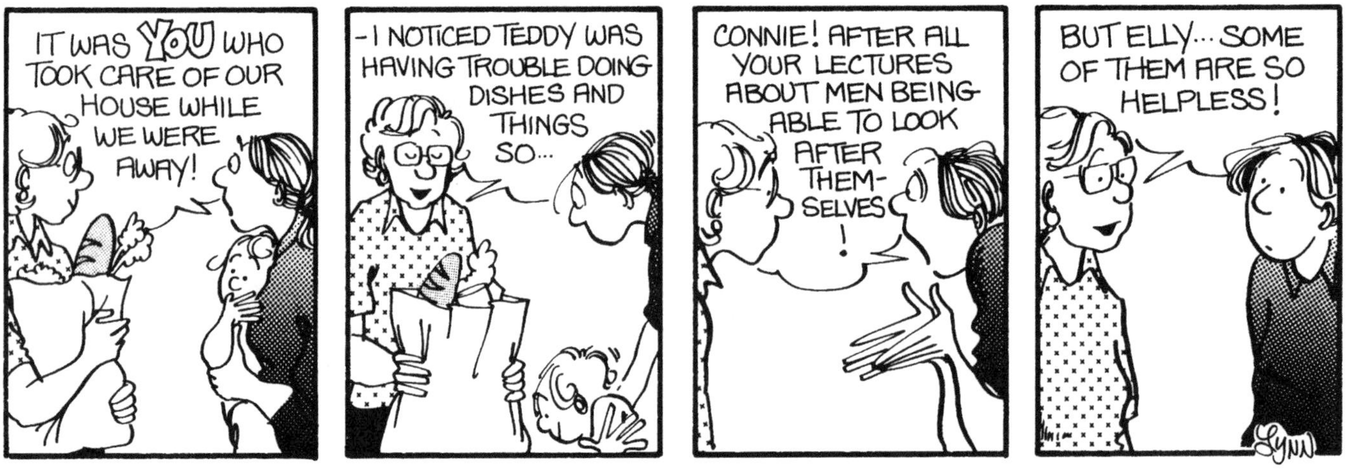
IT WAS YOU WHO TOOK CARE OF OUR HOUSE WHILE WE WERE AWAY!
-I NOTICED TEDDY WAS HAVING TROUBLE DOING DISHES AND THINGS SO...
CONNIE! AFTER ALL YOUR LECTURES ABOUT MEN BEING ABLE TO LOOK AFTER THEMSELVES!
BUT ELLY... SOME OF THEM ARE SO HELPLESS!
LYNN

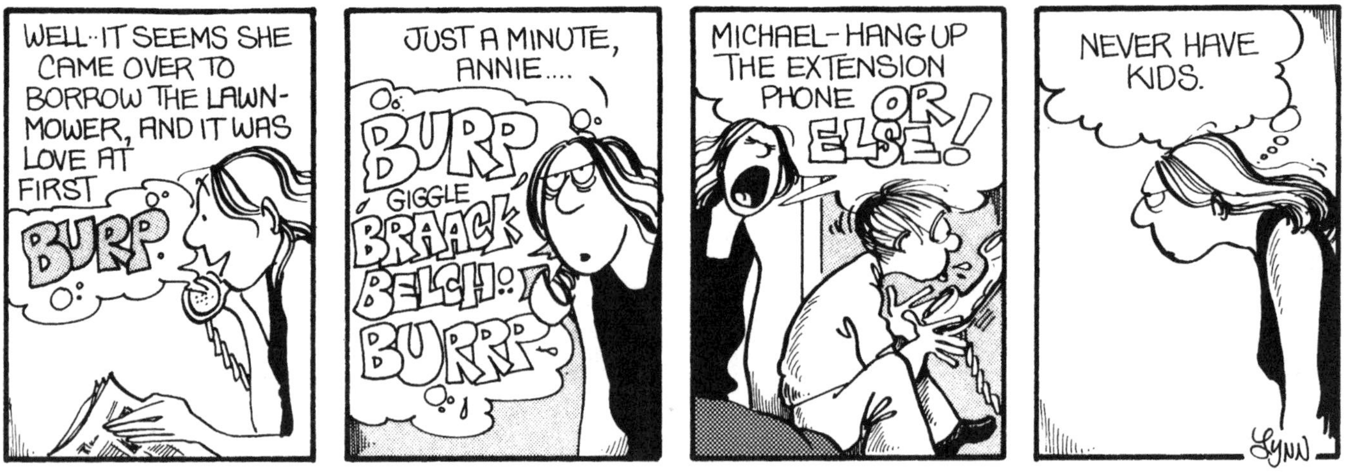
WELL.. IT SEEMS SHE CAME OVER TO BORROW THE LAWN-MOWER, AND IT WAS LOVE AT FIRST
BURP
JUST A MINUTE, ANNIE....
BURP
GIGGLE
BRAACK
BELCH
BURRP
MICHAEL- HANG UP THE EXTENSION PHONE OR ELSE!
NEVER HAVE KIDS.
LYNN

As kids, we had a "party line." Few people had a private phone line at that time. There might be as many as four homes on a party line, and each had a different ring. Ours was two rings, our neighbour was one, and from time to time we knew that the other was listening. The "echo" when another line is open sounds the same now when an extension is off the hook. Even without the sound effects, I knew when the kids were listening in!

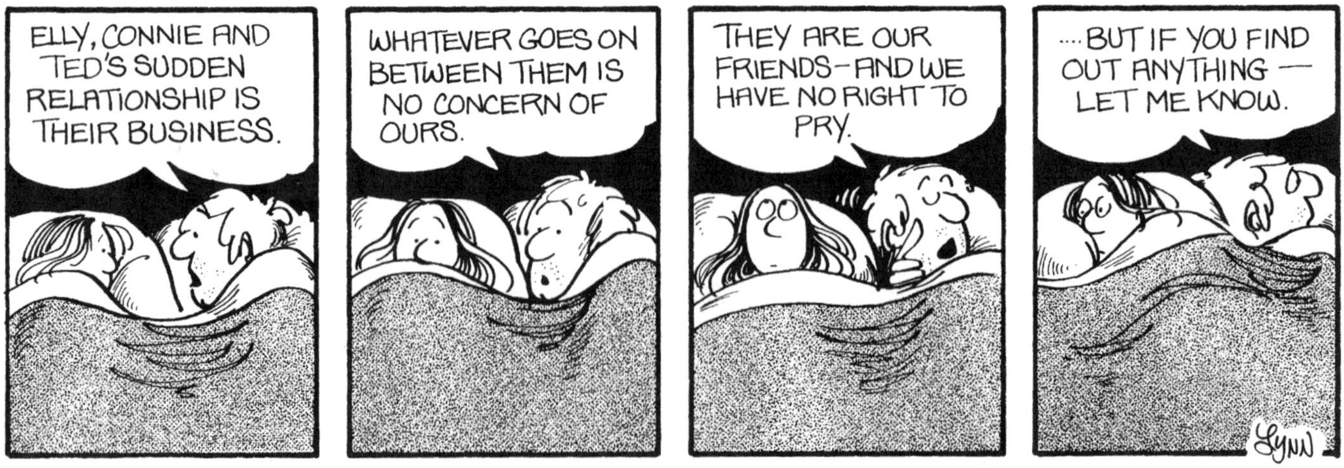
ELLY, CONNIE AND TED'S SUDDEN RELATIONSHIP IS THEIR BUSINESS.
WHATEVER GOES ON BETWEEN THEM IS NO CONCERN OF OURS.
THEY ARE OUR FRIENDS- AND WE HAVE NO RIGHT TO PRY.
....BUT IF YOU FIND OUT ANYTHING — LET ME KNOW.
LYNN

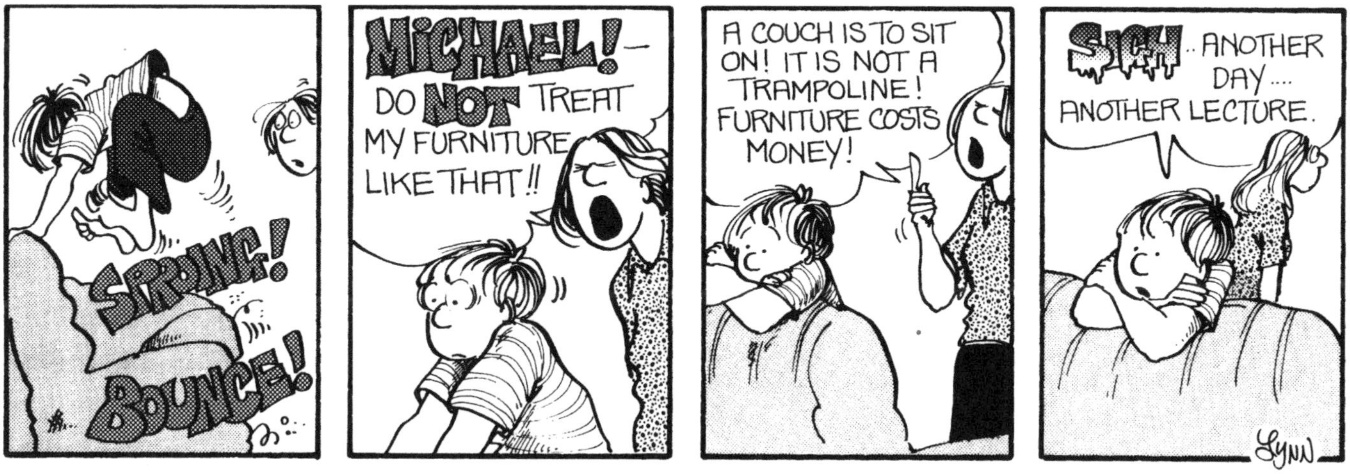
SPRONG!
BOUNCE!
MICHAEL! — DO NOT TREAT MY FURNITURE LIKE THAT!!
A COUCH IS TO SIT ON! IT IS NOT A TRAMPOLINE! FURNITURE COSTS MONEY!
SIGH.. ANOTHER DAY.... ANOTHER LECTURE.
LYNN

My brother and I destroyed our parents' couch the same way our kids destroyed ours. There was no guilt associated with collapsed springs and sagging cushions; we just thought the bounce had gone out of it! Our old striped sofa in Lynn Lake survived until the kids went on to other destructive practices — like denting the car. When we did buy a new couch, it looked beautiful, but somehow ... it lacked the old one's character!

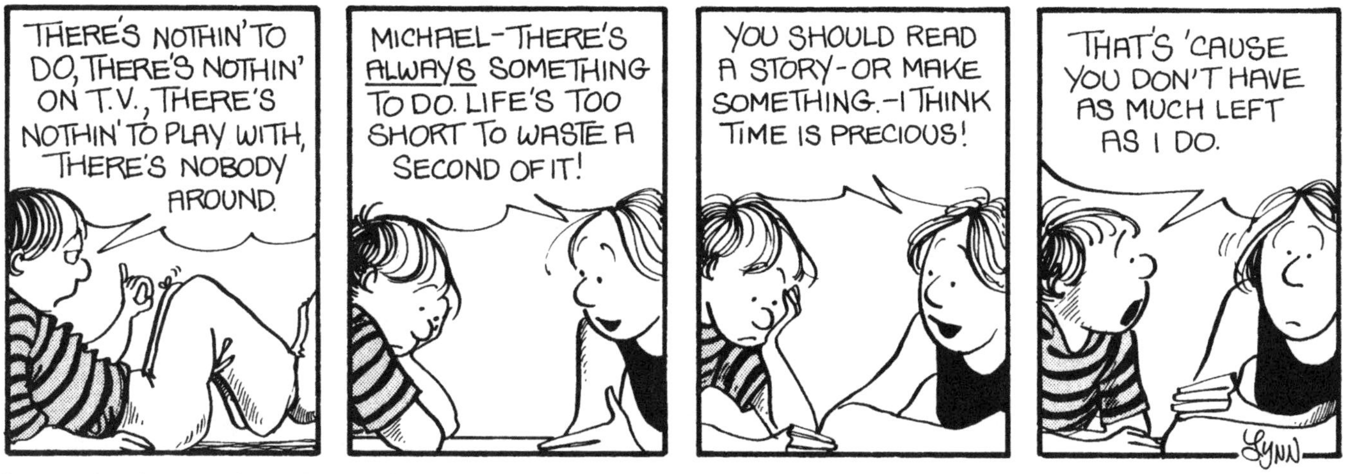
THERE'S NOTHIN' TO DO, THERE'S NOTHIN' ON T.V., THERE'S NOTHIN' TO PLAY WITH, THERE'S NOBODY AROUND.
MICHAEL-THERE'S ALWAYS SOMETHING TO DO. LIFE'S TOO SHORT TO WASTE A SECOND OF IT!
YOU SHOULD READ A STORY-OR MAKE SOMETHING.-I THINK TIME IS PRECIOUS!
THAT'S 'CAUSE YOU DON'T HAVE AS MUCH LEFT AS I DO.
LYNN

I remember being so bored I couldn't stand it. My mother would reason that time went by too fast, and wasn't to be wasted. I thought she was crazy. For kids, a day can be "forever." I knew that my mother's perception of time differed from mine, and although I never said this to her directly, this was my youthful point of view.

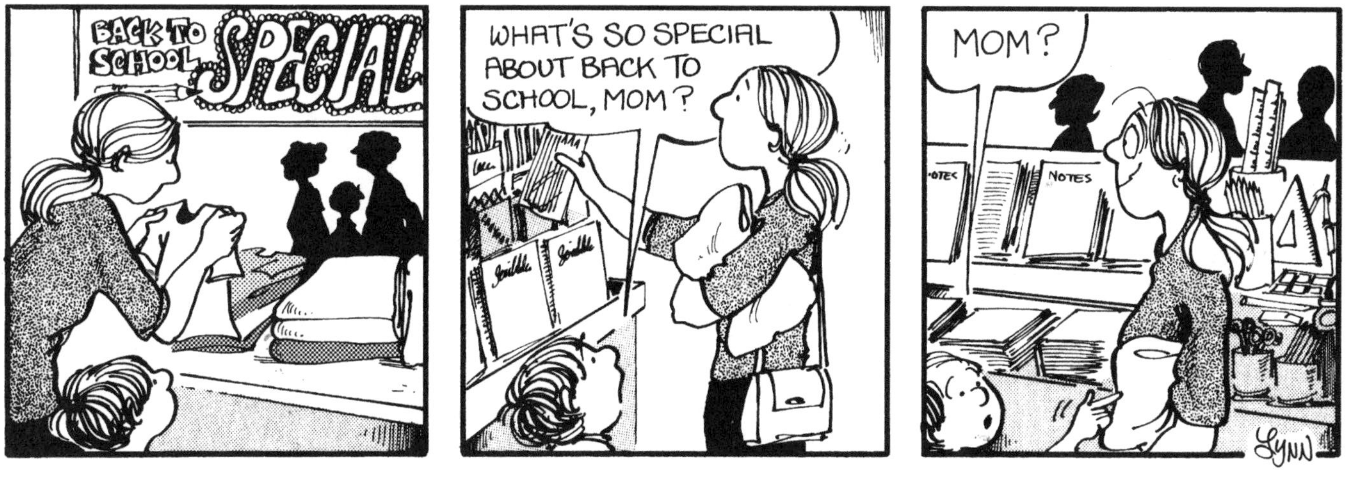
BACK TO SCHOOL SPECIAL
WHAT'S SO SPECIAL ABOUT BACK TO SCHOOL, MOM?
MOM?
NOTES
LYNN

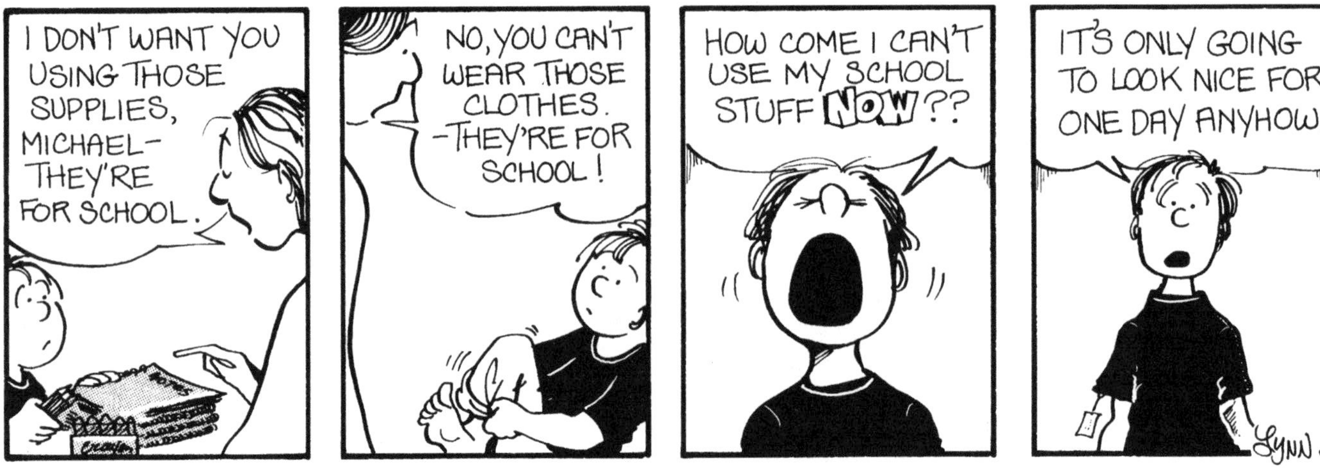
I DON'T WANT YOU USING THOSE SUPPLIES, MICHAEL- THEY'RE FOR SCHOOL.
NO, YOU CAN'T WEAR THOSE CLOTHES. -THEY'RE FOR SCHOOL!
HOW COME I CAN'T USE MY SCHOOL STUFF NOW??
IT'S ONLY GOING TO LOOK NICE FOR ONE DAY ANYHOW.
LYNN

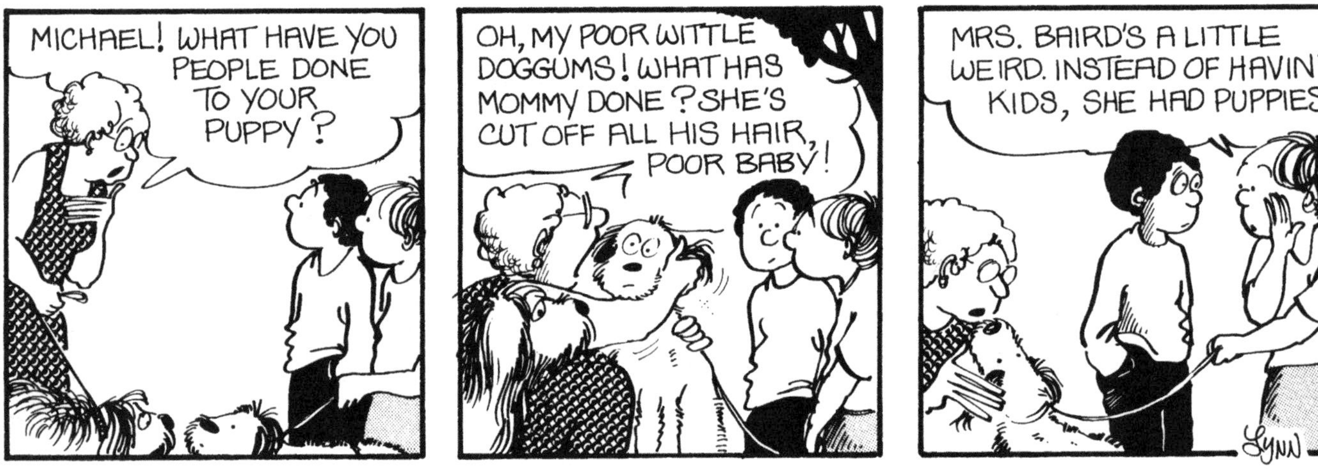
MICHAEL! WHAT HAVE YOU PEOPLE DONE TO YOUR PUPPY?
OH, MY POOR WITTLE DOGGUMS! WHAT HAS MOMMY DONE? SHE'S CUT OFF ALL HIS HAIR, POOR BABY!
MRS. BAIRD'S A LITTLE WEIRD. INSTEAD OF HAVIN' KIDS, SHE HAD PUPPIES.
LYNN

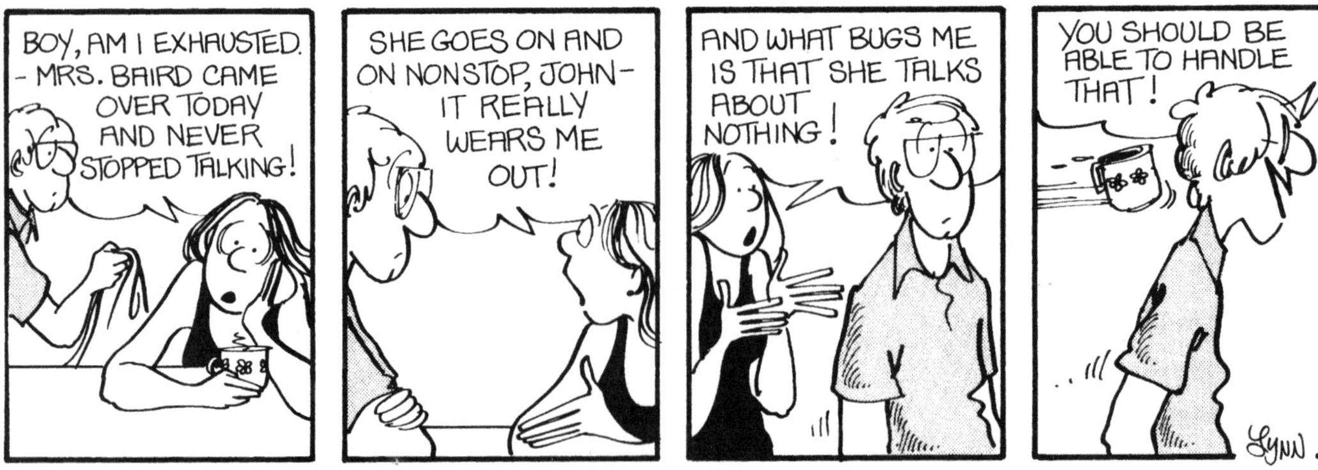
BOY, AM I EXHAUSTED. - MRS. BAIRD CAME OVER TODAY AND NEVER STOPPED TALKING!
SHE GOES ON AND ON NONSTOP, JOHN- IT REALLY WEARS ME OUT!
AND WHAT BUGS ME IS THAT SHE TALKS ABOUT NOTHING!
YOU SHOULD BE ABLE TO HANDLE THAT!
LYNN

Whoa! Here's another one! I have explained before that throwing something at the back of someone's head never really happened. Like the lightbulb over a cartoon character's head, this was old-style symbolism. It was just something I often WANTED to do!

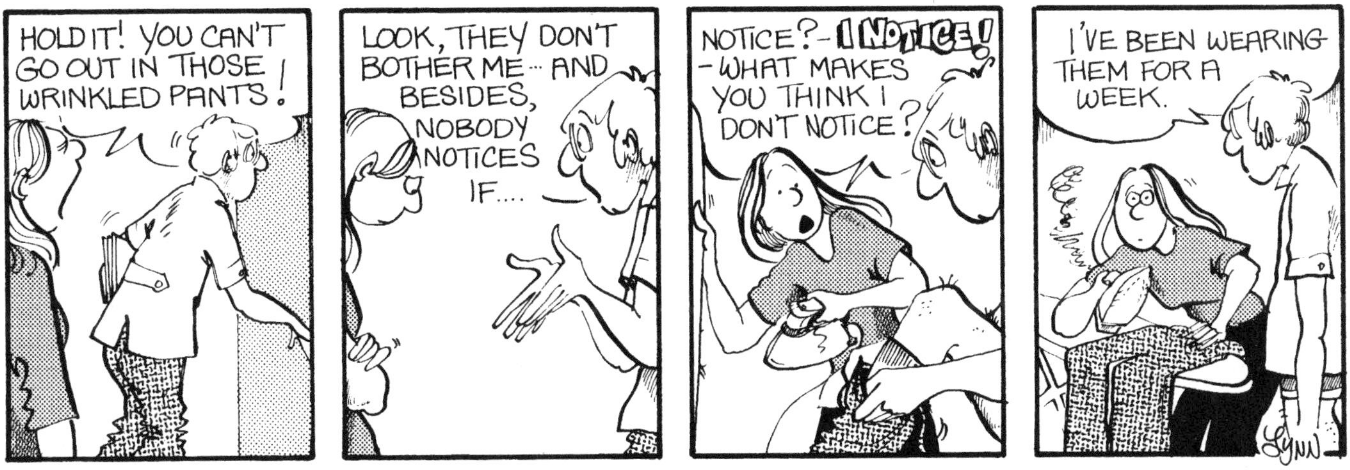
HOLD IT! YOU CAN'T GO OUT IN THOSE WRINKLED PANTS!
LOOK, THEY DON'T BOTHER ME... AND BESIDES, NOBODY NOTICES IF....
NOTICE?- I NOTICE! - WHAT MAKES YOU THINK I DON'T NOTICE?
I'VE BEEN WEARING THEM FOR A WEEK.
LYNN

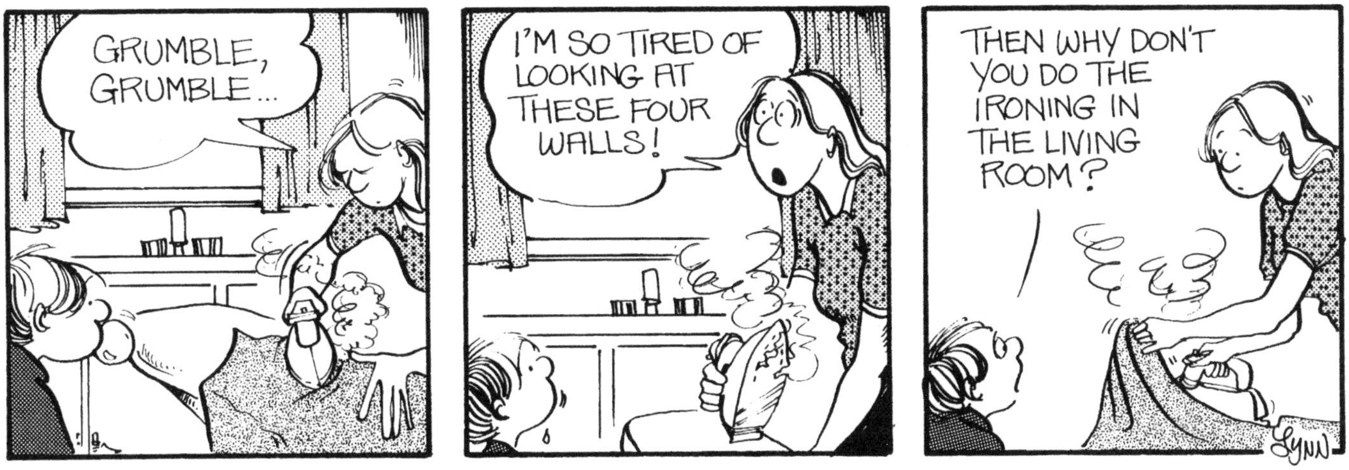
GRUMBLE, GRUMBLE...
I'M SO TIRED OF LOOKING AT THESE FOUR WALLS!
THEN WHY DON'T YOU DO THE IRONING IN THE LIVING ROOM?
LYNN

Of all the household chores, I hate ironing the most. I'll happily wash floors, sweep basements, dust and drudge and polish … but please don't make me iron! Perhaps this stems from the days when there was no such thing as permanent press, and even the sheets had to be done. Whereas others might enjoy the smell, the ease, and the pleasing results, ironing … leaves me flat!

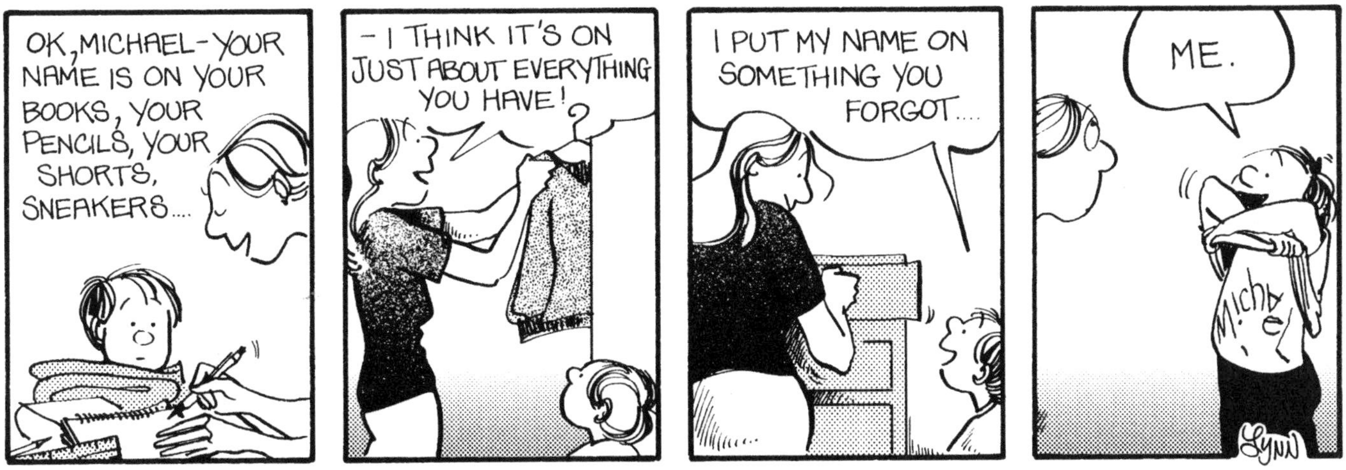
OK, MICHAEL- YOUR NAME IS ON YOUR BOOKS, YOUR PENCILS, YOUR SHORTS, SNEAKERS....
- I THINK IT'S ON JUST ABOUT EVERYTHING YOU HAVE!
I PUT MY NAME ON SOMETHING YOU FORGOT....
ME.
LYNN

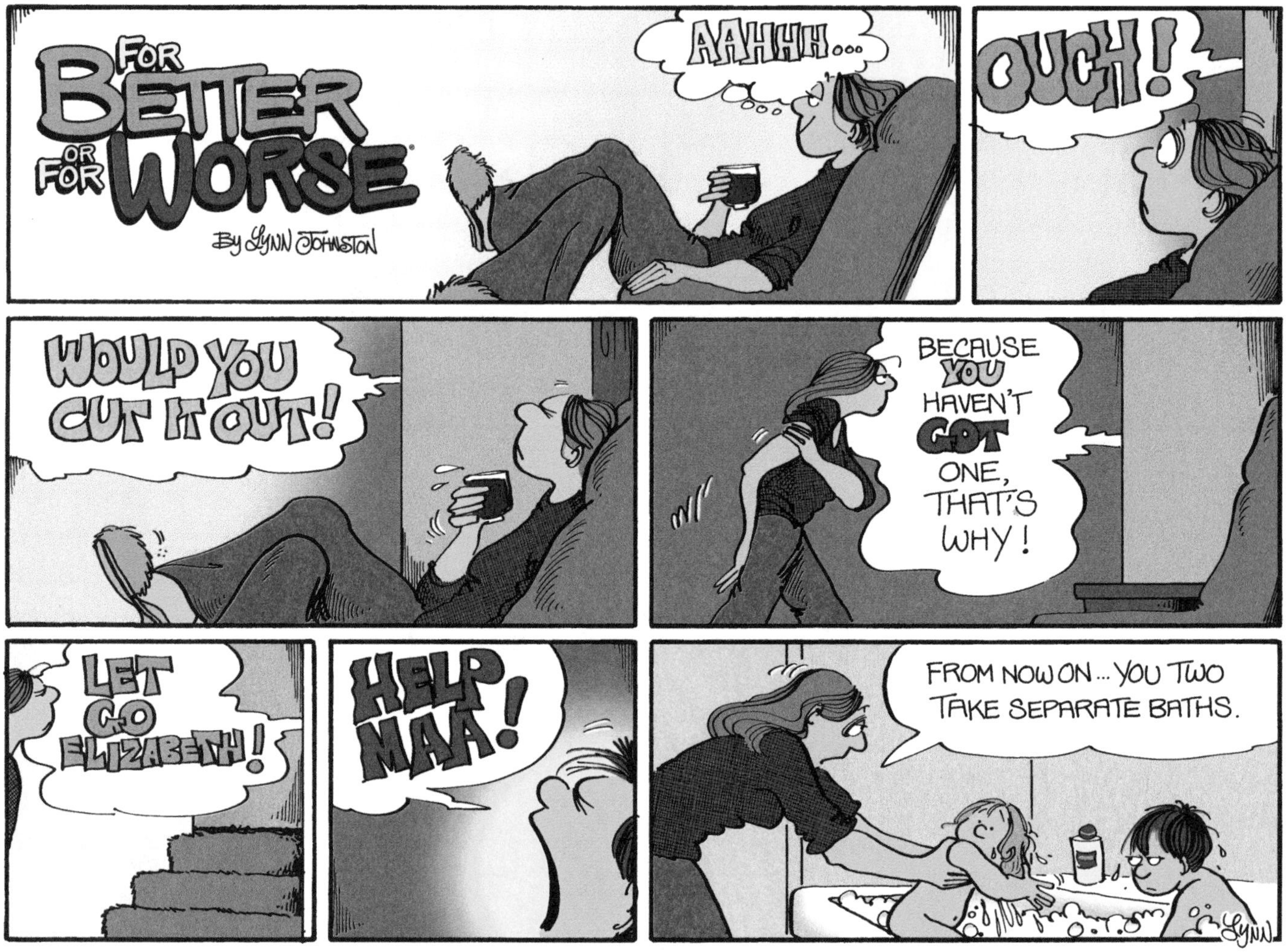
FOR BETTER OR FOR WORSE
BY LYNN JOHNSTON
AAHHH...
OUCH!
WOULD YOU CUT IT OUT!
BECAUSE YOU HAVEN'T GOT ONE, THAT'S WHY!
LET GO ELIZABETH!
HELP MAA!
FROM NOW ON... YOU TWO TAKE SEPARATE BATHS.
LYNN

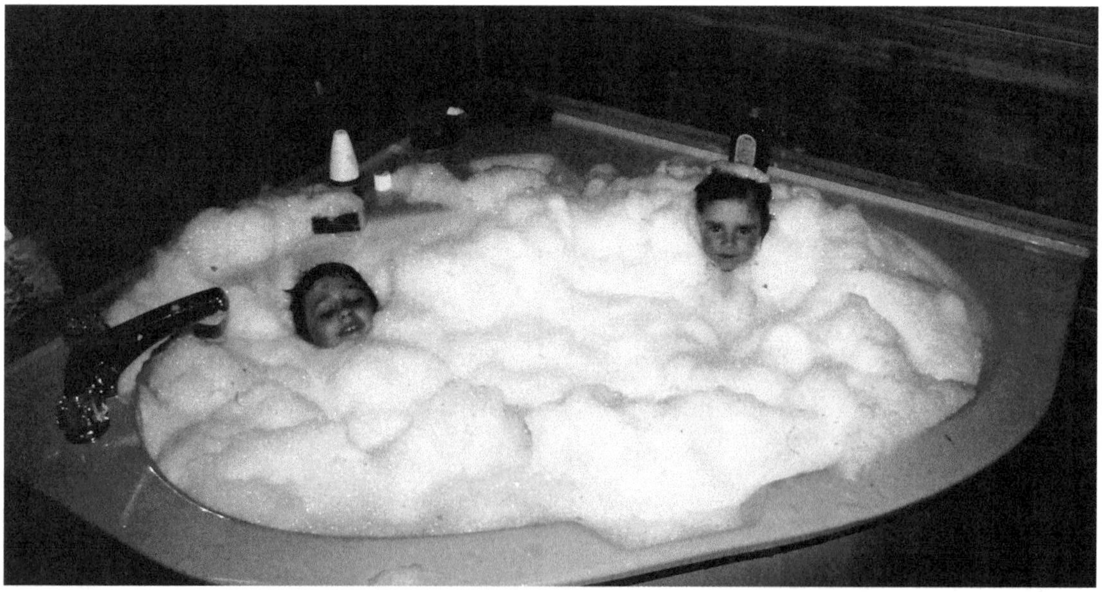

I told Aaron and Kate not to put shampoo into the Jacuzzi, but temptation got the best of them.
I tried to be angry, but took a photo instead.

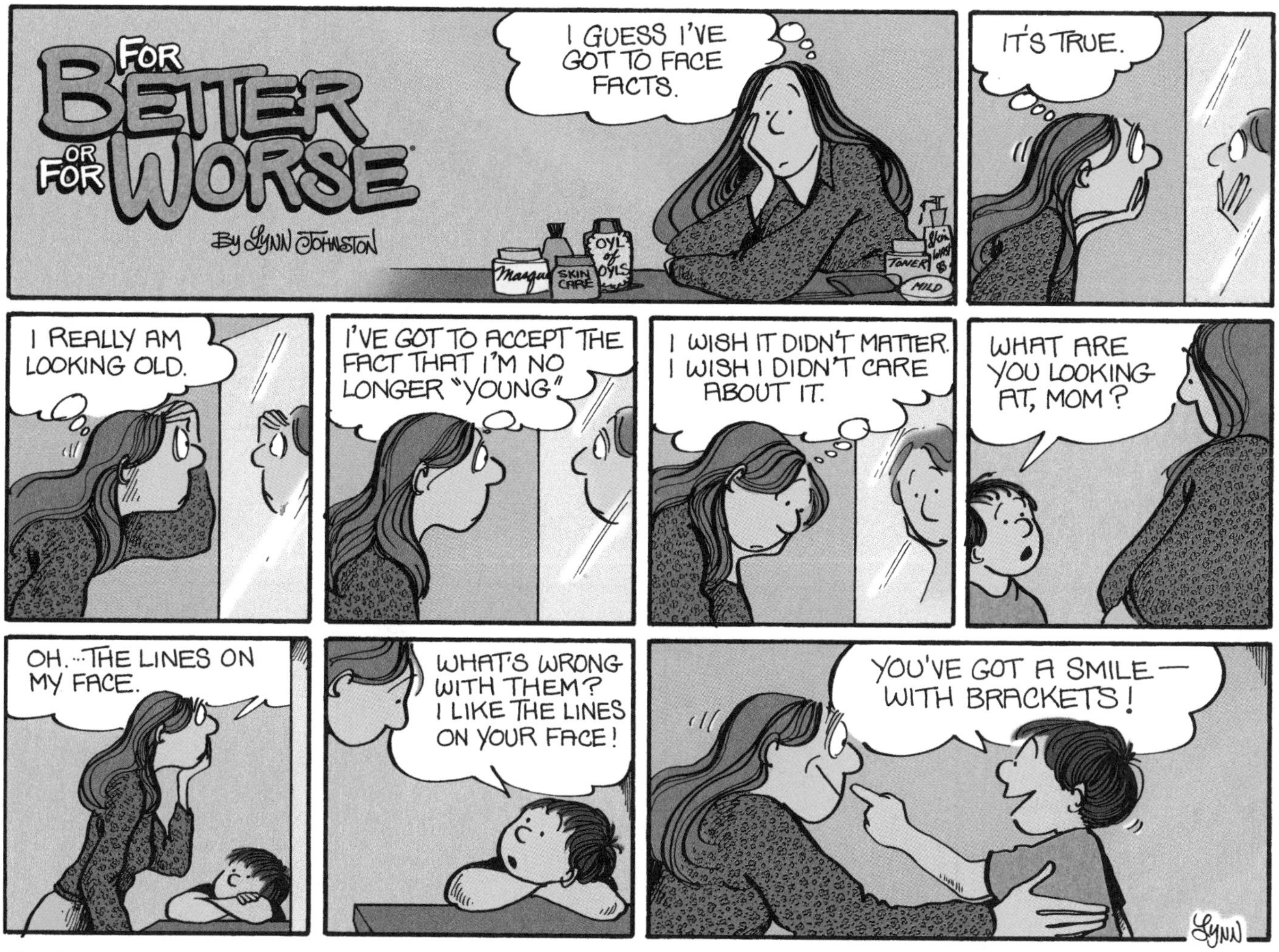
FOR BETTER OR FOR WORSE
BY LYNN JOHNSTON
I GUESS I'VE GOT TO FACE FACTS.
Masque
SKIN CARE
OYL of OYLS
TONER
MILD
IT'S TRUE.
I REALLY AM LOOKING OLD.
I'VE GOT TO ACCEPT THE FACT THAT I'M NO LONGER "YOUNG."
I WISH IT DIDN'T MATTER. I WISH I DIDN'T CARE ABOUT IT.
WHAT ARE YOU LOOKING AT, MOM?
OH.…THE LINES ON MY FACE.
WHAT'S WRONG WITH THEM? I LIKE THE LINES ON YOUR FACE!
YOU'VE GOT A SMILE — WITH BRACKETS!
LYNN

Here's a memory! — I think I was about four years old. My mother and I boarded the bus in North Vancouver. We were going home with some groceries, and the bus was full. Mom told me to go and find a seat somewhere, because we couldn't sit together. I walked up and down the aisle, looking at every face. My mother asked me what I was doing, and I replied, "I want to sit next to someone with smile lines." I remember that day, and it later occurred to me that this was "a smile with brackets." I was later able to incorporate that innocent thought into this Sunday strip.

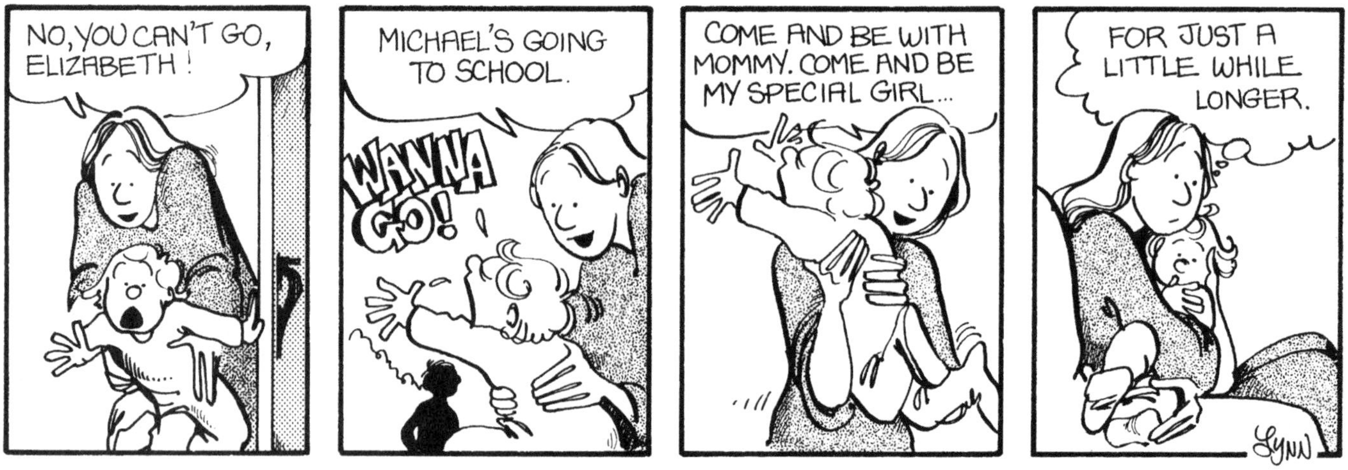
NO, YOU CAN'T GO, ELIZABETH!
MICHAEL'S GOING TO SCHOOL.
WANNA GO!
COME AND BE WITH MOMMY. COME AND BE MY SPECIAL GIRL...
FOR JUST A LITTLE WHILE LONGER.
Lynn

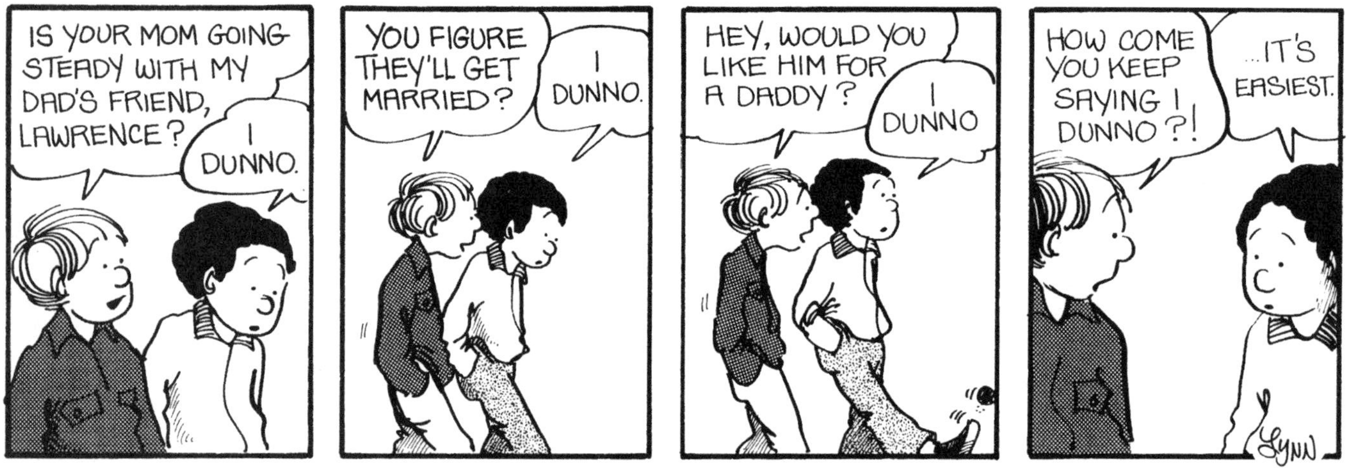
IS YOUR MOM GOING STEADY WITH MY DAD'S FRIEND, LAWRENCE?
I DUNNO.
YOU FIGURE THEY'LL GET MARRIED?
I DUNNO.
HEY, WOULD YOU LIKE HIM FOR A DADDY?
I DUNNO
HOW COME YOU KEEP SAYING I DUNNO?!
...IT'S EASIEST.
Lynn

My friend, Adrienne, and I were single moms together. Both of us had sons, and when we remarried, we wondered how our boys would accept another man in our lives. It wasn't easy. We both dealt with the stress of adjustment, acceptance, and adoption. Our boys did well. It wasn't until they were adults, however, that they told us how difficult it was to share us with someone new.

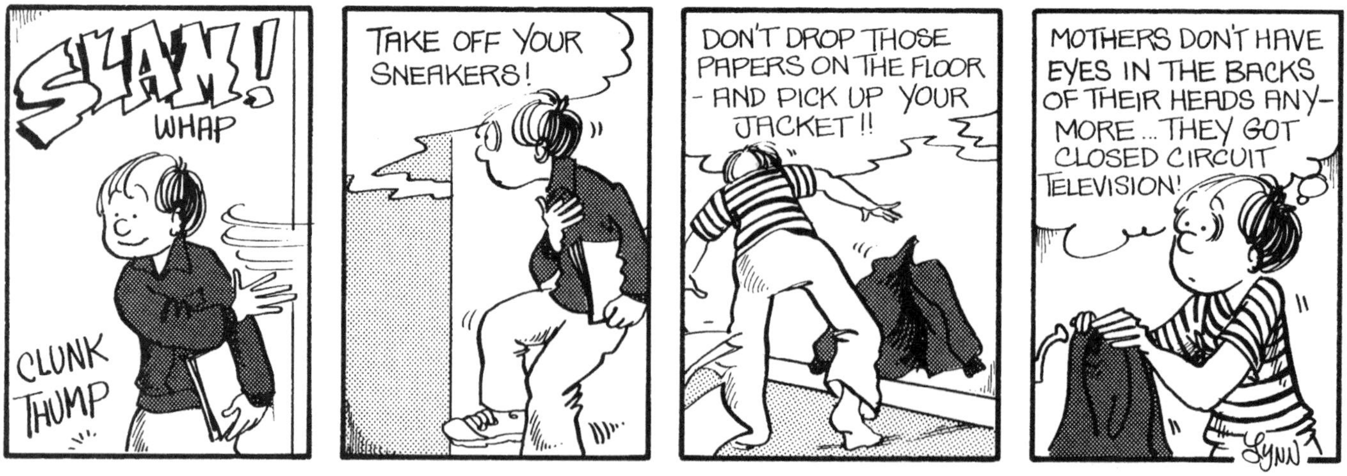
SLAM!
WHAP
CLUNK
THUMP
TAKE OFF YOUR SNEAKERS!
DON'T DROP THOSE PAPERS ON THE FLOOR - AND PICK UP YOUR JACKET!!
MOTHERS DON'T HAVE EYES IN THE BACKS OF THEIR HEADS ANY-MORE... THEY GOT CLOSED CIRCUIT TELEVISION!
Lynn

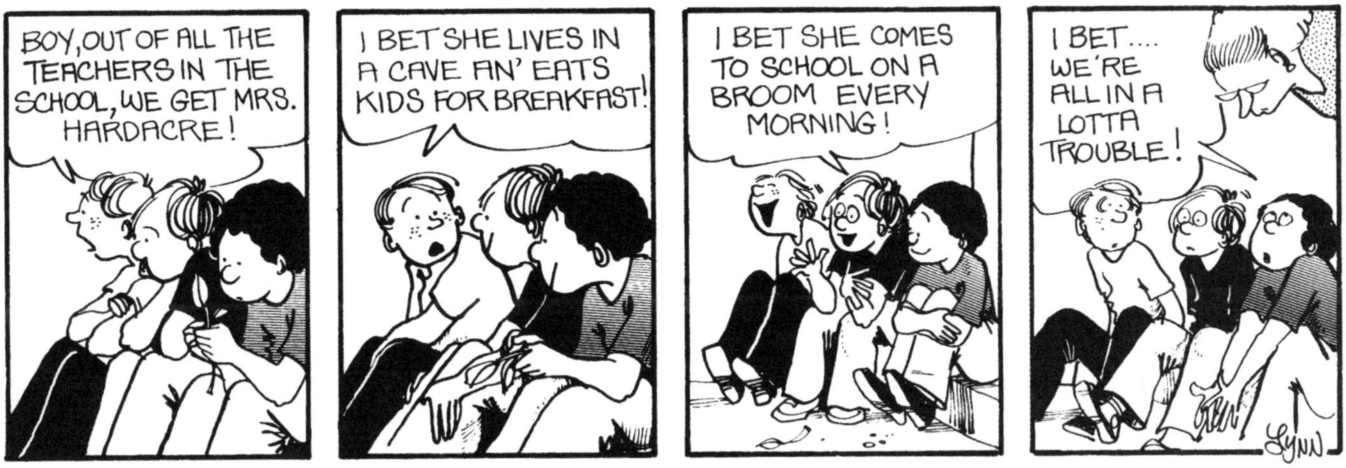
BOY, OUT OF ALL THE TEACHERS IN THE SCHOOL, WE GET MRS. HARDACRE!
I BET SHE LIVES IN A CAVE AN' EATS KIDS FOR BREAKFAST!
I BET SHE COMES TO SCHOOL ON A BROOM EVERY MORNING!
I BET.... WE'RE ALL IN A LOTTA TROUBLE!
LYNN

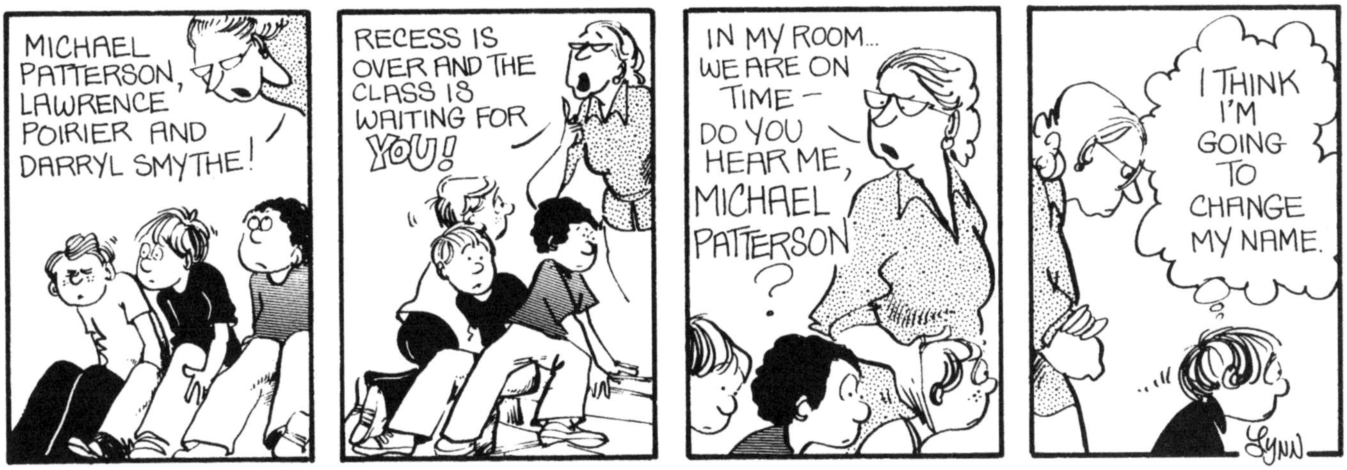
MICHAEL PATTERSON, LAWRENCE POIRIER AND DARRYL SMYTHE!
RECESS IS OVER AND THE CLASS IS WAITING FOR YOU!
IN MY ROOM... WE ARE ON TIME — DO YOU HEAR ME, MICHAEL PATTERSON?
I THINK I'M GOING TO CHANGE MY NAME.
LYNN

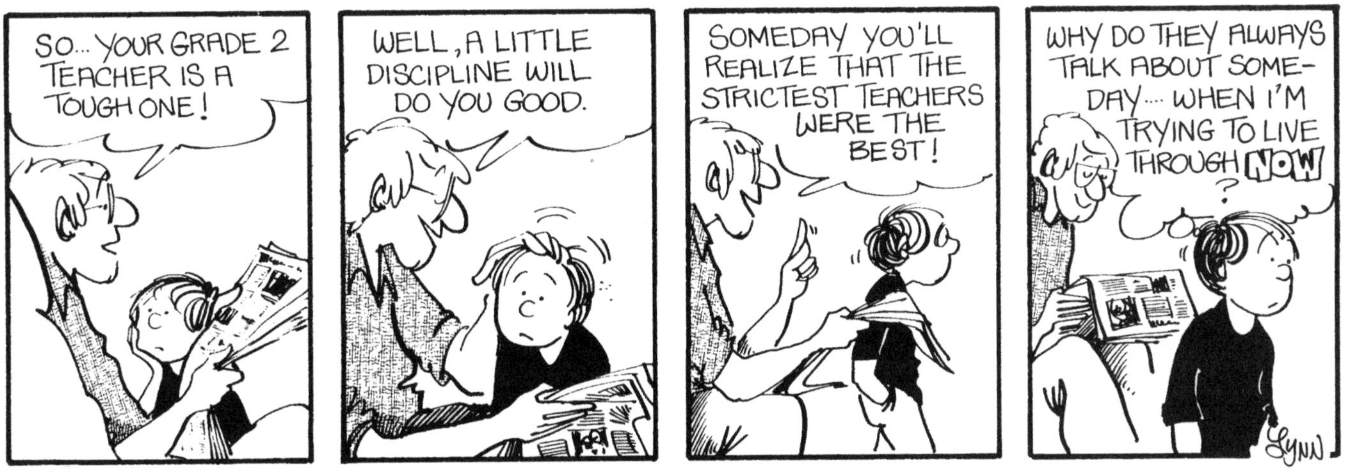
SO... YOUR GRADE 2 TEACHER IS A TOUGH ONE!
WELL, A LITTLE DISCIPLINE WILL DO YOU GOOD.
SOMEDAY YOU'LL REALIZE THAT THE STRICTEST TEACHERS WERE THE BEST!
WHY DO THEY ALWAYS TALK ABOUT SOMEDAY.... WHEN I'M TRYING TO LIVE THROUGH NOW?
LYNN

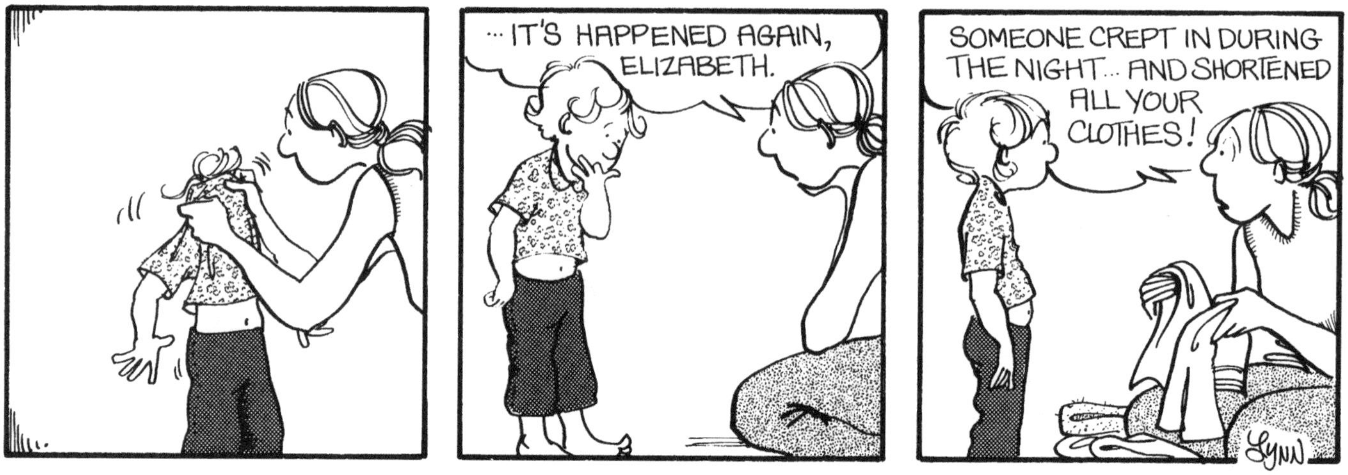
...IT'S HAPPENED AGAIN, ELIZABETH.
SOMEONE CREPT IN DURING THE NIGHT... AND SHORTENED ALL YOUR CLOTHES!
Lynn

I had two piles of clothing for each kid. One pile was too big, and the other they'd grown out of. The duds that fit were filtered through the closet from one pile to the next, and then exchanged with friends. The system went like clockwork. When I saw my friend Nancy looking at overalls in the Hudson's Bay store, I suggested she buy the green ones because they'd suit Katie! I knew they'd hit our "in" pile as soon as her daughter grew out of them!

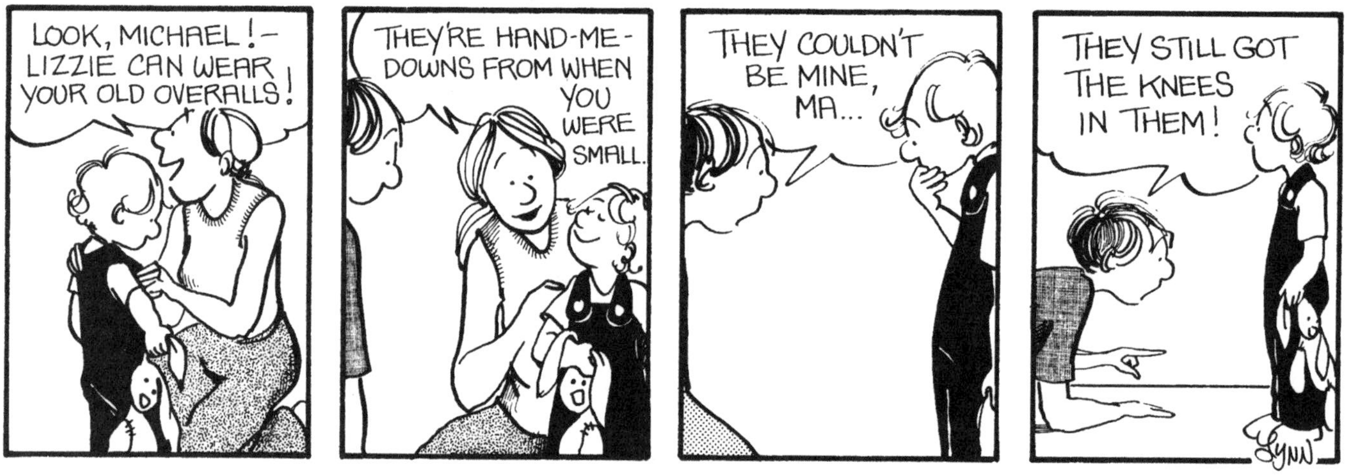
LOOK, MICHAEL! - LIZZIE CAN WEAR YOUR OLD OVERALLS!
THEY'RE HAND-ME-DOWNS FROM WHEN YOU WERE SMALL.
THEY COULDN'T BE MINE, MA...
THEY STILL GOT THE KNEES IN THEM!
Lynn

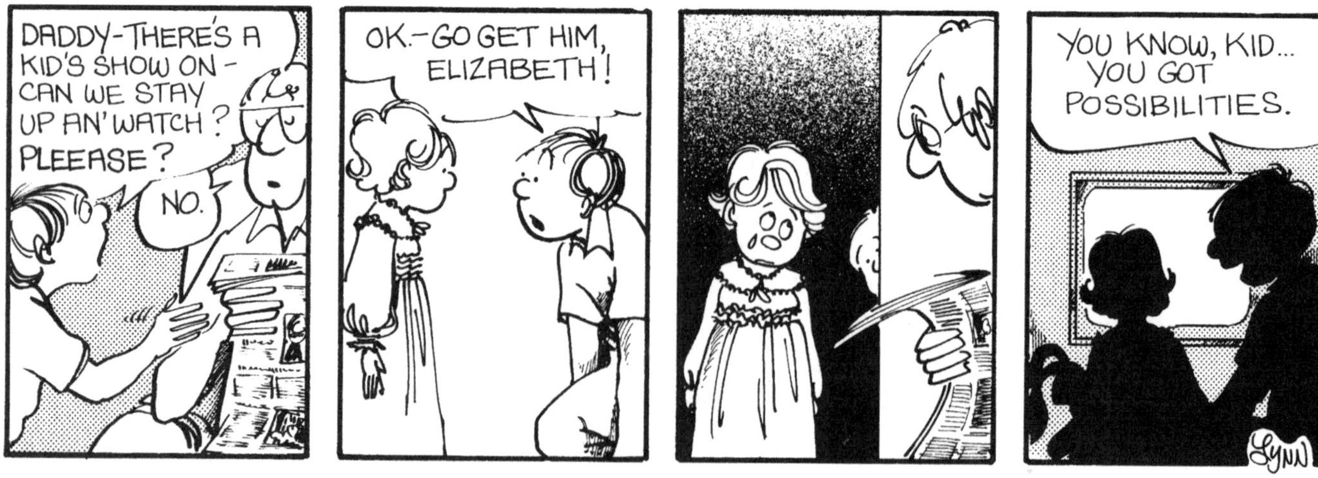
DADDY-THERE'S A KID'S SHOW ON - CAN WE STAY UP AN' WATCH? PLEEASE?
NO.
OK.-GO GET HIM, ELIZABETH!
YOU KNOW, KID... YOU GOT POSSIBILITIES.
Lynn

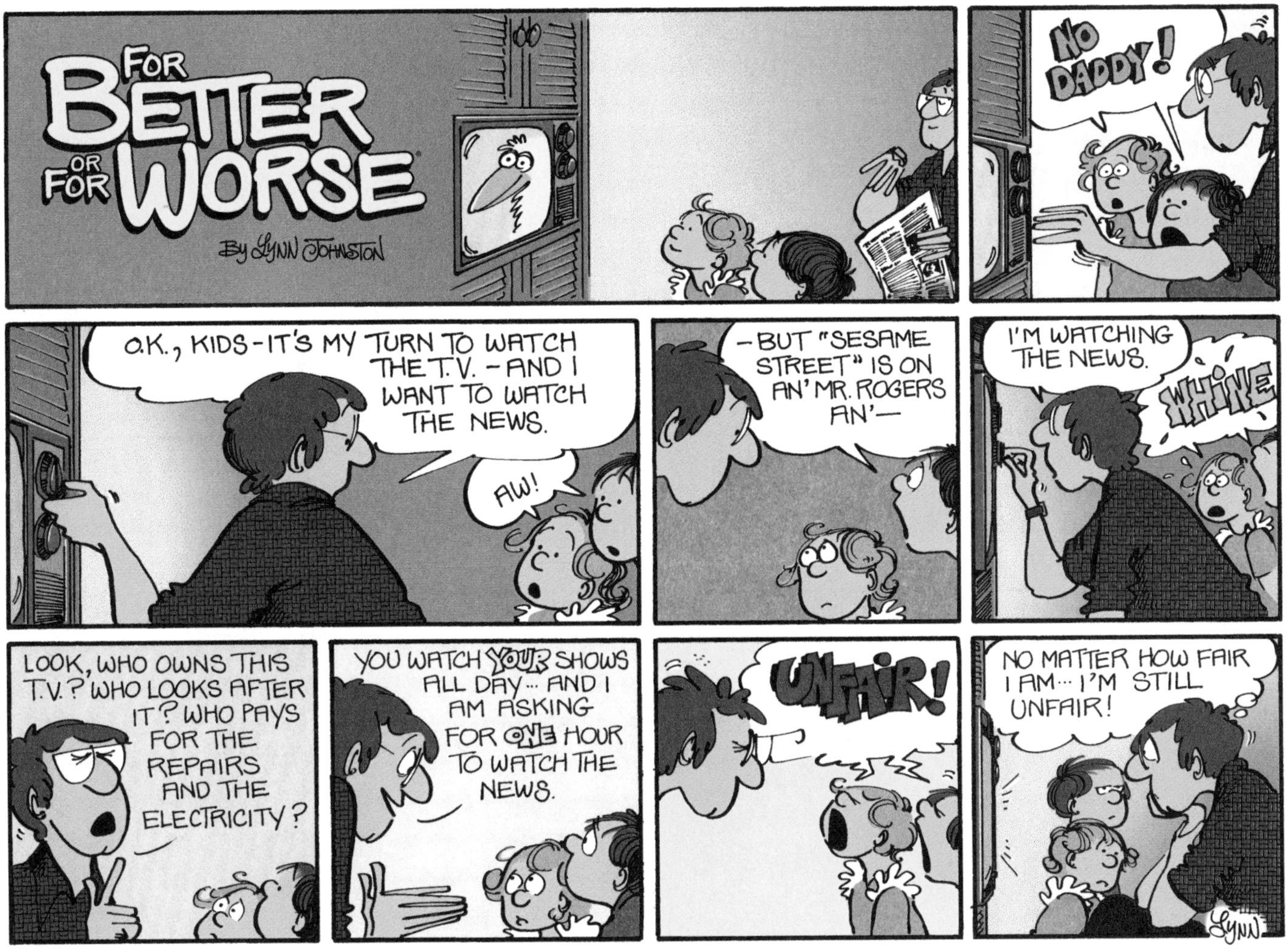
FOR BETTER OR FOR WORSE
BY LYNN JOHNSTON
NO DADDY!
O.K., KIDS - IT'S MY TURN TO WATCH THE T.V. - AND I WANT TO WATCH THE NEWS.
AW!
- BUT "SESAME STREET" IS ON AN' MR. ROGERS AN'—
I'M WATCHING THE NEWS.
WHINE
LOOK, WHO OWNS THIS T.V.? WHO LOOKS AFTER IT? WHO PAYS FOR THE REPAIRS AND THE ELECTRICITY?
YOU WATCH YOUR SHOWS ALL DAY... AND I AM ASKING FOR ONE HOUR TO WATCH THE NEWS.
UNFAIR!
NO MATTER HOW FAIR I AM... I'M STILL UNFAIR!
LYNN

Here is another example of an exchange that really took place. After a long day at the clinic, Rod wanted to watch TV, but had to bargain for the right to do so. The simple logic of who owned the set and who paid for it was not something the kids allowed to register, and as I recall, this was the catalyst that lead to the purchase of a second television.

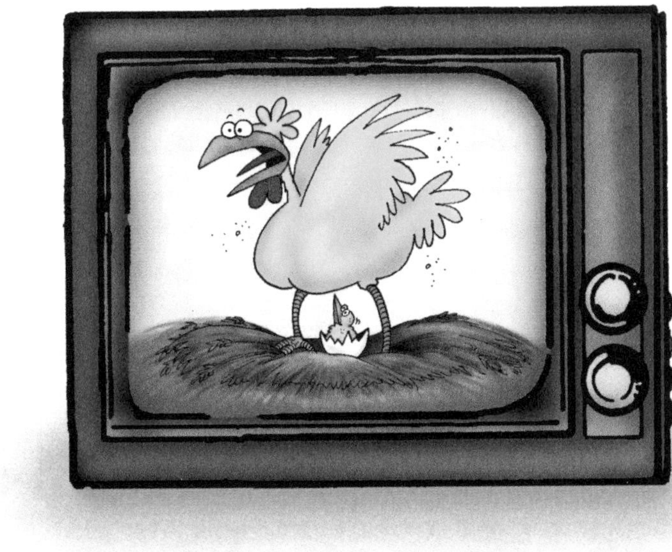

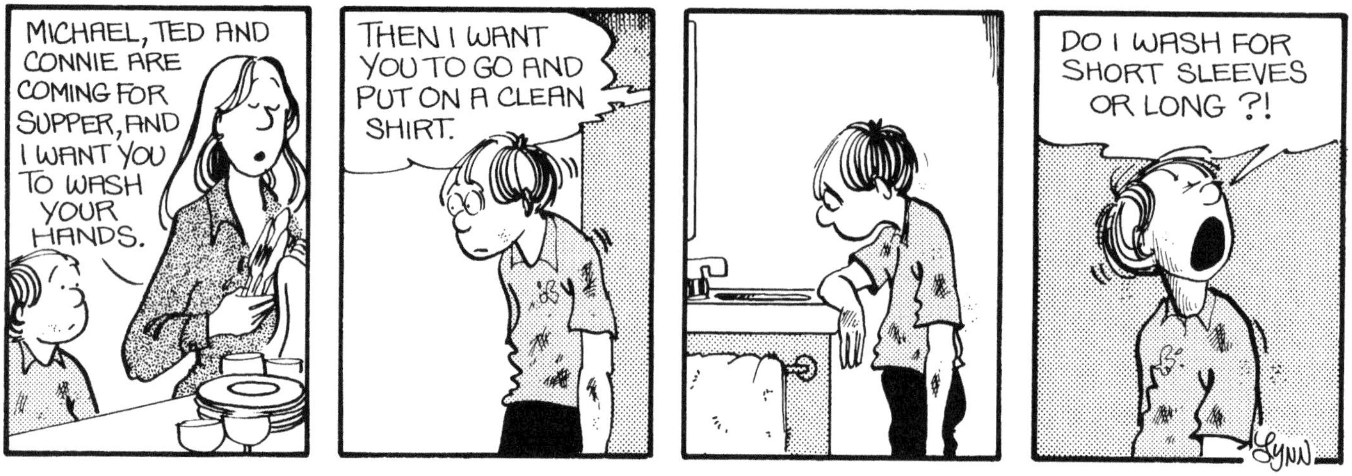
MICHAEL, TED AND CONNIE ARE COMING FOR SUPPER, AND I WANT YOU TO WASH YOUR HANDS.
THEN I WANT YOU TO GO AND PUT ON A CLEAN SHIRT.
DO I WASH FOR SHORT SLEEVES OR LONG ?!
LYNN

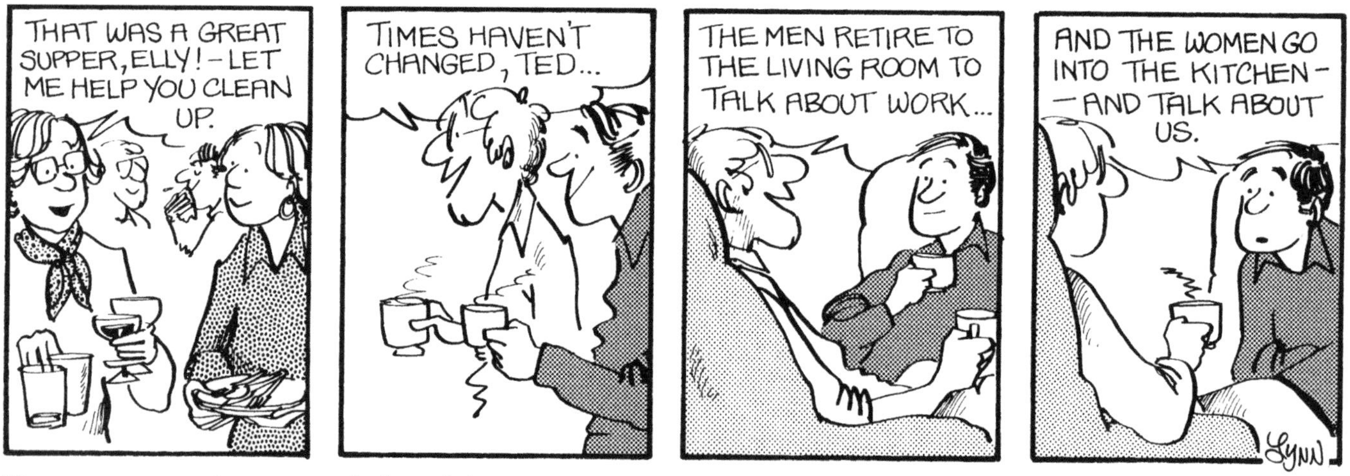
THAT WAS A GREAT SUPPER, ELLY! - LET ME HELP YOU CLEAN UP.
TIMES HAVEN'T CHANGED, TED...
THE MEN RETIRE TO THE LIVING ROOM TO TALK ABOUT WORK...
AND THE WOMEN GO INTO THE KITCHEN - - AND TALK ABOUT US.
LYNN

There were no good restaurants in Lynn Lake, so we got together often with friends for home-cooked meals. The "wimmin" did do the cleaning up, and we did enjoy our private conversations in the kitchen. I don't remember any resentment either — it was our opportunity to kvetch!

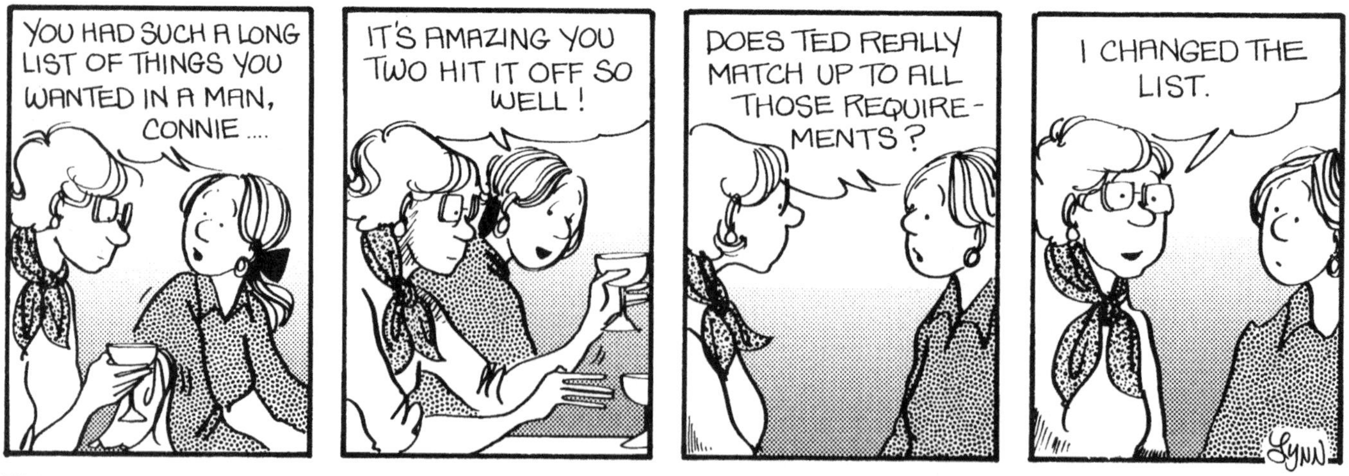
YOU HAD SUCH A LONG LIST OF THINGS YOU WANTED IN A MAN, CONNIE....
IT'S AMAZING YOU TWO HIT IT OFF SO WELL!
DOES TED REALLY MATCH UP TO ALL THOSE REQUIRE-MENTS?
I CHANGED THE LIST.
LYNN

This punch line was one I was particularly proud of. It was true for me. The list I had mentally written changed when I met the man who seemed to be "the one." It's surprising how much we are willing to accept in the name of love. Sadly, the list comes back to haunt us once the commitment has been made!

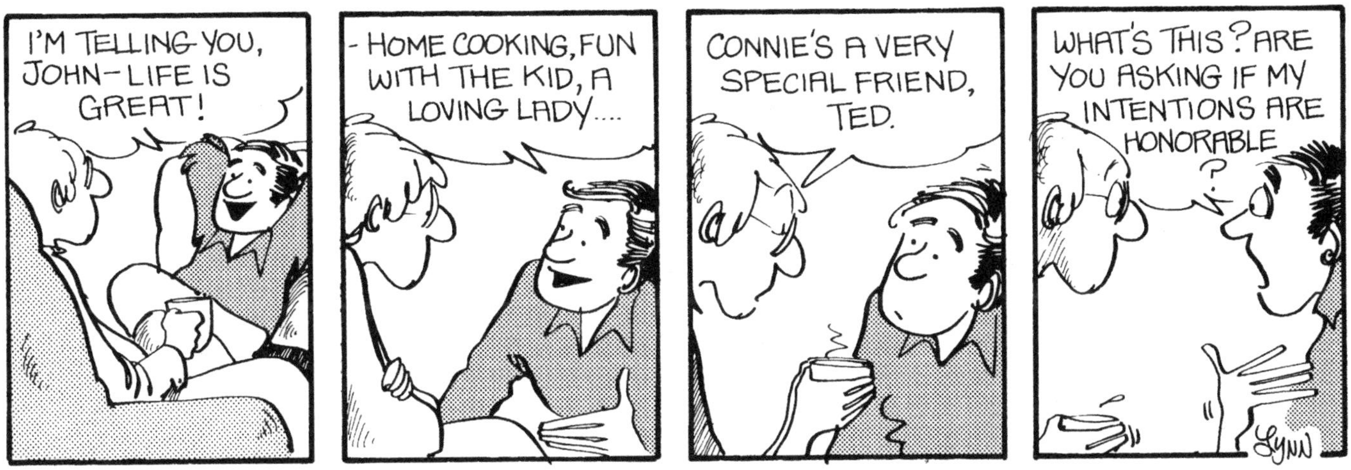
I'M TELLING YOU, JOHN – LIFE IS GREAT!
– HOME COOKING, FUN WITH THE KID, A LOVING LADY....
CONNIE'S A VERY SPECIAL FRIEND, TED.
WHAT'S THIS? ARE YOU ASKING IF MY INTENTIONS ARE HONORABLE?
LYNN

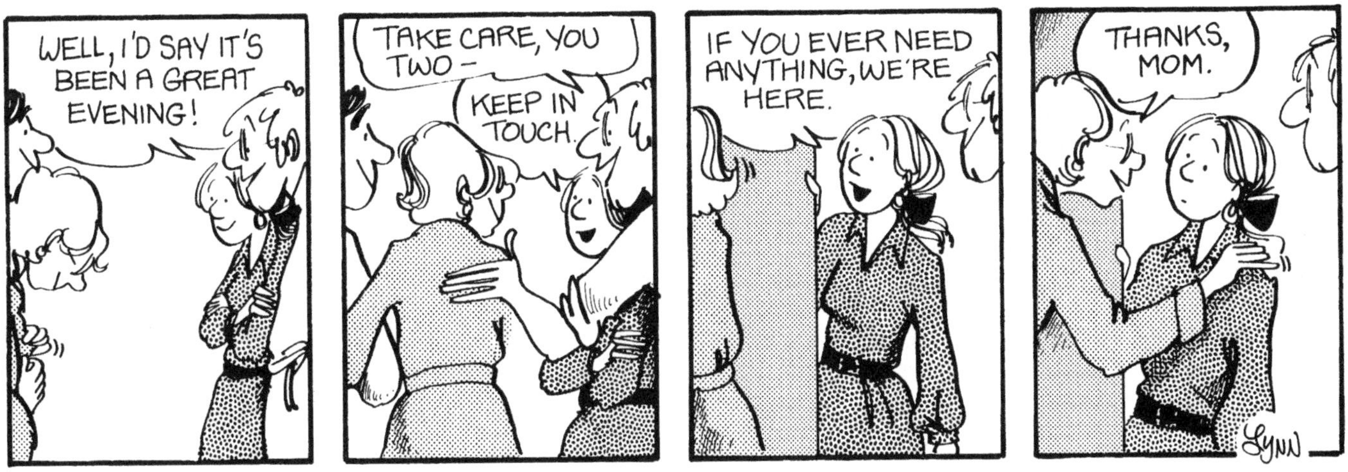
WELL, I'D SAY IT'S BEEN A GREAT EVENING!
TAKE CARE, YOU TWO –
KEEP IN TOUCH.
IF YOU EVER NEED ANYTHING, WE'RE HERE.
THANKS, MOM.
LYNN

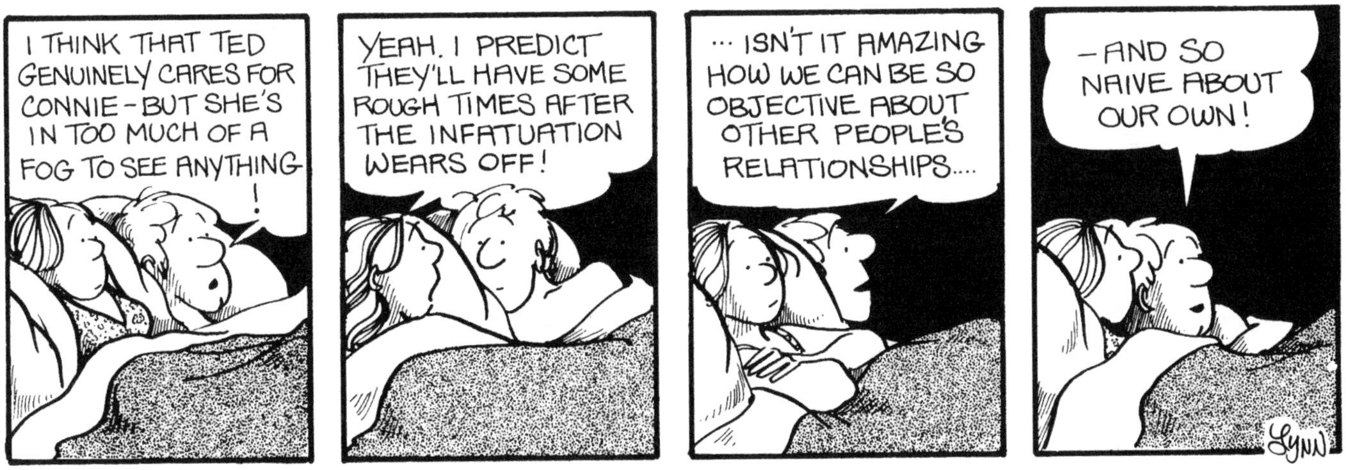
I THINK THAT TED GENUINELY CARES FOR CONNIE – BUT SHE'S IN TOO MUCH OF A FOG TO SEE ANYTHING!
YEAH. I PREDICT THEY'LL HAVE SOME ROUGH TIMES AFTER THE INFATUATION WEARS OFF!
... ISN'T IT AMAZING HOW WE CAN BE SO OBJECTIVE ABOUT OTHER PEOPLE'S RELATIONSHIPS....
– AND SO NAIVE ABOUT OUR OWN!
LYNN

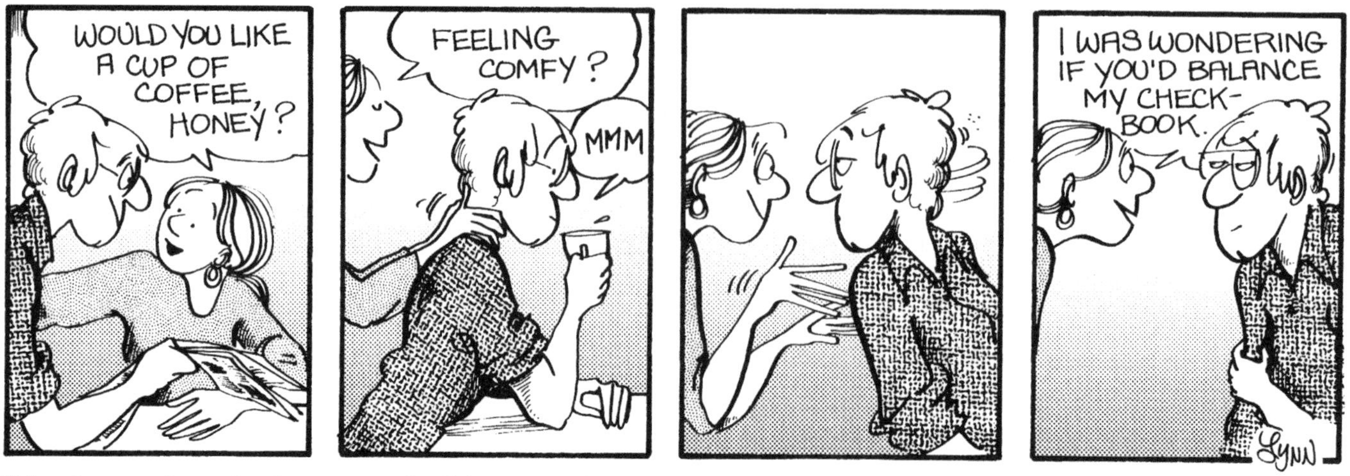
WOULD YOU LIKE A CUP OF COFFEE, HONEY?
FEELING COMFY?
MMM
I WAS WONDERING IF YOU'D BALANCE MY CHECK-BOOK.

Balancing my chequebook was — and still is — one of my least favourite things to do. I'm happy if my cheques don't bounce. My daughter will chase down a discrepancy to the penny, but I prefer to say, "close enough." When I worked for my dad in the jewellry store, I was fine with clients, cleaning, and window displays, but I was kept away from the till. My guess is that even with today's electronic calculators, I would still find ways to make mistakes!

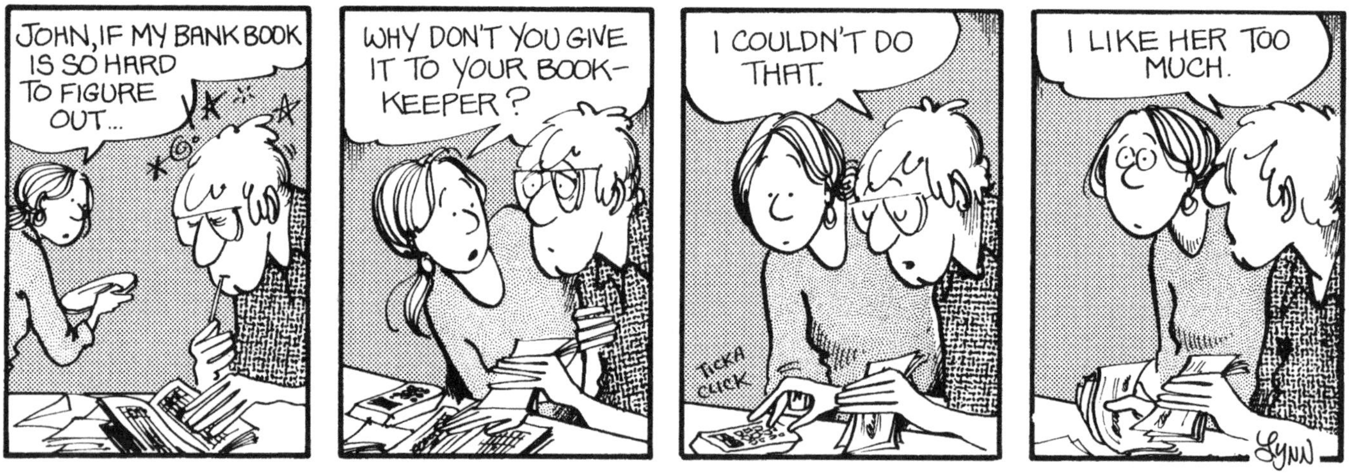
JOHN, IF MY BANK BOOK IS SO HARD TO FIGURE OUT...
WHY DON'T YOU GIVE IT TO YOUR BOOK-KEEPER?
I COULDN'T DO THAT.
TICKA CLICK
I LIKE HER TOO MUCH.

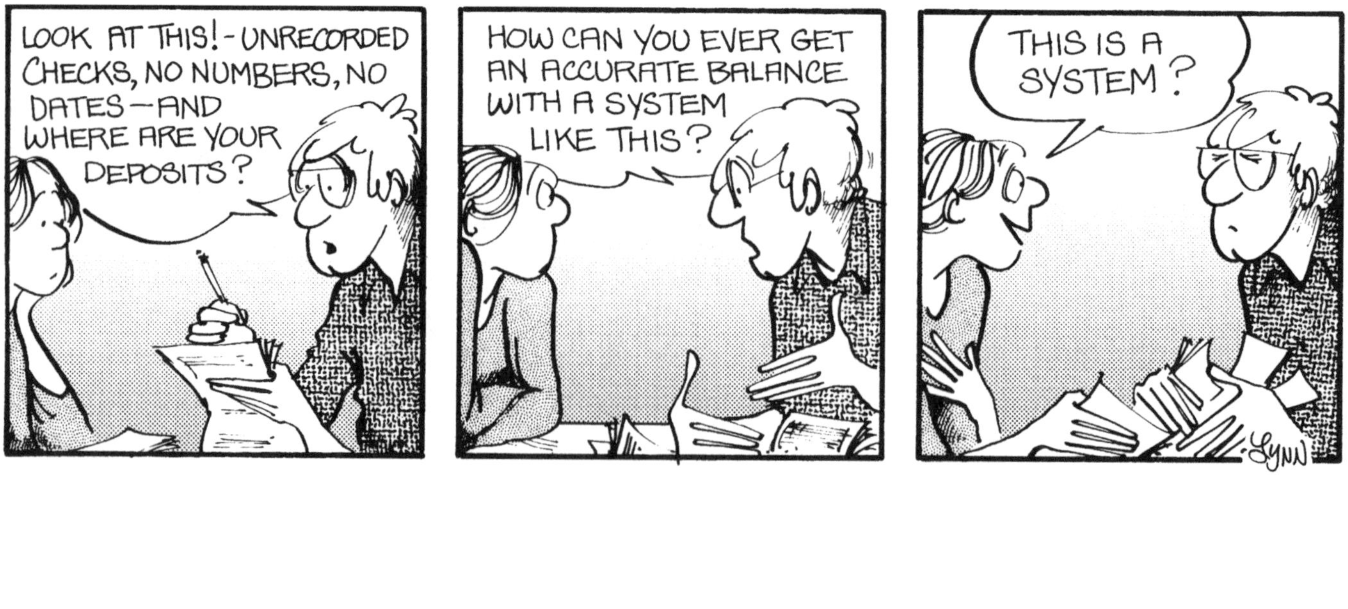
LOOK AT THIS! - UNRECORDED CHECKS, NO NUMBERS, NO DATES — AND WHERE ARE YOUR DEPOSITS?
HOW CAN YOU EVER GET AN ACCURATE BALANCE WITH A SYSTEM LIKE THIS?
THIS IS A SYSTEM?

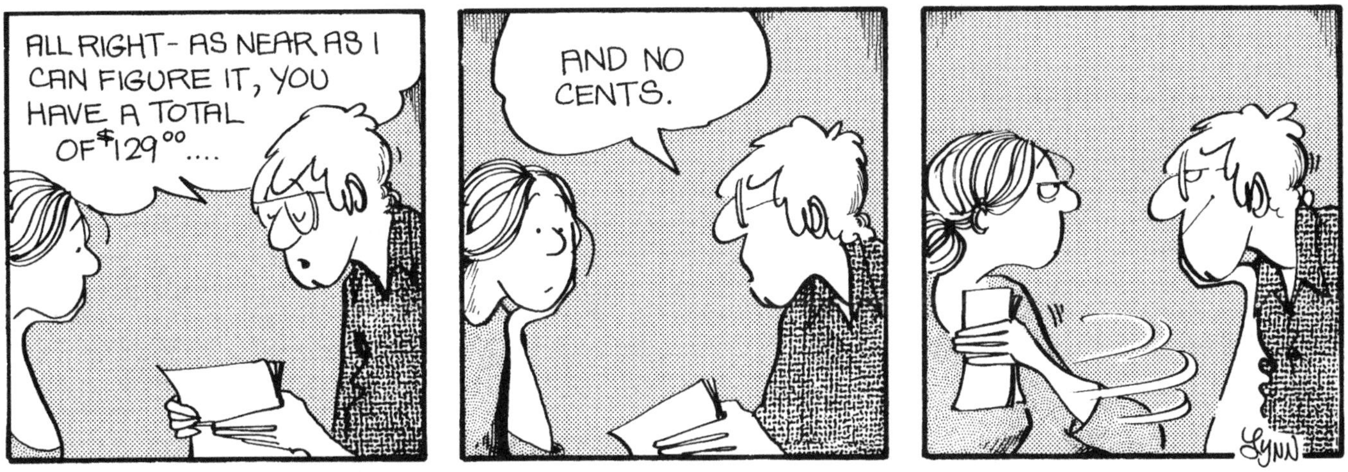
ALL RIGHT- AS NEAR AS I CAN FIGURE IT, YOU HAVE A TOTAL OF $129.00 ....
AND NO CENTS.
Lynn

The subject of money was not as sensitive to me as it was to a friend of mine. I had a full-time job, but she "earned" her income by working at home, and the money she spent was severely regulated by her husband, who "gifted" her with clothing allowances and money for incidentals. I used her situation from time to time when money was an issue with the Pattersons and Elly felt guilty for not "working."

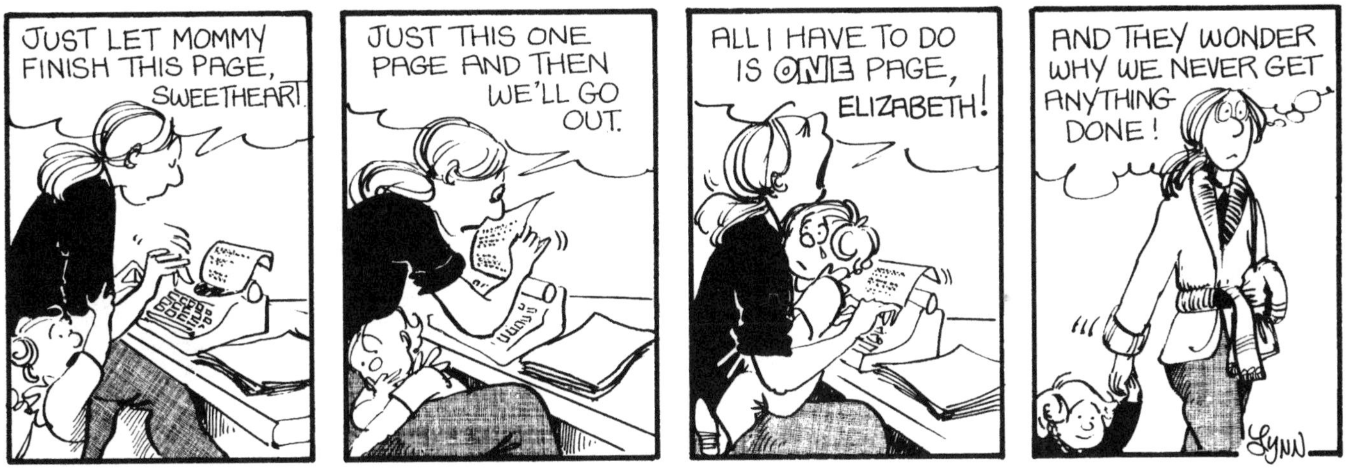
JUST LET MOMMY FINISH THIS PAGE, SWEETHEART.
JUST THIS ONE PAGE AND THEN WE'LL GO OUT.
ALL I HAVE TO DO IS ONE PAGE, ELIZABETH!
AND THEY WONDER WHY WE NEVER GET ANYTHING DONE!
Lynn

There were times when I sat down and tried to figure out what I had actually accomplished during the day. With so many demands on a mom's time, it was hard to account for the hours. Isn't it strange that we call an actual paying job "work" and don't necessarily consider raising children hard work, as well? I confess ... being a good mom is one of the most challenging JOBS on the planet!!

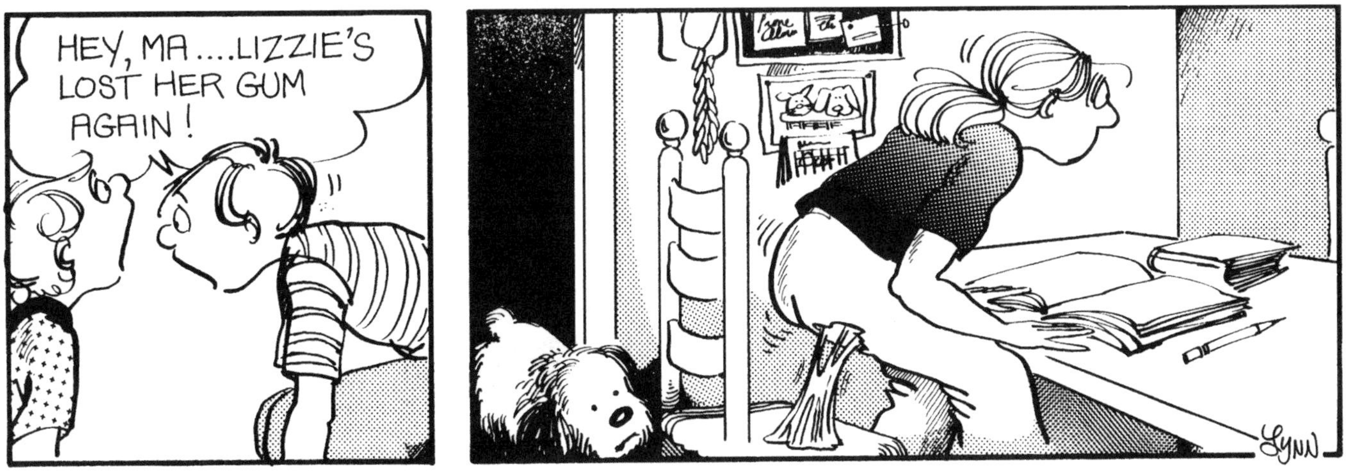
HEY, MA....LIZZIE'S LOST HER GUM AGAIN!
Lynn

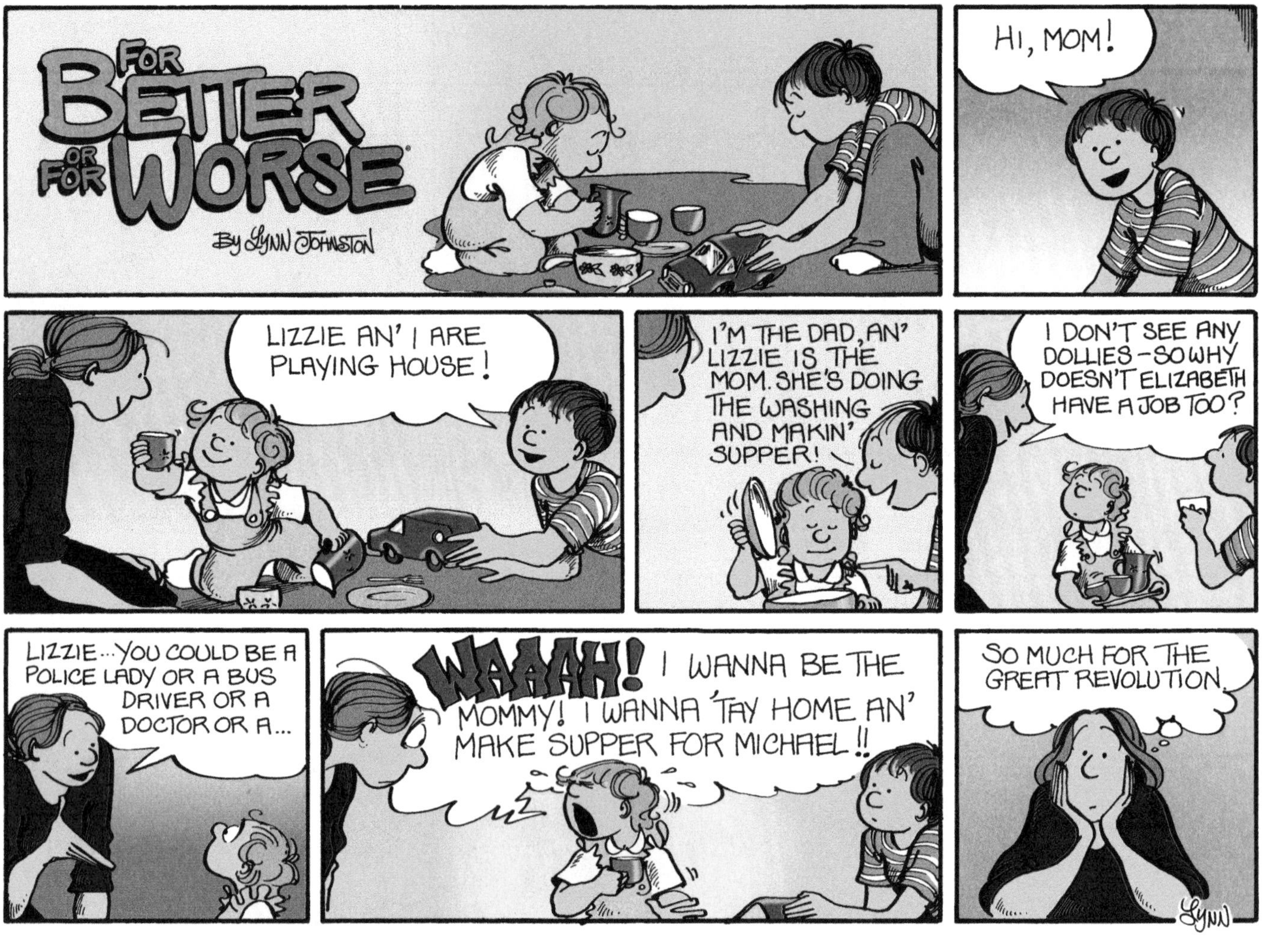
FOR BETTER OR FOR WORSE
BY LYNN JOHNSTON
HI, MOM!
LIZZIE AN' I ARE PLAYING HOUSE!
I'M THE DAD, AN' LIZZIE IS THE MOM. SHE'S DOING THE WASHING AND MAKIN' SUPPER!
I DON'T SEE ANY DOLLIES - SO WHY DOESN'T ELIZABETH HAVE A JOB TOO?
LIZZIE... YOU COULD BE A POLICE LADY OR A BUS DRIVER OR A DOCTOR OR A...
WAAAH! I WANNA BE THE MOMMY! I WANNA 'TAY HOME AN' MAKE SUPPER FOR MICHAEL!!
SO MUCH FOR THE GREAT REVOLUTION.
LYNN

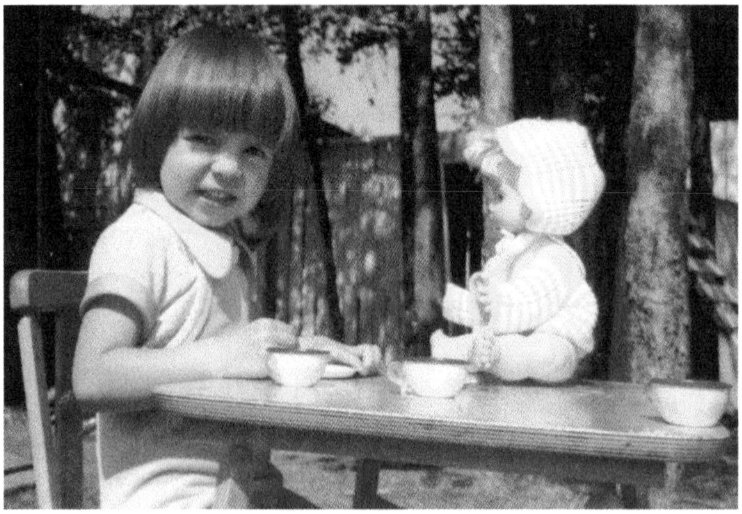

Katie and her tea set in the backyard of our house in Lynn Lake.

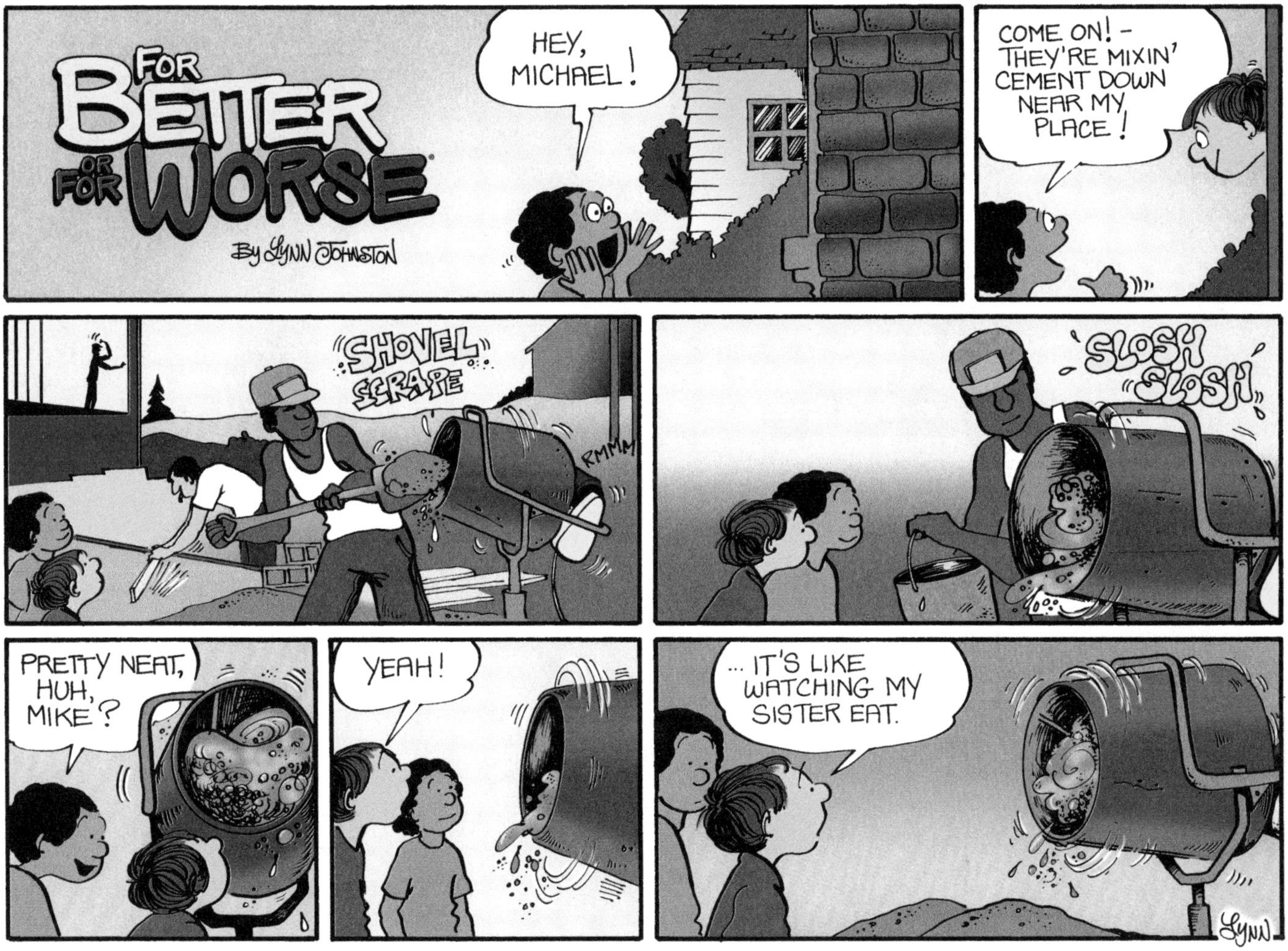
FOR BETTER OR FOR WORSE
BY LYNN JOHNSTON
HEY, MICHAEL!
COME ON! - THEY'RE MIXIN' CEMENT DOWN NEAR MY PLACE!
SHOVEL SCRAPE
RMMM
SLOSH SLOSH
PRETTY NEAT, HUH, MIKE?
YEAH!
... IT'S LIKE WATCHING MY SISTER EAT.
LYNN

In our house, it was of utmost importance to maintain good table manners. My mother went so far as to give us eating lessons. My brother and I learned to sit straight, with yardsticks down our backs and a Golden Book under each arm.

We learned how to use our fork and knife in the English style, cutting with wrists up, dabbing the edibles onto the back of the fork. (Rarely should one "stab" at one's food.) We were never to talk with our mouths full; never to reveal the mastication going on inside. Eating was often an ordeal. The benefits of the lessons, however, came to the fore at summer camp when we were the only kids who could eat comfortably while crushed onto a wooden bench with a line of other campers.

If Mom saw us chewing with our mouths open, there was instant objection. This, of course, made it mandatory that we eat as rudely as possibly when the moment was ripe. This strip was done in memory of those unfettered times.

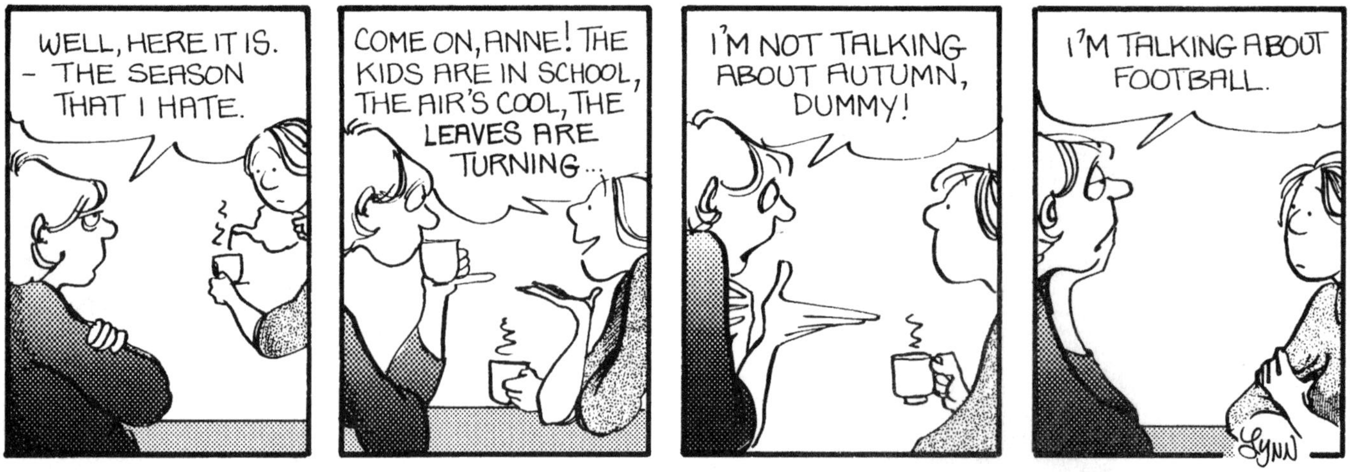
WELL, HERE IT IS. - THE SEASON THAT I HATE.
COME ON, ANNE! THE KIDS ARE IN SCHOOL, THE AIR'S COOL, THE LEAVES ARE TURNING...
I'M NOT TALKING ABOUT AUTUMN, DUMMY!
I'M TALKING ABOUT FOOTBALL.
LYNN

I was once married to a guy who spent so much time on the couch watching televised sports, I suggested we give away the couch, screw legs on him, and use HIM as furniture.

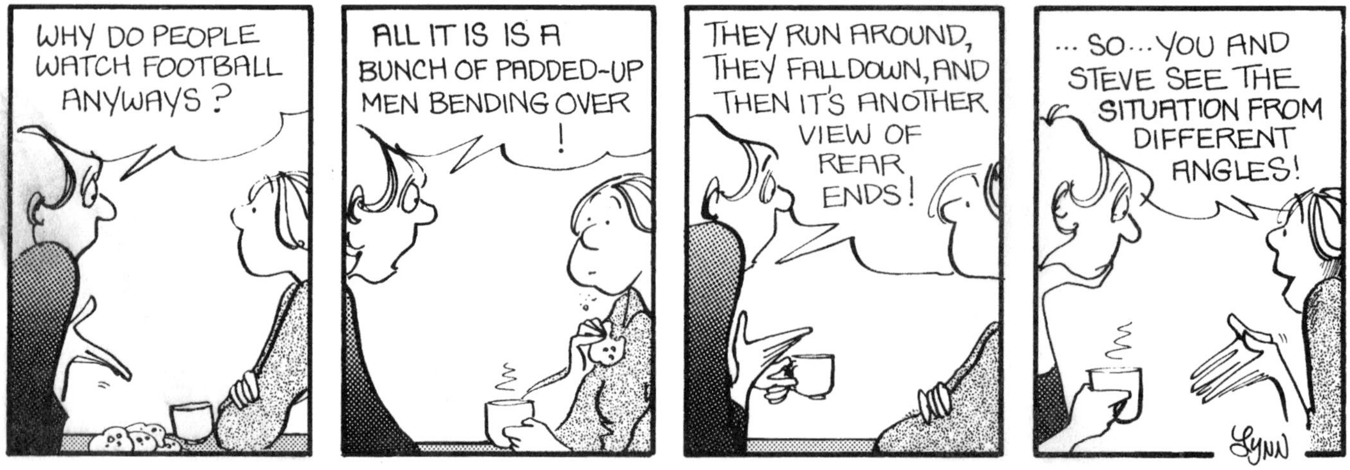
WHY DO PEOPLE WATCH FOOTBALL ANYWAYS?
ALL IT IS IS A BUNCH OF PADDED-UP MEN BENDING OVER!
THEY RUN AROUND, THEY FALL DOWN, AND THEN IT'S ANOTHER VIEW OF REAR ENDS!
... SO... YOU AND STEVE SEE THE SITUATION FROM DIFFERENT ANGLES!
LYNN

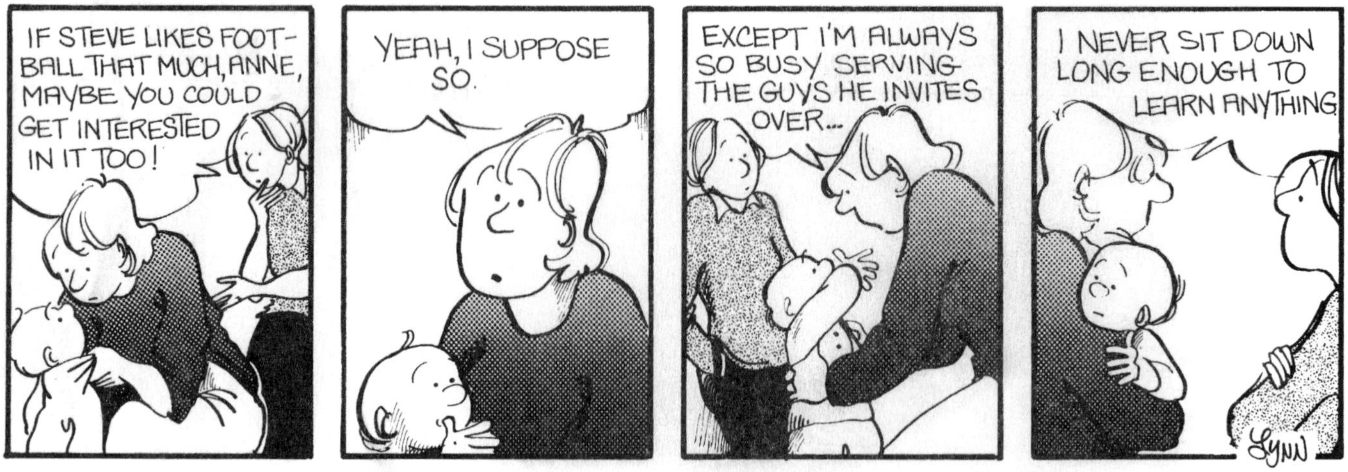
IF STEVE LIKES FOOTBALL THAT MUCH, ANNE, MAYBE YOU COULD GET INTERESTED IN IT TOO!
YEAH, I SUPPOSE SO.
EXCEPT I'M ALWAYS SO BUSY SERVING THE GUYS HE INVITES OVER...
I NEVER SIT DOWN LONG ENOUGH TO LEARN ANYTHING
LYNN

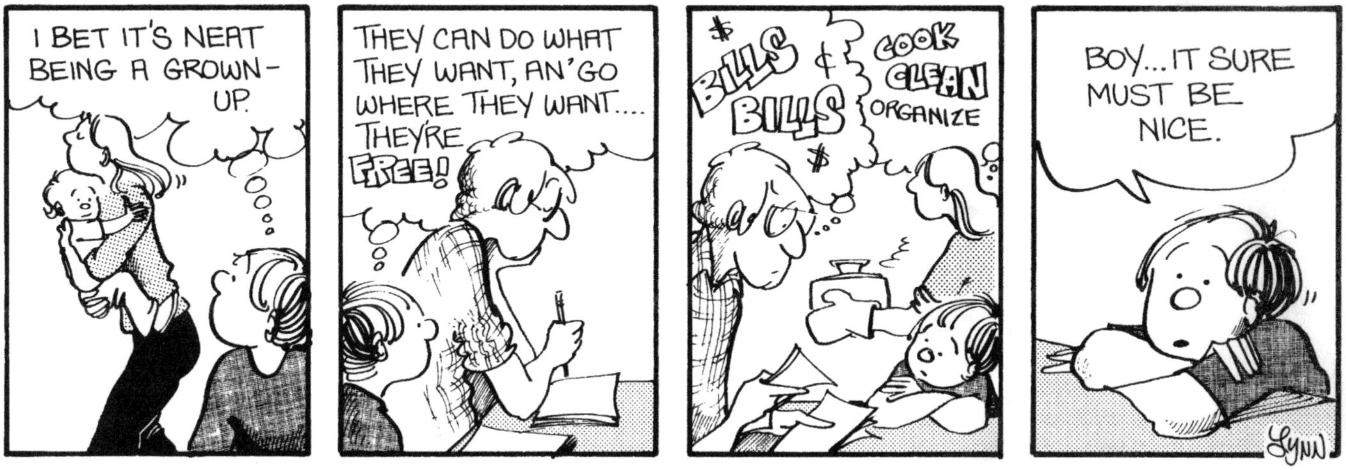
I BET IT'S NEAT BEING A GROWN-UP.
THEY CAN DO WHAT THEY WANT, AN' GO WHERE THEY WANT.... THEY'RE FREE!
BILLS $ BILLS ¢ $
COOK CLEAN ORGANIZE
BOY... IT SURE MUST BE NICE.
LYNN

As a kid, I thought being grown up would be the best thing ever. I thought about the freedom I'd have … And now that I've experienced many years of "freedom" … I wonder why I didn't appreciate those years when somebody ELSE did all the work and the worrying!

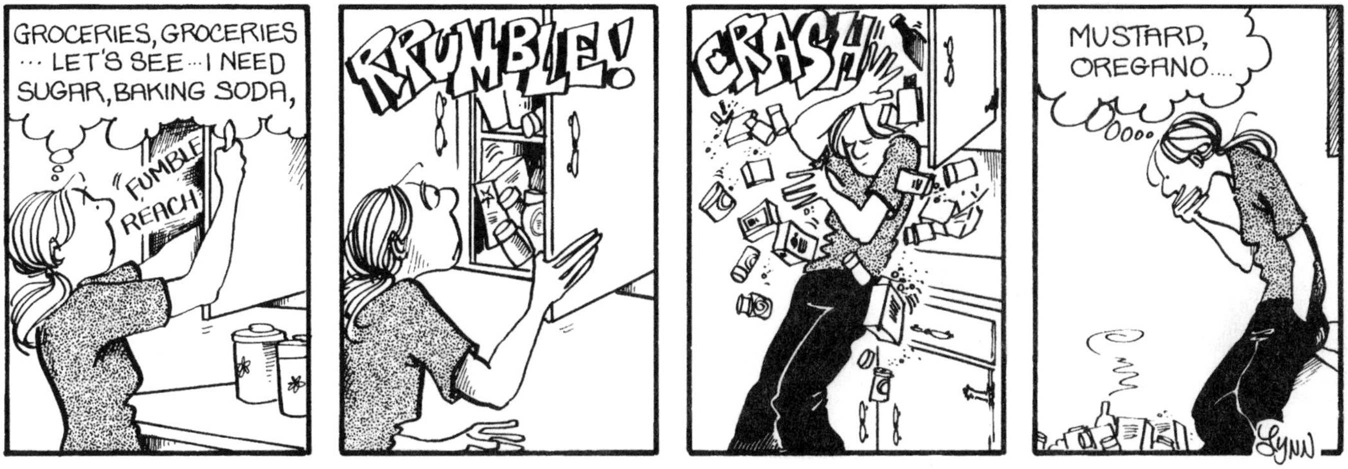
GROCERIES, GROCERIES ... LET'S SEE... I NEED SUGAR, BAKING SODA,
FUMBLE REACH
RRUMBLE!
CRASH!
MUSTARD, OREGANO....
LYNN

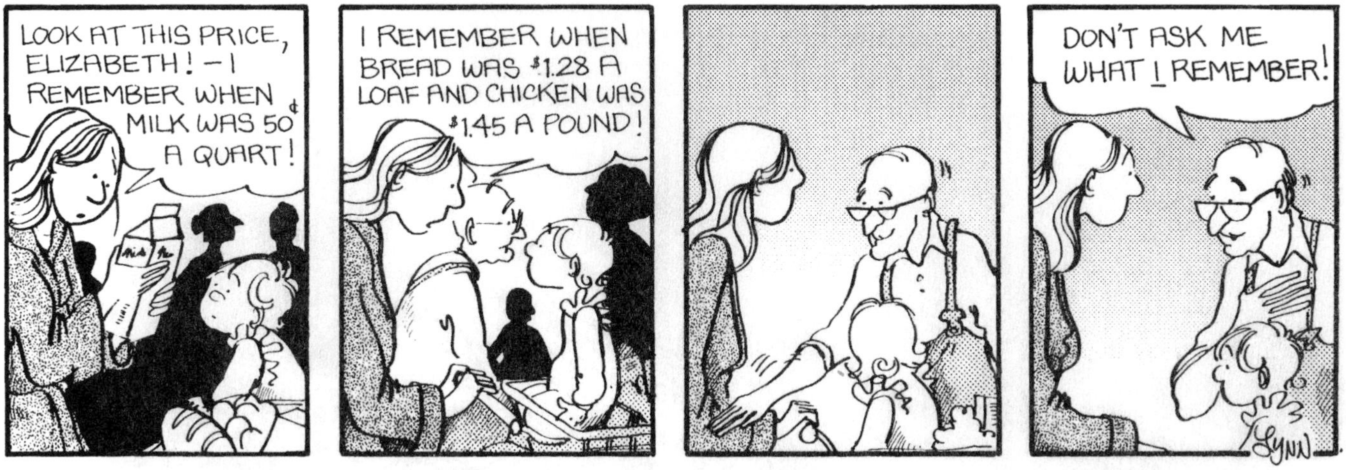
LOOK AT THIS PRICE, ELIZABETH! — I REMEMBER WHEN MILK WAS 50¢ A QUART!
I REMEMBER WHEN BREAD WAS $1.28 A LOAF AND CHICKEN WAS $1.45 A POUND!
DON'T ASK ME WHAT I REMEMBER!
LYNN

This scenario took place word for word as I was grocery shopping with Aaron. I was a single mom on a very tight budget, and if I went over $20 a week for the two of us, I wouldn't be able to pay my mortgage (which was $150 a month at the time).
An older gentleman heard me comparing prices to those of my childhood, and reminded me that times had changed for him, too.
Here I am, now at the age of 64, likely the same age he was … and prices have gone beyond what any of us could have imagined.

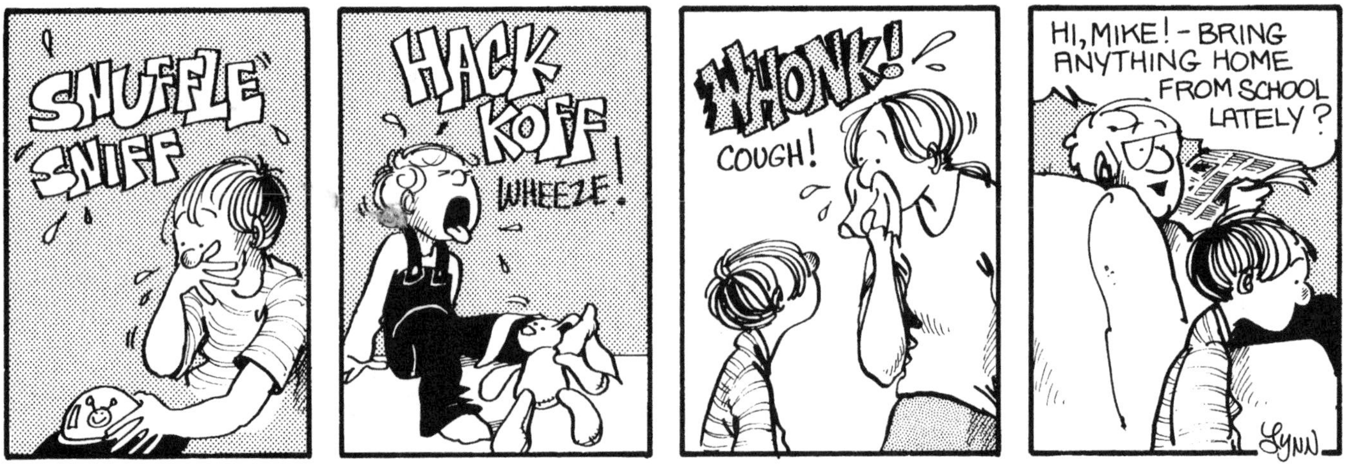
SNUFFLE
SNIFF
HACK
KOFF
WHEEZE!
WHONK!
COUGH!
HI, MIKE! - BRING ANYTHING HOME FROM SCHOOL LATELY?
LYNN

Back to school, always meant "back to bed," as the kids bumbled home with everything from flu to pinkeye. Mine had to be certifiably sick before I'd let them skip school ... none of the "thermometer under the hot water-bottle" stuff ... I wanted proof. Proof of a certified illness usually came in the form of a shared experience as we all came down with whatever was going 'round. "The family that's sick together sticks together," and we did ... under quarantine.

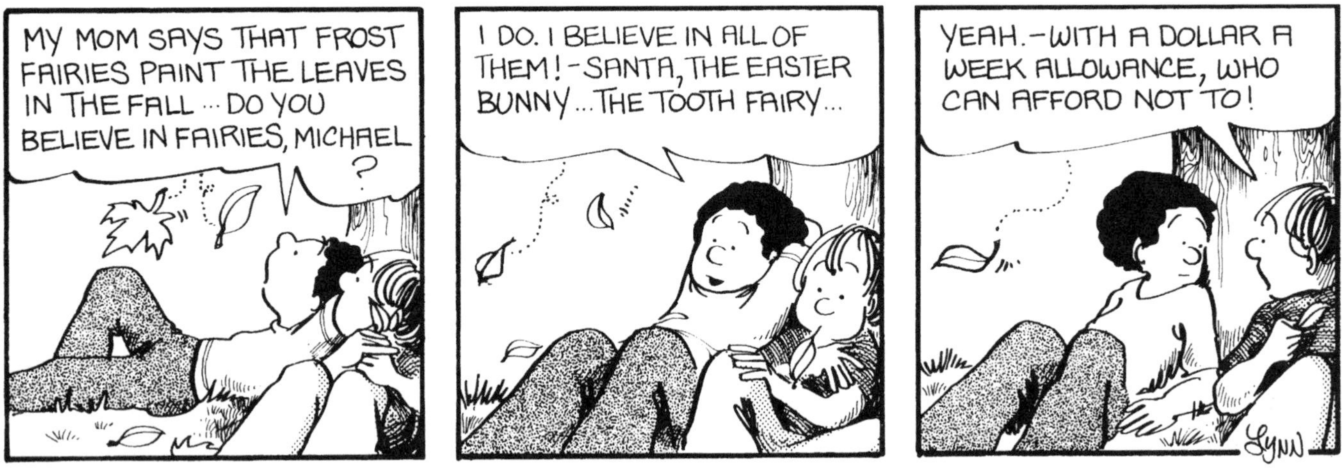
MY MOM SAYS THAT FROST FAIRIES PAINT THE LEAVES IN THE FALL ... DO YOU BELIEVE IN FAIRIES, MICHAEL?
I DO. I BELIEVE IN ALL OF THEM! - SANTA, THE EASTER BUNNY ... THE TOOTH FAIRY ...
YEAH. - WITH A DOLLAR A WEEK ALLOWANCE, WHO CAN AFFORD NOT TO!
LYNN

I don't know what passes for the average allowance now. A buck a week was fine when Kate and Aaron were kids — they seemed to make do. As I recall, however, no matter what the folks decide to bestow ... it's never, ever enough!

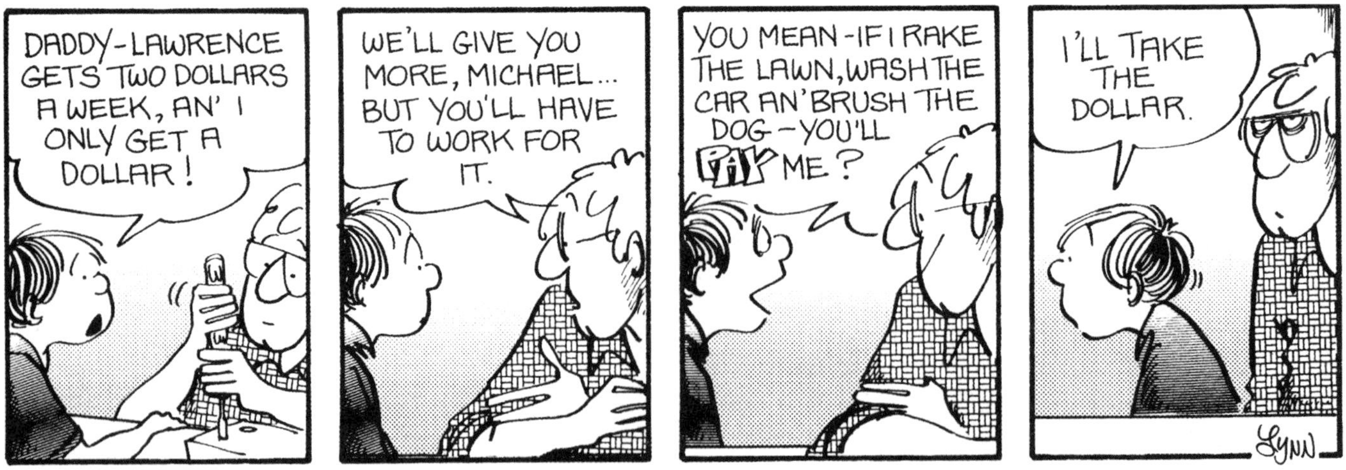
DADDY - LAWRENCE GETS TWO DOLLARS A WEEK, AN' I ONLY GET A DOLLAR!
WE'LL GIVE YOU MORE, MICHAEL ... BUT YOU'LL HAVE TO WORK FOR IT.
YOU MEAN - IF I RAKE THE LAWN, WASH THE CAR AN' BRUSH THE DOG - YOU'LL PAY ME?
I'LL TAKE THE DOLLAR.
LYNN

Negotiating for added income with my dad always involved chores. He rarely gave us extra for breathing ... there was always a lecture about earning, about effort and reward. My brother and I thought he was mean for denying us a free ride. We grumbled through our chores, and imagined we were orphans forced to work under the cruel gaze of a merciless supervisor. When we finally did receive the money, however, we had a real sense of accomplishment in having EARNED it.

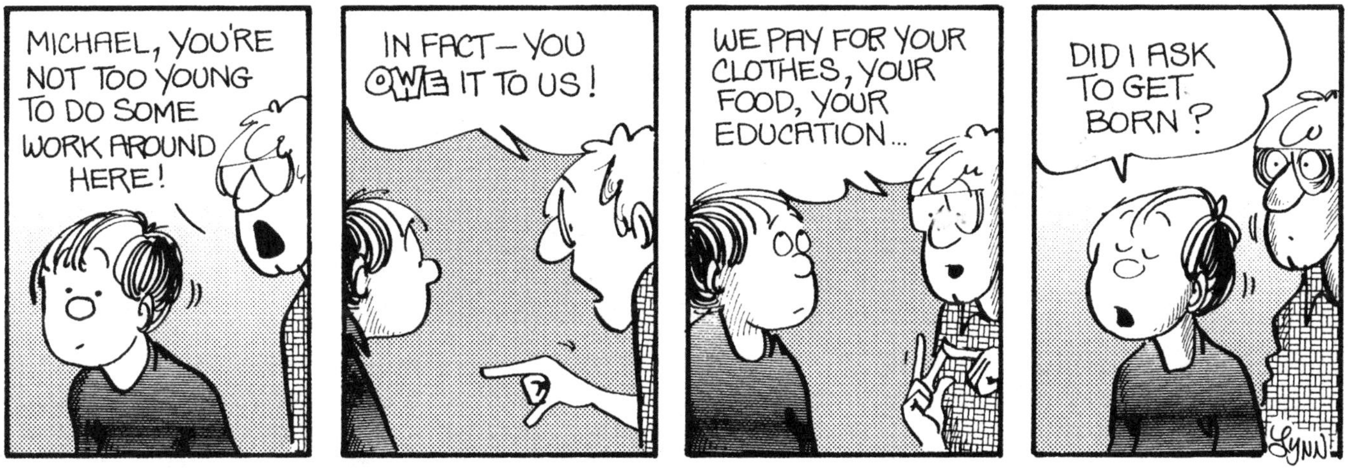
MICHAEL, YOU'RE NOT TOO YOUNG TO DO SOME WORK AROUND HERE!
IN FACT—YOU OWE IT TO US!
WE PAY FOR YOUR CLOTHES, YOUR FOOD, YOUR EDUCATION...
DID I ASK TO GET BORN?
LYNN

More than once I said this to my parents. My mom was especially miffed because if she'd had a choice in the matter, she'd have definitely raised someone other than me. It was a subject I often pondered as a child — how did I get here, in this form, at this time in history. I remember thinking, if I could change my parents for someone else's, who would I choose? After examining the families of friends, I almost always came back to the parents I had ... even though they weren't perfect!

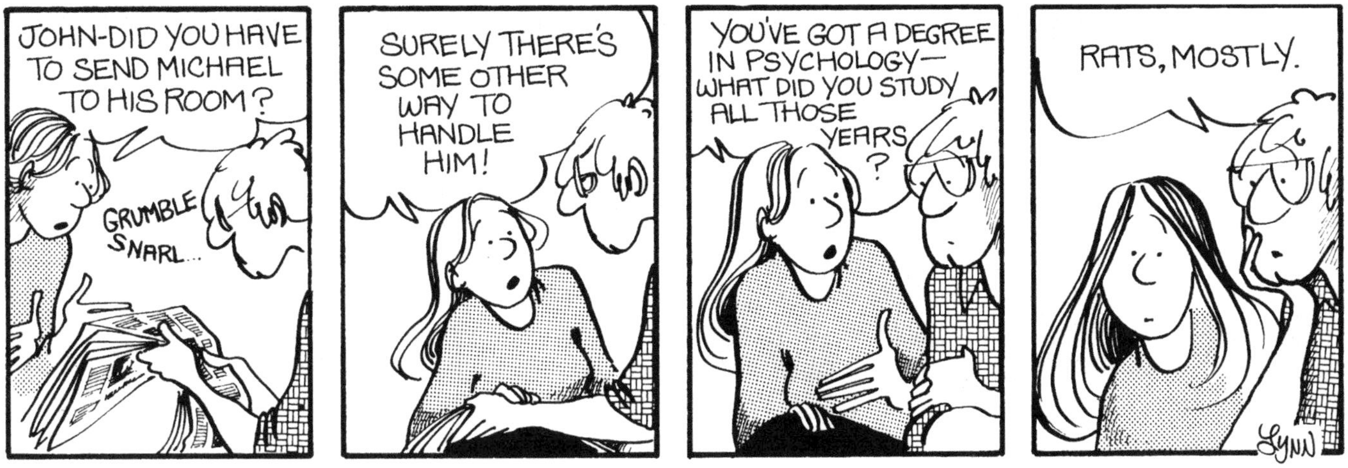
JOHN-DID YOU HAVE TO SEND MICHAEL TO HIS ROOM?
GRUMBLE SNARL...
SURELY THERE'S SOME OTHER WAY TO HANDLE HIM!
YOU'VE GOT A DEGREE IN PSYCHOLOGY—WHAT DID YOU STUDY ALL THOSE YEARS?
RATS, MOSTLY.
LYNN

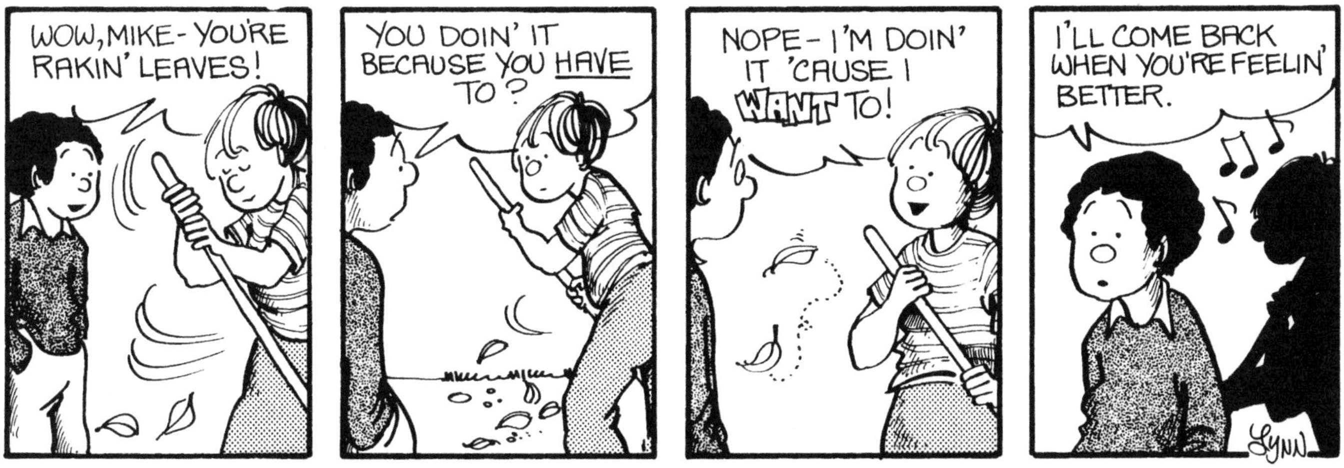
WOW, MIKE- YOU'RE RAKIN' LEAVES!
YOU DOIN' IT BECAUSE YOU HAVE TO?
NOPE- I'M DOIN' IT 'CAUSE I WANT TO!
I'LL COME BACK WHEN YOU'RE FEELIN' BETTER.
LYNN

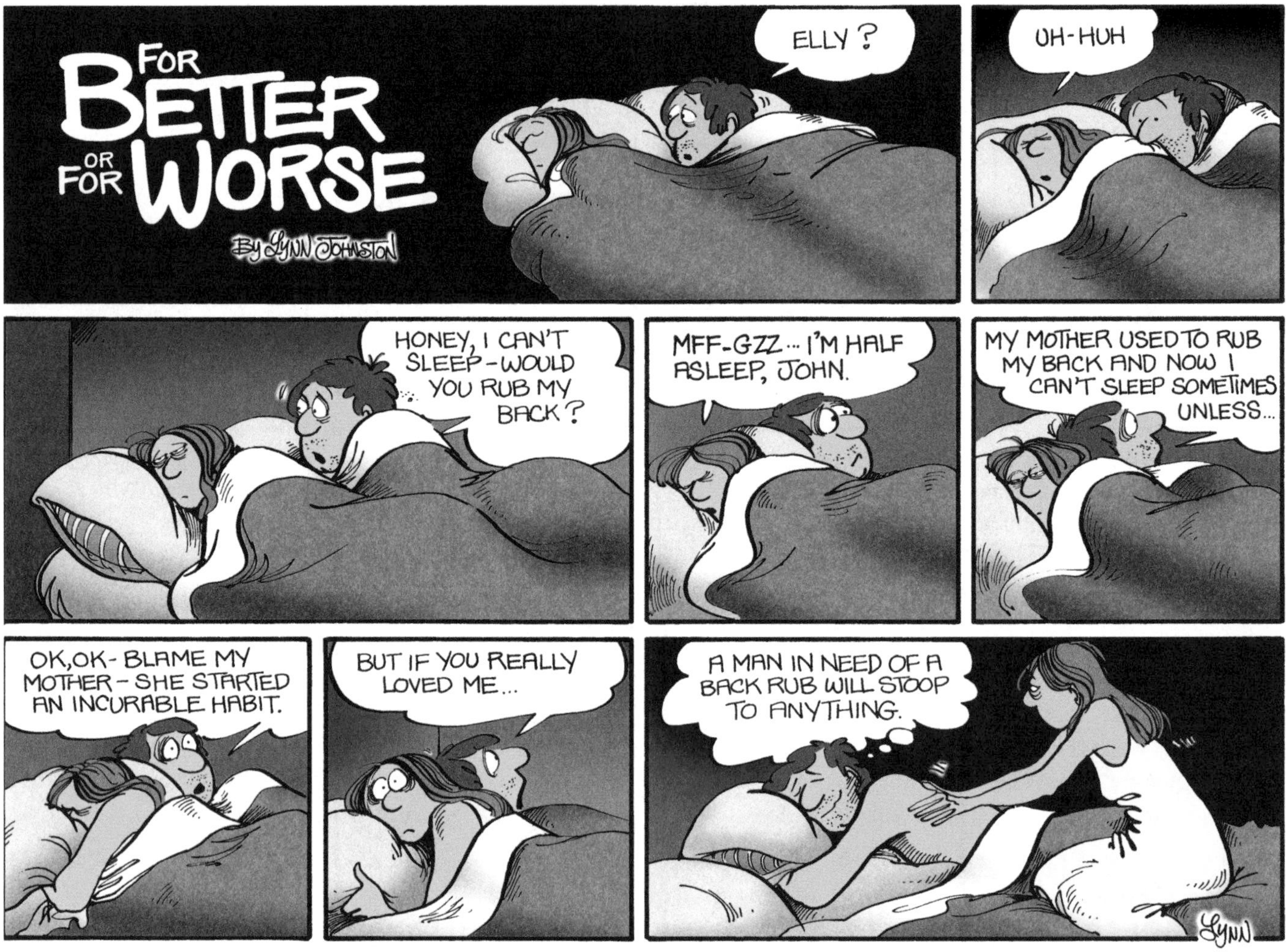
FOR BETTER OR FOR WORSE
BY LYNN JOHNSTON
ELLY?
UH-HUH
HONEY, I CAN'T SLEEP-WOULD YOU RUB MY BACK?
MFF-GZZ... I'M HALF ASLEEP, JOHN.
MY MOTHER USED TO RUB MY BACK AND NOW I CAN'T SLEEP SOMETIMES UNLESS...
OK,OK- BLAME MY MOTHER - SHE STARTED AN INCURABLE HABIT.
BUT IF YOU REALLY LOVED ME...
A MAN IN NEED OF A BACK RUB WILL STOOP TO ANYTHING.
LYNN

My husband grew up enjoying warm back rubs as he went to sleep. When, for some reason, his mom could not, he would bribe his sister to rub his back, and so it went. When we were first married, I continued the practice ... but then ... as life became more stressful, the bedtime back rub disappeared. This was not a good thing. I was reminded from time to time that something was missing — and it was. My advice, then to other newly connected and consenting adults is: If you can't keep something up forever and ever and ever ... don't start in the first place.

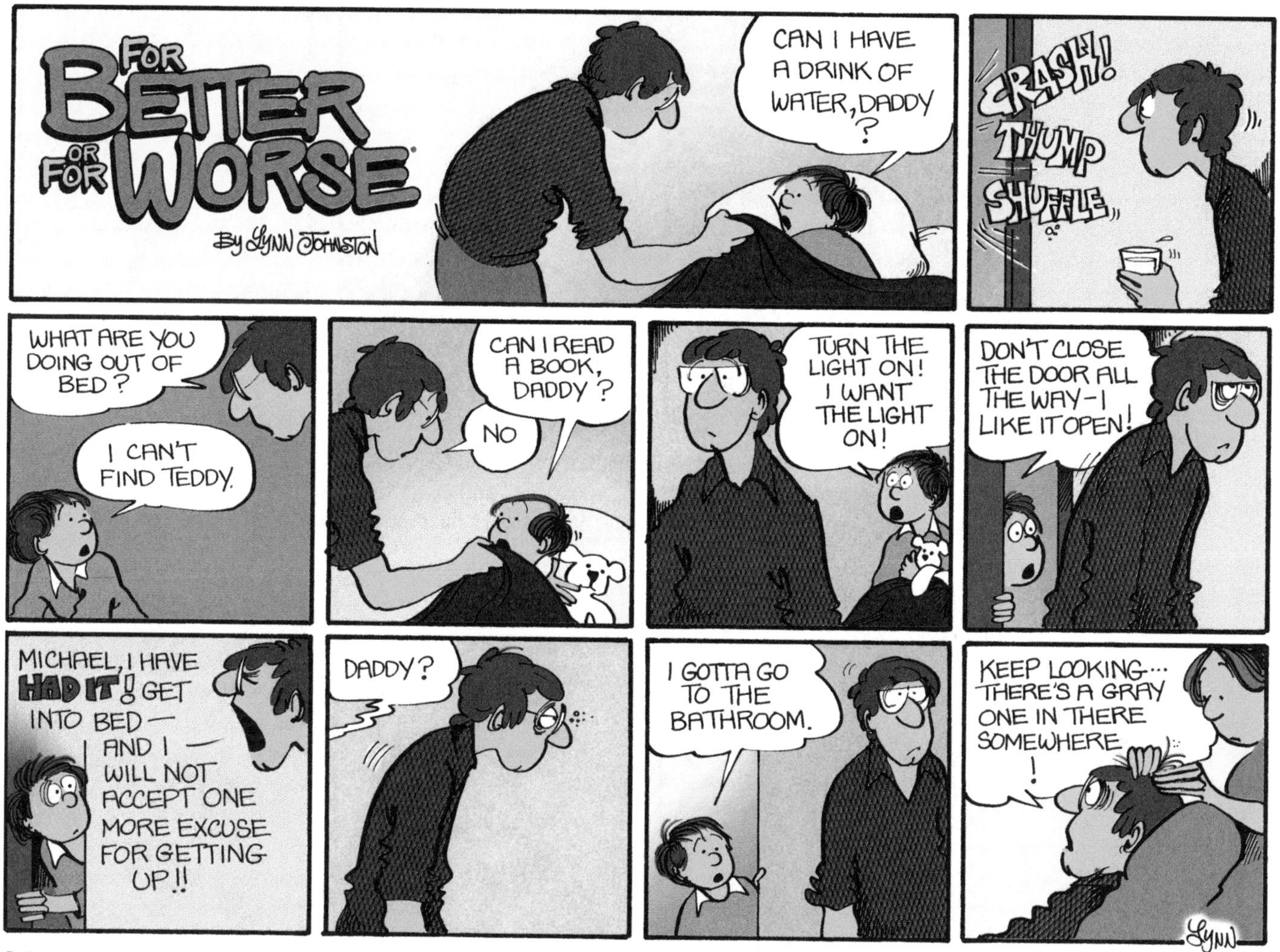
FOR BETTER OR FOR WORSE
By Lynn Johnston
CAN I HAVE A DRINK OF WATER, DADDY ?
CRASH! THUMP SHUFFLE
WHAT ARE YOU DOING OUT OF BED ?
I CAN'T FIND TEDDY.
CAN I READ A BOOK, DADDY ?
NO
TURN THE LIGHT ON! I WANT THE LIGHT ON!
DON'T CLOSE THE DOOR ALL THE WAY—I LIKE IT OPEN!
MICHAEL, I HAVE HAD IT! GET INTO BED—
AND I — WILL NOT ACCEPT ONE MORE EXCUSE FOR GETTING UP!!
DADDY?
I GOTTA GO TO THE BATHROOM.
KEEP LOOKING... THERE'S A GRAY ONE IN THERE SOMEWHERE !
Lynn

I think the idea for this one came more from my babysitting days than it did from our family. The people next door to us on Fifth Street had four little girls. They were sweet, well-behaved kids, but the excuses they made to keep from going to bed were inventive, effective, and unending. When one was down, another was up with a request or a need or a fear or SOMETHING! This was all so frustrating — both because my disciplinary skills were rudimentary, and because Mrs. Benn always left chocolate cake in the fridge, and I couldn't get to it until the kids were asleep. I always wondered how they could stay awake for so long when they were so tired ... but I think we did the same thing to our babysitters ... a rite of passage for the sitters and the sat!

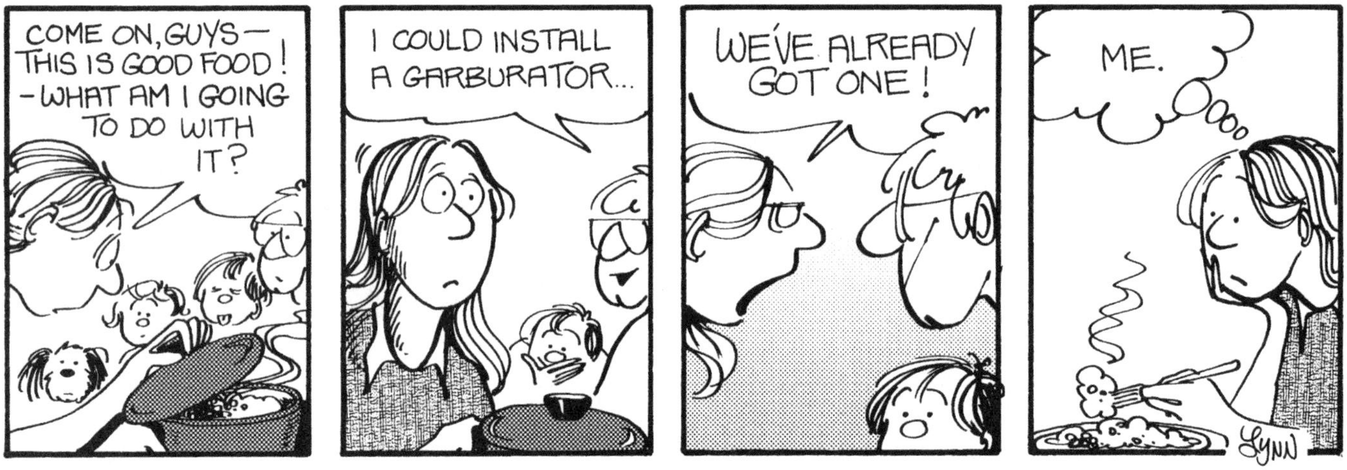
COME ON, GUYS— THIS IS GOOD FOOD! —WHAT AM I GOING TO DO WITH IT?
I COULD INSTALL A GARBURATOR...
WE'VE ALREADY GOT ONE!
ME.

When this strip originally ran, folks asked, "What in the world is a GARBURATOR?" Well, in Canada, that's what we called a garbage disposal installed in the sink. I was told it was called "InSinkErator" and a variety of other things, but I was not about to change a Canadianism, and so, the word stayed. Whatever it's called, I have never owned one. The dog and I took care of the leftovers.

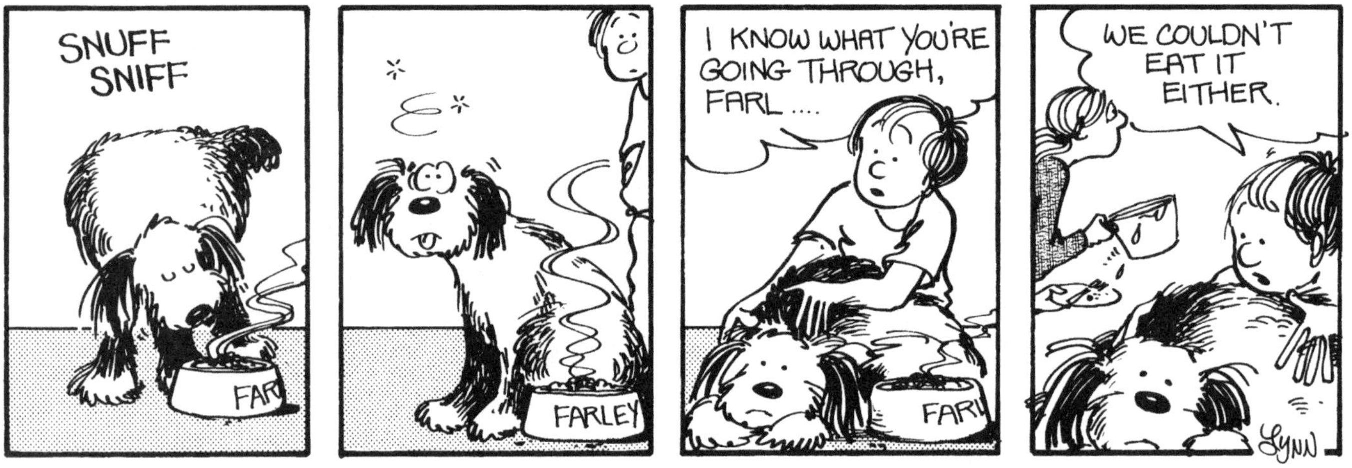
SNUFF SNIFF
FARLEY
I KNOW WHAT YOU'RE GOING THROUGH, FARL....
WE COULDN'T EAT IT EITHER.

When Farley came to live with us, my thinking was "leftovers disposal unit," but my husband had other ideas. A dog was only to eat foods naturally consumed in the wild. This meant regular trips to a mink farm to retrieve fresh meat by-products. This unpleasant stuff, along with a special kind of kibble, was what Farley ate without relish. Whenever I could, I'd break down and slip him a treat. Once he had tasted people food, Farley held out for the GOOD stuff. I didn't blame him one bit!

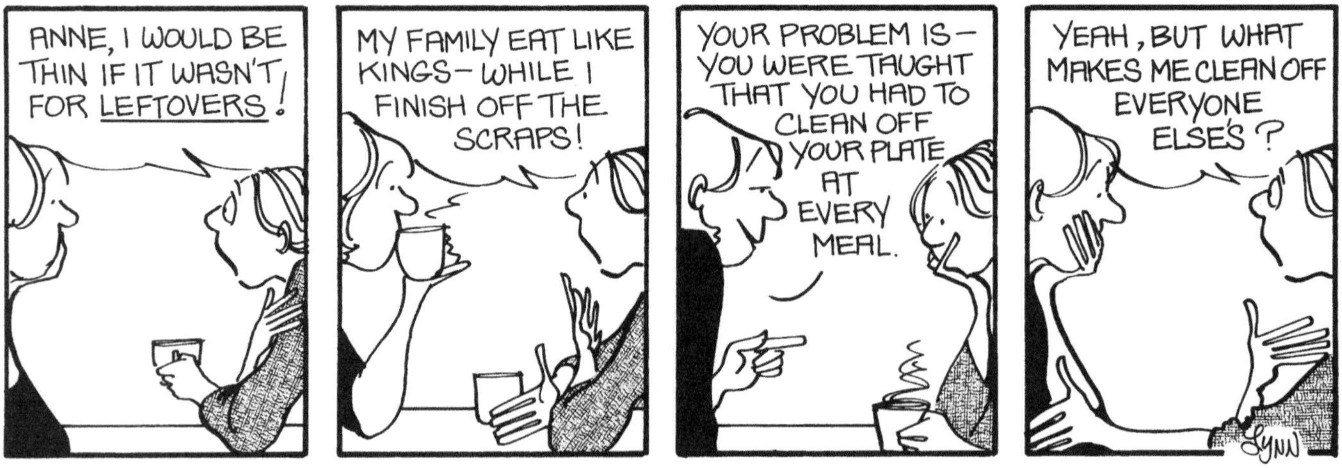
ANNE, I WOULD BE THIN IF IT WASN'T FOR LEFTOVERS!
MY FAMILY EAT LIKE KINGS— WHILE I FINISH OFF THE SCRAPS!
YOUR PROBLEM IS— YOU WERE TAUGHT THAT YOU HAD TO CLEAN OFF YOUR PLATE AT EVERY MEAL.
YEAH, BUT WHAT MAKES ME CLEAN OFF EVERYONE ELSE'S?

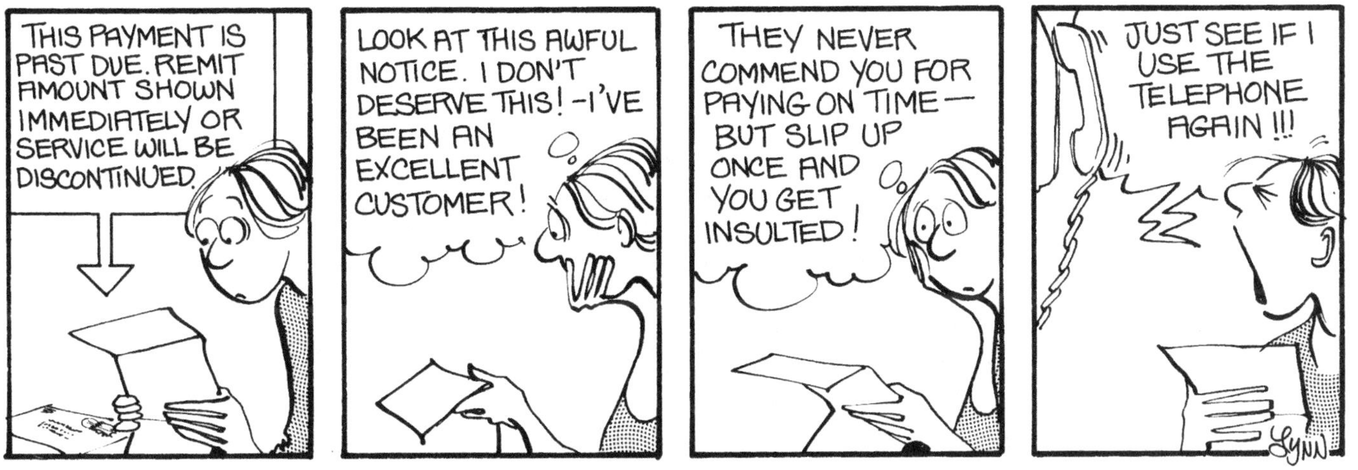
THIS PAYMENT IS PAST DUE. REMIT AMOUNT SHOWN IMMEDIATELY OR SERVICE WILL BE DISCONTINUED.
LOOK AT THIS AWFUL NOTICE. I DON'T DESERVE THIS! -I'VE BEEN AN EXCELLENT CUSTOMER!
THEY NEVER COMMEND YOU FOR PAYING ON TIME— BUT SLIP UP ONCE AND YOU GET INSULTED!
JUST SEE IF I USE THE TELEPHONE AGAIN !!!
LYNN

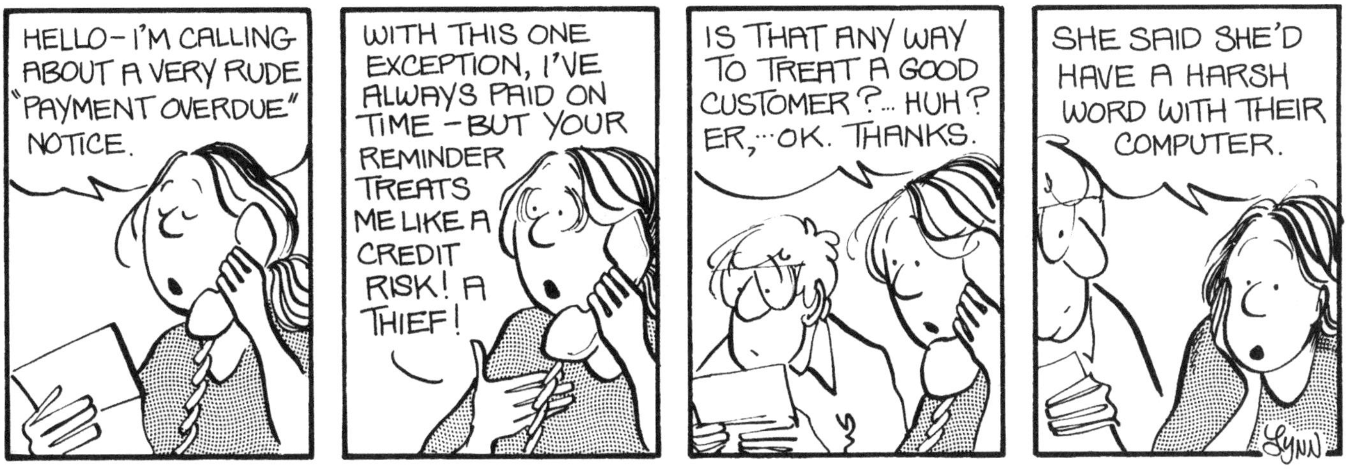
HELLO- I'M CALLING ABOUT A VERY RUDE "PAYMENT OVERDUE" NOTICE.
WITH THIS ONE EXCEPTION, I'VE ALWAYS PAID ON TIME - BUT YOUR REMINDER TREATS ME LIKE A CREDIT RISK! A THIEF!
IS THAT ANY WAY TO TREAT A GOOD CUSTOMER?... HUH? ER,...OK. THANKS.
SHE SAID SHE'D HAVE A HARSH WORD WITH THEIR COMPUTER.
LYNN

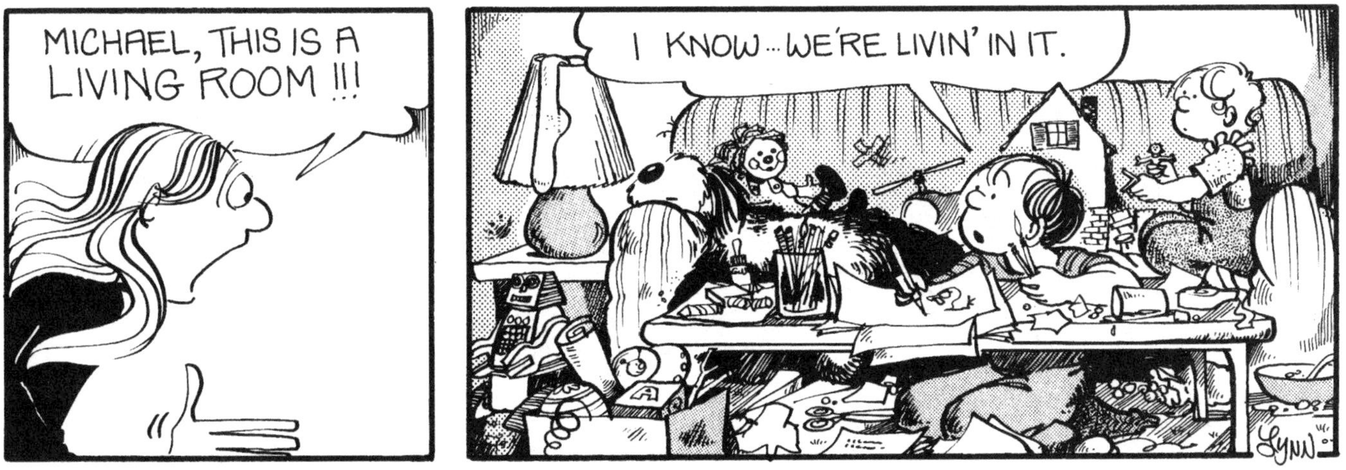
MICHAEL, THIS IS A LIVING ROOM !!!
I KNOW...WE'RE LIVIN' IN IT.
LYNN

This quote I will call an "Aaronism." My son regularly deflected a well-rehearsed tirade because he had better one-liners than I did.

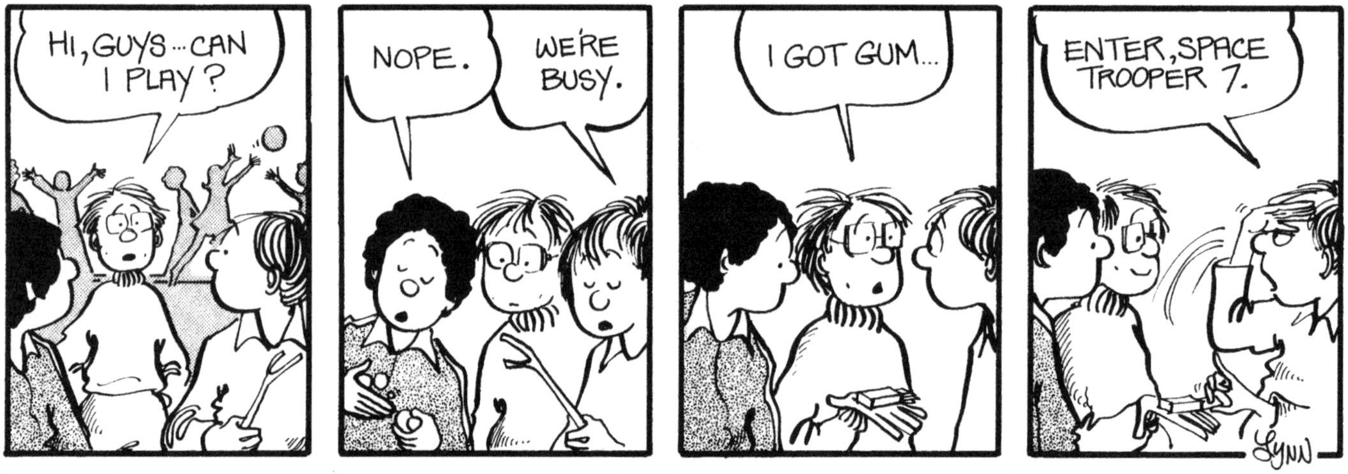
HI, GUYS... CAN I PLAY?
NOPE.
WE'RE BUSY.
I GOT GUM...
ENTER, SPACE TROOPER 7.
Lynn

The old adage "three's a crowd" is never more true than in early grade school. I remember adding a new friend simply because I was offered the opportunity to use a bike or share some candy. I bought into others' friendships, too, when I had stuff to share. Allegiances morphed, changed, and regrouped according to the mood of the day, but the "best friend" was always at the center of the relationship.

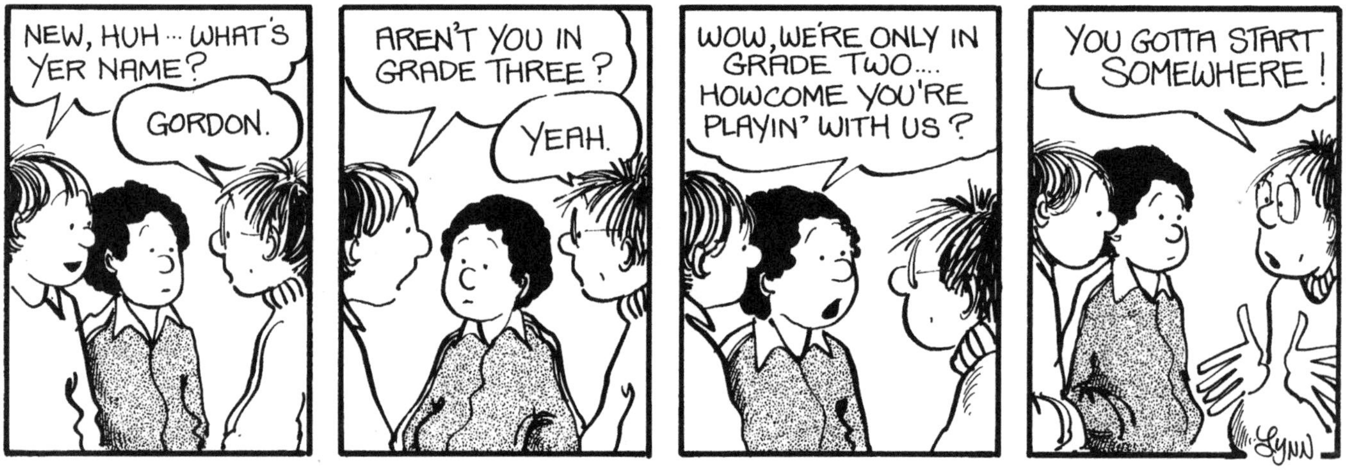
NEW, HUH... WHAT'S YER NAME?
GORDON.
AREN'T YOU IN GRADE THREE?
YEAH.
WOW, WE'RE ONLY IN GRADE TWO.... HOWCOME YOU'RE PLAYIN' WITH US?
YOU GOTTA START SOMEWHERE!
Lynn

Gordon was a year ahead of Mike and Lawrence when they met, but a slow learning curve and troubles at home made schoolwork difficult for him. He was later moved back a year, giving him a chance to catch up. Easy going and nonconfrontational, Gordon was likable. He was the kind of kid who always saw the bright side. He could make the best out of a tough situation. He was a survivor.

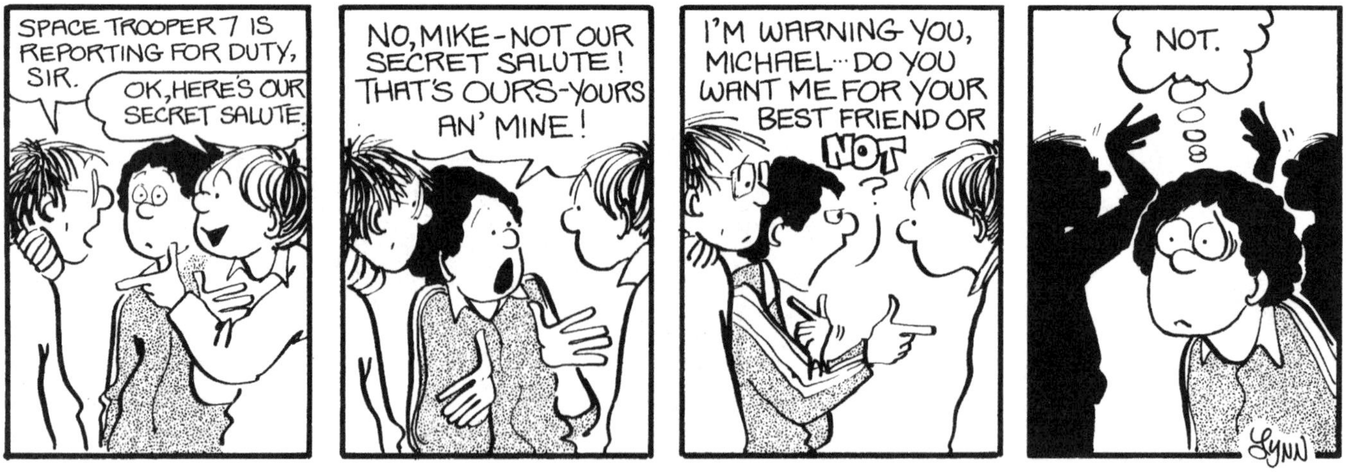
SPACE TROOPER 7 IS REPORTING FOR DUTY, SIR.
OK, HERE'S OUR SECRET SALUTE.
NO, MIKE-NOT OUR SECRET SALUTE! THAT'S OURS-YOURS AN' MINE!
I'M WARNING YOU, MICHAEL... DO YOU WANT ME FOR YOUR BEST FRIEND OR NOT?
NOT.
Lynn

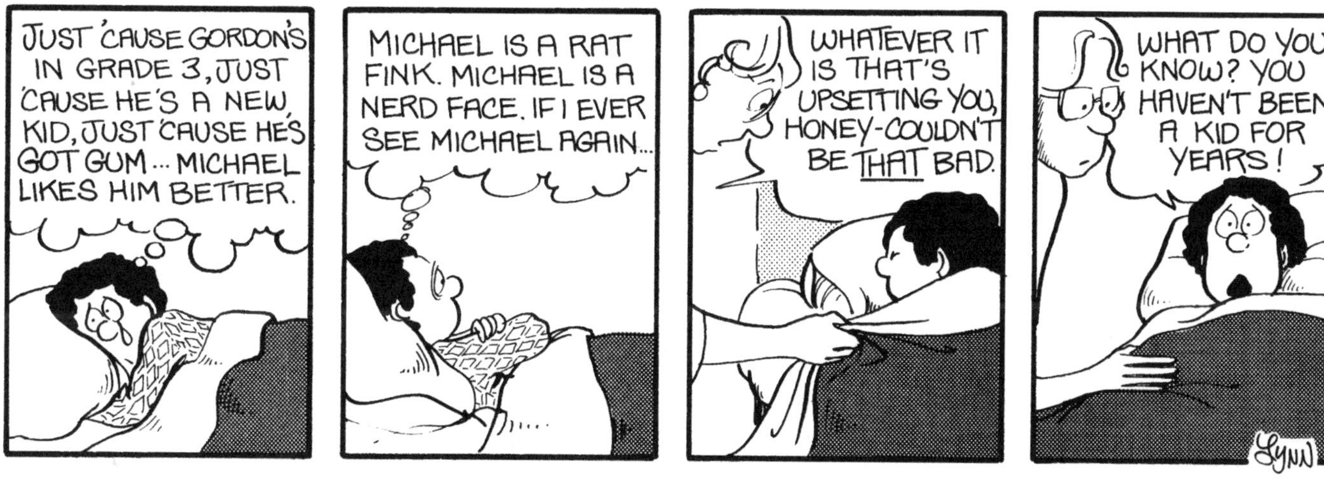
JUST 'CAUSE GORDON'S IN GRADE 3, JUST 'CAUSE HE'S A NEW KID, JUST 'CAUSE HE'S GOT GUM ... MICHAEL LIKES HIM BETTER.
MICHAEL IS A RAT FINK. MICHAEL IS A NERD FACE. IF I EVER SEE MICHAEL AGAIN...
WHATEVER IT IS THAT'S UPSETTING YOU, HONEY-COULDN'T BE THAT BAD.
WHAT DO YOU KNOW? YOU HAVEN'T BEEN A KID FOR YEARS!
LYNN

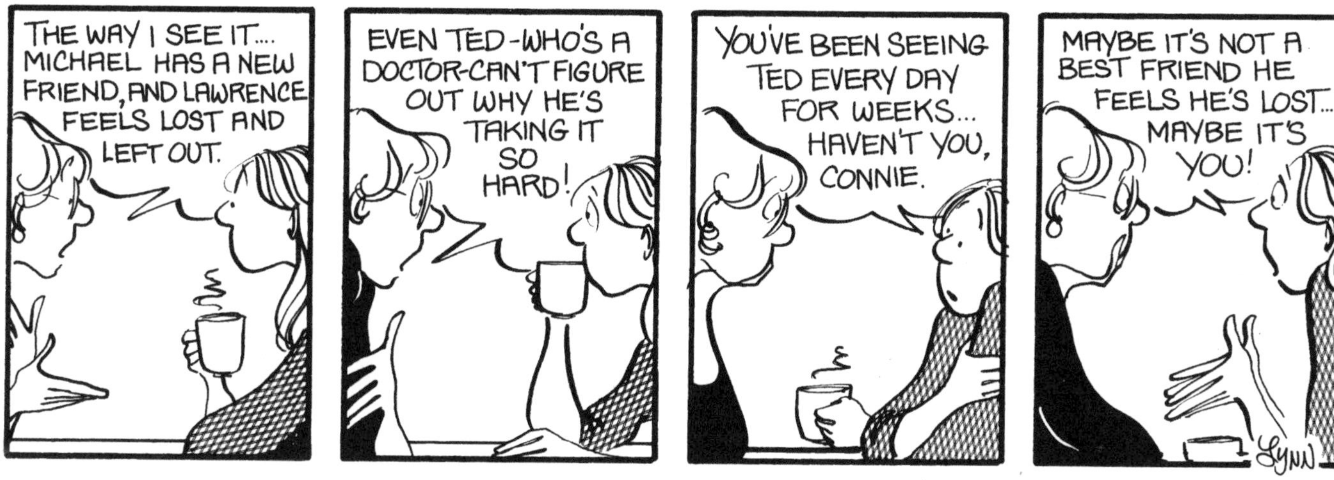
THE WAY I SEE IT.... MICHAEL HAS A NEW FRIEND, AND LAWRENCE FEELS LOST AND LEFT OUT.
EVEN TED-WHO'S A DOCTOR-CAN'T FIGURE OUT WHY HE'S TAKING IT SO HARD!
YOU'VE BEEN SEEING TED EVERY DAY FOR WEEKS... HAVEN'T YOU, CONNIE.
MAYBE IT'S NOT A BEST FRIEND HE FEELS HE'S LOST... MAYBE IT'S YOU!
LYNN

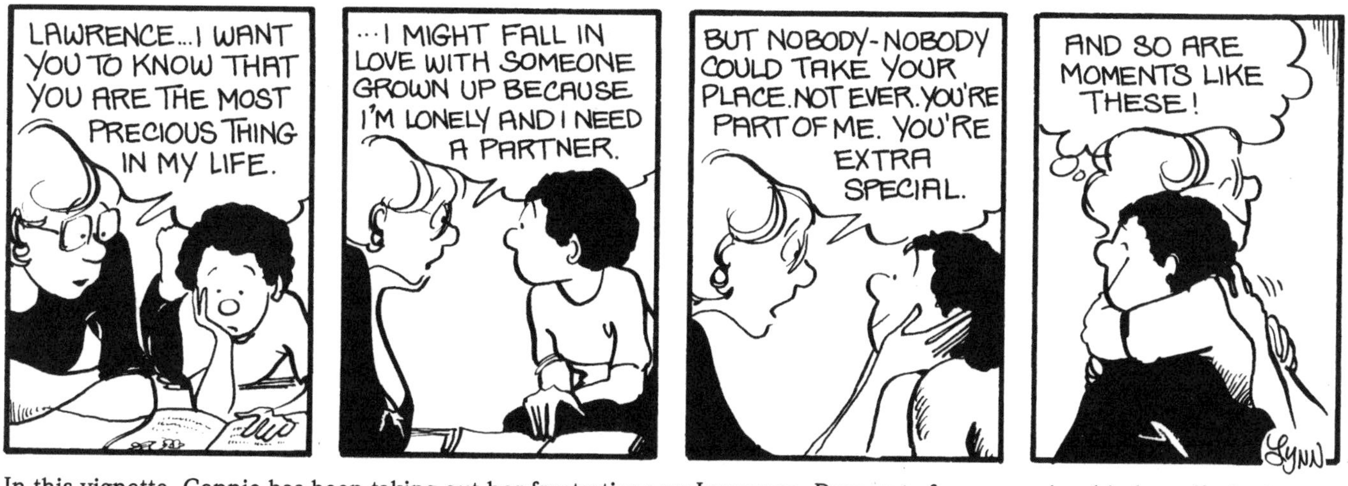
LAWRENCE...I WANT YOU TO KNOW THAT YOU ARE THE MOST PRECIOUS THING IN MY LIFE.
...I MIGHT FALL IN LOVE WITH SOMEONE GROWN UP BECAUSE I'M LONELY AND I NEED A PARTNER.
BUT NOBODY-NOBODY COULD TAKE YOUR PLACE. NOT EVER. YOU'RE PART OF ME. YOU'RE EXTRA SPECIAL.
AND SO ARE MOMENTS LIKE THESE!
LYNN

In this vignette, Connie has been taking out her frustrations on Lawrence. Desperate for companionship herself, she has unwittingly upset her son. Sensing ambivalence and insecurity in his mom, Lawrence had become worried and insecure, as well. There is nothing more rewarding than telling your kids that you're not perfect, you're sorry, and they are so very loved.

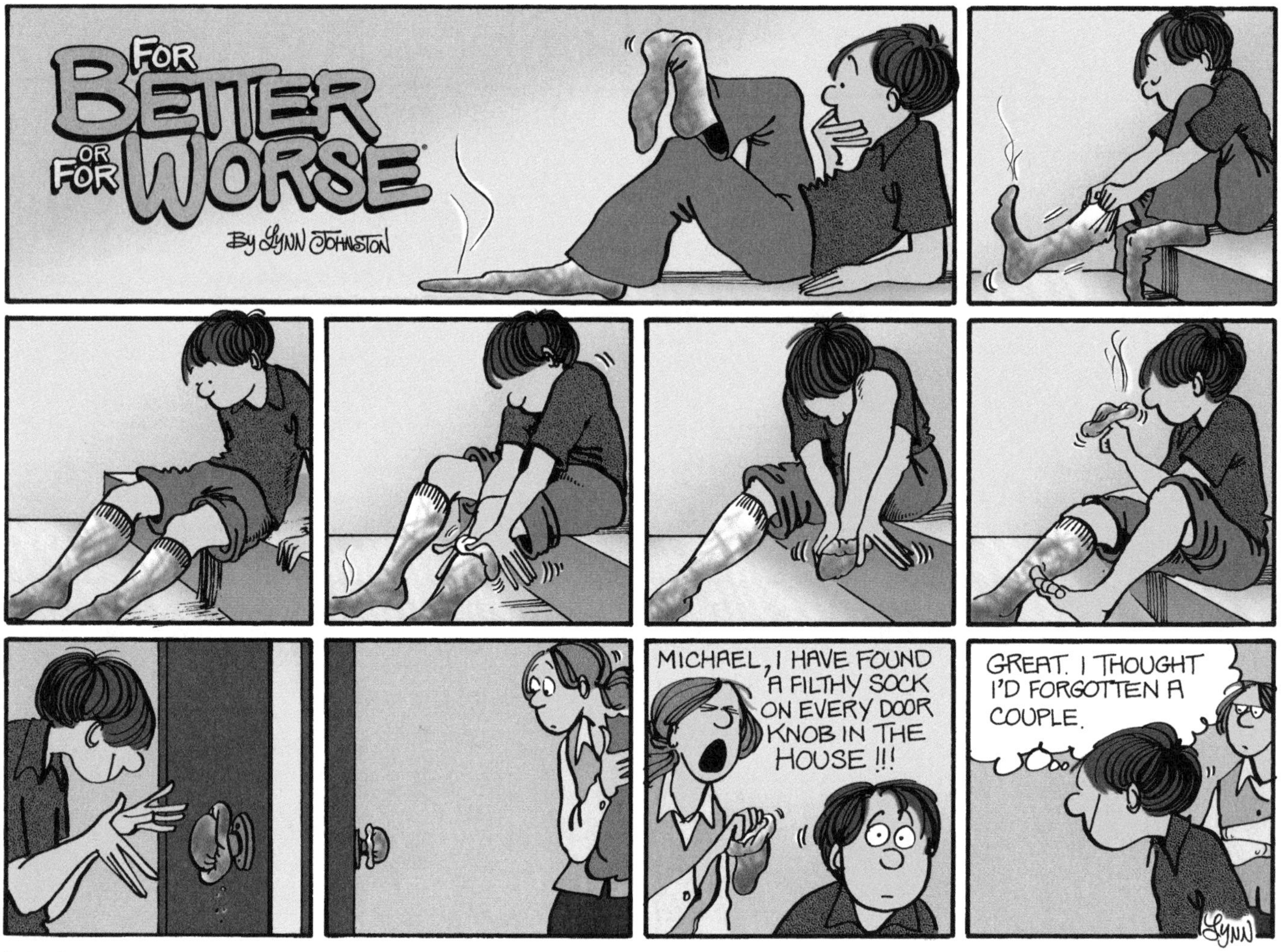
FOR BETTER OR FOR WORSE
By Lynn Johnston
MICHAEL, I HAVE FOUND A FILTHY SOCK ON EVERY DOOR KNOB IN THE HOUSE !!!
GREAT. I THOUGHT I'D FORGOTTEN A COUPLE.
Lynn

I don't know who came up with this disgusting, yet satisfying little prank ... my brother or me. I think I'll take the credit. Mom was a stickler for cleanliness. Long before the clinical admonishment to wash our hands as often as possible, Mom inspected our digits with surgical scrutiny. She once told me that her mother fired a housekeeper because the woman said that making bread was a good way to clean her nails! Mom regularly washed walls, countertops, baseboards, and knobs to make sure we were as germ free as possible. Naturally, it was our prerogative to return these surfaces to their germ-laden norm.

The long socks we wore bore the remnants of rubber, road salt, floorboards, and feet. By day's end they smelled wonderfully wicked. I remember pulling up my dirty socks, rolling them down my leg, and thinking, as the end popped off my foot, that it looked a lot like a fetid kind of hat. When these "hats" didn't do much for my dolls, I decided to put them on the doorknobs — to the great annoyance of Mother, who refused to touch them, much less turn the handle. Her British admonishments were worth hearing: "Dreadful, dreadful, dreadful!" and "You miserable recalcitrant!" and "This is the very LIMIT!" made us giggle behind our hands. I look back at it all now and wonder how she put up with us ... perhaps it's because, despite her militant need for order and discipline, she had a really good sense of humour.

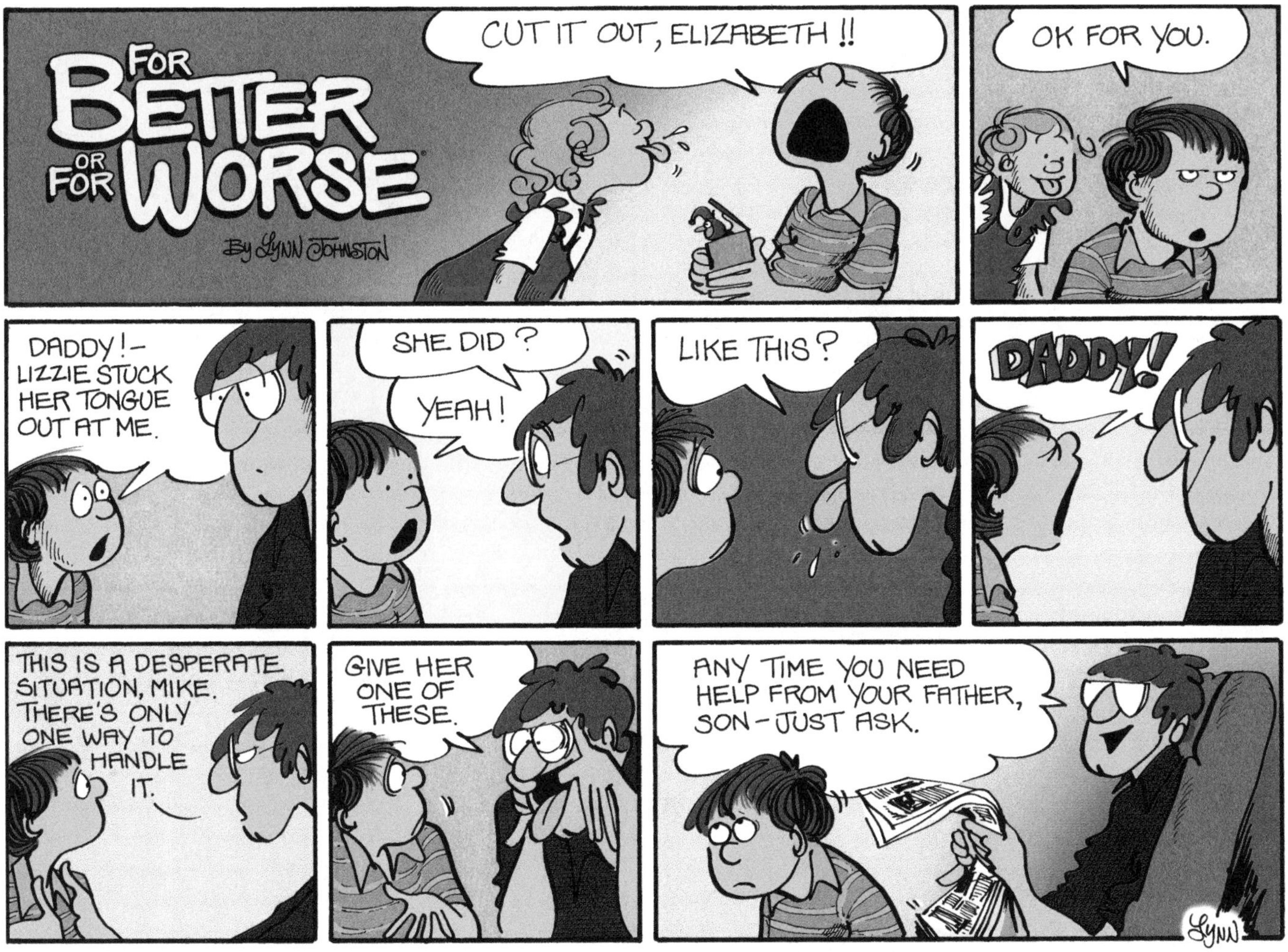
FOR BETTER OR FOR WORSE
By Lynn Johnston
CUT IT OUT, ELIZABETH !!
OK FOR YOU.
DADDY! - LIZZIE STUCK HER TONGUE OUT AT ME.
SHE DID?
YEAH!
LIKE THIS?
DADDY!
THIS IS A DESPERATE SITUATION, MIKE. THERE'S ONLY ONE WAY TO HANDLE IT.
GIVE HER ONE OF THESE.
ANY TIME YOU NEED HELP FROM YOUR FATHER, SON - JUST ASK.
Lynn

My dad was not into discipline, and ran from having to do it. He delivered his style of direction with sarcasm and humour, and more often than not, won the battle hands down. This exchange I remember clearly. On a rainy day, when the cure for boredom was war, Dad intervened with a "raspberry" and a smile, leaving my brother and I in stitches. He was the one who taught us how to pratfall like the comedians in silent films. He could make farting noises with his hand cupped into his armpit, and could whistle like the guys on the ferry dock hauling in the lines. He could burp "God Save the Queen," and he showed us how to spit off the back porch without dribbling on our chins. Stuff like this, other kids had to learn from each other. We were coached by the best. Mom probably knew about our alternate studies with Dad … if she did, she didn't let on. Dad might not have been a disciplinarian, but he sure knew how to get our attention and defuse a fight!

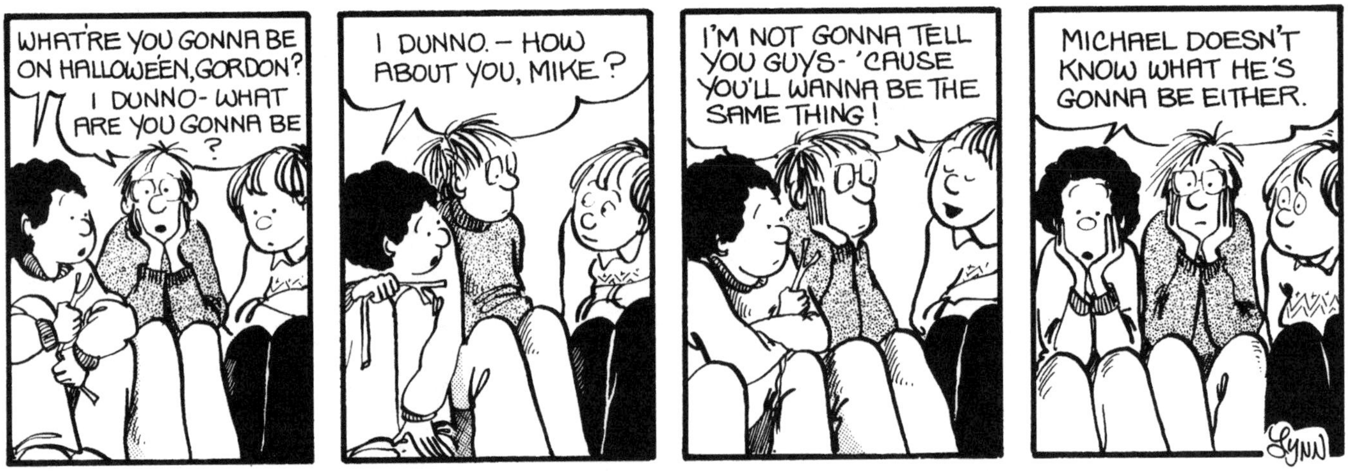
WHAT'RE YOU GONNA BE ON HALLOWEEN, GORDON?
I DUNNO- WHAT ARE YOU GONNA BE ?
I DUNNO. – HOW ABOUT YOU, MIKE ?
I'M NOT GONNA TELL YOU GUYS- 'CAUSE YOU'LL WANNA BE THE SAME THING!
MICHAEL DOESN'T KNOW WHAT HE'S GONNA BE EITHER.
Lynn

Deciding what to be on Halloween was always a challenge. The rainy Vancouver weather was always a factor, but nothing could keep us from our quest to score the most loot on October 31. Our neighbourhood was rich with pickings; lower-middle class, new immigrants, and Canadians "home from the war." The folks around us were generous, kind, and imaginative. All we needed was a costume, a pillowcase, and the energy to run up and down the steep hills of the North Shore.

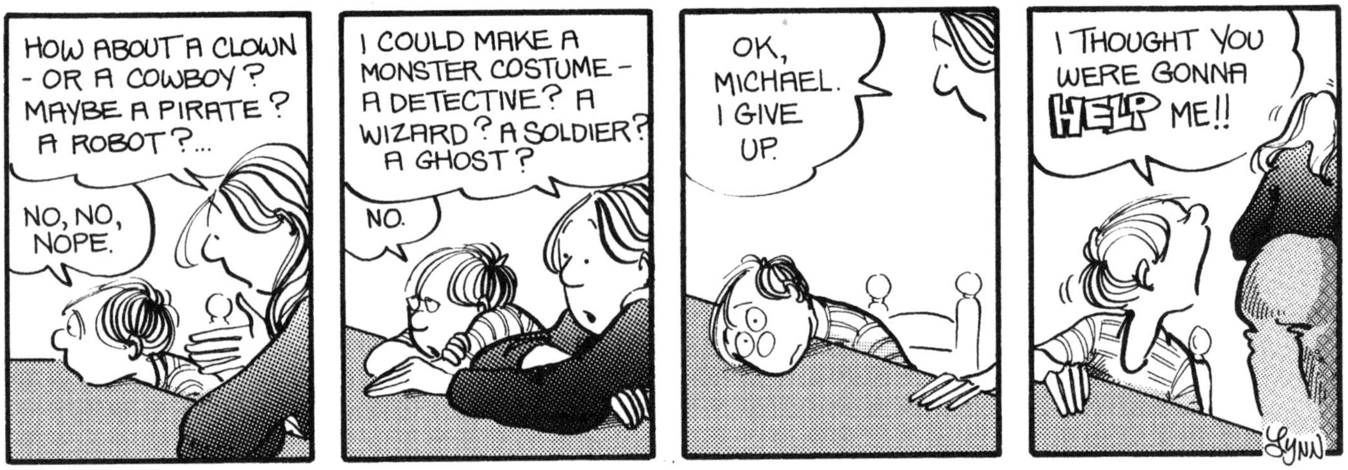
HOW ABOUT A CLOWN - OR A COWBOY? MAYBE A PIRATE? A ROBOT?...
NO, NO, NOPE.
I COULD MAKE A MONSTER COSTUME - A DETECTIVE? A WIZARD? A SOLDIER? A GHOST?
NO.
OK, MICHAEL. I GIVE UP.
I THOUGHT YOU WERE GONNA HELP ME!!
Lynn

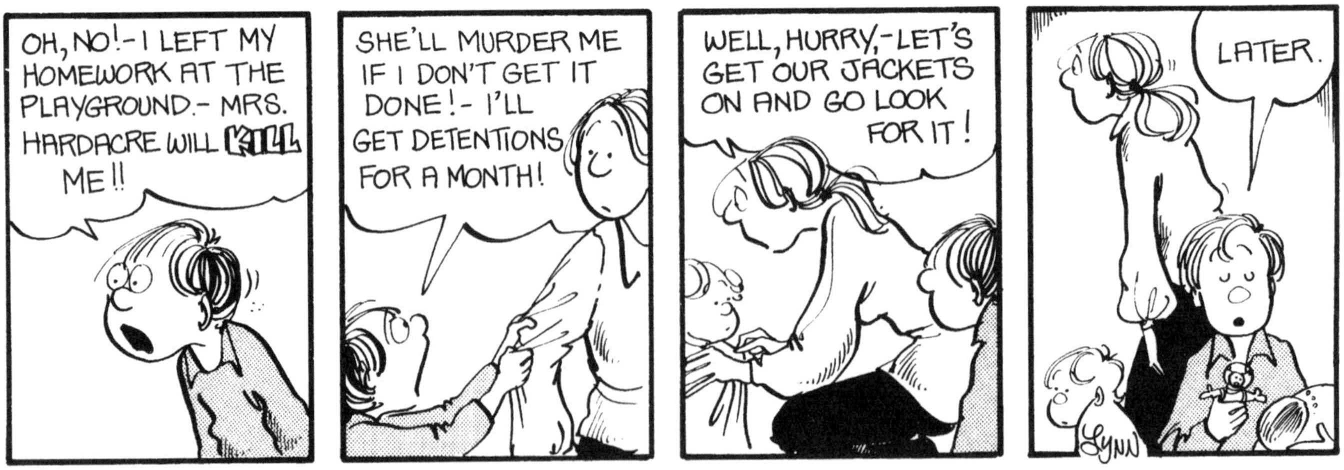
OH, NO!- I LEFT MY HOMEWORK AT THE PLAYGROUND.- MRS. HARDACRE WILL KILL ME!!
SHE'LL MURDER ME IF I DON'T GET IT DONE!- I'LL GET DETENTIONS FOR A MONTH!
WELL, HURRY,- LET'S GET OUR JACKETS ON AND GO LOOK FOR IT!
LATER.
Lynn

Mrs. Hardacre really did exist. This was a salute to a memorable lady and a fine teacher — with an unusual name.

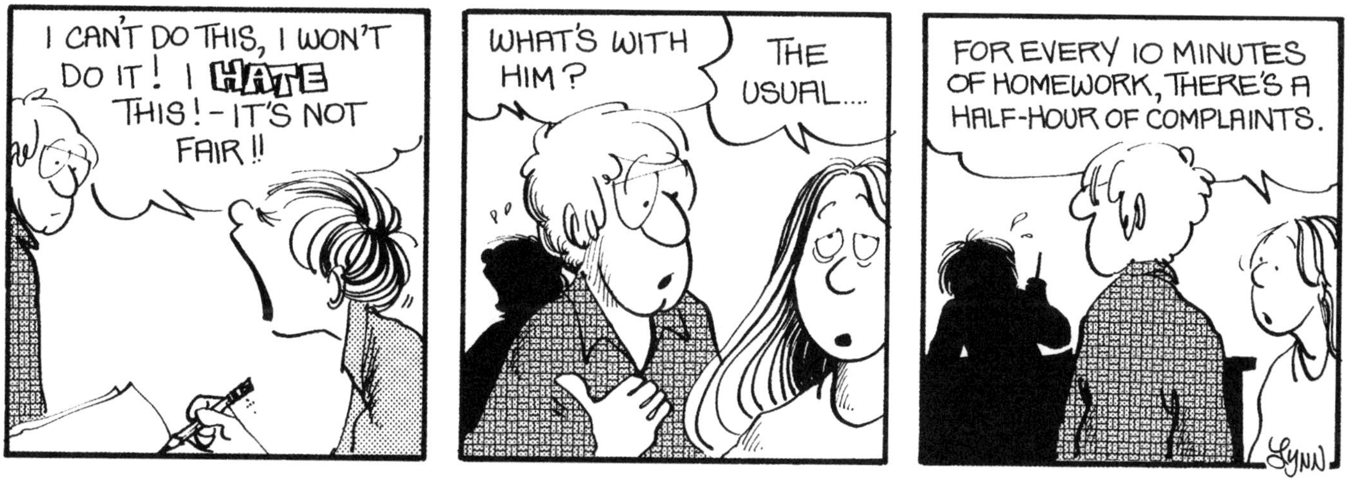
I CAN'T DO THIS, I WON'T DO IT! I HATE THIS! - IT'S NOT FAIR!!
WHAT'S WITH HIM?
THE USUAL....
FOR EVERY 10 MINUTES OF HOMEWORK, THERE'S A HALF-HOUR OF COMPLAINTS.
LYNN

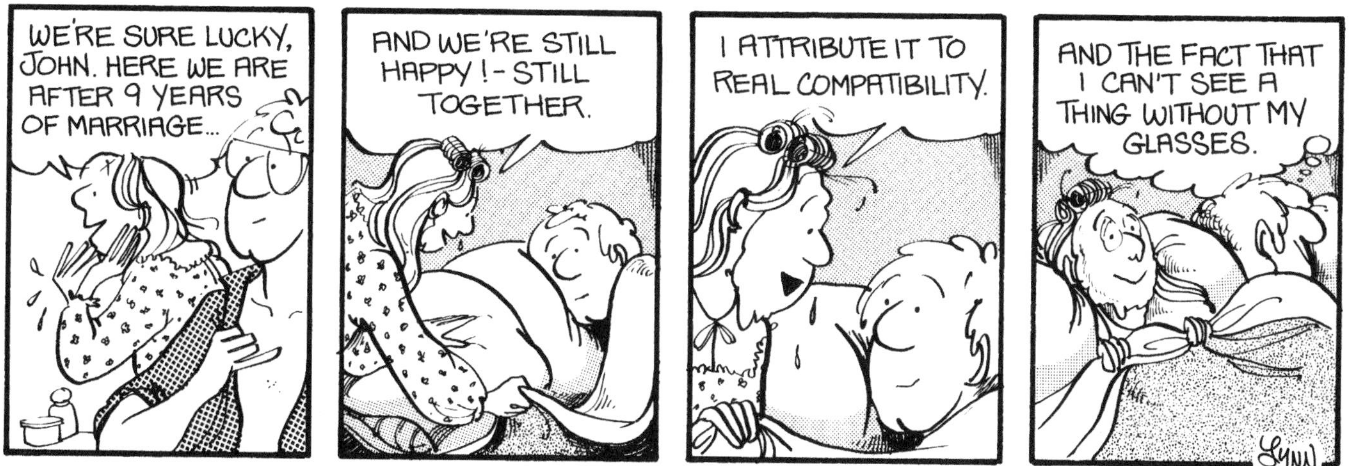
WE'RE SURE LUCKY, JOHN. HERE WE ARE AFTER 9 YEARS OF MARRIAGE...
AND WE'RE STILL HAPPY! - STILL TOGETHER.
I ATTRIBUTE IT TO REAL COMPATIBILITY.
AND THE FACT THAT I CAN'T SEE A THING WITHOUT MY GLASSES.
LYNN

In the early years, I bounced from subject to subject. Other cartoonists did a "gag a day," and I tried to do the same thing. I had, however, found that doing short sequences worked best for me, and in time, I learned how to bring one idea to a close before introducing another. The ups, downs, and dial-tone hums of marriage were always good fodder (and mudder). Although I never did wear face cream to bed, I couldn't resist doing a gag about it.

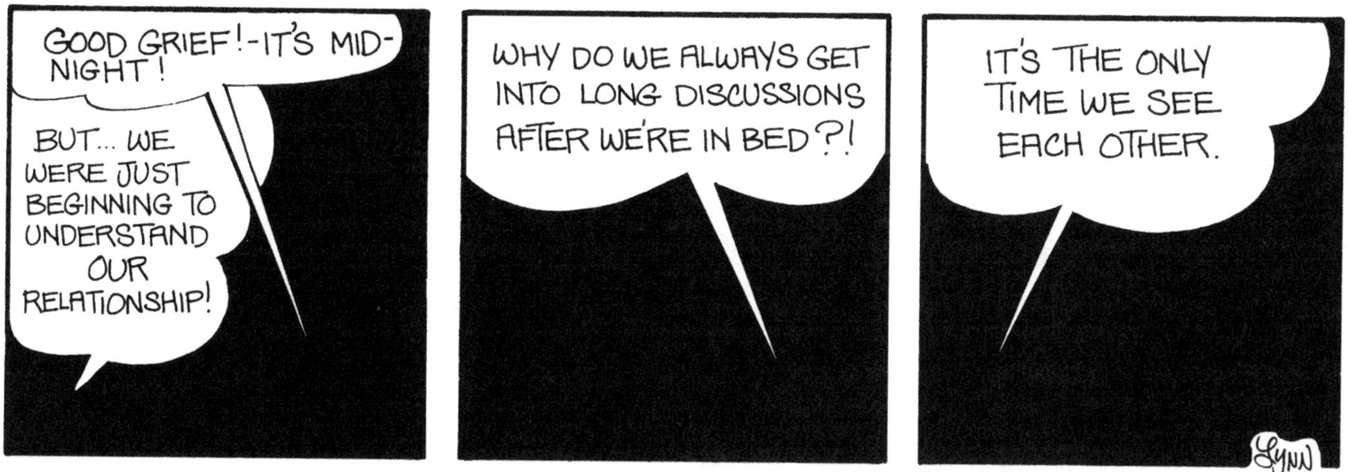
GOOD GRIEF! - IT'S MID-NIGHT!
BUT... WE WERE JUST BEGINNING TO UNDERSTAND OUR RELATIONSHIP!
WHY DO WE ALWAYS GET INTO LONG DISCUSSIONS AFTER WE'RE IN BED?!
IT'S THE ONLY TIME WE SEE EACH OTHER.
LYNN

Still learning the craft, I did a couple of "in the dark" strips, wherein the subjects talk with the lights out and black panels ensue. This is sort of a cop out, since I didn't have to draw anything! It wasn't until this strip was published that I was disappointed in myself for taking such a shortcut. Funny ... when the work was "out there," and I'd see it from the reader's perspective, I'd have a totally different opinion of it. Still, I wonder if the gag would have worked had I drawn everything!

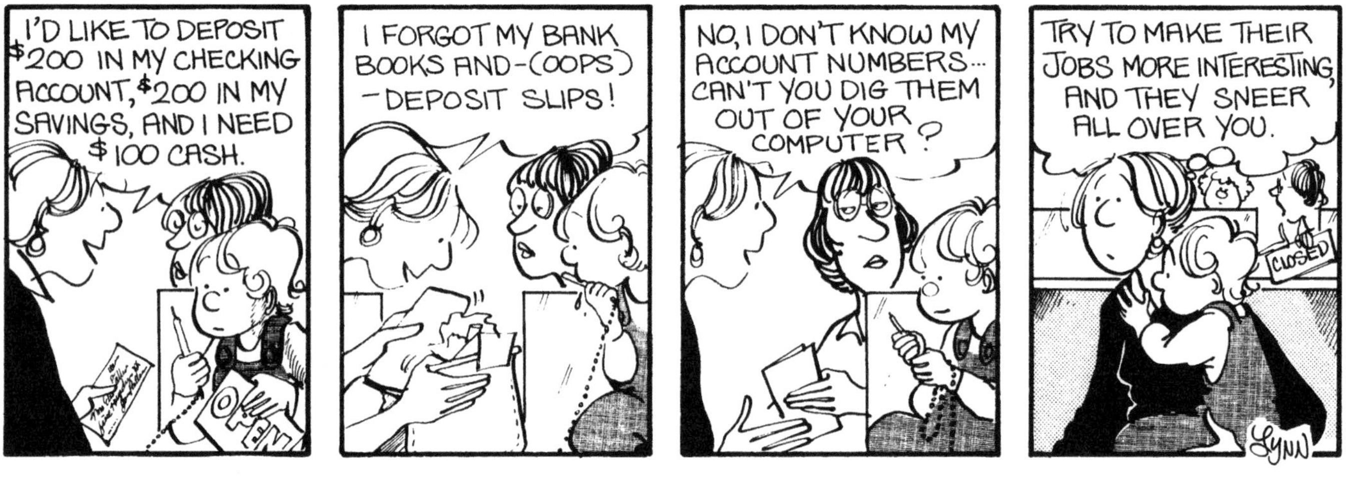
I'D LIKE TO DEPOSIT $200 IN MY CHECKING ACCOUNT, $200 IN MY SAVINGS, AND I NEED $100 CASH.
I FORGOT MY BANK BOOKS AND-(OOPS) -DEPOSIT SLIPS!
NO, I DON'T KNOW MY ACCOUNT NUMBERS... CAN'T YOU DIG THEM OUT OF YOUR COMPUTER?
TRY TO MAKE THEIR JOBS MORE INTERESTING, AND THEY SNEER ALL OVER YOU.
CLOSED
LYNN

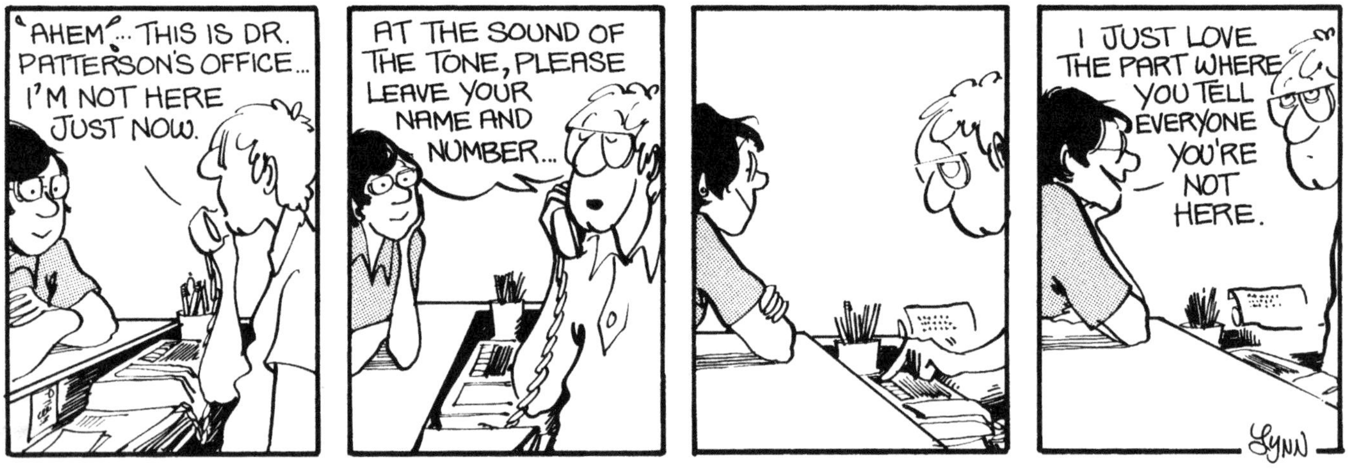
'AHEM'... THIS IS DR. PATTERSON'S OFFICE... I'M NOT HERE JUST NOW.
AT THE SOUND OF THE TONE, PLEASE LEAVE YOUR NAME AND NUMBER...
I JUST LOVE THE PART WHERE YOU TELL EVERYONE YOU'RE NOT HERE.
LYNN

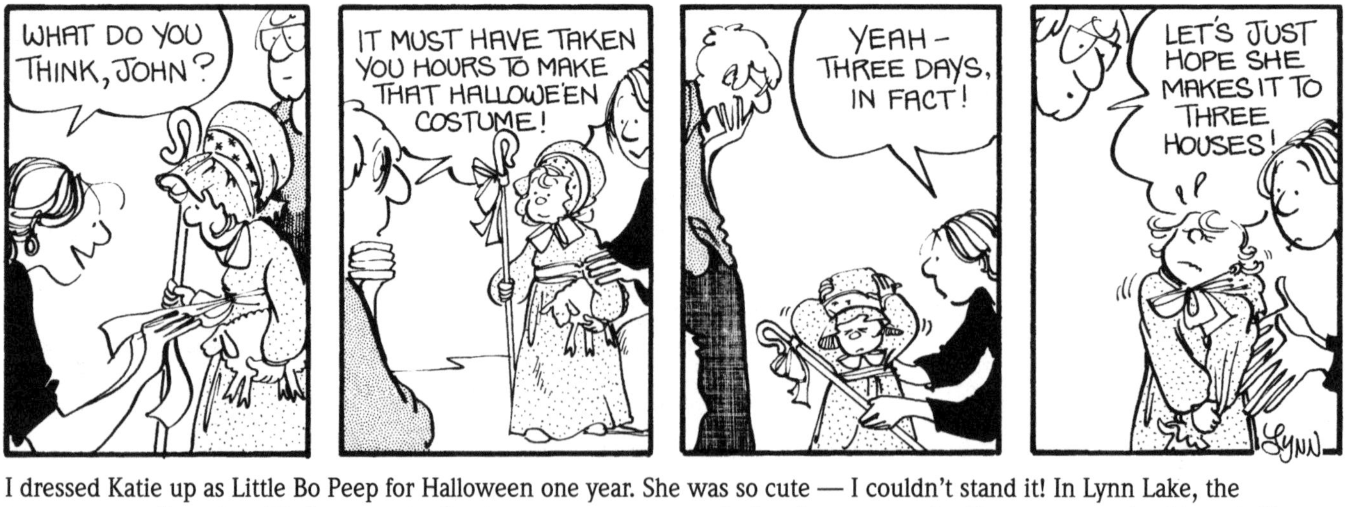
WHAT DO YOU THINK, JOHN?
IT MUST HAVE TAKEN YOU HOURS TO MAKE THAT HALLOWE'EN COSTUME!
YEAH - THREE DAYS, IN FACT!
LET'S JUST HOPE SHE MAKES IT TO THREE HOUSES!
LYNN

I dressed Katie up as Little Bo Peep for Halloween one year. She was so cute — I couldn't stand it! In Lynn Lake, the temperatures dipped well below zero in October, so every costume had to fit over a parka. Kate strenuously objected. She lasted for four blocks ... a good distance for a toddler; not far enough for me — I was just getting into the swing of things! I still have her costume, and some day, if I'm lucky, I'll see it worn again.

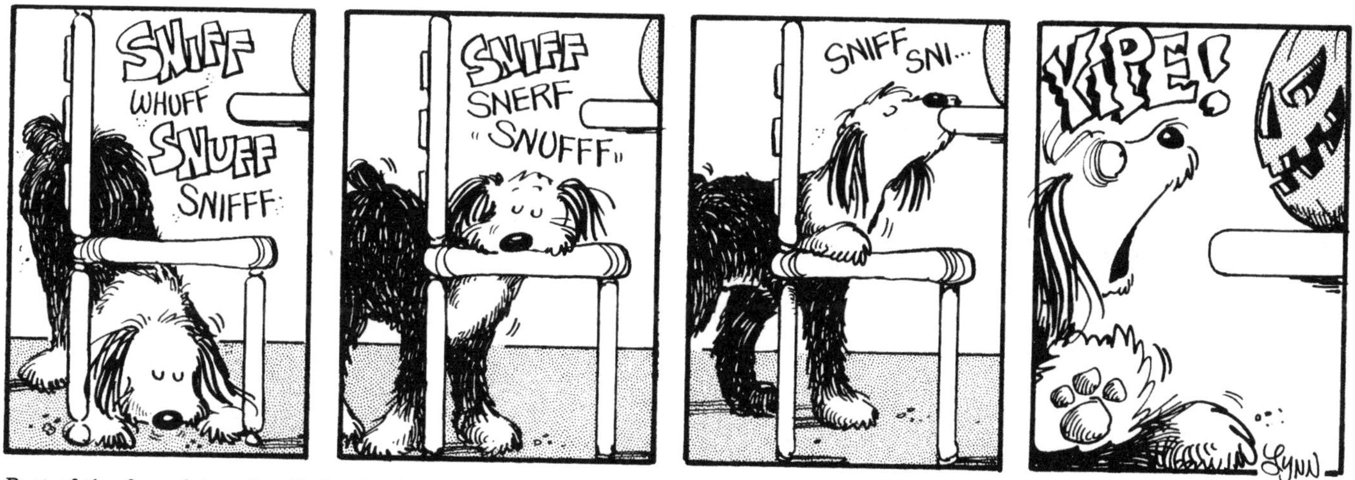
SNIFF
WHUFF
SNUFF
SNIFFF
SNIFF
SNERF
SNUFFF
SNIFF SNI...
YIPE!
LYNN

Part of the fun of drawing Farley is the dirt, the sound effects, and the facial expressions. Humans have to be kept believably human to some extent — especially in a strip that is supposedly realistic — but I could always push the limits when it came to pets. I doubt that a dog would see a pumpkin as a threat, unless it was on fire ... but in this instance, a cartoon dog has a cartoon experience — and I had a laugh drawing it.

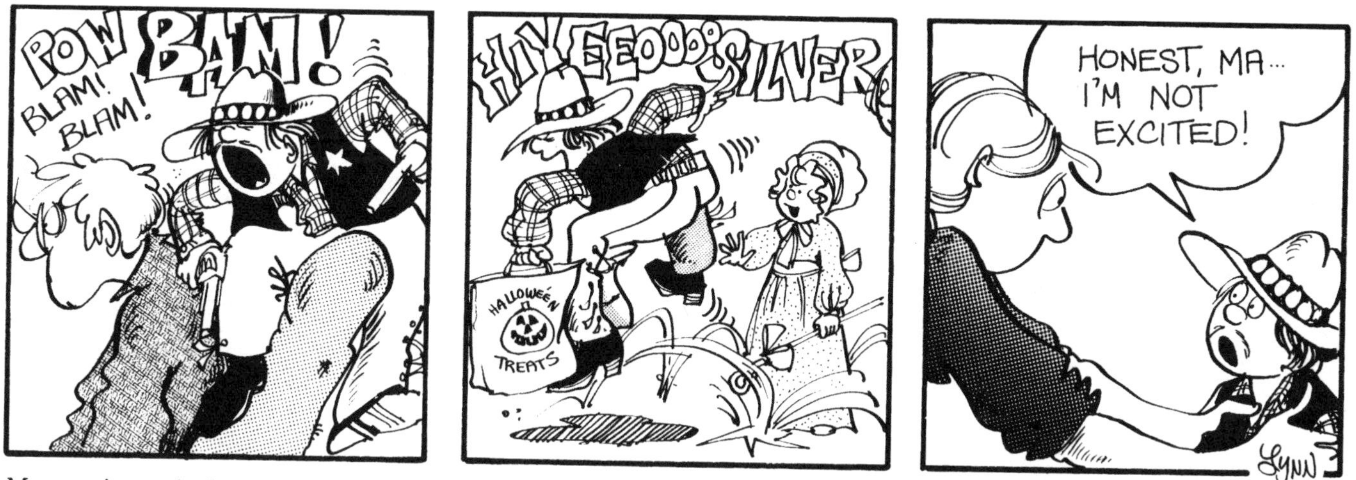
POW
BLAM! BLAM!
BAM!
HI YEEOOO SILVER
HALLOWEEN TREATS
HONEST, MA... I'M NOT EXCITED!
LYNN

My son, Aaron, had a great cowboy costume — right down to the vest, chaps, and six-guns. He'd often dress up and bounce around the house as if he was on a horse. We bought the hat, gun, sheriff's star, and plaid shirt in Winnipeg. I made the chaps, vest, and neck scarf. He was just another kid until the outfit was on, and then he turned into the wildest of the wild. It was his costume of choice, until he grew out of it. This, too, I have preserved, waiting for another kid to make it come to life!

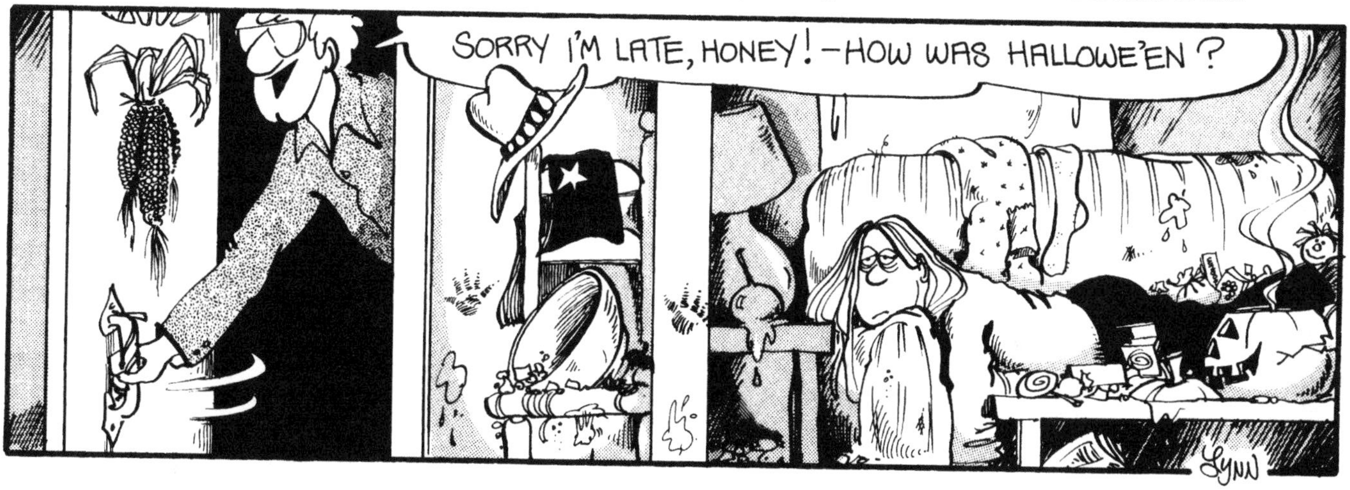
SORRY I'M LATE, HONEY! –HOW WAS HALLOWE'EN ?
LYNN

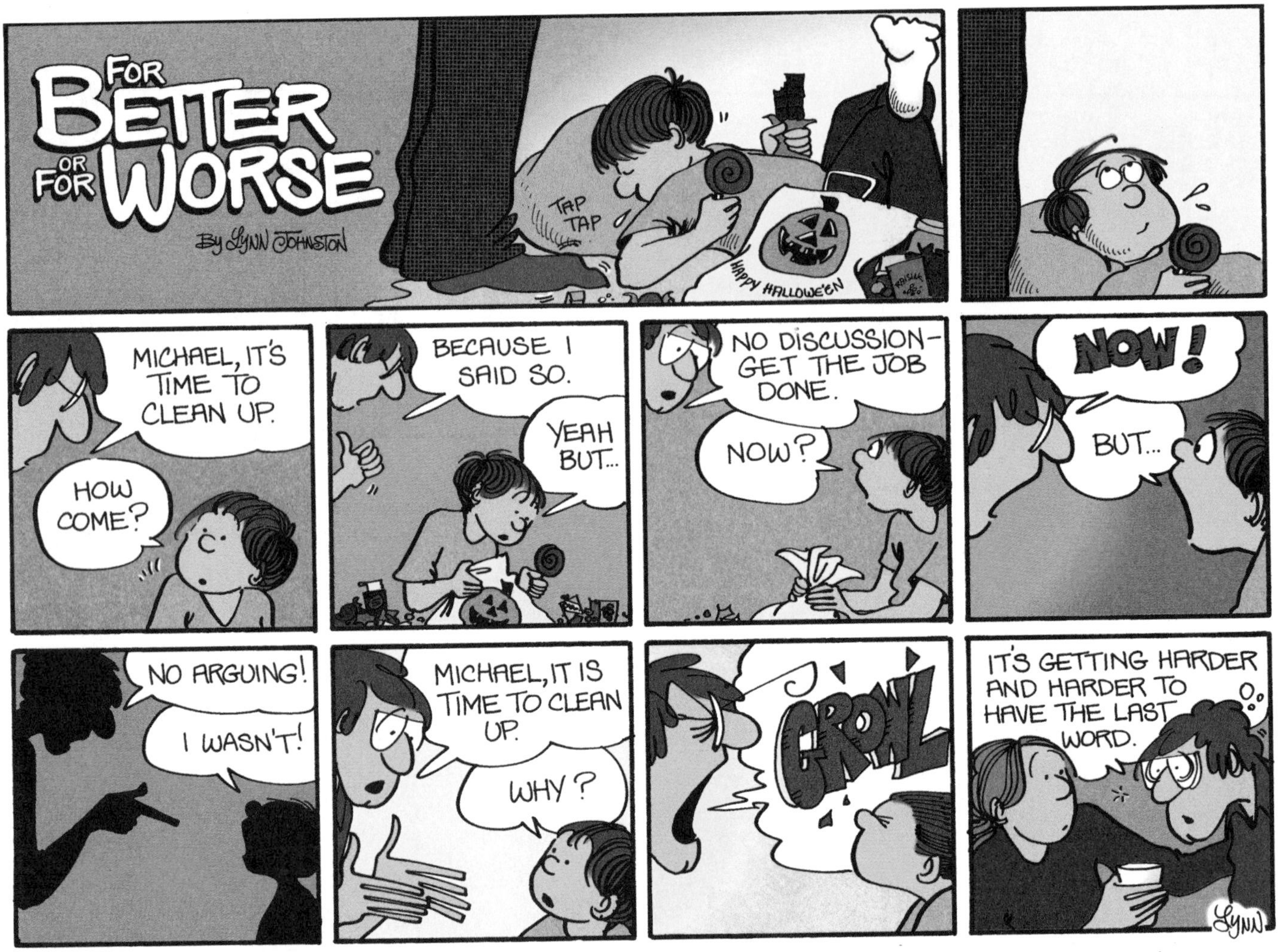
FOR BETTER OR FOR WORSE
By Lynn Johnston
TAP TAP
HAPPY HALLOWE'EN
MICHAEL, IT'S TIME TO CLEAN UP.
HOW COME?
BECAUSE I SAID SO.
YEAH BUT...
NO DISCUSSION- GET THE JOB DONE.
NOW?
NOW!
BUT...
NO ARGUING!
I WASN'T!
MICHAEL, IT IS TIME TO CLEAN UP.
WHY?
GROWL
IT'S GETTING HARDER AND HARDER TO HAVE THE LAST WORD.
Lynn

"Heaven" was lying on our living room couch, eating and watching TV. With the old wood-and-coal furnace, our house was always cold, and the warm spot on the couch was something my brother and I fought over. Yes, we fought over the warm spot! So, once ensconced on the sofa, I hated to remove myself and lose that precious bit of heat! If Dad was the one to order you off the couch, you might be able to beg a few more moments of repose. An order from Mom meant immediate compliance. In this strip, John uses the "ferocious" method of kid removal. I used it, too. When all else fails, we parents often resort to animal behaviour. I stopped at taking them by the scruff of their necks with my teeth, however!

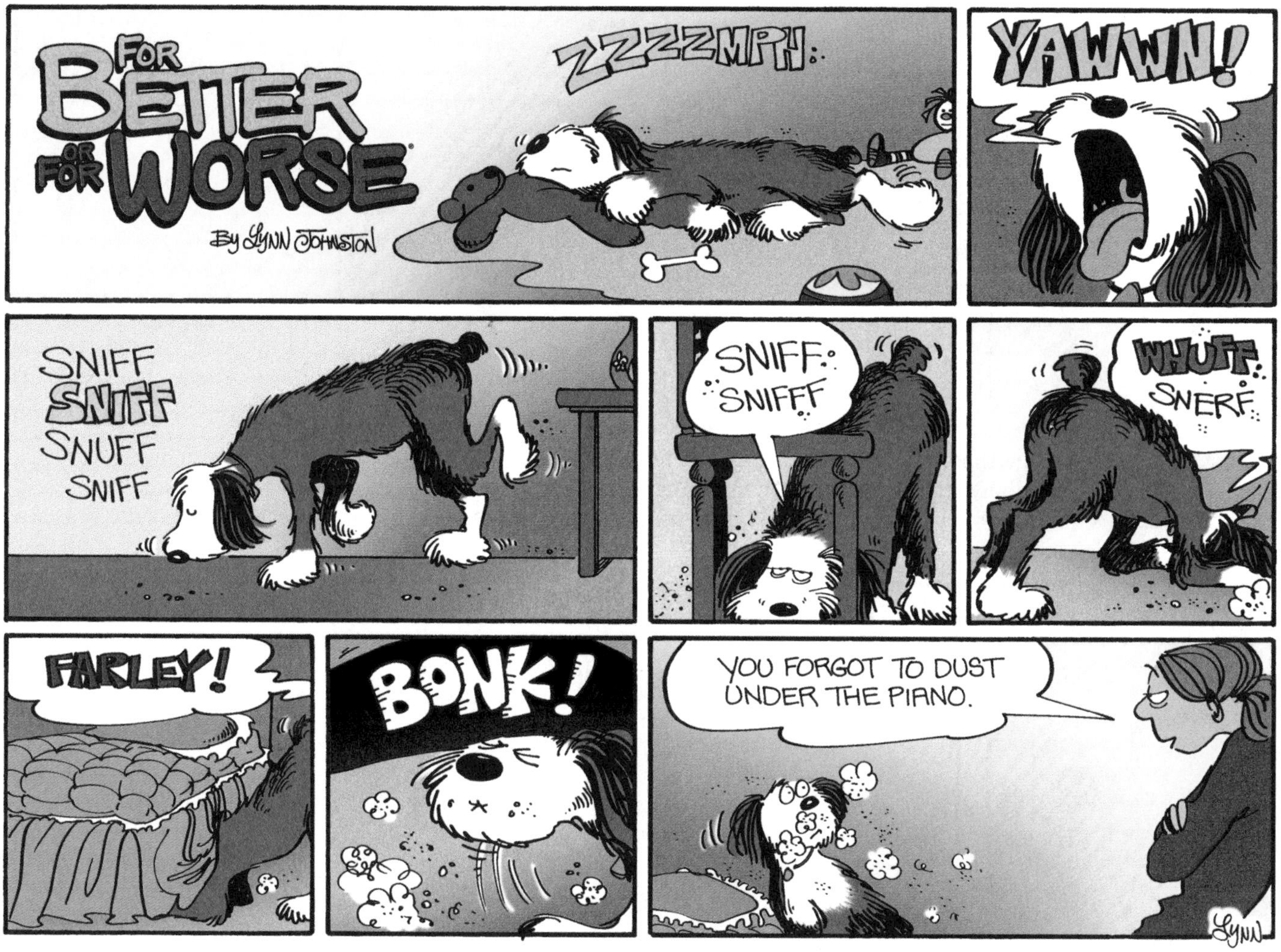
FOR BETTER OR FOR WORSE
BY LYNN JOHNSTON
ZZZZMPH
YAWWN!
SNIFF
SNIFF
SNUFF
SNIFF
SNIFF
SNIFFF
WHUFF
SNERF
FARLEY!
BONK!
YOU FORGOT TO DUST UNDER THE PIANO.
LYNN

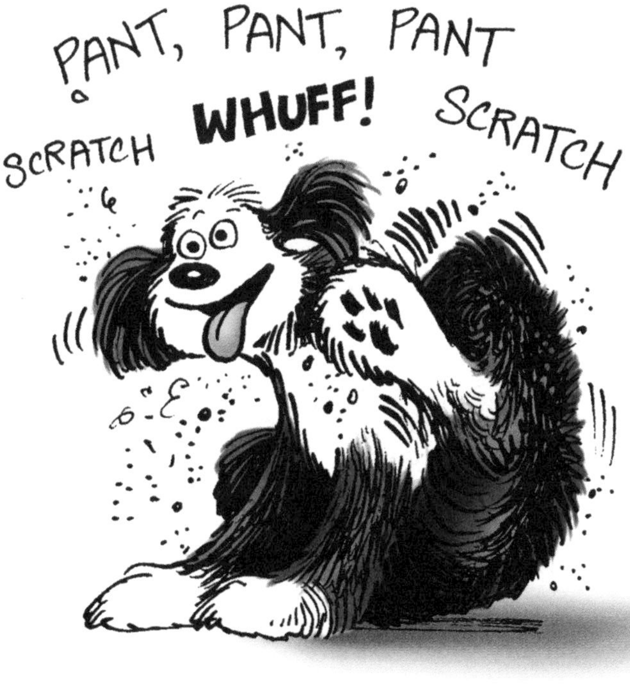
PANT, PANT, PANT
SCRATCH
WHUFF!
SCRATCH

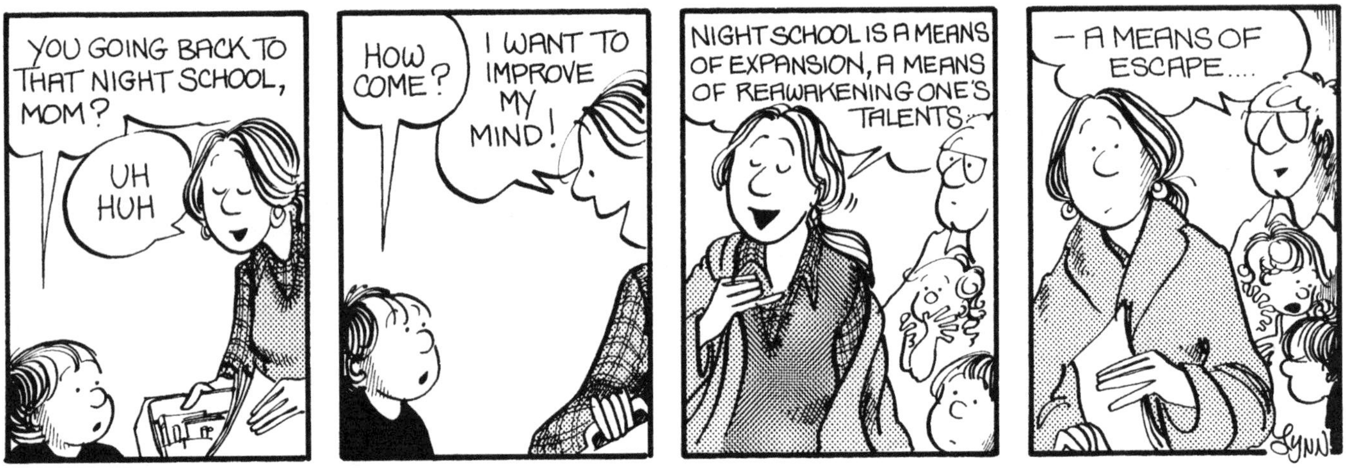
YOU GOING BACK TO THAT NIGHT SCHOOL, MOM?
UH HUH
HOW COME?
I WANT TO IMPROVE MY MIND!
NIGHT SCHOOL IS A MEANS OF EXPANSION, A MEANS OF REAWAKENING ONE'S TALENTS...
— A MEANS OF ESCAPE....
LYNN

During the years when my children were very young, I did not have the option of going back to school, although I would have liked to. My life in a tiny remote mining town in northern Manitoba provided an education of another kind! The character "Elly" is not me. She is someone I MIGHT have been, given other circumstances. My real life wasn't nearly as plausible as Elly Patterson's.

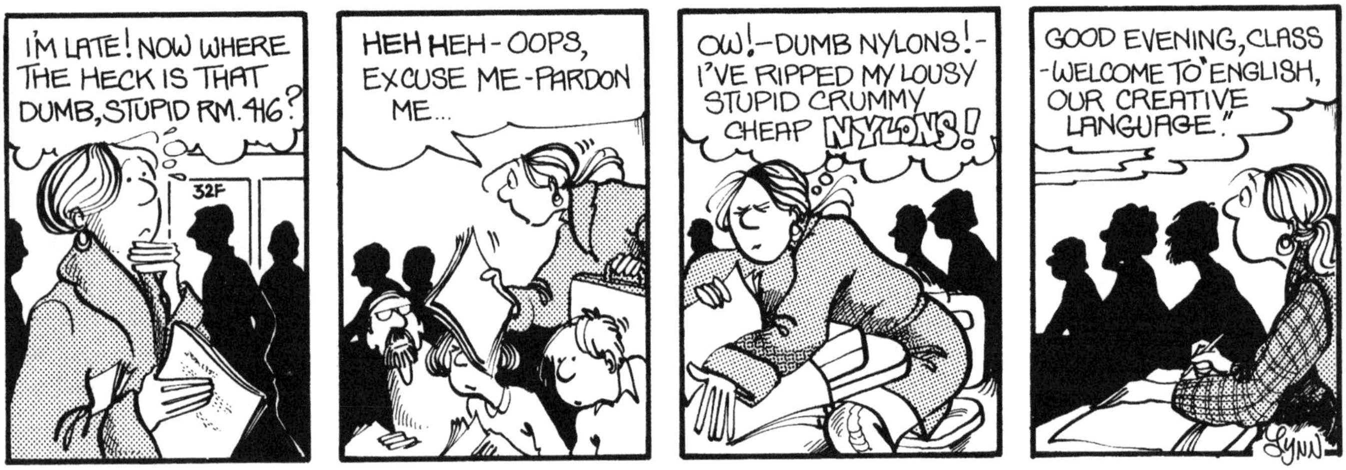
I'M LATE! NOW WHERE THE HECK IS THAT DUMB, STUPID RM. 416?
32F
HEH HEH - OOPS, EXCUSE ME - PARDON ME...
OW! - DUMB NYLONS! - I'VE RIPPED MY LOUSY STUPID CRUMMY CHEAP NYLONS!
GOOD EVENING, CLASS - WELCOME TO "ENGLISH, OUR CREATIVE LANGUAGE."
LYNN

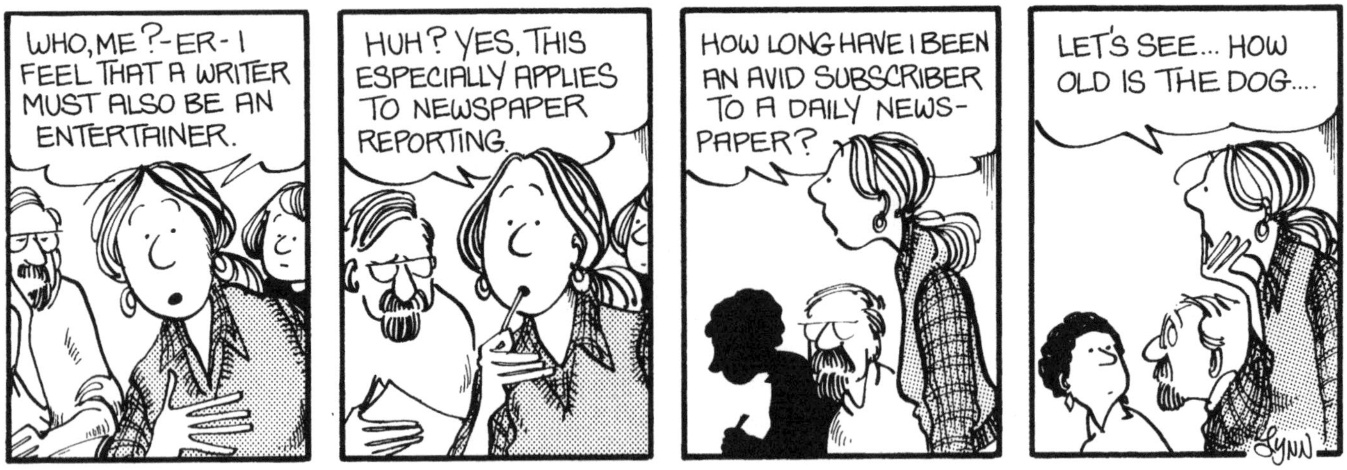
WHO, ME? - ER - I FEEL THAT A WRITER MUST ALSO BE AN ENTERTAINER.
HUH? YES, THIS ESPECIALLY APPLIES TO NEWSPAPER REPORTING.
HOW LONG HAVE I BEEN AN AVID SUBSCRIBER TO A DAILY NEWS-PAPER?
LET'S SEE... HOW OLD IS THE DOG....
LYNN

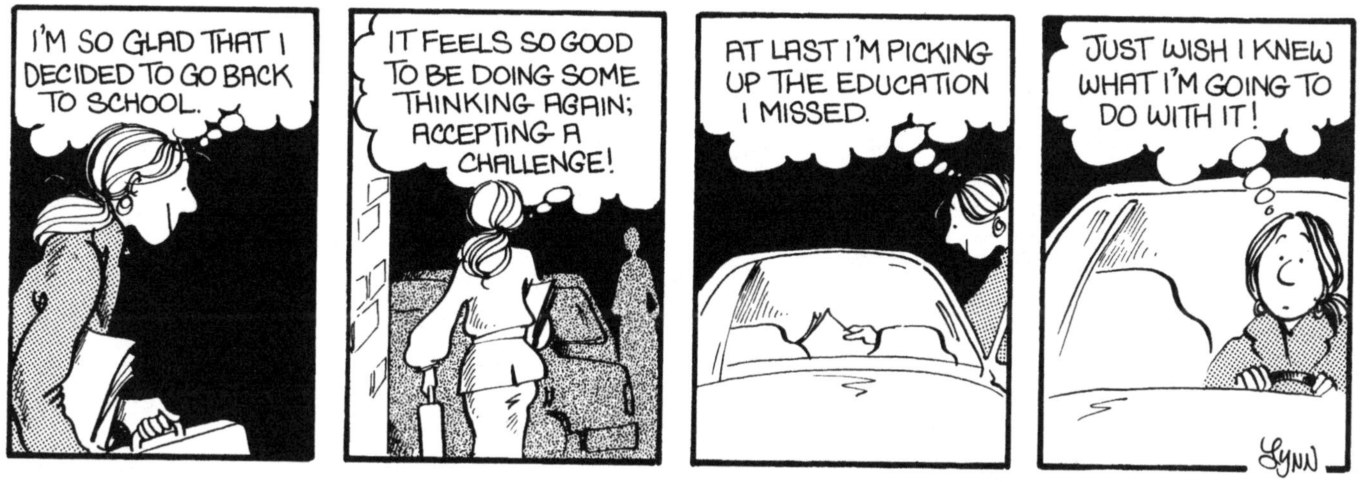
I'M SO GLAD THAT I DECIDED TO GO BACK TO SCHOOL.
IT FEELS SO GOOD TO BE DOING SOME THINKING AGAIN; ACCEPTING A CHALLENGE!
AT LAST I'M PICKING UP THE EDUCATION I MISSED.
JUST WISH I KNEW WHAT I'M GOING TO DO WITH IT!
LYNN

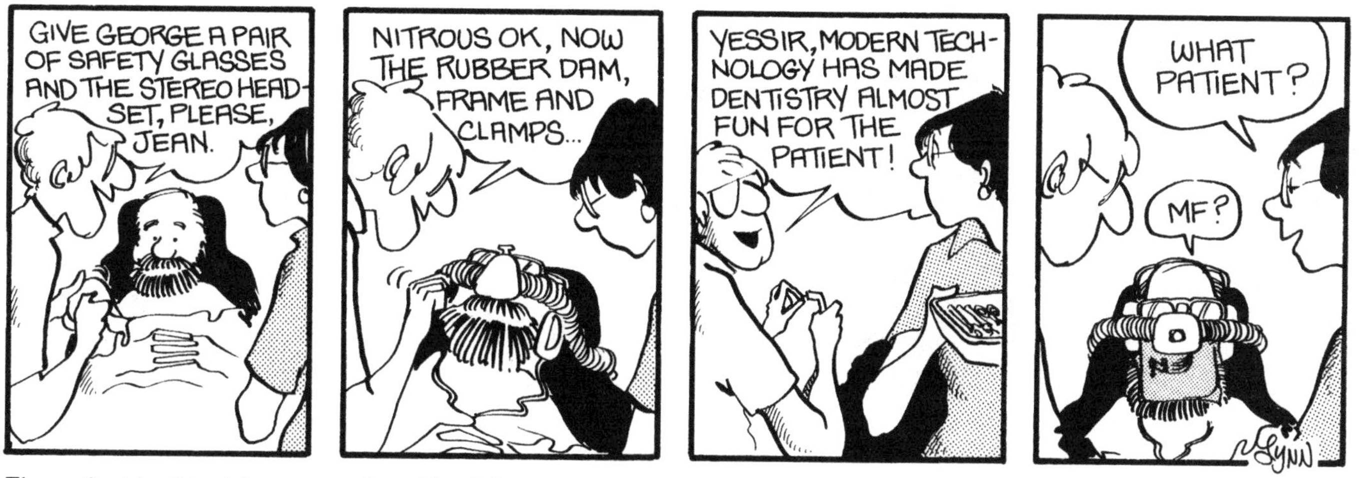
GIVE GEORGE A PAIR OF SAFETY GLASSES AND THE STEREO HEAD-SET, PLEASE, JEAN.
NITROUS OK, NOW THE RUBBER DAM, FRAME AND CLAMPS...
YESSIR, MODERN TECH-NOLOGY HAS MADE DENTISTRY ALMOST FUN FOR THE PATIENT!
WHAT PATIENT?
MF?
LYNN

The patient in this strip was our dear friend George Fast. He and his wife, Sigrid, were our curling partners, and we spent some wonderful times together. I often poked fun at friends by putting them in the strip. Sadly, George passed away far too soon. Seeing this again has brought back some great memories.

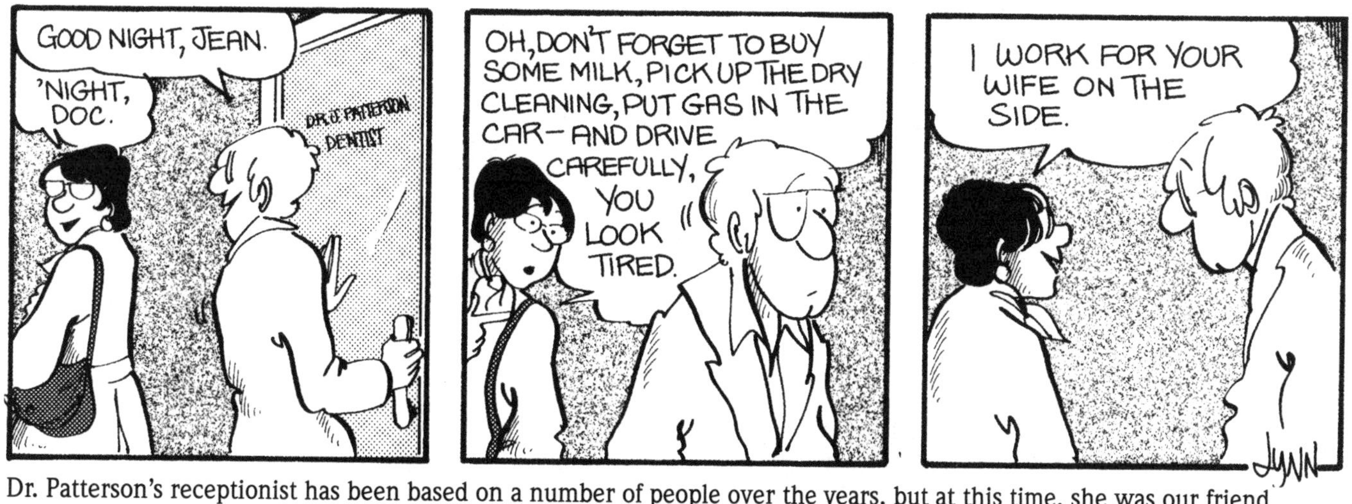
GOOD NIGHT, JEAN.
'NIGHT, DOC.
DR. J. PATTERSON DENTIST
OH, DON'T FORGET TO BUY SOME MILK, PICK UP THE DRY CLEANING, PUT GAS IN THE CAR— AND DRIVE CAREFULLY, YOU LOOK TIRED.
I WORK FOR YOUR WIFE ON THE SIDE.
LYNN

Dr. Patterson's receptionist has been based on a number of people over the years, but at this time, she was our friend Ann-Margret Plummer. Her husband managed the mine, and I think she managed everything else! Efficient, sweet natured, honest, and fair, we relied on her for everything from bookkeeping to bringing home the bacon. Years later, we remain great friends, and see each other as often as possible.

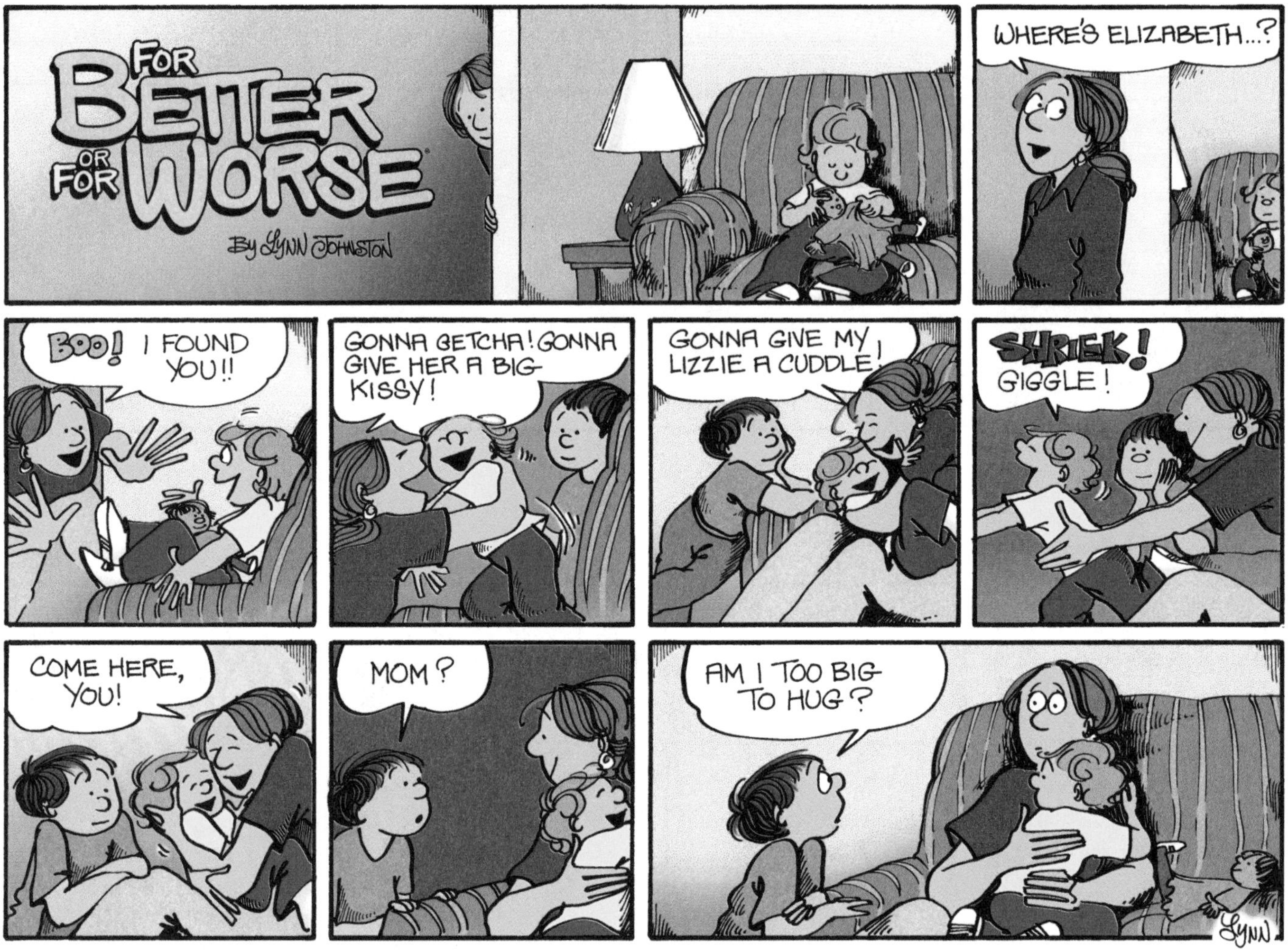
FOR BETTER OR FOR WORSE
By Lynn Johnston
WHERE'S ELIZABETH...?
BOO! I FOUND YOU!!
GONNA GETCHA! GONNA GIVE HER A BIG KISSY!
GONNA GIVE MY LIZZIE A CUDDLE!
SHRIEK! GIGGLE!
COME HERE, YOU!
MOM?
AM I TOO BIG TO HUG?
LYNN

My kids were born almost five years apart. When you have little kids — one you can pick up and cart around and one the size of a St. Bernard, the littlest always seems to get the most affection. Older kids sort of shrug off the hugs and wriggle out of cuddles, but they need them nonetheless. I guess the love wasn't being distributed evenly when Aaron asked this question, and it really hit home. I put Katie down and gave him the biggest cuddle right then and there. A lesson well learned. He's almost 40 now, and still not too big to hug!

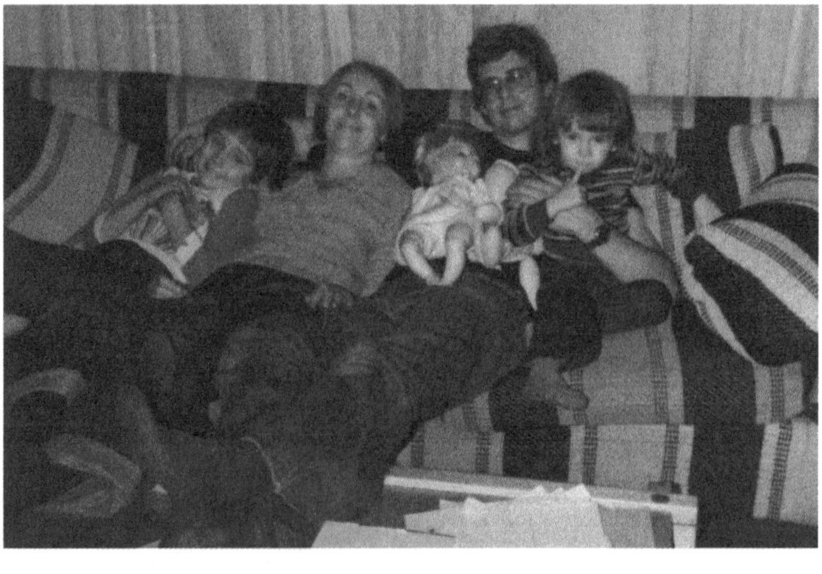

This is us on the old striped couch.

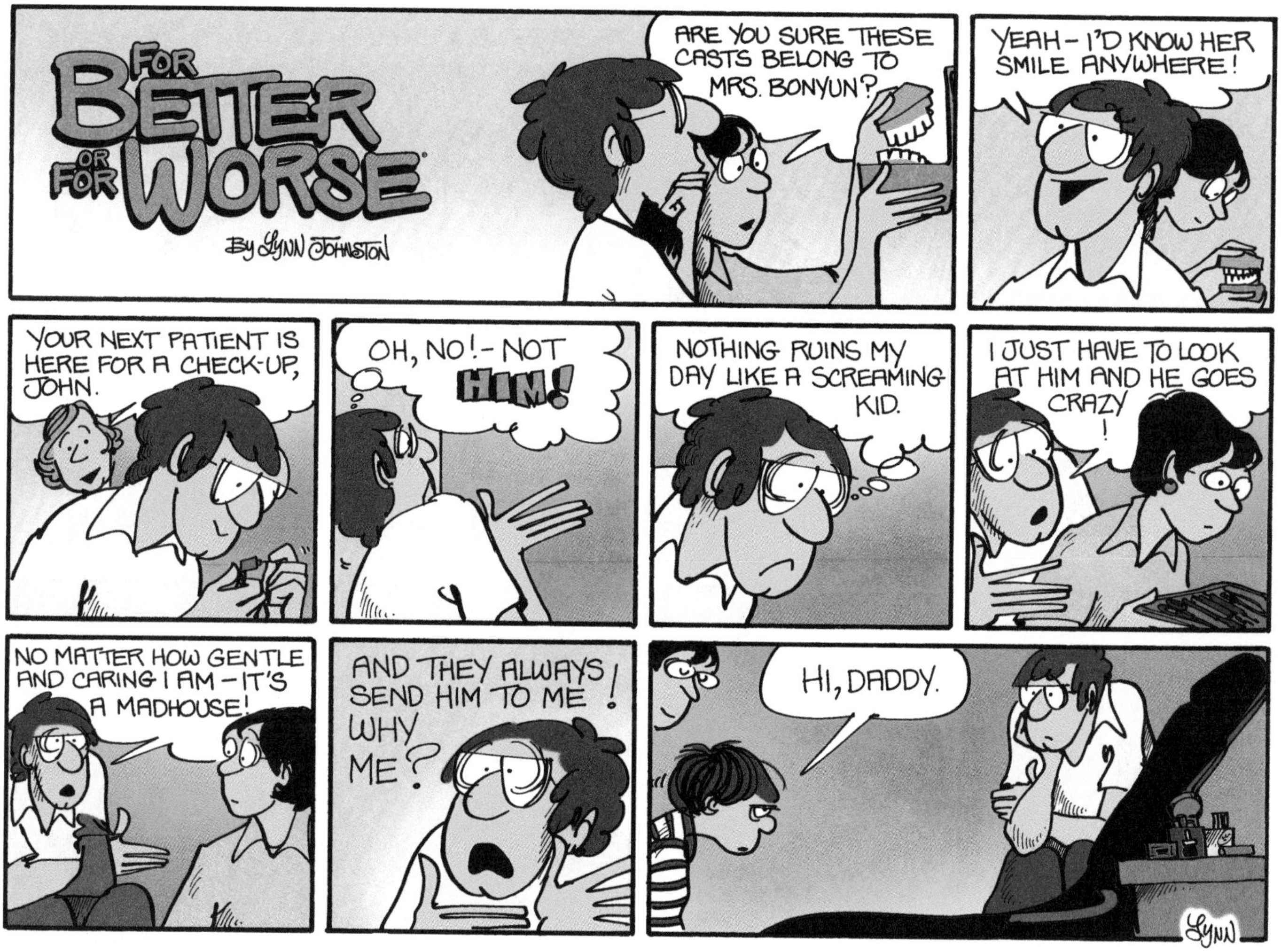
For Better or For Worse
By Lynn Johnston
ARE YOU SURE THESE CASTS BELONG TO MRS. BONYUN?
YEAH - I'D KNOW HER SMILE ANYWHERE!
YOUR NEXT PATIENT IS HERE FOR A CHECK-UP, JOHN.
OH, NO! - NOT HIM!
NOTHING RUINS MY DAY LIKE A SCREAMING KID.
I JUST HAVE TO LOOK AT HIM AND HE GOES CRAZY!
NO MATTER HOW GENTLE AND CARING I AM - IT'S A MADHOUSE!
AND THEY ALWAYS SEND HIM TO ME! WHY ME?
HI, DADDY.
Lynn

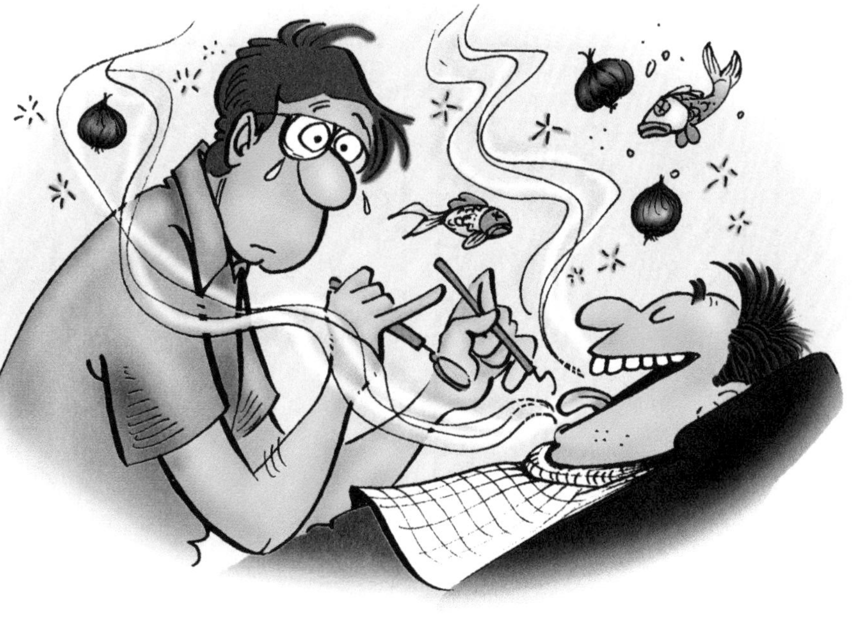

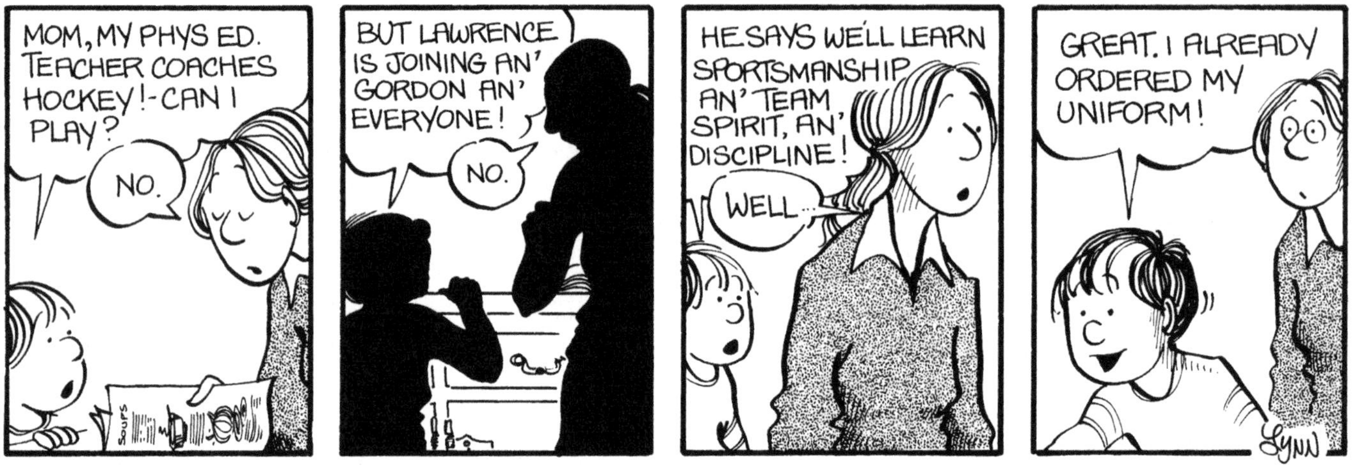
MOM, MY PHYS ED. TEACHER COACHES HOCKEY!-CAN I PLAY?
NO.
BUT LAWRENCE IS JOINING AN' GORDON AN' EVERYONE!
NO.
HE SAYS WE'LL LEARN SPORTSMANSHIP AN' TEAM SPIRIT, AN' DISCIPLINE!
WELL...
GREAT. I ALREADY ORDERED MY UNIFORM!
LYNN

In Lynn Lake, all the kids played hockey. I was surprised when Aaron declared his interest in joining the juniors — he had never been interested in sports before. Aaron played for a few years — until the coaches became serious and really wanted to win. This is when the good players get to play and the kids who are there for the fun of it get to sit on the sidelines.

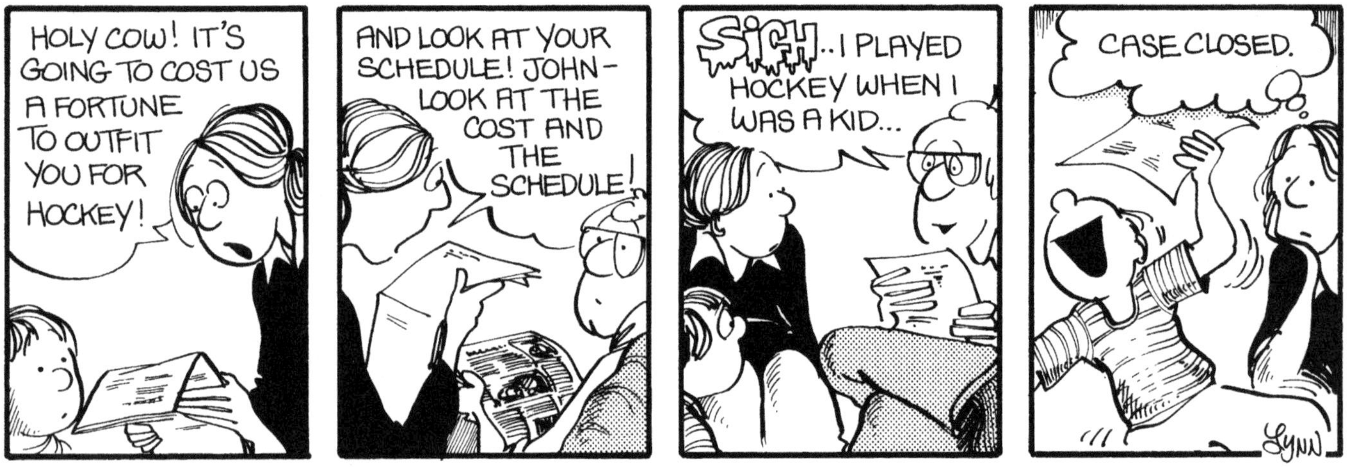
HOLY COW! IT'S GOING TO COST US A FORTUNE TO OUTFIT YOU FOR HOCKEY!
AND LOOK AT YOUR SCHEDULE! JOHN - LOOK AT THE COST AND THE SCHEDULE!
SIGH..I PLAYED HOCKEY WHEN I WAS A KID...
CASE CLOSED.
LYNN

Since there were no sporting-goods shops in town, we all relied on hand-me-downs and the Sears catalog. The sports exchange happened in the church basement; you could tell it was happening as soon as you went in the door just by the smell. Everyone was keen to get there early for the best pickings. If you were lucky, you could make a deal with a neighour before the season began. Despite the availability of secondhand gear, equipping a kid was expensive.

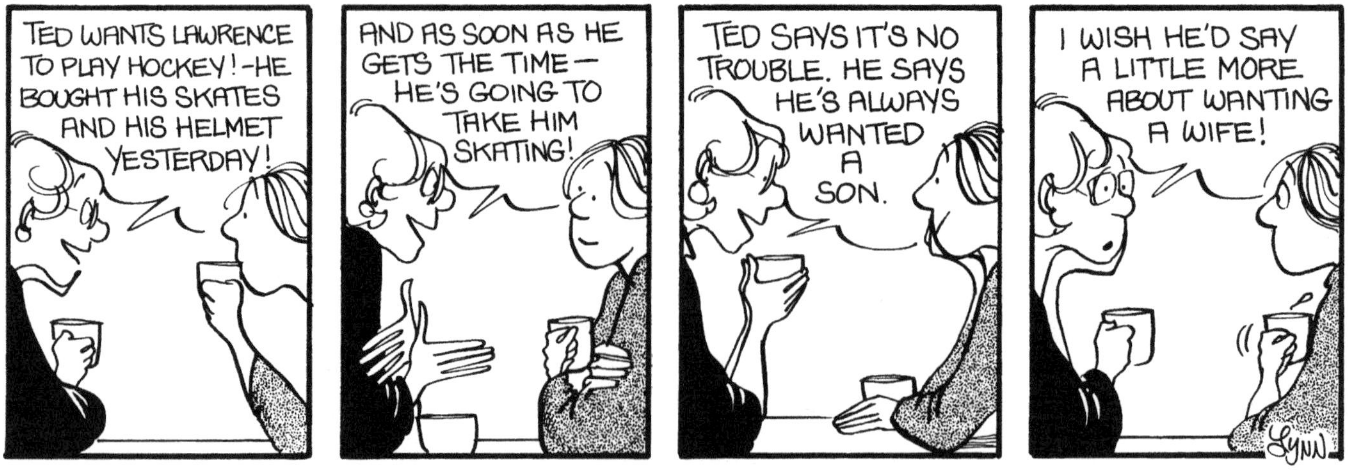
TED WANTS LAWRENCE TO PLAY HOCKEY!-HE BOUGHT HIS SKATES AND HIS HELMET YESTERDAY!
AND AS SOON AS HE GETS THE TIME— HE'S GOING TO TAKE HIM SKATING!
TED SAYS IT'S NO TROUBLE. HE SAYS HE'S ALWAYS WANTED A SON.
I WISH HE'D SAY A LITTLE MORE ABOUT WANTING A WIFE!
LYNN

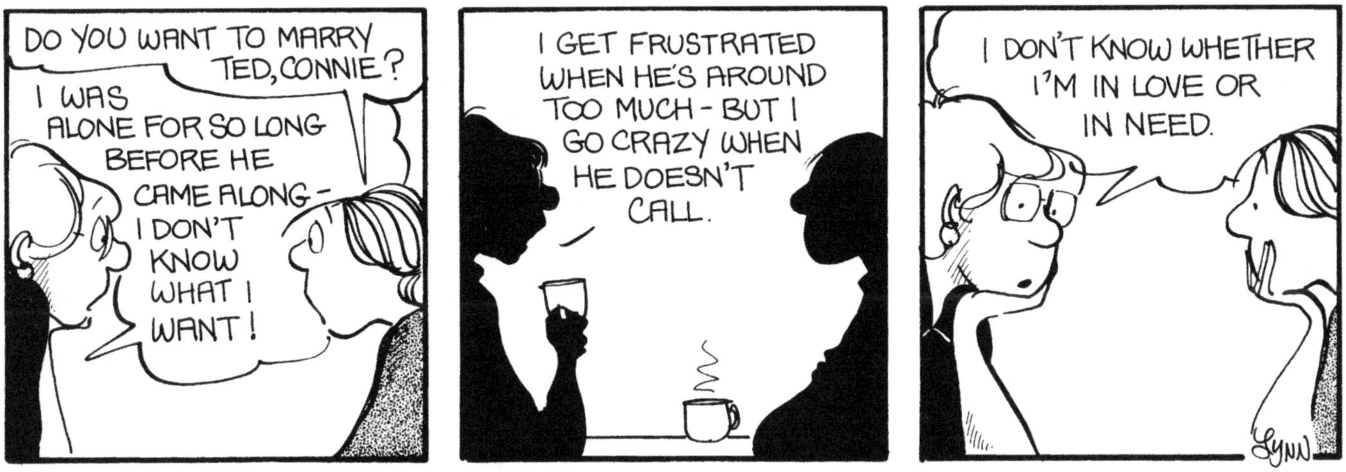
DO YOU WANT TO MARRY TED, CONNIE?
I WAS ALONE FOR SO LONG BEFORE HE CAME ALONG - I DON'T KNOW WHAT I WANT!
I GET FRUSTRATED WHEN HE'S AROUND TOO MUCH - BUT I GO CRAZY WHEN HE DOESN'T CALL.
I DON'T KNOW WHETHER I'M IN LOVE OR IN NEED.
LYNN

The story of Connie and her unhappy relationships, again, is my story. When I was single (the first time) I went through a few frustrating relationships. I had a wonderful friend — a woman I'd met when I was a medical artist at McMaster University. She became my mentor and confidante. While visiting her after a particularly confusing date, I wondered aloud if I should see this man again. Marjorie said: "You have to decide … are you in love or in need?" The answer hurt. I moved on.

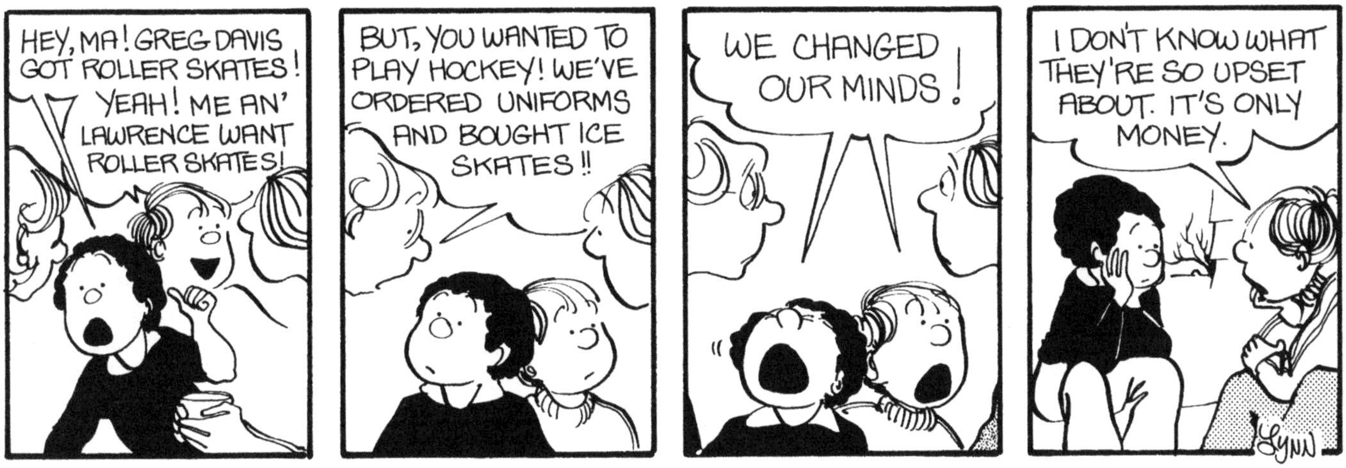
HEY, MA! GREG DAVIS GOT ROLLER SKATES!
YEAH! ME AN' LAWRENCE WANT ROLLER SKATES!
BUT, YOU WANTED TO PLAY HOCKEY! WE'VE ORDERED UNIFORMS AND BOUGHT ICE SKATES!!
WE CHANGED OUR MINDS!
I DON'T KNOW WHAT THEY'RE SO UPSET ABOUT. IT'S ONLY MONEY.
LYNN

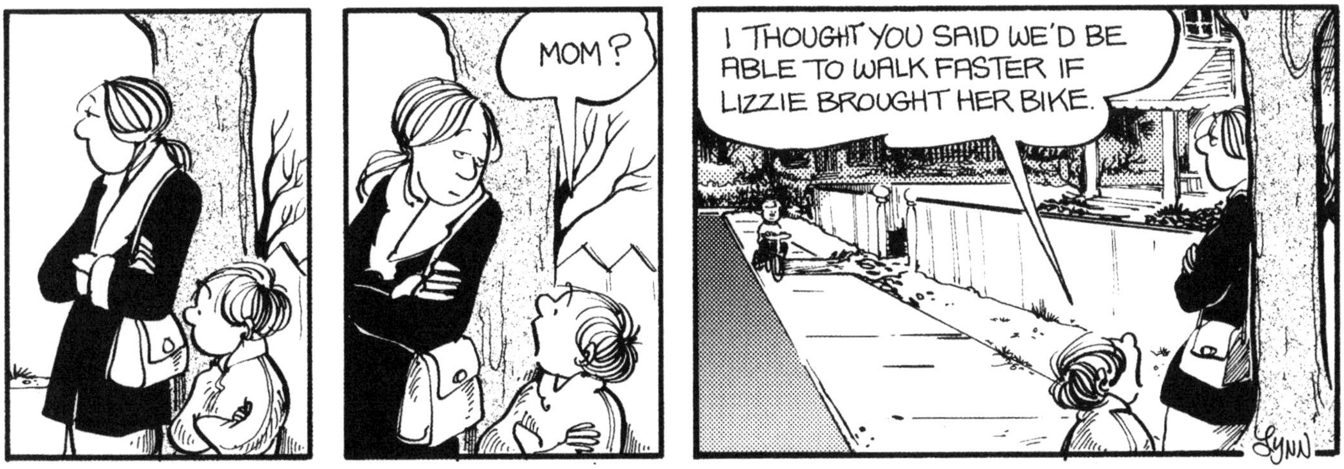
MOM?
I THOUGHT YOU SAID WE'D BE ABLE TO WALK FASTER IF LIZZIE BROUGHT HER BIKE.
LYNN

My brother had a tricycle to which he was welded. He was on it constantly. We didn't own a car so mom trundled us to the corner store — she and I on foot with Alan on his trike. I remember having to wait for him as he sat and watched bugs on the sidewalk or stopped to check out a parked car. It was maddening. Likewise, he would pedal like crazy down the hills and we'd have to run after him. It wasn't until I had kids of my own that I realized how often we'd put Mom's life in danger!

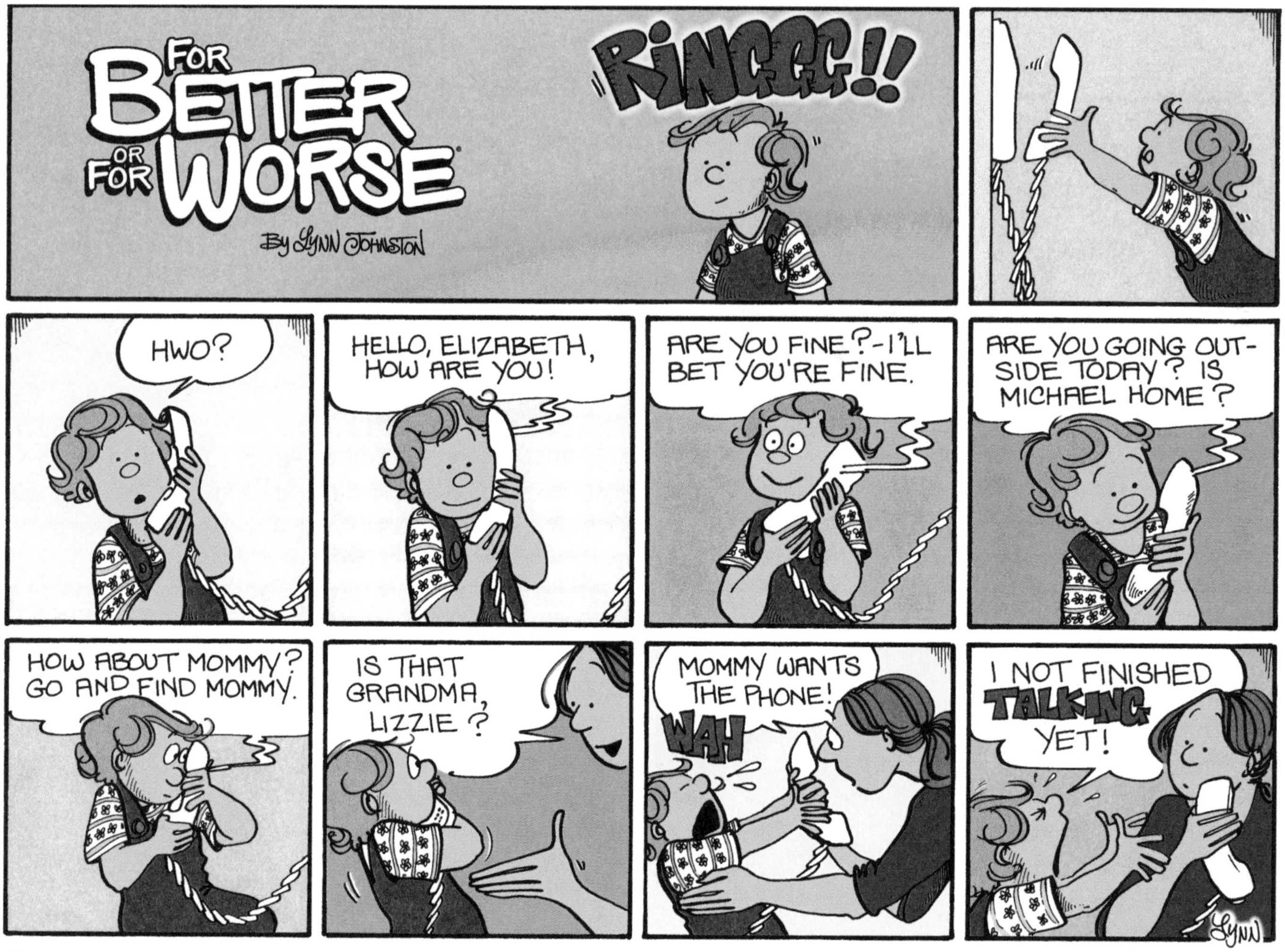
FOR BETTER OR FOR WORSE
BY LYNN JOHNSTON
RINGGG!!
HWO?
HELLO, ELIZABETH, HOW ARE YOU!
ARE YOU FINE?-I'LL BET YOU'RE FINE.
ARE YOU GOING OUT-SIDE TODAY? IS MICHAEL HOME?
HOW ABOUT MOMMY? GO AND FIND MOMMY.
IS THAT GRANDMA, LIZZIE?
MOMMY WANTS THE PHONE!
WAH
I NOT FINISHED TALKING YET!
LYNN

Katie was fascinated by the telephone, and although she didn't catch on to the art of conversation right away, she enjoyed the fun of just hearing someone's voice coming from the receiver. With this in mind, she would sometimes climb onto a chair and press all the numbers. As long as she didn't raise the hand piece, I let her have fun — until we got billed for a call to Hong Kong!!! True story!

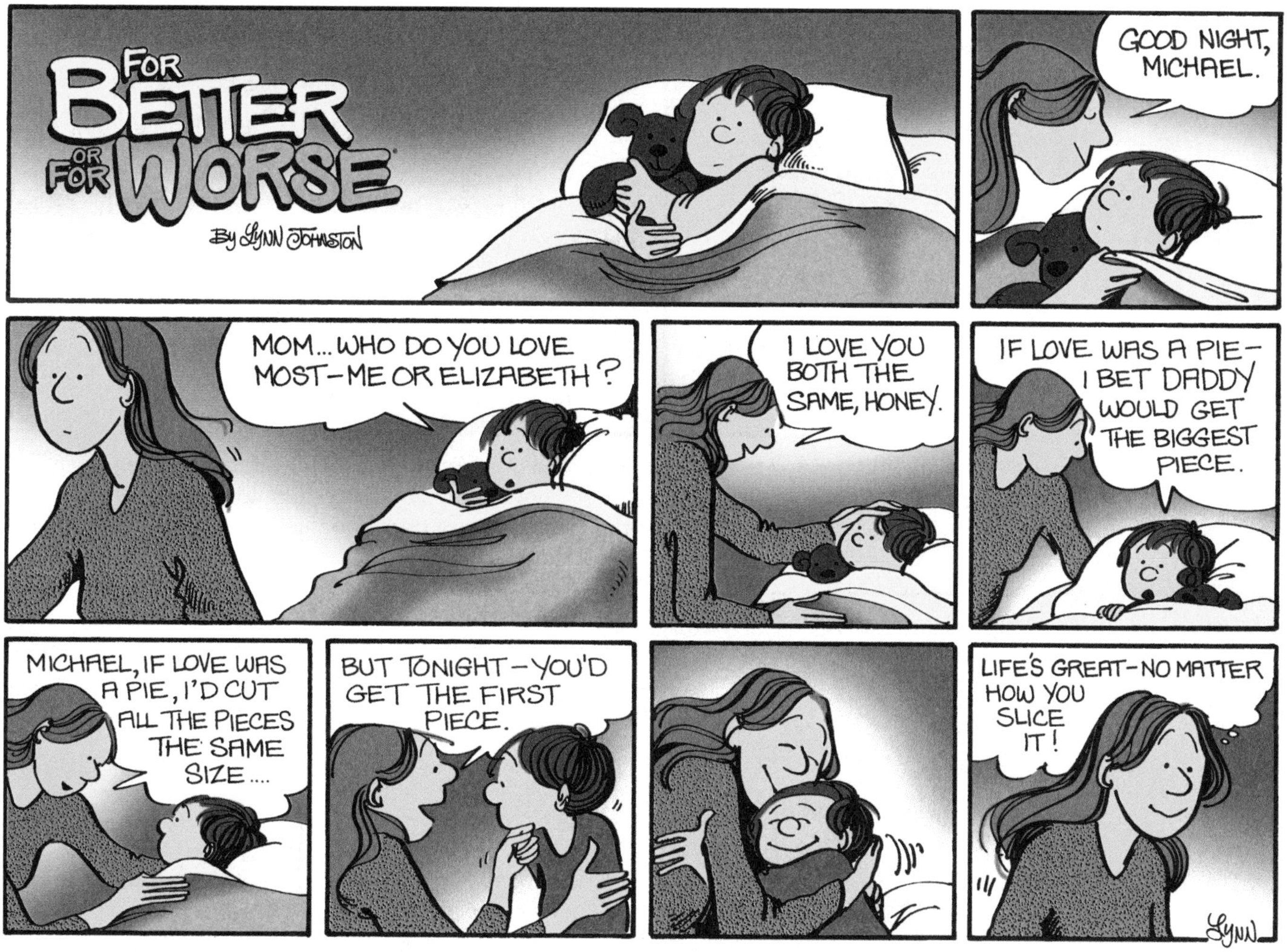
FOR BETTER OR FOR WORSE
BY LYNN JOHNSTON
GOOD NIGHT, MICHAEL.
MOM... WHO DO YOU LOVE MOST-ME OR ELIZABETH?
I LOVE YOU BOTH THE SAME, HONEY.
IF LOVE WAS A PIE-I BET DADDY WOULD GET THE BIGGEST PIECE.
MICHAEL, IF LOVE WAS A PIE, I'D CUT ALL THE PIECES THE SAME SIZE....
BUT TONIGHT-YOU'D GET THE FIRST PIECE.
LIFE'S GREAT-NO MATTER HOW YOU SLICE IT!
LYNN

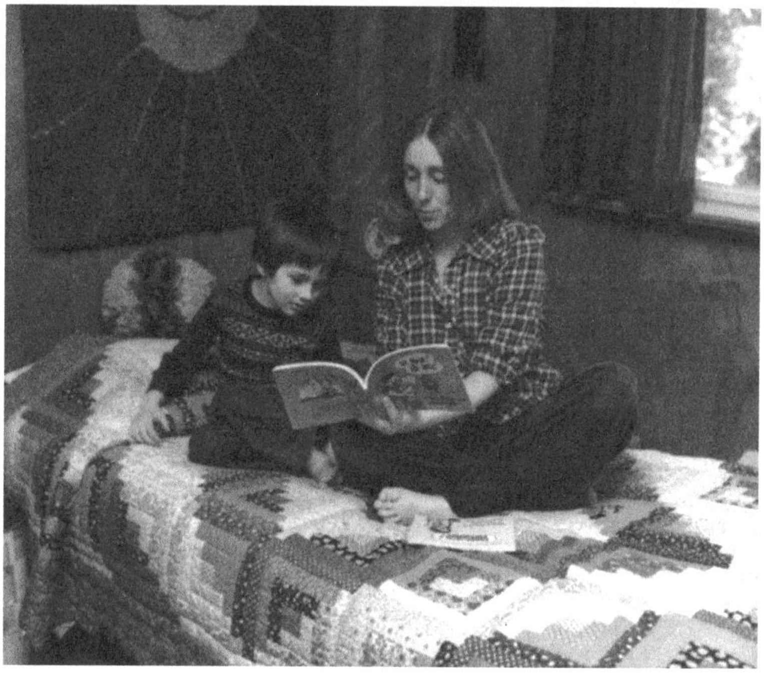

Aaron and me.

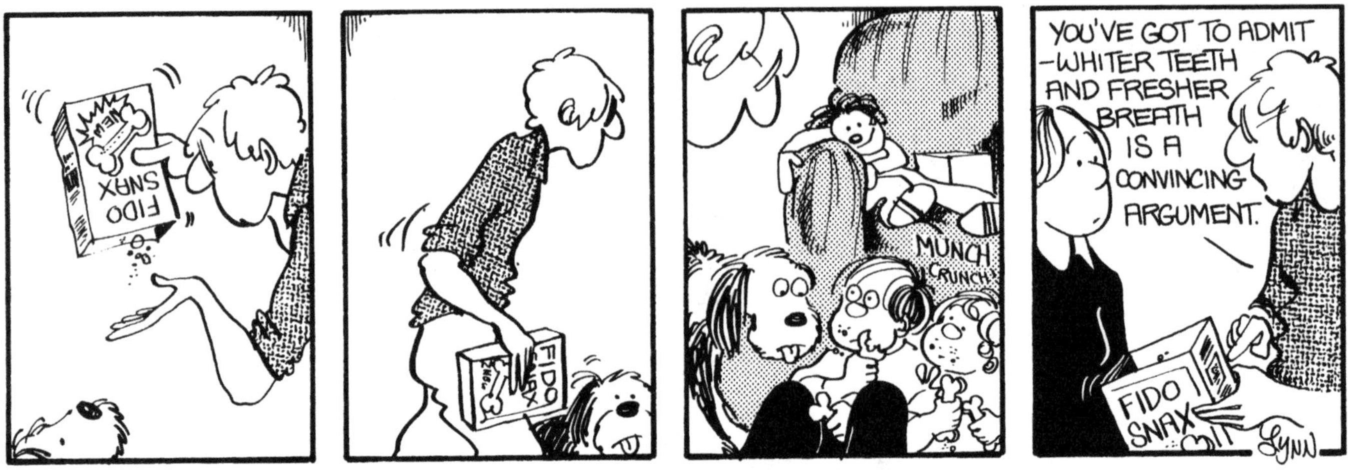
MUNCH
CRUNCH
YOU'VE GOT TO ADMIT —WHITER TEETH AND FRESHER BREATH IS A CONVINCING ARGUMENT.
FIDO SNAX
LYNN

Aaron was crawling around the same time he was teething, so kibble and other Farley fare were readily available. When I discovered Aaron teething on a Milk-Bone and enjoying the grit on his gums, I happily allowed him to indulge. Milk-Bones, after all, didn't disintegrate into mush like other teething biscuits, and they were cheap. The smell of them on the breath of both my charges didn't bother me in the least. Compared with some of the other odors emitted, this was "kissing sweet."

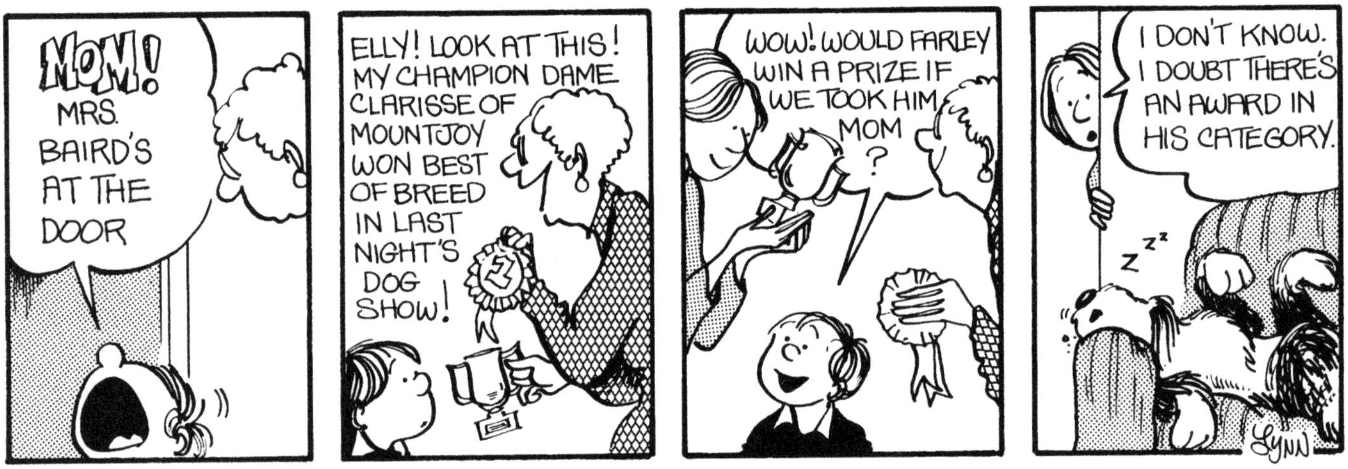
MOM! MRS. BAIRD'S AT THE DOOR
ELLY! LOOK AT THIS! MY CHAMPION DAME CLARISSE OF MOUNTJOY WON BEST OF BREED IN LAST NIGHT'S DOG SHOW!
WOW! WOULD FARLEY WIN A PRIZE IF WE TOOK HIM, MOM?
I DON'T KNOW. I DOUBT THERE'S AN AWARD IN HIS CATEGORY.
Z Z Z
LYNN

Farley the dog — in real life — had come from champion stock. For a while, my first spouse and I belonged to the Old English Sheepdog Owner's Club of Canada. We attended shows, meetings, and picnics, and I did the heading for the monthly newsletter. We thought about breeding Farley. He was a beauty. Unfortunately, he was jealous of baby Aaron, and so we had to find him a new home — it was either the kid or the dog!

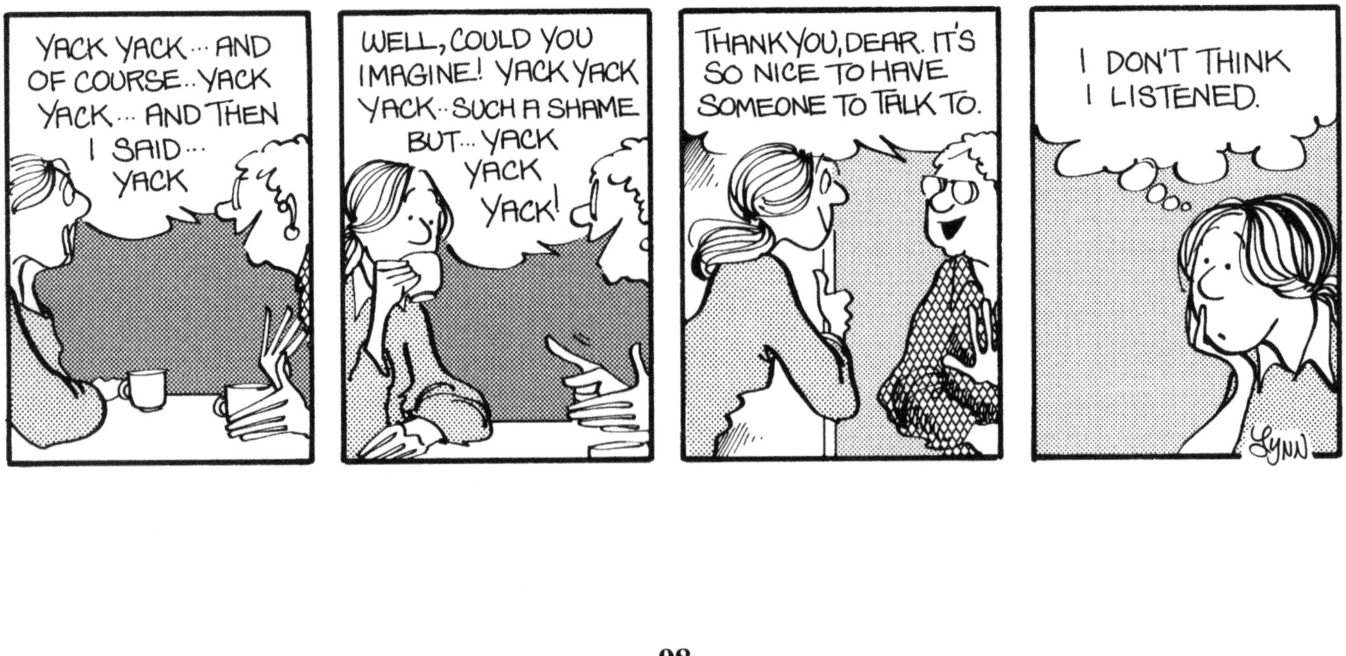
YACK YACK... AND OF COURSE.. YACK YACK... AND THEN I SAID... YACK
WELL, COULD YOU IMAGINE! YACK YACK YACK.. SUCH A SHAME BUT... YACK YACK YACK!
THANK YOU, DEAR. IT'S SO NICE TO HAVE SOMEONE TO TALK TO.
I DON'T THINK I LISTENED.
LYNN

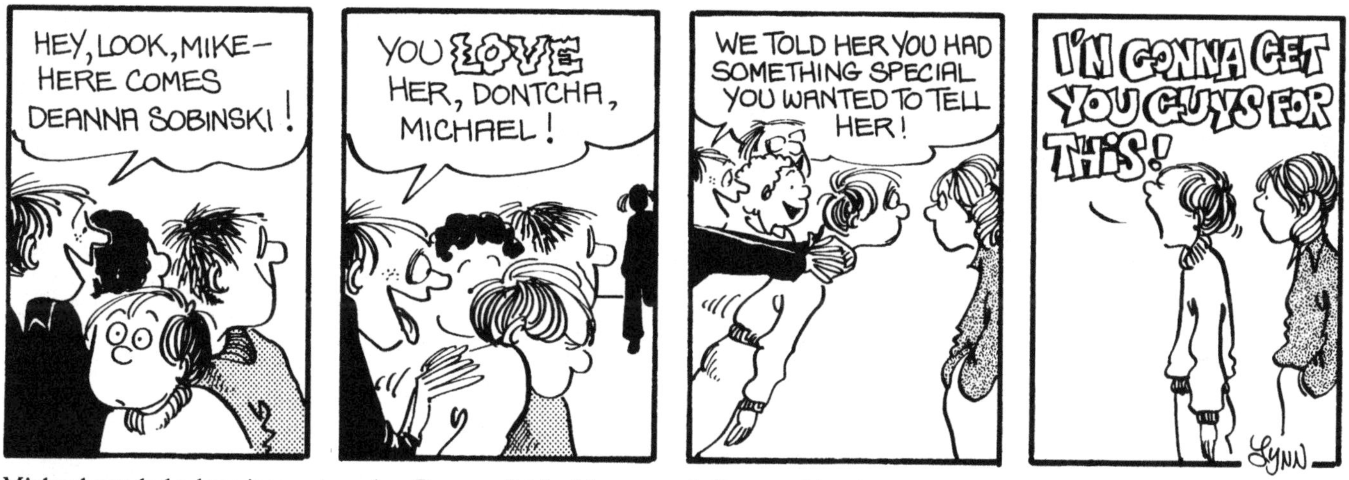
HEY, LOOK, MIKE— HERE COMES DEANNA SOBINSKI!
YOU LOVE HER, DONTCHA, MICHAEL!
WE TOLD HER YOU HAD SOMETHING SPECIAL YOU WANTED TO TELL HER!
I'M GONNA GET YOU GUYS FOR THIS!
LYNN

Michael needed a love interest, and so Deanna Sobinski appeared. She was blond, sweet, slender, smart, and not too interested in his goofy attempts to get her attention. Her first name came from my friend Nancy Lawn's daughter, Deanna — a playmate of Kate. And the name Sobinski was from an art school friend — whose first name, sadly, I forget! I liked the sound of these two names together. It was never my intention to have this relationship be rekindled in later years!

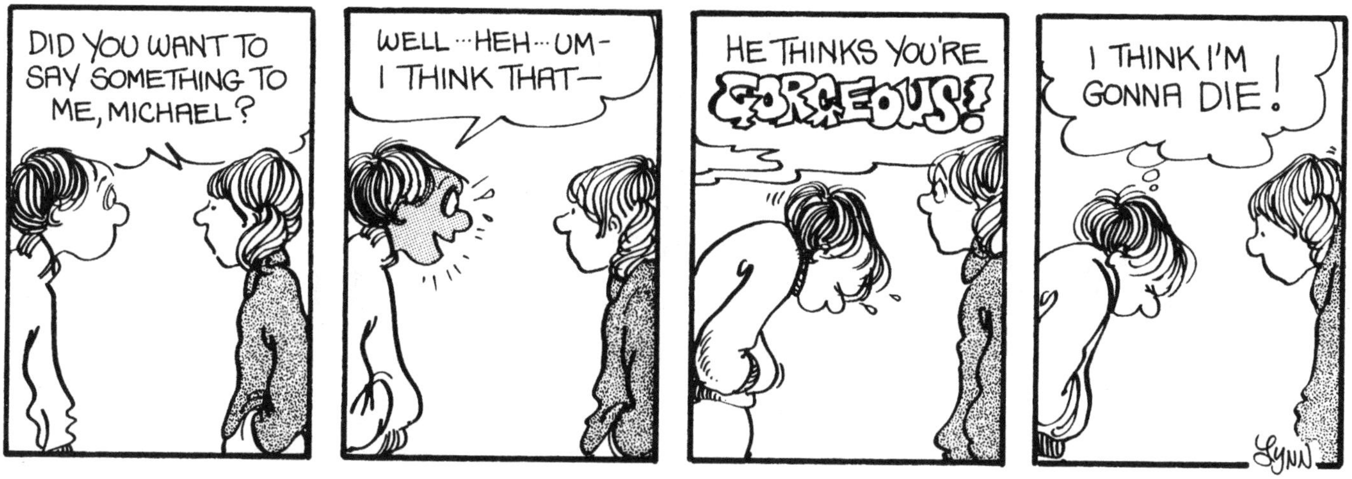
DID YOU WANT TO SAY SOMETHING TO ME, MICHAEL?
WELL···HEH···UM- I THINK THAT—
HE THINKS YOU'RE GORGEOUS!
I THINK I'M GONNA DIE!
LYNN

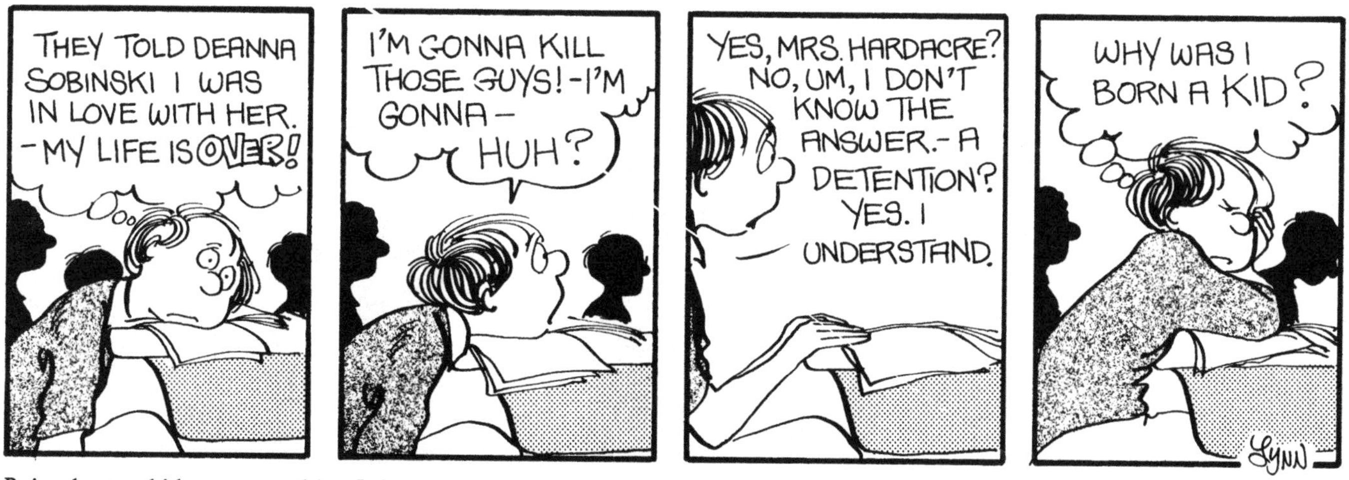
THEY TOLD DEANNA SOBINSKI I WAS IN LOVE WITH HER. -MY LIFE IS OVER!
I'M GONNA KILL THOSE GUYS! -I'M GONNA-
HUH?
YES, MRS. HARDACRE? NO, UM, I DON'T KNOW THE ANSWER.- A DETENTION? YES. I UNDERSTAND.
WHY WAS I BORN A KID?
LYNN

Being born a kid was something I thought about a lot. Adults often treated us as if we didn't understand or were "too young" for things like good explanations to good questions. We quickly separated the dismissive grown-ups from the cool ones, and for these, we'd do our best. Always. Many years later, when I had kids of my own, remembering what it was like to wish I was grown up helped me as a cartoonist — and made me a much better mom.

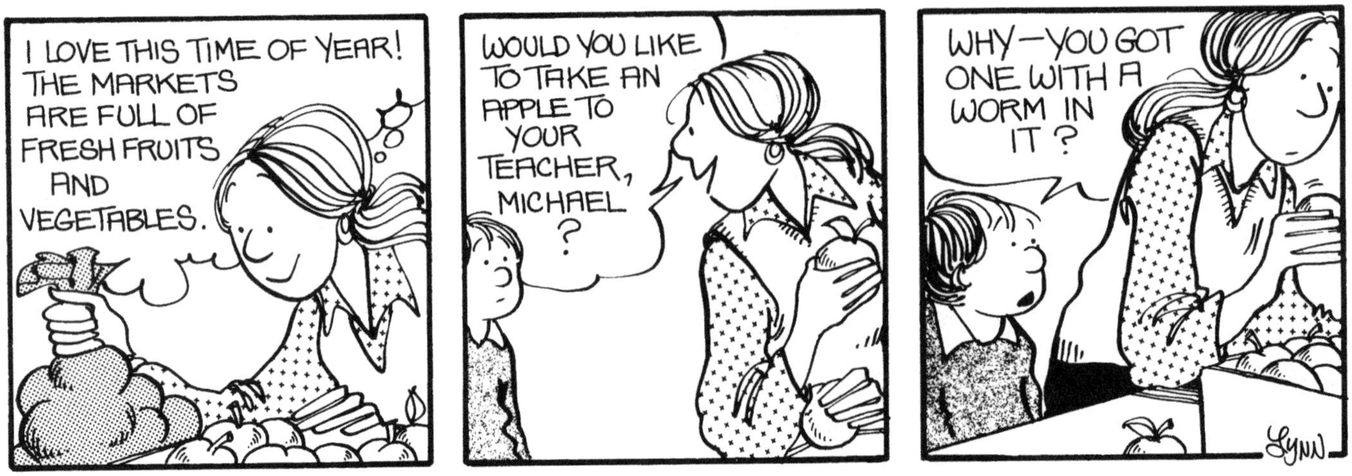
I LOVE THIS TIME OF YEAR! THE MARKETS ARE FULL OF FRESH FRUITS AND VEGETABLES.
WOULD YOU LIKE TO TAKE AN APPLE TO YOUR TEACHER, MICHAEL ?
WHY—YOU GOT ONE WITH A WORM IN IT ?
LYNN

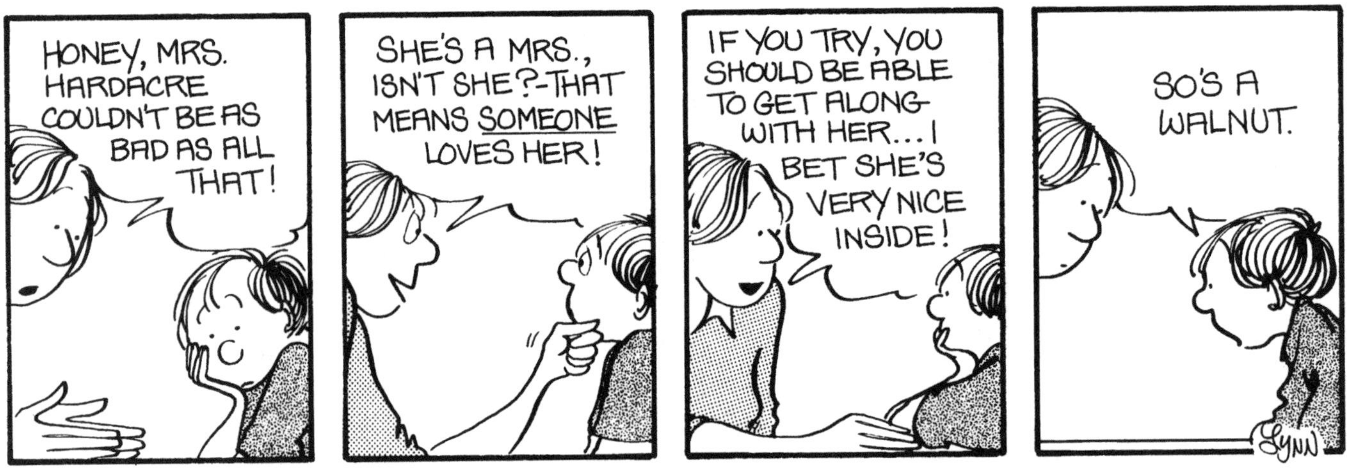
HONEY, MRS. HARDACRE COULDN'T BE AS BAD AS ALL THAT!
SHE'S A MRS., ISN'T SHE?-THAT MEANS SOMEONE LOVES HER!
IF YOU TRY, YOU SHOULD BE ABLE TO GET ALONG WITH HER... I BET SHE'S VERY NICE INSIDE!
SO'S A WALNUT.
LYNN

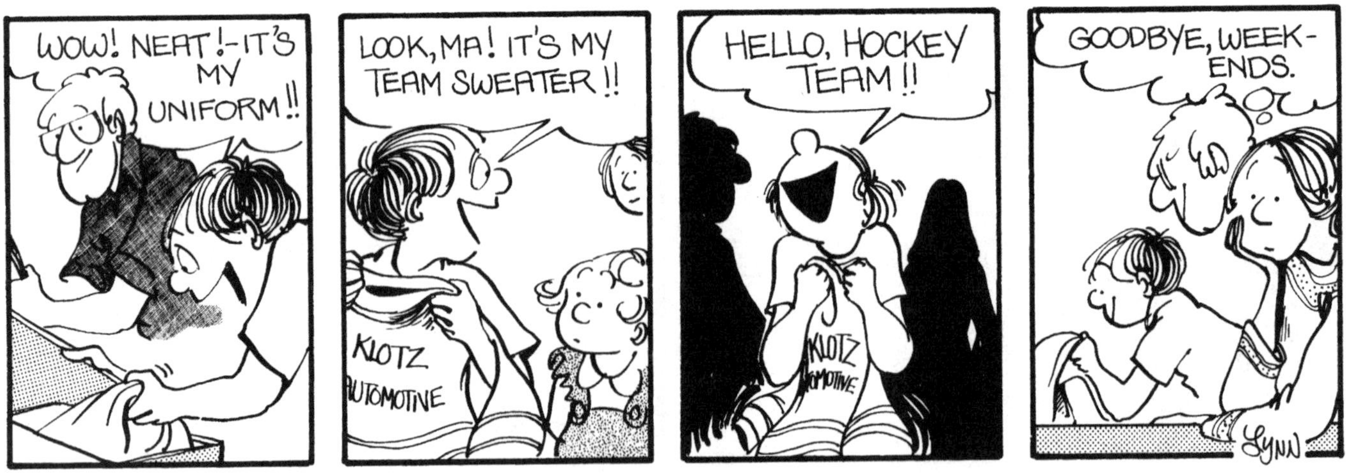
WOW! NEAT!-IT'S MY UNIFORM!!
LOOK, MA! IT'S MY TEAM SWEATER!!
KLOTZ AUTOMOTIVE
HELLO, HOCKEY TEAM!!
KLOTZ AUTOMOTIVE
GOODBYE, WEEK-ENDS.
LYNN

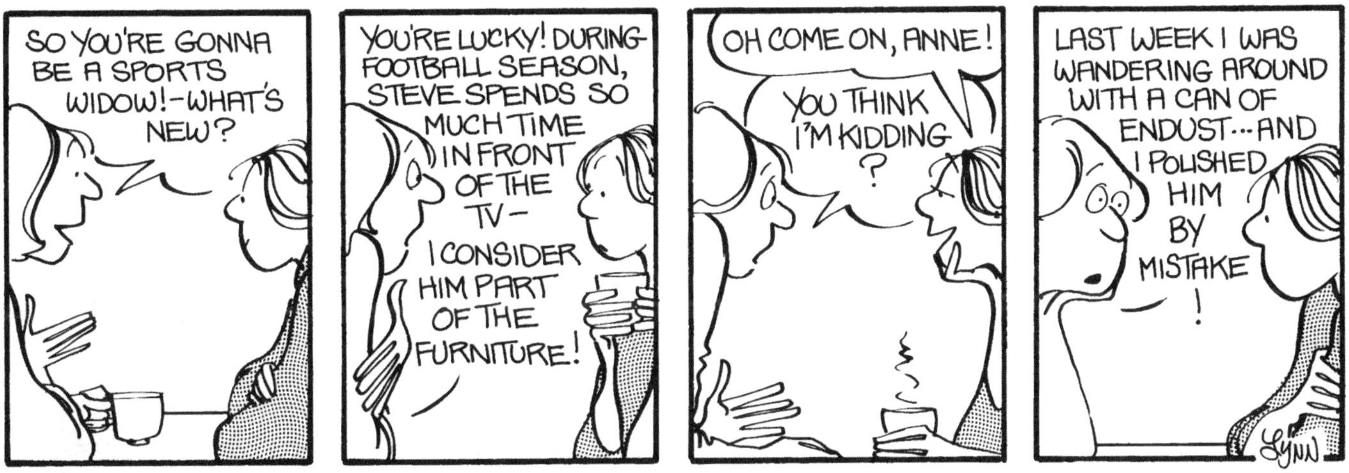
SO YOU'RE GONNA BE A SPORTS WIDOW! - WHAT'S NEW?
YOU'RE LUCKY! DURING FOOTBALL SEASON, STEVE SPENDS SO MUCH TIME IN FRONT OF THE TV -
I CONSIDER HIM PART OF THE FURNITURE!
OH COME ON, ANNE!
YOU THINK I'M KIDDING?
LAST WEEK I WAS WANDERING AROUND WITH A CAN OF ENDUST... AND I POLISHED HIM BY MISTAKE!
LYNN

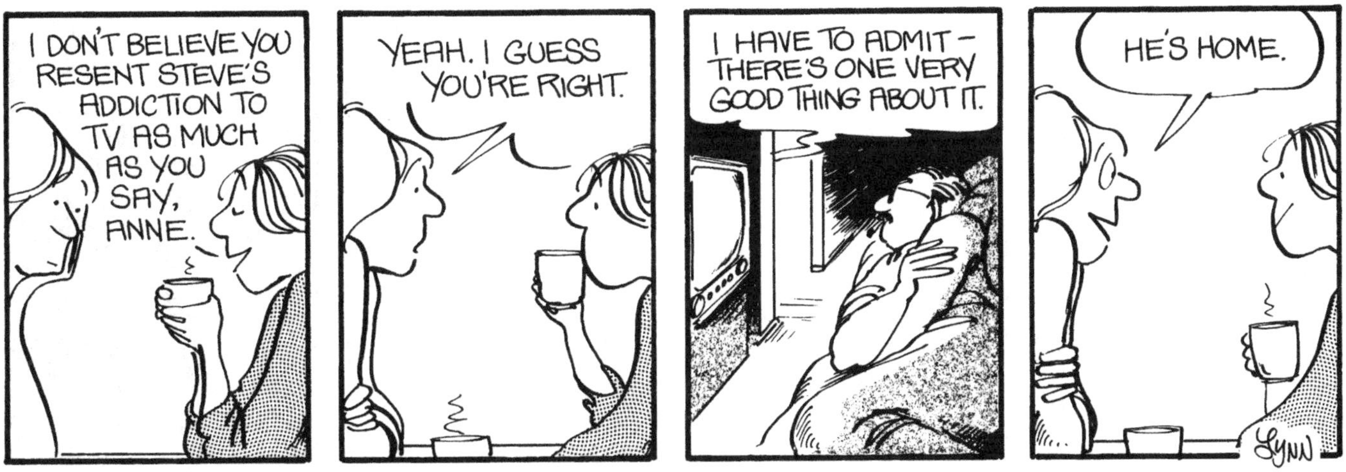
I DON'T BELIEVE YOU RESENT STEVE'S ADDICTION TO TV AS MUCH AS YOU SAY, ANNE.
YEAH. I GUESS YOU'RE RIGHT.
I HAVE TO ADMIT - THERE'S ONE VERY GOOD THING ABOUT IT.
HE'S HOME.
LYNN

Steve Nichols was a character who rarely appeared in FBorFW. As Annie's less-than-perfect spouse, he was to be gossiped about unseen. This is likely the first illustration I did of him. I never put this drawing into my resource files and soon forgot exactly how I'd drawn him! In the next illustration showing Steve, he looked quite different — sans moustache. Nobody ever mentioned this to me and I never noticed until now. Things like this convinced me to keep an accurate character file.

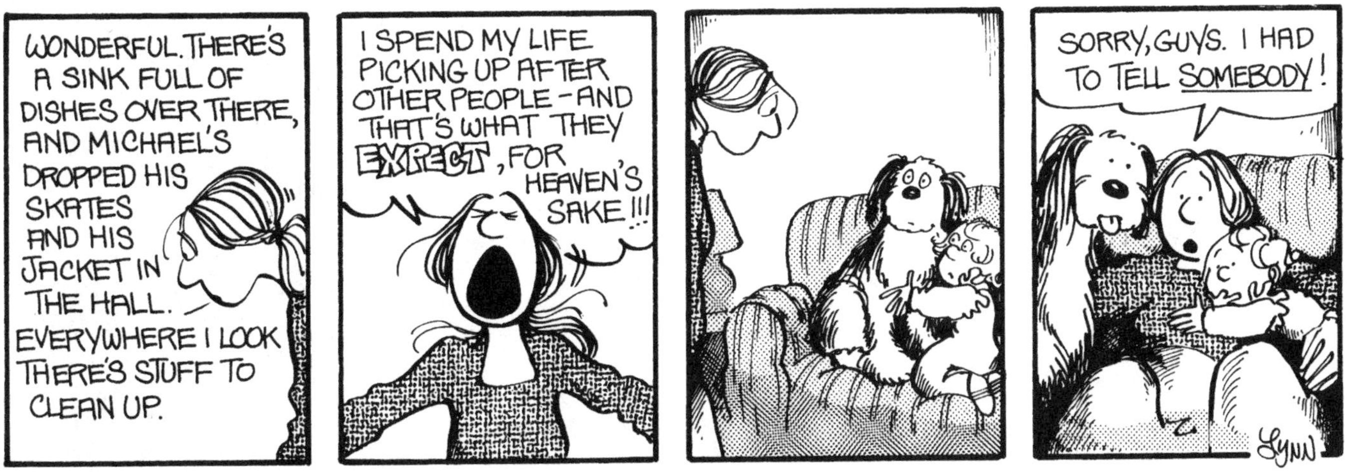
WONDERFUL. THERE'S A SINK FULL OF DISHES OVER THERE, AND MICHAEL'S DROPPED HIS SKATES AND HIS JACKET IN THE HALL. EVERYWHERE I LOOK THERE'S STUFF TO CLEAN UP.
I SPEND MY LIFE PICKING UP AFTER OTHER PEOPLE - AND THAT'S WHAT THEY EXPECT, FOR HEAVEN'S SAKE!!!
SORRY, GUYS. I HAD TO TELL SOMEBODY!
LYNN

Sometimes I let my frustration overflow sending a tsunami towards my kids. I discovered that kids can accept an apology. This wasn't something my folks did too often — an apology was considered a sign of weakness, I guess. For me, it is just plain honesty. When I was at the end of my rope, all I could do was to let the kids know I was human and that I was sorry. I think a sincere apology comes from strength, not weakness. Sometimes it's hard to do but the results, in the end, are wonderful!

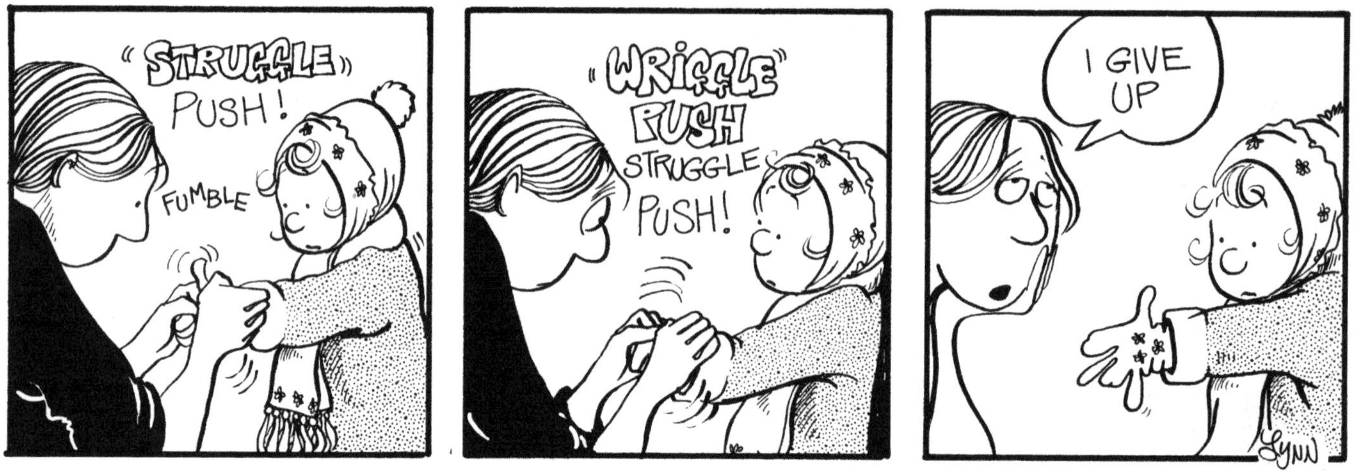
« STRUGGLE »
PUSH!
FUMBLE
" WRIGGLE "
PUSH
STRUGGLE
PUSH!
I GIVE UP
LYNN

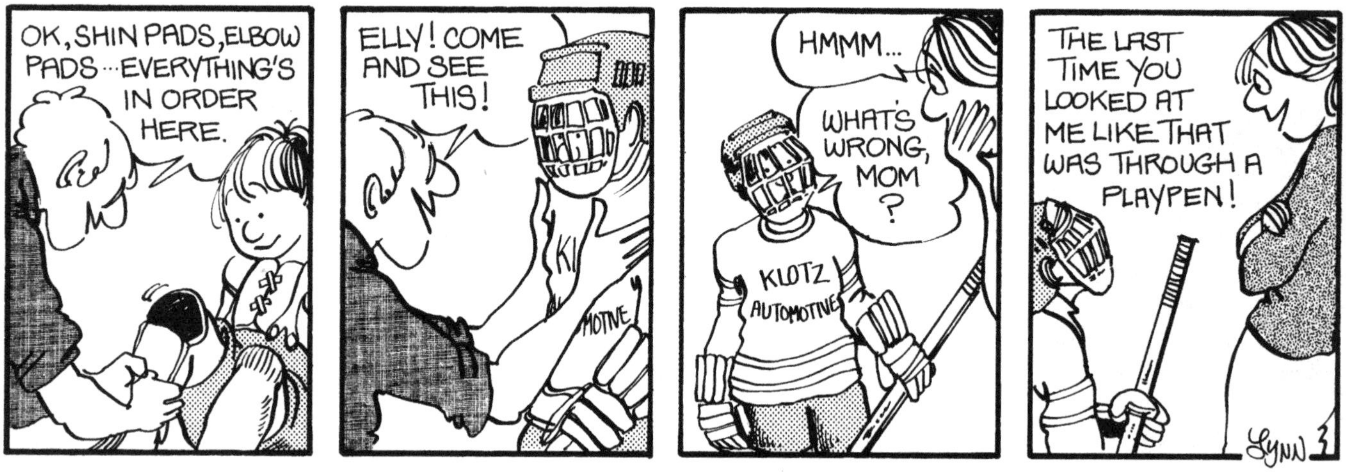
OK, SHIN PADS, ELBOW PADS ... EVERYTHING'S IN ORDER HERE.
ELLY! COME AND SEE THIS!
HMMM...
WHAT'S WRONG, MOM ?
KLOTZ AUTOMOTIVE
THE LAST TIME YOU LOOKED AT ME LIKE THAT WAS THROUGH A PLAYPEN!
LYNN

Liz Klotz and her family lived across the lane from us. They had three adopted kids and fostered others — their house was always busy. From Liz I learned to let the small stuff go, to let kids play and not get upset about the mess of toys and clutter — especially when it was −40 degrees outside and our homes became playgrounds. When I put their name on Mike's hockey jersey, Liz was delighted, but wondered if this meant her husband's small auto repair shop now had to sponsor a local team!

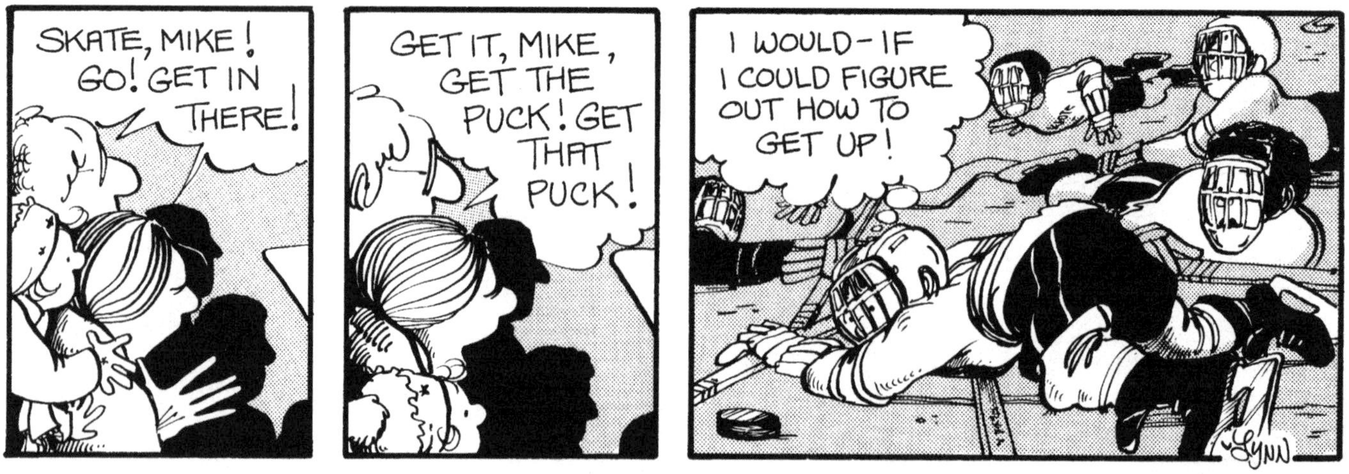
SKATE, MIKE! GO! GET IN THERE!
GET IT, MIKE, GET THE PUCK! GET THAT PUCK!
I WOULD - IF I COULD FIGURE OUT HOW TO GET UP!
LYNN

Watching junior hockey was fun. The kids went as fast as they could with such determination and energy, undeterred by their wobbly legs and restricting gear. All around us, parents who were bent on winning shouted advice and admonishments in a roar that would wake the dead. The rink was a frigid metal building. The small row of heating elements above the bleachers did little more than keep us from freezing to our seats. Cheering was the best thing we could do to stay warm.

Aaron getting ready for a game with the help of his coach.

Myself, Katie, and other supporters cheering on the team.

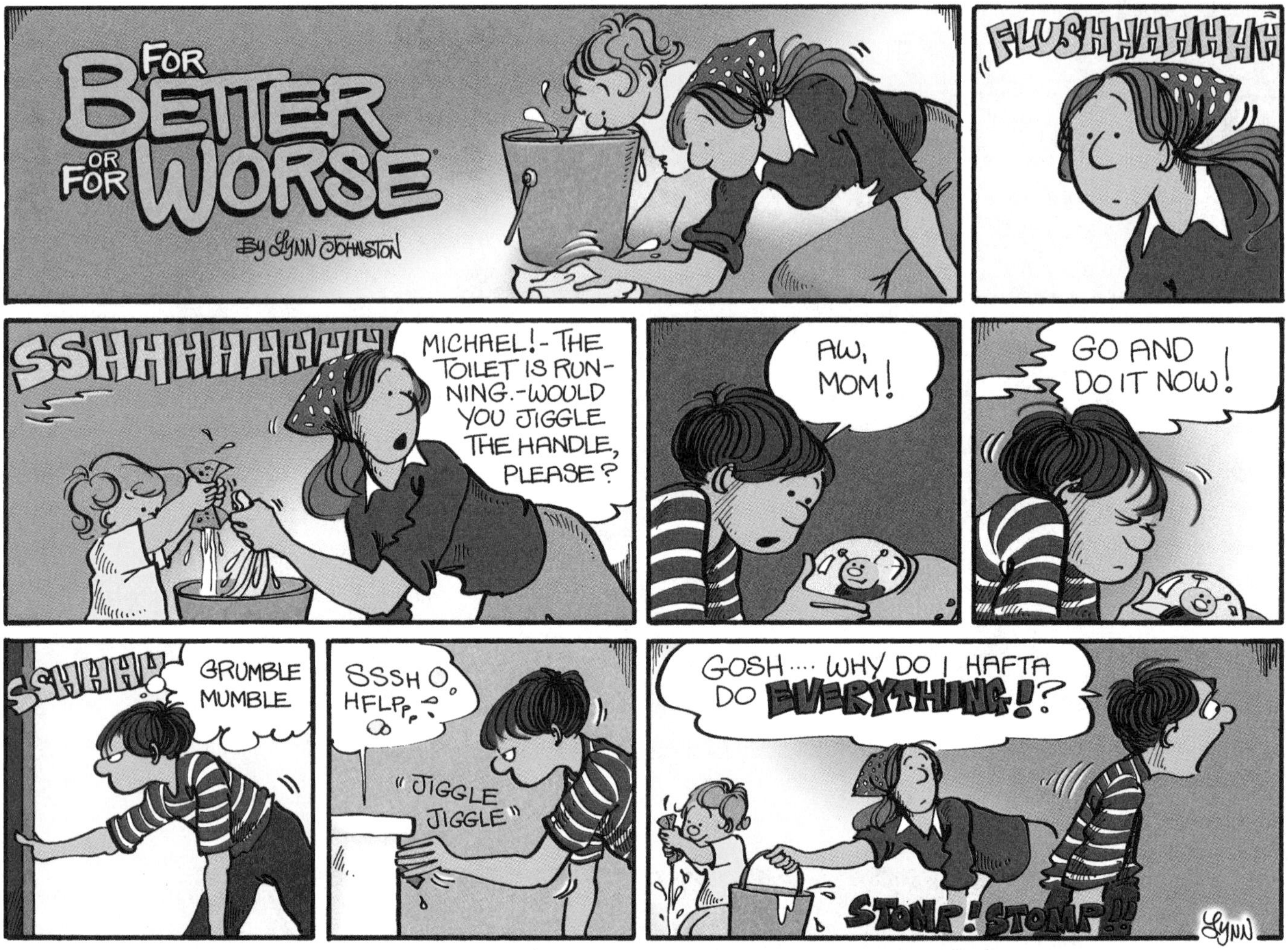

FOR BETTER OR FOR WORSE
BY LYNN JOHNSTON
FLUSHHHHHHH
SSHHHHHHHH
MICHAEL!-THE TOILET IS RUNNING.-WOULD YOU JIGGLE THE HANDLE, PLEASE?
AW, MOM!
GO AND DO IT NOW!
SSHHH
GRUMBLE MUMBLE
SSSH O HFLP
"JIGGLE JIGGLE"
GOSH.... WHY DO I HAFTA DO EVERYTHING!?
STOMP! STOMP!!
LYNN


Like most kids, I was expected to clean up my squalor, help with the dishes, and generally make myself useful. I rebelled. I felt cruelly done by. I lay down on the floor and howled at the injustice of it all. Despite the hardship and the unfairness I felt, I do remember having a distinct sense of pride and satisfaction once a chore was done.

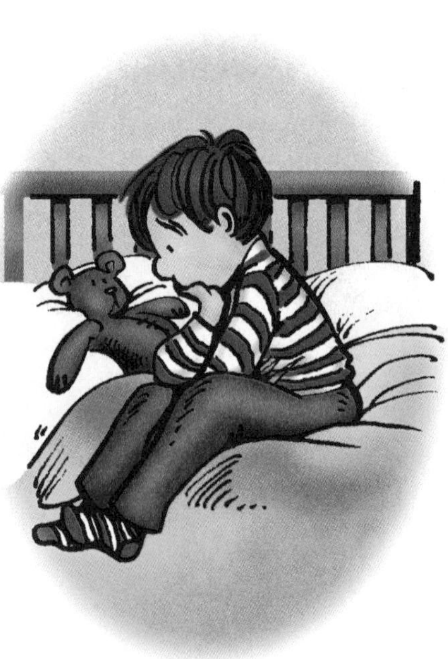

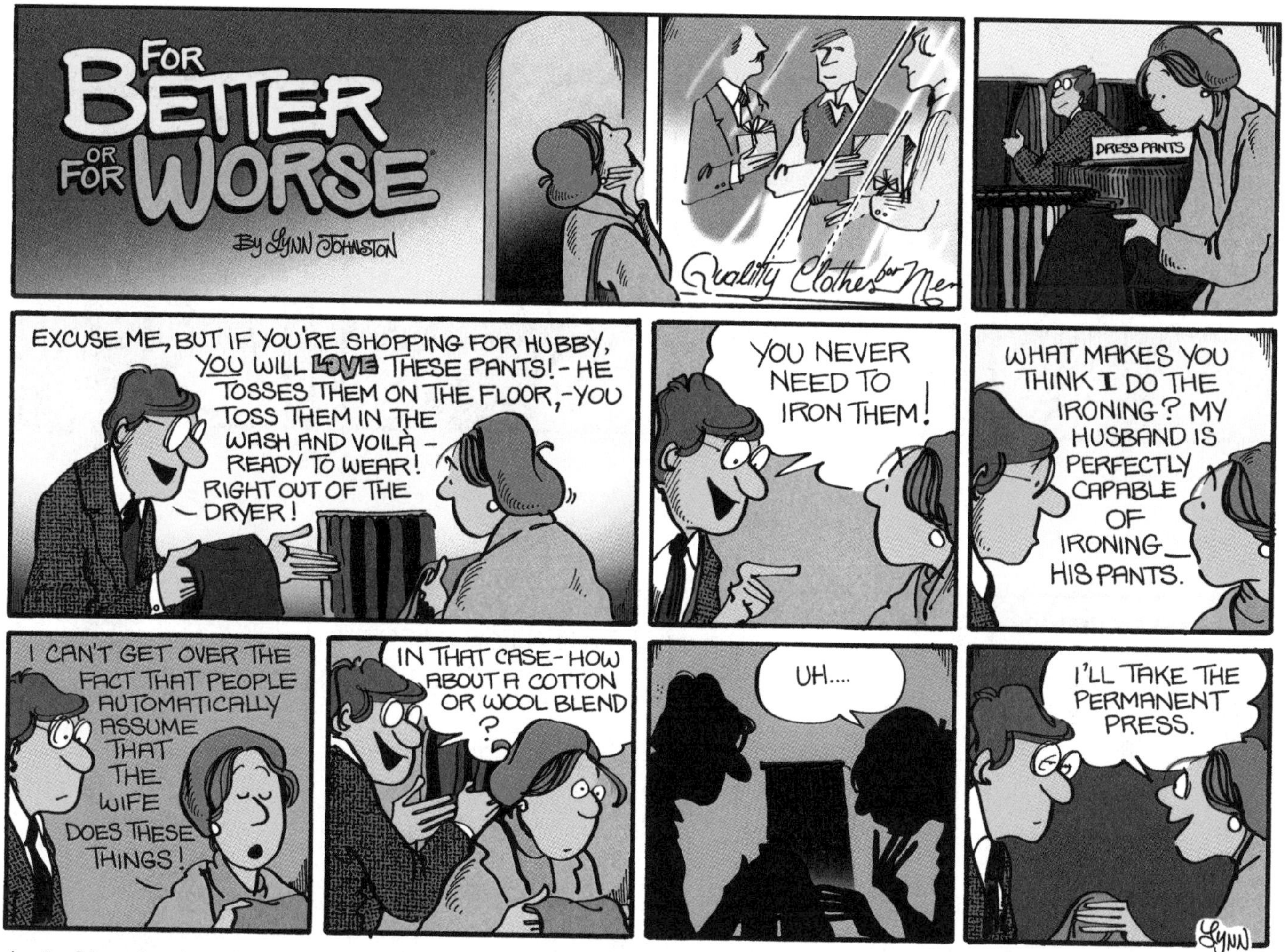
FOR BETTER OR FOR WORSE
BY LYNN JOHNSTON
QUALITY CLOTHES FOR MEN
DRESS PANTS
EXCUSE ME, BUT IF YOU'RE SHOPPING FOR HUBBY, YOU WILL LOVE THESE PANTS! - HE TOSSES THEM ON THE FLOOR, - YOU TOSS THEM IN THE WASH AND VOILÀ - READY TO WEAR! RIGHT OUT OF THE DRYER!
YOU NEVER NEED TO IRON THEM!
WHAT MAKES YOU THINK I DO THE IRONING? MY HUSBAND IS PERFECTLY CAPABLE OF IRONING HIS PANTS.
I CAN'T GET OVER THE FACT THAT PEOPLE AUTOMATICALLY ASSUME THAT THE WIFE DOES THESE THINGS!
IN THAT CASE- HOW ABOUT A COTTON OR WOOL BLEND?
UH....
I'LL TAKE THE PERMANENT PRESS.
LYNN

Again, I hate ironing and I am not alone here … I can hear a cry rising from the masses — men and women alike, screaming "I HATE IRONING!!!" I don't do it unless I absolutely have to. This means hanging stuff in the bathroom as I take a shower — hoping the steam will do the trick. I buy clothes with stripes or patterns to camouflage the wrinkles. I look for clothes that can be stuffed in a suitcase and worn immediately. Anything to keep myself from having to handle that spitting, hissing demon in my laundry room that always seems to have some crud in it. You know … that "scale" or whatever it is that will spit out of those little steam holes onto your cherished garment and stain it permanently with some brown smudge — and always in some really visible place. I hate ironing.

Having said that, however … if I could iron the wrinkles out of my face, I would definitely change my tune. I would embrace that miserable device and use it daily — singing its praises to the end of the earth! But this is not possible. There is no iron for the wrinkles on my countenance … the fabric of my face must remain as nature decrees. I am *au naturel*, gracefully declining in my retirement, accepting wrinkles with confidence and dignity. Right.

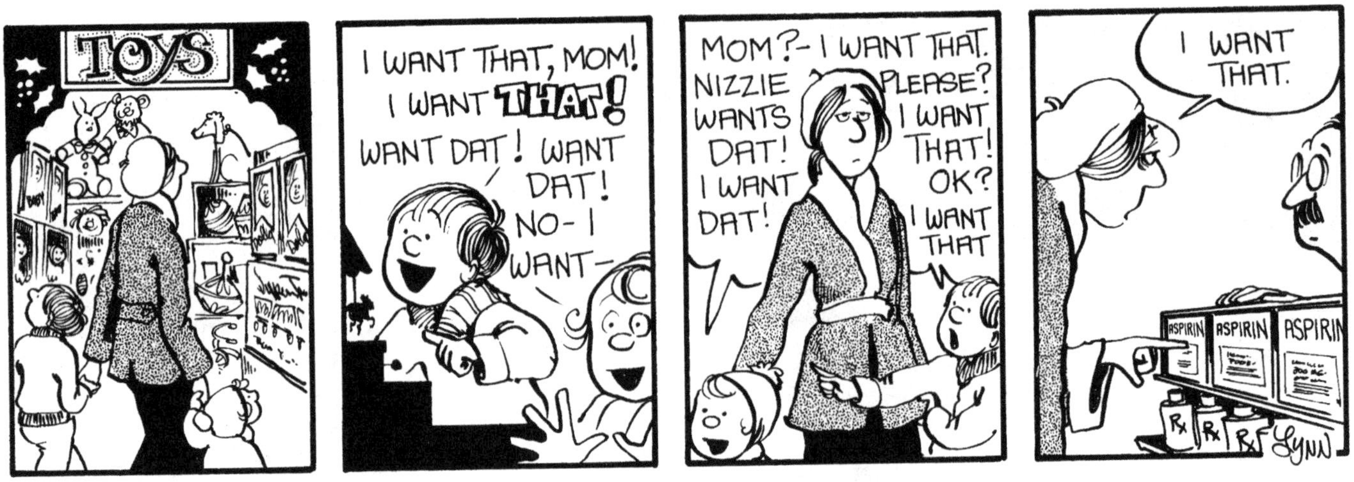
TOYS
I WANT THAT, MOM! I WANT THAT!
WANT DAT! WANT DAT!
NO- I WANT-
MOM?- I WANT THAT.
NIZZIE WANTS DAT! I WANT DAT!
PLEASE? I WANT THAT! OK? I WANT THAT
I WANT THAT.
ASPIRIN
ASPIRIN
ASPIRIN
Lynn

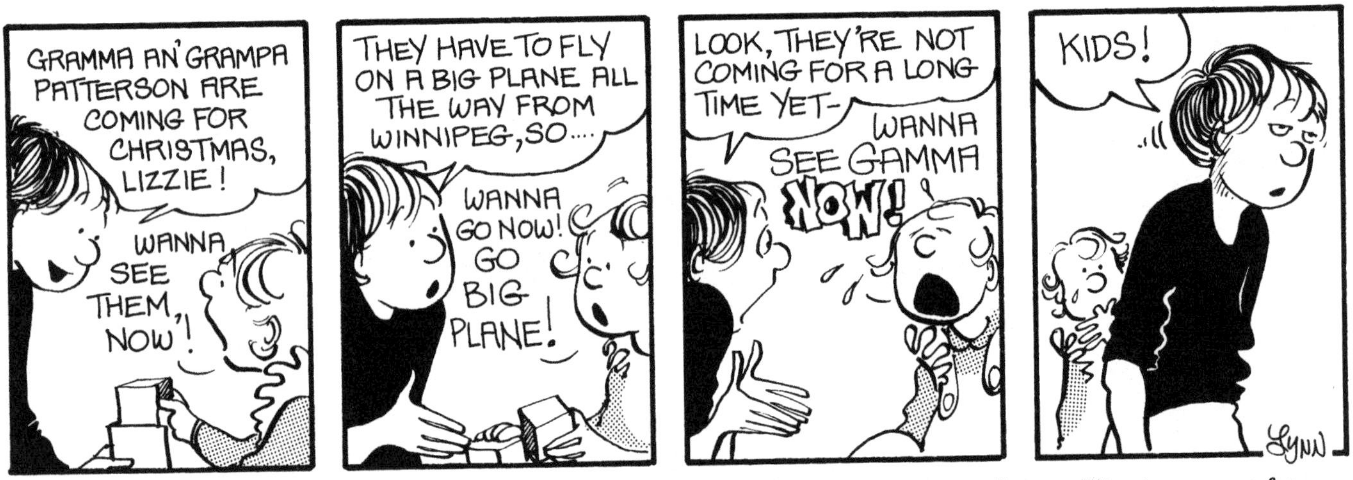
GRAMMA AN' GRAMPA PATTERSON ARE COMING FOR CHRISTMAS, LIZZIE!
WANNA SEE THEM, NOW'!
THEY HAVE TO FLY ON A BIG PLANE ALL THE WAY FROM WINNIPEG, SO....
WANNA GO NOW! GO BIG PLANE!
LOOK, THEY'RE NOT COMING FOR A LONG TIME YET-
WANNA SEE GAMMA NOW!
KIDS!
Lynn

My parents-in-law, Ruth and Tom, lived an easy ten-minute walk away and were the reason I was willing to move so far north. This vignette was a "Patterson" situation. In the strip, both sets of grandparents lived far from the family, so their visits meant juggling bed space and were a welcome adjustment. Having them visit meant I could show the readers who they were and what their personalities were like. I was lucky. I dearly loved my in-laws, and I miss them both very much.

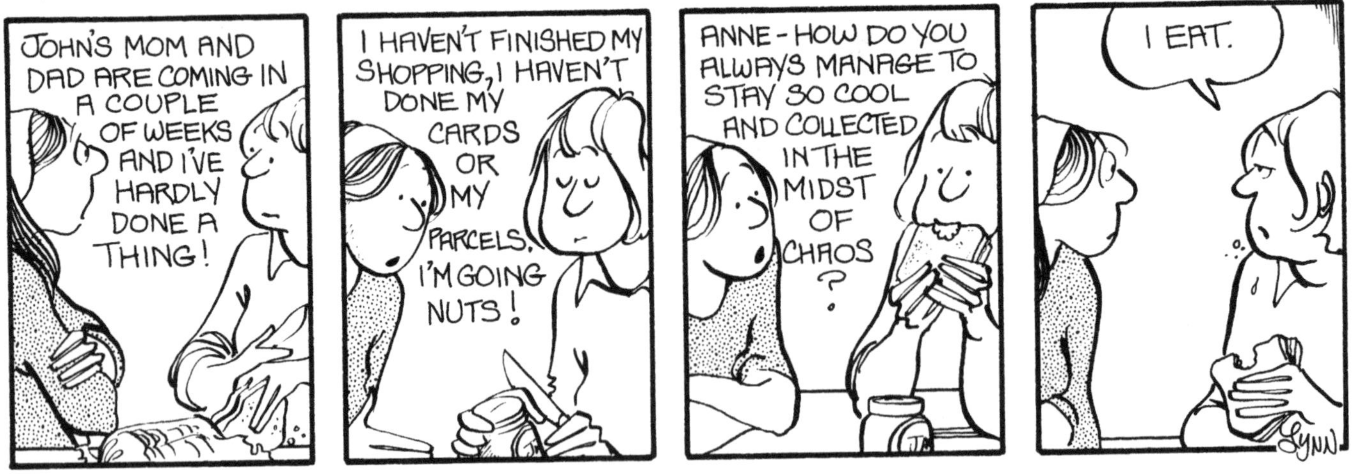
JOHN'S MOM AND DAD ARE COMING IN A COUPLE OF WEEKS AND I'VE HARDLY DONE A THING!
I HAVEN'T FINISHED MY SHOPPING, I HAVEN'T DONE MY CARDS OR MY PARCELS. I'M GOING NUTS!
ANNE - HOW DO YOU ALWAYS MANAGE TO STAY SO COOL AND COLLECTED IN THE MIDST OF CHAOS?
I EAT.
Lynn

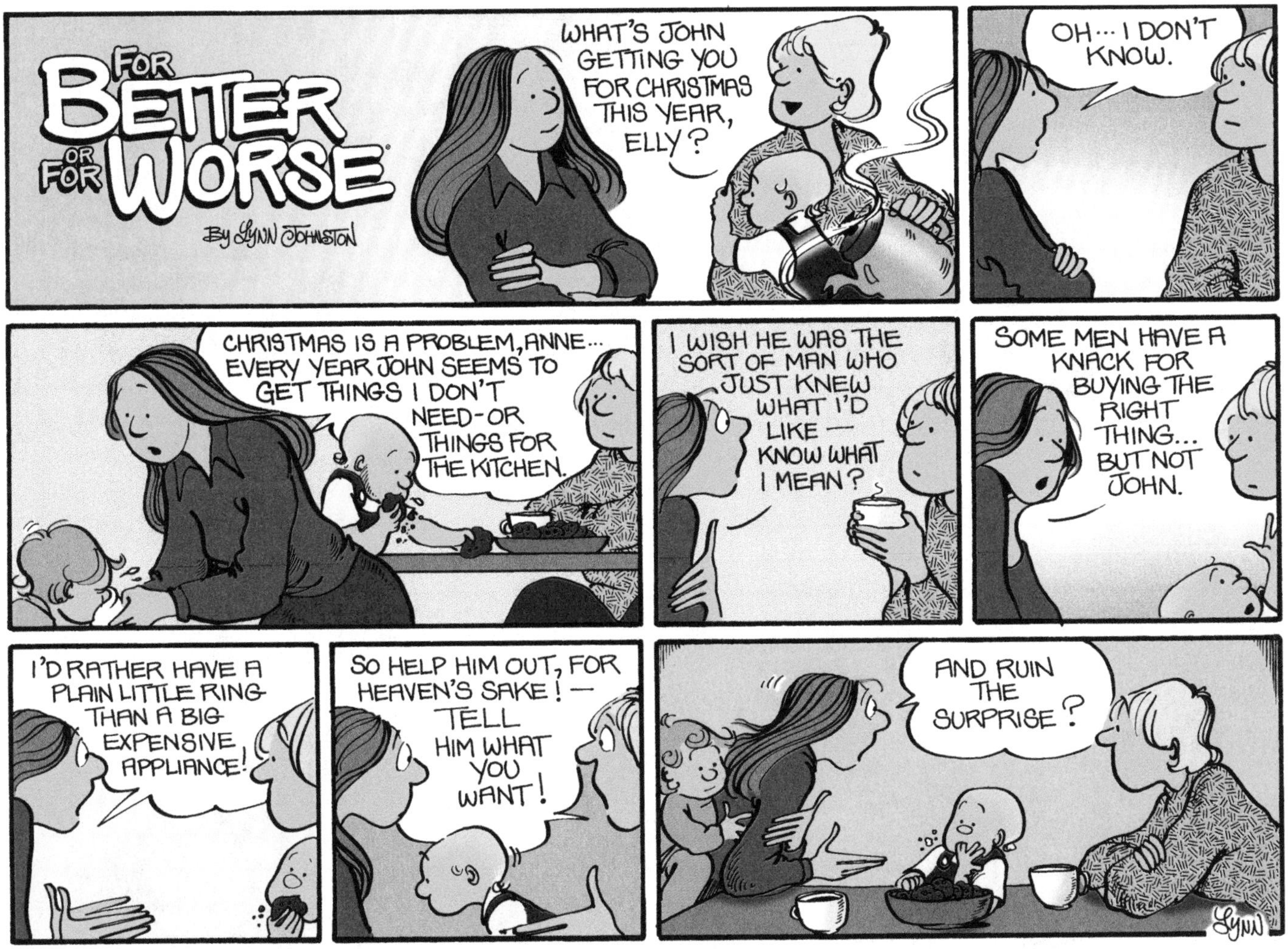
FOR BETTER OR FOR WORSE
BY LYNN JOHNSTON
WHAT'S JOHN GETTING YOU FOR CHRISTMAS THIS YEAR, ELLY?
OH... I DON'T KNOW.
CHRISTMAS IS A PROBLEM, ANNE... EVERY YEAR JOHN SEEMS TO GET THINGS I DON'T NEED-OR THINGS FOR THE KITCHEN.
I WISH HE WAS THE SORT OF MAN WHO JUST KNEW WHAT I'D LIKE — KNOW WHAT I MEAN?
SOME MEN HAVE A KNACK FOR BUYING THE RIGHT THING... BUT NOT JOHN.
I'D RATHER HAVE A PLAIN LITTLE RING THAN A BIG EXPENSIVE APPLIANCE!
SO HELP HIM OUT, FOR HEAVEN'S SAKE! — TELL HIM WHAT YOU WANT!
AND RUIN THE SURPRISE?
LYNN

Mom was an excellent seamstress. She could make anything — even patterns from scratch. I was working at Woodwards in Vancouver, making a salary for the first time, so Dad and I decided to pool our resources and get her a Bernina sewing machine for her birthday. It was the latest thing. It could make designs and buttonholes without a template, and you could use several colours of thread at once. It was expensive, however, and Dad worried that she'd be angry with us for spending so much when we could hardly afford it. He had to tell her our plan. Naturally, she said, "Absolutely not!" She wouldn't have us spending wantonly on something she could well do without. So ... we got her a jewellery box instead. When she opened her gift, we could tell that Mom was bitterly disappointed. "What's the matter?" Dad asked — surprised by her reaction. Pressing a hanky to her eyes, she cried, "I thought I was getting a new sewing machine!!" Go figure. Gift giving was always an awkward time in our family. Any time we did it right — it was a surprise!

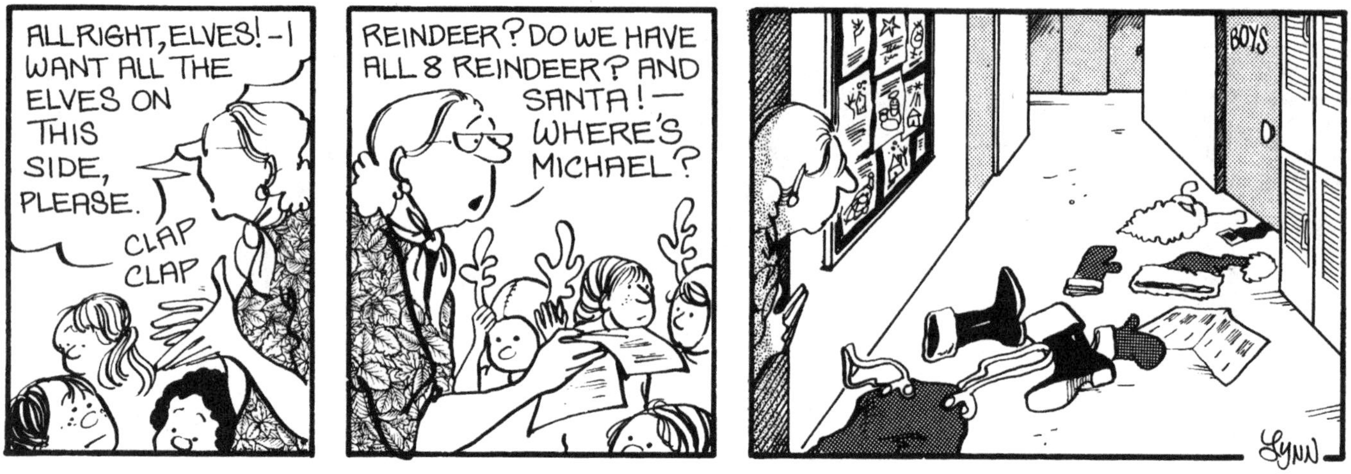
ALLRIGHT, ELVES! - I WANT ALL THE ELVES ON THIS SIDE, PLEASE.
CLAP CLAP
REINDEER? DO WE HAVE ALL 8 REINDEER? AND SANTA! — WHERE'S MICHAEL?
BOYS

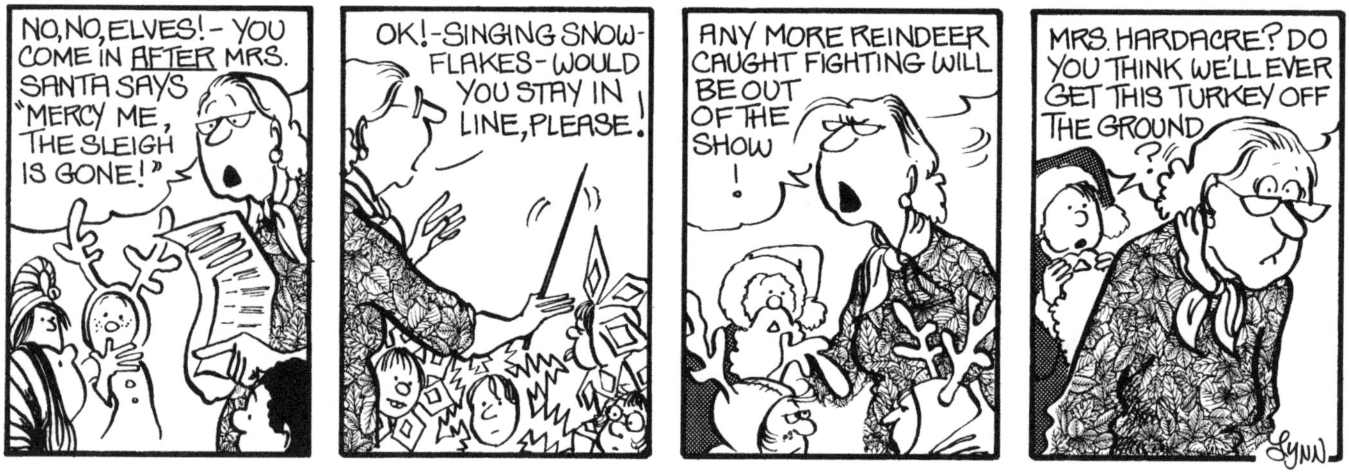
NO, NO, ELVES! - YOU COME IN AFTER MRS. SANTA SAYS "MERCY ME, THE SLEIGH IS GONE!"
OK! - SINGING SNOW-FLAKES - WOULD YOU STAY IN LINE, PLEASE!
ANY MORE REINDEER CAUGHT FIGHTING WILL BE OUT OF THE SHOW!
MRS. HARDACRE? DO YOU THINK WE'LL EVER GET THIS TURKEY OFF THE GROUND?

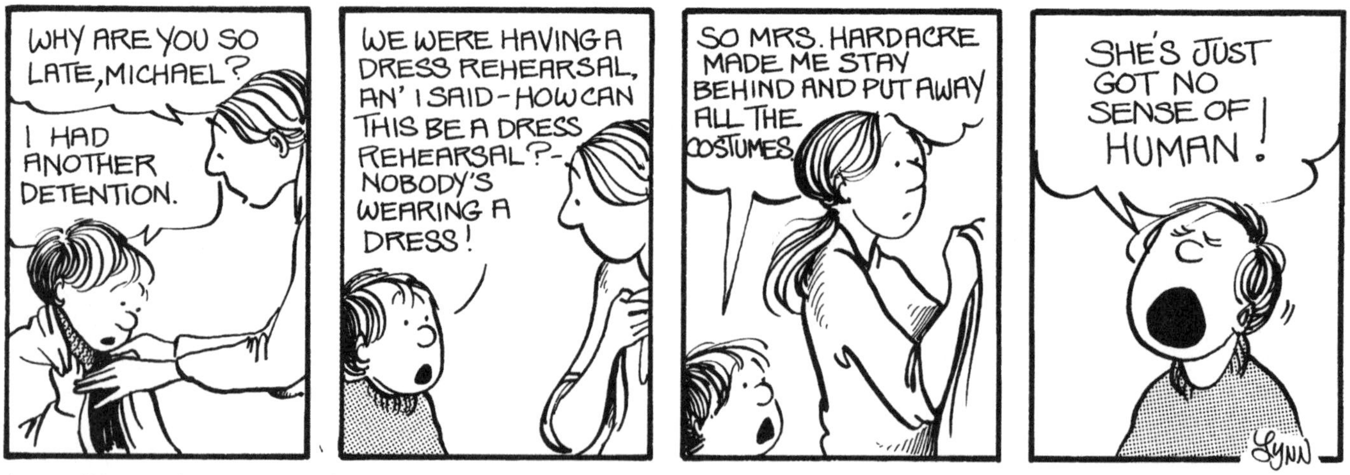
WHY ARE YOU SO LATE, MICHAEL?
I HAD ANOTHER DETENTION.
WE WERE HAVING A DRESS REHEARSAL, AN' I SAID - HOW CAN THIS BE A DRESS REHEARSAL? - NOBODY'S WEARING A DRESS!
SO MRS. HARDACRE MADE ME STAY BEHIND AND PUT AWAY ALL THE COSTUMES.
SHE'S JUST GOT NO SENSE OF HUMAN!

Aaron did come home once and say that his teacher had "no sense of human." His teachers were the best, but like his mother, he managed to push them to their limit. The thing about Aaron was that he was funny. Even if he was completely wrong, he retained a certain aura of acceptance. He enjoyed school and did well in the things he liked, but otherwise he daydreamed, fooled around, and got into trouble. I could understand — this was the way I drifted through elementary school, too.

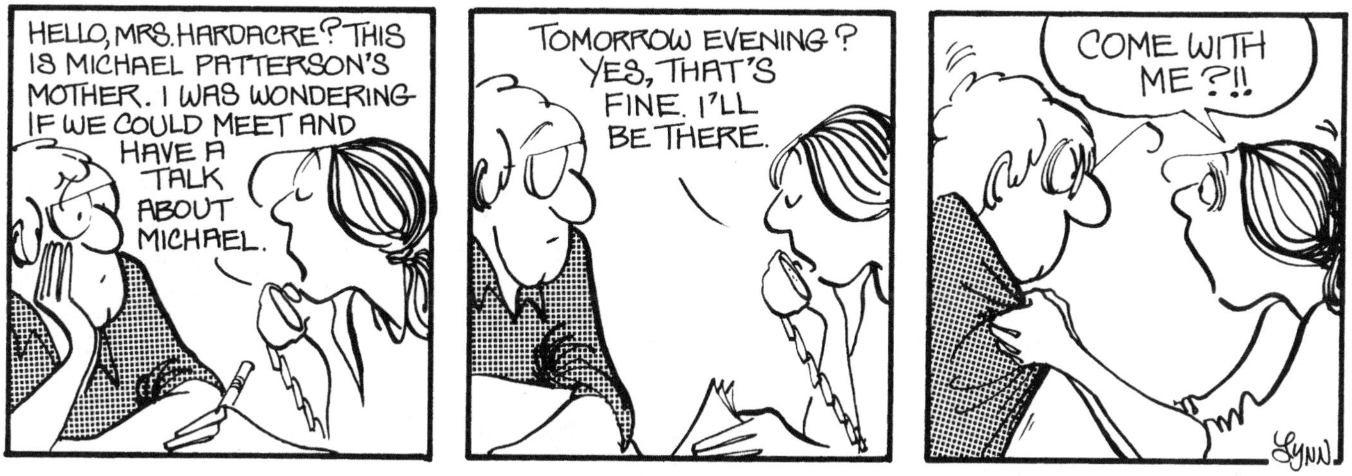
HELLO, MRS. HARDACRE? THIS IS MICHAEL PATTERSON'S MOTHER. I WAS WONDERING IF WE COULD MEET AND HAVE A TALK ABOUT MICHAEL.
TOMORROW EVENING? YES, THAT'S FINE. I'LL BE THERE.
COME WITH ME?!!
LYNN

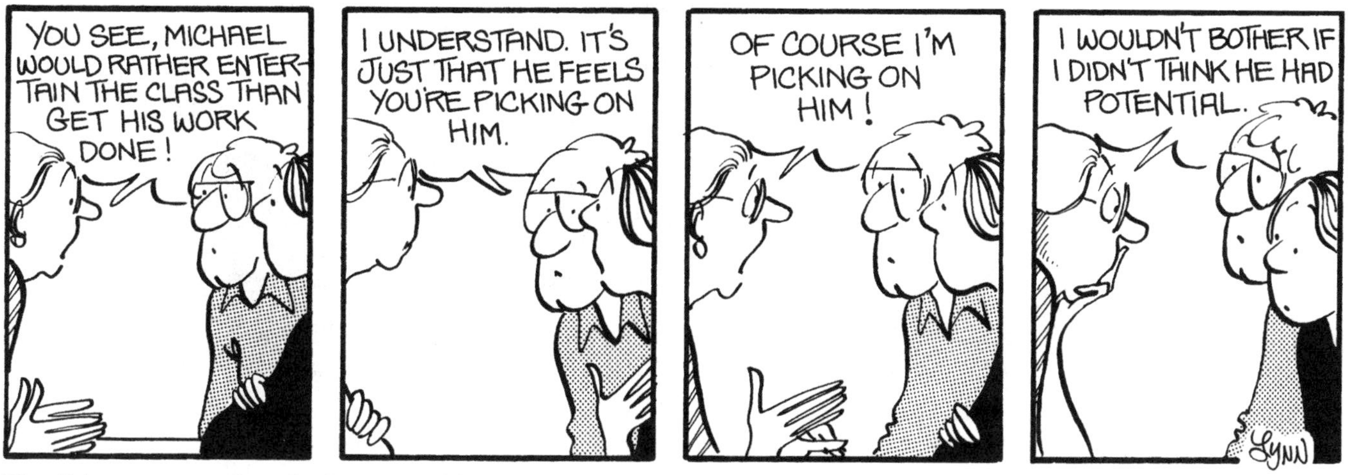
YOU SEE, MICHAEL WOULD RATHER ENTERTAIN THE CLASS THAN GET HIS WORK DONE!
I UNDERSTAND. IT'S JUST THAT HE FEELS YOU'RE PICKING ON HIM.
OF COURSE I'M PICKING ON HIM!
I WOULDN'T BOTHER IF I DIDN'T THINK HE HAD POTENTIAL.
LYNN

The dialogue you see here is almost word for word from a conversation that I had with Mr. Stibbs in grade four. He told me that, yes, he did pick on me and, yes, he did single me out in the class — and that he did so because he knew I could do better. He explained that it took a lot of his time and energy, but he did so because I was worth it. I think he was the first to put a harness on the unruly kid that I was. He showed me that he had respect for my intelligence and, therefore, so should I.

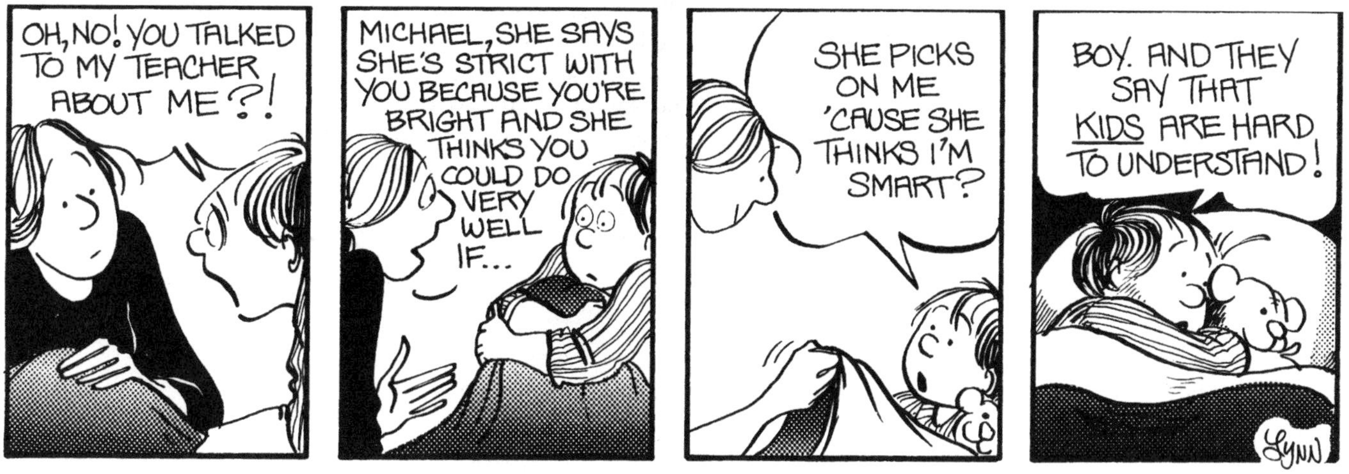
OH, NO! YOU TALKED TO MY TEACHER ABOUT ME?!
MICHAEL, SHE SAYS SHE'S STRICT WITH YOU BECAUSE YOU'RE BRIGHT AND SHE THINKS YOU COULD DO VERY WELL IF...
SHE PICKS ON ME 'CAUSE SHE THINKS I'M SMART?
BOY. AND THEY SAY THAT KIDS ARE HARD TO UNDERSTAND!
LYNN

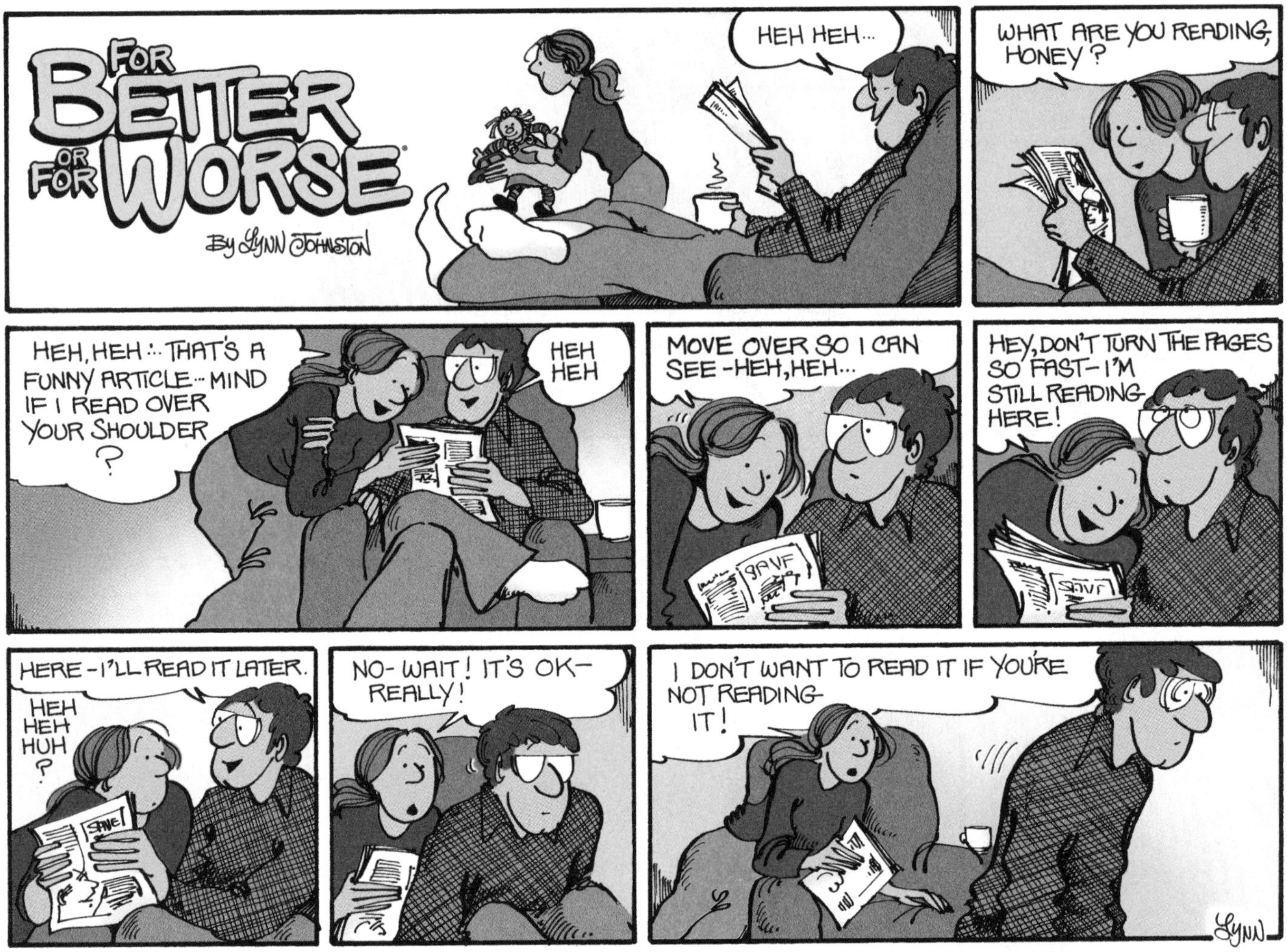
FOR BETTER OR FOR WORSE
BY LYNN JOHNSTON
HEH HEH...
WHAT ARE YOU READING, HONEY?
HEH, HEH... THAT'S A FUNNY ARTICLE... MIND IF I READ OVER YOUR SHOULDER?
HEH HEH
MOVE OVER SO I CAN SEE -HEH, HEH...
HEY, DON'T TURN THE PAGES SO FAST- I'M STILL READING HERE!
HERE - I'LL READ IT LATER.
HEH HEH HUH?
NO- WAIT! IT'S OK- REALLY!
I DON'T WANT TO READ IT IF YOU'RE NOT READING IT!
LYNN

My dad reading the paper while relaxing on the couch is a classic image. Mom always read at the table where she could spread the sheets out evenly — Dad preferred to hold them up to the light. The snap and crackle of him flipping to the next page is a sound I can still hear clearly, recorded in some archive buried deep within my private mental files. It was nice to sit, warm against his side, and read the news with him. My knees on the cushions, my shoulder against his, we'd read together in silence. I learned to read at his fast pace, and when it came to the "funny pages," we studied the panels, the pranks, the precision that made us smile.

Mom, on the other hand, did not like us to read over her shoulder. It bothered her to share what must have been a rare private time and this, of course, offered me the opportunity to ruffle her feathers. I would climb the rung on her chair and read, with my chin on her arm until I could sense a sort of vibration ... an electric exchange that happens between mom and kid that says "That's all I can take!" I knew I was pushing her buttons — the trick was to escape before she blew. Funny isn't it how little things drive folks crazy? My dad loved the company, my mom wanted to be left alone. Both of them loved to read, however — which impressed me greatly. I love to read now, which is a credit to them.

Saturday, Nov. 28, 1981 **PEOPLE** San Francisco Chronicle 11

INTERVIEW

# A Housewife With a Comic Strip Life

*BY SYLVIA RUBIN*

Here's the haggard housewife schlepping the laundry down to the basement just when the baby starts to scream. She puts the laundry down and picks the baby up, but then her 6-year-old is suddenly demanding equal time and a peanut butter on toast sandwich NOW.

For this she went to college?

These sorts of things happen every day to perfectly ordinary people, one of whom is a 34-year-old Canadian cartoonist named Lynn Johnston, the creator of "For Better or for Worse," a strip which appears in more than 200 papers across the country, including The Chronicle.

Like the housewife she draws, Johnston is the mother of two young children (Aaron, 8½, and Katie, 3½) and she has the same long, straight hair and disgruntled sense of humor as Elly Patterson, her cartoon alter ego. Elly's husband John, a chauvinistic dentist, looks very much like Johnston's real-life husband, Rod, a recent dental school graduate who has his own practice.

The Johnstons live in Lynn Lake, Manitoba, a tiny mining community in remote central Canada, where Rod grew up. The town was not named for his wife — "Lynn takes a lot of kidding about that," he said during a recent stop the two made in San Francisco.

Lynn Lake can be described as a "one-horse, no, make that no-horse town," Lynn said. Population, 2000 — "not counting the dogs."

Lynn Johnston, a native of Vancouver, expected she would hate such an isolated life (Winnipeg, the nearest big city, is more than 800 miles away), but she has come to love it as much as her husband does.

"In the morning, my daughter goes off to day care right across the street and my son goes to school down the block. There are some advantages to living in a small town.

"And I kind of need to be insulated from the public because I'm not the type to say 'no.' If I lived in a bigger city, I'd probably be saying yes to all sorts of invitations, and I'd have no time to be home and work on the strip."

Even though Lynn Lake is remote, it is a middle-class, suburban community like many others, Lynn said — except that the temperature can sometimes fall to 70 below on a bad day.

Lynn and her cartoon character Elly are traditional housewives in the sense that they don't work outside the home. But both are liberated enough to know there are other options, and they are gutsy enough to give their husbands a hard time when chauvinism comes shining through.

Although the cartoonist gears her humor toward everyday family situations, Elly and John are not Blondie and Dagwood.

In one strip, Lynn dealt with the issue of her husband's getting a vasectomy, a topic that would have been taboo just a few years ago, and one that will surely never appear in "Blondie."

"I show a toilet in my strip; I show my characters being angry and affectionate with each other," she says. "I show Elly half-dressed in the bedroom. I try to get as close to real life as I can; I push the limits of the censors, but I know I'll be edited if I go too far."

The Johnstons were here, wrapping up a cross-country book tour for a paperback collection of Lynn's cartoons ("I've Got the One-More-Washload Blues . . .")

Their hectic travel schedule seemed to leave them exhausted and not above some good-natured bickering — material that may well show up in future strips. Lynn admits that when Rod comes up with a good line during an argument, she stops everything so she can write it down. "If it's a good enough line," she said, glancing sideways at her husband, "how can I help but use it?"

Drawing a daily strip is the best kind of therapy for her, she said. "The strip is something that I need. It's an outlet for my guilt about being just a housewife. Some people think that women have genetically inherited traits that makes them want to pick up socks, but I felt guilty because I didn't feel like playing Snakes and Ladders with my kids all day."

It was during her first pregnancy that Lynn, who had been a medical illustrator, began to draw a regular cartoon strip to get rid of some of her angst — her marriage to her first husband was on the rocks and being pregnant wasn't helping matters any.

Her obstetrician liked her drawings so much he started projecting them onto the ceiling above his examining table to show his other patients. He encouraged her to pursue a cartooning career.

Now, almost three years after her strip went into syndication, Lynn is earning more than $100,000 a year for her efforts.

She likes to draw in the mornings, she said, from about 9 a.m. until about noon; then it's back to cleaning house. "I never do any housework until noon. I could never have a live-in housekeeper — where would all the material for my strips come from?"

Her husband, unlike John Patterson in the strip, "really does his best about not being chauvinistic. He hates to pick up his clothes, but he really does his share with the kids and the house. He's not just one more kid in my life."

Lynn's characters are composites of many different people she knows. "Sometimes, I'll use people's real names in the strip; Elly's son, Michael, just started to play on a hockey team (so does her son, Aaron), and the name of his sponsor is KLOTZ. Well, that's the name of the guy across the street who has an automotive shop.

"My characters really manipulate me as much as I manipulate them. I sometimes don't know what's going to happen to them."

For instance, there's Ted, a bachelor who has fallen in love with Elly's girlfriend Connie, a divorcee. "I really don't know what will happen with Connie and Ted," Lynn said. "I think I'm going to have Ted be a schmuck for a while; he's a spoiled brat, anyway. I don't want to marry Connie off so soon."

Connie's character gives Lynn the opportunity to sound off about the pros and cons of being single — "Connie is really me when I was a single parent."

The cartoonist admits she was anti-men for quite a while until she met Rod, who, she says, is the romantic in the family. They met at an airport, when Rod, who loves to fly, invited Lynn out for a hamburger and flew her to the nearest town to get one.

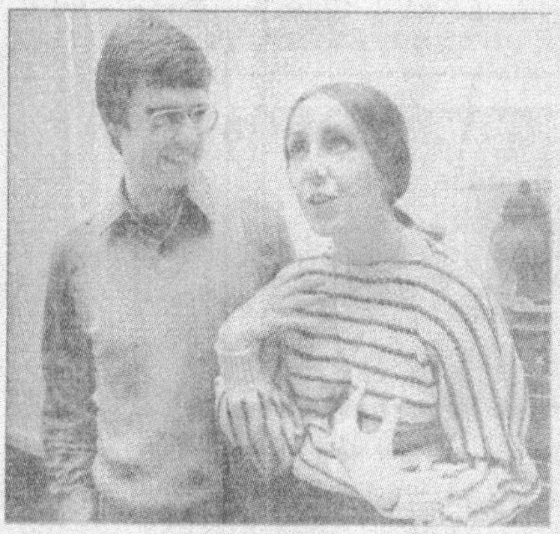

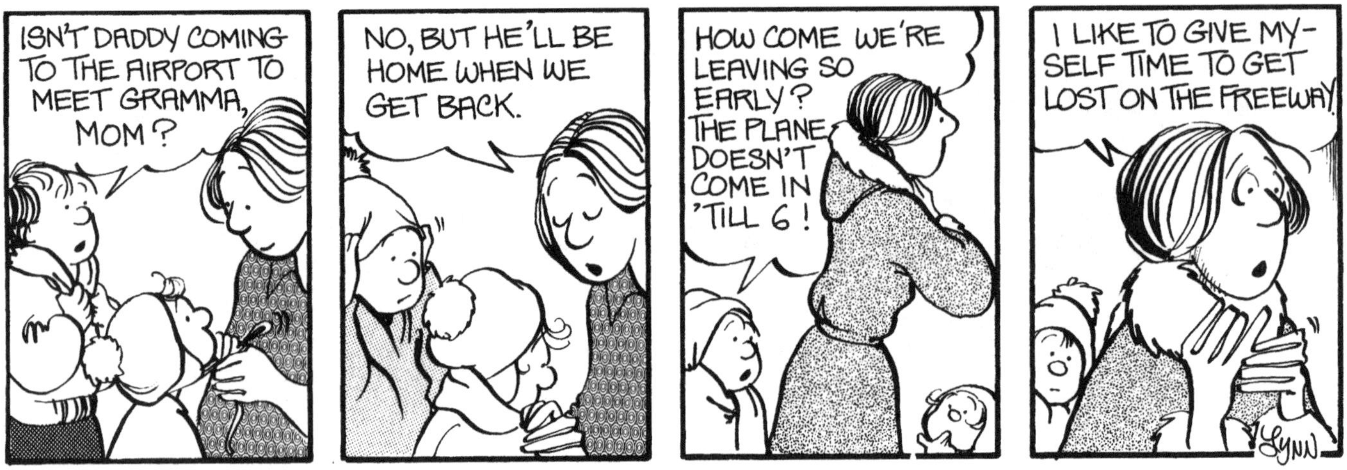
ISN'T DADDY COMING TO THE AIRPORT TO MEET GRAMMA, MOM?
NO, BUT HE'LL BE HOME WHEN WE GET BACK.
HOW COME WE'RE LEAVING SO EARLY? THE PLANE DOESN'T COME IN 'TILL 6!
I LIKE TO GIVE MYSELF TIME TO GET LOST ON THE FREEWAY!
LYNN

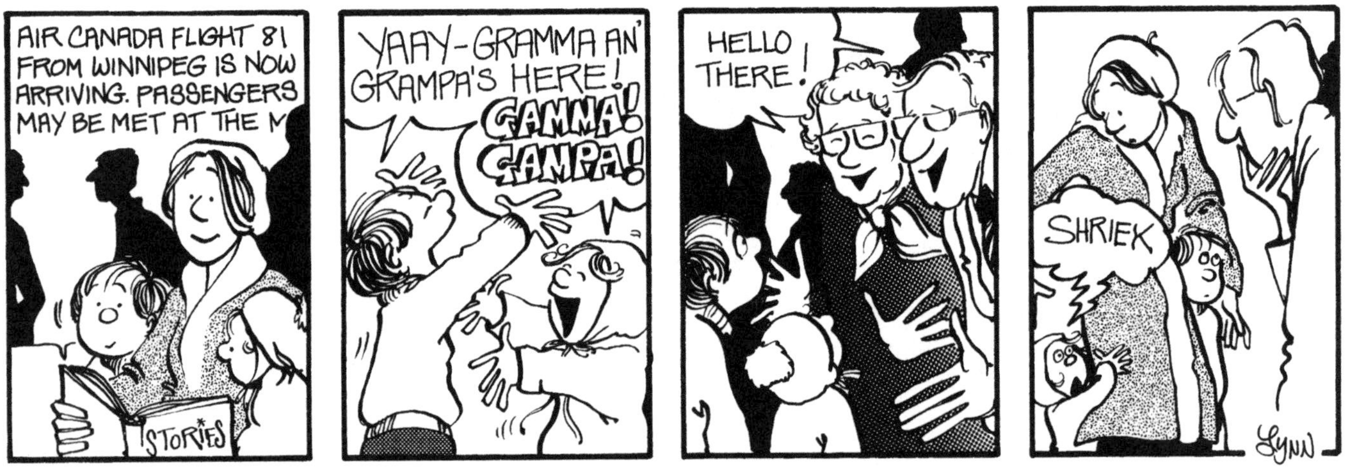
AIR CANADA FLIGHT 81 FROM WINNIPEG IS NOW ARRIVING. PASSENGERS MAY BE MET AT THE M
STORIES
YAAY-GRAMMA AN' GRAMPA'S HERE!
GAMMA! GAMPA!
HELLO THERE!
SHRIEK
LYNN

As I recall, my parents only made the long journey to see us in Manitoba once. Aaron knew them both well, having spent time alone with them at their cottage in Hope, B.C., but to Katie, they were strangers. The joy of our reunion at the small outpost airport was lost on Kate, who hid behind my legs and maintained a wary reserve until they had settled into the house. I can still see her on my dad's knee singing and playing, now aware that she was with family.

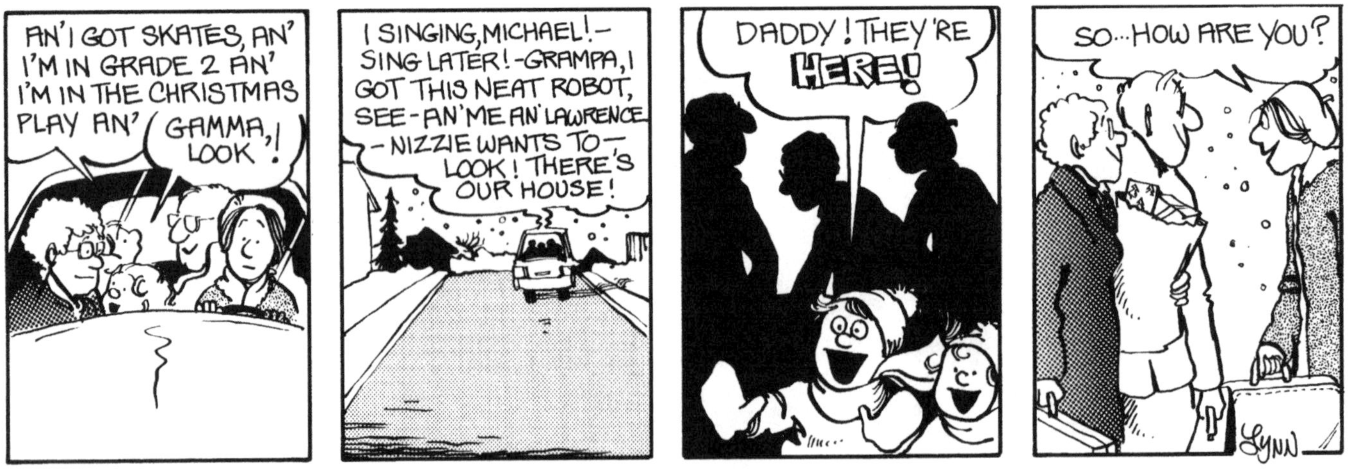
AN' I GOT SKATES, AN' I'M IN GRADE 2 AN' I'M IN THE CHRISTMAS PLAY AN'
GAMMA, LOOK!
I SINGING, MICHAEL!- SING LATER!-GRAMPA, I GOT THIS NEAT ROBOT, SEE-AN' ME AN' LAWRENCE -NIZZIE WANTS TO- LOOK! THERE'S OUR HOUSE!
DADDY! THEY'RE HERE!
SO...HOW ARE YOU?
LYNN

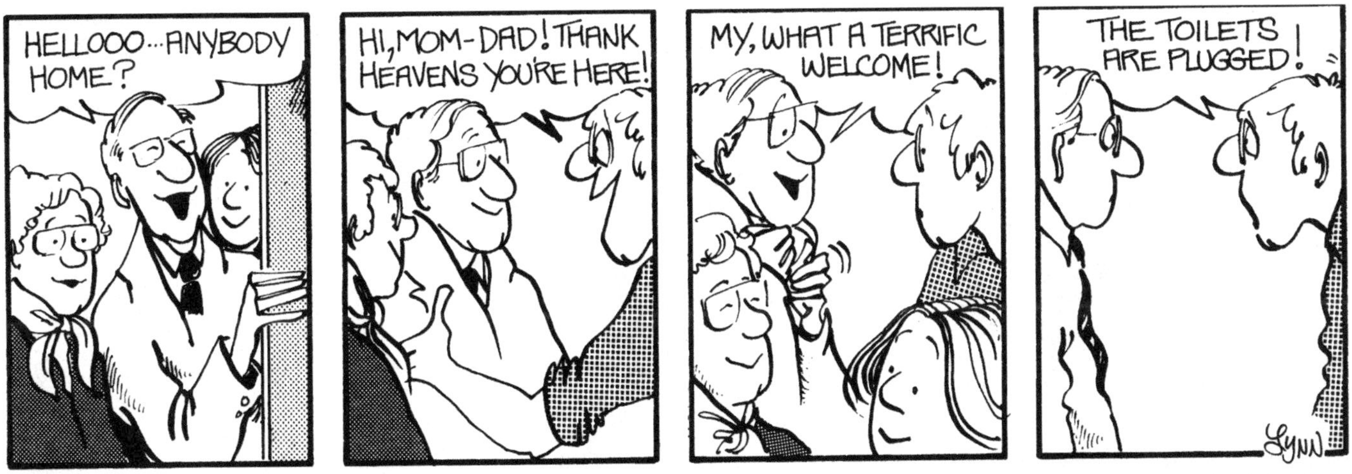
HELLOOO...ANYBODY HOME?
HI, MOM-DAD! THANK HEAVENS YOU'RE HERE!
MY, WHAT A TERRIFIC WELCOME!
THE TOILETS ARE PLUGGED!
Lynn

This story really belongs to my dad. My grandfather (Mom's dad) was a severe man. My dad's family was not as high in the British caste system as he was, and so Gramps treated my father with disdain, often calling him by his last name. We arrived for a visit once only to find a distraught Gramps and an impossibly plugged privy. Dad looked at Gramps and said, "I will unplug your toilet if you will call me by my first name." With some effort, Gramps agreed and the waters flowed once more.

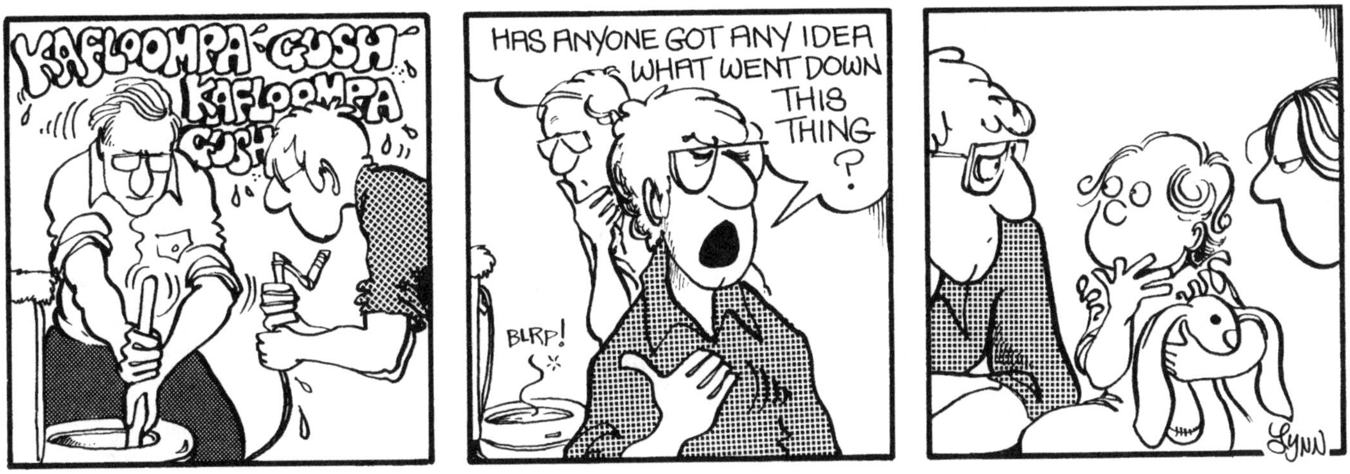
KAFLOOMPA-GUSH
KAFLOOMPA
GUSH
HAS ANYONE GOT ANY IDEA WHAT WENT DOWN THIS THING?
BLRP!
Lynn

"Kafloompa-gush, kafloompa-gush" is my all-time favourite sound effect.

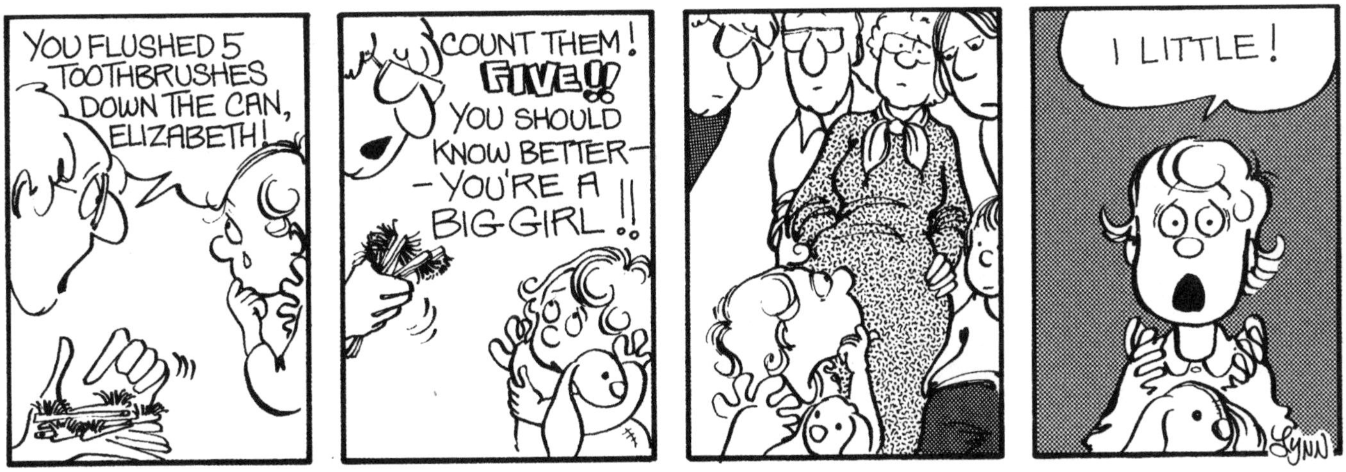
YOU FLUSHED 5 TOOTHBRUSHES DOWN THE CAN, ELIZABETH!
COUNT THEM! FIVE!! YOU SHOULD KNOW BETTER-
-YOU'RE A BIG GIRL!!
I LITTLE!
Lynn

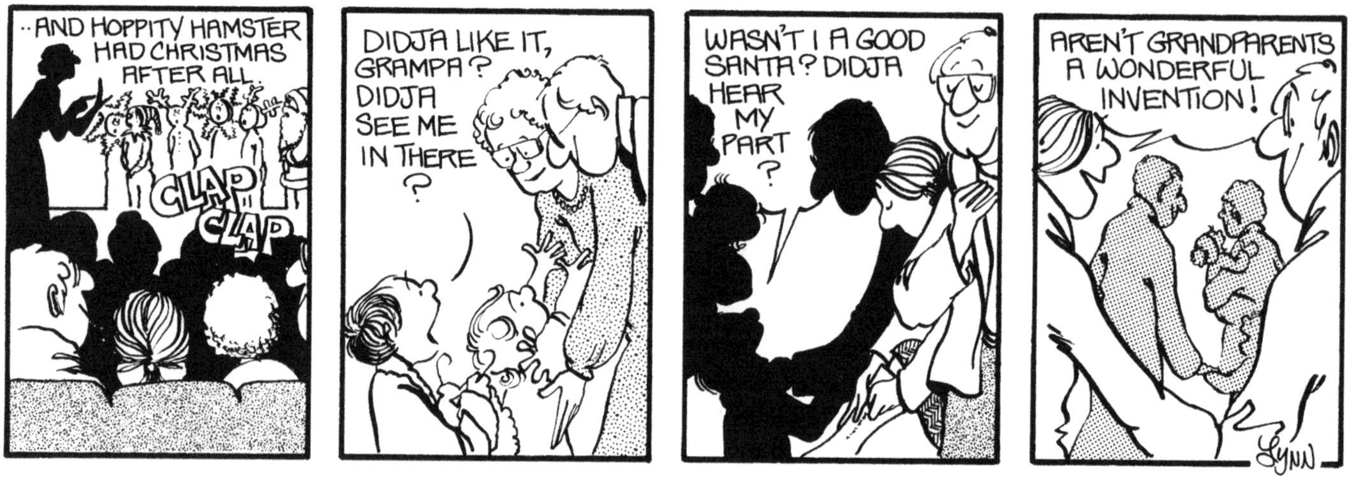
..AND HOPPITY HAMSTER HAD CHRISTMAS AFTER ALL.
CLAP CLAP
DIDJA LIKE IT, GRAMPA? DIDJA SEE ME IN THERE?
WASN'T I A GOOD SANTA? DIDJA HEAR MY PART?
AREN'T GRANDPARENTS A WONDERFUL INVENTION!
LYNN

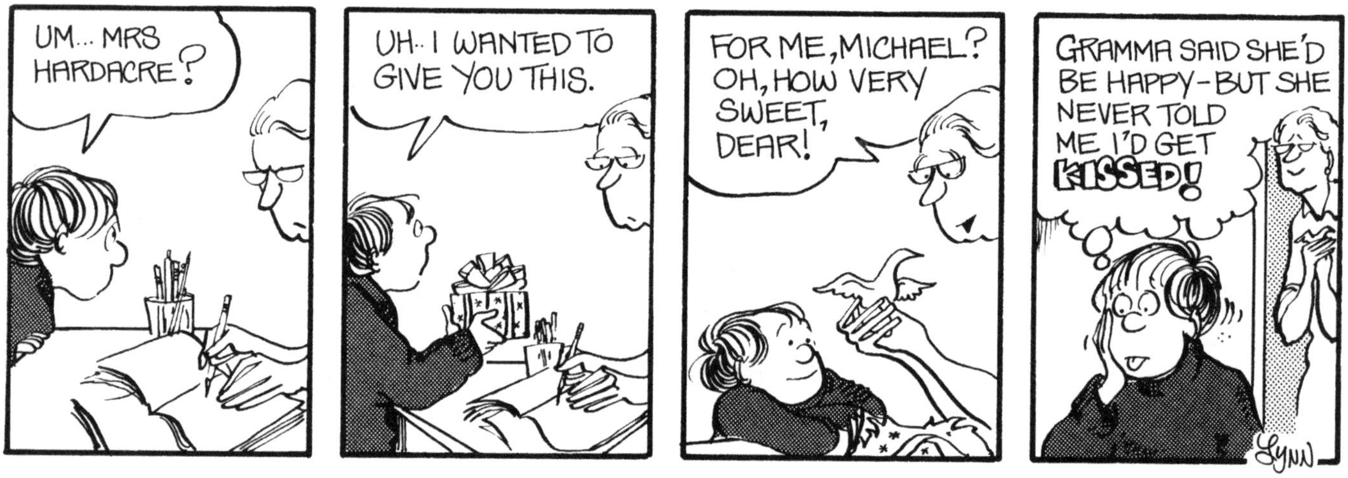
UM... MRS HARDACRE?
UH.. I WANTED TO GIVE YOU THIS.
FOR ME, MICHAEL? OH, HOW VERY SWEET, DEAR!
GRAMMA SAID SHE'D BE HAPPY - BUT SHE NEVER TOLD ME I'D GET KISSED!
LYNN

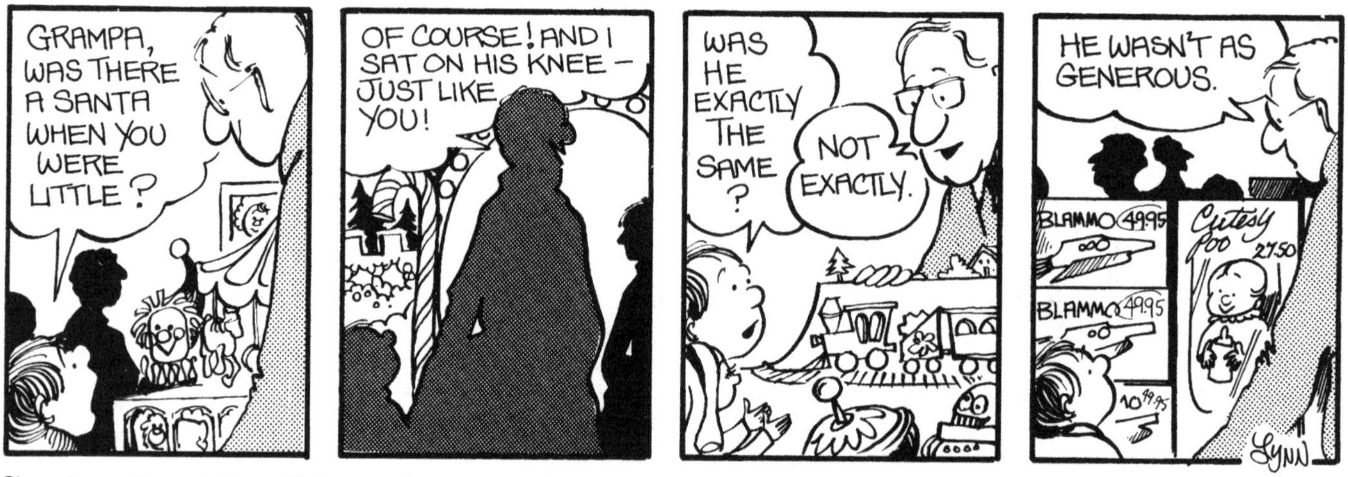
GRAMPA, WAS THERE A SANTA WHEN YOU WERE LITTLE?
OF COURSE! AND I SAT ON HIS KNEE - JUST LIKE YOU!
WAS HE EXACTLY THE SAME?
NOT EXACTLY.
HE WASN'T AS GENEROUS.
BLAMMO 49.95
BLAMMO 49.95
Cutesy Poo 27.50
LYNN

Shopping with my kids at Christmas always reminded me of Christmases at home with my parents. Dad made $47 a week, and if we had something left over by the end of the month, we could go into Vancouver from the North Shore for dinner and a movie. For the four of us, this was a $12 expense and difficult to afford. Christmas was sparse, and yet my parents made it as festive as any, with homemade gifts, hand-sewn clothing, and a turkey dinner to rival any feast in a grand hotel.

*

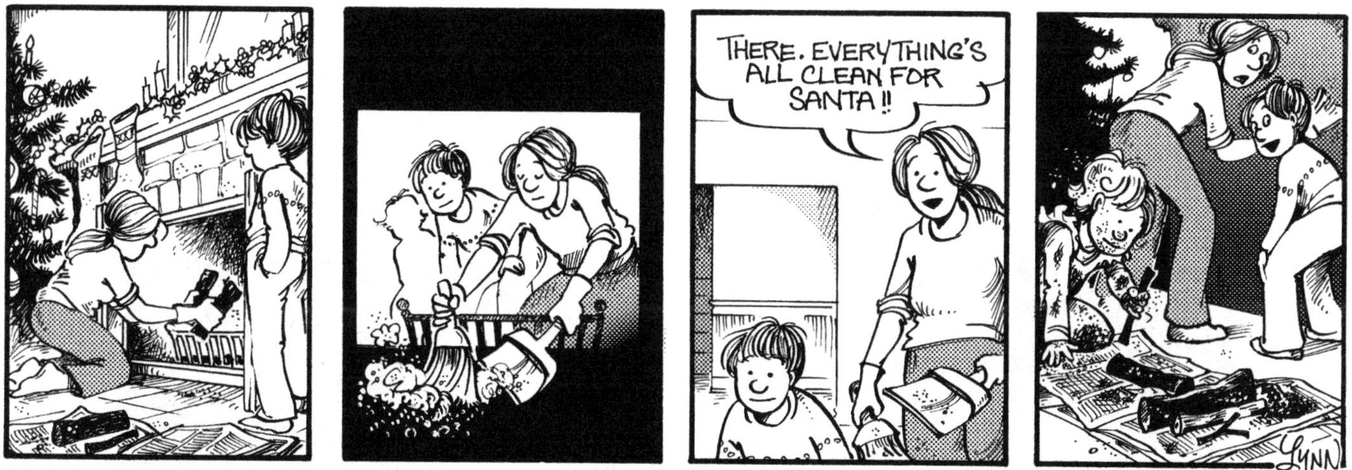
THERE. EVERYTHING'S ALL CLEAN FOR SANTA!!
LYNN

This strip brought back memories of cleaning out the fireplace for Santa's nocturnal arrival. We had a large fireplace in the Lynn Lake house, and sweeping it out was as much of a ritual as cutting the tree — we had to be sure that Santa wouldn't get any soot on the rug. Aaron, being older, already knew about Santa, but it was a long time before the mystery was explained to Katie. I think the best Christmases are the ones we share near a fireplace with people who believe in magic!

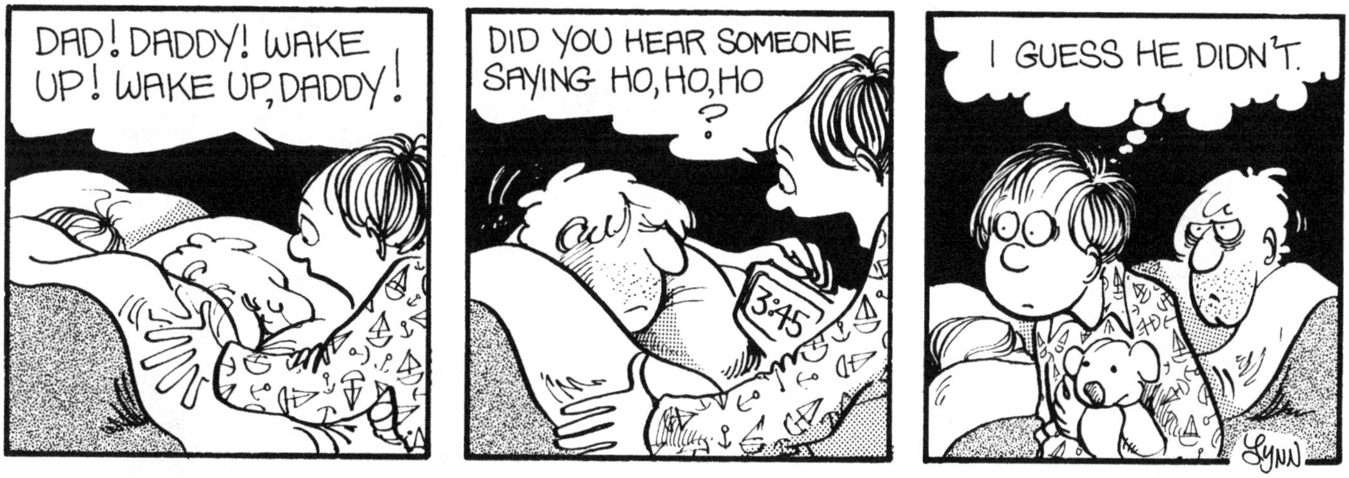
DAD! DADDY! WAKE UP! WAKE UP, DADDY!
DID YOU HEAR SOMEONE SAYING HO, HO, HO?
3:45
I GUESS HE DIDN'T.
LYNN

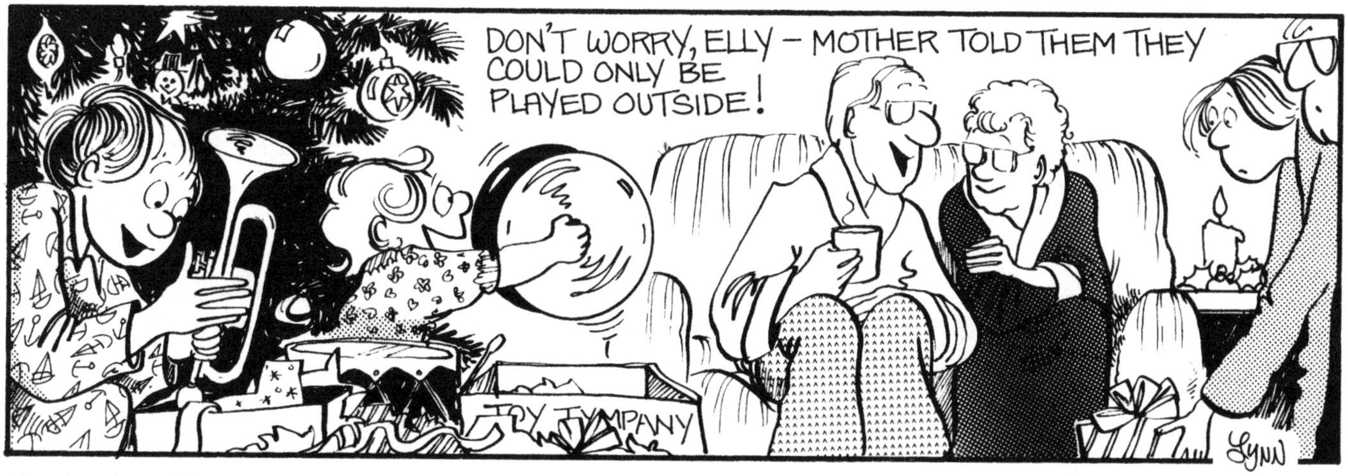
DON'T WORRY, ELLY – MOTHER TOLD THEM THEY COULD ONLY BE PLAYED OUTSIDE!
TOY TYMPANY
LYNN

After lunch on Christmas day, we'd usually walk over to Ruth and Tom's house for more openings and Christmas dinner. My in-laws always gave us practical gifts, so this strip was just for fun. Nobody gave the kids horns and drums — they were noisy enough as it was. Sitting in their living room surrounded by family and food, paper and presents is an image I'll keep with me forever.

Grandparents are a wonderful invention. I was lucky to have had the best parents-in-law one could ask for. Ruth and Tom Johnston were the models for John's parents. I used their photographs to get a likeness, and their personalities were incorporated as well. I was so glad my kids had a rich and healthy connection to at least one set of grandparents. My folks lived on the other side of the country and were not able to see the children too often.

Ruth and Tom Johnston, Lynn Lake, 1977.

My own grandparents were either distant in miles or distant in sentiment. The only recollection I have of my paternal grandfather was "putting him out" when he fell asleep sitting up on the couch in our living room. He would smoke home-rolled cigs, and the paper would be stuck to his bottom lip while the lit end smoldered and dropped hot ashes on his shirt. I remember slight plumes of smoke rising from his chest and Grandma whacking him with a dishcloth to put out the fire! My dad's mom was a round lady with a strong domestic streak who was at home in the kitchen — but I do remember seeing photos of her in buckskins, in the snow, holding a rifle! That's another story.

My mom's folks were British and rather "upper crust." Although they appreciated us, my brother and my cousins and I all had to be seen and not heard. In the strip, I had both sets of grandparents play a meaningful role — even though they lived in Winnipeg and Vancouver. In my imagination, it could all be just the way I wanted it to be!

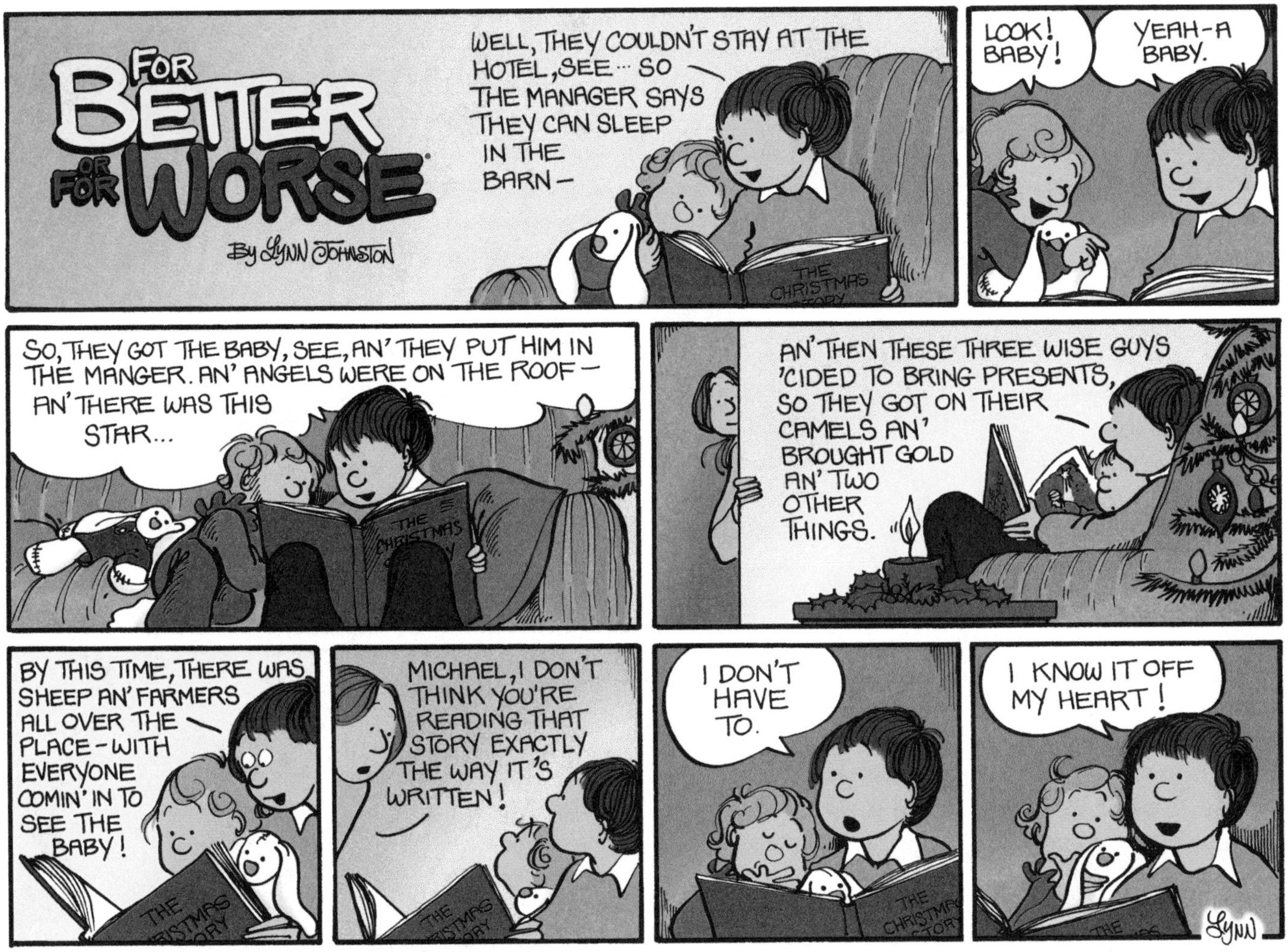

FOR BETTER OR FOR WORSE
BY LYNN JOHNSTON
WELL, THEY COULDN'T STAY AT THE HOTEL, SEE... SO THE MANAGER SAYS THEY CAN SLEEP IN THE BARN –
THE CHRISTMAS STORY
LOOK! BABY!
YEAH – A BABY.
SO, THEY GOT THE BABY, SEE, AN' THEY PUT HIM IN THE MANGER. AN' ANGELS WERE ON THE ROOF – AN' THERE WAS THIS STAR...
AN' THEN THESE THREE WISE GUYS 'CIDED TO BRING PRESENTS, SO THEY GOT ON THEIR CAMELS AN' BROUGHT GOLD AN' TWO OTHER THINGS.
BY THIS TIME, THERE WAS SHEEP AN' FARMERS ALL OVER THE PLACE – WITH EVERYONE COMIN' IN TO SEE THE BABY!
MICHAEL, I DON'T THINK YOU'RE READING THAT STORY EXACTLY THE WAY IT'S WRITTEN!
I DON'T HAVE TO.
I KNOW IT OFF MY HEART!
LYNN


My dad made up words to stories and songs all the time: "When shepherds washed their socks by night," "We three Kings of Orient are trying to smoke a rubber cigar," and "round John Virgin" were all part of our holiday hymns. Naturally, when I read to my brother, it behooved me (a good word at reindeer time) to change the words.

Part of the game was in our having memorized the book or song sheet, so a funny alteration was a challenge and something of an expectation. Every so often I will see a youngster reading from memory, hardly looking at the words, and these scenes come back to me. Thank goodness for memories ... and Christmas memories are some of the best!

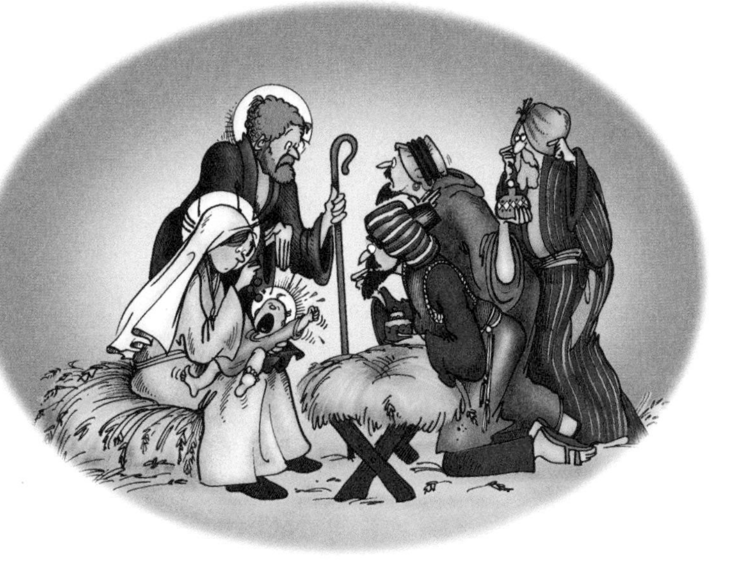

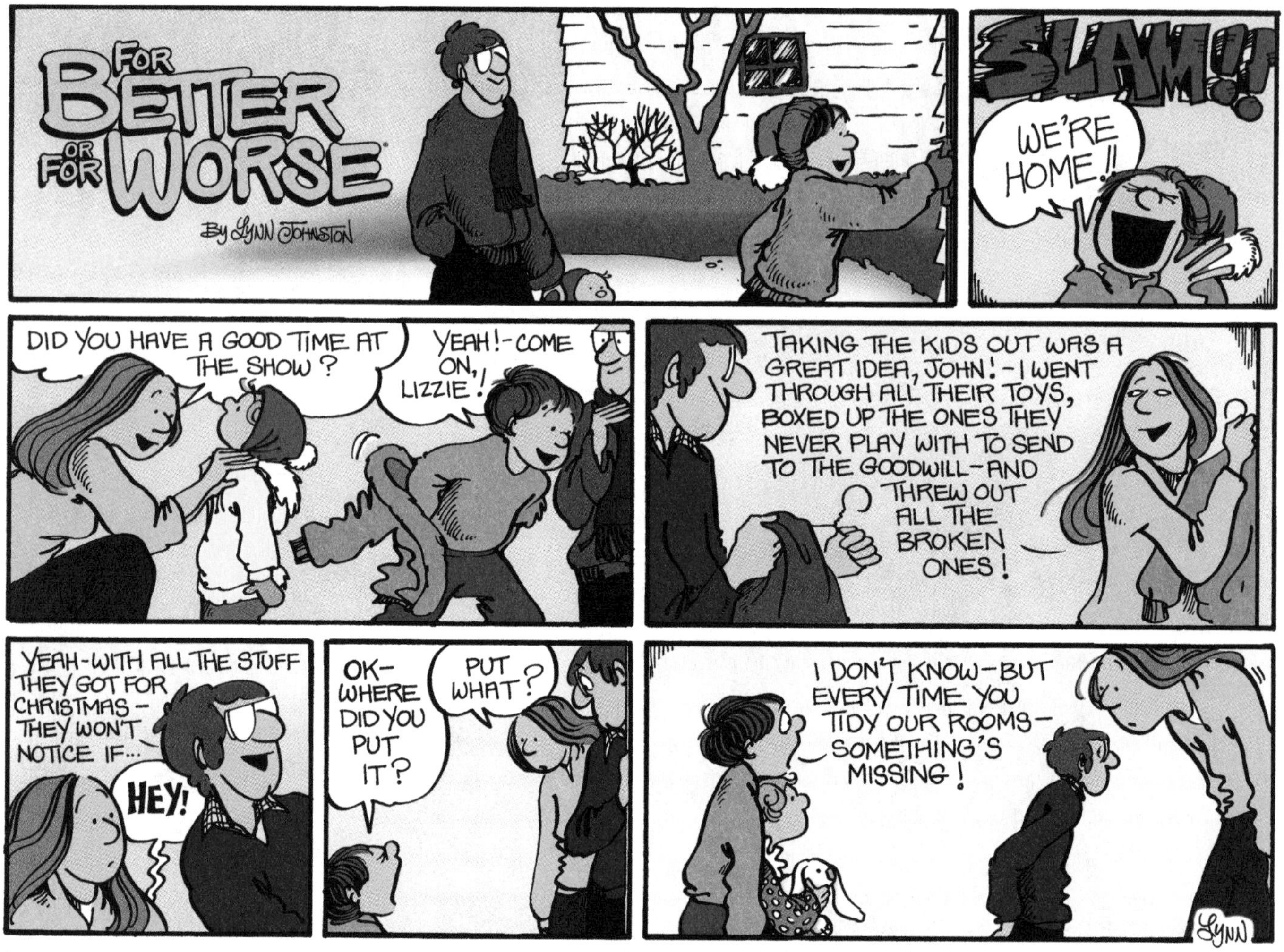
For Better or For Worse
By Lynn Johnston
SLAM!!
WE'RE HOME!!
DID YOU HAVE A GOOD TIME AT THE SHOW?
YEAH!-COME ON, LIZZIE!
TAKING THE KIDS OUT WAS A GREAT IDEA, JOHN! - I WENT THROUGH ALL THEIR TOYS, BOXED UP THE ONES THEY NEVER PLAY WITH TO SEND TO THE GOODWILL - AND THREW OUT ALL THE BROKEN ONES!
YEAH - WITH ALL THE STUFF THEY GOT FOR CHRISTMAS - THEY WON'T NOTICE IF...
HEY!
OK - WHERE DID YOU PUT IT?
PUT WHAT?
I DON'T KNOW - BUT EVERY TIME YOU TIDY OUR ROOMS - SOMETHING'S MISSING!
LYNN

The Lynn Lake theatre was an easy walk from the house. If one of us took the kids to a movie, the other could have a few hours to catch up. One of my favourite things to do is to “organize”! I love to throw things out and often regret having done so. The alternative, though, is to have too much stuff! What a luxurious problem to have.

One day while the kids were out, I did go through their things. I gave much of what I thought was forgotten and ready to recycle to the church for the annual bake and rummage sale. This event was always well attended. I took Katie and Aaron with me to enjoy the tea and the treasure hunt, forgetting there would be a number of their things in the sale. They immediately identified their own toys and I dutifully bought back the things they weren’t ready to part with! I learned to ask first, and to let them choose what to give away and what to save!

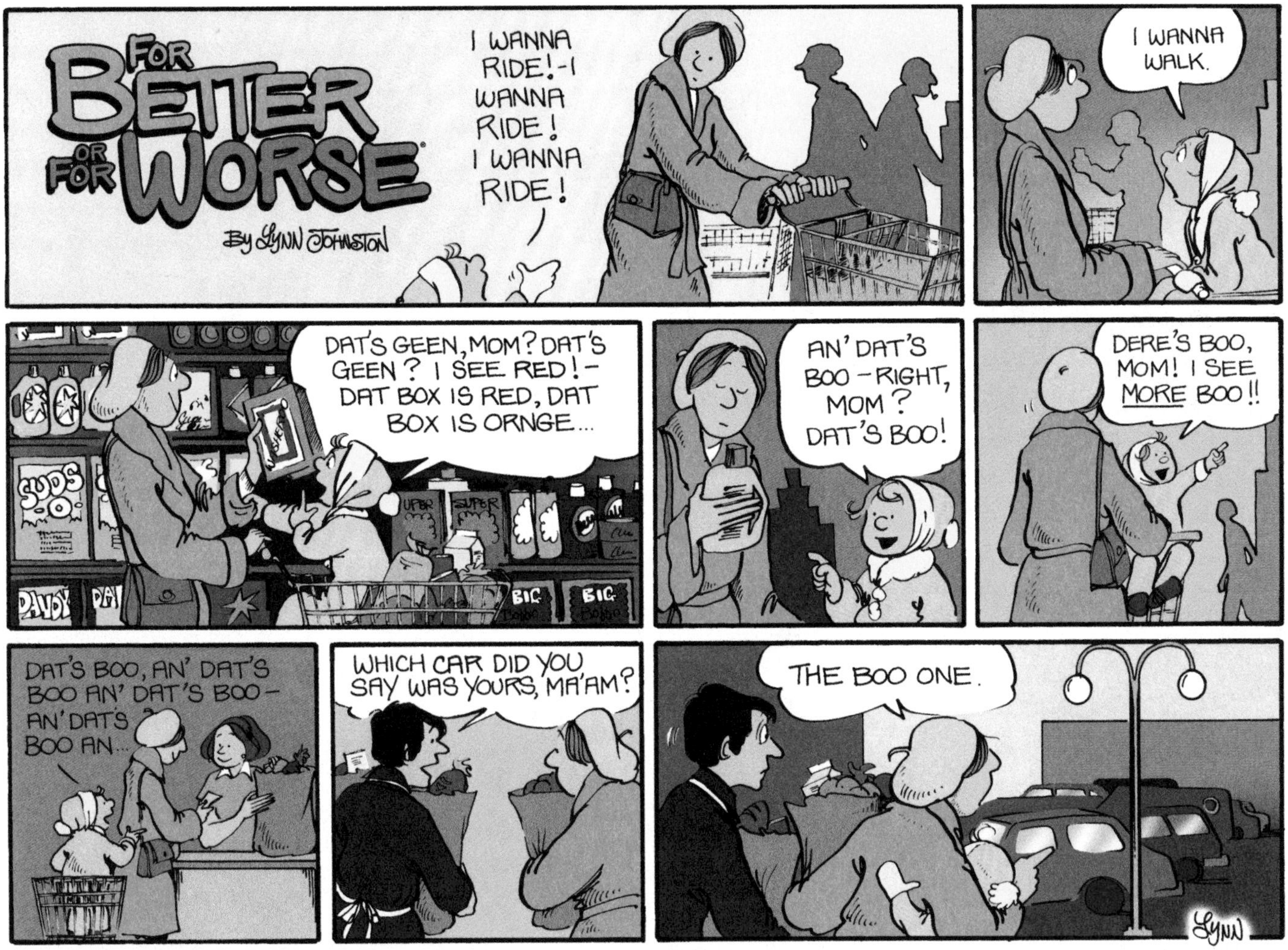
FOR BETTER OR FOR WORSE
BY LYNN JOHNSTON
I WANNA RIDE!-I WANNA RIDE! I WANNA RIDE!
I WANNA WALK.
DAT'S GEEN, MOM? DAT'S GEEN? I SEE RED! - DAT BOX IS RED, DAT BOX IS ORNGE...
SUDS-O
DANDY
BIG
BIG
AN' DAT'S BOO - RIGHT, MOM? DAT'S BOO!
DERE'S BOO, MOM! I SEE MORE BOO!!
DAT'S BOO, AN' DAT'S BOO AN' DAT'S BOO - AN' DAT'S BOO AN...
WHICH CAR DID YOU SAY WAS YOURS, MA'AM?
THE BOO ONE.
LYNN

When I did this, Katie was well into the language learning curve, and her baby talk was a lot of fun. For years, well after her move into adult vocabulary, we used her words ourselves, not wanting to lose the charm and the memory. "Blaffoon" was "bathroom," "puffermink" was "peppermint" and "bleffus" was "breakfast." These were all part of our vocabulary until she went to university! The dialogue in this strip went exactly as written, except that I kept the punch line to myself!

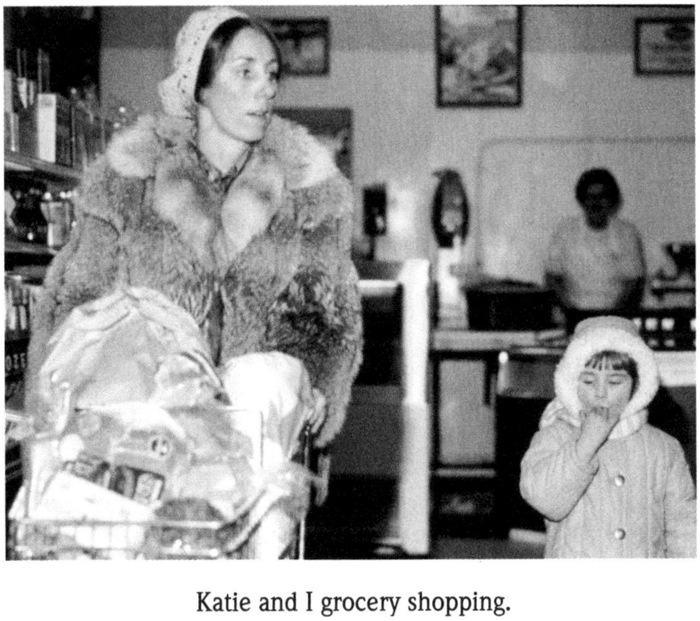

Katie and I grocery shopping.

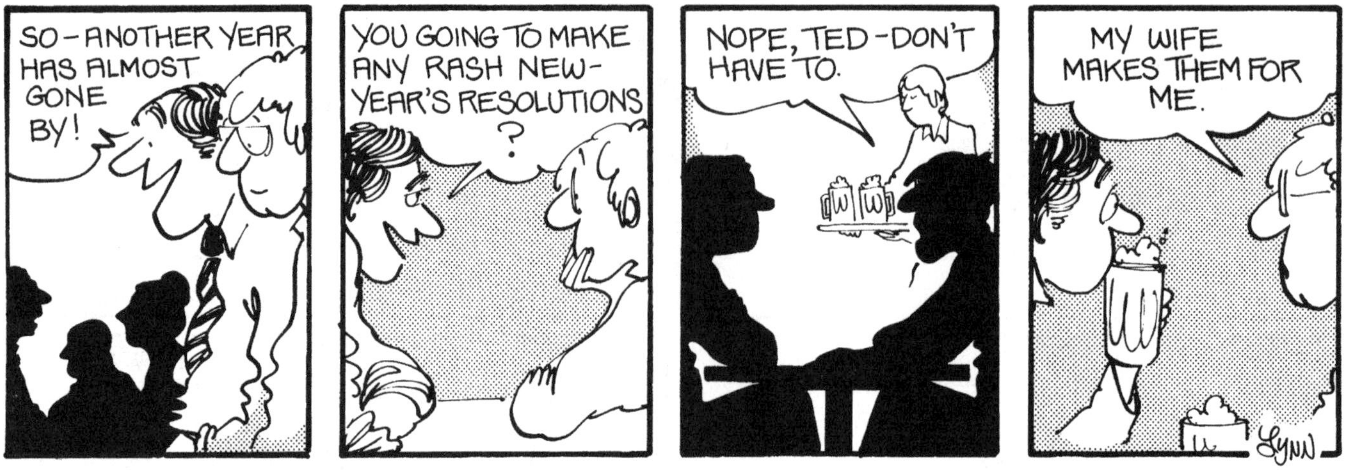
SO - ANOTHER YEAR HAS ALMOST GONE BY!
YOU GOING TO MAKE ANY RASH NEW-YEAR'S RESOLUTIONS?
NOPE, TED - DON'T HAVE TO.
MY WIFE MAKES THEM FOR ME.

I don't remember making too many New Years' resolutions — either for myself or anyone else. I learned long before my kids were born that resolutions, though well intended, rarely come about. Our philosophy then was to do what you could, hope for the best, and to laugh at the things we couldn't change. This we did. We shared laughter with good friends — as often as possible.

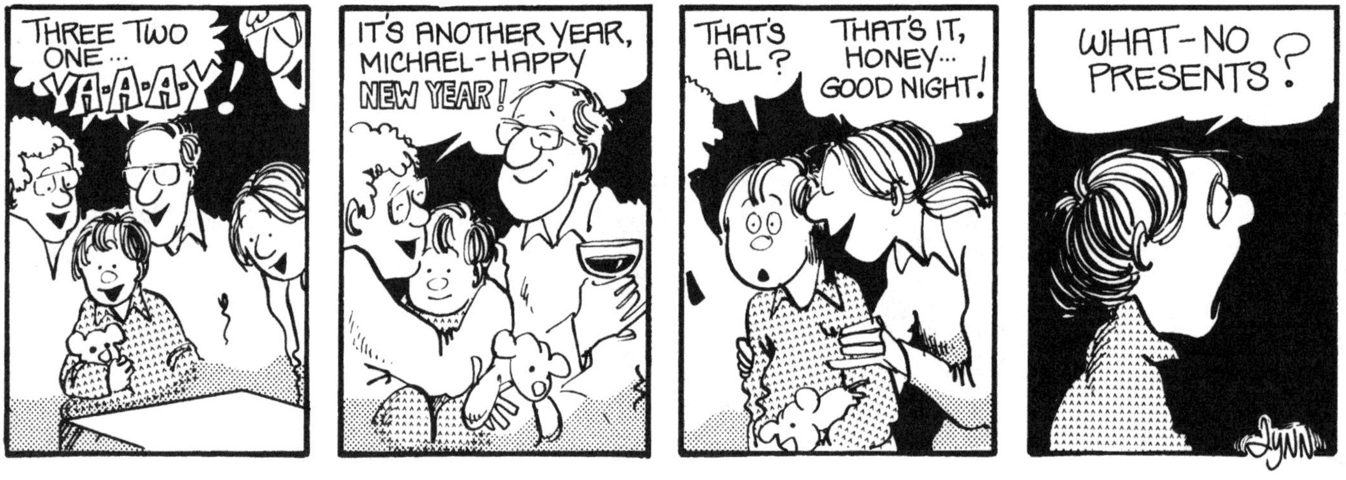
THREE TWO ONE... YA-A-A-Y!
IT'S ANOTHER YEAR, MICHAEL - HAPPY NEW YEAR!
THAT'S ALL?
THAT'S IT, HONEY... GOOD NIGHT!
WHAT - NO PRESENTS?

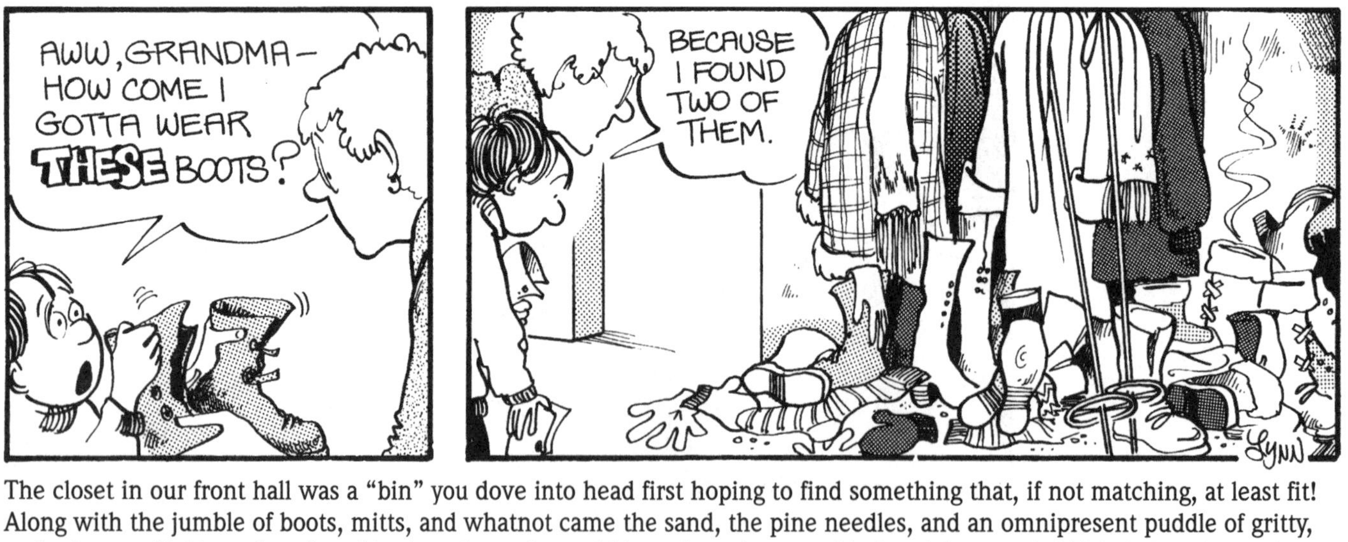
AWW, GRANDMA - HOW COME I GOTTA WEAR THESE BOOTS?
BECAUSE I FOUND TWO OF THEM.

The closet in our front hall was a "bin" you dove into head first hoping to find something that, if not matching, at least fit! Along with the jumble of boots, mitts, and whatnot came the sand, the pine needles, and an omnipresent puddle of gritty, melted snow. If this cache of crud bothered you, it would be a thorn in your side for eight months! This is how long winter lasted in northern Manitoba. You just had to get used to it.

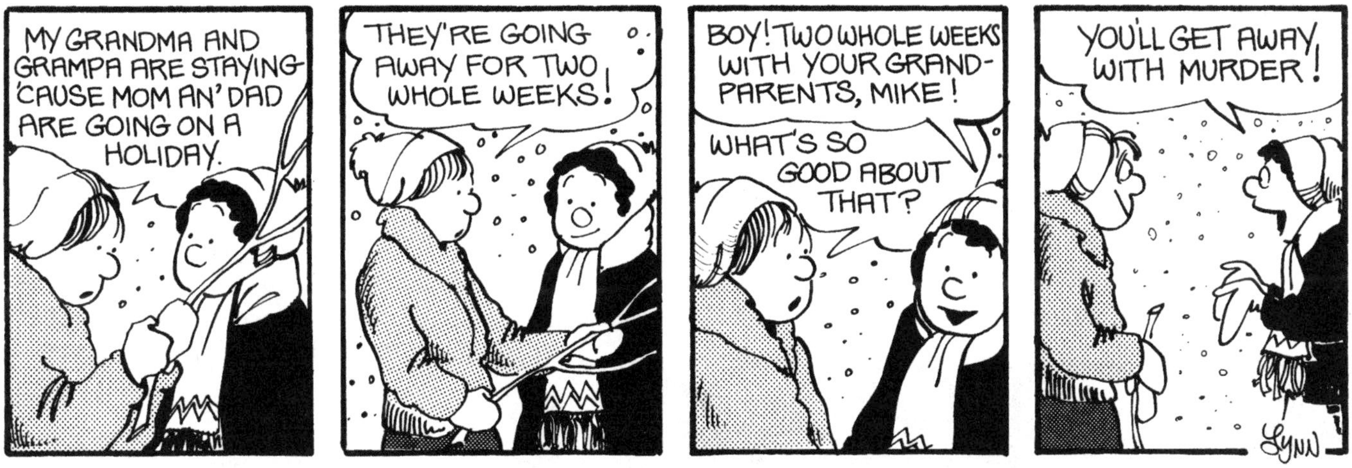
MY GRANDMA AND GRAMPA ARE STAYING 'CAUSE MOM AN' DAD ARE GOING ON A HOLIDAY.
THEY'RE GOING AWAY FOR TWO WHOLE WEEKS!
BOY! TWO WHOLE WEEKS WITH YOUR GRANDPARENTS, MIKE!
WHAT'S SO GOOD ABOUT THAT?
YOU'LL GET AWAY WITH MURDER!
LYNN

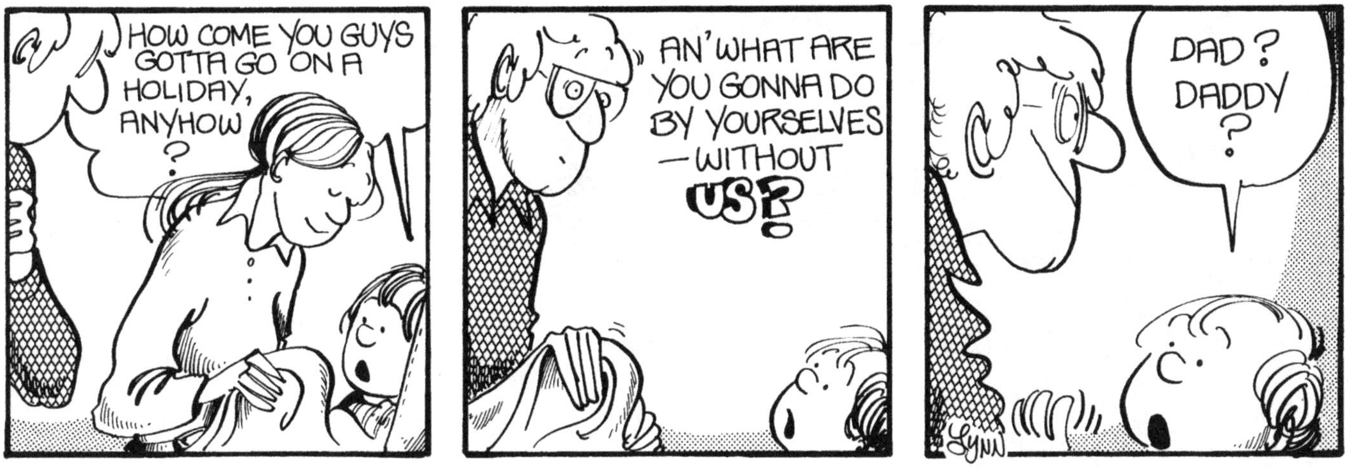
HOW COME YOU GUYS GOTTA GO ON A HOLIDAY, ANYHOW?
AN' WHAT ARE YOU GONNA DO BY YOURSELVES — WITHOUT US?
DAD? DADDY?
LYNN

Telling Aaron we were going on a trip without him wasn't easy. He wanted to go everywhere, see everything — he didn't want to be left out.

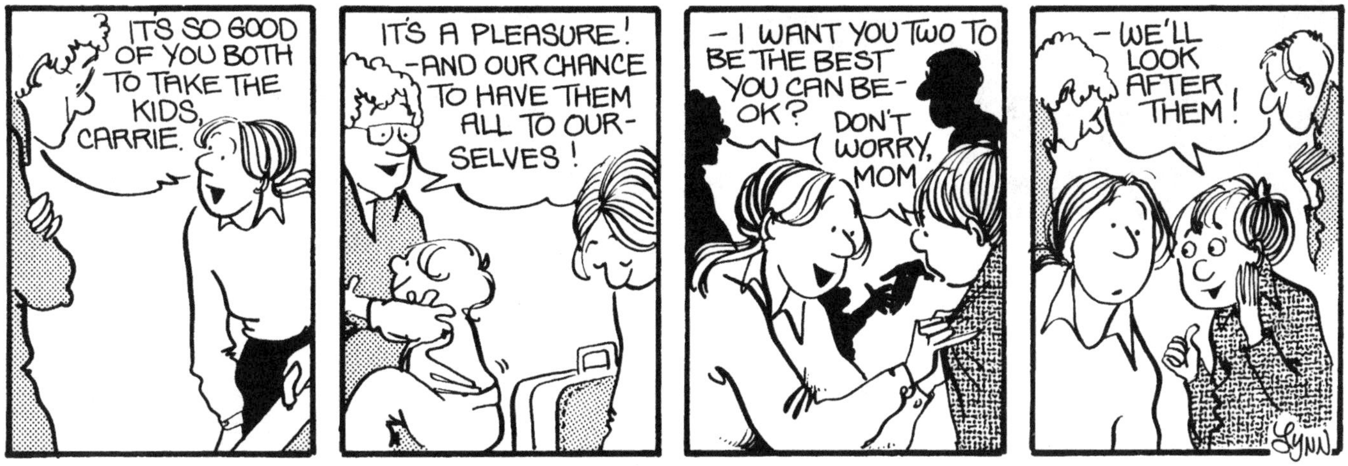
IT'S SO GOOD OF YOU BOTH TO TAKE THE KIDS, CARRIE.
IT'S A PLEASURE! — AND OUR CHANCE TO HAVE THEM ALL TO OURSELVES!
— I WANT YOU TWO TO BE THE BEST YOU CAN BE — OK?
DON'T WORRY, MOM
— WE'LL LOOK AFTER THEM!
LYNN

Our first real vacation was to Barbados the year Katie turned two. Before we went anywhere, I had to work ahead so that the strip would run smoothly and I'd have enough lead time to get back into it again when I got home. To do this, I'd check out our return date then work weekends and evenings until I had six extra weeks of FBorFW done past that date. Travelling, therefore, meant long hours of writing and drawing beforehand, and barking at kids in an airport wasn't going to be part of the scene. We looked forward to the adventure and to the reward of sitting on a warm beach with a cold drink and nothing to do but enjoy. In order to do this, we needed to be kid free — so we made arrangements to leave the kids behind with my in-laws.

Once both kids adjusted to the idea that Mom and Dad were really going to leave them, they settled into Grandma's house without much fuss. Two weeks would go by fast, and maybe we'd bring a few presents when we came home! Aaron took his teddy and Katie took her bunny. Both had been lovingly made by my mom, and were washed so often they had that floppy, misshapen look of a toy well loved. Both of these toys have appeared time and again in the strip.

Aaron and Katie with their favourite toys.

Soon we were on our way, but in order to get there, we had to take a Twin Otter to Thompson, Manitoba, then a jet from there to Winnipeg, where we caught our flight south. For this reason alone, we were glad to be *sans enfants*. It would be a long trip, especially for two young kids.

I did feel guilty for leaving. Aaron especially was aware that we were going away. Katie was just confused. My parents-in-law looked forward to having the kids to themselves. Ruth always had a plan, and this was her opportunity to work on reading habits, table manners, and bathroom toilette. Rather than begrudge the interference, I adored her for her patience and practicality. As we prepared to take off from the Lynn Lake airport, I remember the kids' faces pressed against the airport window, and I wanted to hug them one more time! I knew, however, that they would soon be at Ruth and Tom's house, warm and safe, ready to chow down on homemade buns and hot oatmeal porridge.

Then, we were off — but the thought of warm weather and a sandy beach was still too far away to focus on — we were exhausted from preparing for the trip.

Having no one to leave our outer clothing with, we took with us our parkas, gloves, scarves, and big winter boots. We could have boarded the plane in lighter gear — (there was a heater on board), but living in the north teaches you to be prepared for survival. If anything caused our plane to set down in the bush, we'd be dead without winter clothing.

The trip was a pleasure. We had forgotten what kid-free travelling was like. We didn't have to warm up the plane or prepare a lunch or bring toys or the potty … we just had ourselves to think about. Even though we had to slug suitcases and wait in line and sit for hours, it all seemed like such a luxury!

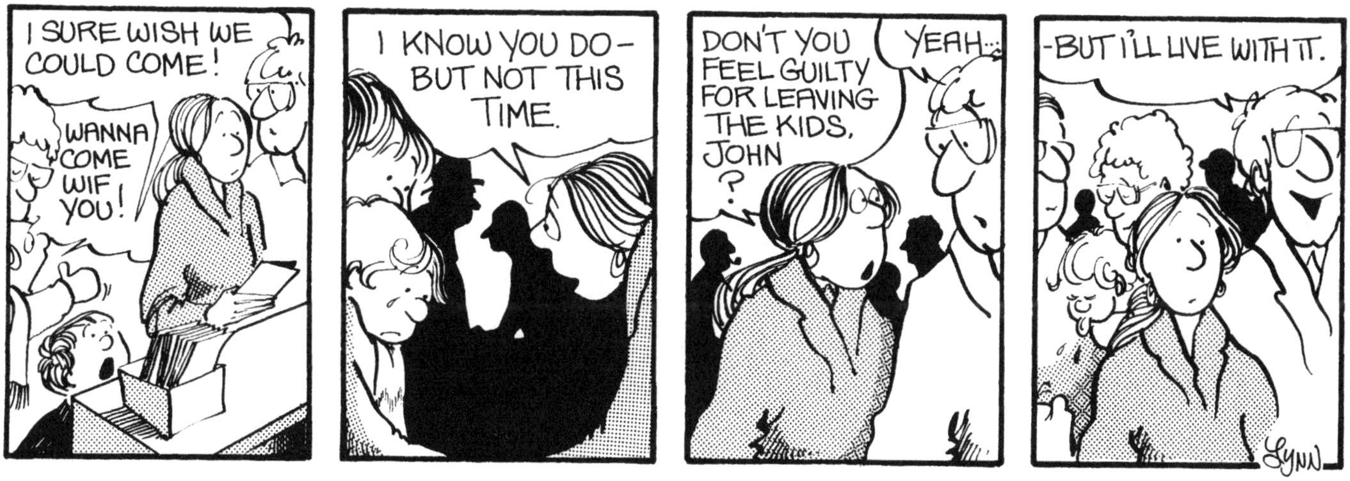
I SURE WISH WE COULD COME!
WANNA COME WIF YOU!
I KNOW YOU DO- BUT NOT THIS TIME.
DON'T YOU FEEL GUILTY FOR LEAVING THE KIDS, JOHN ?
YEAH...
-BUT I'LL LIVE WITH IT.
LYNN

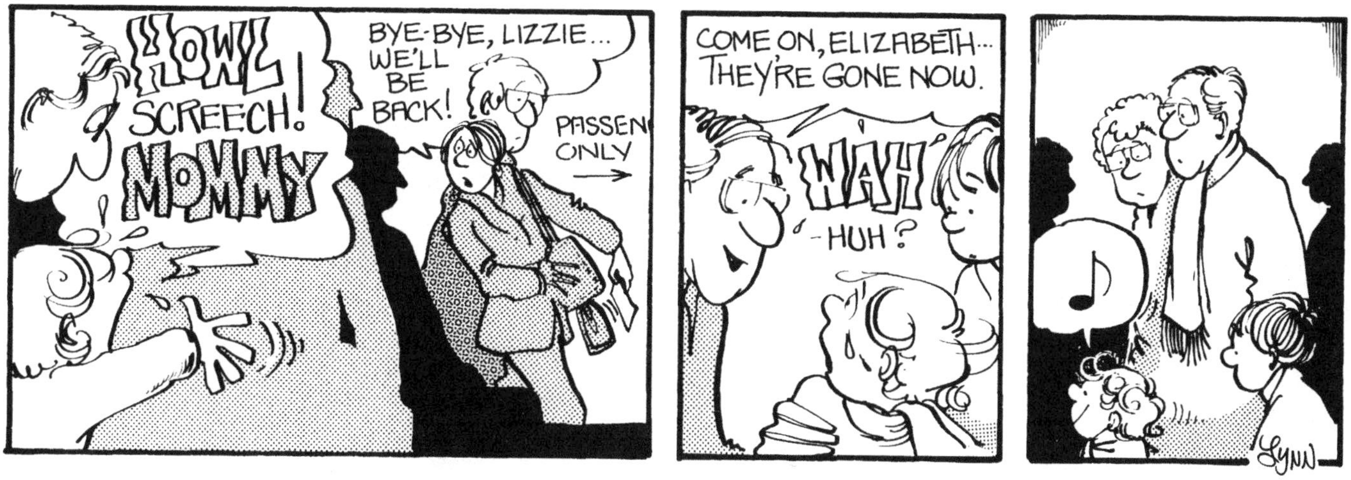
HOWL SCREECH! MOMMY
BYE-BYE, LIZZIE... WE'LL BE BACK!
PASSEN ONLY
COME ON, ELIZABETH... THEY'RE GONE NOW.
WAH
-HUH?
LYNN

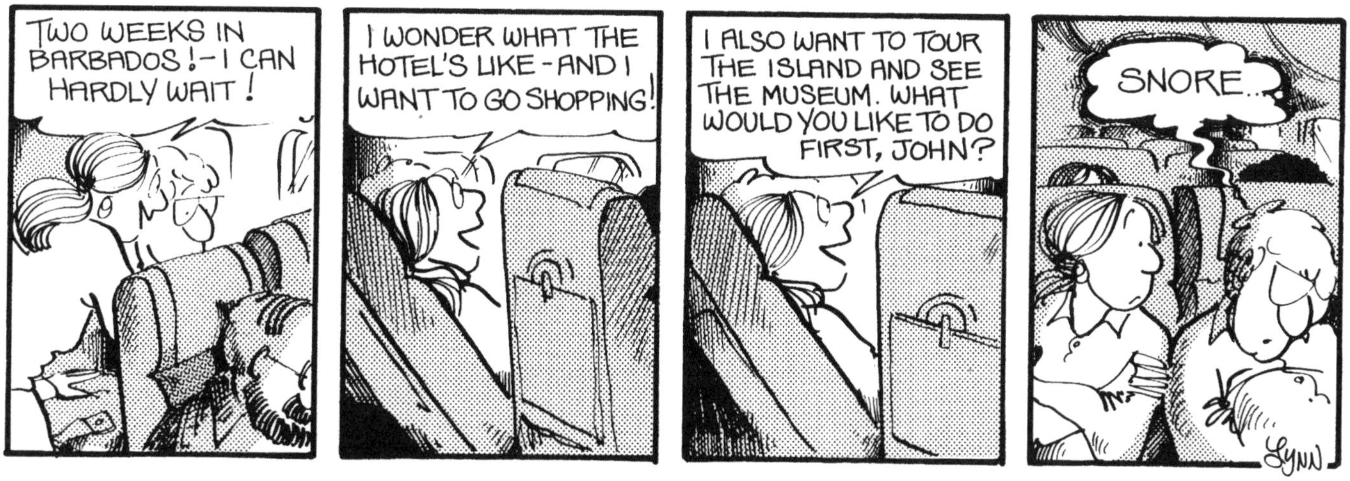
TWO WEEKS IN BARBADOS!-I CAN HARDLY WAIT!
I WONDER WHAT THE HOTEL'S LIKE-AND I WANT TO GO SHOPPING!
I ALSO WANT TO TOUR THE ISLAND AND SEE THE MUSEUM. WHAT WOULD YOU LIKE TO DO FIRST, JOHN?
SNORE...
LYNN

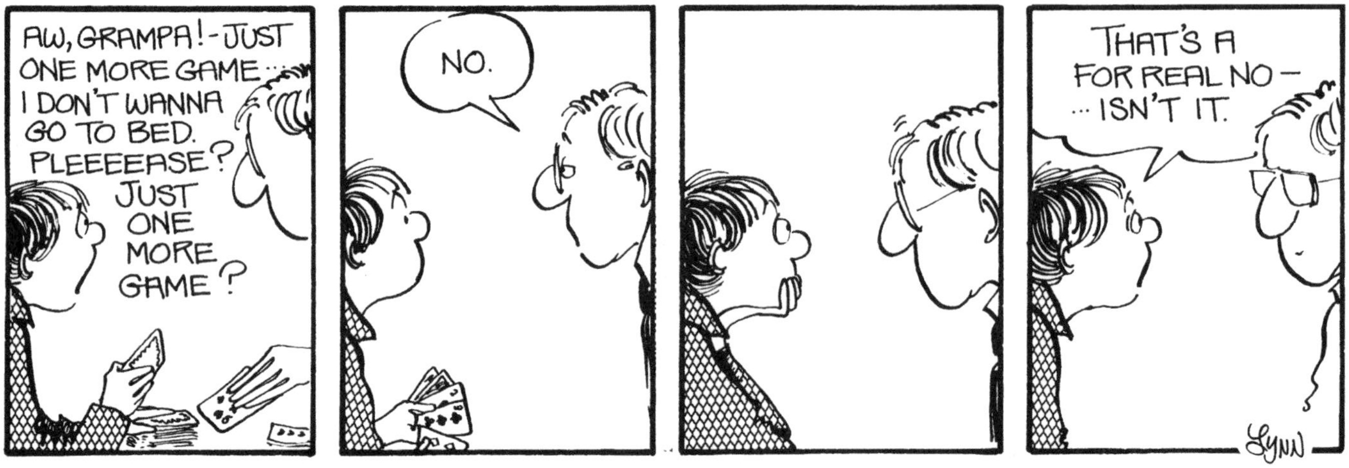
AW, GRAMPA! - JUST ONE MORE GAME... I DON'T WANNA GO TO BED. PLEEEEASE? JUST ONE MORE GAME?
NO.
THAT'S A FOR REAL NO - ...ISN'T IT.
LYNN

Meanwhile, back at the ranch, Aaron and Katie were getting used to Grandma and Grandpa's parenting style — it was clear from the get-go that they had to toe the line, or else! As long as they kept the rules of the house, observed their manners, and went to bed on time, life would be good. At least, that was the plan. It didn't take long for Aaron and Kate to find "chinks in the armour," and their guardians soon found the arrangement to be more than they'd bargained for!

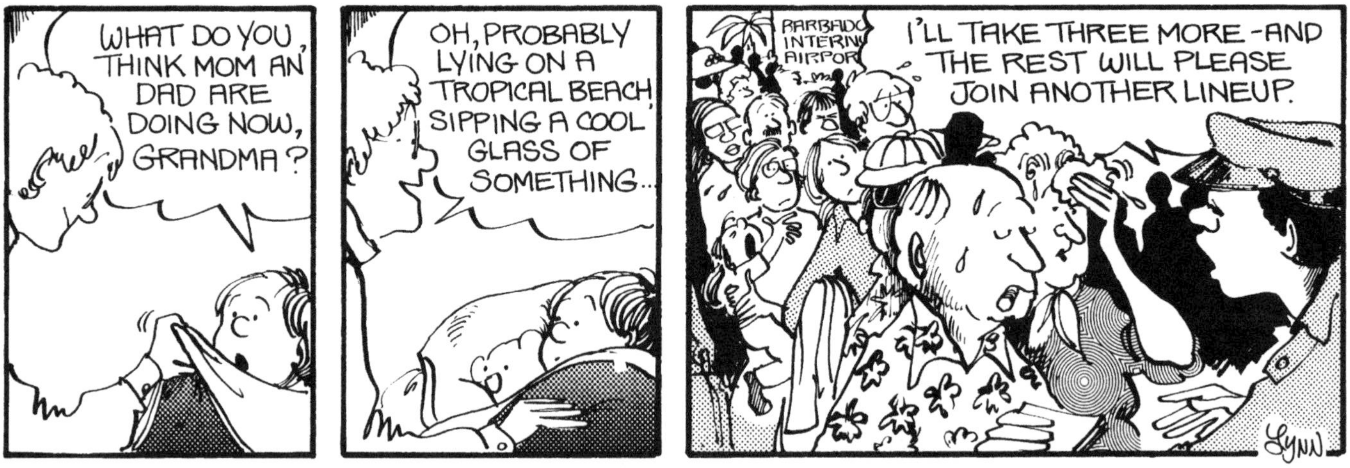
WHAT DO YOU THINK MOM AN' DAD ARE DOING NOW, GRANDMA?
OH, PROBABLY LYING ON A TROPICAL BEACH, SIPPING A COOL GLASS OF SOMETHING...
BARBADO
INTERN
AIRPOR
I'LL TAKE THREE MORE - AND THE REST WILL PLEASE JOIN ANOTHER LINEUP.
LYNN

When we arrived in Barbados, the customs and immigration area was at a standstill and the heat was unbearable. I did this comic strip after we returned. Once it was published, I got a letter from the department of tourism in Barbados! They were quite embarrassed and assured me that their tourist entry control was being reorganized. I don't know if FBorFW can take credit for the modern, efficient, and air-conditioned space they have now — but I'll say that it did and have fun with it!!

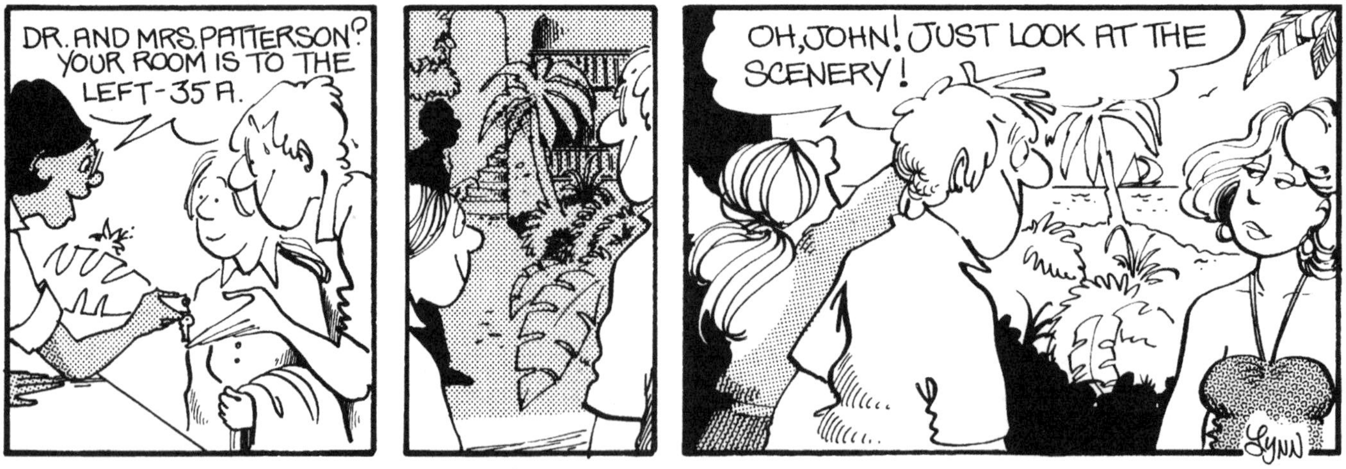
DR. AND MRS. PATTERSON? YOUR ROOM IS TO THE LEFT - 35 A.
OH, JOHN! JUST LOOK AT THE SCENERY!
LYNN

The hotel was a lovely little retreat called "Tamarind Cove." The room we had was 35A. The beach was secluded and the water warm. I grew up next to the ocean, but had never seen this kind of blue before. Rich, pale turquoise ribbons stretched from left to right as far as we could see. Darker blends of greenish blue reflected the clearest sky. The deck chairs beckoned and the first drinks were free. We settled easily into this glorious retreat, wishing that time would stand still.

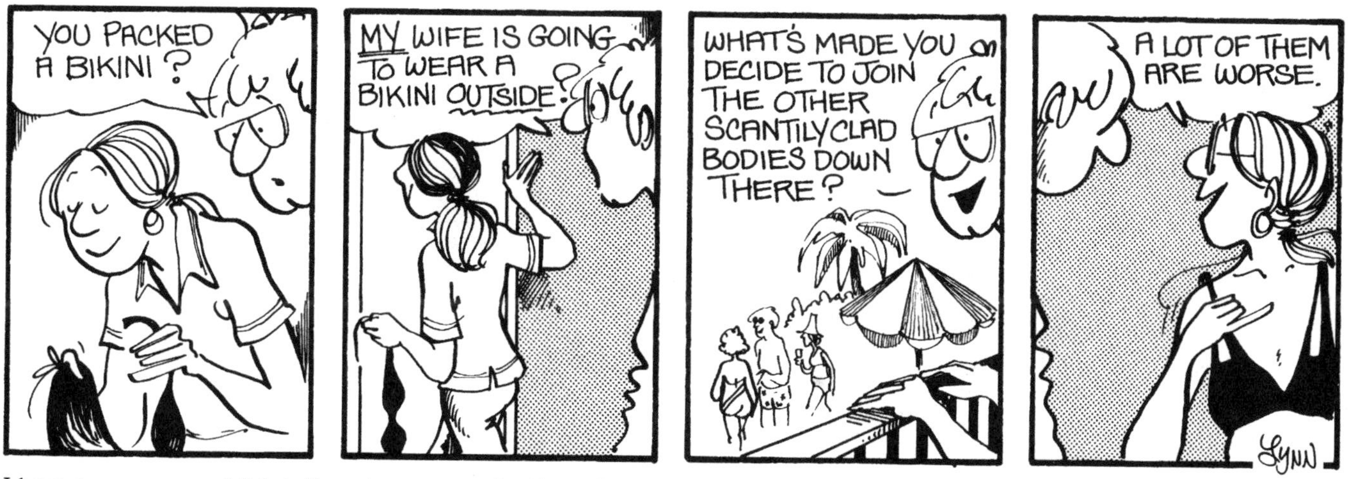
YOU PACKED A BIKINI?
MY WIFE IS GOING TO WEAR A BIKINI OUTSIDE?
WHAT'S MADE YOU DECIDE TO JOIN THE OTHER SCANTILY CLAD BODIES DOWN THERE?
A LOT OF THEM ARE WORSE.
LYNN

I have never worn a bikini. Even in my twenties I was far too self-conscious. In the strip, however, I could wear what I liked. Elly's shape constantly fluctuated. Bulges grew, angles sharpened, and postures slouched and straightened as the moods dictated.

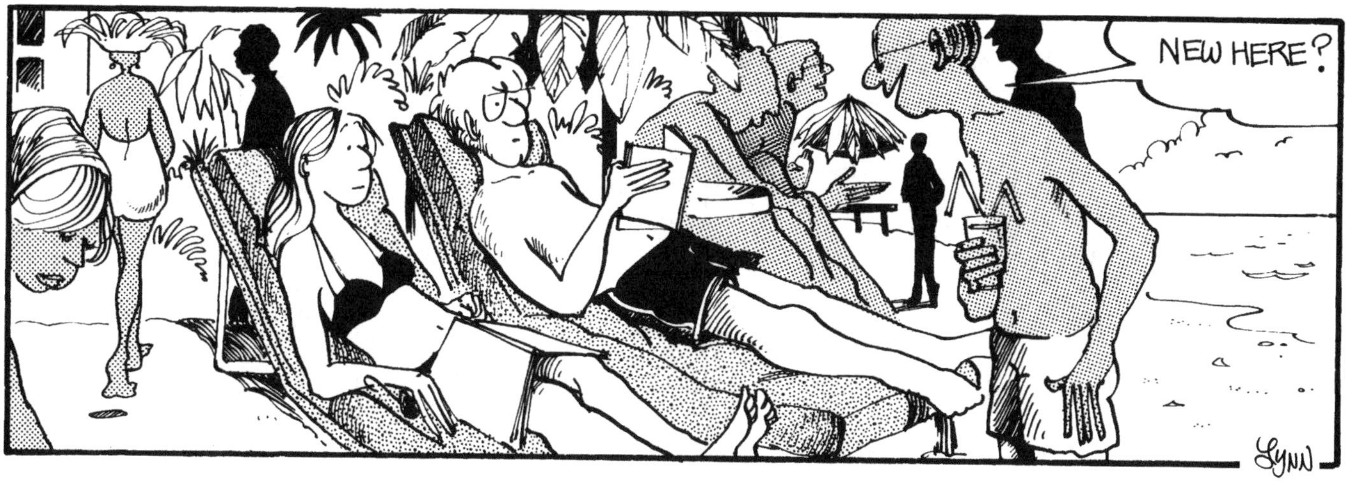
NEW HERE?
LYNN

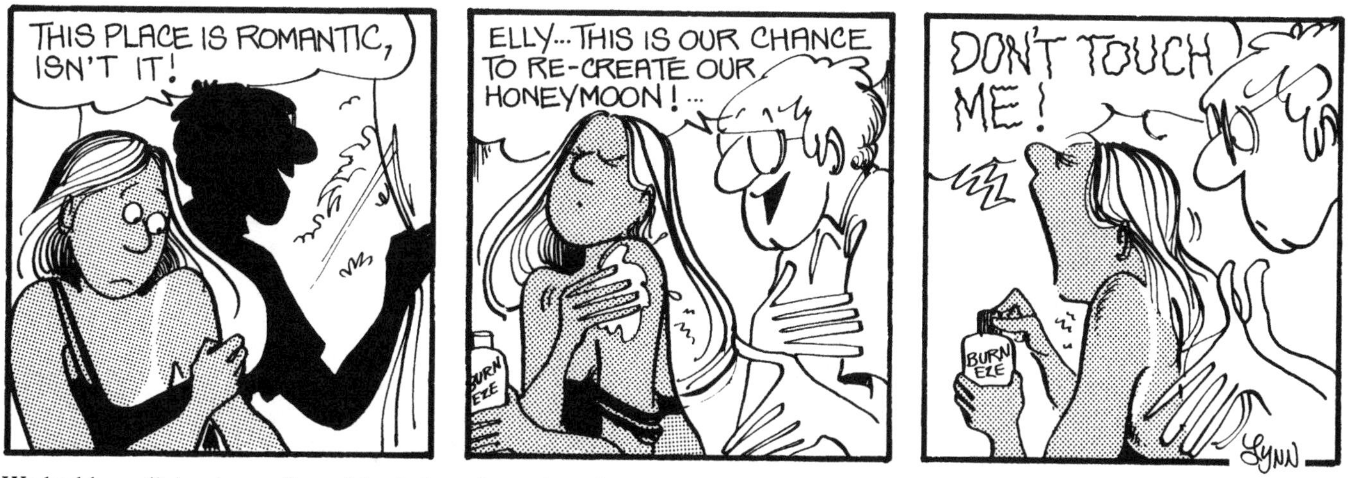
THIS PLACE IS ROMANTIC, ISN'T IT!
ELLY... THIS IS OUR CHANCE TO RE-CREATE OUR HONEYMOON!...
BURN EZE
DON'T TOUCH ME!
BURN EZE
LYNN

We had been living in northern Manitoba, where the winter sun rises around ten in the morning and sets around four in the afternoon. Rod and I were "pale faces"; the only colour being the inevitable frostbite, which reddened our cheeks and made our noses peel. The thought of spending a day on a sandy beach under a warm tropical sun overrode my common sense and inevitably I spent the first few days in agony. What was to have been a second honeymoon became "Don't touch me!"

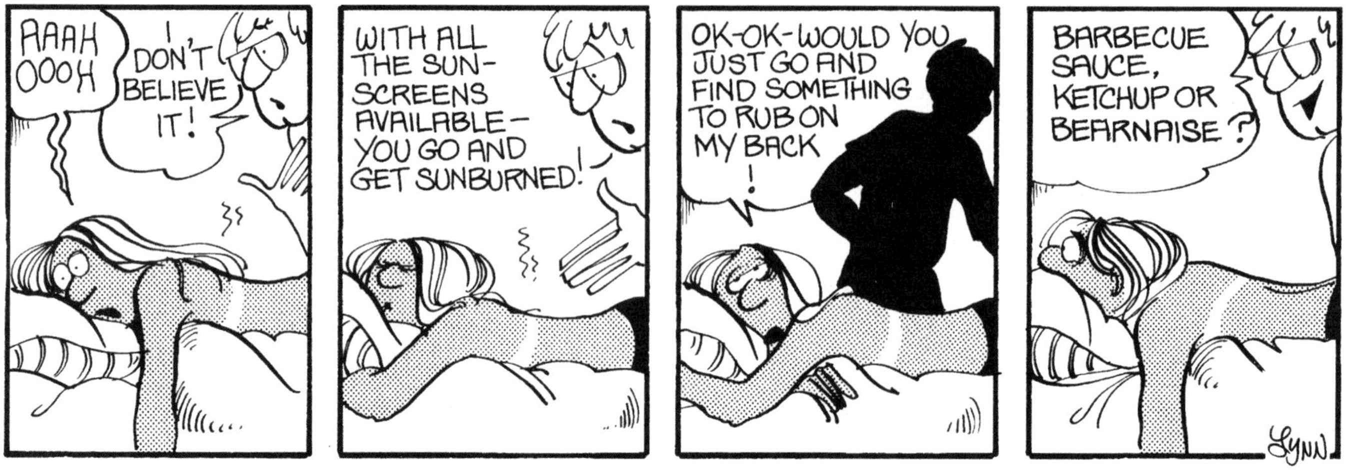
AAAH OOOH
I DON'T BELIEVE IT!
WITH ALL THE SUN-SCREENS AVAILABLE - YOU GO AND GET SUNBURNED!
OK-OK-WOULD YOU JUST GO AND FIND SOMETHING TO RUB ON MY BACK!
BARBECUE SAUCE, KETCHUP OR BEARNAISE?
LYNN

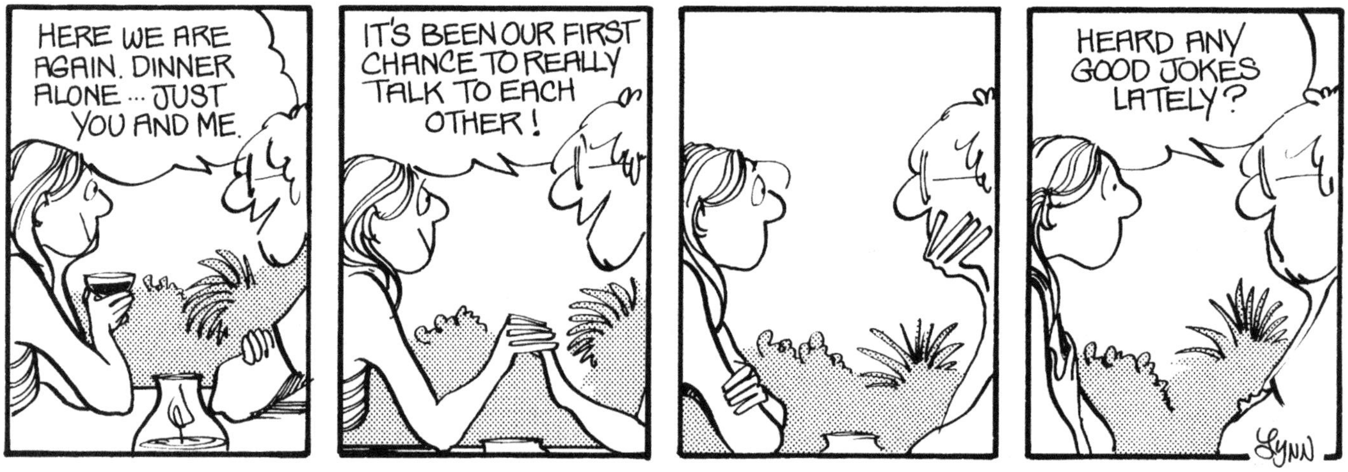
HERE WE ARE AGAIN. DINNER ALONE ... JUST YOU AND ME.
IT'S BEEN OUR FIRST CHANCE TO REALLY TALK TO EACH OTHER!
HEARD ANY GOOD JOKES LATELY?
LYNN

Our first few days alone — *sans* the kids — were surprisingly quiet. We were so used to our conversations being about children that when it came to other subjects, we hardly knew where to begin. Talking about "ME" and "YOU" feels almost selfish when so much of what parents do is for others. It took a few days to get past the need to talk about the kids, and even then, conversation was a novelty!

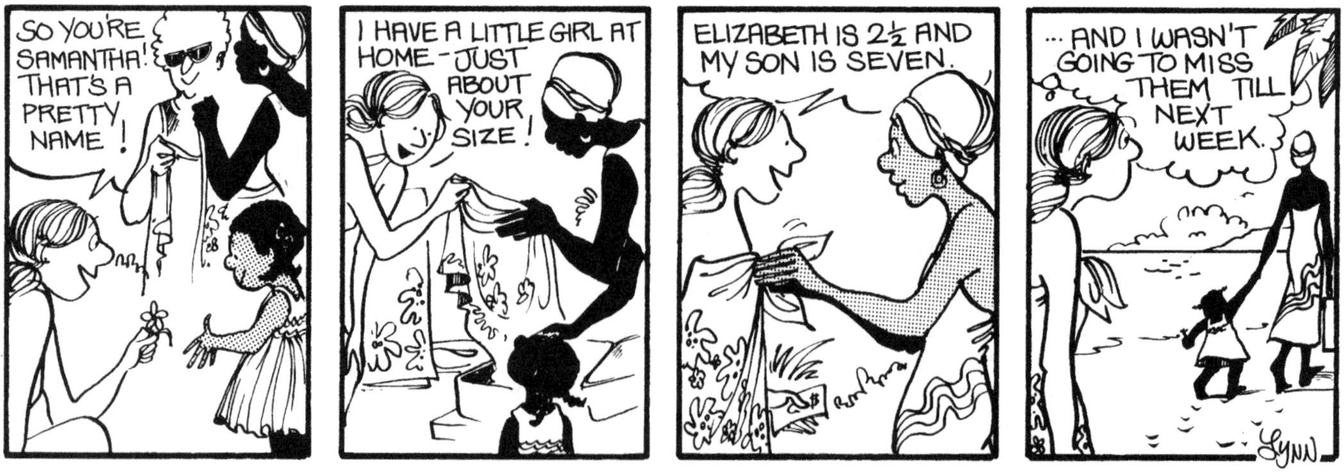
SO YOU'RE SAMANTHA! THAT'S A PRETTY NAME!
I HAVE A LITTLE GIRL AT HOME - JUST ABOUT YOUR SIZE!
ELIZABETH IS 2½ AND MY SON IS SEVEN.
... AND I WASN'T GOING TO MISS THEM TILL NEXT WEEK.
LYNN

Just outside our hotel, a young woman had set up a dress stand. The woman had a little daughter with her — she was about the same age as Katie. I'd watch her and compare the two. Her hair was full of barrettes and her eyes sparkled with mischief. I wondered how the two little girls would get along. For months I had looked forward to being without my children, but it didn't take long before I missed them terribly. I bought two dresses — one for me and one for Katie.

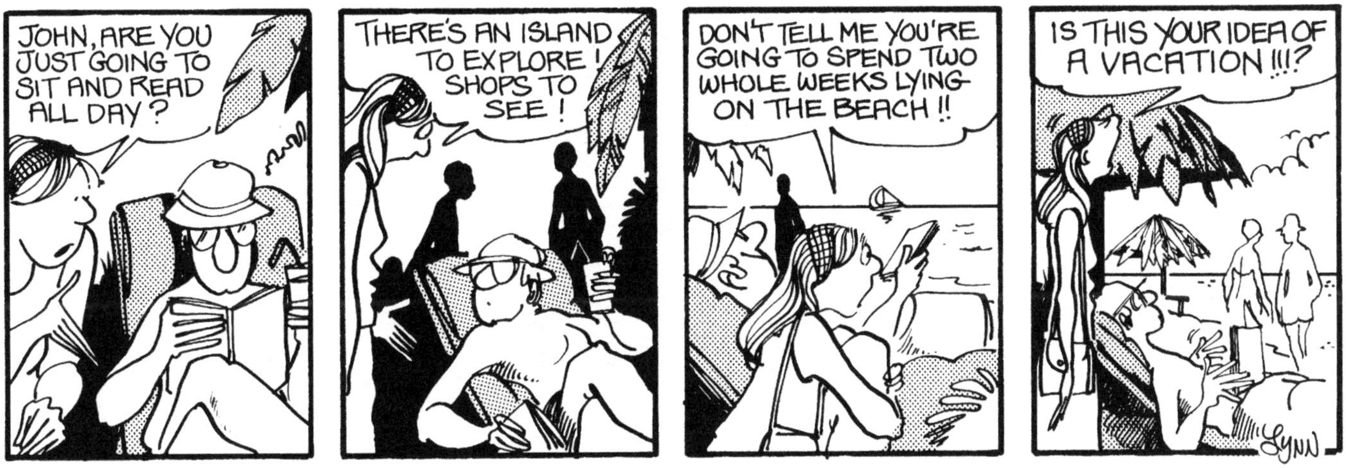

JOHN, ARE YOU JUST GOING TO SIT AND READ ALL DAY?
THERE'S AN ISLAND TO EXPLORE! SHOPS TO SEE!
DON'T TELL ME YOU'RE GOING TO SPEND TWO WHOLE WEEKS LYING ON THE BEACH!!
IS THIS YOUR IDEA OF A VACATION!!!?
LYNN


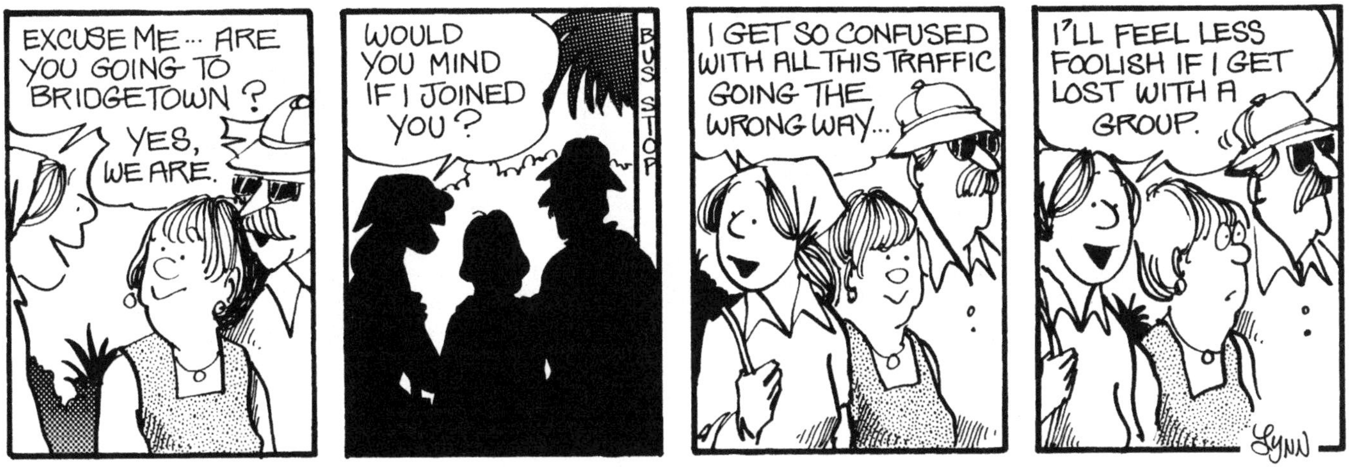

EXCUSE ME... ARE YOU GOING TO BRIDGETOWN?
YES, WE ARE.
WOULD YOU MIND IF I JOINED YOU?
BUS STOP
I GET SO CONFUSED WITH ALL THIS TRAFFIC GOING THE WRONG WAY...
I'LL FEEL LESS FOOLISH IF I GET LOST WITH A GROUP.
LYNN


The local transportation to Bridgetown was not much more than a half-ton truck with an open back into which people literally ran after and jumped into. Since it was a sort of private arrangement, the “bus” was not allowed to stop. When it did come barreling down the road, the other would-be passengers already knew to start running. Needless to say I was not ready to attempt this new and challenging style of travel and waited for the city bus.

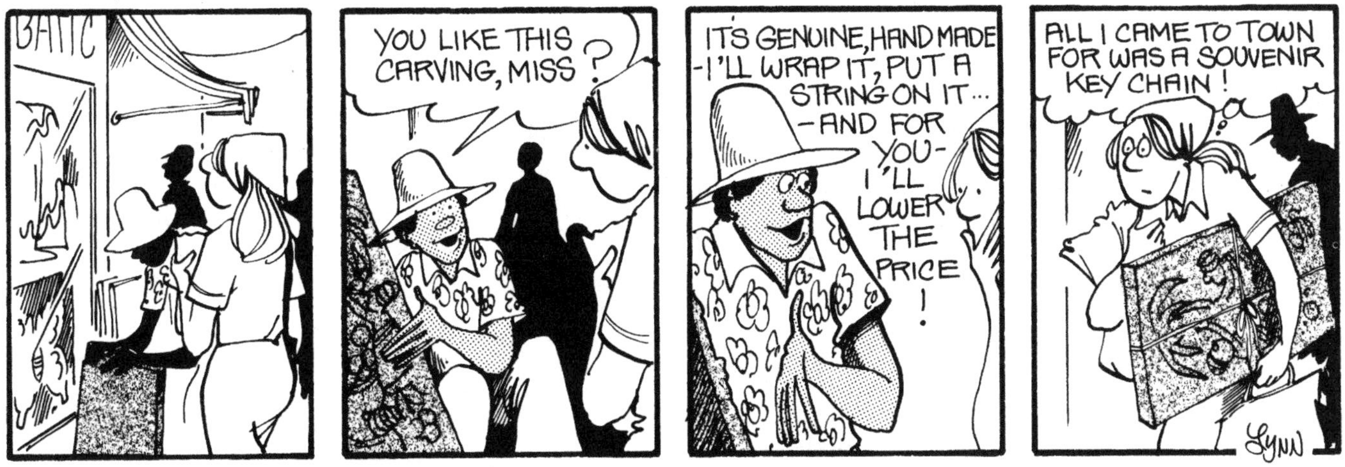

YOU LIKE THIS CARVING, MISS?
IT'S GENUINE, HAND MADE - I'LL WRAP IT, PUT A STRING ON IT... - AND FOR YOU - I'LL LOWER THE PRICE!
ALL I CAME TO TOWN FOR WAS A SOUVENIR KEY CHAIN!
LYNN


In the market, I was surprised to find a woodworker who carved intricate local scenes on discarded planks. His was the only booth in which there was something original and new, so I started a conversation with him. After awhile, I felt rather obliged to support him, so I decided to buy a carving. The one I liked best was about 1½ feet wide and 3 feet high. He wrapped it in newspaper, we shook hands like old chums, and I lugged it back to the hotel.

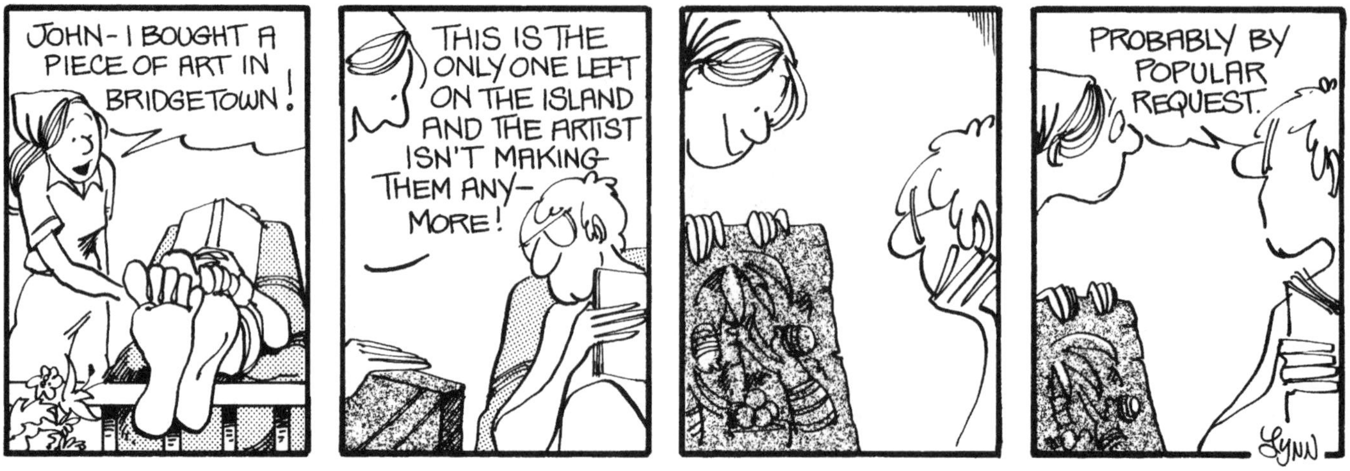
JOHN - I BOUGHT A PIECE OF ART IN BRIDGETOWN!
THIS IS THE ONLY ONE LEFT ON THE ISLAND AND THE ARTIST ISN'T MAKING THEM ANY-MORE!
PROBABLY BY POPULAR REQUEST.
LYNN

Needless to say, my spouse did not see the artistic merit in the work I presented to him and asked that it be put somewhere "reasonable." The carving remained in our basement until we moved from Manitoba to Ontario — and I remember the lady who bought it at my mom-in-law's yard sale saying "How can you get rid of this — it's beautiful!" Goes to show you ... that art is in the eye of the beholder.

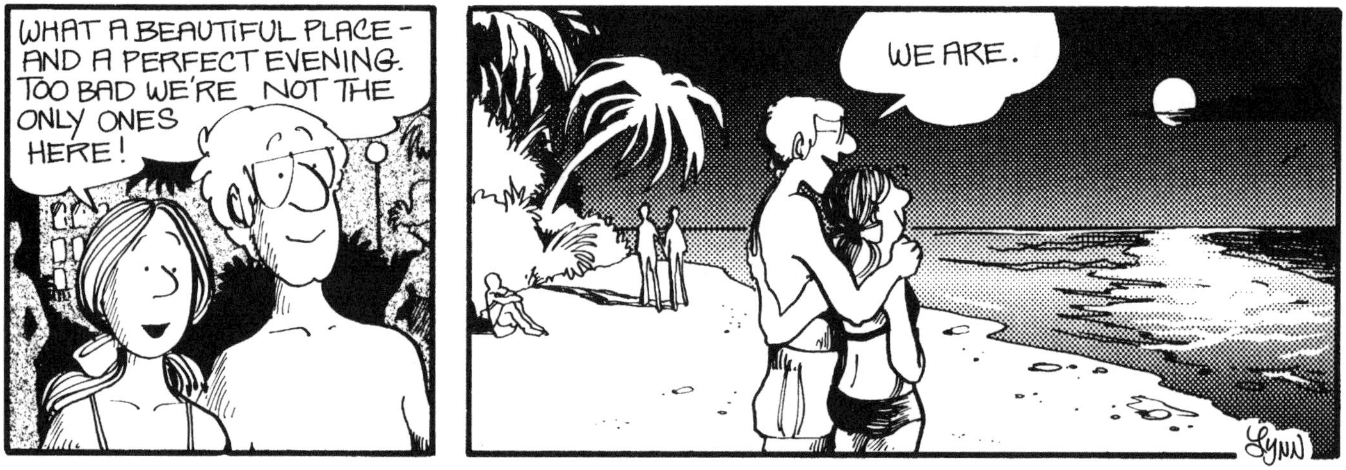
WHAT A BEAUTIFUL PLACE - AND A PERFECT EVENING. TOO BAD WE'RE NOT THE ONLY ONES HERE!
WE ARE.
LYNN

We couldn't believe we were there — back home, it was freezing cold. We had brought our parkas down to Barbados — having no one to store them for us in Winnipeg. One day, just for fun, we decided to wear them on the beach. Standing on the hot sand in our boots and parkas, with the fur hoods low over our faces, we were quite a sight. Even the hotel staff took pictures! They had never seen such clothing and it gave them an idea of the weather we lived in and why we were so glad to be away!

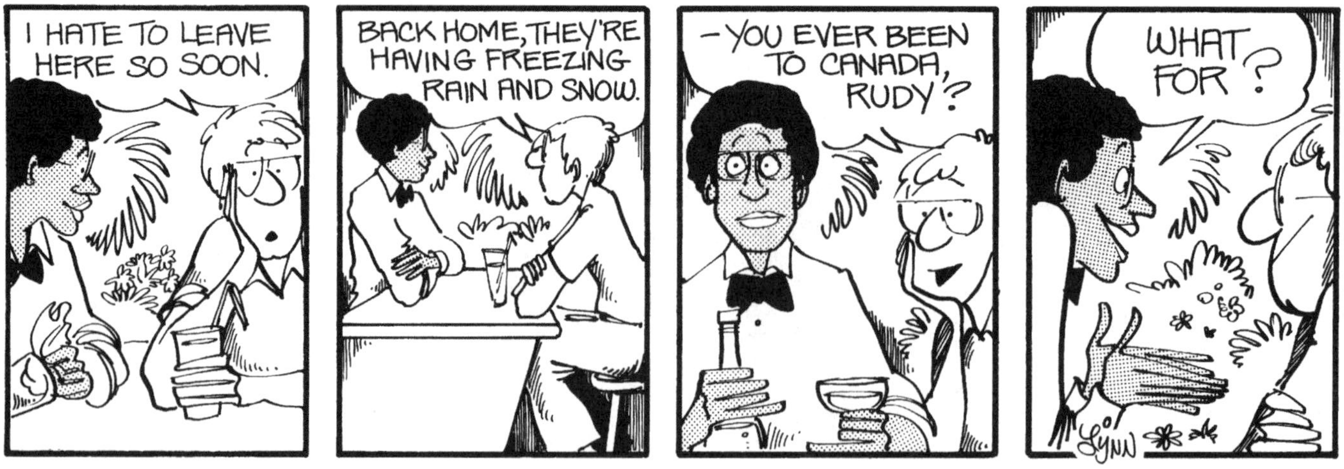
I HATE TO LEAVE HERE SO SOON.
BACK HOME, THEY'RE HAVING FREEZING RAIN AND SNOW.
-YOU EVER BEEN TO CANADA, RUDY?
WHAT FOR?
LYNN

This really was a conversation we had with one of the hotel staff. Rudy had been particularly sweet and we looked forward to seeing him every day. It was as if we had been staying at his house, so naturally we wanted to reciprocate. We asked him if he'd ever been to Canada, thinking we could give him a great tour should he decide to explore our turf, but after seeing us in our parkas and hearing about the weather back home ... this was his response. If you're already in paradise — why leave?!

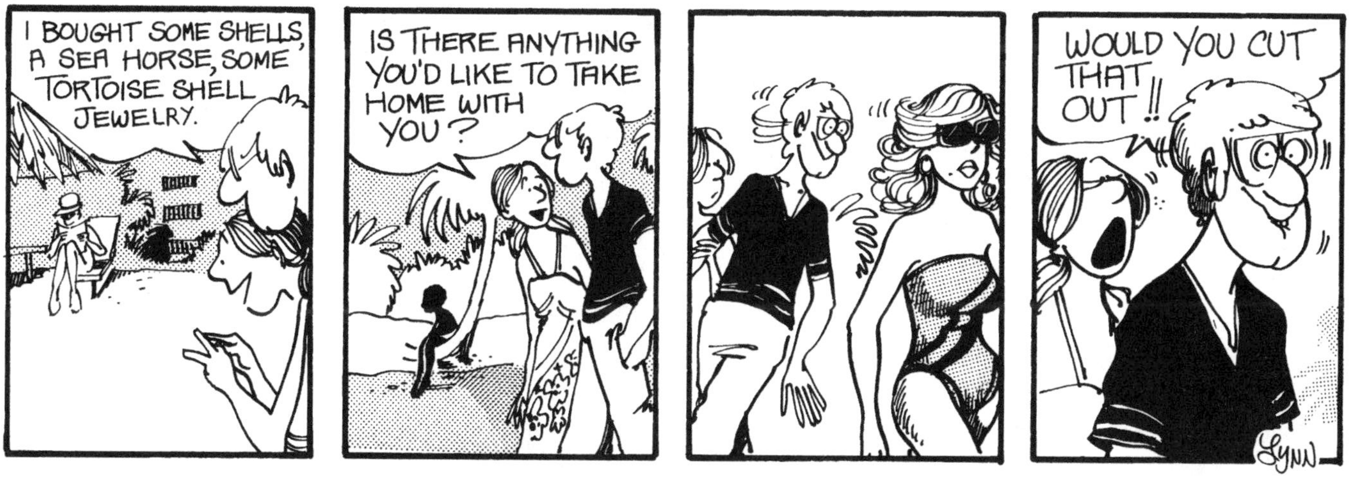
I BOUGHT SOME SHELLS, A SEA HORSE, SOME TORTOISE SHELL JEWELRY.
IS THERE ANYTHING YOU'D LIKE TO TAKE HOME WITH YOU?
WOULD YOU CUT THAT OUT!!
Lynn

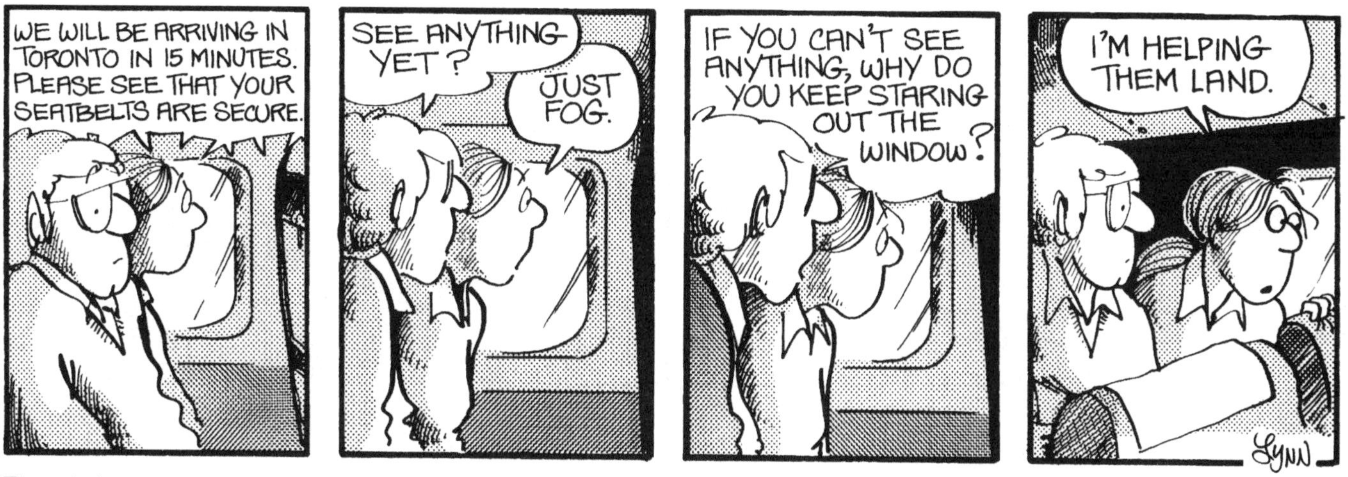
WE WILL BE ARRIVING IN TORONTO IN 15 MINUTES. PLEASE SEE THAT YOUR SEATBELTS ARE SECURE.
SEE ANYTHING YET?
JUST FOG.
IF YOU CAN'T SEE ANYTHING, WHY DO YOU KEEP STARING OUT THE WINDOW?
I'M HELPING THEM LAND.
Lynn

The trip home was a tense one. Our flight was delayed and foggy January conditions made me nervous. I was often more comfortable in our own plane — it felt good to be in control. We could choose not to fly if the weather was bad. Our charter took us back to Winnipeg, but we now had to wait for two more scheduled flights: a small jet to Thompson and the Twin Otter to Lynn Lake. In a commercial aircraft, I had the feeling that I was helping — even if I was just staring at the wing!

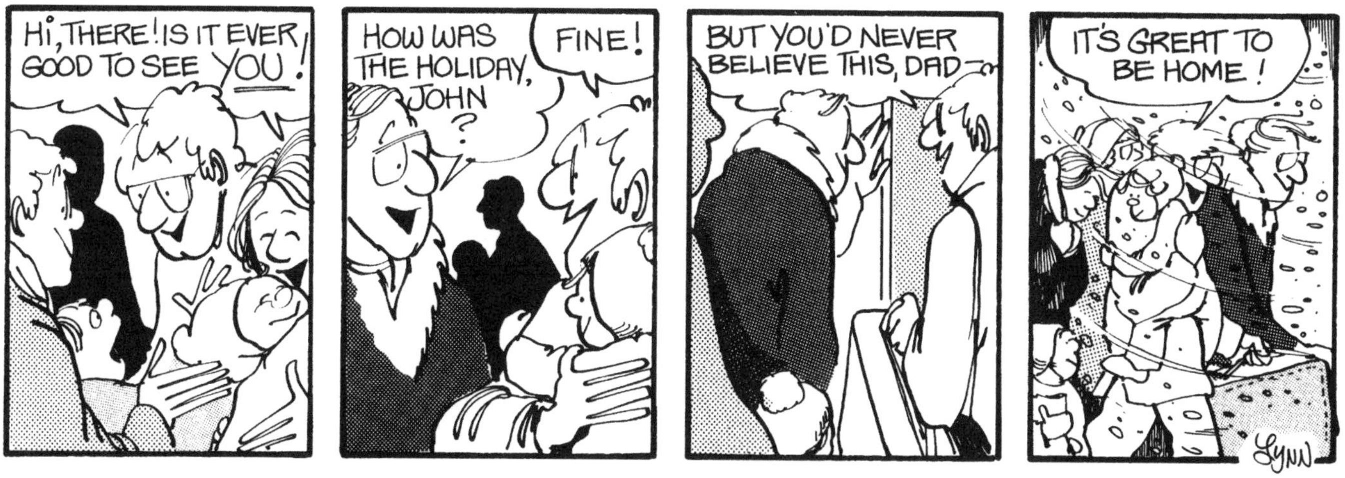
HI, THERE! IS IT EVER GOOD TO SEE YOU!
HOW WAS THE HOLIDAY, JOHN?
FINE!
BUT YOU'D NEVER BELIEVE THIS, DAD—
IT'S GREAT TO BE HOME!
Lynn

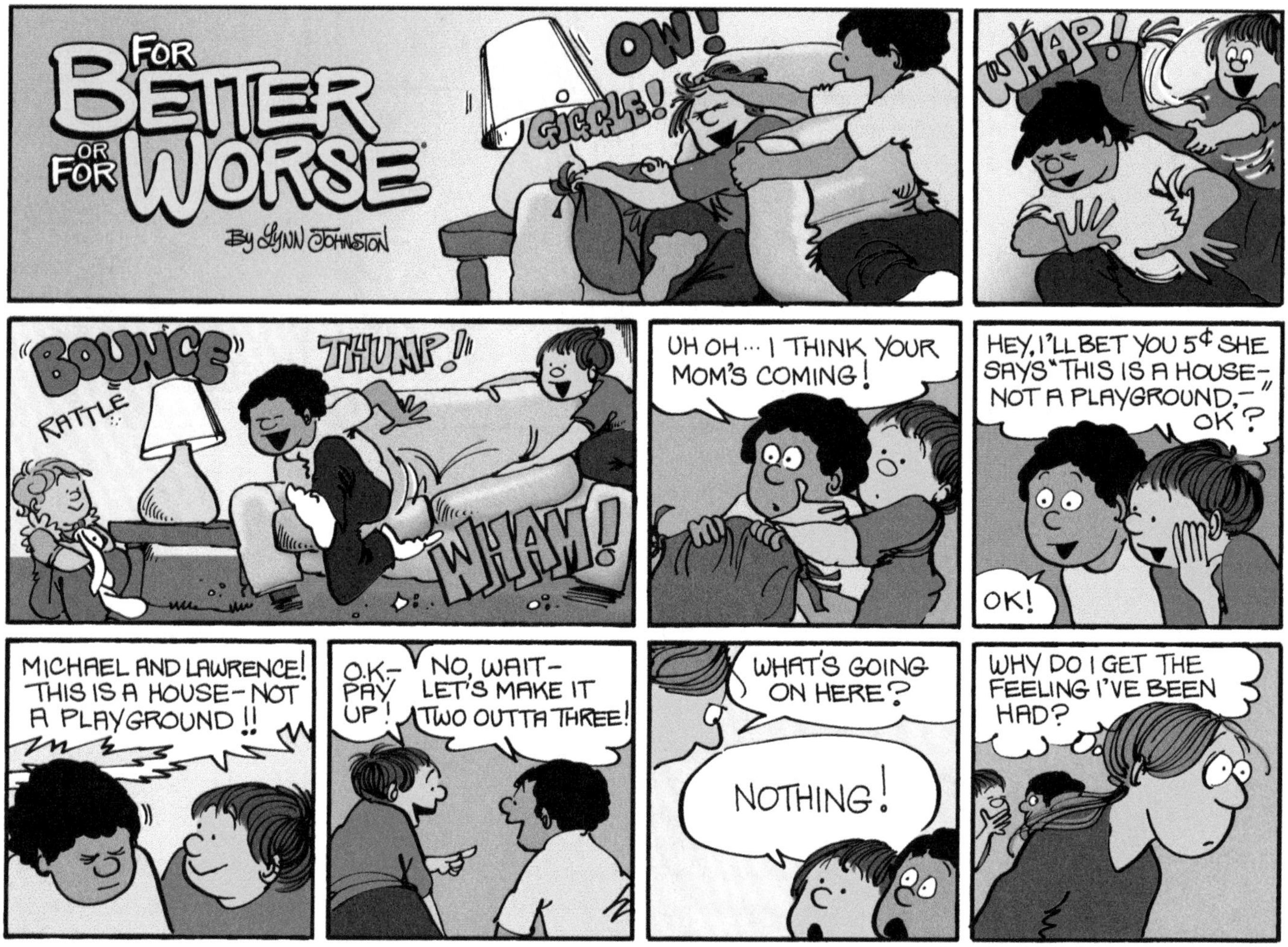
FOR BETTER OR FOR WORSE
BY LYNN JOHNSTON
OW!
GIGGLE!
WHAP!
BOUNCE
THUMP!
RATTLE
WHAM!
UH OH... I THINK YOUR MOM'S COMING!
HEY, I'LL BET YOU 5¢ SHE SAYS "THIS IS A HOUSE - NOT A PLAYGROUND." OK?
OK!
MICHAEL AND LAWRENCE! THIS IS A HOUSE - NOT A PLAYGROUND!!
O.K.- PAY UP!
NO, WAIT- LET'S MAKE IT TWO OUTTA THREE!
WHAT'S GOING ON HERE?
NOTHING!
WHY DO I GET THE FEELING I'VE BEEN HAD?

Our family home in North Vancouver was designed so that a kid could run from the kitchen to the hall, around to the living room, and back into the kitchen again. This made for an excellent track and field event, should it be raining, and it usually was. Mom was long suffering, stoic, and understanding. She let my brother and me blow off steam while she stewed silently, knowing that kids need the exercise. She drew the line at our jumping on the furniture, though, and her admonishments were almost always the same: "This is a house, not a playground!" or "I am sick, sore, fed up, and tired!" Then there was Dad's fave: "Are you cruising for a bruising?" Alan and I could almost mouth the words as they were spoken — but heaven help you if you were caught!

When my own kids took to racing around the house, I heard myself saying the same things my mom said to us — and a new understanding between my mom and I erased some of the wall that had separated us for so long. I knew that my kids had memorized my litany of commands and I now knew how she felt. At long last, my mom was vindicated! Someday ... it will be MY turn!

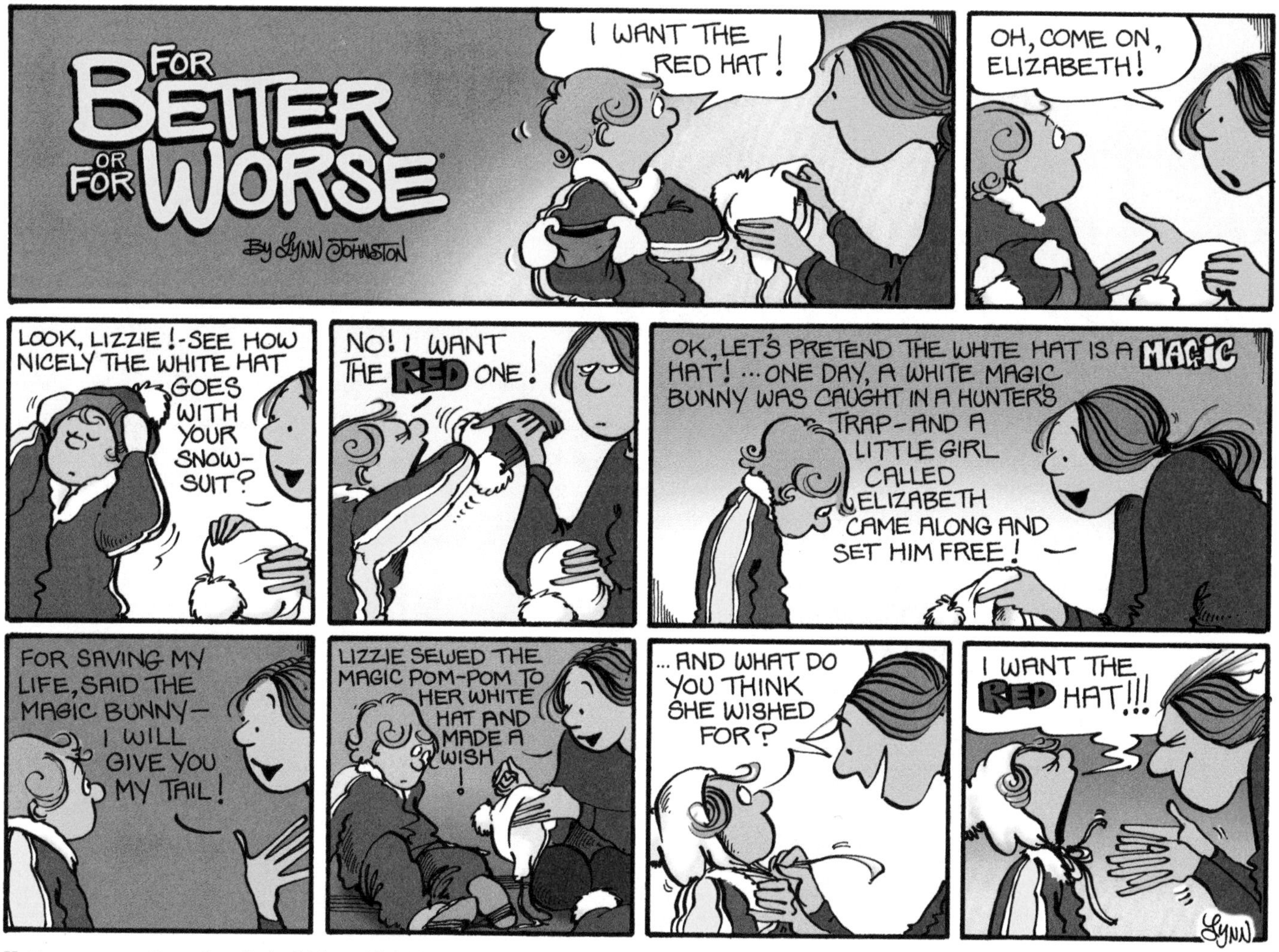
FOR BETTER OR FOR WORSE
BY LYNN JOHNSTON
I WANT THE RED HAT!
OH, COME ON, ELIZABETH!
LOOK, LIZZIE!-SEE HOW NICELY THE WHITE HAT GOES WITH YOUR SNOW-SUIT?
NO! I WANT THE RED ONE!
OK, LET'S PRETEND THE WHITE HAT IS A MAGIC HAT! ...ONE DAY, A WHITE MAGIC BUNNY WAS CAUGHT IN A HUNTER'S TRAP- AND A LITTLE GIRL CALLED ELIZABETH CAME ALONG AND SET HIM FREE!
FOR SAVING MY LIFE, SAID THE MAGIC BUNNY- I WILL GIVE YOU MY TAIL!
LIZZIE SEWED THE MAGIC POM-POM TO HER WHITE HAT AND MADE A WISH!
...AND WHAT DO YOU THINK SHE WISHED FOR?
I WANT THE RED HAT!!!
LYNN

Katie was an attractive little kid and I fell into the "momtrap" of wanting her to look as cute as possible at all times. I had the adorable outfits, the velvet dresses, hats, scarves, and mittens that matched her "girlie" snowsuits. I combed her hair just so and awaited the gooey compliments that come while showing off a preened and perfect princess.

Kate, however, wanted nothing to do with looking cute. Being comfortable was far more important. She wanted to wear what she darned well wanted to wear! She was determined and stubborn, and it was abundantly clear by the time she was three that what she wore would be a compromise. The red hat was actually a patterned toque, and I would have drawn it that way, except that the pattern was too complicated to draw and too hard to colour!

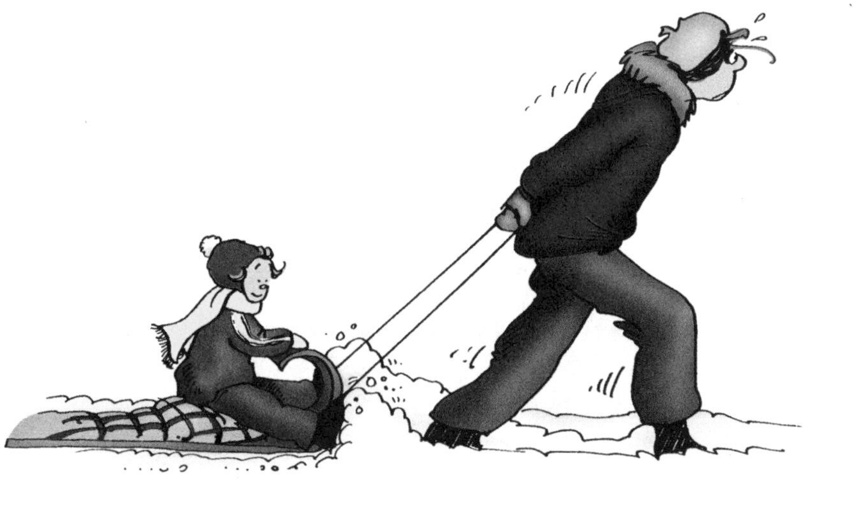

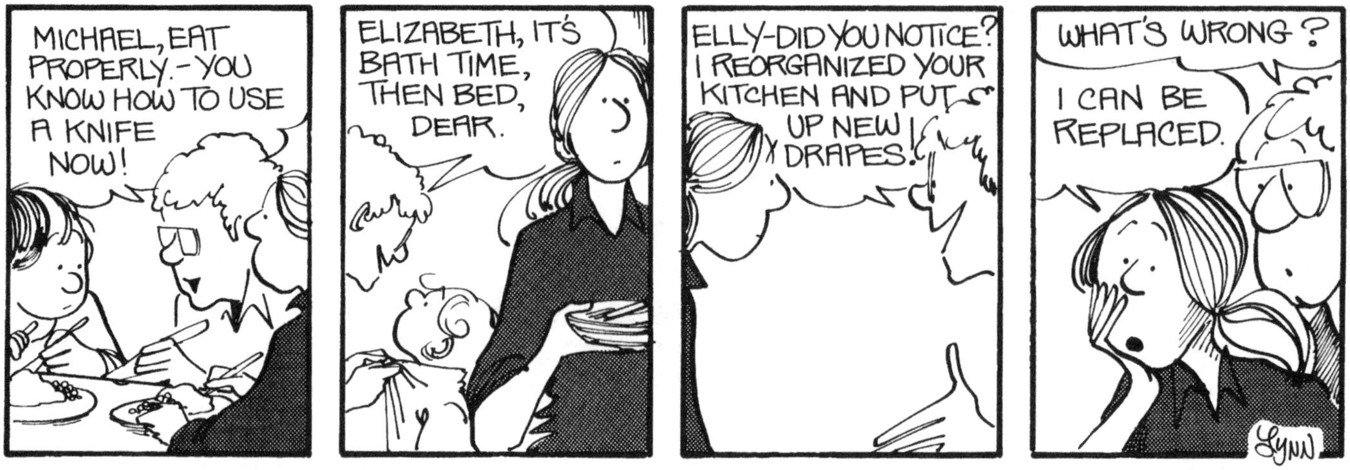
MICHAEL, EAT PROPERLY.-YOU KNOW HOW TO USE A KNIFE NOW!
ELIZABETH, IT'S BATH TIME, THEN BED, DEAR.
ELLY-DID YOU NOTICE? I REORGANIZED YOUR KITCHEN AND PUT UP NEW DRAPES!
WHAT'S WRONG?
I CAN BE REPLACED.
LYNN

After two weeks in her care, Aaron and Katie were now doing things Ruth's way and it took some time before they returned to the nest I had built. Ruth had given them a new routine and some new rules. Ruth's parenting style was something I admired and respected, but it was different. When I came home, I wanted to resume my role as the alpha female! Seeing this in pen and ink was therapeutic. Sometimes the strip provided an outlet that was healing and healthy for all of us.

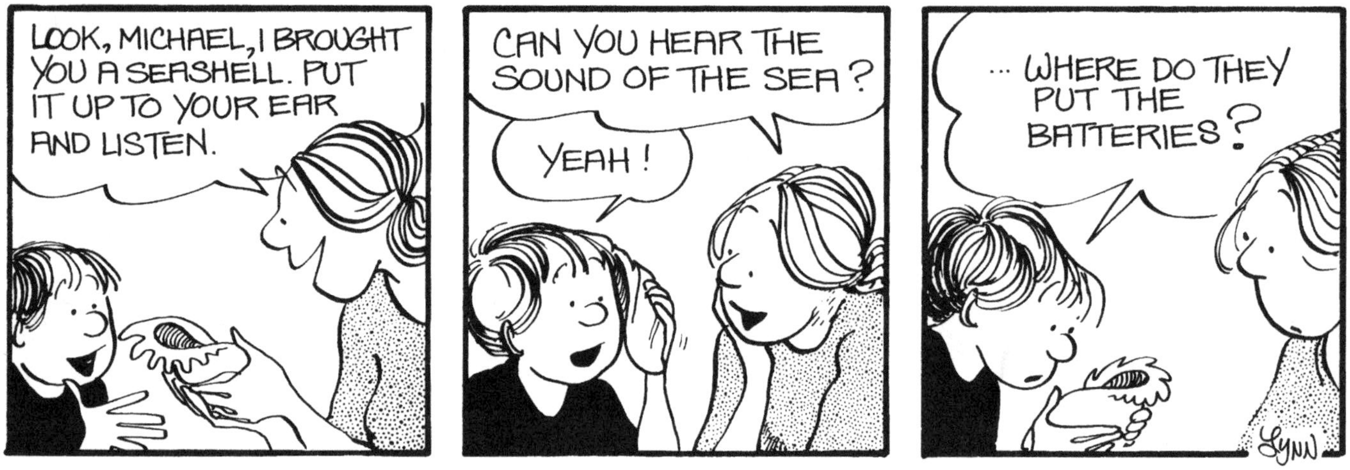
LOOK, MICHAEL, I BROUGHT YOU A SEASHELL. PUT IT UP TO YOUR EAR AND LISTEN.
CAN YOU HEAR THE SOUND OF THE SEA?
YEAH!
... WHERE DO THEY PUT THE BATTERIES?
LYNN

I did bring home a seashell from Barbados. It sits on my bathroom windowsill today as a reminder of the several trips we made to the same pretty hotel. The man who sold it to me explained that conch shells are often too delicate to survive the recovery. They chip easily and the locals remove the roughness by filing away the edge of the shell, making it smooth and even. This one is perfect!

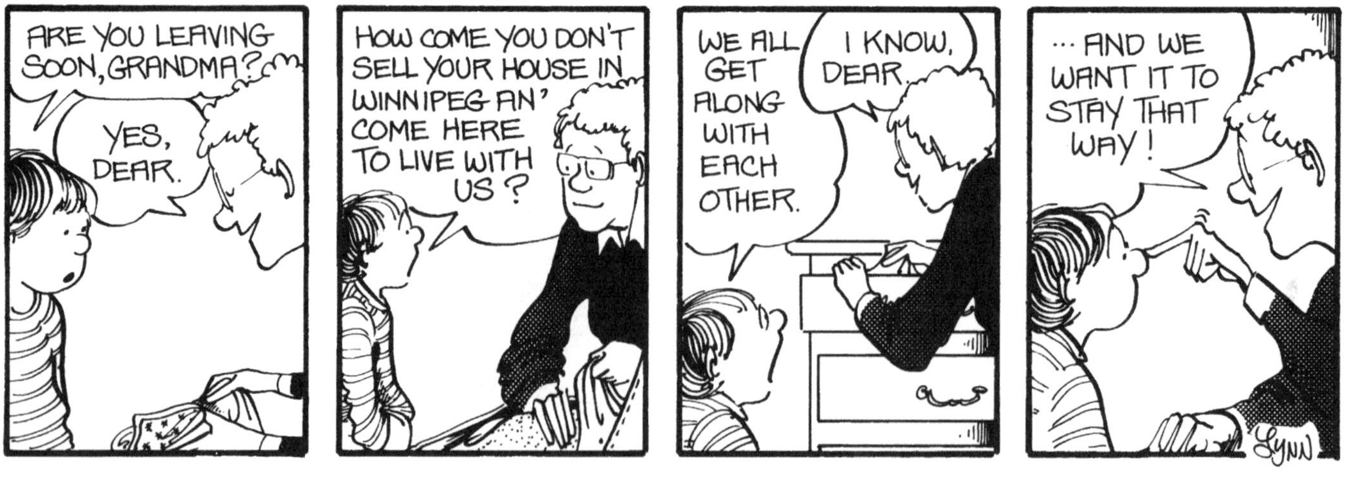
ARE YOU LEAVING SOON, GRANDMA?
YES, DEAR.
HOW COME YOU DON'T SELL YOUR HOUSE IN WINNIPEG AN' COME HERE TO LIVE WITH US?
WE ALL GET ALONG WITH EACH OTHER.
I KNOW, DEAR.
... AND WE WANT IT TO STAY THAT WAY!
LYNN

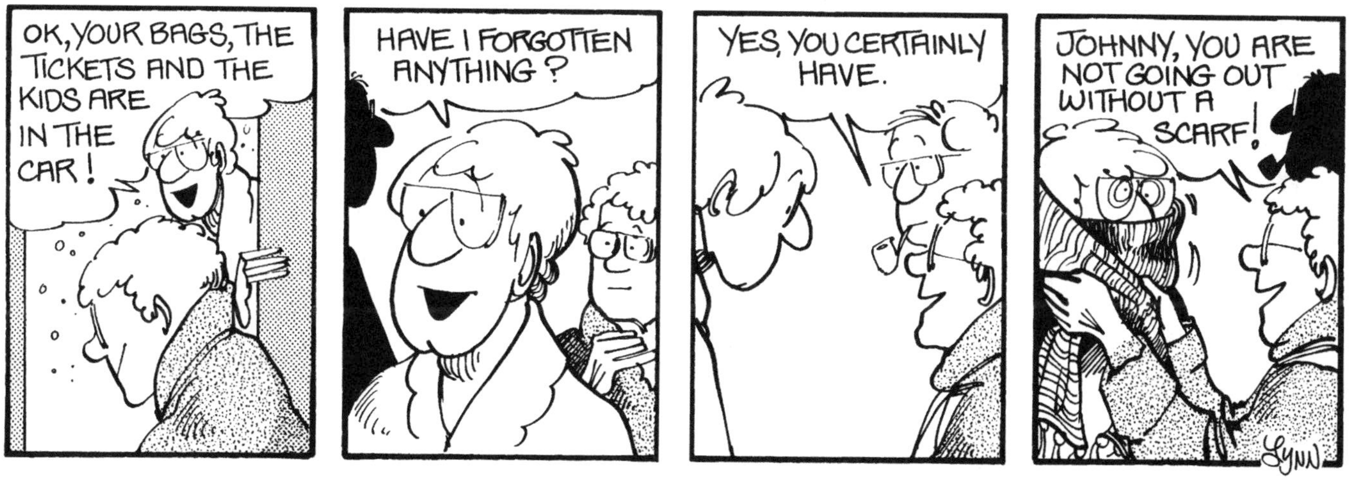
OK, YOUR BAGS, THE TICKETS AND THE KIDS ARE IN THE CAR!
HAVE I FORGOTTEN ANYTHING?
YES, YOU CERTAINLY HAVE.
JOHNNY, YOU ARE NOT GOING OUT WITHOUT A SCARF!
LYNN

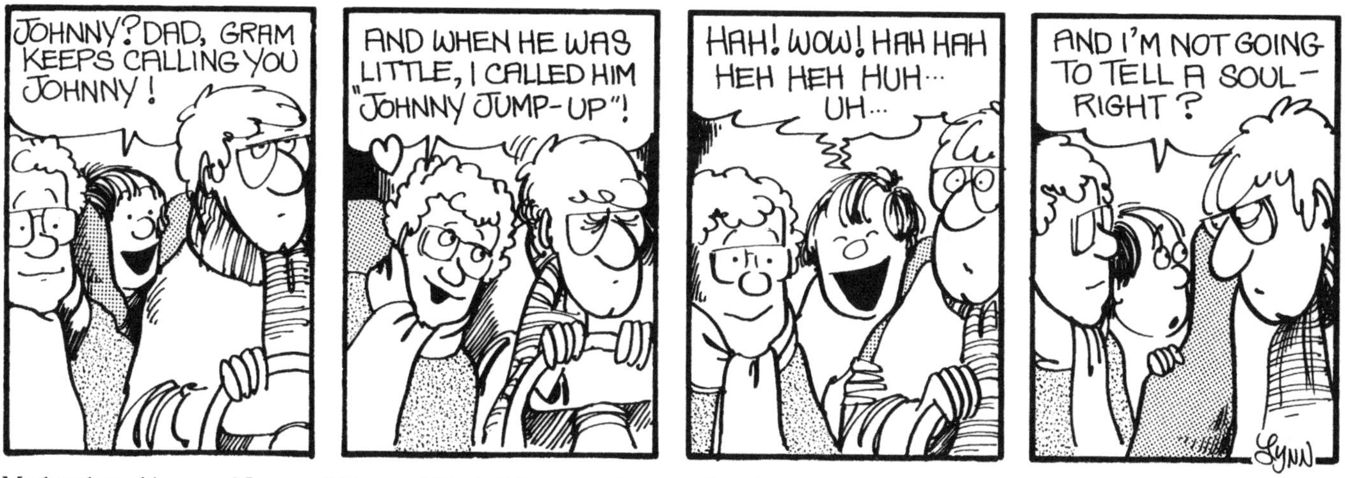
JOHNNY? DAD, GRAM KEEPS CALLING YOU JOHNNY!
AND WHEN HE WAS LITTLE, I CALLED HIM "JOHNNY JUMP-UP"!
HAH! WOW! HAH HAH HEH HEH HUH… UH…
AND I'M NOT GOING TO TELL A SOUL - RIGHT?
LYNN

My brother, Alan, and I were "Alsy and Lindy." I was perhaps eight when I began to hate my nickname. I refused to come if someone called me Lindy and eventually my parents gave in and called me Lynn. These names weren't nearly as irritating as the names we called each other. My brother and I had nicknames that continue to this day — and I won't repeat them. We enjoy an affectionate and peaceful relationship and I don't want that to change!

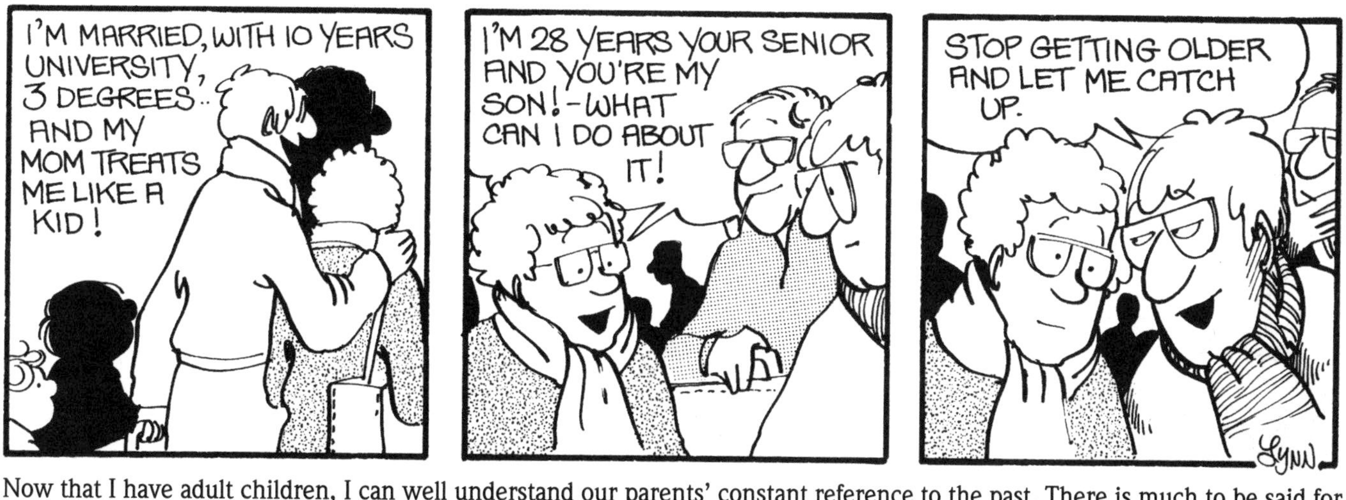
I'M MARRIED, WITH 10 YEARS UNIVERSITY, 3 DEGREES.. AND MY MOM TREATS ME LIKE A KID!
I'M 28 YEARS YOUR SENIOR AND YOU'RE MY SON! - WHAT CAN I DO ABOUT IT!
STOP GETTING OLDER AND LET ME CATCH UP.
LYNN

Now that I have adult children, I can well understand our parents' constant reference to the past. There is much to be said for having passed through the parenting phase and into senior citizenship. I have paid my dues and am enjoying the company of two children I'm proud to see productively out on their own. I consider them my equals — even though I remind them to eat well and keep warm.

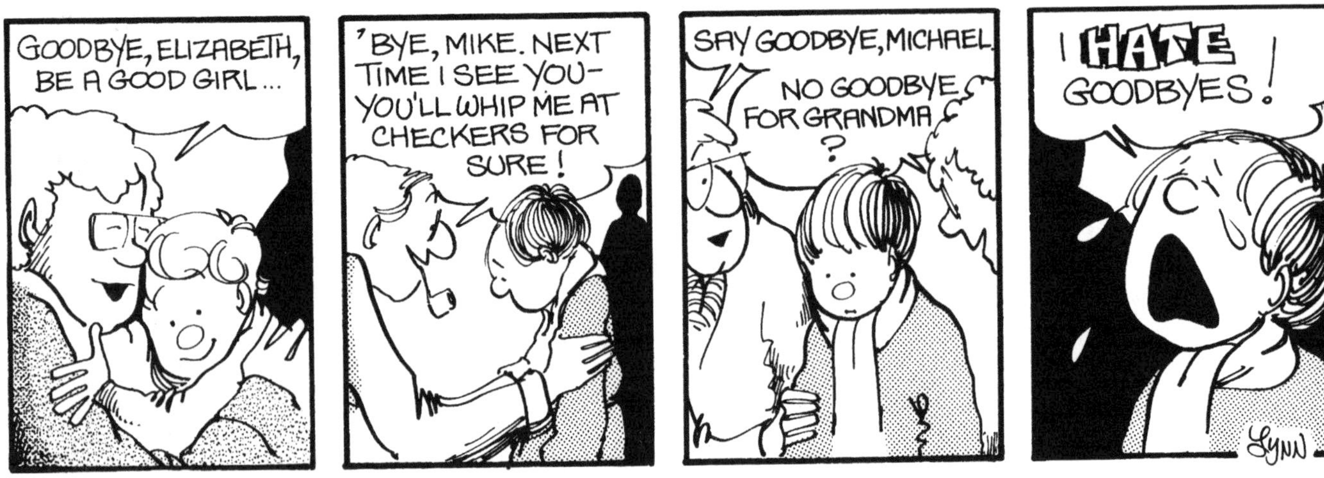
GOODBYE, ELIZABETH, BE A GOOD GIRL...
'BYE, MIKE. NEXT TIME I SEE YOU- YOU'LL WHIP ME AT CHECKERS FOR SURE!
SAY GOODBYE, MICHAEL
NO GOODBYE FOR GRANDMA ?
I HATE GOODBYES!

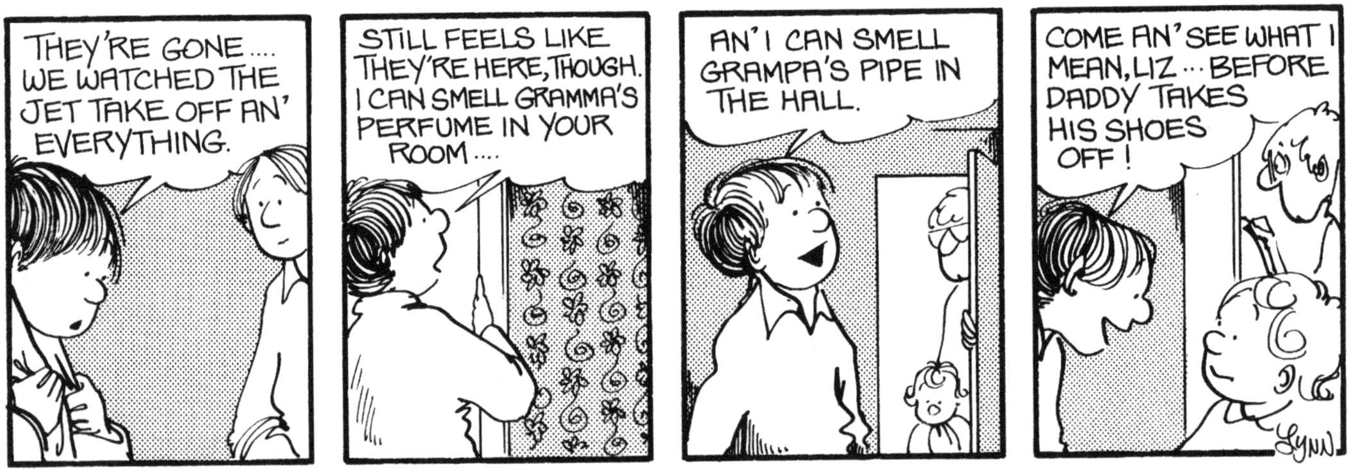
THEY'RE GONE.... WE WATCHED THE JET TAKE OFF AN' EVERYTHING.
STILL FEELS LIKE THEY'RE HERE, THOUGH. I CAN SMELL GRAMMA'S PERFUME IN YOUR ROOM....
AN' I CAN SMELL GRAMPA'S PIPE IN THE HALL.
COME AN' SEE WHAT I MEAN, LIZ... BEFORE DADDY TAKES HIS SHOES OFF!

When I was about fourteen, my father's mother came to stay with us after my grandfather died. She was given my bedroom and I moved into the unfinished basement — a space as famous for its spooks as it was for its spiders. After six long months, Grandma finally returned home. Even though she had gone and I had mucked out my bedroom, the essence of Grandma remained. For some time, her smell lingered in the halls and the living room. This is the memory behind this comic strip!

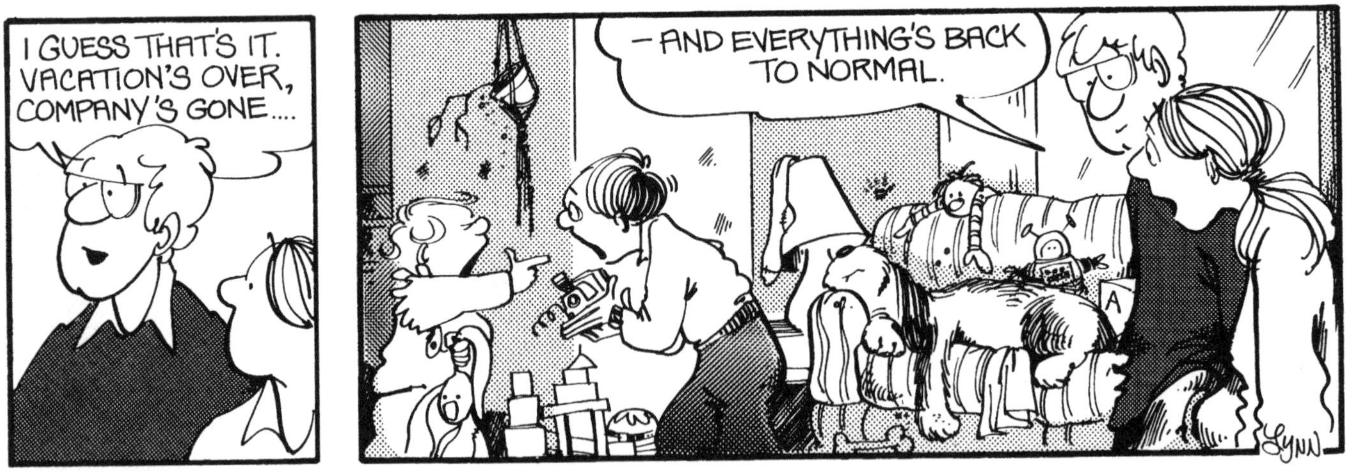
I GUESS THAT'S IT. VACATION'S OVER, COMPANY'S GONE....
—AND EVERYTHING'S BACK TO NORMAL.

They say that "normal" means different things to different people. For us, normal morphed as the kids grew and changed. I recently went to visit friends of my daughter's. Brooke and Matthew have twin daughters, six months old. The girls are just starting to toddle and their small living room is strewn with blankets and toys. Brooke apologized for the mess. I said, "Don't worry, relax — I understand. You have two little kids! ... This is normal!!!"

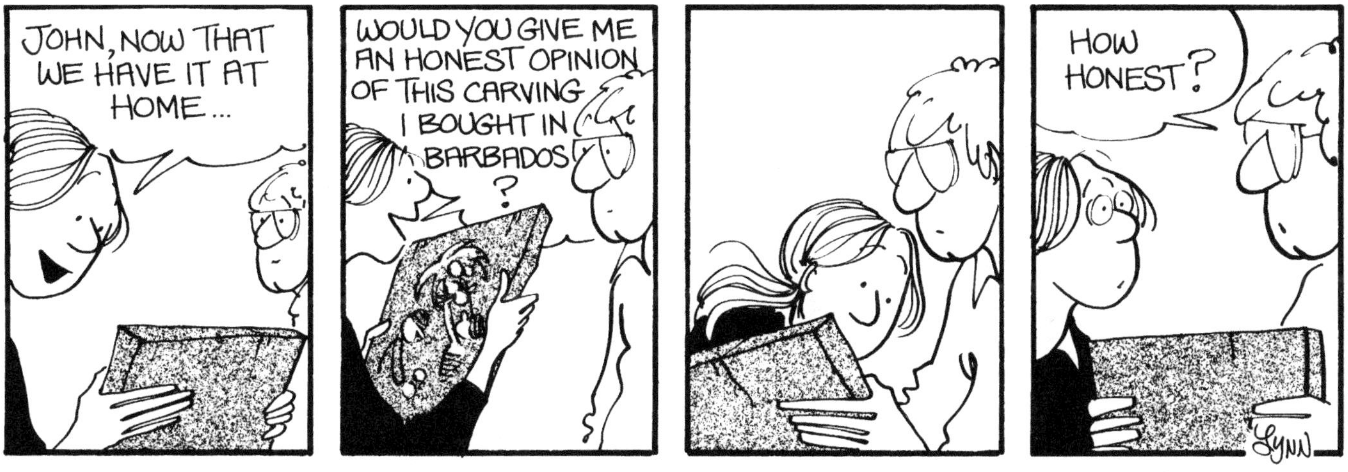
JOHN, NOW THAT WE HAVE IT AT HOME...
WOULD YOU GIVE ME AN HONEST OPINION OF THIS CARVING I BOUGHT IN BARBADOS?
HOW HONEST?
LYNN

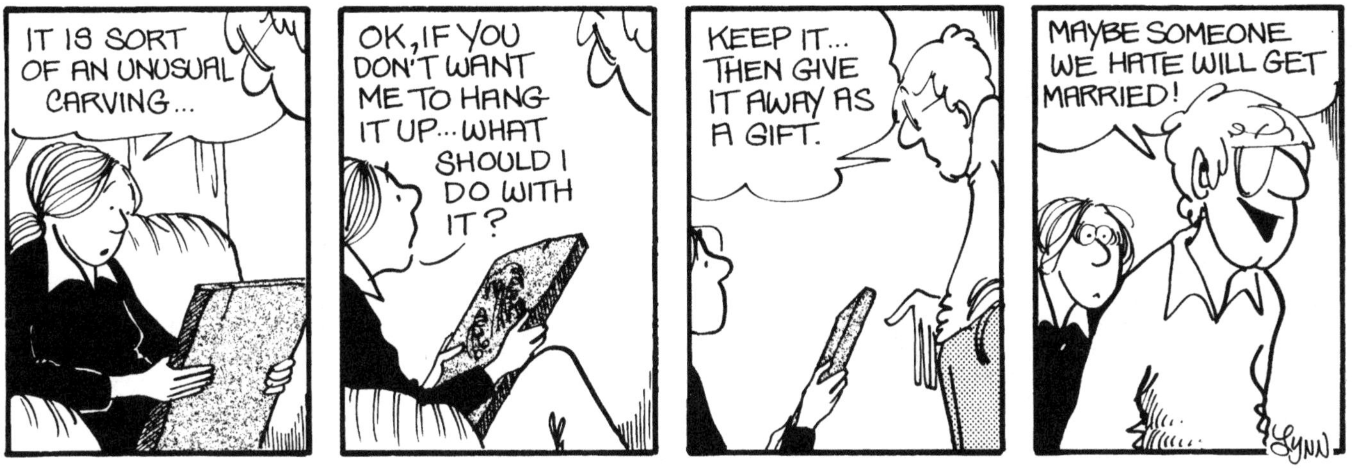
IT IS SORT OF AN UNUSUAL CARVING...
OK, IF YOU DON'T WANT ME TO HANG IT UP... WHAT SHOULD I DO WITH IT?
KEEP IT... THEN GIVE IT AWAY AS A GIFT.
MAYBE SOMEONE WE HATE WILL GET MARRIED!
LYNN

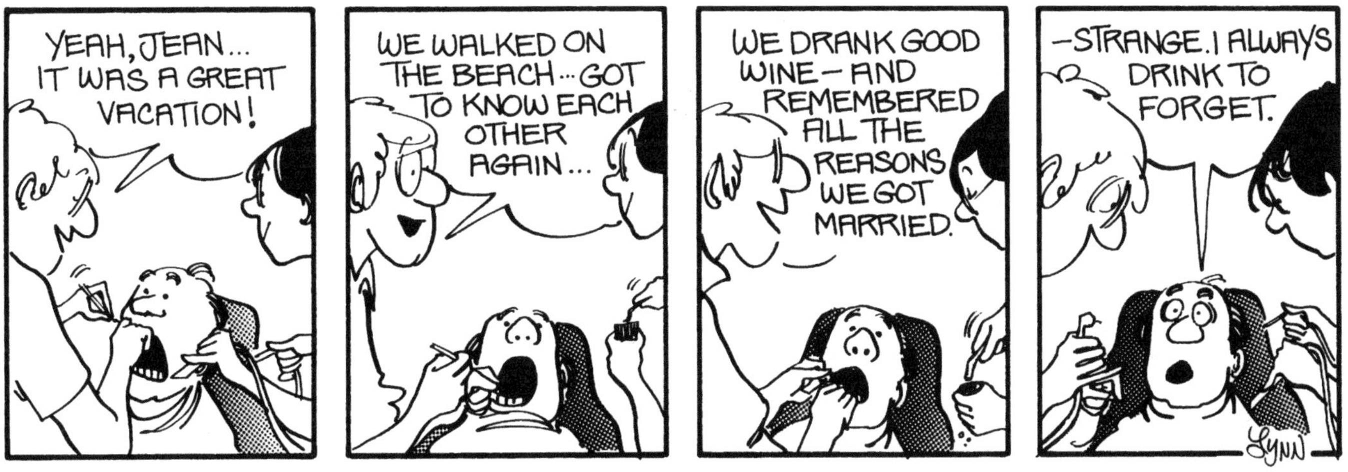
YEAH, JEAN... IT WAS A GREAT VACATION!
WE WALKED ON THE BEACH... GOT TO KNOW EACH OTHER AGAIN...
WE DRANK GOOD WINE — AND REMEMBERED ALL THE REASONS WE GOT MARRIED.
—STRANGE. I ALWAYS DRINK TO FORGET.
LYNN

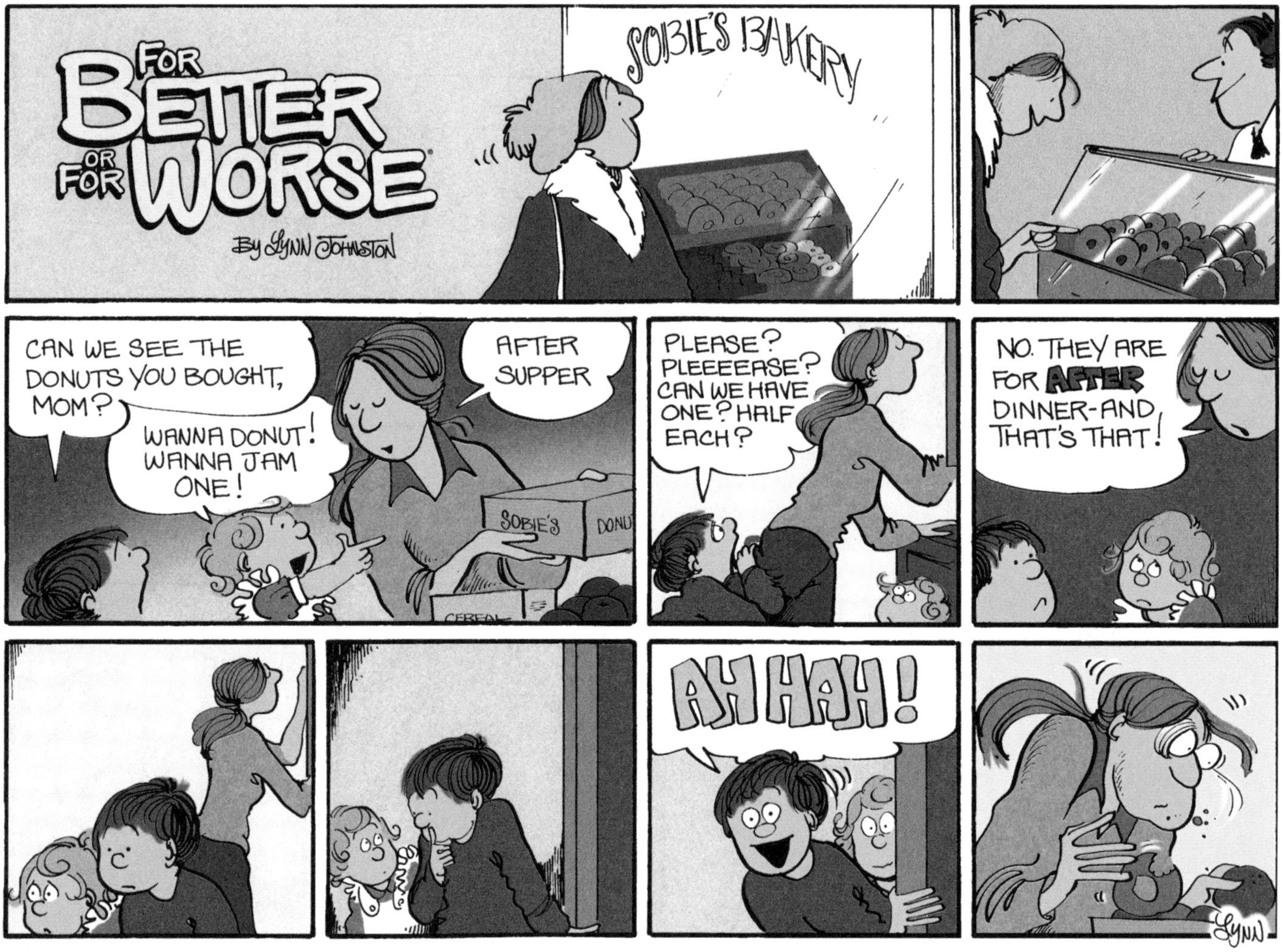

FOR BETTER OR FOR WORSE
By Lynn Johnston
SOBIE'S BAKERY
CAN WE SEE THE DONUTS YOU BOUGHT, MOM?
WANNA DONUT! WANNA JAM ONE!
AFTER SUPPER
SOBIE'S
PLEASE? PLEEEEASE? CAN WE HAVE ONE? HALF EACH?
NO. THEY ARE FOR AFTER DINNER-AND THAT'S THAT!
AH HAH!
Lynn


Sobie's Bakery in Lynn Lake was one of the highlights of the town. Mr. and Mrs. Sobie would be up long before sunrise to get the bread out for the day. You could pick up the scent all the way from the post office. Spice cake was my personal favourite, but their doughnuts came in an easy second. Sobie's was the only bakery for hundreds of miles around. Folks from Leaf Rapids (a 60-mile wilderness drive south) would come all the way to Lynn Lake just to shop at Sobie's. We didn't realize what a gem we had until we moved away. Nobody could decorate with icing like Mrs Sobie. Nobody, except perhaps Grandma Ruth, made better buns.

People would order a spice cake for almost every occasion. I looked forward to these huge, moist desserts covered with cream cheese icing, decorated with coloured artwork — and piped with flowers around the edge. Some, however, got tired of them, and when my friend Nancy Lawn moved to Edmonton, she said, "At least I don't ever have to eat another Sobie's spice cake!"

A year or so later, we decided to fly out west to visit the Lawns in their new home. As a joke, I had Mrs. Sobie make up a big spice cake with double the icing and as ornate as possible. Nancy and Jim met our small plane at the airport. She spied the Sobie's box right away. "That's not a spice cake!" she shouted. "Ahhh!"

I said, "I thought you might need one."

"Have you any idea how much I've MISSED those things?" she cried, opening the box and nicking a fingerful of icing. When we got to her house, she immediately put the cake out of sight, telling us we couldn't have any. "It's OURS," she said. "You can have Sobie's spice cake any time ... you live right there!"

I think I gave the Sobie family the original of this cartoon. I don't think I ever told them how much I missed their bakery, but I hope they remember me as fondly as I remember them.

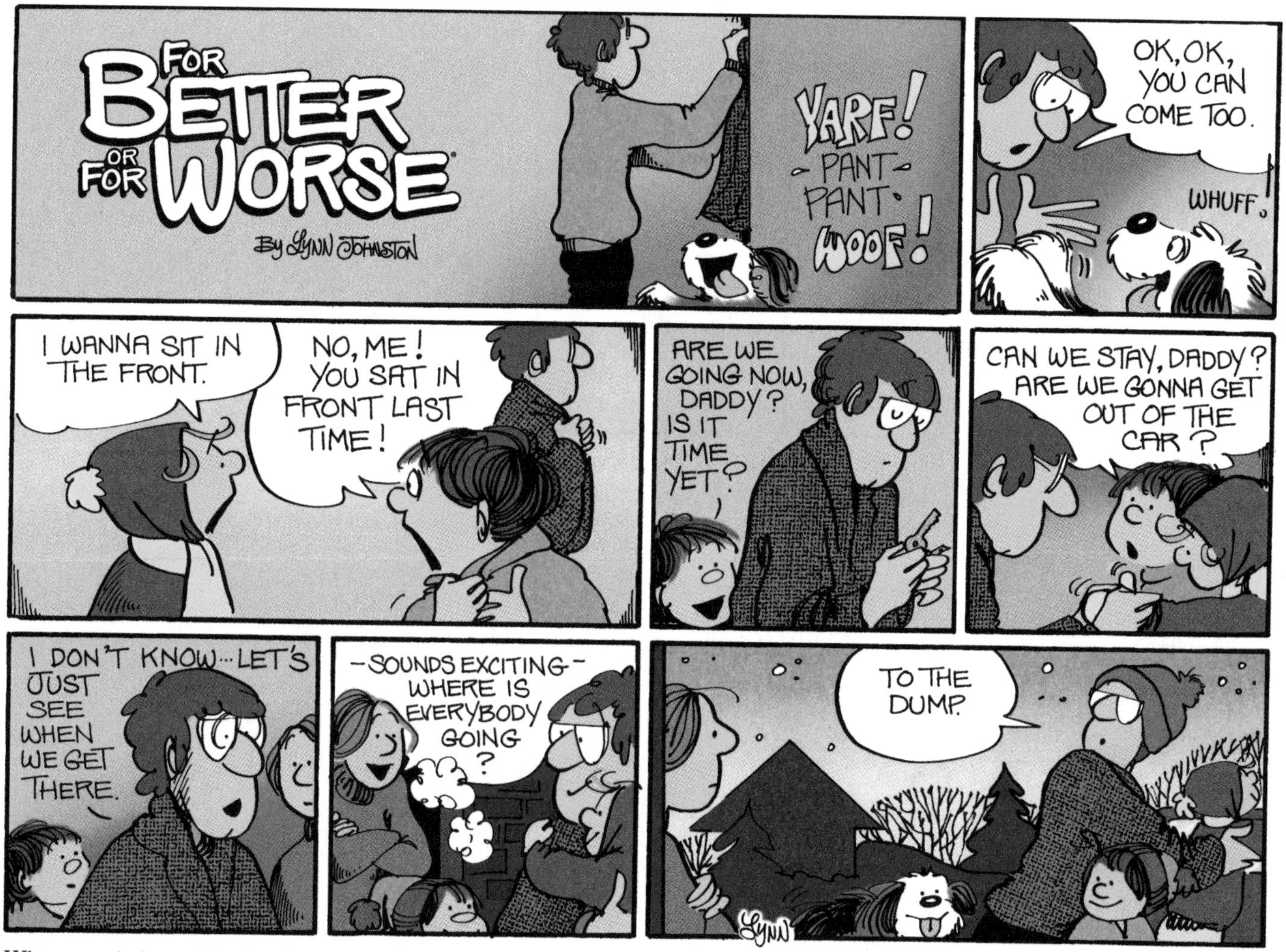
FOR BETTER OR FOR WORSE
BY LYNN JOHNSTON
YARF! PANT PANT WOOF!
OK, OK, YOU CAN COME TOO.
WHUFF.
I WANNA SIT IN THE FRONT.
NO, ME! YOU SAT IN FRONT LAST TIME!
ARE WE GOING NOW, DADDY? IS IT TIME YET?
CAN WE STAY, DADDY? ARE WE GONNA GET OUT OF THE CAR?
I DON'T KNOW... LET'S JUST SEE WHEN WE GET THERE.
-SOUNDS EXCITING- WHERE IS EVERYBODY GOING?
TO THE DUMP.
LYNN

When my dad went to the dump, we always wondered if he'd bring home more than he left there. The North Vancouver dump was about six miles from home, then a circuitous drive down a long dirt road. Going there was as exciting as anything we ever did on a weekend, and my brother and I would fight for the front seat when we saw the folks pitching stuff into the back end of the car.

A great chain-link fence ran around the "nuisance grounds," and the "dump man" would meet us at the gate. He'd roll his cigarette to the side of his mouth and ask what we were bringing in. Then he'd direct us to the appropriate space in the compound, and Dad would steer the old green Volvo into position for the drop. After we'd made our deposit, we were free to check out the scattered offerings, hoping to find some treasure. The smell of wet paper, burning fabric, and decay was not too bad — considering the fact that stuff here was FREE, so we happily climbed over the rubble on our quest for the perfect thing to rescue and take home.

The dump man was cool. He didn't have a uniform, but he had a sort of military air. He enjoyed his place of authority, and the fact that Dad brought him a beer now and then improved our chances of getting out with something big!

The score I remember most was the gooseneck lamp that Dad found. It was a greeny-grey ... brass, I think, and not too badly scarred from the fire. The cord and plug looked good, and Pop figured this was just the thing to go on his workbench downstairs. Mom, of course, was unimpressed, and quietly told me later that she expected it would be gone in a fortnight — if she had anything to do with it.

When our parents passed away, there in the basement on Dad's workbench was the gooseneck lamp. It had followed them for forty years, and was now an heirloom. The trouble with heirlooms is ... the heirs have to decide what to do with them. Alan and I thought about taking it to the dump, but we couldn't.

Alan is retired from teaching now and has a workshop in his basement. He makes one-of-a-kind kayaks and canoes. He has a nice workbench where he cuts wood and copper, which he carefully sets into the sides of his kayaks. Illuminating his workbench is the gooseneck lamp.

*

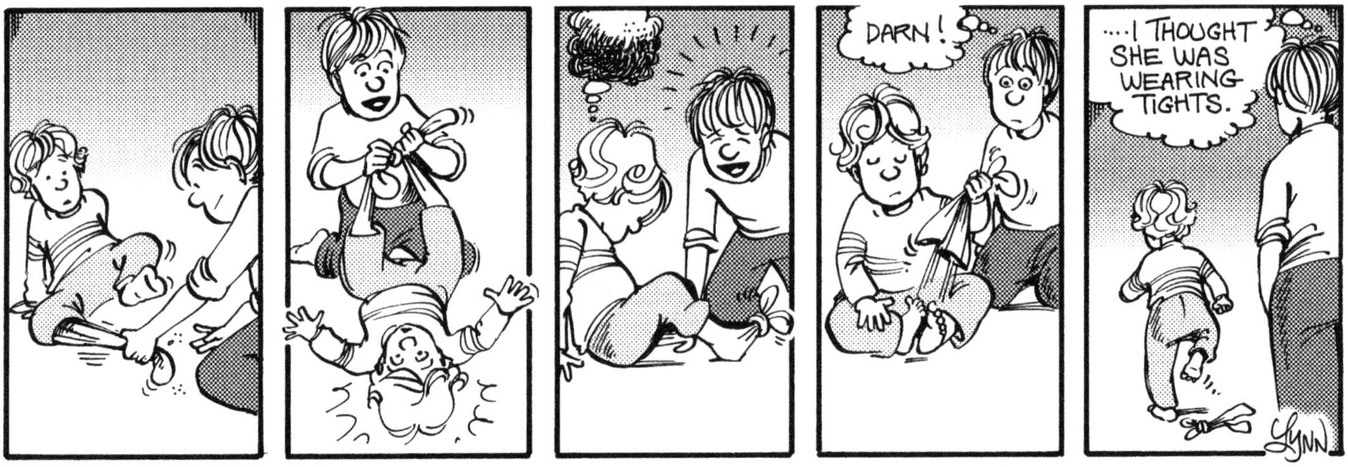
DARN!
...I THOUGHT SHE WAS WEARING TIGHTS.
LYNN

For some reason, we lost a week of dailies. We looked in the archives, pulled out old negatives and checked the collection books — and still, six days out of this year were missing. We discovered that the week had never been published. Terrible winter weather caused shipping problems, so this week never made it to the syndicate, and has been lost forever. Now we send the strips electronically and don't have that problem anymore.

*

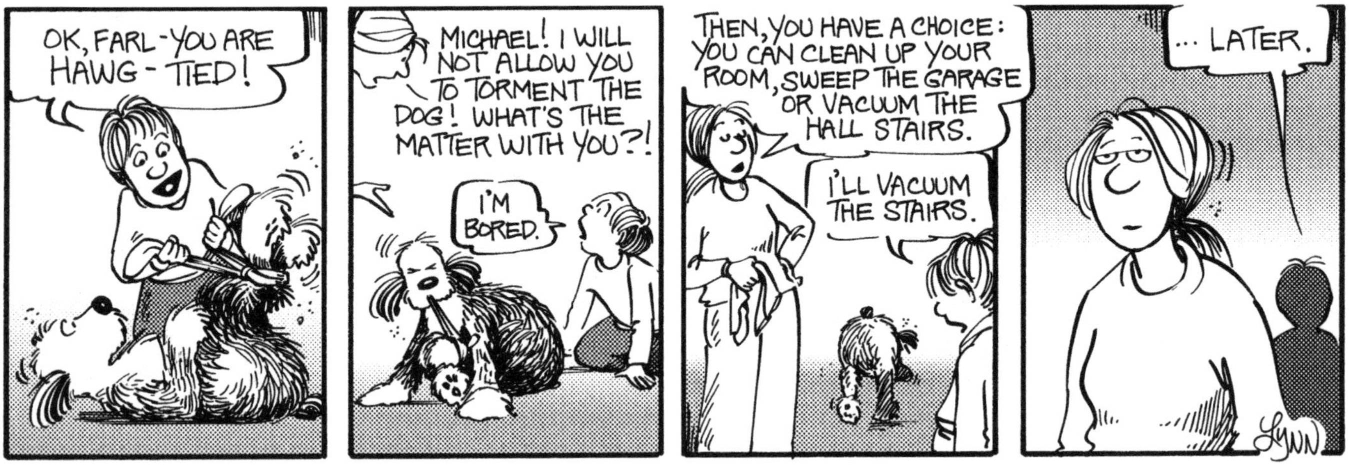
OK, FARL-YOU ARE HAWG-TIED!
MICHAEL! I WILL NOT ALLOW YOU TO TORMENT THE DOG! WHAT'S THE MATTER WITH YOU?!
I'M BORED.
THEN, YOU HAVE A CHOICE: YOU CAN CLEAN UP YOUR ROOM, SWEEP THE GARAGE OR VACUUM THE HALL STAIRS.
I'LL VACUUM THE STAIRS.
... LATER.
LYNN

Kevin called and asked me to draw up a new week of dailies to fill in the space. This is the week! It was fun to do. I haven't had to produce new FBorFW material for a while and I was surprised by how easy it was to get back into the routine. The trouble is — what used to take me a few hours now takes me a few days.

*

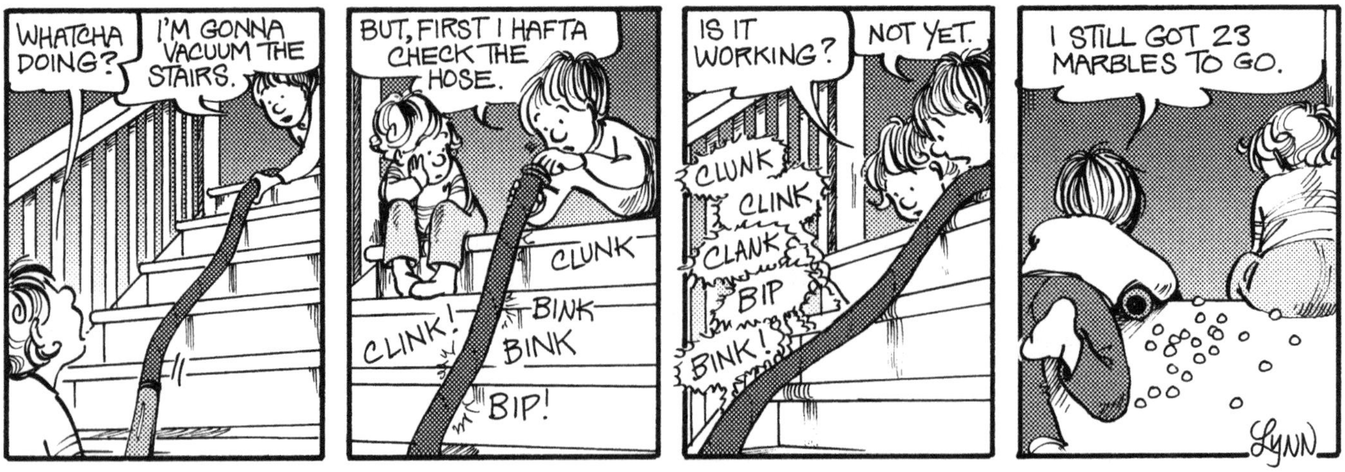
WHATCHA DOING?
I'M GONNA VACUUM THE STAIRS.
BUT, FIRST I HAFTA CHECK THE HOSE.
CLUNK
CLINK!
BINK
BINK
BIP!
IS IT WORKING?
NOT YET.
CLUNK
CLINK
CLANK
BIP
BINK!
I STILL GOT 23 MARBLES TO GO.
LYNN

When I was a kid, we had a dark maroon vacuum cleaner. My mother, having given in to anything "safe" that would keep us occupied, allowed my brother and me to roll marbles down the hose into the basement. Coins, buttons, stones, and gumballs took the plunge. The exhaust end of the vacuum was another source of entertainment. We tried to inflate balloons, kitchen gloves, and the bulb on the turkey baster — imaginary missiles we hoped to inflict on the neighbourhood. Those were the days!

*

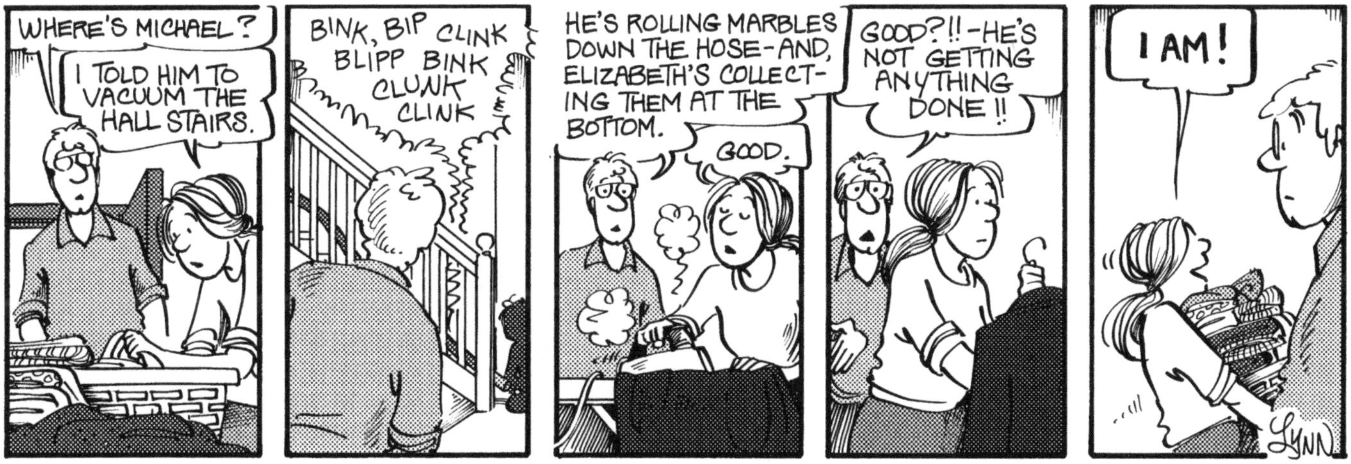
WHERE'S MICHAEL?
I TOLD HIM TO VACUUM THE HALL STAIRS.
BINK, BIP CLINK BLIPP BINK CLUNK CLINK
HE'S ROLLING MARBLES DOWN THE HOSE-AND, ELIZABETH'S COLLECT-ING THEM AT THE BOTTOM.
GOOD.
GOOD?!! -HE'S NOT GETTING ANYTHING DONE!!
I AM!
LYNN

*

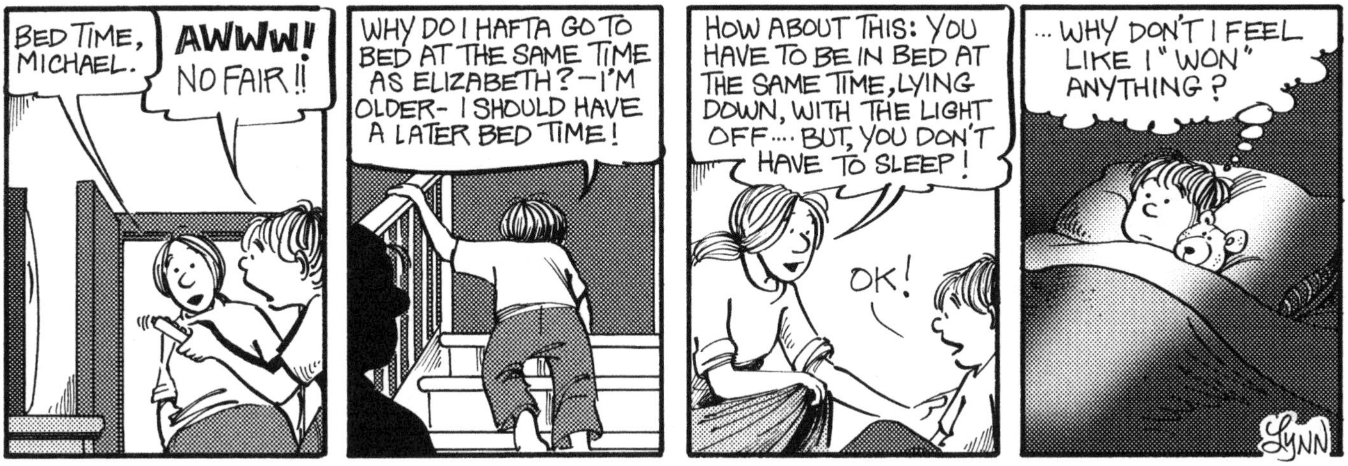
BED TIME, MICHAEL.
AWWW! NO FAIR!!
WHY DO I HAFTA GO TO BED AT THE SAME TIME AS ELIZABETH? -I'M OLDER- I SHOULD HAVE A LATER BED TIME!
HOW ABOUT THIS: YOU HAVE TO BE IN BED AT THE SAME TIME, LYING DOWN, WITH THE LIGHT OFF.... BUT, YOU DON'T HAVE TO SLEEP!
OK!
...WHY DON'T I FEEL LIKE I "WON" ANYTHING?
LYNN

*

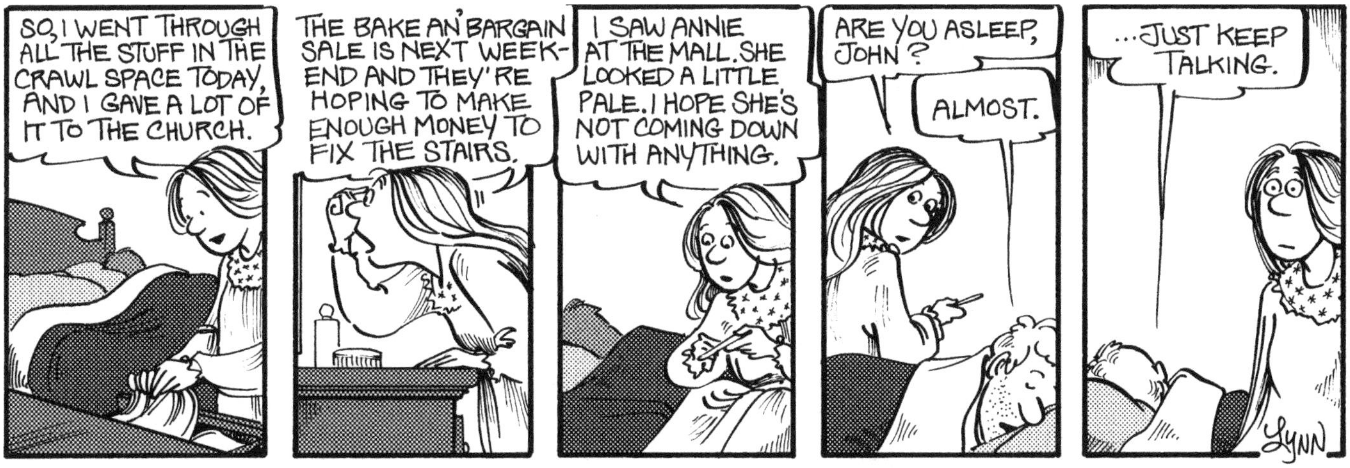
SO, I WENT THROUGH ALL THE STUFF IN THE CRAWL SPACE TODAY, AND I GAVE A LOT OF IT TO THE CHURCH.
THE BAKE AN' BARGAIN SALE IS NEXT WEEK-END AND THEY'RE HOPING TO MAKE ENOUGH MONEY TO FIX THE STAIRS.
I SAW ANNIE AT THE MALL. SHE LOOKED A LITTLE PALE. I HOPE SHE'S NOT COMING DOWN WITH ANYTHING.
ARE YOU ASLEEP, JOHN?
ALMOST.
...JUST KEEP TALKING.
LYNN

If I can't sleep, I will often turn the radio on to the CBC. The droning of interviews, the endless ardent and erudite guests, sends me into a haze unequalled since high school. When a lecture was lengthy and the room was warm, I slept easily sitting in a hard wooden desk with my head on a textbook. To me, the sound of someone talking can become like the hum of an aircraft engine, and I just drift away.

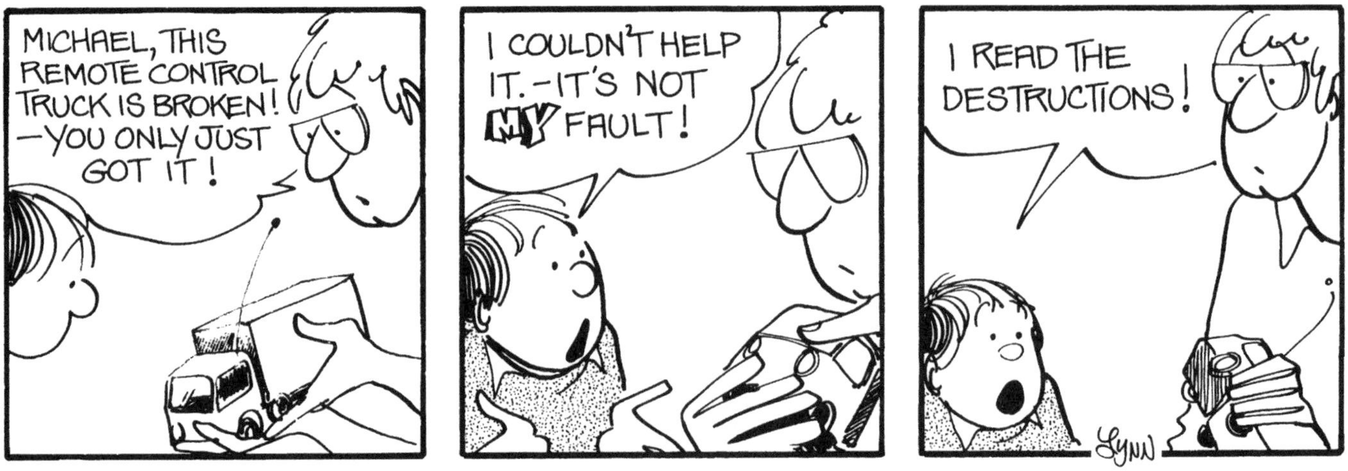
MICHAEL, THIS REMOTE CONTROL TRUCK IS BROKEN! —YOU ONLY JUST GOT IT!
I COULDN'T HELP IT.-IT'S NOT MY FAULT!
I READ THE DESTRUCTIONS!
LYNN

Aaron's "punch lines" were a gift. He would unwittingly change an expression or a turn of phrase that would then become part of *For Better or For Worse*. Kids say funny things all the time, but some are just prone to wordplay, and Aaron trumped them all. There were times he would be "let off the hook" if his remarks got a laugh, and I had to be careful not to encourage him too much or the discipline we managed to instill would go whizzing down the drain.

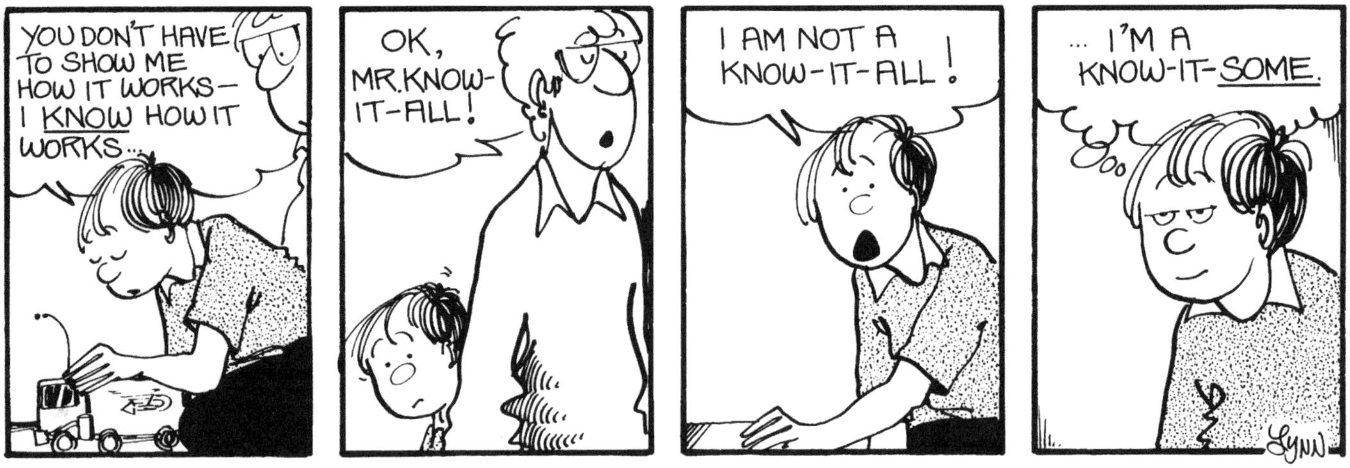
YOU DON'T HAVE TO SHOW ME HOW IT WORKS— I KNOW HOW IT WORKS...
OK, MR. KNOW-IT-ALL!
I AM NOT A KNOW-IT-ALL!
... I'M A KNOW-IT-SOME.
LYNN

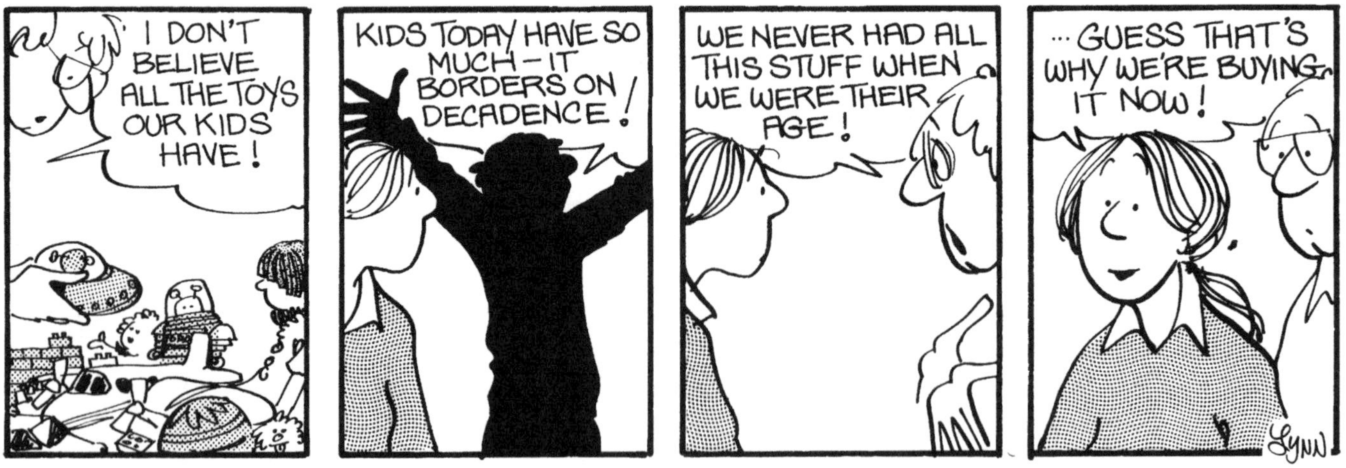
I DON'T BELIEVE ALL THE TOYS OUR KIDS HAVE!
KIDS TODAY HAVE SO MUCH—IT BORDERS ON DECADENCE!
WE NEVER HAD ALL THIS STUFF WHEN WE WERE THEIR AGE!
...GUESS THAT'S WHY WE'RE BUYING IT NOW!
LYNN

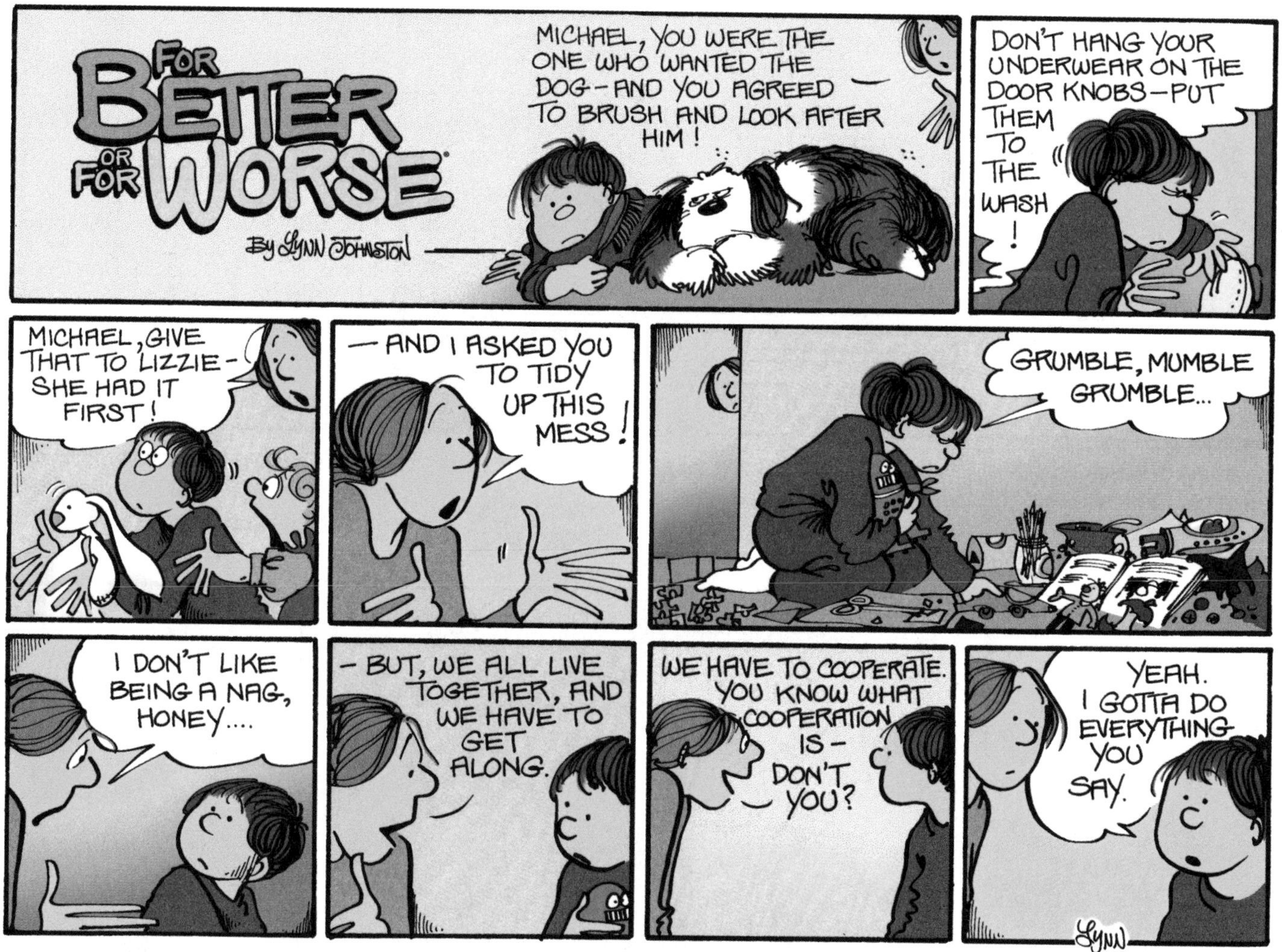
FOR BETTER OR FOR WORSE
BY LYNN JOHNSTON
MICHAEL, YOU WERE THE ONE WHO WANTED THE DOG – AND YOU AGREED TO BRUSH AND LOOK AFTER HIM!
DON'T HANG YOUR UNDERWEAR ON THE DOOR KNOBS – PUT THEM TO THE WASH!
MICHAEL, GIVE THAT TO LIZZIE – SHE HAD IT FIRST!
– AND I ASKED YOU TO TIDY UP THIS MESS!
GRUMBLE, MUMBLE GRUMBLE...
I DON'T LIKE BEING A NAG, HONEY....
– BUT, WE ALL LIVE TOGETHER, AND WE HAVE TO GET ALONG.
WE HAVE TO COOPERATE. YOU KNOW WHAT COOPERATION IS – DON'T YOU?
YEAH. I GOTTA DO EVERYTHING YOU SAY.
LYNN

My mother used to nag me constantly! Seems there was always something better to do than play or draw or watch television. The way I saw it, my room was my room and if I had to climb over a Vesuvius of moldering junk to find the bed I slept in, then that was my problem. Clean and ironed clothing was not a priority, nor was washing behind bodily protuberances. I longed for the day when I could do what I wanted to do, eat what and when I wanted to, have my own space, my own money, and my own rules.

That didn't happen until I was 20 and married for the first time. Then, I amazed even myself. I became a stickler for cleanliness. My apartment was spotless. Clothes were immaculate, ironed, and sorted into their exact compartments. The bed was made, the carpets lint free, and the kitchen was a neat, organized workspace. Aahhh … the change that comes with independence!

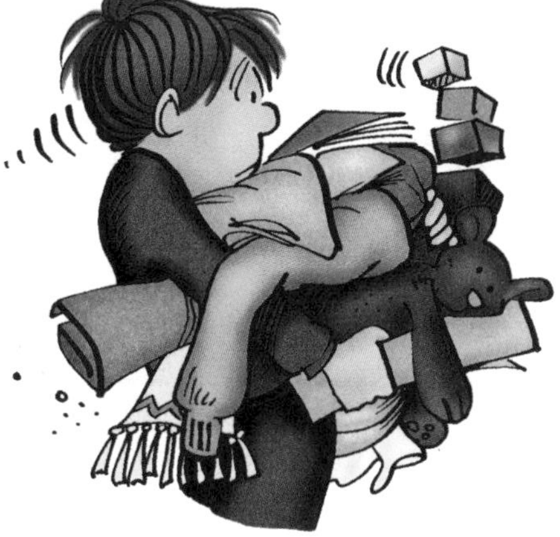

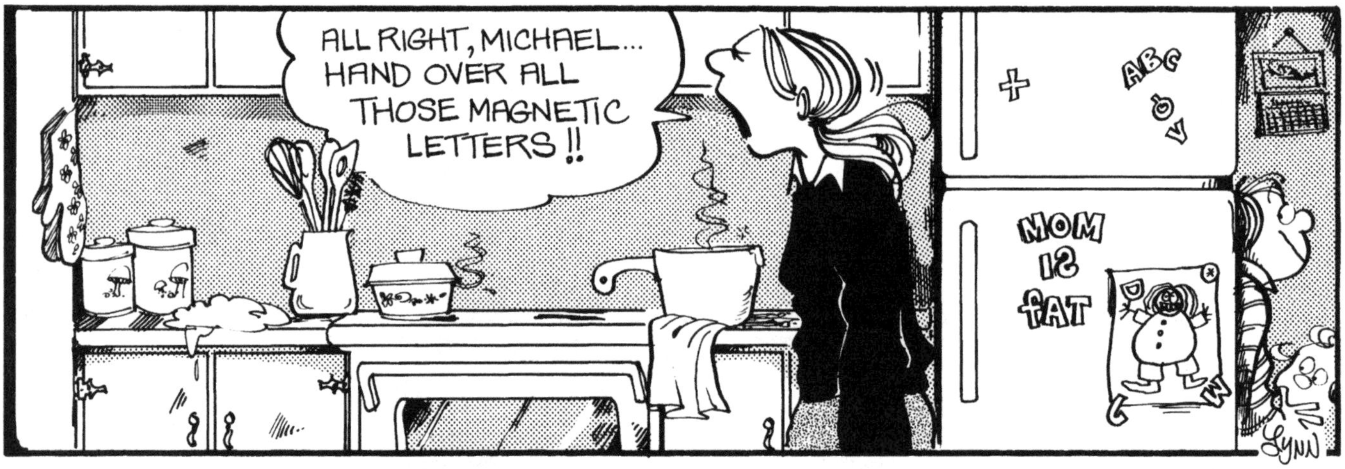
ALL RIGHT, MICHAEL... HAND OVER ALL THOSE MAGNETIC LETTERS !!
ABC
MOM IS fAT
LYNN

We ordered a new fridge from the Sears catalogue shortly after moving to Lynn Lake. My new fridge was a beauty. I organized it and put some colourful alphabet magnets on the door in preparation for the photos, notes, and doodles I looked forward to hanging there. Kate, who was toddling and full of mischief, saw the magnets and, before I could stop her, started to "scrub" them around, scratching the surface of my new fridge. I had only had it one day before it was "broken" in.

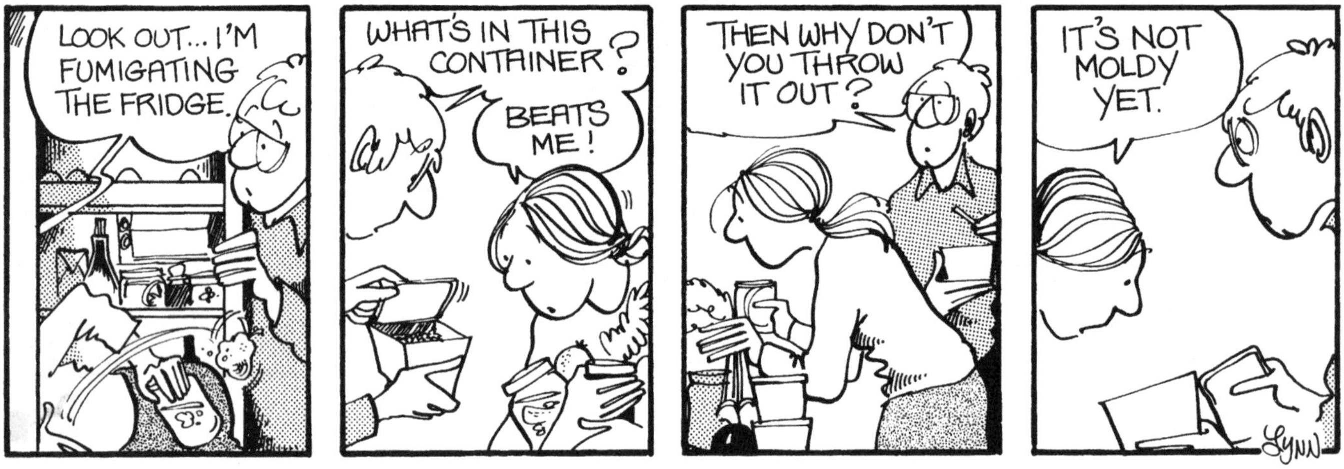
LOOK OUT... I'M FUMIGATING THE FRIDGE.
WHAT'S IN THIS CONTAINER?
BEATS ME!
THEN WHY DON'T YOU THROW IT OUT?
IT'S NOT MOLDY YET.
LYNN

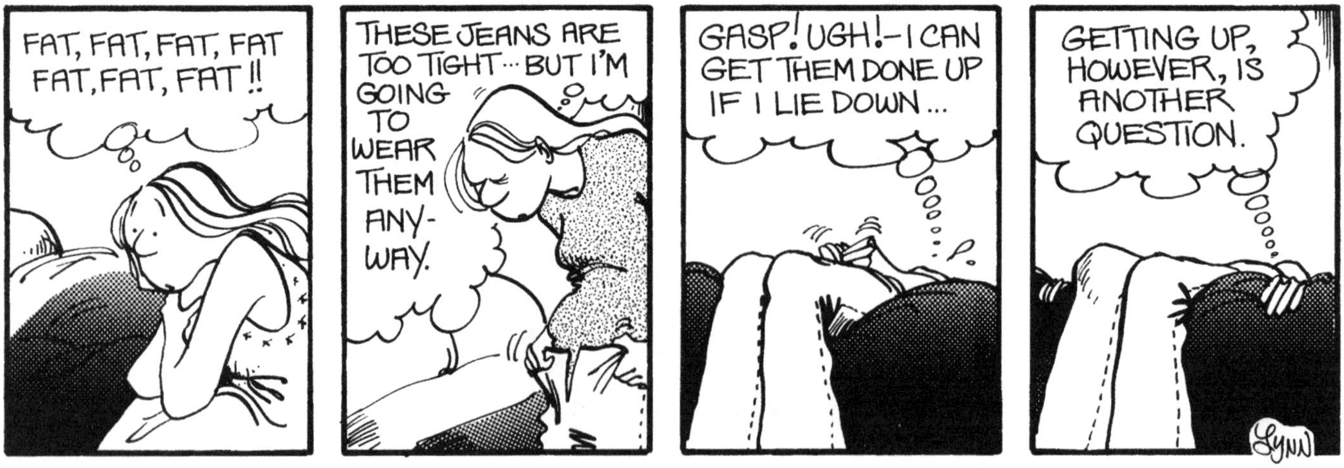
FAT, FAT, FAT, FAT FAT, FAT, FAT !!
THESE JEANS ARE TOO TIGHT... BUT I'M GOING TO WEAR THEM ANY-WAY.
GASP! UGH! - I CAN GET THEM DONE UP IF I LIE DOWN...
GETTING UP, HOWEVER, IS ANOTHER QUESTION.
LYNN

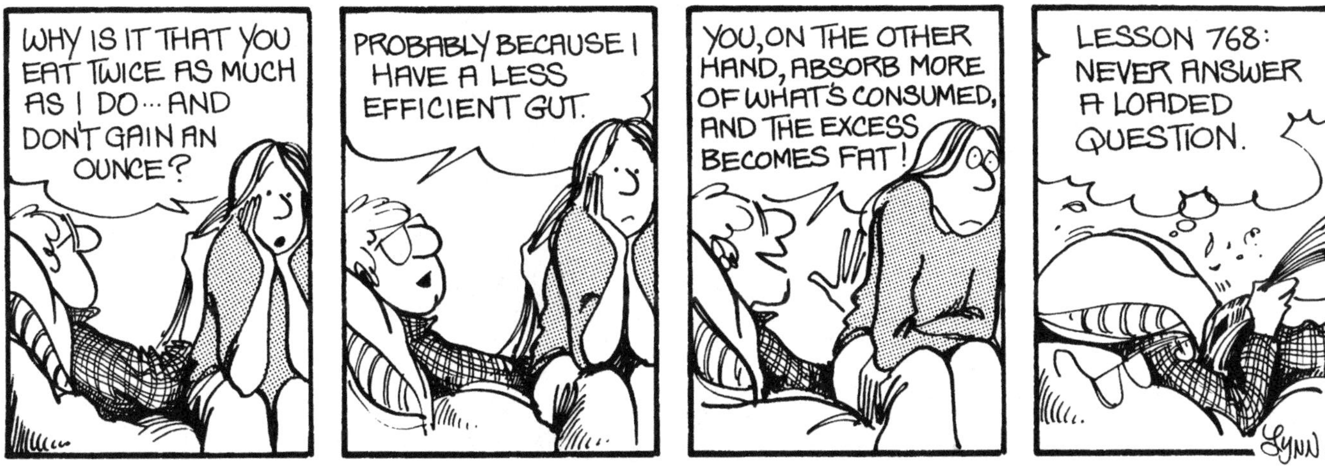
WHY IS IT THAT YOU EAT TWICE AS MUCH AS I DO... AND DON'T GAIN AN OUNCE?
PROBABLY BECAUSE I HAVE A LESS EFFICIENT GUT.
YOU, ON THE OTHER HAND, ABSORB MORE OF WHAT'S CONSUMED, AND THE EXCESS BECOMES FAT!
LESSON 768: NEVER ANSWER A LOADED QUESTION.
LYNN

This was my mother's argument. The suggestion that she and I had more efficient metaboli and were therefore able to retain more of the nutrients we consumed was supposed to make us feel OK about weight gain. My dad and my brother didn't have to think about this. They burned off everything they ate! We were fortunate, she said. If she and I were ever marooned on a desert island with a group of people and little food, we would outlive everyone who needed to eat more than we did.

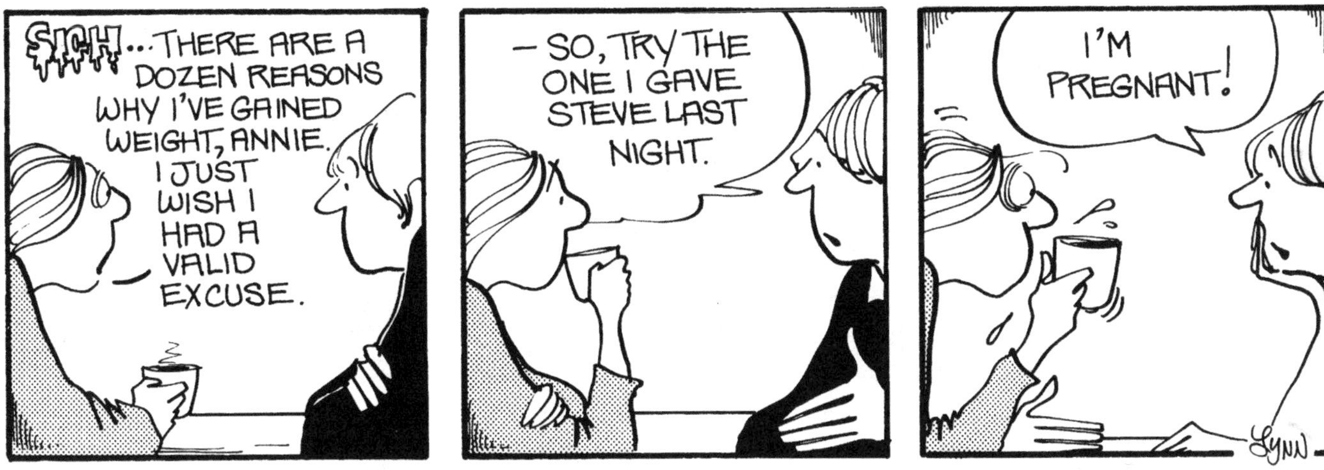
SIGH... THERE ARE A DOZEN REASONS WHY I'VE GAINED WEIGHT, ANNIE. I JUST WISH I HAD A VALID EXCUSE.
– SO, TRY THE ONE I GAVE STEVE LAST NIGHT.
I'M PREGNANT!
LYNN

I toyed with the thought of adding to our family. After some intense discussion, we decided that two was enough, so Annie in the strip got pregnant instead!

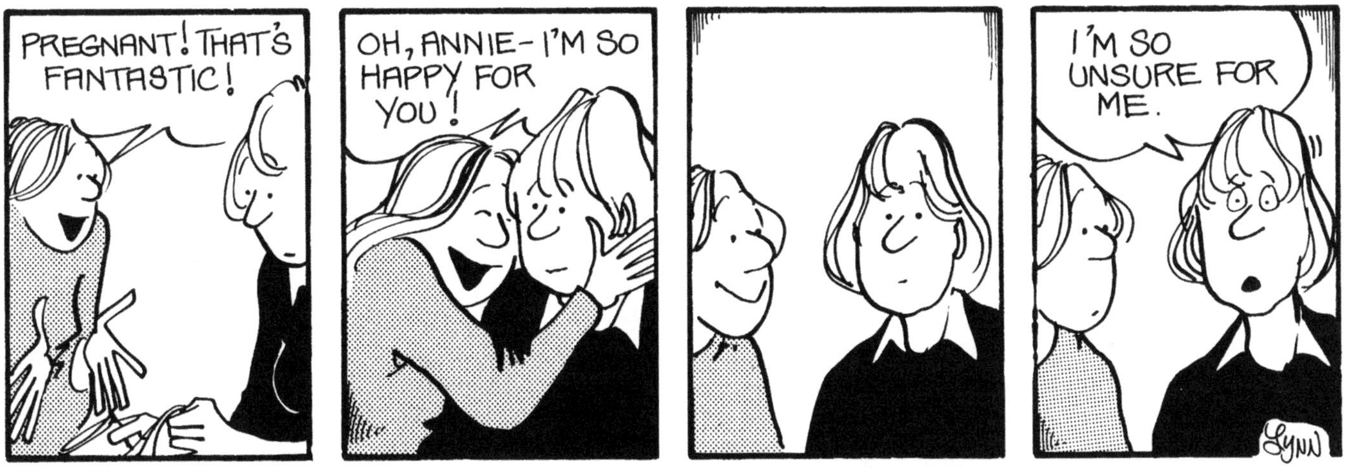
PREGNANT! THAT'S FANTASTIC!
OH, ANNIE– I'M SO HAPPY FOR YOU!
I'M SO UNSURE FOR ME.
LYNN

I knew a lot about Annie that the readers didn't know. I knew that she had her hands full — especially with another baby on the way. And, something she suspected but didn't want to know; that her husband was serially unfaithful. It was challenging to write about and draw people in an ordinary neighbourhood, dealing with ordinary things all the time. So, adding new elements of interest made FBorFW come alive for me and made the whole story more exciting.

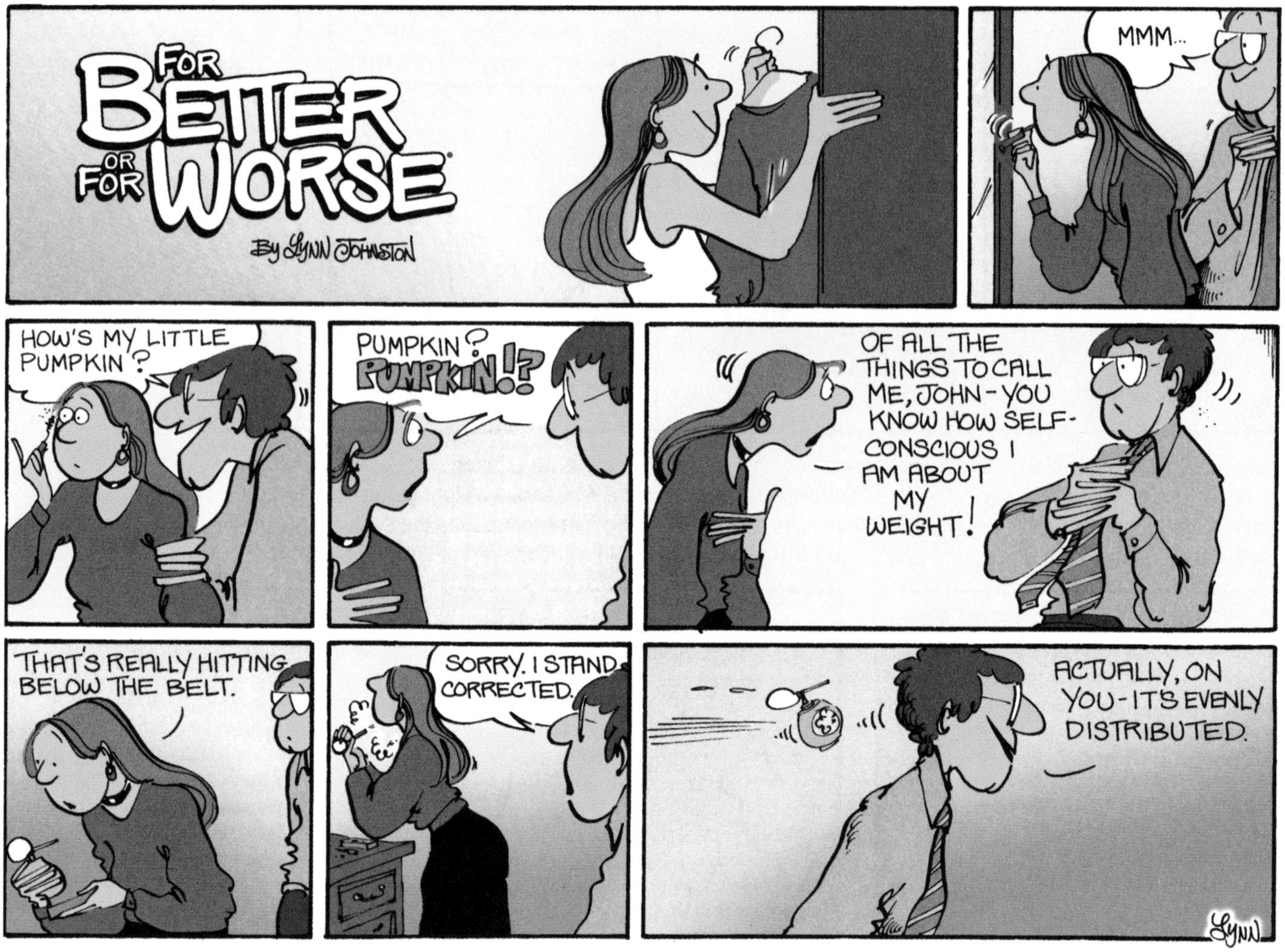
FOR BETTER OR FOR WORSE
BY LYNN JOHNSTON
MMM...
HOW'S MY LITTLE PUMPKIN?
PUMPKIN? PUMPKIN!?
OF ALL THE THINGS TO CALL ME, JOHN - YOU KNOW HOW SELF-CONSCIOUS I AM ABOUT MY WEIGHT!
THAT'S REALLY HITTING BELOW THE BELT.
SORRY. I STAND CORRECTED.
ACTUALLY, ON YOU - IT'S EVENLY DISTRIBUTED.
LYNN

With a comic strip to get out and personal baggage to exploit therein, I often drew Elly large-nosed, slumped over, and bottom heavy. It was OK to do this. As long as I was critical of myself, the household ambience remained stable. Should someone ELSE deliver the blow, however, even as a joke, I was instantly rushed back in time to my moody adolescence when image was everything and a full-length mirror was dangerous to one's health.

Now, at the ripening age of 64, I'm no longer as obsessed with my waistline as I was then. I've gone beyond wanting to look like one of those angular sylphs in the catalogues. I'm comfortable with the way I am. I'm at ease with the woman within. I'm able to look at myself objectively and positively with confidence and cool. But ... should anyone joke about my wrinkles ... WATCH OUT!!!!

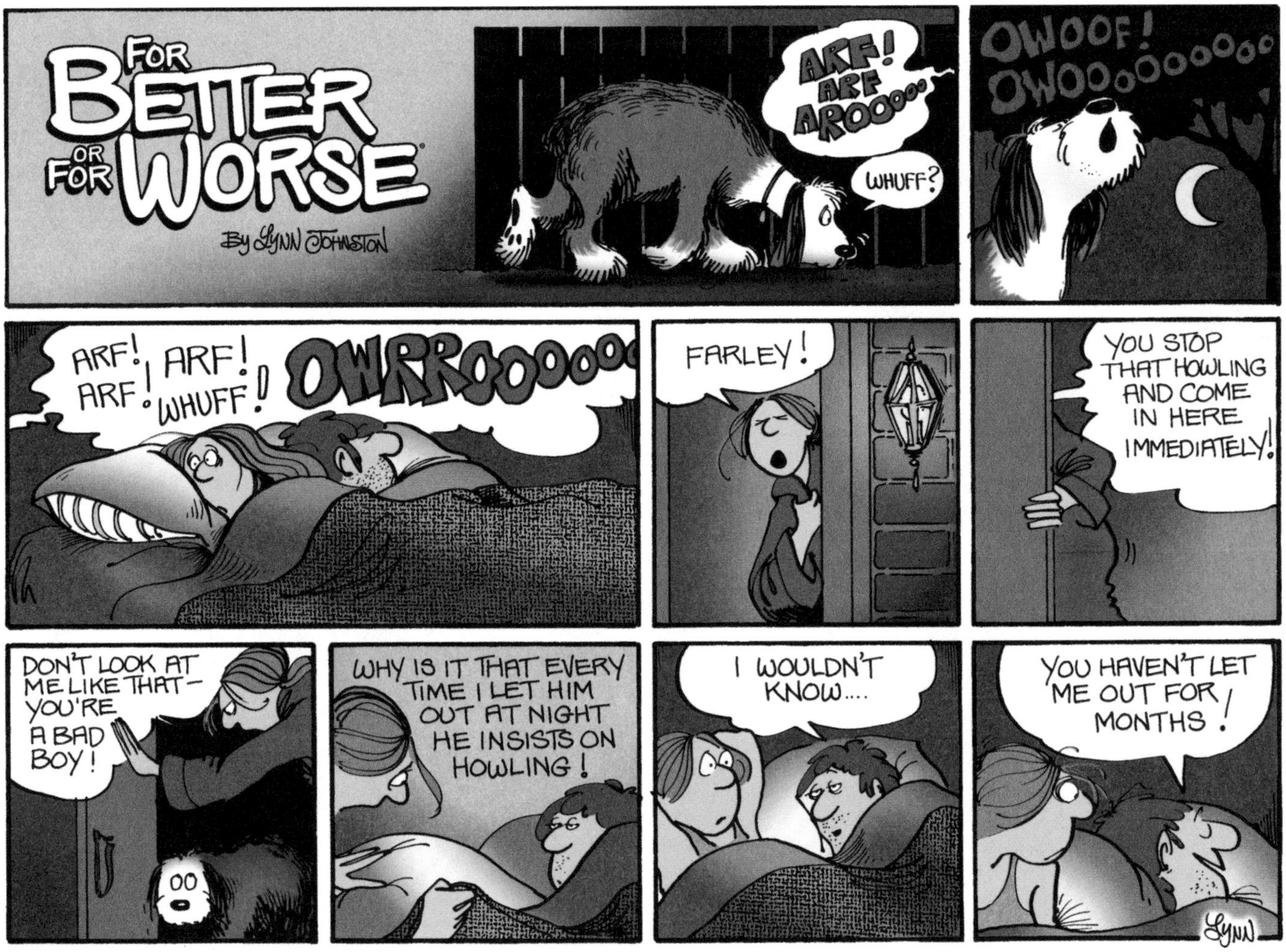
FOR BETTER OR FOR WORSE
BY LYNN JOHNSTON
ARF! ARF AROOOoo
WHUFF?
OWOOF! OWOOoOoooooo
ARF! ARF!
ARF! WHUFF!
OWRROOOOOO
FARLEY!
YOU STOP THAT HOWLING AND COME IN HERE IMMEDIATELY!
DON'T LOOK AT ME LIKE THAT— YOU'RE A BAD BOY!
WHY IS IT THAT EVERY TIME I LET HIM OUT AT NIGHT HE INSISTS ON HOWLING!
I WOULDN'T KNOW....
YOU HAVEN'T LET ME OUT FOR MONTHS!
LYNN

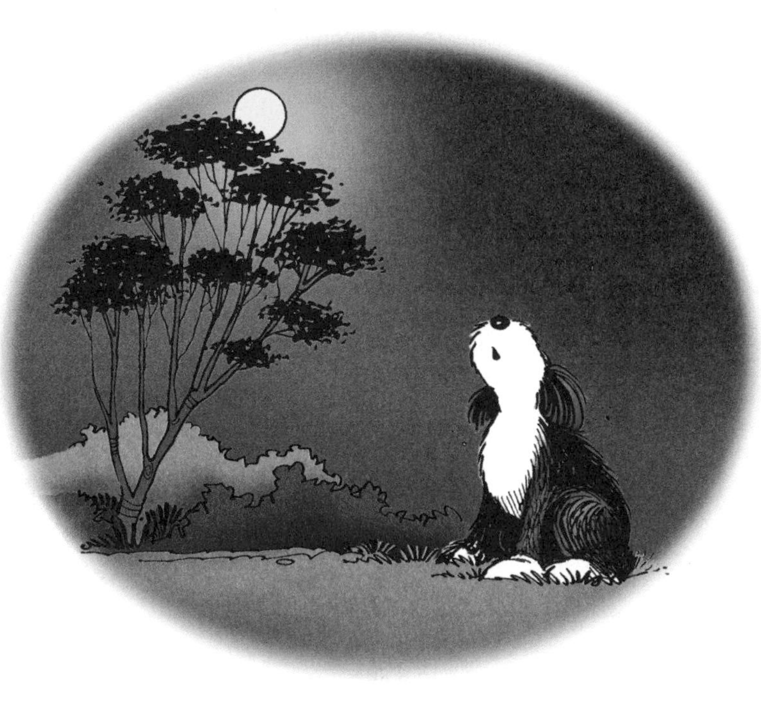

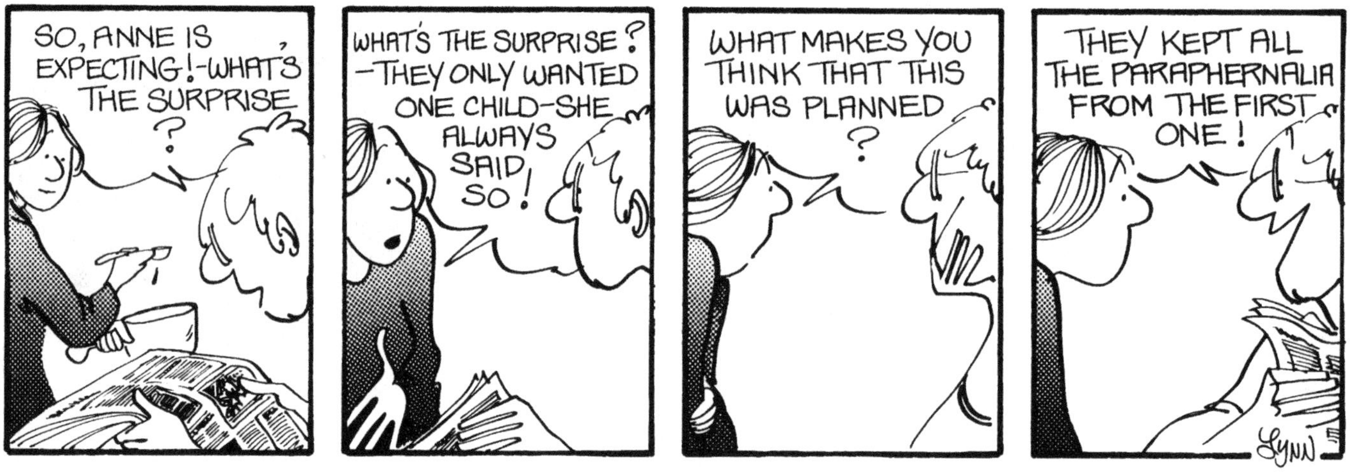
SO, ANNE IS EXPECTING!-WHAT'S THE SURPRISE?
WHAT'S THE SURPRISE? -THEY ONLY WANTED ONE CHILD-SHE ALWAYS SAID SO!
WHAT MAKES YOU THINK THAT THIS WAS PLANNED?
THEY KEPT ALL THE PARAPHERNALIA FROM THE FIRST ONE!
LYNN

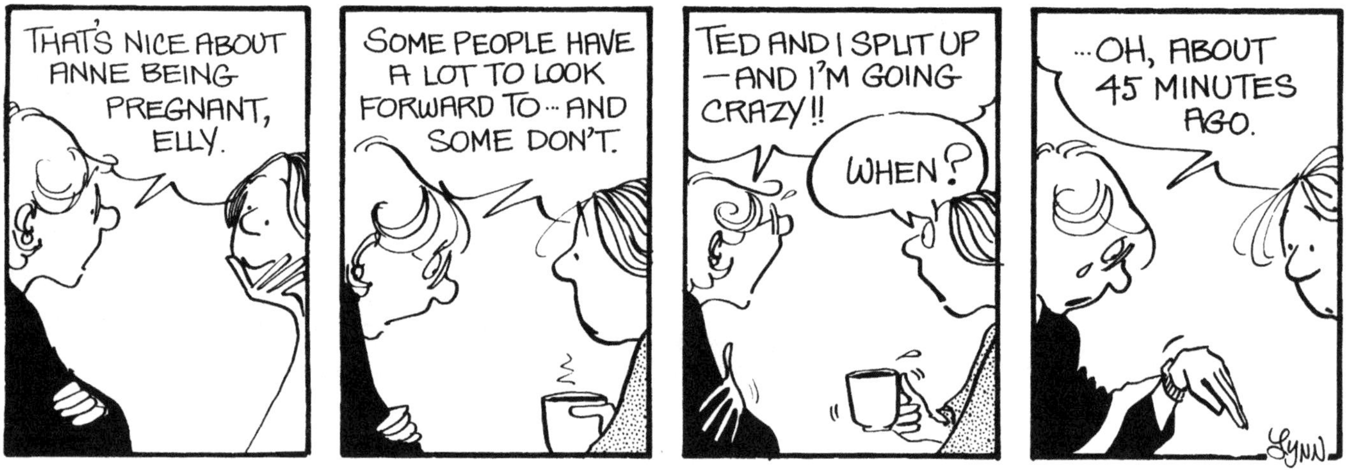
THAT'S NICE ABOUT ANNE BEING PREGNANT, ELLY.
SOME PEOPLE HAVE A LOT TO LOOK FORWARD TO... AND SOME DON'T.
TED AND I SPLIT UP—AND I'M GOING CRAZY!!
WHEN?
...OH, ABOUT 45 MINUTES AGO.
LYNN

In the early eighties, I was still learning how to make my thirty seconds a day morph into a story. I wanted there to be a rift between Connie and Ted, partly because I thought he was a schmuck, and just to keep things interesting. Had I been doing this segment today, I would have told their story in detail.

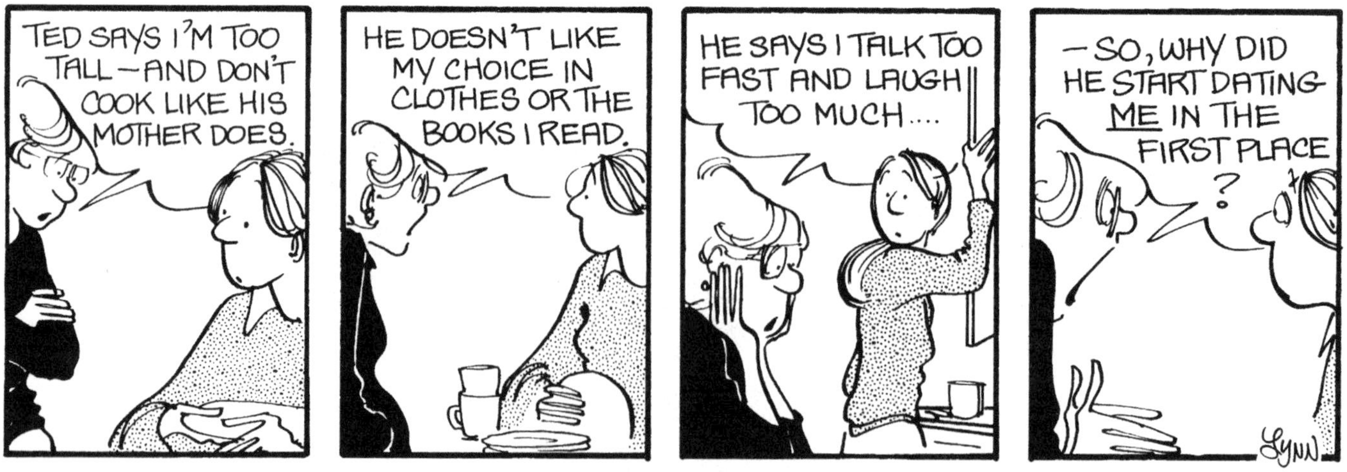
TED SAYS I'M TOO TALL—AND DON'T COOK LIKE HIS MOTHER DOES.
HE DOESN'T LIKE MY CHOICE IN CLOTHES OR THE BOOKS I READ.
HE SAYS I TALK TOO FAST AND LAUGH TOO MUCH....
—SO, WHY DID HE START DATING ME IN THE FIRST PLACE?
LYNN

The way I saw it ... Ted lived with an overbearing mother. There would never be a woman good enough for her son, and she saw to it that Connie was a reject, even before the relationship got off the ground. In my head I knew what had happened and how the breakup had taken place, but I never told the story to the readers. At the time, I thought I could get away with such instant info, but it's hard for an audience to buy into something they haven't witnessed for themselves.

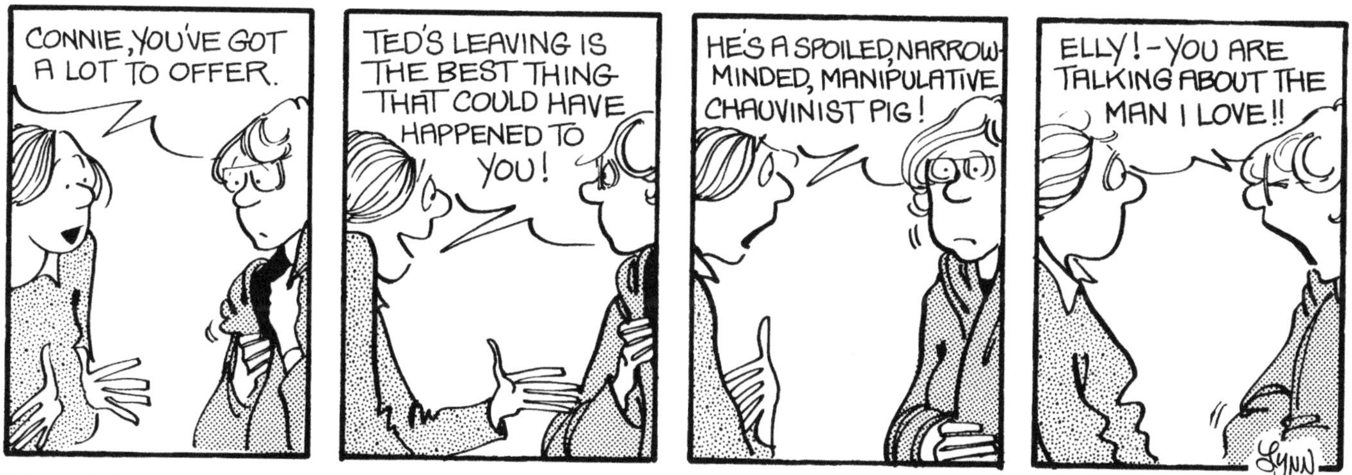
CONNIE, YOU'VE GOT A LOT TO OFFER.
TED'S LEAVING IS THE BEST THING THAT COULD HAVE HAPPENED TO YOU!
HE'S A SPOILED, NARROW-MINDED, MANIPULATIVE CHAUVINIST PIG!
ELLY! - YOU ARE TALKING ABOUT THE MAN I LOVE!!
Lynn

I learned the hard way to not tell a friend what I really thought of her husband. My friend Alice was married to a fellow I thought was a genuine cad! When he left her for another woman, I told her that she was better off without him. Six months later, she and her husband reconciled and I was out of the picture. It's safer to console without criticism!

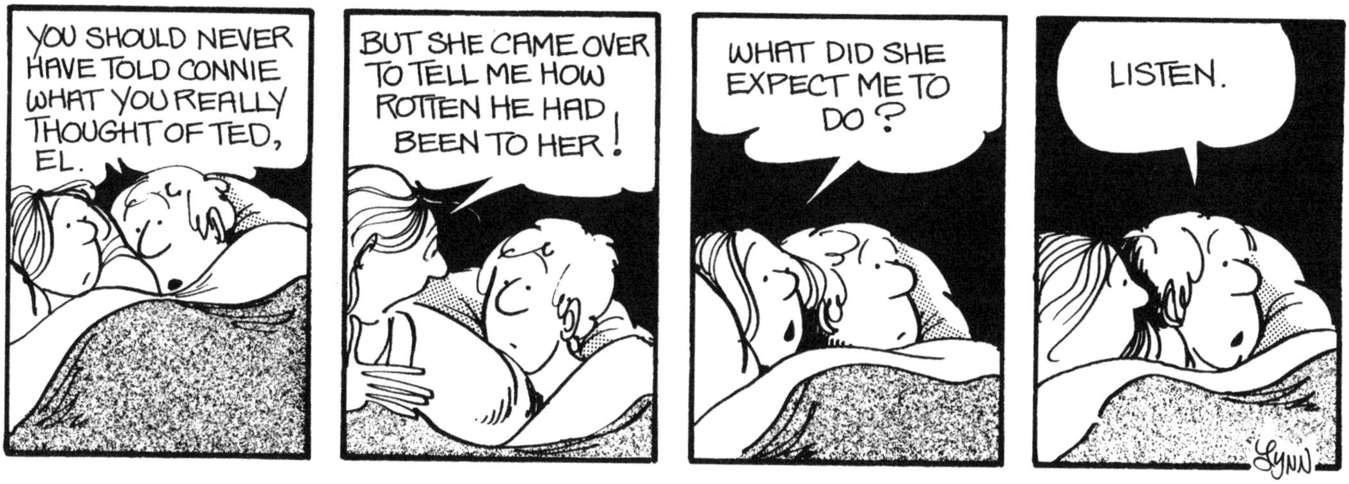
YOU SHOULD NEVER HAVE TOLD CONNIE WHAT YOU REALLY THOUGHT OF TED, EL.
BUT SHE CAME OVER TO TELL ME HOW ROTTEN HE HAD BEEN TO HER!
WHAT DID SHE EXPECT ME TO DO?
LISTEN.
Lynn

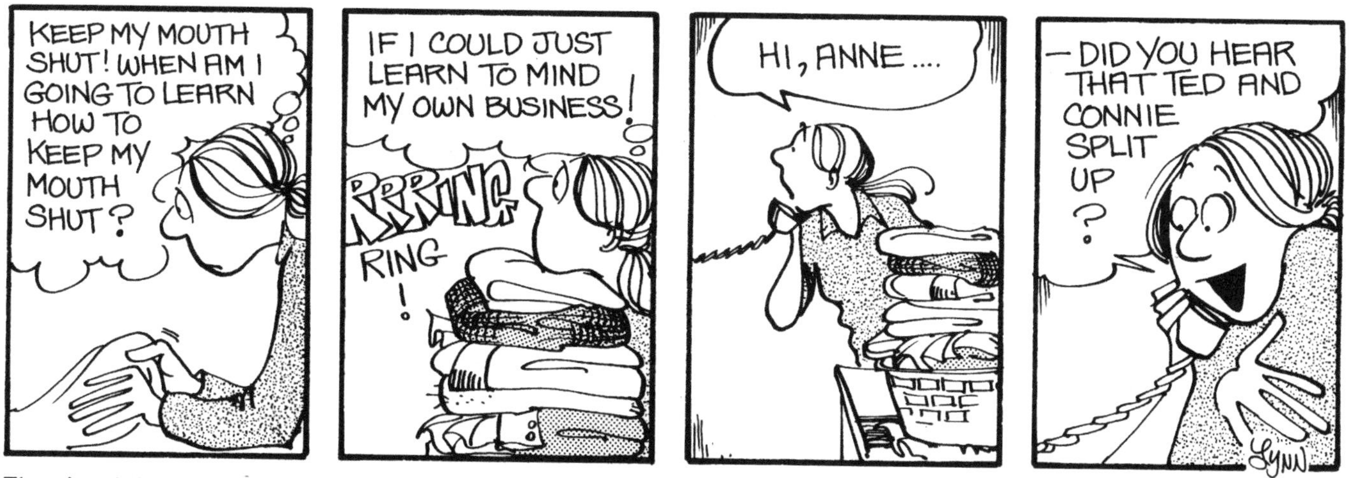
KEEP MY MOUTH SHUT! WHEN AM I GOING TO LEARN HOW TO KEEP MY MOUTH SHUT?
IF I COULD JUST LEARN TO MIND MY OWN BUSINESS!
RRRING
RING!
HI, ANNE....
—DID YOU HEAR THAT TED AND CONNIE SPLIT UP?
Lynn

There's a difference between news and gossip, and in a small town it didn't take me long to learn that you had to be careful with both. Lynn Lake was such a small town that gossip came back to you the same day. It was fun to hear the latest community news, as long as you weren't part of it!

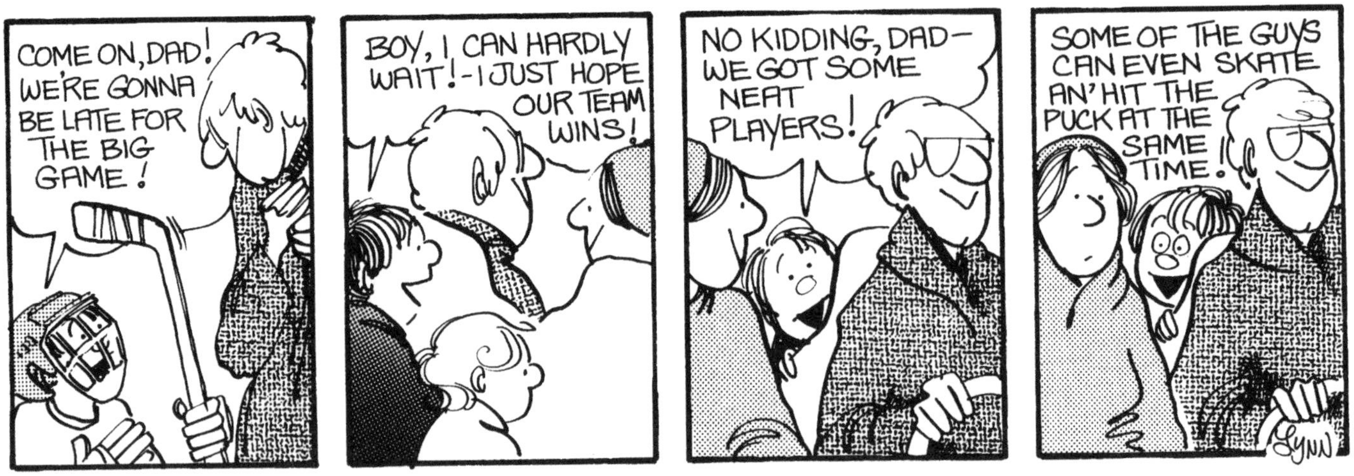
COME ON, DAD! WE'RE GONNA BE LATE FOR THE BIG GAME!
BOY, I CAN HARDLY WAIT! - I JUST HOPE OUR TEAM WINS!
NO KIDDING, DAD - WE GOT SOME NEAT PLAYERS!
SOME OF THE GUYS CAN EVEN SKATE AN' HIT THE PUCK AT THE SAME TIME!
LYNN

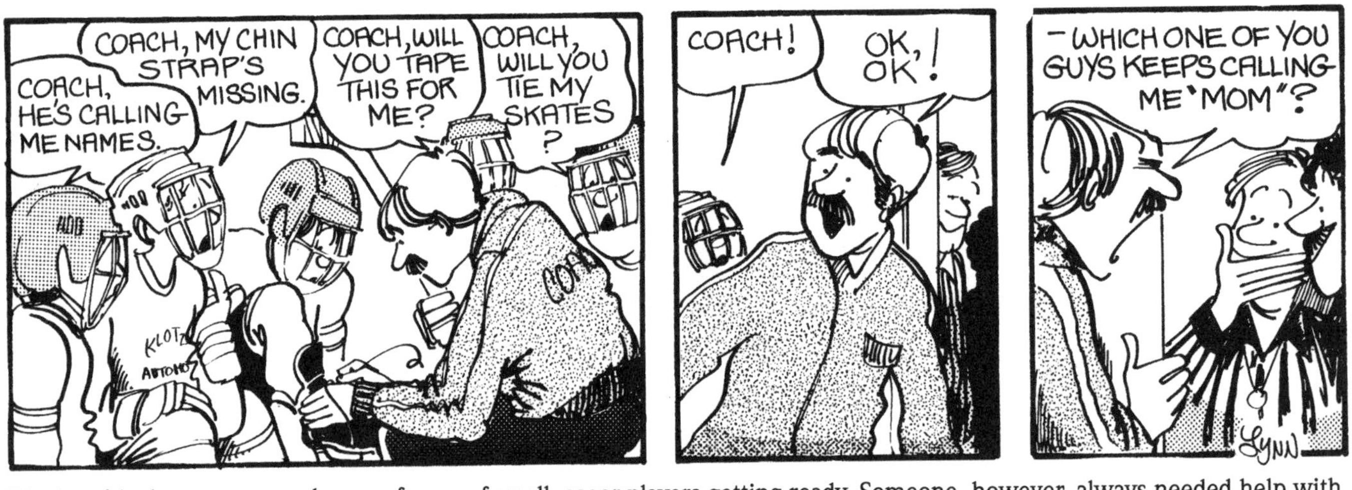
COACH, MY CHIN STRAP'S MISSING.
COACH, HE'S CALLING ME NAMES.
COACH, WILL YOU TAPE THIS FOR ME?
COACH, WILL YOU TIE MY SKATES?
COACH!
OK, OK!
- WHICH ONE OF YOU GUYS KEEPS CALLING ME "MOM"?
LYNN

The boys' locker room was always a frenzy of small, eager players getting ready. Someone, however, always needed help with something! The men who coached junior hockey were such patient, caring, and hardworking guys. Even the ones who were not fathers yet had what it takes to be great role models. When the coach tied laces he did it in a way that said, "Anything you need, man, just let me know!" I'm grateful to the people who take on the challenge of coaching minor hockey!

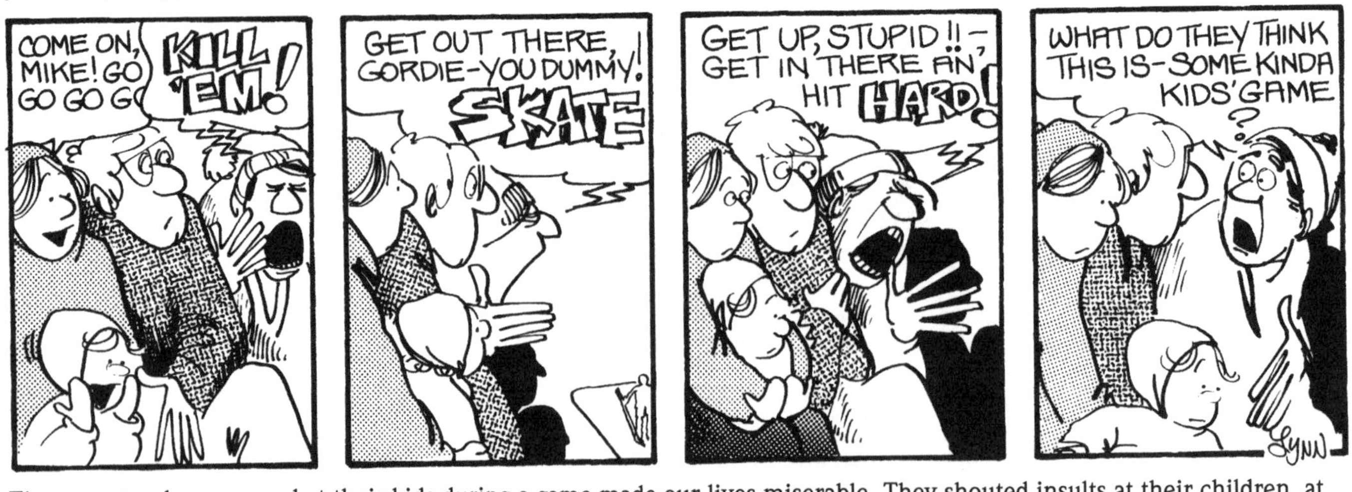
COME ON, MIKE! GO GO GO G
KILL 'EM!
GET OUT THERE, GORDIE - YOU DUMMY!
SKATE
GET UP, STUPID!! - GET IN THERE AN' HIT HARD!
WHAT DO THEY THINK THIS IS - SOME KINDA KIDS' GAME?
LYNN

The parents who screamed at their kids during a game made our lives miserable. They shouted insults at their children, at other peoples' children, at the coaches, and at each other — I could never figure it out. These people were shopkeepers, community leaders, patients, and acquaintances in town. So, if you did start something at the rink with another parent, it often came back to bite you later. Rules of good sportsmanship aren't just for the players — they apply to audiences too!

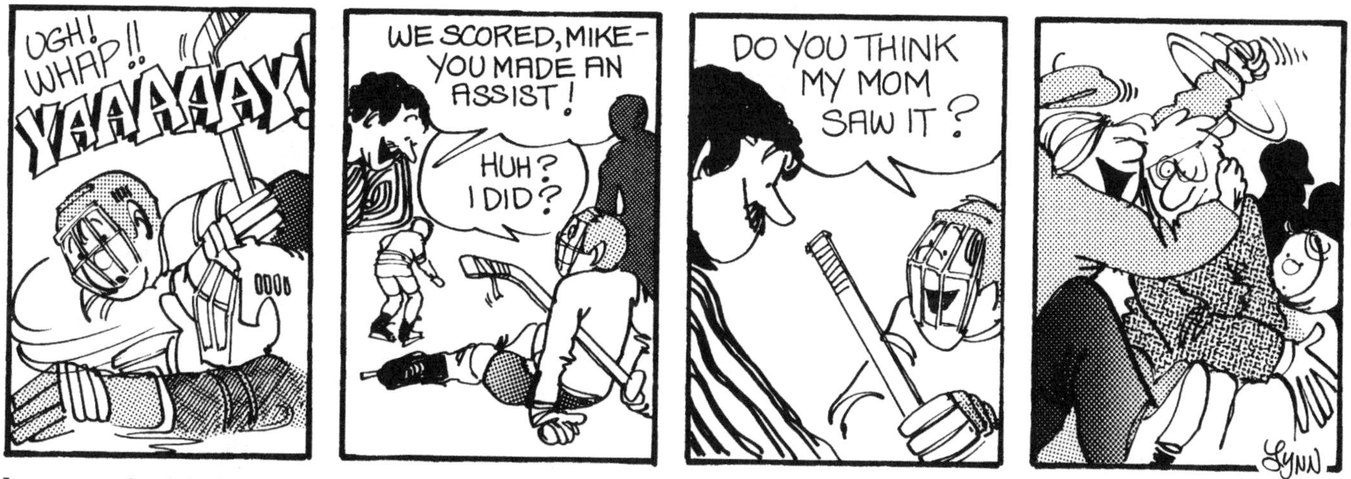
UGH!
WHAP!!
YAAAAAY!
WE SCORED, MIKE- YOU MADE AN ASSIST!
HUH? I DID?
DO YOU THINK MY MOM SAW IT?
LYNN

I was one of a tight-knit group of hockey moms who always sat in the same place. No matter how fast he was skating or how complex the play, Aaron knew where I was in the stands. We dutifully watched our boys skate their hearts out — for the team and for us. I never looked forward to the 6 a.m. practices, but I'll always be glad I was there.

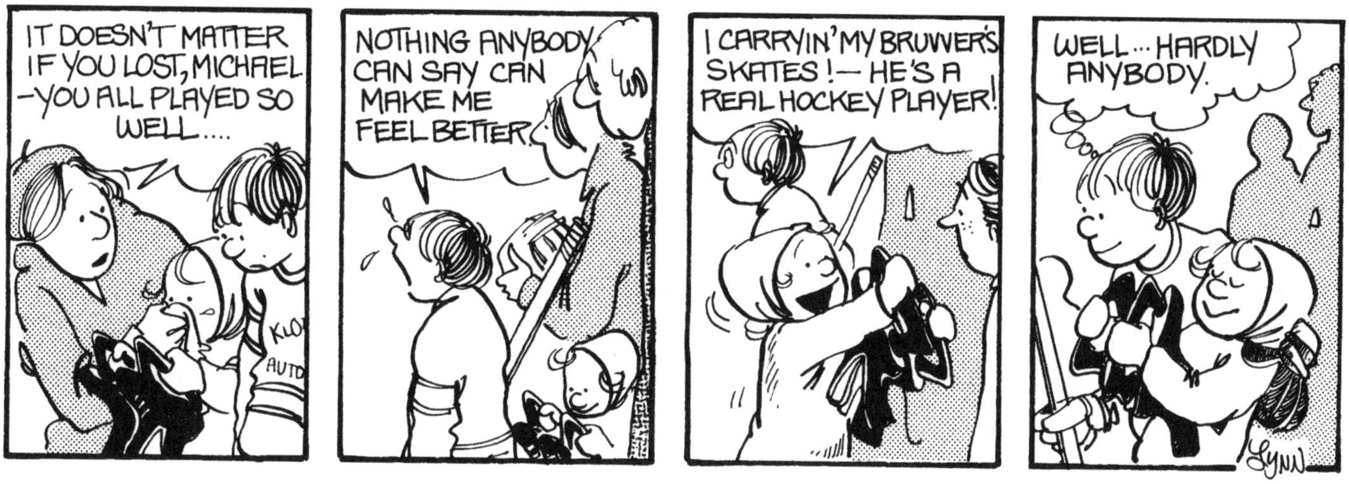
IT DOESN'T MATTER IF YOU LOST, MICHAEL -YOU ALL PLAYED SO WELL....
NOTHING ANYBODY CAN SAY CAN MAKE ME FEEL BETTER.
I CARRYIN' MY BRUVVER'S SKATES!— HE'S A REAL HOCKEY PLAYER!
WELL... HARDLY ANYBODY.
LYNN

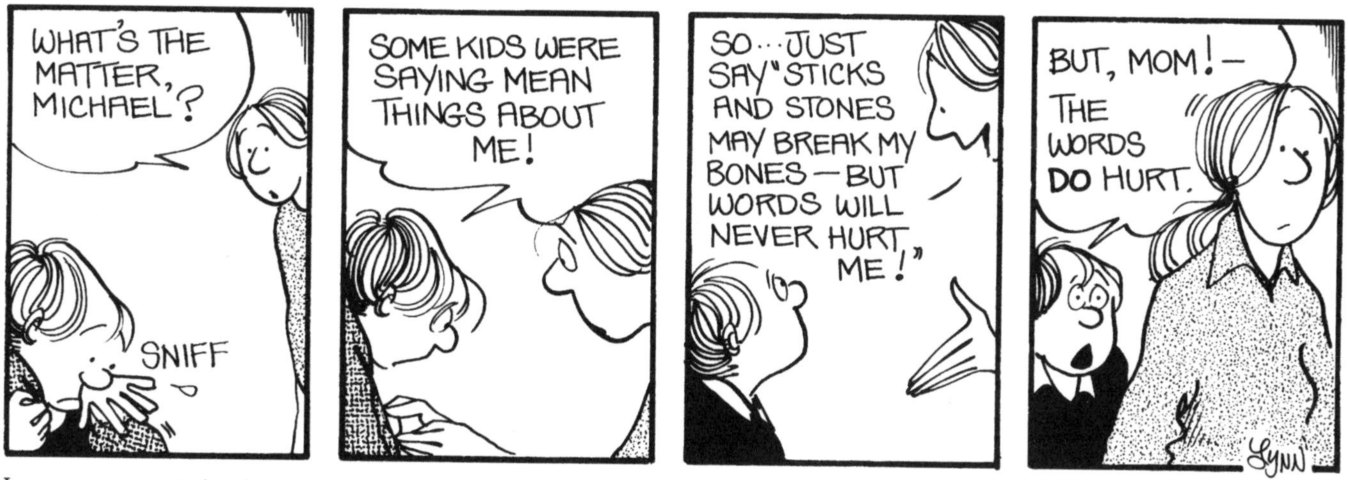
WHAT'S THE MATTER, MICHAEL?
SNIFF
SOME KIDS WERE SAYING MEAN THINGS ABOUT ME!
SO...JUST SAY "STICKS AND STONES MAY BREAK MY BONES — BUT WORDS WILL NEVER HURT ME!"
BUT, MOM!— THE WORDS DO HURT.
LYNN

I was a smartmouth when I was a kid. I enjoyed a good verbal fight and could dish out some pretty cruel remarks. I wasn't so good at being on the receiving end, however. I remember my mother telling me the "sticks and stones" thing and thinking, as the tears ran down my face, that words hurt more than a pounding — and lasted longer than a bruise!

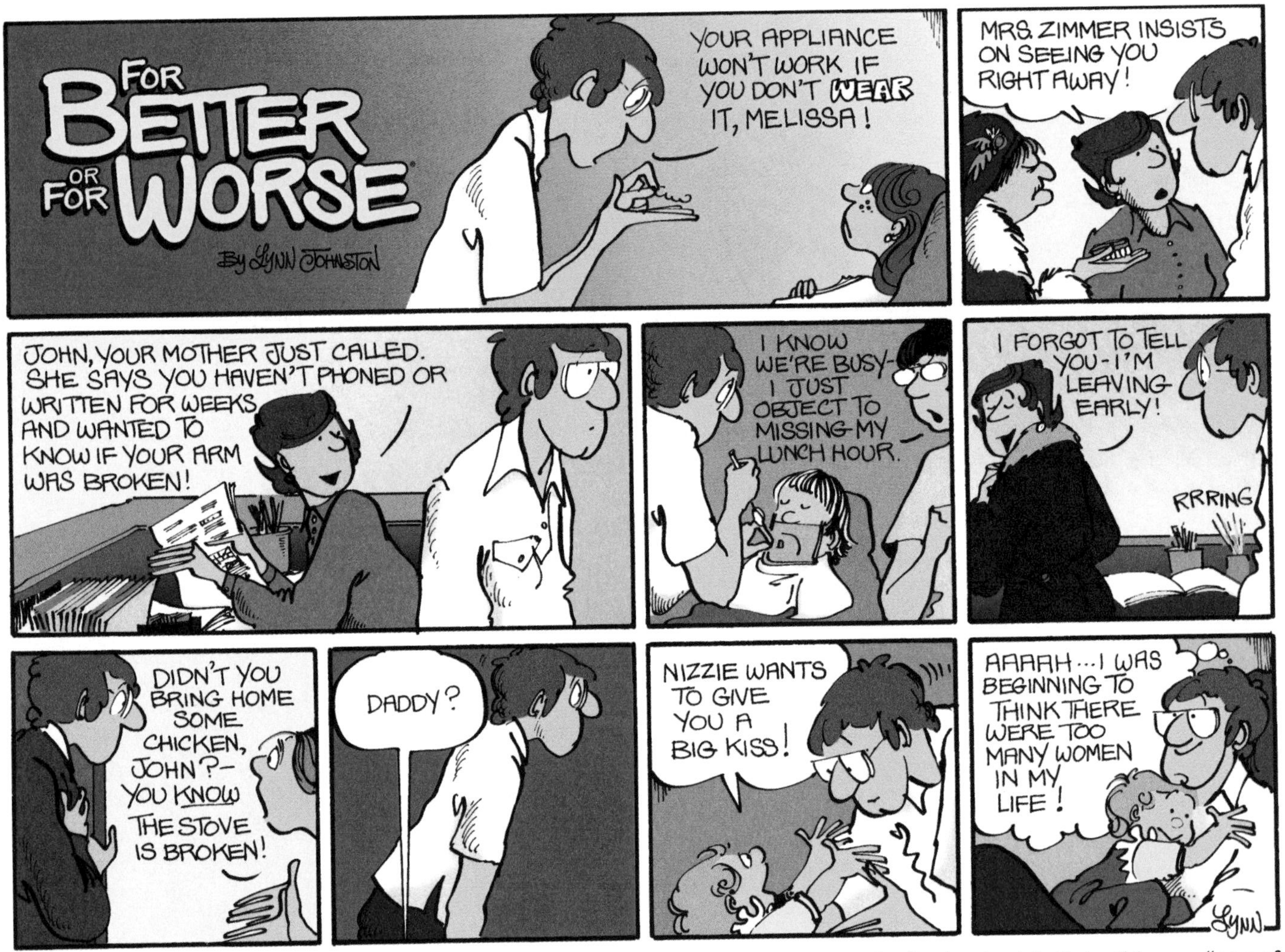
FOR BETTER OR FOR WORSE
BY LYNN JOHNSTON
YOUR APPLIANCE WON'T WORK IF YOU DON'T WEAR IT, MELISSA!
MRS. ZIMMER INSISTS ON SEEING YOU RIGHT AWAY!
JOHN, YOUR MOTHER JUST CALLED. SHE SAYS YOU HAVEN'T PHONED OR WRITTEN FOR WEEKS AND WANTED TO KNOW IF YOUR ARM WAS BROKEN!
I KNOW WE'RE BUSY- I JUST OBJECT TO MISSING MY LUNCH HOUR.
I FORGOT TO TELL YOU - I'M LEAVING EARLY!
RRRING
DIDN'T YOU BRING HOME SOME CHICKEN, JOHN?- YOU KNOW THE STOVE IS BROKEN!
DADDY?
NIZZIE WANTS TO GIVE YOU A BIG KISS!
AAAAH...I WAS BEGINNING TO THINK THERE WERE TOO MANY WOMEN IN MY LIFE!
LYNN

As in any profession, there are days when everything is a hassle and nothing goes right. In the dental clinic, this was "one of those days." The great thing about living with a dentist was the stories that he came home with. Cartoons about life in the clinic were often based on real events and real people. Fortunately for me, these folks never recognized themselves … which is where funny faces and funny names came in. Both Rod and I had stressful jobs and constant deadlines, which might have contributed to more stress at home. We were lucky we had a good sense of humour, good friends, and a great family.

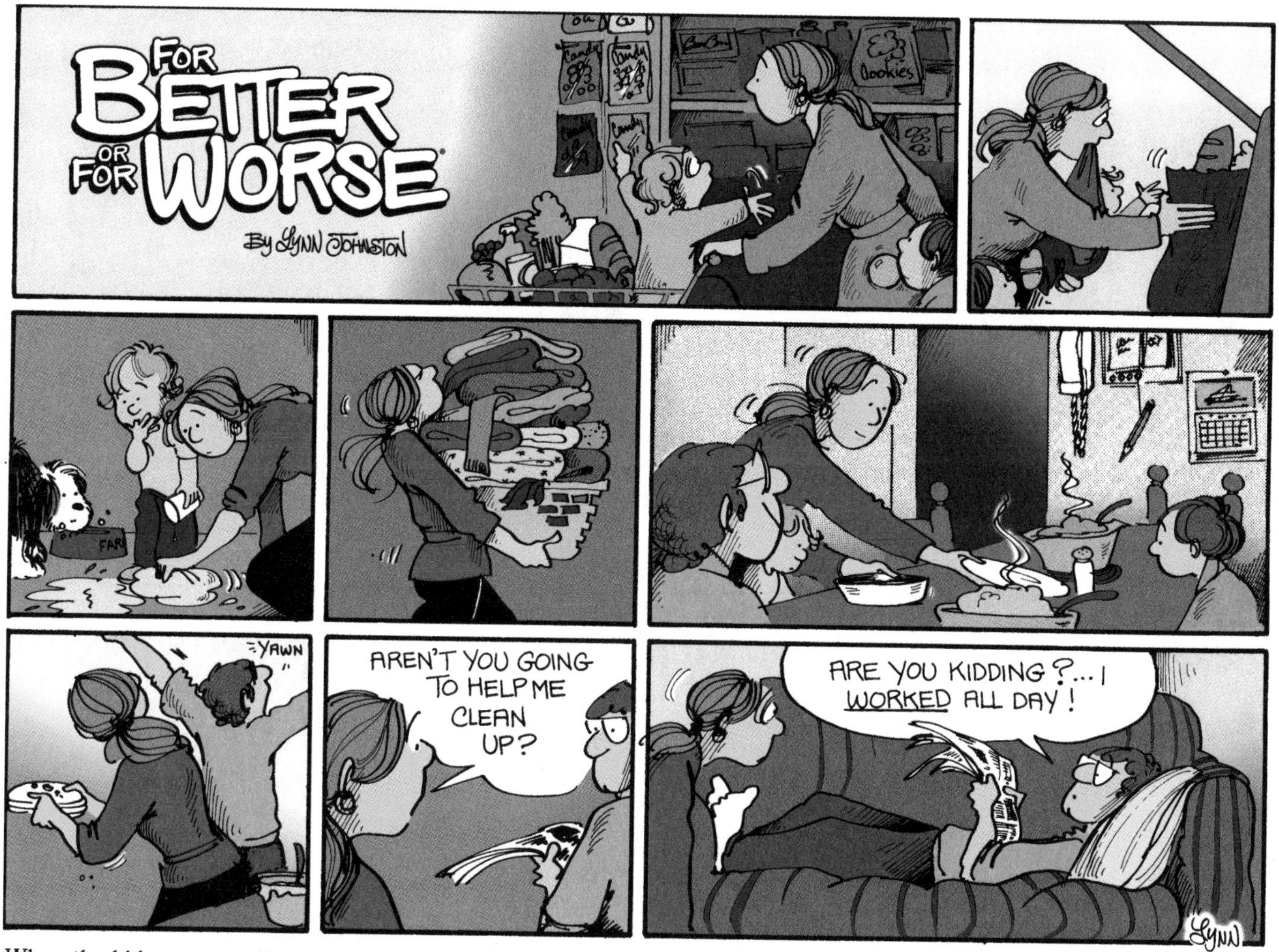
FOR BETTER OR FOR WORSE
BY LYNN JOHNSTON
Cookies
YAWN
AREN'T YOU GOING TO HELP ME CLEAN UP?
ARE YOU KIDDING?... I WORKED ALL DAY!
LYNN

When the kids were small, the work never ended. By suppertime when laundry, cleaning, shopping, and meals were done, I wondered where the time had gone. It wasn't until the dishes were done and the kids in bed that I could sit down — without guilt — and enjoy the paper.

Being a "housewife" is a full-time job. Add parenting to this and you have an all-encompassing career. I was lucky enough to have a job that allowed me to work at home. I had two jobs! Strips like this one were done to support all the smart, productive, and caring moms I knew who were struggling to stay sane. These comic strip complaints also made me less resentful of my own responsibilities. It felt amazingly good to confide my feelings to an unseen community of friends!

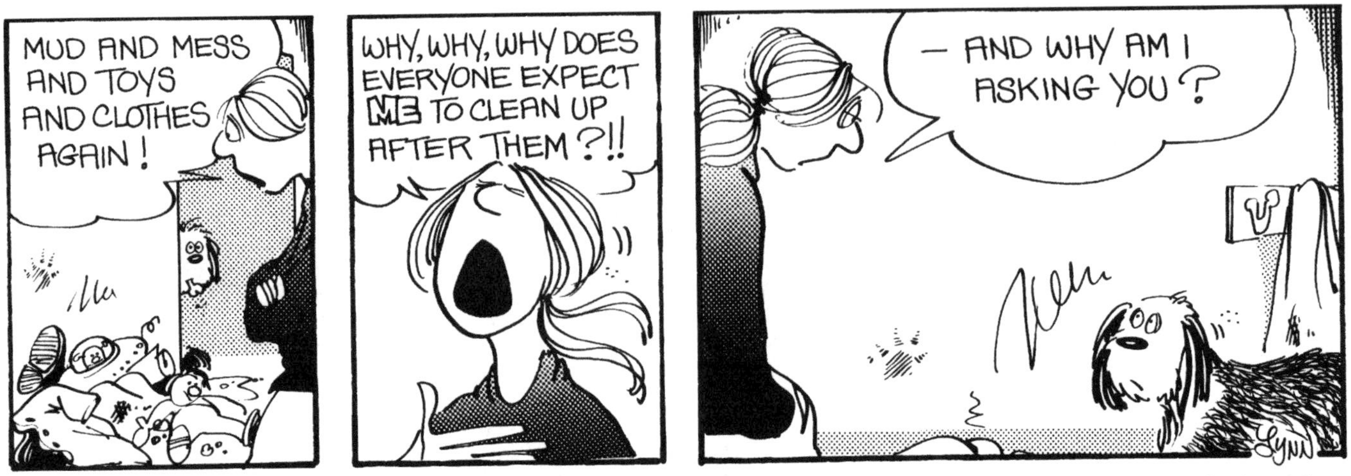
MUD AND MESS AND TOYS AND CLOTHES AGAIN!
WHY, WHY, WHY DOES EVERYONE EXPECT ME TO CLEAN UP AFTER THEM?!!
— AND WHY AM I ASKING YOU?

I actually enjoy cleaning and organizing stuff … but the thrill is lost as soon as the door opens and someone walks in with a wad of crud on his boots. Looking back, I wonder why I even tried to keep a tidy house. Nobody really cared but me.

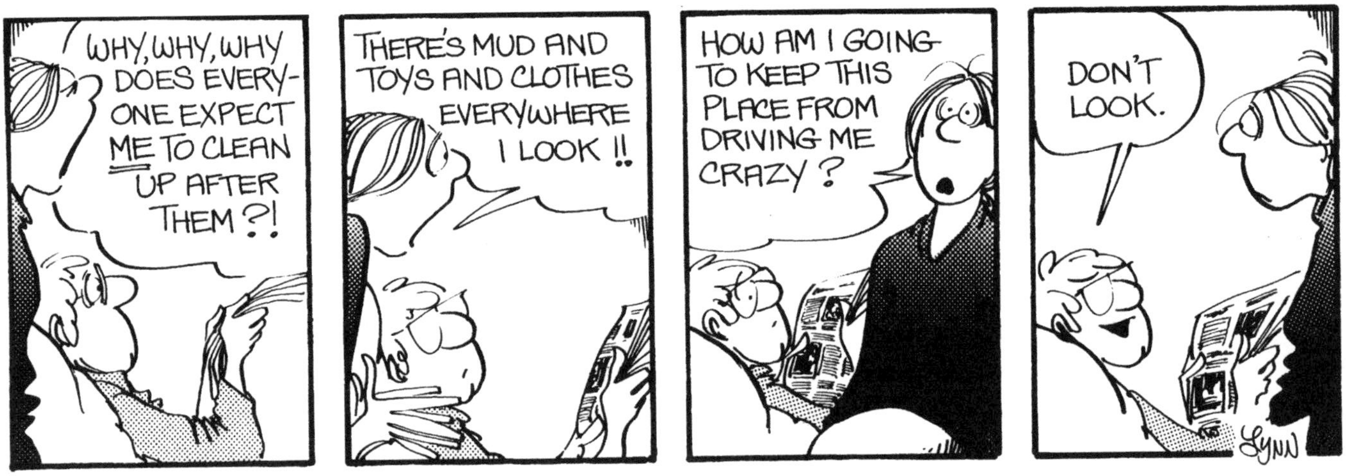
WHY, WHY, WHY DOES EVERY-ONE EXPECT ME TO CLEAN UP AFTER THEM?!
THERE'S MUD AND TOYS AND CLOTHES EVERYWHERE I LOOK!!
HOW AM I GOING TO KEEP THIS PLACE FROM DRIVING ME CRAZY?
DON'T LOOK.

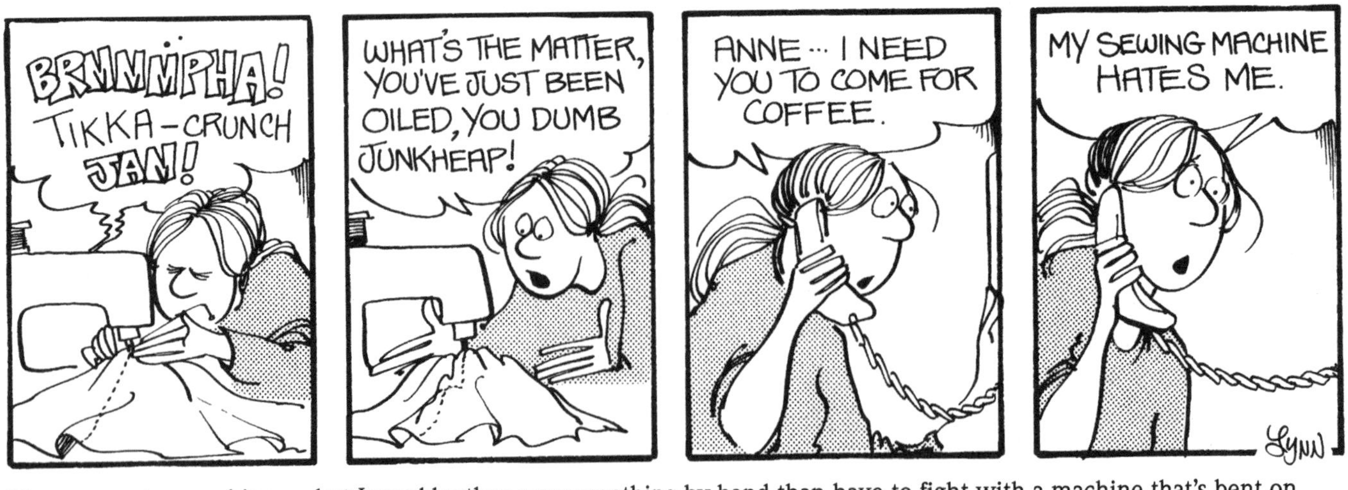
BRNNMPHA!
TIKKA-CRUNCH
JAM!
WHAT'S THE MATTER, YOU'VE JUST BEEN OILED, YOU DUMB JUNKHEAP!
ANNE … I NEED YOU TO COME FOR COFFEE.
MY SEWING MACHINE HATES ME.

I have a sewing machine — but I would rather sew something by hand than have to fight with a machine that's bent on destroying my dignity. So … if there's a rip, tear, hem, or whatnot to repair and it can't be done with a handheld needle and thread, then it waits. Sometimes for years!

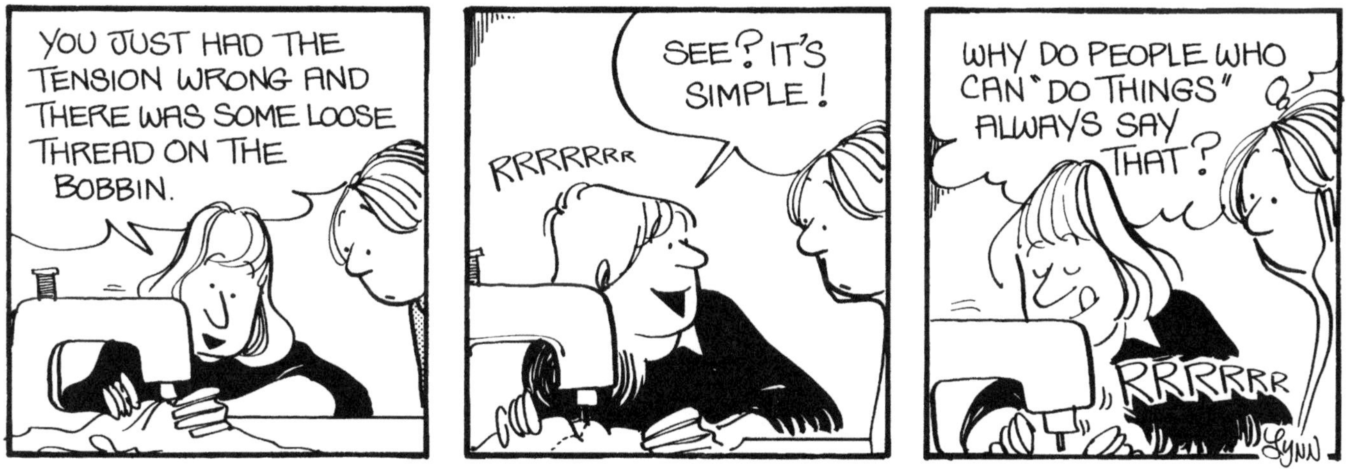
YOU JUST HAD THE TENSION WRONG AND THERE WAS SOME LOOSE THREAD ON THE BOBBIN.
RRRRRRRR
SEE? IT'S SIMPLE!
WHY DO PEOPLE WHO CAN "DO THINGS" ALWAYS SAY THAT?
RRRRRRR
Lynn

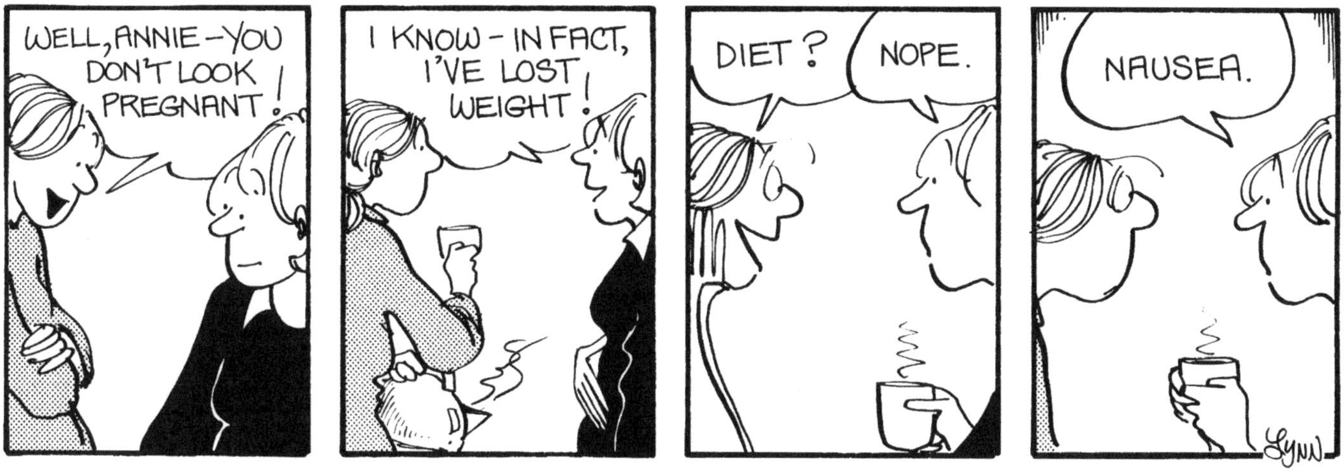
WELL, ANNIE-YOU DON'T LOOK PREGNANT!
I KNOW-IN FACT, I'VE LOST WEIGHT!
DIET?
NOPE.
NAUSEA.
Lynn

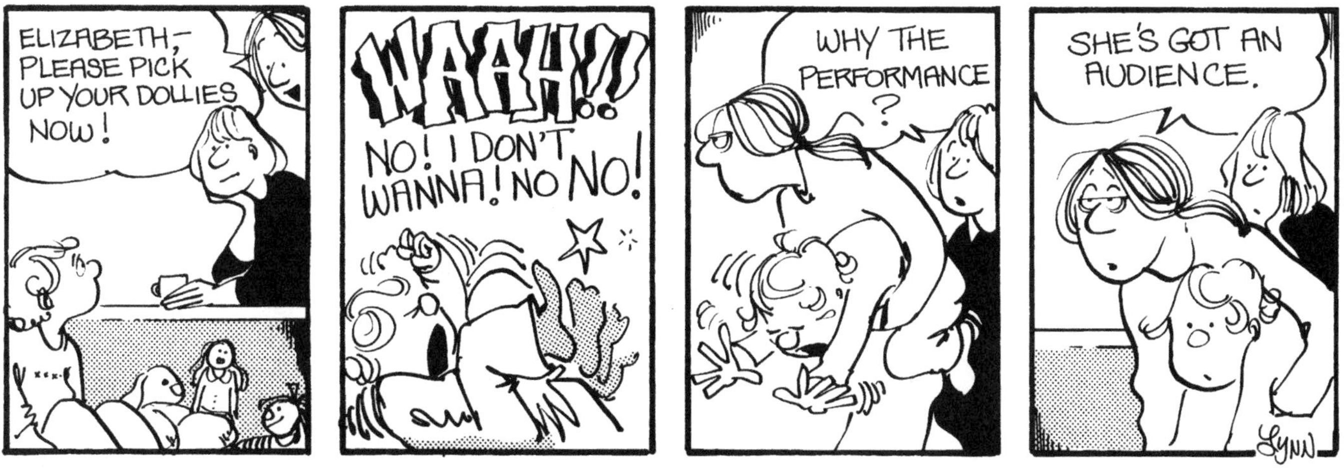
ELIZABETH,-PLEASE PICK UP YOUR DOLLIES NOW!
WAAH!!
NO! I DON'T WANNA! NO NO!
WHY THE PERFORMANCE?
SHE'S GOT AN AUDIENCE.
Lynn

Aaron could have earned an academy award for drama. It wasn't unusual for him to collapse onto the floor in an all-out fit as he faced the job of putting his Lego back in its box or picking up his shoes. From friends, I learned about an amazing secondary use for the egg timer — the TIME-OUT! Rather than fight with him, I'd set the timer and send him to his room until the timer ran out. If he continued to sulk, I would add a few more minutes. This was a lifesaver for both of us.

The GAZETTE, Montreal, Saturday, March 13, 1982

# Montrealer thrilled to be in the funnies

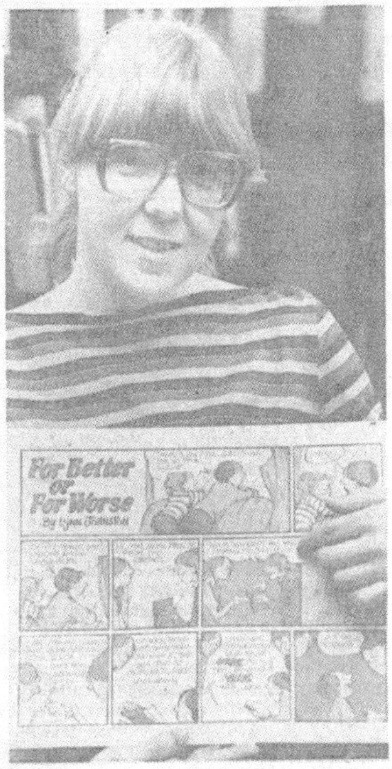
For Better or For Worse

Gazette, Jean Pierre Rivest

**Monique Prescott and her comic strip.**

**By SUSAN SCHWARTZ of The Gazette**

The 50 million North Americans who turn to the color funny pages this morning will meet a new character in *For Better or For Worse* — a character based on and named after a Montreal library clerk.

And Montrealer Monique Prescott will see her dream come true.

Prescott, 30, was written into the strip by its creator, Lynn Johnston, after telling the CTV television program *Thrill of a Lifetime* of her dream to meet the Canadian cartoonist and appear in her strip.

Johnston, 34, is a lot like Elly Patterson, the harried and over-houseworked but lovable mother and wife in the strip, according to Prescott, who recently returned from a visit with Johnston and her family at their home in Lynn Lake, Man., a small town about 840 km northwest of Winnipeg.

"Physically, Lynn Johnston is almost the same person as the cartoon character," she said.

## Believable strip

"She is really easy to meet, very down-to-earth and very friendly," said Prescott, who had been wanting to meet Johnston ever since reading an article about her in *Canadian Weekend* magazine (Dec. 1, 1979) three months after the launching of *For Better or For Worse.*

Johnston admits that her own family is the subject for her wrily funny, sensitive and very believable strip, said Prescott.

Johnston told Prescott that she often discusses ideas for the strip with her dentist husband Rod (who looks remarkably like John, Elly's husband) and 9-year-old son Aaron (Michael in the strip; the Johnstons have a 4-year-old daughter, Katie, who is Lizzie in the strip).

"You could see she likes to *live* in her house. There were eight people in the house for a full day (*Thrill of a Lifetime* television crew). She never said things like 'Don't put that on this table' or 'Wipe your feet.' She never apologized, like saying 'I'm sorry my house isn't clean.' "

## All the way

Prescott found Johnston "more outgoing and more sure of herself" than the Elly Patterson character.

"I thought she would be shy because she is a housewife and stays home a lot. She is not. She's not a shrinking violet. She is very confident of herself; you can see that," she said.

Several people, including Johnston, were surprised at Prescott's choice of thrill of a lifetime.

"I was surprised that anyone would come all the way up to Lynn Lake," Johnston told *The Gazette* in a telephone interview this week.

"I was just hoping it was someone I would instantly like and she was such a genuine person. It was such a pleasure to meet her," she said. "And I could see she was genuinely excited to be here."

Coming up with a way to incorporate Prescott in the strip took some mulling over, said Johnston.

In the strip, which appears in the color comics of today's *Gazette*, the character Monique Prescott from the library turns up at the Patterson home with Michael's math work, which he had forgotten yet again, this time at the library.

"I had to come up with an idea of someone new coming into the house, bring in the fact that she was a librarian and have the family encountering a librarian, — I just made it up as I went along and hoped I'd come up with a punch line and I did," she said.

## Central library

Appearing in the strip is important to Prescott, who works at the City of Montreal's central library.

Prescott married but has no children. Even so, she says she identifies with Elly Patterson as a woman.

"Even if you don't have children, you can love her cartoons.

"I feel what the woman in the cartoon feels for everyone else."

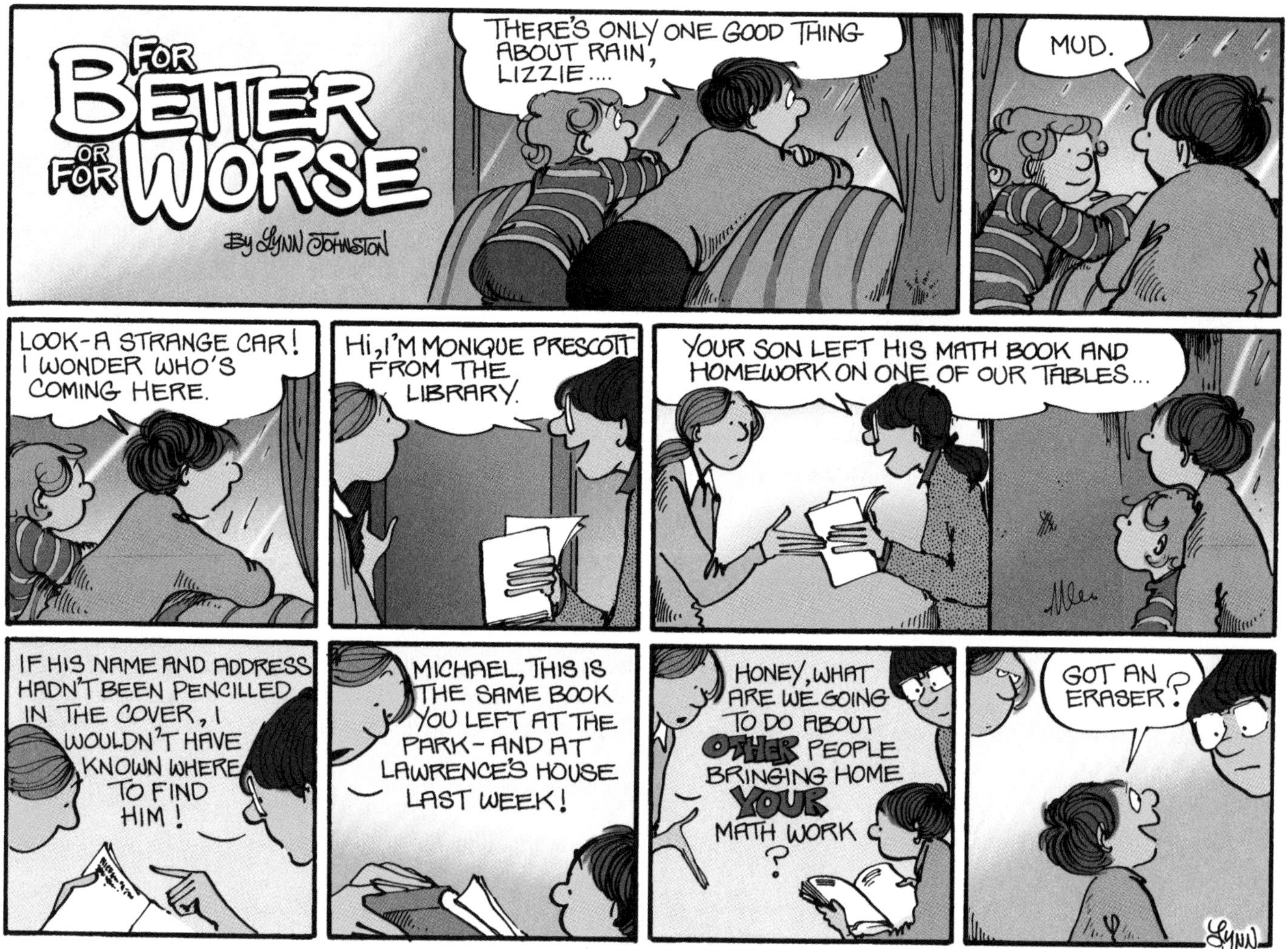
FOR BETTER OR FOR WORSE
BY LYNN JOHNSTON
THERE'S ONLY ONE GOOD THING ABOUT RAIN, LIZZIE....
MUD.
LOOK-A STRANGE CAR! I WONDER WHO'S COMING HERE.
Hi, I'M MONIQUE PRESCOTT FROM THE LIBRARY.
YOUR SON LEFT HIS MATH BOOK AND HOMEWORK ON ONE OF OUR TABLES...
IF HIS NAME AND ADDRESS HADN'T BEEN PENCILLED IN THE COVER, I WOULDN'T HAVE KNOWN WHERE TO FIND HIM!
MICHAEL, THIS IS THE SAME BOOK YOU LEFT AT THE PARK - AND AT LAWRENCE'S HOUSE LAST WEEK!
HONEY, WHAT ARE WE GOING TO DO ABOUT OTHER PEOPLE BRINGING HOME YOUR MATH WORK ?
GOT AN ERASER?
LYNN

I thoroughly enjoyed meeting Monique Prescott — a sweet and enthusiastic young woman. With her ready smile, thick hair, and glasses, she made a fine cartoon character! She stayed for the day, I drew the strip, we had dinner together, and she left the following morning. We promised to keep in touch — which we did for a while. I later met her for dinner in Montreal, but our time together was interrupted and I regret not being able to get to know her better.

Monique, if you're still in Montreal, I'd love to hear from you and find out what you've been doing after all these years!

OH, NO - NOT AGAIN!
IT'S AMAZING HOW MUCH TOOTHPASTE THERE IS IN THE ECONO-TUBE!
LYNN

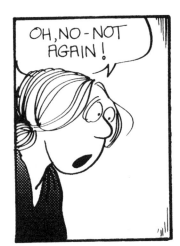

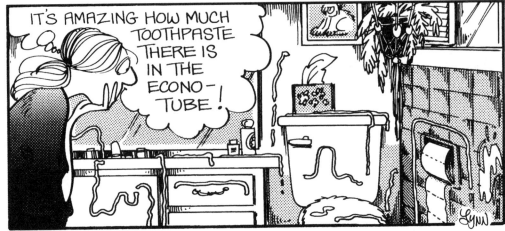

One morning, I was making my bed and Katie was playing in her room. Between the two rooms was our upstairs communal privy. It was a place that held endless fascination for both kids — what with a tub for water sports and a porcelain receptacle guaranteed to "disappear" stuff, the bathroom was, hands down, the room of choice for indoor recreation. Above the sink our hard-to-reach medicine cabinet was filled with forbidden fruit. It wasn't locked, but it took some jungle athletics to reach it and a strong pull to get it open.

Believing she was dressing up dolls, I continued to putter until the "mom's sixth sense" kicked in. I decided to check on her. Katie, having climbed the biff cabinet drawers like a staircase, had achieved the countertop plateau and was trying to open the medicine cabinet. This wasn't the only thing I discovered ... an entire tube of toothpaste had been squeezed onto virtually every surface of the room, and she was on a mission to find more. Katie loved toothpaste, and heaven knows we had access to lots of it.

I removed her from the scene and spent the rest of the day cleaning out the can. The good thing about this event was ... the bathroom smelled great for weeks afterwards!

Katie climbing bathroom "staircase."

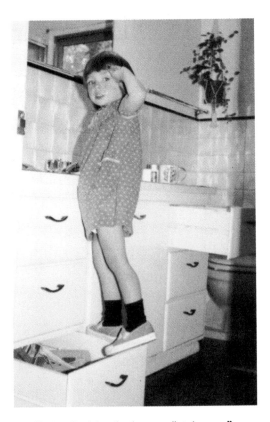

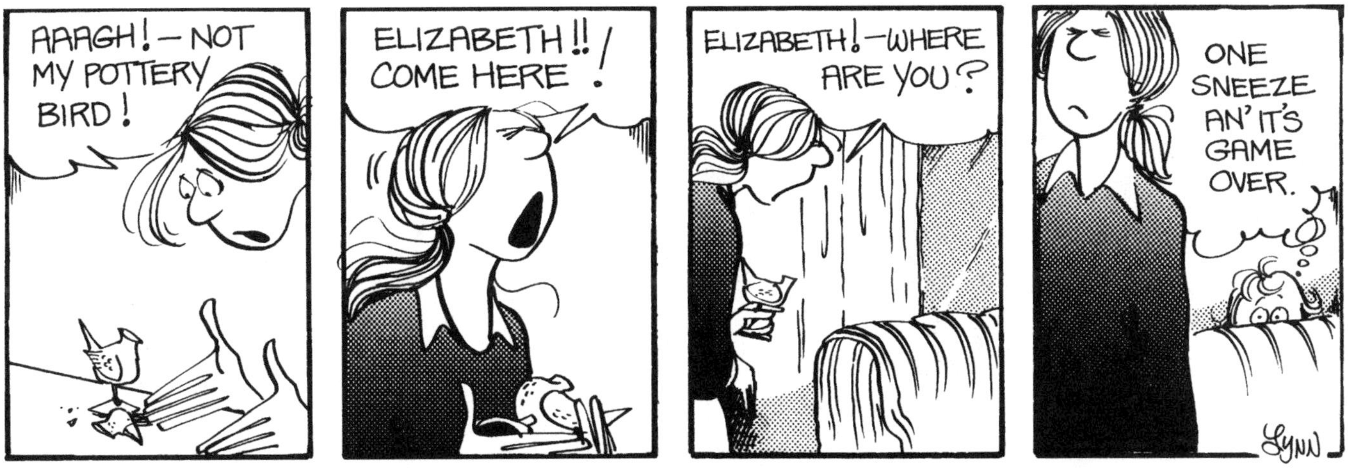
AAAGH! – NOT MY POTTERY BIRD!
ELIZABETH!! COME HERE!
ELIZABETH! – WHERE ARE YOU?
ONE SNEEZE AN' IT'S GAME OVER.

Katie was not only adept at scaling cabinetry, she was able to conceal the damage that ensued. After finding a broken figurine carefully hidden under the couch, I asked her why she didn't tell me right away. She looked at me as if I was crazy; why confess when a punishment could be deferred until … who knows? I could understand her reasoning, but I still wanted my kids to respect my property and ME! I look forward to the day she has kids of her own — I'm going to give her some china!

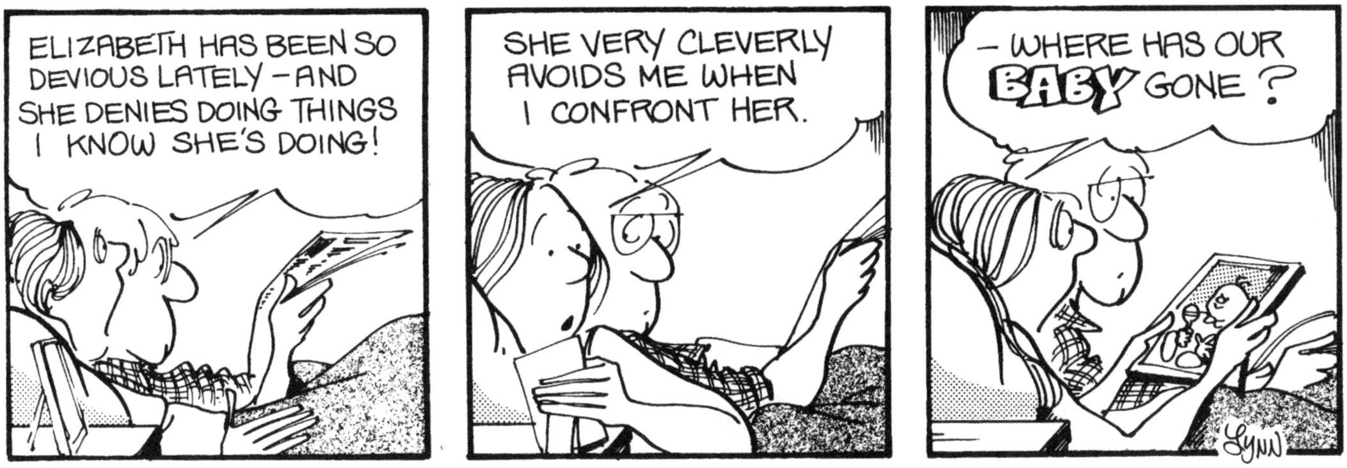
ELIZABETH HAS BEEN SO DEVIOUS LATELY – AND SHE DENIES DOING THINGS I KNOW SHE'S DOING!
SHE VERY CLEVERLY AVOIDS ME WHEN I CONFRONT HER.
– WHERE HAS OUR BABY GONE?

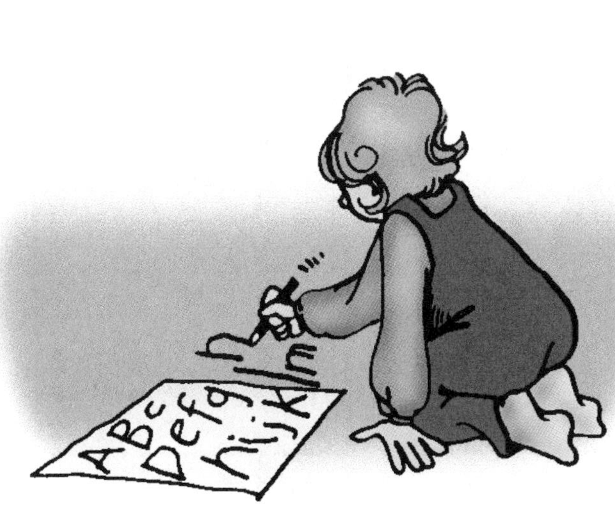

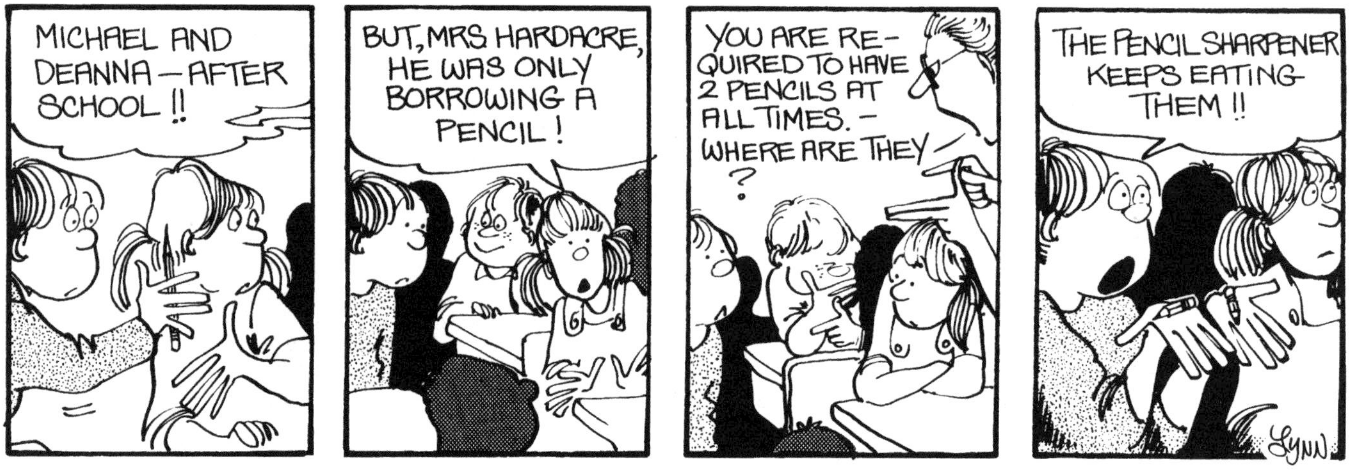
MICHAEL AND DEANNA — AFTER SCHOOL !!
BUT, MRS HARDACRE, HE WAS ONLY BORROWING A PENCIL !
YOU ARE REQUIRED TO HAVE 2 PENCILS AT ALL TIMES. — WHERE ARE THEY ?
THE PENCIL SHARPENER KEEPS EATING THEM !!
LYNN

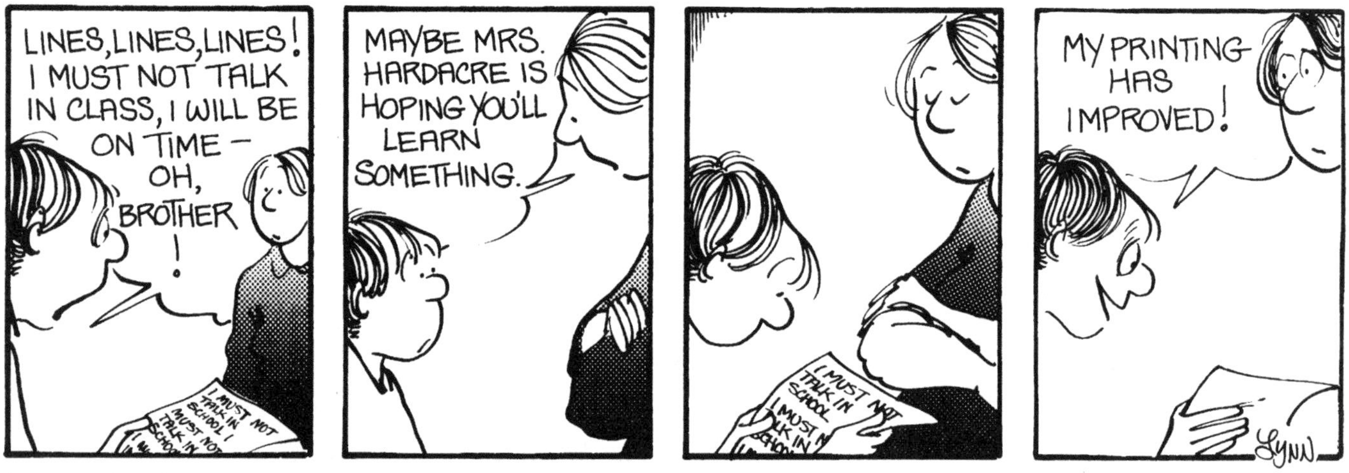
LINES, LINES, LINES! I MUST NOT TALK IN CLASS, I WILL BE ON TIME — OH, BROTHER !
MAYBE MRS. HARDACRE IS HOPING YOU'LL LEARN SOMETHING.
MY PRINTING HAS IMPROVED!
LYNN

Among other things, my mom worked as a calligrapher for my grandfather — a philatelist who dealt in rare stamps and forgeries. It was fascinating to watch her do the beautiful handwritten text that went with each "cover." Occasionally, she would patiently sit and teach me the art of fine lettering. I just loved to write. I loved to write lessons and poems and copy stuff from the blackboard. If I was told to write lines after school, I didn't mind at all — it gave me a chance to show off!

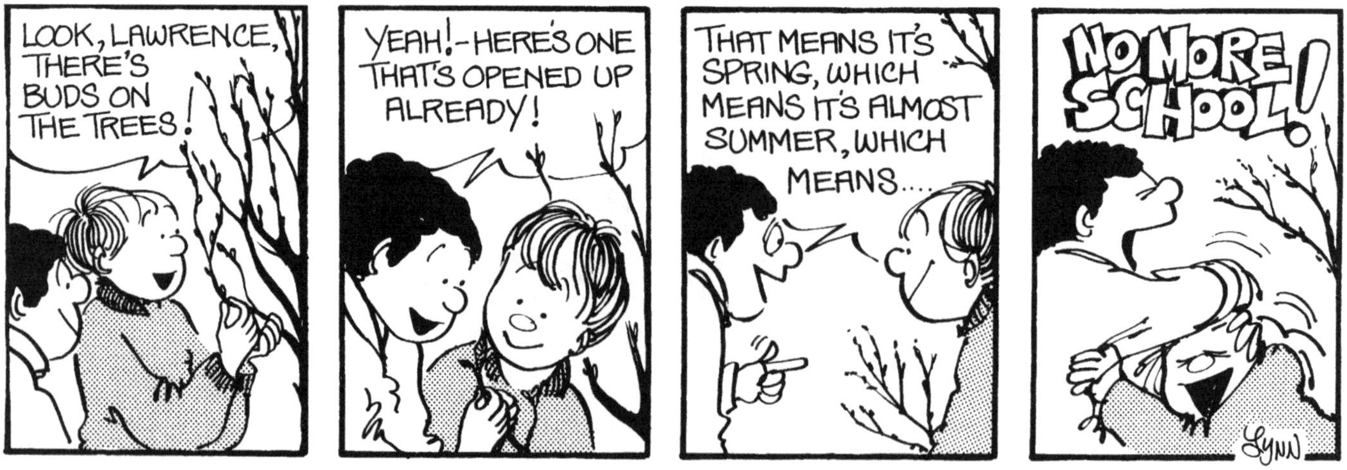
LOOK, LAWRENCE, THERE'S BUDS ON THE TREES!
YEAH! - HERE'S ONE THAT'S OPENED UP ALREADY!
THAT MEANS IT'S SPRING, WHICH MEANS IT'S ALMOST SUMMER, WHICH MEANS....
NO MORE SCHOOL!
LYNN

Summer in North Vancouver meant running down to the ferry dock and fishing for crabs or riding our bikes up to Lynn Canyon and swinging on the suspension bridge. It meant taking the bus to Stanley Park, English Bay, walking around the sea wall, taking the ferry to Bowen Island, and going to summer camp. There was so much to do, and we couldn't wait for school to be finished so we could get out and do it!

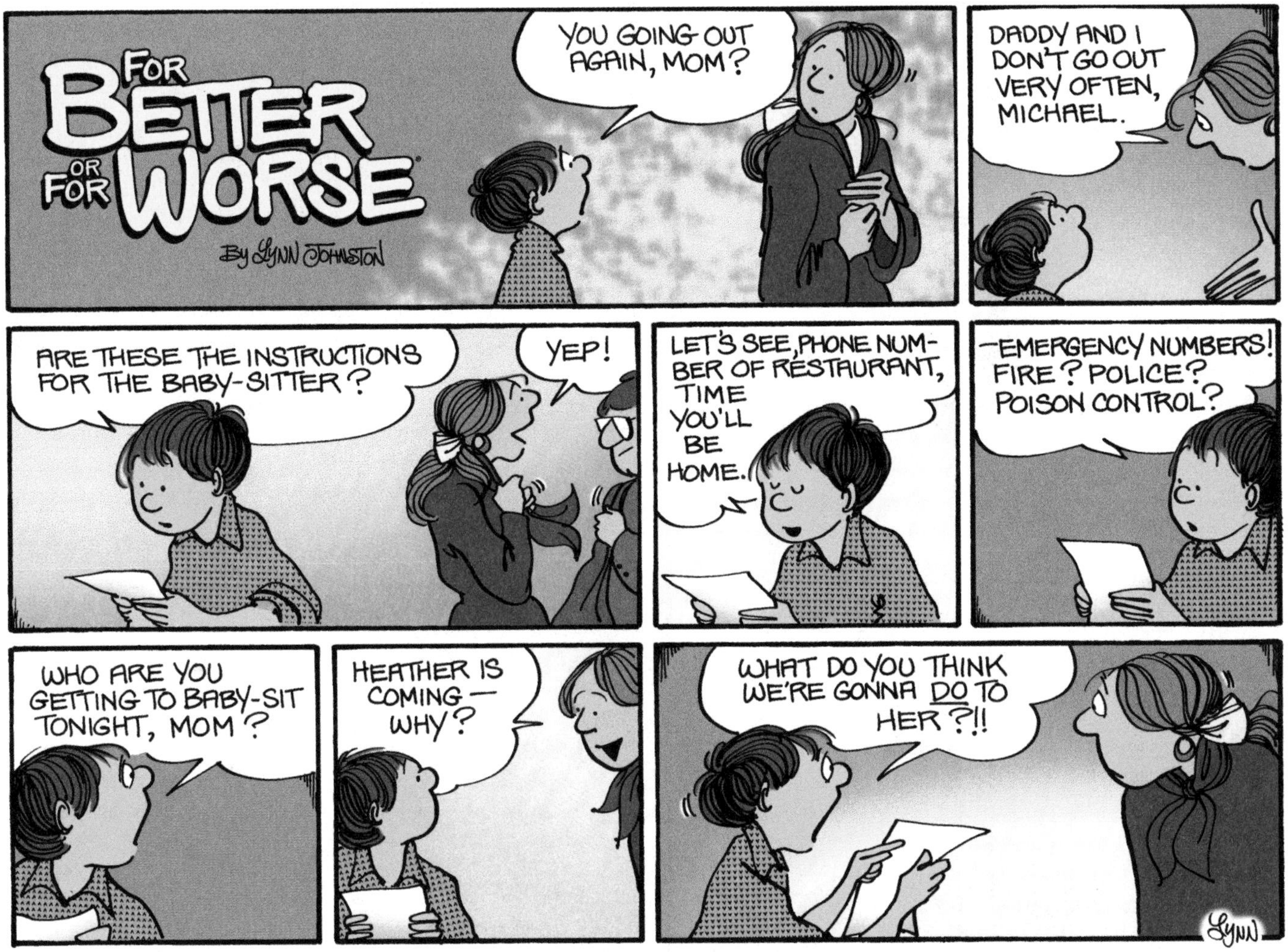
FOR BETTER OR FOR WORSE
BY LYNN JOHNSTON
YOU GOING OUT AGAIN, MOM?
DADDY AND I DON'T GO OUT VERY OFTEN, MICHAEL.
ARE THESE THE INSTRUCTIONS FOR THE BABY-SITTER?
YEP!
LET'S SEE, PHONE NUMBER OF RESTAURANT, TIME YOU'LL BE HOME.
—EMERGENCY NUMBERS! FIRE? POLICE? POISON CONTROL?
WHO ARE YOU GETTING TO BABY-SIT TONIGHT, MOM?
HEATHER IS COMING— WHY?
WHAT DO YOU THINK WE'RE GONNA DO TO HER?!!
LYNN

Tootie Arbuckle babysat for my brother and me. She lived next door, and I thought she was cool because she had the preserved fetus of a calf in a jar on her bedside table. She also had chickens and frogs on which she would perform experiments. She fed the chickens coloured grain to see if they would lay coloured eggs, and she found out that frogs ate each other as readily as they ate flies. She showed us how dragonfly larvae chewed up tadpoles, and helped us boil a dead raccoon to get the bones for science class. Tootie was from a tough family and was made of solid stuff. Nonetheless, Alan and I gave her a run for her money when she babysat.

It was important for us to know our sitters' soft spots, what buttons to push, and where we could get her down. It's no wonder that our folks had a hard time finding people hardy enough to suffer through an evening with "the Ridgway kids," but Tootie tried. She was strong and she needed the money. I remember her asking my parents exactly where they would be and when they'd be home and looking at us as if to say "Try anything and you're toast!"

One evening after the folks had gone to their place of reprieve, Alan and I started our reign of terror. Tootie tried to get the upper hand but gave up and went to the phone.

"Are you calling our dad?" (Our dad was a notorious softie.)

"No" she said. "I'm calling MINE!"

Within minutes, George Arbuckle, a short, stocky man with a very short fuse, came in the kitchen door and slammed it shut. He worked in the shipyards and took "no guff from nobody." He cruised around us, slapping his fist into the palm of his hand and soon had the two of us cowering in our beds with the threat of a pounding as security.

The next morning, my folks said that Tootie's report had been favourable, that we had been "as good as gold," and from now on Tootie would be our regular sitter. I don't think they ever found out about Mr. Arbuckle's influence on our behaviour, and we never pushed Tootie that far again!

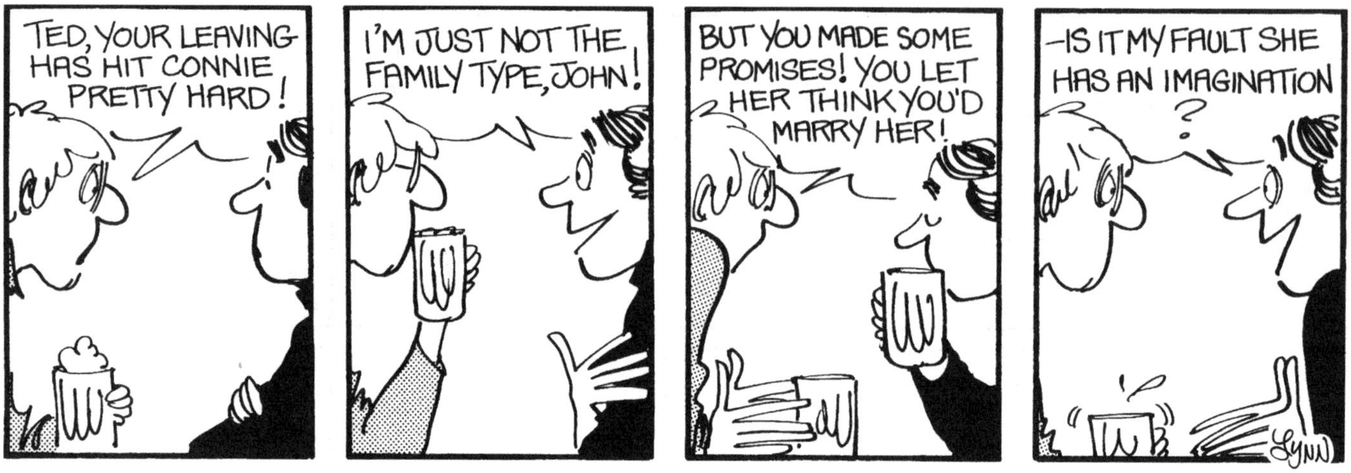
TED, YOUR LEAVING HAS HIT CONNIE PRETTY HARD!
I'M JUST NOT THE FAMILY TYPE, JOHN!
BUT YOU MADE SOME PROMISES! YOU LET HER THINK YOU'D MARRY HER!
–IS IT MY FAULT SHE HAS AN IMAGINATION
?
LYNN

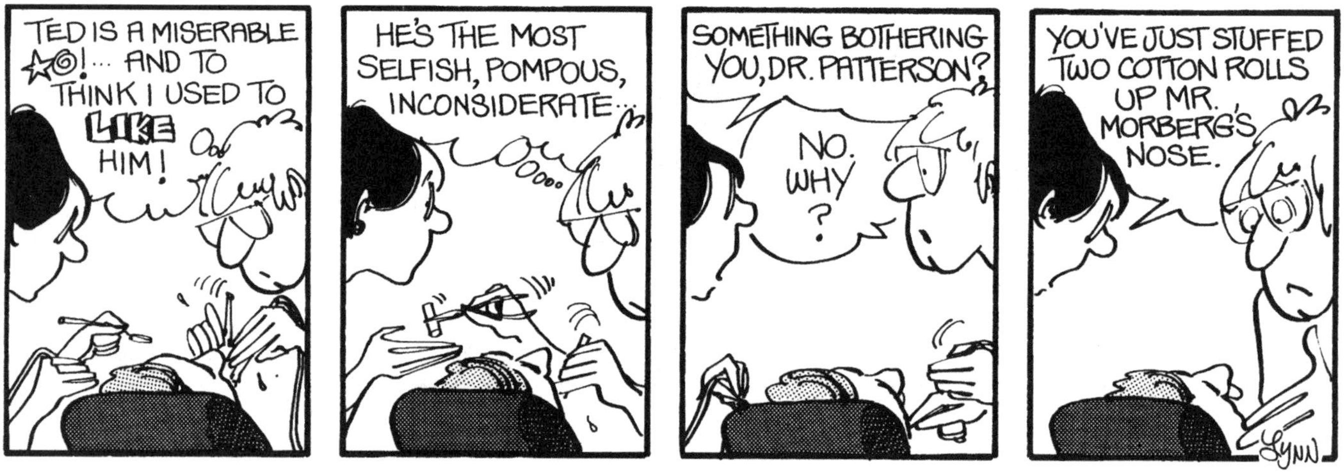
TED IS A MISERABLE ☆@!... AND TO THINK I USED TO LIKE HIM!
HE'S THE MOST SELFISH, POMPOUS, INCONSIDERATE...
SOMETHING BOTHERING YOU, DR. PATTERSON?
NO. WHY?
YOU'VE JUST STUFFED TWO COTTON ROLLS UP MR. MORBERG'S NOSE.
LYNN

Here I used the name of a friend who had started a busy flight service in northern Manitoba — CALM Air was Carl Arnold Lawrence Morberg's "baby" and he ran it well. His family and friends called him as soon as they saw his name in the paper — he was able to reconnect with folks he hadn't seen in years!

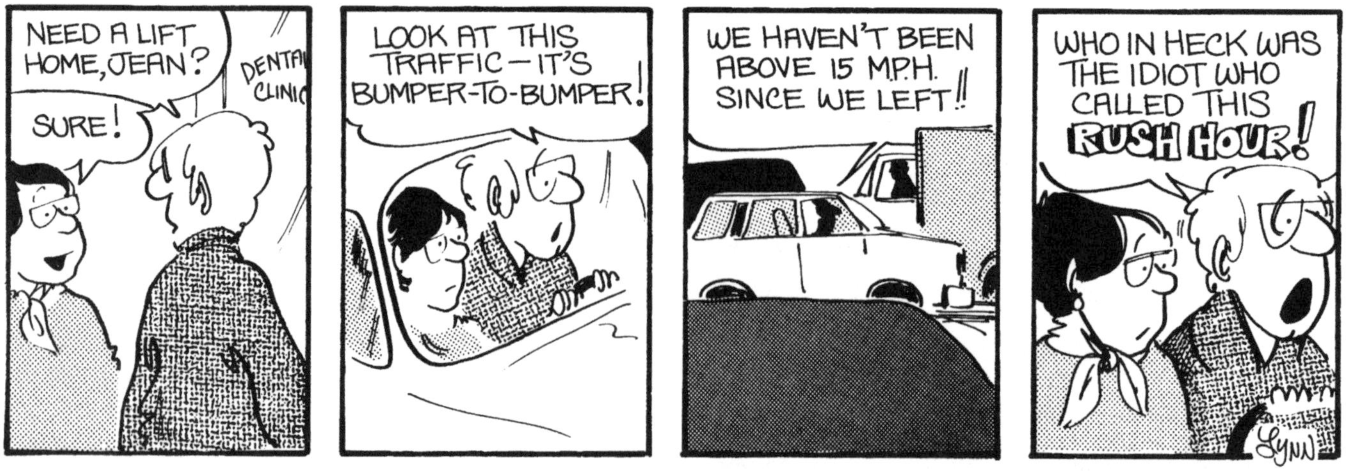
NEED A LIFT HOME, JEAN?
SURE!
LOOK AT THIS TRAFFIC – IT'S BUMPER-TO-BUMPER!
WE HAVEN'T BEEN ABOVE 15 M.P.H. SINCE WE LEFT!!
WHO IN HECK WAS THE IDIOT WHO CALLED THIS RUSH HOUR!
LYNN

Lynn Lake was so small that everyone but the miners walked to work. "Rush hour" was what we called the after-work lineup at the pub!

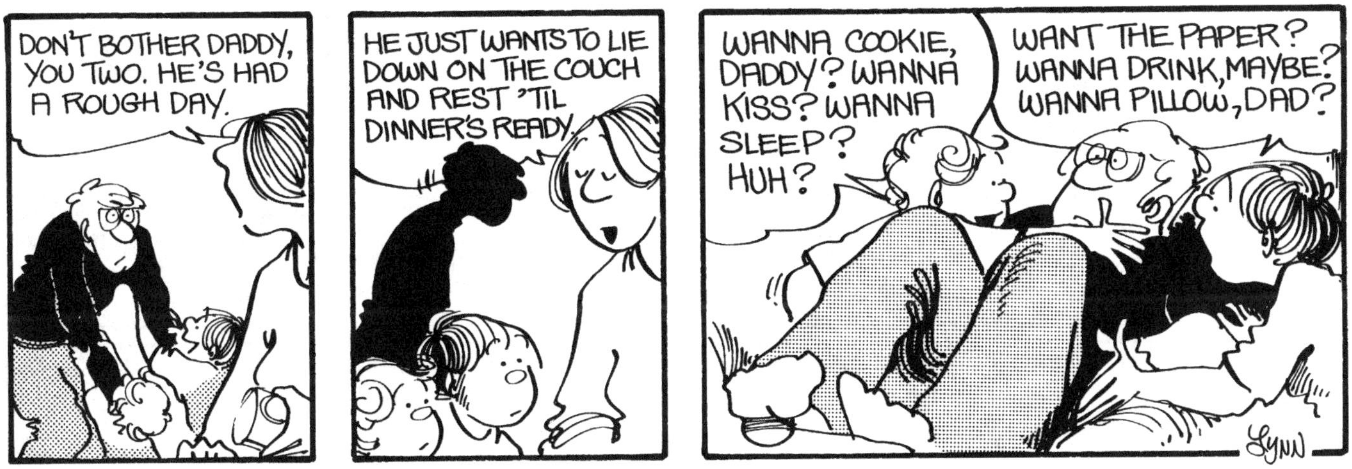
DON'T BOTHER DADDY, YOU TWO. HE'S HAD A ROUGH DAY.
HE JUST WANTS TO LIE DOWN ON THE COUCH AND REST 'TIL DINNER'S READY.
WANNA COOKIE, DADDY? WANNA KISS? WANNA SLEEP? HUH?
WANT THE PAPER? WANNA DRINK, MAYBE? WANNA PILLOW, DAD?
LYNN

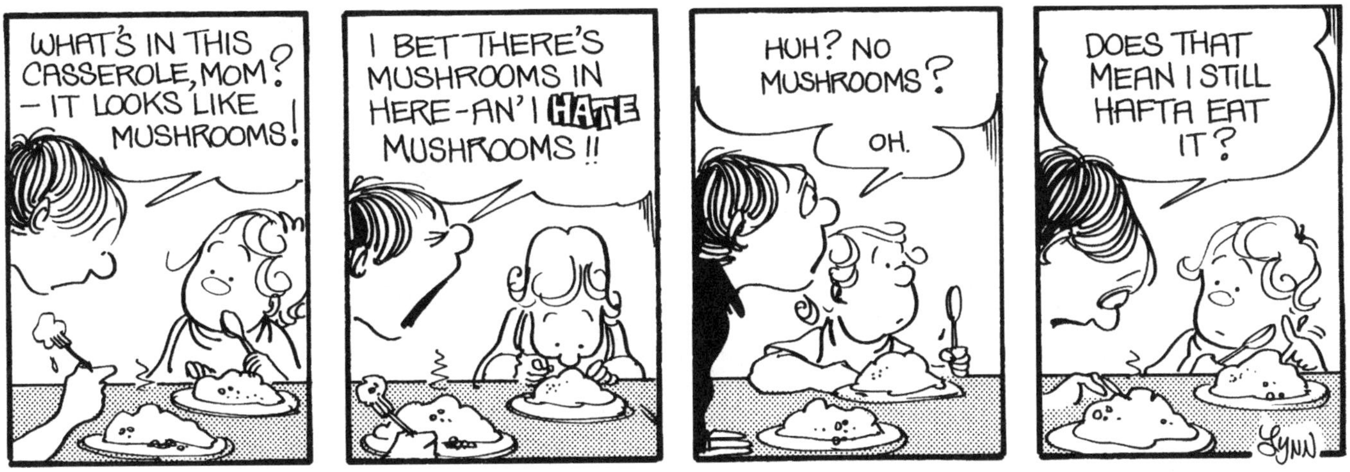
WHAT'S IN THIS CASSEROLE, MOM? – IT LOOKS LIKE MUSHROOMS!
I BET THERE'S MUSHROOMS IN HERE–AN' I HATE MUSHROOMS!!
HUH? NO MUSHROOMS?
OH.
DOES THAT MEAN I STILL HAFTA EAT IT?
LYNN

The two local grocery stores in Lynn Lake did their best to supply fresh meat, but fresh veggies were something of a luxury. Aaron was not a fan of mushrooms (and still isn't), but if I could lay my hands on a fresh pack of mushies, by jove, we were gonna eat them. He has a tongue that can locate and isolate a mushroom faster than a dog spits out pills! I wasn't going to make fungus-free meals just for HIM! "I hate mushrooms" was uttered more than once around our dinner table.

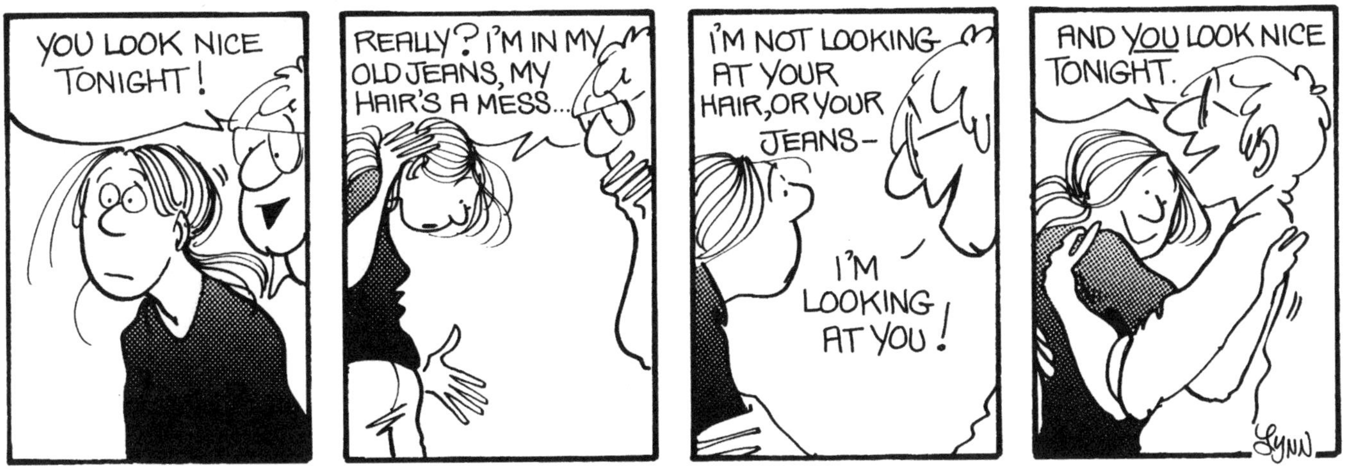
YOU LOOK NICE TONIGHT!
REALLY? I'M IN MY OLD JEANS, MY HAIR'S A MESS...
I'M NOT LOOKING AT YOUR HAIR, OR YOUR JEANS–
I'M LOOKING AT YOU!
AND YOU LOOK NICE TONIGHT.
LYNN

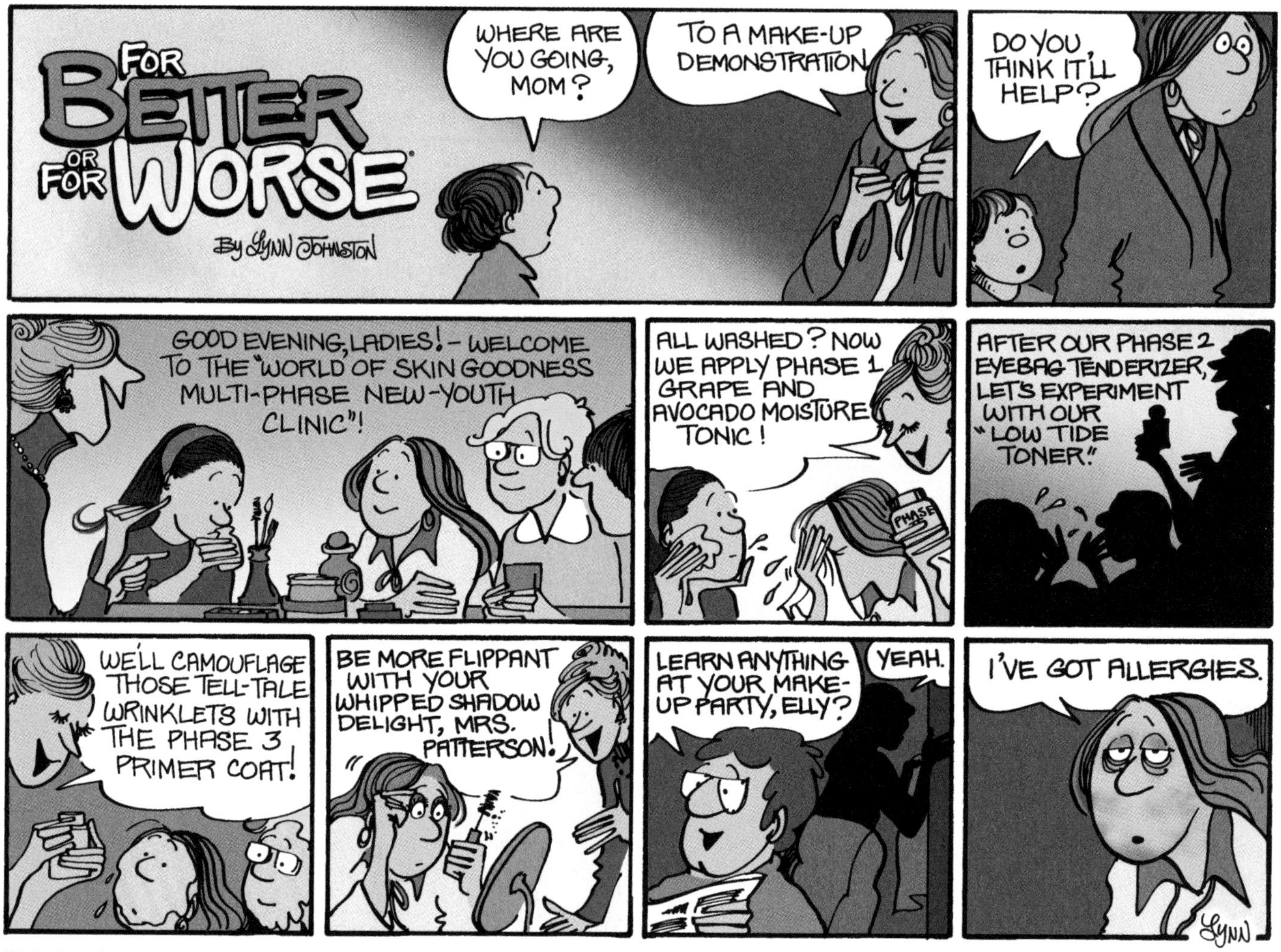
FOR BETTER OR FOR WORSE
BY LYNN JOHNSTON
WHERE ARE YOU GOING, MOM?
TO A MAKE-UP DEMONSTRATION.
DO YOU THINK IT'LL HELP?
GOOD EVENING, LADIES! - WELCOME TO THE "WORLD OF SKIN GOODNESS MULTI-PHASE NEW-YOUTH CLINIC"!
ALL WASHED? NOW WE APPLY PHASE 1, GRAPE AND AVOCADO MOISTURE TONIC!
PHASE
AFTER OUR PHASE 2 EYEBAG TENDERIZER, LET'S EXPERIMENT WITH OUR "LOW TIDE TONER."
WE'LL CAMOUFLAGE THOSE TELL-TALE WRINKLETS WITH THE PHASE 3 PRIMER COAT!
BE MORE FLIPPANT WITH YOUR WHIPPED SHADOW DELIGHT, MRS. PATTERSON!
LEARN ANYTHING AT YOUR MAKE-UP PARTY, ELLY?
YEAH.
I'VE GOT ALLERGIES.
LYNN

This Sunday page was done as a result of a television program. The National Film Board had started a sort of documentary on *FBorFW*, and a crew had been sent to Lynn Lake to record the local "colour." One of the things we ladies did for fun was to attend different demonstrations at each other's homes. Small private sales events were as popular then as they are now. We went to Tupperware and candle sales, clothing shows, cooking and makeup demonstrations — anything that would get us out of the house and into an adult environment. Booze was optional, but certainly helped augment the ambiance and the sales.

For the sake of the Film Board, I agreed to host a makeup demonstration in my home. The process required the participants to allow their hair to be tied back so that a variety of goops and granules could be spread on their faces. This was not appreciated by some of the ladies who had never been on television and didn't want their debut to be mid-toilette.

After a bit of cajoling and a few drinks, we proceeded to give the NFB the inside scoop on the home facial demo ... doing what we could to make this the highlight of the film. It took hours and many applications of facial stuff before we could call it quits. The ladies departed with grateful thanks from all involved, and I promised them a copy of the video if it ever came to be. It did. The all-day makeup demonstration, with retakes, reasks, and redos, however, was reduced to a few seconds of the film. No one complained. It was fun to do, but none of us was really too keen to see the results — some things are best left on the cutting room floor!

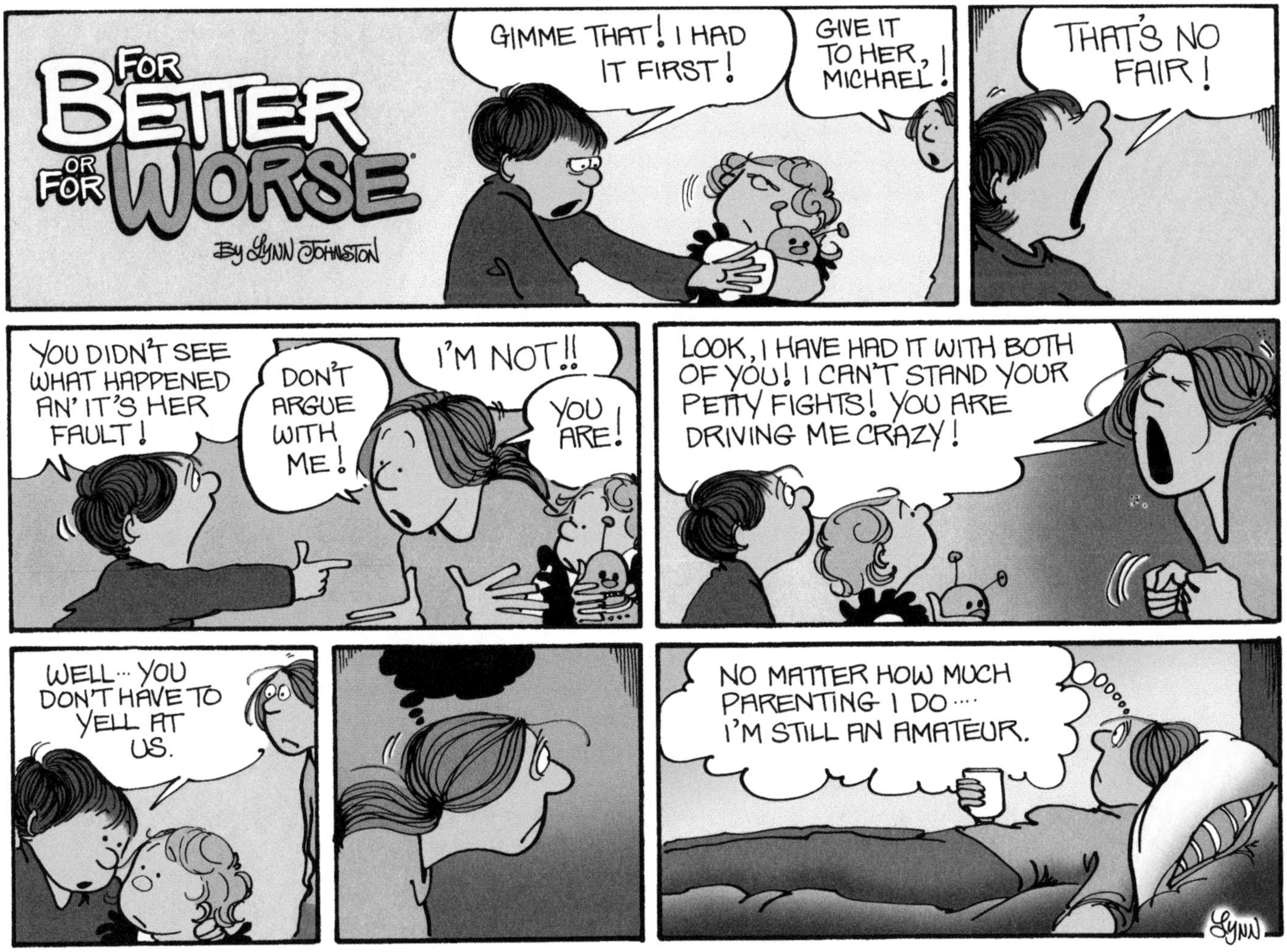
FOR BETTER OR FOR WORSE
BY LYNN JOHNSTON
GIMME THAT! I HAD IT FIRST!
GIVE IT TO HER, MICHAEL!
THAT'S NO FAIR!
YOU DIDN'T SEE WHAT HAPPENED AN' IT'S HER FAULT!
DON'T ARGUE WITH ME!
I'M NOT!!
YOU ARE!
LOOK, I HAVE HAD IT WITH BOTH OF YOU! I CAN'T STAND YOUR PETTY FIGHTS! YOU ARE DRIVING ME CRAZY!
WELL... YOU DON'T HAVE TO YELL AT US.
NO MATTER HOW MUCH PARENTING I DO.... I'M STILL AN AMATEUR.
LYNN

I don't know how many times I sat alone after some frustrating bout with the kids, wishing I had "done it better." It's hard to do something better if you're doing it for the first time — and considering how many "firsts" there are in parenting, we're bound to make a few mistakes along the way. Books, professionals, friends, and family can give advice, but in the end this is our responsibility, our environment, our rules — and everyone has to learn to get along.

Even though I did my best, I made some awful errors; I shouted, I cried, I fought, and I did things that weren't fair. I remember some tearful times when I had to admit I had not handled something well and I told my children I was truly sorry.

Noisy and fanciful, naive and full of mischief, children are still people. They know what's fair and what's not. They can detect a lie. They can sniff out insincerity and they appreciate an apology as much as anyone else. Parenting is sure a challenge, but I wouldn't give it up for anything!

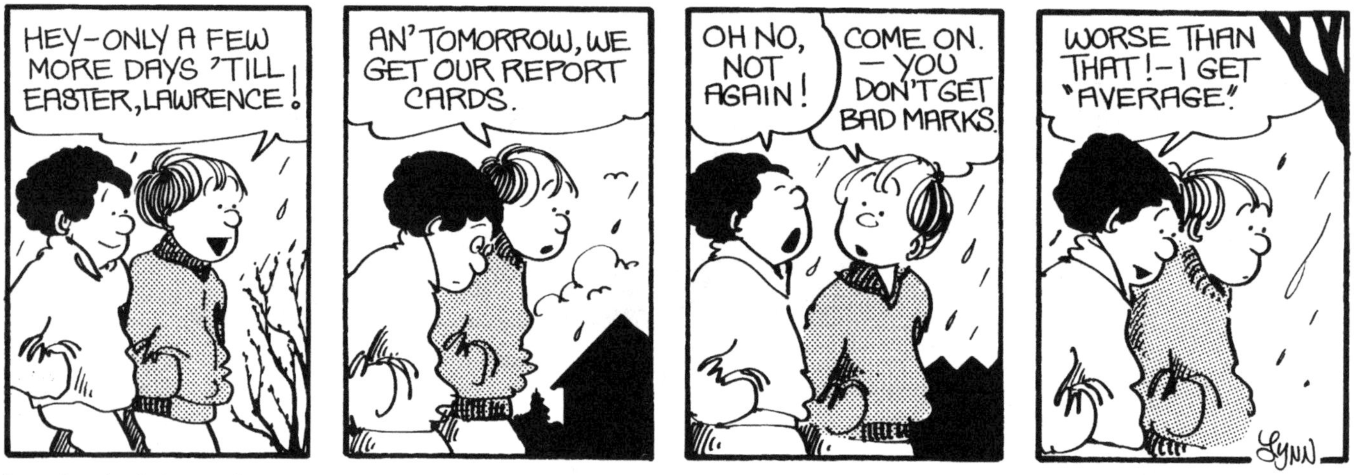
HEY-ONLY A FEW MORE DAYS 'TILL EASTER, LAWRENCE!
AN' TOMORROW, WE GET OUR REPORT CARDS.
OH NO, NOT AGAIN!
COME ON. — YOU DON'T GET BAD MARKS.
WORSE THAN THAT!-I GET "AVERAGE."
LYNN

I used to look forward to getting my report cards. My marks would always be: A in art and reading, B in everything else but math and sports — in those subjects I was lucky to get a pass.

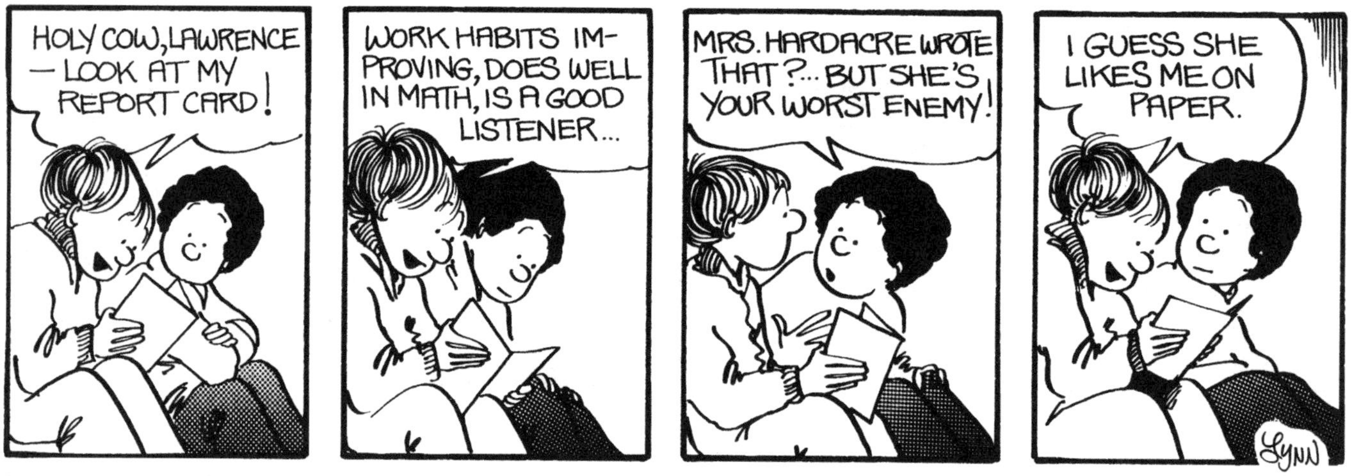
HOLY COW, LAWRENCE — LOOK AT MY REPORT CARD!
WORK HABITS IMPROVING, DOES WELL IN MATH, IS A GOOD LISTENER...
MRS. HARDACRE WROTE THAT?... BUT SHE'S YOUR WORST ENEMY!
I GUESS SHE LIKES ME ON PAPER.
LYNN

In the teacher's comment column, I could expect "Excellent work in the subjects she enjoys, does not apply herself in math and sports. Does not concentrate. Likes to be the class clown." I was content with my educational prowess, much to the chagrin of my parents and teachers, who tried to persuade me to do better. The best comment I can remember came from my grade four teacher George Stibbs, who said that I "made the class fun and interesting."

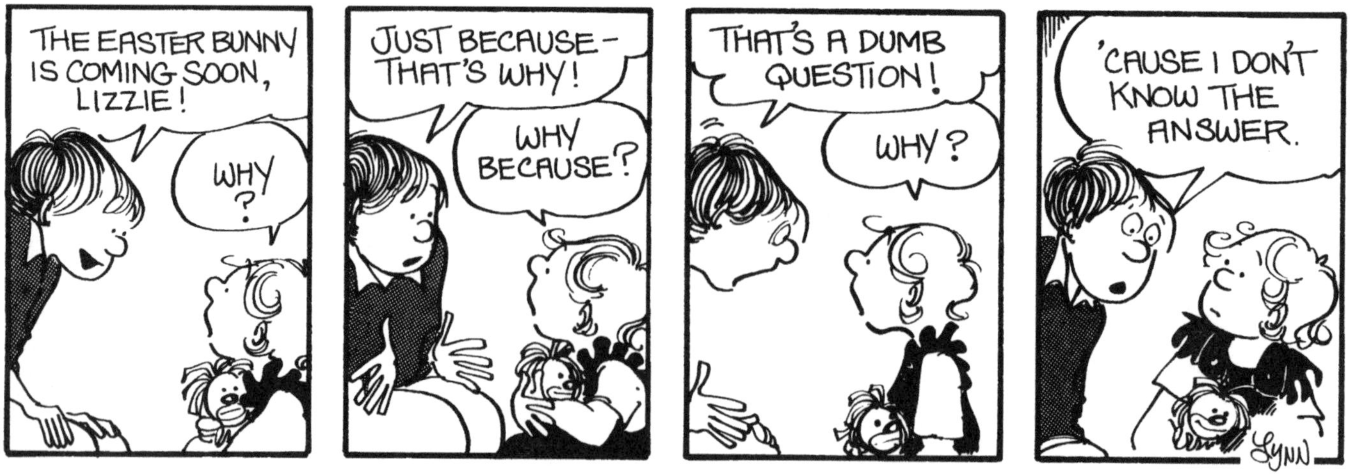
THE EASTER BUNNY IS COMING SOON, LIZZIE!
WHY?
JUST BECAUSE-THAT'S WHY!
WHY BECAUSE?
THAT'S A DUMB QUESTION!
WHY?
'CAUSE I DON'T KNOW THE ANSWER.
LYNN

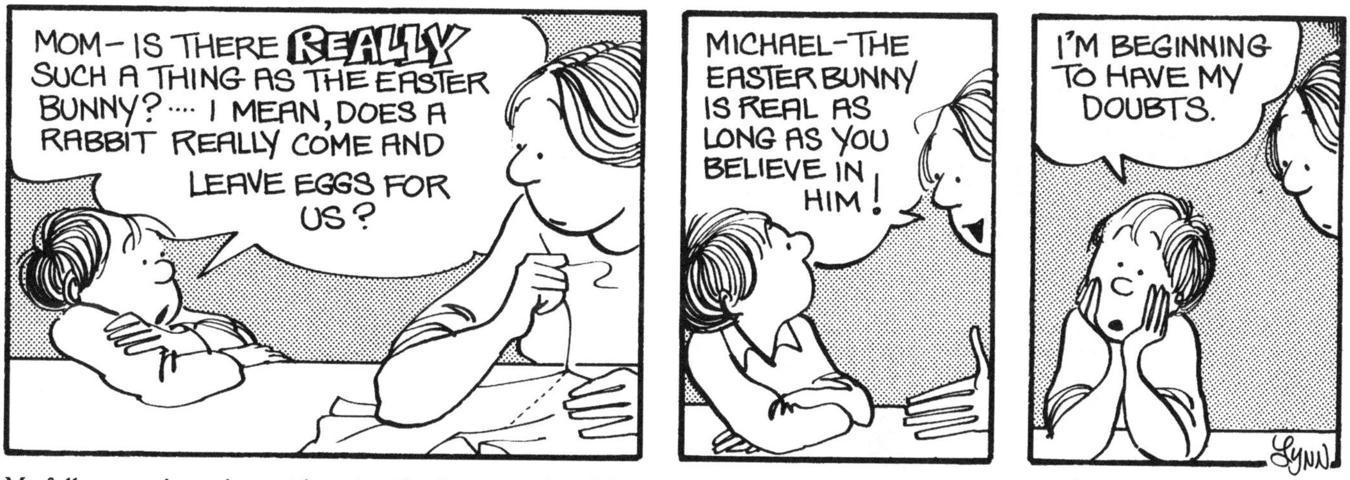
MOM– IS THERE REALLY SUCH A THING AS THE EASTER BUNNY? .... I MEAN, DOES A RABBIT REALLY COME AND LEAVE EGGS FOR US?
MICHAEL–THE EASTER BUNNY IS REAL AS LONG AS YOU BELIEVE IN HIM!
I'M BEGINNING TO HAVE MY DOUBTS.
LYNN

My folks were ingenious at keeping the fantasy going. My mother, though eager to teach us everything about science and nature, went far beyond the old "As long as you believe, he exists" thing and asked us to prove the Easter Bunny did NOT exist, which, until we were at the skeptical age of eight, was pretty hard to do. The fact was that it was fun to believe and there was always the fear that if the spell was broken, we wouldn't get chocolate anymore!

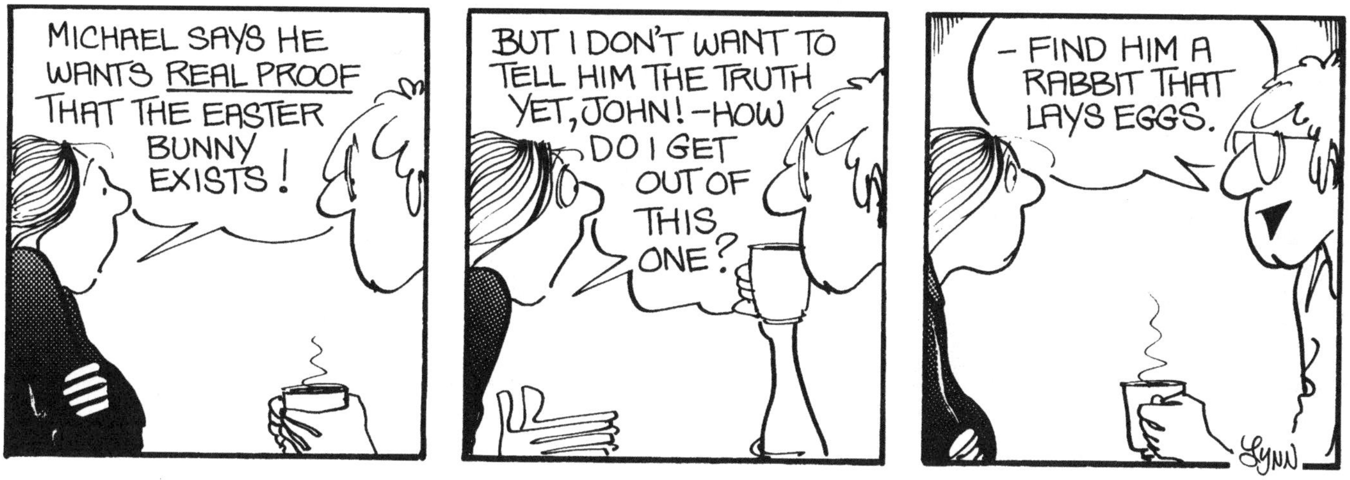
MICHAEL SAYS HE WANTS REAL PROOF THAT THE EASTER BUNNY EXISTS!
BUT I DON'T WANT TO TELL HIM THE TRUTH YET, JOHN! –HOW DO I GET OUT OF THIS ONE?
– FIND HIM A RABBIT THAT LAYS EGGS.
LYNN

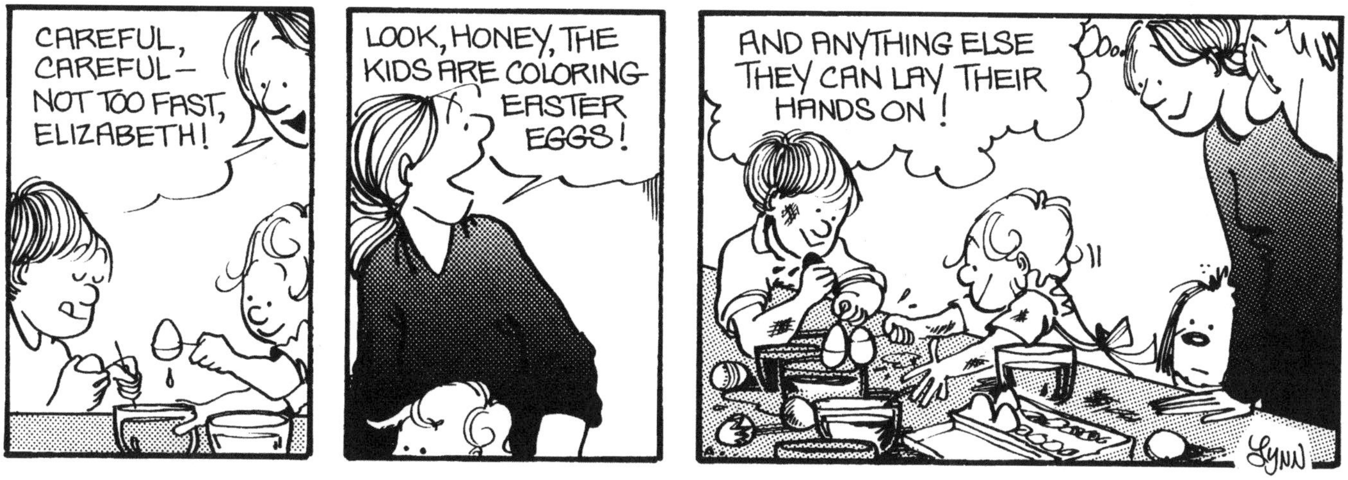
CAREFUL, CAREFUL– NOT TOO FAST, ELIZABETH!
LOOK, HONEY, THE KIDS ARE COLORING EASTER EGGS!
AND ANYTHING ELSE THEY CAN LAY THEIR HANDS ON!
LYNN

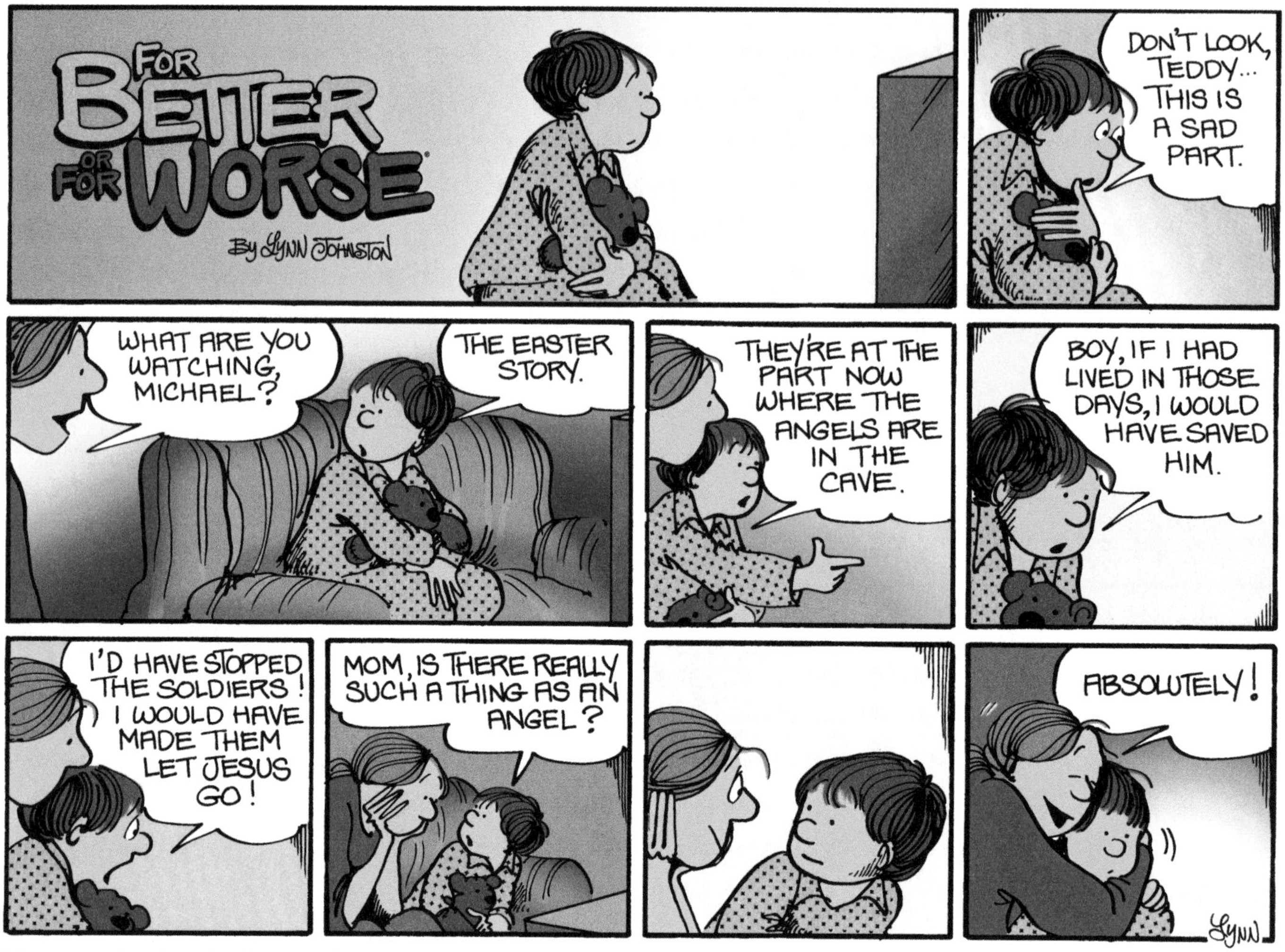
FOR BETTER OR FOR WORSE
BY LYNN JOHNSTON
DON'T LOOK, TEDDY... THIS IS A SAD PART.
WHAT ARE YOU WATCHING, MICHAEL?
THE EASTER STORY.
THEY'RE AT THE PART NOW WHERE THE ANGELS ARE IN THE CAVE.
BOY, IF I HAD LIVED IN THOSE DAYS, I WOULD HAVE SAVED HIM.
I'D HAVE STOPPED THE SOLDIERS! I WOULD HAVE MADE THEM LET JESUS GO!
MOM, IS THERE REALLY SUCH A THING AS AN ANGEL?
ABSOLUTELY!
LYNN

These are the thoughts I had as I sat in church with my mother listening to the Easter morning service. Our Anglican minister put a heavy focus on the death of Jesus, and we were all made to feel responsible! "It's because of YOU that he died! You are all SINNERS!!! You nailed Him to the cross!" I was eight years old and I thought ... "But, I wasn't there! I wasn't responsible! I wasn't even BORN yet!"

Years later, when my children asked to know more about the Easter story, I tried to tell it in a way that they could understand by putting the blame on a time when people were often unjustly condemned. I think this helped to separate them from a tragedy that occurred two thousand years ago and allowed them to focus on the message, the meaning, and what was achieved.

This cartoon was done after Aaron and I had watched a movie together — I think it was *Ben Hur*. He was so moved by the crucifixion that he wished he had been there to prevent it. It was an exceptional moment that we shared together and we talked about it for some time. This is one instance when I had an opportunity to talk about some really serious concepts with my son and in the strip as well.

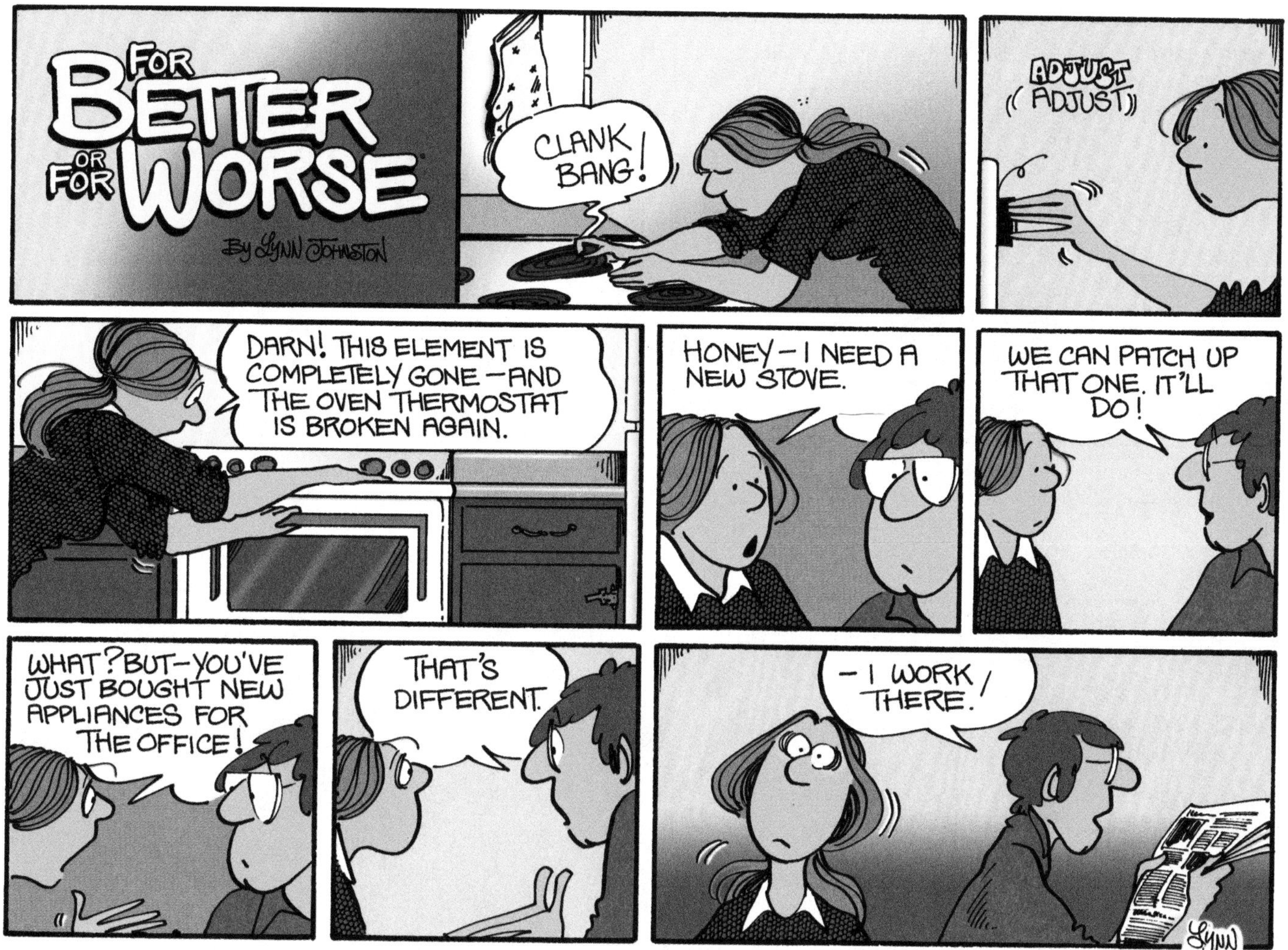
FOR BETTER OR FOR WORSE
BY LYNN JOHNSTON
CLANK BANG!
ADJUST (( ADJUST ))
DARN! THIS ELEMENT IS COMPLETELY GONE — AND THE OVEN THERMOSTAT IS BROKEN AGAIN.
HONEY — I NEED A NEW STOVE.
WE CAN PATCH UP THAT ONE. IT'LL DO!
WHAT? BUT — YOU'VE JUST BOUGHT NEW APPLIANCES FOR THE OFFICE!
THAT'S DIFFERENT.
— I WORK THERE!
LYNN

Neither one of us was adept at fixing things, although we tried. In the north, if there were no spare parts, you had to wait for something to come by mail or hope there was a similar machine at the dump. This made duct tape and bailing twine common supplies for repair.

My kitchen appliance décor was that peculiar shade of yellow they called "harvest gold" … but it was closer to the colour of cottage cheese, well past the expiry date — which describes the appliances as well. My stove had one of those ceramic tops — a source of interest and considerable invention. Not only did we cook directly on it, but I found that I could repair paperback books by running the spine quickly across the cooking surface to melt the glue — voilà, no more loose pages! The oven was often used to dry wet winter boots — something we only forgot about once; the memory of hot felt and scorched rubber still comes to mind.

The future of the town was so uncertain that buying anything new meant we might be removing it soon after it was installed. The question of whether to repair or replace was always a challenge to answer. I remember being quite miffed that the machinery at the clinic was always in top working order and our home equipment was not. I guess … "patients are a virtue!!"

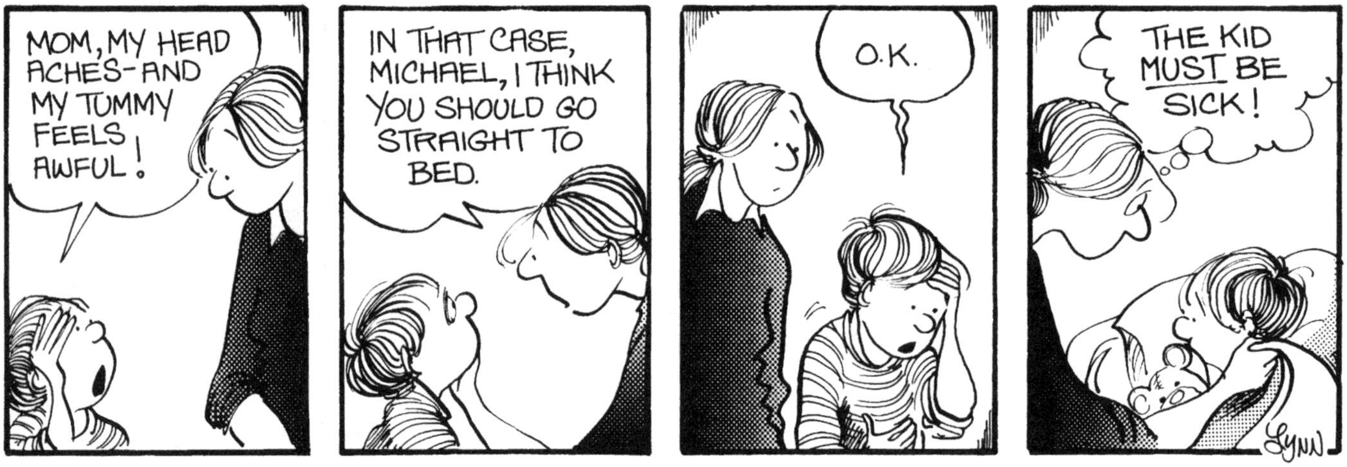
MOM, MY HEAD ACHES-AND MY TUMMY FEELS AWFUL!
IN THAT CASE, MICHAEL, I THINK YOU SHOULD GO STRAIGHT TO BED.
O.K.
THE KID MUST BE SICK!

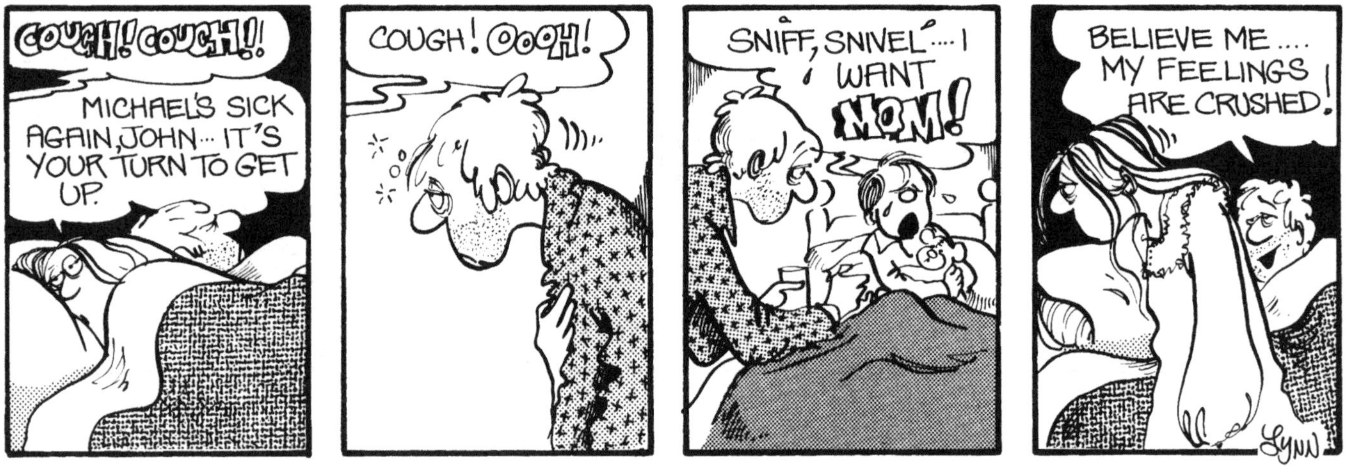
COUGH! COUGH!!
MICHAEL'S SICK AGAIN, JOHN... IT'S YOUR TURN TO GET UP.
COUGH! OOOH!
SNIFF, SNIVEL.... I WANT MOM!
BELIEVE ME.... MY FEELINGS ARE CRUSHED!

My mom always wanted a career in medicine, so heaven help you if you felt sick. She had a remedy for everything. We went to bed wearing diapers pinned to our chests, spread with hot mustard. With towels over our heads, we breathed fumes from a bowl of boiling water and camphor. We drank hot milk and rum, gagged on malt extract and cod liver oil, and when she was really stumped, there was always the dreaded enema! Despite the awful concoctions, we knew she really cared.

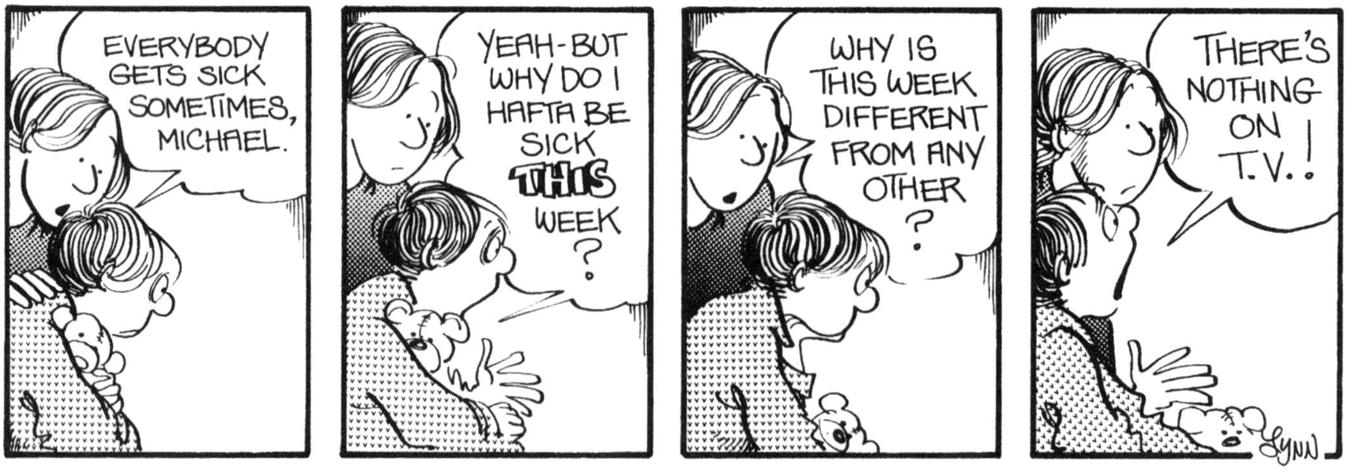
EVERYBODY GETS SICK SOMETIMES, MICHAEL.
YEAH-BUT WHY DO I HAFTA BE SICK THIS WEEK?
WHY IS THIS WEEK DIFFERENT FROM ANY OTHER?
THERE'S NOTHING ON T.V.!

Mom worked full time at our jewellery shop on Lonsdale, but if either Alan or I was seriously down for the count, she'd drop everything and stay home. At these times, nothing was as soothing as having someone read to me. My mother read us wonderful stories from The Brothers Grimm to Rupert Bear, the Golden Books and Dickens. She read well, putting life and drama into everything. Sad to say that when my kids were home sick, they preferred to watch television!

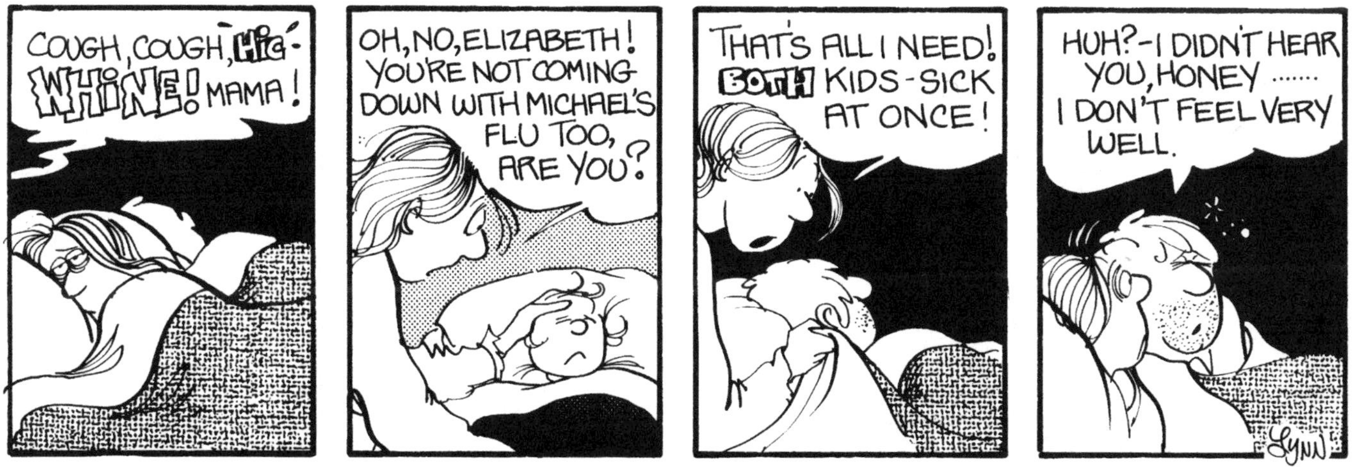
COUGH, COUGH, HIC-
WHINE! MAMA!
OH, NO, ELIZABETH! YOU'RE NOT COMING DOWN WITH MICHAEL'S FLU TOO, ARE YOU?
THAT'S ALL I NEED! BOTH KIDS-SICK AT ONCE!
HUH?-I DIDN'T HEAR YOU, HONEY ....... I DON'T FEEL VERY WELL.
LYNN

With school-aged kids, the whole family was exposed to whatever was going around. Luckily, I didn't have to work outside the home and so I was available to prescribe the home remedies (without resorting to mustard plasters) to whoever needed them. We managed to pull through whatever came down the pipe (as they say). It makes me realize how lucky we are not to be living in the Middle Ages; if you didn't die then from the illness, you were likely to croak from the cure!

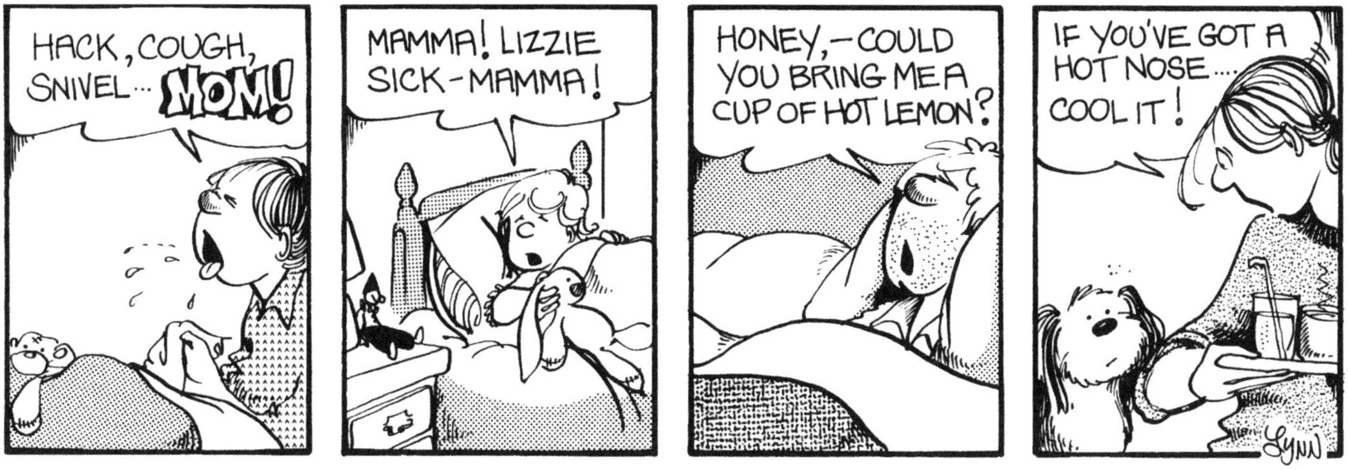
HACK, COUGH, SNIVEL... MOM!
MAMMA! LIZZIE SICK-MAMMA!
HONEY,-COULD YOU BRING ME A CUP OF HOT LEMON?
IF YOU'VE GOT A HOT NOSE.... COOL IT!
LYNN

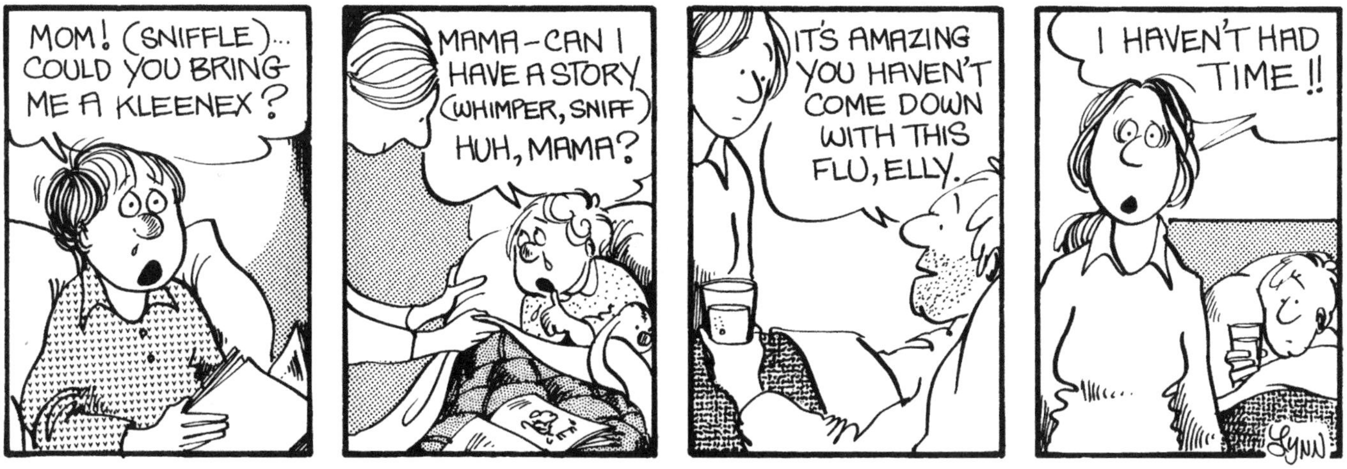
MOM! (SNIFFLE)... COULD YOU BRING ME A KLEENEX?
MAMA-CAN I HAVE A STORY (WHIMPER, SNIFF) HUH, MAMA?
IT'S AMAZING YOU HAVEN'T COME DOWN WITH THIS FLU, ELLY.
I HAVEN'T HAD TIME!!
LYNN

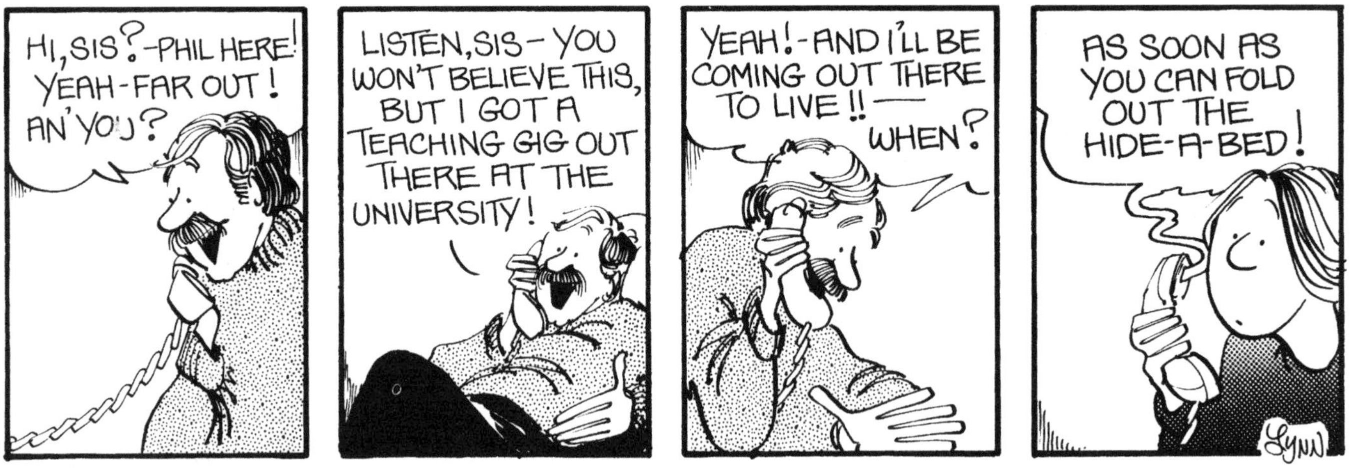
HI, SIS?-PHIL HERE! YEAH-FAR OUT! AN' YOU?
LISTEN, SIS - YOU WON'T BELIEVE THIS, BUT I GOT A TEACHING GIG OUT THERE AT THE UNIVERSITY!
YEAH!-AND I'LL BE COMING OUT THERE TO LIVE!! — WHEN?
AS SOON AS YOU CAN FOLD OUT THE HIDE-A-BED!
LYNN

After my first divorce, I was living in a small house in Dundas, learning how to raise a baby on my own. Aaron and I survived on my freelance artwork until I got a job doing graphics for a packaging firm in Hamilton. Money was tight, and when my brother, Alan, said he was moving to town and wanted to stay with me, I saw it as an opportunity for companionship, some help around the house and, perhaps, some extra cash.

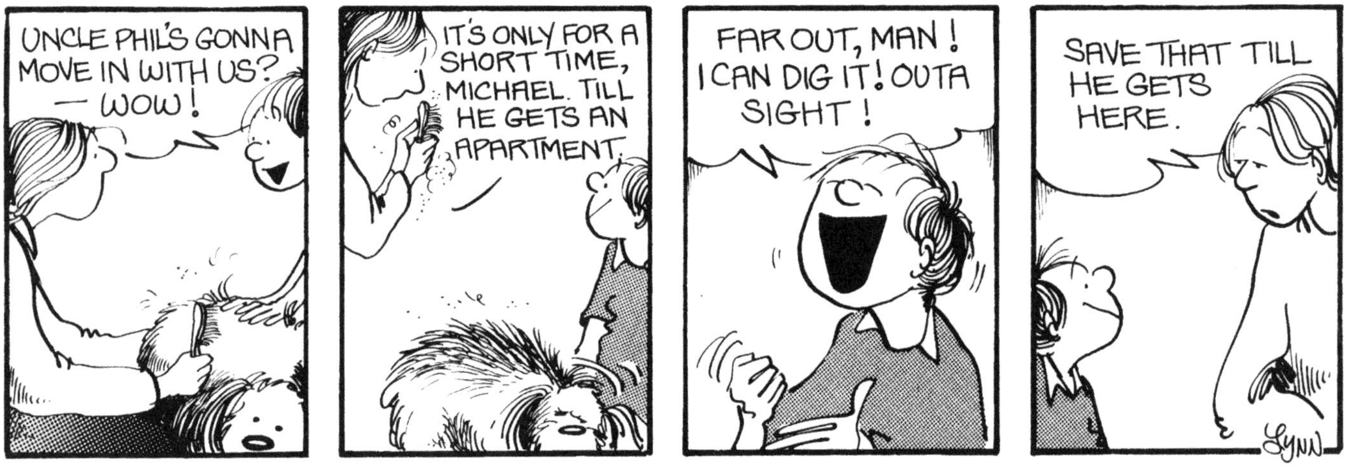
UNCLE PHIL'S GONNA MOVE IN WITH US? — WOW!
IT'S ONLY FOR A SHORT TIME, MICHAEL. TILL HE GETS AN APARTMENT.
FAR OUT, MAN! I CAN DIG IT! OUTA SIGHT!
SAVE THAT TILL HE GETS HERE.
LYNN

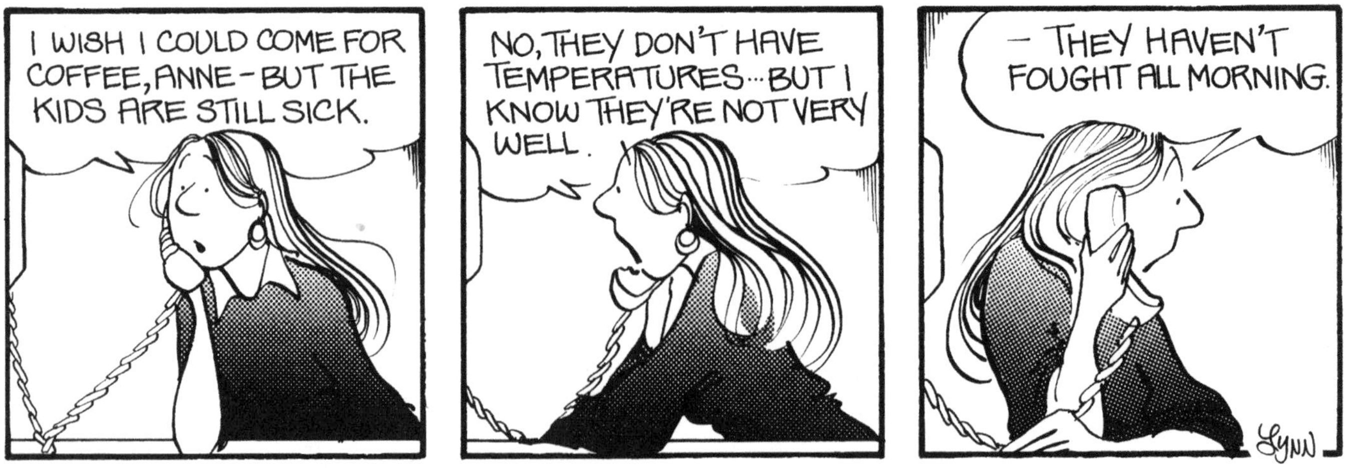
I WISH I COULD COME FOR COFFEE, ANNE - BUT THE KIDS ARE STILL SICK.
NO, THEY DON'T HAVE TEMPERATURES...BUT I KNOW THEY'RE NOT VERY WELL.
- THEY HAVEN'T FOUGHT ALL MORNING.
LYNN

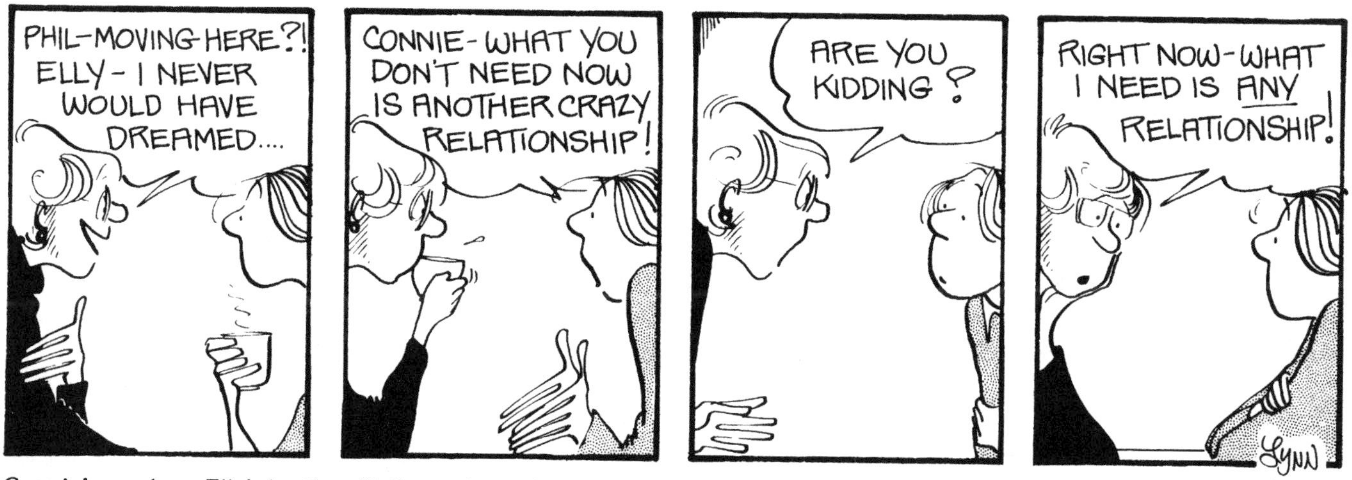
PHIL-MOVING HERE?! ELLY- I NEVER WOULD HAVE DREAMED....
CONNIE- WHAT YOU DON'T NEED NOW IS ANOTHER CRAZY RELATIONSHIP!
ARE YOU KIDDING?
RIGHT NOW- WHAT I NEED IS ANY RELATIONSHIP!
LYNN

Connie's crush on Elly's brother, Phil, was just a fun idea and good fodder for the strip — it had no reflection on my brother's love life at the time. I had no plans for where this relationship would lead; I let the story go where it wanted to go. In fact, Connie's loneliness came wholly from my own experience as a single mother — everything she said came from some painful places I guess I needed to visit again.

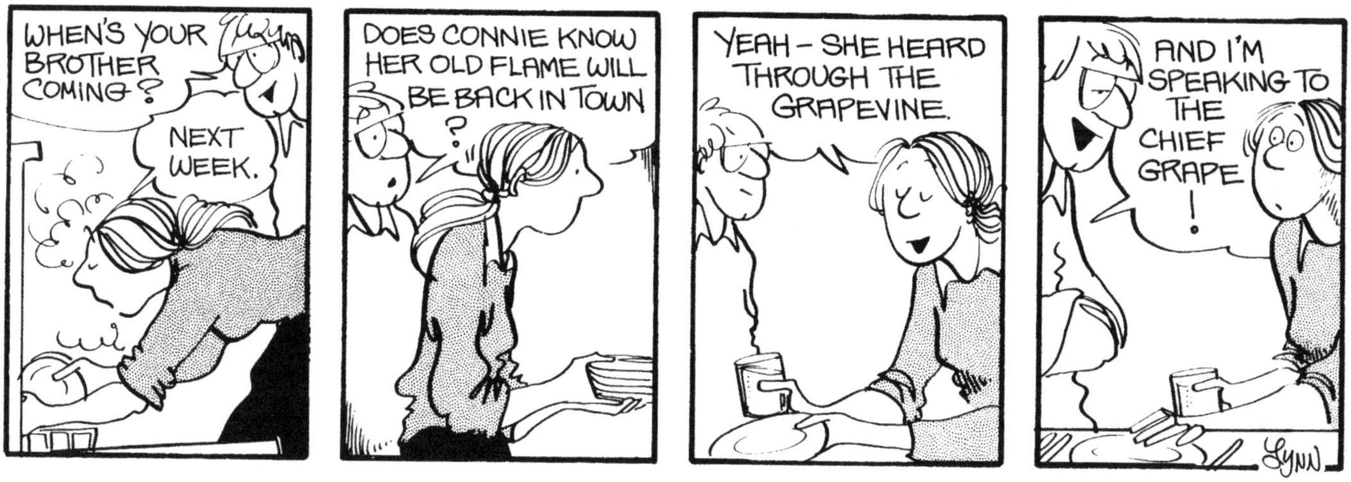
WHEN'S YOUR BROTHER COMING?
NEXT WEEK.
DOES CONNIE KNOW HER OLD FLAME WILL BE BACK IN TOWN?
YEAH - SHE HEARD THROUGH THE GRAPEVINE.
AND I'M SPEAKING TO THE CHIEF GRAPE!
LYNN

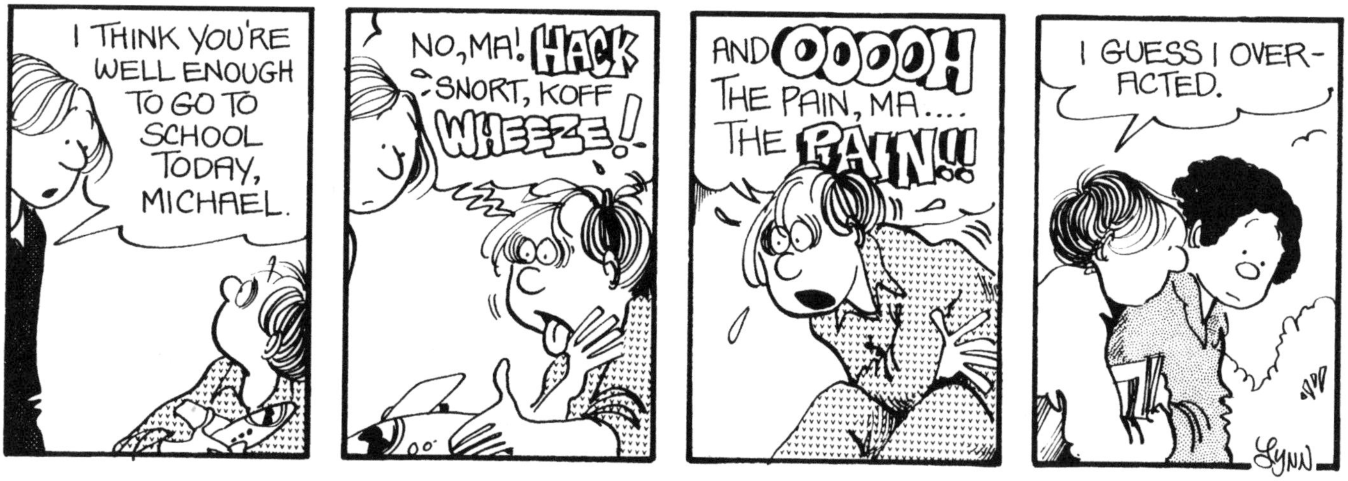
I THINK YOU'RE WELL ENOUGH TO GO TO SCHOOL TODAY, MICHAEL.
NO, MA! HACK SNORT, KOFF WHEEZE!
AND OOOOH THE PAIN, MA.... THE PAIN!!
I GUESS I OVER-ACTED.
LYNN

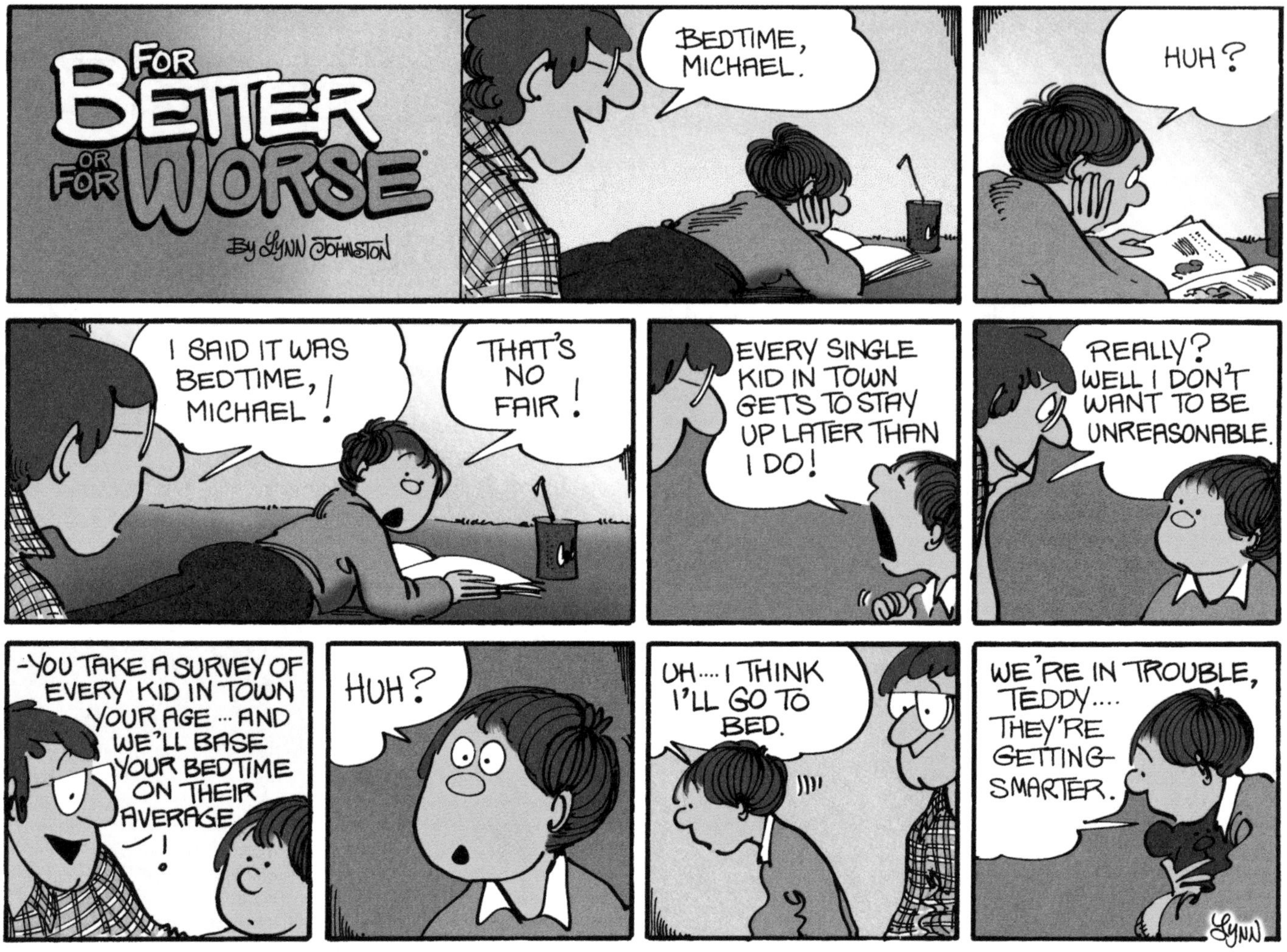
FOR BETTER OR FOR WORSE
BY LYNN JOHNSTON
BEDTIME, MICHAEL.
HUH?
I SAID IT WAS BEDTIME, MICHAEL!
THAT'S NO FAIR!
EVERY SINGLE KID IN TOWN GETS TO STAY UP LATER THAN I DO!
REALLY? WELL I DON'T WANT TO BE UNREASONABLE.
-YOU TAKE A SURVEY OF EVERY KID IN TOWN YOUR AGE ... AND WE'LL BASE YOUR BEDTIME ON THEIR AVERAGE!
HUH?
UH.... I THINK I'LL GO TO BED.
WE'RE IN TROUBLE, TEDDY.... THEY'RE GETTING SMARTER.
LYNN

My kids negotiated their bedtime, as did my brother and I. With the passion and forethought of seasoned debaters, we plied our folks with every possible reason, suggestion, and excuse for why we should stay up longer — always to no avail. Now it was my turn to set the rules.

Aaron was especially keen to see us give in. It was the challenge that made his entreaties a ritual. By the time dinner ended, he was devising yet another way to add a few more seconds to the deadline of eight o'clock, and the ruses began with his disappearance. Not one to be unnoticed, he would slip into the basement to do "stuff" or head outside and down the lane, where he'd melt into the network of sheds, fences, and open back doors. This was particularly frustrating in the summer, when the sun went down around midnight and there seemed to be no reason to hit the sack in broad daylight. Bringing him home hollering, "No fair," when neighbours were outside washing their cars and chatting over coffee seemed, well … no fair! Still, a tired kid is not something you want to mess with in the morning.

Aaron is almost forty, now. He's still a night owl and often hits the sack well after 2 a.m. He's convinced me that this is his natural rhythm and that he was never meant to go to bed at eight o'clock. Even as a kid, he tells me he was often awake late into the night and that I should have let him stay up until he was tired. Perhaps he's right. But he was a kid then, and as parents, we had our rules — some of which were meant to save our sanity!!

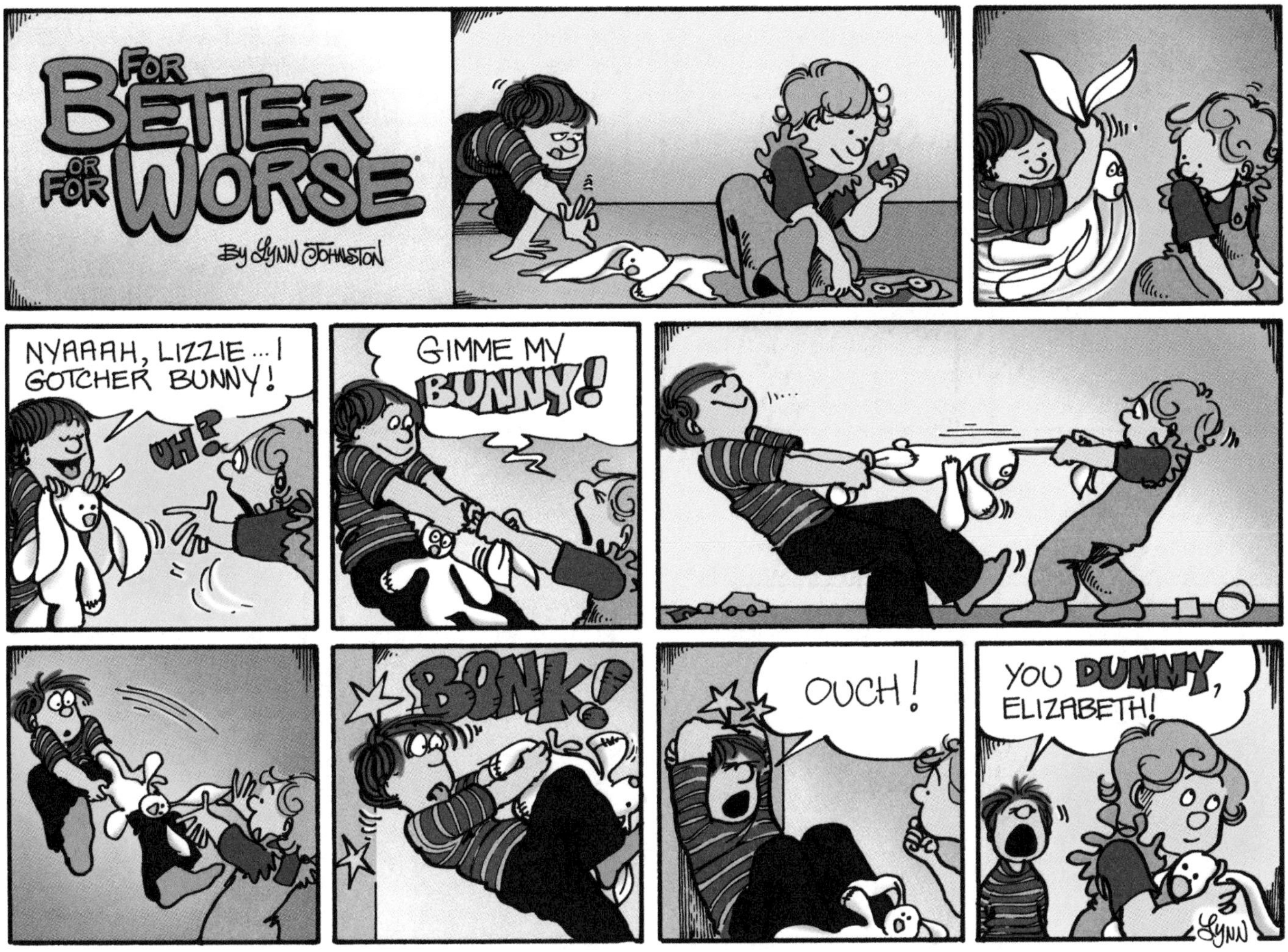
FOR BETTER OR FOR WORSE
BY LYNN JOHNSTON
NYAAAH, LIZZIE... I GOTCHER BUNNY!
UH?
GIMME MY BUNNY!
BONK!
OUCH!
YOU DUMMY, ELIZABETH!
LYNN

Katie's white stuffed bunny was her favourite toy; it went everywhere with her. And, because it was so important to her, "Bunny" became a target for Aaron. He'd hide it, throw it, or otherwise mistreat it just to get a rise out of Kate. Fortunately, Bunny was well made and survived everything from the bathtub to the sandbox to travelling all over the continent. Still, I worried that he'd somehow disappear and asked my mom to make a spare, just in case. Mom made two more bunnies — a boy and a girl. She made outfits for both, and eventually all three bunnies were essential to Kate's day. We still have these. Tattered and worn from washing and play, they are family treasures. They were made from scraps, but they're worth far more than I can say!

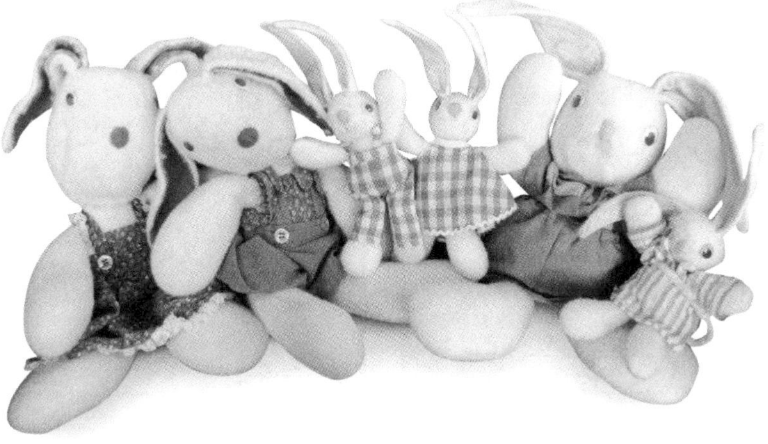

Kate's bunnies — they multiplied over the years.

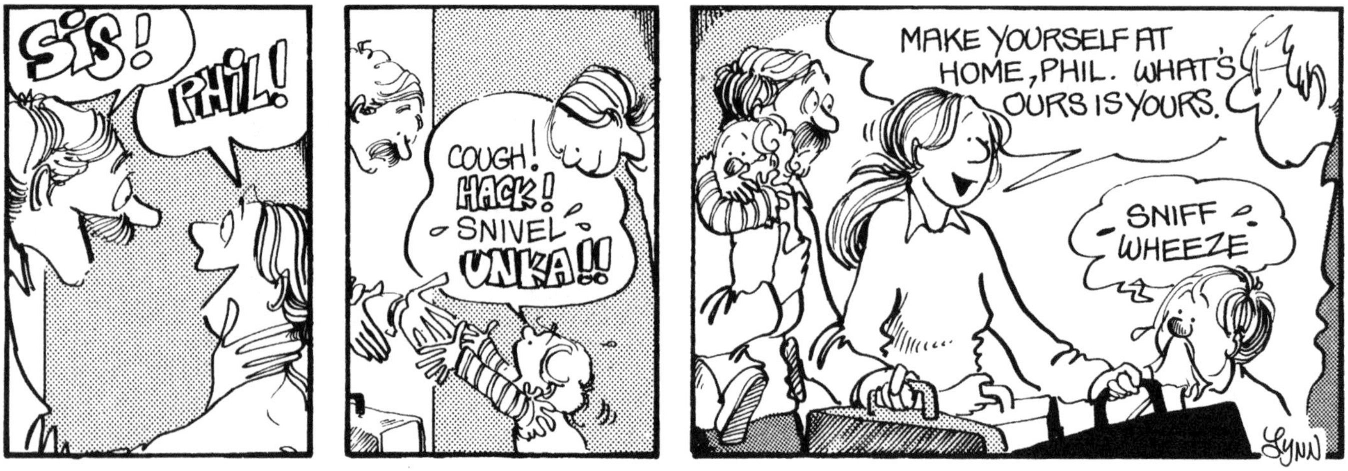
SIS!
PHIL!
COUGH! HACK! SNIVEL UNKA!!
MAKE YOURSELF AT HOME, PHIL. WHAT'S OURS IS YOURS.
SNIFF WHEEZE
LYNN

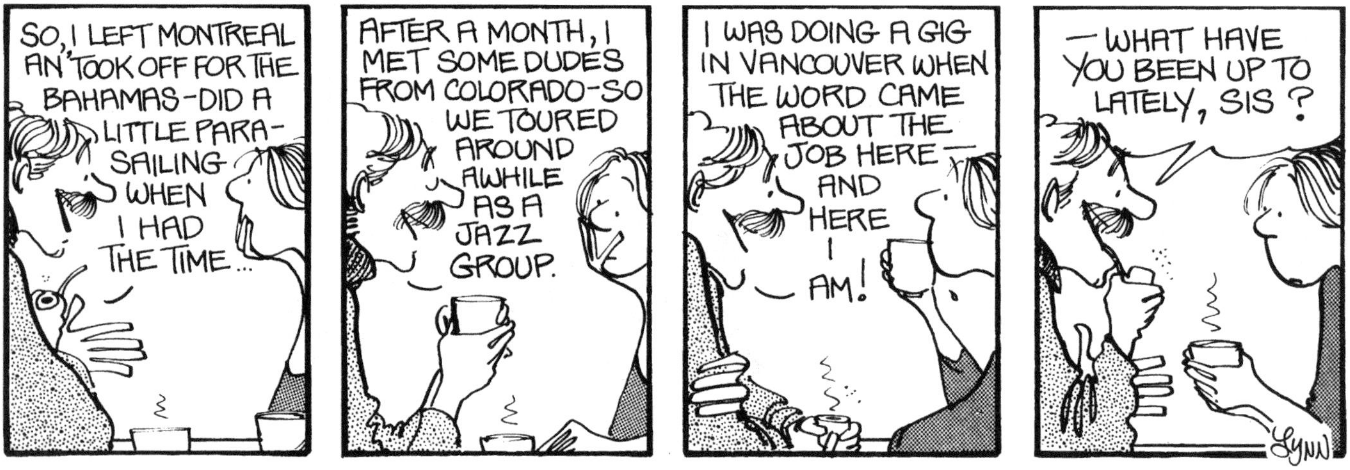
SO, I LEFT MONTREAL AN' TOOK OFF FOR THE BAHAMAS-DID A LITTLE PARA-SAILING WHEN I HAD THE TIME...
AFTER A MONTH, I MET SOME DUDES FROM COLORADO-SO WE TOURED AROUND AWHILE AS A JAZZ GROUP.
I WAS DOING A GIG IN VANCOUVER WHEN THE WORD CAME ABOUT THE JOB HERE-AND HERE I AM!
—WHAT HAVE YOU BEEN UP TO LATELY, SIS?
LYNN

I have to admit that I was a bit jealous of Alan's freedom and his casual ways; no kids, no demanding career, no mortgage, no commitments, no hassles, or headaches. I imagined his life to be ideal. To talk to him now, he remembers it very differently. For him it was unsettling to be living in my house without a steady job. He felt lost and lonely and wanted the stability I seemed to have.

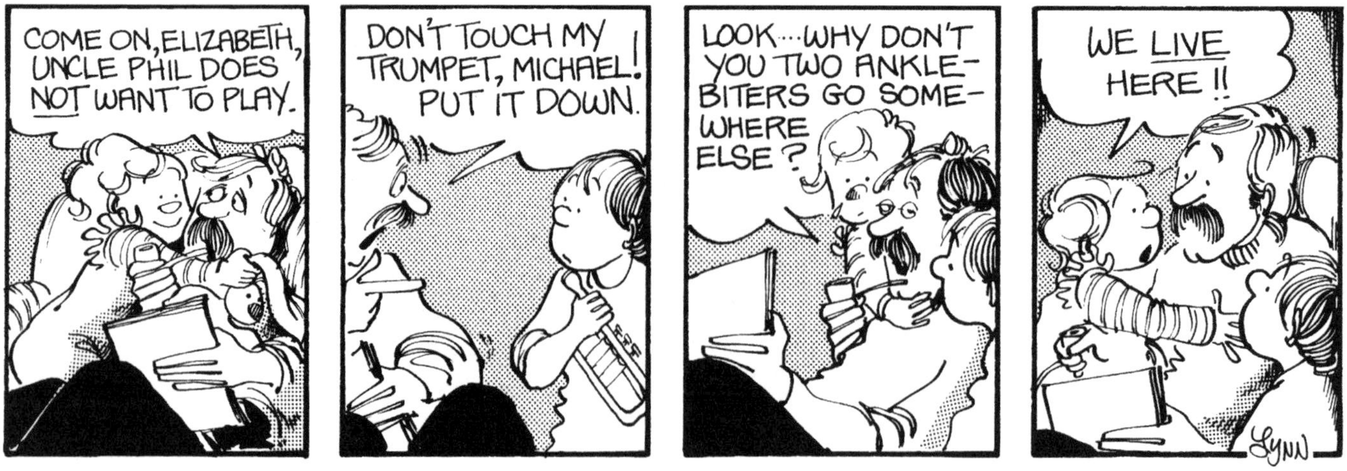
COME ON, ELIZABETH, UNCLE PHIL DOES NOT WANT TO PLAY.
DON'T TOUCH MY TRUMPET, MICHAEL! PUT IT DOWN.
LOOK...WHY DON'T YOU TWO ANKLE-BITERS GO SOME-WHERE ELSE?
WE LIVE HERE!!
LYNN

Before Alan came to live with me, I was learning to be a single mom and a homeowner. We had little to live on, but I was determined to carry my own load. I had a very tight budget; if I spent more than $20 a week on groceries, I'd be unable to pay the mortgage. Along with the mortgage came the taxes, repairs, maintenance, and other bills — all of which meant that I really needed another source of income. My friend, Fran, was renting our spare room, which helped a lot. She also took care of Aaron and did much of the cooking.

Having my brother come to stay seemed like a good solution, but I had to find a space for him. My house was a tiny two-bedroom bungalow with no basement, so the plan was for Alan to live in the garage. It wasn't a great space, but it was winterized and the doors could be boarded over. I moved my car outside, cleaned and organized, and made it as habitable as possible. This was going to be an experiment and we all hoped it would work out well.

Alan was leaving Vancouver and moving to Ontario. He was and still is a professional musician: a trumpet player. At the time, he was looking for work as an electrician while he scoped out possibilities in the Ontario music scene. The garage gave him a place to live and to practice.

Aaron was just a baby when Alan became a roommate. Aaron was thrilled to have a man around; one with a sense of humour and the time to play rough and tumble with him. It was surprising to see how well they got along together. Today, Aaron and Alan are still the best of friends.

Alan loved the time he spent playing and visiting with Aaron and Katie, but he was always keen to burrow into a book or fly the coop when the noise and the chaos got the best of him.

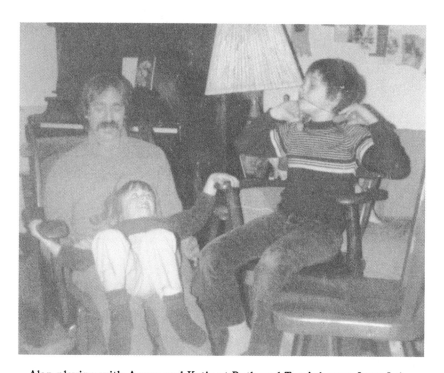

Alan playing with Aaron and Katie at Ruth and Tom's house, Lynn Lake.

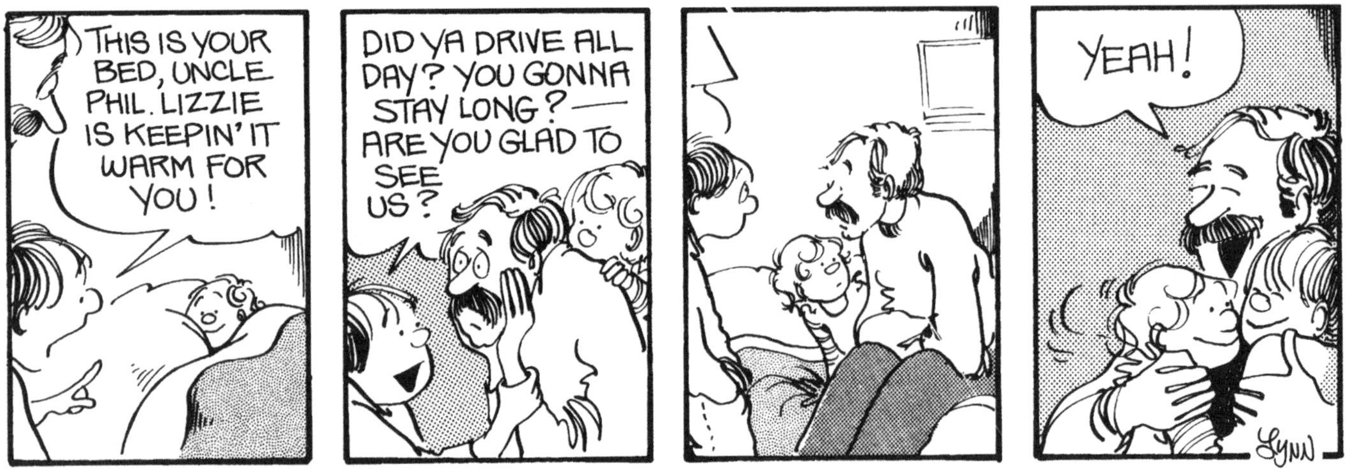
THIS IS YOUR BED, UNCLE PHIL. LIZZIE IS KEEPIN' IT WARM FOR YOU!
DID YA DRIVE ALL DAY? YOU GONNA STAY LONG? — ARE YOU GLAD TO SEE US?
YEAH!
Lynn

Our house in Lynn Lake had a spare room, but the house the Pattersons lived in didn't. The idea of Uncle Phil taking over Elizabeth's room was more fun and provided more opportunity for comedy than had he stayed in more comfortable digs. Later I was asked to draw a floor plan of the Patterson's house. I found that much of it didn't make sense based on the stories and drawings I had previously done but, once I started an idea, the deadlines forced me to carry on no matter what!

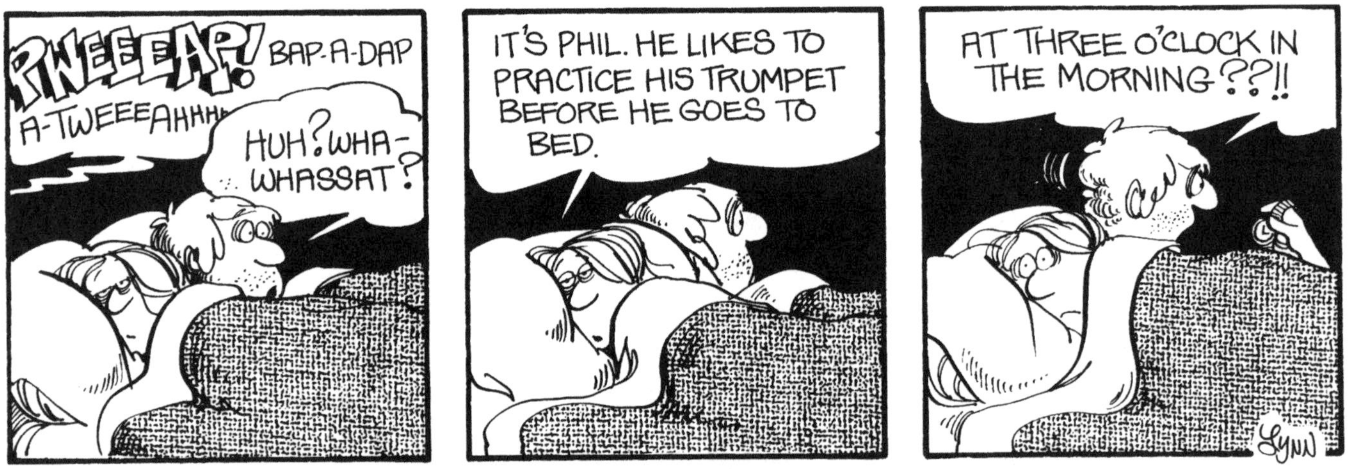
PWEEEAP! BAP-A-DAP
A-TWEEEAHHH
HUH? WHA-WHASSAT?
IT'S PHIL. HE LIKES TO PRACTICE HIS TRUMPET BEFORE HE GOES TO BED.
AT THREE O'CLOCK IN THE MORNING??!!
Lynn

Al had regular performances, which often kept him out until 2 a.m. He played classical and Baroque and when he wasn't playing for an event, he practiced. It wasn't unusual after a performance for him to practice in the garage well into the morning hours, and if I asked him to lower the sound, he used his mouthpiece. This made a Donald Duck kind of "kwakking" sound — this was fine if I was awake and sensible, but not so cool at a bewitching hour.

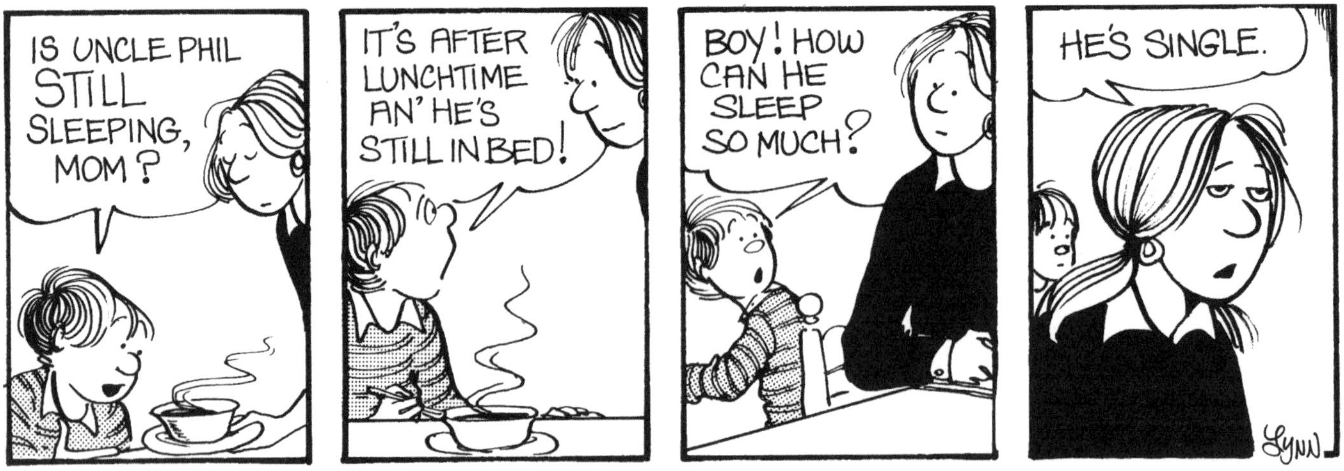
IS UNCLE PHIL STILL SLEEPING, MOM?
IT'S AFTER LUNCHTIME AN' HE'S STILL IN BED!
BOY! HOW CAN HE SLEEP SO MUCH?
HE'S SINGLE.
Lynn

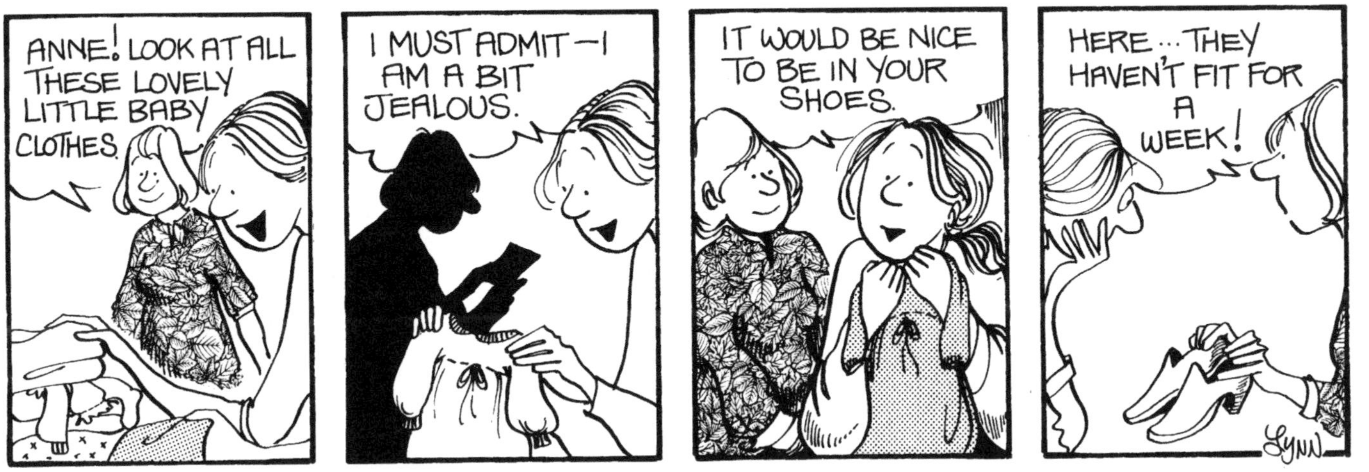
ANNE! LOOK AT ALL THESE LOVELY LITTLE BABY CLOTHES.
I MUST ADMIT—I AM A BIT JEALOUS.
IT WOULD BE NICE TO BE IN YOUR SHOES.
HERE ... THEY HAVEN'T FIT FOR A WEEK!
LYNN

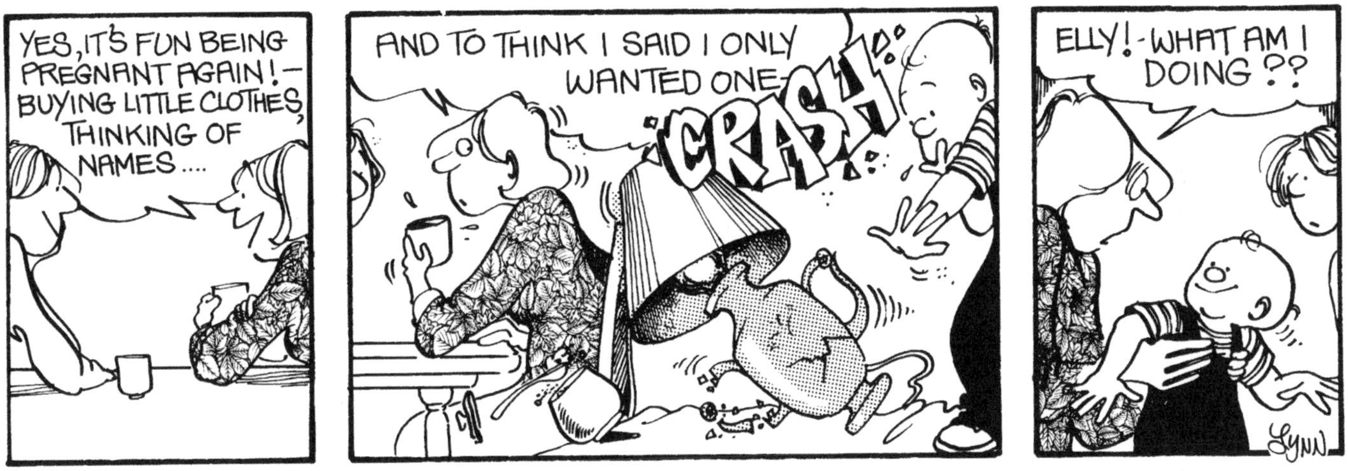
YES, IT'S FUN BEING PREGNANT AGAIN!—BUYING LITTLE CLOTHES, THINKING OF NAMES ....
AND TO THINK I SAID I ONLY WANTED ONE—
CRASH
ELLY!-WHAT AM I DOING??
LYNN

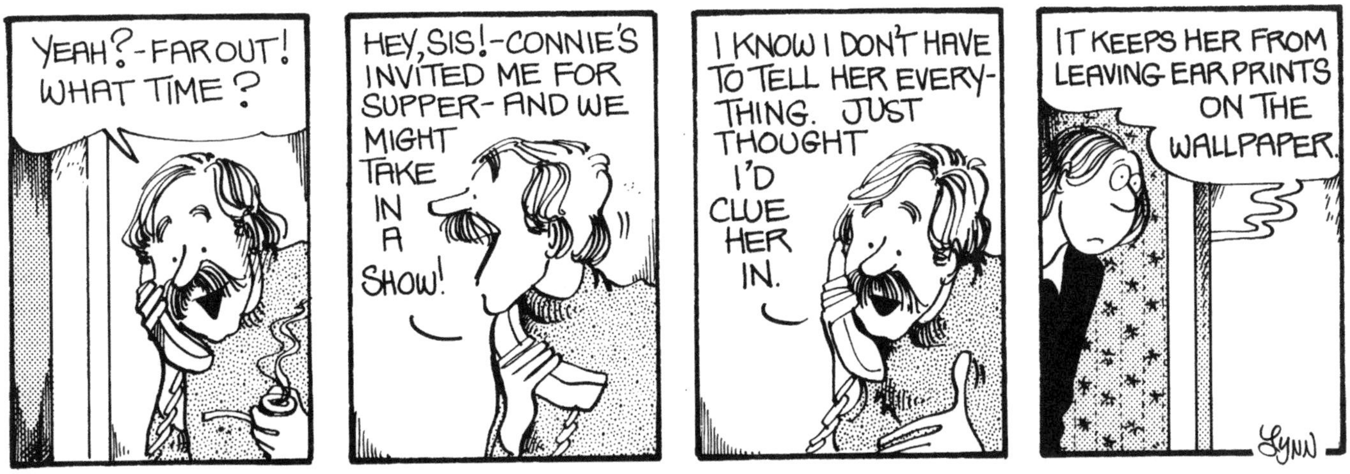
YEAH?-FAR OUT! WHAT TIME?
HEY, SIS!-CONNIE'S INVITED ME FOR SUPPER- AND WE MIGHT TAKE IN A SHOW!
I KNOW I DON'T HAVE TO TELL HER EVERYTHING. JUST THOUGHT I'D CLUE HER IN.
IT KEEPS HER FROM LEAVING EAR PRINTS ON THE WALLPAPER.
LYNN

Naturally, Elly was intrigued by her brother's affairs. Because he was living in her home and dating her close friend, she felt it was ... let's say "her responsibility" to find out what was going on. When my brother lived with me, however, I didn't ask about his personal life — I would wait until he confided in my other roommate, Fran, and I'd worm the information out of her!

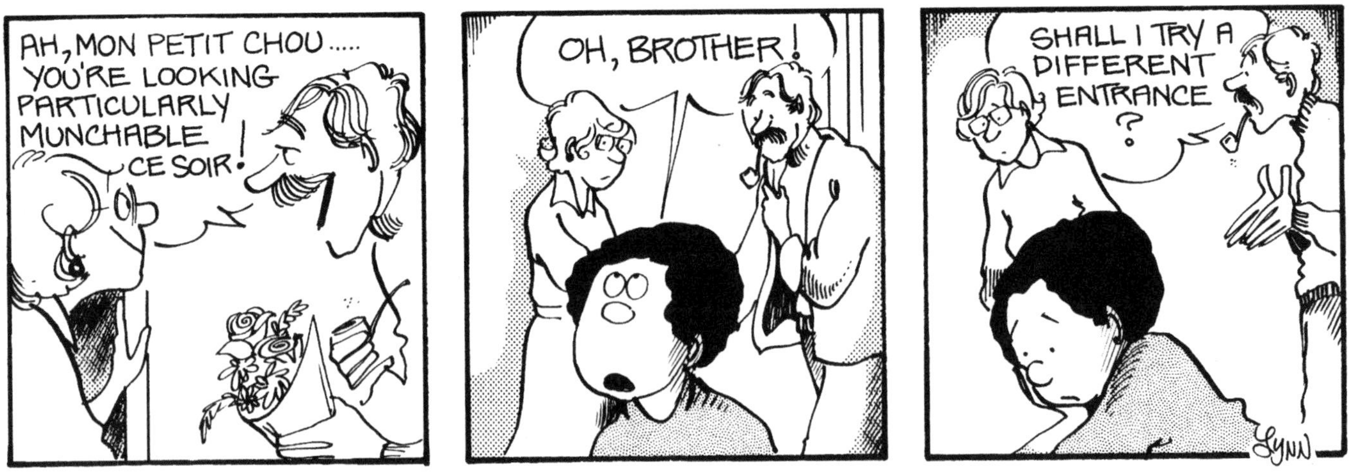
AH, MON PETIT CHOU..... YOU'RE LOOKING PARTICULARLY MUNCHABLE CE SOIR!
OH, BROTHER!
SHALL I TRY A DIFFERENT ENTRANCE?
LYNN

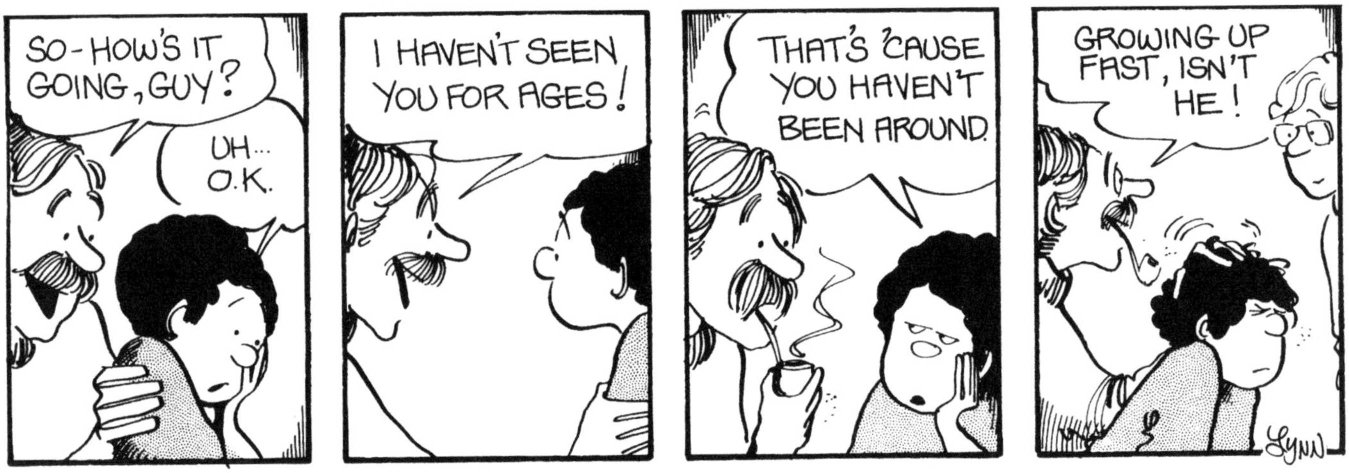
SO-HOW'S IT GOING, GUY?
UH... O.K.
I HAVEN'T SEEN YOU FOR AGES!
THAT'S 'CAUSE YOU HAVEN'T BEEN AROUND.
GROWING UP FAST, ISN'T HE!
LYNN

Never ask a kid a direct question unless you're prepared to hear an equally direct answer!

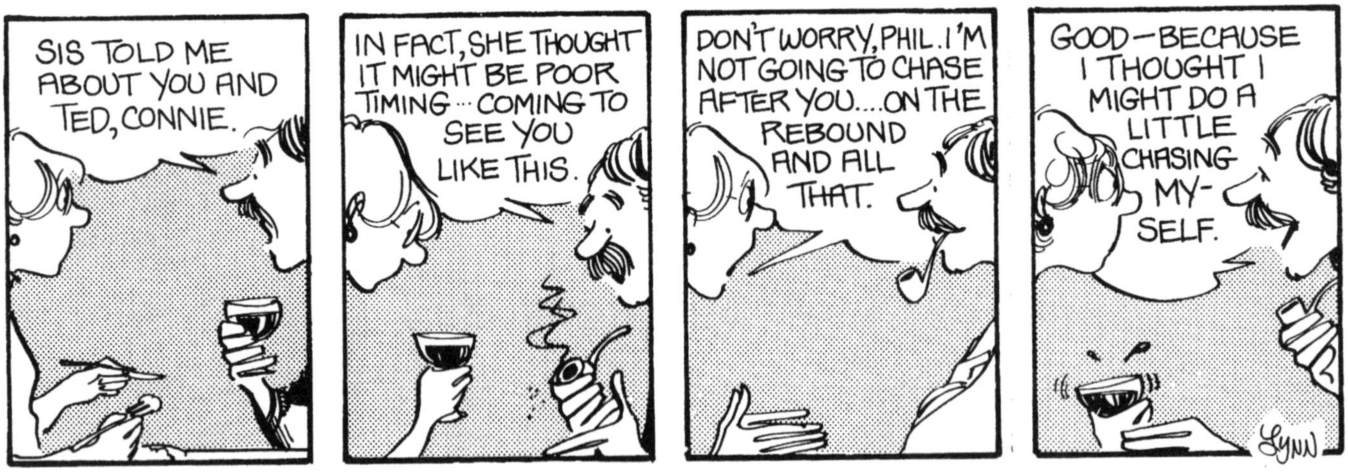
SIS TOLD ME ABOUT YOU AND TED, CONNIE.
IN FACT, SHE THOUGHT IT MIGHT BE POOR TIMING... COMING TO SEE YOU LIKE THIS.
DON'T WORRY, PHIL. I'M NOT GOING TO CHASE AFTER YOU.... ON THE REBOUND AND ALL THAT.
GOOD—BECAUSE I THOUGHT I MIGHT DO A LITTLE CHASING MY-SELF.
LYNN

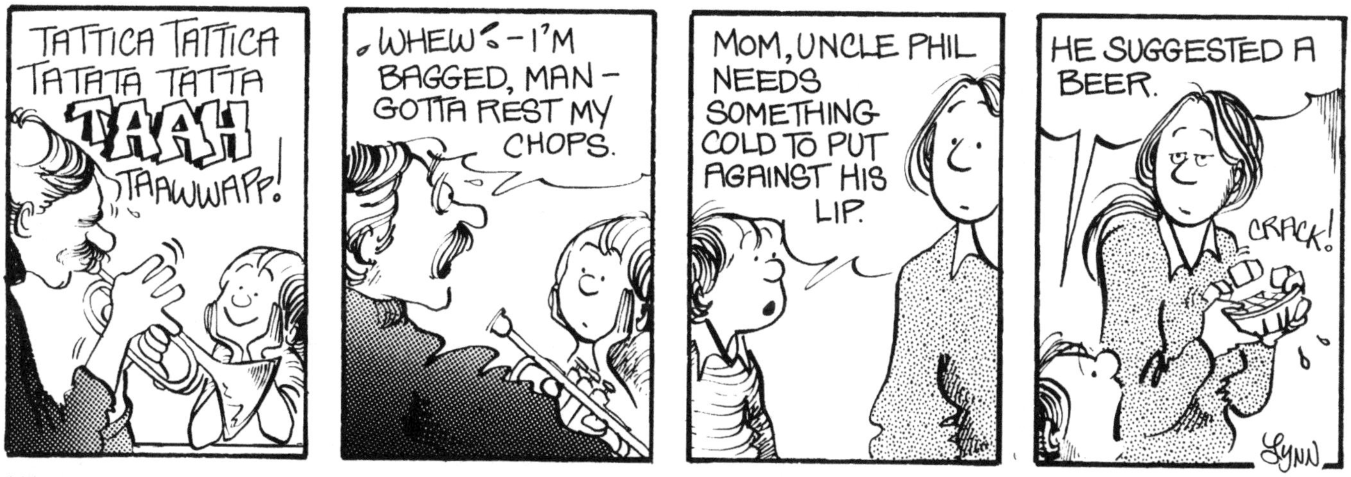
TATTICA TATTICA TATATA TATTA TAAH TAAWWAPP!
WHEW! - I'M BAGGED, MAN - GOTTA REST MY CHOPS.
MOM, UNCLE PHIL NEEDS SOMETHING COLD TO PUT AGAINST HIS LIP.
HE SUGGESTED A BEER.
CRACK!
LYNN

Alan has been playing the trumpet since he was about nine years old. He'd sit on the old blue couch in our folks' living room and with unyielding dedication he'd practice until he was exhausted. We all admired his tenacity. Eventually, our basement became a rehearsal hall for Al and his musical friends. The refrigerator emptied "faster than lard through a goose" (a quote from Dad). Beer was never a staple in our family, but it soon became the weekend libation of choice.

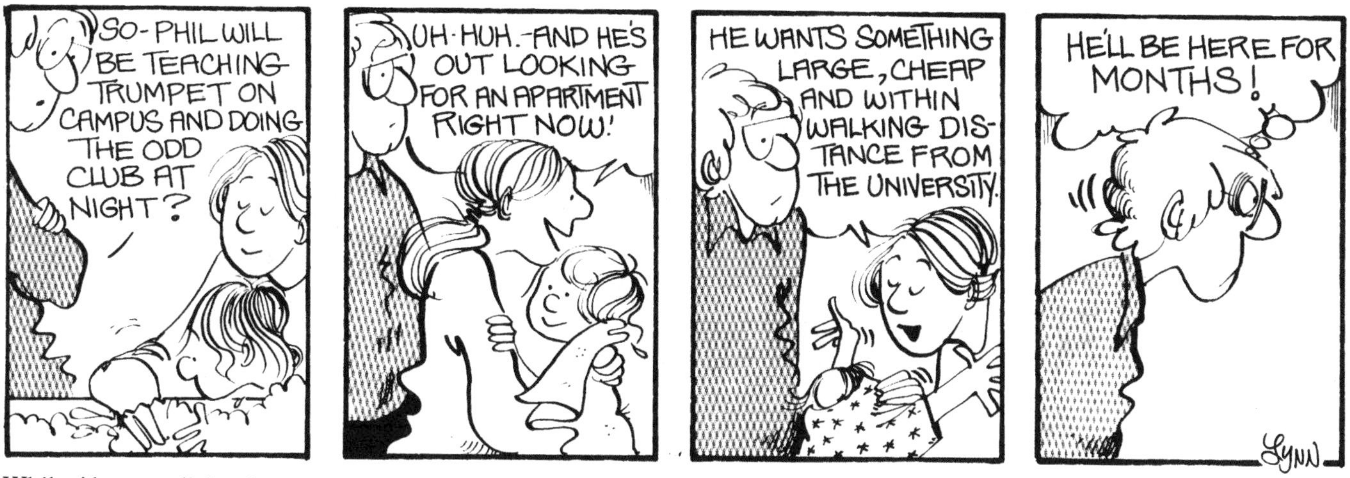
SO-PHIL WILL BE TEACHING TRUMPET ON CAMPUS AND DOING THE ODD CLUB AT NIGHT?
UH-HUH.-AND HE'S OUT LOOKING FOR AN APARTMENT RIGHT NOW!
HE WANTS SOMETHING LARGE, CHEAP AND WITHIN WALKING DISTANCE FROM THE UNIVERSITY.
HE'LL BE HERE FOR MONTHS!
LYNN

While Alan was living in my garage, the quest for a cheap, clean apartment was ongoing. Everything from distance to parking to price thwarted his efforts, and then there was the noise. Where could one practice the trumpet at all hours without being thrown out? Despite the dreary ambiance of my garage, it provided him with cheap digs, a place to practice, and easy access to a full fridge.

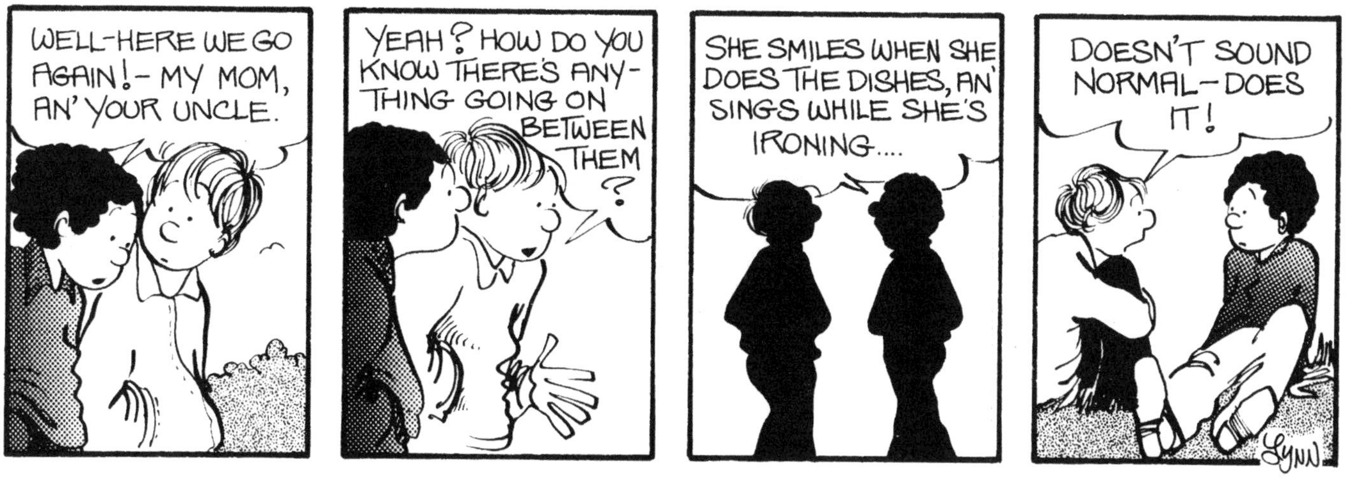
WELL-HERE WE GO AGAIN! - MY MOM, AN' YOUR UNCLE.
YEAH? HOW DO YOU KNOW THERE'S ANYTHING GOING ON BETWEEN THEM?
SHE SMILES WHEN SHE DOES THE DISHES, AN' SINGS WHILE SHE'S IRONING....
DOESN'T SOUND NORMAL - DOES IT!
LYNN

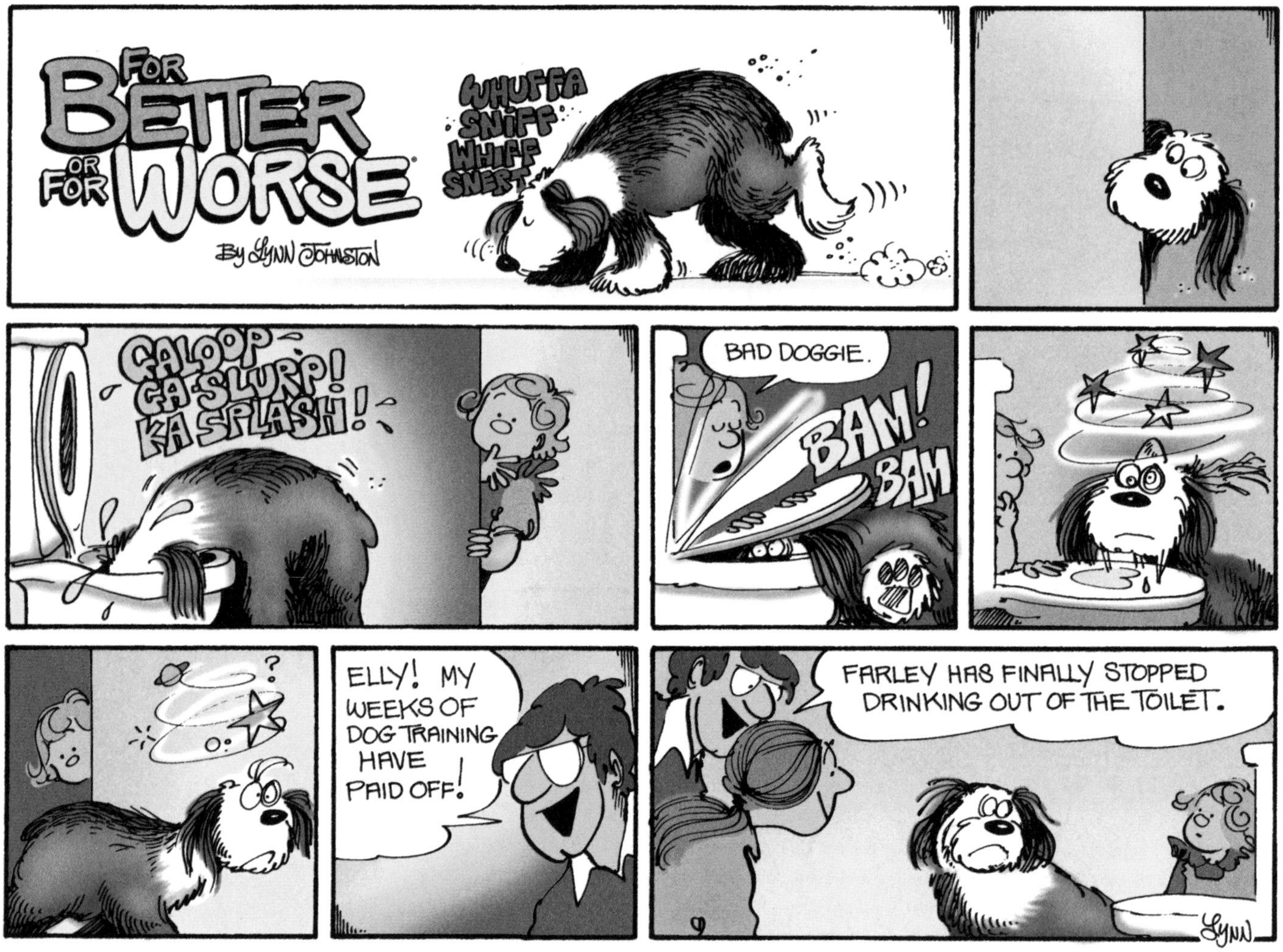
FOR BETTER OR FOR WORSE
BY LYNN JOHNSTON
WHUFFA SNIFF WHIFF SNERT
GALOOP GA-SLURP! KA SPLASH!
BAD DOGGIE.
BAM! BAM
ELLY! MY WEEKS OF DOG TRAINING HAVE PAID OFF!
FARLEY HAS FINALLY STOPPED DRINKING OUT OF THE TOILET.
LYNN

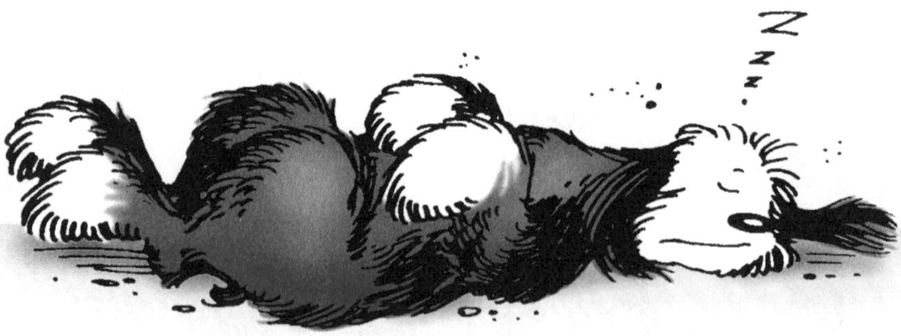

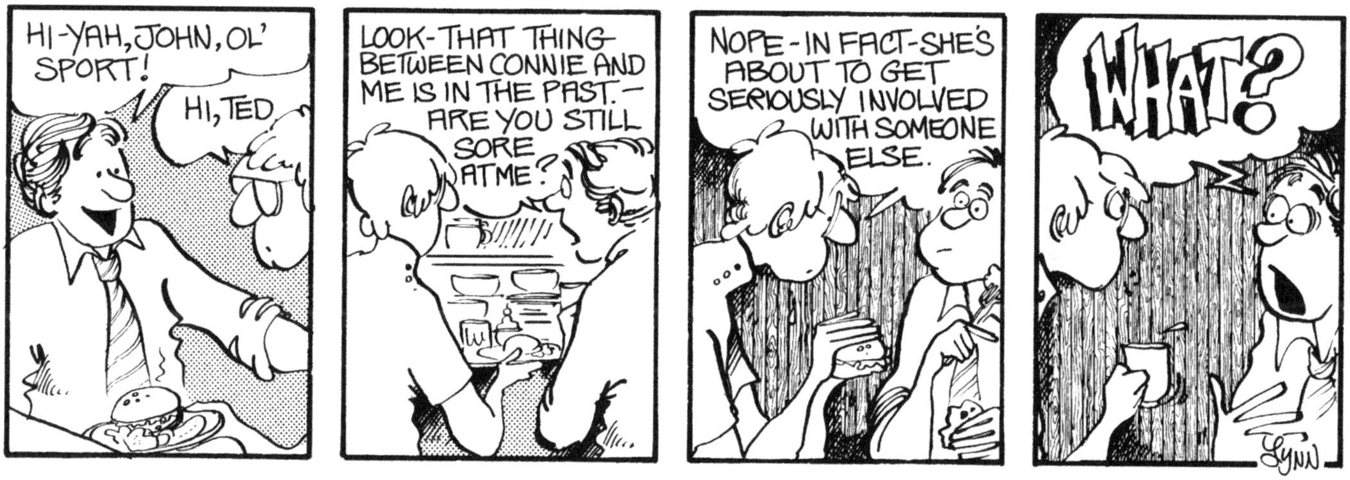
HI-YAH, JOHN, OL' SPORT!
HI, TED
LOOK-THAT THING BETWEEN CONNIE AND ME IS IN THE PAST.—ARE YOU STILL SORE AT ME?
NOPE-IN FACT-SHE'S ABOUT TO GET SERIOUSLY INVOLVED WITH SOMEONE ELSE.
WHAT?

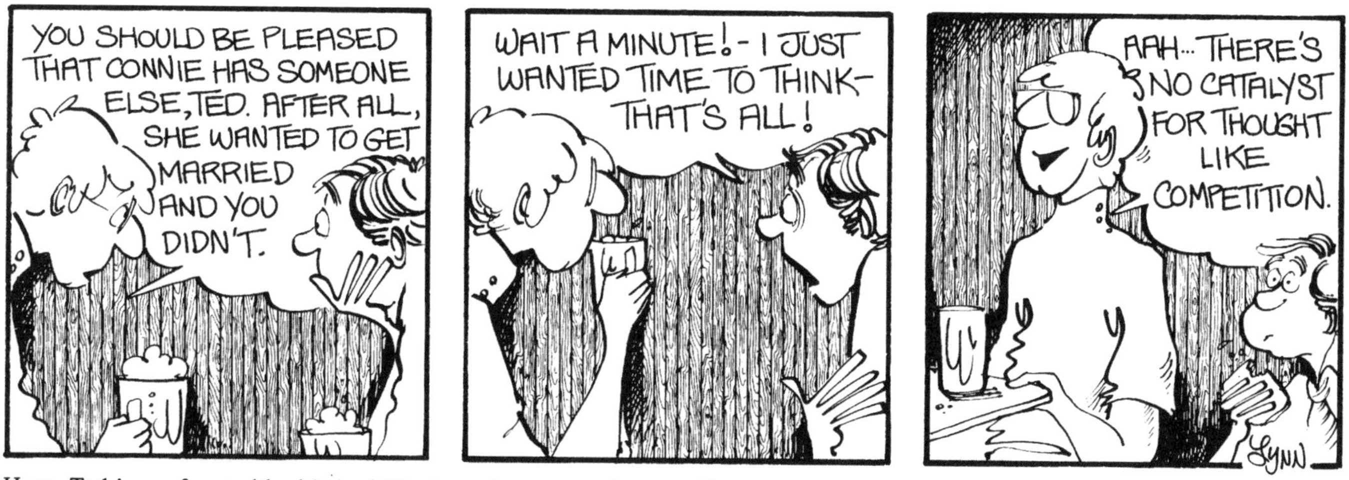
YOU SHOULD BE PLEASED THAT CONNIE HAS SOMEONE ELSE, TED. AFTER ALL, SHE WANTED TO GET MARRIED AND YOU DIDN'T.
WAIT A MINUTE!- I JUST WANTED TIME TO THINK- THAT'S ALL!
AAH... THERE'S NO CATALYST FOR THOUGHT LIKE COMPETITION.

Here, Ted is confronted by his inability to make a commitment. The story eventually ended without his ever having had a strong, long-term relationship.

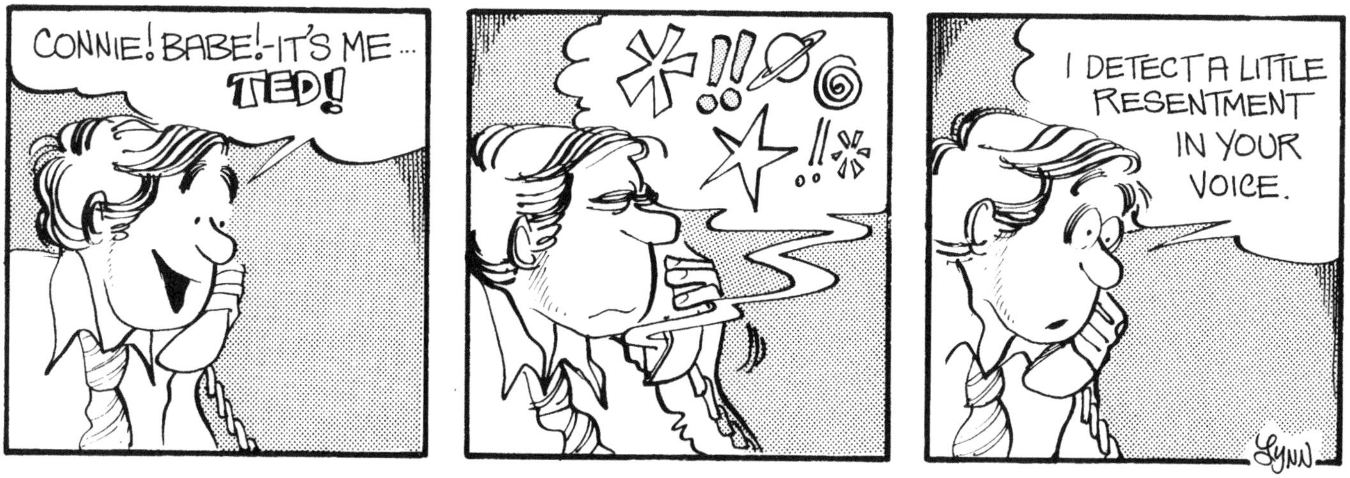
CONNIE! BABE!-IT'S ME... TED!
I DETECT A LITTLE RESENTMENT IN YOUR VOICE.

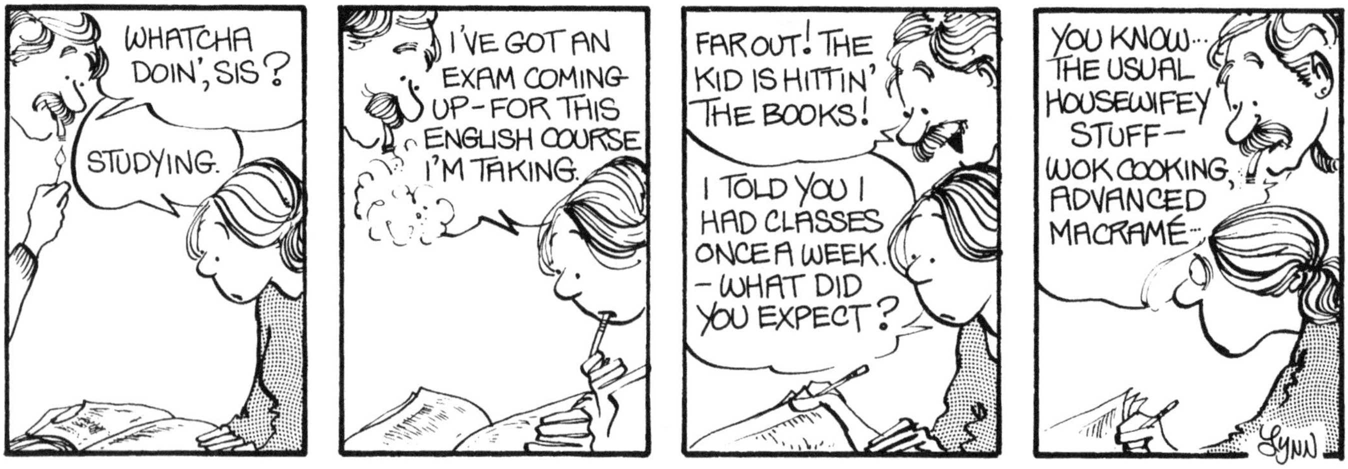
WHATCHA DOIN', SIS?
STUDYING.
I'VE GOT AN EXAM COMING UP-FOR THIS ENGLISH COURSE I'M TAKING.
FAR OUT! THE KID IS HITTIN' THE BOOKS!
I TOLD YOU I HAD CLASSES ONCE A WEEK. -WHAT DID YOU EXPECT?
YOU KNOW... THE USUAL HOUSEWIFEY STUFF— WOK COOKING, ADVANCED MACRAMÉ...
LYNN

My friend Adrienne went back to school when she was thirty — she finished her grade twelve and went on to become a lab technician in the blood lab at McMaster University. She was a single mom with more courage and determination than most. She made me realize that you can do anything at any age — if you really want to. With "Andie" in mind, I had Elly go back to school and take some of the courses she had missed.

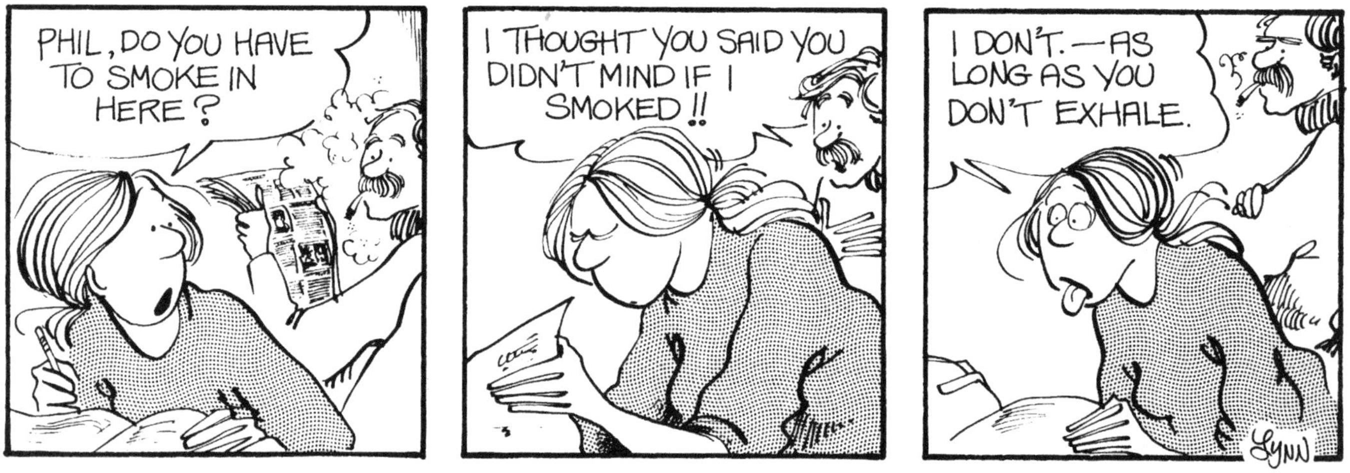
PHIL, DO YOU HAVE TO SMOKE IN HERE?
I THOUGHT YOU SAID YOU DIDN'T MIND IF I SMOKED!!
I DON'T. —AS LONG AS YOU DON'T EXHALE.
Lynn

Both my folks smoked, and it was my job to clean the ashtrays. It seemed as though we had an ashtray on every surface — it was a chore I hated! The ceiling above Dad's chair was yellow, and the curtains had the stale smell of smoke. I would kneel on the couch, looking out the window through the sheers, and vow that one day there would be no smoking in my house. It was, therefore, a bone of contention between Alan and me when he moved in with his habit and his reluctance to smoke outside.

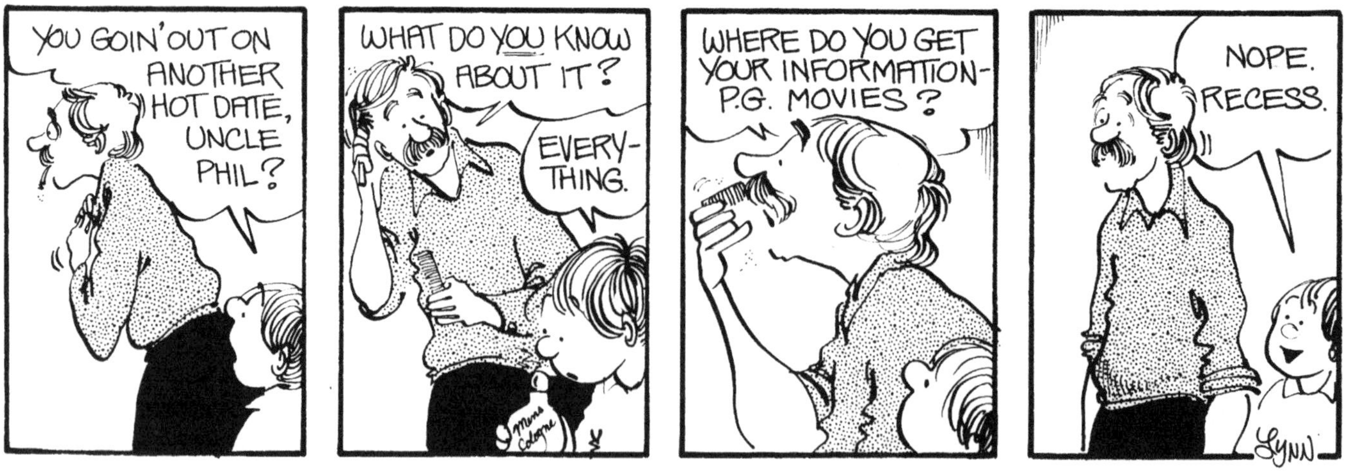
YOU GOIN' OUT ON ANOTHER HOT DATE, UNCLE PHIL?
WHAT DO YOU KNOW ABOUT IT?
EVERY-THING.
WHERE DO YOU GET YOUR INFORMATION- P.G. MOVIES?
NOPE. RECESS.
Lynn

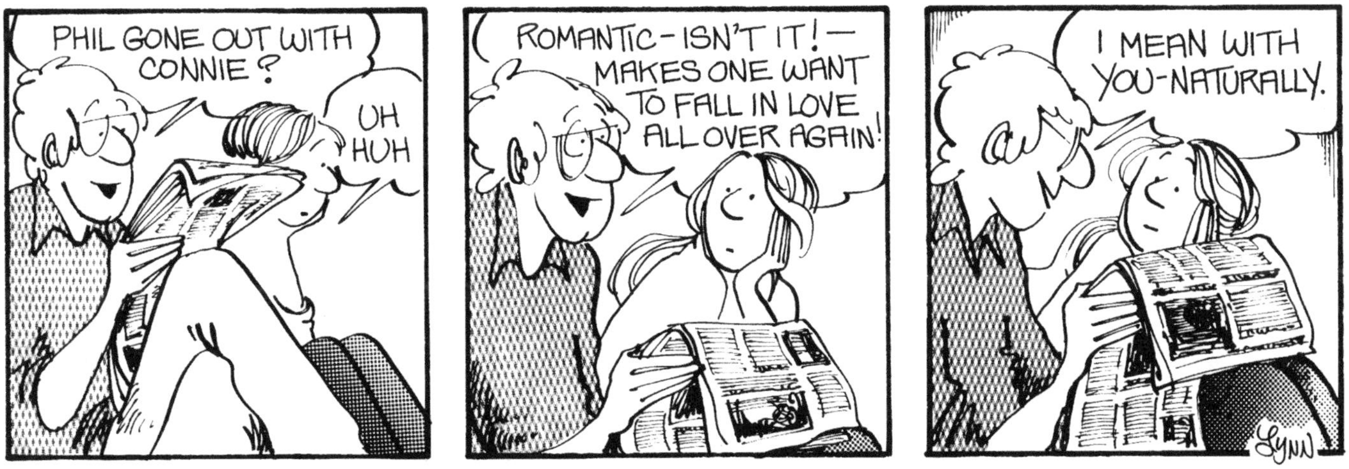
PHIL GONE OUT WITH CONNIE?
UH HUH
ROMANTIC - ISN'T IT! — MAKES ONE WANT TO FALL IN LOVE ALL OVER AGAIN!
I MEAN WITH YOU - NATURALLY.
LYNN

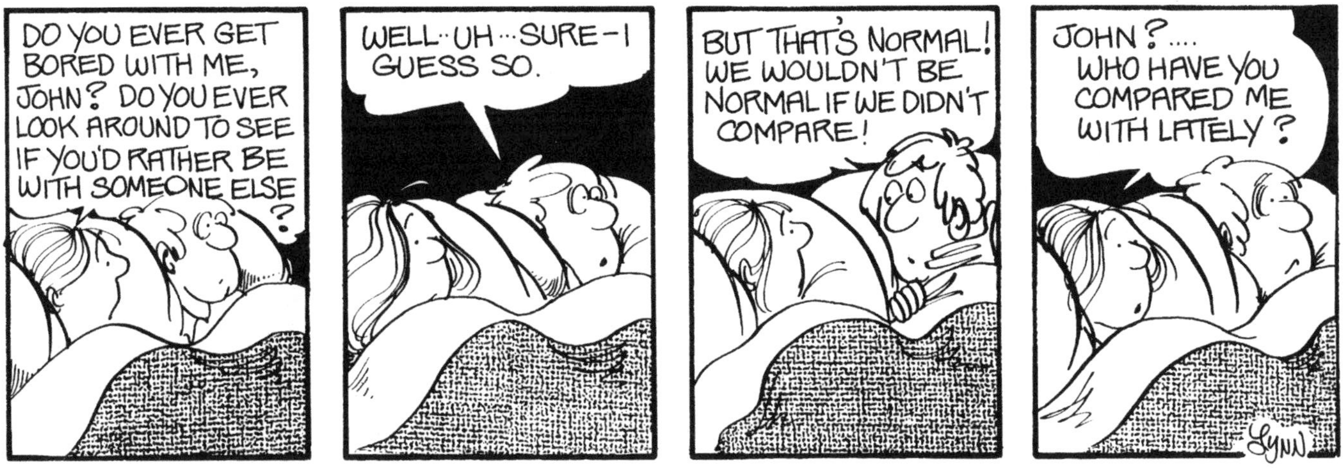
DO YOU EVER GET BORED WITH ME, JOHN? DO YOU EVER LOOK AROUND TO SEE IF YOU'D RATHER BE WITH SOMEONE ELSE?
WELL·· UH ··· SURE - I GUESS SO.
BUT THAT'S NORMAL! WE WOULDN'T BE NORMAL IF WE DIDN'T COMPARE!
JOHN?.... WHO HAVE YOU COMPARED ME WITH LATELY?
LYNN

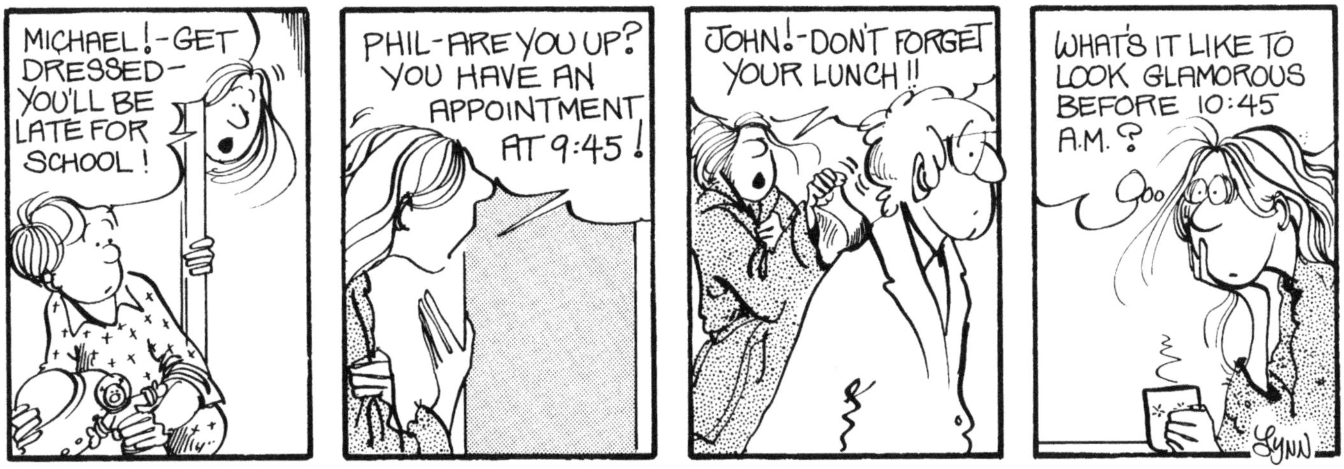
MICHAEL! - GET DRESSED - YOU'LL BE LATE FOR SCHOOL!
PHIL - ARE YOU UP? YOU HAVE AN APPOINTMENT AT 9:45!
JOHN! - DON'T FORGET YOUR LUNCH!!
WHAT'S IT LIKE TO LOOK GLAMOROUS BEFORE 10:45 A.M.?
Ooo
LYNN

When we accept the role of Mom, we become a nurse, a psychologist, a short-order cook, a laundress, and an alarm clock. Our day seems to belong to everyone else, and there's rarely time for makeup and hair spray.

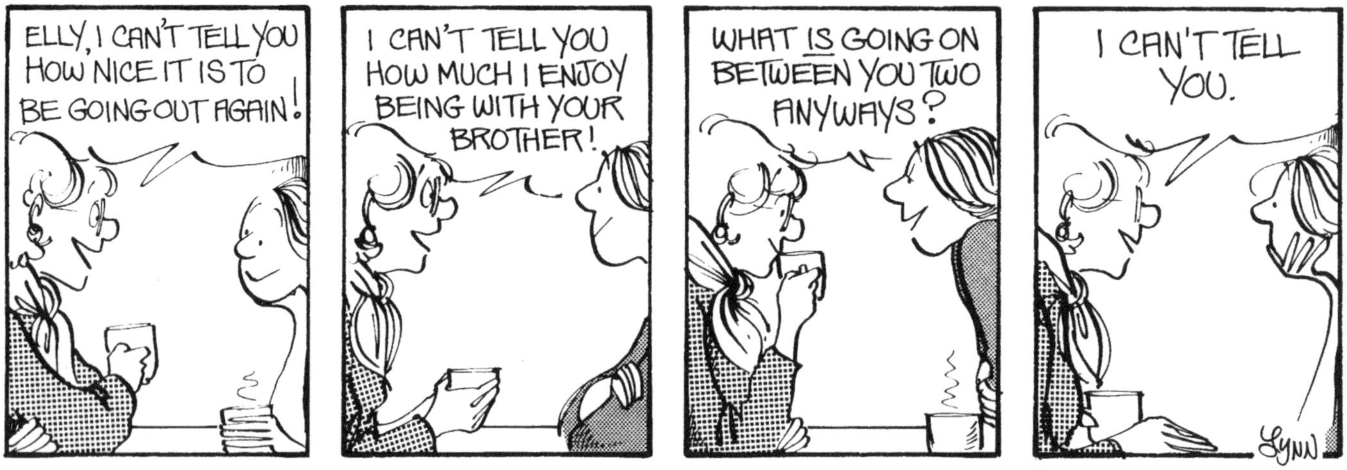
ELLY, I CAN'T TELL YOU HOW NICE IT IS TO BE GOING OUT AGAIN!
I CAN'T TELL YOU HOW MUCH I ENJOY BEING WITH YOUR BROTHER!
WHAT IS GOING ON BETWEEN YOU TWO ANYWAYS?
I CAN'T TELL YOU.
LYNN

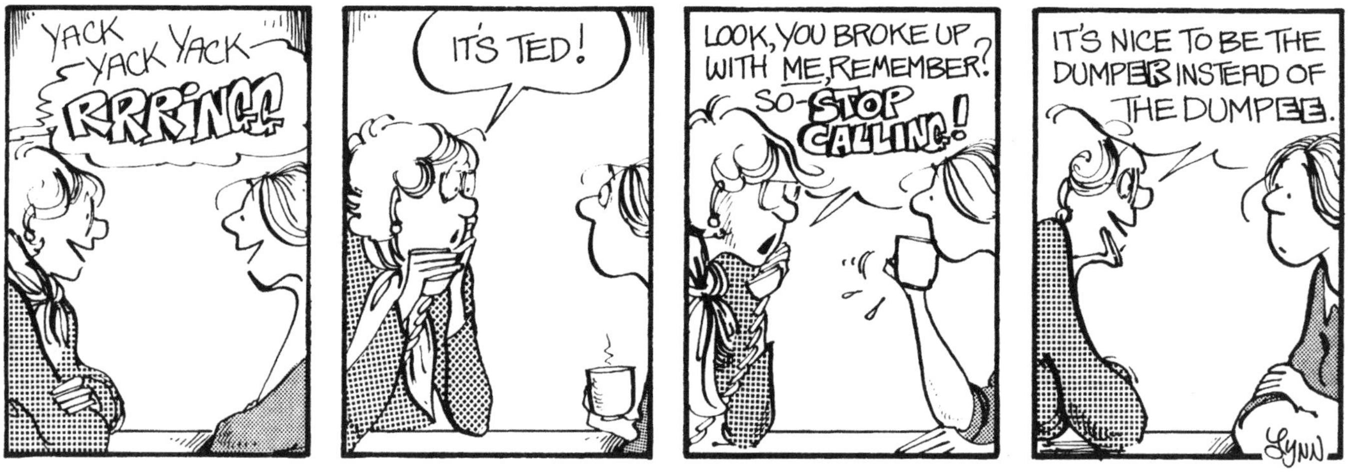
YACK YACK YACK—
RRRINGG
IT'S TED!
LOOK, YOU BROKE UP WITH ME, REMEMBER? SO- STOP CALLING!
IT'S NICE TO BE THE DUMPER INSTEAD OF THE DUMPEE.
LYNN

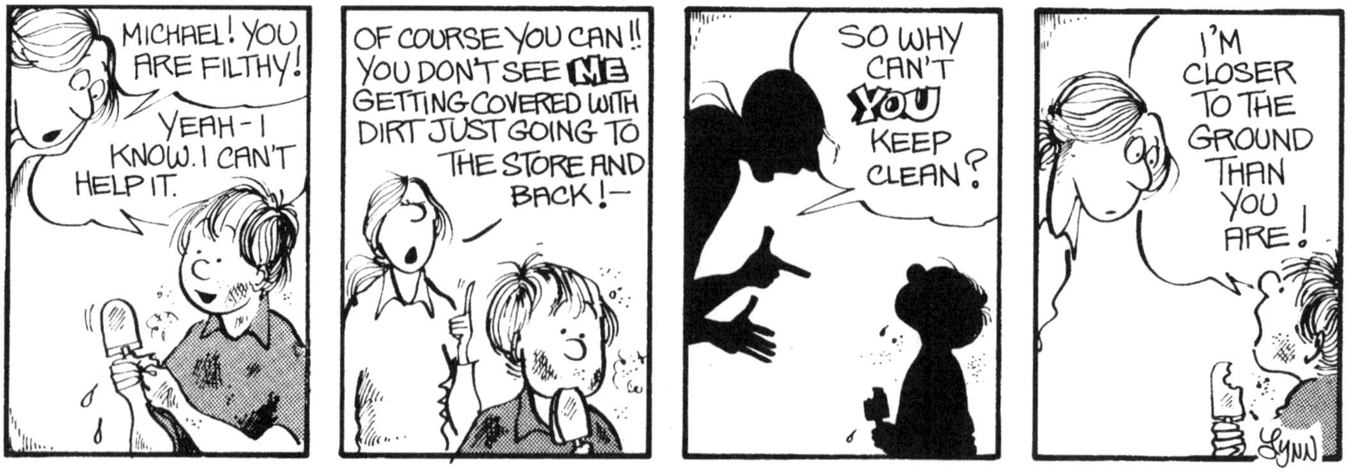
MICHAEL! YOU ARE FILTHY!
YEAH - I KNOW. I CAN'T HELP IT.
OF COURSE YOU CAN!! YOU DON'T SEE ME GETTING COVERED WITH DIRT JUST GOING TO THE STORE AND BACK!—
SO WHY CAN'T YOU KEEP CLEAN?
I'M CLOSER TO THE GROUND THAN YOU ARE!
LYNN

I wish this had been another one of Aaron's lines — but it was mine! Aaron did, however, carry a constant dusting of grime wherever he went.

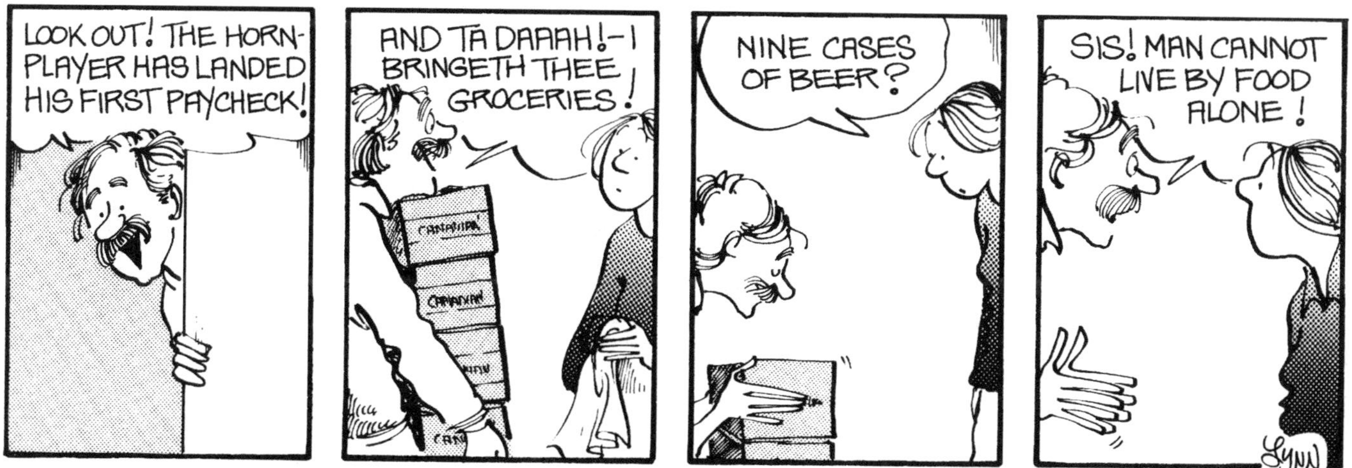
LOOK OUT! THE HORN-PLAYER HAS LANDED HIS FIRST PAYCHECK!
AND TA DAAAH!—I BRINGETH THEE GROCERIES!
NINE CASES OF BEER?
SIS! MAN CANNOT LIVE BY FOOD ALONE!
LYNN

My brother's idea of a grocery contribution was several cases of beer. He still brings beer when he comes to visit now, but it's a more expensive brand!

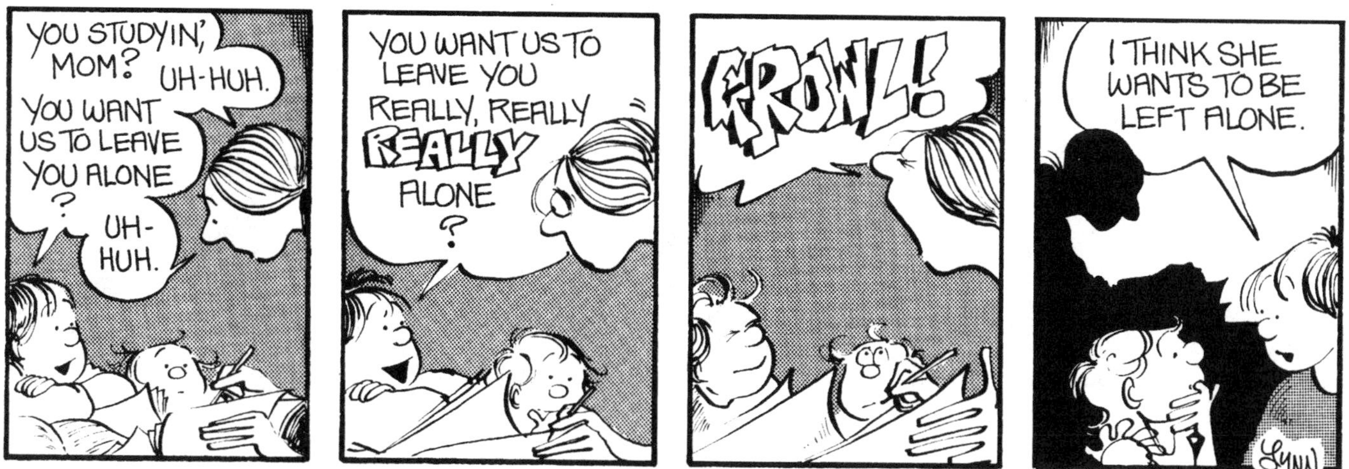
YOU STUDYIN', MOM?
UH-HUH.
YOU WANT US TO LEAVE YOU ALONE?
UH-HUH.
YOU WANT US TO LEAVE YOU REALLY, REALLY REALLY ALONE?
GROWL!
I THINK SHE WANTS TO BE LEFT ALONE.
LYNN

This was a regular scenario for us. My studio was in the house, and the kids knew when I was so into my work that I was "gone." They were pretty good about it, but now and then, they let me know, in a way kids do, that it was time to come out of the zone and be Mom again!

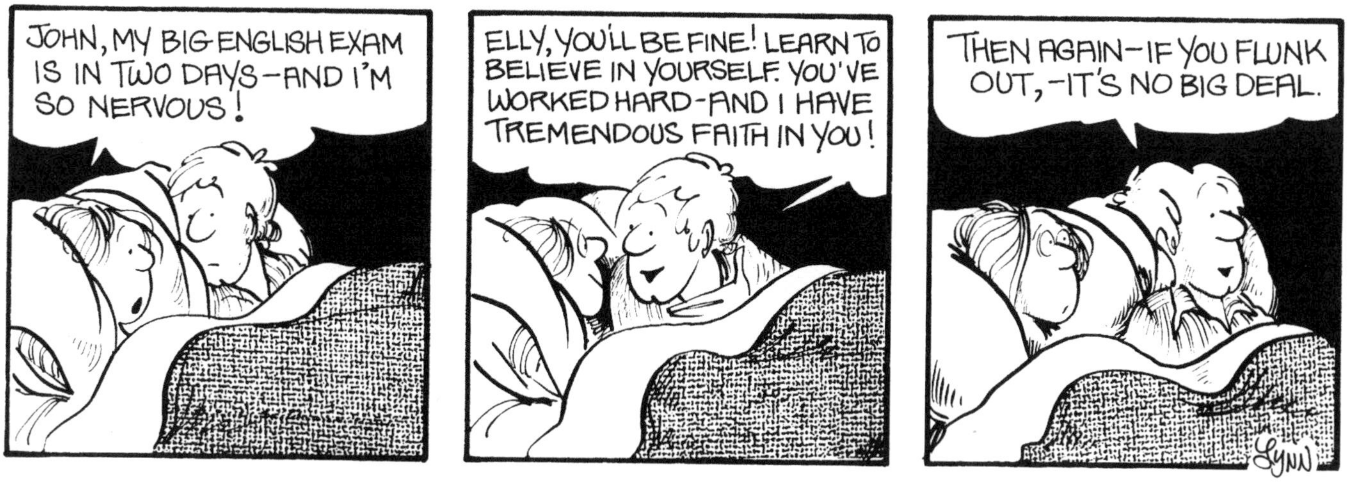
JOHN, MY BIG ENGLISH EXAM IS IN TWO DAYS—AND I'M SO NERVOUS!
ELLY, YOU'LL BE FINE! LEARN TO BELIEVE IN YOURSELF. YOU'VE WORKED HARD—AND I HAVE TREMENDOUS FAITH IN YOU!
THEN AGAIN—IF YOU FLUNK OUT,—IT'S NO BIG DEAL.
LYNN

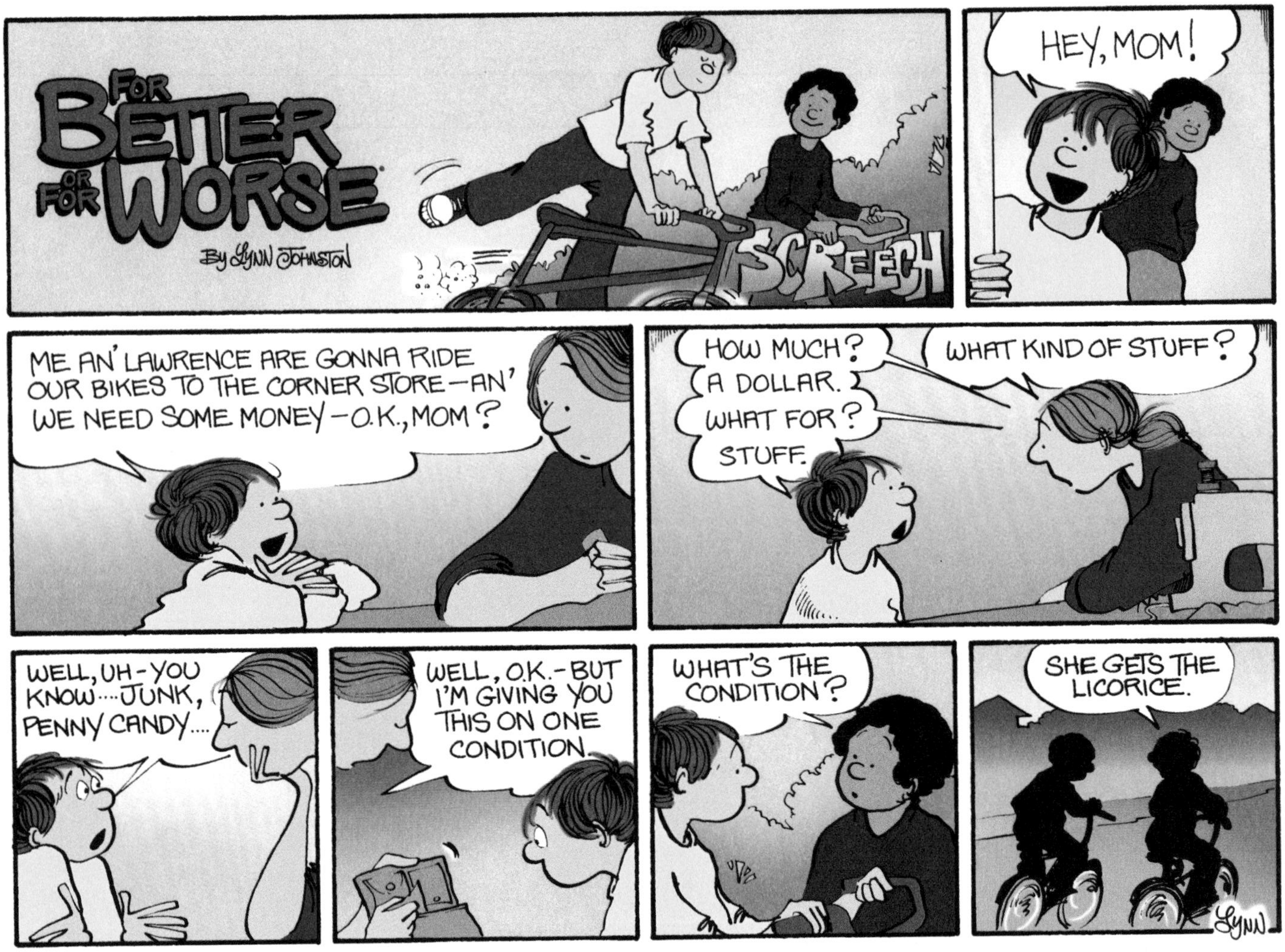
FOR BETTER OR FOR WORSE
BY LYNN JOHNSTON
SCREECH
HEY, MOM!
ME AN' LAWRENCE ARE GONNA RIDE OUR BIKES TO THE CORNER STORE—AN' WE NEED SOME MONEY—O.K., MOM?
HOW MUCH?
A DOLLAR.
WHAT FOR?
STUFF.
WHAT KIND OF STUFF?
WELL, UH-YOU KNOW....JUNK, PENNY CANDY....
WELL, O.K.-BUT I'M GIVING YOU THIS ON ONE CONDITION.
WHAT'S THE CONDITION?
SHE GETS THE LICORICE.
LYNN

Here, word for word, is a true exchange. Aaron and his friend Roy were allowed to go down to “Fergie’s” — the local corner store, pool hall, and hangout. Fergie’s motto was “Buy or bye-bye.” Fergie made his money on pop and penny candy. Despite the difficulty in getting fresh produce into the north, Fergie’s licorice was always fresh. Licorice, ginger, and chocolate are my favourite diet-breakers, and the kids knew I’d shell out a few bucks if they’d be sure to return with “the goods.”

Licorice was my grandfather’s favourite, my mother’s favourite, and Charles Schulz liked it, too; I took him a bag of licorice allsorts when he was in the hospital, and he lit up with a smile. This is what we munched on as we spoke for the last time. He died not long afterward, and every time I see licorice allsorts, I think of him.

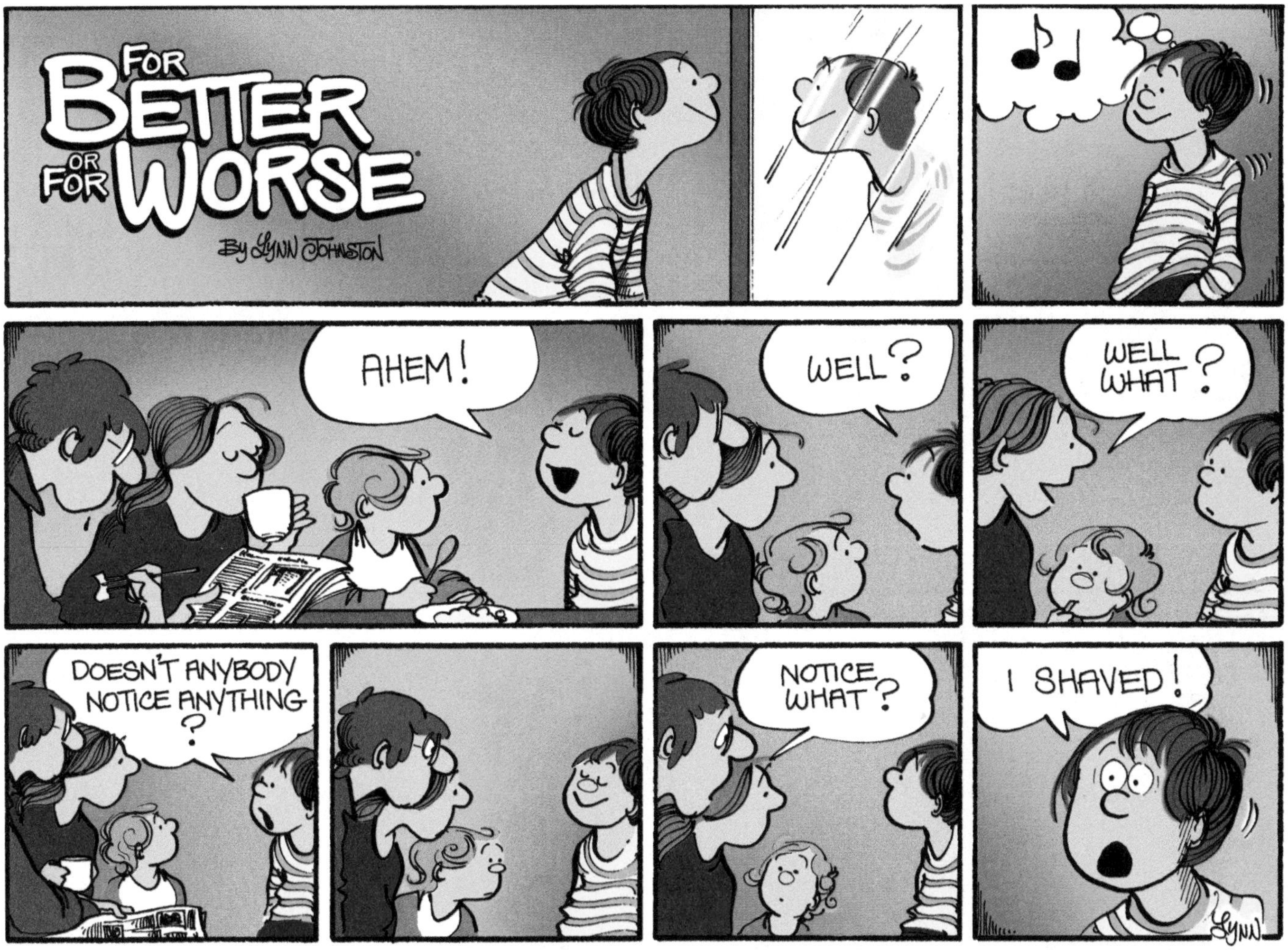
FOR BETTER OR FOR WORSE
By Lynn Johnston
AHEM!
WELL?
WELL WHAT?
DOESN'T ANYBODY NOTICE ANYTHING?
NOTICE WHAT?
I SHAVED!
Lynn

This scenario is straight from my past. My dad used a blade razor for years until electric shavers became efficient and more popular. In fact, he sold them at the store, which had become a sort of high-end gift shop by the time I was in my teens. I think the first one he ever came home with was a Ronco shaver.

We had one small communal bathroom, so nothing was secret, sacred, or safe! When Dad left the new shaver on the sink, it was only a matter of hours before Alan and I were shaving ourselves, each other, and the carpet in the hall. I remember taking it apart and tapping the debris into the sink. Dad was never as miffed as Mom was by the things we did. Dad could fix anything, and when the Ronco jammed, he'd find a way to get it humming again.

Lady's shavers were introduced soon after the men's became popular, but Mom refused to have one. She said she preferred a blade on her legs. We put this down to her great practicality until one day, when she thought she was alone in the house, I saw her shaving her chin with Dad's electric shaver!

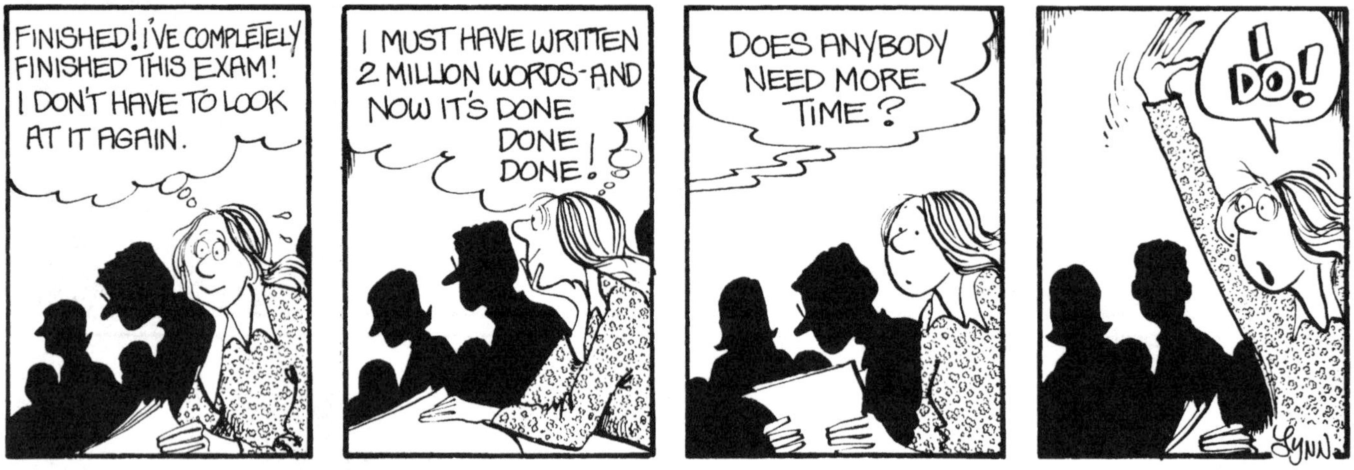
FINISHED! I'VE COMPLETELY FINISHED THIS EXAM! I DON'T HAVE TO LOOK AT IT AGAIN.
I MUST HAVE WRITTEN 2 MILLION WORDS - AND NOW IT'S DONE DONE! DONE!
DOES ANYBODY NEED MORE TIME?
I DO!
LYNN

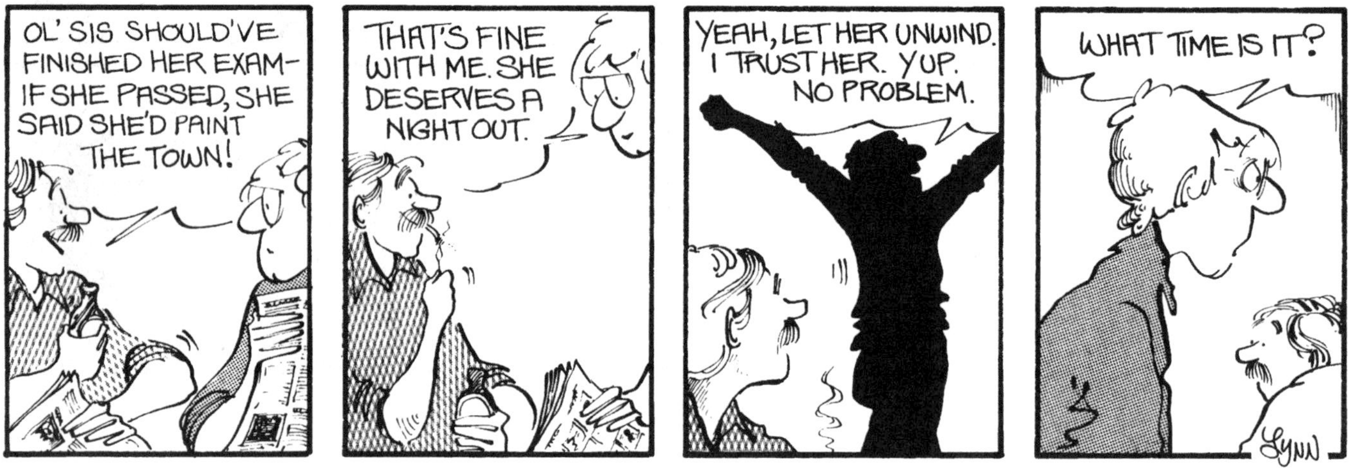
OL' SIS SHOULD'VE FINISHED HER EXAM - IF SHE PASSED, SHE SAID SHE'D PAINT THE TOWN!
THAT'S FINE WITH ME. SHE DESERVES A NIGHT OUT.
YEAH, LET HER UNWIND. I TRUST HER. YUP. NO PROBLEM.
WHAT TIME IS IT?
LYNN

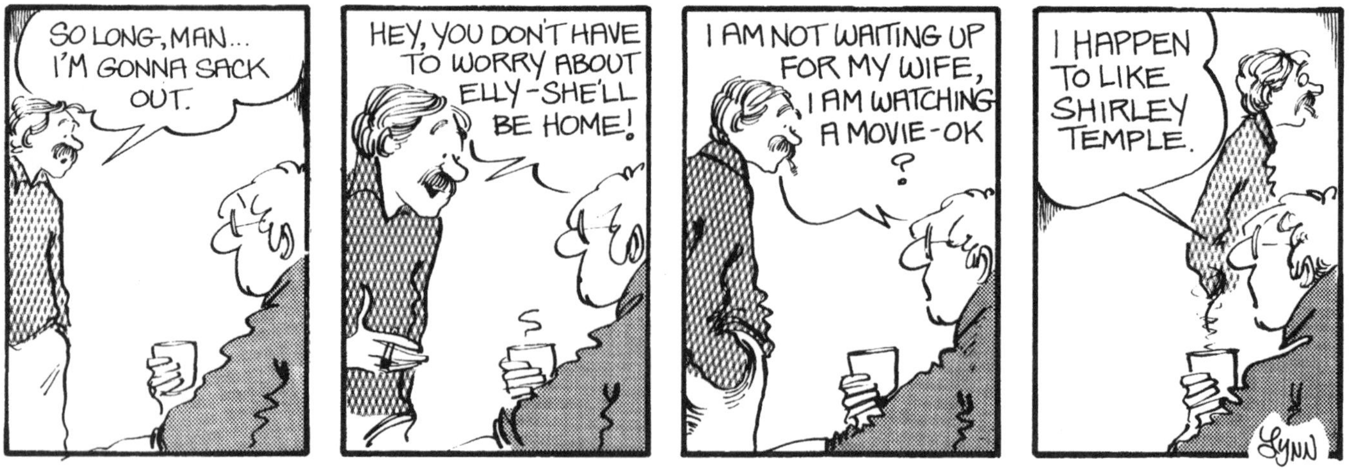
SO LONG, MAN... I'M GONNA SACK OUT.
HEY, YOU DON'T HAVE TO WORRY ABOUT ELLY - SHE'LL BE HOME!
I AM NOT WAITING UP FOR MY WIFE, I AM WATCHING A MOVIE - OK?
I HAPPEN TO LIKE SHIRLEY TEMPLE.
LYNN

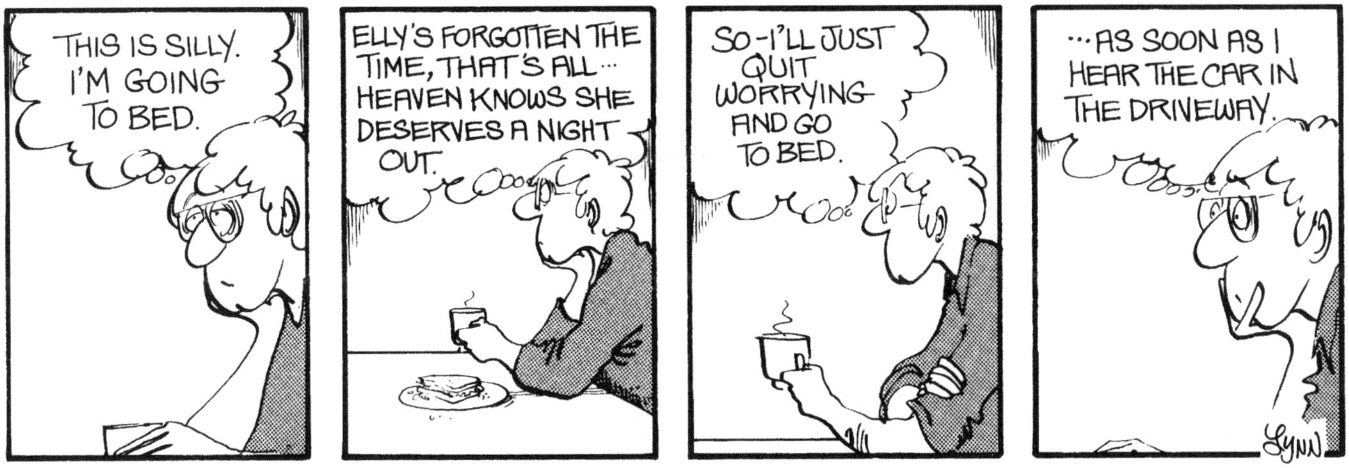
THIS IS SILLY. I'M GOING TO BED.
ELLY'S FORGOTTEN THE TIME, THAT'S ALL... HEAVEN KNOWS SHE DESERVES A NIGHT OUT.
SO-I'LL JUST QUIT WORRYING AND GO TO BED.
...AS SOON AS I HEAR THE CAR IN THE DRIVEWAY.
LYNN

Before my first marriage ended, I spent a lot of time at night listening for our car to come down the driveway. I instinctively knew the sound of the engine and the pattern the headlights made on the walls. I'd feel guilty for being mistrustful, but then again, my husband was doing things I'd never do to him, and his excuses never seemed to resolve things. I often used the strip to "vent" about the past.

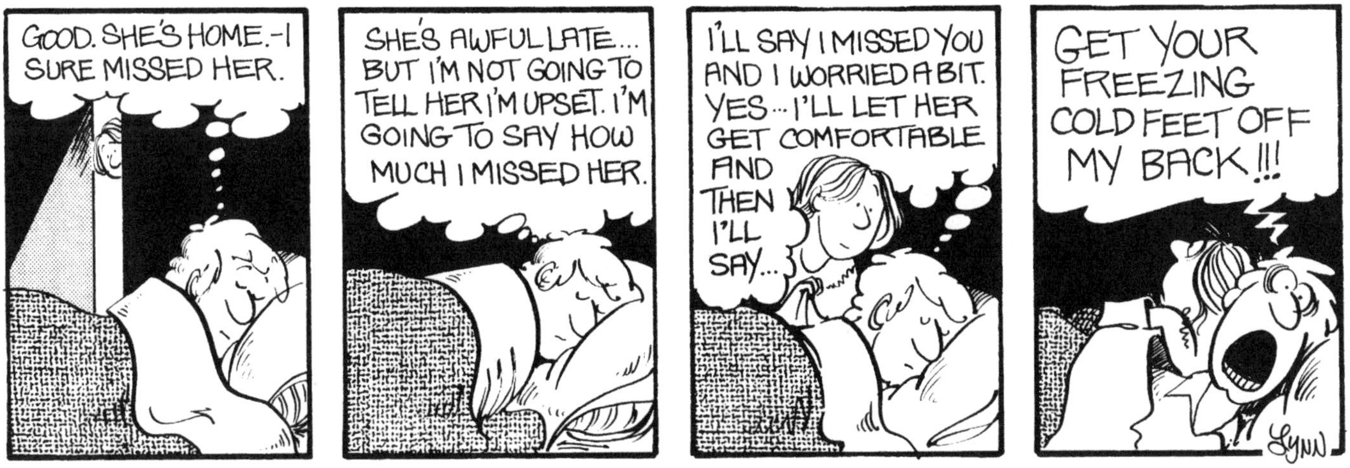
GOOD. SHE'S HOME.-I SURE MISSED HER.
SHE'S AWFUL LATE... BUT I'M NOT GOING TO TELL HER I'M UPSET. I'M GOING TO SAY HOW MUCH I MISSED HER.
I'LL SAY I MISSED YOU AND I WORRIED A BIT. YES... I'LL LET HER GET COMFORTABLE AND THEN I'LL SAY...
GET YOUR FREEZING COLD FEET OFF MY BACK!!!
LYNN

Before the onset of menopause, my feet were always cold. I wore long cotton nightgowns and slept with my socks on. I don't think I pulled this trick too many times, but the idea was funny, and it was fun to draw; any opportunity to show a character hollering with a mouth wide open like this made my day!

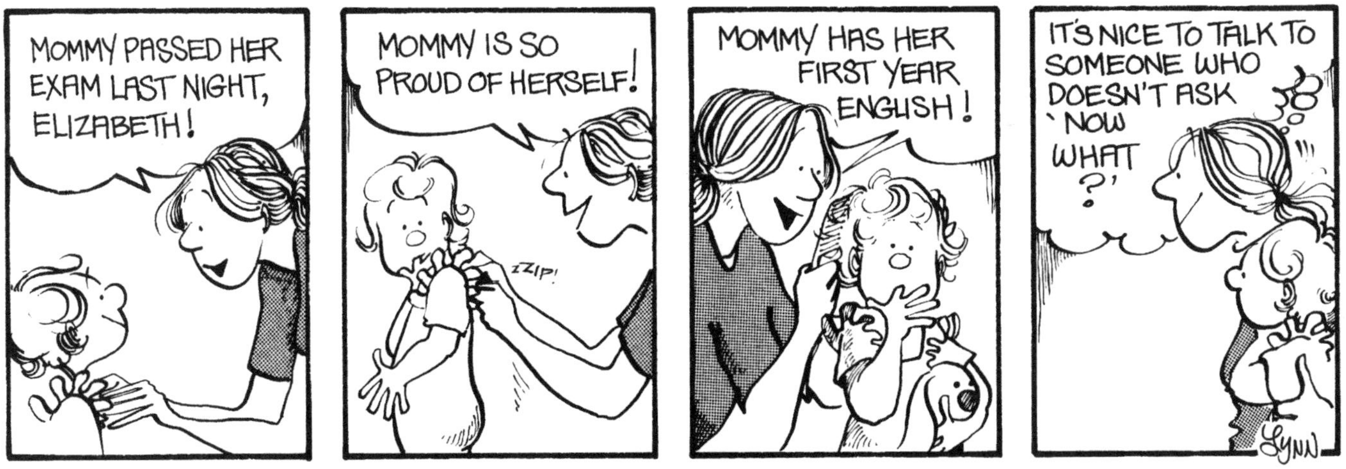
MOMMY PASSED HER EXAM LAST NIGHT, ELIZABETH!
MOMMY IS SO PROUD OF HERSELF!
ZZIP!
MOMMY HAS HER FIRST YEAR ENGLISH!
IT'S NICE TO TALK TO SOMEONE WHO DOESN'T ASK 'NOW WHAT?'
LYNN

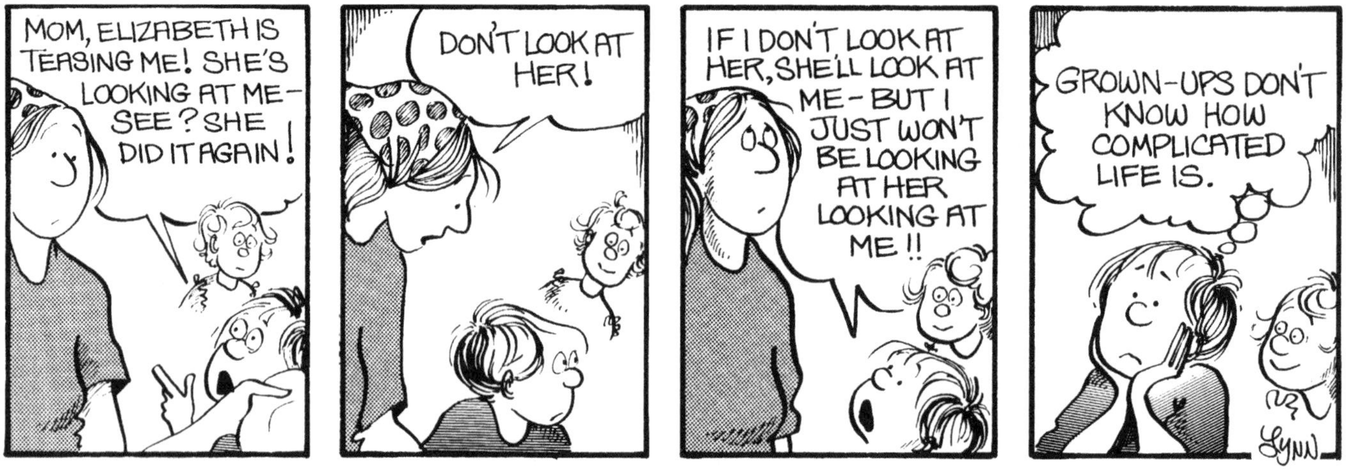
MOM, ELIZABETH IS TEASING ME! SHE'S LOOKING AT ME - SEE? SHE DID IT AGAIN!
DON'T LOOK AT HER!
IF I DON'T LOOK AT HER, SHE'LL LOOK AT ME - BUT I JUST WON'T BE LOOKING AT HER LOOKING AT ME!!
GROWN-UPS DON'T KNOW HOW COMPLICATED LIFE IS.
LYNN

This was a "game" my brother and I played. It was a subtle kind of teasing that involved eye contact — or the lack thereof. We'd stare at each other — glaring, menacing, then calmly look away when a parent came by. We would enrage each other, and it's awfully hard to plead your case when there's no evidence of wrongdoing.

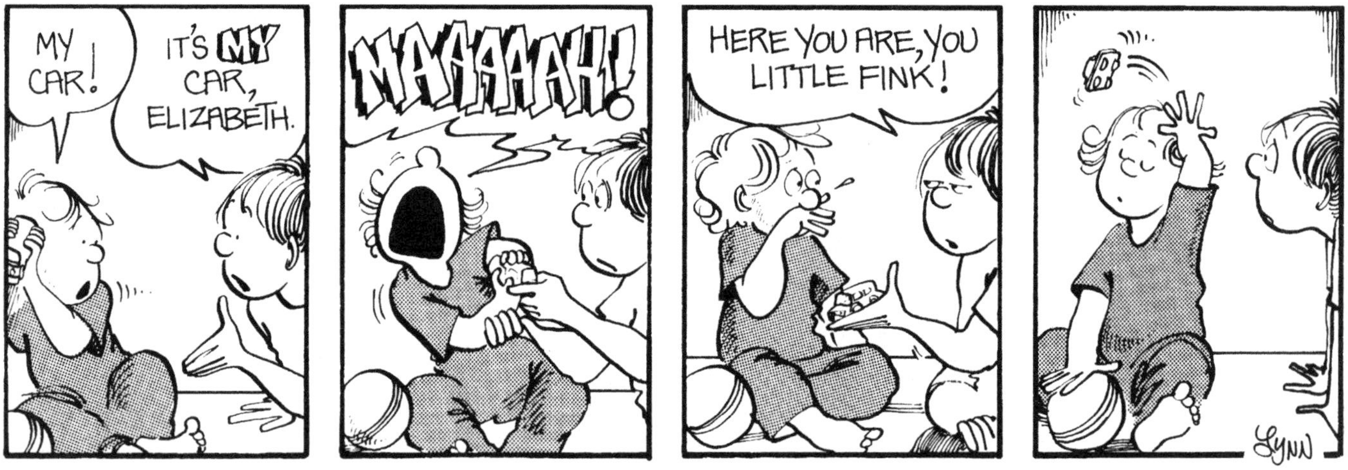
MY CAR!
IT'S MY CAR, ELIZABETH.
MAAAAAH!
HERE YOU ARE, YOU LITTLE FINK!
LYNN

Alan and I couldn't pass up an opportunity to upset one another, and this lasted well into our teens. No wonder our folks were so pleased when we moved out!

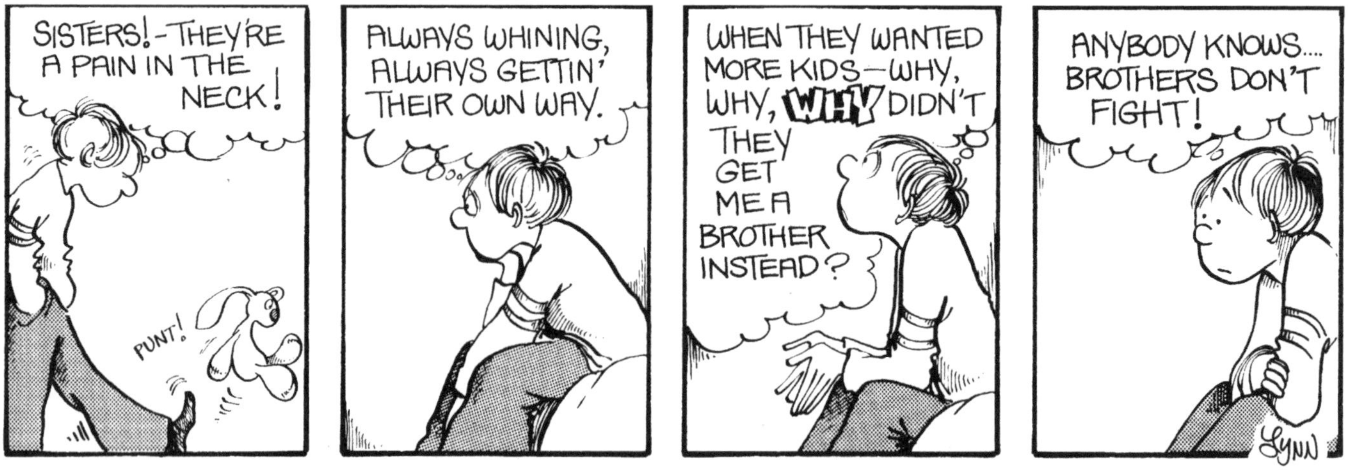
SISTERS! - THEY'RE A PAIN IN THE NECK!
PUNT!
ALWAYS WHINING, ALWAYS GETTIN' THEIR OWN WAY.
WHEN THEY WANTED MORE KIDS—WHY, WHY, WHY DIDN'T THEY GET ME A BROTHER INSTEAD?
ANYBODY KNOWS.... BROTHERS DON'T FIGHT!
LYNN

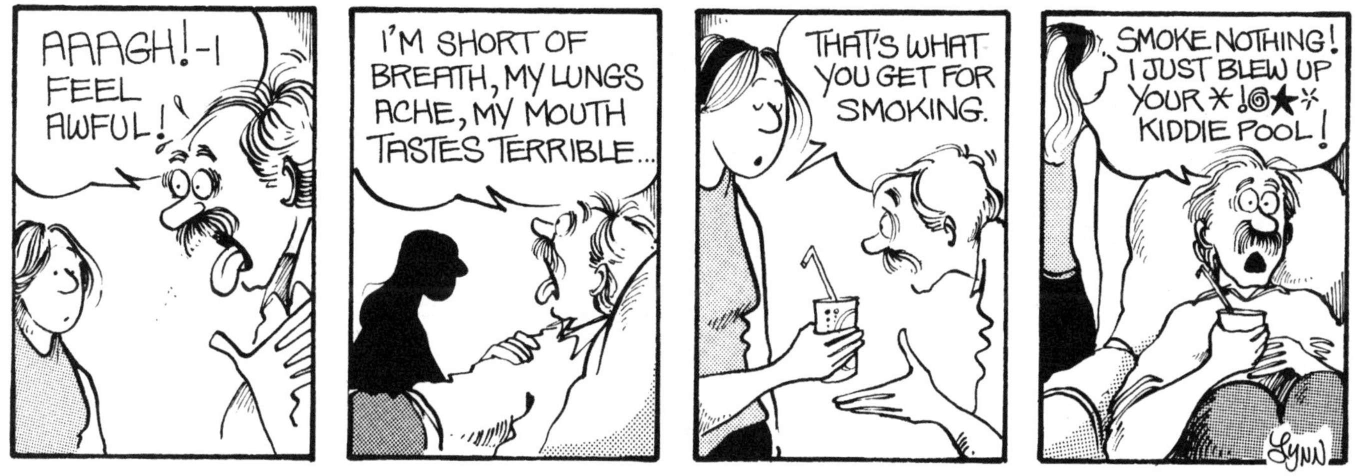
AAAGH! - I FEEL AWFUL!
I'M SHORT OF BREATH, MY LUNGS ACHE, MY MOUTH TASTES TERRIBLE...
THAT'S WHAT YOU GET FOR SMOKING.
SMOKE NOTHING! I JUST BLEW UP YOUR *!@★*: KIDDIE POOL!
LYNN

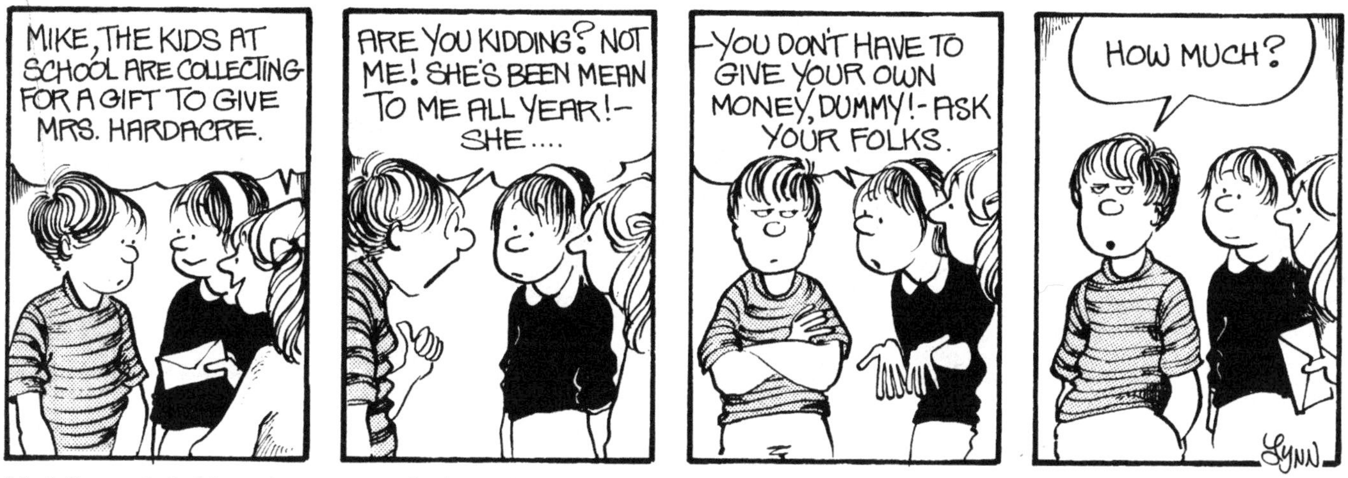
MIKE, THE KIDS AT SCHOOL ARE COLLECTING FOR A GIFT TO GIVE MRS. HARDACRE.
ARE YOU KIDDING? NOT ME! SHE'S BEEN MEAN TO ME ALL YEAR! - SHE....
- YOU DON'T HAVE TO GIVE YOUR OWN MONEY, DUMMY! - ASK YOUR FOLKS.
HOW MUCH?
LYNN

My folks carried china, glassware, and other gift items in the jewellery store. This meant they were often asked to provide gifts for our teacher, and I had to help them decide. It was difficult to choose something for a teacher I wasn't fond of, and the first thing that came to mind was to select something DUMB! I found myself, instead, choosing something beautiful, and in so doing, I would rethink my feelings for the person it was for.

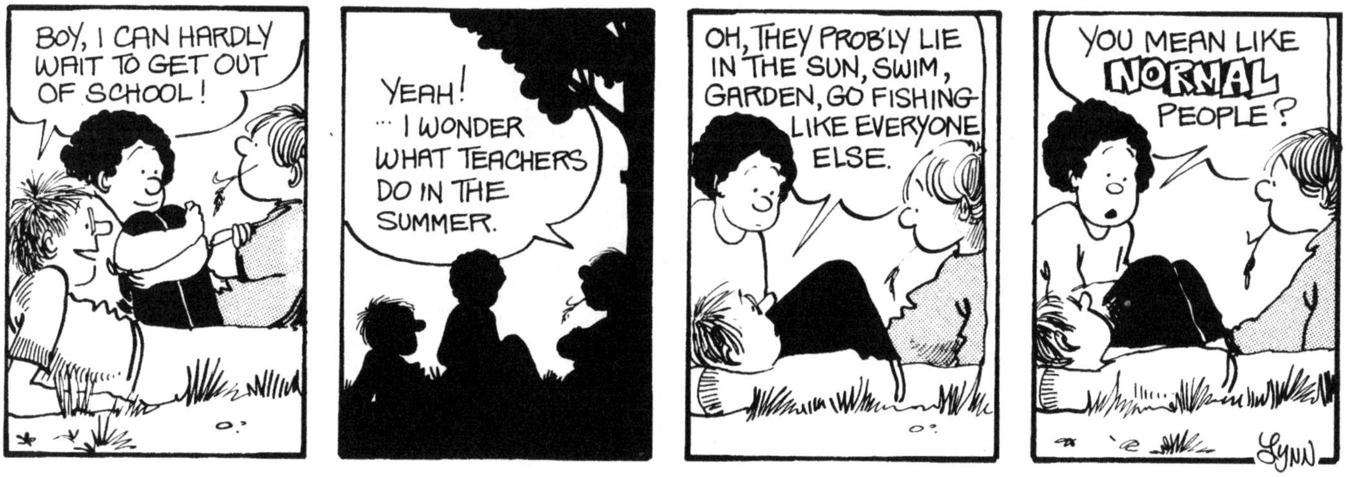
BOY, I CAN HARDLY WAIT TO GET OUT OF SCHOOL!
YEAH! ... I WONDER WHAT TEACHERS DO IN THE SUMMER.
OH, THEY PROB'LY LIE IN THE SUN, SWIM, GARDEN, GO FISHING LIKE EVERYONE ELSE.
YOU MEAN LIKE NORMAL PEOPLE?
LYNN

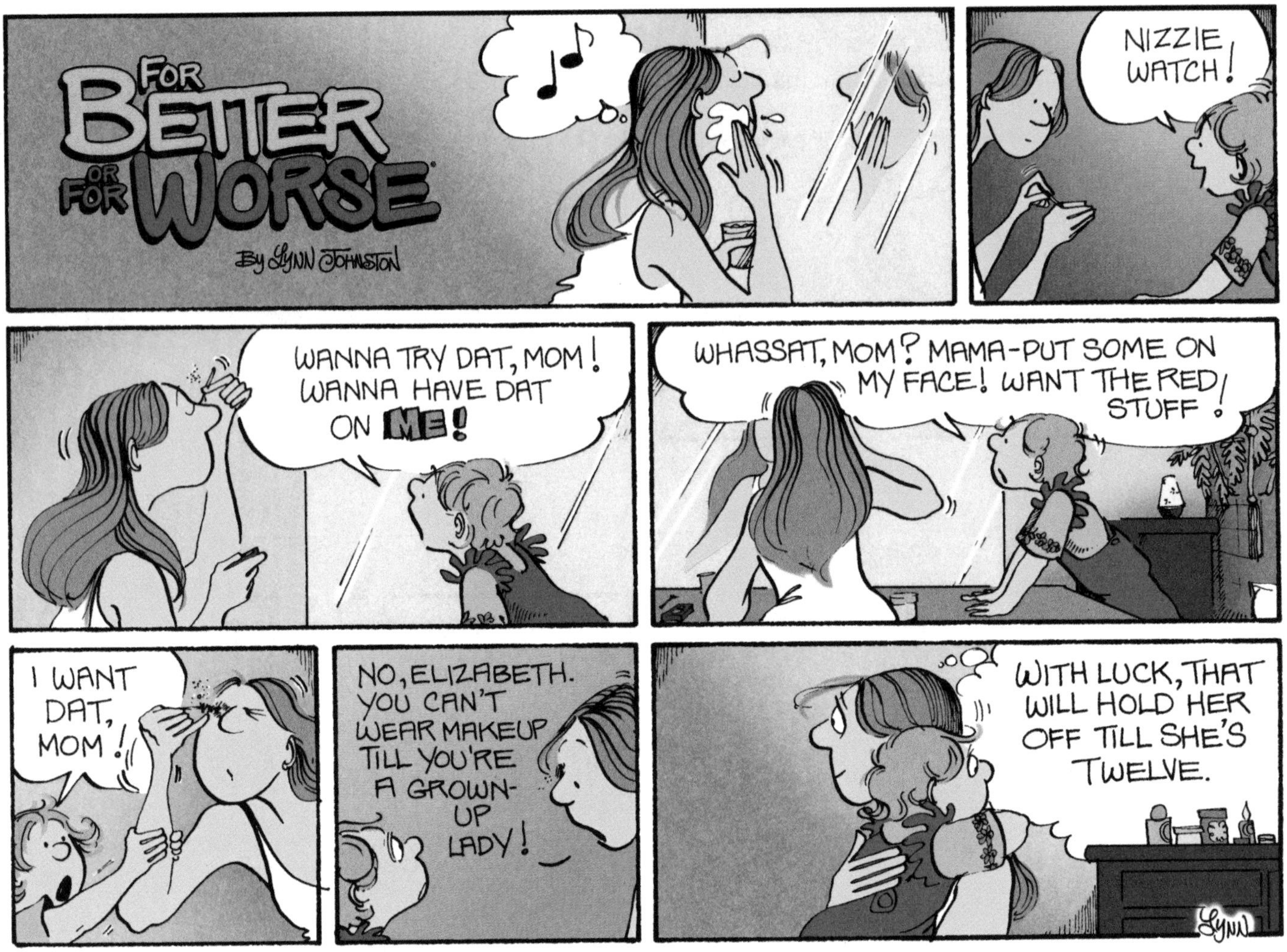
FOR BETTER OR FOR WORSE
BY LYNN JOHNSTON
NIZZIE WATCH!
WANNA TRY DAT, MOM! WANNA HAVE DAT ON ME!
WHASSAT, MOM? MAMA-PUT SOME ON MY FACE! WANT THE RED STUFF!
I WANT DAT, MOM!
NO, ELIZABETH. YOU CAN'T WEAR MAKEUP TILL YOU'RE A GROWN-UP LADY!
WITH LUCK, THAT WILL HOLD HER OFF TILL SHE'S TWELVE.
LYNN

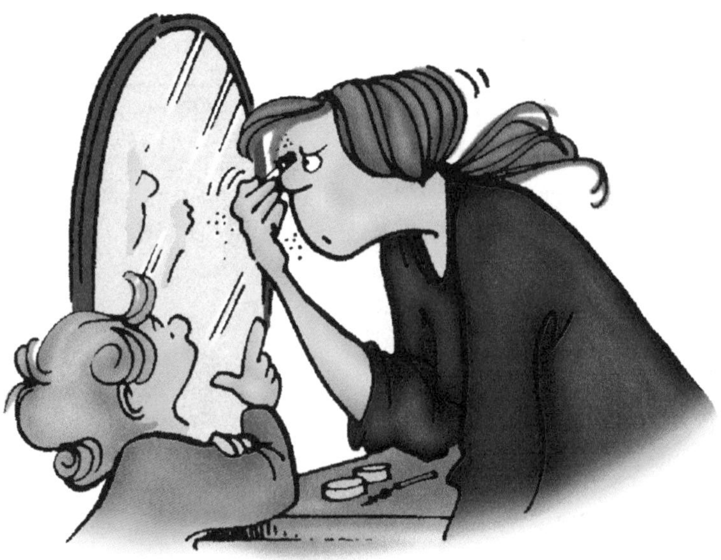

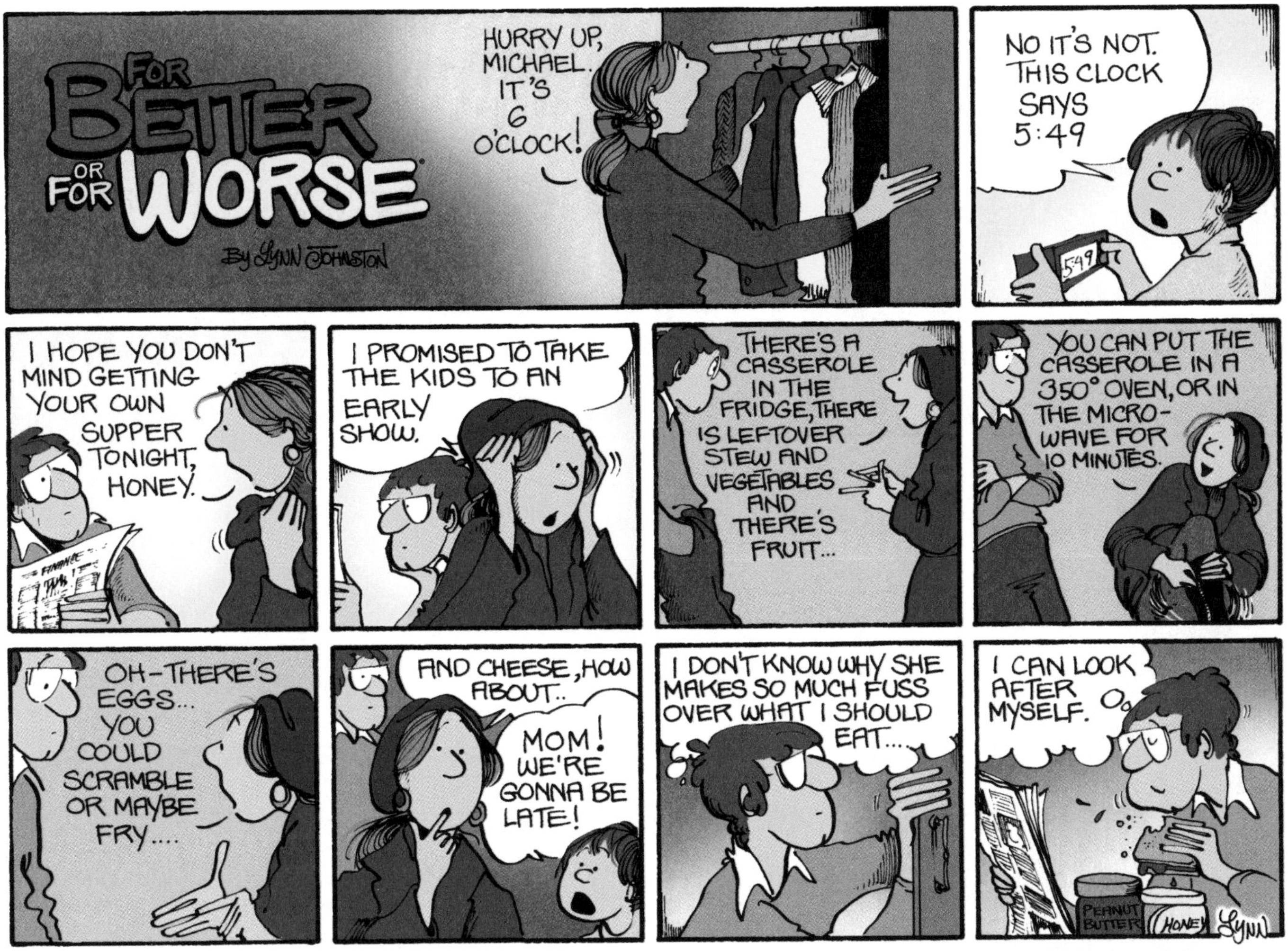
FOR BETTER OR FOR WORSE
BY LYNN JOHNSTON
HURRY UP, MICHAEL. IT'S 6 O'CLOCK!
NO IT'S NOT. THIS CLOCK SAYS 5:49
5:49
I HOPE YOU DON'T MIND GETTING YOUR OWN SUPPER TONIGHT, HONEY.
I PROMISED TO TAKE THE KIDS TO AN EARLY SHOW.
THERE'S A CASSEROLE IN THE FRIDGE, THERE IS LEFTOVER STEW AND VEGETABLES AND THERE'S FRUIT...
YOU CAN PUT THE CASSEROLE IN A 350° OVEN, OR IN THE MICRO-WAVE FOR 10 MINUTES.
OH-THERE'S EGGS... YOU COULD SCRAMBLE OR MAYBE FRY....
AND CHEESE, HOW ABOUT..
MOM! WE'RE GONNA BE LATE!
I DON'T KNOW WHY SHE MAKES SO MUCH FUSS OVER WHAT I SHOULD EAT....
I CAN LOOK AFTER MYSELF.
PEANUT BUTTER
HONEY
LYNN

Here is a scenario that would play out many times in my housewifely career. My job often required me to be away. In preparation for each trip, I'd make easy meals that covered all the food groups and leave them in the fridge to be accessed by the troops. Without a second thought, they bypassed my well-organized and clearly labelled containers … and ate JUNK! On my return from wherever it was I went, I'd find my beautifully prepared grub reduced to dried, mouldering leftovers — having never seen plate nor palate.

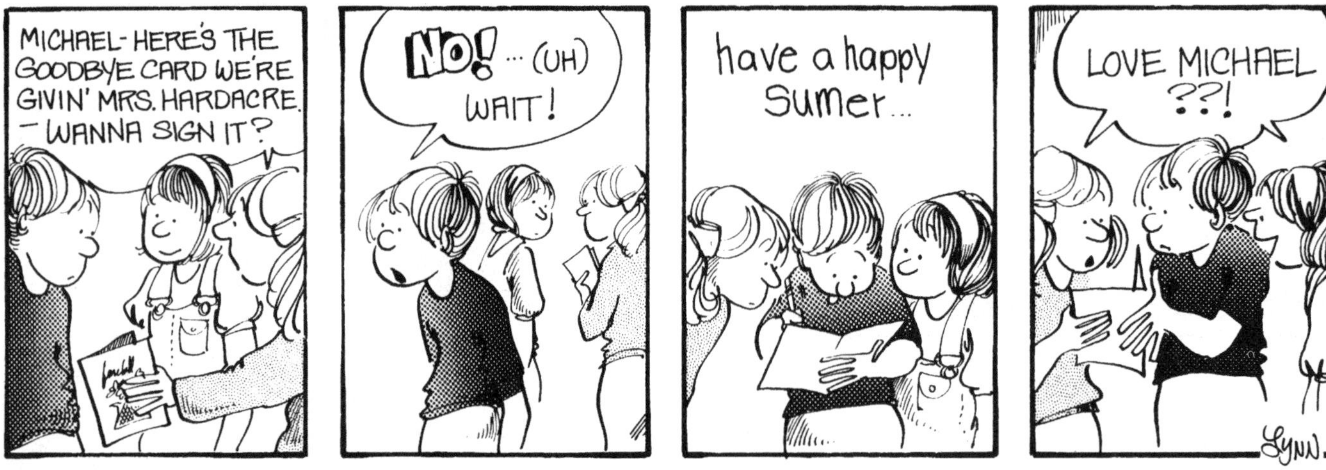
MICHAEL- HERE'S THE GOODBYE CARD WE'RE GIVIN' MRS. HARDACRE. - WANNA SIGN IT?
NO! ...(UH) WAIT!
have a happy Sumer...
LOVE MICHAEL ??!
LYNN

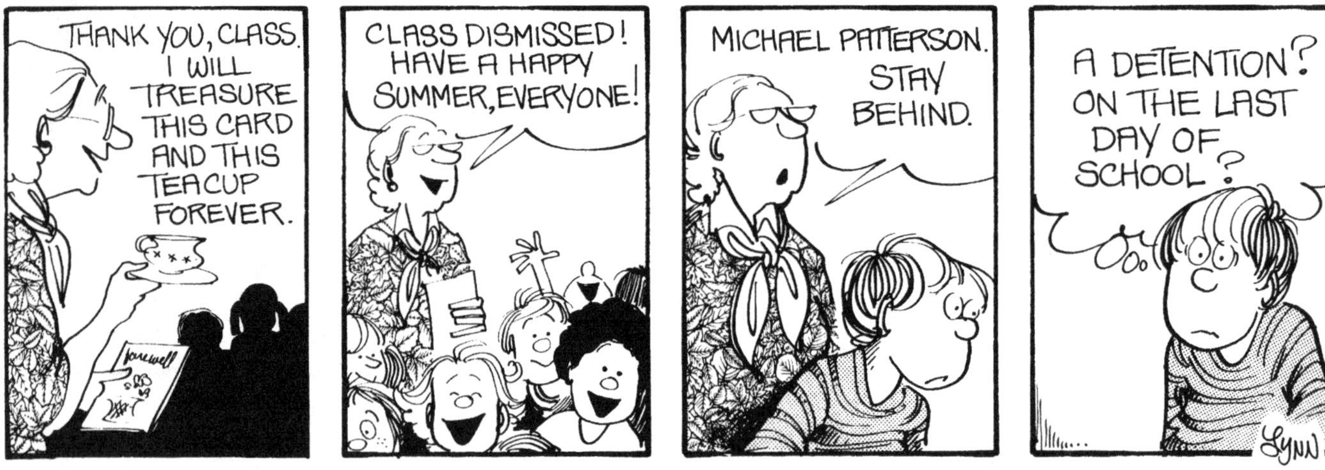
THANK YOU, CLASS. I WILL TREASURE THIS CARD AND THIS TEACUP FOREVER.
CLASS DISMISSED! HAVE A HAPPY SUMMER, EVERYONE!
MICHAEL PATTERSON. STAY BEHIND.
A DETENTION? ON THE LAST DAY OF SCHOOL?
LYNN

My grade three teacher kept me after school on the last day to tell me that, after all the conflict we had endured together during the year, she thought I was basically a good kid. This was the attitude that most of my teachers had … and when Aaron's teachers gave him "the talk," I knew exactly where they were coming from.

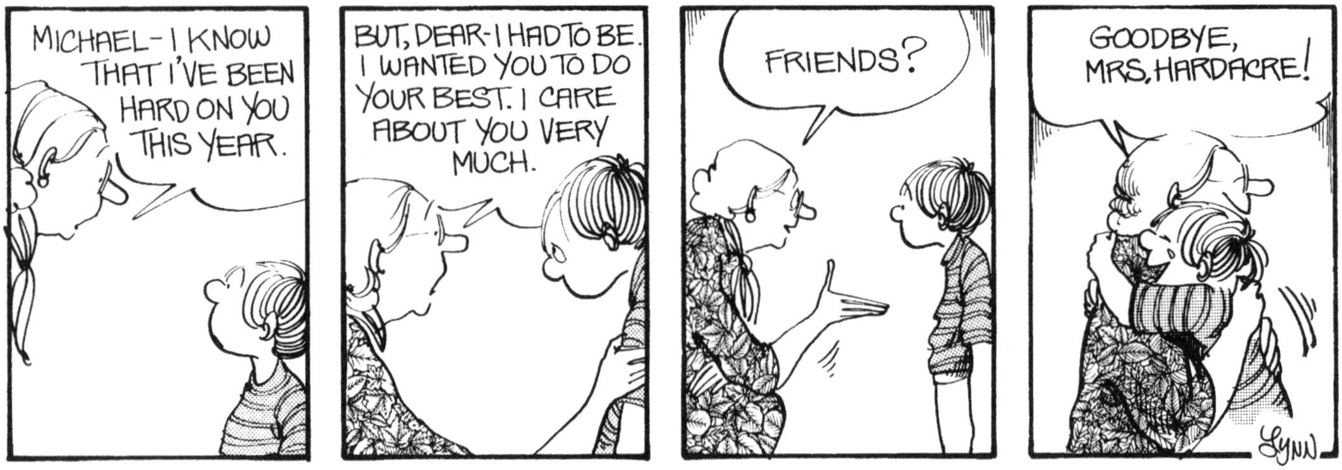
MICHAEL- I KNOW THAT I'VE BEEN HARD ON YOU THIS YEAR.
BUT, DEAR- I HAD TO BE. I WANTED YOU TO DO YOUR BEST. I CARE ABOUT YOU VERY MUCH.
FRIENDS?
GOODBYE, MRS. HARDACRE!
LYNN

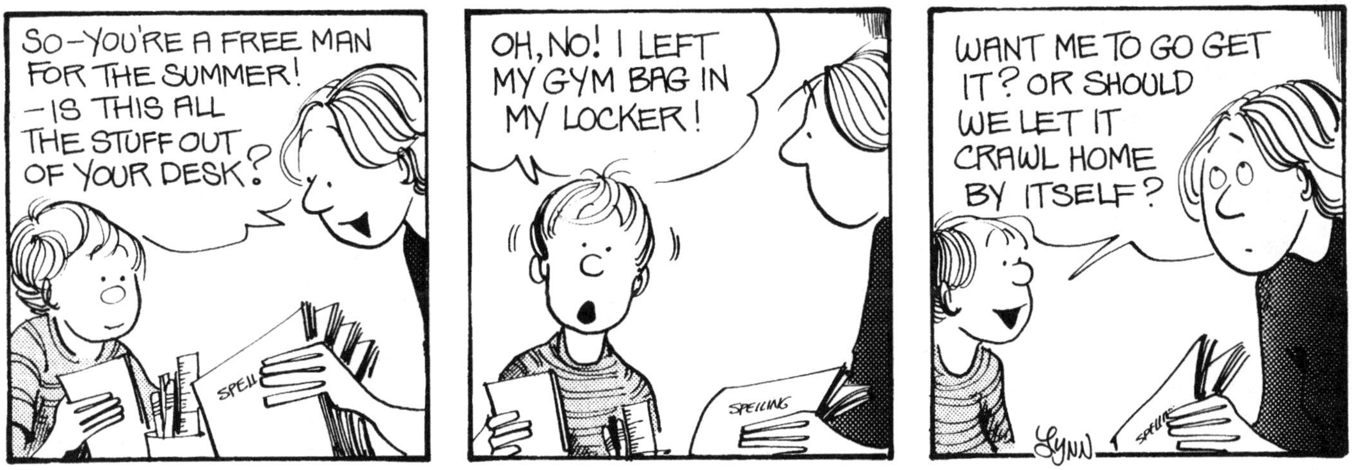
SO-YOU'RE A FREE MAN FOR THE SUMMER! -IS THIS ALL THE STUFF OUT OF YOUR DESK?
OH, NO! I LEFT MY GYM BAG IN MY LOCKER!
WANT ME TO GO GET IT? OR SHOULD WE LET IT CRAWL HOME BY ITSELF?

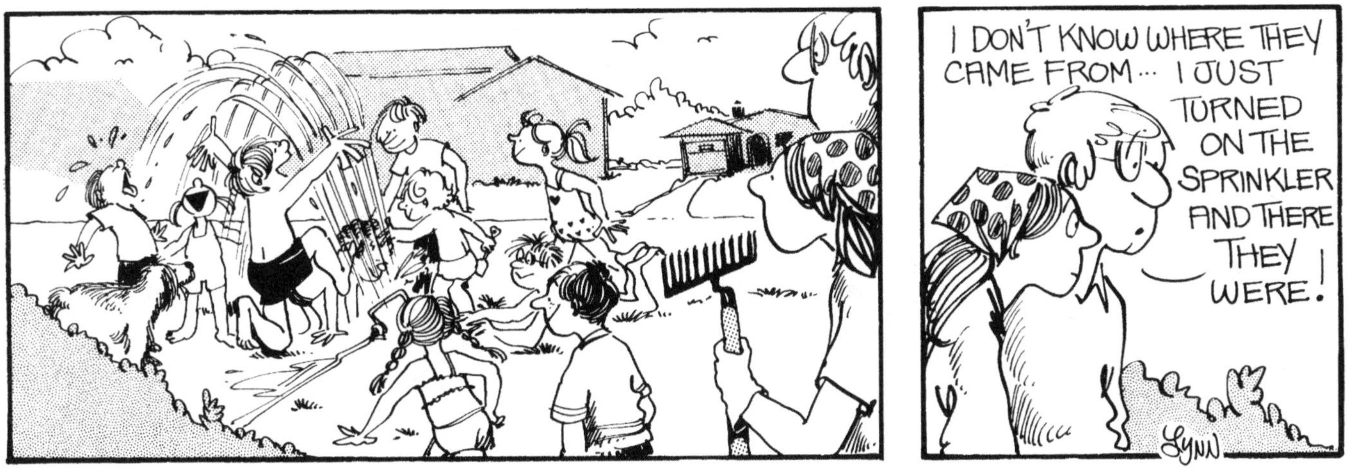
I DON'T KNOW WHERE THEY CAME FROM... I JUST TURNED ON THE SPRINKLER AND THERE THEY WERE!

Our childhood home on Fifth and Lonsdale in North Vancouver was where all the neighbourhood kids seemed to congregate. When our sprinkler was on, it meant food, fun, and a bathroom — if we remembered to use it! My folks were tolerant and welcoming, and everyone took their generosity for granted. They rarely complained. They wanted to be able to look out the window and know where we were!

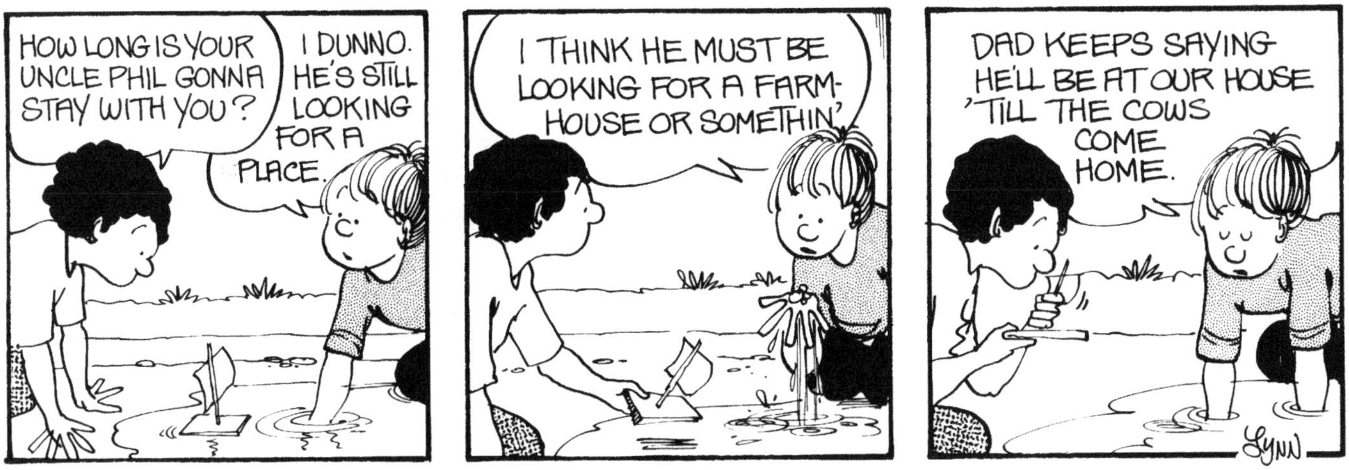
HOW LONG IS YOUR UNCLE PHIL GONNA STAY WITH YOU?
I DUNNO. HE'S STILL LOOKING FOR A PLACE.
I THINK HE MUST BE LOOKING FOR A FARM-HOUSE OR SOMETHIN'.
DAD KEEPS SAYING HE'LL BE AT OUR HOUSE 'TILL THE COWS COME HOME.

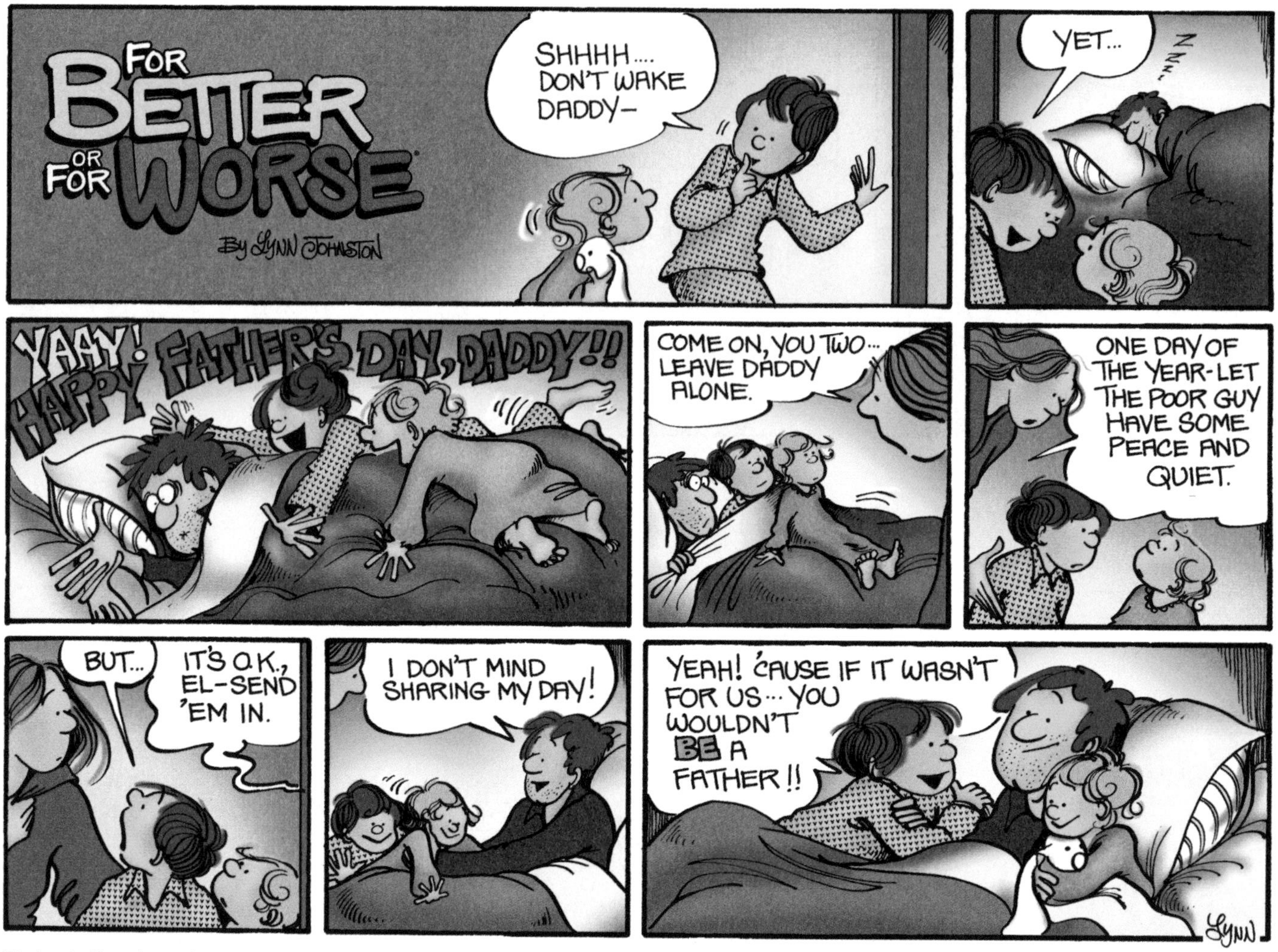
FOR BETTER OR FOR WORSE
BY LYNN JOHNSTON
SHHHH.... DON'T WAKE DADDY–
YET...
Z Z Z
YAAY! HAPPY FATHER'S DAY, DADDY!!
COME ON, YOU TWO... LEAVE DADDY ALONE.
ONE DAY OF THE YEAR- LET THE POOR GUY HAVE SOME PEACE AND QUIET.
BUT...
IT'S O.K., EL- SEND 'EM IN.
I DON'T MIND SHARING MY DAY!
YEAH! 'CAUSE IF IT WASN'T FOR US... YOU WOULDN'T BE A FATHER!!
LYNN

Father's Day has always been one of the more challenging Sunday comics to produce. We never really made too much of it when I was a kid; and later, when my two were small, it was a day when the best "present" was to let Dad spend the day in his workshop! Still, it's a day that puts the spotlight on dads and children, no matter what the marital dynamics are — which is a good thing. We need more Father's Days and Mother's Days, if you ask me. Heaven knows — there's nothing more rewarding than being recognized and appreciated for doing a difficult job well!

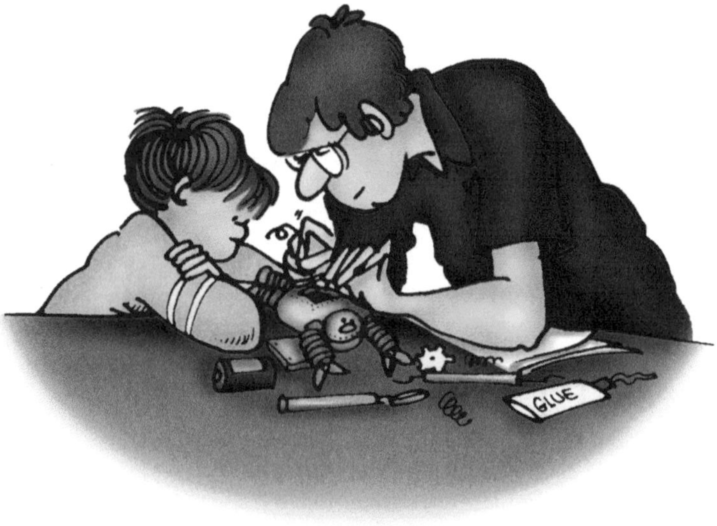
GLUE

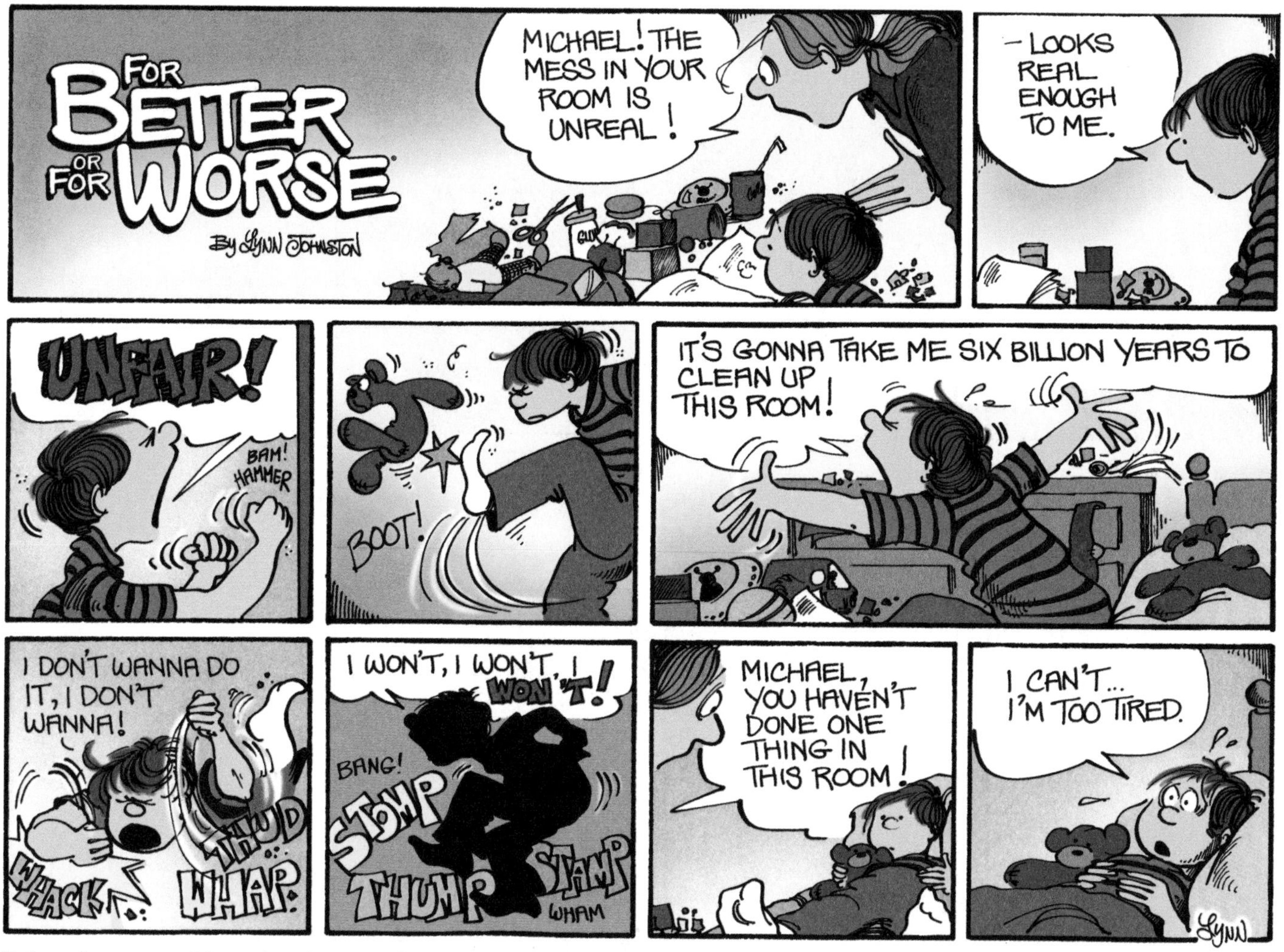
FOR BETTER OR FOR WORSE
By Lynn Johnston
MICHAEL! THE MESS IN YOUR ROOM IS UNREAL!
– LOOKS REAL ENOUGH TO ME.
UNFAIR!
BAM! HAMMER
BOOT!
IT'S GONNA TAKE ME SIX BILLION YEARS TO CLEAN UP THIS ROOM!
I DON'T WANNA DO IT, I DON'T WANNA!
WHACK
THUD
WHAP
I WON'T, I WON'T, I WON'T!
BANG!
STOMP
THUMP
STAMP
WHAM
MICHAEL, YOU HAVEN'T DONE ONE THING IN THIS ROOM!
I CAN'T... I'M TOO TIRED.
LYNN

I shared a room with my brother until I was about ten. When Alan moved into a newly built room in the basement, I finally had a space to myself. My room was both a refuge and a cell; I was either there of my own volition or was sent there to dwell on various misdeeds until I'd done penance and was released. When my room was a place of chastisement, it made no difference to me if it was a wreck or not. I had no interest in tidying up a "jail." When my room was my "apartment," making it tidy wasn't so difficult.

I remember having real fits of rage in that room. Breaking something would result in some serious punishment, so pounding the bed and pummelling toys took care of the worst of it. The thing about being a kid is you know you're miserable, but you can't figure out why! You're not able to sift through the events of the day, identify the exact reason for your snit; and this kind of adds to the fury ... and I could be furious!

After awhile, I'd wear myself out. Exhausted, I'd crawl into bed — and, in the end, a good sleep was probably what I had needed in the first place!

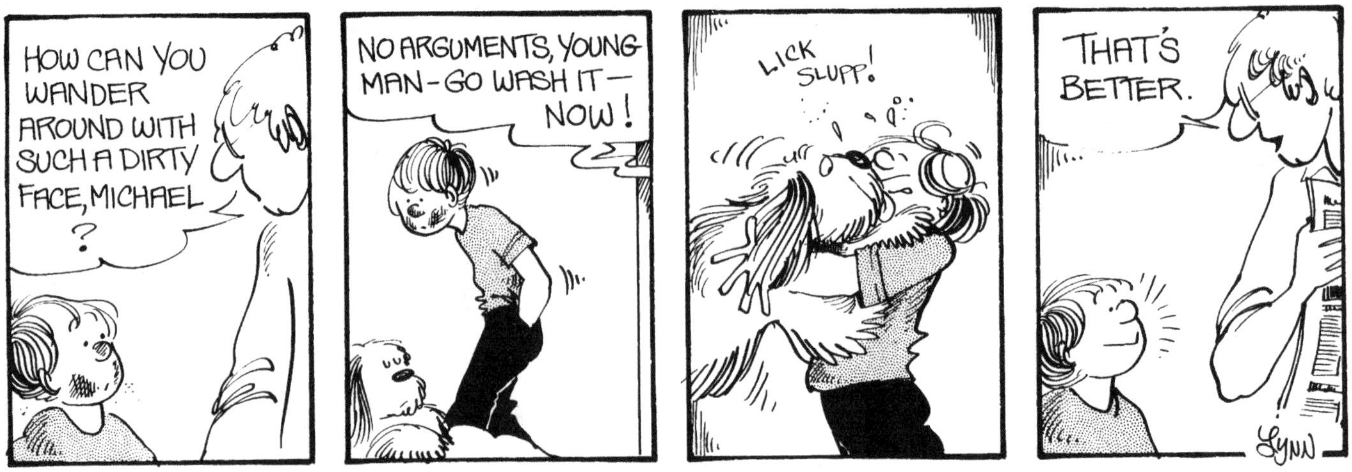
HOW CAN YOU WANDER AROUND WITH SUCH A DIRTY FACE, MICHAEL?
NO ARGUMENTS, YOUNG MAN - GO WASH IT — NOW!
LICK SLUPP!
THAT'S BETTER.

Aaron was a baby when Farley freely roamed the house, and because he was my dog, I was used to him — I didn't panic when he'd sidle to the jolly jumper and remove Aaron's lunch from his face with his big, wet tongue. When I see a dog licking a baby's face today, I cringe.

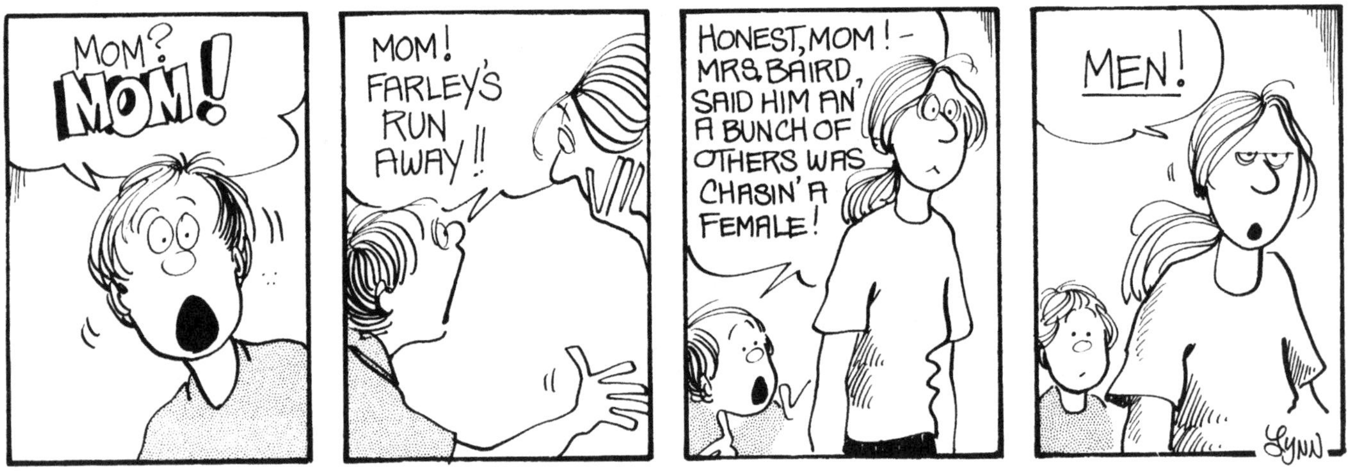
MOM? MOM!
MOM! FARLEY'S RUN AWAY!!
HONEST, MOM! - MRS. BAIRD, SAID HIM AN' A BUNCH OF OTHERS WAS CHASIN' A FEMALE!
MEN!

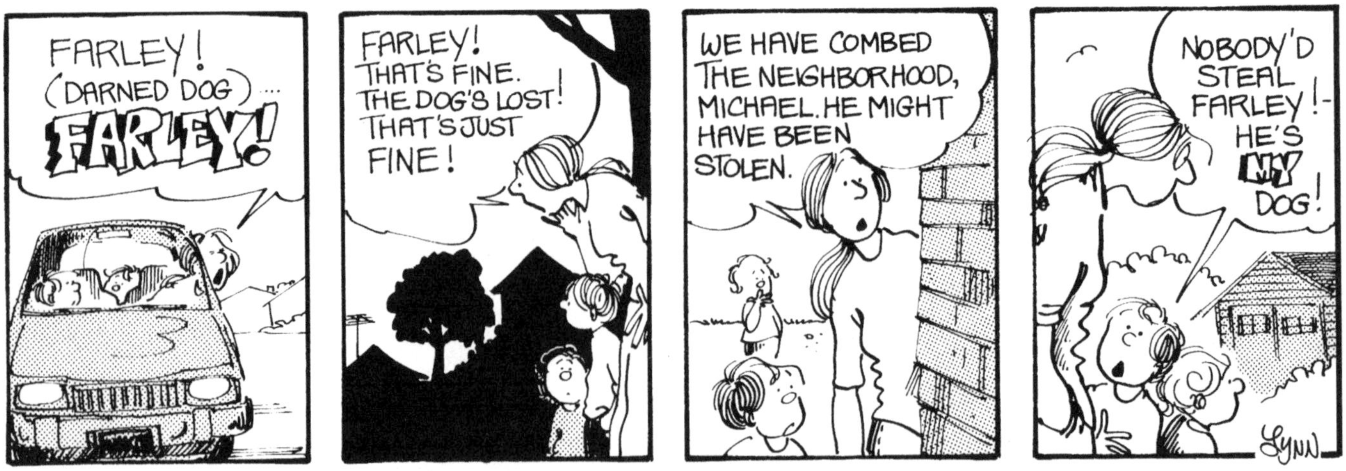
FARLEY! (DARNED DOG).... FARLEY!
FARLEY! THAT'S FINE. THE DOG'S LOST! THAT'S JUST FINE!
WE HAVE COMBED THE NEIGHBORHOOD, MICHAEL. HE MIGHT HAVE BEEN STOLEN.
NOBODY'D STEAL FARLEY! - HE'S MY DOG!

The real Farley rarely left the property, but if he did decide to go AWOL, he'd be gone for the day. It was hard to find him in our housing complex, and there was a ravine to get into as well. It was the highway close by that really worried me. He was big and cuddly, but a pretty dim bulb. On one occasion when he disappeared, I wondered if he had been stolen — but somehow the idea of someone loading his dirty, hairy, odiferous butt into their vehicle was pretty hard to imagine!

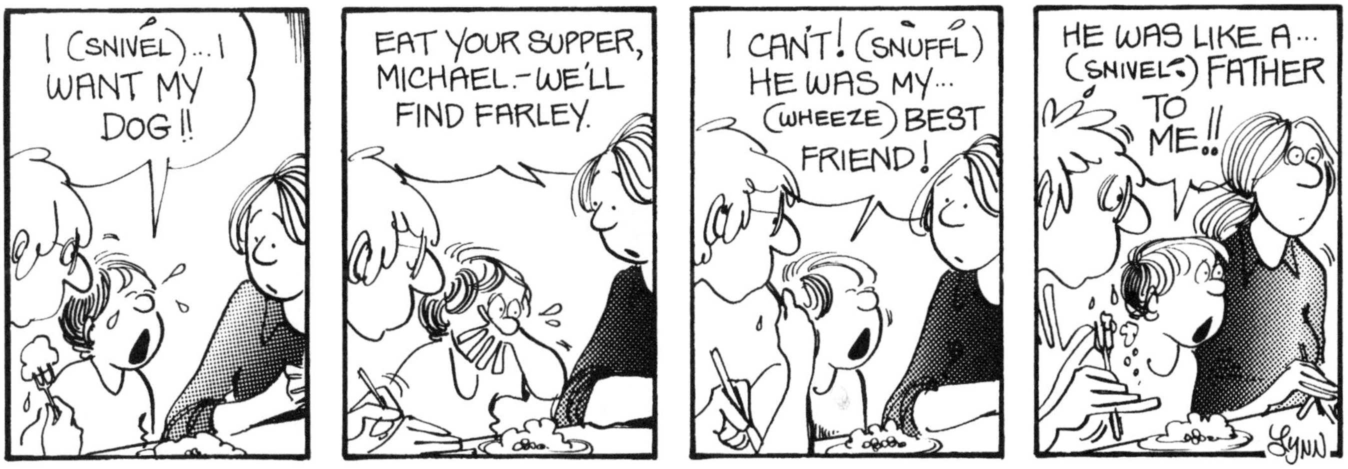
I (SNIVEL)... I WANT MY DOG!!
EAT YOUR SUPPER, MICHAEL.-WE'LL FIND FARLEY.
I CAN'T! (SNUFFL) HE WAS MY... (WHEEZE) BEST FRIEND!
HE WAS LIKE A... (SNIVEL) FATHER TO ME!!
LYNN

This was based on a scenario that once kept my neighbours Marg and Kenny up all night. Their small dog named "Pixie" took off for parts unknown. Marg was so upset that she had to be sedated. Meanwhile, police, firemen, neighbours, and family combed the area without success. Pixie later appeared on her own. She had been under the porch, too afraid to come out with all the crying and commotion going on.

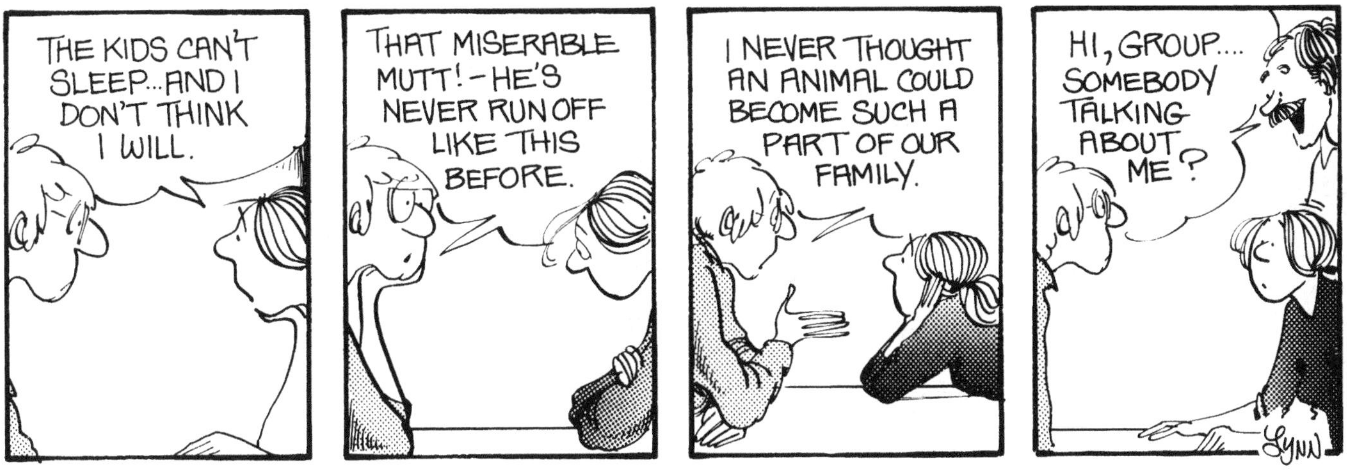
THE KIDS CAN'T SLEEP...AND I DON'T THINK I WILL.
THAT MISERABLE MUTT!-HE'S NEVER RUN OFF LIKE THIS BEFORE.
I NEVER THOUGHT AN ANIMAL COULD BECOME SUCH A PART OF OUR FAMILY.
HI, GROUP.... SOMEBODY TALKING ABOUT ME?
LYNN

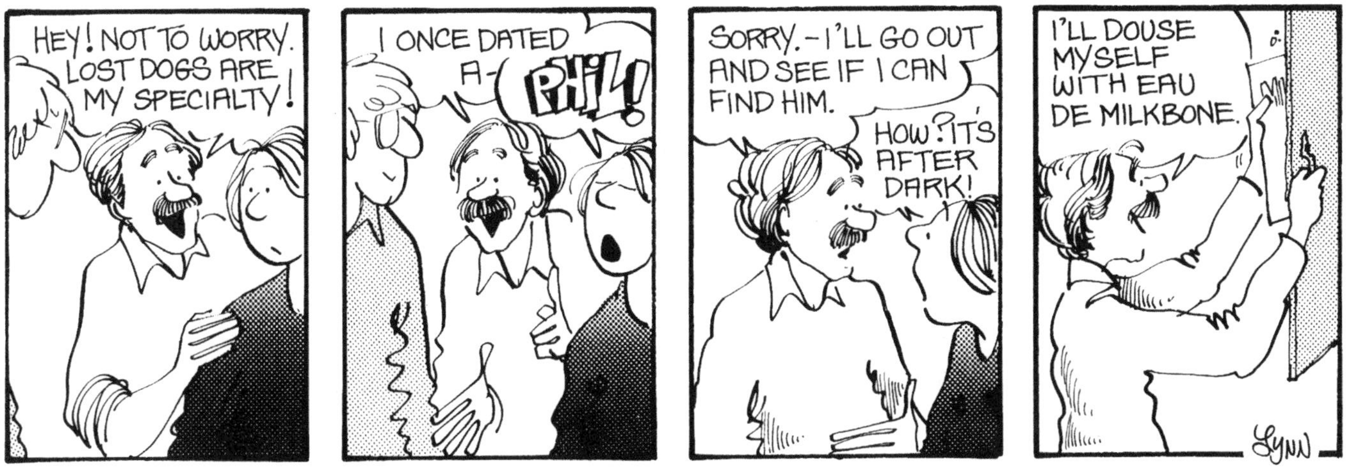
HEY! NOT TO WORRY. LOST DOGS ARE MY SPECIALTY!
I ONCE DATED A-
PHIL!
SORRY.-I'LL GO OUT AND SEE IF I CAN FIND HIM.
HOW? IT'S AFTER DARK!
I'LL DOUSE MYSELF WITH EAU DE MILKBONE.
LYNN

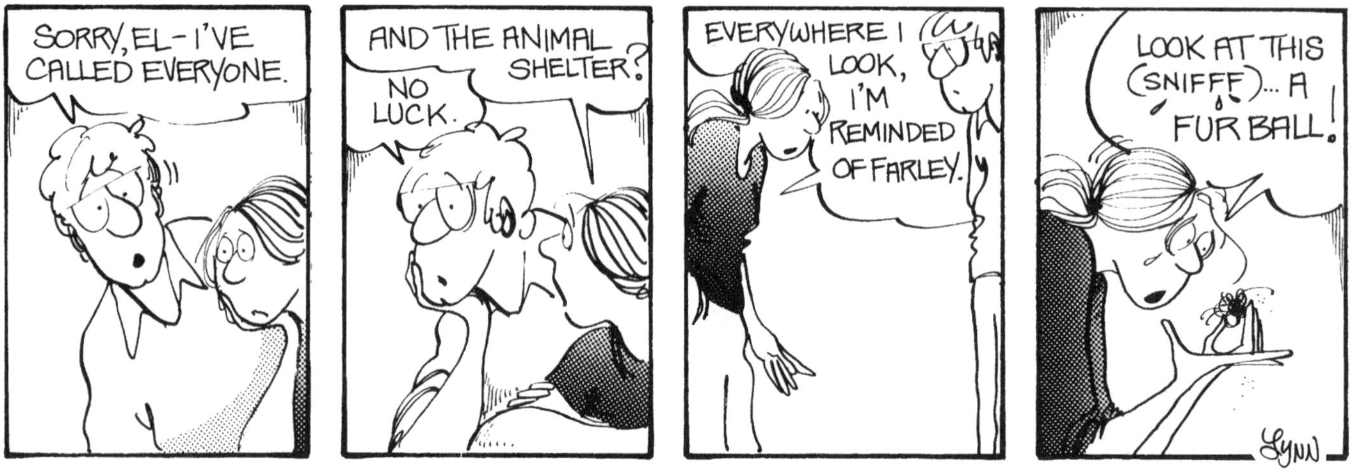
SORRY, EL - I'VE CALLED EVERYONE.
AND THE ANIMAL SHELTER?
NO LUCK.
EVERYWHERE I LOOK, I'M REMINDED OF FARLEY.
LOOK AT THIS (SNIFFF)... A FUR BALL!
LYNN

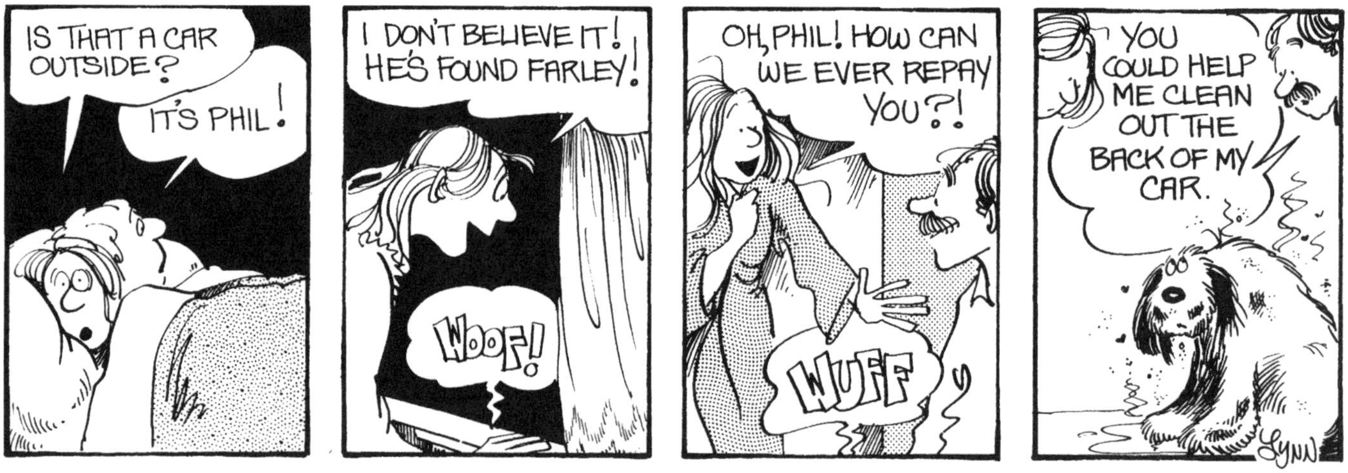
IS THAT A CAR OUTSIDE?
IT'S PHIL!
I DON'T BELIEVE IT! HE'S FOUND FARLEY!
WOOF!
OH, PHIL! HOW CAN WE EVER REPAY YOU?!
WUFF
YOU COULD HELP ME CLEAN OUT THE BACK OF MY CAR.
LYNN

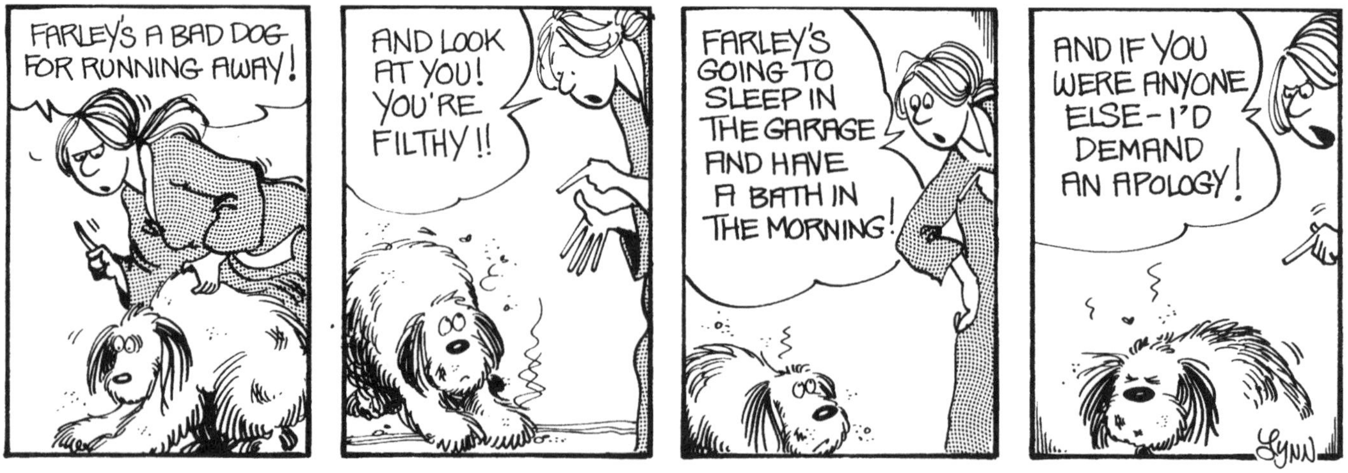
FARLEY'S A BAD DOG FOR RUNNING AWAY!
AND LOOK AT YOU! YOU'RE FILTHY!!
FARLEY'S GOING TO SLEEP IN THE GARAGE AND HAVE A BATH IN THE MORNING!
AND IF YOU WERE ANYONE ELSE - I'D DEMAND AN APOLOGY!
LYNN

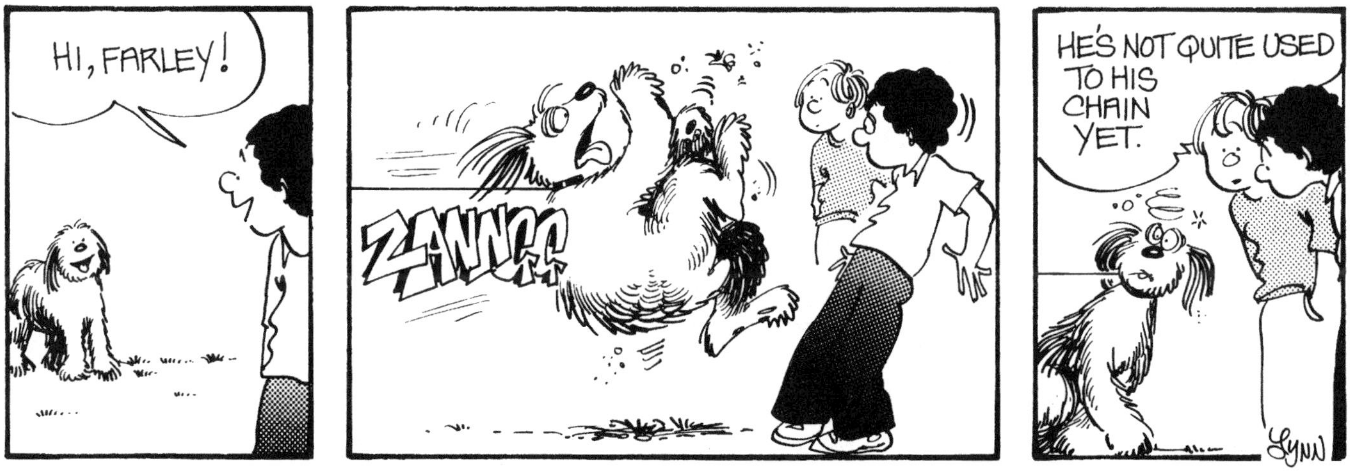
HI, FARLEY!
ZANNGG
HE'S NOT QUITE USED TO HIS CHAIN YET.
LYNN

We tried everything with Farley, even obedience school, but he was really hard to train. We tried tying him up, but he howled pitifully, and we didn't want to annoy the neighbours. Despite our efforts, he never did get the concept of being on a leash. By the end ... I was at the end of my rope.

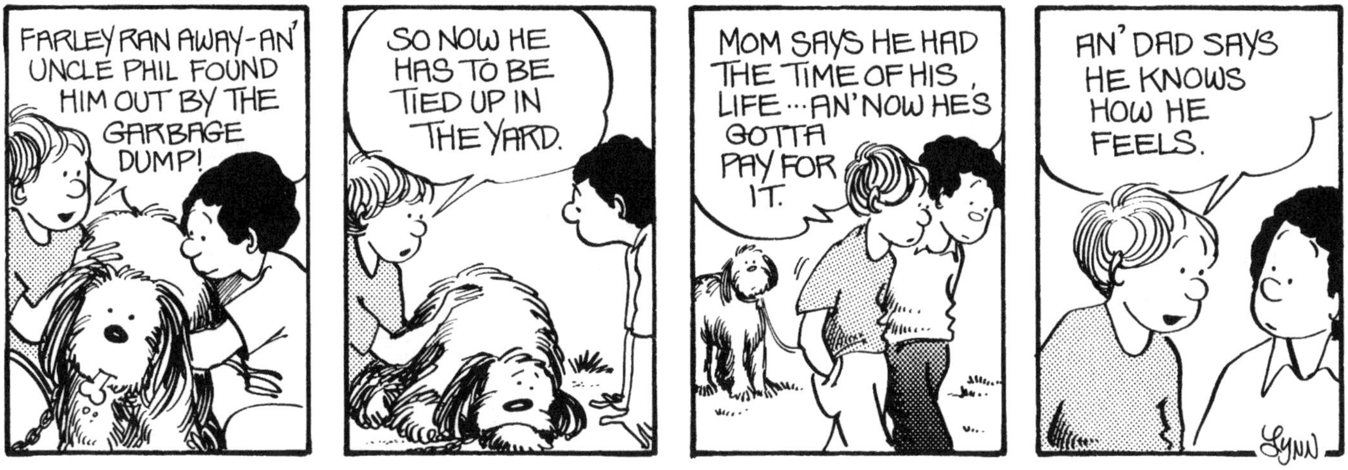
FARLEY RAN AWAY-AN' UNCLE PHIL FOUND HIM OUT BY THE GARBAGE DUMP!
SO NOW HE HAS TO BE TIED UP IN THE YARD.
MOM SAYS HE HAD THE TIME OF HIS LIFE... AN' NOW HE'S GOTTA PAY FOR IT.
AN' DAD SAYS HE KNOWS HOW HE FEELS.
LYNN

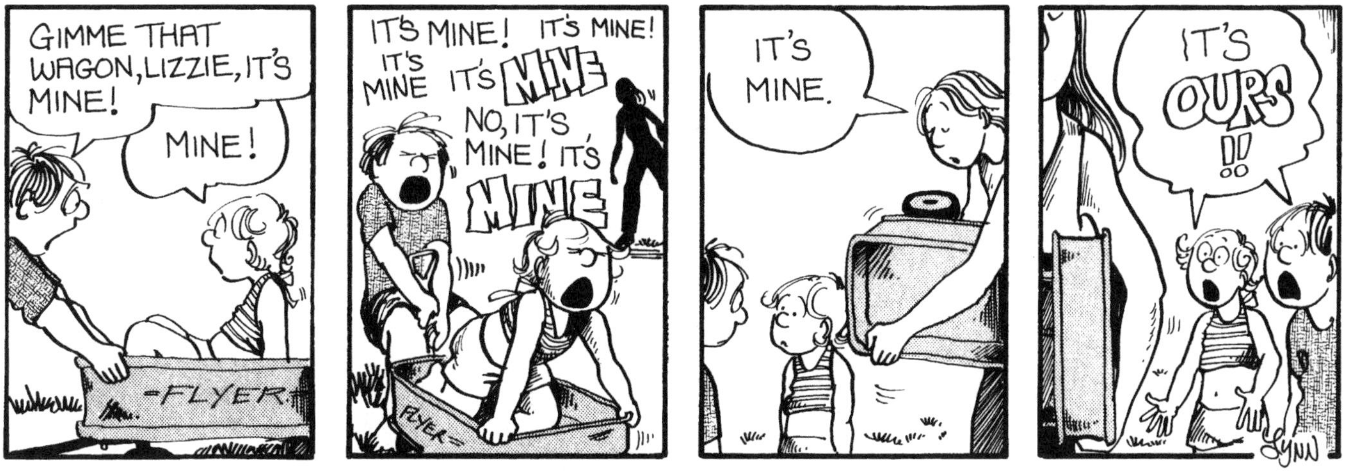
GIMME THAT WAGON, LIZZIE, IT'S MINE!
MINE!
FLYER
IT'S MINE! IT'S MINE! IT'S MINE IT'S MINE NO, IT'S MINE! IT'S MINE
FLYER
IT'S MINE.
IT'S OURS!!
LYNN

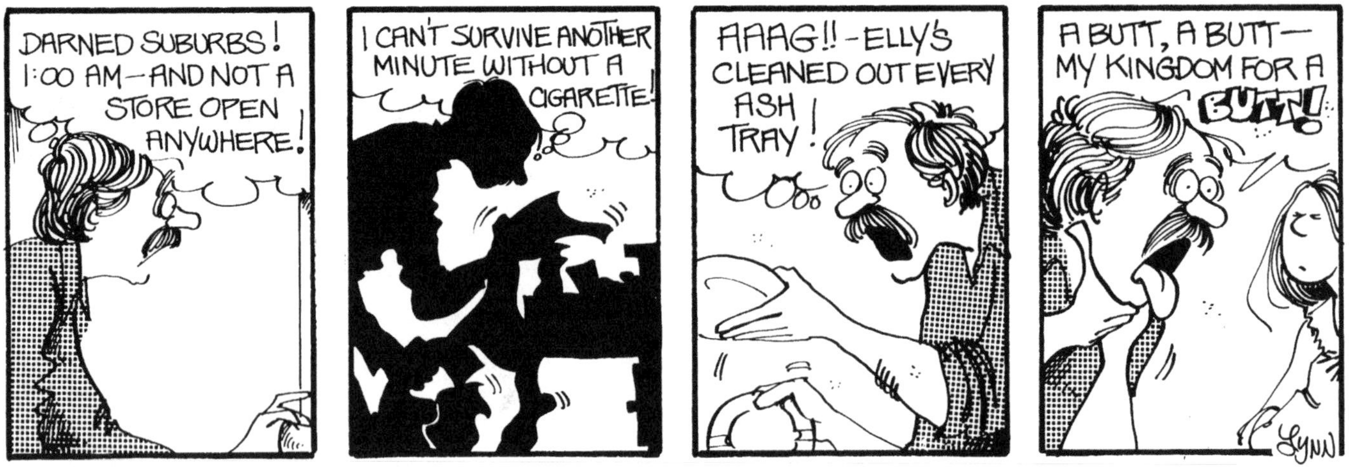
DARNED SUBURBS! 1:00 AM—AND NOT A STORE OPEN ANYWHERE!
I CAN'T SURVIVE ANOTHER MINUTE WITHOUT A CIGARETTE!
AAAG!! -ELLY'S CLEANED OUT EVERY ASH TRAY!
A BUTT, A BUTT— MY KINGDOM FOR A BUTT!
LYNN

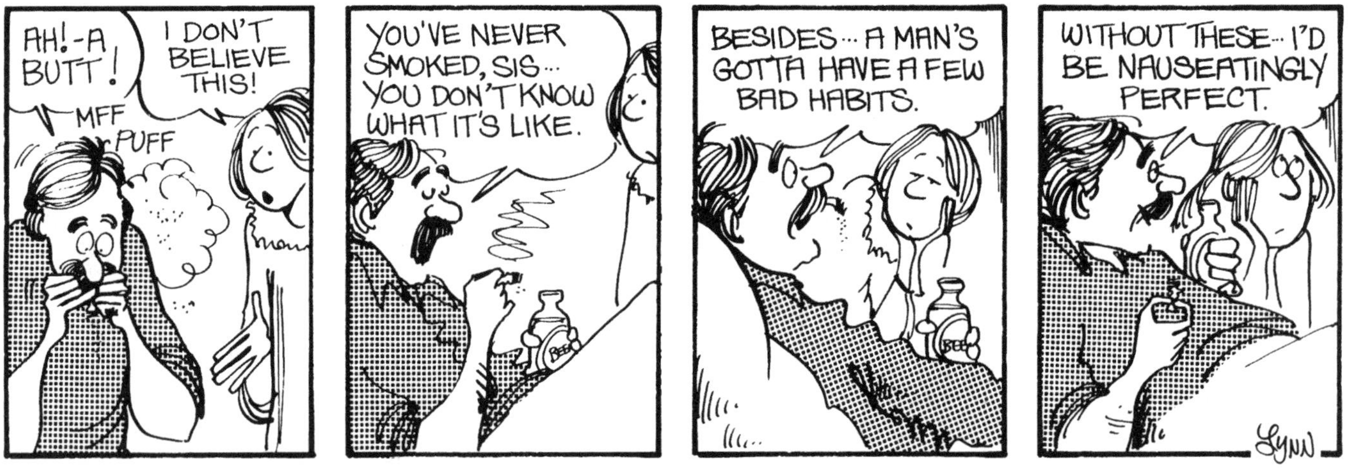
AH! -A BUTT!
MFF
PUFF
I DON'T BELIEVE THIS!
YOU'VE NEVER SMOKED, SIS... YOU DON'T KNOW WHAT IT'S LIKE.
BESIDES... A MAN'S GOTTA HAVE A FEW BAD HABITS.
WITHOUT THESE... I'D BE NAUSEATINGLY PERFECT.
LYNN

Alan was always trying to quit. This and a serious lack of funds kept him without a reliable supply of smokes. He might say I'm making this up … but I do remember him sifting through the household refuse looking for salvageable butts. This is clear in my memory because, despite my objection to smoking, I felt truly sorry for him!

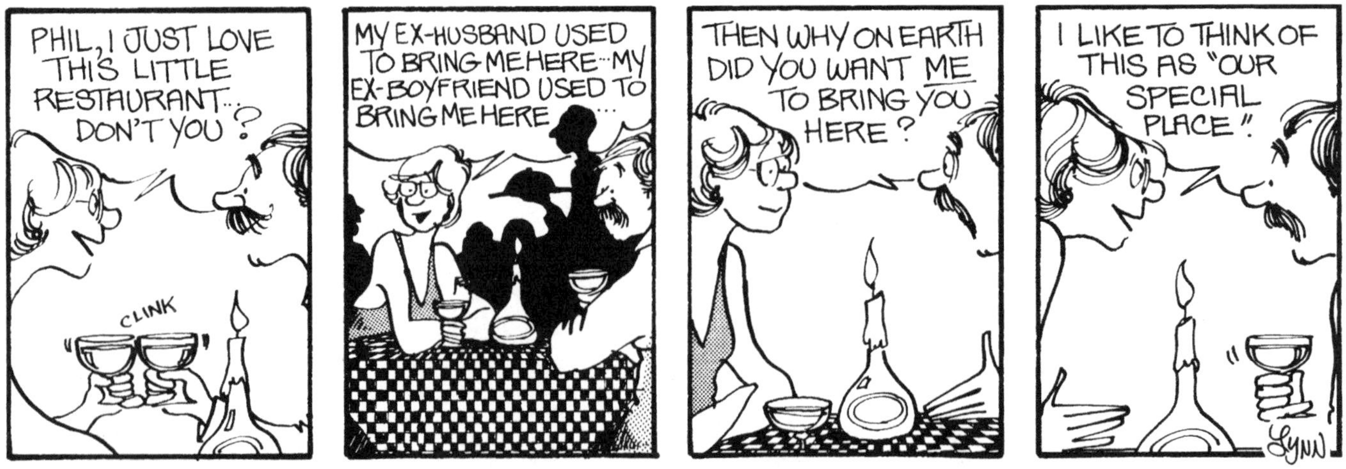
PHIL, I JUST LOVE THIS LITTLE RESTAURANT... DON'T YOU?
CLINK
MY EX-HUSBAND USED TO BRING ME HERE... MY EX-BOYFRIEND USED TO BRING ME HERE...
THEN WHY ON EARTH DID YOU WANT ME TO BRING YOU HERE?
I LIKE TO THINK OF THIS AS "OUR SPECIAL PLACE."
LYNN

I moved Connie and Phil together and apart as I pleased. Their relationship was in no way a reflection of my brother's love life. Alan would read the stories in the newspaper six weeks after I'd written and drawn them. To his great credit, he never seriously objected to my taking such liberties with a character who everyone knew was "him"!

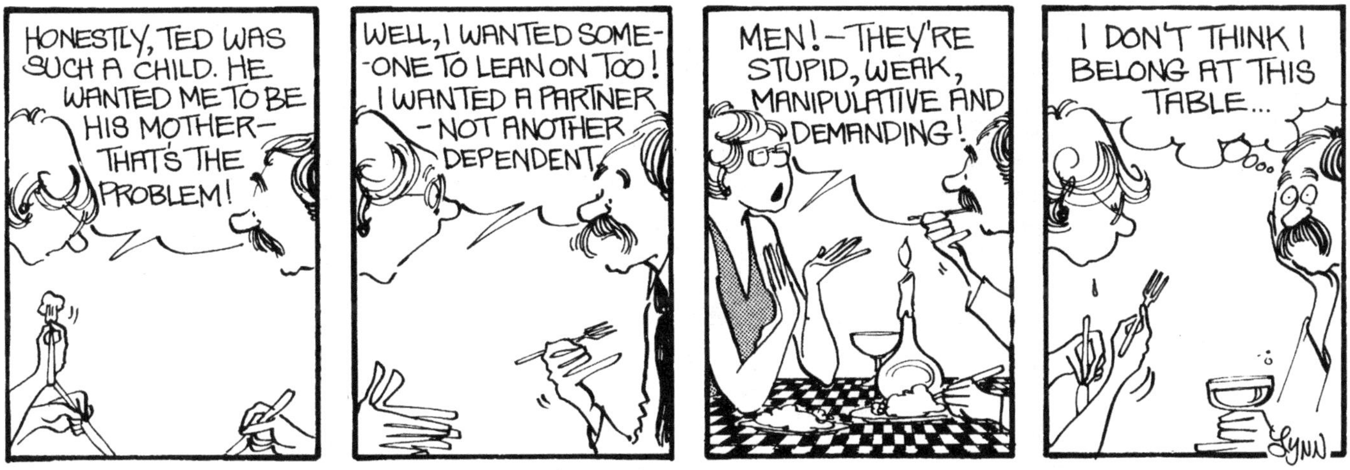
HONESTLY, TED WAS SUCH A CHILD. HE WANTED ME TO BE HIS MOTHER—THAT'S THE PROBLEM!
WELL, I WANTED SOME-ONE TO LEAN ON TOO! I WANTED A PARTNER—NOT ANOTHER DEPENDENT.
MEN!—THEY'RE STUPID, WEAK, MANIPULATIVE AND DEMANDING!
I DON'T THINK I BELONG AT THIS TABLE...
LYNN

When I was a newly single mom, I dated men long before I was ready to enter into another relationship. Still reeling from deceit and divorce, I'd tell my suitor details of the past — things I should have kept to myself. I figure it takes about three years for the dust to settle after a marriage breakup — but when you're young, insecure, and lonely, you just don't have time!

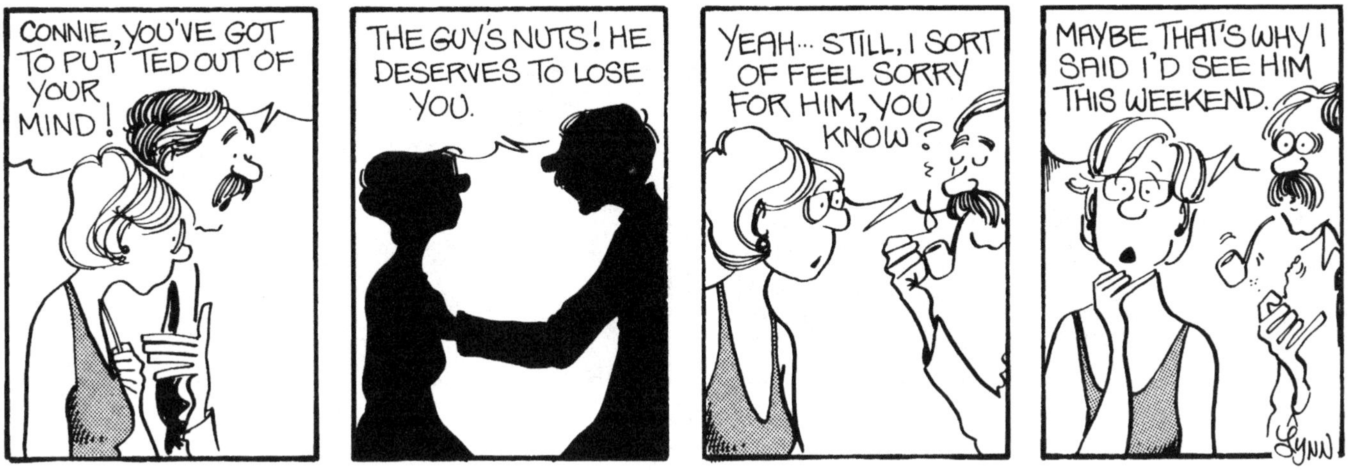
CONNIE, YOU'VE GOT TO PUT TED OUT OF YOUR MIND!
THE GUY'S NUTS! HE DESERVES TO LOSE YOU.
YEAH... STILL, I SORT OF FEEL SORRY FOR HIM, YOU KNOW?
MAYBE THAT'S WHY I SAID I'D SEE HIM THIS WEEKEND.
LYNN

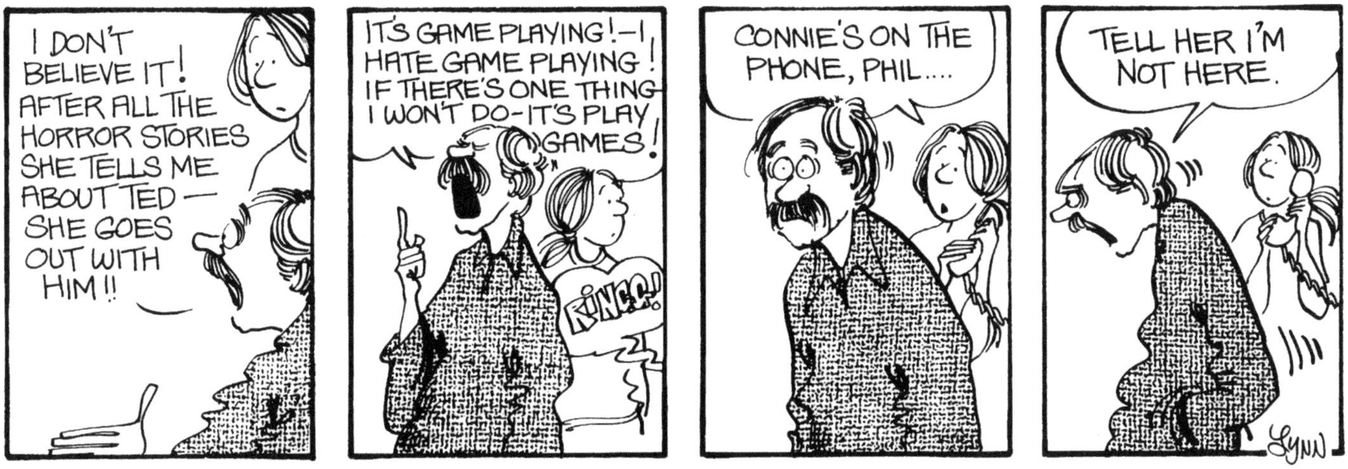
I DON'T BELIEVE IT! AFTER ALL THE HORROR STORIES SHE TELLS ME ABOUT TED—SHE GOES OUT WITH HIM!!
IT'S GAME PLAYING!—I HATE GAME PLAYING! IF THERE'S ONE THING I WON'T DO—IT'S PLAY GAMES!
RING!
CONNIE'S ON THE PHONE, PHIL....
TELL HER I'M NOT HERE.
LYNN

I think this was one of my favourite lines, because we have all been guilty of "game-playing" at some point in our lives. It is especially evident in a new relationship, when the emotional tug of war to establish where the other stands gets the better of us. Although I consider myself a straight shooter, I've indulged in these wars of wit, and worry, too.

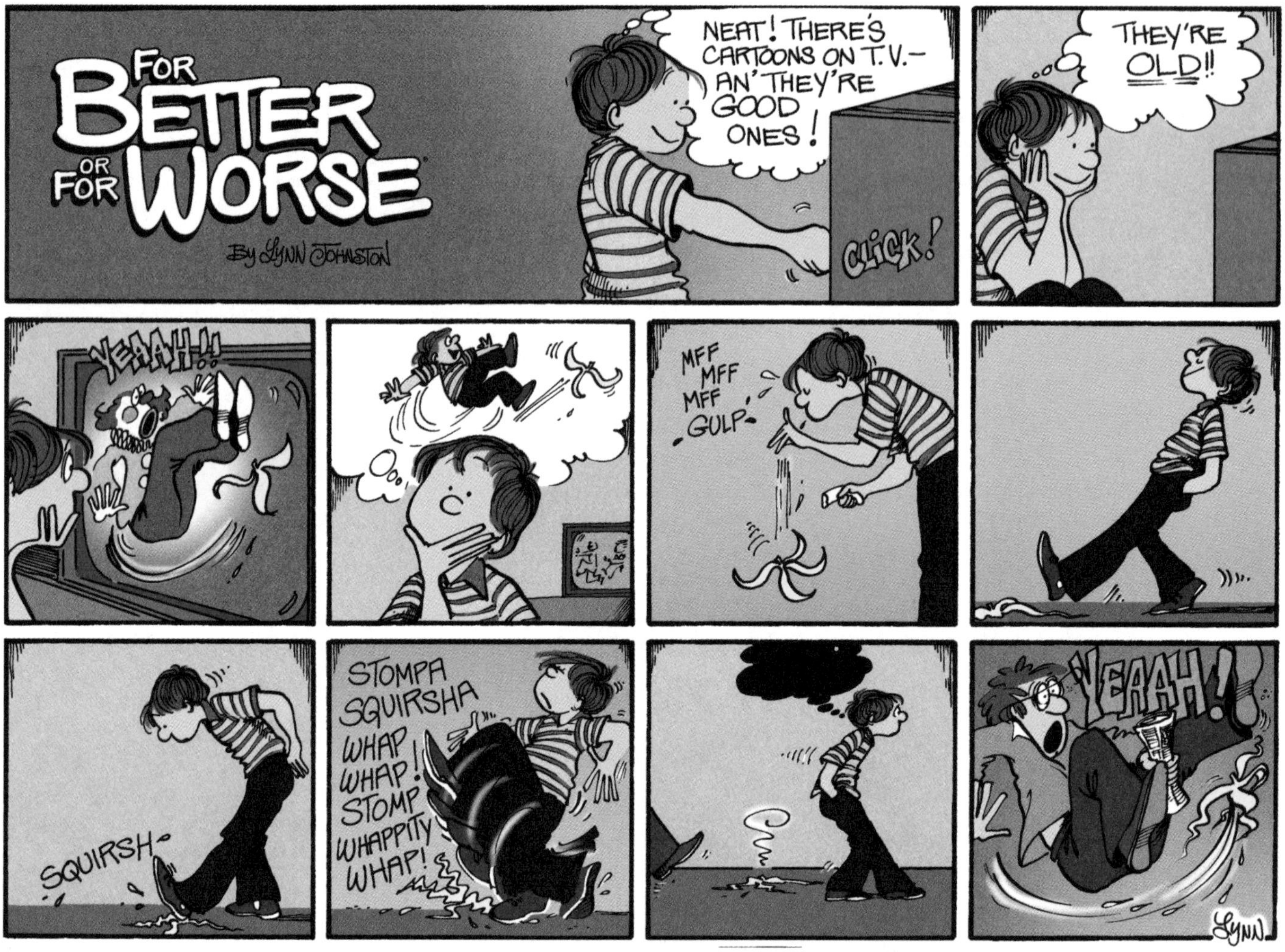
FOR BETTER OR FOR WORSE
By Lynn Johnston
NEAT! THERE'S CARTOONS ON T.V.– AN' THEY'RE GOOD ONES!
CLICK!
THEY'RE OLD!!
YEAAAH!!
MFF MFF MFF GULP
SQUIRSH
STOMPA SQUIRSHA WHAP WHAP! STOMP WHAPPITY WHAP!
YEAAH!
LYNN

I loved slapstick movies. Good animated cartoons kept me glued to the screen at the Odeon Theatre every Saturday afternoon when I was a kid. One of the most overrated gag ideas has always been the "slip on a banana peel." This pratfall was something my brother and I tried unsuccessfully to re-create many times. You need: a ripe peel, a slippery linoleum floor, and a bozo who doesn't look where he's going. All three are hard to put in the same place at the same time without deliberate and calculated effort. Unsuccessful with the surprise attack, we tried the stunt on each other, our buddies, and our dad. (Mom would have whacked the both of us for doing something so stupid, so she was out of the scene altogether.) We never did re-create the wonderful slip, slide, and landing that was so funny in the theatre. It was therefore important, once I had the freedom of a comic strip at hand, to complete this elusive gag in the newspapers and fulfill a lifelong quest.

FOR BETTER OR FOR WORSE
By Lynn Johnston
AAACGH!
AAGH!!! NOT AGAIN!
STUPID, DUMB, CRUMMY
CRASH!!
NO! AAH! I DON'T WANNA GO TO BED! WAAAH!!
MOM? AREN'T YOU GONNA KISS ME GOODNIGHT?
TO TELL YOU THE TRUTH, MIKE, WHEN YOU ACT LIKE THAT.... I JUST DON'T FEEL LIKE KISSING YOU AT ALL!
BUT, MOM.... THAT'S WHEN I NEED IT MOST!
Lynn

When I was about ten, I remember being in such a state that I stabbed the desk in my room repeatedly with a pair of scissors. Sounds drastic, but that's what I did. I still lose my temper like this on occasion, but I don't destroy stuff! I holler, fume, storm about the house, and … then I need to talk to someone!

We all know how it feels to be beyond angry, and to do something that is really out of character. In remembering how I felt when I destroyed my desk, I tried to love my kids just a bit more and hug them just a little tighter when they were at their (and my) wits' end. This calmed us both down enough to be able to talk about what was wrong, and we'd share a long, loving hug. Sometimes the most unlikely response to bad behaviour is the one that works.

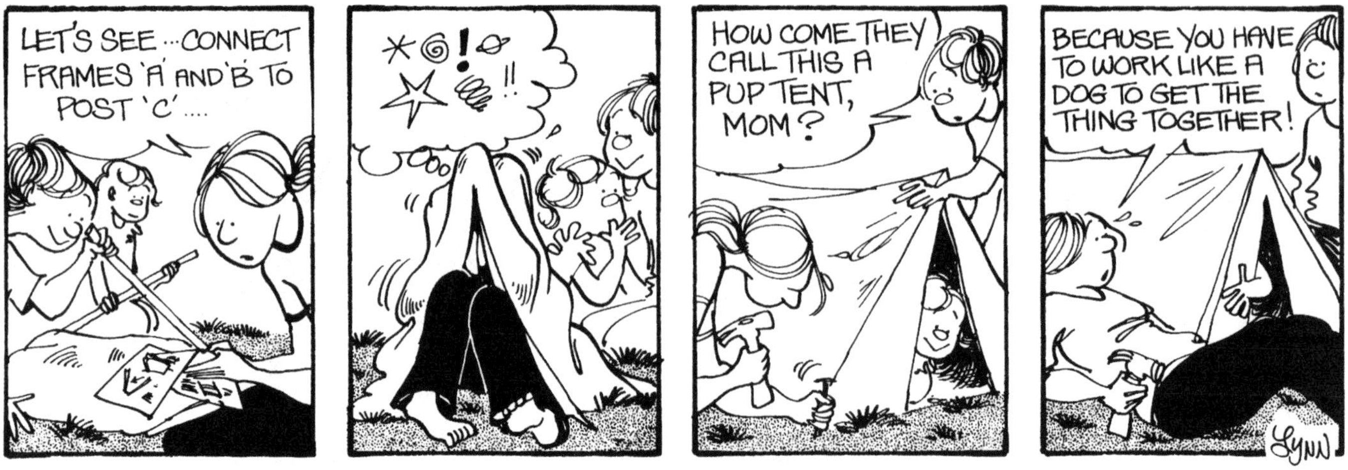
LET'S SEE ... CONNECT FRAMES 'A' AND 'B' TO POST 'C' ....
HOW COME THEY CALL THIS A PUP TENT, MOM?
BECAUSE YOU HAVE TO WORK LIKE A DOG TO GET THE THING TOGETHER!
LYNN

This was my dad trying to assemble one of those wicked mind traps we used to buy from Woolworths — with the hope it would turn into a tent. The metal poles bent, the fabric wouldn't stretch, and when you finally did get a shelter to come out of it, you were too mad to enjoy it!

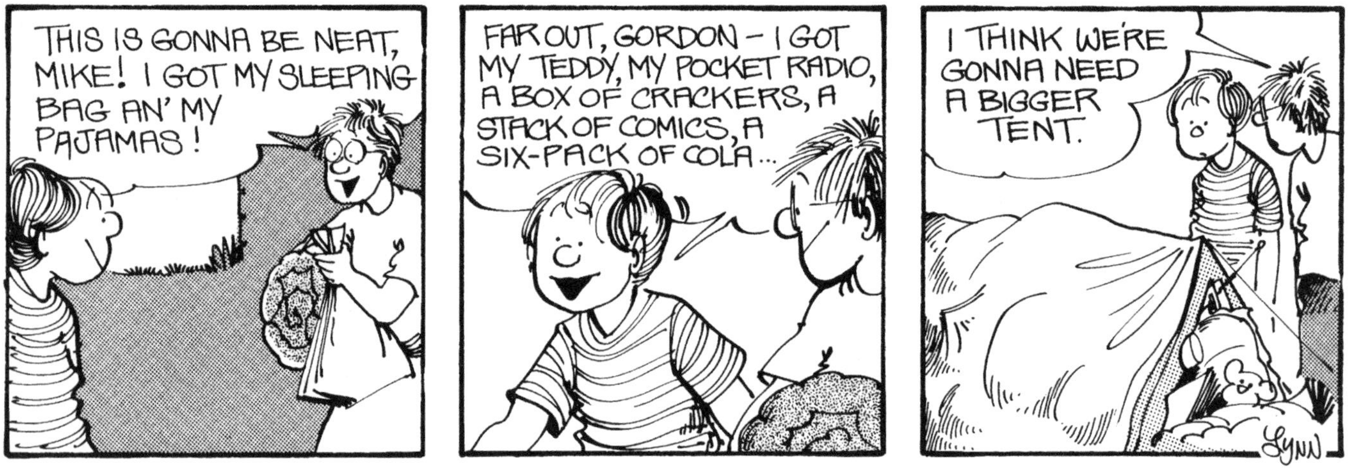
THIS IS GONNA BE NEAT, MIKE! I GOT MY SLEEPING BAG AN' MY PAJAMAS!
FAR OUT, GORDON – I GOT MY TEDDY, MY POCKET RADIO, A BOX OF CRACKERS, A STACK OF COMICS, A SIX-PACK OF COLA ...
I THINK WE'RE GONNA NEED A BIGGER TENT.
LYNN

Every summer Alan and I would sleep outside in the backyard. We'd look forward to the adventure of being outdoors (forgetting the mosquitoes — which instantly filled the floorless space as soon as the thing was rigged). With blankets, food, transistor radio, toys, and bedrolls, we more than filled the enclosure. Between bickering and bug bites, we were lucky if we could last two nights.

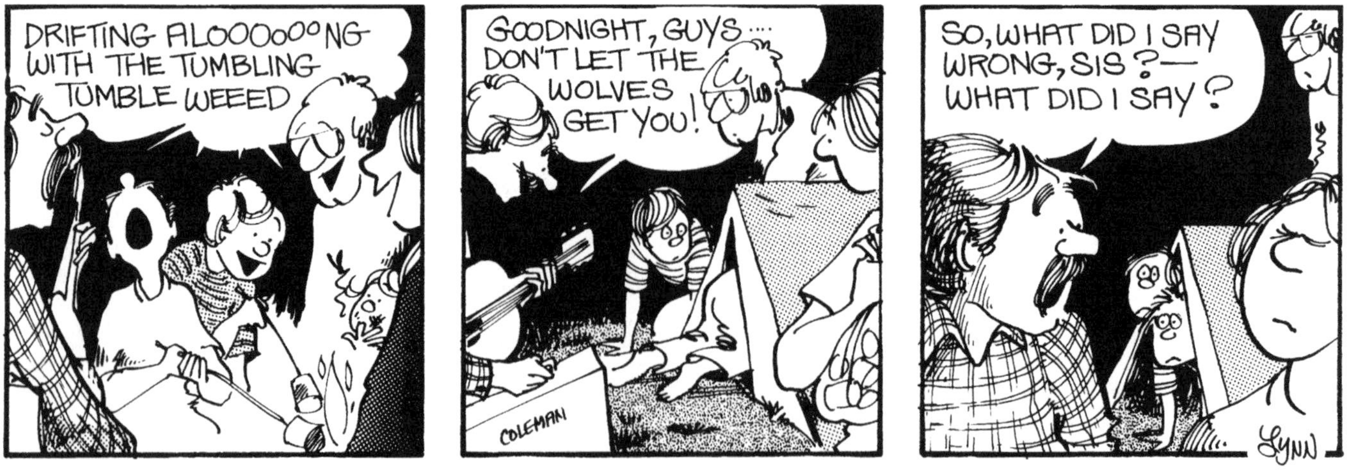
DRIFTING ALOOOOoooNG WITH THE TUMBLING TUMBLE WEEED
GOODNIGHT, GUYS .... DON'T LET THE WOLVES GET YOU!
COLEMAN
SO, WHAT DID I SAY WRONG, SIS? — WHAT DID I SAY?
LYNN

We didn't have a bonfire in the backyard, but we did have deck chairs, flashlights, and food. Dad played the guitar. He knew every camp and military ditty by heart, and my brother and I thought he was absolutely wonderful.

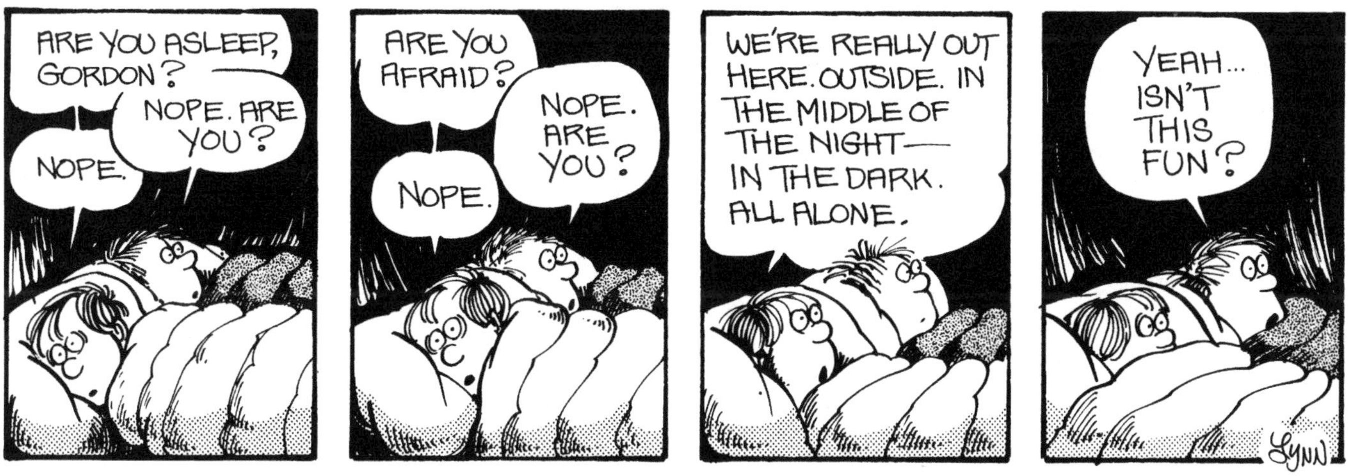
ARE YOU ASLEEP, GORDON?
NOPE. ARE YOU?
NOPE.
ARE YOU AFRAID?
NOPE. ARE YOU?
NOPE.
WE'RE REALLY OUT HERE. OUTSIDE. IN THE MIDDLE OF THE NIGHT— IN THE DARK. ALL ALONE.
YEAH... ISN'T THIS FUN?
LYNN

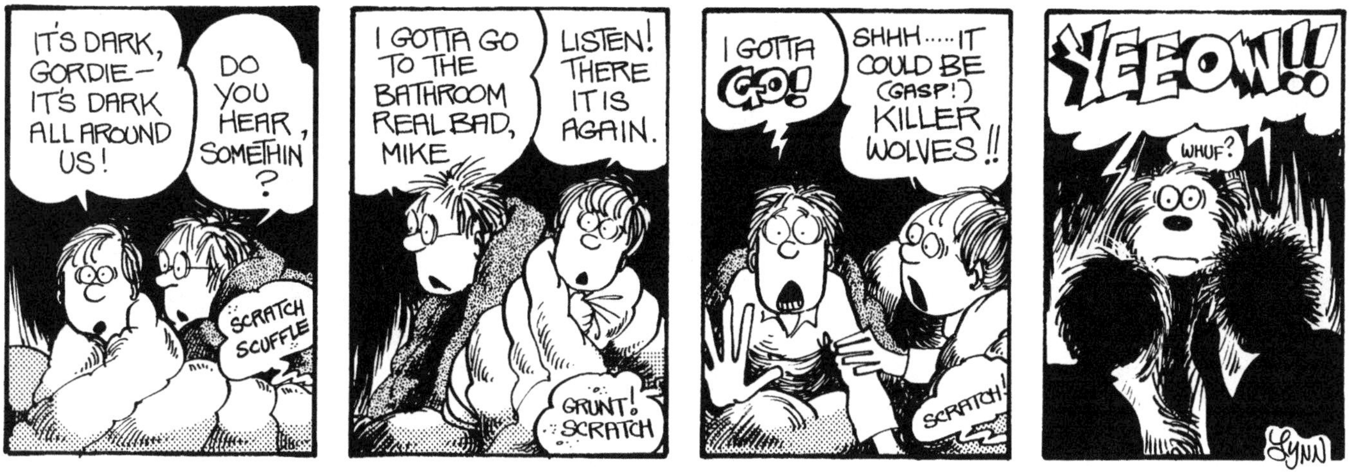
IT'S DARK, GORDIE— IT'S DARK ALL AROUND US!
DO YOU HEAR, SOMETHIN'?
SCRATCH SCUFFLE
I GOTTA GO TO THE BATHROOM REAL BAD, MIKE
LISTEN! THERE IT IS AGAIN.
GRUNT! SCRATCH
I GOTTA GO!
SHHH..... IT COULD BE (GASP!) KILLER WOLVES!!
SCRATCH!
YEEOW!!
WHUF?
LYNN

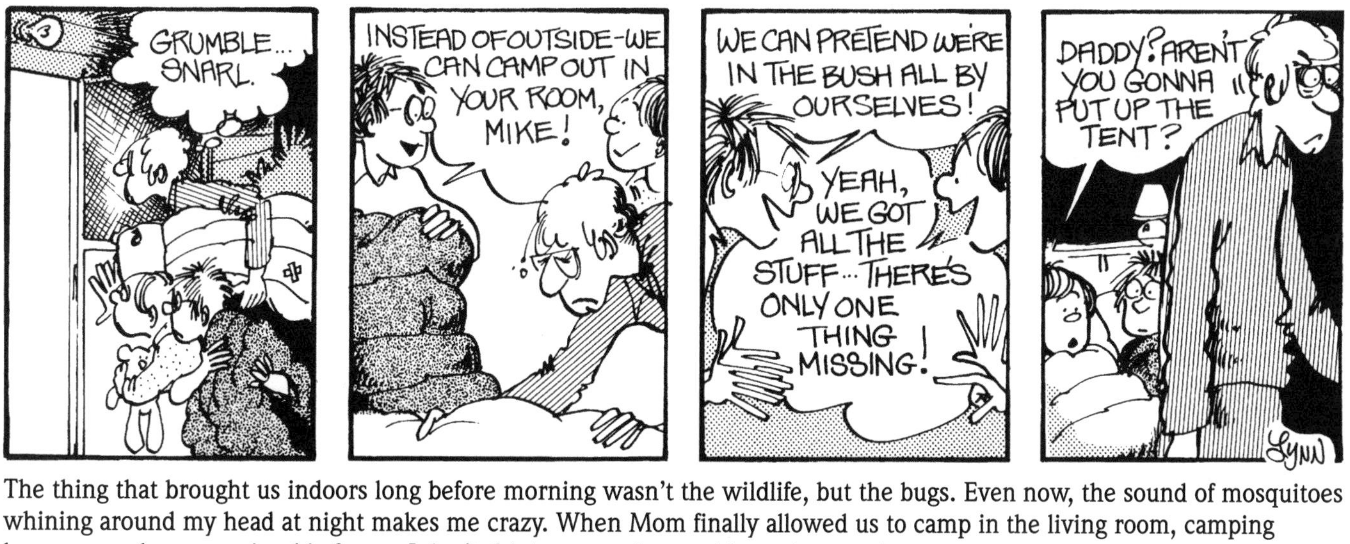
GRUMBLE... SNARL.
INSTEAD OF OUTSIDE—WE CAN CAMP OUT IN YOUR ROOM, MIKE!
WE CAN PRETEND WE'RE IN THE BUSH ALL BY OURSELVES!
YEAH, WE GOT ALL THE STUFF... THERE'S ONLY ONE THING MISSING!
DADDY? AREN'T YOU GONNA PUT UP THE TENT?
LYNN

The thing that brought us indoors long before morning wasn't the wildlife, but the bugs. Even now, the sound of mosquitoes whining around my head at night makes me crazy. When Mom finally allowed us to camp in the living room, camping became much more enjoyable for us. I don't think my mother could say the same!

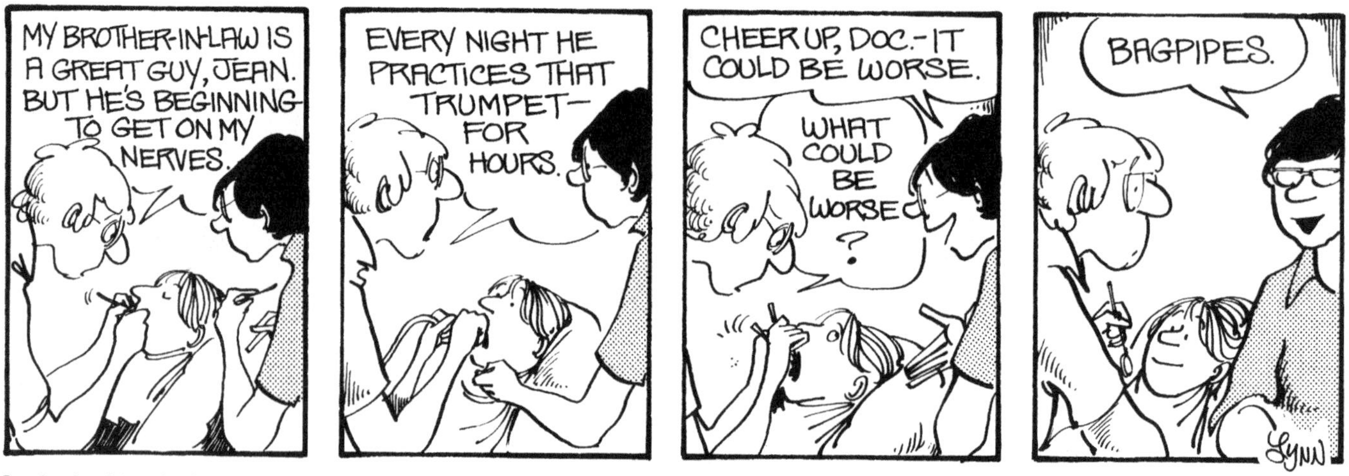
MY BROTHER-IN-LAW IS A GREAT GUY, JEAN. BUT HE'S BEGINNING TO GET ON MY NERVES.
EVERY NIGHT HE PRACTICES THAT TRUMPET— FOR HOURS.
CHEER UP, DOC.- IT COULD BE WORSE.
WHAT COULD BE WORSE?
BAGPIPES.
LYNN

I asked a friend of ours who played the bagpipes if he'd show me how they worked. After dinner one evening, he and I went to the churchyard to practice. After about half an hour of my trying to get the bag inflated and the chanter to play, we gave up. The next day, I was stopped by a neighbour, who asked if I'd heard the "squalling in the churchyard last night"! She was sure some animal had been caught and strangled — she had almost called the cops.

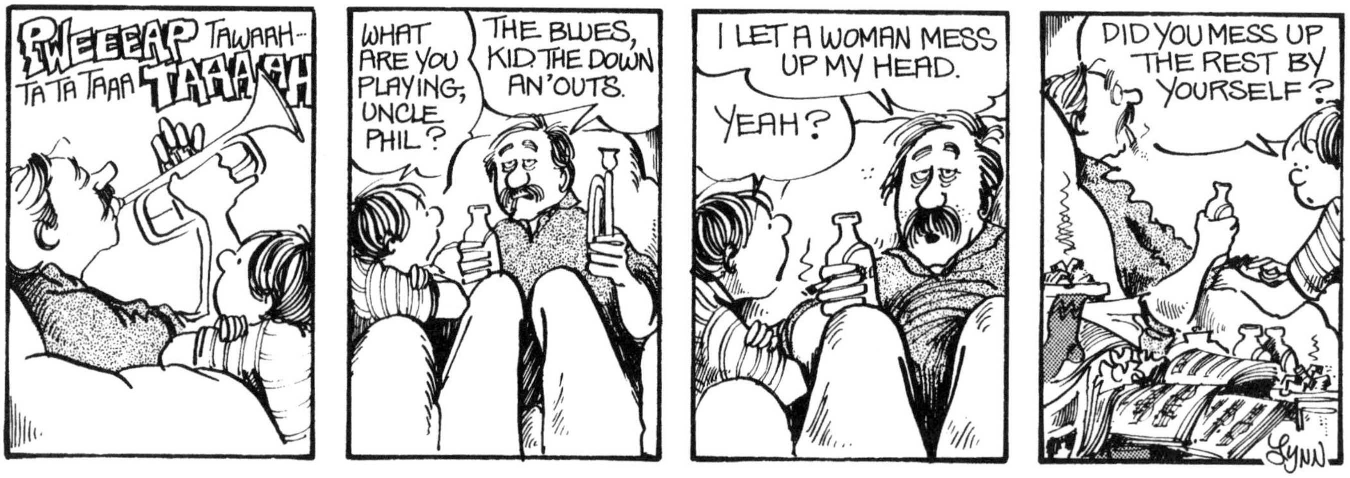
PWEEEAP TAWAAH...
TA TA TAAA TAAAAH
WHAT ARE YOU PLAYING, UNCLE PHIL?
THE BLUES, KID. THE DOWN AN'OUTS.
I LET A WOMAN MESS UP MY HEAD.
YEAH?
DID YOU MESS UP THE REST BY YOURSELF?
LYNN

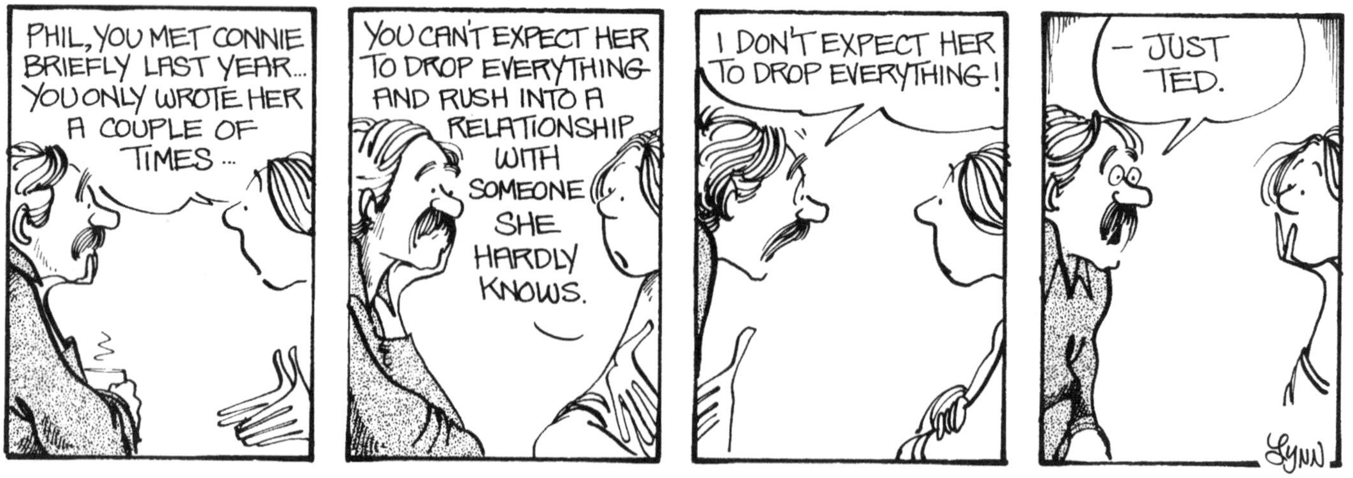
PHIL, YOU MET CONNIE BRIEFLY LAST YEAR... YOU ONLY WROTE HER A COUPLE OF TIMES...
YOU CAN'T EXPECT HER TO DROP EVERYTHING AND RUSH INTO A RELATIONSHIP WITH SOMEONE SHE HARDLY KNOWS.
I DON'T EXPECT HER TO DROP EVERYTHING!
— JUST TED.
LYNN

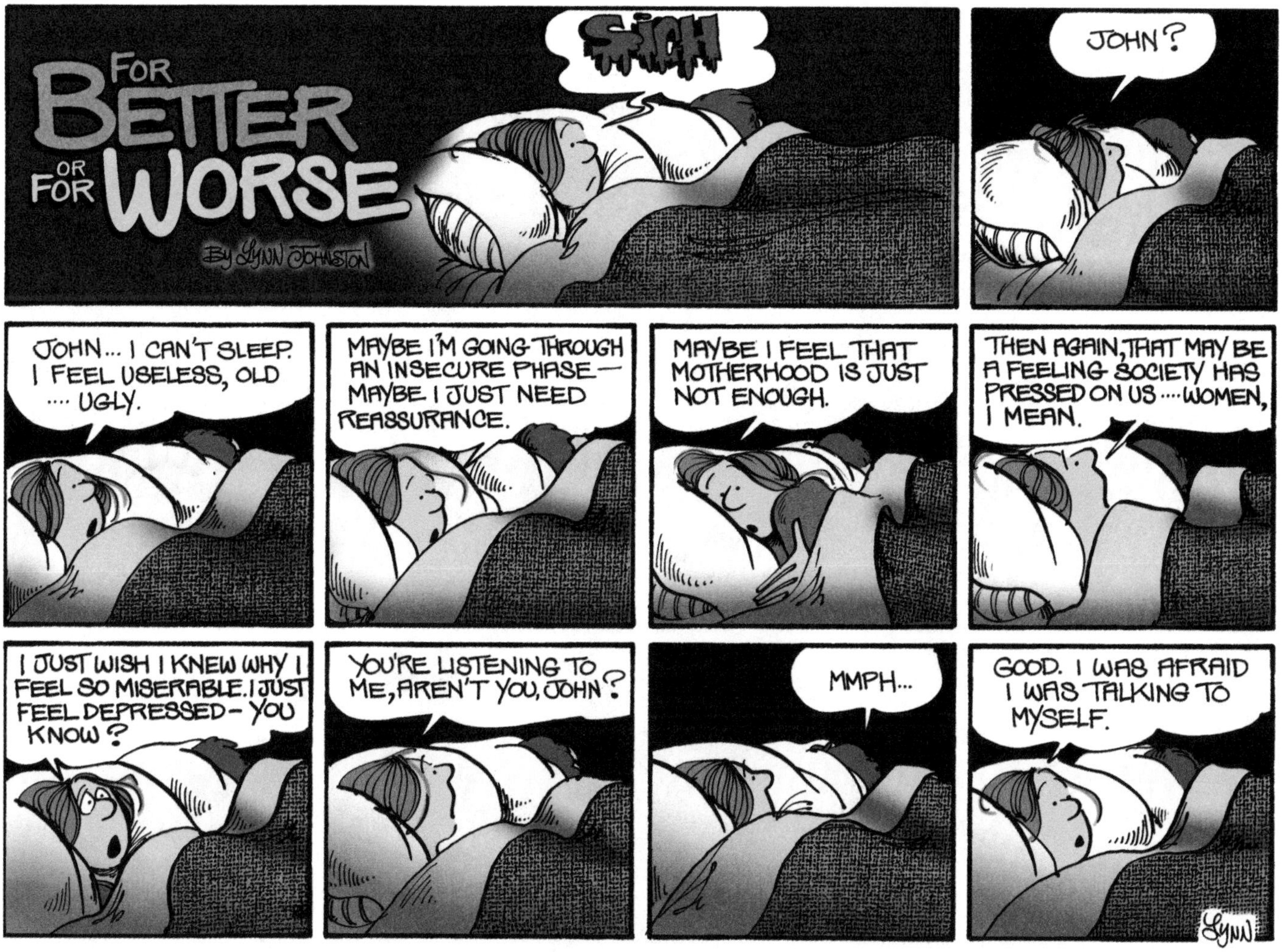
FOR BETTER OR FOR WORSE
BY LYNN JOHNSTON
SIGH
JOHN?
JOHN... I CAN'T SLEEP. I FEEL USELESS, OLD .... UGLY.
MAYBE I'M GOING THROUGH AN INSECURE PHASE— MAYBE I JUST NEED REASSURANCE.
MAYBE I FEEL THAT MOTHERHOOD IS JUST NOT ENOUGH.
THEN AGAIN, THAT MAY BE A FEELING SOCIETY HAS PRESSED ON US ....WOMEN, I MEAN.
I JUST WISH I KNEW WHY I FEEL SO MISERABLE. I JUST FEEL DEPRESSED - YOU KNOW?
YOU'RE LISTENING TO ME, AREN'T YOU, JOHN?
MMPH...
GOOD. I WAS AFRAID I WAS TALKING TO MYSELF.
LYNN

In 1974, after my first divorce, I dated a psychiatrist. One of his standby pieces of advice was to NOT think about serious things after midnight. This, he said, was a twilight zone where emotional fatigue and the onset of dreaming make sensible, rational thought all but impossible. He said it was best to not go to bed angry. The chances of problem solving when you're tired are slim.

The "twilight zone" thing has stayed with me since then, and I have given others this same advice. The problem is ... your problems all seem to surface when you're relaxed, have the day's chores behind you, and the kids are asleep. Sometimes you HAVE to talk things over when you and your partner are in bed because, in today's busy household, there are few other opportunities! So, despite the warning from my sweet psychiatrist, I would open up after dark and talk about whatever it was that was bothering me. Fortunately, the broaching of sensitive topics never resulted in late-night fisticuffs — my husband, sedated by the sound of my voice, happily slept right through it!

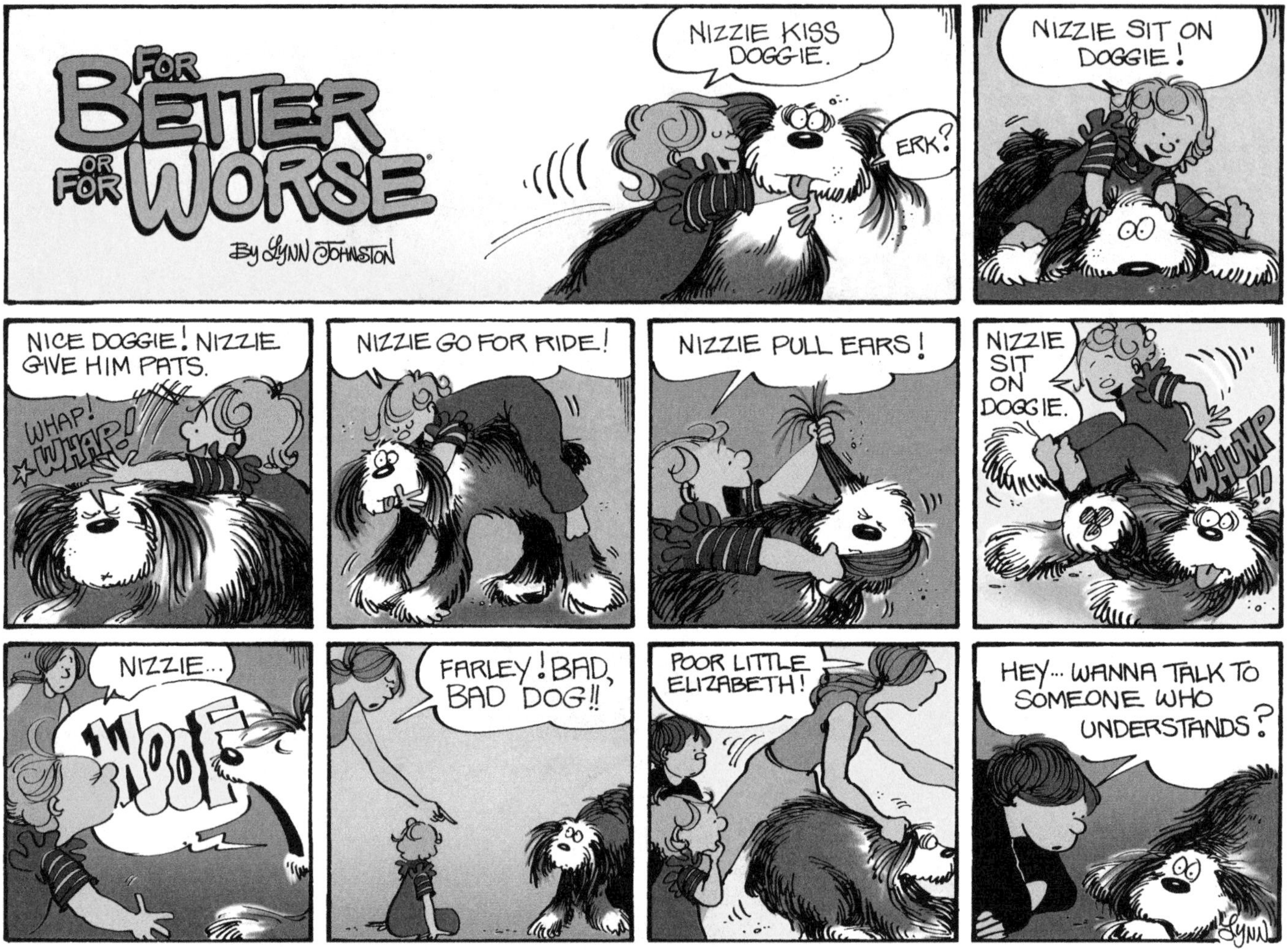
FOR BETTER OR FOR WORSE
BY LYNN JOHNSTON
NIZZIE KISS DOGGIE.
ERK?
NIZZIE SIT ON DOGGIE!
NICE DOGGIE! NIZZIE GIVE HIM PATS.
WHAP! WHAP!
NIZZIE GO FOR RIDE!
NIZZIE PULL EARS!
NIZZIE SIT ON DOGGIE.
WHUMP!!
NIZZIE...
WOOF
FARLEY! BAD, BAD DOG!!
POOR LITTLE ELIZABETH!
HEY... WANNA TALK TO SOMEONE WHO UNDERSTANDS?
LYNN

It amazes me how resilient and stoic some dogs are with young children. They put up with being sat on, pulled at, and strangled. Their patience and good humour is remarkable. They seem to instinctively know that babies don't know any better. On the other hand, some dogs can't tolerate young children at all. Some bark and snarl, some just ignore kids and walk away. Amazing, isn't it ... to see how often dogs behave like people!

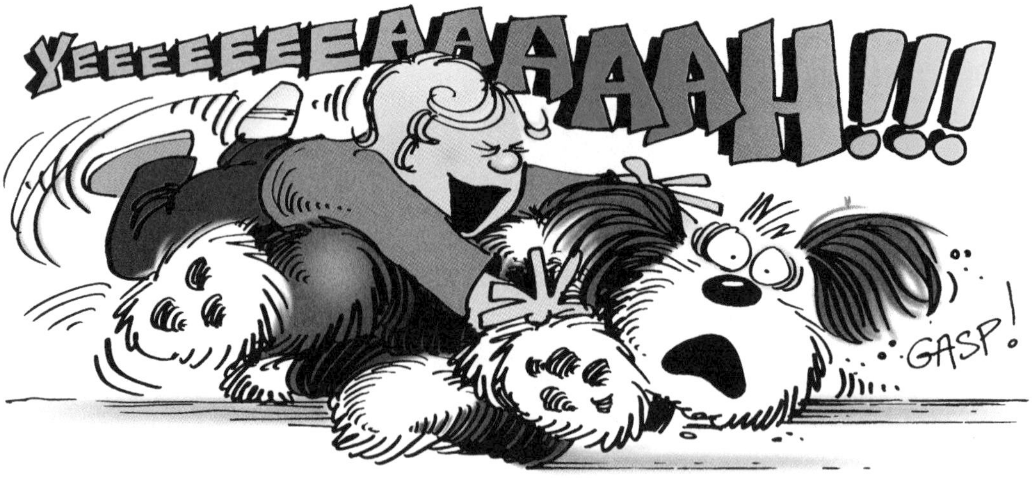
YEEEEEEEAAAAAAH!!!!
GASP!

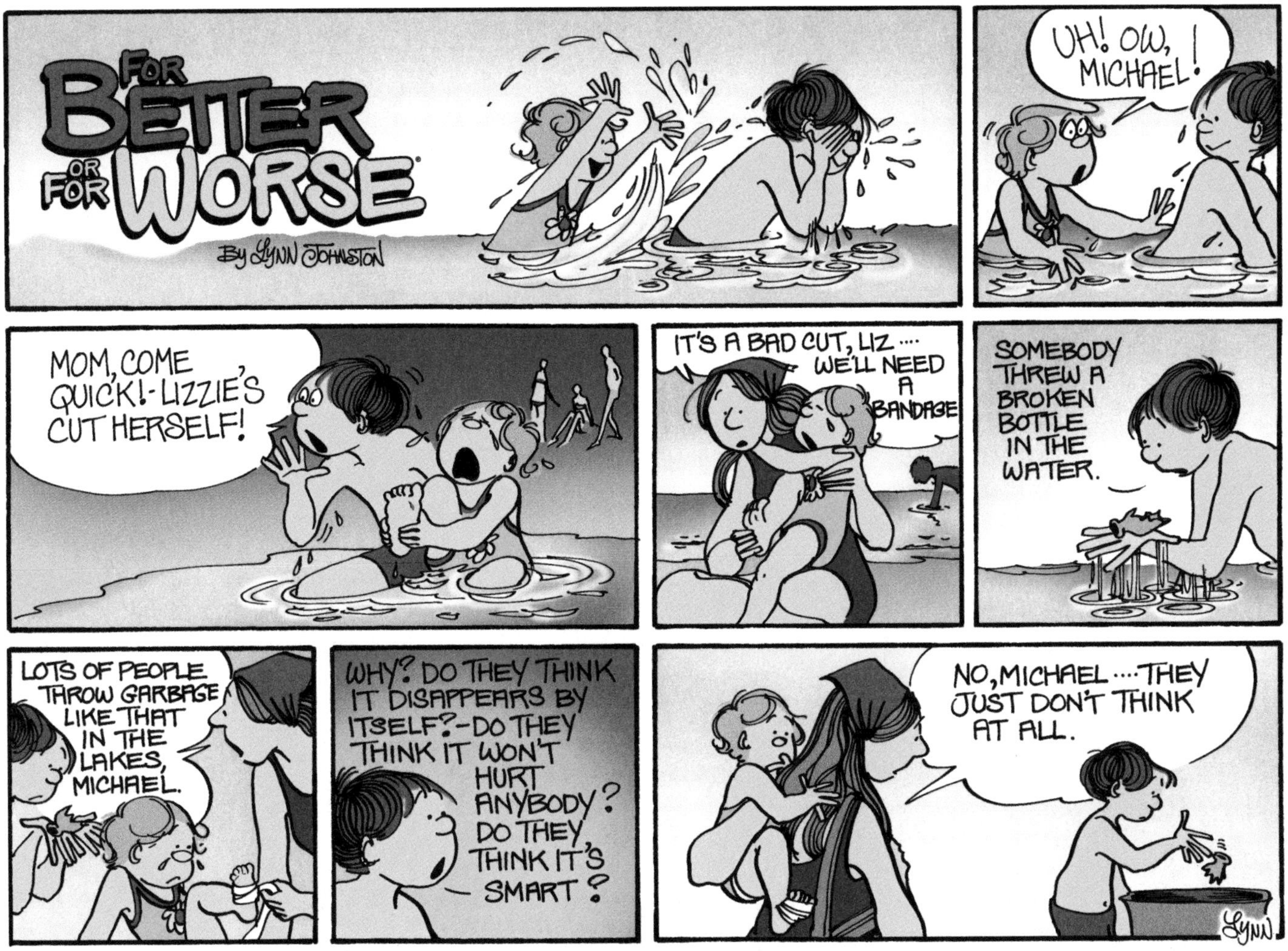
For Better or For Worse
By Lynn Johnston
UH! OW, MICHAEL!
MOM, COME QUICK! - LIZZIE'S CUT HERSELF!
IT'S A BAD CUT, LIZ .... WE'LL NEED A BANDAGE
SOMEBODY THREW A BROKEN BOTTLE IN THE WATER.
LOTS OF PEOPLE THROW GARBAGE LIKE THAT IN THE LAKES, MICHAEL.
WHY? DO THEY THINK IT DISAPPEARS BY ITSELF? - DO THEY THINK IT WON'T HURT ANYBODY? DO THEY THINK IT'S SMART?
NO, MICHAEL .... THEY JUST DON'T THINK AT ALL.
Lynn

Cartoonists are discouraged from using comic strips as a platform for preaching reform — but every now and then, something really got under my skin, and I simply had to write about it. For me, littering is a red flag. If I ruled the world, all convicted litterists would receive a stiff fine, a broom, and a dustpan. They would be sentenced to cleaning the community streets, parks, and beaches for as long as it took to reform them — and even then, they would be on parole. When Katie cut her foot on a broken beer bottle at the beach one weekend, I penned this Sunday page. The response was immediate — I received a lot of mail from folks who felt the same way I did. It occurred to me … with so many people angry, frustrated, and disgusted by littering, why do we still have so darned much of it??!!

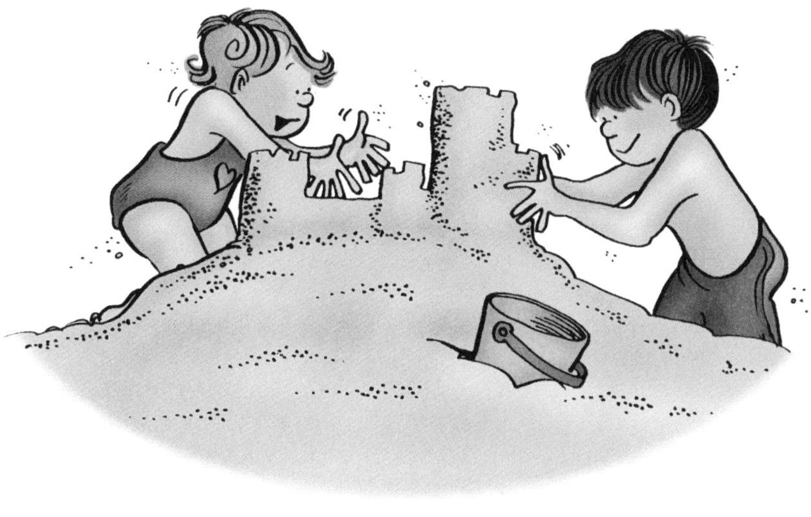

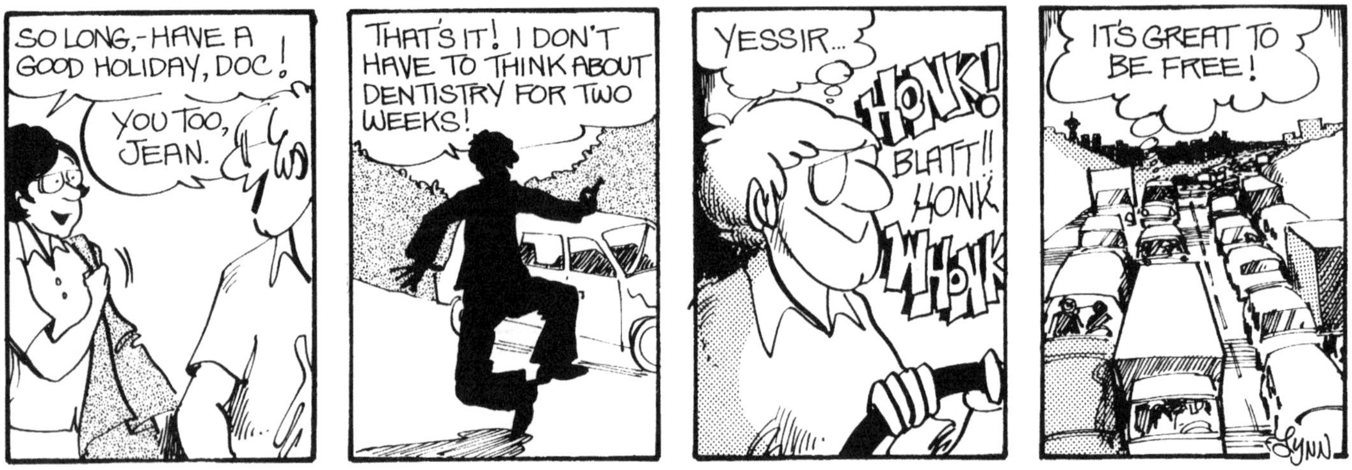
SO LONG,-HAVE A GOOD HOLIDAY, DOC!
YOU TOO, JEAN.
THAT'S IT! I DON'T HAVE TO THINK ABOUT DENTISTRY FOR TWO WEEKS!
YESSIR...
HONK!
BLATT!!
HONK
WHONK
IT'S GREAT TO BE FREE!
LYNN

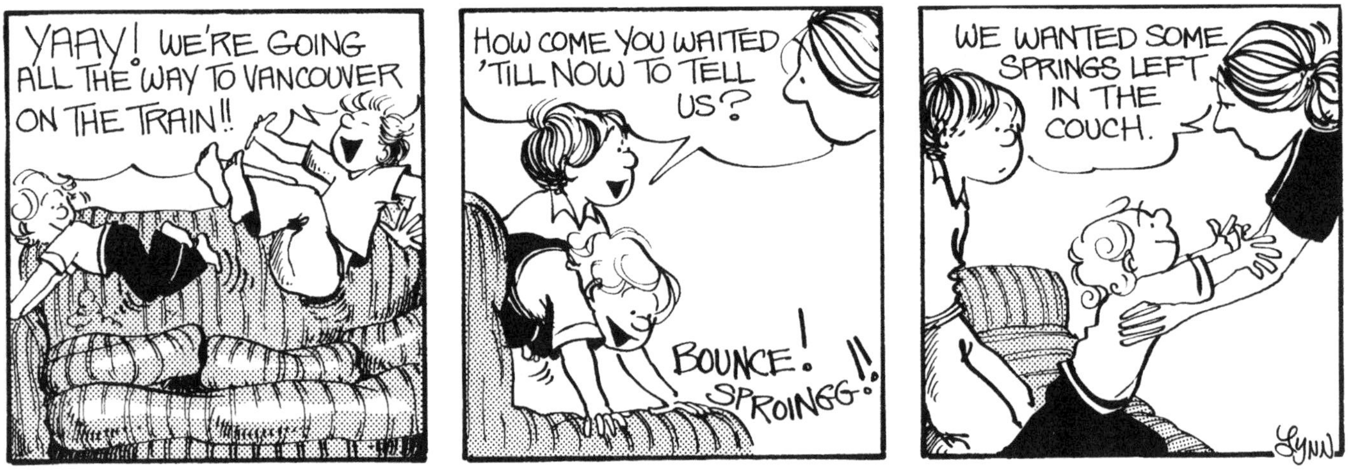
YAAY! WE'RE GOING ALL THE WAY TO VANCOUVER ON THE TRAIN!!
HOW COME YOU WAITED 'TILL NOW TO TELL US?
BOUNCE!
SPROINGG!!
WE WANTED SOME SPRINGS LEFT IN THE COUCH.
LYNN

The trip we took by train from Winnipeg to Vancouver was quite a journey. It began with telling the kids (far too soon) that we were going on a holiday. It was so memorable that I just couldn't resist having the Pattersons experience the same adventures.

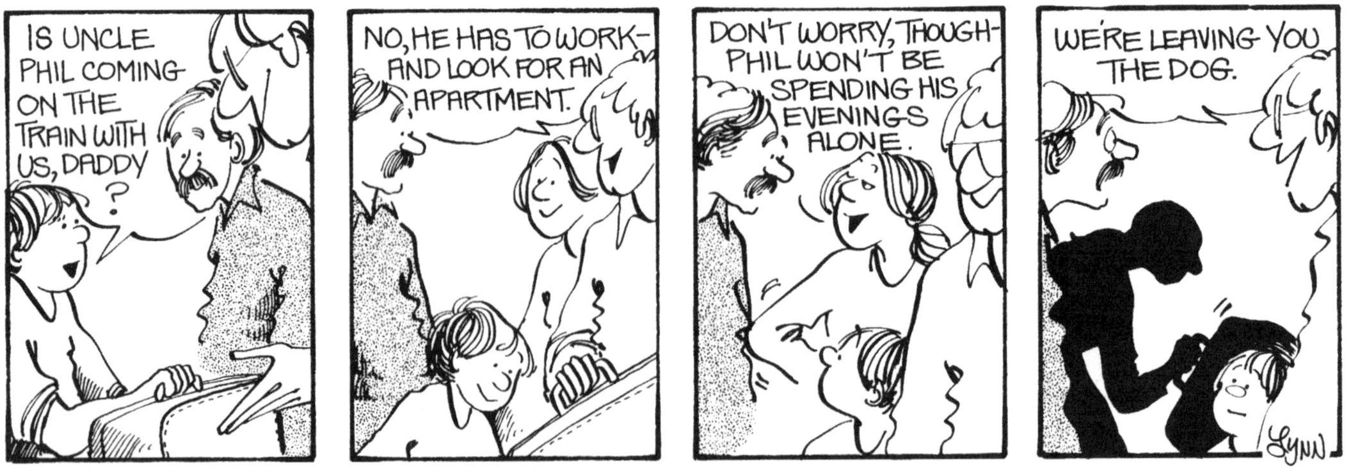
IS UNCLE PHIL COMING ON THE TRAIN WITH US, DADDY?
NO, HE HAS TO WORK- AND LOOK FOR AN APARTMENT.
DON'T WORRY, THOUGH- PHIL WON'T BE SPENDING HIS EVENINGS ALONE.
WE'RE LEAVING YOU THE DOG.
LYNN

Having Uncle Phil stay in the house while the Pattersons left for Vancouver meant that I didn't have to find a kennel for Farley. (Even cartoon dogs have to be taken care of.)

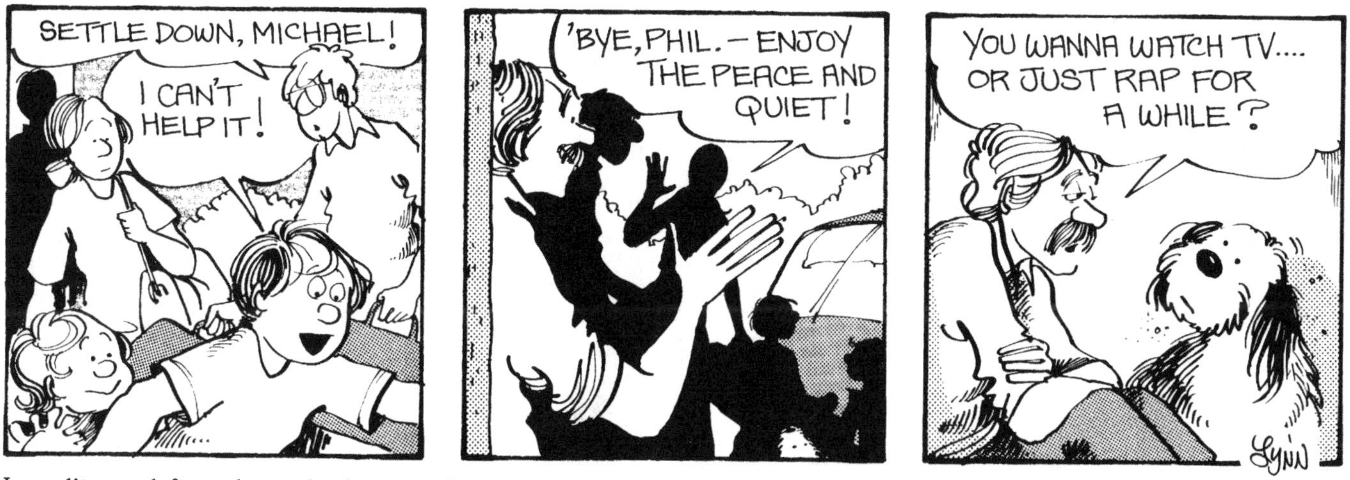
SETTLE DOWN, MICHAEL!
I CAN'T HELP IT!
'BYE, PHIL. – ENJOY THE PEACE AND QUIET!
YOU WANNA WATCH TV.... OR JUST RAP FOR A WHILE?
LYNN

In reality, we left our house in the care of neighbours and family, and took off for what we hoped would be an easy and enjoyable two weeks away from home. Like a canoe in the rapids with nowhere to go but the flow, our trip had begun.

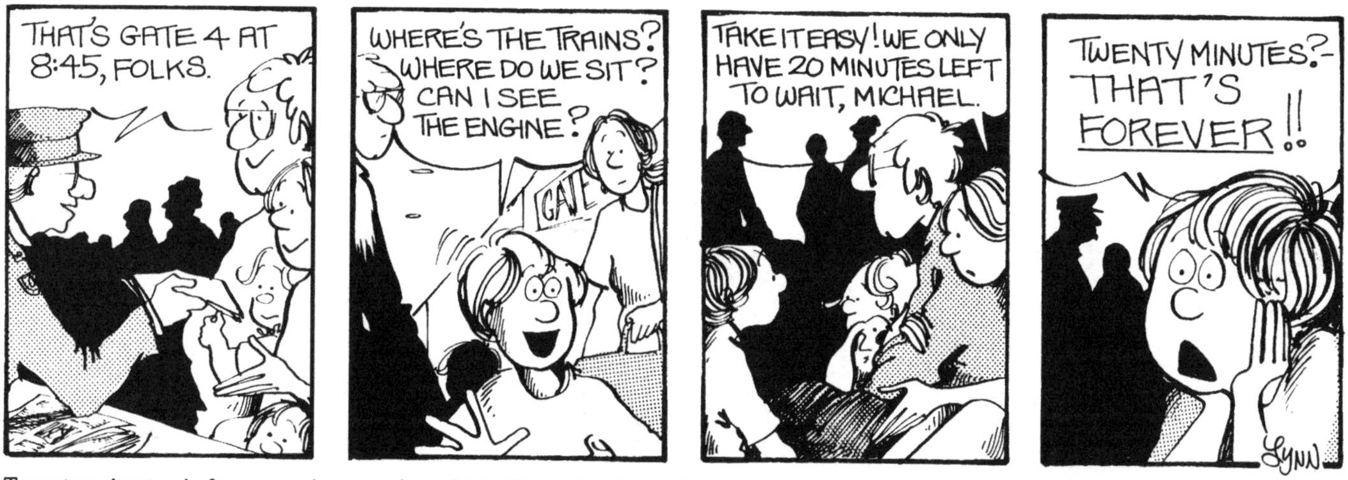
THAT'S GATE 4 AT 8:45, FOLKS.
WHERE'S THE TRAINS? WHERE DO WE SIT? CAN I SEE THE ENGINE?
GATE
TAKE IT EASY! WE ONLY HAVE 20 MINUTES LEFT TO WAIT, MICHAEL.
TWENTY MINUTES?– THAT'S FOREVER!!
LYNN

Twenty minutes is forever when you're a kid. We sat in the train station trying to keep Aaron occupied until we could board and get settled in our rooms. Katie was an easy traveller. If she was restless, you could settle her down with a book or a puzzle, and she'd often fall asleep. Aaron, on the other hand, was a ball of pent-up energy, and required all of our attention, patience, and creativity.

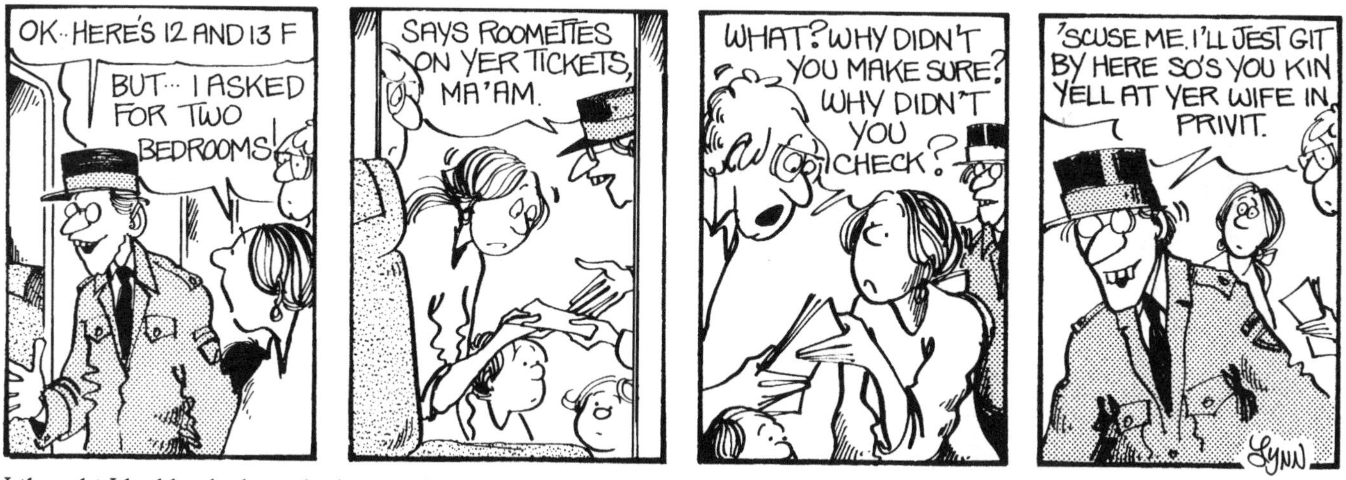
OK.. HERE'S 12 AND 13 F
BUT... I ASKED FOR TWO BEDROOMS!
SAYS ROOMETTES ON YER TICKETS, MA'AM.
WHAT? WHY DIDN'T YOU MAKE SURE? WHY DIDN'T YOU CHECK?
'SCUSE ME. I'LL JEST GIT BY HERE SO'S YOU KIN YELL AT YER WIFE IN PRIVIT.
LYNN

I thought I had booked two bedrooms, but in error I'd booked roomettes. These tiny spaces had a bench seat, which converted to a single bed for sleeping — under which, inconveniently stored, was ... the loo. I had planned for the "boys" to share one compartment, and Katie and I would share the other. The roomettes were so confining, however, that in order for us all to fit, the kids were exchanged. Kate stayed with her dad, and Aaron stayed with me.

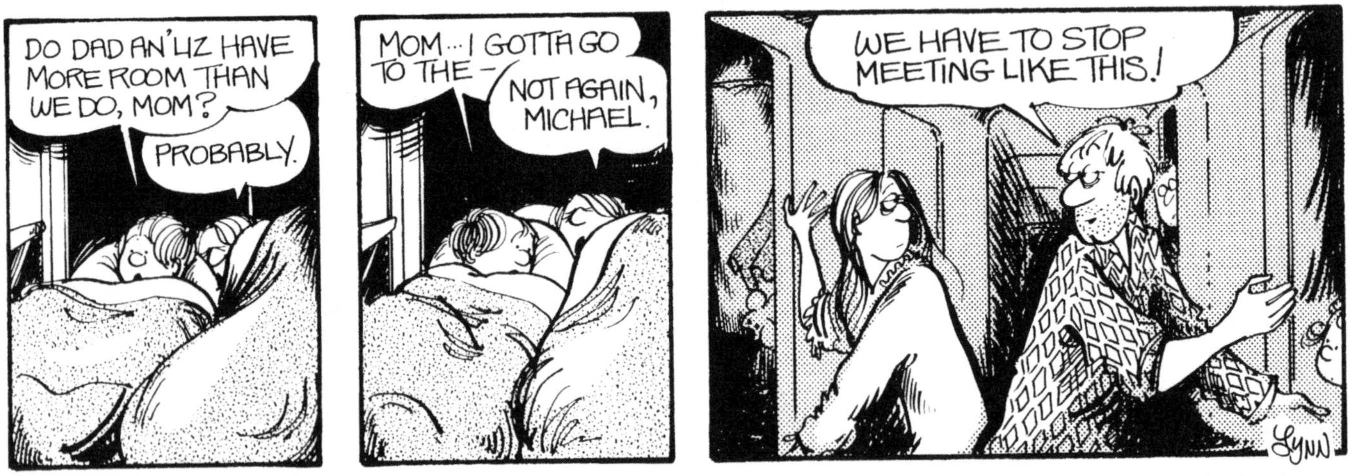
DO DAD AN' LIZ HAVE MORE ROOM THAN WE DO, MOM?
PROBABLY.
MOM...I GOTTA GO TO THE –
NOT AGAIN, MICHAEL.
WE HAVE TO STOP MEETING LIKE THIS!
LYNN

Despite watering both kids before bedtime, they both had to use the facilities during the night. This meant we had to leave the privacy of the compartment, lift the bed up, expose the lavatory, close the door, and "go." The process was reversed when everyone got back into bed. I was not the most popular "travel agent," and heard a lot about what I "should have done."

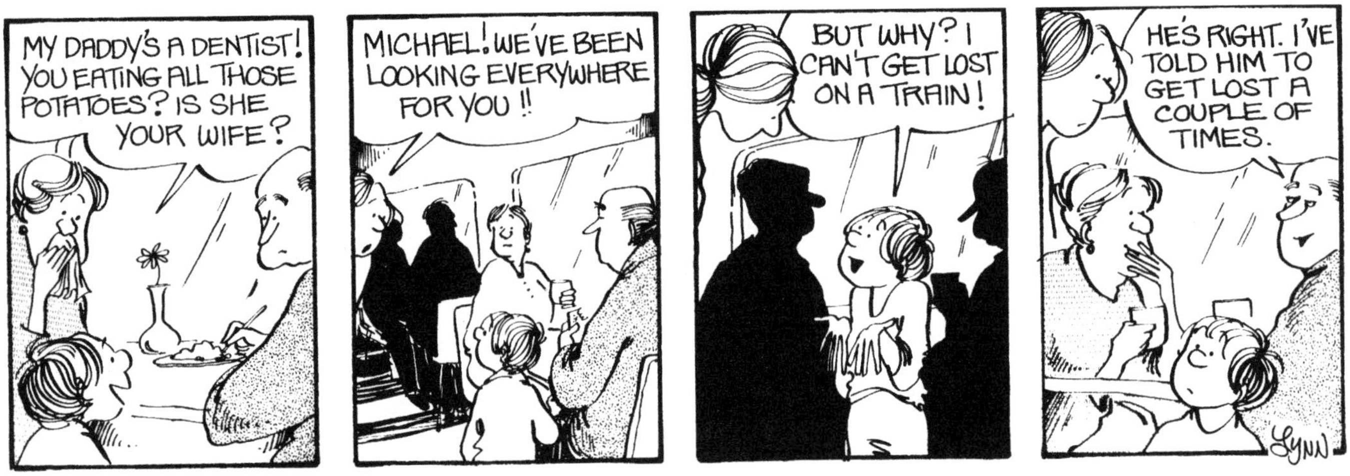
MY DADDY'S A DENTIST! YOU EATING ALL THOSE POTATOES? IS SHE YOUR WIFE?
MICHAEL! WE'VE BEEN LOOKING EVERYWHERE FOR YOU!!
BUT WHY? I CAN'T GET LOST ON A TRAIN!
HE'S RIGHT. I'VE TOLD HIM TO GET LOST A COUPLE OF TIMES.
LYNN

Aaron was extremely social, and enjoyed walking up and down the cars, talking to the other passengers. He was well-behaved, and didn't get into trouble until the novelty wore off. His favourite place was the dining room where, if he was lucky, he'd score an extra dessert.

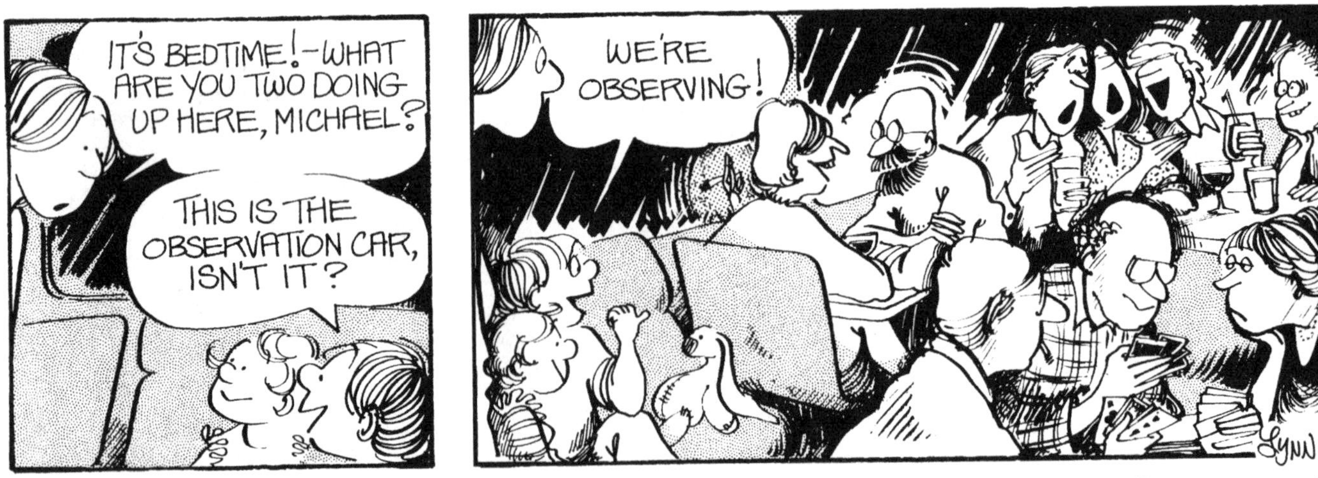
IT'S BEDTIME! – WHAT ARE YOU TWO DOING UP HERE, MICHAEL?
THIS IS THE OBSERVATION CAR, ISN'T IT?
WE'RE OBSERVING!
LYNN

The bar car was also the observation car, and even though kids weren't supposed to be in an area where liquor was served, there seemed to be a double standard on the train. Kids sat with their parents, and when it got too dark to enjoy the scenery, youngsters watched the grown-ups lose their cool and happily act like children!

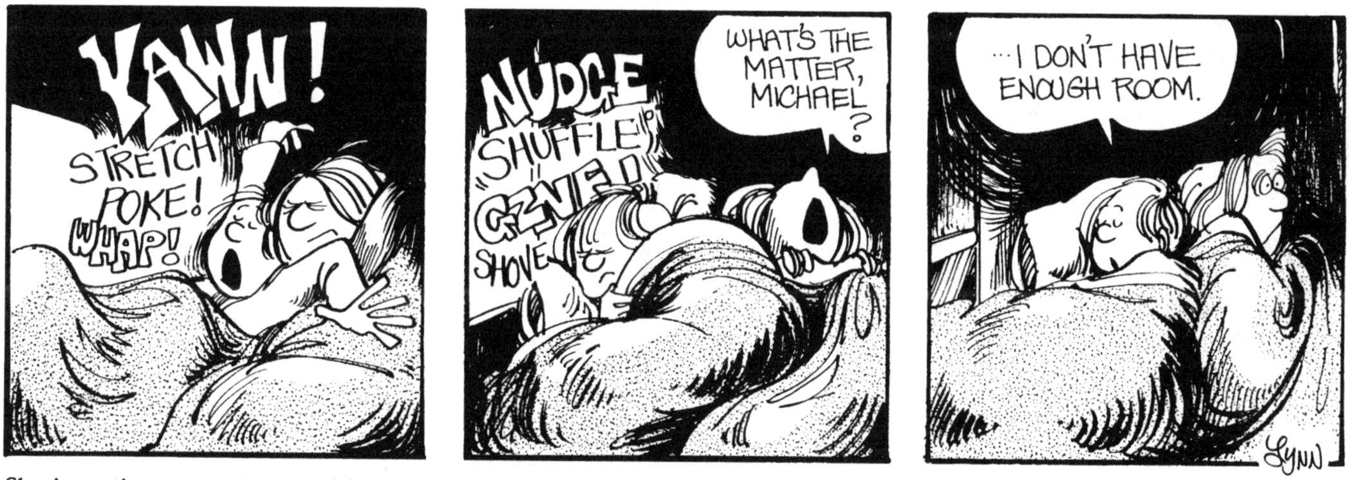
YAWN!
STRETCH
POKE!
WHAP!
NUDGE
SHUFFLE
SHOVE
WHAT'S THE MATTER, MICHAEL?
...I DON'T HAVE ENOUGH ROOM.

Sharing a tiny compartment with my son was a challenge. The only time he really fell asleep was when the train was in motion. The rocking and the click of the rails nicely put him under — but as soon as we stopped on a siding, he was ready for action, wanting to know exactly where we were.

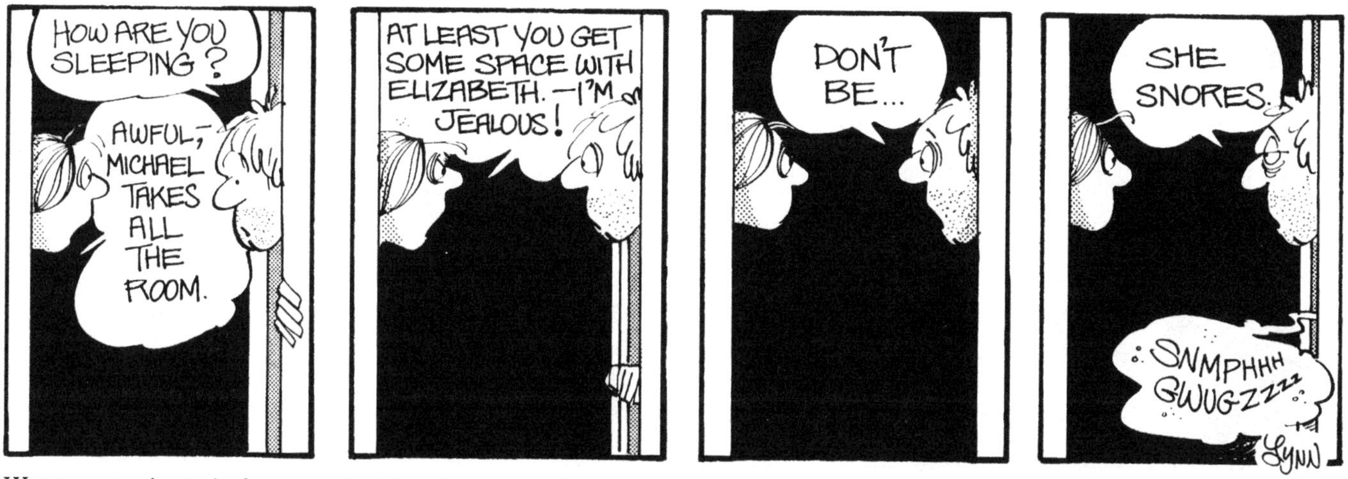
HOW ARE YOU SLEEPING?
AWFUL,- MICHAEL TAKES ALL THE ROOM.
AT LEAST YOU GET SOME SPACE WITH ELIZABETH. -I'M JEALOUS!
DON'T BE...
SHE SNORES.
SNMPHHH GWUG-ZZZZ

We were on the train for several nights. Even though the kids were the best they could be, they tossed and turned. And their constant up and down to the toilet made each night a real challenge. We also met others in the hallway as they reorganized themselves into these confined spaces — and more than once we heard, "Why didn't you a book a compartment instead of a roomette?"

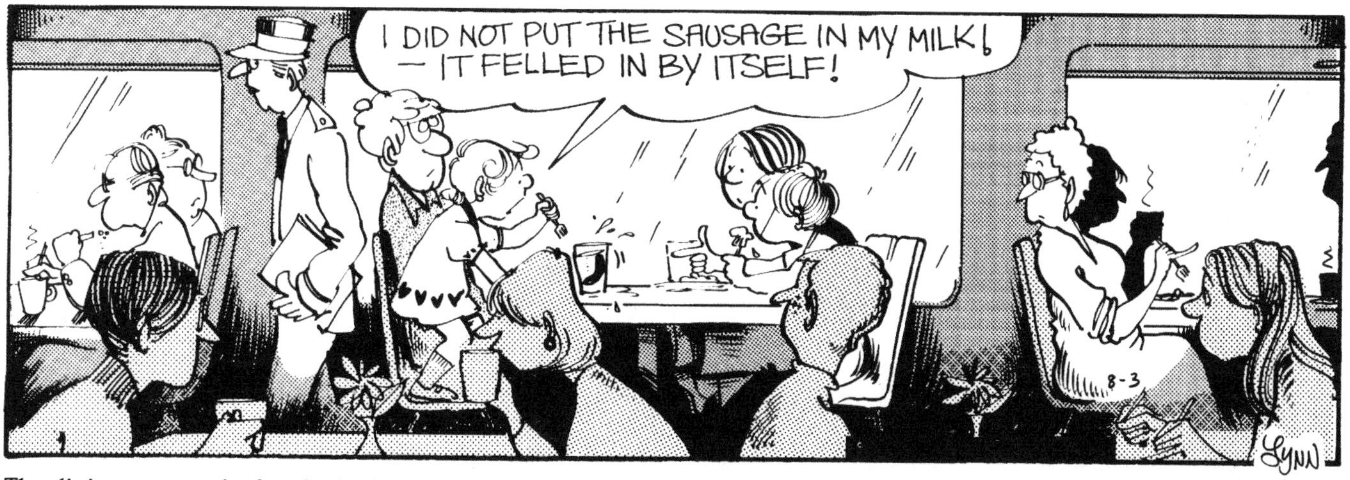
I DID NOT PUT THE SAUSAGE IN MY MILK! — IT FELLED IN BY ITSELF!

The dining car was, by far, the highlight of the trip. At the time, Canadian National Railway was still into "elegance." We had tables with cloths, nice dishes, good cutlery — and even the children behaved better in this classic and refined dining room. This is one of the rare strips in which I showed them being more of a handful than they really were!

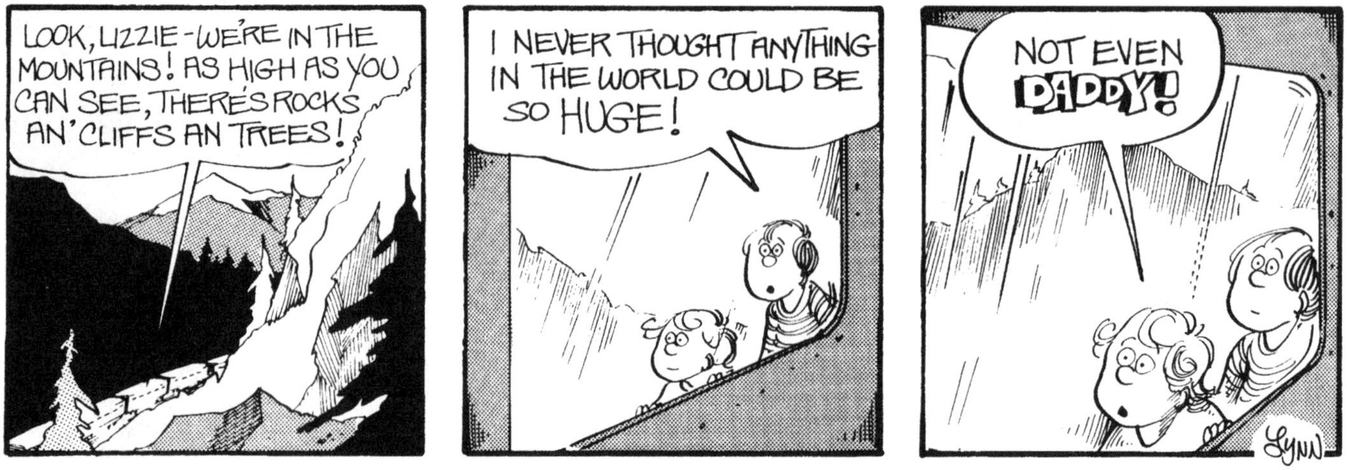
LOOK, LIZZIE - WE'RE IN THE MOUNTAINS! AS HIGH AS YOU CAN SEE, THERE'S ROCKS AN' CLIFFS AN TREES!
I NEVER THOUGHT ANYTHING IN THE WORLD COULD BE SO HUGE!
NOT EVEN DADDY!
LYNN

For a number of years, the passenger train was scheduled to go through the Rocky Mountains late at night. This astounded us, as the most breathtaking view in Canada was there, and we didn't want to sleep through it! Eventually they realized they were making a mistake and changed the schedule. Over time, we eventually forgot the discomfort of the small sleeping quarters — but we'll never forget the view!

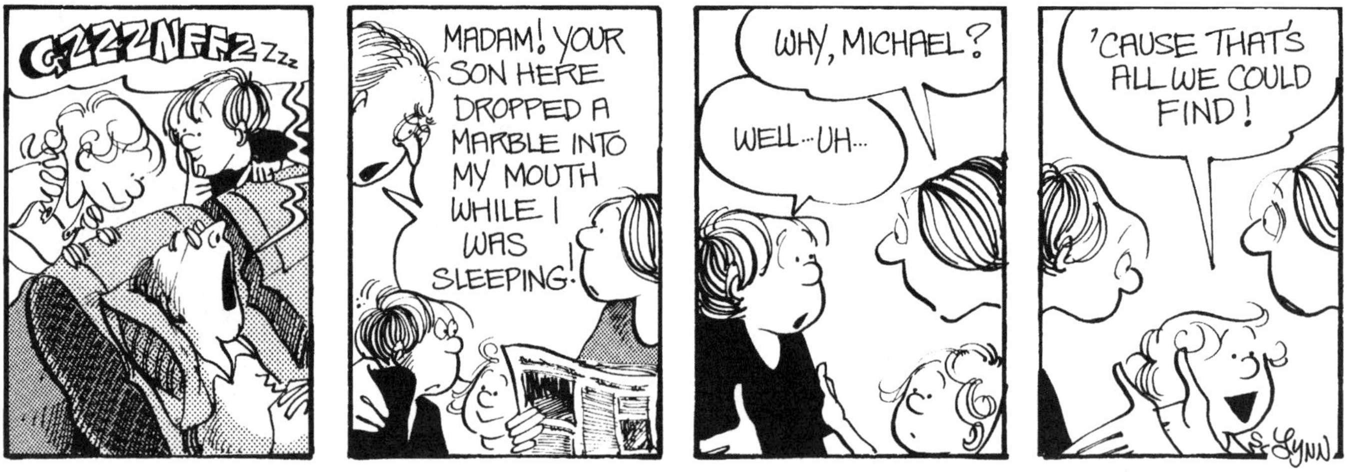
GZZZNFFZ Zzz
MADAM! YOUR SON HERE DROPPED A MARBLE INTO MY MOUTH WHILE I WAS SLEEPING!
WHY, MICHAEL?
WELL...UH...
'CAUSE THAT'S ALL WE COULD FIND!
LYNN

Aaron did not put a marble in a man's mouth — but he thought about it. He was standing on a seat, looking into this snoring aperture. It was an open invitation to neatly drop something in. I caught Aaron's eye just before he let go of the marble he was holding. We both smiled. It was almost too tempting to resist, but resist he must ... and we both laughed out loud just thinking about it.

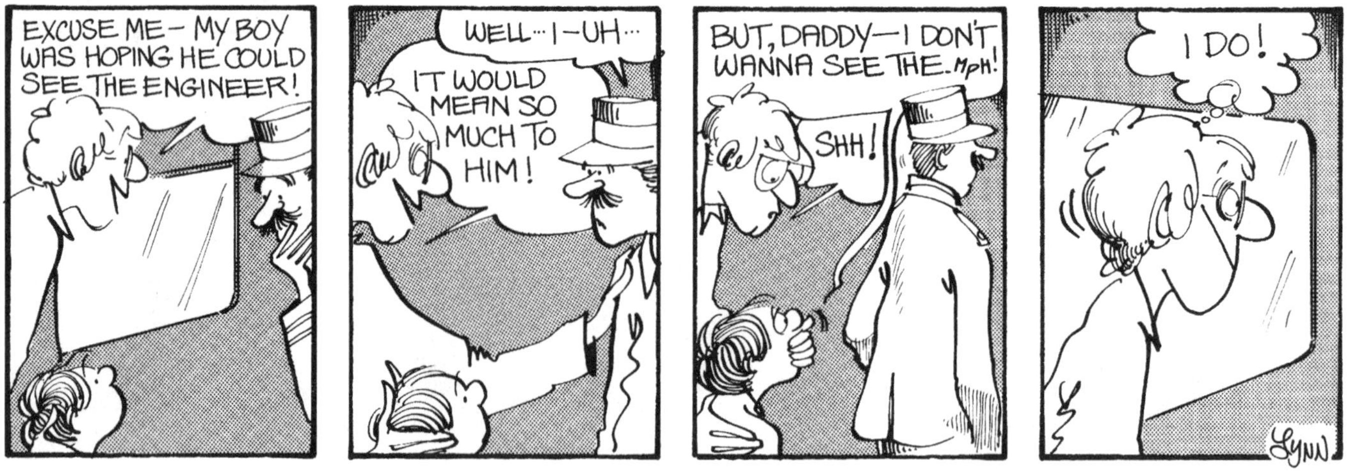
EXCUSE ME - MY BOY WAS HOPING HE COULD SEE THE ENGINEER!
WELL... I - UH...
IT WOULD MEAN SO MUCH TO HIM!
BUT, DADDY—I DON'T WANNA SEE THE... MPH!
SHH!
I DO!
LYNN

Aaron wasn't really all that interested in going to visit the engineer, but his father was. Rod had loved trains since his childhood in Lynn Lake. Sometimes, when you really want to do something but are too shy to ask, it's nice to have a child to hide behind!

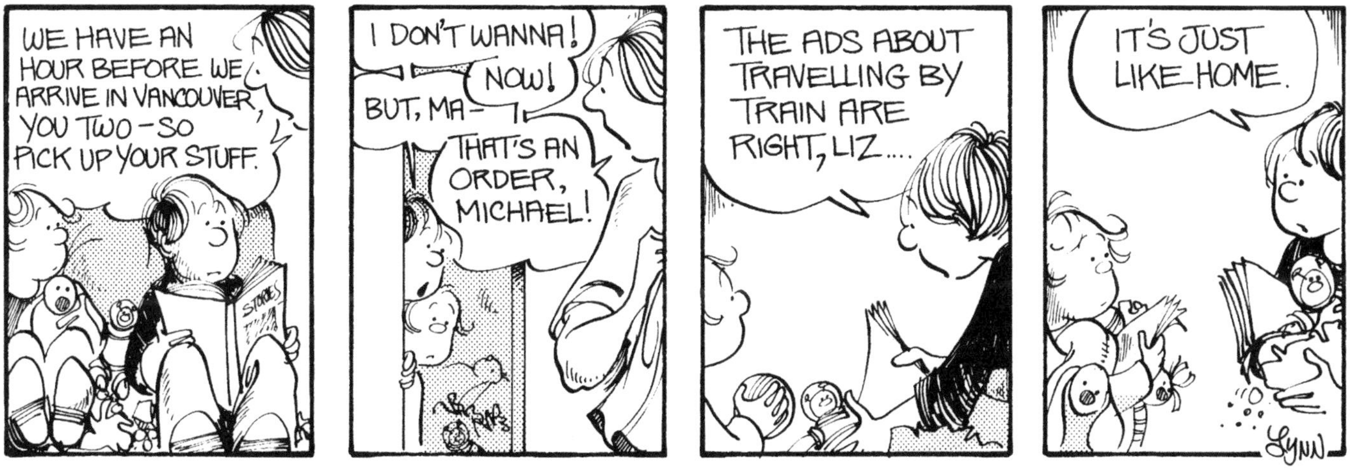
WE HAVE AN HOUR BEFORE WE ARRIVE IN VANCOUVER, YOU TWO - SO PICK UP YOUR STUFF.
STORIES
I DON'T WANNA!
NOW!
BUT, MA-
THAT'S AN ORDER, MICHAEL!
THE ADS ABOUT TRAVELLING BY TRAIN ARE RIGHT, LIZ....
IT'S JUST LIKE HOME.
LYNN

All told, the trip by train was a great adventure. We had spent quality time together in an environment of constant change, and we saw our country from a different perspective. It's something I hope we can do again one day ... but next time, I'll know the difference between roomettes and cabins!

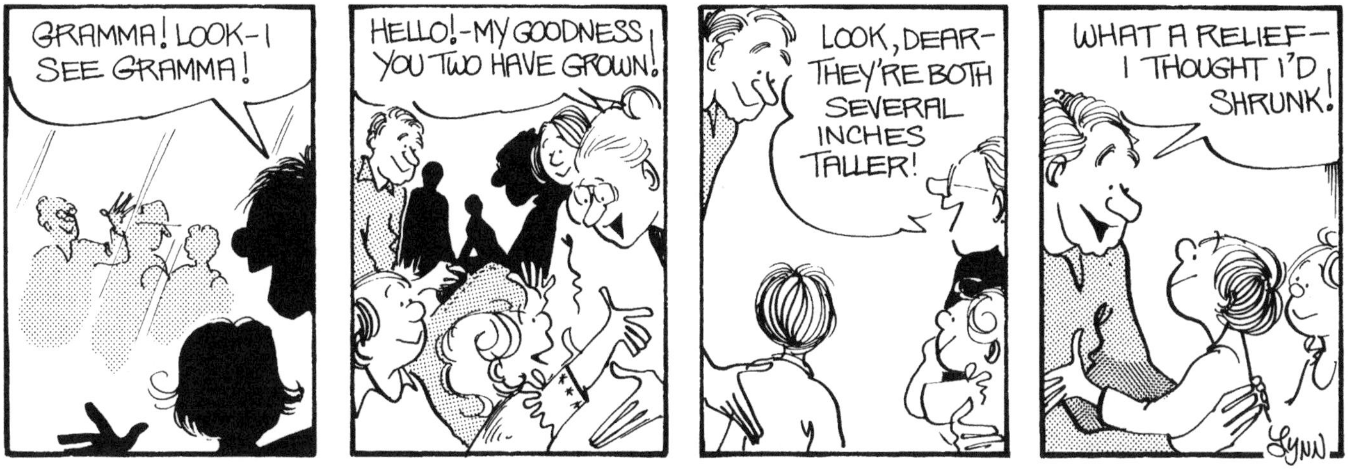
GRAMMA! LOOK - I SEE GRAMMA!
HELLO! - MY GOODNESS YOU TWO HAVE GROWN!
LOOK, DEAR - THEY'RE BOTH SEVERAL INCHES TALLER!
WHAT A RELIEF - I THOUGHT I'D SHRUNK!
LYNN

My parents had a cottage in Hope, B.C. We got off the train in Hope and drove to Kawkawa Lake with them. We saw my parents perhaps once a year, but the kids always remembered them. Even though "they were not going to be spoiled," Aaron and Katie were the centre of attention and had a wonderful time.

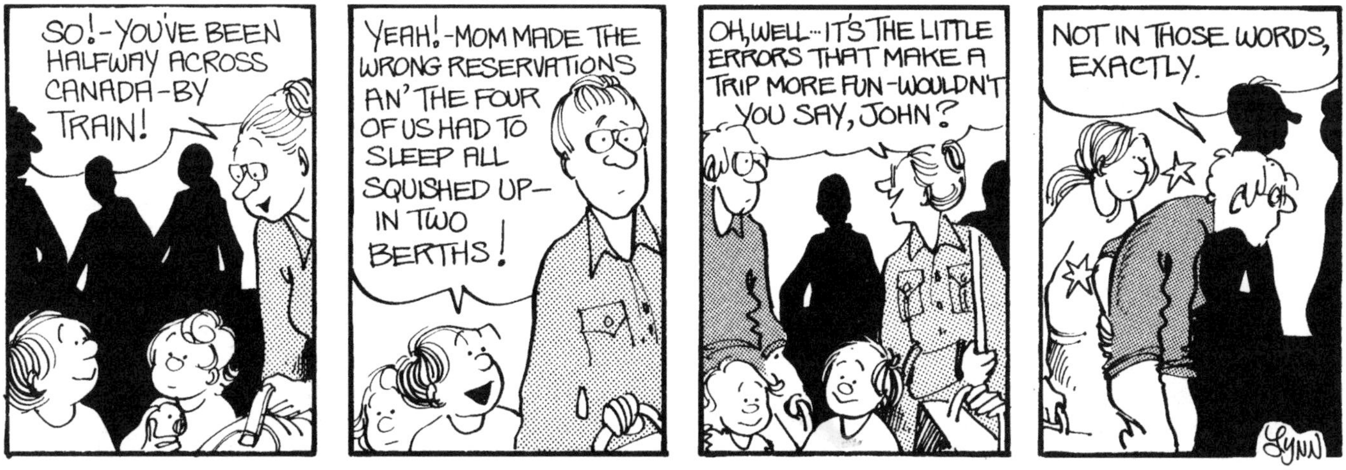
SO! - YOU'VE BEEN HALFWAY ACROSS CANADA - BY TRAIN!
YEAH! - MOM MADE THE WRONG RESERVATIONS AN' THE FOUR OF US HAD TO SLEEP ALL SQUISHED UP - IN TWO BERTHS!
OH, WELL... IT'S THE LITTLE ERRORS THAT MAKE A TRIP MORE FUN - WOULDN'T YOU SAY, JOHN?
NOT IN THOSE WORDS, EXACTLY.
LYNN

We were totally beat by the time we made it to my folks' place. It was such a relief to turn our two busy offspring over to healthy, active grandparents. Mom and Dad weren't used to having such busy kids about, but they soon managed to get into the swing of things. It was fun for me to see them being parents again — from the vantage point of being a parent, now, myself!

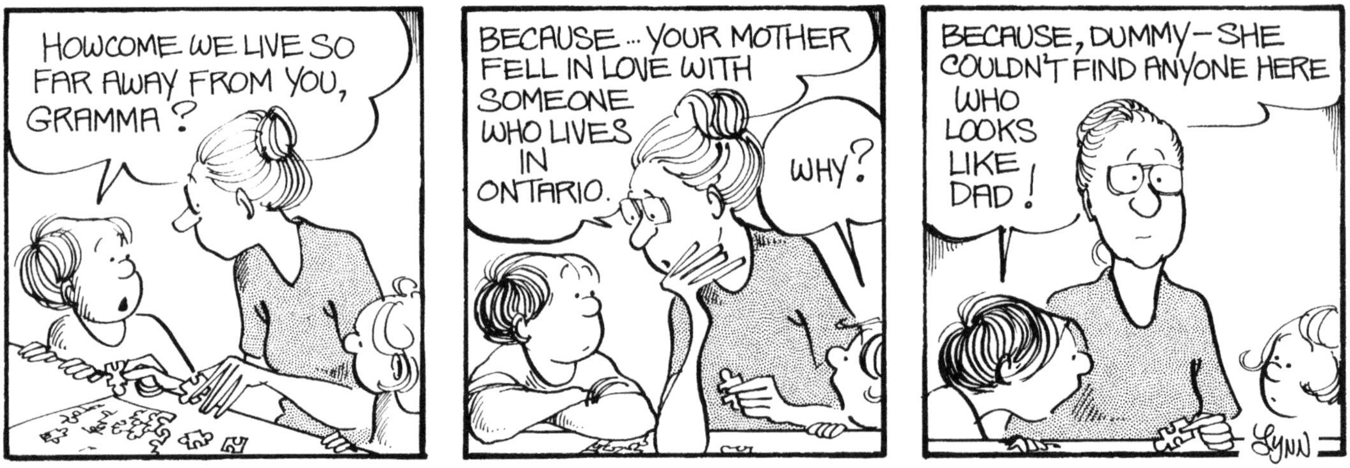
HOWCOME WE LIVE SO FAR AWAY FROM YOU, GRAMMA?
BECAUSE... YOUR MOTHER FELL IN LOVE WITH SOMEONE WHO LIVES IN ONTARIO.
WHY?
BECAUSE, DUMMY—SHE COULDN'T FIND ANYONE HERE WHO LOOKS LIKE DAD!
Lynn

Having a long-distance relationship with my family was difficult. I was getting to know my in-laws very well, and the kids were at home with everyone on "the other side of the family," but I missed my own. Both of my parents were creative and would have been happy to play a larger role in the children's lives, but time and the cost of travel separated us. Every visit was filled with activities, and the time always flew by far too fast.

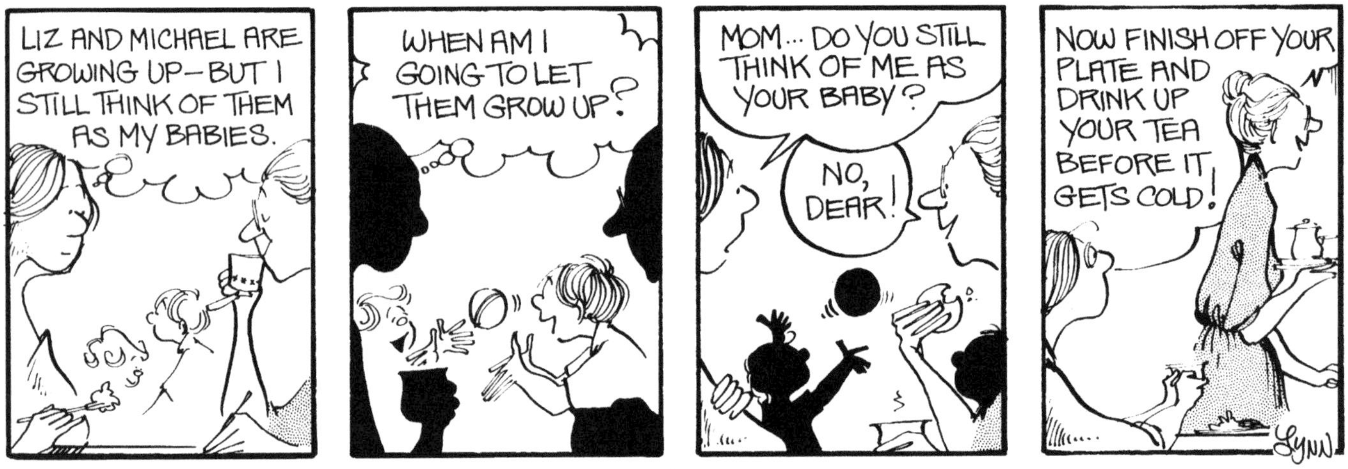
LIZ AND MICHAEL ARE GROWING UP—BUT I STILL THINK OF THEM AS MY BABIES.
WHEN AM I GOING TO LET THEM GROW UP?
MOM... DO YOU STILL THINK OF ME AS YOUR BABY?
NO, DEAR!
NOW FINISH OFF YOUR PLATE AND DRINK UP YOUR TEA BEFORE IT GETS COLD!
Lynn

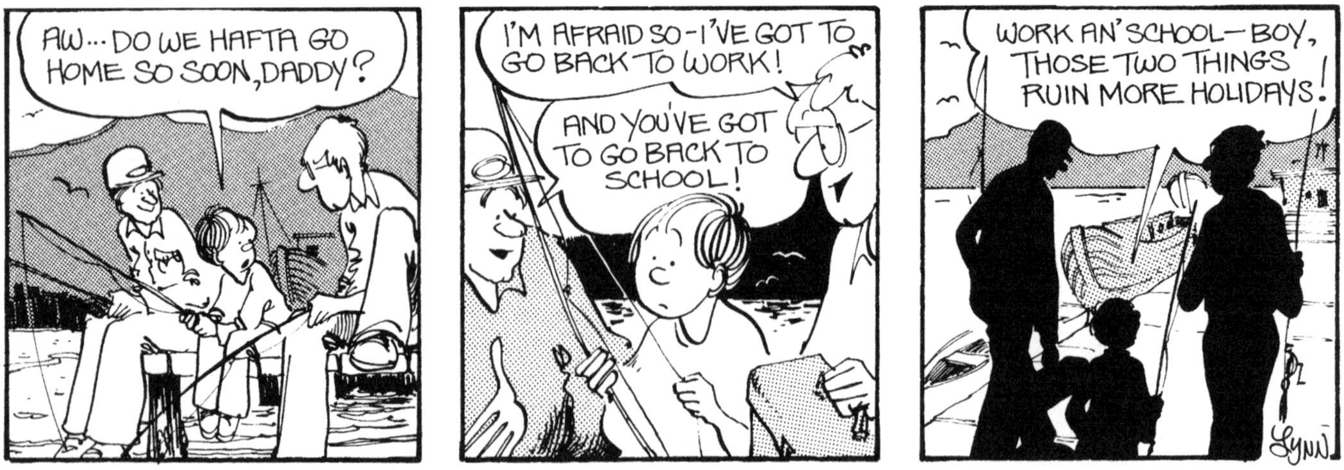
AW... DO WE HAFTA GO HOME SO SOON, DADDY?
I'M AFRAID SO-I'VE GOT TO GO BACK TO WORK!
AND YOU'VE GOT TO GO BACK TO SCHOOL!
WORK AN' SCHOOL—BOY, THOSE TWO THINGS RUIN MORE HOLIDAYS!
Lynn

There's nothing like being at the lake to keep kids happy. Aaron and Katie learned to swim at Kawkawa, and even though the fishing was limited to minnows, it was exhilarating just to catch one and let it go. "The boys" would go out in my dad's old canoe, and if they were lucky, there'd be something to photograph and some tall tales to tell. It was a wonderful time, and the kids never wanted to leave.

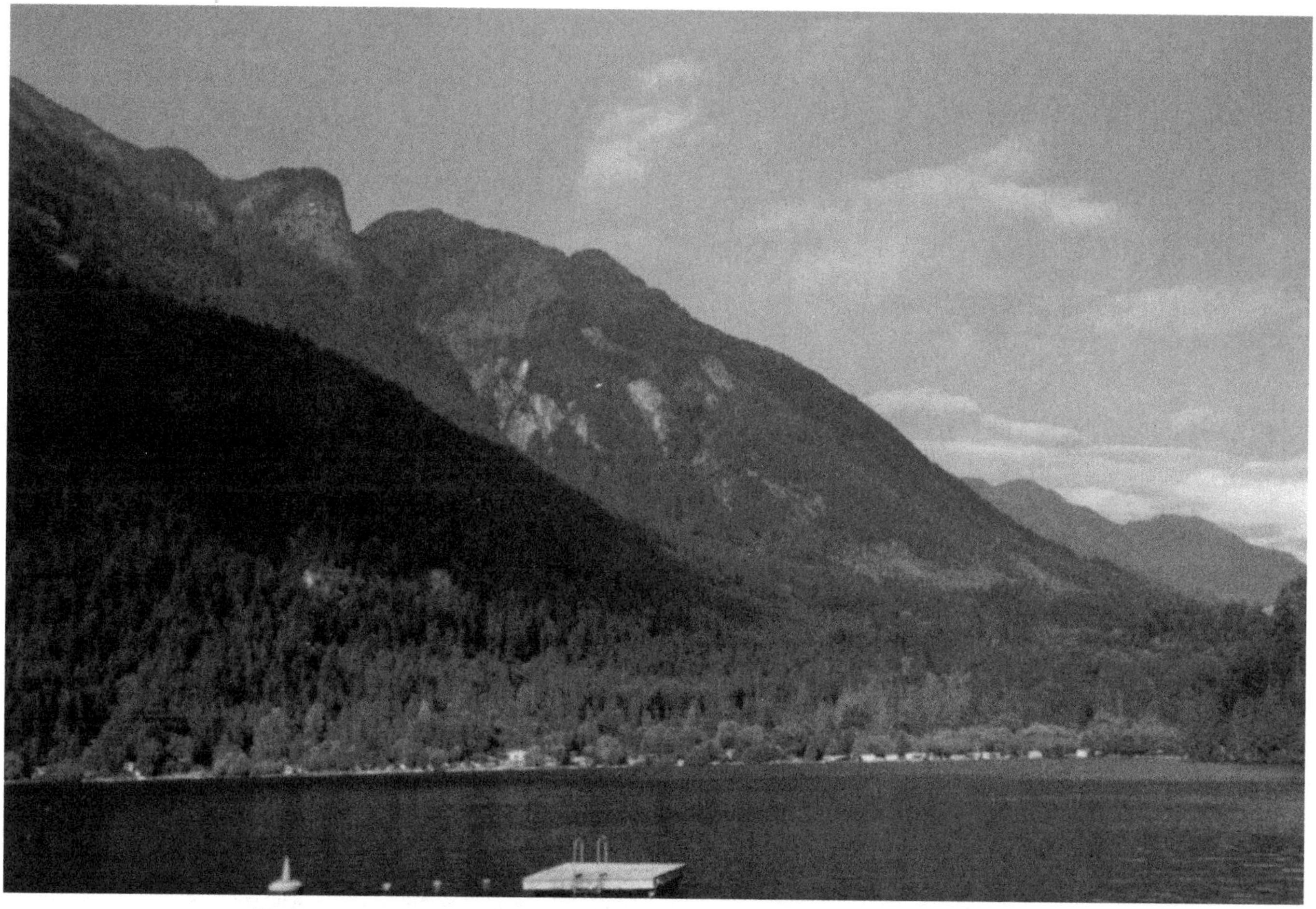

The beautiful view from my parents' place on Kawkawa Lake, Hope, B.C.

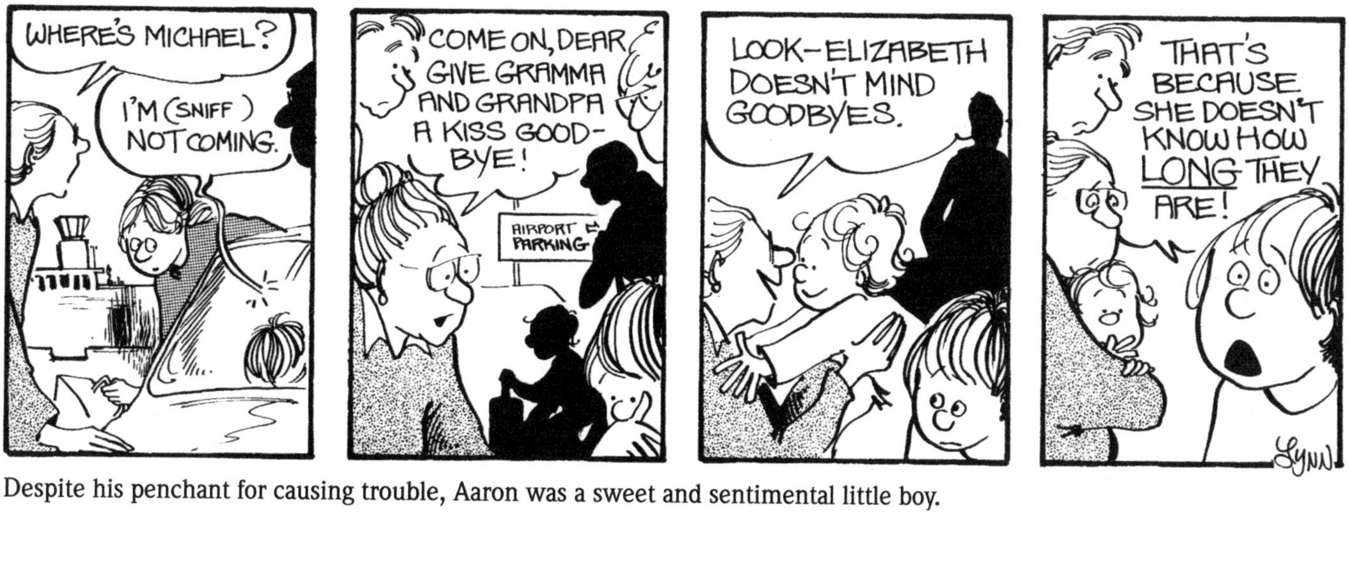
WHERE'S MICHAEL?
I'M (SNIFF) NOT COMING.
COME ON, DEAR GIVE GRAMMA AND GRANDPA A KISS GOOD-BYE!
AIRPORT PARKING
LOOK-ELIZABETH DOESN'T MIND GOODBYES.
THAT'S BECAUSE SHE DOESN'T KNOW HOW LONG THEY ARE!
LYNN

Despite his penchant for causing trouble, Aaron was a sweet and sentimental little boy.

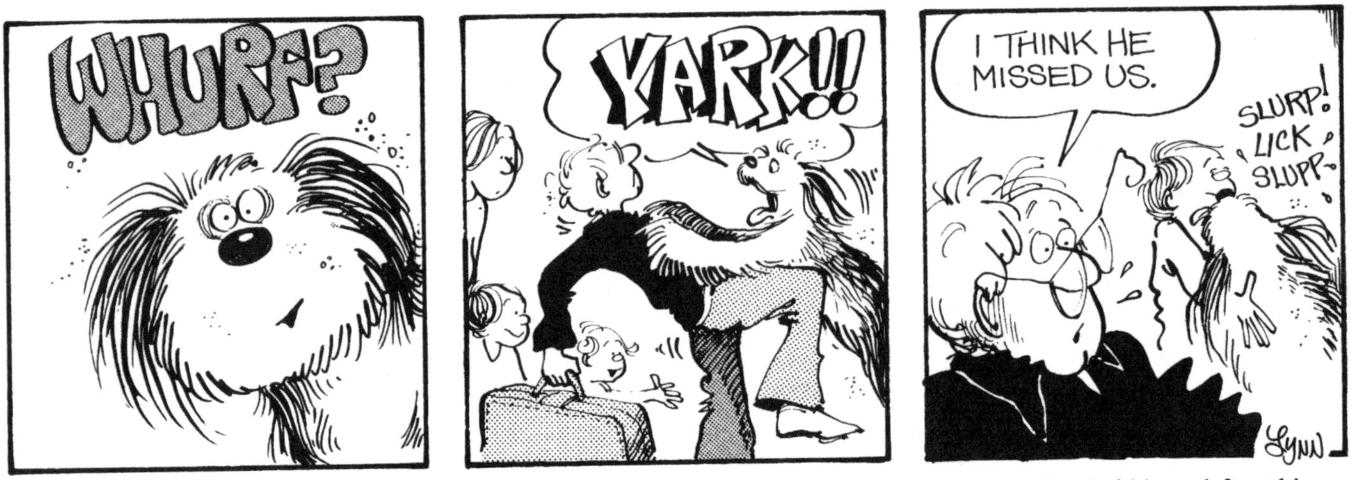
WHURF?
YARK!!
I THINK HE MISSED US.
SLURP! LICK SLUPP
LYNN

I remember the face-licking, body-slamming, seat-wagging welcome that Farley used to give us after he'd been left on his own for a while. It was a greeting so filled with joy and expectation that you couldn't fault him for almost knocking you down!

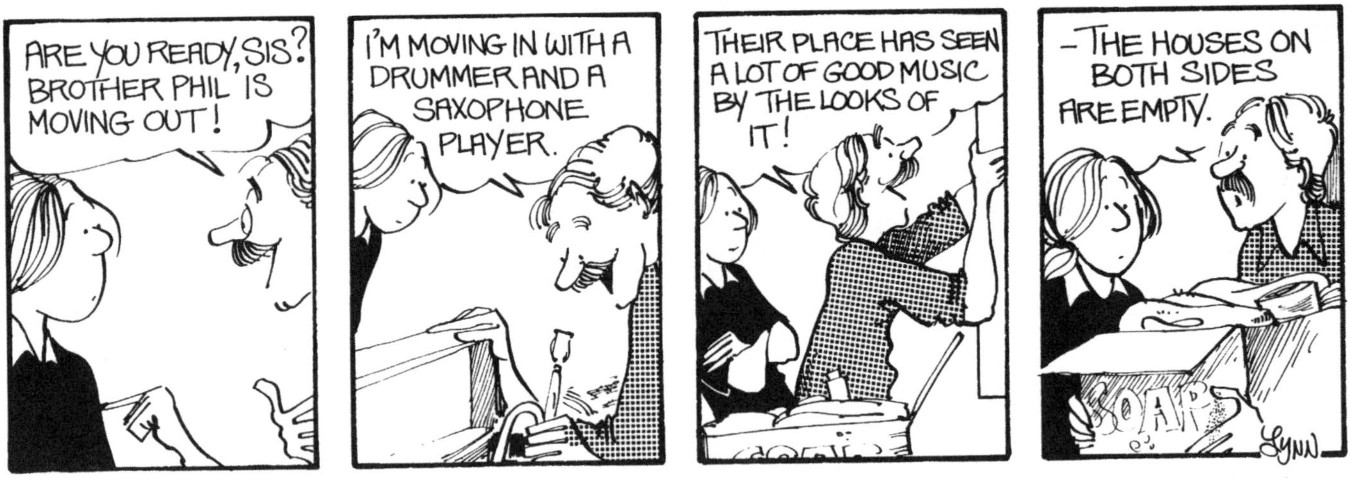
ARE YOU READY, SIS? BROTHER PHIL IS MOVING OUT!
I'M MOVING IN WITH A DRUMMER AND A SAXOPHONE PLAYER.
THEIR PLACE HAS SEEN A LOT OF GOOD MUSIC BY THE LOOKS OF IT!
-THE HOUSES ON BOTH SIDES ARE EMPTY.
SOAP
LYNN

After living in my garage for more than a year, my brother, Alan, moved to Hamilton, and then to Stratford, Ontario, where he played for Stratford's Festival Theatre. My roommate, Fran, moved to Calgary to continue her studies, and I was suddenly alone in the house. I helped Alan move to his new apartment, and wished him well. Although I was happy to have the place to myself again, I missed their company terribly.

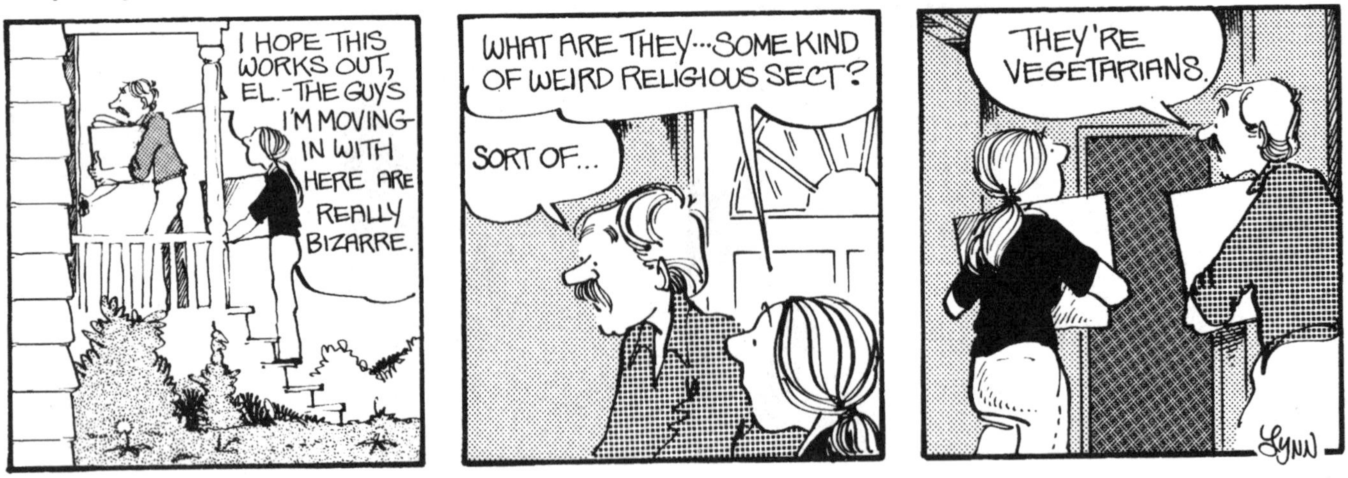
I HOPE THIS WORKS OUT, EL.-THE GUYS I'M MOVING IN WITH HERE ARE REALLY BIZARRE.
WHAT ARE THEY...SOME KIND OF WEIRD RELIGIOUS SECT?
SORT OF...
THEY'RE VEGETARIANS.
LYNN

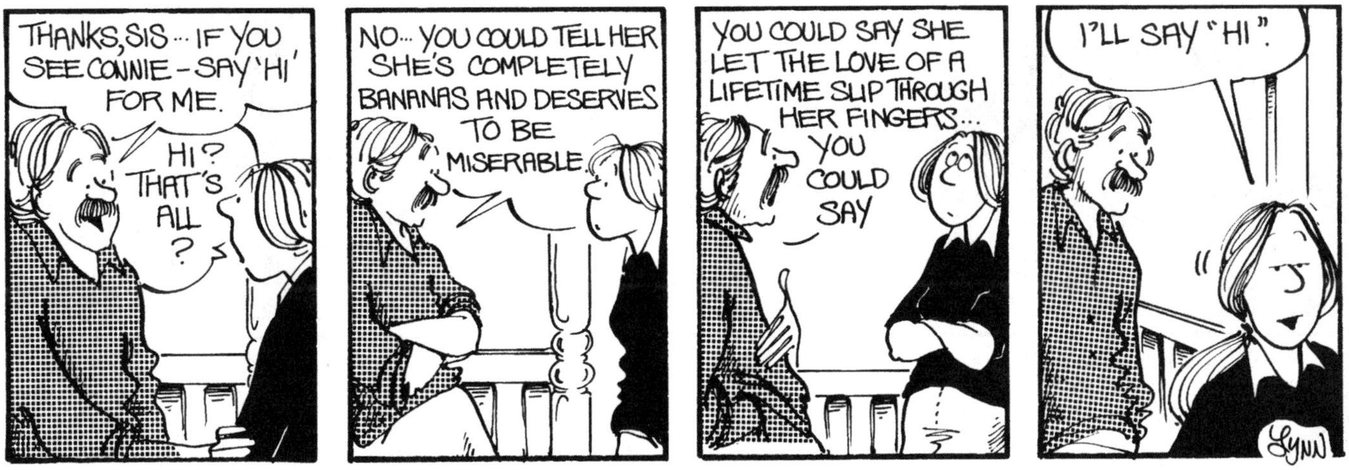
THANKS, SIS... IF YOU SEE CONNIE - SAY 'HI' FOR ME.
HI? THAT'S ALL?
NO... YOU COULD TELL HER SHE'S COMPLETELY BANANAS AND DESERVES TO BE MISERABLE.
YOU COULD SAY SHE LET THE LOVE OF A LIFETIME SLIP THROUGH HER FINGERS...
YOU COULD SAY
I'LL SAY "HI".
LYNN

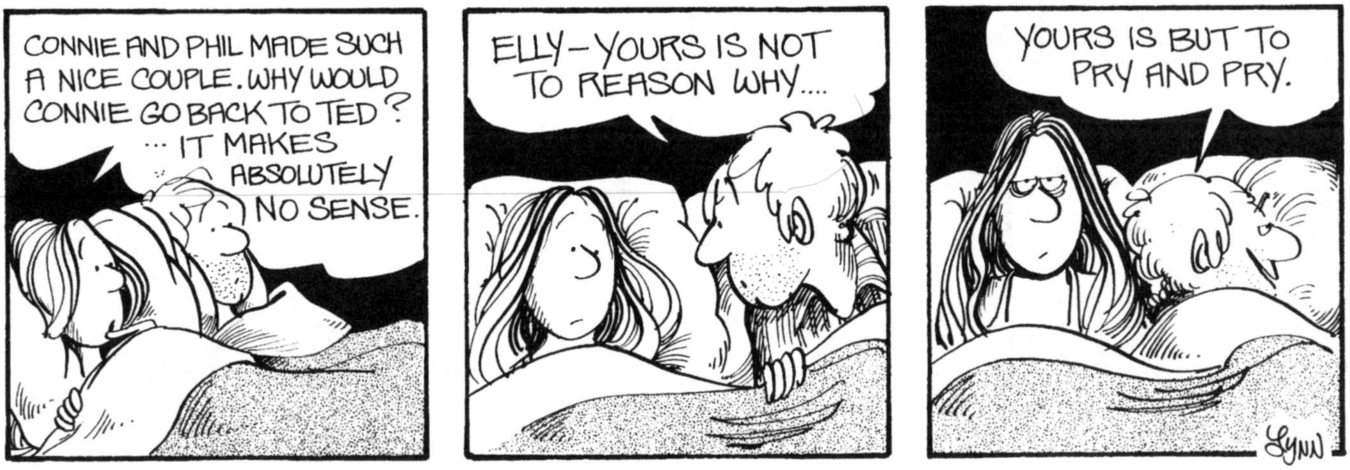
CONNIE AND PHIL MADE SUCH A NICE COUPLE. WHY WOULD CONNIE GO BACK TO TED? ... IT MAKES ABSOLUTELY NO SENSE.
ELLY - YOURS IS NOT TO REASON WHY....
YOURS IS BUT TO PRY AND PRY.
LYNN

My efforts to pry had never been too successful.

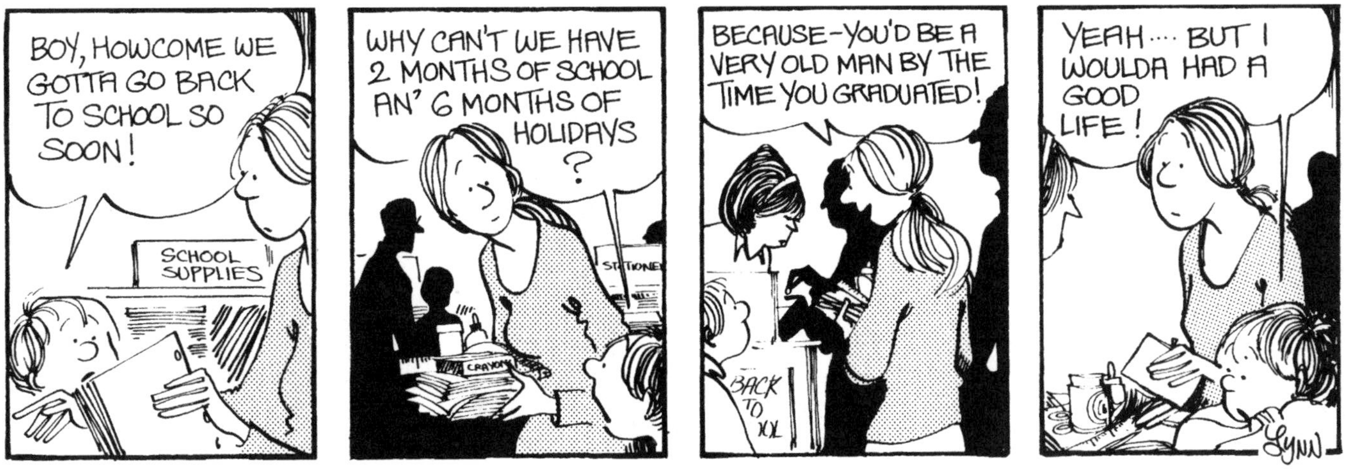
BOY, HOWCOME WE GOTTA GO BACK TO SCHOOL SO SOON!
SCHOOL SUPPLIES
WHY CAN'T WE HAVE 2 MONTHS OF SCHOOL AN' 6 MONTHS OF HOLIDAYS?
BECAUSE - YOU'D BE A VERY OLD MAN BY THE TIME YOU GRADUATED!
YEAH.... BUT I WOULDA HAD A GOOD LIFE!
LYNN

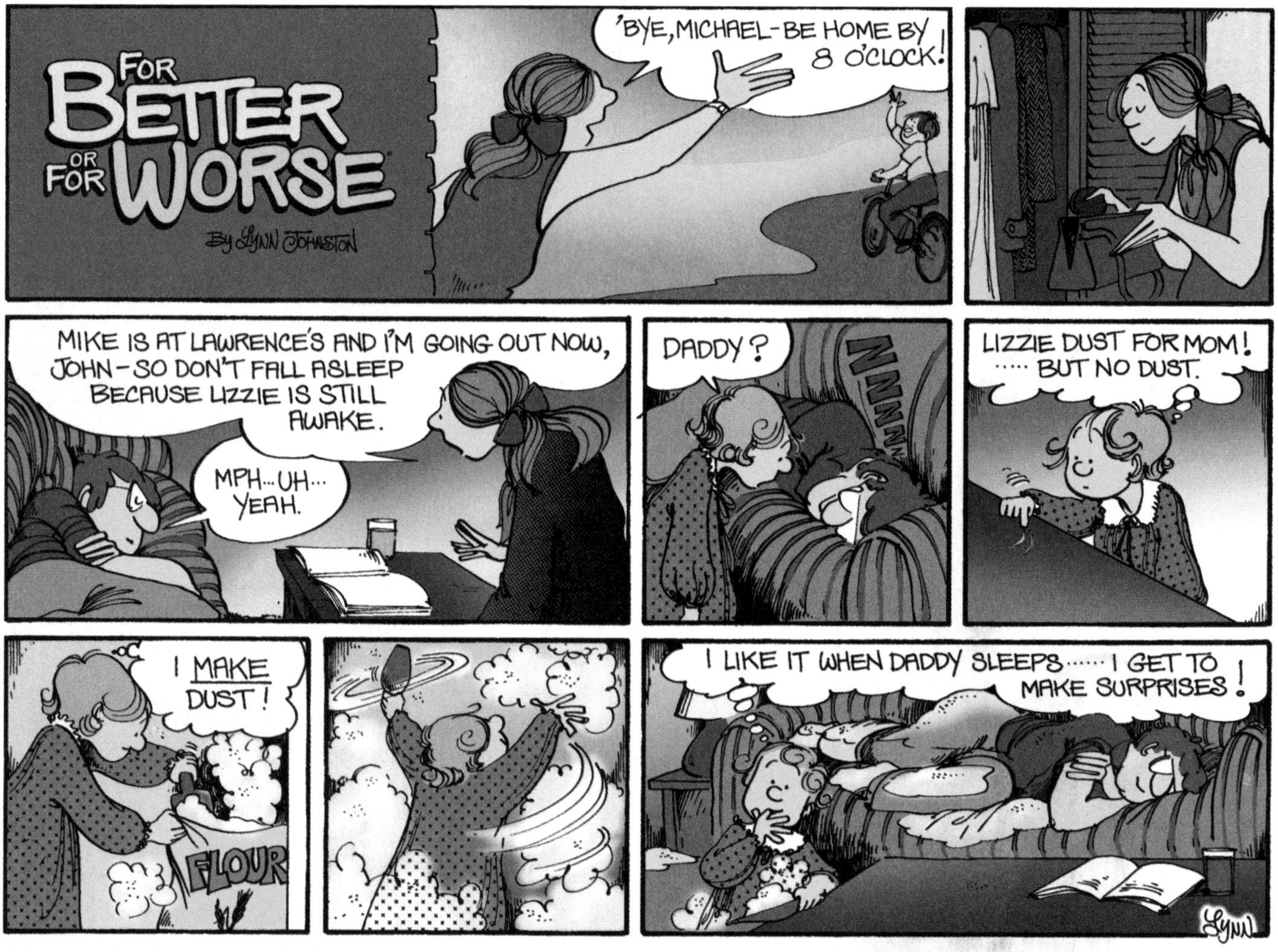
FOR BETTER OR FOR WORSE
By Lynn Johnston
'BYE, MICHAEL- BE HOME BY 8 O'CLOCK!
MIKE IS AT LAWRENCE'S AND I'M GOING OUT NOW, JOHN - SO DON'T FALL ASLEEP BECAUSE LIZZIE IS STILL AWAKE.
MPH... UH... YEAH.
DADDY?
LIZZIE DUST FOR MOM! ..... BUT NO DUST.
I MAKE DUST!
FLOUR
I LIKE IT WHEN DADDY SLEEPS...... I GET TO MAKE SURPRISES!
Lynn

Aaron used to be up and running at four or five in the morning. Food and dressing took an hour, but there were usually two hours left before I took him to daycare. Exhausted, I'd lie on the couch as he ran from room to room, jumped on the furniture and on me. Sometimes, I'd actually fall asleep — this was when he'd go into the kitchen cupboards and find the stuff he shouldn't have. This scenario really happened ... and both of us survived to tell the tale!

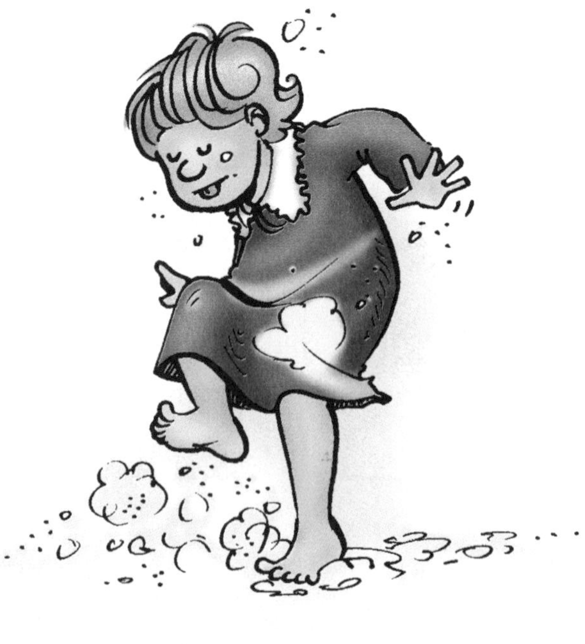

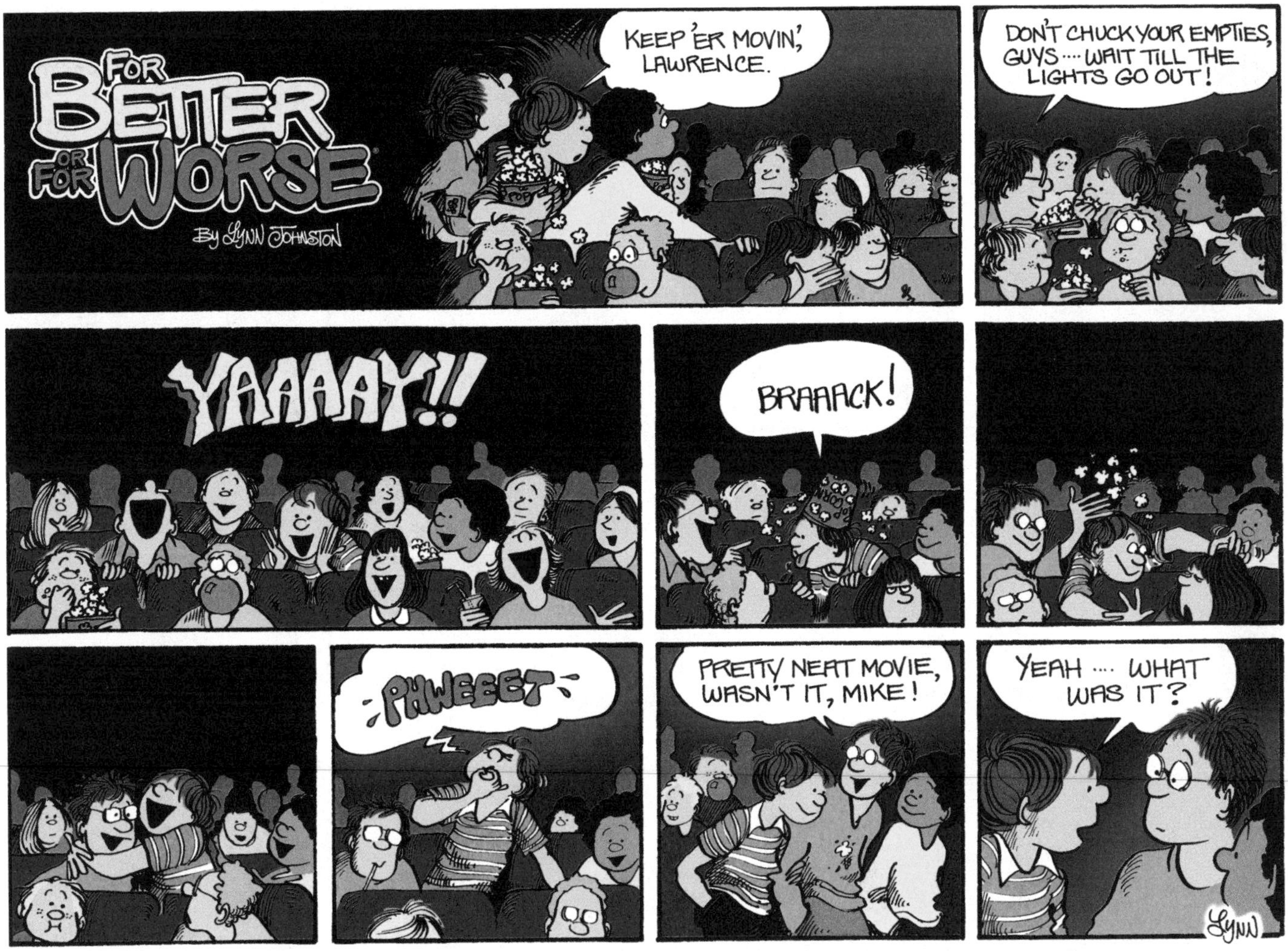
FOR BETTER OR FOR WORSE
By Lynn Johnston
KEEP 'ER MOVIN', LAWRENCE.
DON'T CHUCK YOUR EMPTIES, GUYS .... WAIT TILL THE LIGHTS GO OUT!
YAAAAY!!
BRAAACK!
PHWEEEET
PRETTY NEAT MOVIE, WASN'T IT, MIKE!
YEAH .... WHAT WAS IT?
Lynn

The Odeon Theatre was a two-mile walk from my house in North Vancouver. The Saturday afternoon matinee was always packed with kids looking forward to a double bill, which was separated by a cartoon, a newsreel, and a commercial. This was the arena into which we crushed ourselves: rich, poor, native, and new immigrants; to tease, shove, joke, and annoy each other until the screen lit up with whatever Hollywood had to offer.

My routine was to go early and be first in line, so I could get the pick of the seats. Somewhere in the sixth row near the middle was best, and if the crowd exceeded the seating, then wooden orange crates were set out in front of the screen for the slackers. I once watched Tarzan from the orange crates. All I could see was Johnny Weismuller's enormous feet and tiny head — all out of focus.

We talked through the dialogue, cheered with the action, groaned when the kissing started, and laughed at the cartoons till we wet our seats. This was kid heaven. Here at the theatre, we were all equals. The movies brought us together at a time when so many things tore us apart. The old Odeon Theatre is gone, now. This Sunday cartoon brought it back to me!

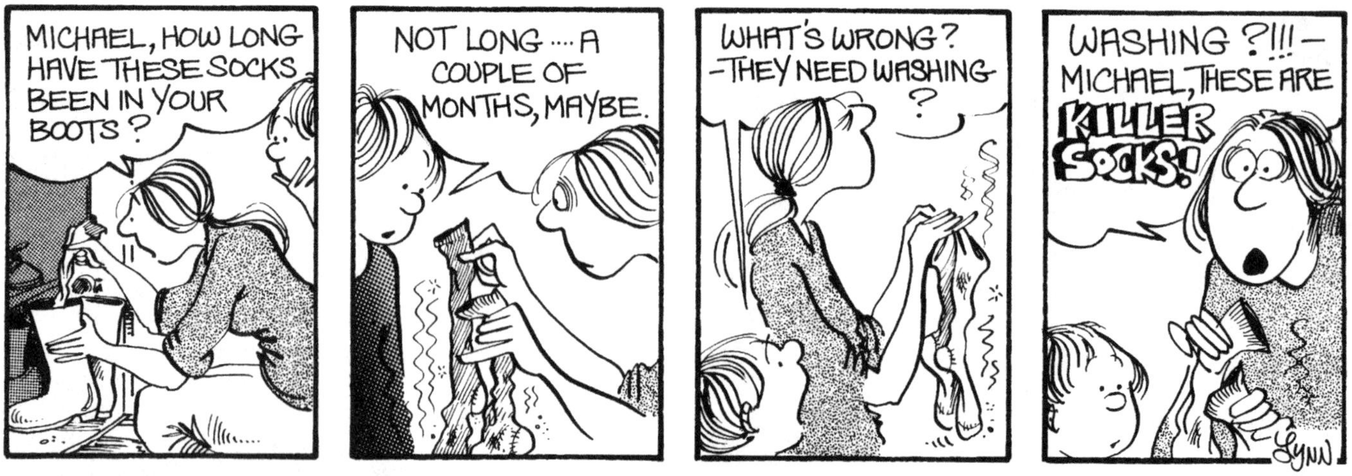
MICHAEL, HOW LONG HAVE THESE SOCKS BEEN IN YOUR BOOTS?
NOT LONG.... A COUPLE OF MONTHS, MAYBE.
WHAT'S WRONG? -THEY NEED WASHING?
WASHING?!!!- MICHAEL, THESE ARE KILLER SOCKS!
LYNN

For some reason, stinking socks are funny … much like burps and toots. In truth, the fact that kids' footwear did give off noxious gasses surprised me. But, then again, kids and odours go together like dogs and fleas. My son could wear a pair of socks until they were stiff, and no amount of washing could restore the colour, no matter what it was. I dragged dirty socks into the text several times, and each time, readers reacted with comments like, "Whoa! This happens at your house, too?!"

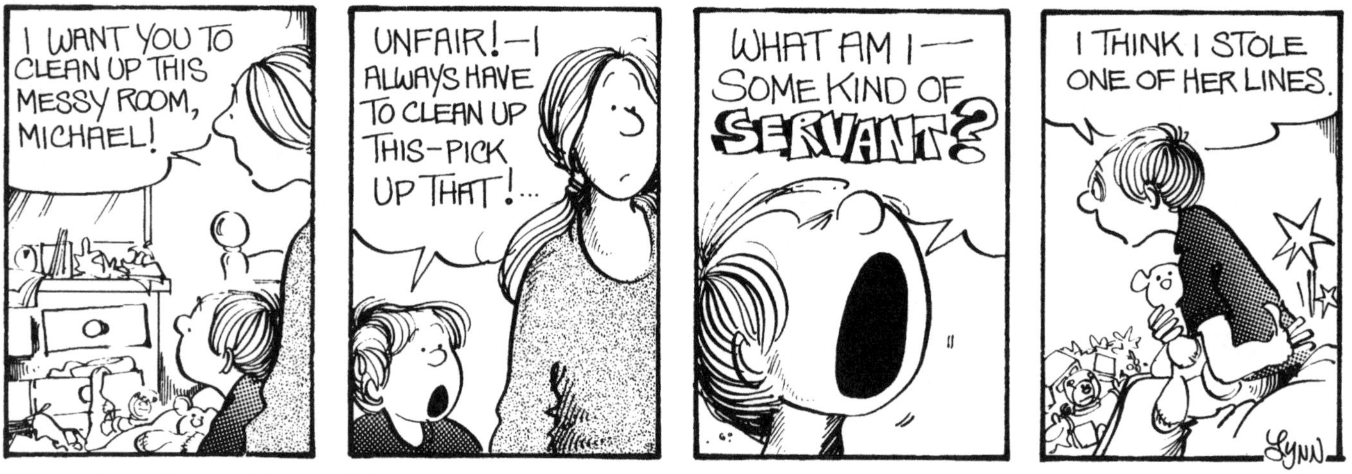
I WANT YOU TO CLEAN UP THIS MESSY ROOM, MICHAEL!
UNFAIR!-I ALWAYS HAVE TO CLEAN UP THIS-PICK UP THAT!...
WHAT AM I— SOME KIND OF SERVANT?
I THINK I STOLE ONE OF HER LINES.
LYNN

This exchange is, word for word, from my own childhood. I knew if I said to my mom, "Do you think I'm some kind of servant?" she'd go completely off her nut. Why did I say it? I don't know. I have always enjoyed a punch line — even if it meant getting a punch in return! So, I said it, and she swatted me and put me in my room. I hoped that when she saw this strip, she'd be vindicated … once more!

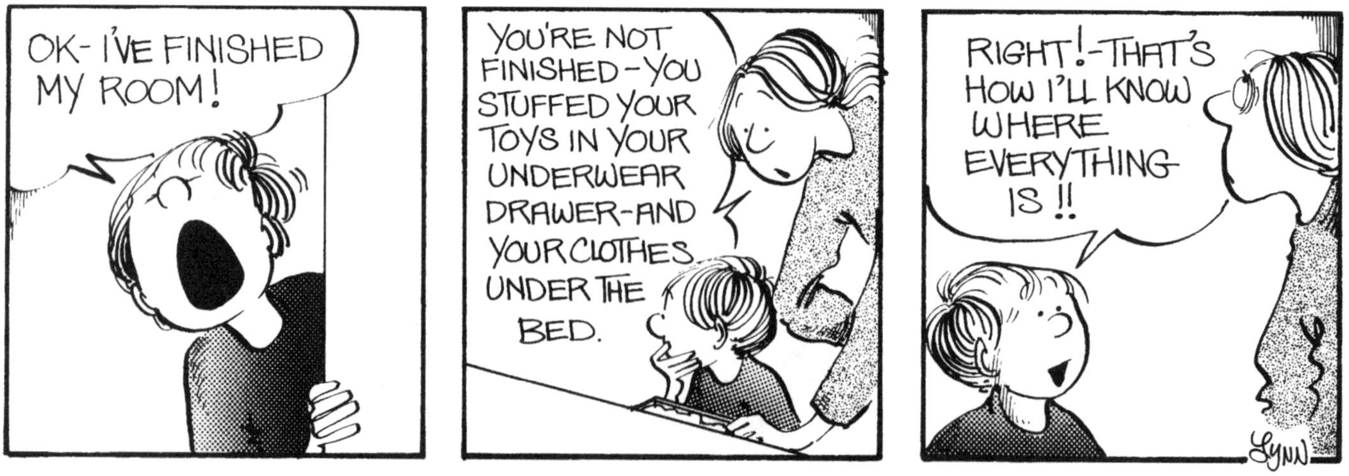
OK- I'VE FINISHED MY ROOM!
YOU'RE NOT FINISHED-YOU STUFFED YOUR TOYS IN YOUR UNDERWEAR DRAWER-AND YOUR CLOTHES UNDER THE BED.
RIGHT!-THAT'S HOW I'LL KNOW WHERE EVERYTHING IS!!
LYNN

I absolutely hated cleaning my room. I couldn't see the point. Why make my bed just to sleep in it and mess it up again? Why put stuff away when I'm just going to get it out again? Nobody lives in my room but me, and if I don't care. … None of my arguments held water with my mom, who would stand at the door like a jailhouse warden and watch me tidy up. "There," she'd say, "isn't that better?" Honestly, I couldn't say that it was. *Sigh.* The things you have to do to please your parents!

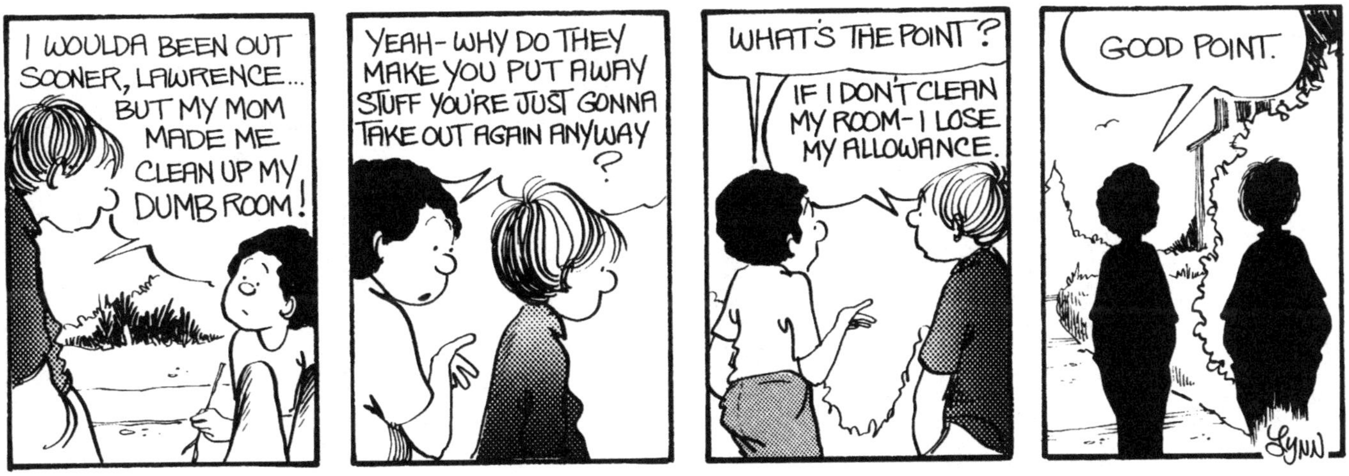
I WOULDA BEEN OUT SOONER, LAWRENCE... BUT MY MOM MADE ME CLEAN UP MY DUMB ROOM!
YEAH- WHY DO THEY MAKE YOU PUT AWAY STUFF YOU'RE JUST GONNA TAKE OUT AGAIN ANYWAY?
WHAT'S THE POINT?
IF I DON'T CLEAN MY ROOM- I LOSE MY ALLOWANCE.
GOOD POINT.
LYNN

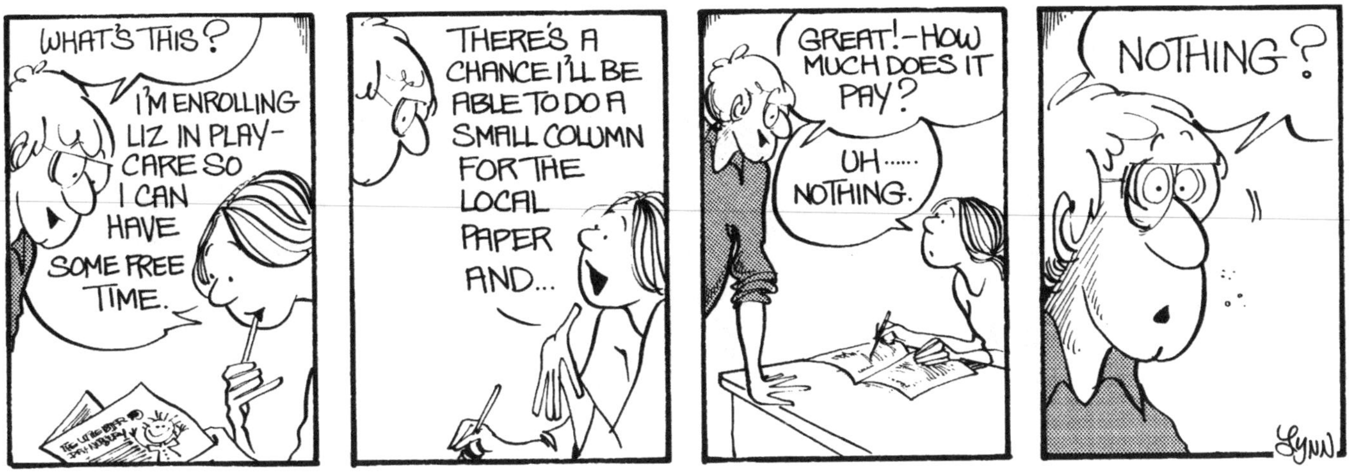
WHAT'S THIS?
I'M ENROLLING LIZ IN PLAY-CARE SO I CAN HAVE SOME FREE TIME.
THERE'S A CHANCE I'LL BE ABLE TO DO A SMALL COLUMN FOR THE LOCAL PAPER AND...
GREAT!-HOW MUCH DOES IT PAY?
UH...... NOTHING.
NOTHING?
LYNN

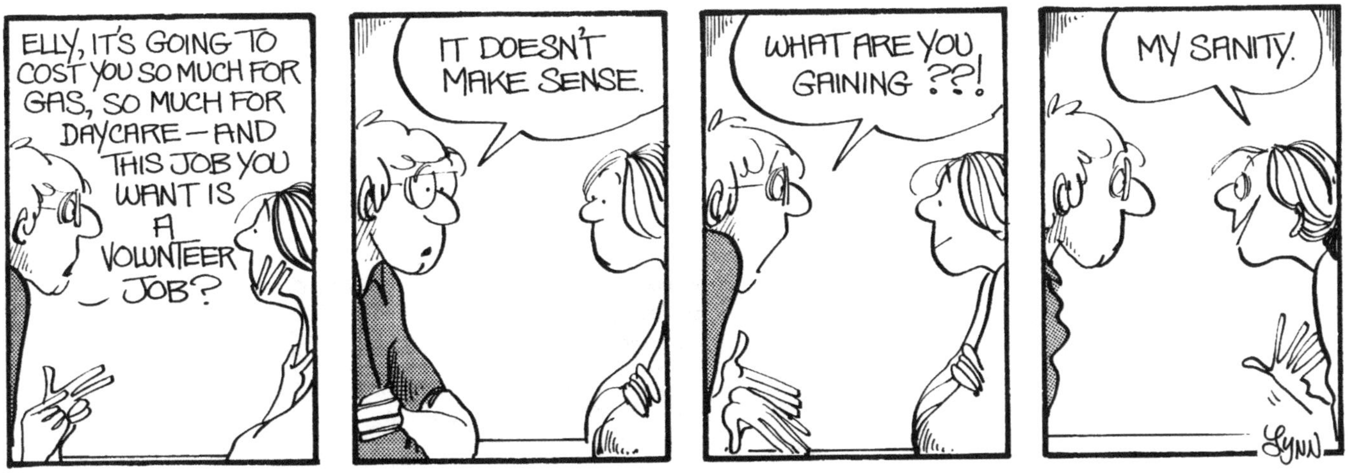
ELLY, IT'S GOING TO COST YOU SO MUCH FOR GAS, SO MUCH FOR DAYCARE—AND THIS JOB YOU WANT IS A VOLUNTEER JOB?
IT DOESN'T MAKE SENSE.
WHAT ARE YOU GAINING??!
MY SANITY.
LYNN

It's important for young artists to see their work published. In the early days, I volunteered a lot. I did posters, bookmarks, and signs for the library. I learned about borders and lettering, and ways to get the most from two plates on the press. It was an opportunity to learn and to make up a good folio. When I hear people complain that they have to volunteer, I remember my dad saying, "You pay for an education, don't you?" Well, this was an education, and I was getting it for free!

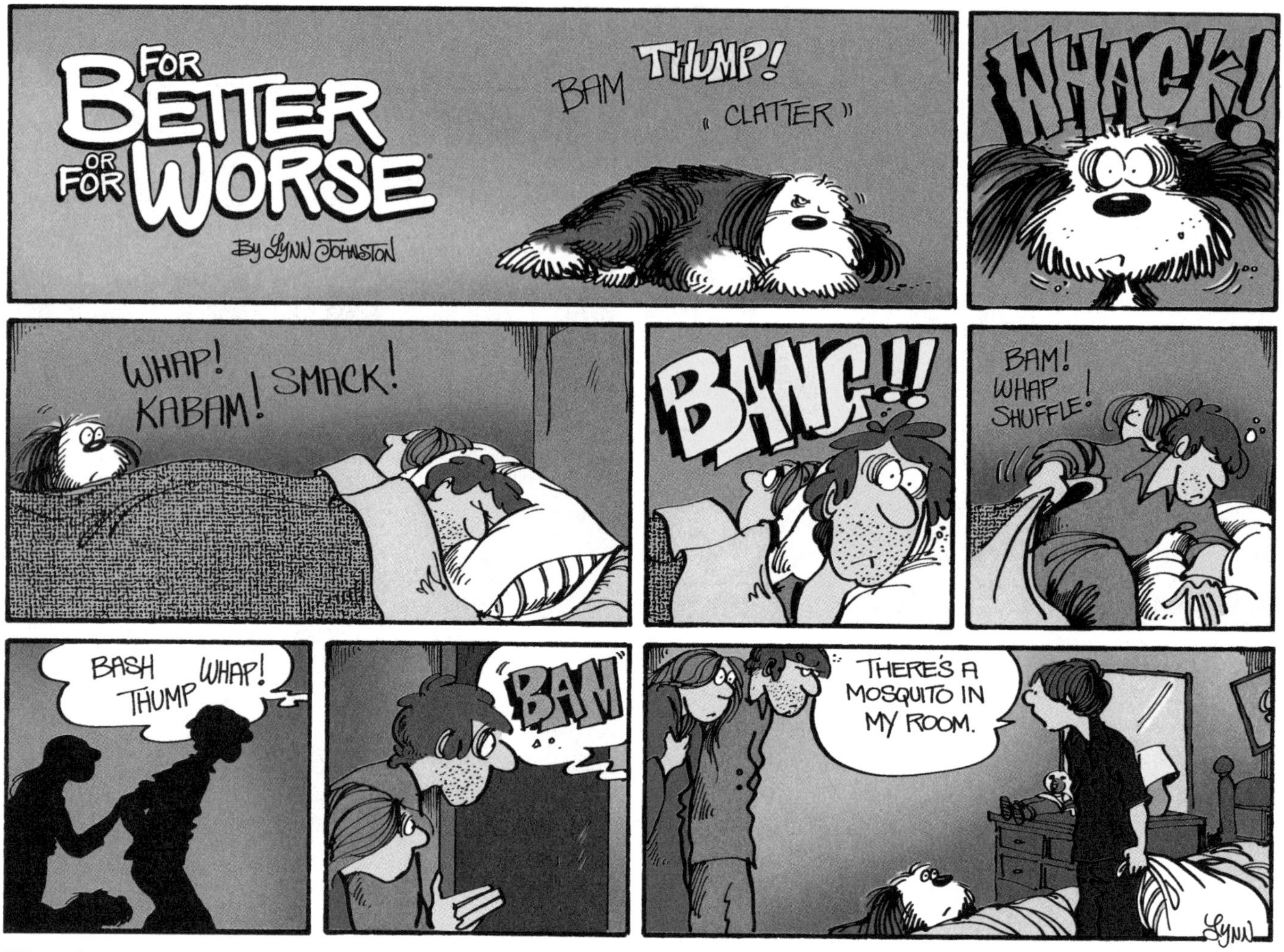
FOR BETTER OR FOR WORSE
By Lynn Johnston
BAM THUMP!
"CLATTER"
WHACK!
WHAP! KABAM! SMACK!
BANG!!
BAM! WHAP SHUFFLE!
BASH THUMP WHAP!
BAM
THERE'S A MOSQUITO IN MY ROOM.
Lynn

When I was married, a mosquito in the room meant a 50 percent chance of being bitten, and I could sleep quite comfortably. When I was a kid, however, the high-pitched whine of a hungry insect drove me nuts. I'd turn on the light and take whatever time it required to hunt it down and do it in. I considered myself to be an excellent sniper. I'd wait for however long it took for the prey to appear and SMACKKK!!! I won. I fairly ruled the summer night, until my brother showed me an article that said, statistically, we eat at least three spiders in our lifetime — they crawl into our open mouths while sleeping. AAAAAUGH!!!!!!

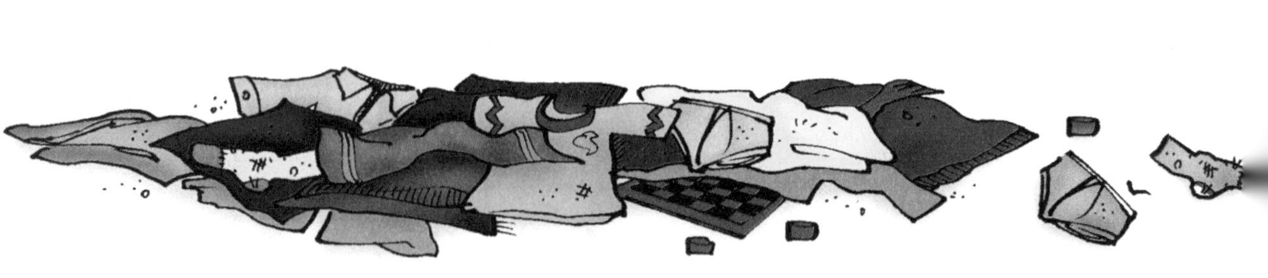

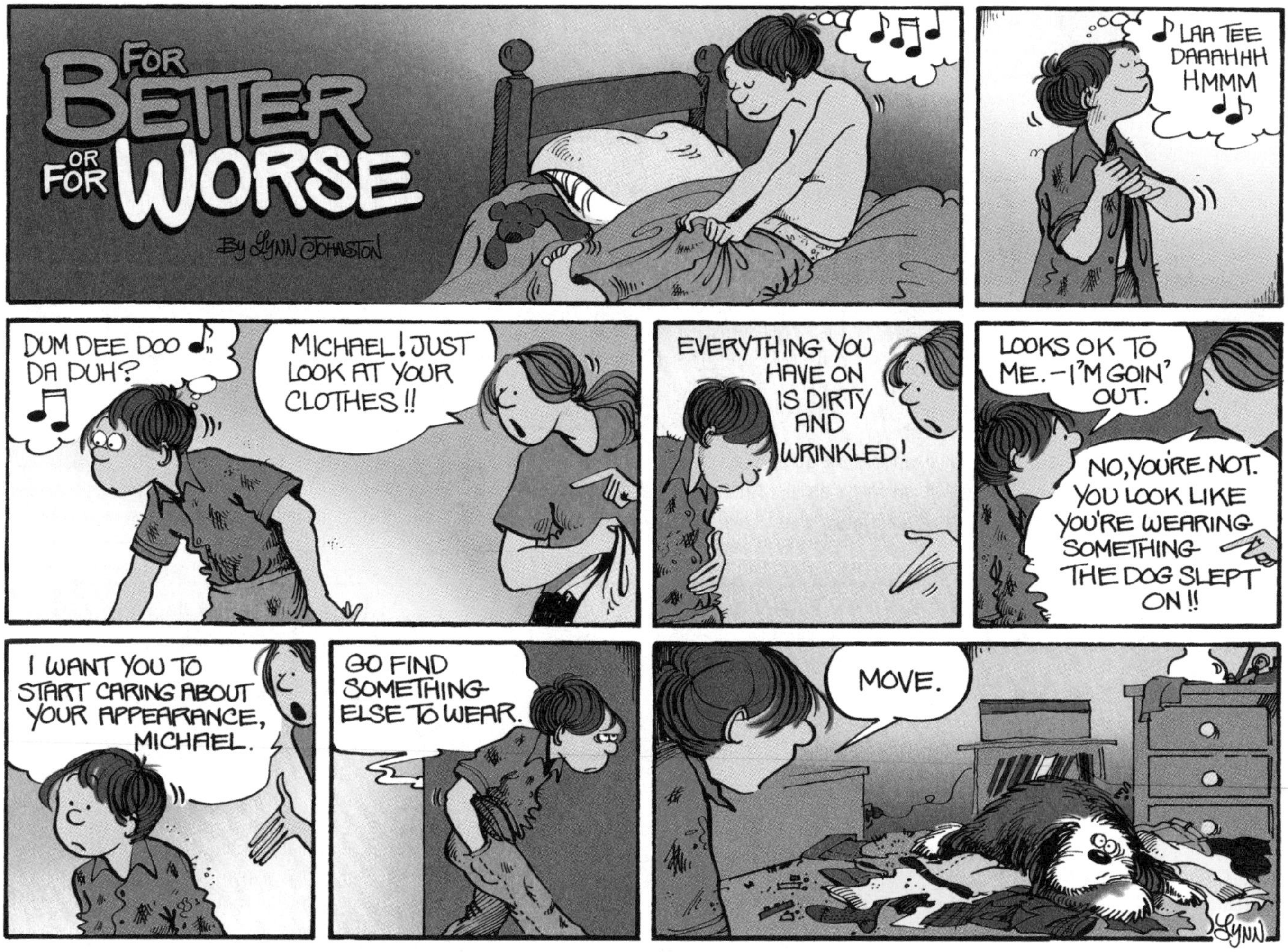
FOR BETTER OR FOR WORSE
By Lynn Johnston
LAA TEE DAAAHHH HMMM
DUM DEE DOO DA DUH?
MICHAEL! JUST LOOK AT YOUR CLOTHES !!
EVERYTHING YOU HAVE ON IS DIRTY AND WRINKLED!
LOOKS OK TO ME. - I'M GOIN' OUT.
NO, YOU'RE NOT. YOU LOOK LIKE YOU'RE WEARING SOMETHING THE DOG SLEPT ON !!
I WANT YOU TO START CARING ABOUT YOUR APPEARANCE, MICHAEL.
GO FIND SOMETHING ELSE TO WEAR.
MOVE.
Lynn

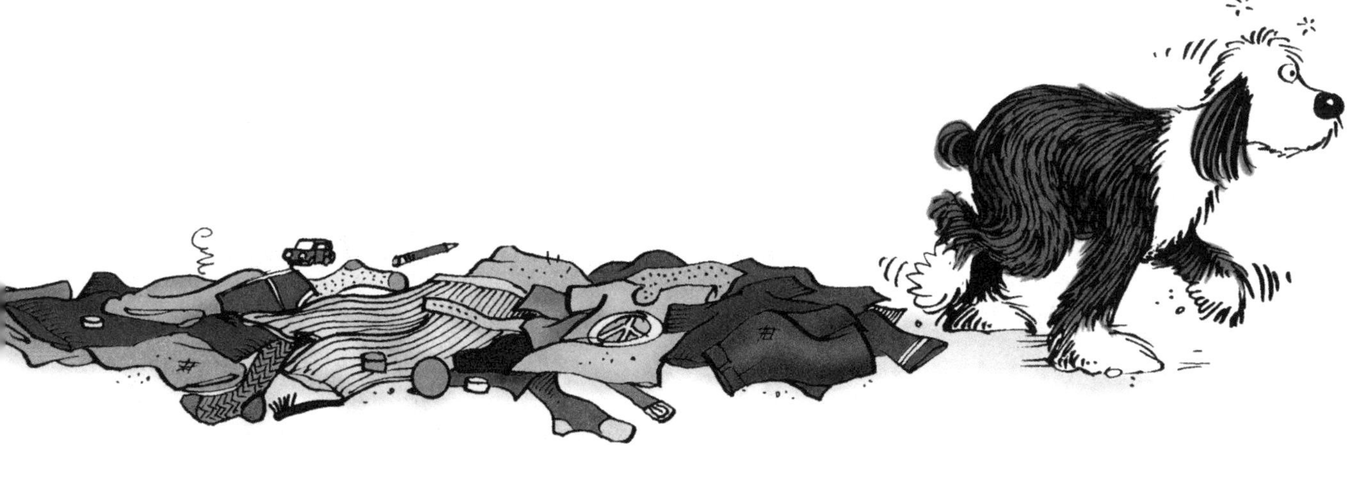

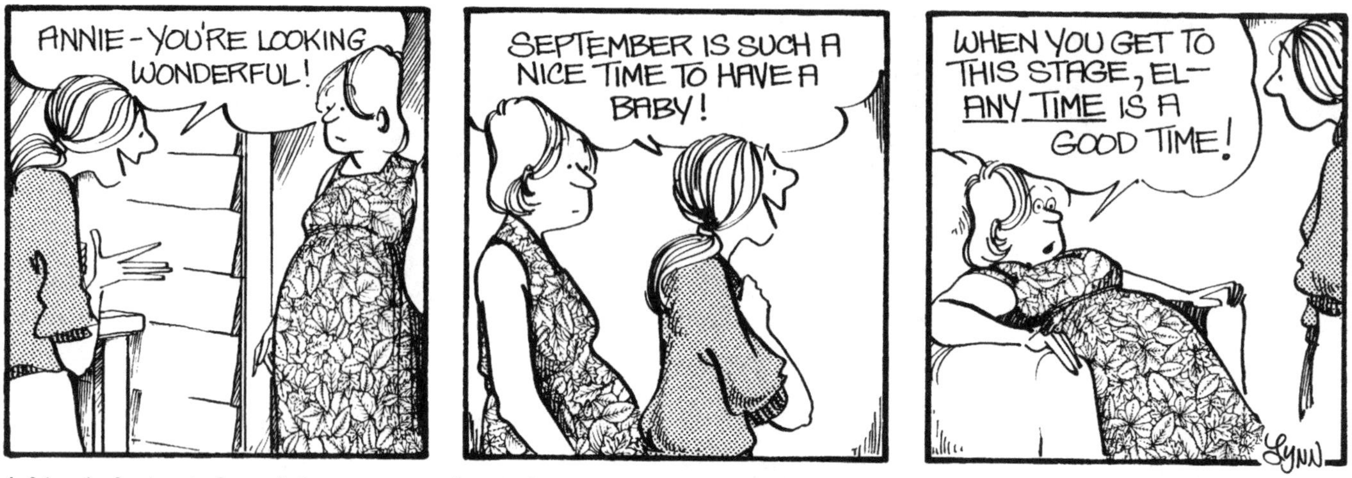
ANNIE - YOU'RE LOOKING WONDERFUL!
SEPTEMBER IS SUCH A NICE TIME TO HAVE A BABY!
WHEN YOU GET TO THIS STAGE, EL- ANY TIME IS A GOOD TIME!
LYNN

A friend of mine in Lynn Lake was expecting at the same time as Annie was, and her input was priceless. I could capture the way she walked and shuffled in slippers as her feet swelled. I watched her shape expand in all directions. She was more than happy to play a role in my research and, even though I remembered going through it myself, having another mom to talk to made all the difference.

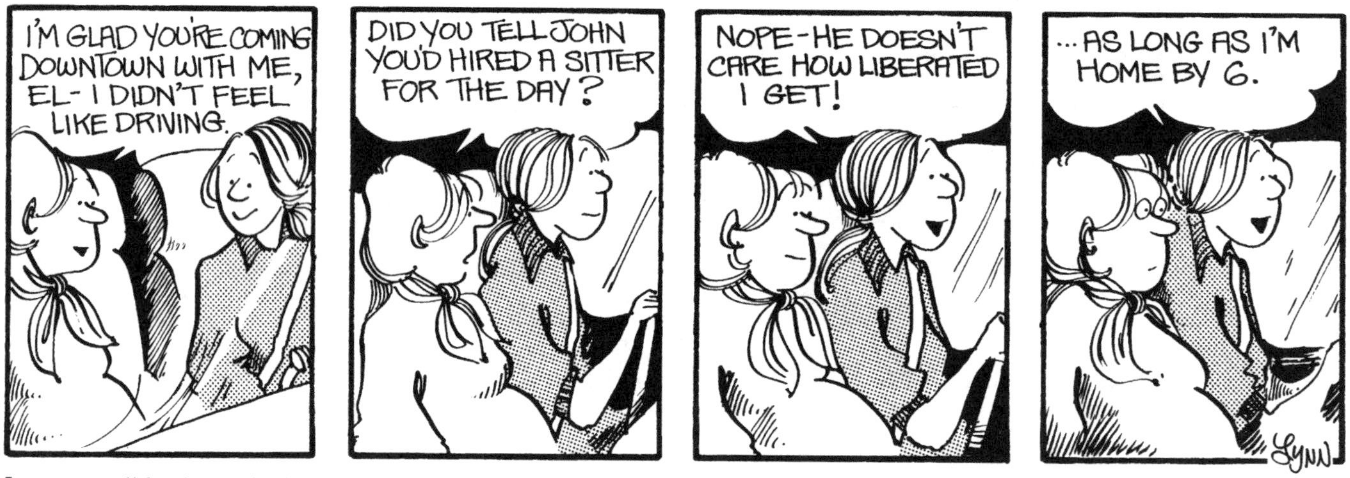
I'M GLAD YOU'RE COMING DOWNTOWN WITH ME, EL- I DIDN'T FEEL LIKE DRIVING.
DID YOU TELL JOHN YOU'D HIRED A SITTER FOR THE DAY?
NOPE-HE DOESN'T CARE HOW LIBERATED I GET!
...AS LONG AS I'M HOME BY 6.
LYNN

I ran a small business, had my own income, and made my own decisions, but I wanted Elly to be more like the person I might have been. I loaded her with some of the baggage that I might have carried, and made her a bit pathetic at times. Maybe it was an effort to separate her from me — or maybe there was something else. I don't know, but that's the way it was!

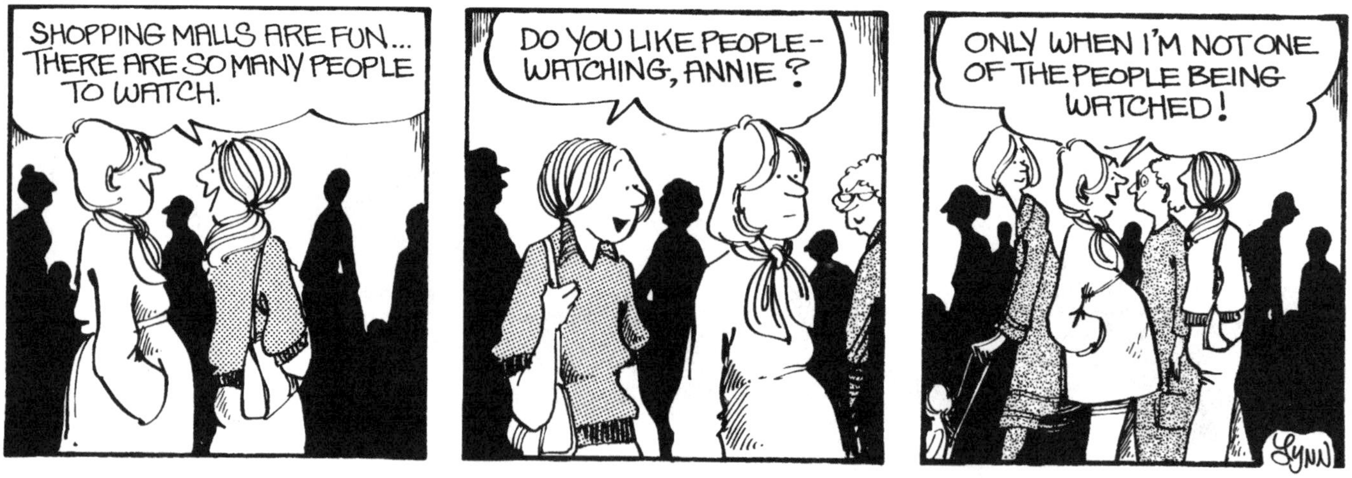
SHOPPING MALLS ARE FUN... THERE ARE SO MANY PEOPLE TO WATCH.
DO YOU LIKE PEOPLE-WATCHING, ANNIE?
ONLY WHEN I'M NOT ONE OF THE PEOPLE BEING WATCHED!
LYNN

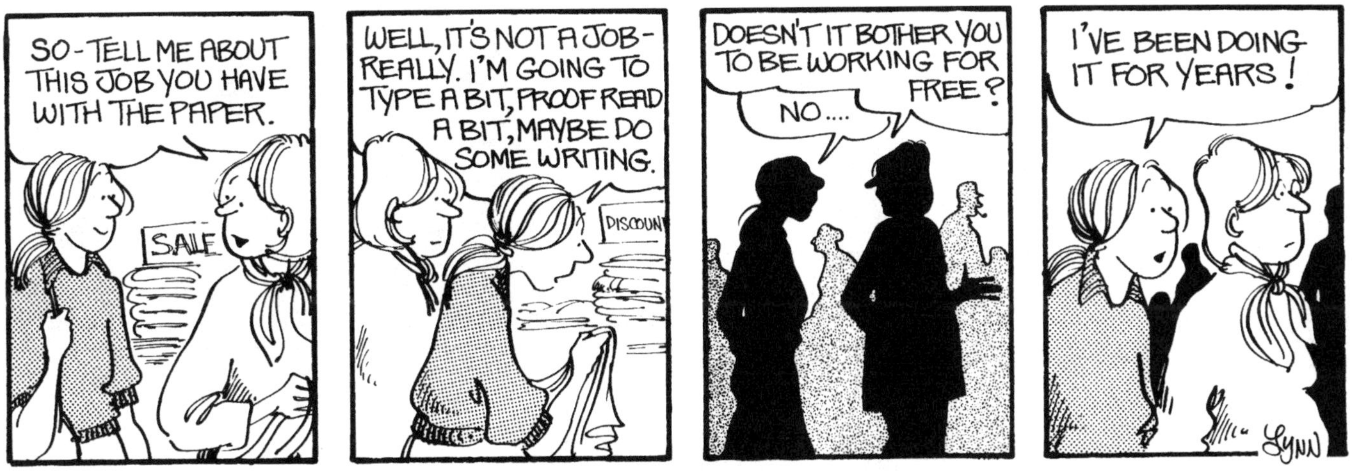
SO-TELL ME ABOUT THIS JOB YOU HAVE WITH THE PAPER.
WELL, IT'S NOT A JOB-REALLY. I'M GOING TO TYPE A BIT, PROOF READ A BIT, MAYBE DO SOME WRITING.
SALE
DISCOUN
DOESN'T IT BOTHER YOU TO BE WORKING FOR FREE?
NO....
I'VE BEEN DOING IT FOR YEARS!
LYNN

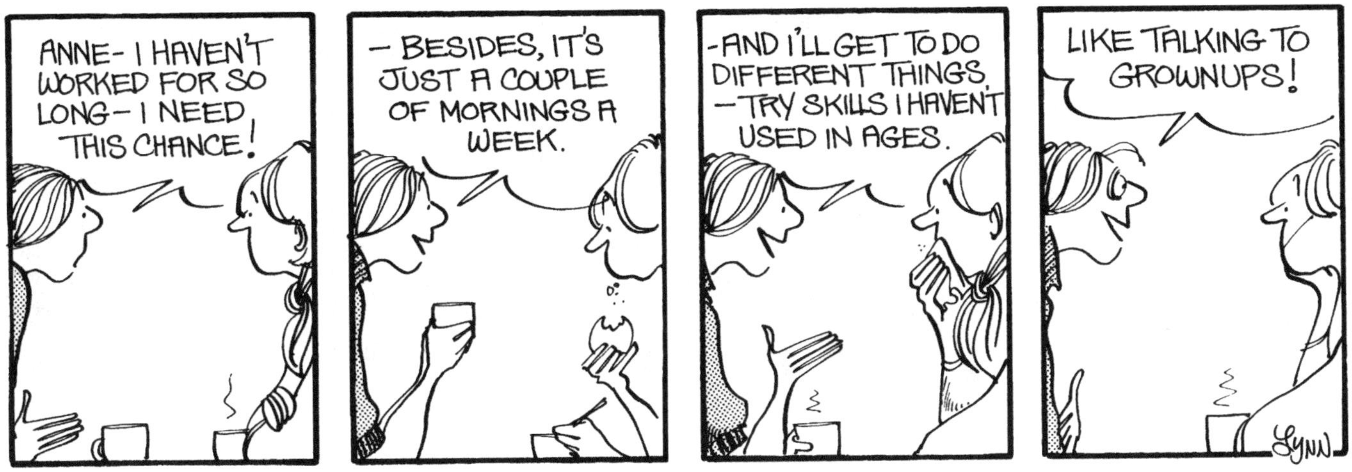
ANNE- I HAVEN'T WORKED FOR SO LONG- I NEED THIS CHANCE!
- BESIDES, IT'S JUST A COUPLE OF MORNINGS A WEEK.
-AND I'LL GET TO DO DIFFERENT THINGS, -TRY SKILLS I HAVEN'T USED IN AGES.
LIKE TALKING TO GROWNUPS!
LYNN

I loved my children, but talking to toddlers all day fried my mind. I so desperately needed the company of grown-ups, I'd go shopping just so I could exchange a few sentences that didn't contain "poo-poo" or "don't wanna!!" If Elly had a chance to work, even for free a couple of times a week, I figured she'd take it, even if it meant paying someone else to take Elizabeth. A mom's gotta do what a mom's gotta do.

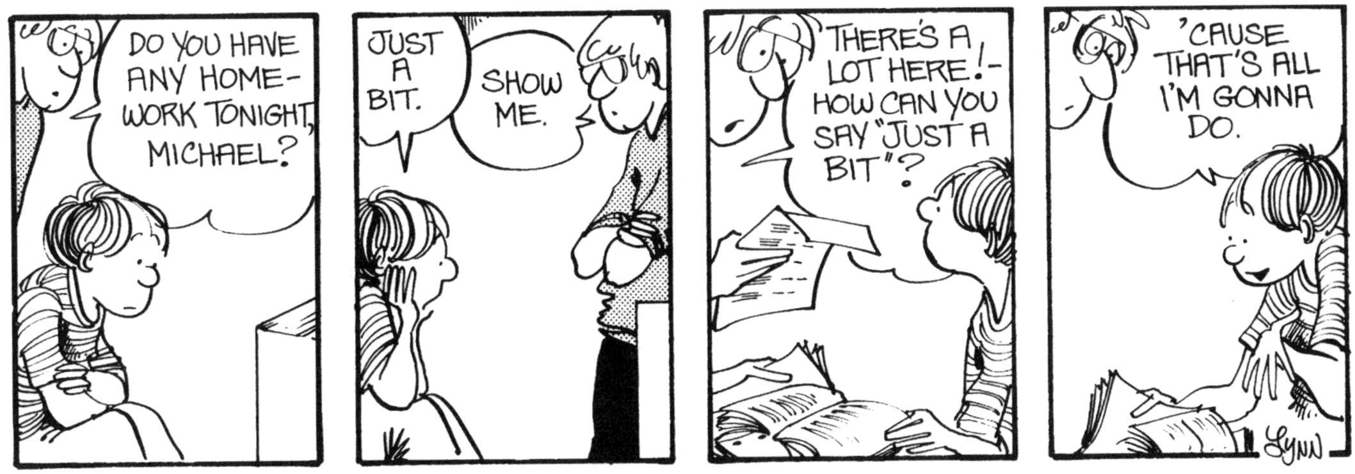
DO YOU HAVE ANY HOME-WORK TONIGHT, MICHAEL?
JUST A BIT.
SHOW ME.
THERE'S A LOT HERE!- HOW CAN YOU SAY "JUST A BIT"?
'CAUSE THAT'S ALL I'M GONNA DO.
LYNN

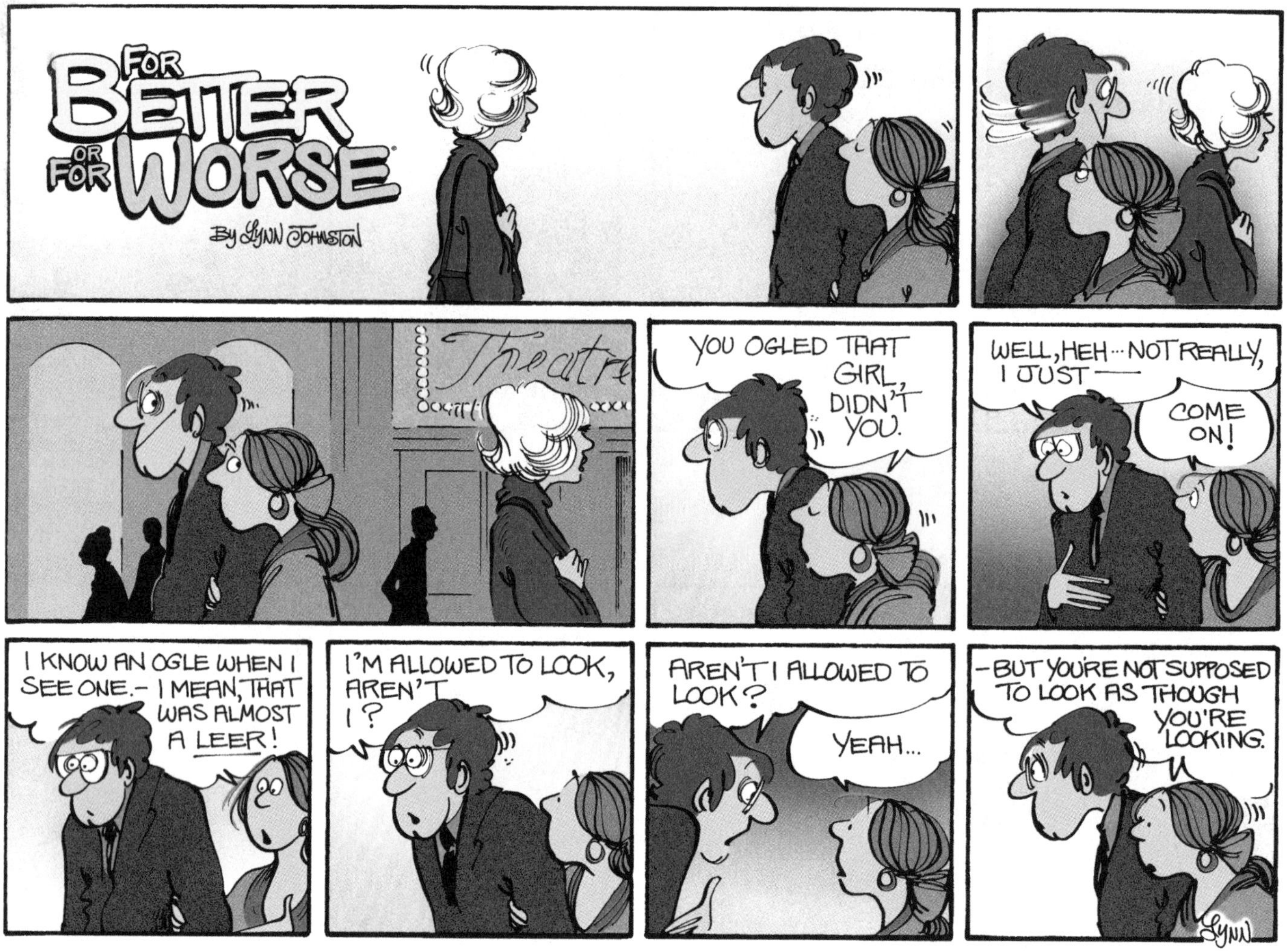
FOR BETTER OR FOR WORSE
BY LYNN JOHNSTON
Theatre
YOU OGLED THAT GIRL, DIDN'T YOU.
WELL, HEH... NOT REALLY, I JUST —
COME ON!
I KNOW AN OGLE WHEN I SEE ONE.– I MEAN, THAT WAS ALMOST A LEER!
I'M ALLOWED TO LOOK, AREN'T I?
AREN'T I ALLOWED TO LOOK?
YEAH...
–BUT YOU'RE NOT SUPPOSED TO LOOK AS THOUGH YOU'RE LOOKING.
LYNN

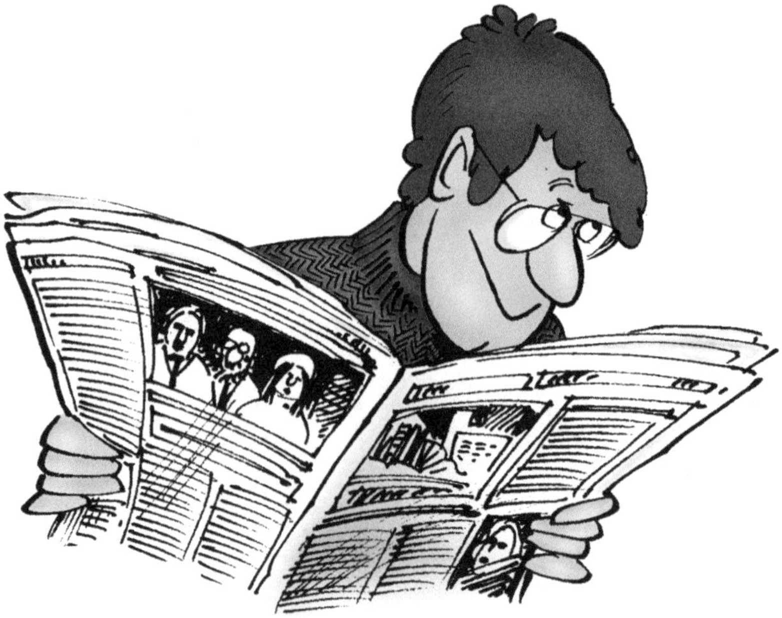

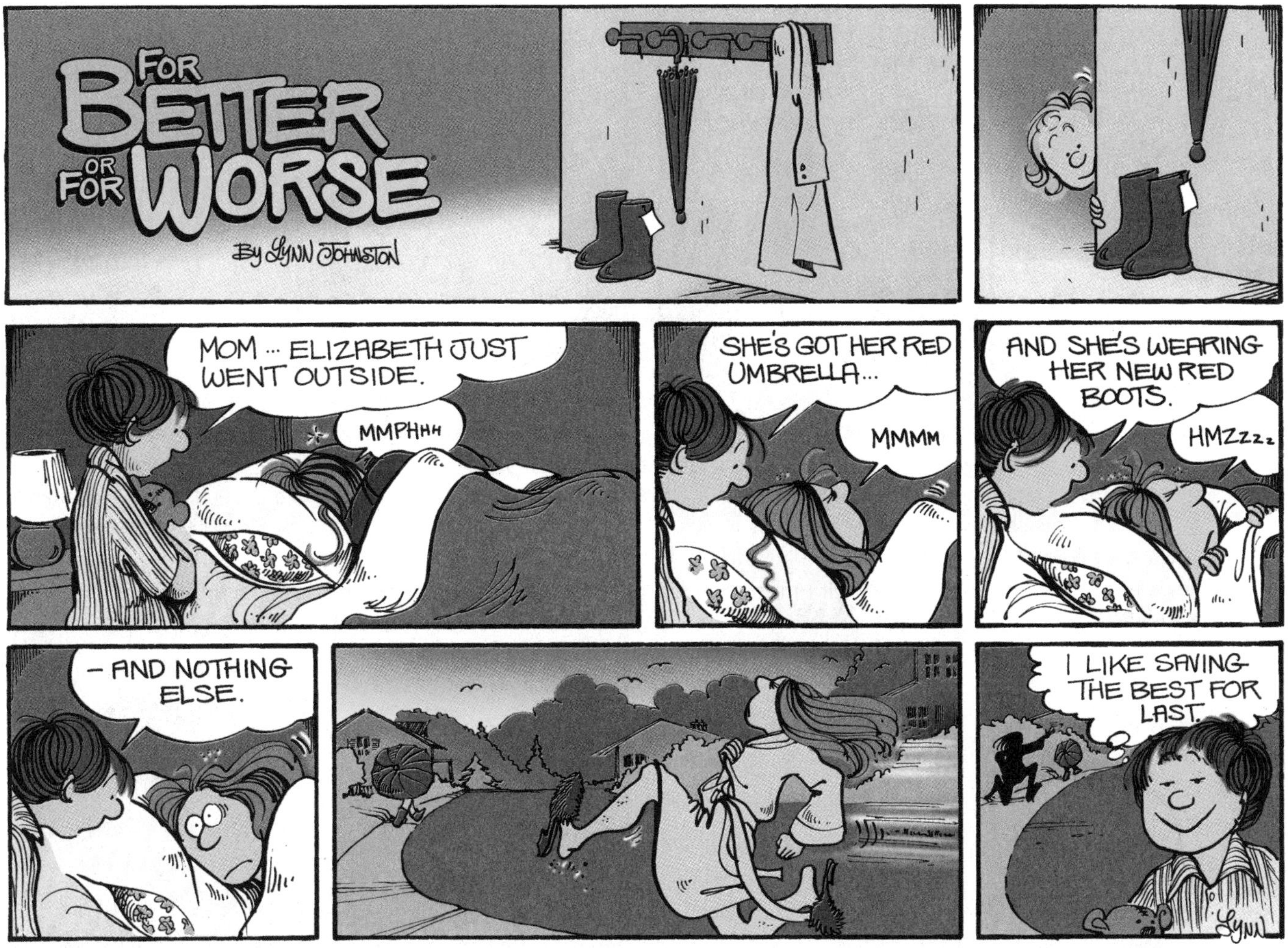
FOR BETTER OR FOR WORSE
By Lynn Johnston
MOM ... ELIZABETH JUST WENT OUTSIDE.
MMPHHH
SHE'S GOT HER RED UMBRELLA...
MMMM
AND SHE'S WEARING HER NEW RED BOOTS.
HMZzzz
- AND NOTHING ELSE.
I LIKE SAVING THE BEST FOR LAST.
LYNN

This has to be one of my favourite Sunday pages. Aaron often came into my room early in the morning and talked to me while I was half asleep. Katie had no reservations about running outside in the buff. Combine these two elements, and I had a good gag. I had fun with the illustration — most of all, I loved doing the expressions on the faces of the characters. Facial expressions and body language are as important as the punch line — I erased Michael's sly smile several times before it was right on! Sunday comics like this one were fun to read when they came out in the paper; I would read this strip as if I were a stranger who'd never seen it before. If it made me laugh again, then I knew I had a good one!

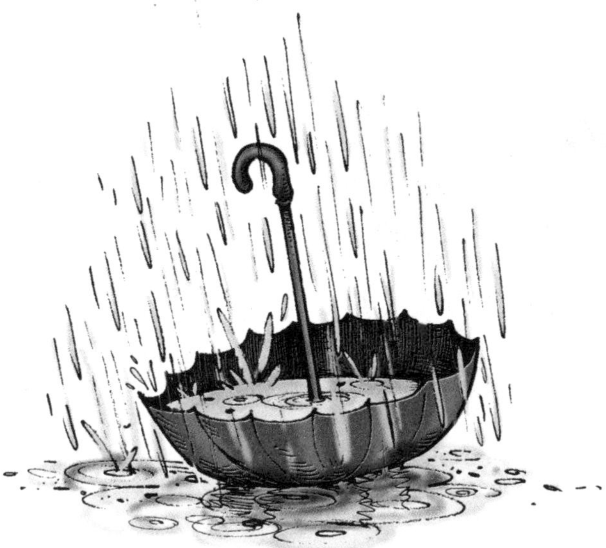

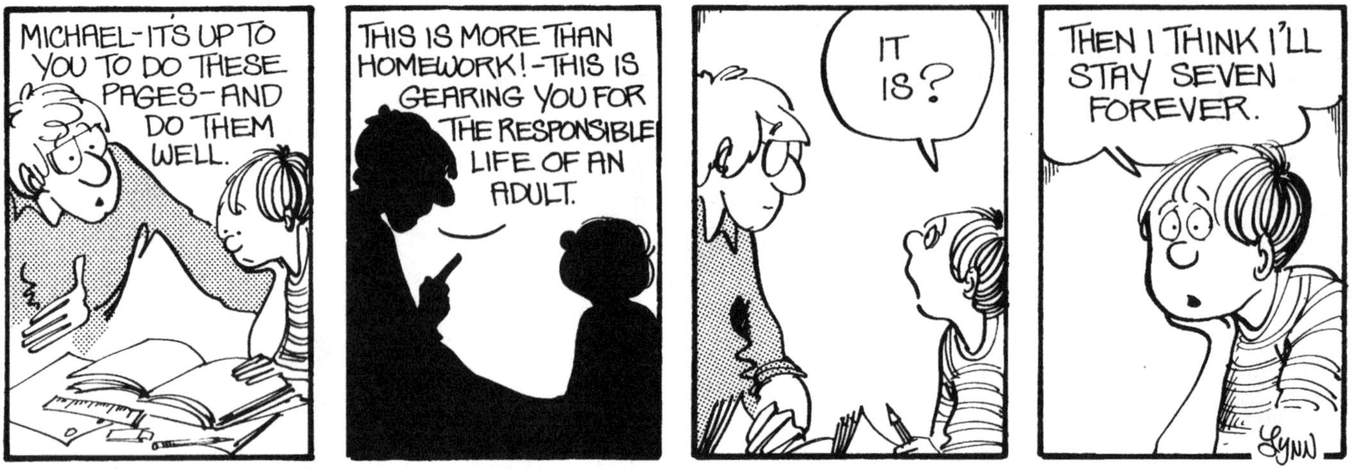
MICHAEL-IT'S UP TO YOU TO DO THESE PAGES-AND DO THEM WELL.
THIS IS MORE THAN HOMEWORK!-THIS IS GEARING YOU FOR THE RESPONSIBLE LIFE OF AN ADULT.
IT IS?
THEN I THINK I'LL STAY SEVEN FOREVER.
Lynn

Homework was a subject that riled us all. If Aaron had something to do for school, there'd be a stalemate right away. He might get out all the equipment. He might even start. But within a few minutes, he'd be miserable. I don't know how many times we sat and did his work with him — lesson by lesson, page by page. When some kids graduate to the next level of their education, their parents should get a promotion, too!

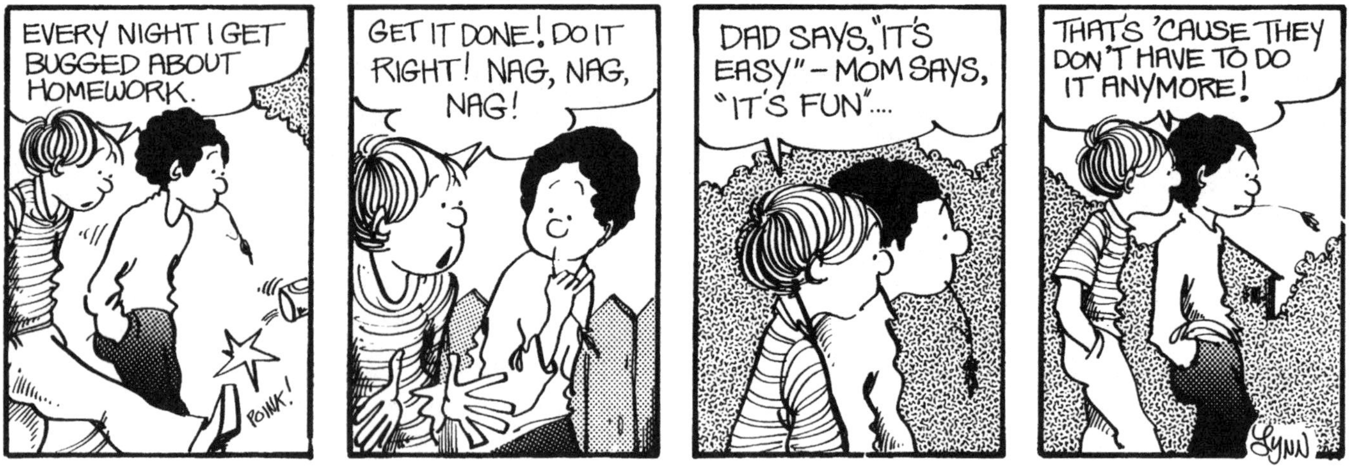
EVERY NIGHT I GET BUGGED ABOUT HOMEWORK.
POINK!
GET IT DONE! DO IT RIGHT! NAG, NAG, NAG!
DAD SAYS, "IT'S EASY" - MOM SAYS, "IT'S FUN"....
THAT'S 'CAUSE THEY DON'T HAVE TO DO IT ANYMORE!
Lynn

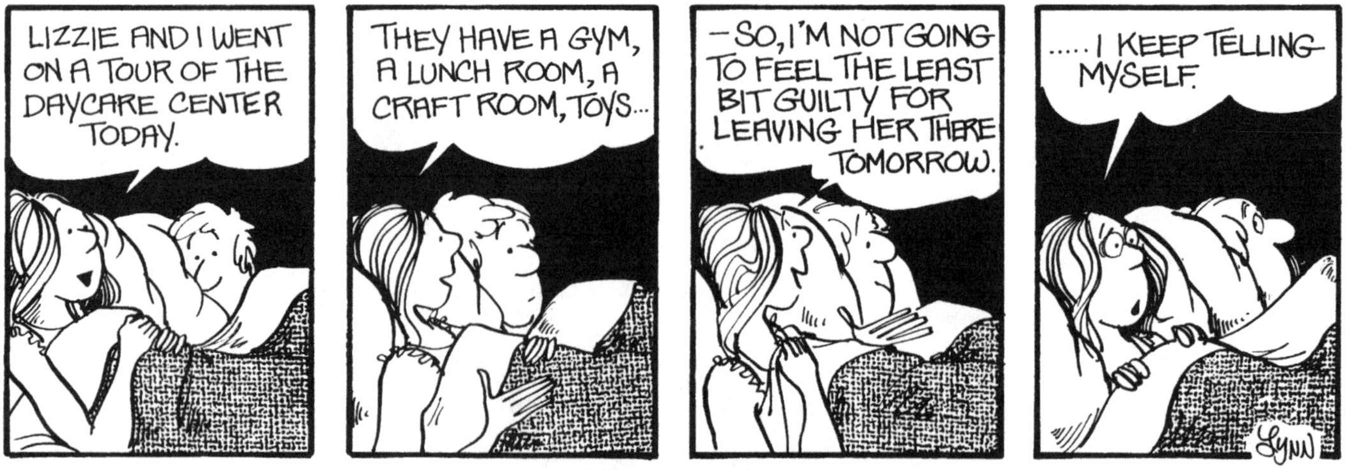
LIZZIE AND I WENT ON A TOUR OF THE DAYCARE CENTER TODAY.
THEY HAVE A GYM, A LUNCH ROOM, A CRAFT ROOM, TOYS...
-SO, I'M NOT GOING TO FEEL THE LEAST BIT GUILTY FOR LEAVING HER THERE TOMORROW.
.....I KEEP TELLING MYSELF.
Lynn

When I couldn't support myself and Aaron as a freelance artist, I accepted a job at Standard Engravers — a packaging company in Hamilton, Ontario. Aaron attended the Dundas, Ontario, daycare, courtesy of the Canadian welfare system, for which I'll be eternally grateful! Before his first full day, we went for an introduction. He was so excited about the toys and the company that he left me immediately and blended in. There was no separation anxiety, and I think I was just a little hurt by that!

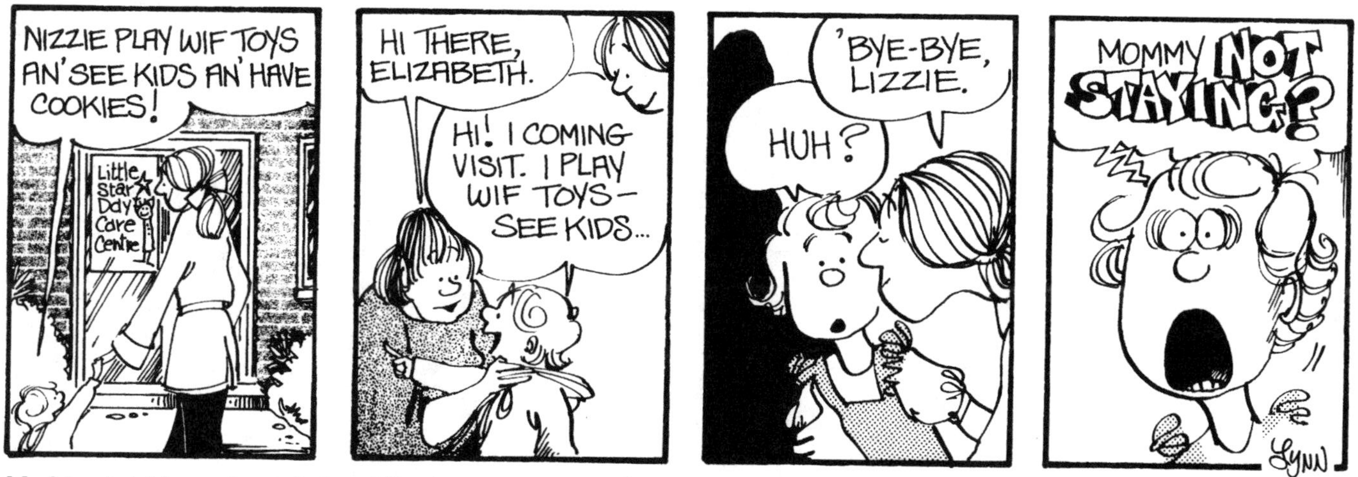
NIZZIE PLAY WIF TOYS AN' SEE KIDS AN' HAVE COOKIES!
Little Star Day Care Centre
HI THERE, ELIZABETH.
HI! I COMING VISIT. I PLAY WIF TOYS— SEE KIDS...
'BYE-BYE, LIZZIE.
HUH?
MOMMY NOT STAYING?
LYNN

My friends told me about their toddlers' reluctance to being left at the daycare centre, but Aaron was a social kid who couldn't wait to get into the stuff and the food and the excitement of new surroundings. Later, when Katie went to a sitter while I worked, she was also happy to have my friend Marian's attention, and never made a fuss. I was lucky!

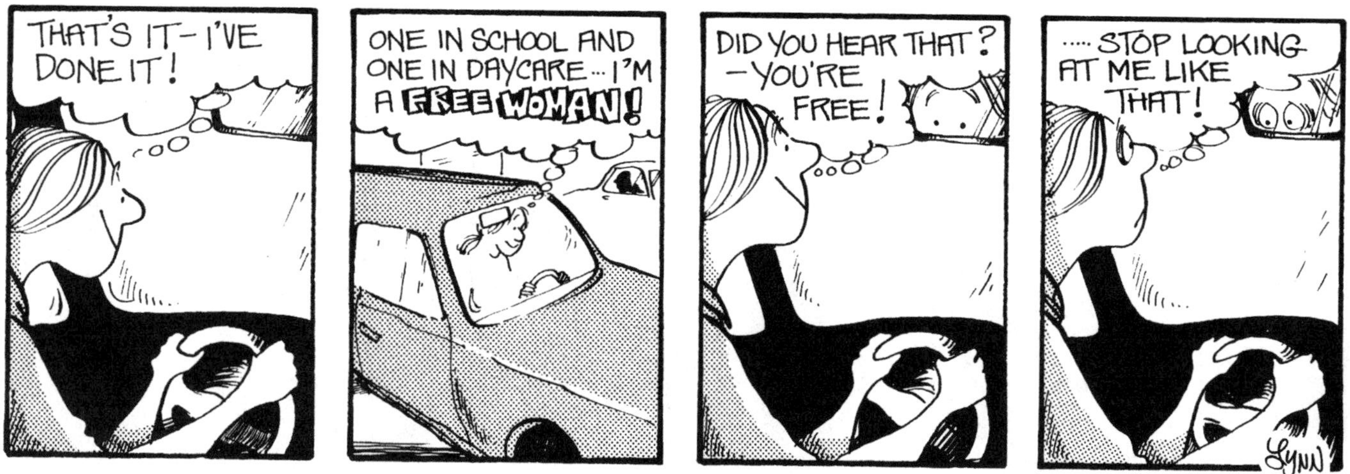
THAT'S IT— I'VE DONE IT!
ONE IN SCHOOL AND ONE IN DAYCARE... I'M A FREE WOMAN!
DID YOU HEAR THAT? —YOU'RE FREE!
..... STOP LOOKING AT ME LIKE THAT!
LYNN

I did not feel guilty for leaving Aaron at the Dundas daycare centre. Not until he was sick! Nothing makes you feel negligent and helpless like a call from the daycare to say your child is sick and asking for you. I was lucky to have an understanding boss. Looking at my reflection in the rearview mirror, I remember thinking, "To heck with all the powers they come up with in the comic books — a REAL superhero would be someone who could be in two places at once!"

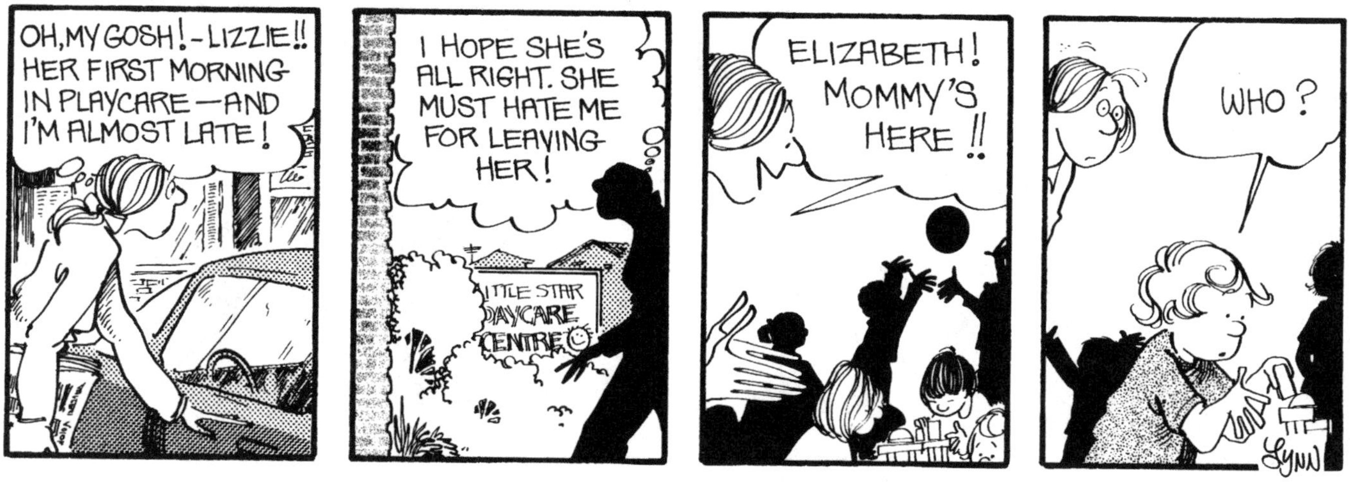
OH, MY GOSH! - LIZZIE!! HER FIRST MORNING IN PLAYCARE—AND I'M ALMOST LATE!
I HOPE SHE'S ALL RIGHT. SHE MUST HATE ME FOR LEAVING HER!
LITTLE STAR DAYCARE CENTRE
ELIZABETH! MOMMY'S HERE!!
WHO?
LYNN

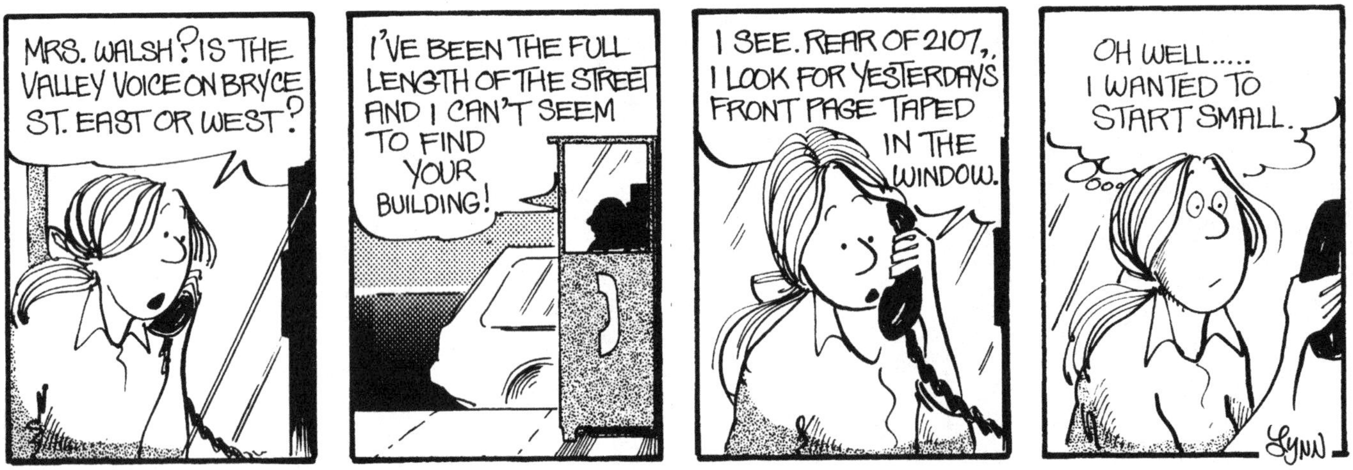
MRS. WALSH? IS THE VALLEY VOICE ON BRYCE ST. EAST OR WEST?
I'VE BEEN THE FULL LENGTH OF THE STREET AND I CAN'T SEEM TO FIND YOUR BUILDING!
I SEE. REAR OF 2107,, I LOOK FOR YESTERDAYS FRONT PAGE TAPED IN THE WINDOW.
OH WELL..... I WANTED TO START SMALL.
Lynn

Dundas is a small suburb of Hamilton, Ontario, where I lived for about four years. I would go to the *Dundas Valley Journal* and see if they needed any cartoons and, eventually, they bought a weekly panel from me for $10 apiece. Elly and her quest for a column in her local paper was based on this.

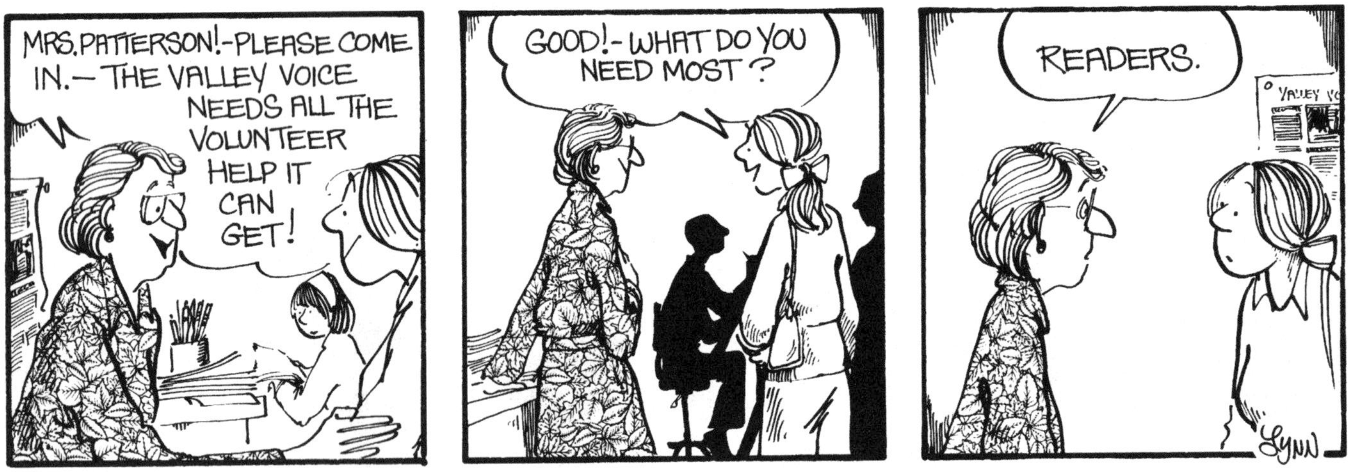
MRS. PATTERSON! - PLEASE COME IN. — THE VALLEY VOICE NEEDS ALL THE VOLUNTEER HELP IT CAN GET!
GOOD! - WHAT DO YOU NEED MOST?
READERS.
Lynn

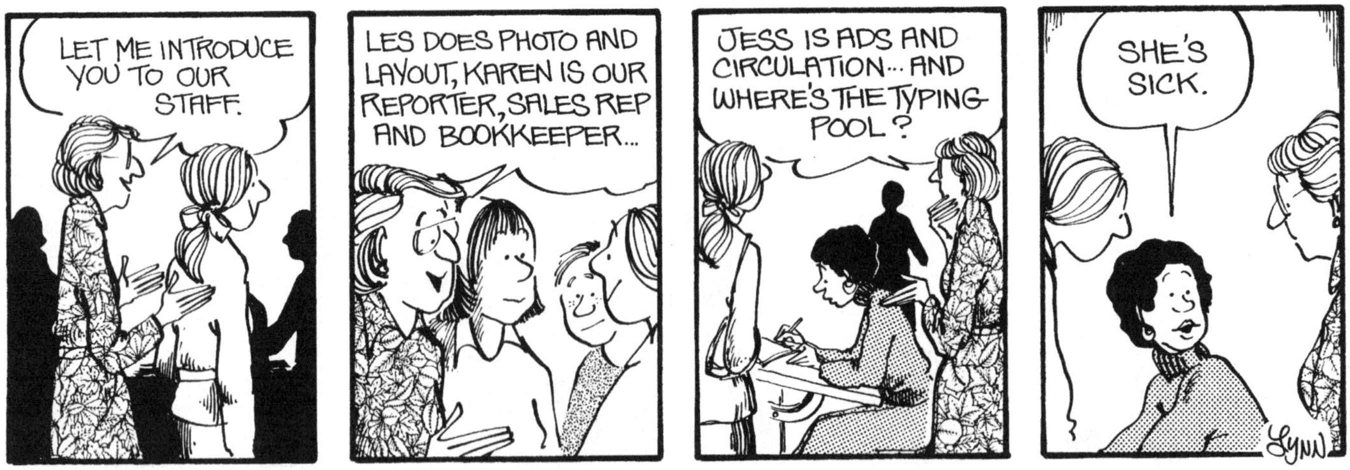
LET ME INTRODUCE YOU TO OUR STAFF.
LES DOES PHOTO AND LAYOUT, KAREN IS OUR REPORTER, SALES REP AND BOOKKEEPER...
JESS IS ADS AND CIRCULATION... AND WHERE'S THE TYPING POOL?
SHE'S SICK.
Lynn

The *Dundas Valley Journal* was a small-town newspaper in every way; a great place to begin if you wanted to get to know and work in each facet of the business! The *DVJ* was a popular weekly rag, but despite strong local support, the publisher had a hard time staying in the black and white!

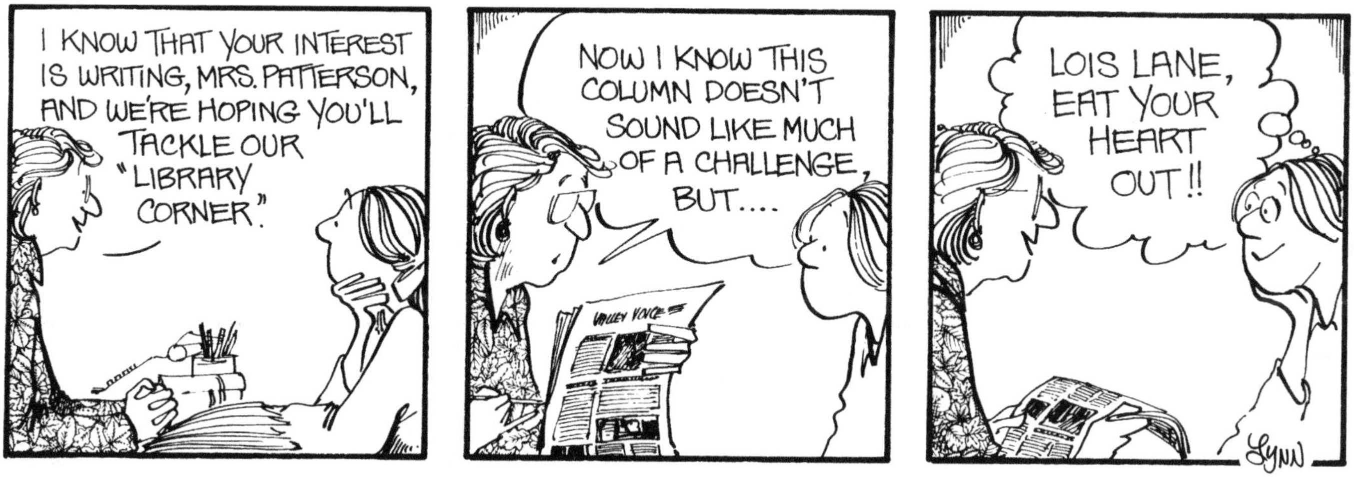
I KNOW THAT YOUR INTEREST IS WRITING, MRS. PATTERSON, AND WE'RE HOPING YOU'LL TACKLE OUR "LIBRARY CORNER."
NOW I KNOW THIS COLUMN DOESN'T SOUND LIKE MUCH OF A CHALLENGE, BUT....
VALLEY VOICE
LOIS LANE, EAT YOUR HEART OUT!!
LYNN

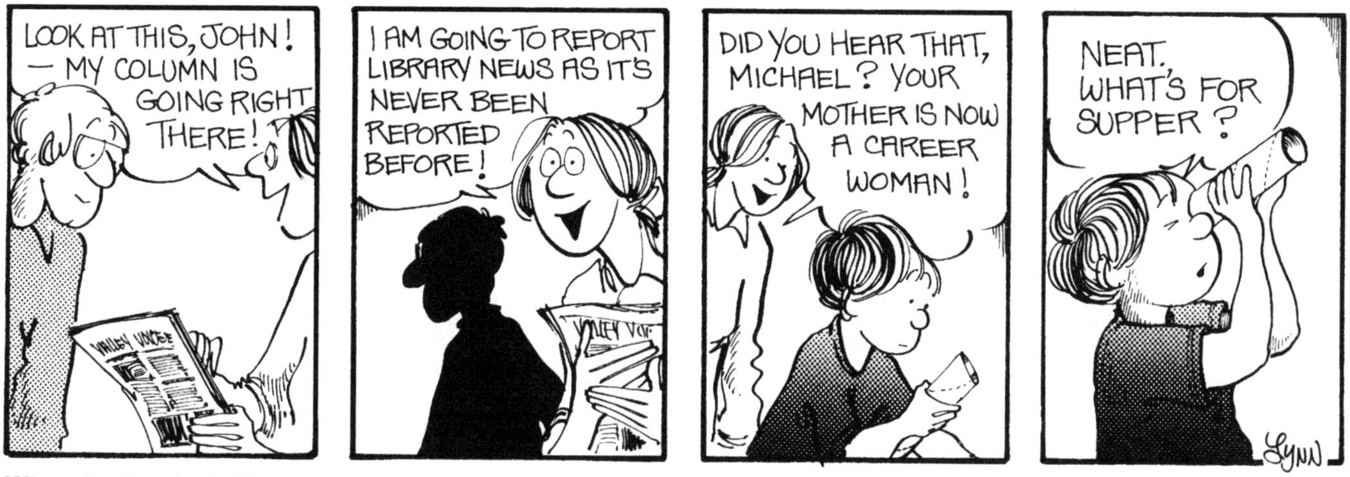
LOOK AT THIS, JOHN! — MY COLUMN IS GOING RIGHT THERE!
VALLEY VOICE
I AM GOING TO REPORT LIBRARY NEWS AS IT'S NEVER BEEN REPORTED BEFORE!
DID YOU HEAR THAT, MICHAEL? YOUR MOTHER IS NOW A CAREER WOMAN!
NEAT. WHAT'S FOR SUPPER?
LYNN

When the *Dundas Valley Journal* accepted my first cartoons, I was thrilled. To see my work in print in a local paper was wonderful. I was working at the packaging company in town, and freelancing for McMaster University, as well. As far as an education in graphic arts goes, I was doing it all.

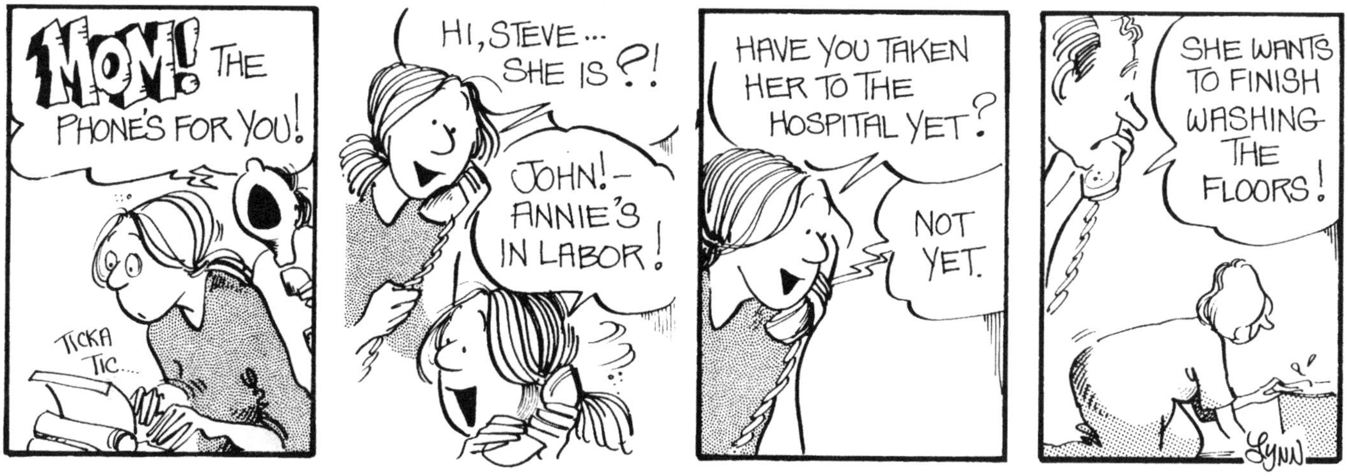
MOM! THE PHONE'S FOR YOU!
TICKA TIC....
HI, STEVE... SHE IS?!
JOHN! – ANNIE'S IN LABOR!
HAVE YOU TAKEN HER TO THE HOSPITAL YET?
NOT YET.
SHE WANTS TO FINISH WASHING THE FLOORS!
LYNN

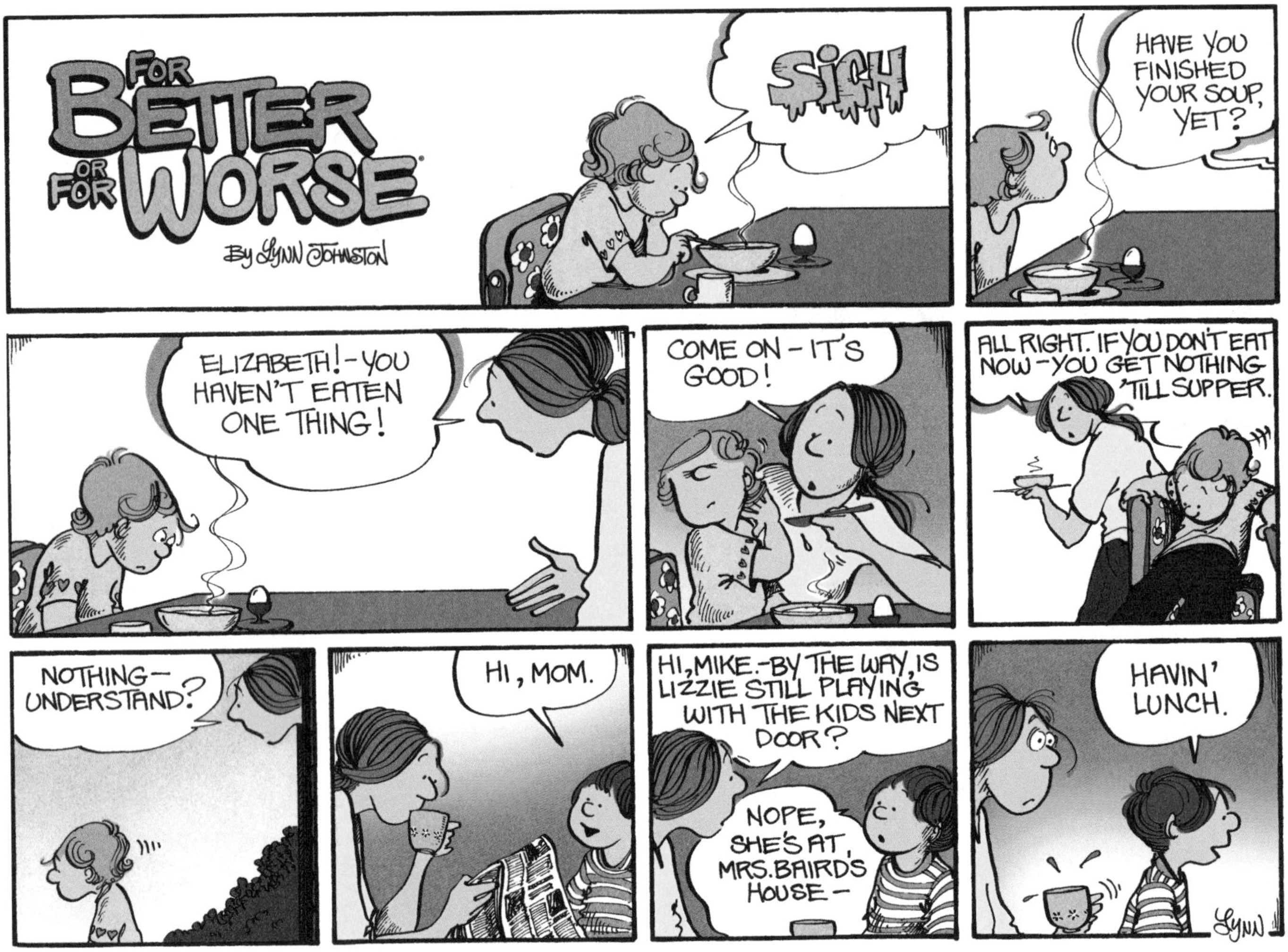
FOR BETTER OR FOR WORSE
BY LYNN JOHNSTON
SIGH
HAVE YOU FINISHED YOUR SOUP, YET?
ELIZABETH! - YOU HAVEN'T EATEN ONE THING!
COME ON - IT'S GOOD!
ALL RIGHT. IF YOU DON'T EAT NOW - YOU GET NOTHING 'TILL SUPPER.
NOTHING - UNDERSTAND?
HI, MOM.
HI, MIKE. - BY THE WAY, IS LIZZIE STILL PLAYING WITH THE KIDS NEXT DOOR?
NOPE, SHE'S AT MRS. BAIRD'S HOUSE -
HAVIN' LUNCH.
LYNN

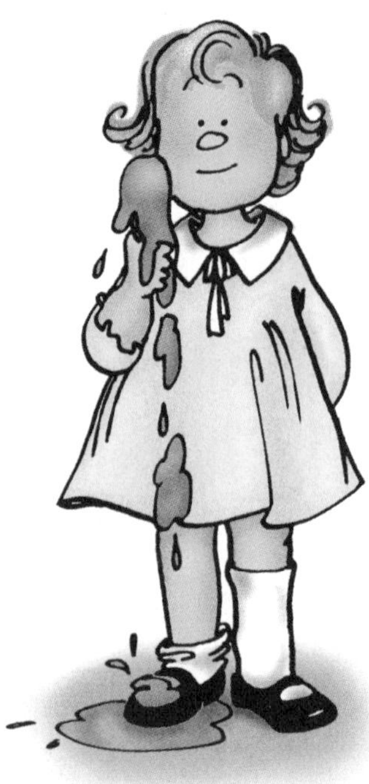

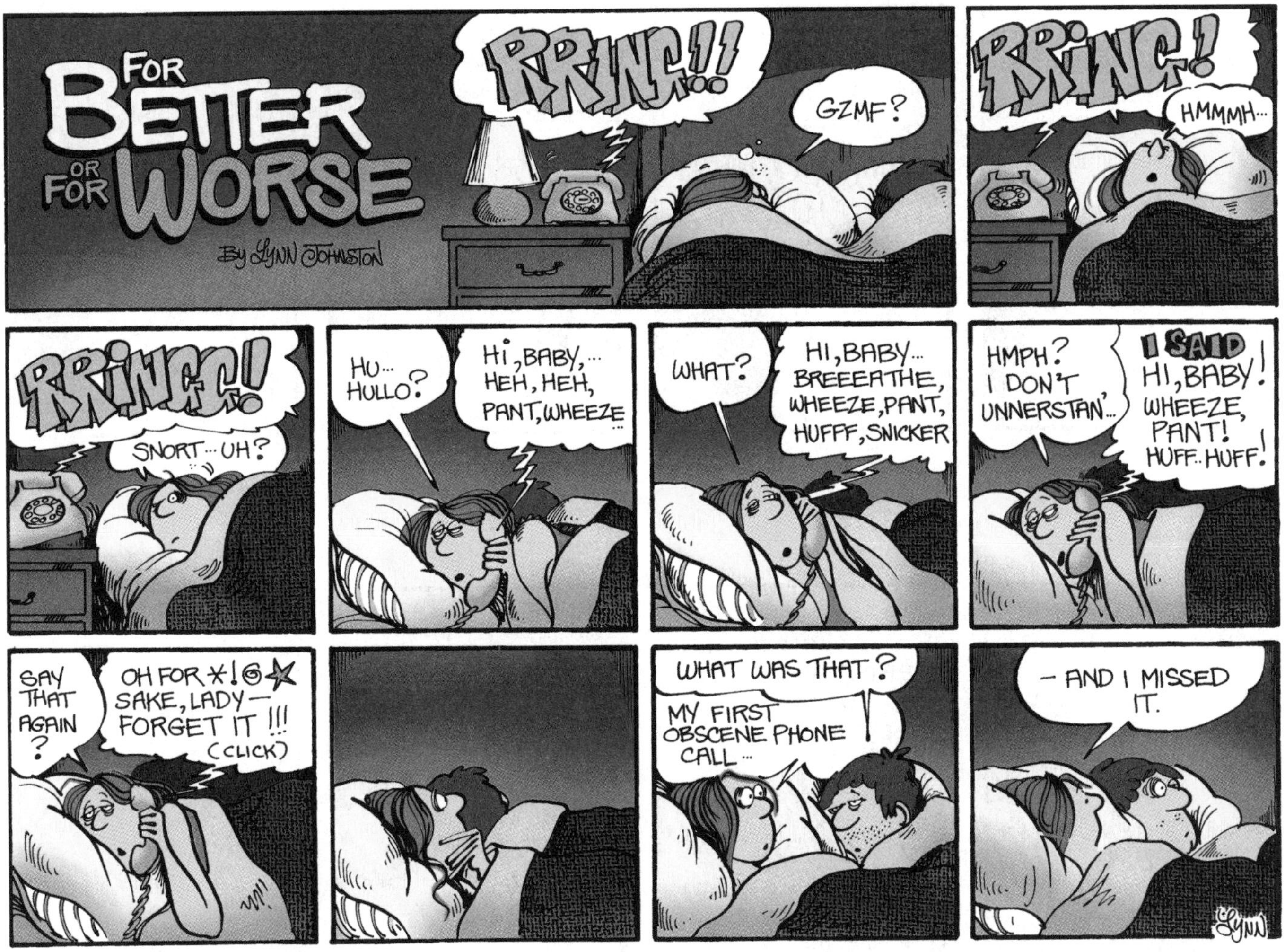
FOR BETTER OR FOR WORSE
BY LYNN JOHNSTON
RRING!!!
GZMF?
RRING!
HMMMH...
RRINGG!
SNORT...UH?
HU... HULLO?
HI, BABY,... HEH, HEH, PANT, WHEEZE...
WHAT?
HI, BABY... BREEEATHE, WHEEZE, PANT, HUFFF, SNICKER
HMPH? I DON'T UNNERSTAN'...
I SAID HI, BABY! WHEEZE, PANT! HUFF..HUFF!
SAY THAT AGAIN?
OH FOR *!@★ SAKE, LADY— FORGET IT !!! (CLICK)
WHAT WAS THAT?
MY FIRST OBSCENE PHONE CALL...
—AND I MISSED IT.
LYNN

We were living in a log house and having renovations done. A number of workmen, strangers to me, were coming and going at the time. One night the phone rang. The receiver was on my side of the bed. I answered, expecting it to be the dental "on call" service, but a man's voice said something I couldn't quite understand. I had been in a deep sleep, and wasn't prepared for a conversation. "What??" I asked. He repeated whatever it was, but I still couldn't understand. He said something vaguely suggestive, but I wasn't able to pick up the thread. He eventually gave up, and asked if I knew who it was. I said I did not, and he seemed surprised. At this point, I just wanted to go back to sleep, but he asked again if I recognized his voice, and I said I didn't. Satisfied that he'd remain unknown, he hung up.

The next day I was convinced it had been one of the guys who was working on the house. One, in particular, was a bit of a wild card, and I wondered if it had been him. It amazed me to think how vulnerable and anxious I felt, even though the call had been clumsy and short. Somebody was "watching" me in an unhealthy way, and it made me nervous and wary until the project was over and the strangers were gone. I tried to imagine what someone who had been seriously threatened would feel, and how long, if ever, they would take to get over it.

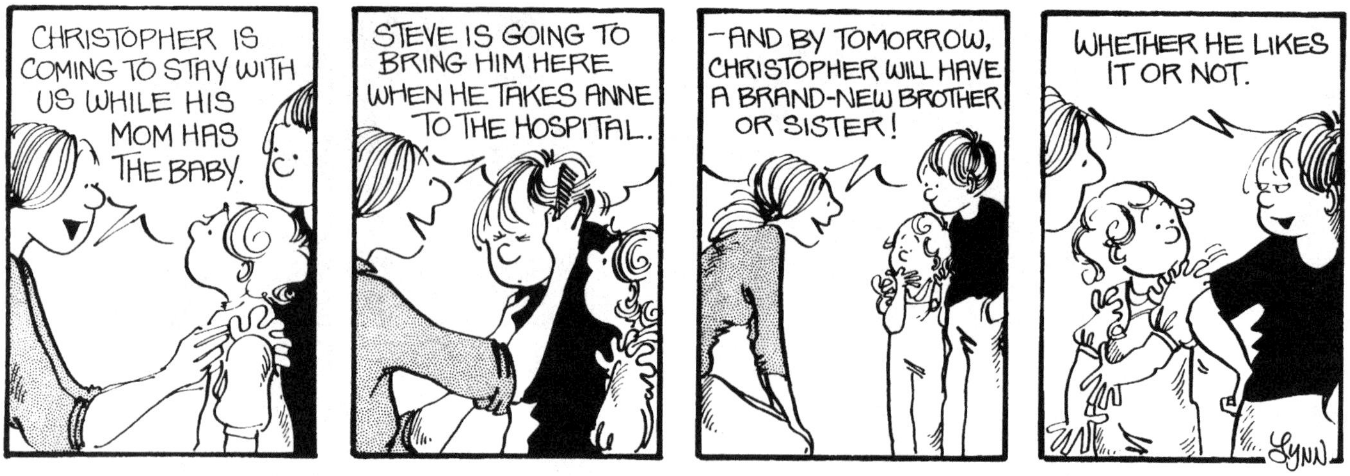
CHRISTOPHER IS COMING TO STAY WITH US WHILE HIS MOM HAS THE BABY.
STEVE IS GOING TO BRING HIM HERE WHEN HE TAKES ANNE TO THE HOSPITAL.
–AND BY TOMORROW, CHRISTOPHER WILL HAVE A BRAND-NEW BROTHER OR SISTER!
WHETHER HE LIKES IT OR NOT.

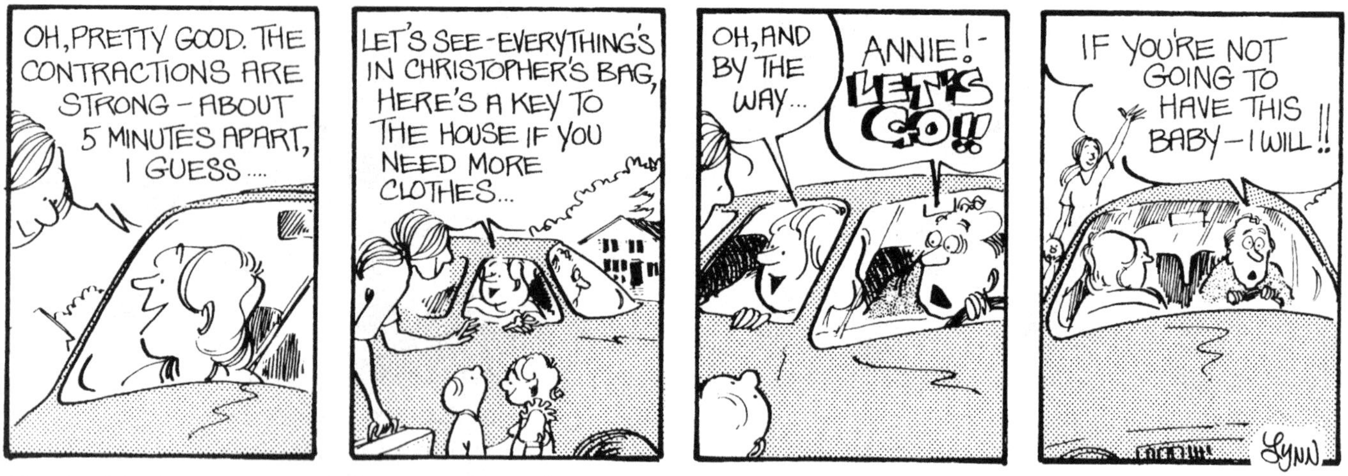
OH, PRETTY GOOD. THE CONTRACTIONS ARE STRONG – ABOUT 5 MINUTES APART, I GUESS....
LET'S SEE - EVERYTHING'S IN CHRISTOPHER'S BAG, HERE'S A KEY TO THE HOUSE IF YOU NEED MORE CLOTHES...
OH, AND BY THE WAY...
ANNIE! - LET'S GO!!
IF YOU'RE NOT GOING TO HAVE THIS BABY – I WILL!!

My friend Audrey was as nonchalant as could be when it came to delivering her baby. It was her husband who panicked! When she said she thought it might be time to leave for the hospital, Mack ran out to the car with her overnight bag and almost forgot her. Then he backed into a post on the way out of the driveway. Audrey ended up driving to the hospital and checking herself in. We laughed when she said she'd told the orderly to put Mack in the wheelchair for the ride to the room!

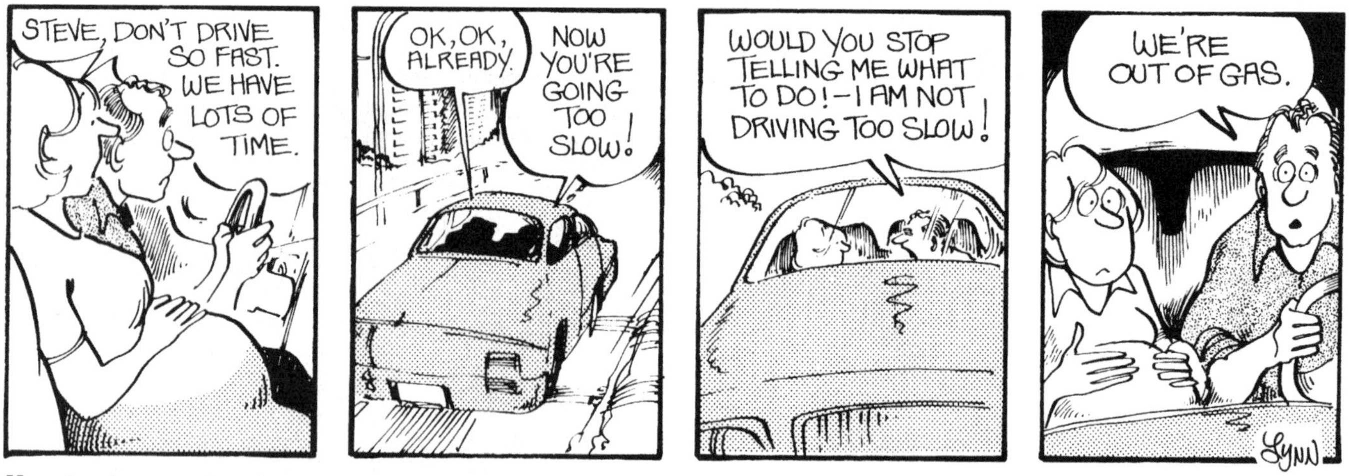
STEVE, DON'T DRIVE SO FAST. WE HAVE LOTS OF TIME.
OK, OK, ALREADY.
NOW YOU'RE GOING TOO SLOW!
WOULD YOU STOP TELLING ME WHAT TO DO! – I AM NOT DRIVING TOO SLOW!
WE'RE OUT OF GAS.

Here is where my imagination took me for a ride. Running out of gas on the way to the hospital appealed to me. Typically, I had no idea what the outcome of my contrived situations would be, so this was like living through the real incident: "What happens now?"

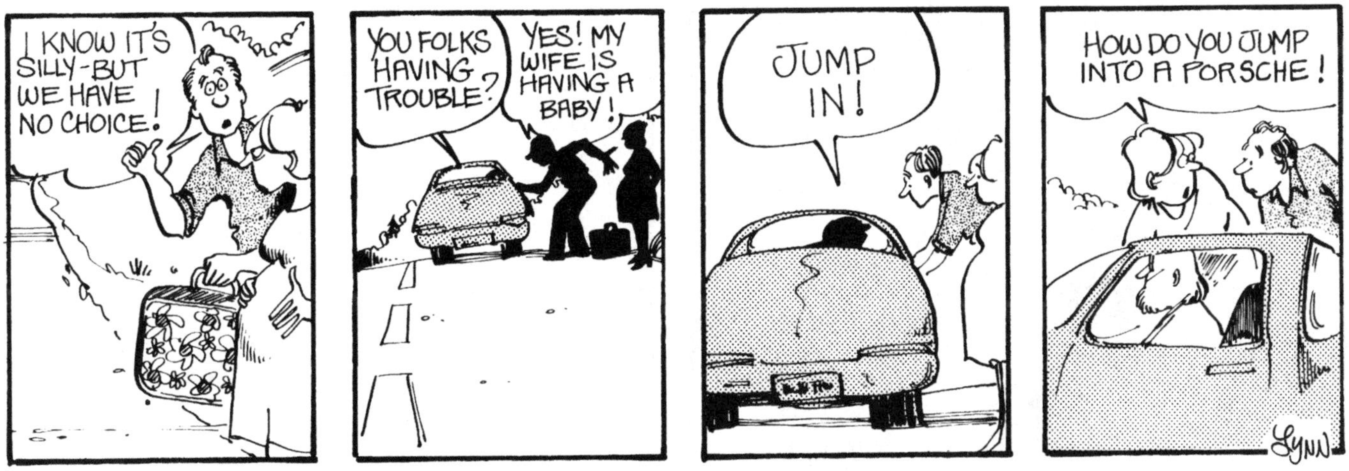
I KNOW IT'S SILLY-BUT WE HAVE NO CHOICE!
YOU FOLKS HAVING TROUBLE?
YES! MY WIFE IS HAVING A BABY!
JUMP IN!
HOW DO YOU JUMP INTO A PORSCHE!
Lynn

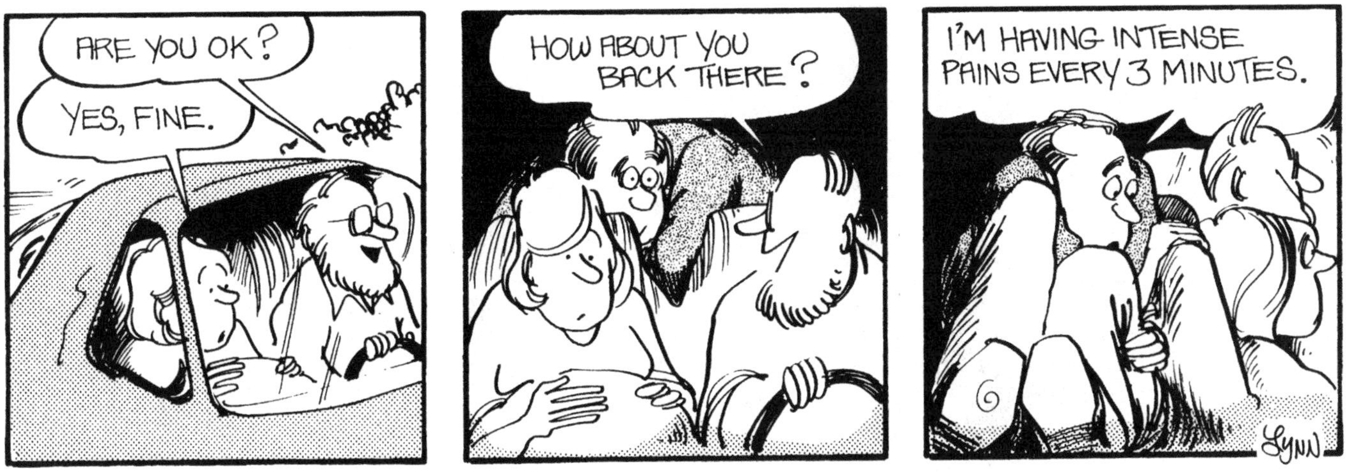
ARE YOU OK?
YES, FINE.
HOW ABOUT YOU BACK THERE?
I'M HAVING INTENSE PAINS EVERY 3 MINUTES.
Lynn

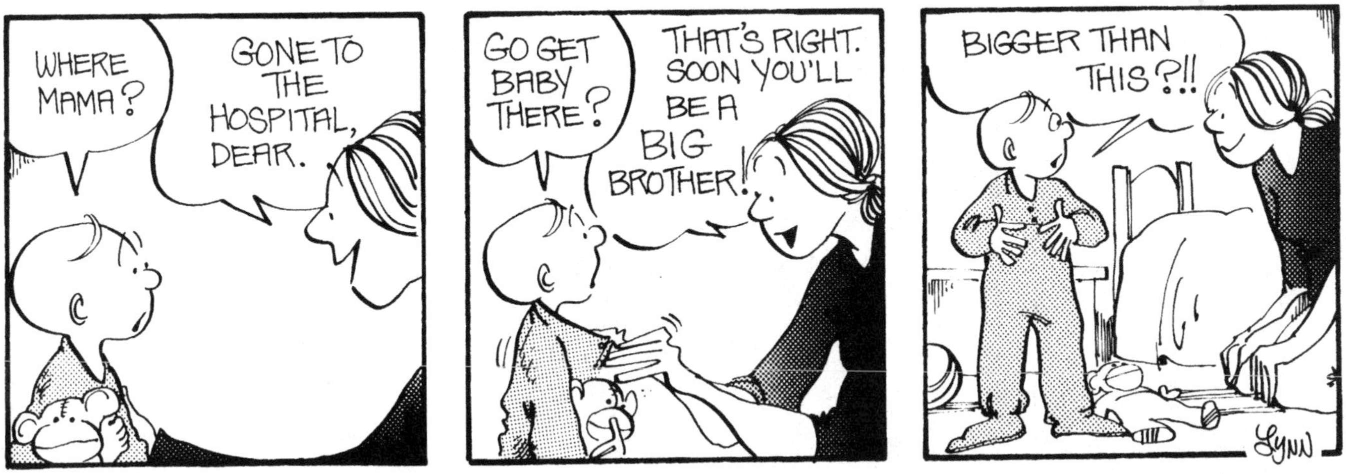
WHERE MAMA?
GONE TO THE HOSPITAL, DEAR.
GO GET BABY THERE?
THAT'S RIGHT. SOON YOU'LL BE A BIG BROTHER!
BIGGER THAN THIS?!!
Lynn

When I was about to have Katie, it was important to spend as much time as I could with Aaron to reassure him that even though a new baby was coming, he was still the first, and was very special. I told him he would be a big brother, that he'd be the older one, and be able to teach his new brother or sister all kinds of things. What he remembered most, however, was that his friends said he might get presents!

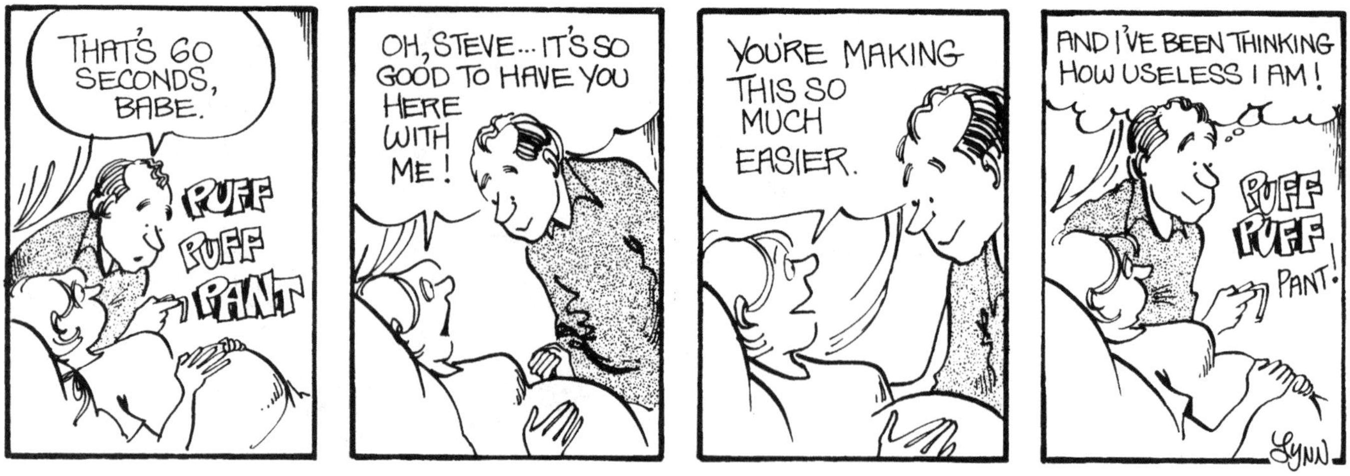
THAT'S 60 SECONDS, BABE.
PUFF
PUFF
PANT
OH, STEVE... IT'S SO GOOD TO HAVE YOU HERE WITH ME!
YOU'RE MAKING THIS SO MUCH EASIER.
AND I'VE BEEN THINKING HOW USELESS I AM!
PUFF
PUFF
PANT!
LYNN

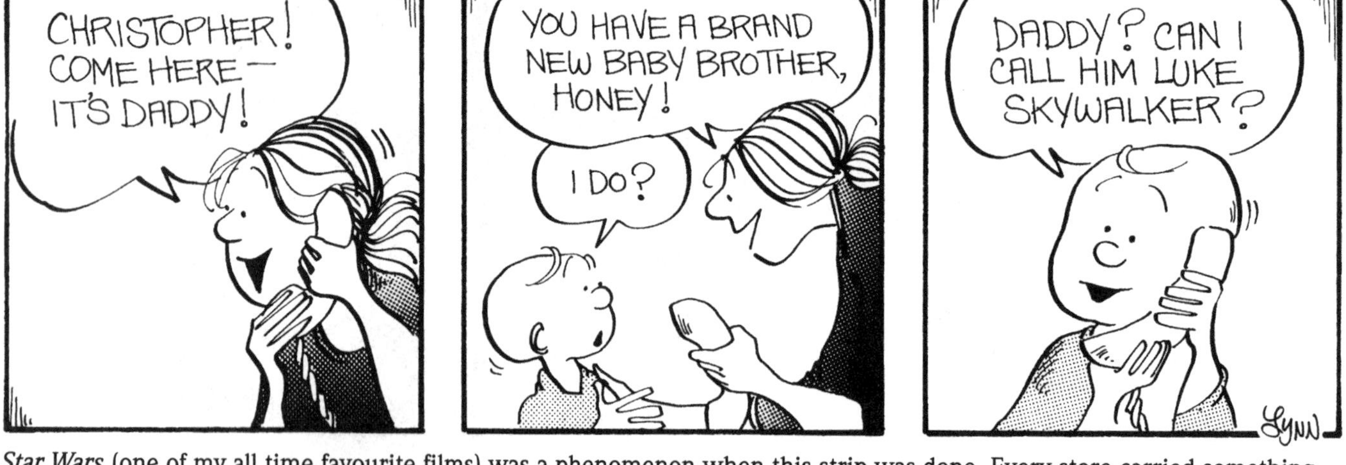
CHRISTOPHER! COME HERE— IT'S DADDY!
YOU HAVE A BRAND NEW BABY BROTHER, HONEY!
I DO?
DADDY? CAN I CALL HIM LUKE SKYWALKER?
LYNN

*Star Wars* (one of my all time favourite films) was a phenomenon when this strip was done. Every store carried something relating to this wonderful fantasy, and Aaron was caught up in it, too. What he wanted was a pet, and he said if we got one, he'd call it "Luke Skywalker." To me, it sounded like a good name for a housefly!

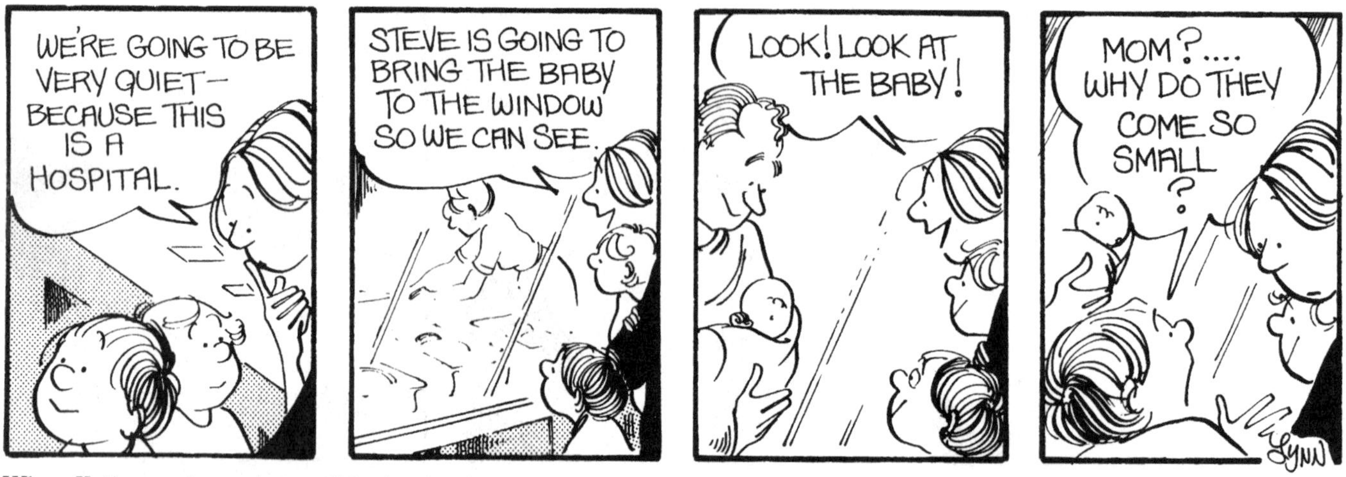
WE'RE GOING TO BE VERY QUIET— BECAUSE THIS IS A HOSPITAL.
STEVE IS GOING TO BRING THE BABY TO THE WINDOW SO WE CAN SEE.
LOOK! LOOK AT THE BABY!
MOM?.... WHY DO THEY COME SO SMALL?
LYNN

When Katie was born, Aaron did ask why she was so small. Having just pushed her out of my nether regions, and with walking and sitting still a quivering thought, I told him it was extremely good engineering, and that was that. I don't think I gave a full explanation until he stopped believing in Santa Claus!

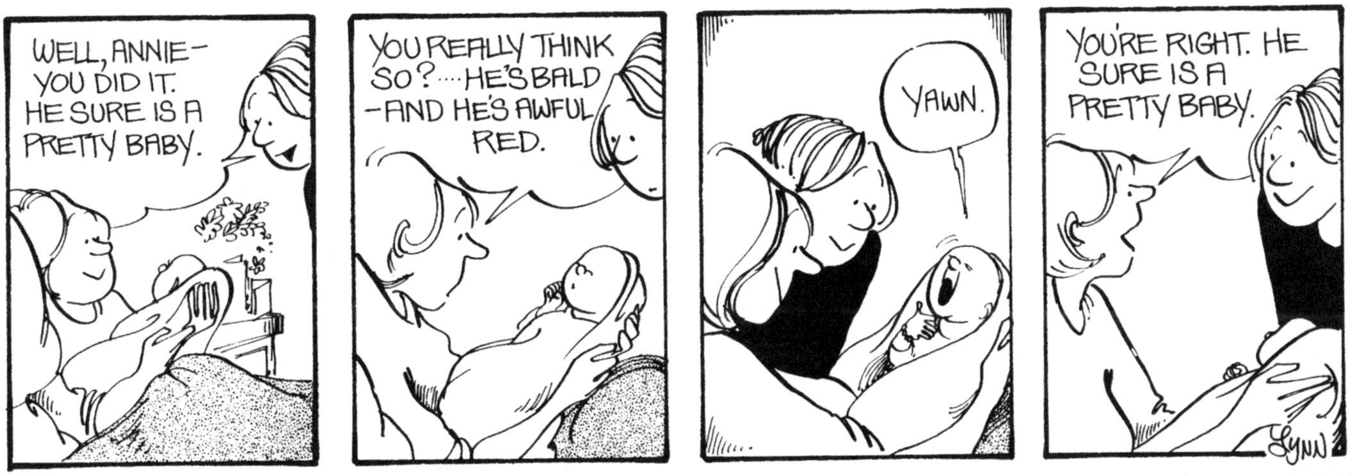
WELL, ANNIE- YOU DID IT. HE SURE IS A PRETTY BABY.
YOU REALLY THINK SO?.... HE'S BALD -AND HE'S AWFUL RED.
YAWN.
YOU'RE RIGHT. HE SURE IS A PRETTY BABY.
LYNN

No matter what, your baby is the most beautiful thing on the planet. I remember looking at mine as soon as they were out of the chute and thinking, "miracle!" Red, blotchy, and crying, they are the culmination of nine months of concern, protection, discomfort, worry, and joy. They are also a grunt to produce. I often thought that if it was an easy process, we might not appreciate them as much as we do!

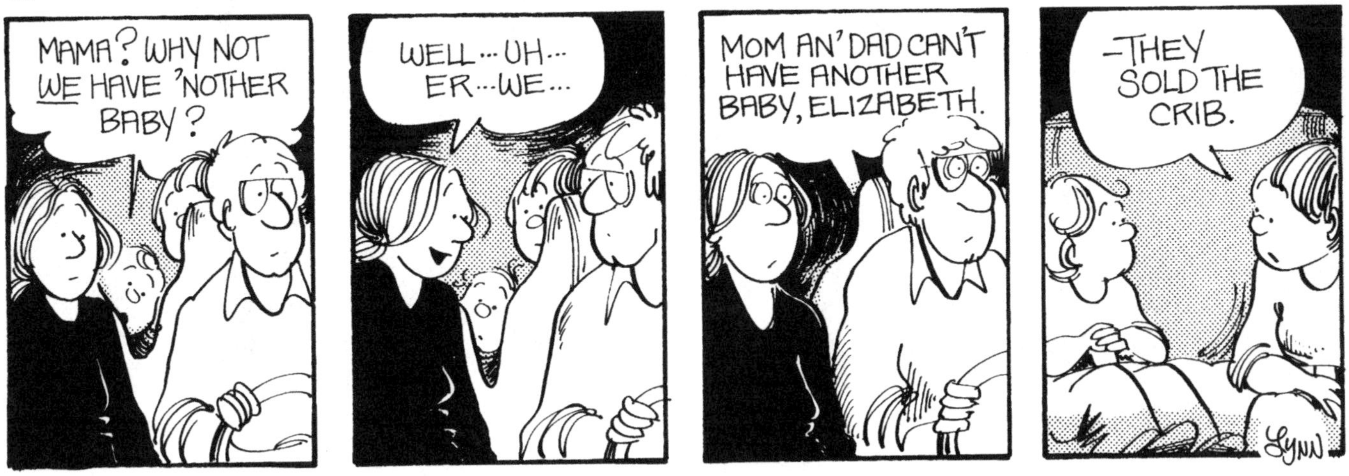
MAMA? WHY NOT WE HAVE 'NOTHER BABY?
WELL... UH... ER... WE...
MOM AN' DAD CAN'T HAVE ANOTHER BABY, ELIZABETH.
-THEY SOLD THE CRIB.
LYNN

Aaron did ask why we didn't have another baby, and my explanation was that we had sold the crib. In a way, it's true. If you have even the slightest positive thought about having another, you store the stuff. With this in mind, however, I have friends who kept everything "just in case," and are now offering cribs and jolly jumpers to their married, adult children!

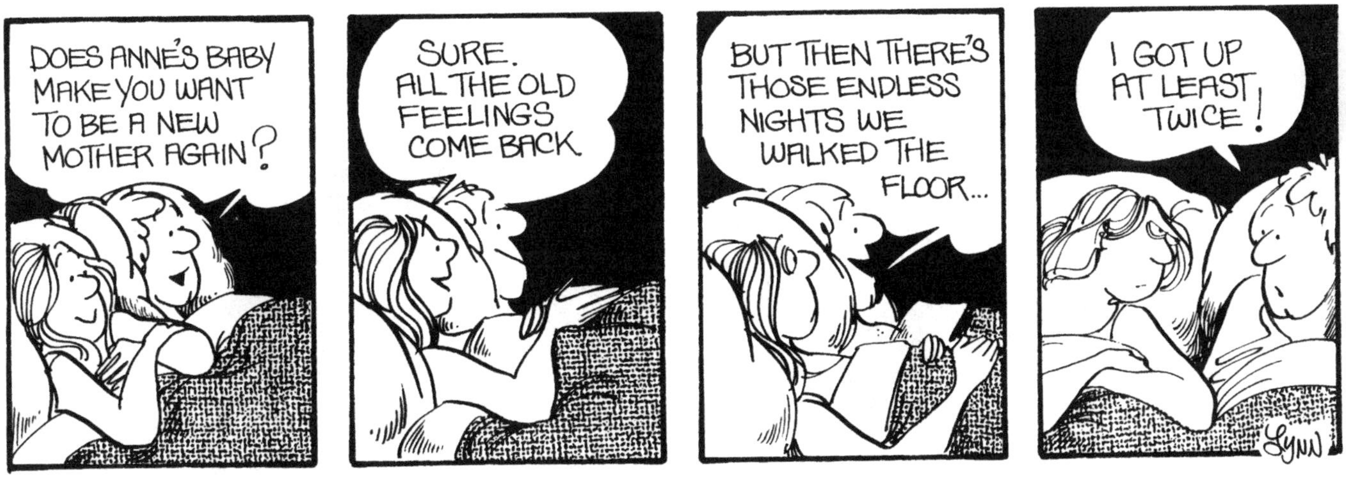
DOES ANNE'S BABY MAKE YOU WANT TO BE A NEW MOTHER AGAIN?
SURE. ALL THE OLD FEELINGS COME BACK.
BUT THEN THERE'S THOSE ENDLESS NIGHTS WE WALKED THE FLOOR...
I GOT UP AT LEAST TWICE!
LYNN

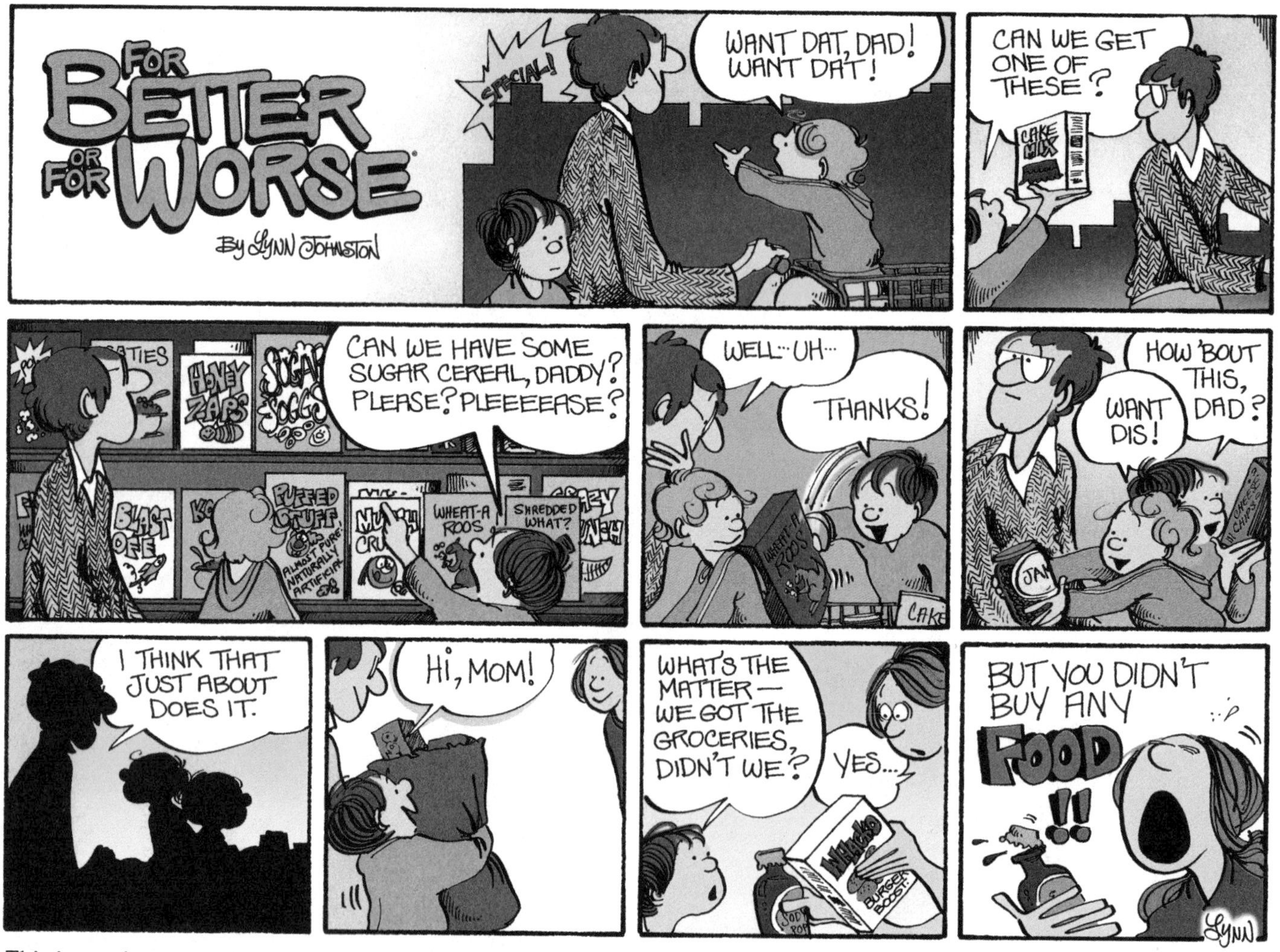
FOR BETTER OR FOR WORSE
BY LYNN JOHNSTON
SPECIAL!
WANT DAT, DAD! WANT DAT!
CAN WE GET ONE OF THESE?
CAKE MIX
HONEY ZAPS
CAN WE HAVE SOME SUGAR CEREAL, DADDY? PLEASE? PLEEEEEASE?
BLAST OFF
PUFFED STUFF
ALMOST PURE! NATURALLY ARTIFICIAL
WHEAT-A ROOS
SHREDDED WHAT?
WELL... UH...
THANKS!
WHEAT-A ROOS
CAKE
HOW 'BOUT THIS, DAD?
WANT DIS!
I THINK THAT JUST ABOUT DOES IT.
HI, MOM!
WHAT'S THE MATTER — WE GOT THE GROCERIES, DIDN'T WE?
YES...
BURGER BOOST
BUT YOU DIDN'T BUY ANY
FOOD
!!
LYNN

This is another example of something I just made up. In fact, I don't remember my husband taking the kids to buy groceries — this was my job and I enjoyed it. This is a gag that I knew had been done by other cartoonists, and yet, I did it again.

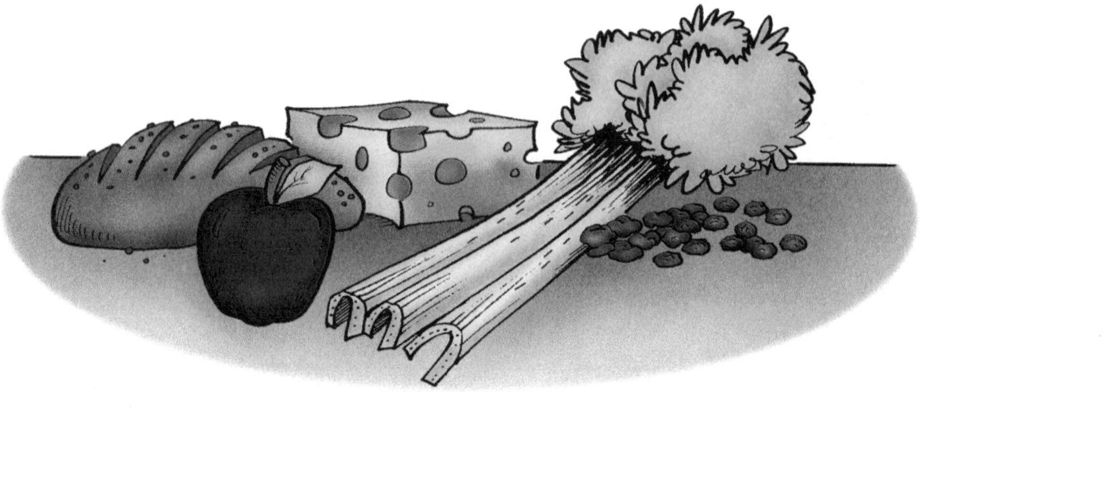

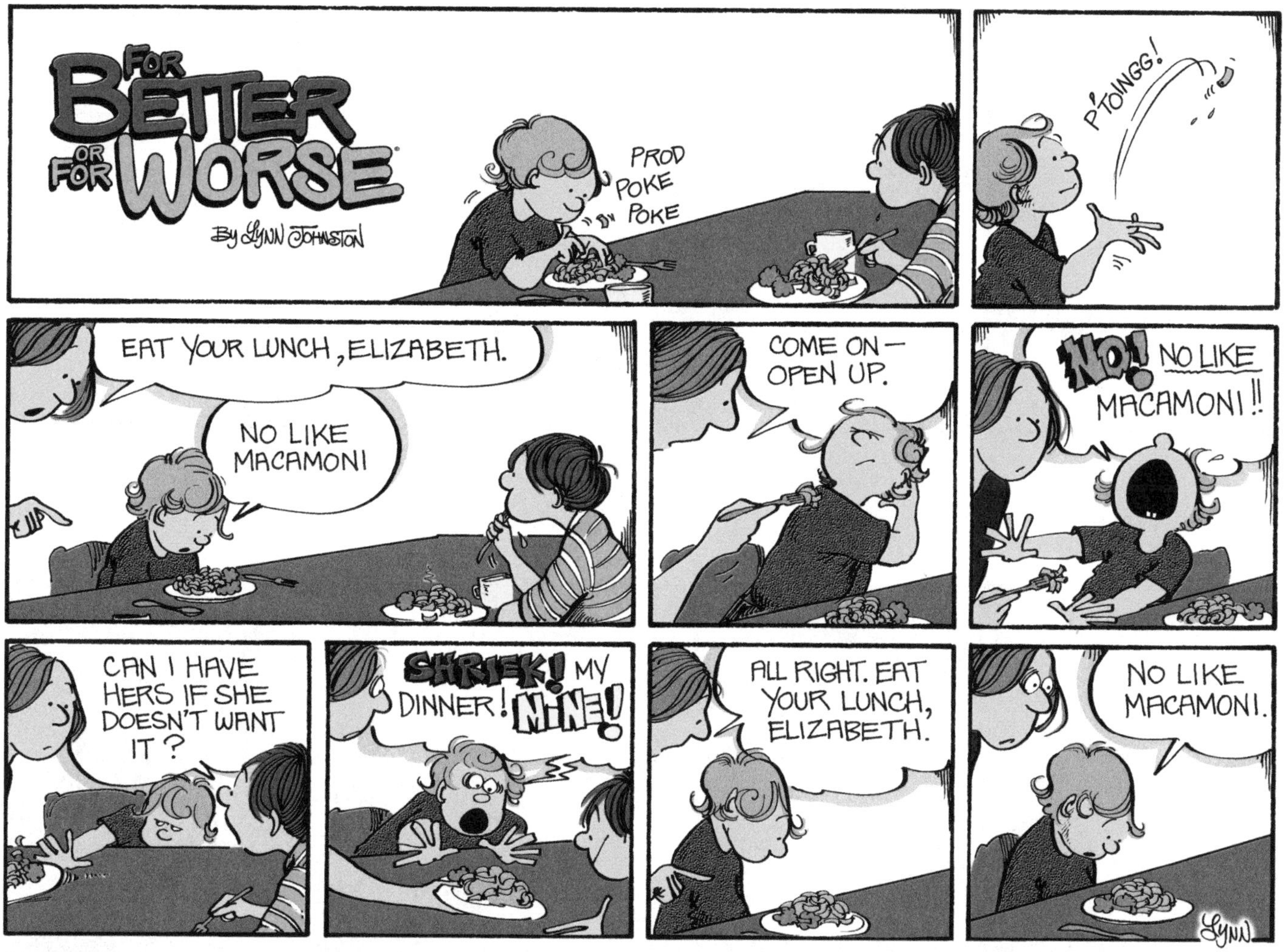
FOR BETTER OR FOR WORSE
BY LYNN JOHNSTON
PROD POKE POKE
P'TOINGG!
EAT YOUR LUNCH, ELIZABETH.
NO LIKE MACAMONI
COME ON — OPEN UP.
NO! NO LIKE MACAMONI!!
CAN I HAVE HERS IF SHE DOESN'T WANT IT?
SHRIEK! MY DINNER! MINE!
ALL RIGHT. EAT YOUR LUNCH, ELIZABETH.
NO LIKE MACAMONI.
LYNN

My method for writing strips was to stretch out on the couch with a lined pad of paper on my lap and imagine myself in the Patterson kitchen at suppertime. It didn't take long for the characters to begin a conversation, and I would listen in. Like a tape recorder, I could run the commentary back and forth, change or modify the answers, and if luck was with me, I'd get a funny line. I remember being particularly happy with this one, and wondering, again, where the idea had come from. It was too good (I thought) to have come from ME!

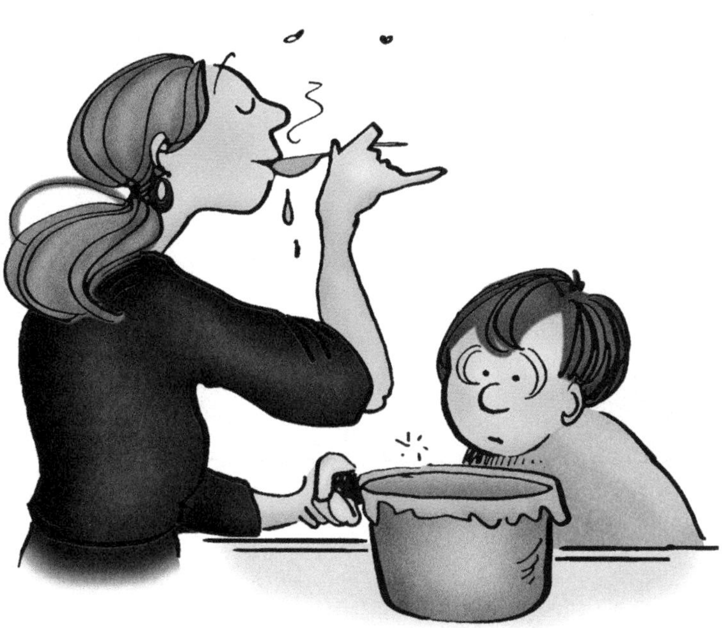

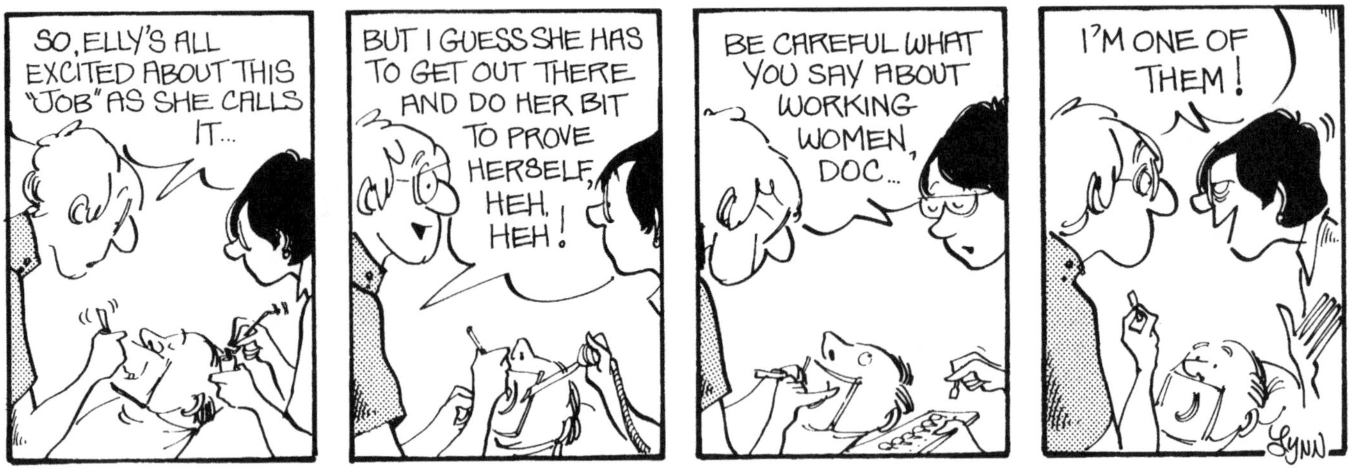
SO, ELLY'S ALL EXCITED ABOUT THIS "JOB" AS SHE CALLS IT...
BUT I GUESS SHE HAS TO GET OUT THERE AND DO HER BIT TO PROVE HERSELF, HEH, HEH!
BE CAREFUL WHAT YOU SAY ABOUT WORKING WOMEN, DOC...
I'M ONE OF THEM!
LYNN

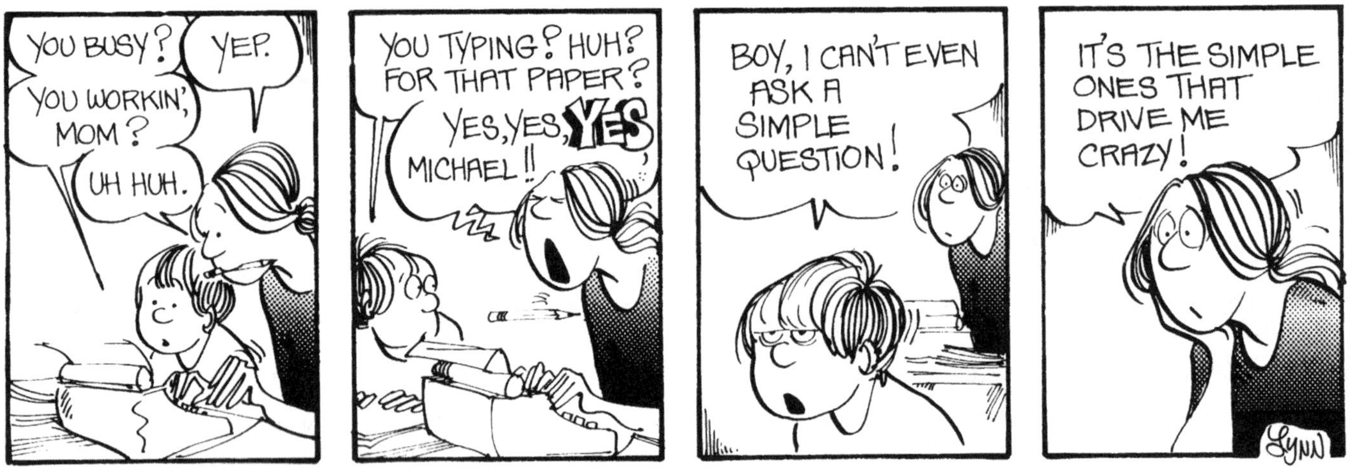
YOU BUSY?
YEP.
YOU WORKIN', MOM?
UH HUH.
YOU TYPING? HUH? FOR THAT PAPER?
YES, YES, YES MICHAEL!!
BOY, I CAN'T EVEN ASK A SIMPLE QUESTION!
IT'S THE SIMPLE ONES THAT DRIVE ME CRAZY!
LYNN

I have always welcomed questions from my kids. It's an opportunity to share knowledge and to show them that I value their intelligence. It's just that they always seemed to ask me stuff when I had no time to answer. It didn't matter what I was up to; they always wanted an answer NOW! Do kids do this because they want our undivided attention all of the time, or because they enjoy hearing the often ridiculous, spur-of-the-moment responses that we come up with? Either way, it drove me crazy.

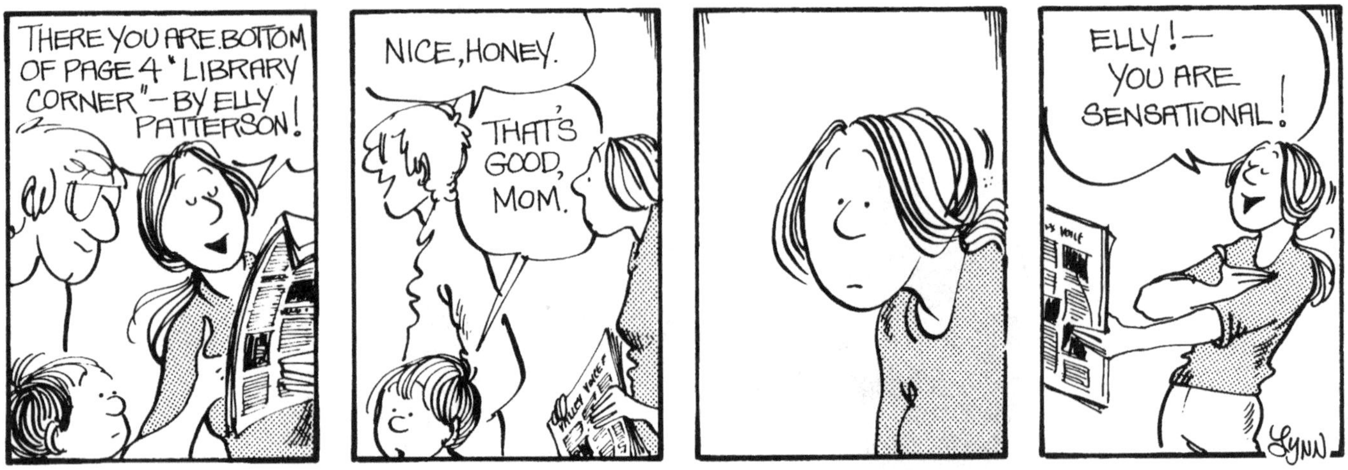
THERE YOU ARE. BOTTOM OF PAGE 4 "LIBRARY CORNER" – BY ELLY PATTERSON!
NICE, HONEY.
THAT'S GOOD, MOM.
ELLY! — YOU ARE SENSATIONAL!
LYNN

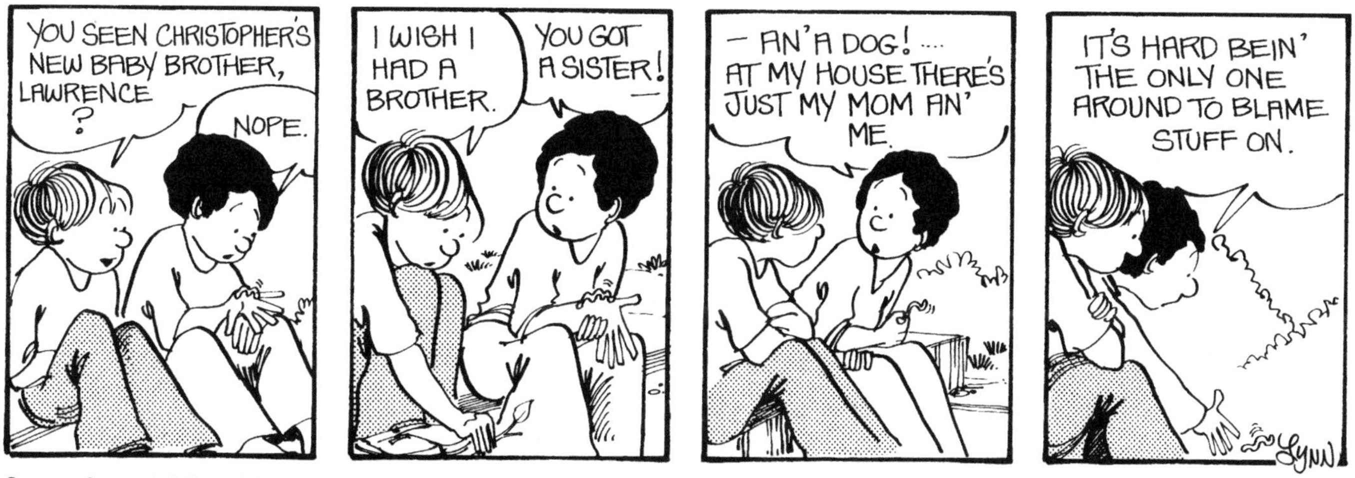
YOU SEEN CHRISTOPHER'S NEW BABY BROTHER, LAWRENCE ?
NOPE.
I WISH I HAD A BROTHER.
YOU GOT A SISTER!
— AN' A DOG! .... AT MY HOUSE THERE'S JUST MY MOM AN' ME.
IT'S HARD BEIN' THE ONLY ONE AROUND TO BLAME STUFF ON.
Lynn

Some of my childhood friends were only children. They often told me how lucky I was to have a brother. From my standpoint, I'd have gladly traded places with them — or exchanged my brother for something more practical, like a bike or a movie projector. The only time Alan and I really got along was in the face of a common enemy. We might have belted each other about, but we always came to each other's defence.

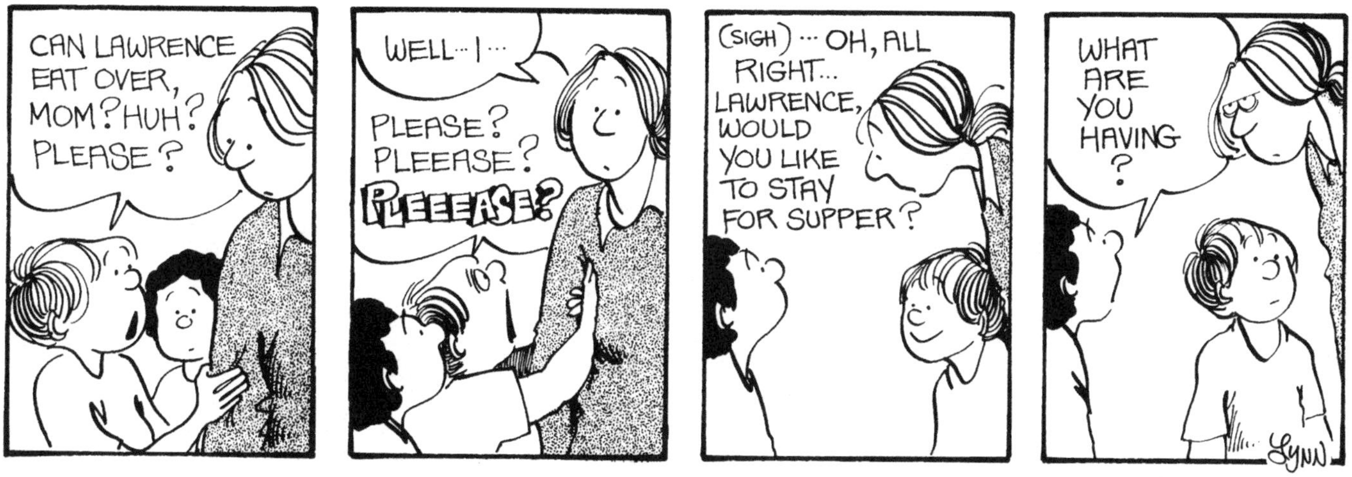
CAN LAWRENCE EAT OVER, MOM? HUH? PLEASE?
WELL ... I ...
PLEASE? PLEEASE? PLEEEEASE?
(SIGH) ... OH, ALL RIGHT... LAWRENCE, WOULD YOU LIKE TO STAY FOR SUPPER?
WHAT ARE YOU HAVING ?
Lynn

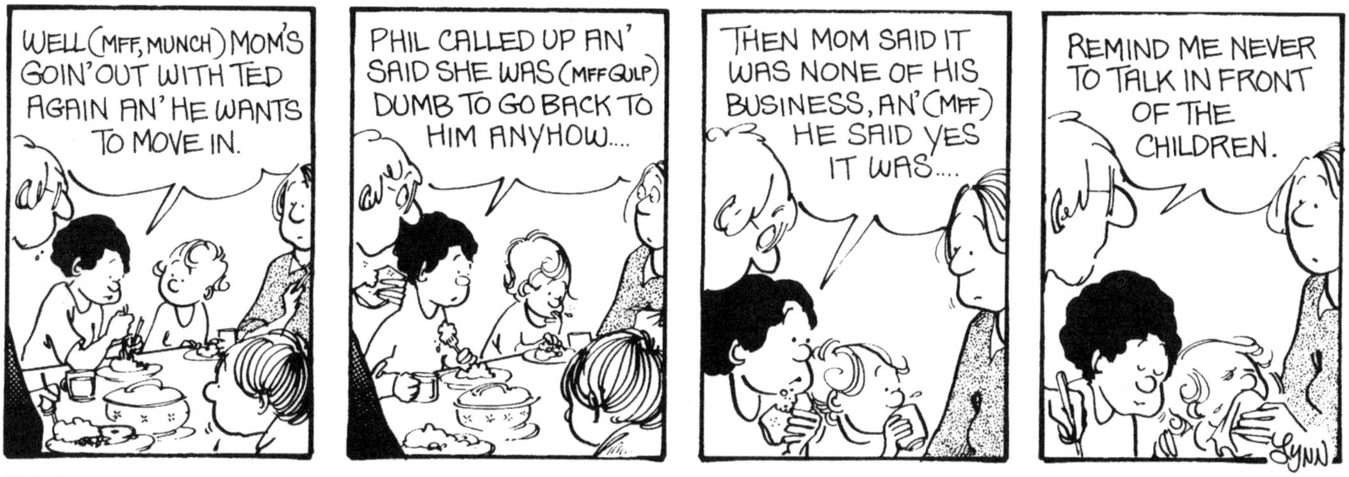
WELL (MFF, MUNCH) MOM'S GOIN' OUT WITH TED AGAIN AN' HE WANTS TO MOVE IN.
PHIL CALLED UP AN' SAID SHE WAS (MFF GULP) DUMB TO GO BACK TO HIM ANYHOW....
THEN MOM SAID IT WAS NONE OF HIS BUSINESS, AN' (MFF) HE SAID YES IT WAS....
REMIND ME NEVER TO TALK IN FRONT OF THE CHILDREN.
Lynn

This is an example of how to fill the audience in on a lot of information with one strip. If I didn't have time to show the audience what had transpired, I could trust one of the characters to "tell all" in a sequence like this.

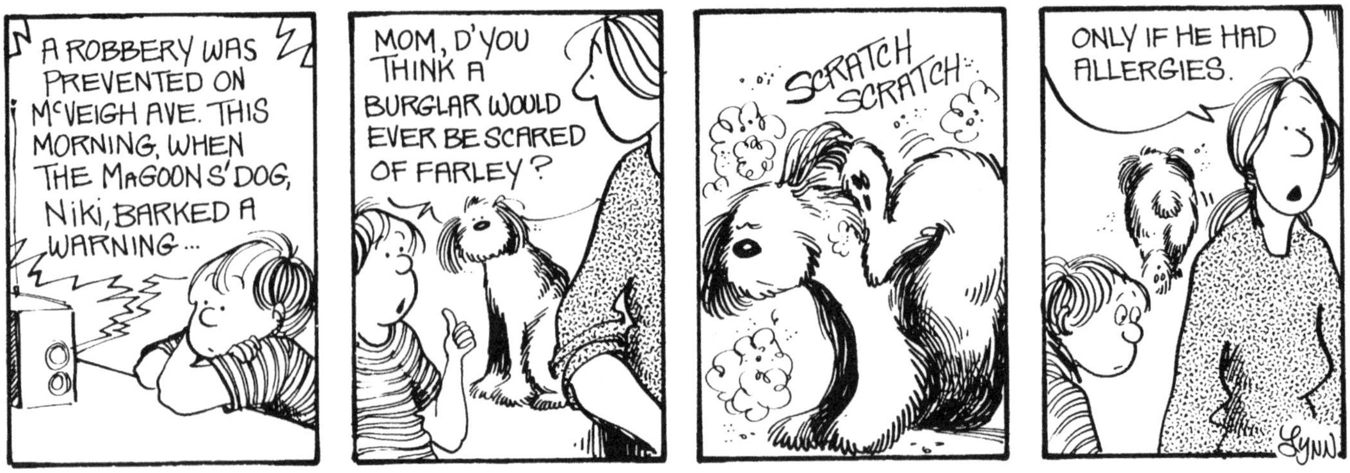
A ROBBERY WAS PREVENTED ON McVEIGH AVE. THIS MORNING, WHEN THE MAGOONS' DOG, NIKI, BARKED A WARNING...
MOM, D'YOU THINK A BURGLAR WOULD EVER BE SCARED OF FARLEY?
SCRATCH SCRATCH
ONLY IF HE HAD ALLERGIES.
LYNN

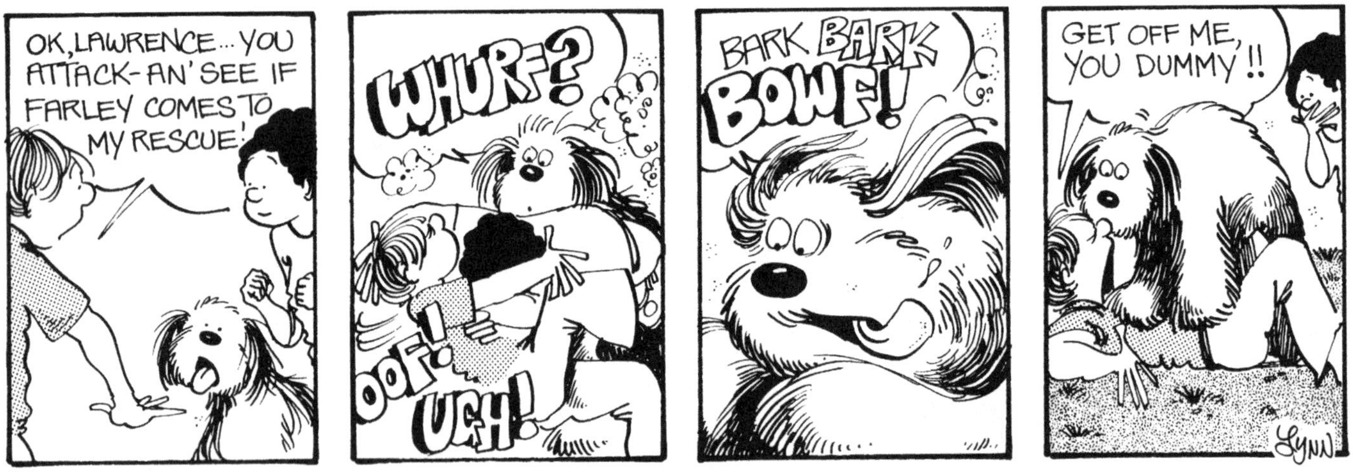
OK, LAWRENCE... YOU ATTACK- AN' SEE IF FARLEY COMES TO MY RESCUE!
WHURF?
OOF!
UGH!
BARK BARK BOWF!
GET OFF ME, YOU DUMMY!!
LYNN

One of my childhood neighbours had a dog that was specifically trained to defend his owners. The result was that their young daughter would march down the road, dog in tow, and insult us all — knowing that we'd be unable to touch her. She was particularly mean, and so was the dog. Eventually this family moved, but even with them gone, we kids were very nervous around large dogs for a long time to come.

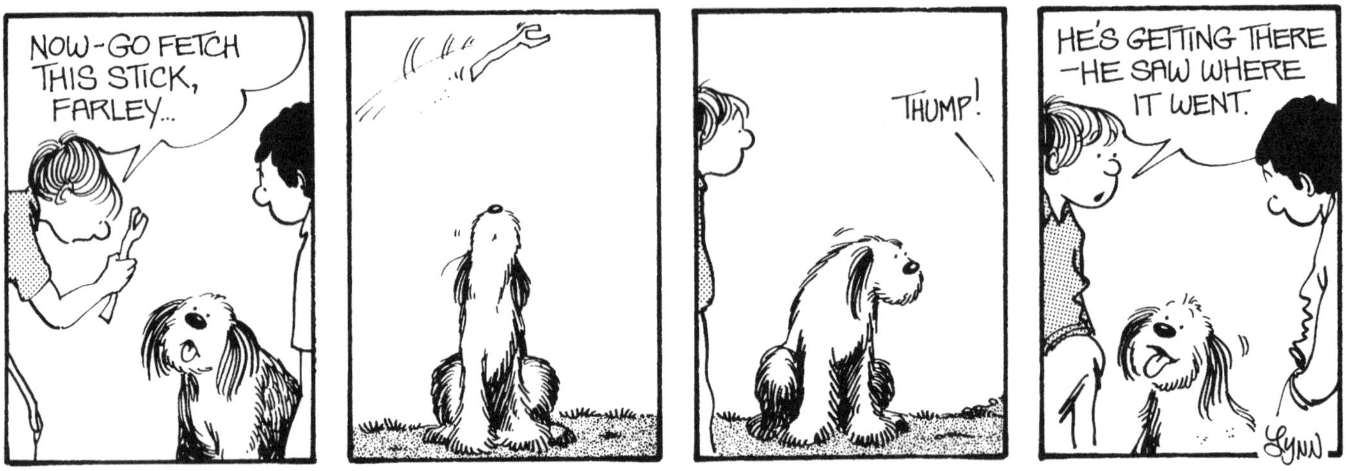
NOW-GO FETCH THIS STICK, FARLEY...
THUMP!
HE'S GETTING THERE -HE SAW WHERE IT WENT.
LYNN

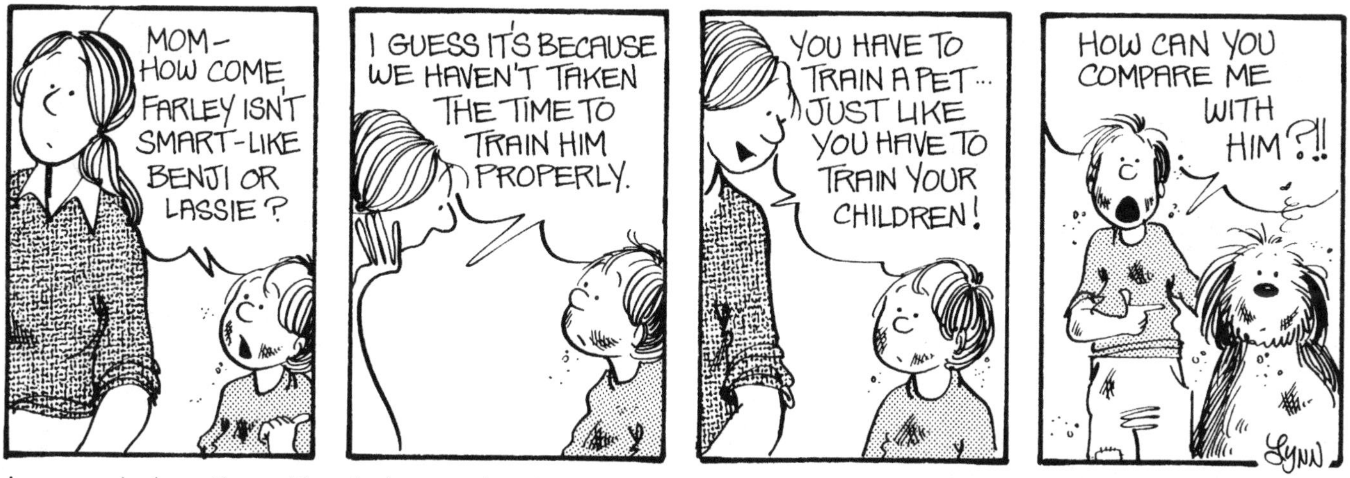
MOM– HOW COME FARLEY ISN'T SMART–LIKE BENJI OR LASSIE?
I GUESS IT'S BECAUSE WE HAVEN'T TAKEN THE TIME TO TRAIN HIM PROPERLY.
YOU HAVE TO TRAIN A PET... JUST LIKE YOU HAVE TO TRAIN YOUR CHILDREN!
HOW CAN YOU COMPARE ME WITH HIM?!!
LYNN

As a new single mother, with nobody around to give me advice, I often turned to the one instruction manual I was familiar with: *How to Train Your Puppy*. This booklet got us through much of Aaron's toddlerhood, and I don't think it warped his psyche too much. He grew up to be a fairly normal adult. ... He still does, however, stop and point when he sees ducks.

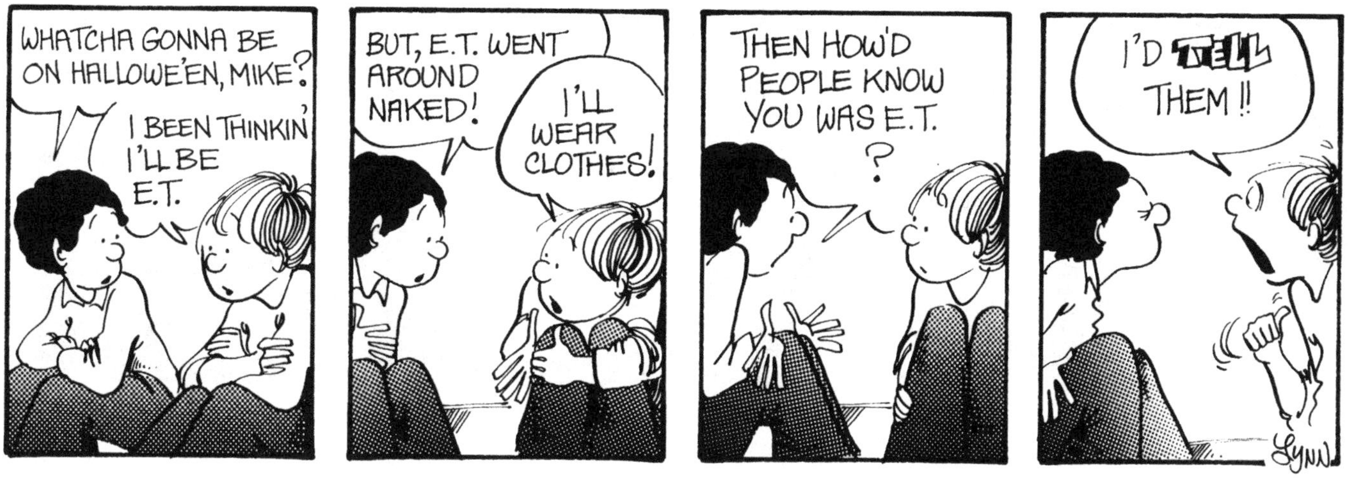
WHATCHA GONNA BE ON HALLOWE'EN, MIKE?
I BEEN THINKIN' I'LL BE E.T.
BUT, E.T. WENT AROUND NAKED!
I'LL WEAR CLOTHES!
THEN HOW'D PEOPLE KNOW YOU WAS E.T.?
I'D TELL THEM!!
LYNN

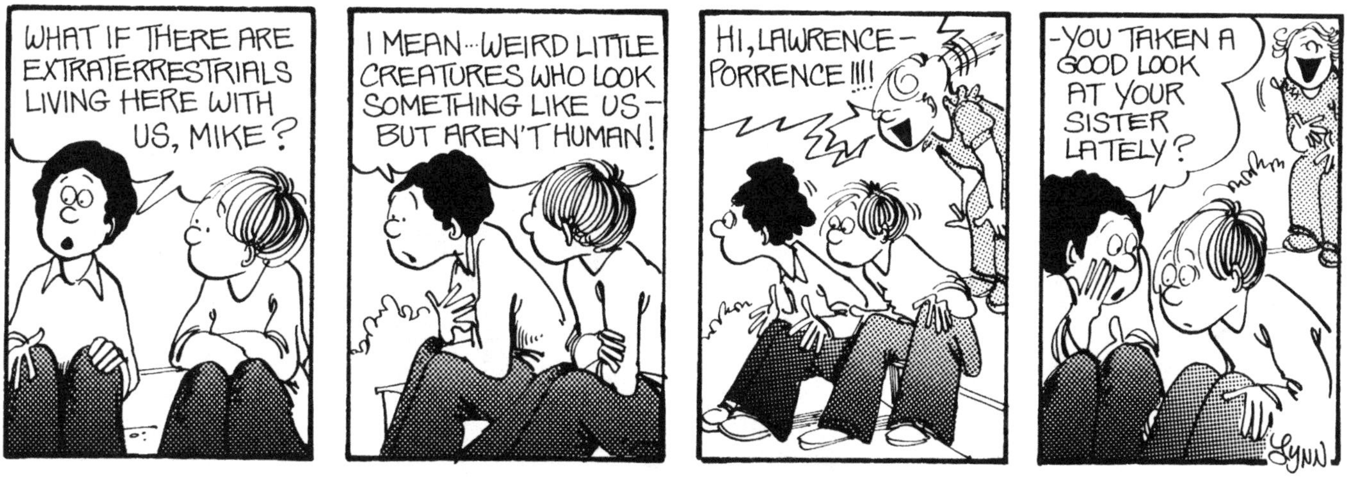
WHAT IF THERE ARE EXTRATERRESTRIALS LIVING HERE WITH US, MIKE?
I MEAN...WEIRD LITTLE CREATURES WHO LOOK SOMETHING LIKE US– BUT AREN'T HUMAN!
HI, LAWRENCE– PORRENCE!!!!
–YOU TAKEN A GOOD LOOK AT YOUR SISTER LATELY?
LYNN

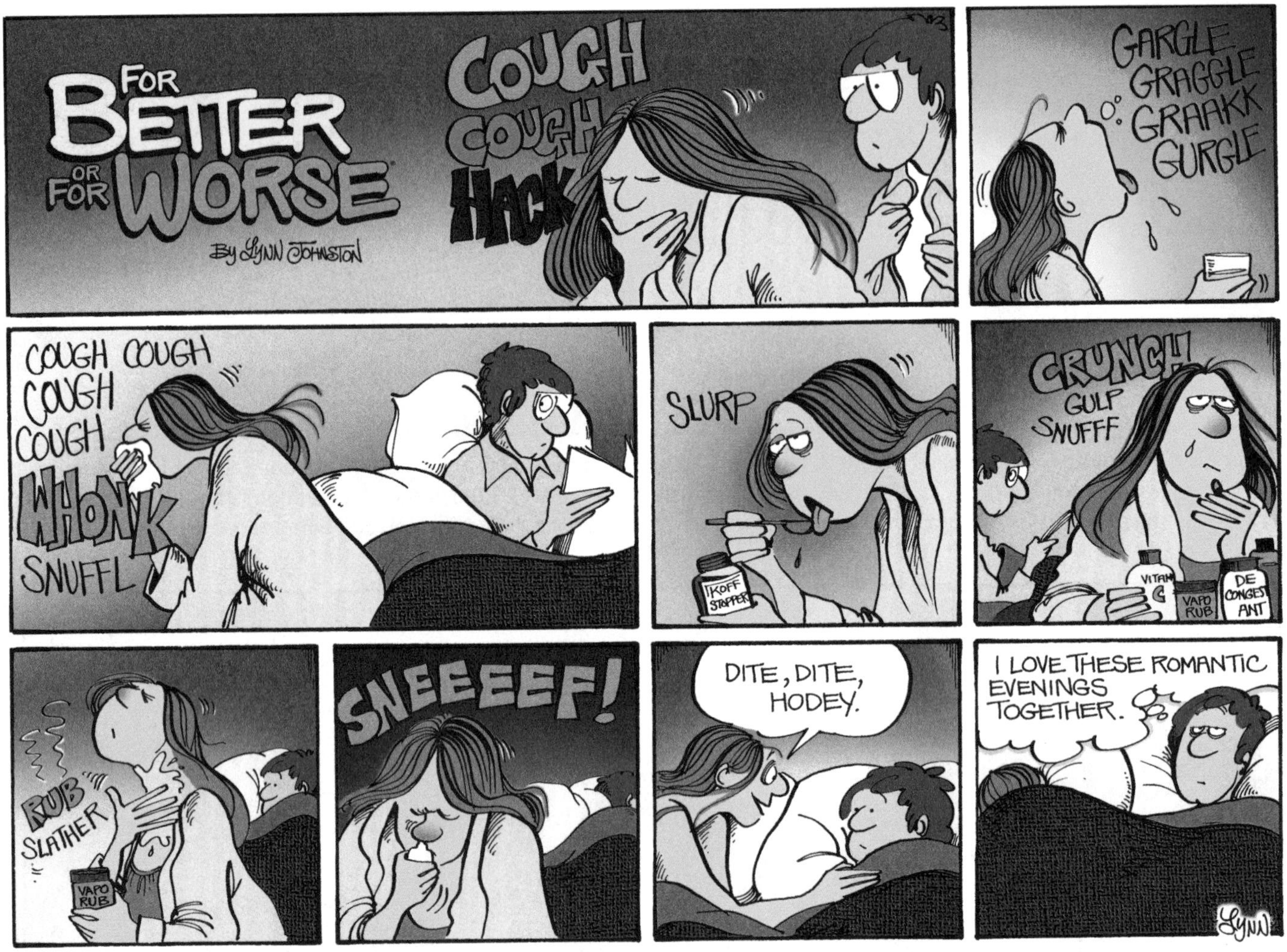
FOR BETTER OR FOR WORSE
BY LYNN JOHNSTON
COUGH COUGH HACK
GARGLE GRAGGLE GRAAKK GURGLE
COUGH COUGH COUGH COUGH WHONK SNUFFL
SLURP
KOFF STAPPER
CRUNCH GULP SNUFFF
VITAM C
VAPO RUB
DE CONGEST ANT
RUB SLATHER
VAPO RUB
SNEEEEF!
DITE, DITE, HODEY.
I LOVE THESE ROMANTIC EVENINGS TOGETHER.
LYNN

Any intimate partnership must pass the "sick" test before it can be called a serious relationship. Cohabitation requires us to accept, endure, and be considerate of our significant others' health concerns.

Your partner's audible woe is an opportunity: Every sympathetic gesture, every coo of understanding, and every expression of concern that you offer are bankable brownie points to be redeemed when it's YOUR turn to be sick. And misery, as we all know, loves company!

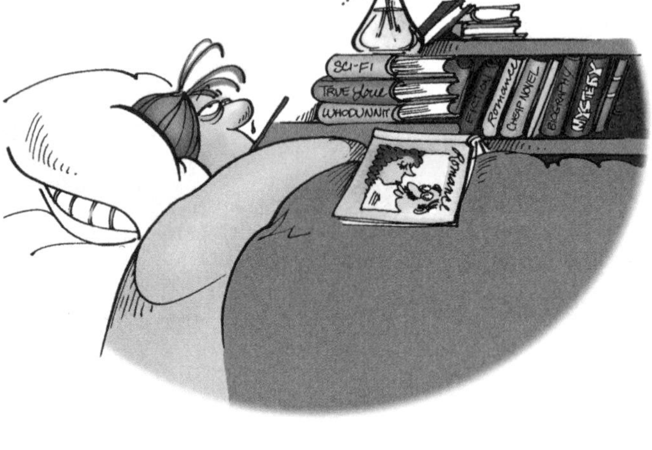
SCI-FI
TRUE LOVE
WHODUNNIT
CHEAP NOVEL
BIOGRAPHY
MYSTERY
Romance

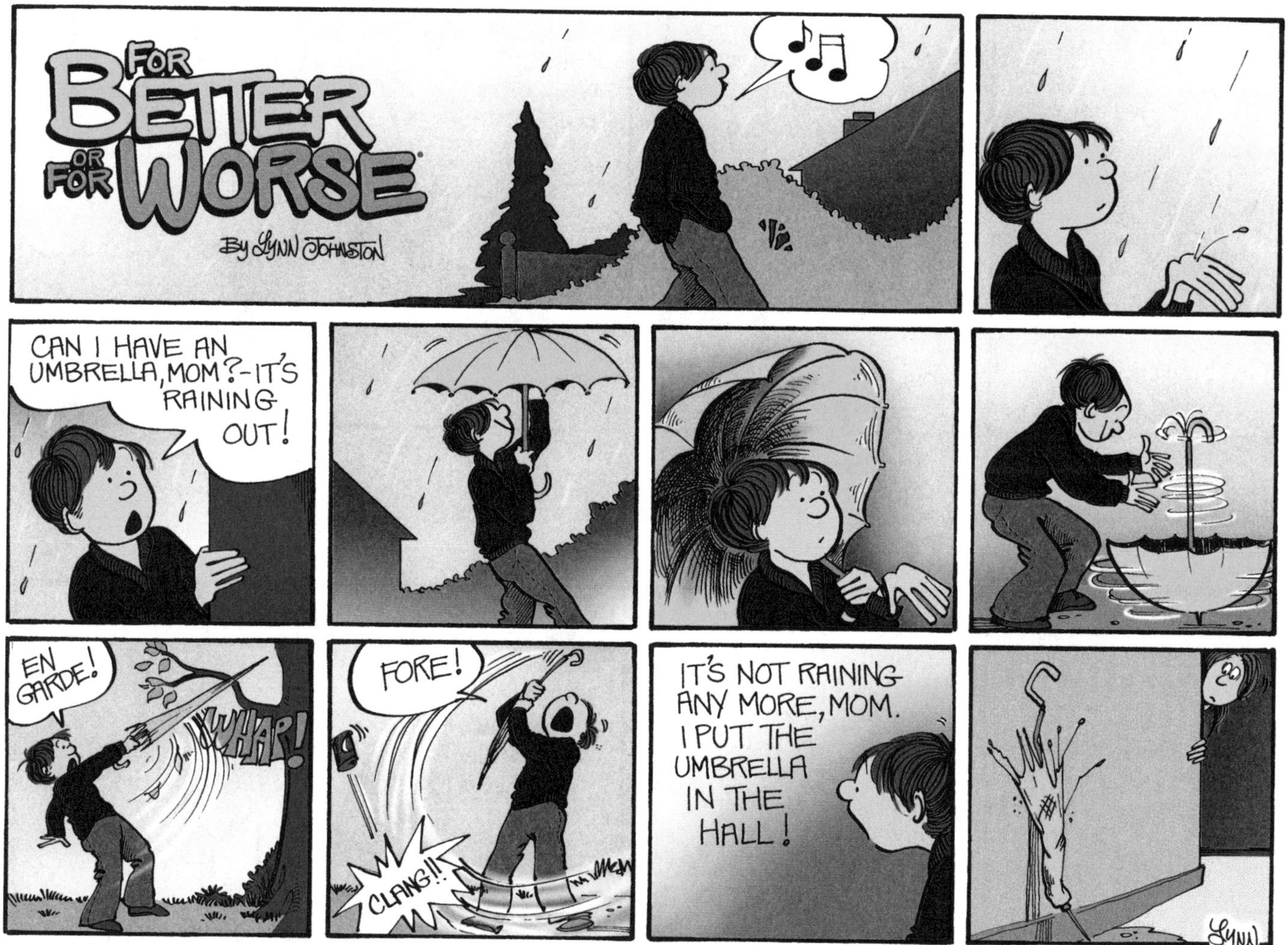
FOR BETTER OR FOR WORSE
BY LYNN JOHNSTON
CAN I HAVE AN UMBRELLA, MOM?-IT'S RAINING OUT!
EN GARDE!
WHAP!
FORE!
CLANG!!
IT'S NOT RAINING ANY MORE, MOM. I PUT THE UMBRELLA IN THE HALL!
LYNN

Vancouverites always have an umbrella somewhere handy — ready to use at a moment's notice. My folks had a stand in the front hall full of them. We used them as swords, canes, and crutches. We filled them with water, and we let the wind blow them inside out. I was always surprised by how much abuse they could take and still do the job. Much like mothers, umbrellas are always there when you need them!

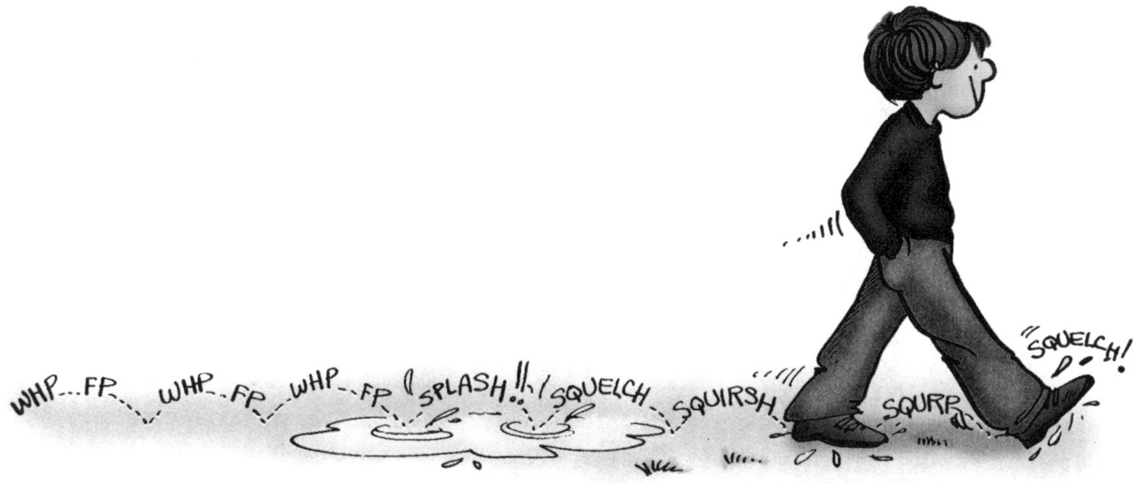
WHP...FP WHP..FP WHP..FP SPLASH!! SQUELCH SQUIRSH SQURP SQUELCH!

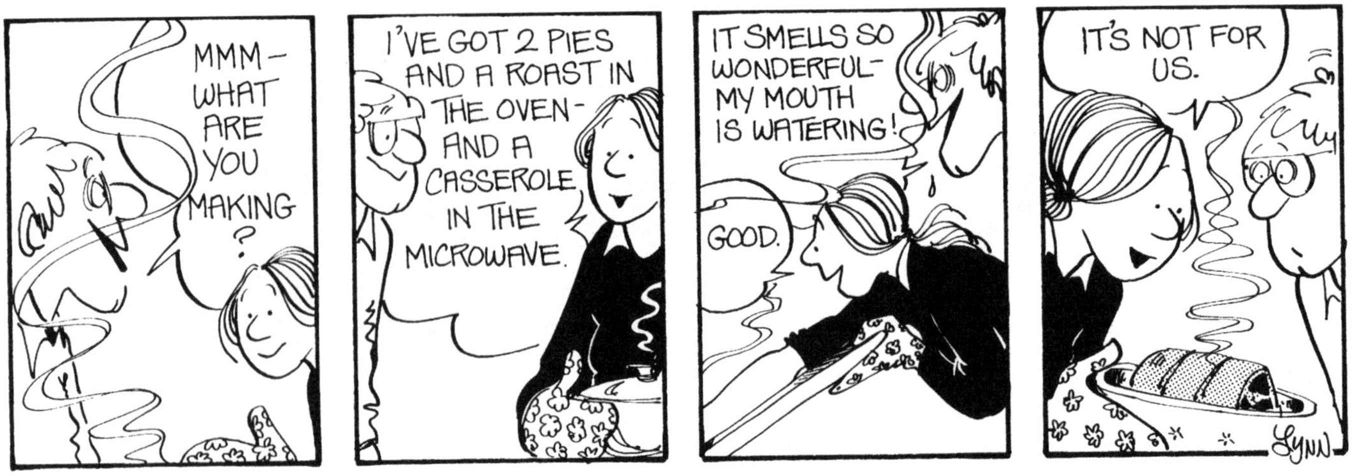
MMM– WHAT ARE YOU MAKING?
I'VE GOT 2 PIES AND A ROAST IN THE OVEN– AND A CASSEROLE IN THE MICROWAVE.
IT SMELLS SO WONDERFUL– MY MOUTH IS WATERING!
GOOD.
IT'S NOT FOR US.
LYNN

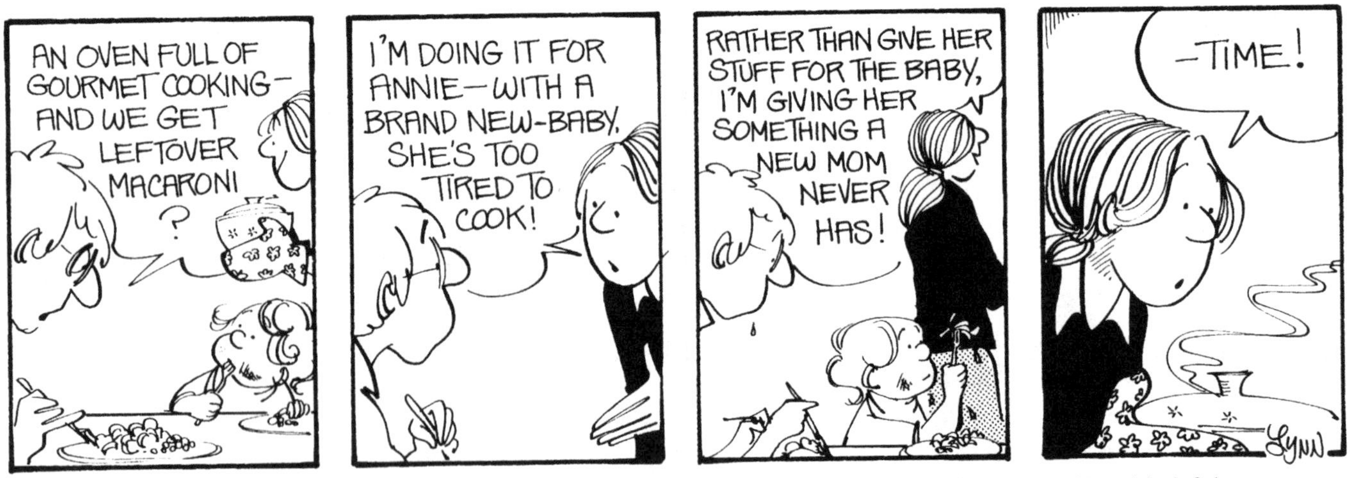
AN OVEN FULL OF GOURMET COOKING– AND WE GET LEFTOVER MACARONI?
I'M DOING IT FOR ANNIE–WITH A BRAND NEW-BABY, SHE'S TOO TIRED TO COOK!
RATHER THAN GIVE HER STUFF FOR THE BABY, I'M GIVING HER SOMETHING A NEW MOM NEVER HAS!
–TIME!
LYNN

When my second child came along, I was living a different life, enjoying the company of new friends and helpful neighbours. They all got together and filled my freezer with great meals that could be easily thawed and served. Even when you're exhausted from pushing a kid out of your nether parts, sleep deprived, and sore enough to want serious drugs, you're still expected to create in the kitchen.

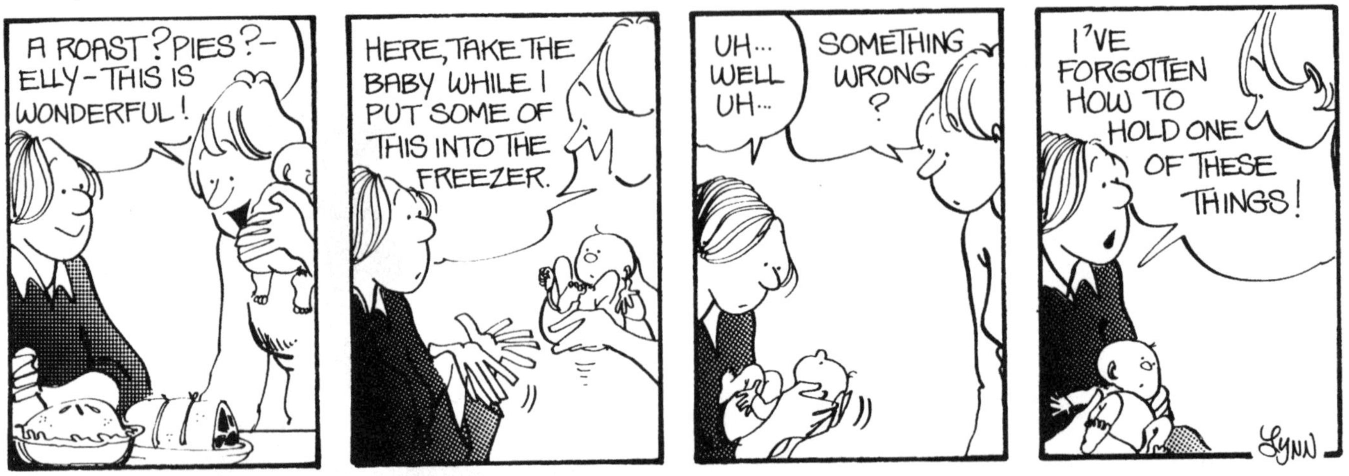
A ROAST? PIES?– ELLY–THIS IS WONDERFUL!
HERE, TAKE THE BABY WHILE I PUT SOME OF THIS INTO THE FREEZER.
UH... WELL UH...
SOMETHING WRONG?
I'VE FORGOTTEN HOW TO HOLD ONE OF THESE THINGS!
LYNN

It's true. I have no idea how to handle a newborn now. I have friends who automatically rip into the mother role; they know how to pick up, turn over, bathe, feed, and bundle a tiny baby, while I just sit by helplessly and watch. Strange … I had no problem handling my own children. I had no trouble changing them, either. I guess when they're yours, it's different. At least it was for me!

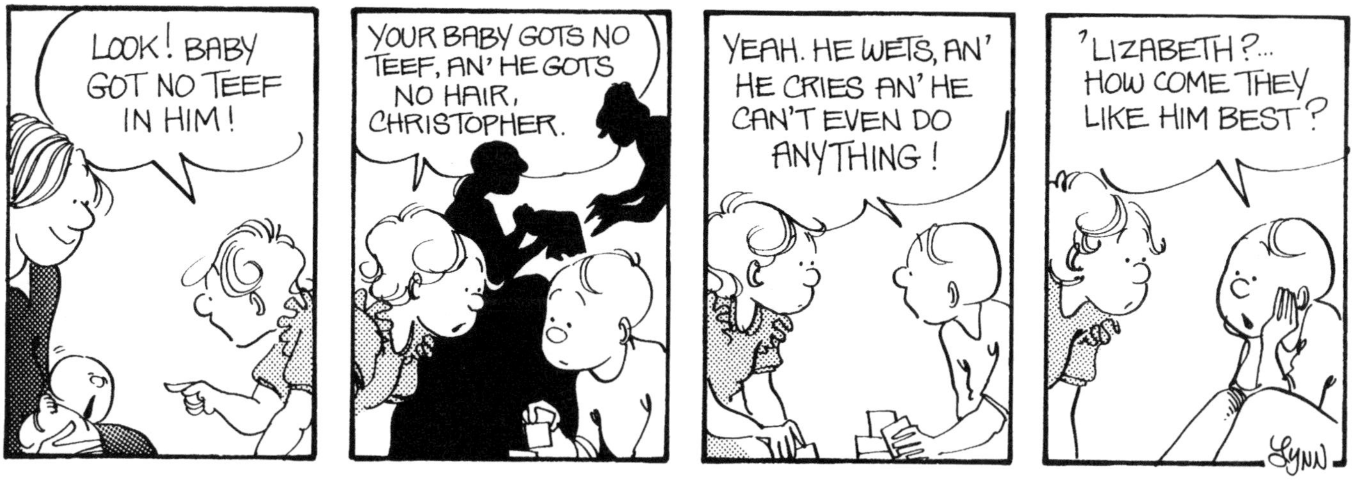
LOOK! BABY GOT NO TEEF IN HIM!
YOUR BABY GOTS NO TEEF, AN' HE GOTS NO HAIR, CHRISTOPHER.
YEAH. HE WETS, AN' HE CRIES AN' HE CAN'T EVEN DO ANYTHING!
'LIZABETH?... HOW COME THEY LIKE HIM BEST?
LYNN

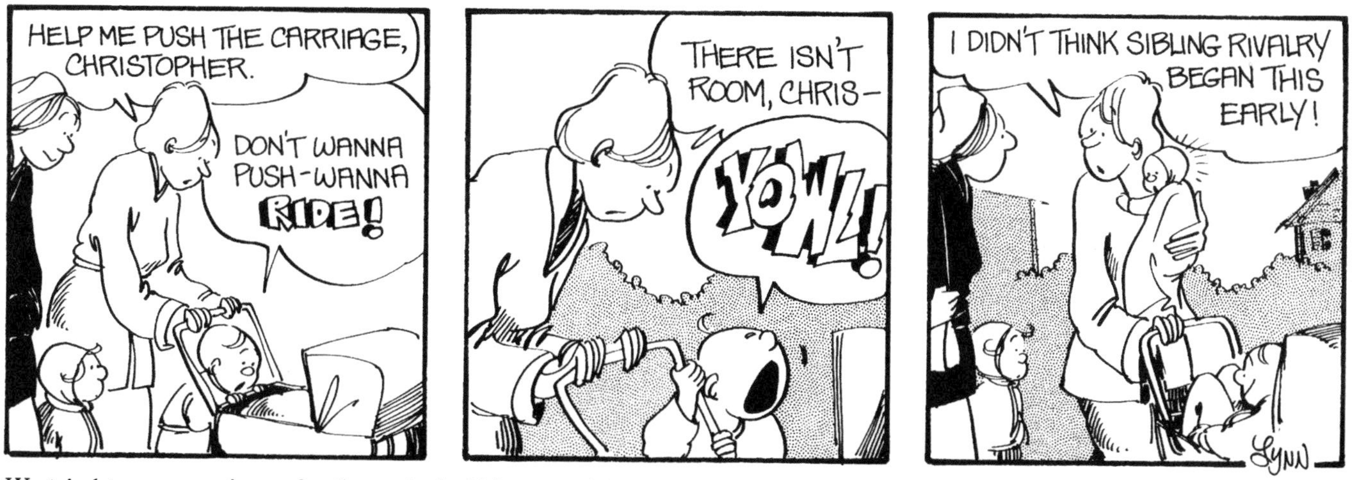
HELP ME PUSH THE CARRIAGE, CHRISTOPHER.
DON'T WANNA PUSH-WANNA RIDE!
THERE ISN'T ROOM, CHRIS-
YOWL!
I DIDN'T THINK SIBLING RIVALRY BEGAN THIS EARLY!
LYNN

We tried to prepare Aaron for the arrival of his new sibling by telling him his position in the family would be elevated to "Big Brother" status. We also said he could have bunk beds when we moved to Lynn Lake. He wanted to sleep up high, he said. Maybe he wanted a place that was safe from toddlers!

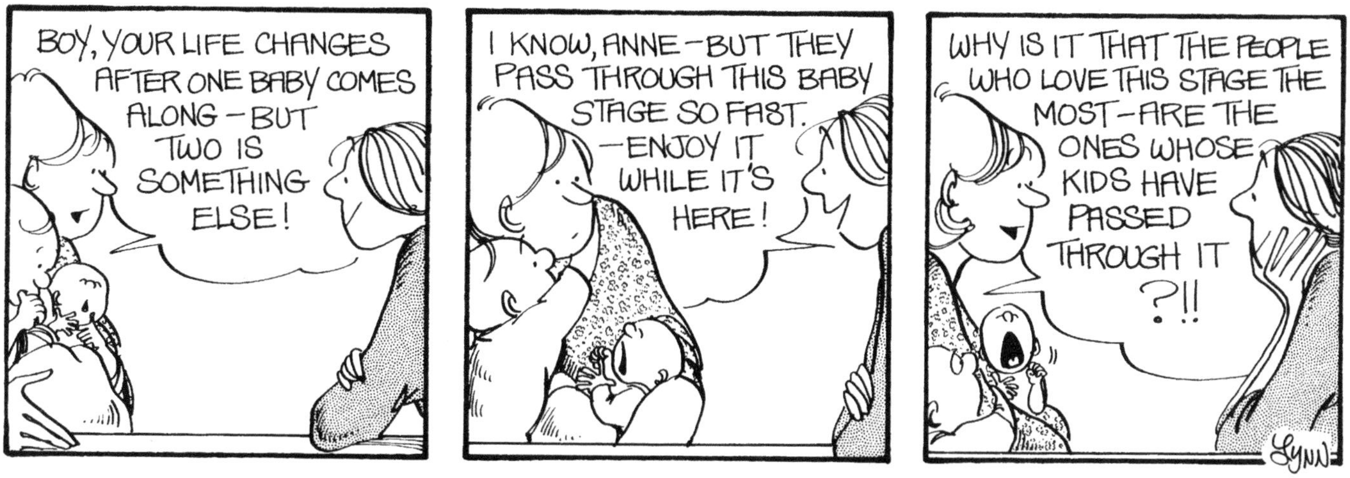
BOY, YOUR LIFE CHANGES AFTER ONE BABY COMES ALONG-BUT TWO IS SOMETHING ELSE!
I KNOW, ANNE-BUT THEY PASS THROUGH THIS BABY STAGE SO FAST. -ENJOY IT WHILE IT'S HERE!
WHY IS IT THAT THE PEOPLE WHO LOVE THIS STAGE THE MOST-ARE THE ONES WHOSE KIDS HAVE PASSED THROUGH IT ?!!
LYNN

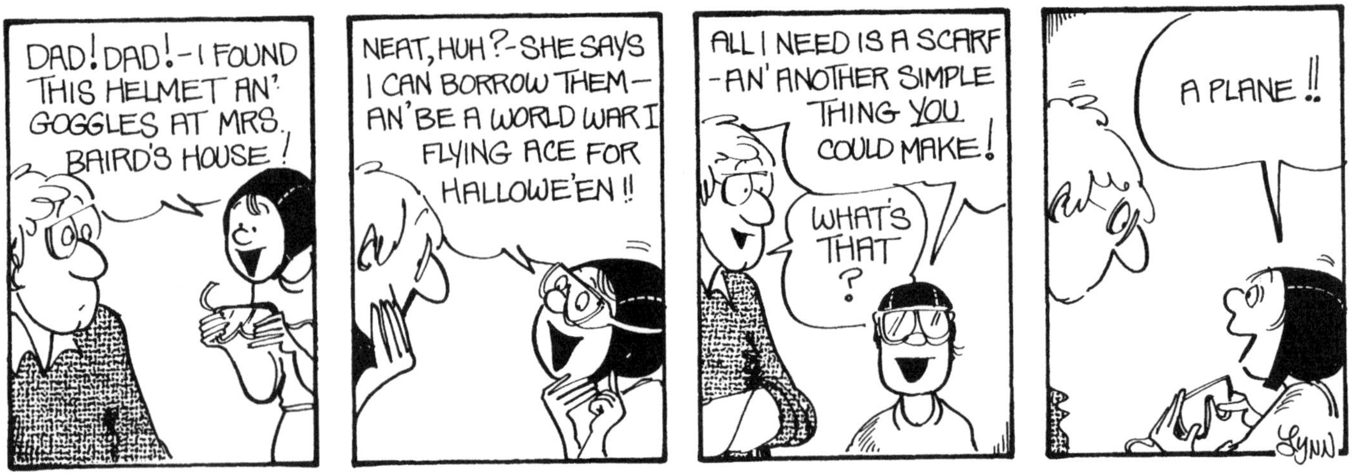
DAD! DAD! - I FOUND THIS HELMET AN' GOGGLES AT MRS. BAIRD'S HOUSE!
NEAT, HUH? - SHE SAYS I CAN BORROW THEM - AN' BE A WORLD WAR I FLYING ACE FOR HALLOWE'EN!!
ALL I NEED IS A SCARF - AN' ANOTHER SIMPLE THING YOU COULD MAKE!
WHAT'S THAT?
A PLANE!!
LYNN

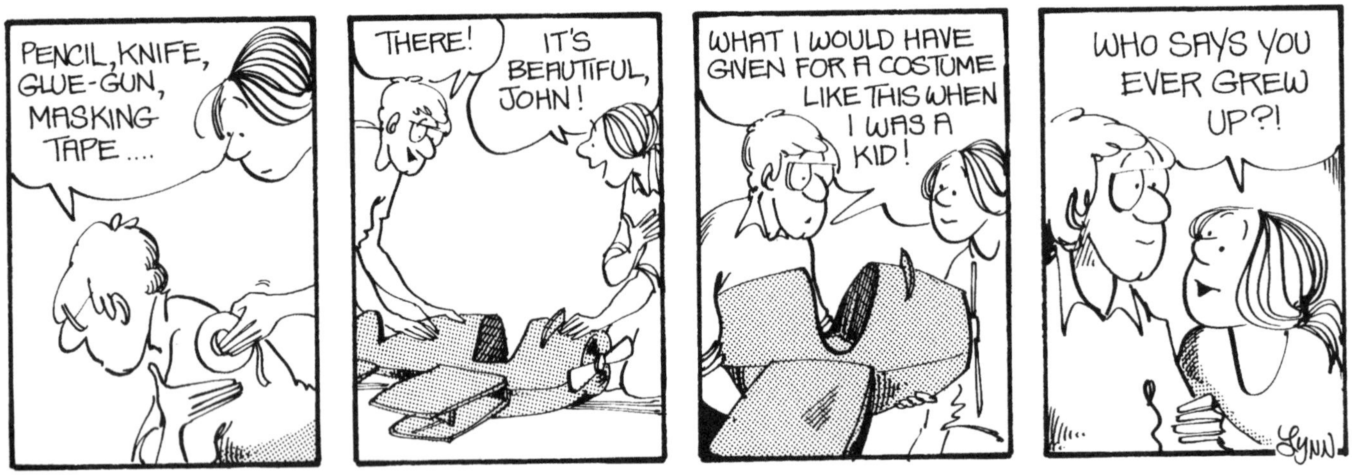
PENCIL, KNIFE, GLUE-GUN, MASKING TAPE....
THERE!
IT'S BEAUTIFUL, JOHN!
WHAT I WOULD HAVE GIVEN FOR A COSTUME LIKE THIS WHEN I WAS A KID!
WHO SAYS YOU EVER GREW UP?!
LYNN

One Halloween, we did make Aaron an airplane costume. It was an ambitious project, as it had to fit over his snowsuit and be easy to walk around in.

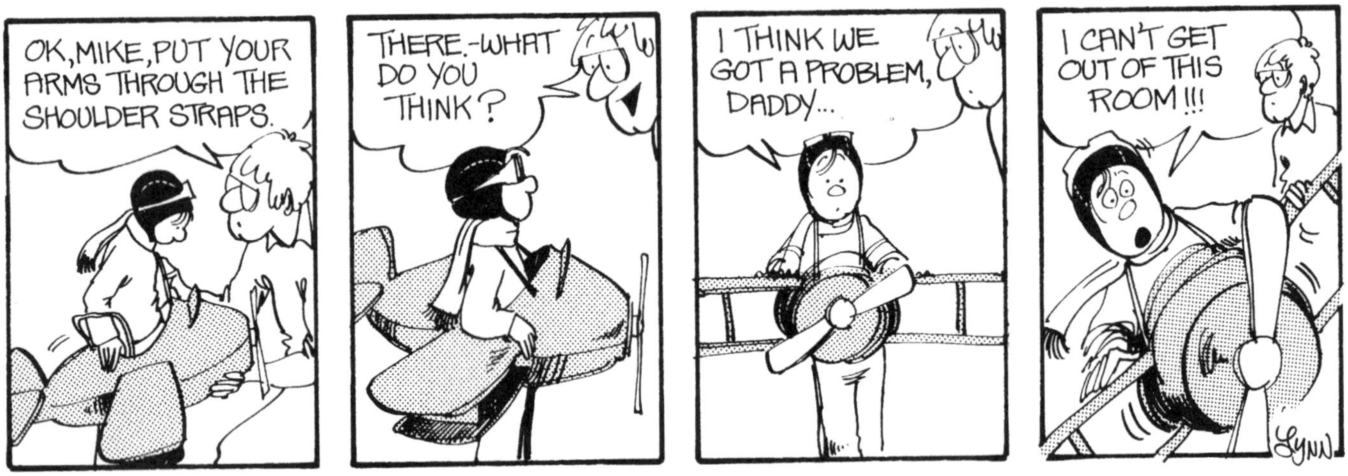
OK, MIKE, PUT YOUR ARMS THROUGH THE SHOULDER STRAPS.
THERE. - WHAT DO YOU THINK?
I THINK WE GOT A PROBLEM, DADDY...
I CAN'T GET OUT OF THIS ROOM!!!
LYNN

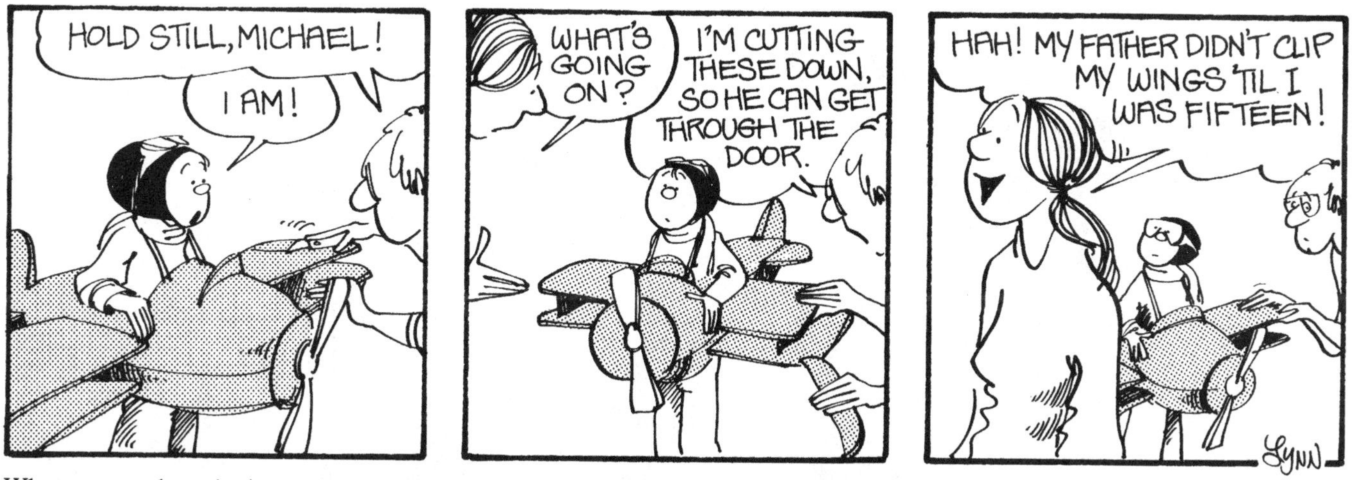
HOLD STILL, MICHAEL!
I AM!
WHAT'S GOING ON?
I'M CUTTING THESE DOWN, SO HE CAN GET THROUGH THE DOOR.
HAH! MY FATHER DIDN'T CLIP MY WINGS 'TIL I WAS FIFTEEN!
Lynn

What you see here is the exact costume with the dilemma of having to shorten the wings so our hero could get out through the door. This was one time when I was able to give a real glimpse into our private lives and the family didn't mind a bit.

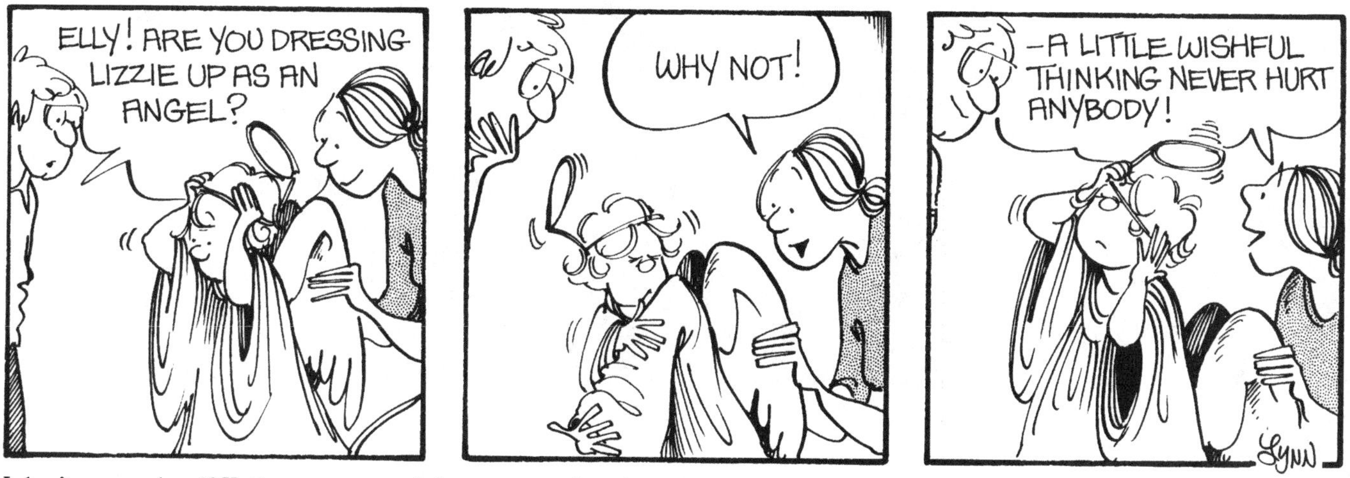
ELLY! ARE YOU DRESSING LIZZIE UP AS AN ANGEL?
WHY NOT!
-A LITTLE WISHFUL THINKING NEVER HURT ANYBODY!
Lynn

I don't remember if Katie was an angel that year — there's a good chance she was!

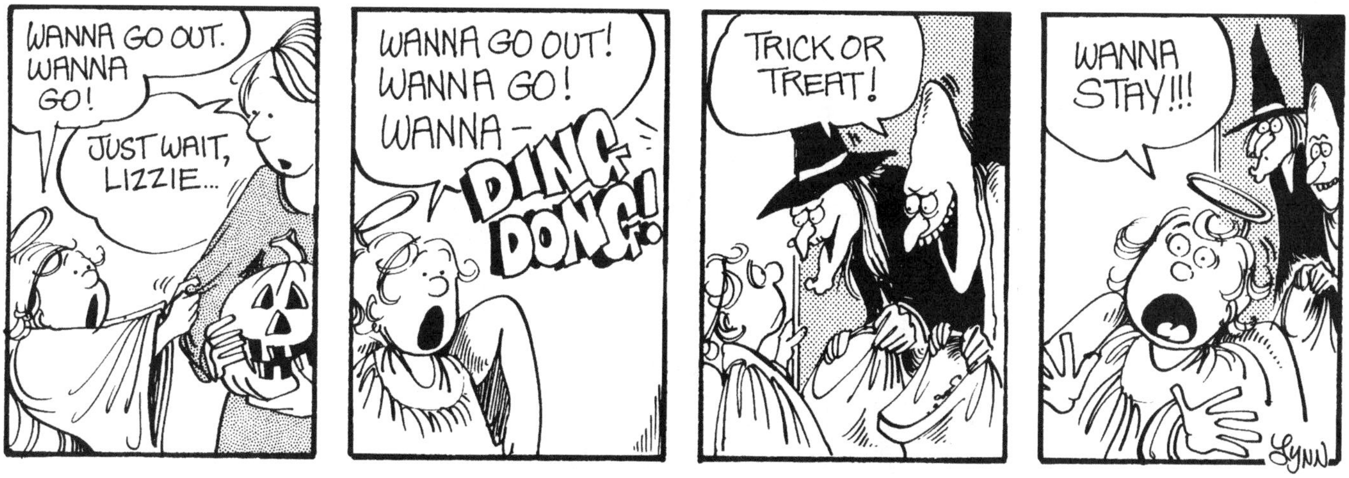
WANNA GO OUT. WANNA GO!
JUST WAIT, LIZZIE...
WANNA GO OUT! WANNA GO! WANNA -
DING DONG!
TRICK OR TREAT!
WANNA STAY!!!
Lynn

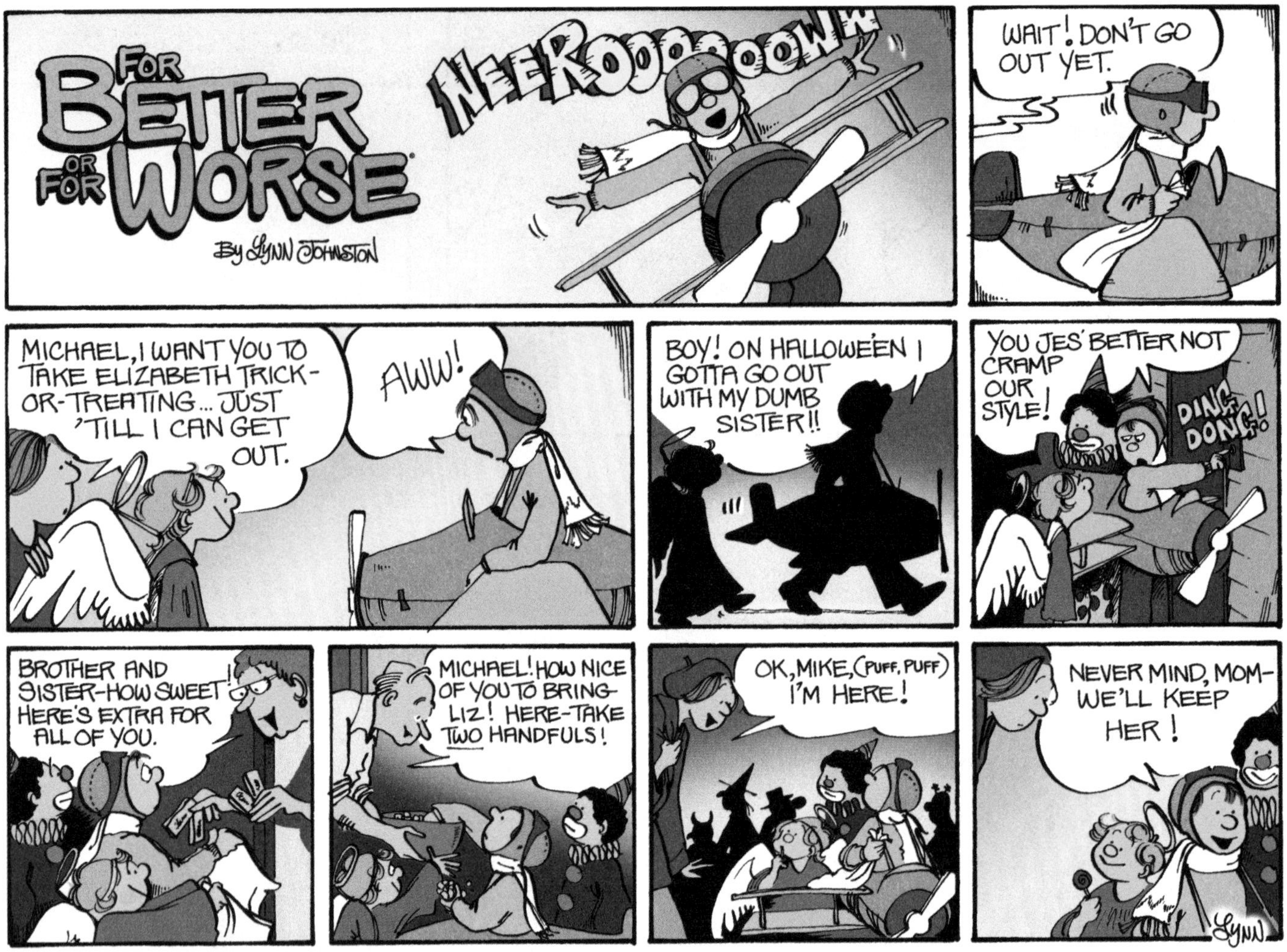
FOR BETTER OR FOR WORSE
BY LYNN JOHNSTON
NEEROOOOOOWN
WAIT! DON'T GO OUT YET.
MICHAEL, I WANT YOU TO TAKE ELIZABETH TRICK-OR-TREATING... JUST 'TILL I CAN GET OUT.
AWW!
BOY! ON HALLOWEEN I GOTTA GO OUT WITH MY DUMB SISTER!!
YOU JES' BETTER NOT CRAMP OUR STYLE!
DING DONG!
BROTHER AND SISTER-HOW SWEET! HERE'S EXTRA FOR ALL OF YOU.
MICHAEL! HOW NICE OF YOU TO BRING LIZ! HERE-TAKE TWO HANDFULS!
OK, MIKE, (PUFF, PUFF) I'M HERE!
NEVER MIND, MOM-WE'LL KEEP HER!
LYNN

The town of Lynn Lake was small enough that kids could be out on their own and you knew they wouldn't be much more than a block away. Even so, one of us always accompanied the trick or treaters — as much for the social interaction as for their safety. Aaron resented having Kate along — he didn't like to be slowed down. So this didn't happen. This was another "what if" moment. What if Lizzie's appearance resulted in more loot?

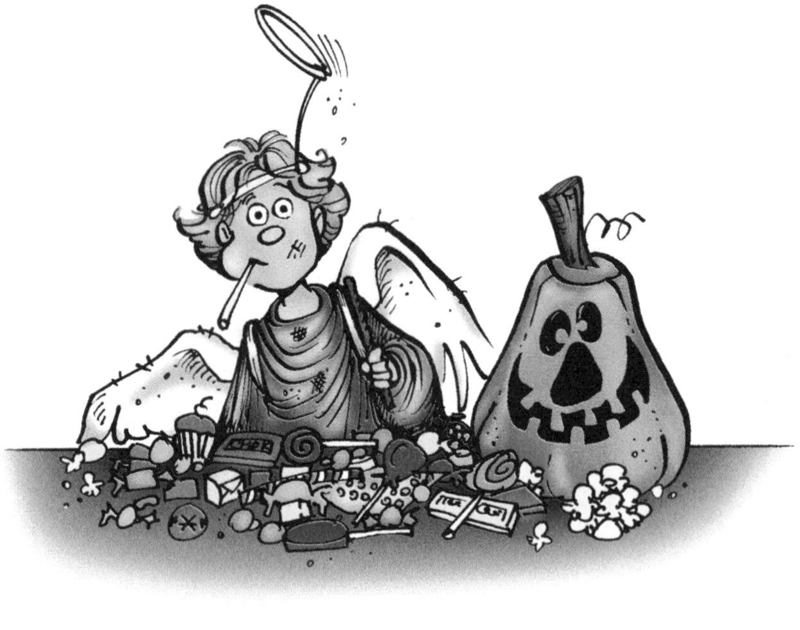

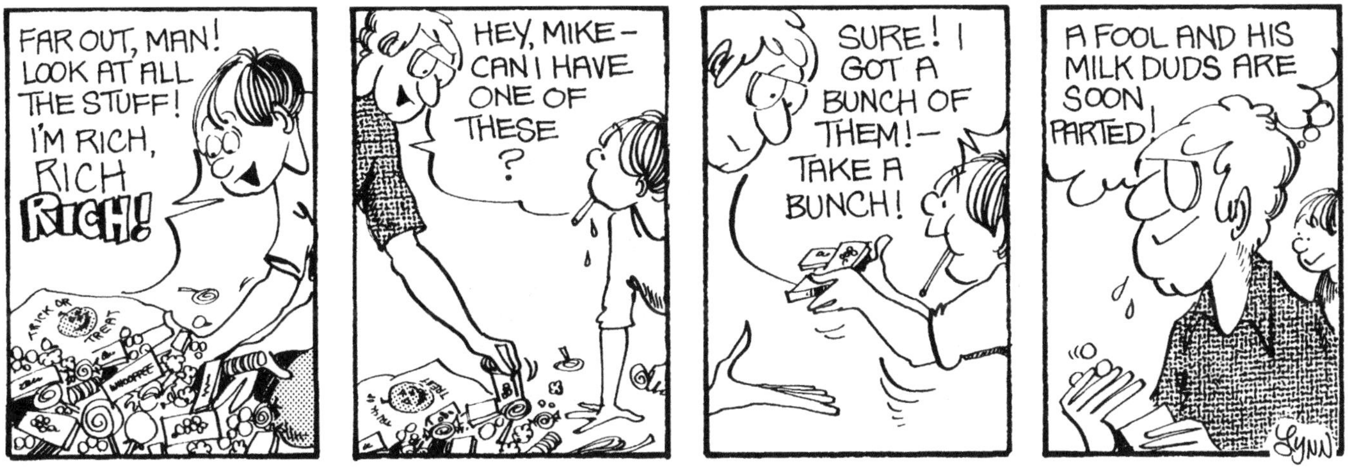
FAR OUT, MAN! LOOK AT ALL THE STUFF! I'M RICH, RICH RICH!
HEY, MIKE – CAN I HAVE ONE OF THESE ?
SURE! I GOT A BUNCH OF THEM! – TAKE A BUNCH!
A FOOL AND HIS MILK DUDS ARE SOON PARTED!
LYNN

It's funny. My husband, the dentist, had the sweetest tooth in the family!

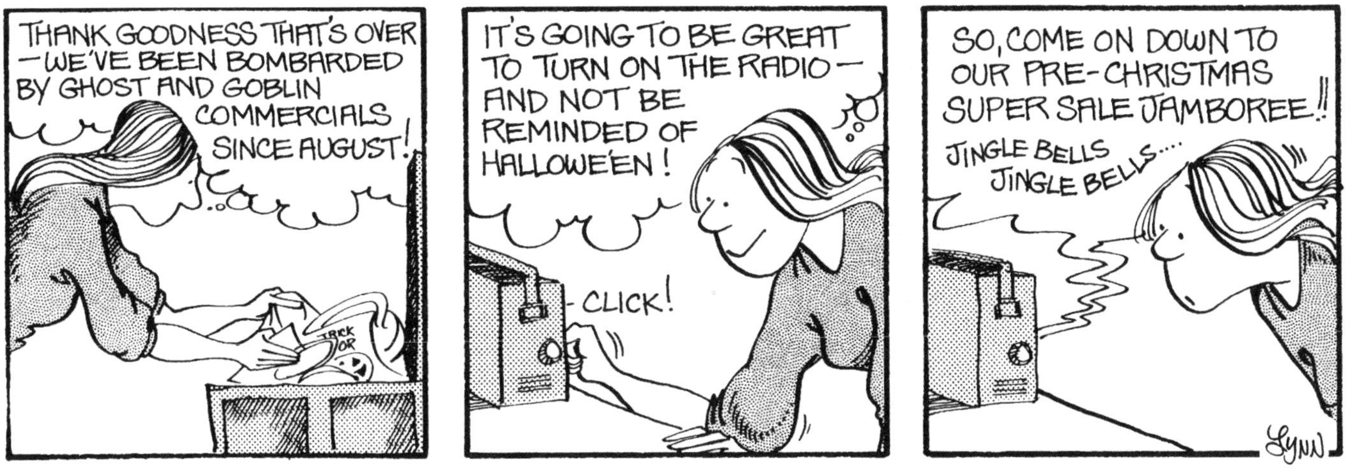
THANK GOODNESS THAT'S OVER – WE'VE BEEN BOMBARDED BY GHOST AND GOBLIN COMMERCIALS SINCE AUGUST!
IT'S GOING TO BE GREAT TO TURN ON THE RADIO – AND NOT BE REMINDED OF HALLOWE'EN!
CLICK!
SO, COME ON DOWN TO OUR PRE-CHRISTMAS SUPER SALE JAMBOREE!!
JINGLE BELLS JINGLE BELLS....
LYNN

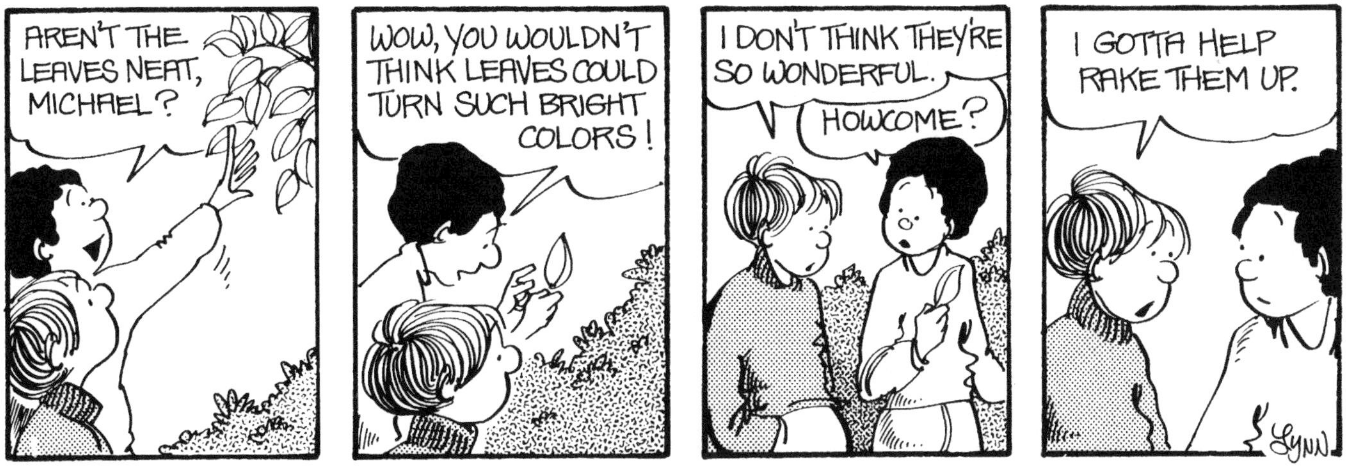
AREN'T THE LEAVES NEAT, MICHAEL?
WOW, YOU WOULDN'T THINK LEAVES COULD TURN SUCH BRIGHT COLORS!
I DON'T THINK THEY'RE SO WONDERFUL.
HOWCOME?
I GOTTA HELP RAKE THEM UP.
LYNN

Raking leaves was not much of a problem in Lynn Lake. The few trees we did have didn't shed much, and the rest were bare by the end of September.

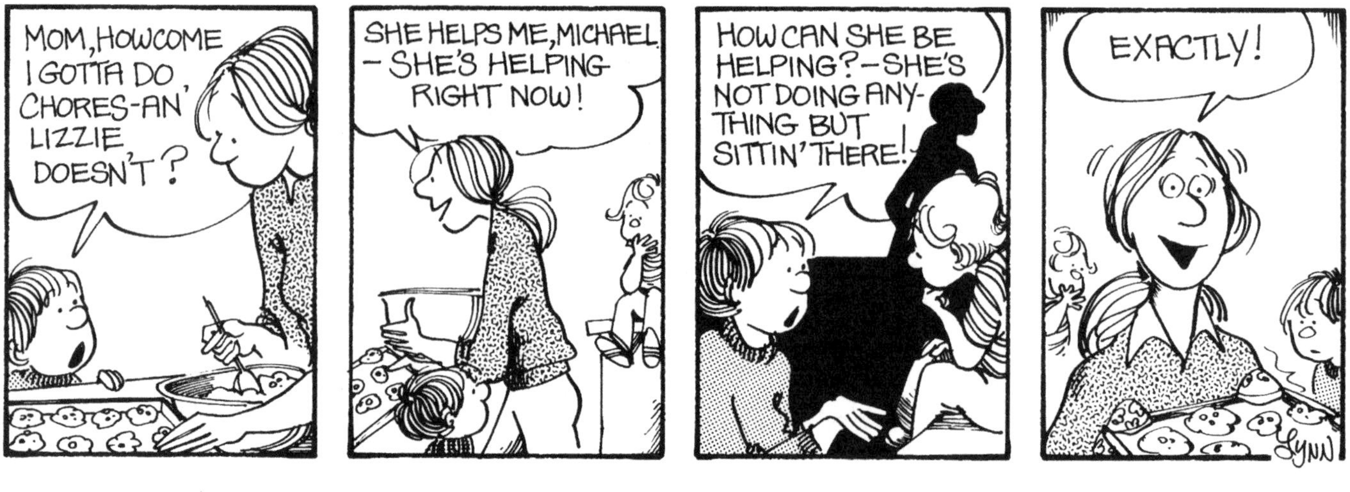
MOM, HOWCOME I GOTTA DO CHORES-AN' LIZZIE DOESN'T?
SHE HELPS ME, MICHAEL - SHE'S HELPING RIGHT NOW!
HOW CAN SHE BE HELPING?-SHE'S NOT DOING ANYTHING BUT SITTIN' THERE!
EXACTLY!
LYNN

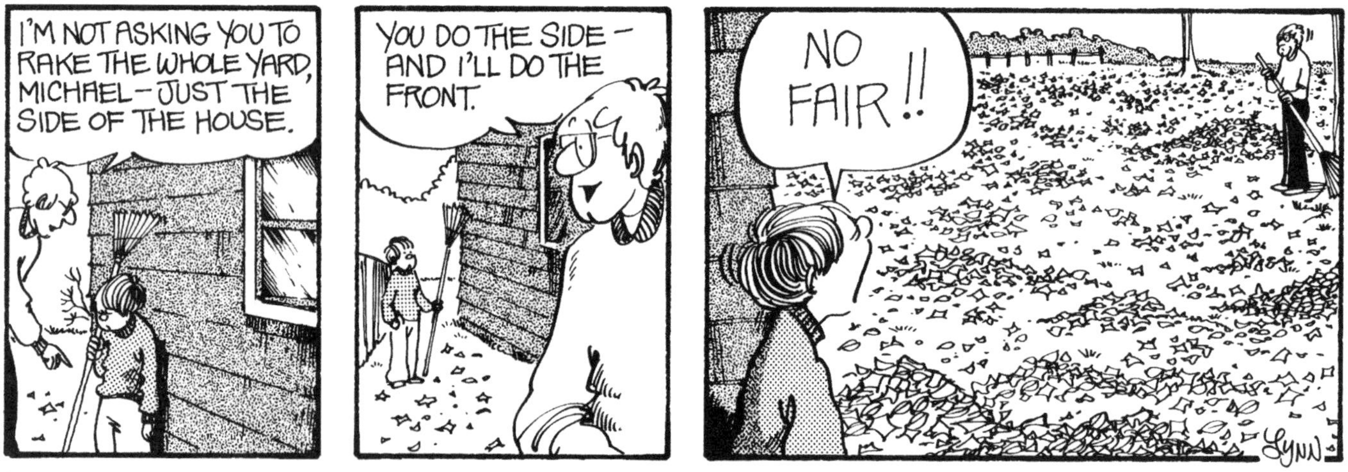
I'M NOT ASKING YOU TO RAKE THE WHOLE YARD, MICHAEL - JUST THE SIDE OF THE HOUSE.
YOU DO THE SIDE - AND I'LL DO THE FRONT.
NO FAIR!!
LYNN

The yard I drew here was the yard in front of our house on Tally Ho Road in Dundas. We had a number of big, leafy trees, and the amount of raking to be done in the fall was overwhelming. The good thing was that they created a wonderful playground. We could bury Aaron and each other in the leaves. We rolled in them, used the leaf bags as beanbag chairs, and enjoyed the crackle, the colour, and the smell.

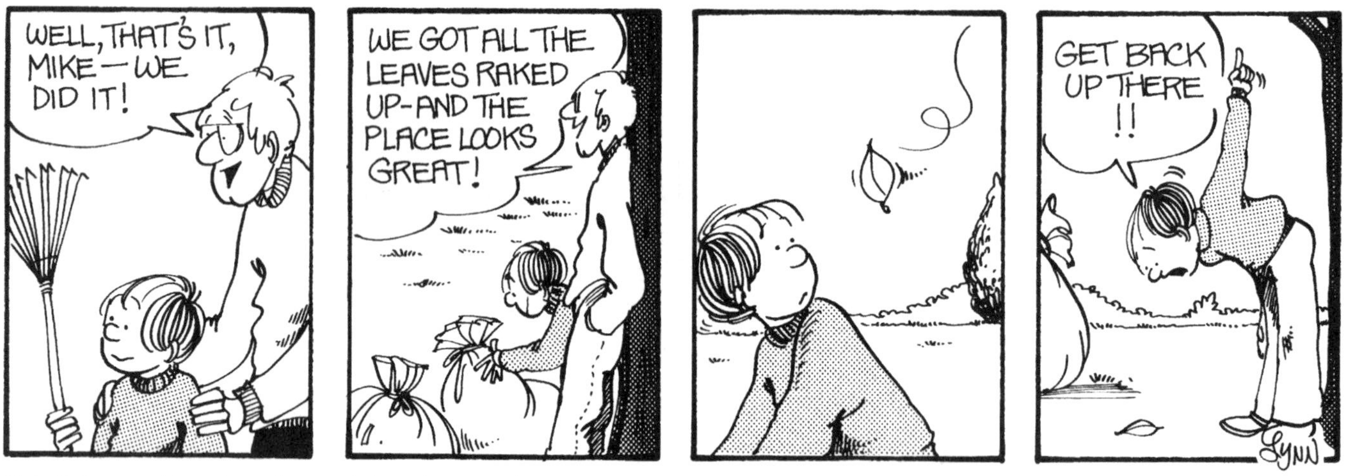
WELL, THAT'S IT, MIKE — WE DID IT!
WE GOT ALL THE LEAVES RAKED UP-AND THE PLACE LOOKS GREAT!
GET BACK UP THERE !!
LYNN

This little one-liner I used once before in a single-panel cartoon, which I submitted to the *Dundas Valley Journal*.

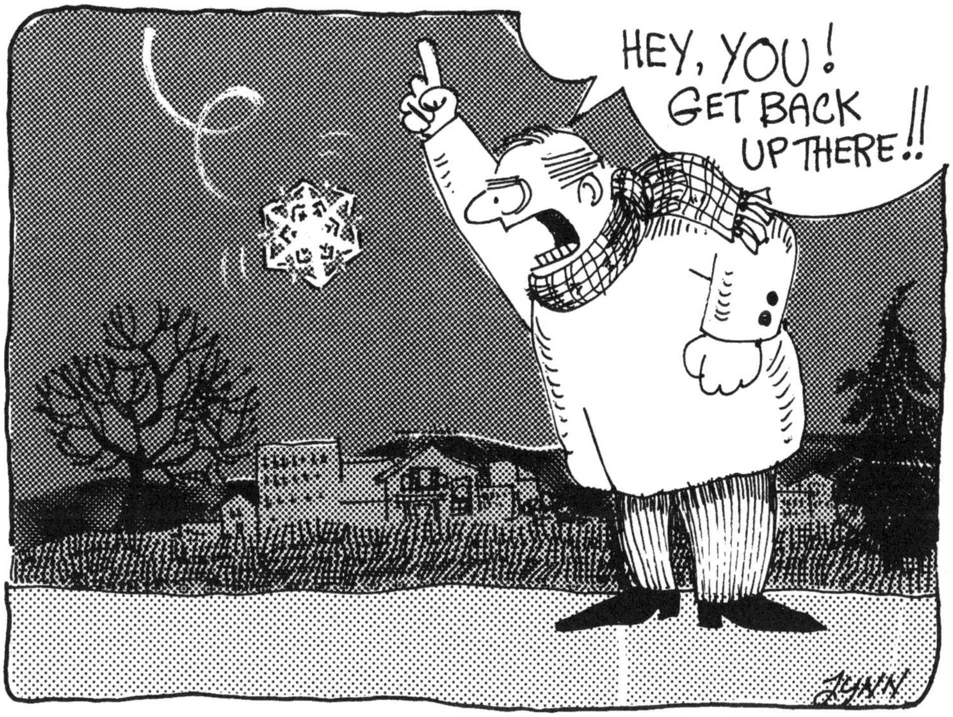
HEY, YOU! GET BACK UP THERE!!
LYNN

This is the actual cartoon, which appeared circa 1973 — it was the first cartoon I had published in a newspaper. Here are some other cartoons that were published around the same time. ...

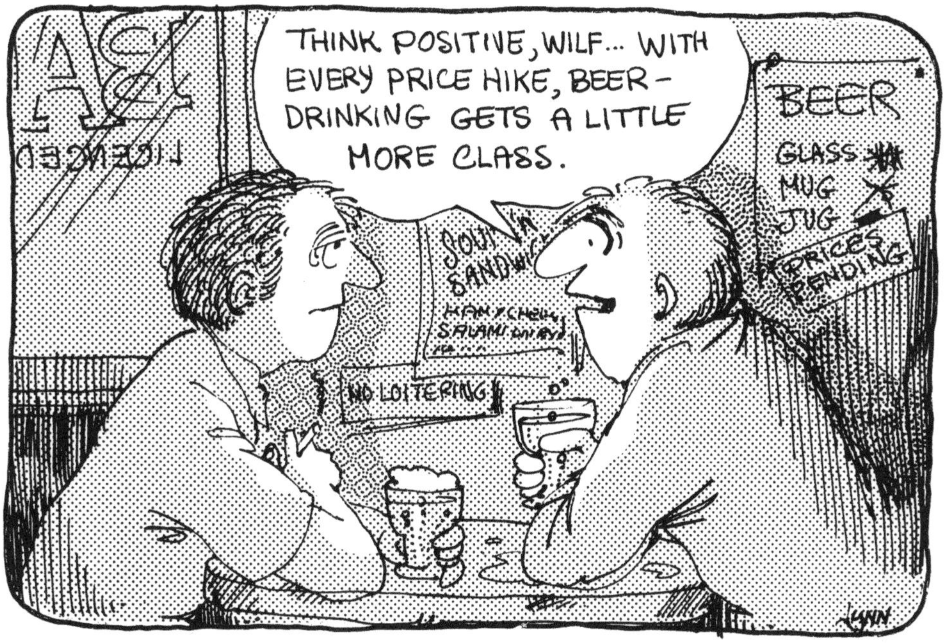
THINK POSITIVE, WILF... WITH EVERY PRICE HIKE, BEER-DRINKING GETS A LITTLE MORE CLASS.
BEER
GLASS
MUG
JUG
PRICES PENDING
NO LOITERING
LYNN

A hike in beer prices was the catalyst for this panel.

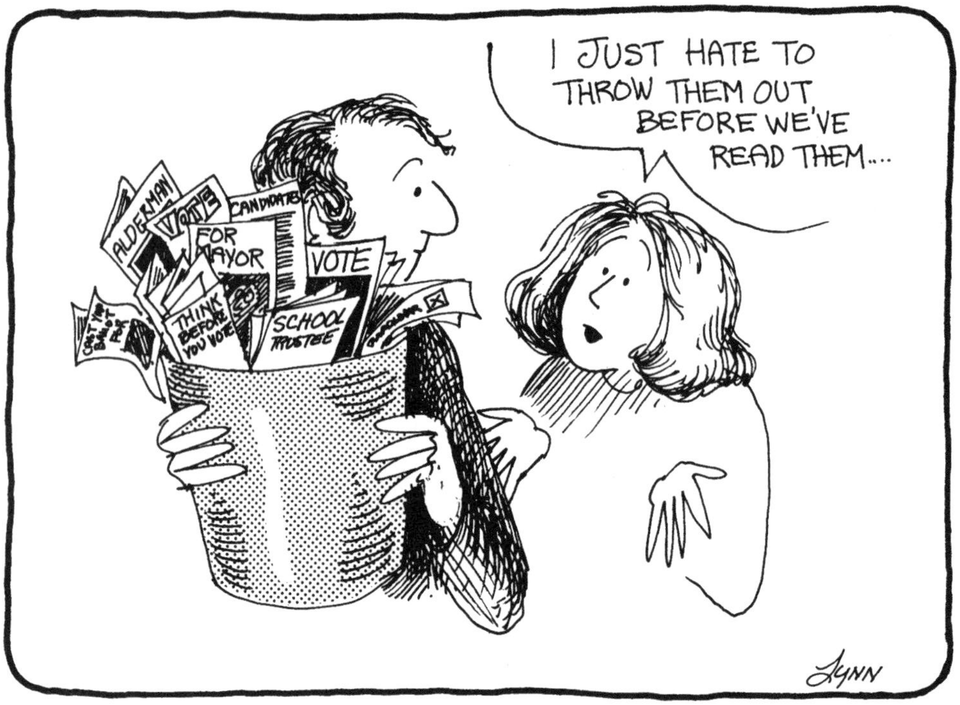
I JUST HATE TO THROW THEM OUT BEFORE WE'VE READ THEM....
ALDERMAN
VOTE
CANDIDATES
FOR MAYOR
VOTE
THINK BEFORE YOU VOTE
SCHOOL TRUSTEE
LYNN

After an election, friends told me they had voted, but knew nothing about the candidates.

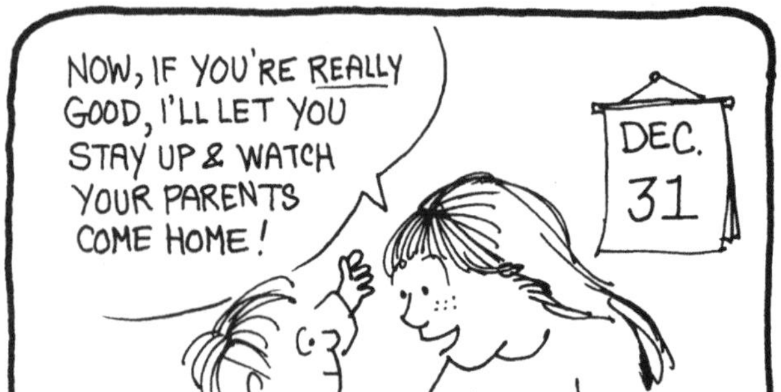
NOW, IF YOU'RE REALLY GOOD, I'LL LET YOU STAY UP & WATCH YOUR PARENTS COME HOME!
DEC. 31
LYNN

I rather like this one!

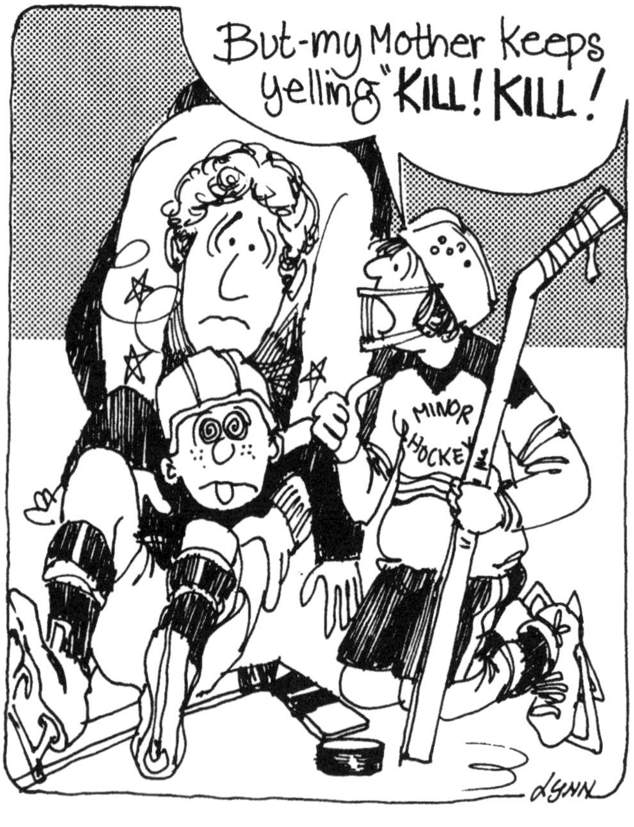
But-my Mother keeps yelling "KILL! KILL!
MINOR HOCKEY
LYNN

It's been almost forty years ... and nothing's changed.

DUNDAS CALLED "CACTUS CAPITAL"...
HE'S NO BUDDING GENIUS, HARRIET.... BUT THE BOY'S GOT SPINE.
HOME GROAN.... BY LYNN JOHNSTON.

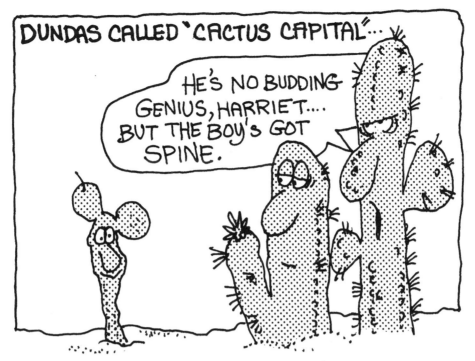

In Dundas, the Veldhuis family had a garden centre that was well known for its amazing and beautiful cactus plants.

SURELY THERE'S ANOTHER WAY OF KEEPING THE SQUIRRELS FROM YOUR BIRDSEED, MOTHER....

When I was a kid, my mom used a slingshot!

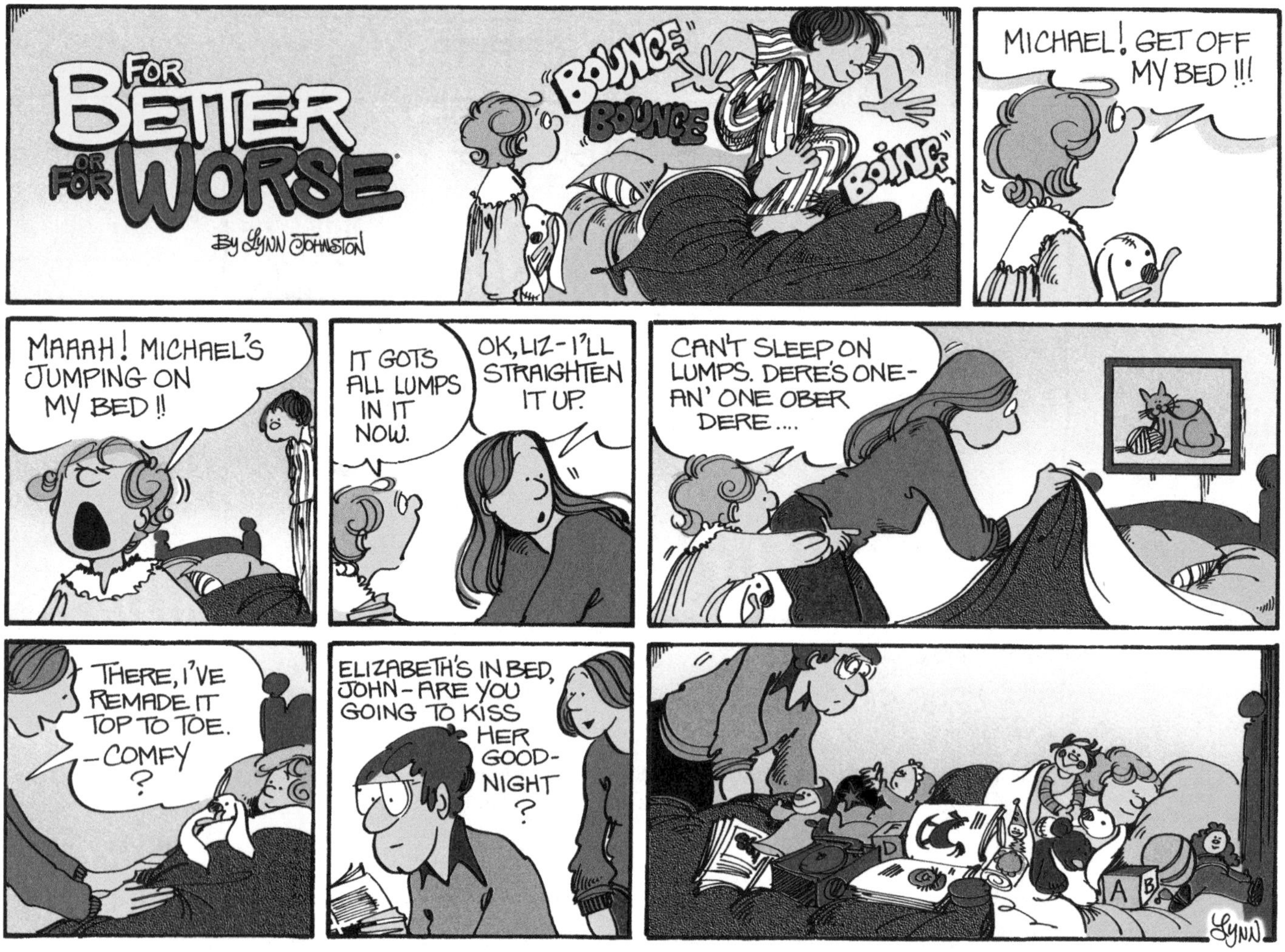
FOR BETTER OR FOR WORSE
BY LYNN JOHNSTON
"BOUNCE"
BOUNCE
"BOING"
MICHAEL! GET OFF MY BED !!!
MAAAH! MICHAEL'S JUMPING ON MY BED !!
IT GOTS ALL LUMPS IN IT NOW.
OK, LIZ - I'LL STRAIGHTEN IT UP.
CAN'T SLEEP ON LUMPS. DERE'S ONE- AN' ONE OBER DERE....
THERE, I'VE REMADE IT TOP TO TOE. -COMFY ?
ELIZABETH'S IN BED, JOHN - ARE YOU GOING TO KISS HER GOOD-NIGHT ?
LYNN

Kate and Aaron each had a favourite toy they slept with. I filled my bed with stuffed animals and slept around them when I was a kid. My favourite was a koala bear that my grandmother brought back from Tasmania for me. It was made with real kangaroo hide, and I loved him until his fur was almost gone. My brother stole him away from me once, insisted on sleeping with him, and then wet his bed. Mom couldn't wash my koala because he was leather, so her advice was to let him sit on the windowsill and air out. "In time he will be less whiffy," she said. But he stank for years, so "Whiffy" was what I called him. I still have old "Whiff" in my what-not cabinet. He's sweeter smelling now, and still loved.

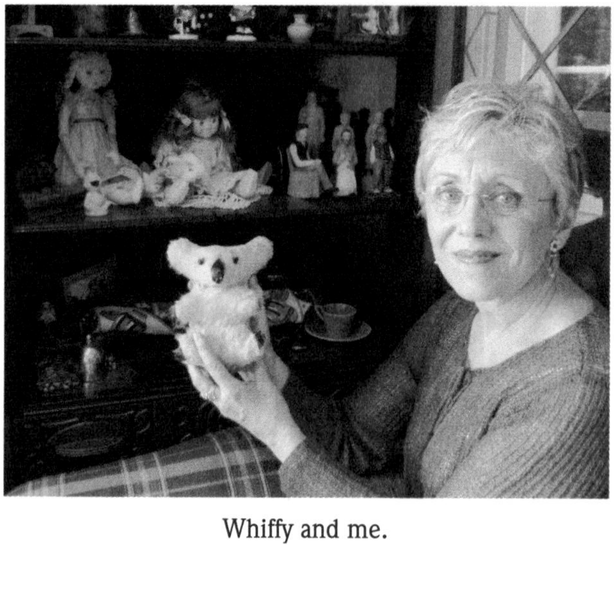

Whiffy and me.

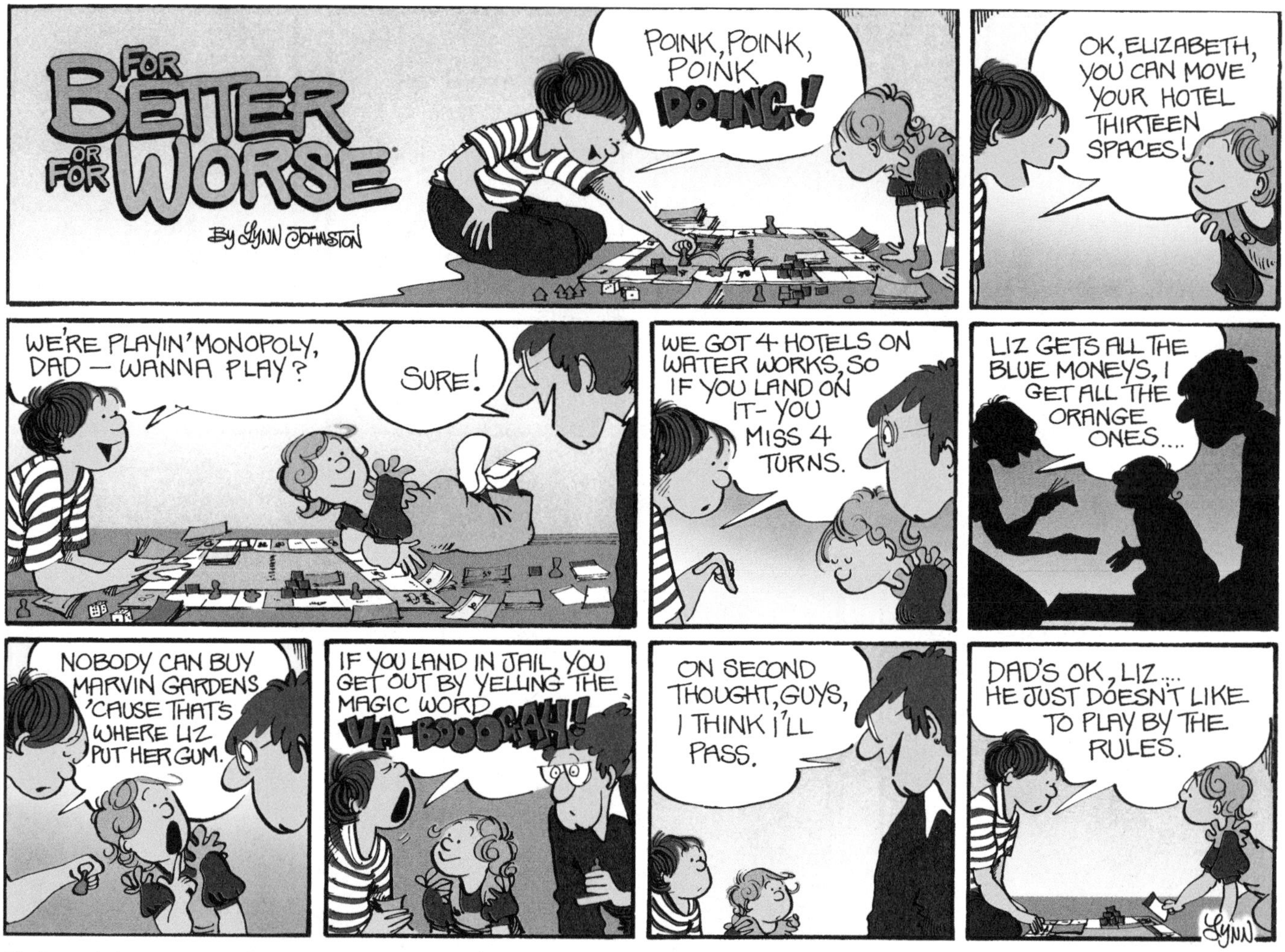
For Better or For Worse
By Lynn Johnston
POINK, POINK, POINK
DOING!
OK, ELIZABETH, YOU CAN MOVE YOUR HOTEL THIRTEEN SPACES!
WE'RE PLAYIN' MONOPOLY, DAD — WANNA PLAY?
SURE!
WE GOT 4 HOTELS ON WATER WORKS, SO IF YOU LAND ON IT- YOU MISS 4 TURNS.
LIZ GETS ALL THE BLUE MONEYS, I GET ALL THE ORANGE ONES....
NOBODY CAN BUY MARVIN GARDENS 'CAUSE THAT'S WHERE LIZ PUT HER GUM.
IF YOU LAND IN JAIL, YOU GET OUT BY YELLING THE MAGIC WORD
VA-BOOOGAH!
ON SECOND THOUGHT, GUYS, I THINK I'LL PASS.
DAD'S OK, LIZ.... HE JUST DOESN'T LIKE TO PLAY BY THE RULES.
LYNN

Katie and Aaron made their own Monopoly rules when the ones that came with the game didn't suit them. This is a shortened version of their game, including "Va-Boogah!", which was best shouted through a mouthful of Cheezies. These were the days before interactive video games, and I often wonder if this was more fun.

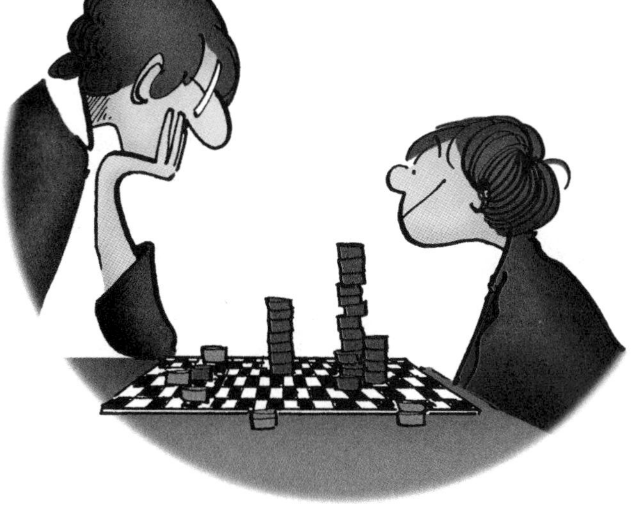

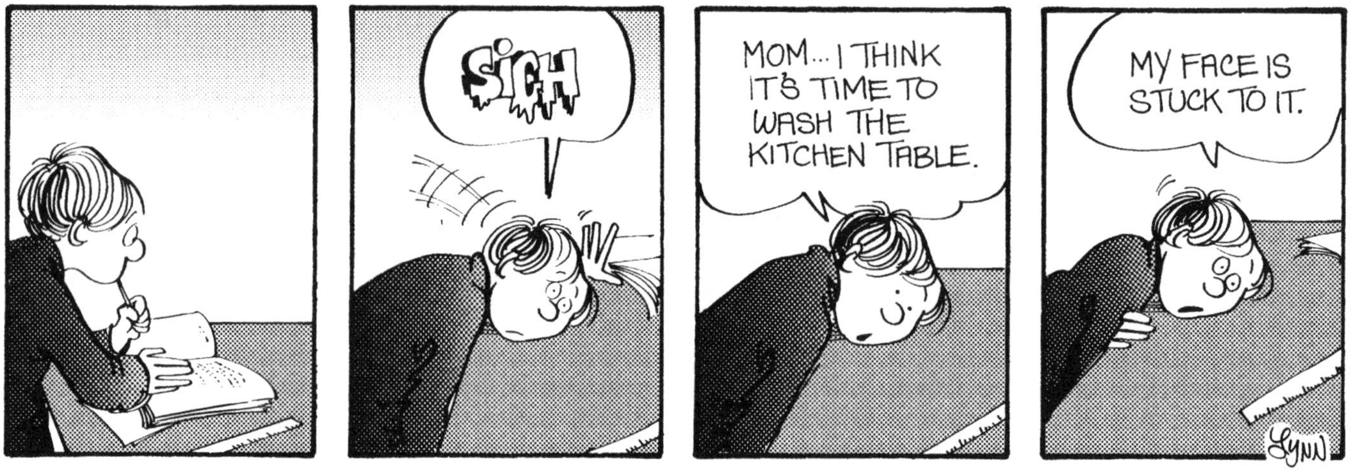
SIGH
MOM... I THINK IT'S TIME TO WASH THE KITCHEN TABLE.
MY FACE IS STUCK TO IT.
LYNN

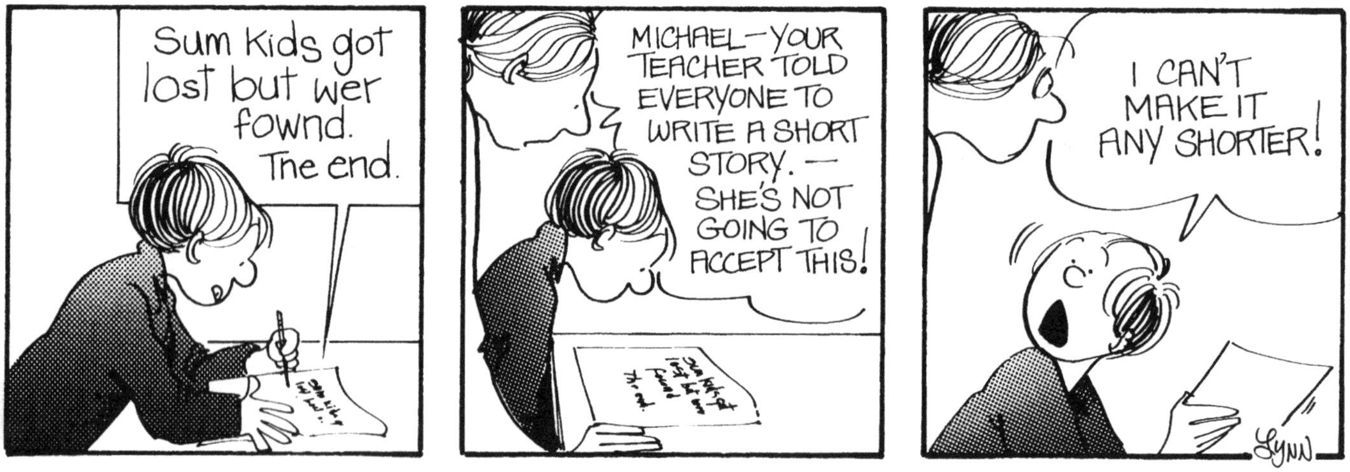
Sum kids got lost but wer fownd. The end.
MICHAEL—YOUR TEACHER TOLD EVERYONE TO WRITE A SHORT STORY.—SHE'S NOT GOING TO ACCEPT THIS!
I CAN'T MAKE IT ANY SHORTER!
LYNN

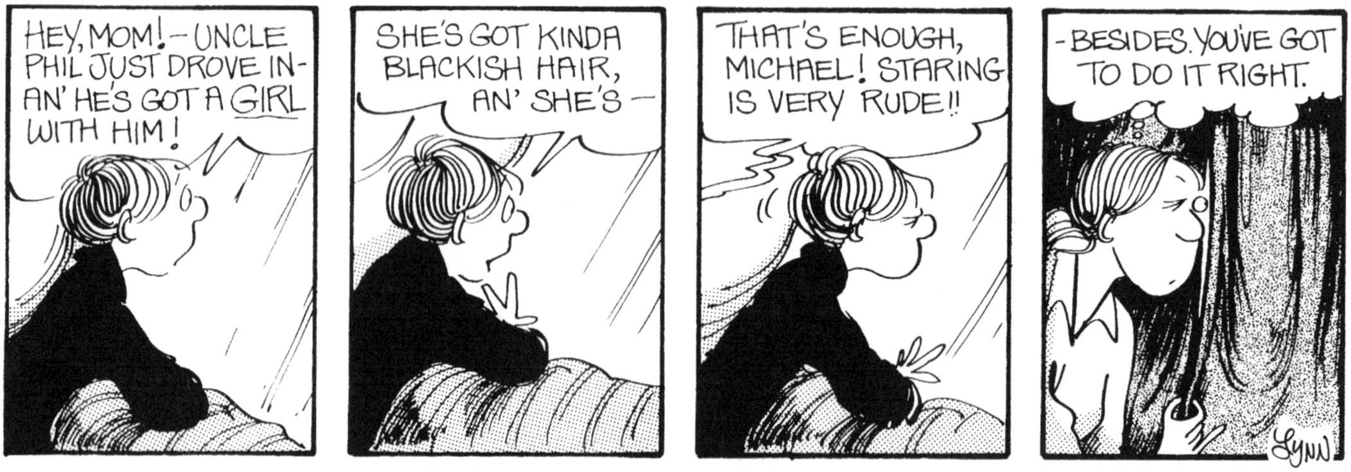
HEY, MOM!—UNCLE PHIL JUST DROVE IN—AN' HE'S GOT A GIRL WITH HIM!
SHE'S GOT KINDA BLACKISH HAIR, AN' SHE'S—
THAT'S ENOUGH, MICHAEL! STARING IS VERY RUDE!!
-BESIDES. YOU'VE GOT TO DO IT RIGHT.
LYNN

Every house on Eldon Avenue in Lynn Lake was close to the road, and folks could easily see into the windows. We had sheers over ours both for privacy and for the luxury of watching while not being seen.

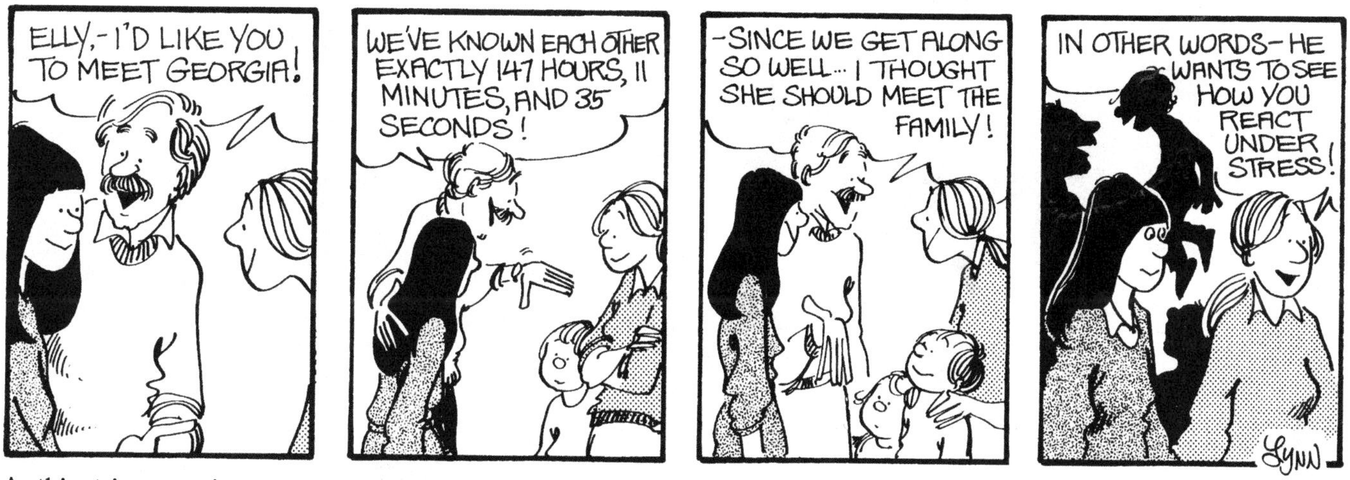
ELLY,- I'D LIKE YOU TO MEET GEORGIA!
WE'VE KNOWN EACH OTHER EXACTLY 147 HOURS, 11 MINUTES, AND 35 SECONDS!
-SINCE WE GET ALONG SO WELL... I THOUGHT SHE SHOULD MEET THE FAMILY!
IN OTHER WORDS- HE WANTS TO SEE HOW YOU REACT UNDER STRESS!
LYNN

As this strip was going to press, my brother, Alan, had started to go out with a lovely lady named Joan. I had been so close to guessing details about his relationships in the strip that, when he saw this, he asked me not to have Phil and Georgia get married until after he married Joan!

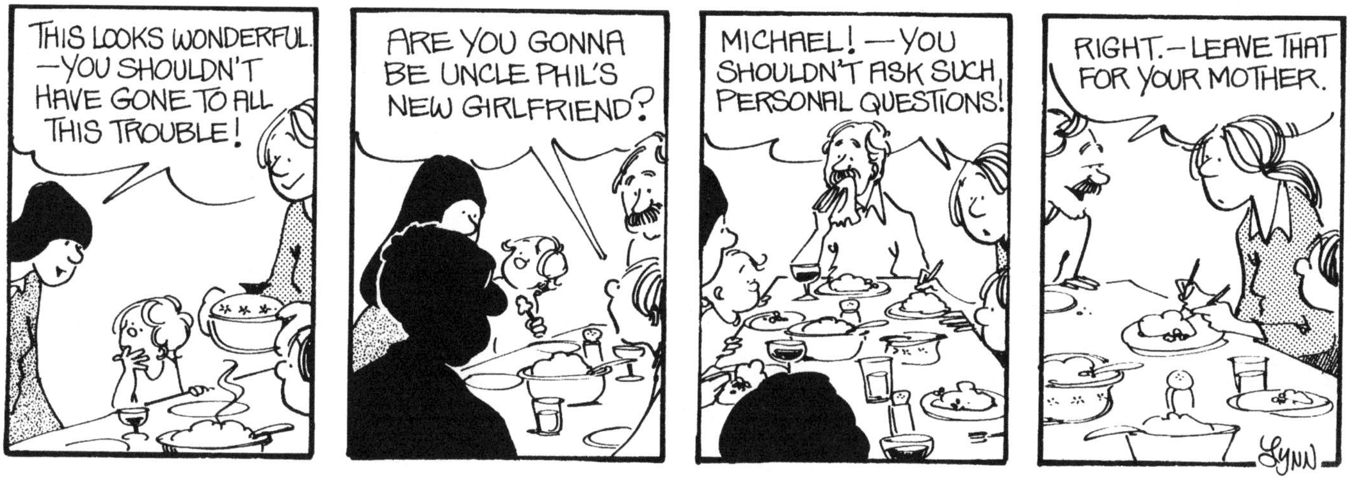
THIS LOOKS WONDERFUL. —YOU SHOULDN'T HAVE GONE TO ALL THIS TROUBLE!
ARE YOU GONNA BE UNCLE PHIL'S NEW GIRLFRIEND?
MICHAEL! —YOU SHOULDN'T ASK SUCH PERSONAL QUESTIONS!
RIGHT.– LEAVE THAT FOR YOUR MOTHER.
LYNN

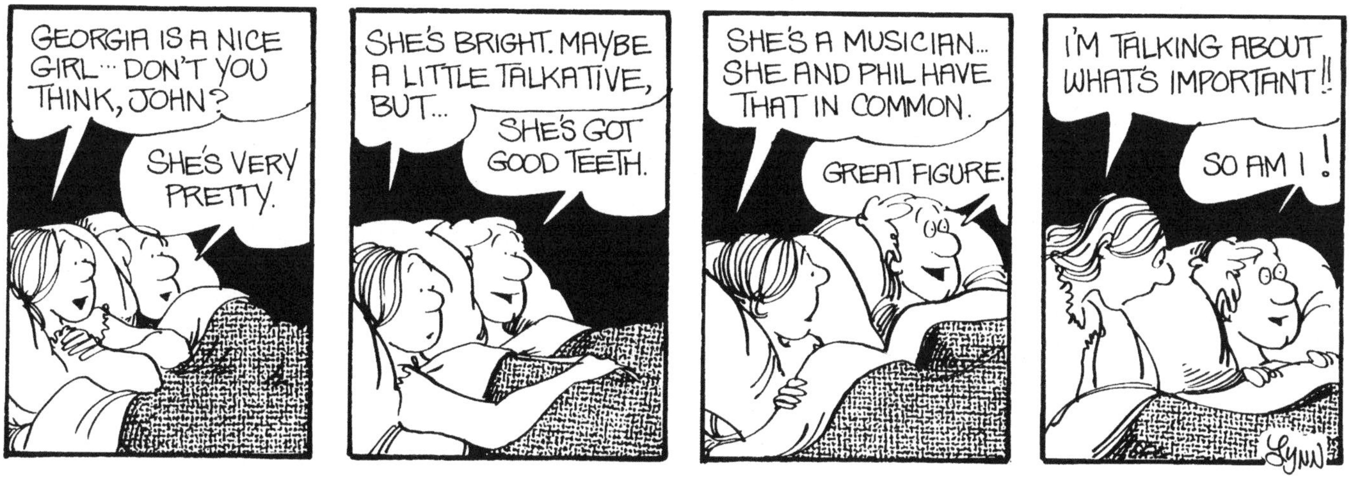
GEORGIA IS A NICE GIRL... DON'T YOU THINK, JOHN?
SHE'S VERY PRETTY.
SHE'S BRIGHT. MAYBE A LITTLE TALKATIVE, BUT...
SHE'S GOT GOOD TEETH.
SHE'S A MUSICIAN... SHE AND PHIL HAVE THAT IN COMMON.
GREAT FIGURE.
I'M TALKING ABOUT WHAT'S IMPORTANT!!
SO AM I!
LYNN

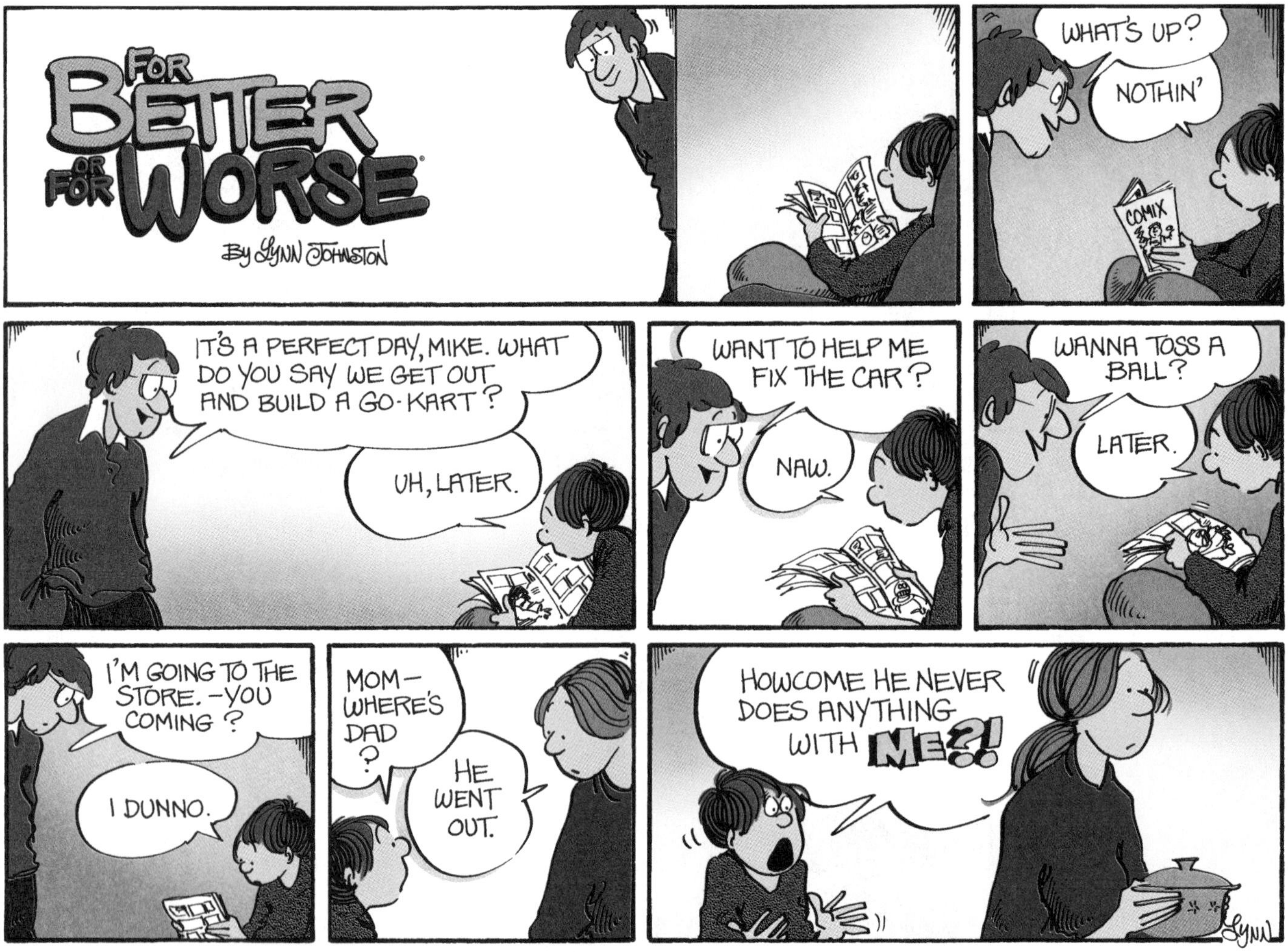
FOR BETTER OR FOR WORSE
BY LYNN JOHNSTON
WHAT'S UP?
NOTHIN'
COMIX
IT'S A PERFECT DAY, MIKE. WHAT DO YOU SAY WE GET OUT AND BUILD A GO-KART?
UH, LATER.
WANT TO HELP ME FIX THE CAR?
NAW.
WANNA TOSS A BALL?
LATER.
I'M GOING TO THE STORE. -YOU COMING?
I DUNNO.
MOM— WHERE'S DAD?
HE WENT OUT.
HOWCOME HE NEVER DOES ANYTHING WITH ME?!
LYNN

This is another glimpse from my childhood. My dad was the kind of guy who loved to build go-karts and tree houses and water slides on the lawn. Even though it wasn't cool to do stuff with your parents, a day with Dad always ended with a trophy of some kind: something built or found or eaten. When we weren't building stuff, we were hitting the dump or scrounging in the workshop, and after that, we'd go to the Dairy Queen. The BIG cone cost a quarter, and was almost too big to eat. It was when we had grown up a bit that we stopped hanging out with Dad. We'd give him excuses for why we weren't into making stuff or going out, and it hurt him to see us change. I do remember him taking the neighbour's kid out for an ice cream cone and wondering, "Why isn't he taking me?" — knowing full well that I'd cut him out of my circle of friends. I just wanted him to be a dad. What I didn't know was that he was being a dad — and he was exceptional!

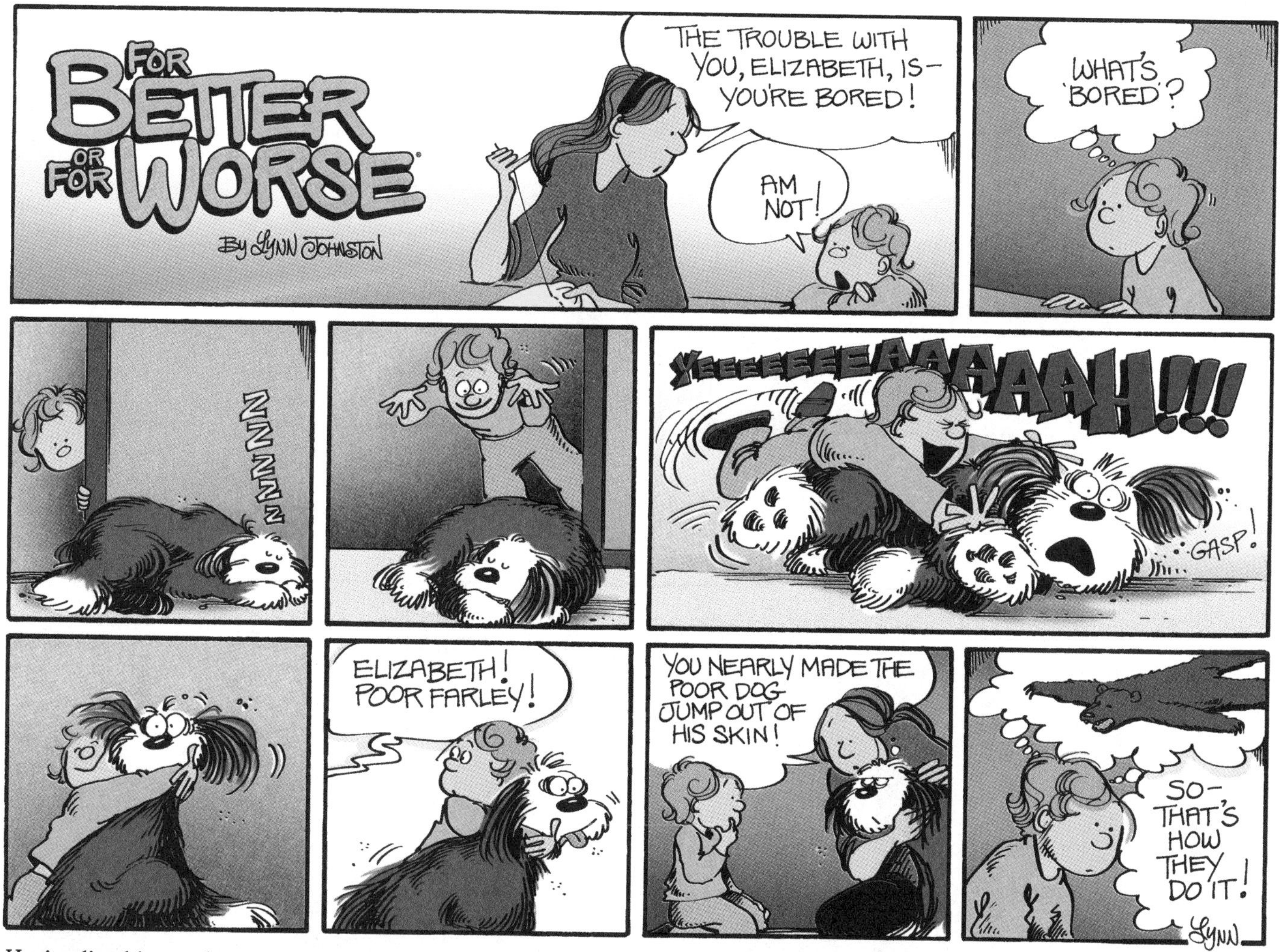
FOR BETTER OR FOR WORSE
BY LYNN JOHNSTON
THE TROUBLE WITH YOU, ELIZABETH, IS— YOU'RE BORED!
AM NOT!
WHAT'S 'BORED'?
ZZZZZZ
YEEEEEEEAAAAAAH!!!!
GASP!
ELIZABETH! POOR FARLEY!
YOU NEARLY MADE THE POOR DOG JUMP OUT OF HIS SKIN!
SO— THAT'S HOW THEY DO IT!
LYNN

Having lived in northern communities for most of my adult life, I have been exposed to the fur trade from the trappers' point of view. It isn't unusual to see samples of pelts made into rugs, and some are pretty vicious looking. In fact, we owned one ourselves in Lynn Lake. It was a "cross fox" pelt, which lay in front of our fireplace. When this Sunday page appeared, I had quite a number of complaints from animal-rights activists. They were understandably concerned. It's just that, this is the way it was for us, and still is. Katie did ask how and why the rug had come to be. I had purchased the pelt to support a family living in the bush — and I felt no guilt in doing so. This is not the best cartoon I ever did — it's probably one of the more forgettable ones … but when you have a relentless deadline, you go with whatever you can think up and run with it. Then … you wait for the flack to come later!

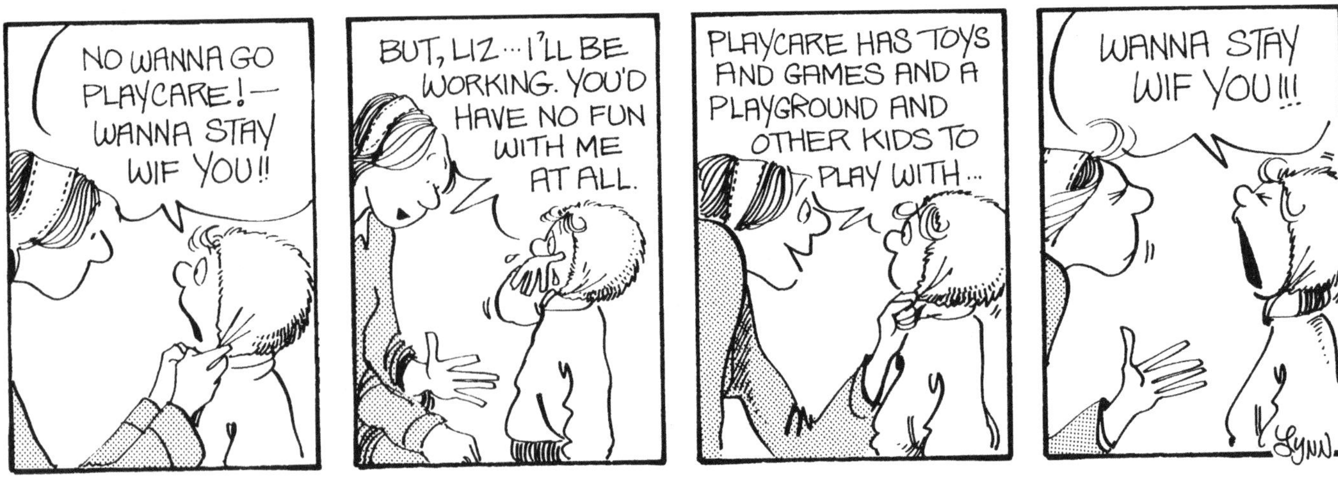
NO WANNA GO PLAYCARE!— WANNA STAY WIF YOU!!
BUT, LIZ... I'LL BE WORKING. YOU'D HAVE NO FUN WITH ME AT ALL.
PLAYCARE HAS TOYS AND GAMES AND A PLAYGROUND AND OTHER KIDS TO PLAY WITH...
WANNA STAY WIF YOU!!!
LYNN

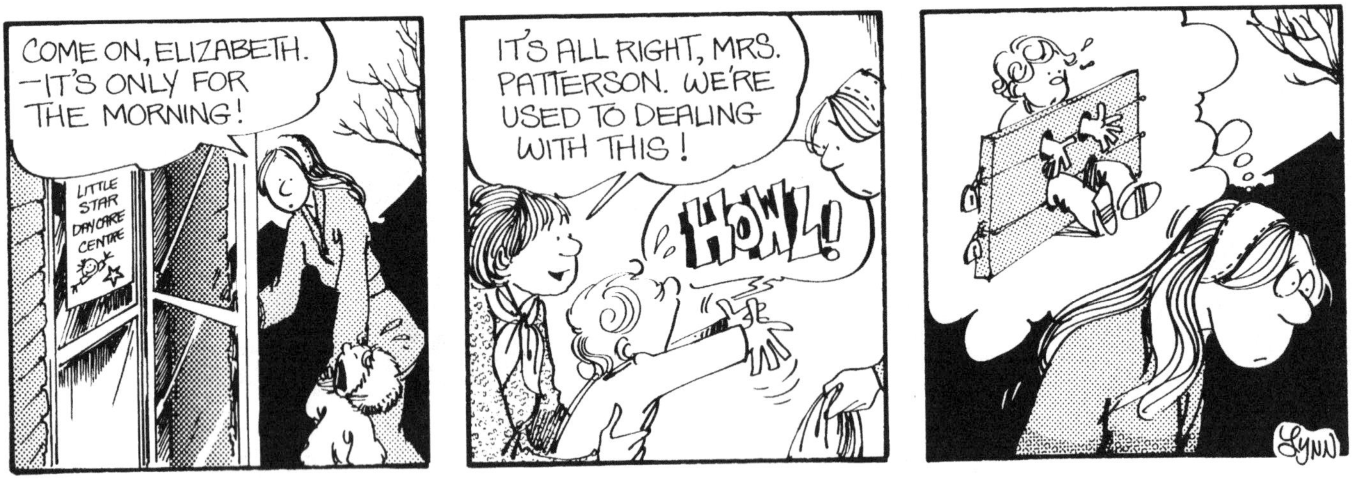
COME ON, ELIZABETH. —IT'S ONLY FOR THE MORNING!
LITTLE STAR DAYCARE CENTRE
IT'S ALL RIGHT, MRS. PATTERSON. WE'RE USED TO DEALING WITH THIS!
HOWL!
LYNN

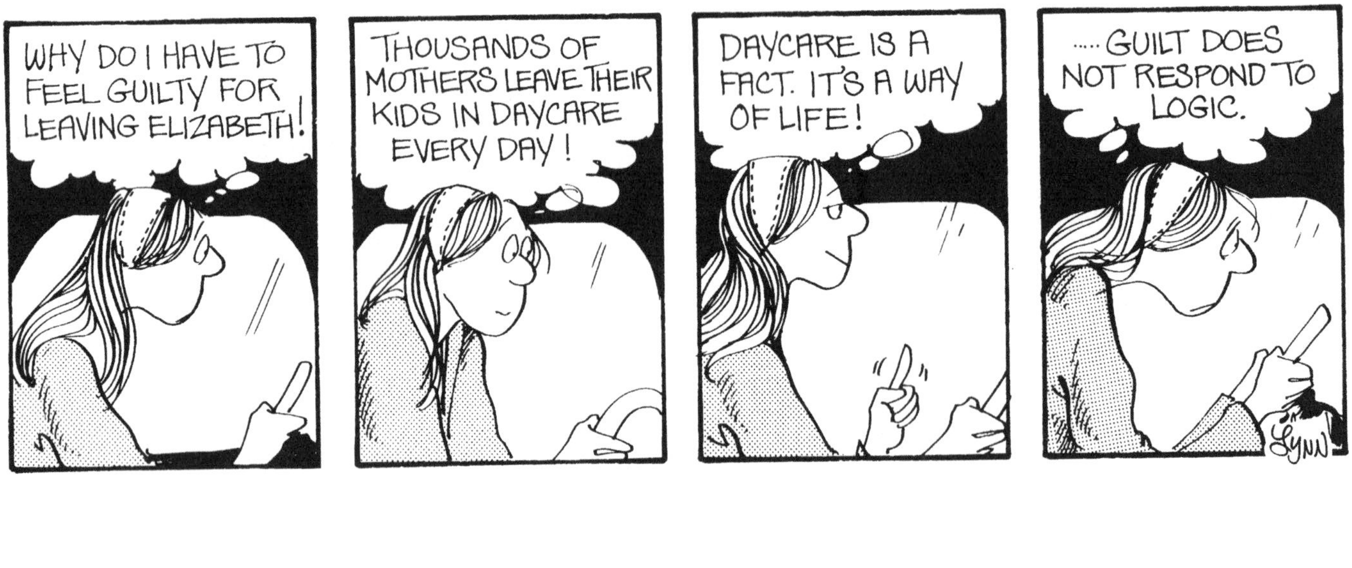
WHY DO I HAVE TO FEEL GUILTY FOR LEAVING ELIZABETH!
THOUSANDS OF MOTHERS LEAVE THEIR KIDS IN DAYCARE EVERY DAY!
DAYCARE IS A FACT. IT'S A WAY OF LIFE!
.....GUILT DOES NOT RESPOND TO LOGIC.
LYNN

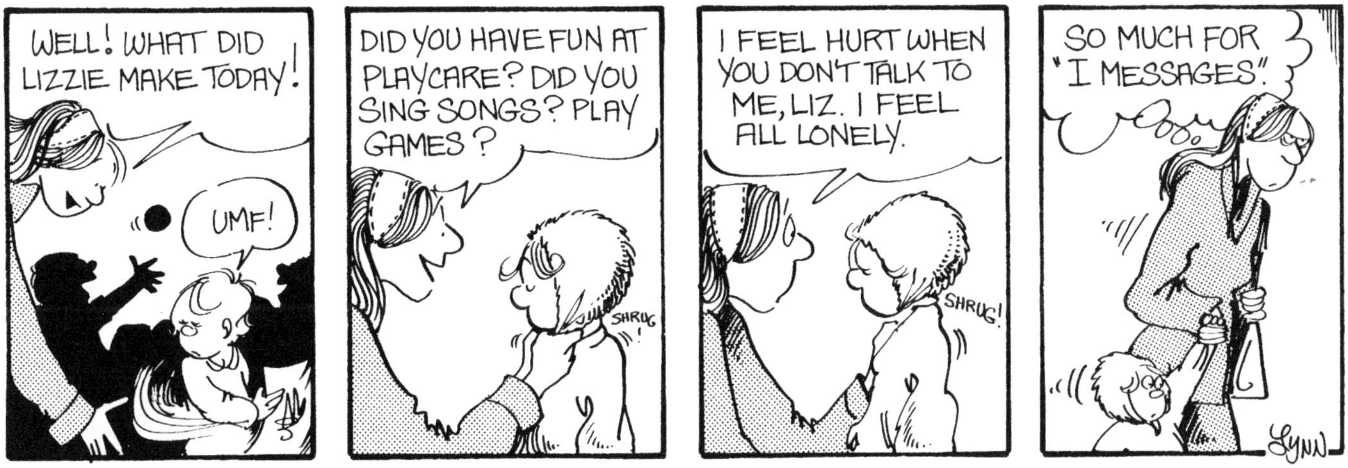
WELL! WHAT DID LIZZIE MAKE TODAY!
UMF!
DID YOU HAVE FUN AT PLAYCARE? DID YOU SING SONGS? PLAY GAMES?
SHRUG!
I FEEL HURT WHEN YOU DON'T TALK TO ME, LIZ. I FEEL ALL LONELY.
SHRUG!
SO MUCH FOR "I MESSAGES".
Lynn

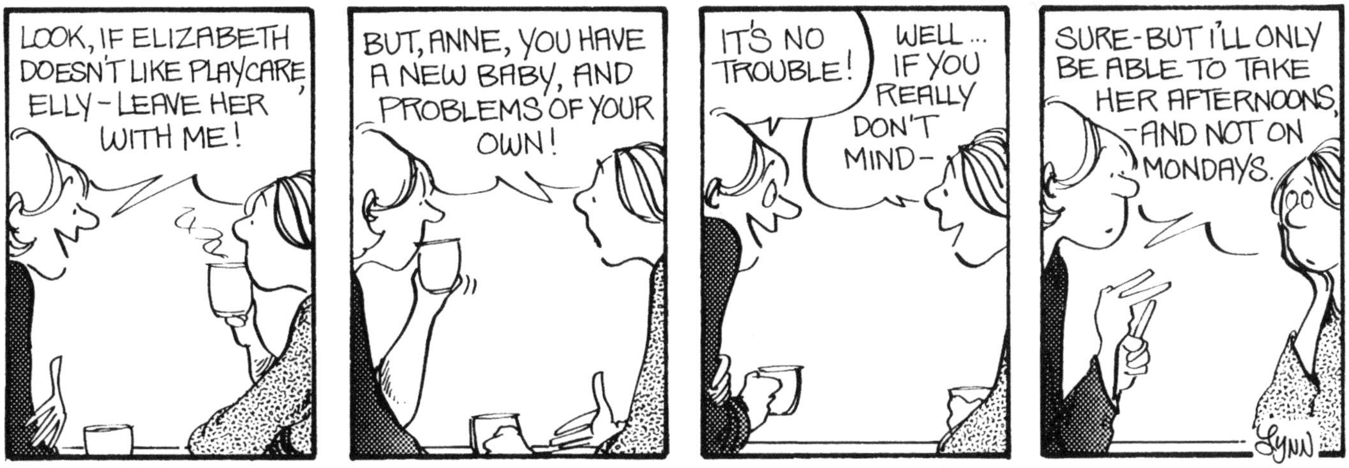
LOOK, IF ELIZABETH DOESN'T LIKE PLAYCARE, ELLY - LEAVE HER WITH ME!
BUT, ANNE, YOU HAVE A NEW BABY, AND PROBLEMS OF YOUR OWN!
IT'S NO TROUBLE!
WELL... IF YOU REALLY DON'T MIND-
SURE - BUT I'LL ONLY BE ABLE TO TAKE HER AFTERNOONS, - AND NOT ON MONDAYS.
Lynn

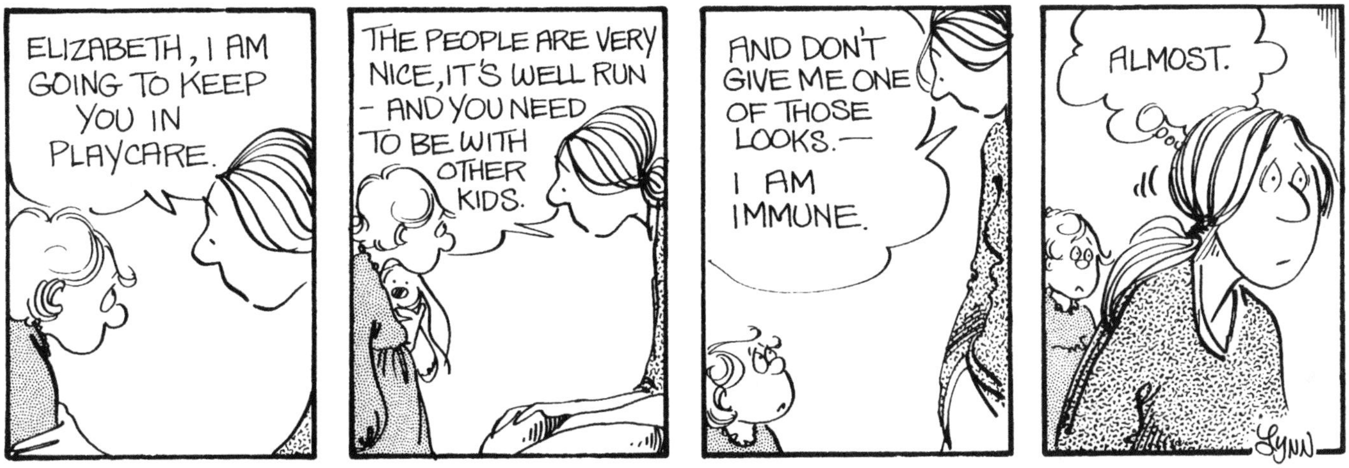
ELIZABETH, I AM GOING TO KEEP YOU IN PLAYCARE.
THE PEOPLE ARE VERY NICE, IT'S WELL RUN - AND YOU NEED TO BE WITH OTHER KIDS.
AND DON'T GIVE ME ONE OF THOSE LOOKS.— I AM IMMUNE.
ALMOST.
Lynn

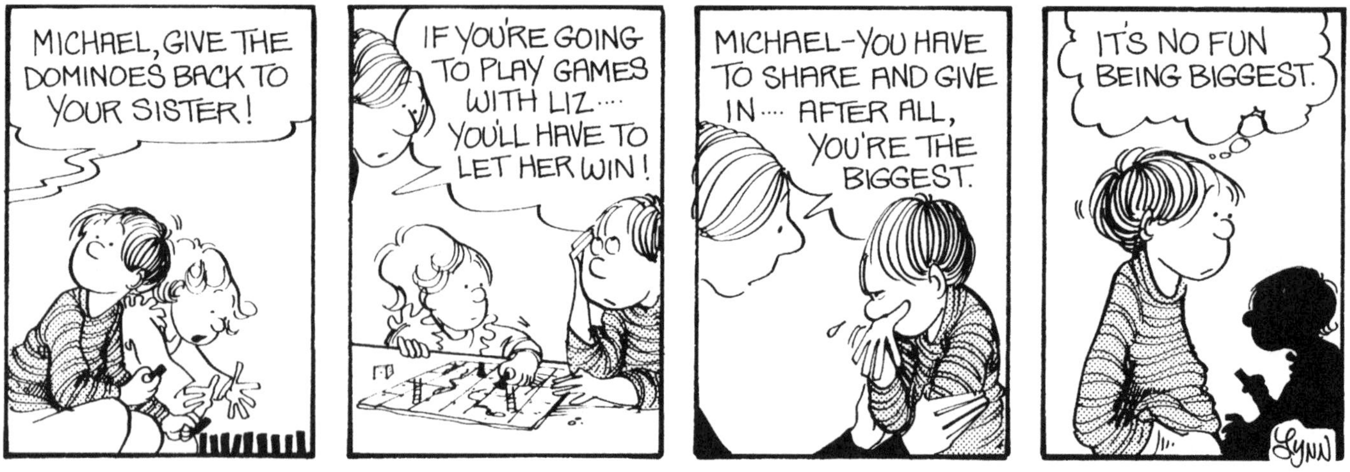
MICHAEL, GIVE THE DOMINOES BACK TO YOUR SISTER!
IF YOU'RE GOING TO PLAY GAMES WITH LIZ.... YOU'LL HAVE TO LET HER WIN!
MICHAEL-YOU HAVE TO SHARE AND GIVE IN.... AFTER ALL, YOU'RE THE BIGGEST.
IT'S NO FUN BEING BIGGEST.
LYNN

There's nothing like knowing all the rules to make you feel superior. I remember being told to let my brother win if I was teaching him a card game, but it was hard to do. So, I didn't! Later, when Alan became proficient with chess, I asked him to teach me — but I never learned. Playing with my brother drove me crazy. Alan made sure that he always won!

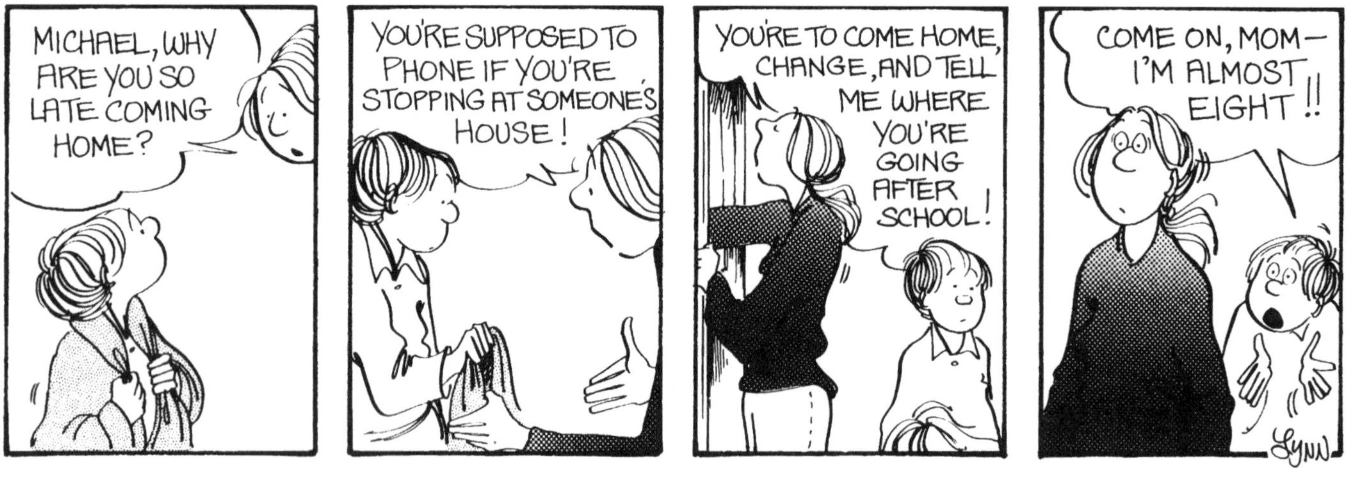
MICHAEL, WHY ARE YOU SO LATE COMING HOME?
YOU'RE SUPPOSED TO PHONE IF YOU'RE STOPPING AT SOMEONE'S HOUSE!
YOU'RE TO COME HOME, CHANGE, AND TELL ME WHERE YOU'RE GOING AFTER SCHOOL!
COME ON, MOM— I'M ALMOST EIGHT!!
LYNN

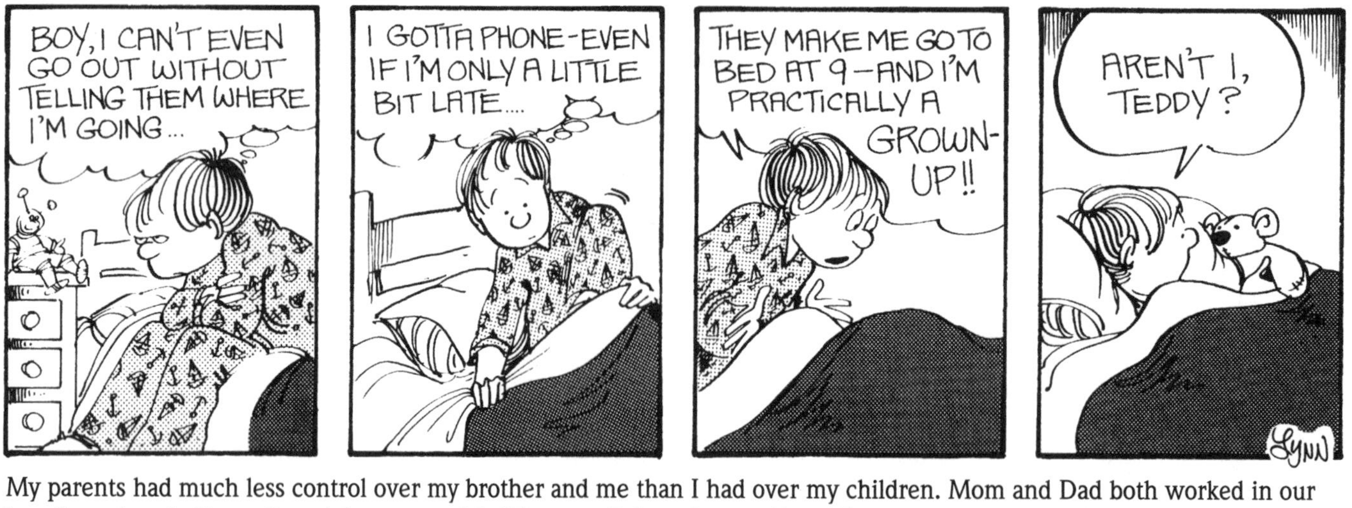
BOY, I CAN'T EVEN GO OUT WITHOUT TELLING THEM WHERE I'M GOING...
I GOTTA PHONE-EVEN IF I'M ONLY A LITTLE BIT LATE....
THEY MAKE ME GO TO BED AT 9—AND I'M PRACTICALLY A GROWN-UP!!
AREN'T I, TEDDY?
LYNN

My parents had much less control over my brother and me than I had over my children. Mom and Dad both worked in our jewellery shop in Upper Lonsdale — a good half-hour walk from home. Al and I were on our own a lot. We could do just about anything as long as dinner was ready by six and nothing in the house was busted or burning. I became the cook at about age ten, and Al just had to keep out of my way. Life was complicated. I knew what it was like to be "grown up" in my head and a kid in stature!

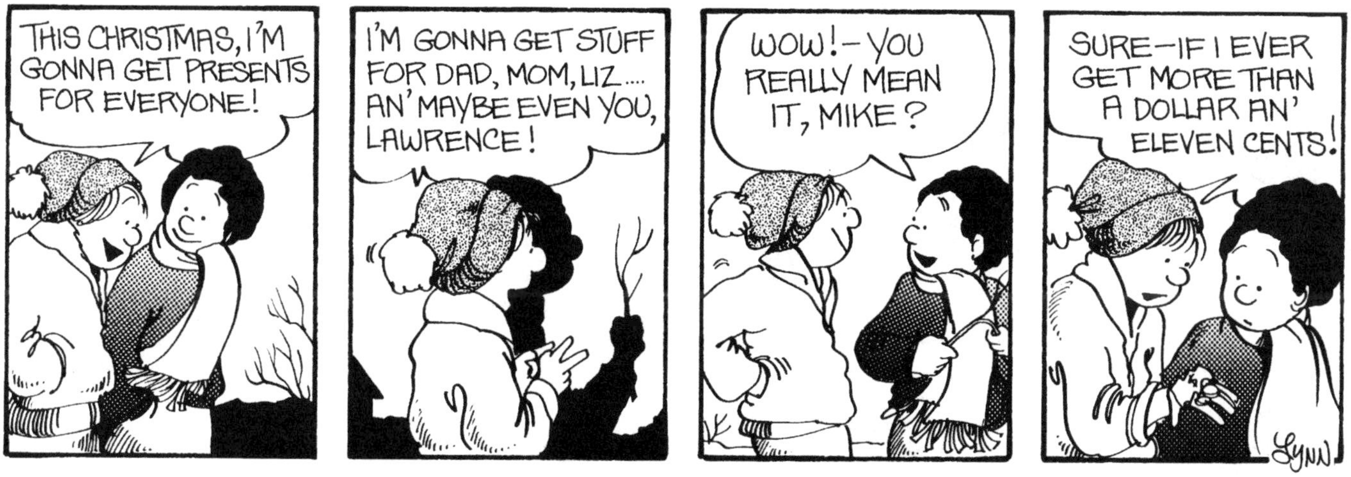
THIS CHRISTMAS, I'M GONNA GET PRESENTS FOR EVERYONE!
I'M GONNA GET STUFF FOR DAD, MOM, LIZ.... AN' MAYBE EVEN YOU, LAWRENCE!
WOW! - YOU REALLY MEAN IT, MIKE?
SURE - IF I EVER GET MORE THAN A DOLLAR AN' ELEVEN CENTS!
LYNN

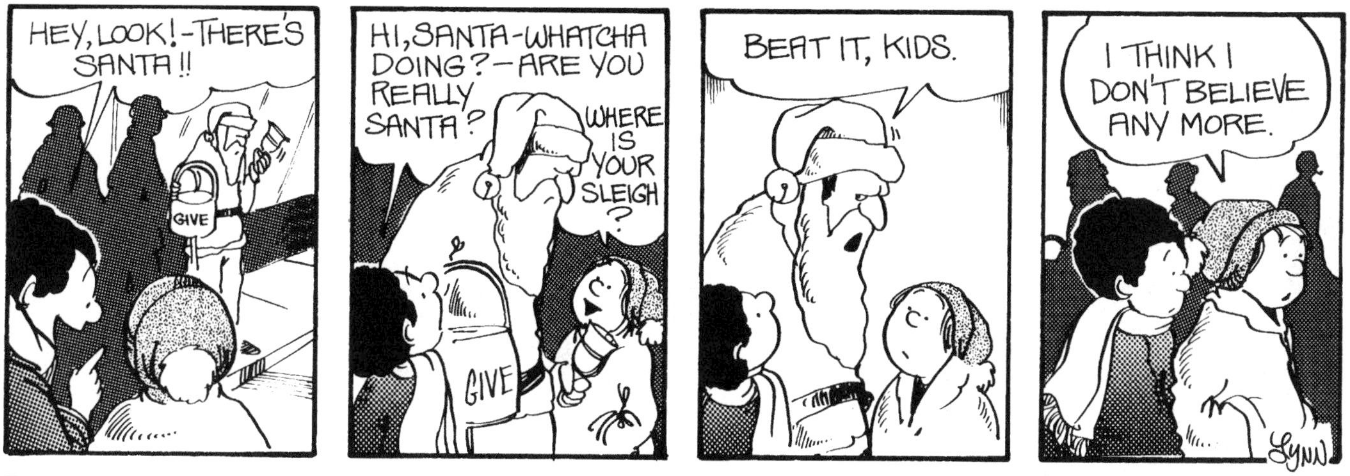
HEY, LOOK! - THERE'S SANTA!!
GIVE
HI, SANTA - WHATCHA DOING? - ARE YOU REALLY SANTA?
WHERE IS YOUR SLEIGH?
GIVE
BEAT IT, KIDS.
I THINK I DON'T BELIEVE ANY MORE.
LYNN

This happened to me outside Woodward's department store when I was small. My folks were standing close to the curb, watching for the bus to come. I was next to the window checking out the Christmas display and watching the Salvation Army Santa. He wasn't doing much, so I started to ask him questions (not in a disrespectful way) and he barked at me! This was very un-Santa-like behaviour, and was the catalyst for my gradual withdrawal from his list of believers!

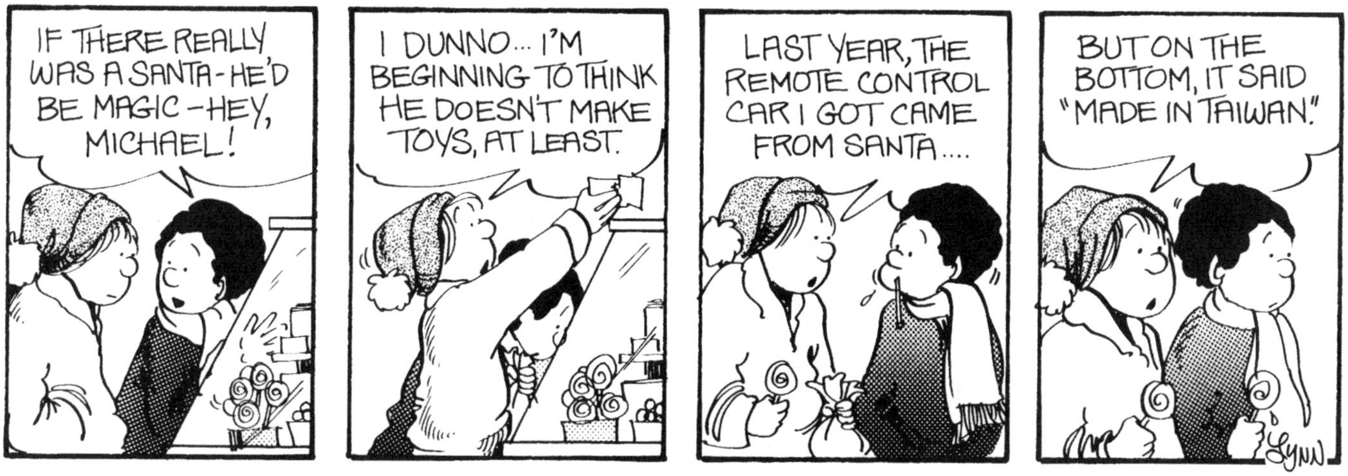
IF THERE REALLY WAS A SANTA - HE'D BE MAGIC - HEY, MICHAEL!
I DUNNO... I'M BEGINNING TO THINK HE DOESN'T MAKE TOYS, AT LEAST.
LAST YEAR, THE REMOTE CONTROL CAR I GOT CAME FROM SANTA....
BUT ON THE BOTTOM, IT SAID "MADE IN TAIWAN."
LYNN

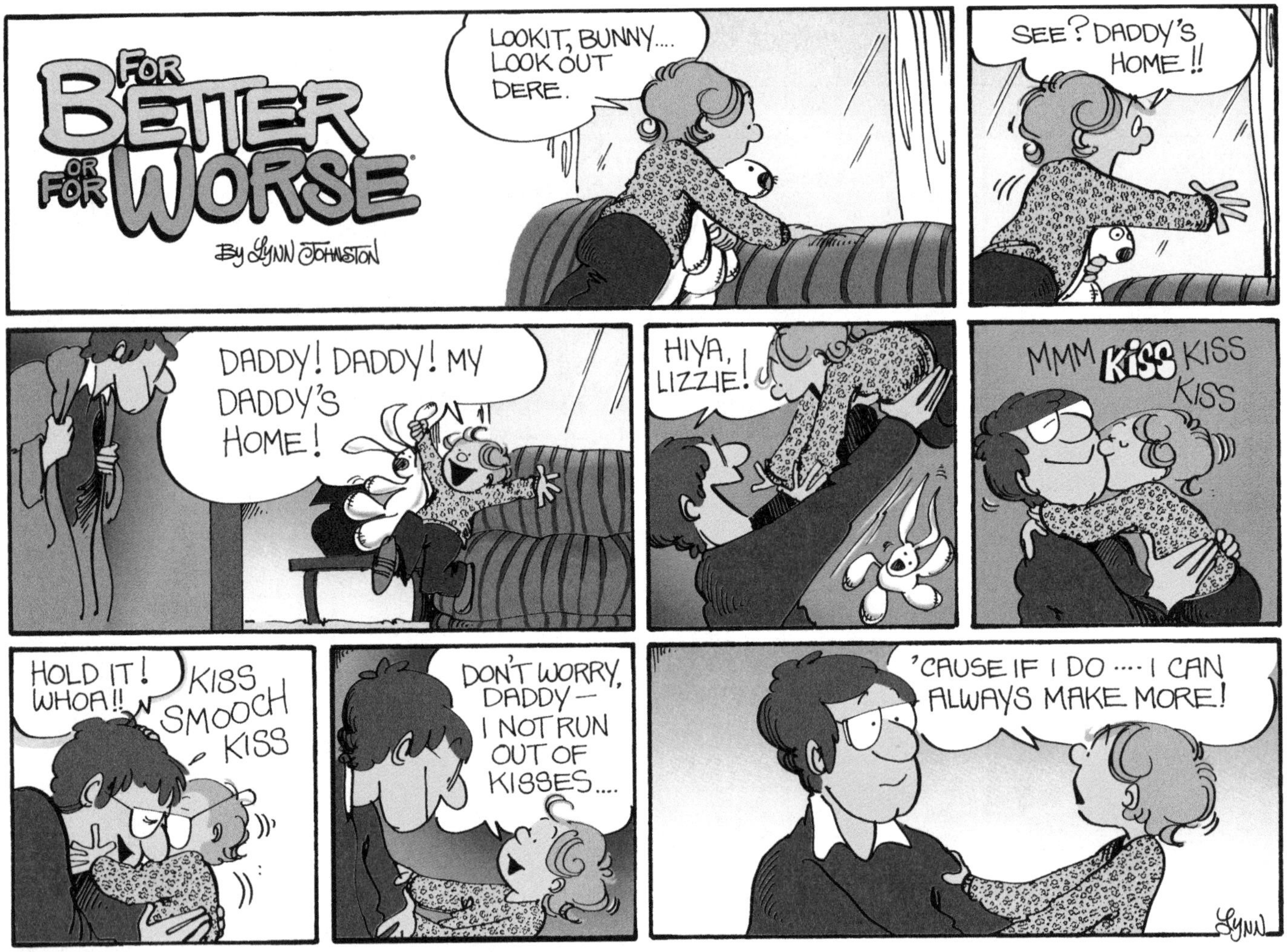
FOR BETTER OR FOR WORSE
BY LYNN JOHNSTON
LOOKIT, BUNNY.... LOOK OUT DERE.
SEE? DADDY'S HOME!!
DADDY! DADDY! MY DADDY'S HOME!
HIYA, LIZZIE!
MMM KISS KISS KISS
HOLD IT! WHOA!!
KISS SMOOCH KISS
DON'T WORRY, DADDY— I NOT RUN OUT OF KISSES....
'CAUSE IF I DO .... I CAN ALWAYS MAKE MORE!
LYNN

Before my folks took over Shore's Jewellers in North Vancouver, my dad worked for the main store on Hastings Street. Every morning he'd walk to the bottom of Lonsdale and take the ferry into the city. Like clockwork, he'd come back on the return ferry at 5:30 and be home on the dot of 6:00 p.m. We knew exactly when he'd be home. Alan and I would wait like two giddy, wagging dogs, ready to pounce on him. His arrival was a big part of the family routine. It heralded a call to dinner, then (after homework) an evening of board games or TV. We'd watch something like *Gunsmoke* or *Walt Disney Presents* before going to bed. How lucky we were. I still remember the smell of my dad's raincoat as I buried my face in it. I remember being picked up so I could look directly into his eyes, and thinking it must be wonderful to be so tall. I remember him kissing me and hugging me and swinging me around when he came home. When I drew this strip, I thought about how much I loved him, and how love never runs out.

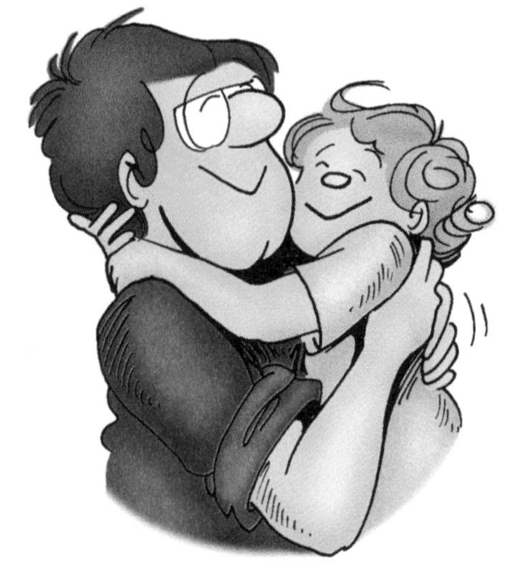

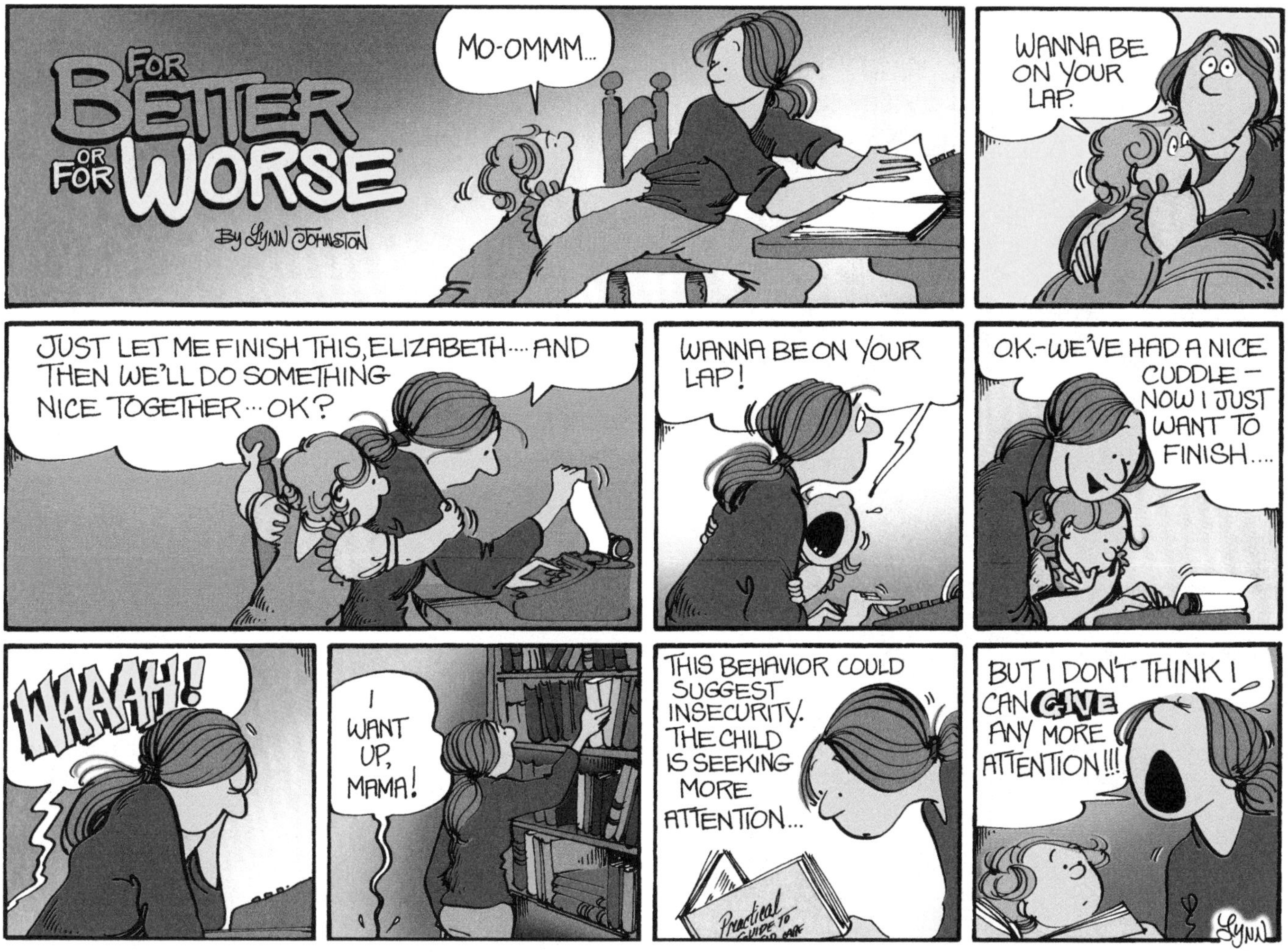
FOR BETTER OR FOR WORSE
BY LYNN JOHNSTON
MO-OMMM...
WANNA BE ON YOUR LAP.
JUST LET ME FINISH THIS, ELIZABETH.... AND THEN WE'LL DO SOMETHING NICE TOGETHER... OK?
WANNA BE ON YOUR LAP!
O.K.-WE'VE HAD A NICE CUDDLE - NOW I JUST WANT TO FINISH....
WAAAH!
I WANT UP, MAMA!
THIS BEHAVIOR COULD SUGGEST INSECURITY. THE CHILD IS SEEKING MORE ATTENTION...
Practical GUIDE TO
BUT I DON'T THINK I CAN GIVE ANY MORE ATTENTION!!!
LYNN

Here is where my folks differed a great deal: My dad was always up for a hug; Mom was not. She needed her space and didn't appreciate being interrupted when she was in the middle of something — even for a bit of cuddling. She was always very busy. Life wasn't easy for the moms of the '50s. We had no car. We had a wringer washer, a leaky icebox, and a gas stove that required an engineering degree to operate. She made bread regularly, and most of our clothing. She canned fruit, grew a vegetable and flower garden, and did all the paperwork for the family and the business. She shopped and cooked and cleaned and took care of two active kids, so when she did get a few minutes to herself, she wanted to be left alone — Please!

She had endless patience. She could do or fix or make just about anything. She was an artist and a writer, and she should have gone to university — except that her father didn't believe in educating women! To him, it was a waste of money and time. What she couldn't learn at school, she taught herself. Mom was an amazing person. We respected and admired her. But, it wasn't until I was a mom myself that I truly appreciated all she did for us.

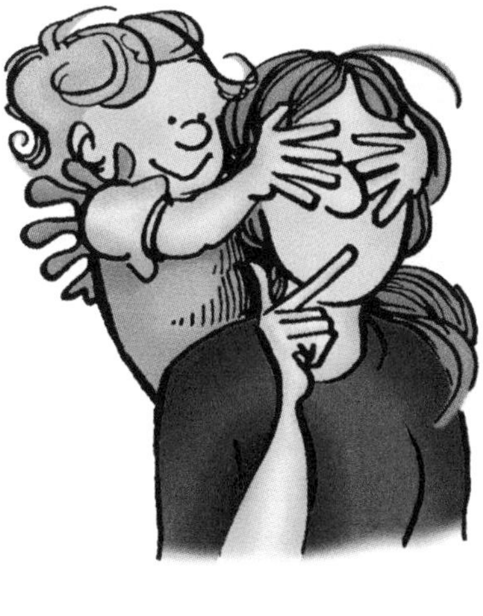

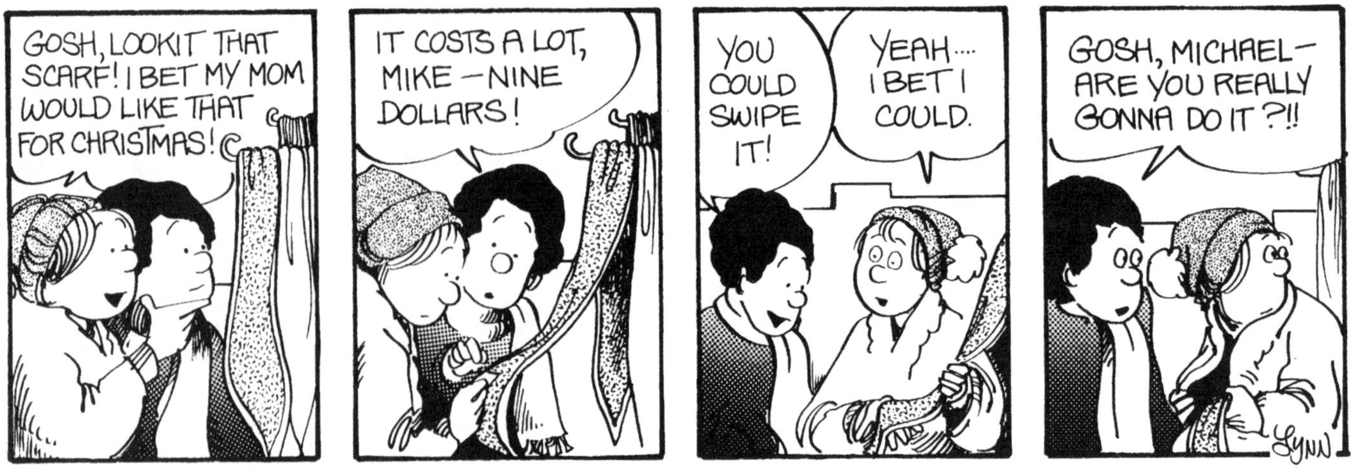
GOSH, LOOKIT THAT SCARF! I BET MY MOM WOULD LIKE THAT FOR CHRISTMAS!
IT COSTS A LOT, MIKE — NINE DOLLARS!
YOU COULD SWIPE IT!
YEAH.... I BET I COULD.
GOSH, MICHAEL— ARE YOU REALLY GONNA DO IT?!!
LYNN

This short vignette was done after I discovered that Aaron had taken a toy from a shop in town.

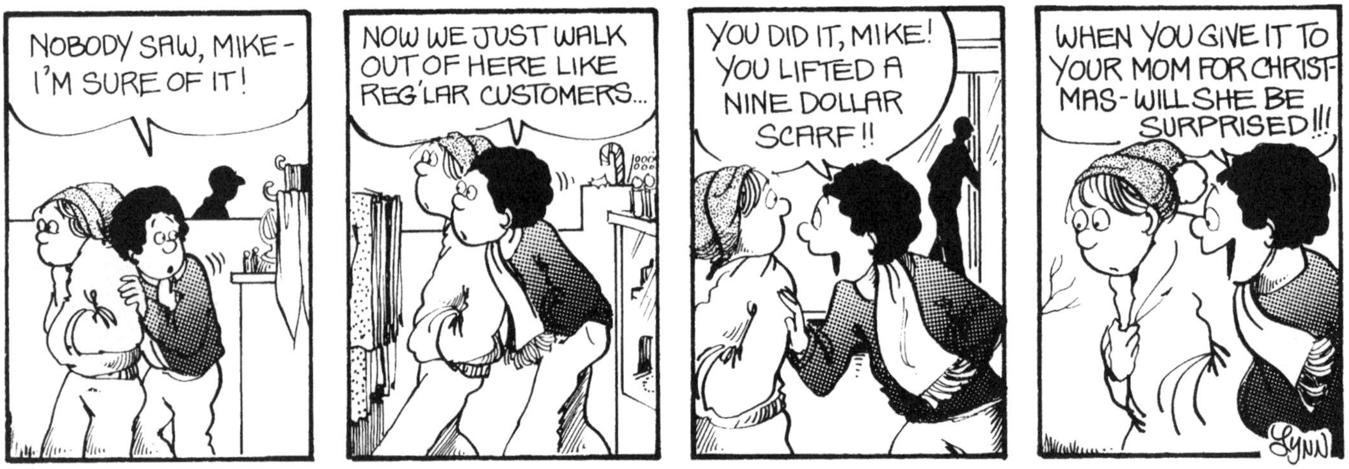
NOBODY SAW, MIKE— I'M SURE OF IT!
NOW WE JUST WALK OUT OF HERE LIKE REG'LAR CUSTOMERS...
YOU DID IT, MIKE! YOU LIFTED A NINE DOLLAR SCARF!!
WHEN YOU GIVE IT TO YOUR MOM FOR CHRISTMAS- WILL SHE BE SURPRISED!!!
LYNN

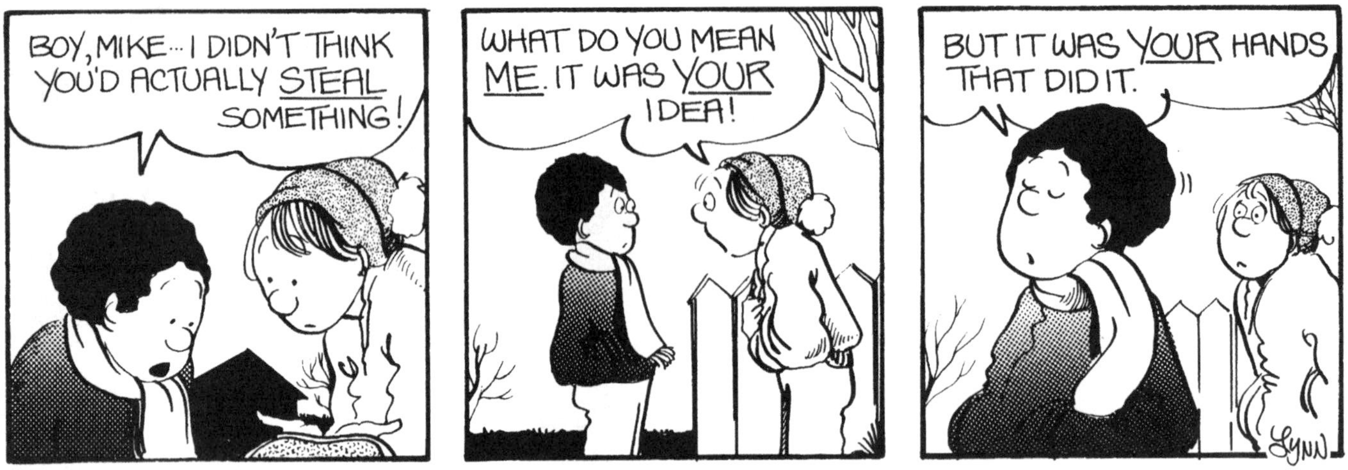
BOY, MIKE... I DIDN'T THINK YOU'D ACTUALLY STEAL SOMETHING!
WHAT DO YOU MEAN ME. IT WAS YOUR IDEA!
BUT IT WAS YOUR HANDS THAT DID IT.
LYNN

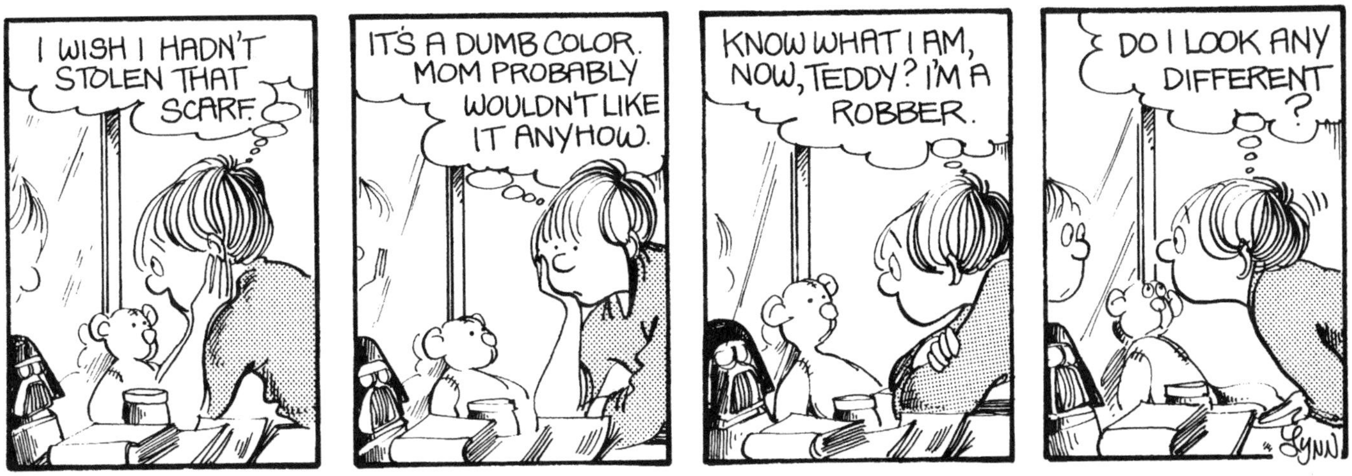
I WISH I HADN'T STOLEN THAT SCARF.
IT'S A DUMB COLOR. MOM PROBABLY WOULDN'T LIKE IT ANYHOW.
KNOW WHAT I AM, NOW, TEDDY? I'M A ROBBER.
DO I LOOK ANY DIFFERENT?
LYNN

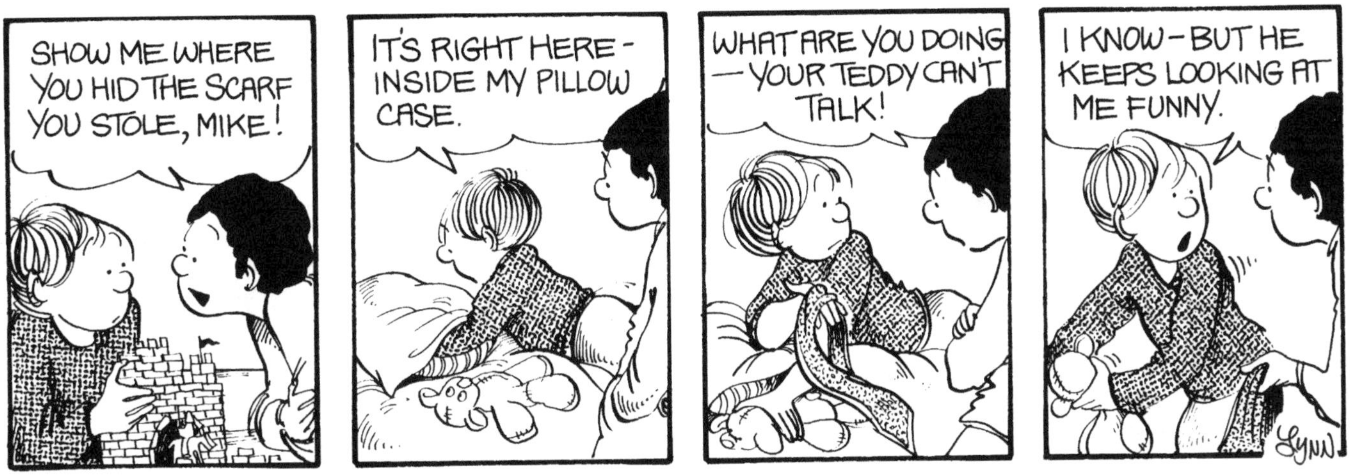
SHOW ME WHERE YOU HID THE SCARF YOU STOLE, MIKE!
IT'S RIGHT HERE - INSIDE MY PILLOW CASE.
WHAT ARE YOU DOING — YOUR TEDDY CAN'T TALK!
I KNOW - BUT HE KEEPS LOOKING AT ME FUNNY.
LYNN

I found it in his room under his bedsheets with the price tag still on.

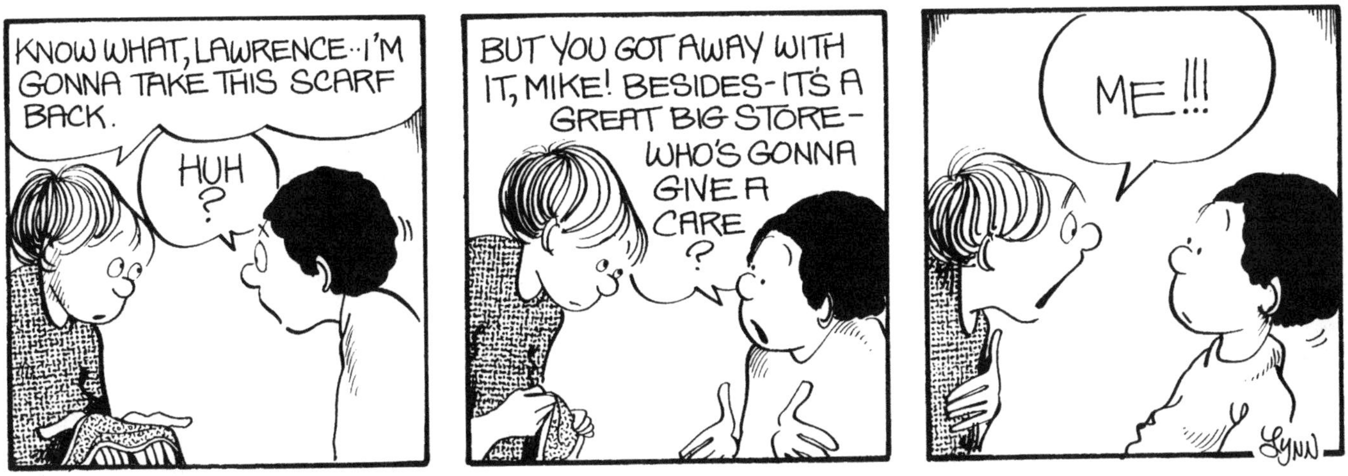
KNOW WHAT, LAWRENCE.. I'M GONNA TAKE THIS SCARF BACK.
HUH?
BUT YOU GOT AWAY WITH IT, MIKE! BESIDES - IT'S A GREAT BIG STORE - WHO'S GONNA GIVE A CARE?
ME!!!
LYNN

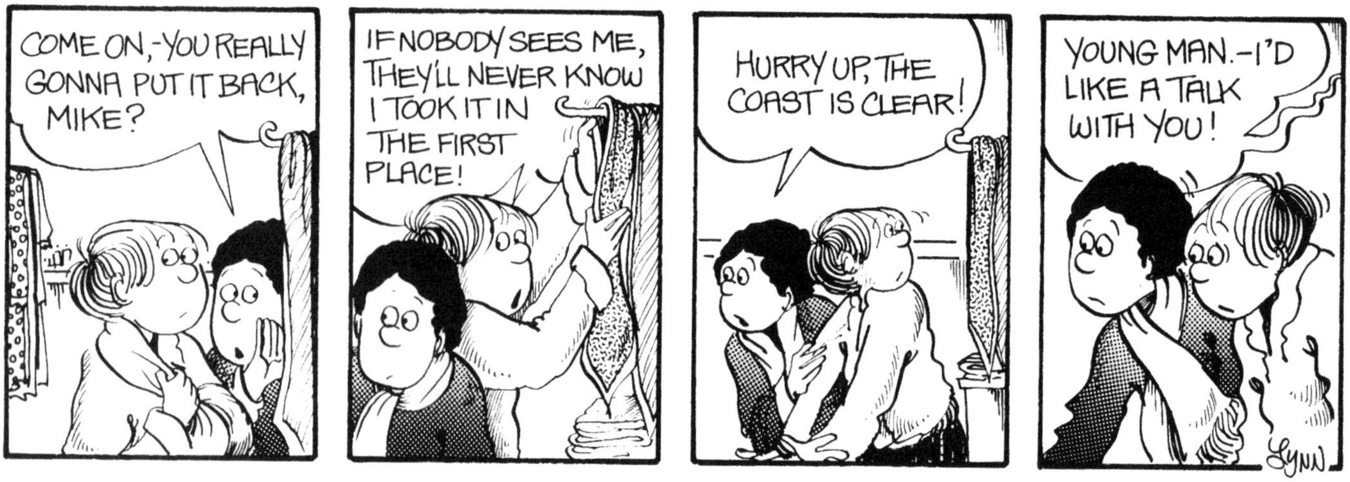
COME ON, -YOU REALLY GONNA PUT IT BACK, MIKE?
IF NOBODY SEES ME, THEY'LL NEVER KNOW I TOOK IT IN THE FIRST PLACE!
HURRY UP, THE COAST IS CLEAR!
YOUNG MAN. -I'D LIKE A TALK WITH YOU!
LYNN

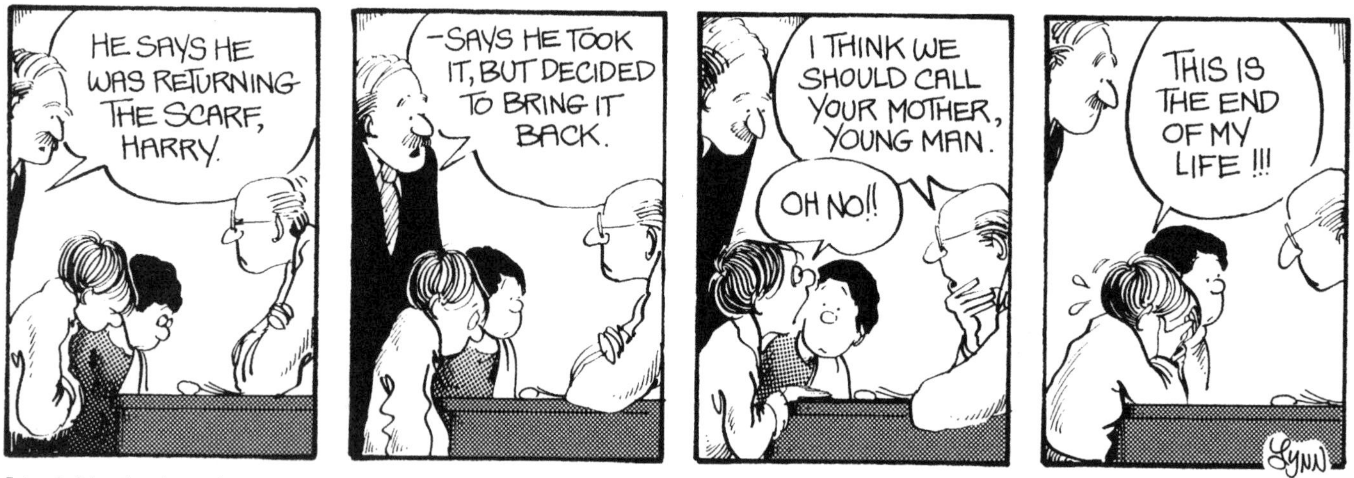
HE SAYS HE WAS RETURNING THE SCARF, HARRY.
-SAYS HE TOOK IT, BUT DECIDED TO BRING IT BACK.
I THINK WE SHOULD CALL YOUR MOTHER, YOUNG MAN.
OH NO!!
THIS IS THE END OF MY LIFE !!!
LYNN

I took him back to the store to return the item, and together we talked to the manager of the toy department.

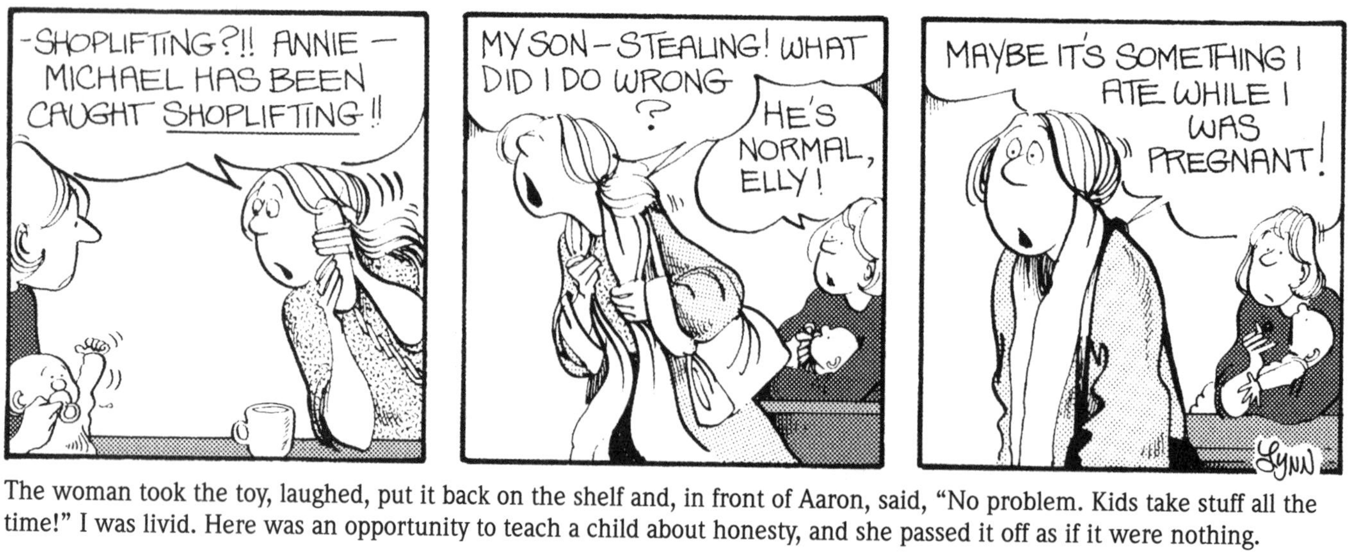
-SHOPLIFTING?!! ANNIE - MICHAEL HAS BEEN CAUGHT SHOPLIFTING!!
MY SON - STEALING! WHAT DID I DO WRONG?
HE'S NORMAL, ELLY!
MAYBE IT'S SOMETHING I ATE WHILE I WAS PREGNANT!
LYNN

The woman took the toy, laughed, put it back on the shelf and, in front of Aaron, said, "No problem. Kids take stuff all the time!" I was livid. Here was an opportunity to teach a child about honesty, and she passed it off as if it were nothing.

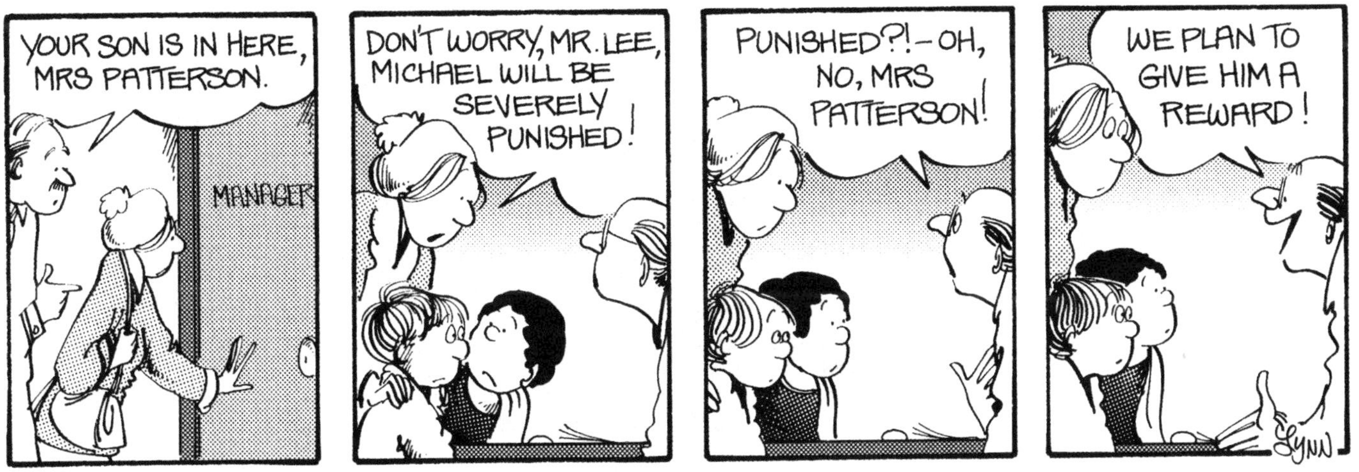
YOUR SON IS IN HERE, MRS PATTERSON.
MANAGER
DON'T WORRY, MR. LEE, MICHAEL WILL BE SEVERELY PUNISHED!
PUNISHED?! – OH, NO, MRS PATTERSON!
WE PLAN TO GIVE HIM A REWARD!
Lynn

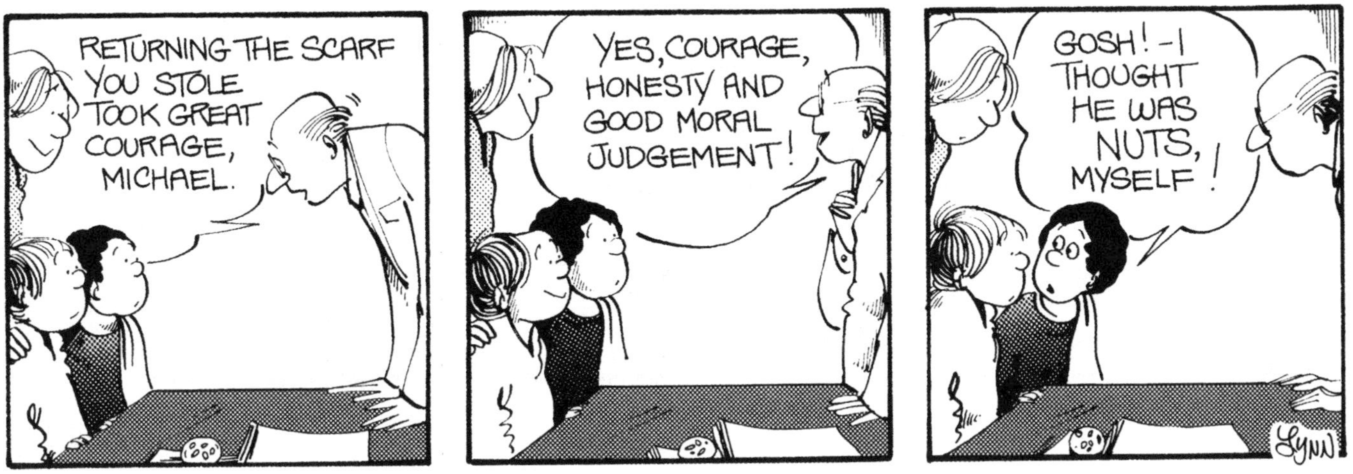
RETURNING THE SCARF YOU STOLE TOOK GREAT COURAGE, MICHAEL.
YES, COURAGE, HONESTY AND GOOD MORAL JUDGEMENT!
GOSH! – I THOUGHT HE WAS NUTS, MYSELF!
Lynn

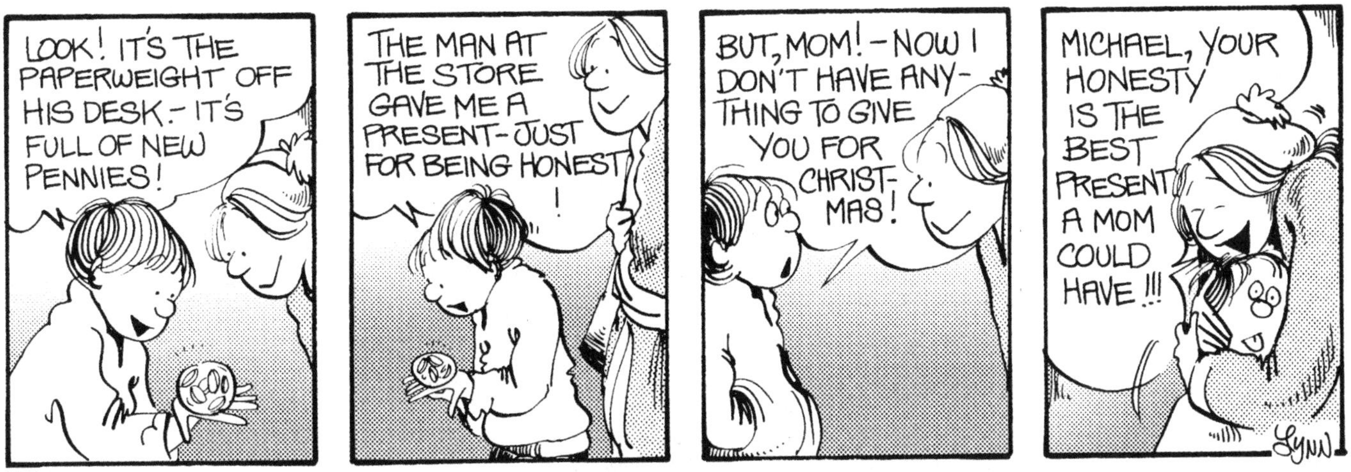
LOOK! IT'S THE PAPERWEIGHT OFF HIS DESK – IT'S FULL OF NEW PENNIES!
THE MAN AT THE STORE GAVE ME A PRESENT – JUST FOR BEING HONEST!
BUT, MOM! – NOW I DON'T HAVE ANY-THING TO GIVE YOU FOR CHRIST-MAS!
MICHAEL, YOUR HONESTY IS THE BEST PRESENT A MOM COULD HAVE!!!
Lynn

In retaliation, I did this short storyline about theft and guilt and honesty, and sent it in. As Farley Mowat said (when I asked him if everything he wrote in his books was true), "If it didn't happen, it SHOULD have!" My thoughts exactly!

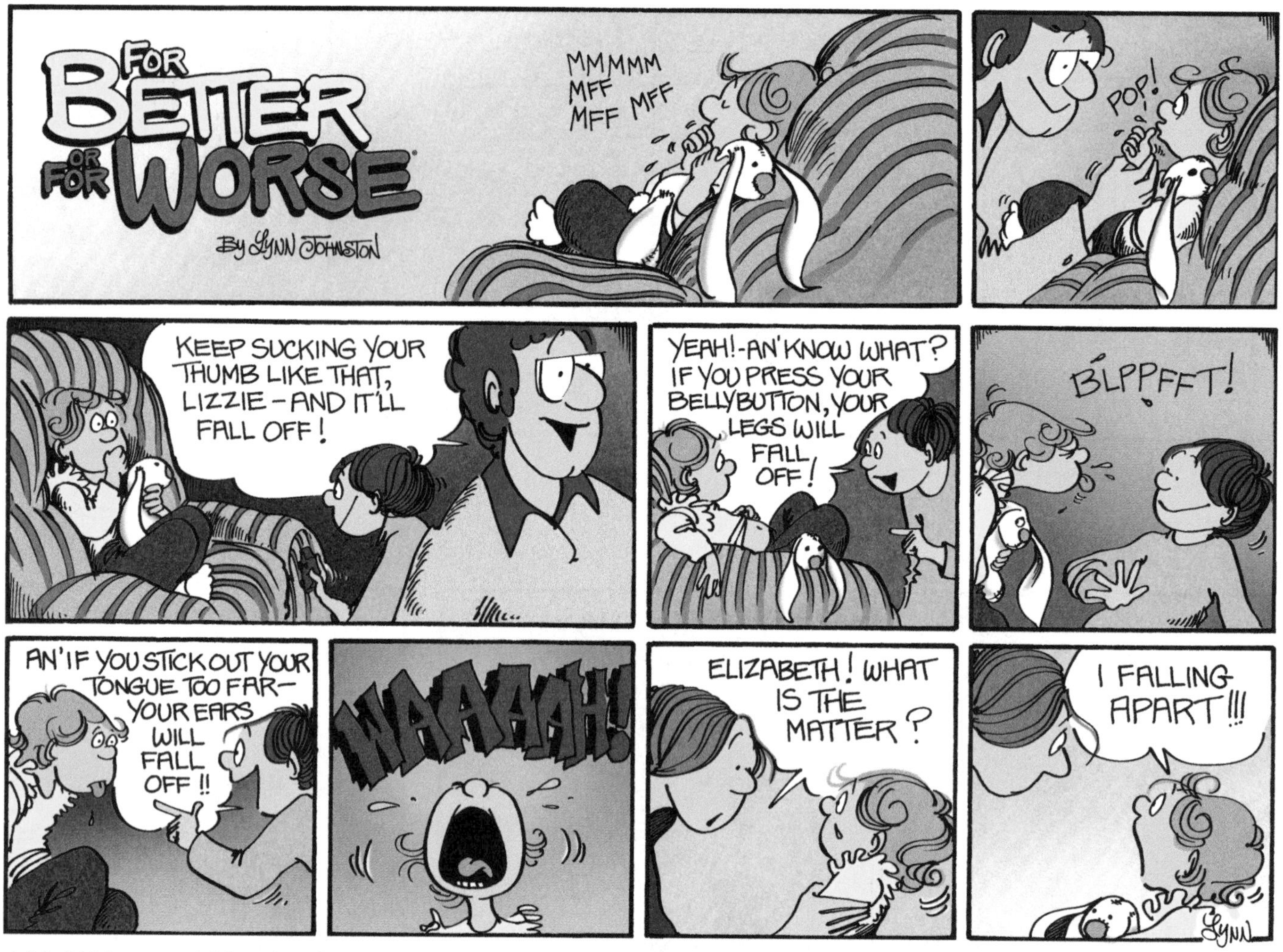
FOR BETTER OR FOR WORSE
BY LYNN JOHNSTON
MMMMM MFF MFF MFF
POP!
KEEP SUCKING YOUR THUMB LIKE THAT, LIZZIE - AND IT'LL FALL OFF!
YEAH! - AN' KNOW WHAT? IF YOU PRESS YOUR BELLYBUTTON, YOUR LEGS WILL FALL OFF!
BLPPFFT!
AN' IF YOU STICK OUT YOUR TONGUE TOO FAR - YOUR EARS WILL FALL OFF!!
WAAAAH!
ELIZABETH! WHAT IS THE MATTER?
I FALLING APART!!!
LYNN

A big kid in my neighbourhood once told me that my butt would fall off if I unscrewed my belly button. I believed him. I have an "inny," and it was hard to see just how the "button" was engineered in there. In fear of dire consequences, I asked my dad if this was true, and he laughed out loud. He assured me that my belly button was a permanent decoration and I was not to worry about losing my behind. He did tell me, however, that if I screwed up my face ... it would stay that way.

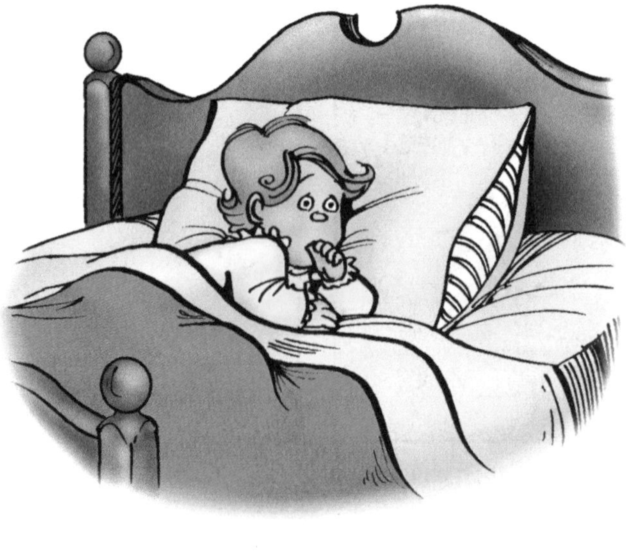

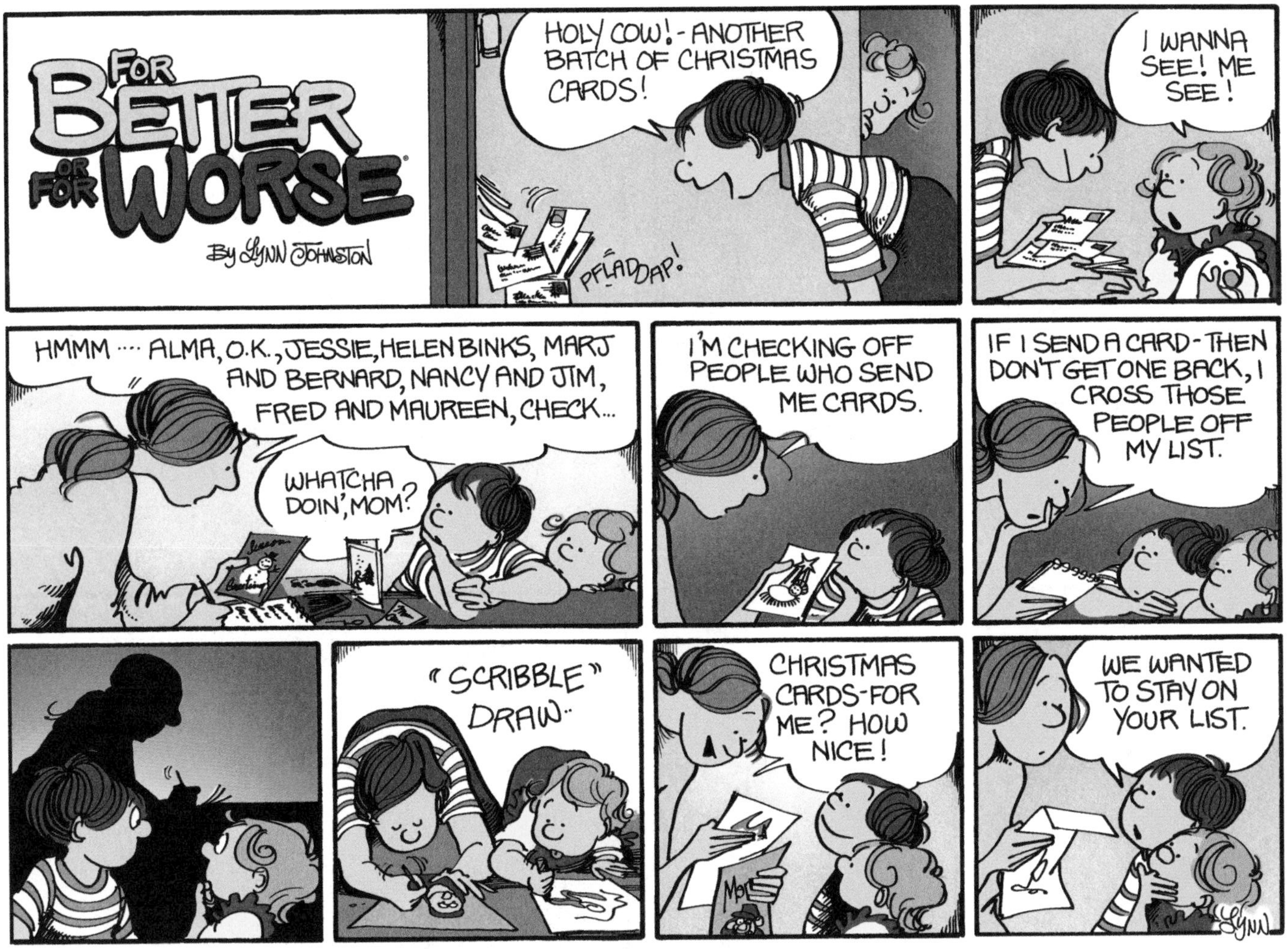
FOR BETTER OR FOR WORSE
BY LYNN JOHNSTON
HOLY COW! - ANOTHER BATCH OF CHRISTMAS CARDS!
PFLADDAP!
I WANNA SEE! ME SEE!
HMMM .... ALMA, O.K., JESSIE, HELEN BINKS, MARJ AND BERNARD, NANCY AND JIM, FRED AND MAUREEN, CHECK...
WHATCHA DOIN', MOM?
I'M CHECKING OFF PEOPLE WHO SEND ME CARDS.
IF I SEND A CARD - THEN DON'T GET ONE BACK, I CROSS THOSE PEOPLE OFF MY LIST.
"SCRIBBLE" DRAW..
CHRISTMAS CARDS - FOR ME? HOW NICE!
WE WANTED TO STAY ON YOUR LIST.
LYNN

By listing their names, I was able to say “hello” to a number of dear friends in this strip. When it appeared in the paper, I looked forward to their inevitable calls. So often my friends would say, “You'd better not put me in the paper!” But when I did, they were always thrilled.

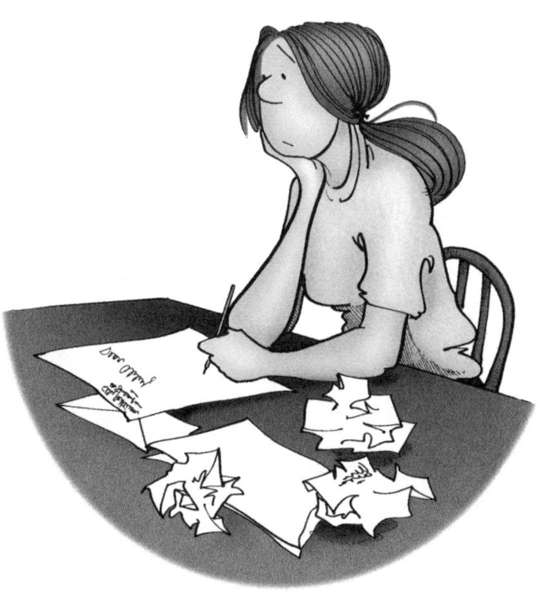

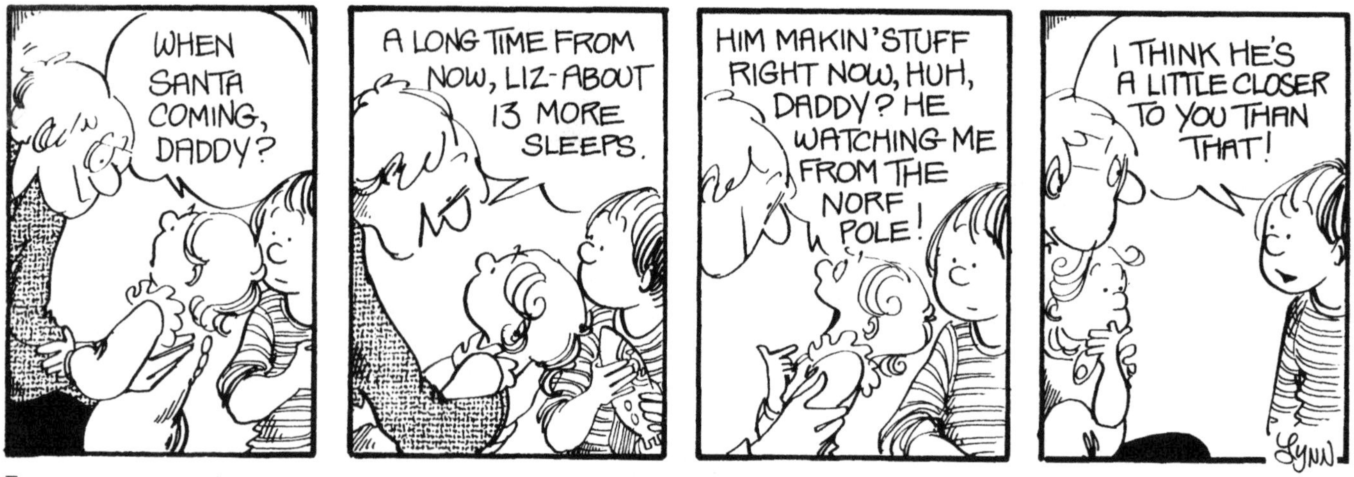
WHEN SANTA COMING, DADDY?
A LONG TIME FROM NOW, LIZ-ABOUT 13 MORE SLEEPS.
HIM MAKIN'STUFF RIGHT NOW, HUH, DADDY? HE WATCHING ME FROM THE NORF POLE!
I THINK HE'S A LITTLE CLOSER TO YOU THAN THAT!
LYNN

For some parents, the magic of Santa and the fantasy surrounding the season is hard to let go of — long after their kids have stopped believing.

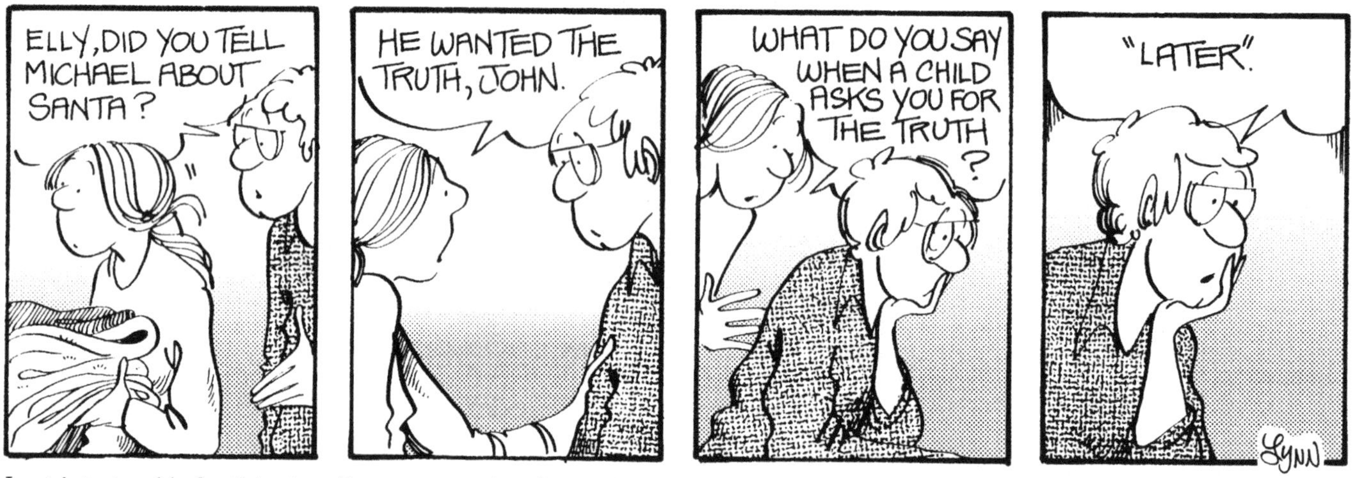
ELLY, DID YOU TELL MICHAEL ABOUT SANTA?
HE WANTED THE TRUTH, JOHN.
WHAT DO YOU SAY WHEN A CHILD ASKS YOU FOR THE TRUTH?
"LATER".
LYNN

I got into trouble for this story line, too; people who read the comics to their children didn't want to have to explain the origin of the Santa species. But, I figured if the kid was old enough to read and understand the comics page, he likely had the Santa thing figured out, anyway. Not so, apparently!

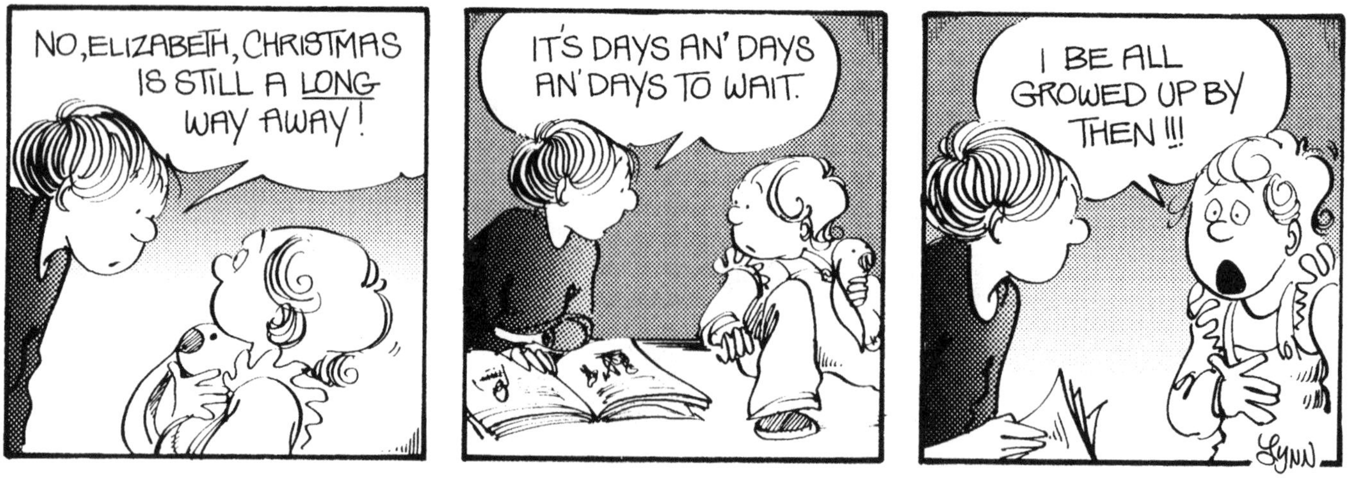
NO, ELIZABETH, CHRISTMAS IS STILL A LONG WAY AWAY!
IT'S DAYS AN' DAYS AN' DAYS TO WAIT.
I BE ALL GROWED UP BY THEN!!!
LYNN

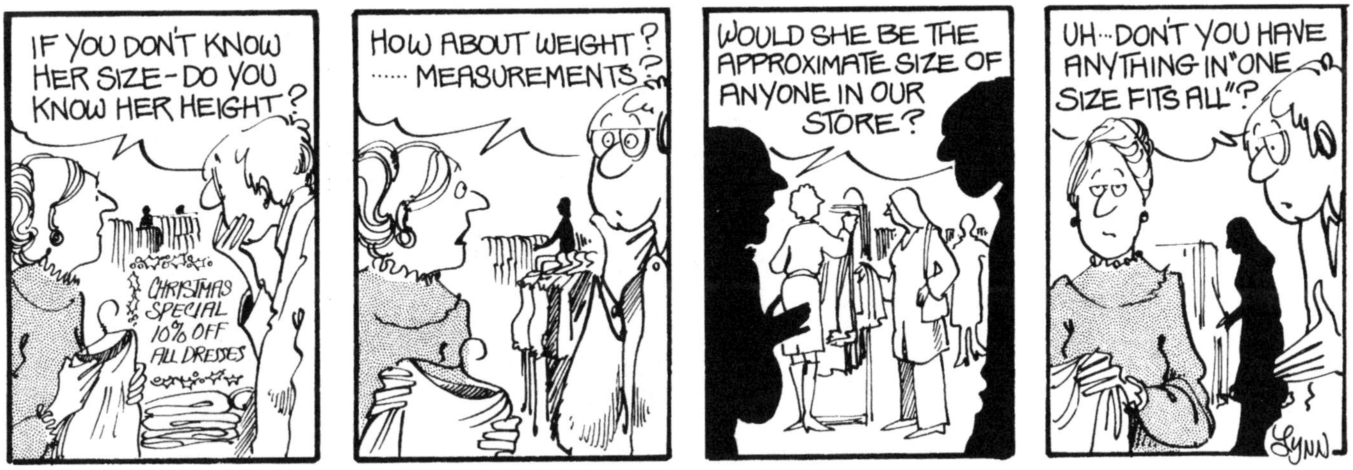
IF YOU DON'T KNOW HER SIZE-DO YOU KNOW HER HEIGHT?
CHRISTMAS SPECIAL 10% OFF ALL DRESSES
HOW ABOUT WEIGHT? ...... MEASUREMENTS?
WOULD SHE BE THE APPROXIMATE SIZE OF ANYONE IN OUR STORE?
UH...DON'T YOU HAVE ANYTHING IN "ONE SIZE FITS ALL"?
LYNN

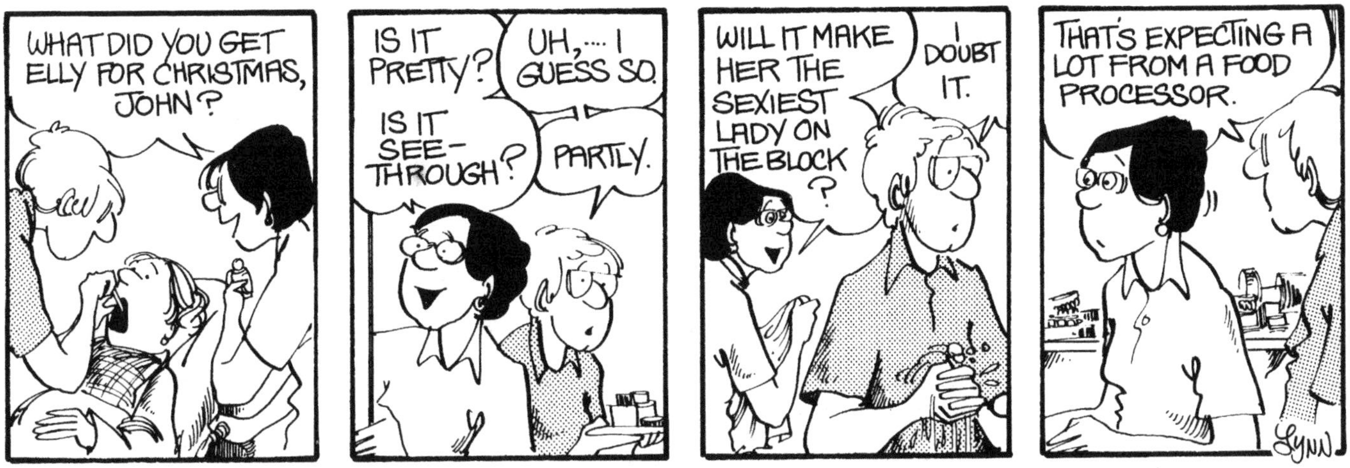
WHAT DID YOU GET ELLY FOR CHRISTMAS, JOHN?
IS IT PRETTY?
UH,.... I GUESS SO.
IS IT SEE-THROUGH?
PARTLY.
WILL IT MAKE HER THE SEXIEST LADY ON THE BLOCK?
I DOUBT IT.
THAT'S EXPECTING A LOT FROM A FOOD PROCESSOR.
LYNN

I don't know about you ladies out there, but I'd much rather get a food processor for Christmas than a nightgown that was chosen by my husband!

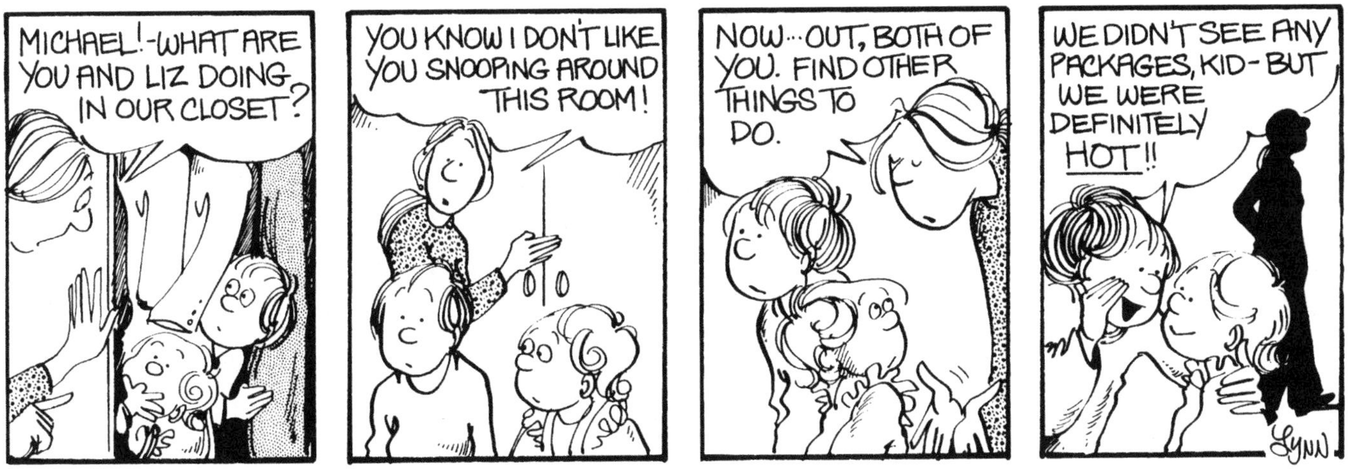
MICHAEL!-WHAT ARE YOU AND LIZ DOING IN OUR CLOSET?
YOU KNOW I DON'T LIKE YOU SNOOPING AROUND THIS ROOM!
NOW...OUT, BOTH OF YOU. FIND OTHER THINGS TO DO.
WE DIDN'T SEE ANY PACKAGES, KID-BUT WE WERE DEFINITELY HOT!!
LYNN

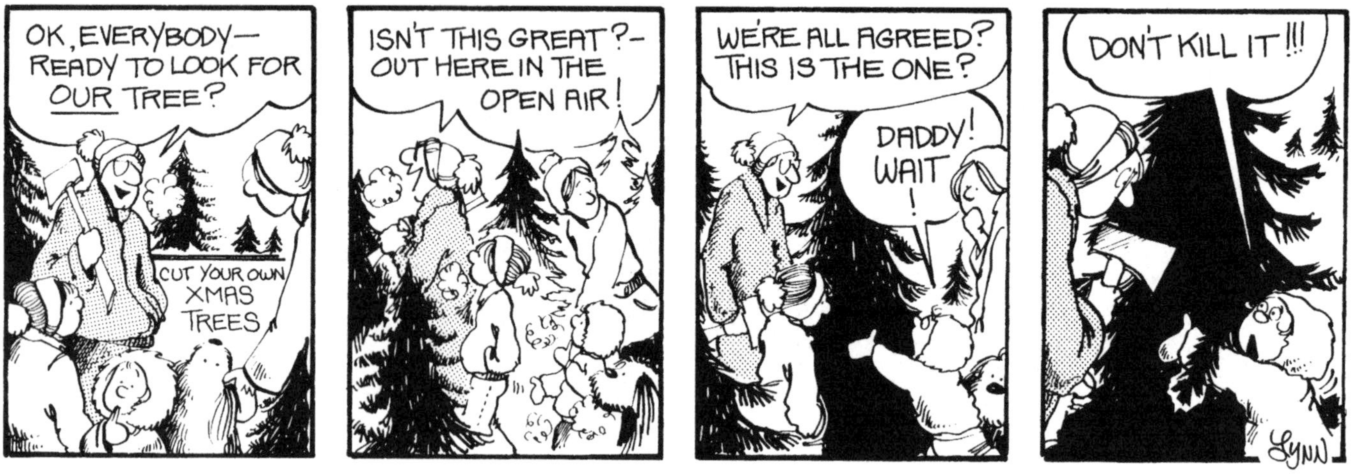
OK, EVERYBODY— READY TO LOOK FOR OUR TREE?
CUT YOUR OWN XMAS TREES
ISN'T THIS GREAT?— OUT HERE IN THE OPEN AIR!
WE'RE ALL AGREED? THIS IS THE ONE?
DADDY! WAIT!
DON'T KILL IT!!!
LYNN

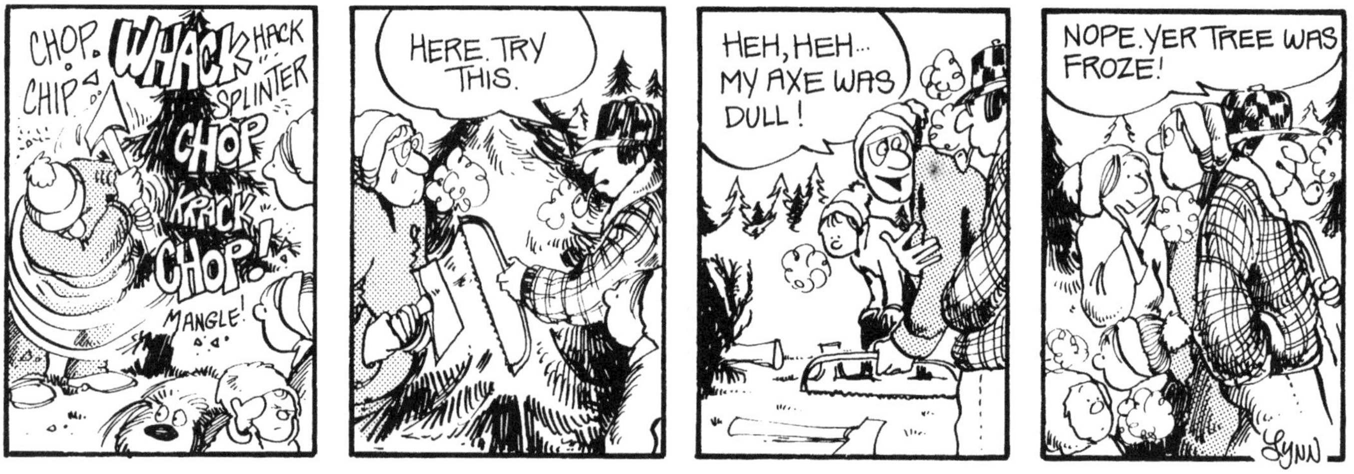
CHOP CHIP WHACK HACK SPLINTER CHOP KRACK CHOP! MANGLE!
HERE. TRY THIS.
HEH, HEH... MY AXE WAS DULL!
NOPE. YER TREE WAS FROZE!
LYNN

The annual trek into the bush to get our Christmas tree was a Lynn Lake ritual. The trouble was that the good trees were only visible in the summer. You'd have to tag the tree and hope some schmuck didn't cut it down before you did! December temperatures would often dip below -40°C, so you had to know where you were going and take your tree fast — before you froze to the spot where you were standing. A frozen trunk wasn't always the easiest thing to chop or saw through, either!

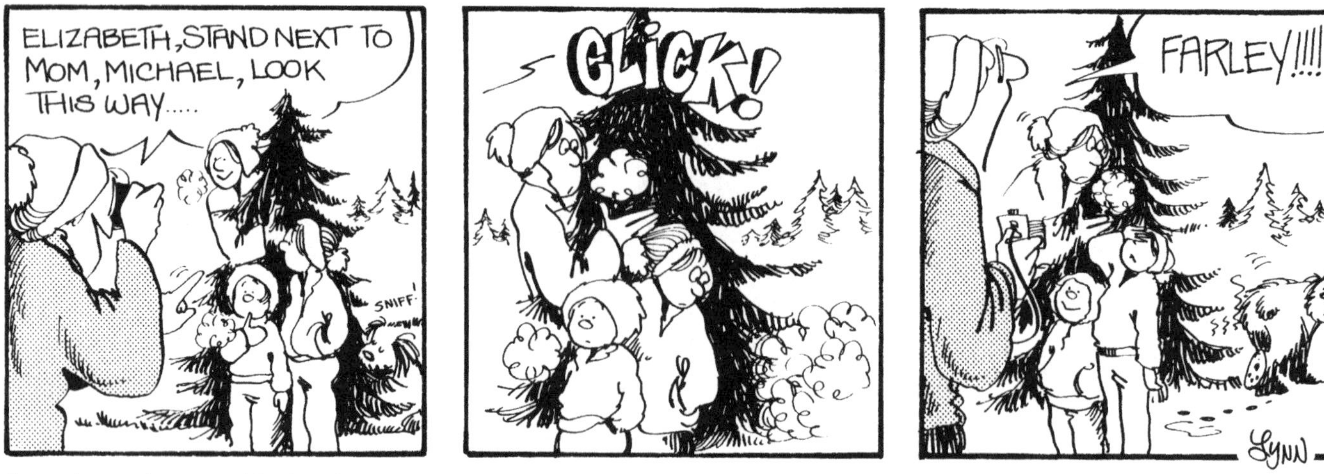
ELIZABETH, STAND NEXT TO MOM, MICHAEL, LOOK THIS WAY.....
SNIFF
CLICK!
FARLEY!!!!
LYNN

A good tree, harvested by hand, was something to celebrate. In this strip, Farley is giving the yuletide conifer a canine-style christening — another event that never happened, but should have!

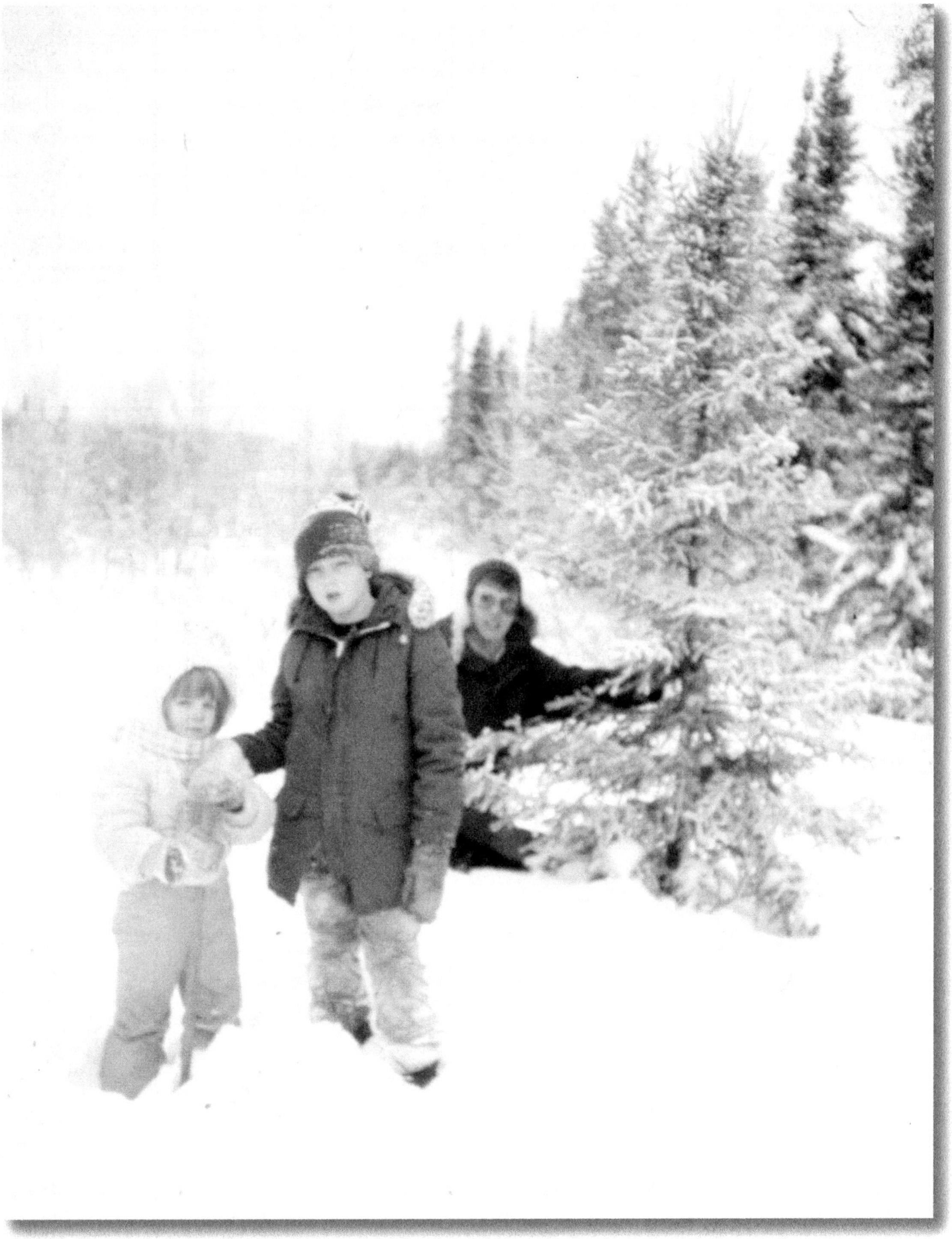

Kate, Aaron, and Rod in search of a perfect Christmas tree.

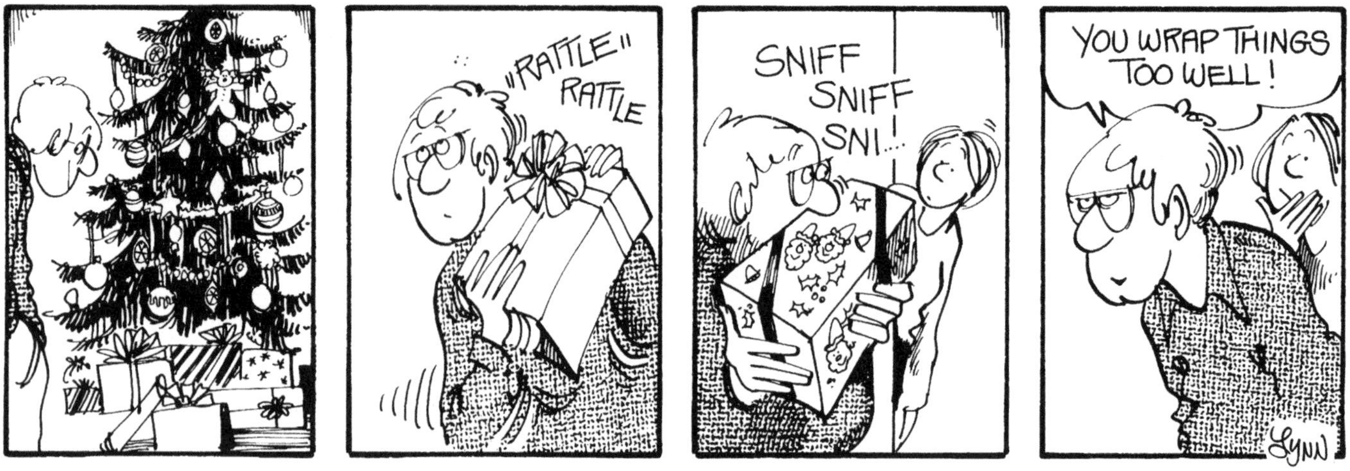
"RATTLE" RATTLE
SNIFF SNIFF SNI...
YOU WRAP THINGS TOO WELL!
LYNN

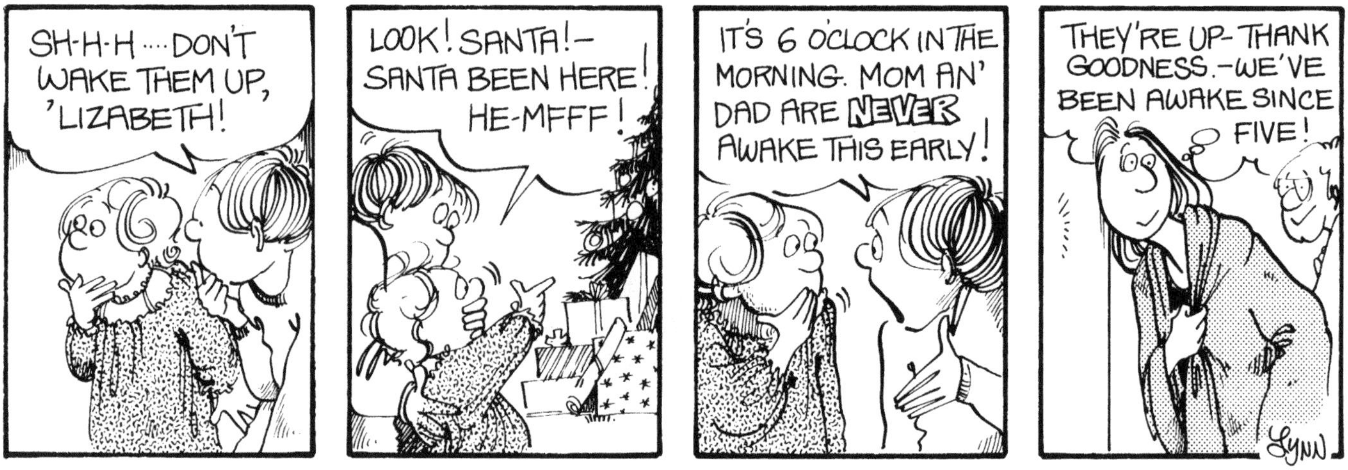
SH-H-H .... DON'T WAKE THEM UP, 'LIZABETH!
LOOK! SANTA! - SANTA BEEN HERE! HE-MFFF!
IT'S 6 O'CLOCK IN THE MORNING. MOM AN' DAD ARE NEVER AWAKE THIS EARLY!
THEY'RE UP - THANK GOODNESS. - WE'VE BEEN AWAKE SINCE FIVE!
LYNN

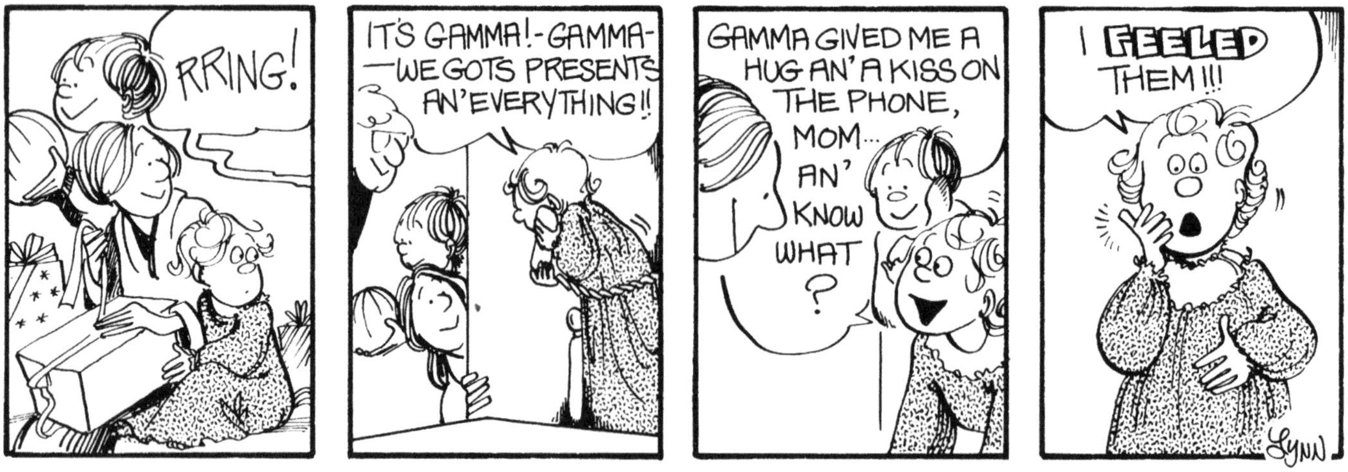
RRING!
IT'S GAMMA! - GAMMA - WE GOTS PRESENTS AN' EVERYTHING!!
GAMMA GIVED ME A HUG AN' A KISS ON THE PHONE, MOM... AN' KNOW WHAT?
I FEELED THEM!!!
LYNN

I wished that my parents hadn't lived so far away. Christmastime, especially, would have been better if the other set of "grands" had been there to share it with. The telephone was the next best thing, and the bill became our annual gifts to each other.

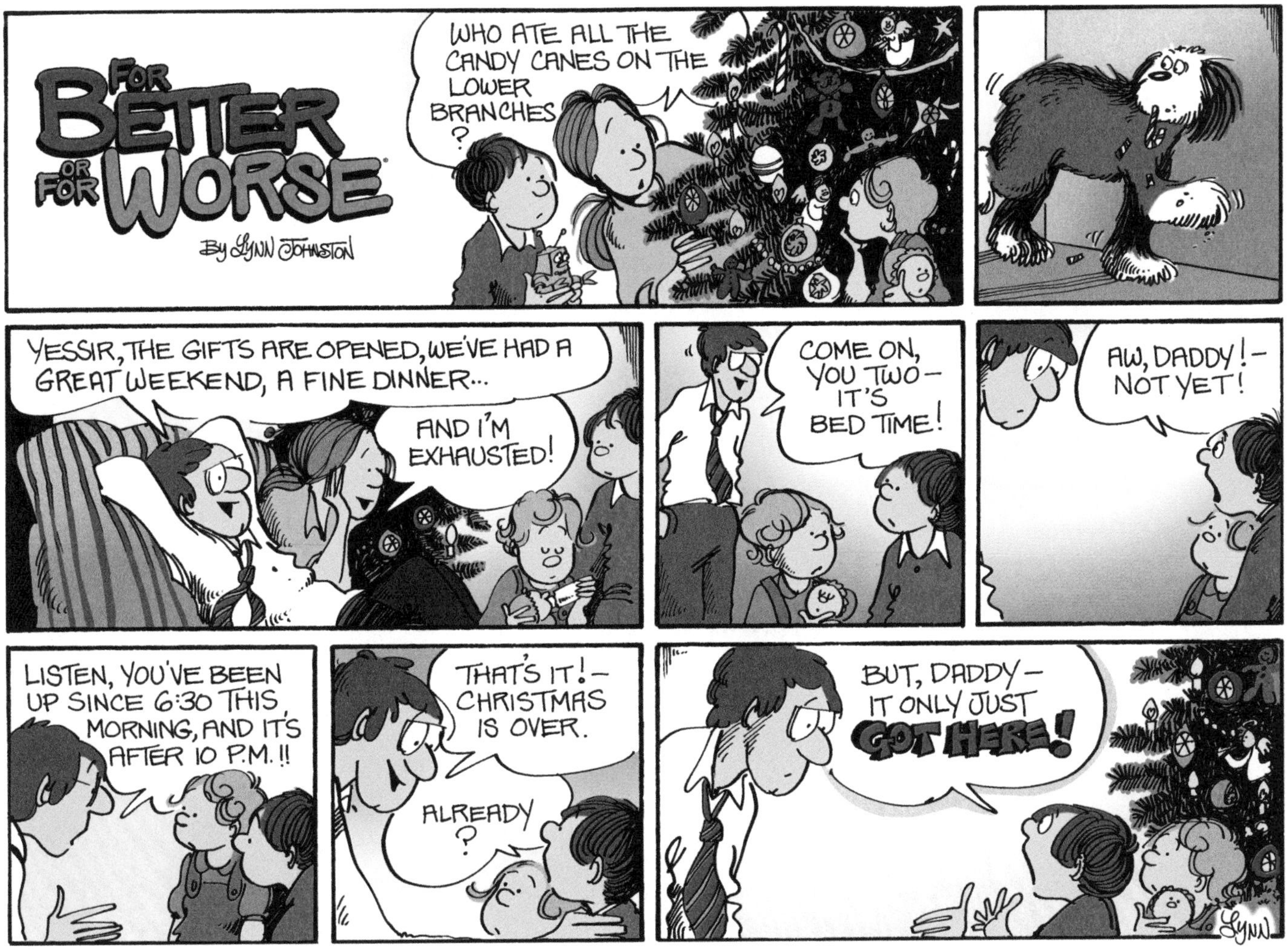
FOR BETTER OR FOR WORSE
BY LYNN JOHNSTON
WHO ATE ALL THE CANDY CANES ON THE LOWER BRANCHES ?
YESSIR, THE GIFTS ARE OPENED, WE'VE HAD A GREAT WEEKEND, A FINE DINNER...
AND I'M EXHAUSTED!
COME ON, YOU TWO— IT'S BED TIME!
AW, DADDY!— NOT YET!
LISTEN, YOU'VE BEEN UP SINCE 6:30 THIS MORNING, AND IT'S AFTER 10 P.M.!!
THAT'S IT!— CHRISTMAS IS OVER.
ALREADY ?
BUT, DADDY— IT ONLY JUST GOT HERE!
LYNN

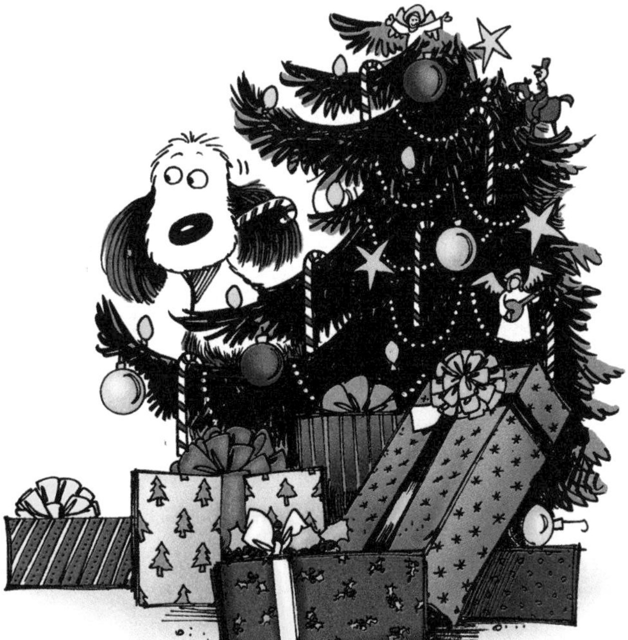

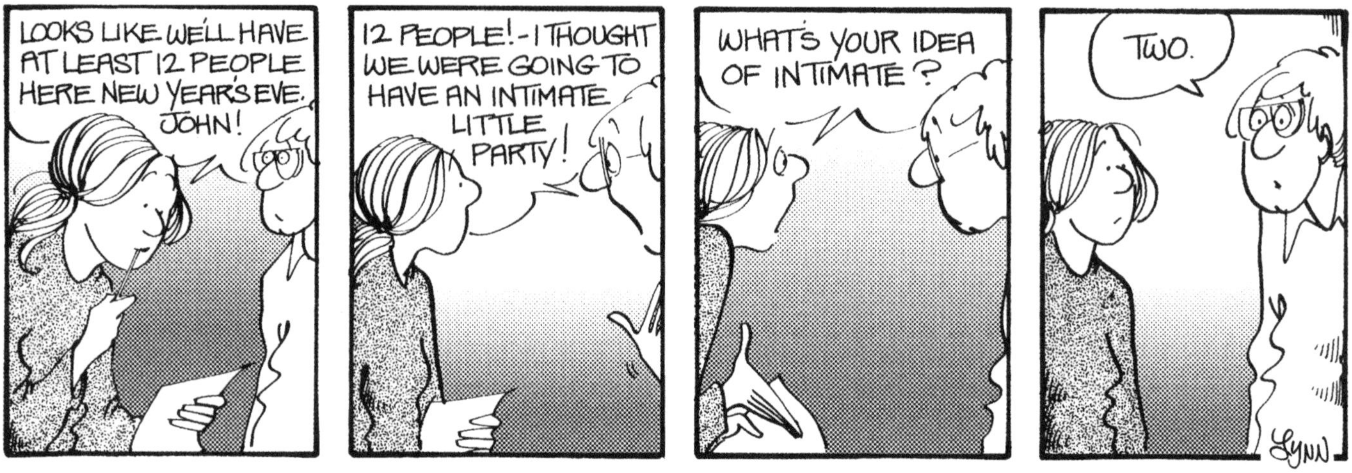
LOOKS LIKE WE'LL HAVE AT LEAST 12 PEOPLE HERE NEW YEAR'S EVE, JOHN!
12 PEOPLE! - I THOUGHT WE WERE GOING TO HAVE AN INTIMATE LITTLE PARTY!
WHAT'S YOUR IDEA OF INTIMATE?
TWO.
LYNN

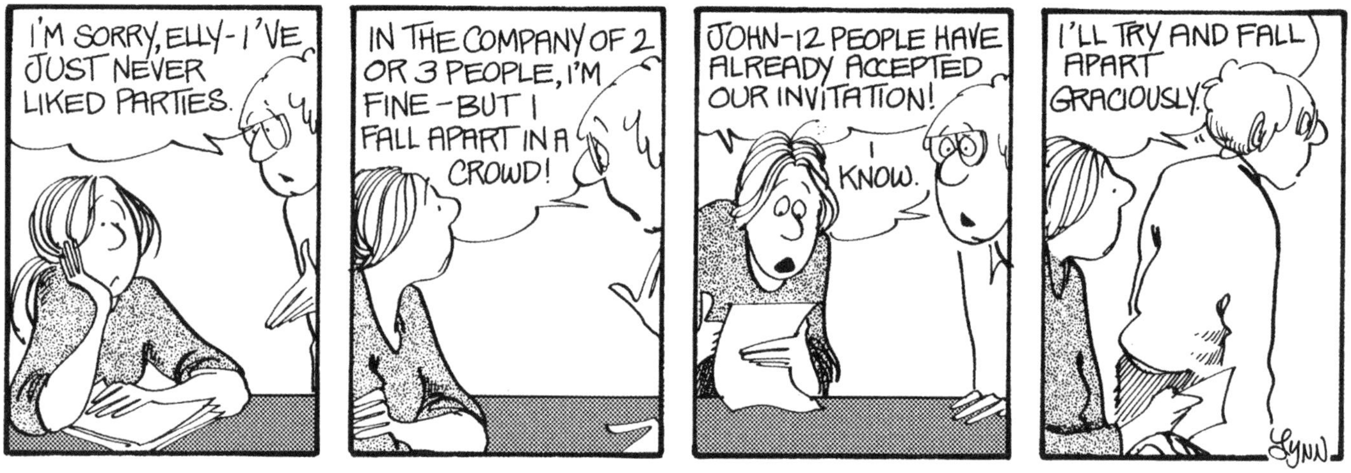
I'M SORRY, ELLY - I'VE JUST NEVER LIKED PARTIES.
IN THE COMPANY OF 2 OR 3 PEOPLE, I'M FINE - BUT I FALL APART IN A CROWD!
JOHN - 12 PEOPLE HAVE ALREADY ACCEPTED OUR INVITATION!
I KNOW.
I'LL TRY AND FALL APART GRACIOUSLY.
LYNN

In reality, it was I who felt uncomfortable in a crowd. My husband fit nicely into any large group and could dig into any conversation easily. If the gathering was at our place, I knew my role. But if it was elsewhere, however, I would rather help the hostess in the kitchen than try and fit in with the guests. Despite the public speaking and all the travelling I do, I'm still out of my element when I'm in a crowd!

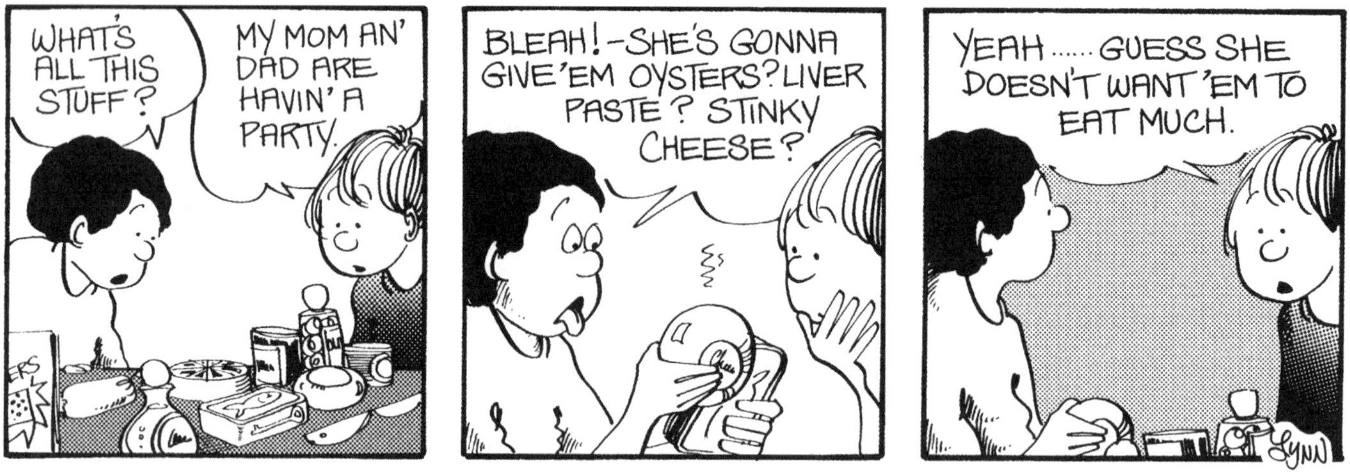
WHAT'S ALL THIS STUFF?
MY MOM AN' DAD ARE HAVIN' A PARTY.
BLEAH! - SHE'S GONNA GIVE 'EM OYSTERS? LIVER PASTE? STINKY CHEESE?
YEAH ...... GUESS SHE DOESN'T WANT 'EM TO EAT MUCH.
LYNN

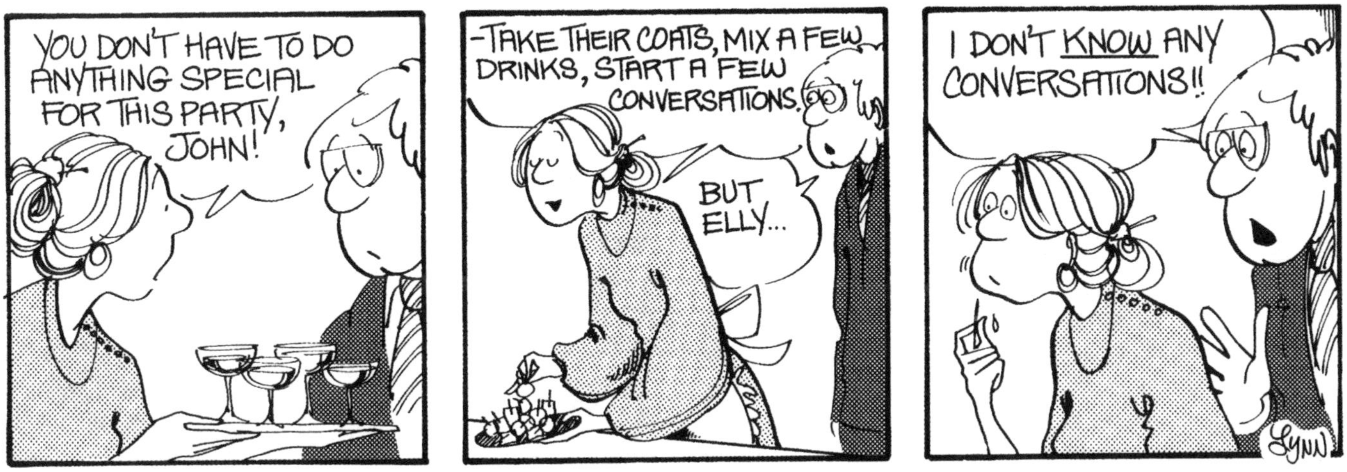
YOU DON'T HAVE TO DO ANYTHING SPECIAL FOR THIS PARTY, JOHN!
-TAKE THEIR COATS, MIX A FEW DRINKS, START A FEW CONVERSATIONS.
BUT ELLY...
I DON'T KNOW ANY CONVERSATIONS!!
LYNN

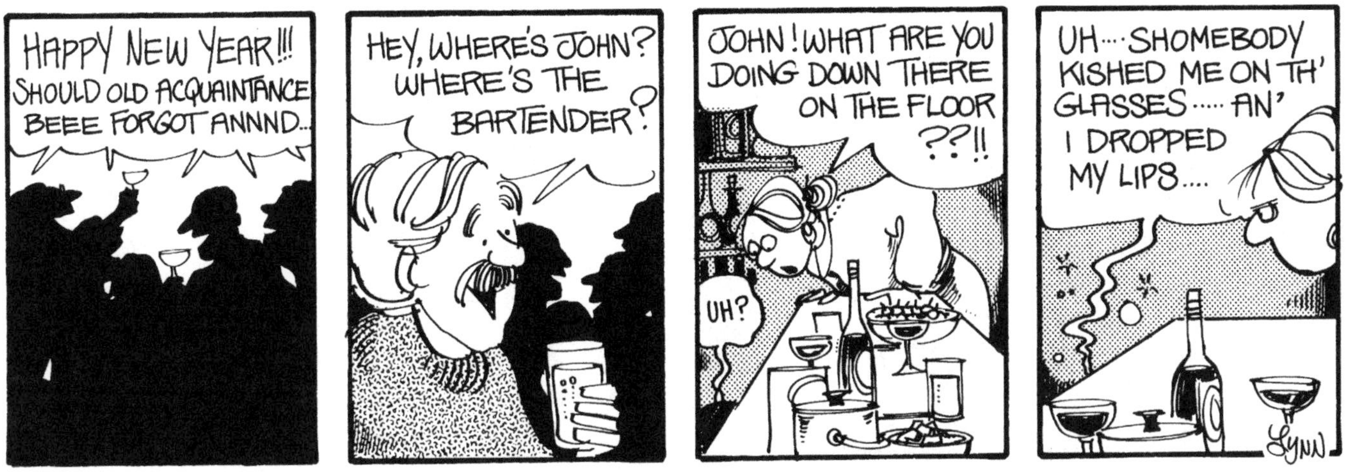
HAPPY NEW YEAR!!! SHOULD OLD ACQUAINTANCE BEEE FORGOT ANNND...
HEY, WHERE'S JOHN? WHERE'S THE BARTENDER?
JOHN! WHAT ARE YOU DOING DOWN THERE ON THE FLOOR ??!!
UH?
UH.... SHOMEBODY KISHED ME ON TH' GLASSES..... AN' I DROPPED MY LIPS....
LYNN

The town pharmacist hosted the first New Year's Eve party we ever attended in Lynn Lake. Because the liquor store was in the pharmacy, libation flowed. It didn't take long before my husband was leaning dangerously. Fearing we'd make a scene in front of the town's professionals, I insisted we walk home. As we shuffled the six blocks between buildings, we heard a truck behind us. It was the pharmacist and all the guys from the party. They were hanging out the windows … wildly cheering us on!

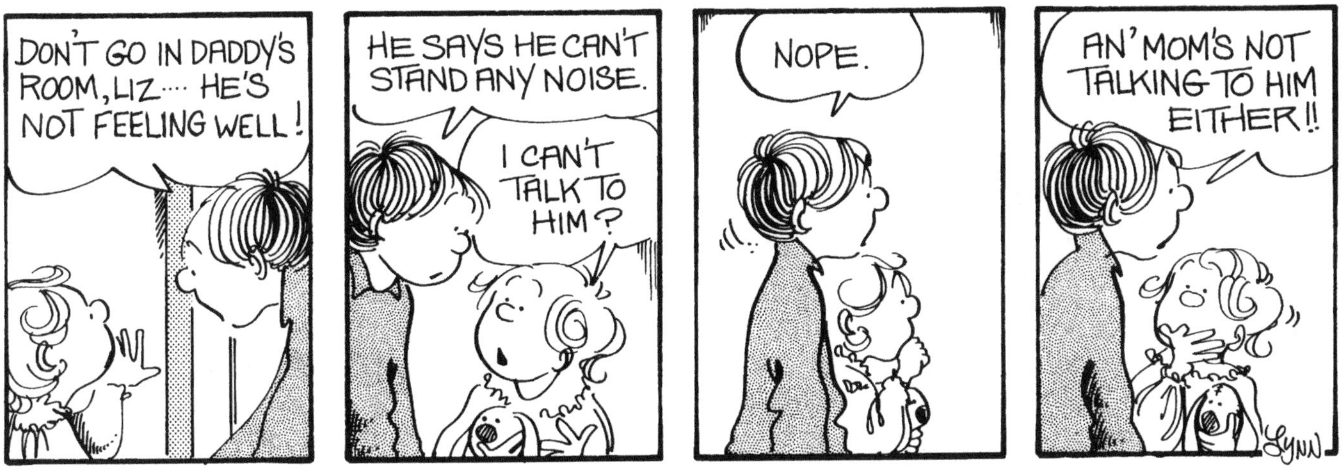
DON'T GO IN DADDY'S ROOM, LIZ.... HE'S NOT FEELING WELL!
HE SAYS HE CAN'T STAND ANY NOISE.
I CAN'T TALK TO HIM?
NOPE.
AN' MOM'S NOT TALKING TO HIM EITHER!!
LYNN

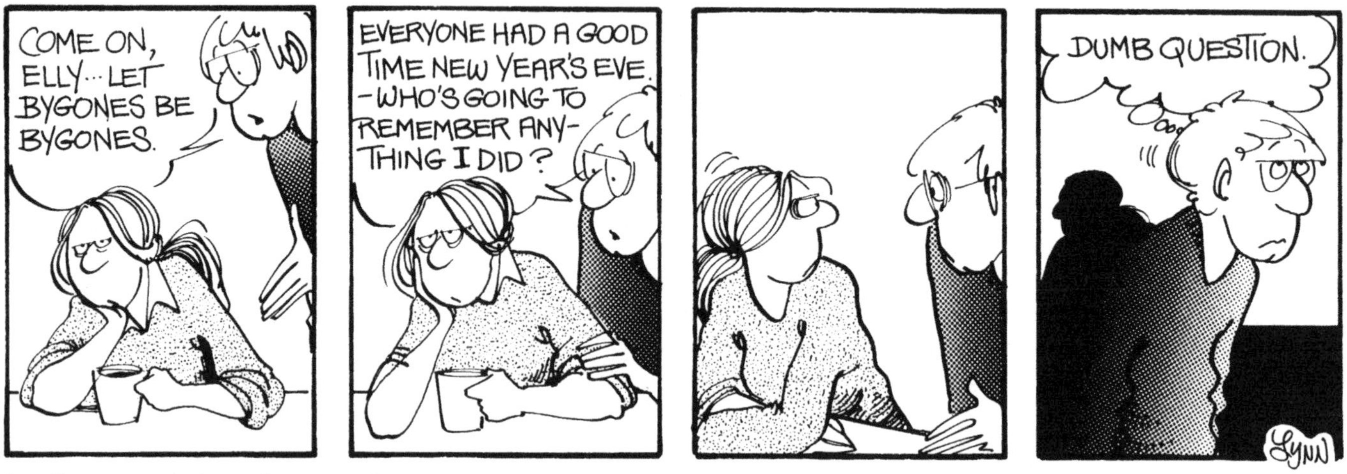
COME ON, ELLY... LET BYGONES BE BYGONES.
EVERYONE HAD A GOOD TIME NEW YEAR'S EVE. -WHO'S GOING TO REMEMBER ANY-THING I DID?
DUMB QUESTION.
LYNN

I really was mad about that party. I wanted to make a good impression on people we were meeting socially for the first time. I needn't have worried. After a year of living there, we knew the best and the worst about everyone and they knew as much about us. Nobody remembered anything about the party — other than my snit and the guys following us home.

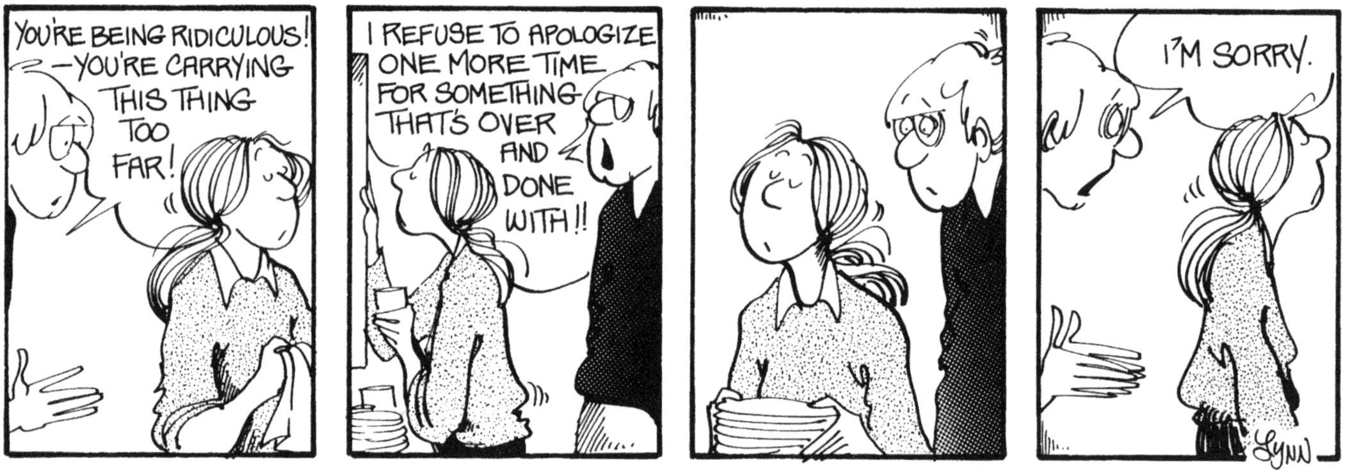
YOU'RE BEING RIDICULOUS! —YOU'RE CARRYING THIS THING TOO FAR!
I REFUSE TO APOLOGIZE ONE MORE TIME FOR SOMETHING THAT'S OVER AND DONE WITH!!
I'M SORRY.
LYNN

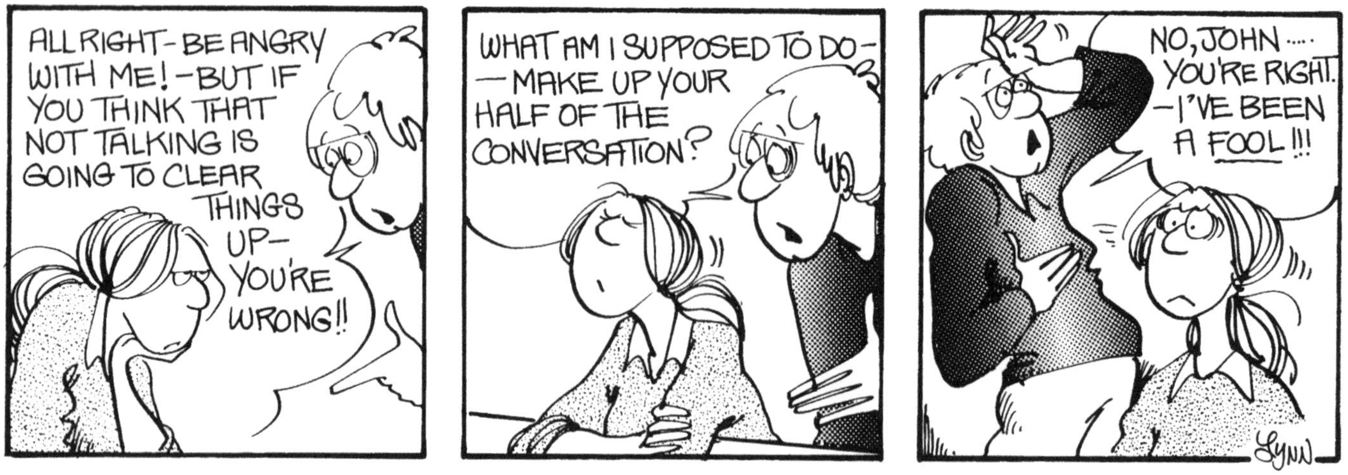
ALL RIGHT- BE ANGRY WITH ME! -BUT IF YOU THINK THAT NOT TALKING IS GOING TO CLEAR THINGS UP- YOU'RE WRONG!!
WHAT AM I SUPPOSED TO DO- —MAKE UP YOUR HALF OF THE CONVERSATION?
NO, JOHN..... YOU'RE RIGHT. -I'VE BEEN A FOOL!!!
LYNN

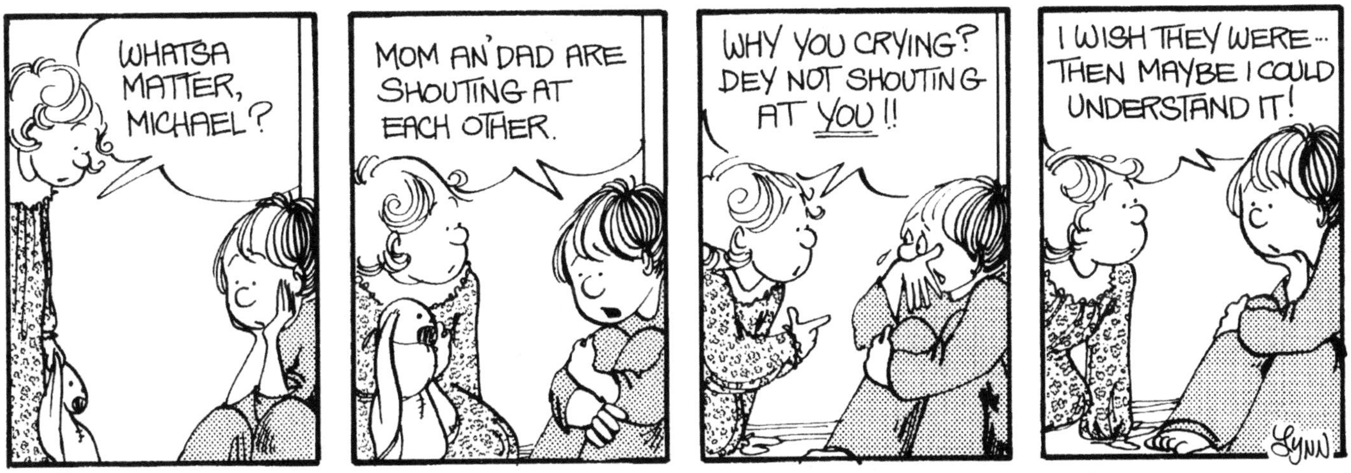
WHATSA MATTER, MICHAEL?
MOM AN' DAD ARE SHOUTING AT EACH OTHER.
WHY YOU CRYING? DEY NOT SHOUTING AT YOU !!
I WISH THEY WERE... THEN MAYBE I COULD UNDERSTAND IT!
LYNN

I knew the kids suffered anytime we fought. We didn't disagree too often, but when we did, Kate and Aaron felt it was somehow their fault. We usually don't talk to them about the issues, we don't explain what's happening and why we're mad, so kids try and unravel the puzzle the best way they know how. To a child, the world revolves around them — and if this is the case, it must be their fault if the world leaves its axis and gets wobbly sometimes! I tried to show that here.

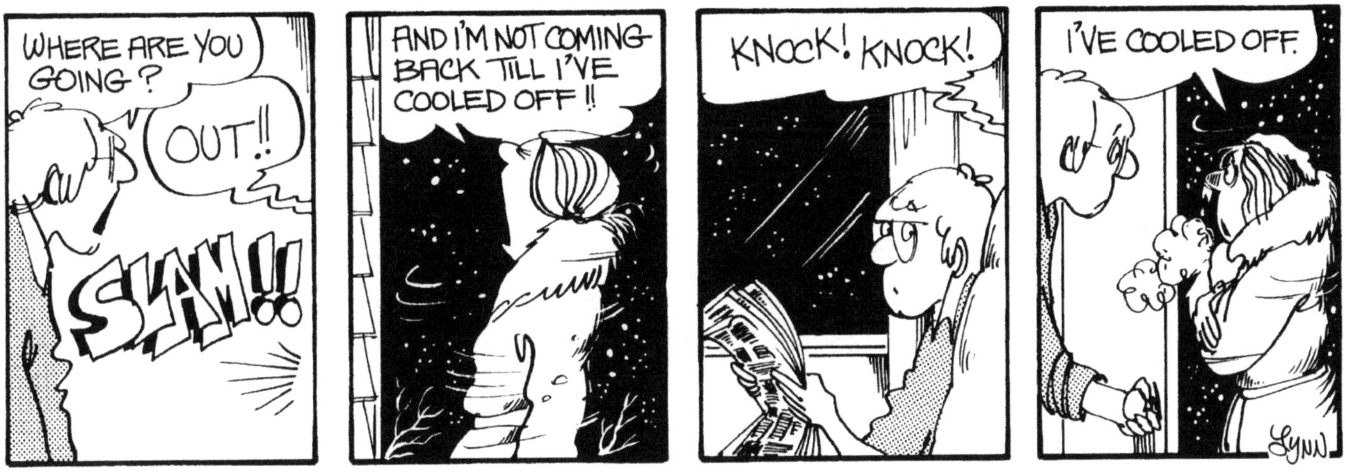
WHERE ARE YOU GOING?
OUT!!
SLAM!!
AND I'M NOT COMING BACK TILL I'VE COOLED OFF!!
KNOCK! KNOCK!
I'VE COOLED OFF.
LYNN

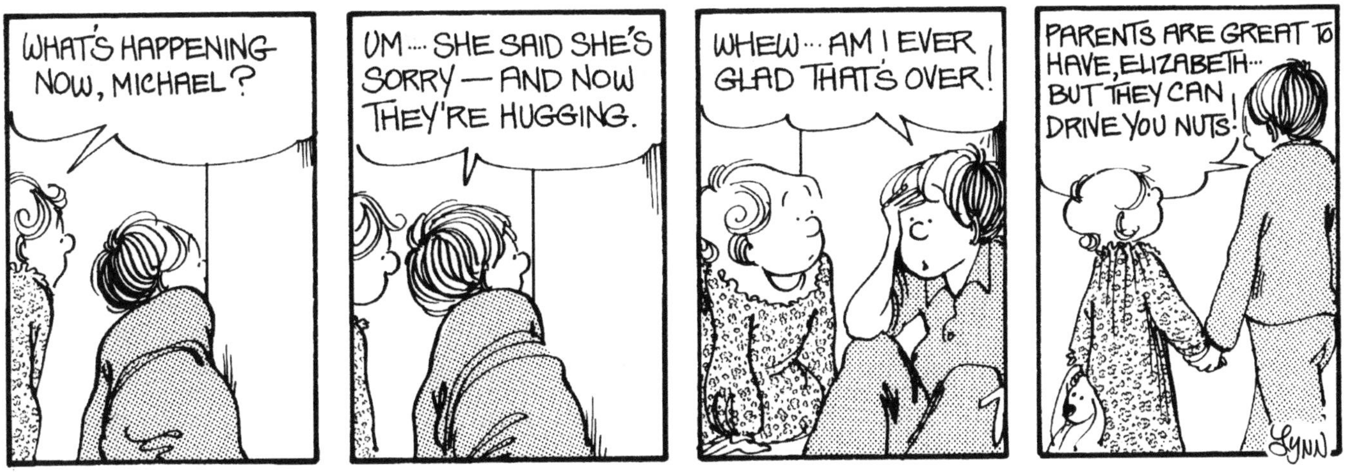
WHAT'S HAPPENING NOW, MICHAEL?
UM.... SHE SAID SHE'S SORRY — AND NOW THEY'RE HUGGING.
WHEW... AM I EVER GLAD THAT'S OVER!
PARENTS ARE GREAT TO HAVE, ELIZABETH... BUT THEY CAN DRIVE YOU NUTS!
LYNN

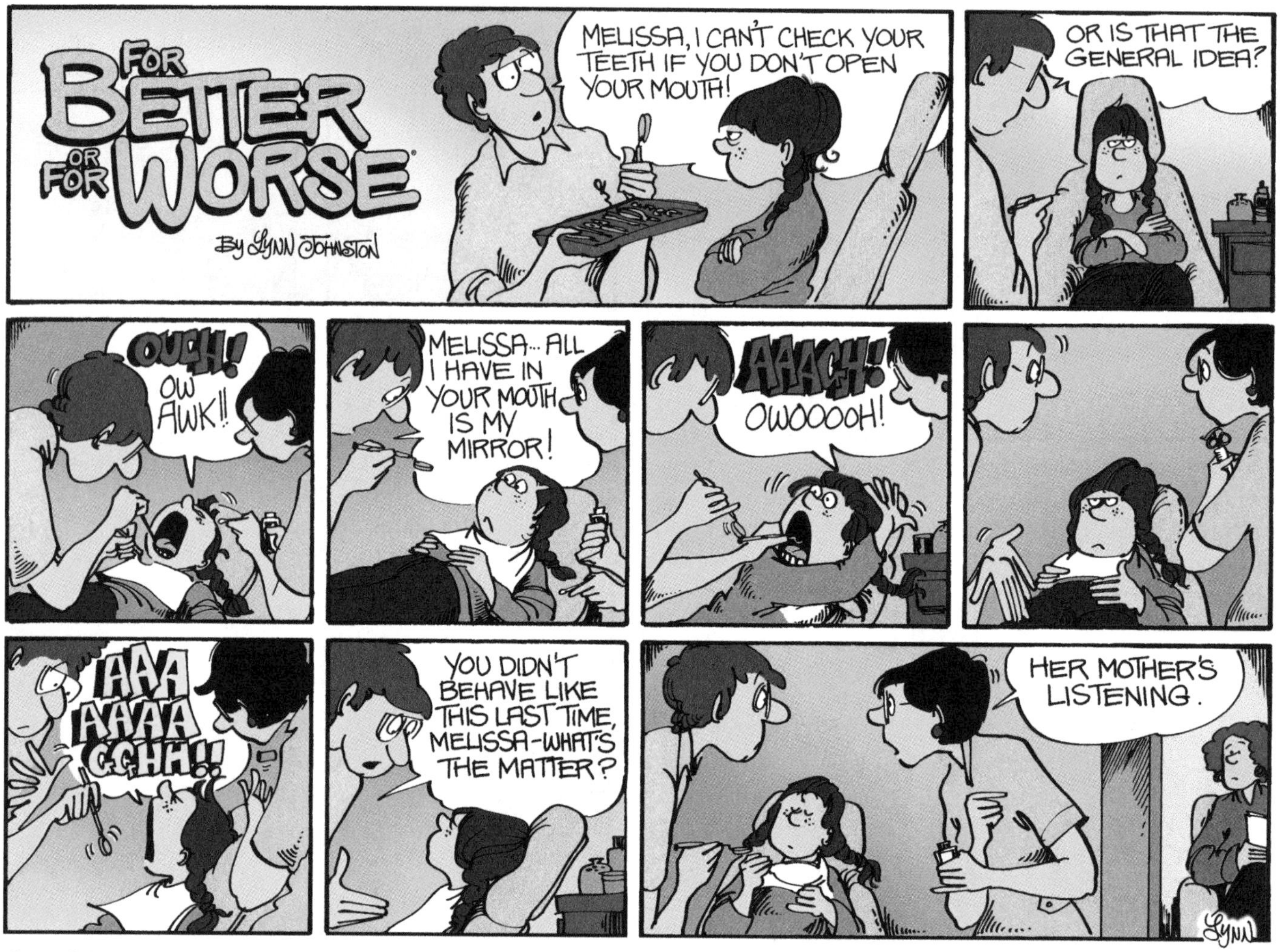
FOR BETTER OR FOR WORSE
BY LYNN JOHNSTON
MELISSA, I CAN'T CHECK YOUR TEETH IF YOU DON'T OPEN YOUR MOUTH!
OR IS THAT THE GENERAL IDEA?
OUCH! OW AWK!!
MELISSA... ALL I HAVE IN YOUR MOUTH IS MY MIRROR!
AAACH! OWOOOOH!
AAA AAAA GGHH!!
YOU DIDN'T BEHAVE LIKE THIS LAST TIME, MELISSA-WHAT'S THE MATTER?
HER MOTHER'S LISTENING.
LYNN

One of the concerns my husband had at the dental clinic was well-meaning moms wanting to be in the operatory to "help calm the children." Typically, the child would be fine with the dental staff and the doctor, but Mom would insist on being there — that's when the problems began. I remember him telling me about a mother who watched the procedure in silence until he was ready to inject the anaesthetic. Then she said to her son in a singsong voice, "Here comes the needle!!" The child immediately started to howl, and the process was delayed until he settled down. Just knowing that Mom was listening in might be enough for a nervous or high-maintenance kid to start a row. So the farther the parent was separated from the patient, the better.

I did this strip a few months after this actual incident occurred. The characters were changed to protect the identities of the patient and his mom. As far as I know, they never did see the connection!

FOR BETTER OR FOR WORSE
By Lynn Johnston
GIMME THAT, ELIZABETH!
NO!
IT'S MINE!
IT'S MINE!
IT'S MINE!
IT'S MINE!
IT'S MINE!
JOHN, DON'T JUST SIT THERE - DO SOMETHING WITH THOSE TWO!
I'M BUSY UP HERE - AND CAN'T BE EXPECTED TO DO EVERYTHING!
I GET TO CHOOSE A STORY FIRST!
NO, ME!
STORY TIME
JOHN, WHEN YOU'RE DONE THERE, I NEED A NEW SHELF MADE FOR THE LAUNDRY ROOM!
DID YOU HEAR ME, HONEY? - AND THE SINK STILL LEAKS!
MORE STORIES, DADDY.... WANT MORE!
I BELIEVE THIS IS WHY PRIMITIVE MAN STARTED TO HUNT.
Lynn

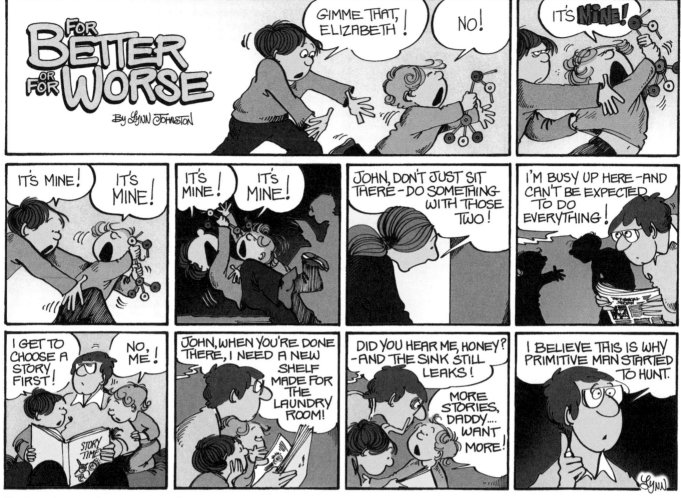

Settling disputes between the offspring usually fell to me, and there were times when I had no patience left to work with. I was so tired of the constant, petty squabbles to care. If the kids could go outside, they'd be too occupied to start a row, but inside, the tug-of-war waged on, and I would often be at the "end of my rope."

I would envy the guys who disappeared into their workshops to "get stuff done." It was hard to deny them the time they spent over an oily valve or a piece of lumber or a broken pipe. This was, after all, essential to the household maintenance. The cool, quiet ambience of the workshop was a perfect place to spend an afternoon. Guys dropping by to give advice or lend a hand were welcome. They'd lean comfortably against the doorframe, chewing the fat, and hoping for a beer to materialize. Sometimes they even got sandwiches and cake! It might take a day to fix a gadget or repair a hose — time well spent, according to the menfolk, but ... an entire day?!!

Some of my friends had hunters/fishermen in the family, and when the weekend came, their menfolk would go off to the call of the wild. The women kept the home fires burning and the small fry in line. When we came into contact with each other, we'd compare notes about the absent spouses. What did the guys REALLY do while we held down the fort? Mystery loves company. So, while I went along with the social flow, I resented it, as well. Situations like this found their way into *For Better or For Worse,* and I was always comforted by the positive responses from other moms. It was wonderful to know I wasn't alone.

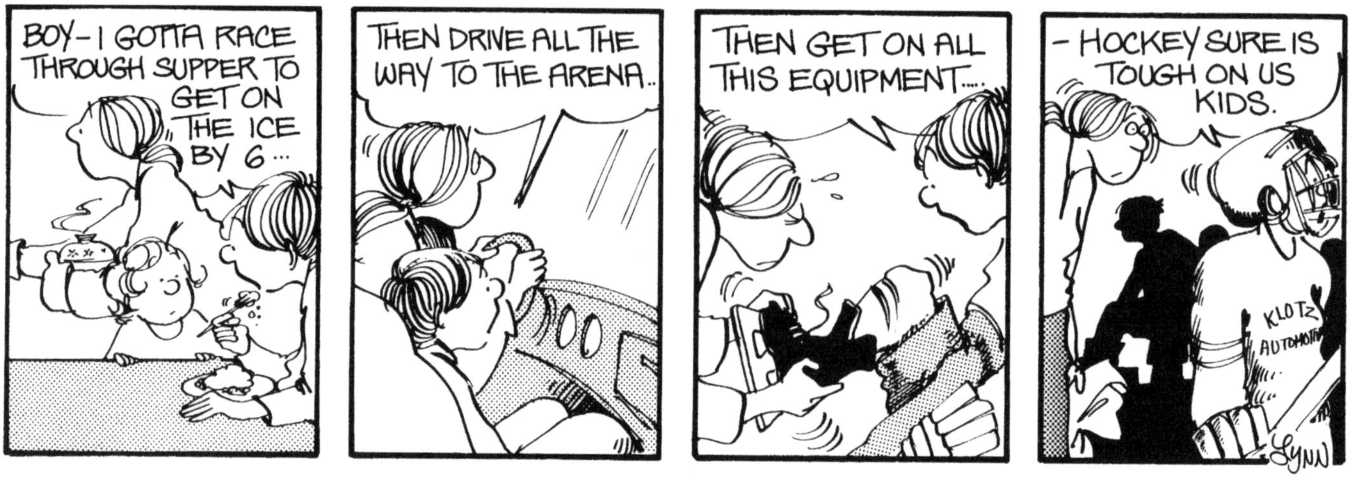
BOY- I GOTTA RACE THROUGH SUPPER TO GET ON THE ICE BY 6...
THEN DRIVE ALL THE WAY TO THE ARENA..
THEN GET ON ALL THIS EQUIPMENT.....
- HOCKEY SURE IS TOUGH ON US KIDS.
KLOTZ AUTOMOTIVE
LYNN

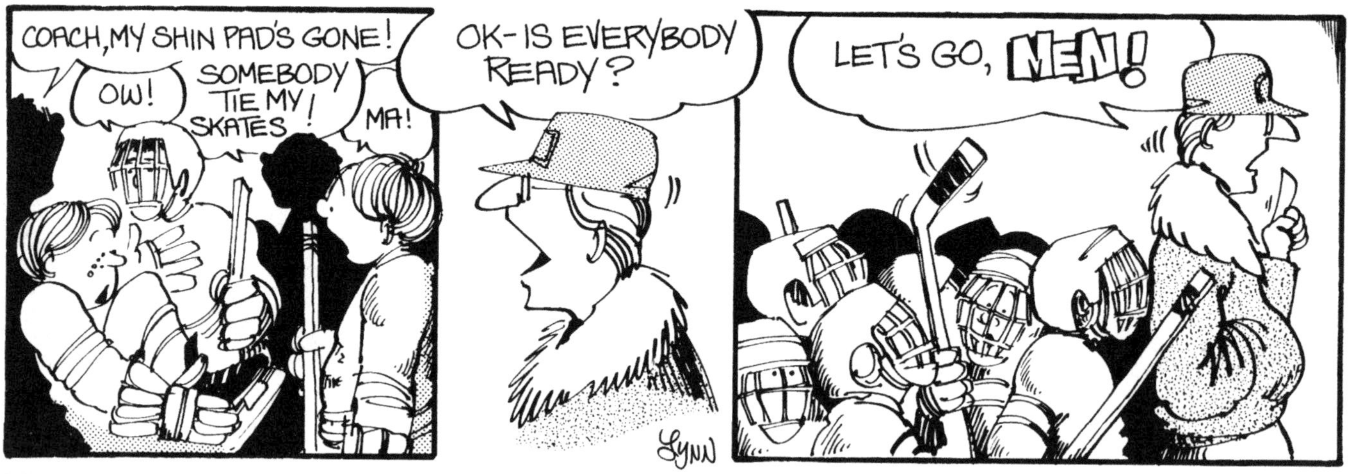
COACH, MY SHIN PAD'S GONE!
OW!
SOMEBODY TIE MY SKATES!
MA!
OK- IS EVERYBODY READY?
LET'S GO, MEN!
LYNN

When the kids were suited up and ready to do battle, they were serious. Being part of a team was so important. They learned everything from good sportsmanship to how to lose a game graciously. And knowing the position they played gave them purpose, focus, and pride.

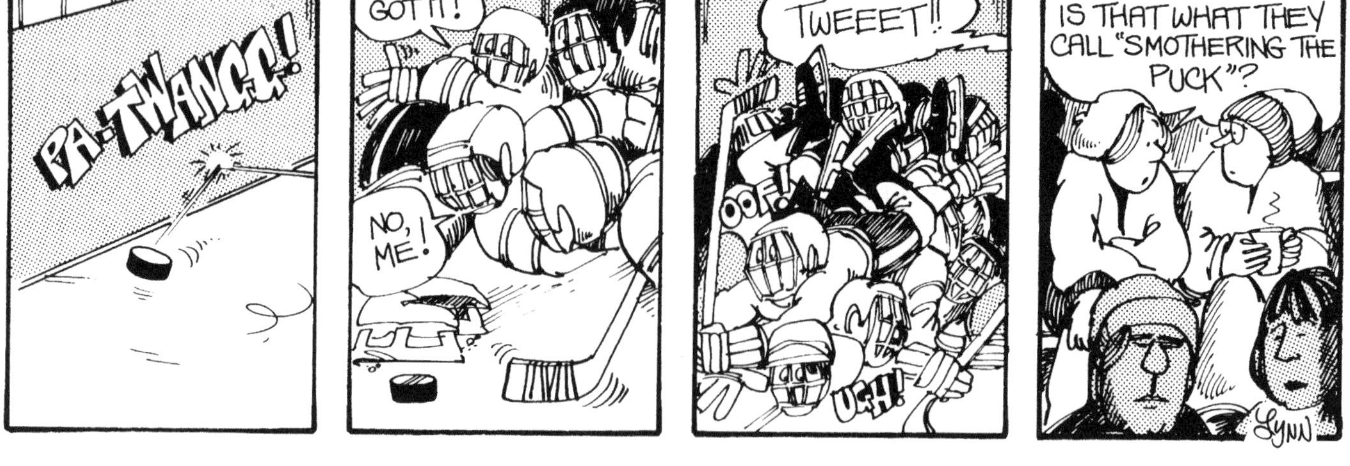
PA-TWANGG!
GOT IT!
NO, ME!
TWEEEET!!
UGH!
IS THAT WHAT THEY CALL "SMOTHERING THE PUCK"?
LYNN

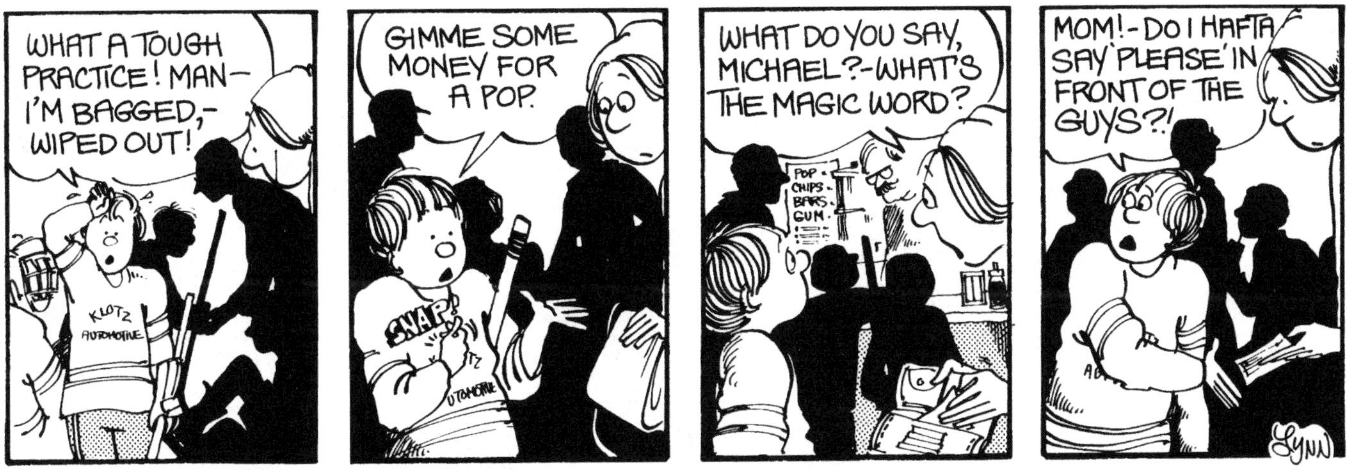
WHAT A TOUGH PRACTICE! MAN– I'M BAGGED,– WIPED OUT!
KLOTZ AUTOMOTIVE
GIMME SOME MONEY FOR A POP.
SNAP
WHAT DO YOU SAY, MICHAEL?–WHAT'S THE MAGIC WORD?
POP CHIPS BARS GUM
MOM!–DO I HAFTA SAY 'PLEASE' IN FRONT OF THE GUYS?!
LYNN

We had to make sure the kids maintained their good manners, even though they imagined themselves hitting the big leagues, then hitting the bars, and hitting each other! The contrast between the confident team player and the immature little boy was enormous — it was hard not to "parent" a youngster who was trying so hard to be a man.

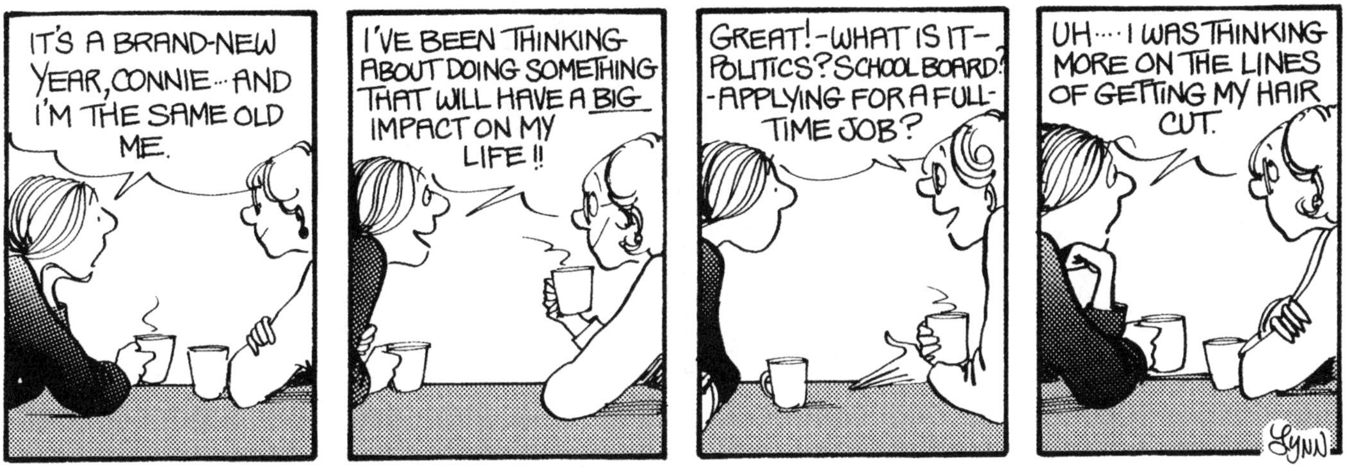
IT'S A BRAND-NEW YEAR, CONNIE... AND I'M THE SAME OLD ME.
I'VE BEEN THINKING ABOUT DOING SOMETHING THAT WILL HAVE A BIG IMPACT ON MY LIFE!!
GREAT!–WHAT IS IT– POLITICS? SCHOOL BOARD? –APPLYING FOR A FULL-TIME JOB?
UH.... I WAS THINKING MORE ON THE LINES OF GETTING MY HAIR CUT.
LYNN

Readers never tired of telling me that Elly Patterson should cut her hair. "Why," they asked, "does she look so frowsy?" My response was always the same: "Because she has a LOOK that has to be consistent." Even in a situation comedy, the performers maintain a consistent look. They might make a few changes, but generally they have to stay in character. Comic strips are the same. Besides, I couldn't draw well enough at the time to change Elly's hair and still have her look like Elly!

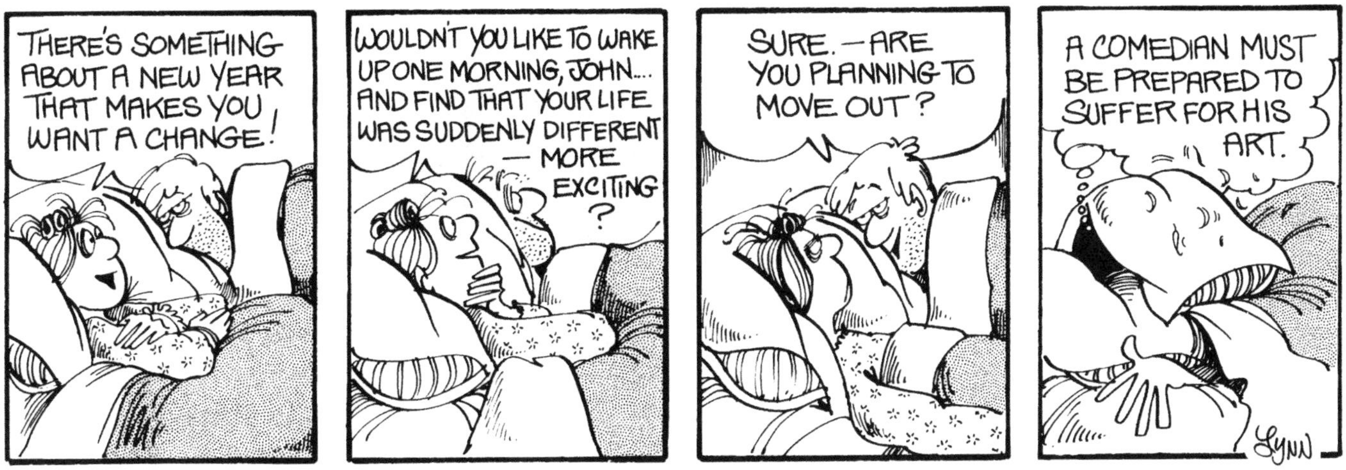
THERE'S SOMETHING ABOUT A NEW YEAR THAT MAKES YOU WANT A CHANGE!
WOULDN'T YOU LIKE TO WAKE UP ONE MORNING, JOHN... AND FIND THAT YOUR LIFE WAS SUDDENLY DIFFERENT — MORE EXCITING?
SURE. — ARE YOU PLANNING TO MOVE OUT?
A COMEDIAN MUST BE PREPARED TO SUFFER FOR HIS ART.
LYNN

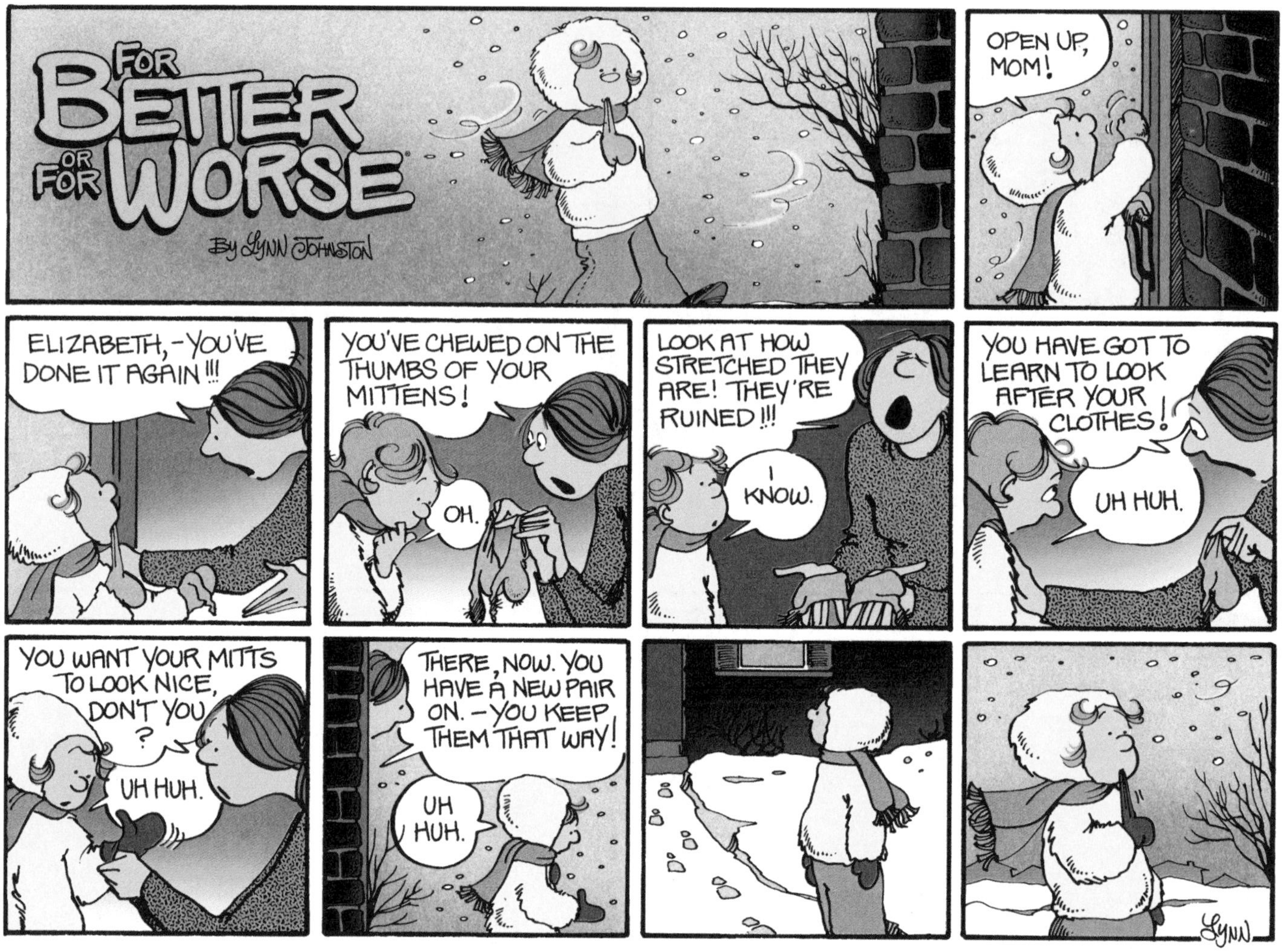
FOR BETTER OR FOR WORSE
BY LYNN JOHNSTON
OPEN UP, MOM!
ELIZABETH, -YOU'VE DONE IT AGAIN !!!
YOU'VE CHEWED ON THE THUMBS OF YOUR MITTENS!
OH.
LOOK AT HOW STRETCHED THEY ARE! THEY'RE RUINED !!!
I KNOW.
YOU HAVE GOT TO LEARN TO LOOK AFTER YOUR CLOTHES!
UH HUH.
YOU WANT YOUR MITTS TO LOOK NICE, DON'T YOU?
UH HUH.
THERE, NOW. YOU HAVE A NEW PAIR ON. -YOU KEEP THEM THAT WAY!
UH HUH.
LYNN

Katie did chew her mittens — right through the thumb. This strip was another cry of angst from her mom. My kids were often lucky that I could "use" this material!

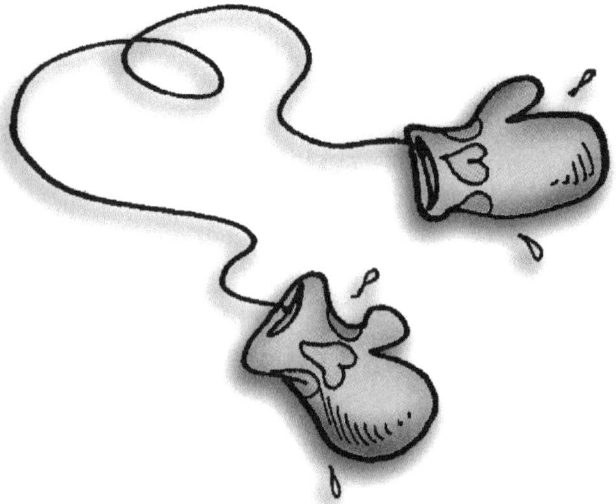

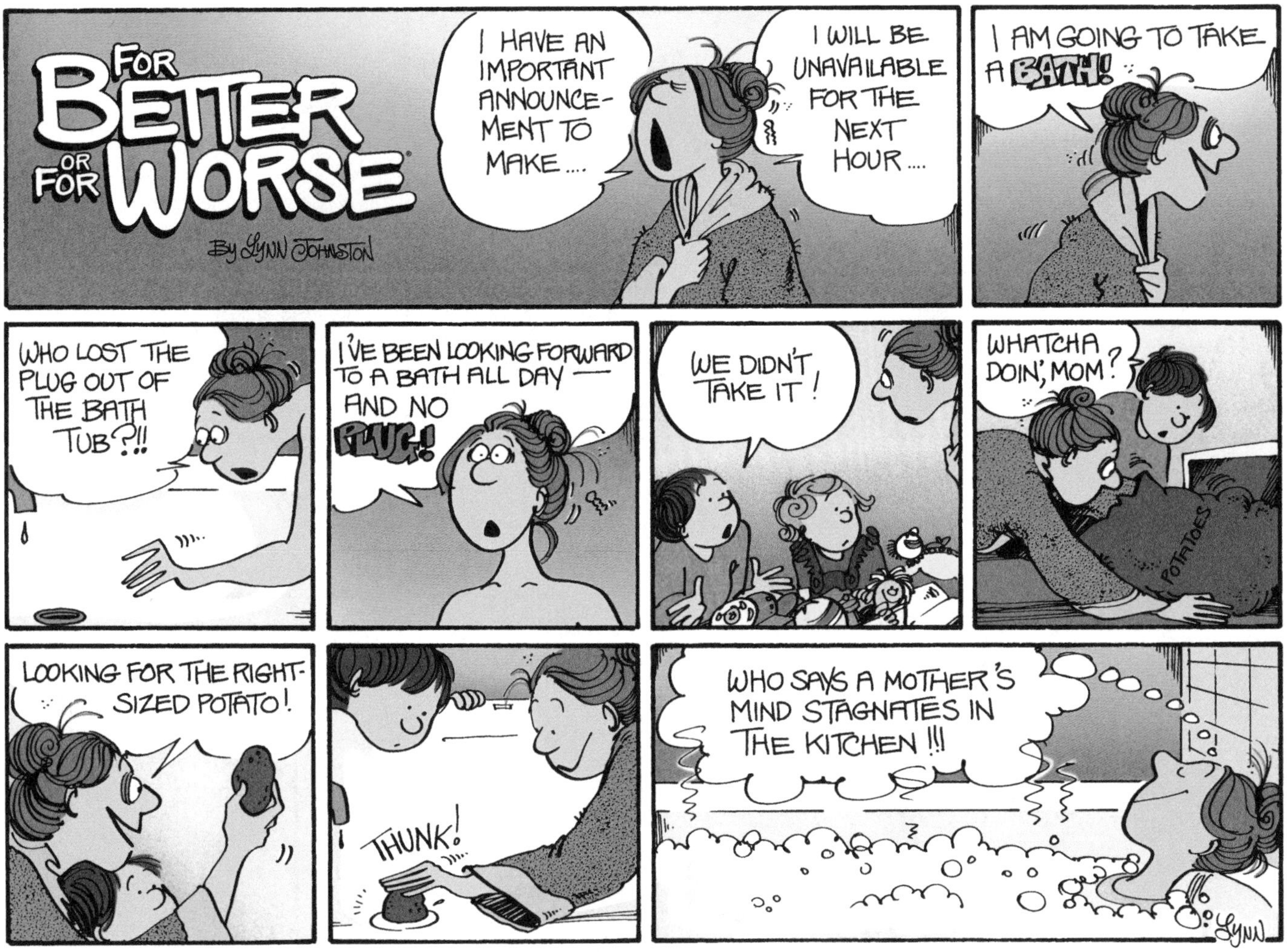
FOR BETTER OR FOR WORSE
BY LYNN JOHNSTON
I HAVE AN IMPORTANT ANNOUNCE-MENT TO MAKE....
I WILL BE UNAVAILABLE FOR THE NEXT HOUR....
I AM GOING TO TAKE A BATH!
WHO LOST THE PLUG OUT OF THE BATH TUB?!!
I'VE BEEN LOOKING FORWARD TO A BATH ALL DAY — AND NO PLUG!
WE DIDN'T TAKE IT!
WHATCHA DOIN', MOM?
POTATOES
LOOKING FOR THE RIGHT-SIZED POTATO!
THUNK!
WHO SAYS A MOTHER'S MIND STAGNATES IN THE KITCHEN!!!
LYNN

After looking for the bathtub plug for some time, I once settled on a spud that fit right into the hole. I'll do anything to have a nice, hot bath! Years later, I was visiting friends in Cuba. A neighbour kindly invited us to her house for dinner, and when we went to do the dishes afterwards, there was no plug in the sink. She was about to use a soup pot to wash up in when I saw a basket of fresh potatoes under the counter. I selected one the right size and popped it into the hole. Potato is *papa* in Spanish, and the word for plug is *tapa*. So, I said, "Look! You have a *papa* for a *tapa*!" She laughed, and I promised her that I would bring her a plug the next day. My friends and I went to every hardware store in Havana and could not find a simple rubber stopper for a sink! There were a number of things we couldn't find: a large garbage pail with a lid, a good pair of scissors, and masking tape — these things are found everywhere back home. I couldn't believe that these small, useful items that we all took for granted were so hard to find.

The following year, I went back to Cuba. I took our friend a plug for her sink and a number of other things. She was more than pleased — she was grateful. Circumstances there are different now. Cuba has opened up, and stores are able to carry more products. I still visit my friends, and we always recall the time I used a *papa* for a *tapa* ... a little trick I brought from home.

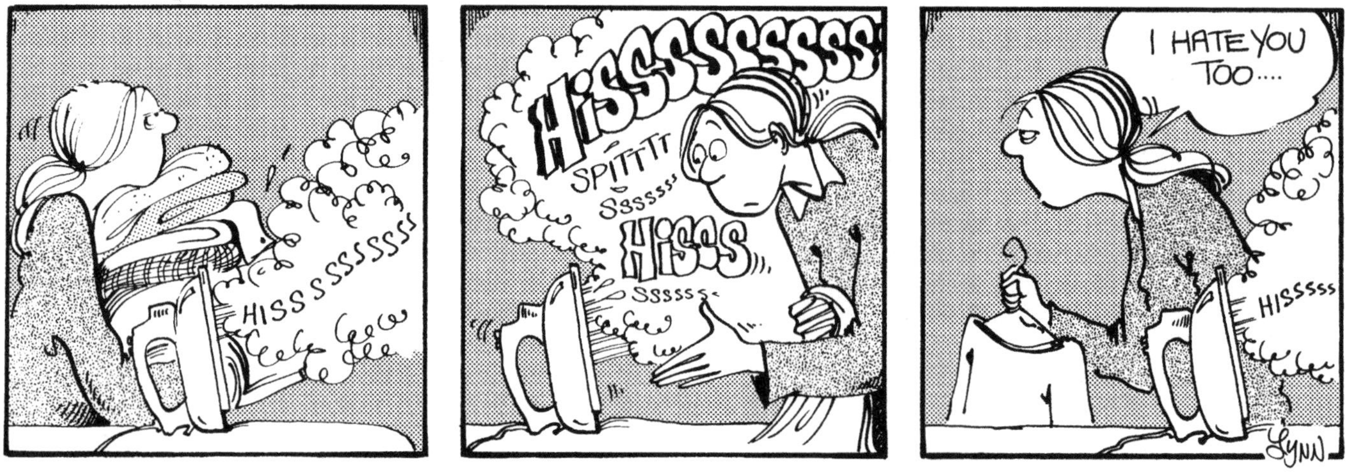
HISSSSSSSSS
HiSSSSSSSSSS
SPITTTT
SSSSSS
HiSSS
SSSSSS
I HATE YOU TOO....
HISSSSS
LYNN

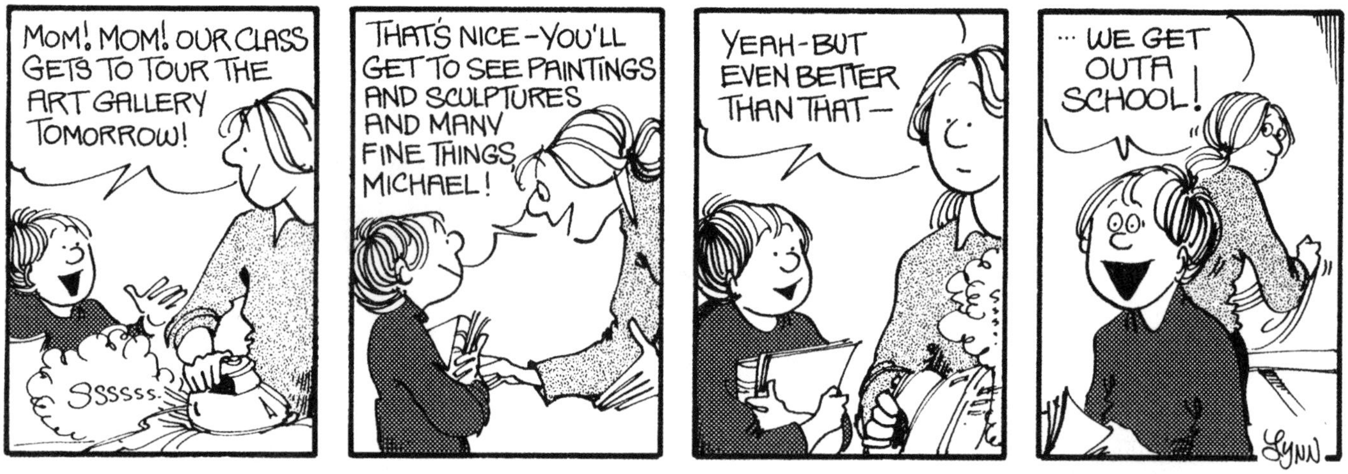
MOM! MOM! OUR CLASS GETS TO TOUR THE ART GALLERY TOMORROW!
SSSSSS.
THAT'S NICE -YOU'LL GET TO SEE PAINTINGS AND SCULPTURES AND MANY FINE THINGS MICHAEL!
YEAH-BUT EVEN BETTER THAN THAT-
...WE GET OUTA SCHOOL!
LYNN

There was little in the way of "displays" in Lynn Lake for the children to go to, so when we went down to Winnipeg, we made sure they got to see the museum, the art gallery, and live theatre — if we were lucky. Aaron knew his way around the museum as well as the docents did. The gallery provided him and Katie with new sights and ideas, and I was always pleased to see how respectful they were of both facilities. When you don't have something like this near you — the real thing is almost a "shrine!"

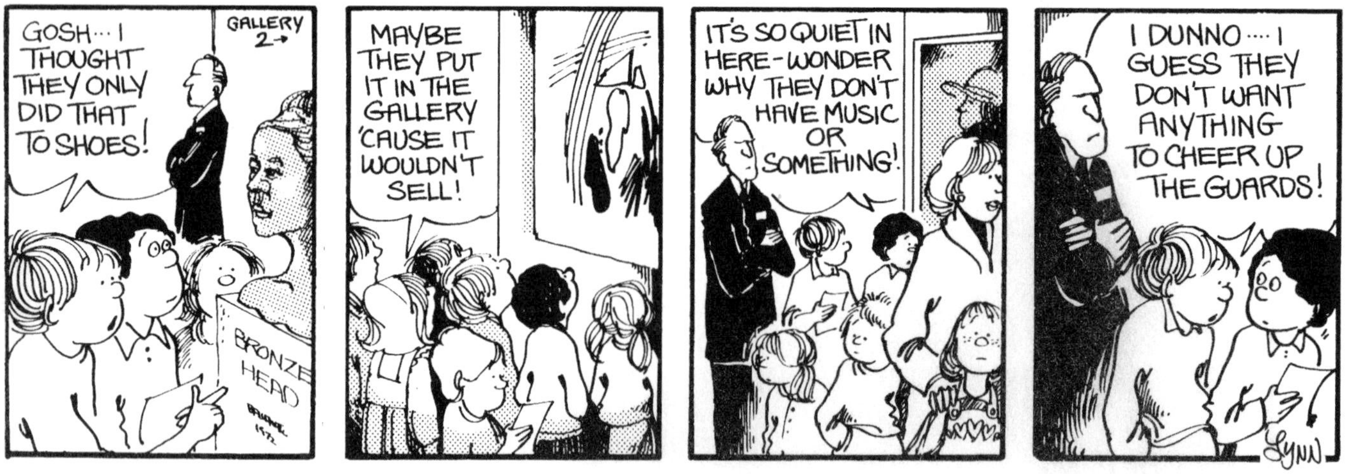
GOSH... I THOUGHT THEY ONLY DID THAT TO SHOES!
GALLERY 2→
BRONZE HEAD
MAYBE THEY PUT IT IN THE GALLERY 'CAUSE IT WOULDN'T SELL!
IT'S SO QUIET IN HERE-WONDER WHY THEY DON'T HAVE MUSIC OR SOMETHING!
I DUNNO.... I GUESS THEY DON'T WANT ANYTHING TO CHEER UP THE GUARDS!
LYNN

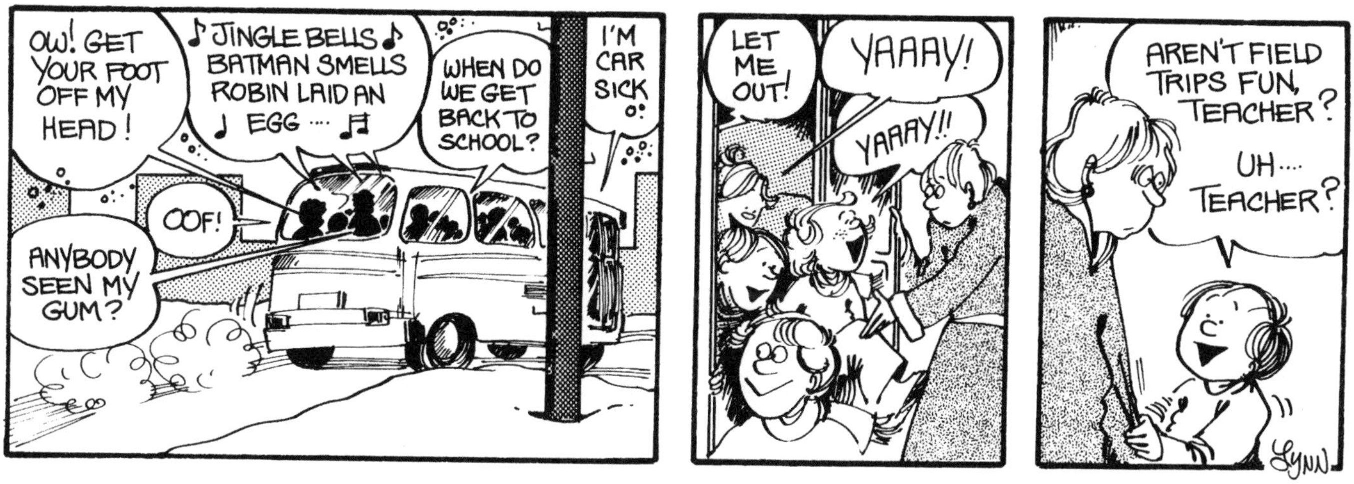
OW! GET YOUR FOOT OFF MY HEAD!
♪ JINGLE BELLS ♪ BATMAN SMELLS ROBIN LAID AN ♩ EGG .... ♬
WHEN DO WE GET BACK TO SCHOOL?
I'M CAR SICK
OOF!
ANYBODY SEEN MY GUM?
LET ME OUT!
YAAAY!
YAAAY!!
AREN'T FIELD TRIPS FUN, TEACHER?
UH.... TEACHER?
LYNN

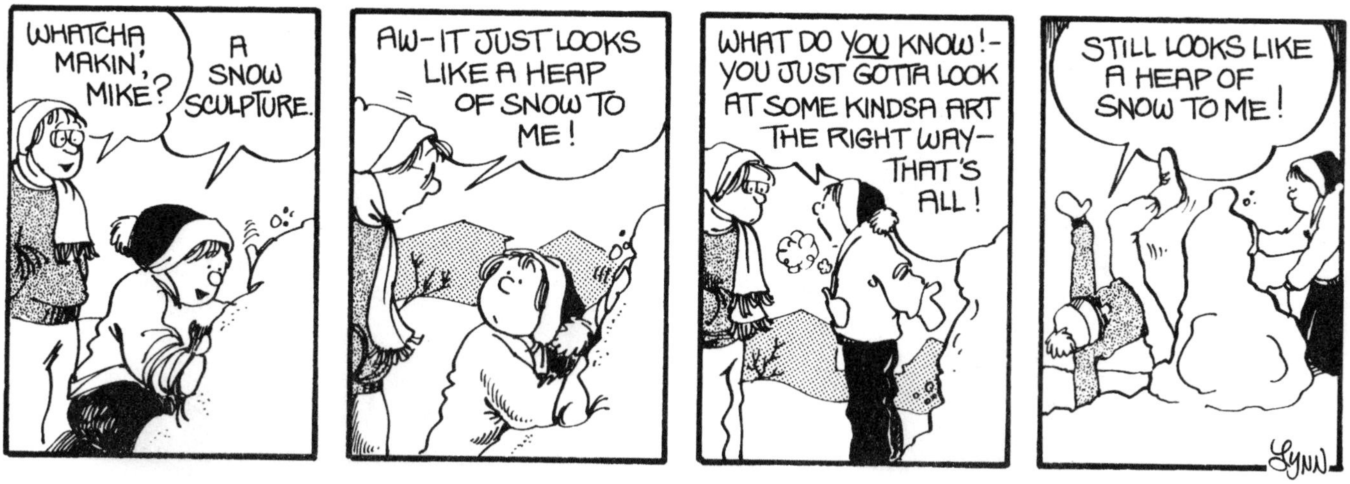
WHATCHA MAKIN', MIKE?
A SNOW SCULPTURE.
AW- IT JUST LOOKS LIKE A HEAP OF SNOW TO ME!
WHAT DO YOU KNOW! - YOU JUST GOTTA LOOK AT SOME KINDSA ART THE RIGHT WAY- THAT'S ALL!
STILL LOOKS LIKE A HEAP OF SNOW TO ME!
LYNN

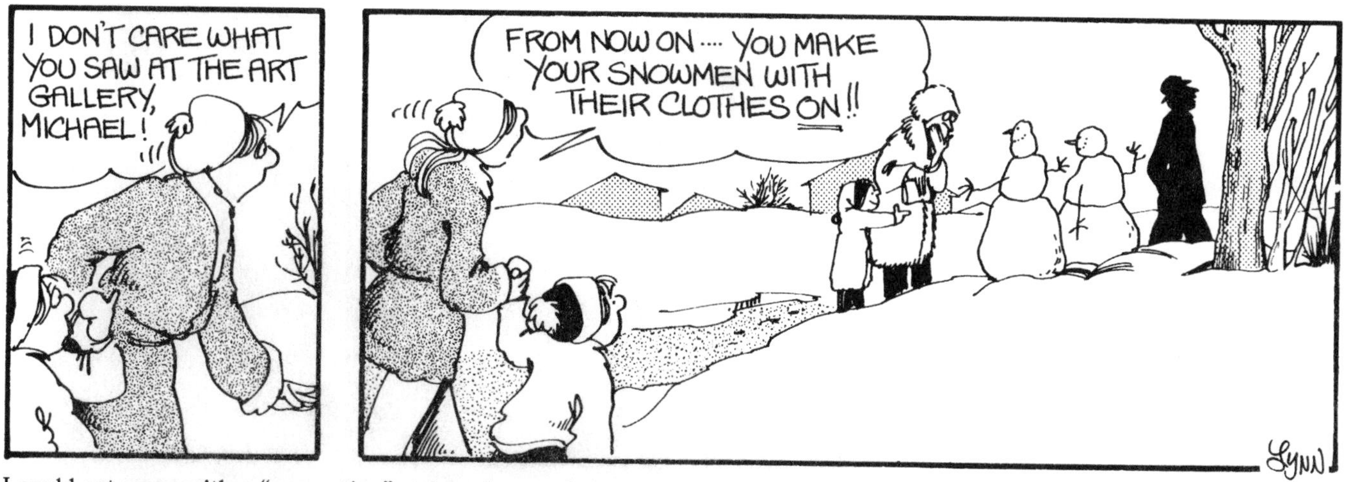
I DON'T CARE WHAT YOU SAW AT THE ART GALLERY, MICHAEL!
FROM NOW ON .... YOU MAKE YOUR SNOWMEN WITH THEIR CLOTHES ON!!
LYNN

I could get away with a "suggestive" strip as long as I didn't show the details!

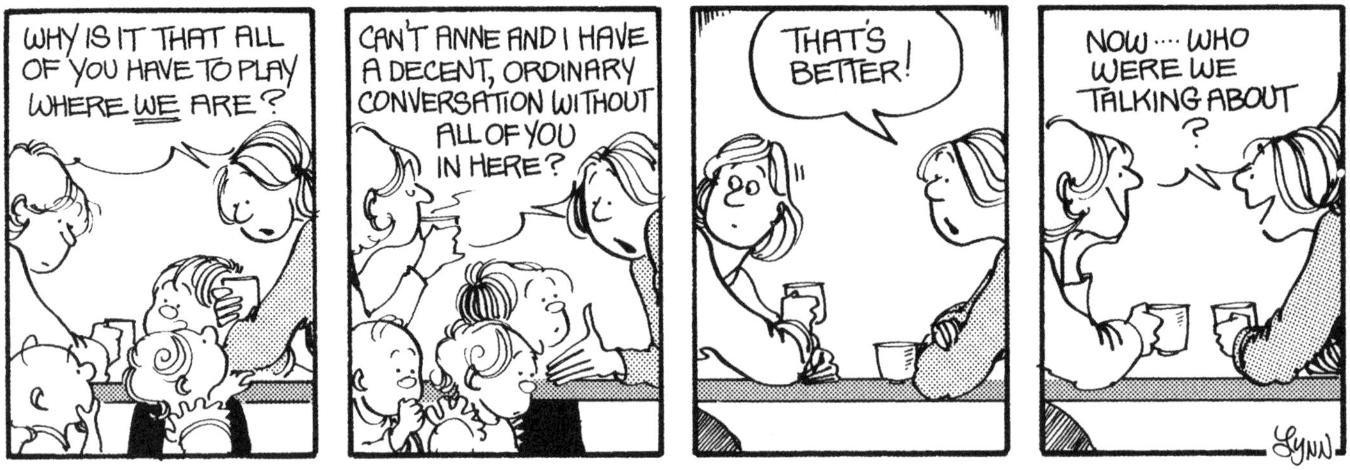
WHY IS IT THAT ALL OF YOU HAVE TO PLAY WHERE WE ARE?
CAN'T ANNE AND I HAVE A DECENT, ORDINARY CONVERSATION WITHOUT ALL OF YOU IN HERE?
THAT'S BETTER!
NOW .... WHO WERE WE TALKING ABOUT?
Lynn

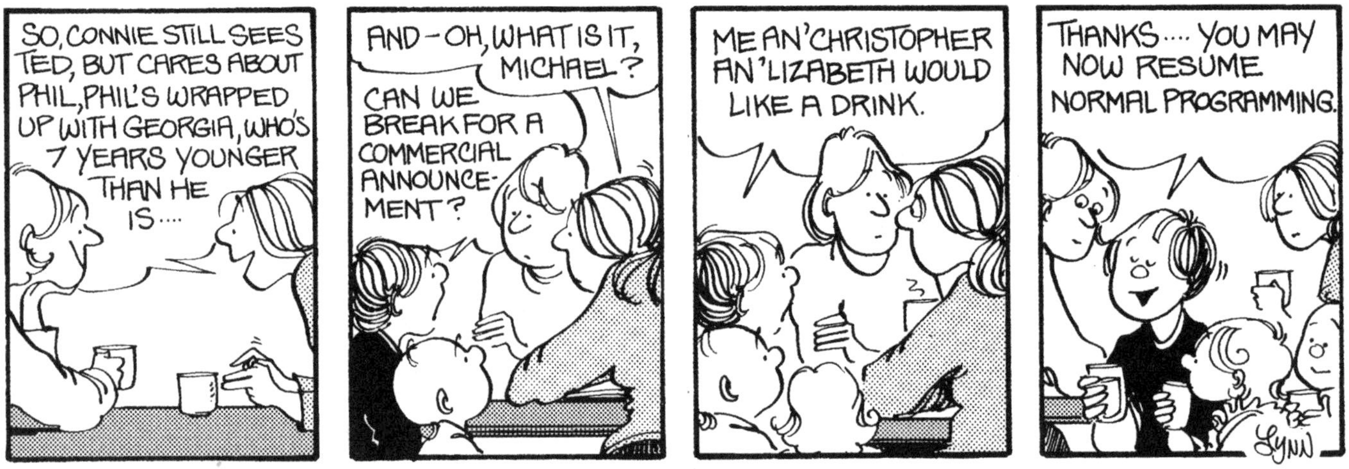
SO, CONNIE STILL SEES TED, BUT CARES ABOUT PHIL, PHIL'S WRAPPED UP WITH GEORGIA, WHO'S 7 YEARS YOUNGER THAN HE IS....
AND - OH, WHAT IS IT, MICHAEL?
CAN WE BREAK FOR A COMMERCIAL ANNOUNCE-MENT?
ME AN' CHRISTOPHER AN' LIZABETH WOULD LIKE A DRINK.
THANKS.... YOU MAY NOW RESUME NORMAL PROGRAMMING.
Lynn

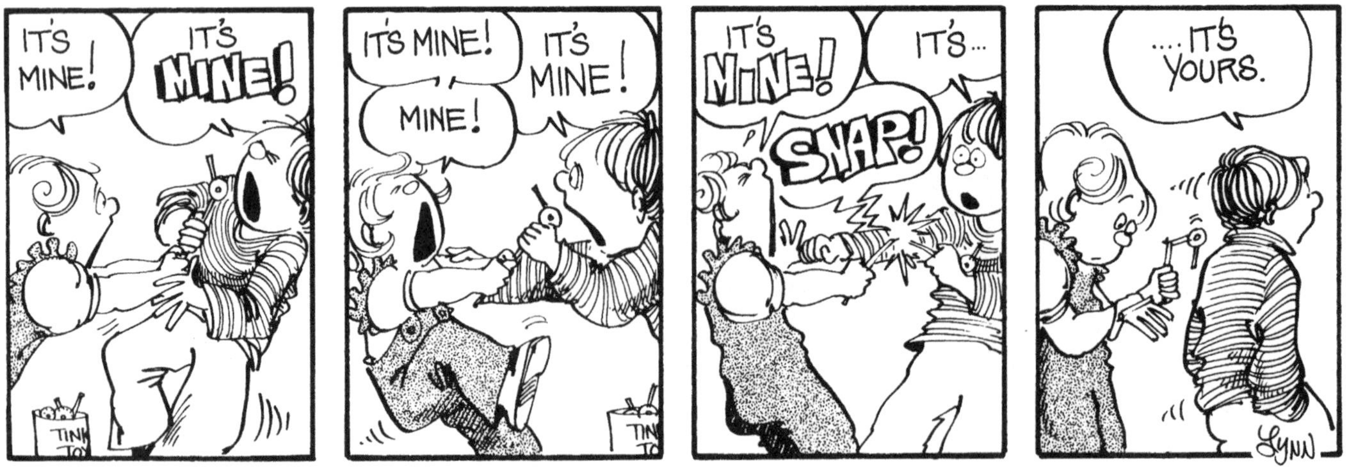
IT'S MINE!
IT'S MINE!
IT'S MINE!
IT'S MINE!
MINE!
IT'S MINE!
IT'S...
SNAP!
....IT'S YOURS.
Lynn

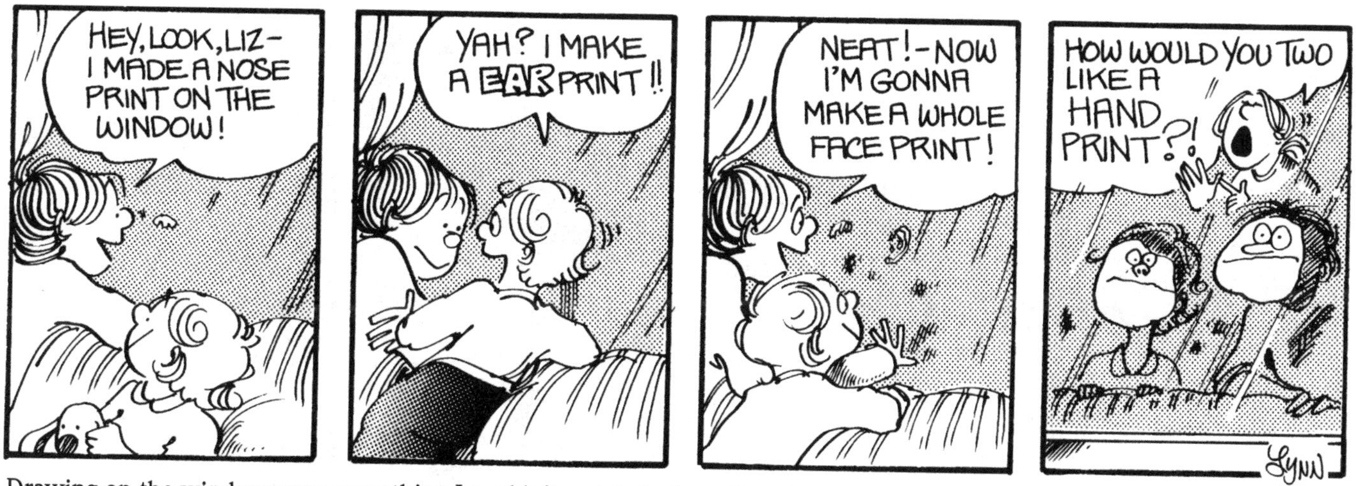
HEY, LOOK, LIZ- I MADE A NOSE PRINT ON THE WINDOW!
YAH? I MAKE A EAR PRINT!!
NEAT! - NOW I'M GONNA MAKE A WHOLE FACE PRINT!
HOW WOULD YOU TWO LIKE A HAND PRINT?!
Lynn

Drawing on the windows was something I couldn't resist. As far as I was concerned, the art disappeared, so what was the problem? I never saw the greasy lines and ugly smudges I left behind. Only my mom could see these things — she was far too particular in my eyes. A steamy living room window was an endless canvas put there for an artist (me) to draw on. Later, when I was older and smarter, I learned to hide my fingerprints by wiping the windows with the sheers.

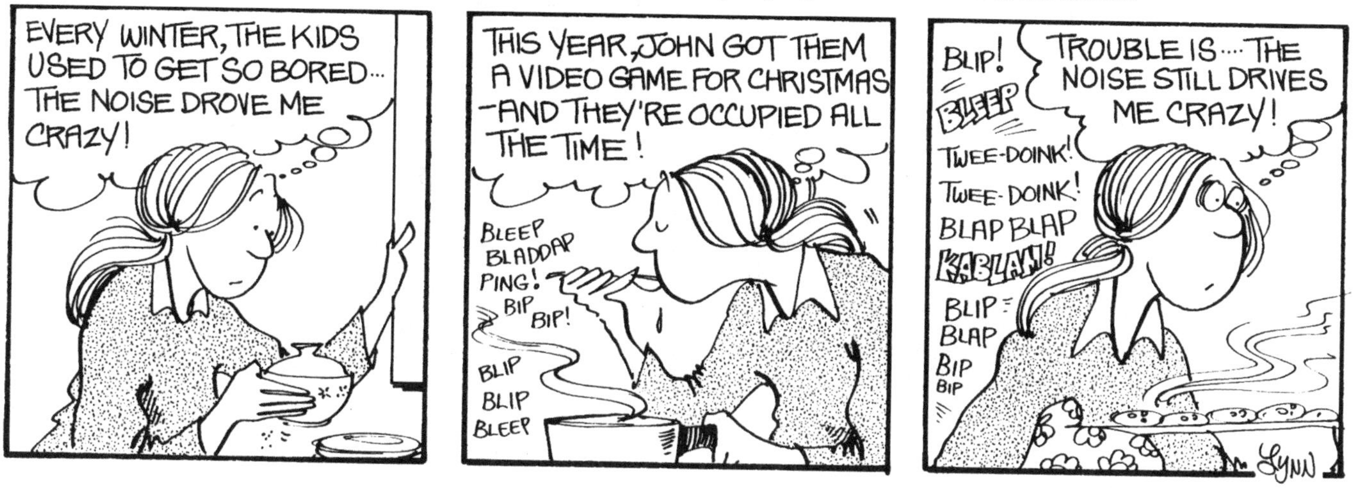
EVERY WINTER, THE KIDS USED TO GET SO BORED... THE NOISE DROVE ME CRAZY!
THIS YEAR, JOHN GOT THEM A VIDEO GAME FOR CHRISTMAS -AND THEY'RE OCCUPIED ALL THE TIME!
BLEEP BLADDAP PING! BIP BIP!
BLIP BLIP BLEEP
BLIP! BLEEP
TROUBLE IS.... THE NOISE STILL DRIVES ME CRAZY!
TWEE-DOINK! TWEE-DOINK! BLAP BLAP KABLAM!
BLIP BLAP BIP BIP
Lynn

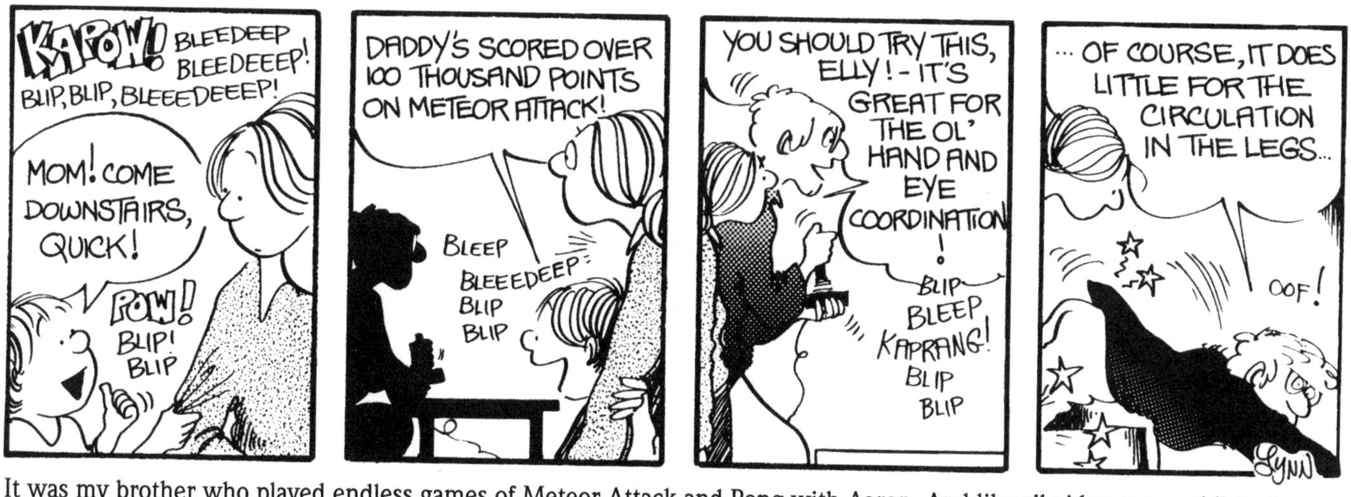
KAPOW! BLEEDEEP BLEEDEEEP! BLIP, BLIP, BLEEEDEEEP!
MOM! COME DOWNSTAIRS, QUICK!
POW! BLIP! BLIP
DADDY'S SCORED OVER 100 THOUSAND POINTS ON METEOR ATTACK!
BLEEP BLEEEDEEP BLIP BLIP
YOU SHOULD TRY THIS, ELLY! - IT'S GREAT FOR THE OL' HAND AND EYE COORDINATION!
BLIP BLEEP KAPRANG! BLIP BLIP
... OF COURSE, IT DOES LITTLE FOR THE CIRCULATION IN THE LEGS...
OOF!
Lynn

It was my brother who played endless games of Meteor Attack and Pong with Aaron. And like all video game addicts, he suffered. Today's players have trouble with their thumbs; back then, it was the lower extremities from sitting on the floor too long. Whatever the ailment, I confess, I have absolutely no sympathy.

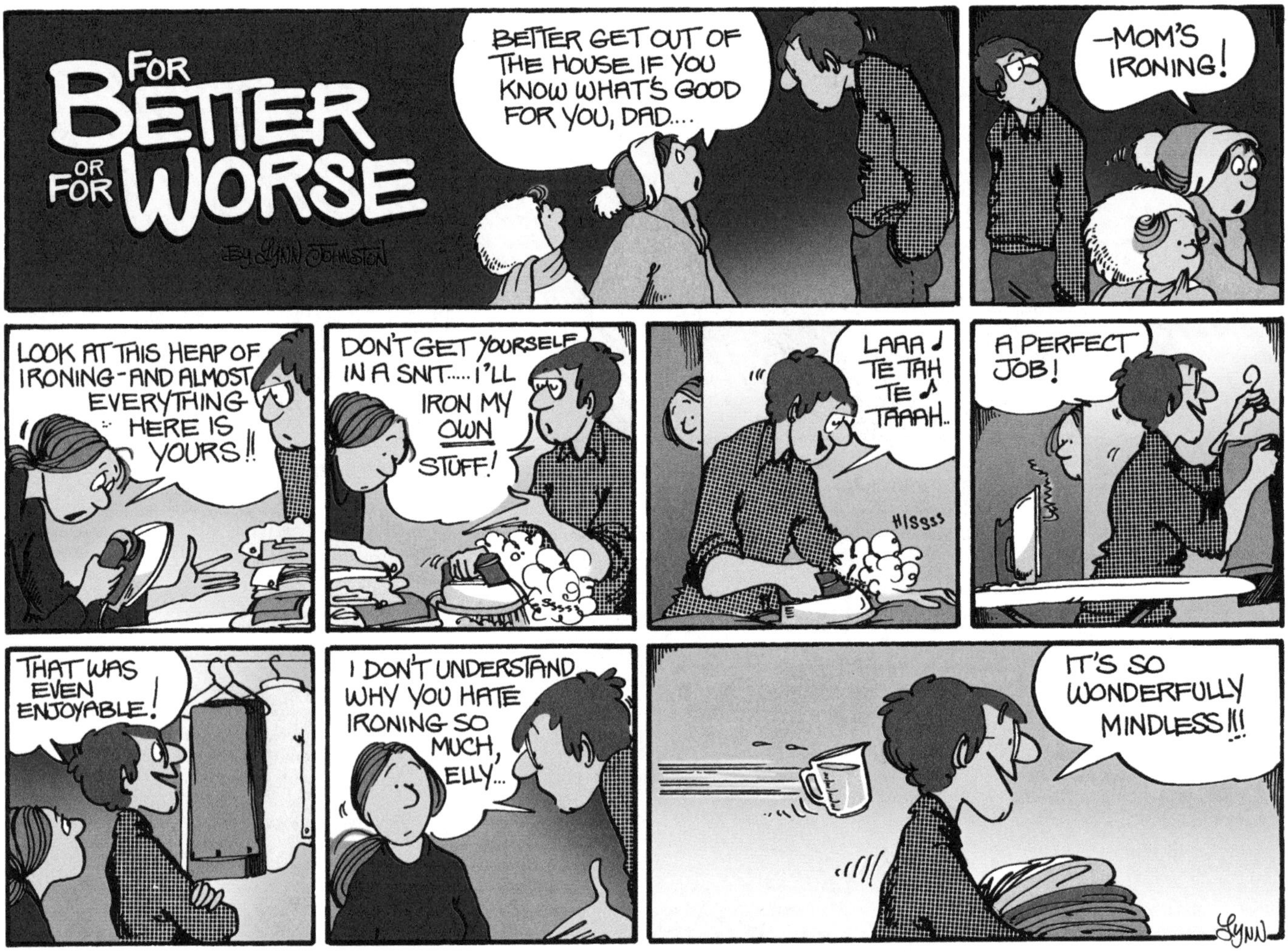
FOR BETTER OR FOR WORSE
By Lynn Johnston
BETTER GET OUT OF THE HOUSE IF YOU KNOW WHAT'S GOOD FOR YOU, DAD....
–MOM'S IRONING!
LOOK AT THIS HEAP OF IRONING - AND ALMOST EVERYTHING HERE IS YOURS!!
DON'T GET YOURSELF IN A SNIT..... I'LL IRON MY OWN STUFF!
LAAA TE TAH TE TAAAH..
HISSSS
A PERFECT JOB!
THAT WAS EVEN ENJOYABLE!
I DON'T UNDERSTAND WHY YOU HATE IRONING SO MUCH, ELLY...
IT'S SO WONDERFULLY MINDLESS!!!
Lynn

Here is another word-for-word exchange between my husband and me. The punch line was exactly as written. I didn't toss a measuring cup — but I sure wanted to. This resulted in his taking over the pressing of his own shirts and clinic gowns — until we hired a housekeeper, who came once a week and actually enjoyed ironing!

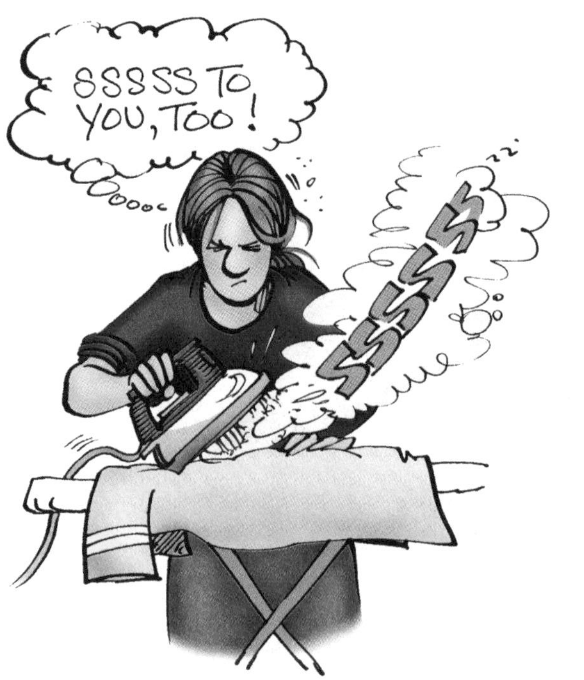
SSSSS TO YOU, TOO!
SSSSS

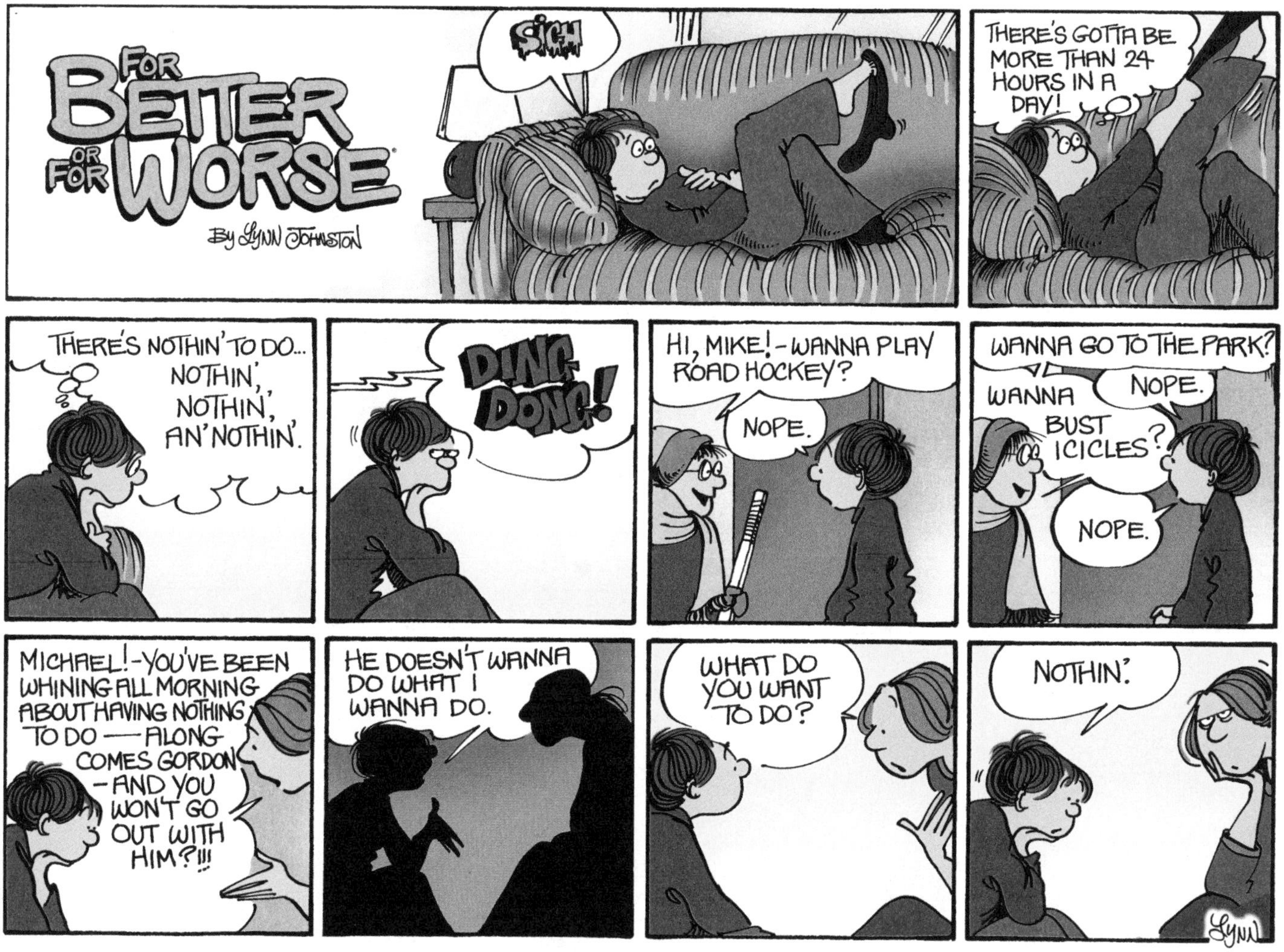
FOR BETTER OR FOR WORSE
BY LYNN JOHNSTON
SIGH
THERE'S GOTTA BE MORE THAN 24 HOURS IN A DAY!
THERE'S NOTHIN' TO DO... NOTHIN', NOTHIN', AN' NOTHIN'.
DING-DONG!
HI, MIKE! - WANNA PLAY ROAD HOCKEY?
NOPE.
WANNA GO TO THE PARK?
NOPE.
WANNA BUST ICICLES?
NOPE.
MICHAEL! - YOU'VE BEEN WHINING ALL MORNING ABOUT HAVING NOTHING TO DO — ALONG COMES GORDON - AND YOU WON'T GO OUT WITH HIM?!!!
HE DOESN'T WANNA DO WHAT I WANNA DO.
WHAT DO YOU WANT TO DO?
NOTHIN'.
LYNN

This is me. These are my words. This is also my mother and her logic. I could waste an entire day lying on the couch, wishing I was someone else, somewhere else, wondering why I had to wait so long to be out of the house and on my own. I wasn't even a teenager at the time — I was in elementary school.

As a teen, I was involved in too many projects and clubs and activities to be bored. As a child, I was either off in a world of fantasy or trying to figure out why life was the way it was. I wanted to know why I was there, what I was going to do when I grew up, and I wanted to get started NOW! A day was so long and a week was forever. I figured I was wasting time. It wasn't until I was sent to the Vancouver School of Art for Saturday morning classes that I felt secure. For some kids, it's sports that get them out and energized. For me and for many of my friends, it was art that filled us with a sense of purpose.

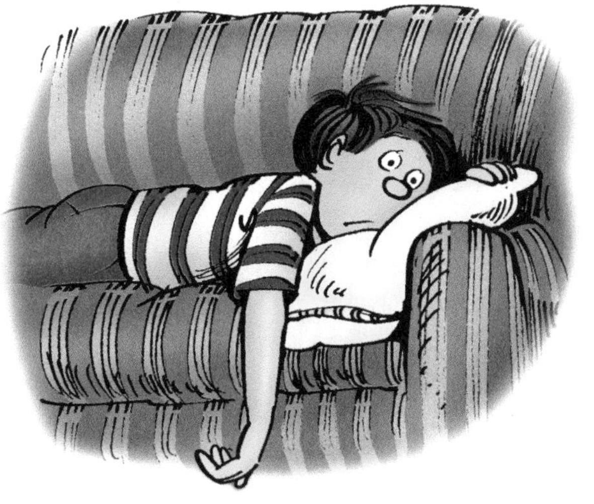

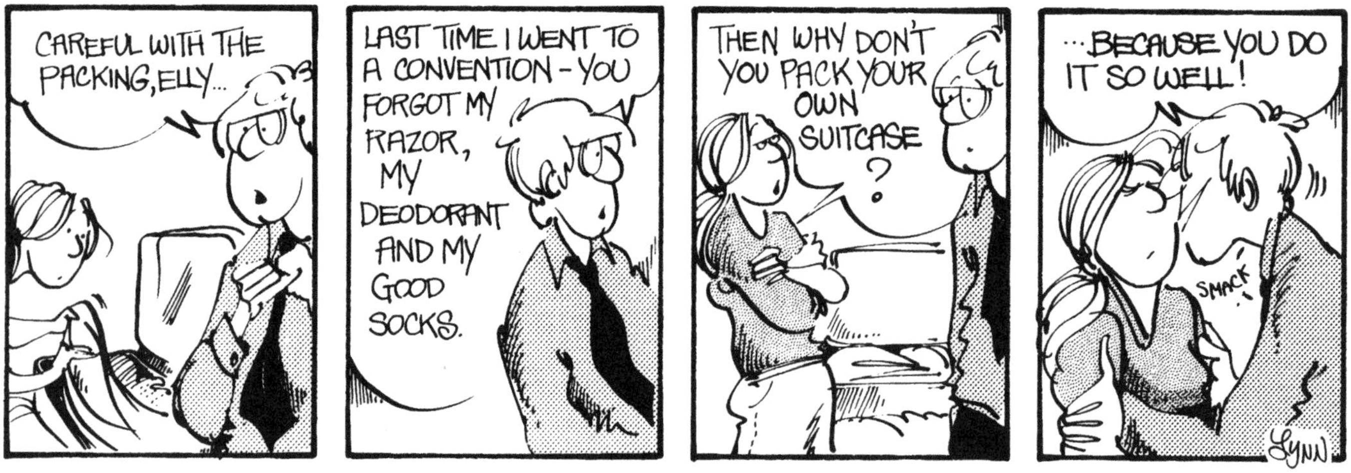
CAREFUL WITH THE PACKING, ELLY...
LAST TIME I WENT TO A CONVENTION - YOU FORGOT MY RAZOR, MY DEODORANT AND MY GOOD SOCKS.
THEN WHY DON'T YOU PACK YOUR OWN SUITCASE ?
...BECAUSE YOU DO IT SO WELL!
SMACK!
Lynn

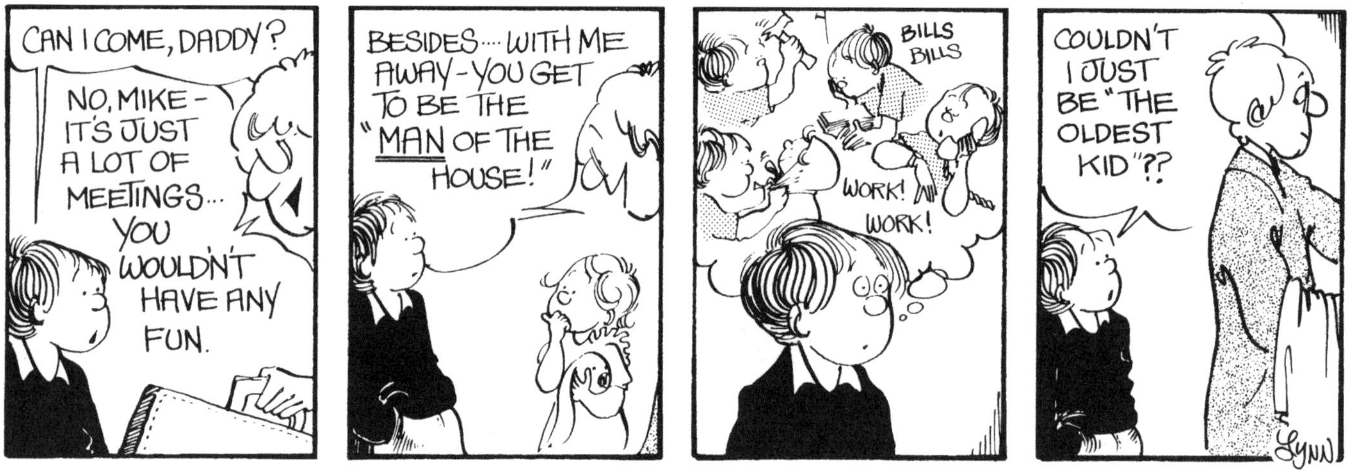
CAN I COME, DADDY?
NO, MIKE - IT'S JUST A LOT OF MEETINGS... YOU WOULDN'T HAVE ANY FUN.
BESIDES.... WITH ME AWAY - YOU GET TO BE THE "MAN OF THE HOUSE!"
BILLS BILLS
WORK! WORK!
COULDN'T I JUST BE "THE OLDEST KID"??
Lynn

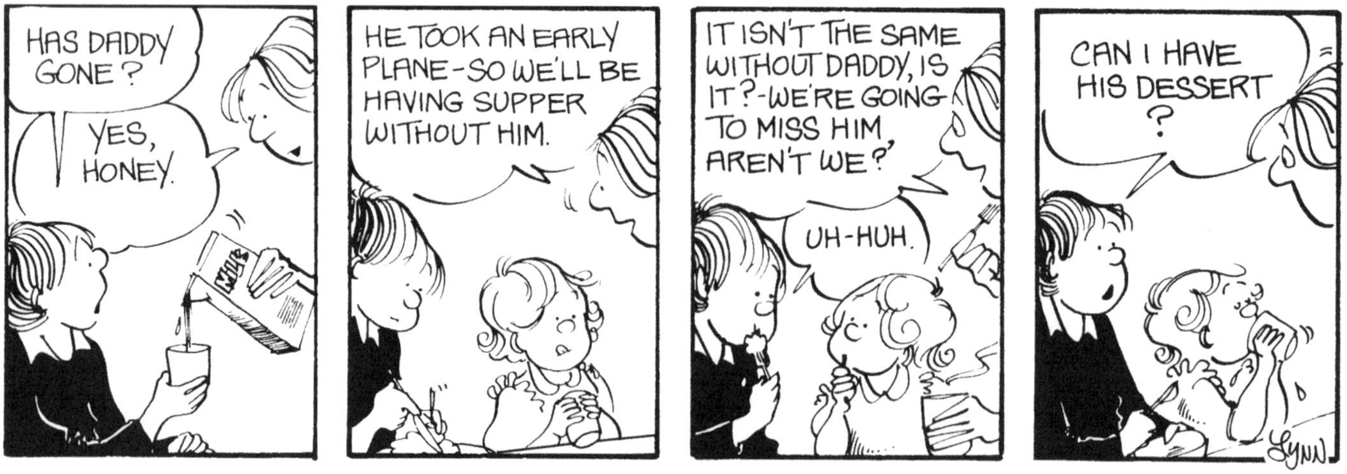
HAS DADDY GONE ?
YES, HONEY.
MILK
HE TOOK AN EARLY PLANE - SO WE'LL BE HAVING SUPPER WITHOUT HIM.
IT ISN'T THE SAME WITHOUT DADDY, IS IT? - WE'RE GOING TO MISS HIM AREN'T WE?
UH-HUH.
CAN I HAVE HIS DESSERT ?
Lynn

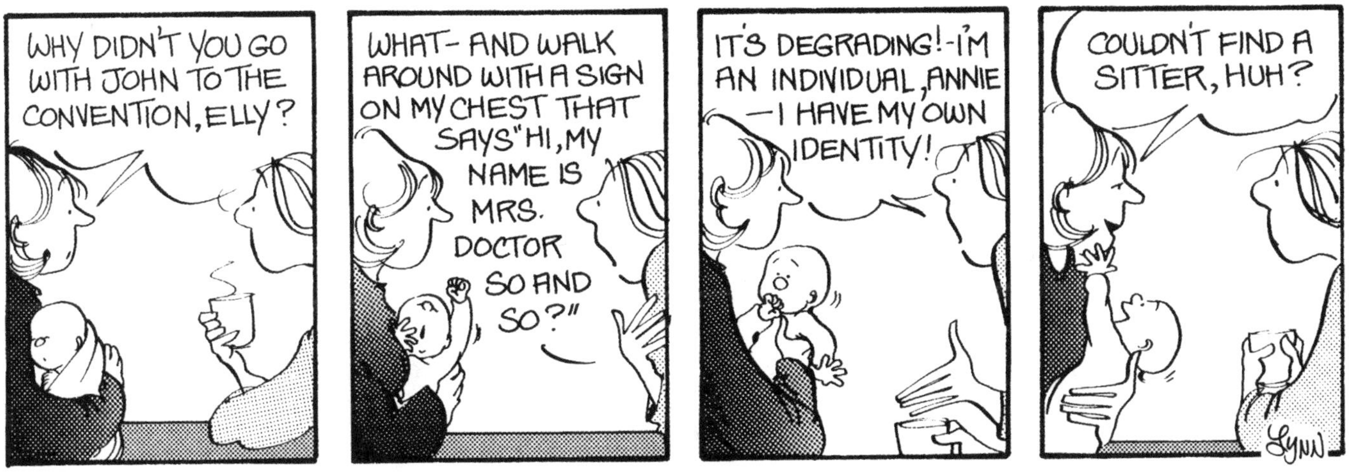
WHY DIDN'T YOU GO WITH JOHN TO THE CONVENTION, ELLY?
WHAT- AND WALK AROUND WITH A SIGN ON MY CHEST THAT SAYS "HI, MY NAME IS MRS. DOCTOR SO AND SO?"
IT'S DEGRADING! - I'M AN INDIVIDUAL, ANNIE — I HAVE MY OWN IDENTITY!
COULDN'T FIND A SITTER, HUH?
LYNN

Because of our jobs, one of us always seemed to be on the road. I still keep a suitcase partially packed for the next trip somewhere. Rod did go to a few conventions without me, but I was used to these absences and he was used to mine. We had his mom and dad close by, and great neighbours, as well, to count on. I imagined here how Elly would react to a few days on her own with the kids, how she would see her role, and how she would explain staying home to her friends.

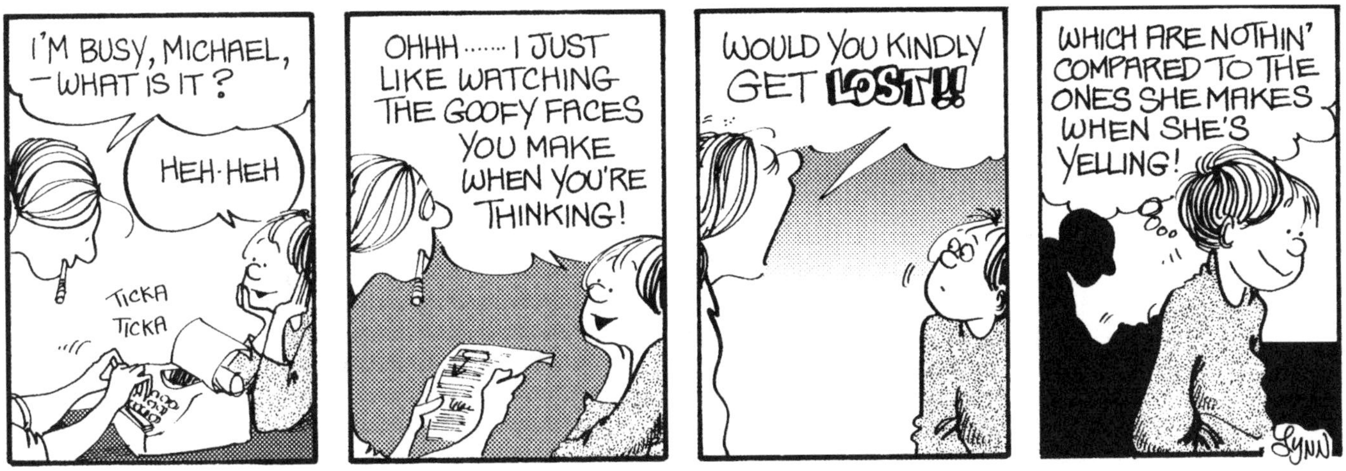
I'M BUSY, MICHAEL, — WHAT IS IT?
HEH·HEH
TICKA TICKA
OHHH...... I JUST LIKE WATCHING THE GOOFY FACES YOU MAKE WHEN YOU'RE THINKING!
WOULD YOU KINDLY GET LOST!!
WHICH ARE NOTHIN' COMPARED TO THE ONES SHE MAKES WHEN SHE'S YELLING!
LYNN

When I'm working, I will make the same faces as the characters I'm drawing. It was funny for the kids to watch me — especially if the face I was drawing was screaming or just plain mad!

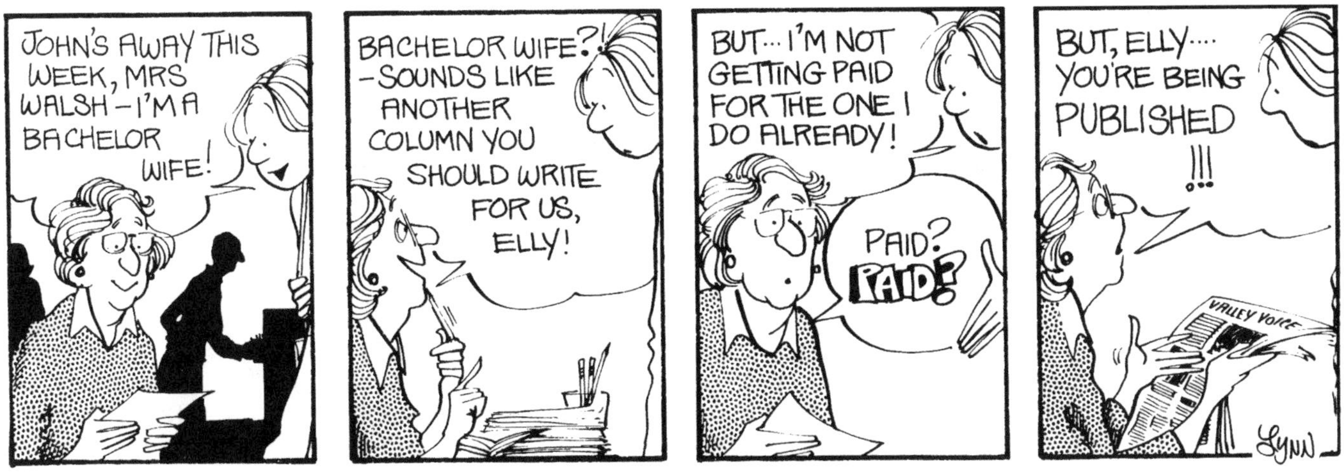
JOHN'S AWAY THIS WEEK, MRS WALSH - I'M A BACHELOR WIFE!
BACHELOR WIFE?! - SOUNDS LIKE ANOTHER COLUMN YOU SHOULD WRITE FOR US, ELLY!
BUT... I'M NOT GETTING PAID FOR THE ONE I DO ALREADY!
PAID? PAID?
BUT, ELLY.... YOU'RE BEING PUBLISHED !!!
VALLEY VOICE
LYNN

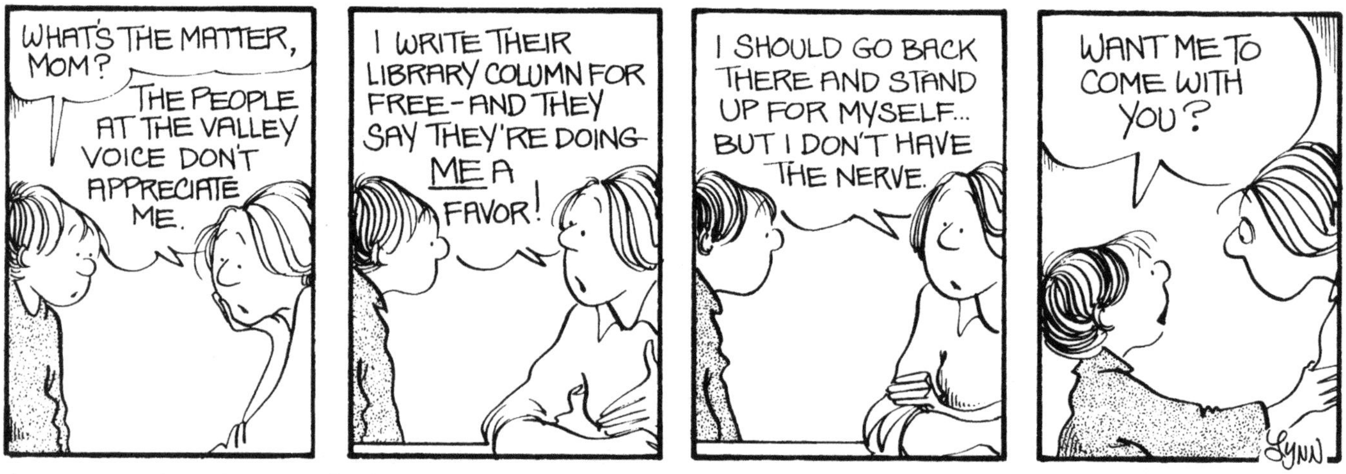
WHAT'S THE MATTER, MOM?
THE PEOPLE AT THE VALLEY VOICE DON'T APPRECIATE ME.
I WRITE THEIR LIBRARY COLUMN FOR FREE - AND THEY SAY THEY'RE DOING ME A FAVOR!
I SHOULD GO BACK THERE AND STAND UP FOR MYSELF... BUT I DON'T HAVE THE NERVE.
WANT ME TO COME WITH YOU?
LYNN

As a young artist trying to get freelance work anywhere I could, I often found myself doing things for clients who offered to pay me, but when it came time to do so, had no money. It was hard to defend myself against such people, so I just kept producing and taking my lumps. I did a lot of illustration for a small local publisher when I was young. When I pleaded with him to pay me the money he owed me, he said I should be happy just to see my work in print!

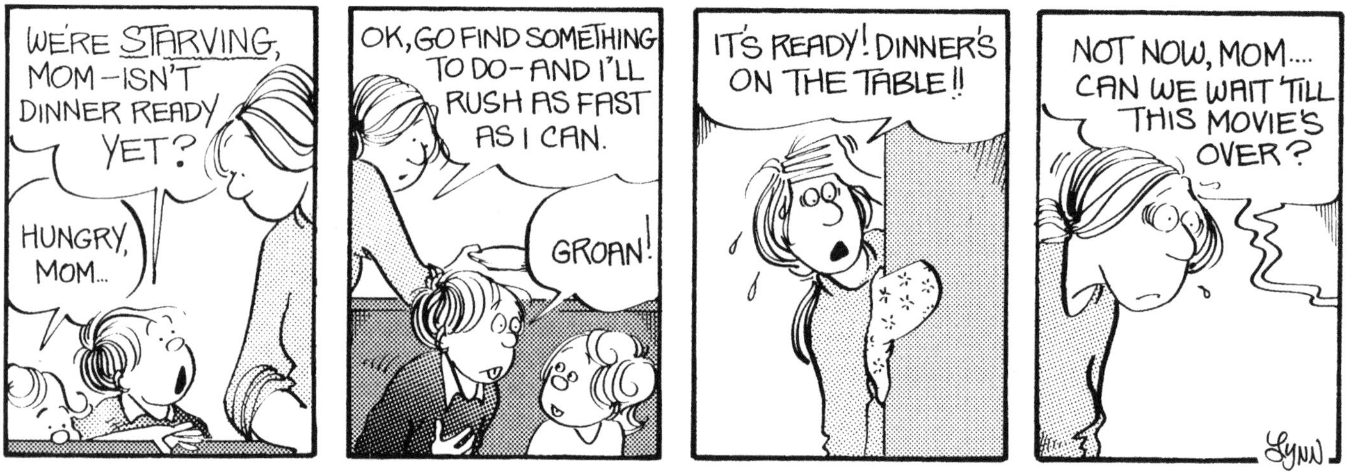
WE'RE STARVING, MOM - ISN'T DINNER READY YET?
HUNGRY, MOM...
OK, GO FIND SOMETHING TO DO - AND I'LL RUSH AS FAST AS I CAN.
GROAN!
IT'S READY! DINNER'S ON THE TABLE!!
NOT NOW, MOM.... CAN WE WAIT 'TILL THIS MOVIE'S OVER?
LYNN

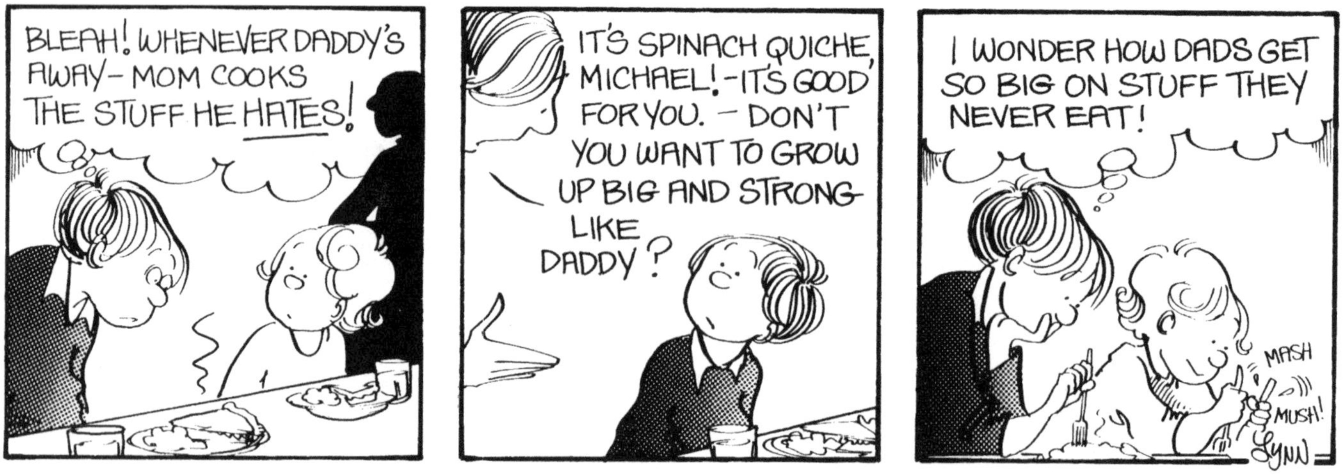
BLEAH! WHENEVER DADDY'S AWAY - MOM COOKS THE STUFF HE HATES!
IT'S SPINACH QUICHE, MICHAEL! - IT'S GOOD FOR YOU. - DON'T YOU WANT TO GROW UP BIG AND STRONG LIKE DADDY?
I WONDER HOW DADS GET SO BIG ON STUFF THEY NEVER EAT!
MASH
MUSH!
LYNN

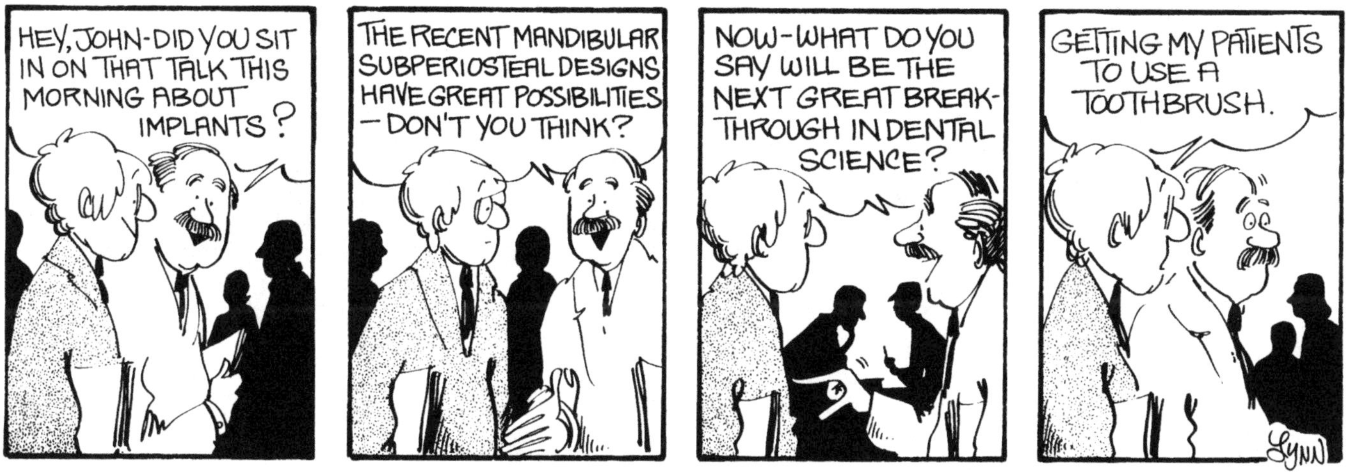
HEY, JOHN-DID YOU SIT IN ON THAT TALK THIS MORNING ABOUT IMPLANTS?
THE RECENT MANDIBULAR SUBPERIOSTEAL DESIGNS HAVE GREAT POSSIBILITIES — DON'T YOU THINK?
NOW-WHAT DO YOU SAY WILL BE THE NEXT GREAT BREAK-THROUGH IN DENTAL SCIENCE?
GETTING MY PATIENTS TO USE A TOOTHBRUSH.
LYNN

This is a serious point, and I wanted to make it. People can avoid so much pain and expense if they just brush and floss their teeth regularly!

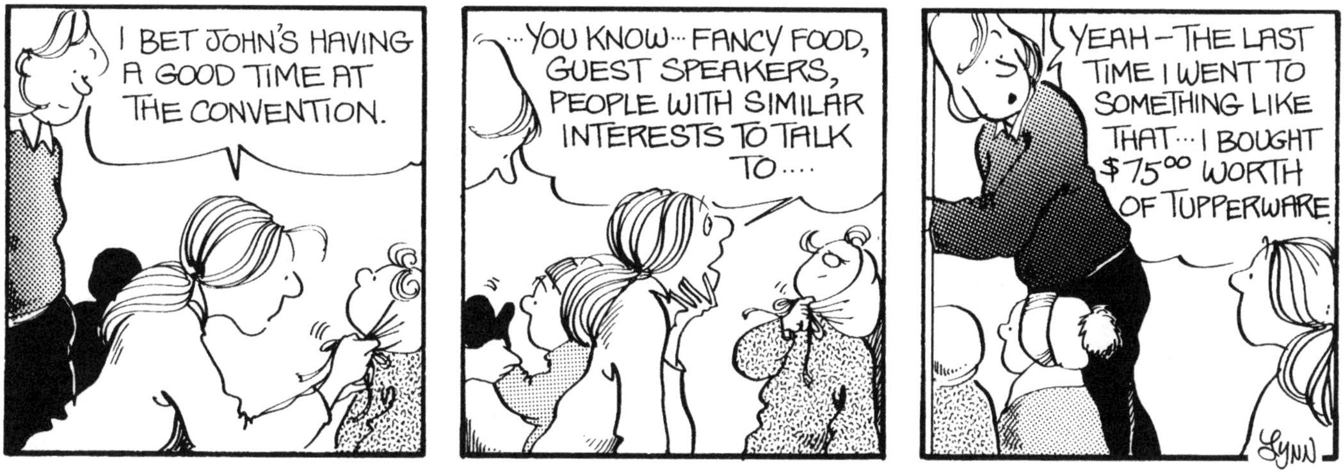
I BET JOHN'S HAVING A GOOD TIME AT THE CONVENTION.
...YOU KNOW... FANCY FOOD, GUEST SPEAKERS, PEOPLE WITH SIMILAR INTERESTS TO TALK TO....
YEAH — THE LAST TIME I WENT TO SOMETHING LIKE THAT... I BOUGHT $75.00 WORTH OF TUPPERWARE.
LYNN

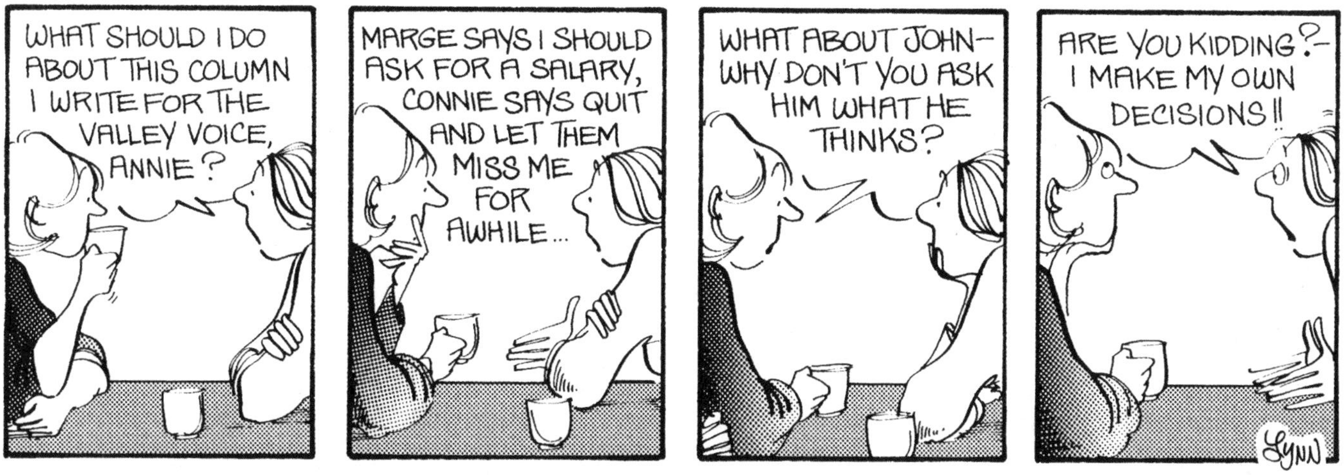
WHAT SHOULD I DO ABOUT THIS COLUMN I WRITE FOR THE VALLEY VOICE, ANNIE?
MARGE SAYS I SHOULD ASK FOR A SALARY, CONNIE SAYS QUIT AND LET THEM MISS ME FOR AWHILE...
WHAT ABOUT JOHN— WHY DON'T YOU ASK HIM WHAT HE THINKS?
ARE YOU KIDDING?— I MAKE MY OWN DECISIONS!!
LYNN

When I did the weekly comic panel for the *Dundas Valley Journal*, they paid me $10 for each one. At the time, I was living on a shoestring and was desperate for a few dollars more. When I asked if they would increase my rate to $15, they refused. This is when I started doing cartoons for my obstetrician — preferring the approval from his patients and staff to the paper. I guess my pride was more important than my pocketbook.

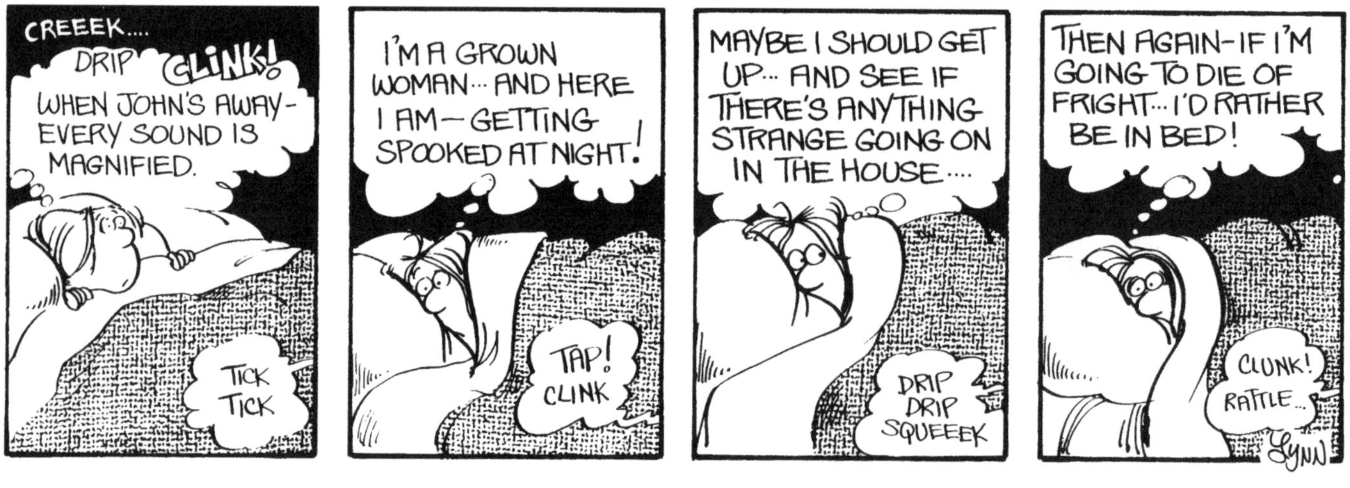
CREEEK....
DRIP
CLINK!
WHEN JOHN'S AWAY-
EVERY SOUND IS
MAGNIFIED.
TICK
TICK
I'M A GROWN
WOMAN... AND HERE
I AM — GETTING
SPOOKED AT NIGHT!
TAP!
CLINK
MAYBE I SHOULD GET
UP... AND SEE IF
THERE'S ANYTHING
STRANGE GOING ON
IN THE HOUSE....
DRIP
DRIP
SQUEEEK
THEN AGAIN-IF I'M
GOING TO DIE OF
FRIGHT... I'D RATHER
BE IN BED!
CLUNK!
RATTLE...
Lynn

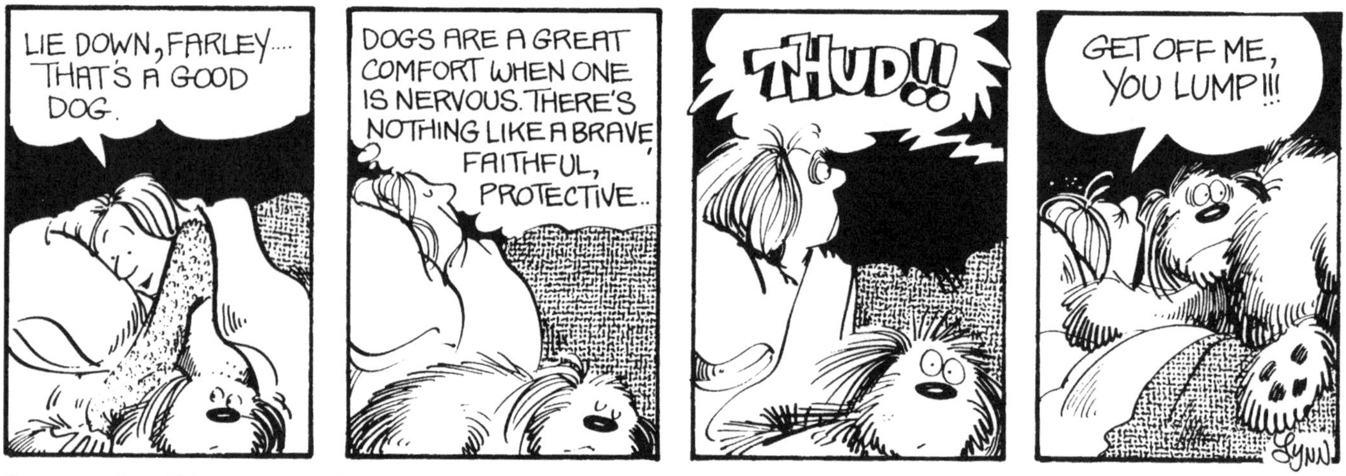
LIE DOWN, FARLEY....
THAT'S A GOOD
DOG.
DOGS ARE A GREAT
COMFORT WHEN ONE
IS NERVOUS. THERE'S
NOTHING LIKE A BRAVE,
FAITHFUL,
PROTECTIVE...
THUD!!
GET OFF ME,
YOU LUMP!!!
Lynn

Every so often, I'd realize that I had not featured Farley in the strip for a while, so I'd find a way to write him in. Although I never slept with any of my pets, this is how I imagined sharing my space with a character like Farley.

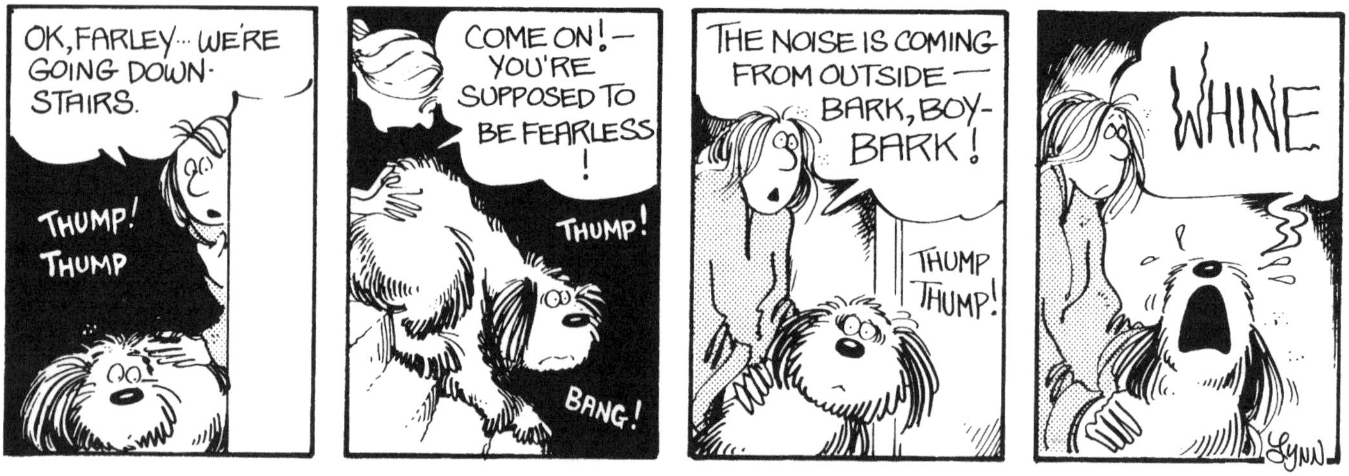
OK, FARLEY... WE'RE
GOING DOWN-
STAIRS.
THUMP!
THUMP
COME ON! —
YOU'RE
SUPPOSED TO
BE FEARLESS
!
THUMP!
BANG!
THE NOISE IS COMING
FROM OUTSIDE —
BARK, BOY-
BARK!
THUMP
THUMP!
WHINE
Lynn

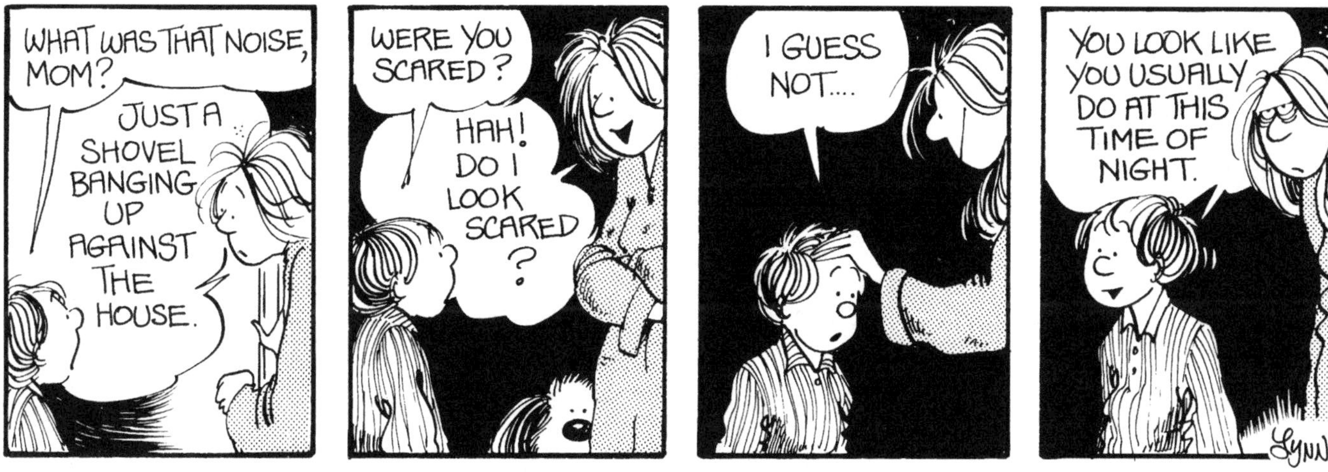
WHAT WAS THAT NOISE, MOM?
JUST A SHOVEL BANGING UP AGAINST THE HOUSE.
WERE YOU SCARED?
HAH! DO I LOOK SCARED?
I GUESS NOT....
YOU LOOK LIKE YOU USUALLY DO AT THIS TIME OF NIGHT.
LYNN

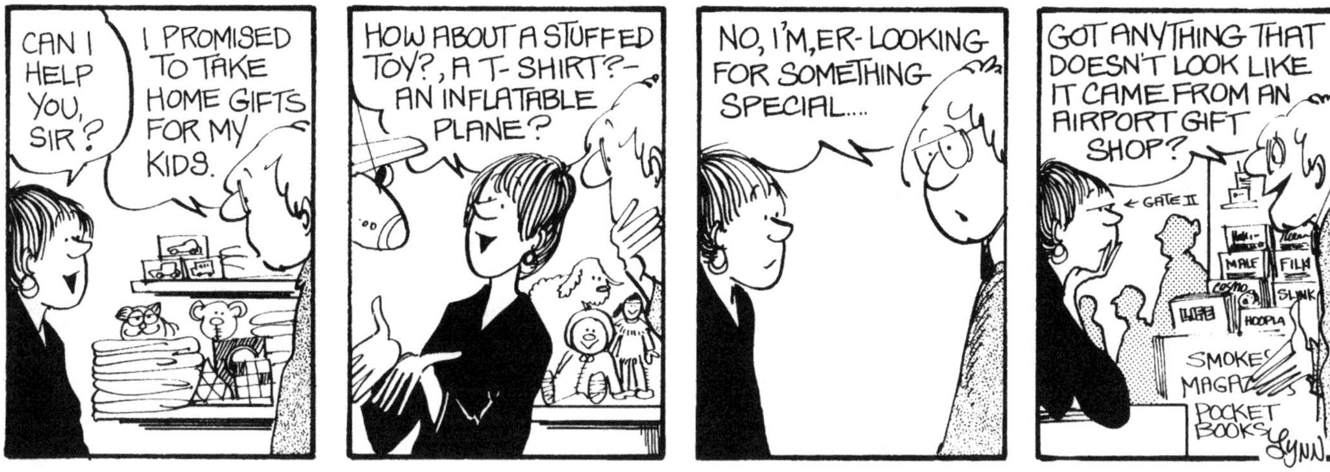
CAN I HELP YOU, SIR?
I PROMISED TO TAKE HOME GIFTS FOR MY KIDS.
HOW ABOUT A STUFFED TOY?, A T-SHIRT?- AN INFLATABLE PLANE?
NO, I'M, ER- LOOKING FOR SOMETHING SPECIAL....
GOT ANYTHING THAT DOESN'T LOOK LIKE IT CAME FROM AN AIRPORT GIFT SHOP?
← GATE II
MALE
FILM
LIFE
HOOPLA
POCKET BOOKS
LYNN

The gift from the airport gift shop was a subject that brought a number of responses. Some letters came from travellers who bemoaned the fact that a small gift was expected. Others enjoyed shopping for treasure and the surprise it would bring. It was a really divisive subject, and I learned that when it comes to gifts and the business traveller, it's much better to receive. Personally, I love to shop for "gifties," and sometimes the airport has the best shops!

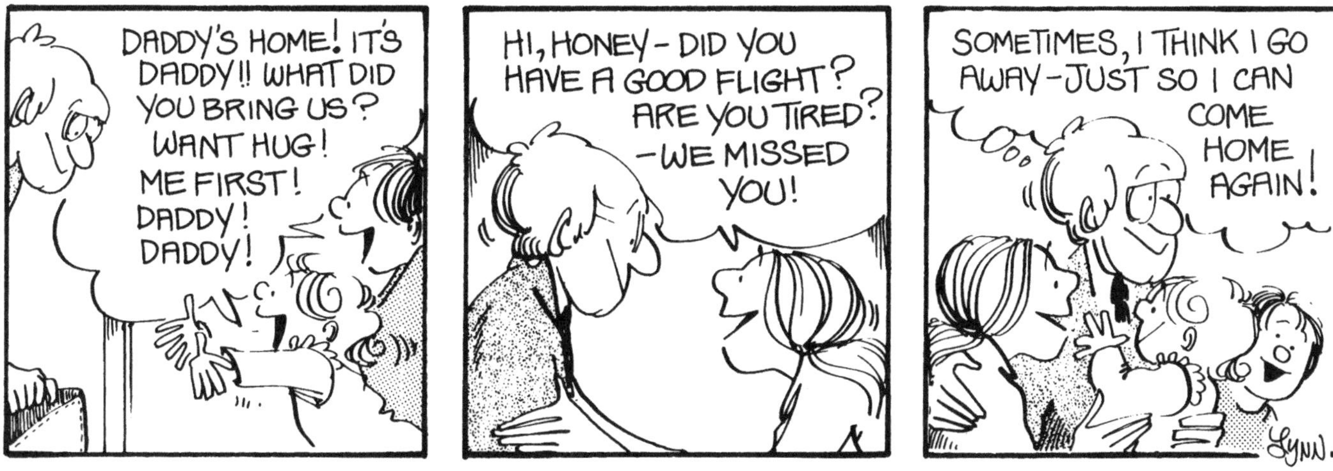
DADDY'S HOME! IT'S DADDY!! WHAT DID YOU BRING US? WANT HUG! ME FIRST! DADDY! DADDY!
HI, HONEY- DID YOU HAVE A GOOD FLIGHT? ARE YOU TIRED? -WE MISSED YOU!
SOMETIMES, I THINK I GO AWAY- JUST SO I CAN COME HOME AGAIN!
LYNN

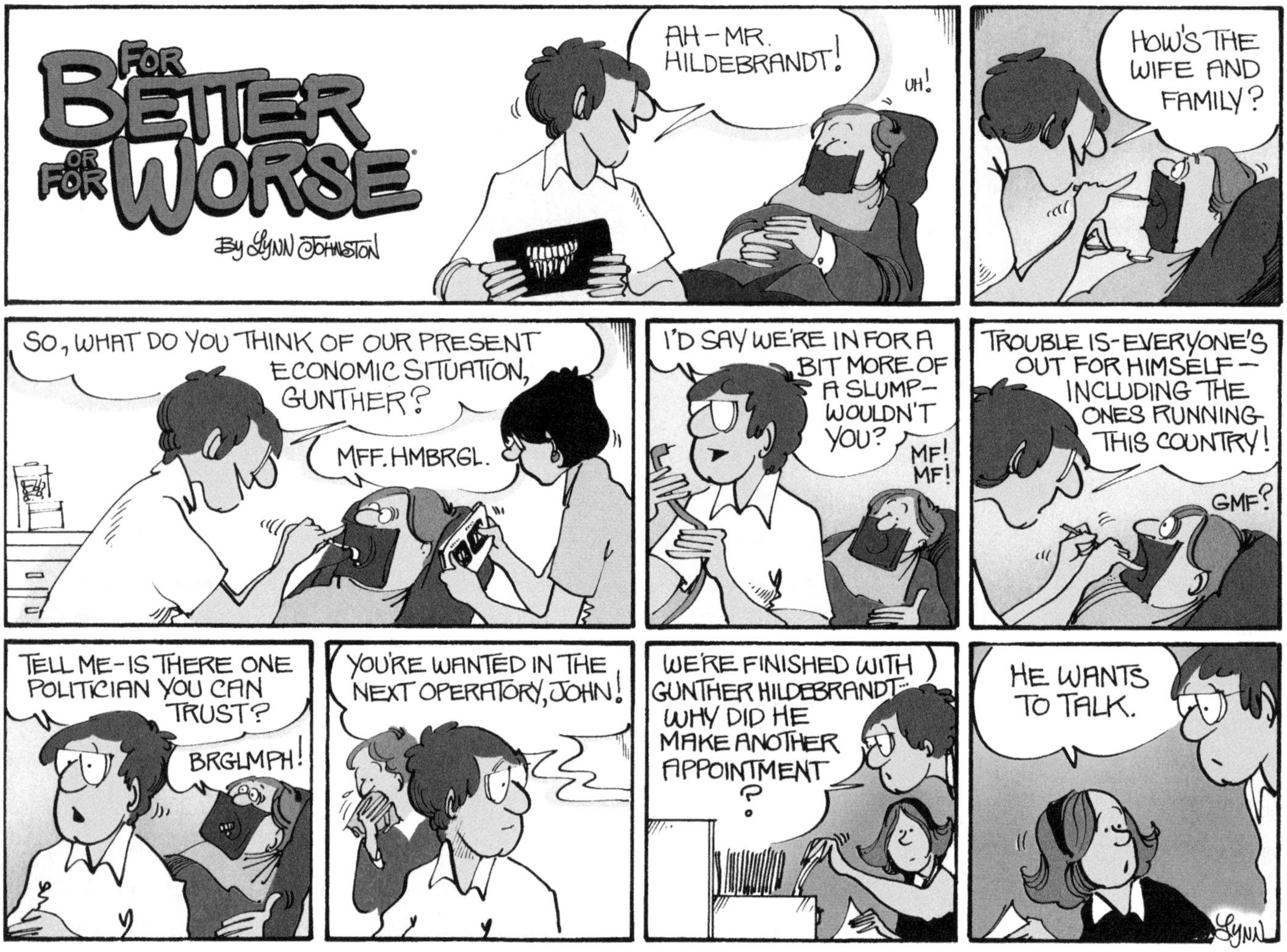
FOR BETTER OR FOR WORSE
By Lynn Johnston
AH - MR. HILDEBRANDT!
UH!
HOW'S THE WIFE AND FAMILY?
SO, WHAT DO YOU THINK OF OUR PRESENT ECONOMIC SITUATION, GUNTHER?
MFF. HMBRGL.
I'D SAY WE'RE IN FOR A BIT MORE OF A SLUMP- WOULDN'T YOU?
MF! MF!
TROUBLE IS-EVERYONE'S OUT FOR HIMSELF - INCLUDING THE ONES RUNNING THIS COUNTRY!
GMF?
TELL ME-IS THERE ONE POLITICIAN YOU CAN TRUST?
BRGLMPH!
YOU'RE WANTED IN THE NEXT OPERATORY, JOHN!
WE'RE FINISHED WITH GUNTHER HILDEBRANDT... WHY DID HE MAKE ANOTHER APPOINTMENT?
HE WANTS TO TALK.
Lynn

This was an inside joke between Gunther Hildebrandt, a longtime family friend, and ourselves. Gunther enjoyed reading the news and discussing current events, especially with my father-in-law. Together, they would solve the problems of the world. Gunther loved to talk, so in this strip I am having a bit of fun at his expense. The dental clinic was never the place to have a really good conversation, especially for the patient.

Gunther was a good sport. In fact, friends and family always enjoyed seeing their names, and it undoubtedly resulted in mail and phone calls from their own friends and family, from all across the continent, saying, "I saw you in the funny papers!"

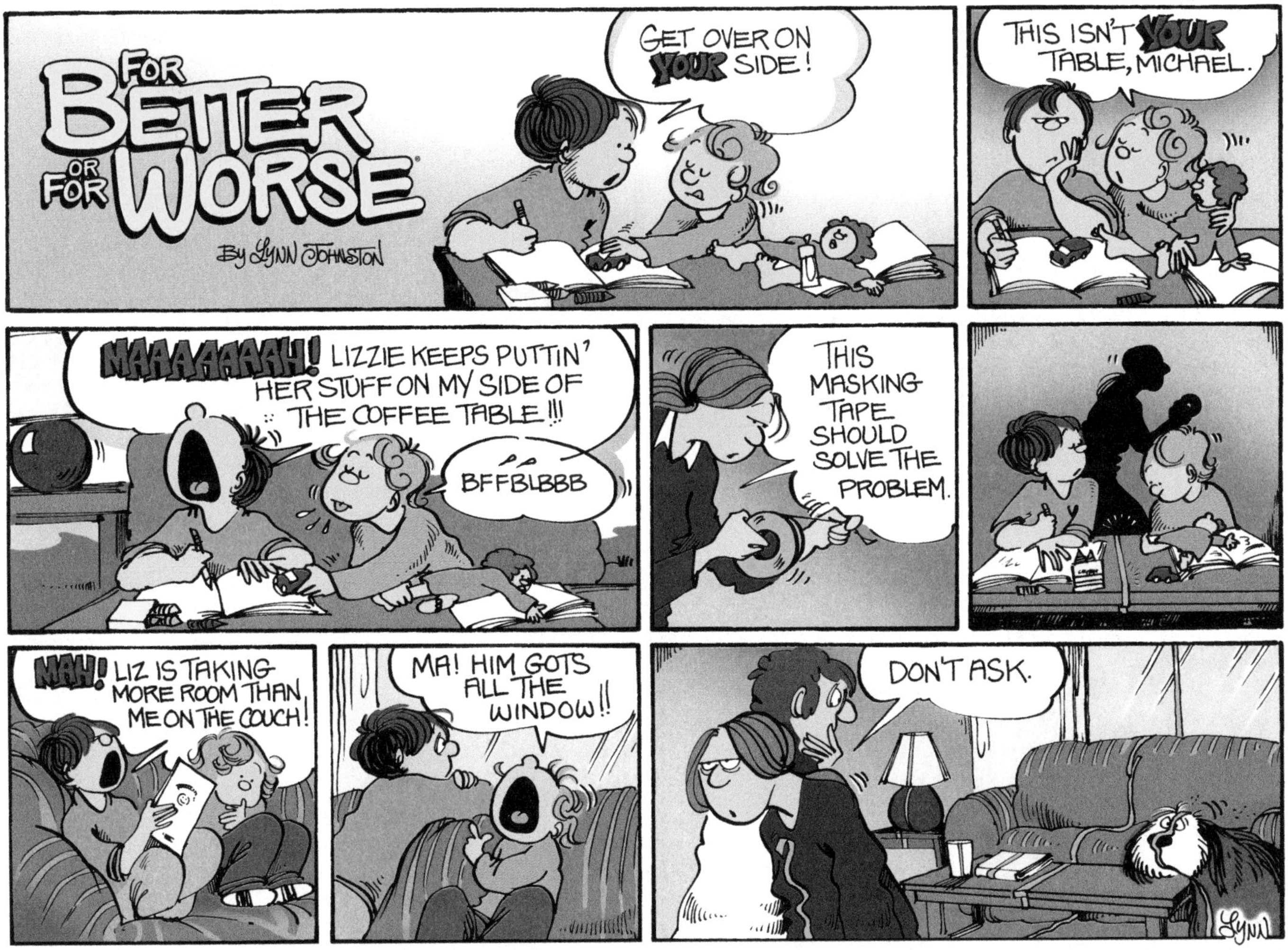
FOR BETTER OR FOR WORSE
By Lynn Johnston
GET OVER ON YOUR SIDE!
THIS ISN'T YOUR TABLE, MICHAEL.
MAAAAAAAH! LIZZIE KEEPS PUTTIN' HER STUFF ON MY SIDE OF THE COFFEE TABLE!!!
BFFBLBBB
THIS MASKING TAPE SHOULD SOLVE THE PROBLEM.
MAH! LIZ IS TAKING MORE ROOM THAN ME ON THE COUCH!
MA! HIM GOTS ALL THE WINDOW!!
DON'T ASK.
Lynn

To end a dispute between Kate and Aaron, I did divide the kitchen table so that each child had their own side. I then divided the couch and Aaron himself divided the living room. This bit of biblical rectitude resulted in a deep interest in equality. Both kids then wanted to divide the house, the hallways, and the stairwell into "what's yours" and "what's mine." The task was not a small one, but they were determined. It gave them something to do together and the price of a roll of masking tape was a small price to pay for silence. I decided to use this in a Sunday strip. The thought that they might even have tried to divide the dog had me smiling for days!

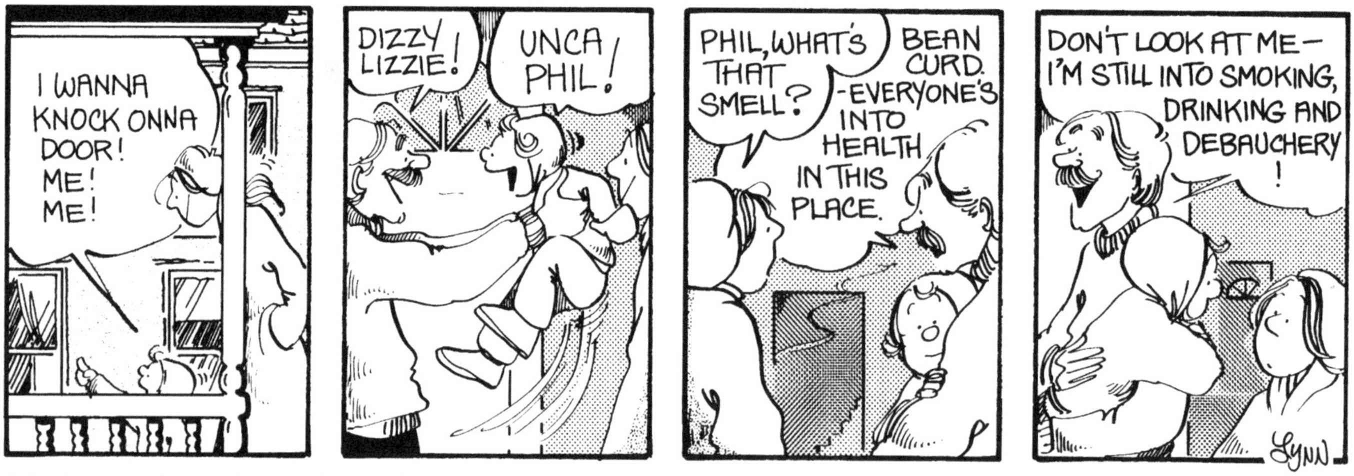
I WANNA KNOCK ONNA DOOR! ME! ME!
DIZZY LIZZIE!
UNCA PHIL!
PHIL, WHAT'S THAT SMELL?
BEAN CURD. -EVERYONE'S INTO HEALTH IN THIS PLACE.
DON'T LOOK AT ME- I'M STILL INTO SMOKING, DRINKING AND DEBAUCHERY!
LYNN

I don't remember seeing my brother's first apartment, so I made up this entrance. After he moved, I turned his living space back into a garage, and focused on trying to make ends meet. It was awhile before we got together again. After living together, Alan and I needed a break from each other!

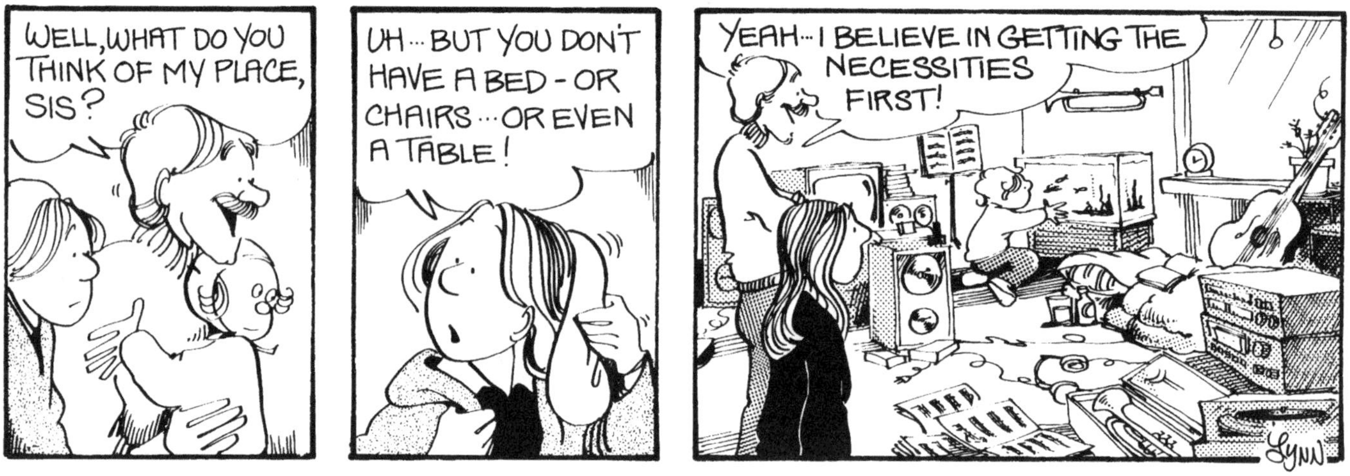
WELL, WHAT DO YOU THINK OF MY PLACE, SIS?
UH... BUT YOU DON'T HAVE A BED - OR CHAIRS... OR EVEN A TABLE!
YEAH... I BELIEVE IN GETTING THE NECESSITIES FIRST!
LYNN

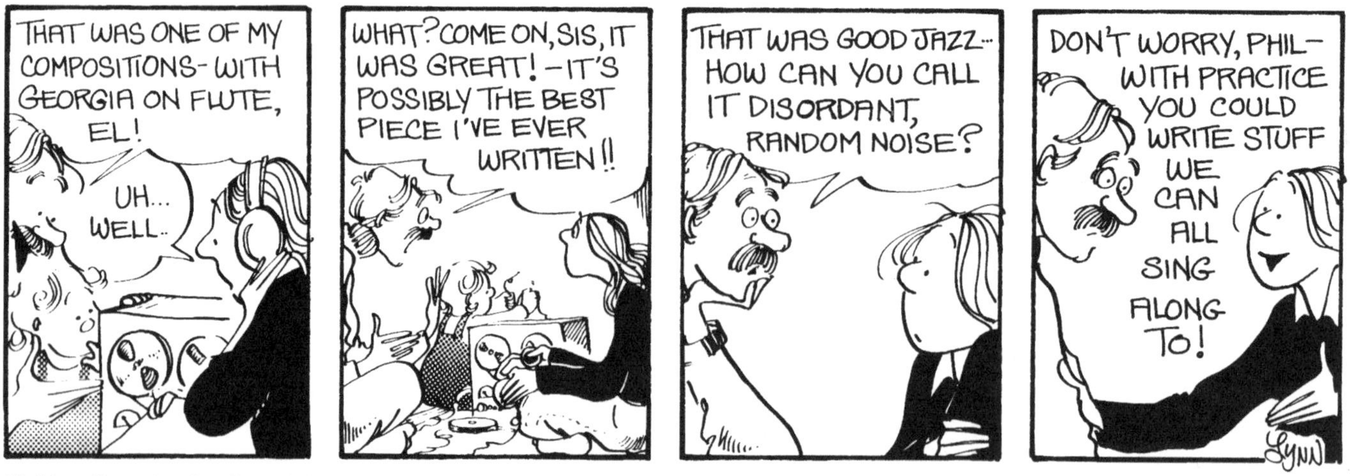
THAT WAS ONE OF MY COMPOSITIONS- WITH GEORGIA ON FLUTE, EL!
UH... WELL..
WHAT? COME ON, SIS, IT WAS GREAT! -IT'S POSSIBLY THE BEST PIECE I'VE EVER WRITTEN!!
THAT WAS GOOD JAZZ... HOW CAN YOU CALL IT DISORDANT, RANDOM NOISE?
DON'T WORRY, PHIL- WITH PRACTICE YOU COULD WRITE STUFF WE CAN ALL SING ALONG TO!
LYNN

Making Georgia play flute delivered me from having to say how and where she and Phil met.

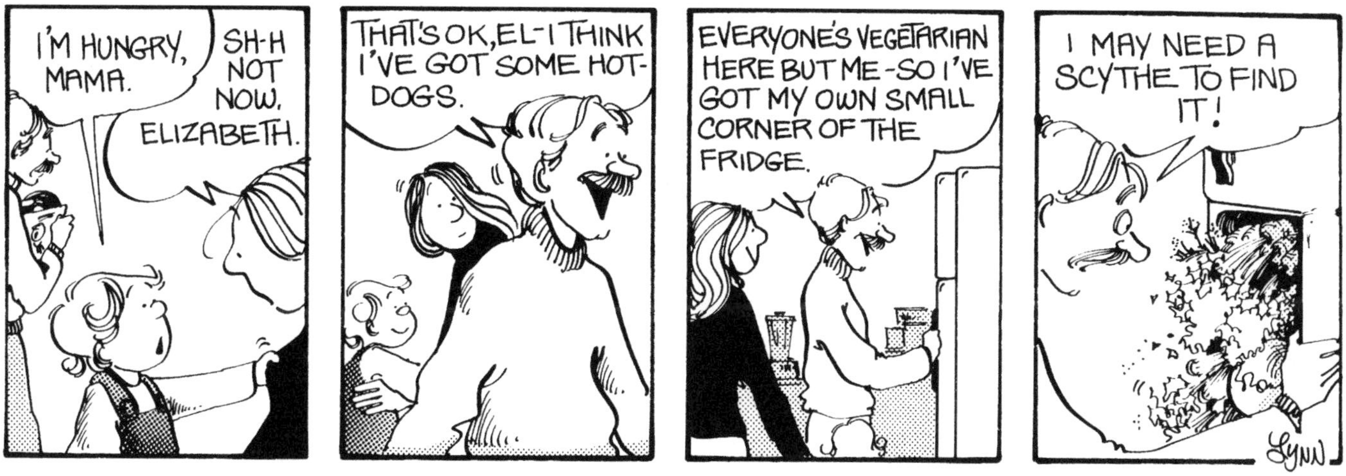
I'M HUNGRY, MAMA.
SH-H NOT NOW, ELIZABETH.
THAT'S OK, EL-I THINK I'VE GOT SOME HOT-DOGS.
EVERYONE'S VEGETARIAN HERE BUT ME-SO I'VE GOT MY OWN SMALL CORNER OF THE FRIDGE.
I MAY NEED A SCYTHE TO FIND IT!
LYNN

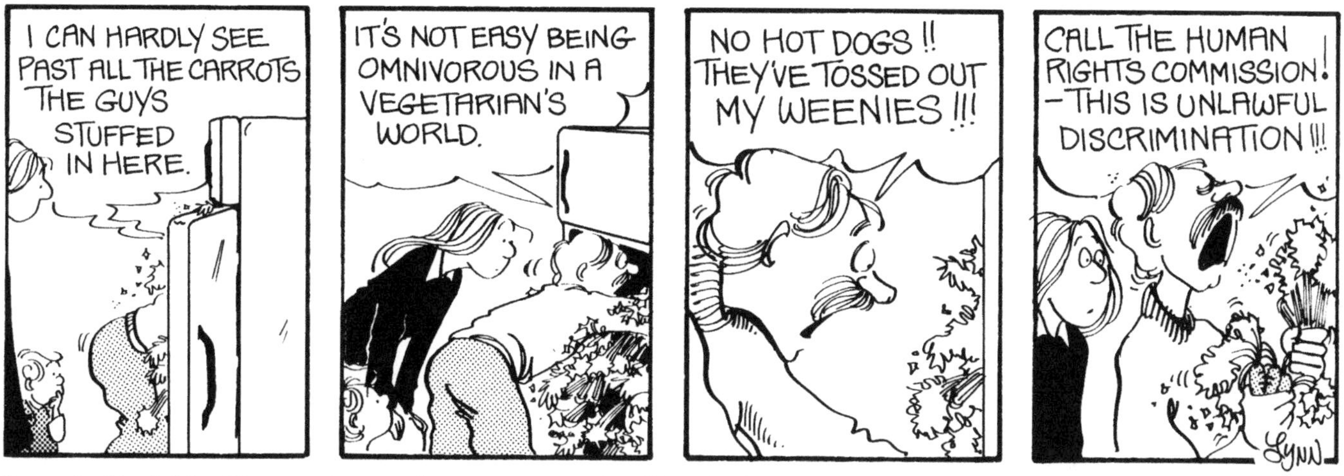
I CAN HARDLY SEE PAST ALL THE CARROTS THE GUYS STUFFED IN HERE.
IT'S NOT EASY BEING OMNIVOROUS IN A VEGETARIAN'S WORLD.
NO HOT DOGS!! THEY'VE TOSSED OUT MY WEENIES!!!
CALL THE HUMAN RIGHTS COMMISSION! -THIS IS UNLAWFUL DISCRIMINATION!!!
LYNN

It was in Alan's Hamilton apartment where vegan roomies filled the fridge with greens. He remembers giving them some money for groceries, and all they brought home were carrots!

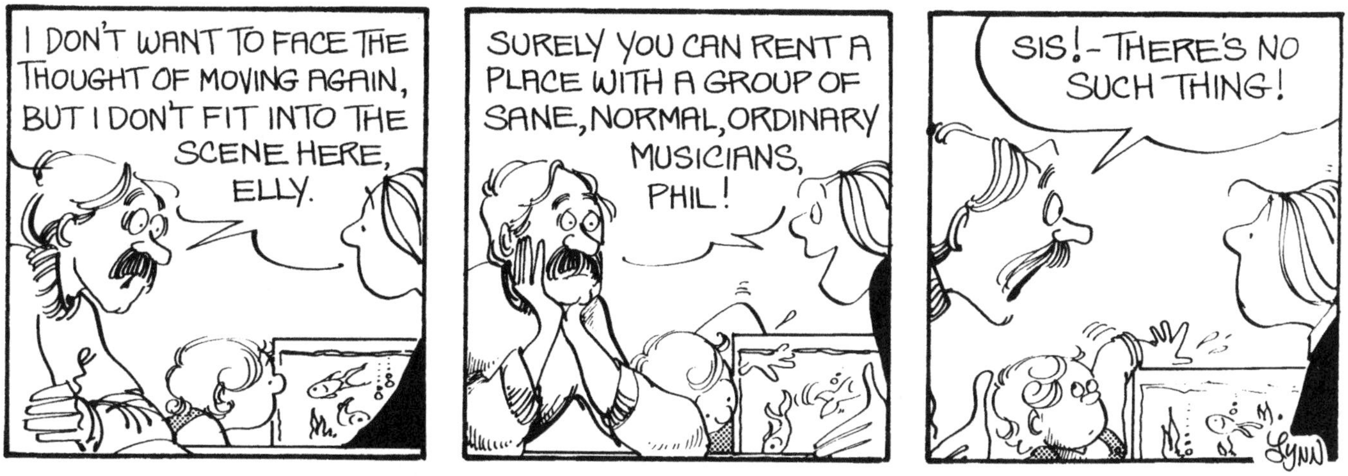
I DON'T WANT TO FACE THE THOUGHT OF MOVING AGAIN, BUT I DON'T FIT INTO THE SCENE HERE, ELLY.
SURELY YOU CAN RENT A PLACE WITH A GROUP OF SANE, NORMAL, ORDINARY MUSICIANS, PHIL!
SIS!-THERE'S NO SUCH THING!
LYNN

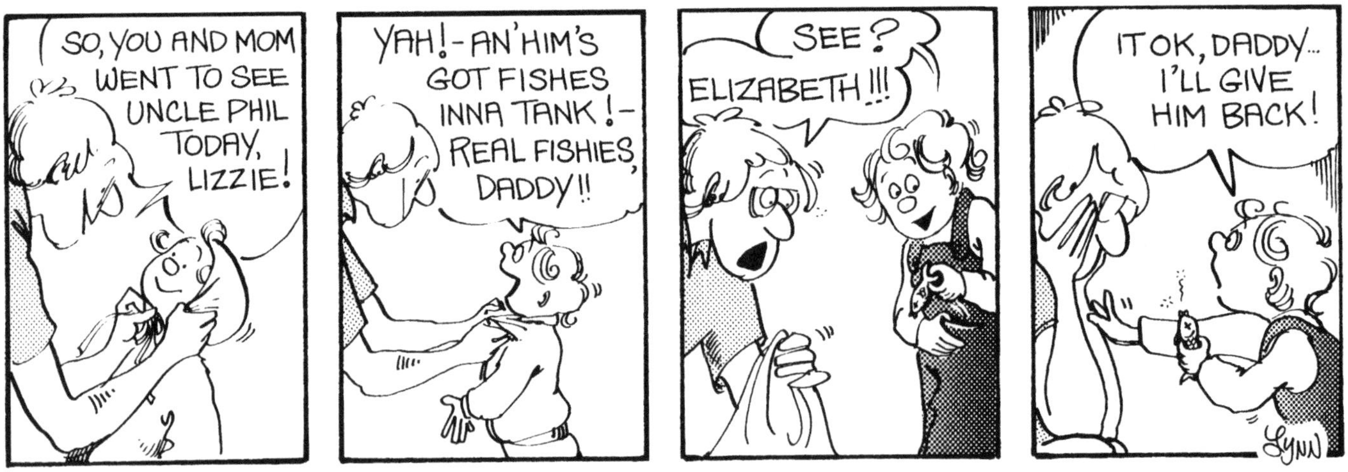
SO, YOU AND MOM WENT TO SEE UNCLE PHIL TODAY, LIZZIE!
YAH!-AN'HIM'S GOT FISHES INNA TANK!-REAL FISHIES, DADDY!!
SEE?
ELIZABETH!!!
IT OK, DADDY... I'LL GIVE HIM BACK!
LYNN

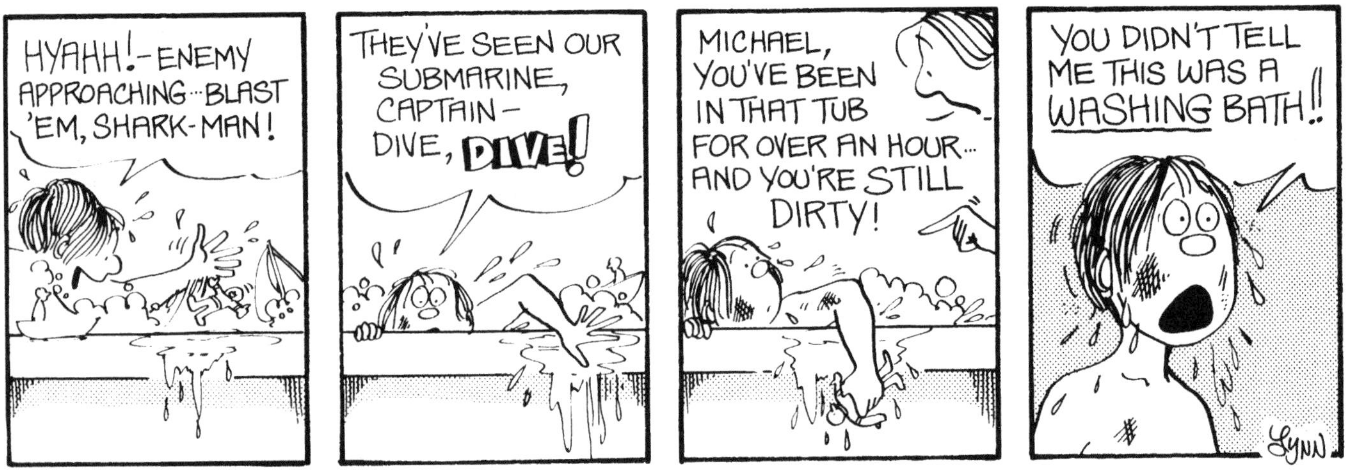
HYAHH!-ENEMY APPROACHING...BLAST 'EM, SHARK-MAN!
THEY'VE SEEN OUR SUBMARINE, CAPTAIN-DIVE, DIVE!
MICHAEL, YOU'VE BEEN IN THAT TUB FOR OVER AN HOUR... AND YOU'RE STILL DIRTY!
YOU DIDN'T TELL ME THIS WAS A WASHING BATH!!
LYNN

Another unmistakable "Aaronism."

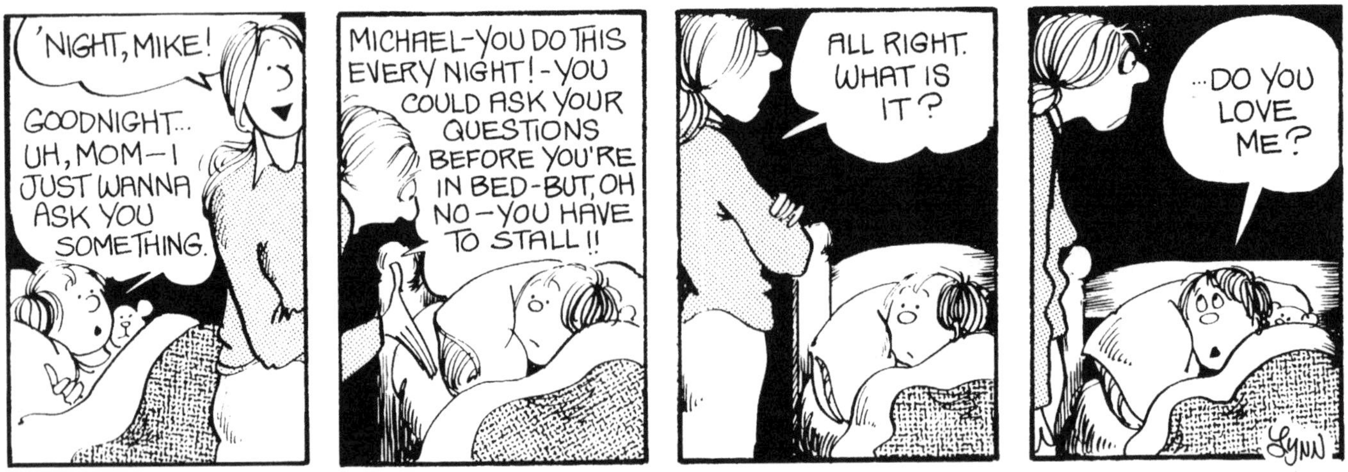
'NIGHT, MIKE!
GOODNIGHT... UH, MOM-I JUST WANNA ASK YOU SOMETHING.
MICHAEL-YOU DO THIS EVERY NIGHT!-YOU COULD ASK YOUR QUESTIONS BEFORE YOU'RE IN BED-BUT, OH NO-YOU HAVE TO STALL!!
ALL RIGHT. WHAT IS IT?
...DO YOU LOVE ME?
LYNN

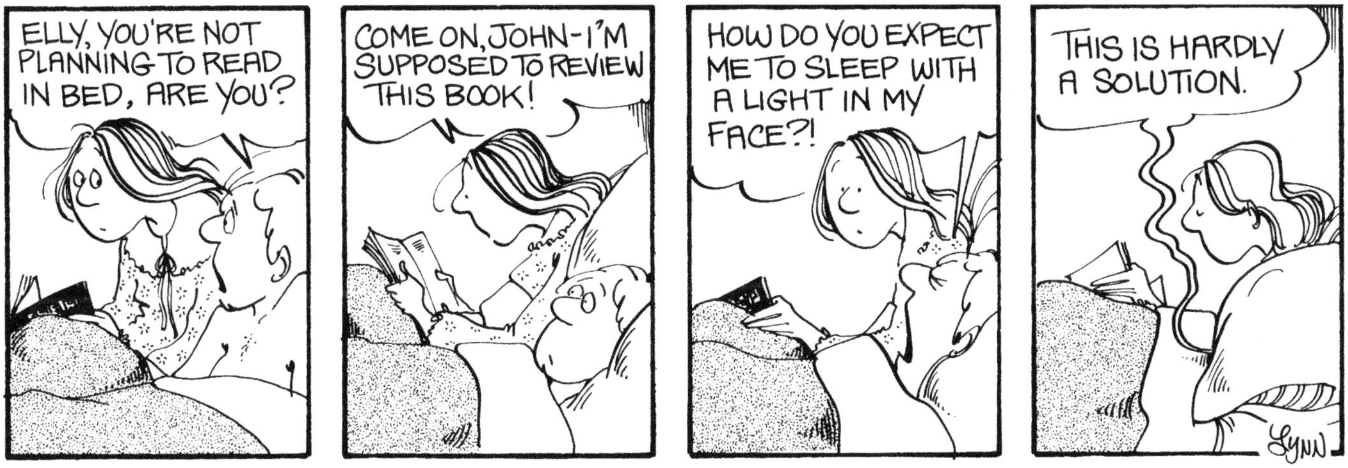
ELLY, YOU'RE NOT PLANNING TO READ IN BED, ARE YOU?
COME ON, JOHN - I'M SUPPOSED TO REVIEW THIS BOOK!
HOW DO YOU EXPECT ME TO SLEEP WITH A LIGHT IN MY FACE?!
THIS IS HARDLY A SOLUTION.
LYNN

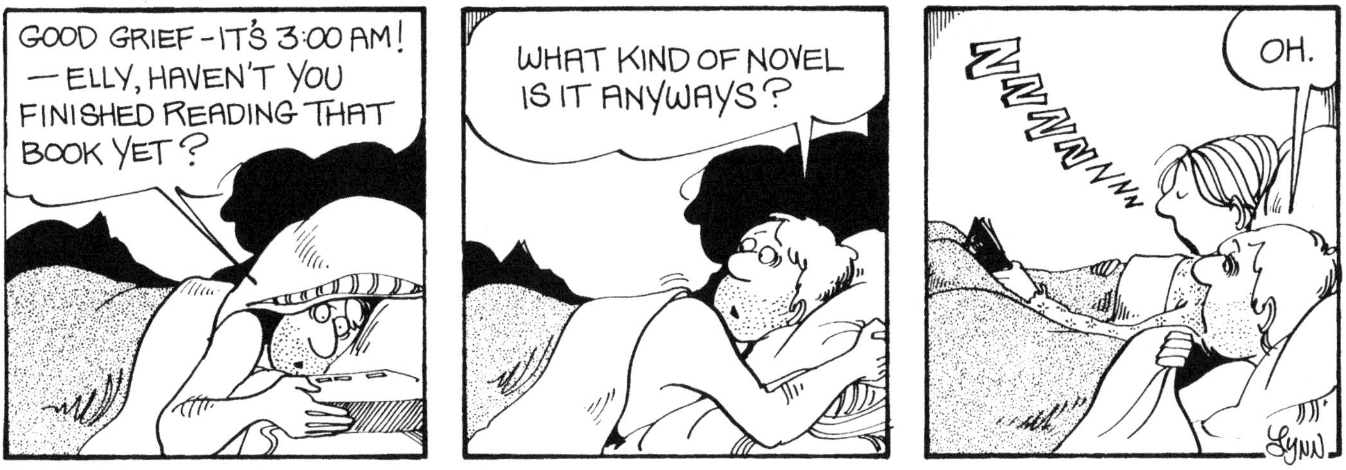
GOOD GRIEF - IT'S 3:00 AM! — ELLY, HAVEN'T YOU FINISHED READING THAT BOOK YET?
WHAT KIND OF NOVEL IS IT ANYWAYS?
ZZZZZZZZZ
OH.
LYNN

I have never been one to read in bed. This is an insight into one of my neighbour's relationships, and yes, I asked if I could use it!

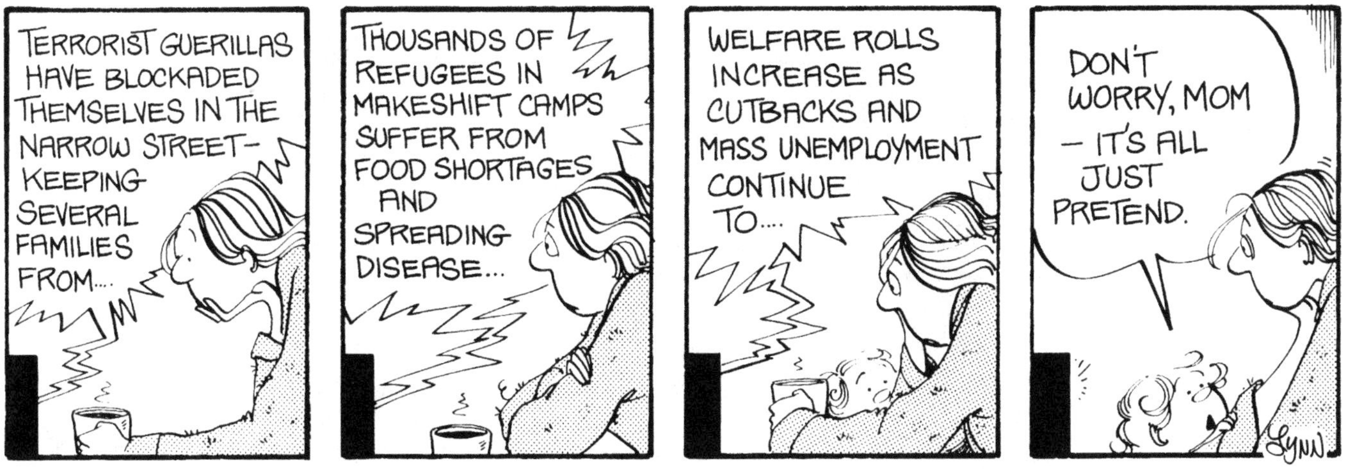
TERRORIST GUERILLAS HAVE BLOCKADED THEMSELVES IN THE NARROW STREET- KEEPING SEVERAL FAMILIES FROM...
THOUSANDS OF REFUGEES IN MAKESHIFT CAMPS SUFFER FROM FOOD SHORTAGES AND SPREADING DISEASE...
WELFARE ROLLS INCREASE AS CUTBACKS AND MASS UNEMPLOYMENT CONTINUE TO....
DON'T WORRY, MOM - IT'S ALL JUST PRETEND.
LYNN

I had hoped that by the time my children were grown, this type of news would be a thing of the past.

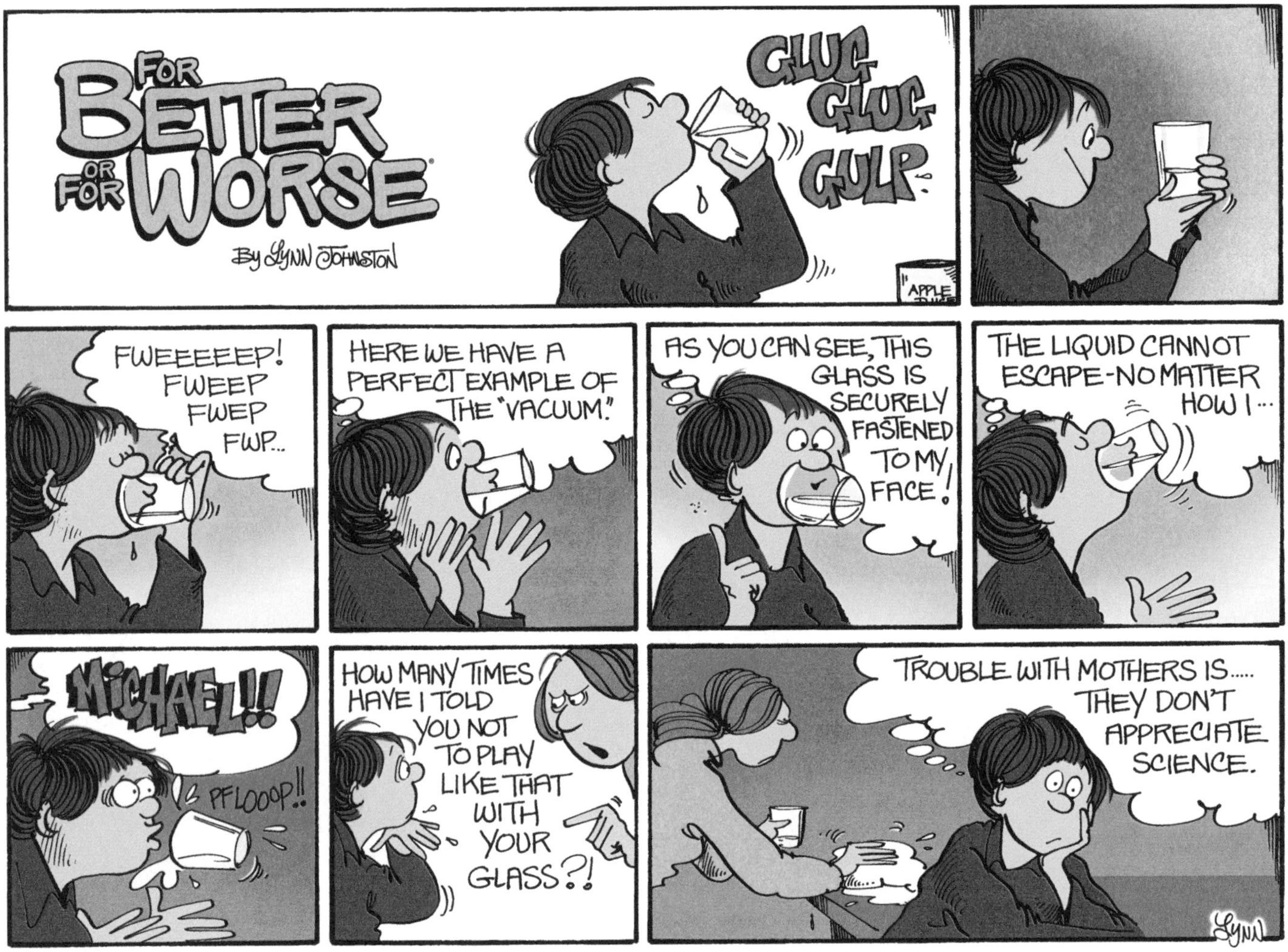
FOR BETTER OR FOR WORSE
BY LYNN JOHNSTON
GLUG GLUG GULP
APPLE
FWEEEEEEP! FWEEP FWEP FWP...
HERE WE HAVE A PERFECT EXAMPLE OF THE "VACUUM."
AS YOU CAN SEE, THIS GLASS IS SECURELY FASTENED TO MY FACE!
THE LIQUID CANNOT ESCAPE-NO MATTER HOW I...
MICHAEL!!
PFLOOOP!!
HOW MANY TIMES HAVE I TOLD YOU NOT TO PLAY LIKE THAT WITH YOUR GLASS?!
TROUBLE WITH MOTHERS IS..... THEY DON'T APPRECIATE SCIENCE.
LYNN

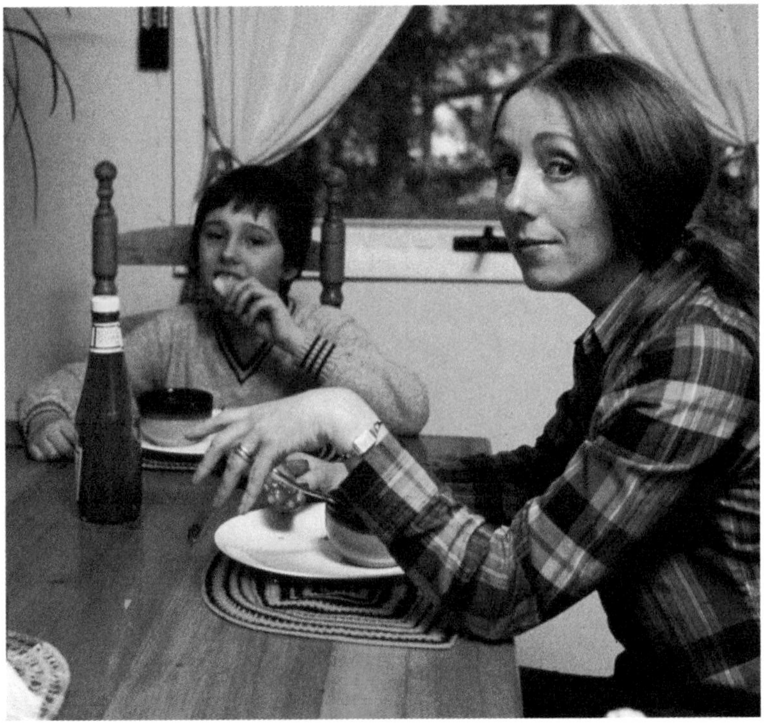

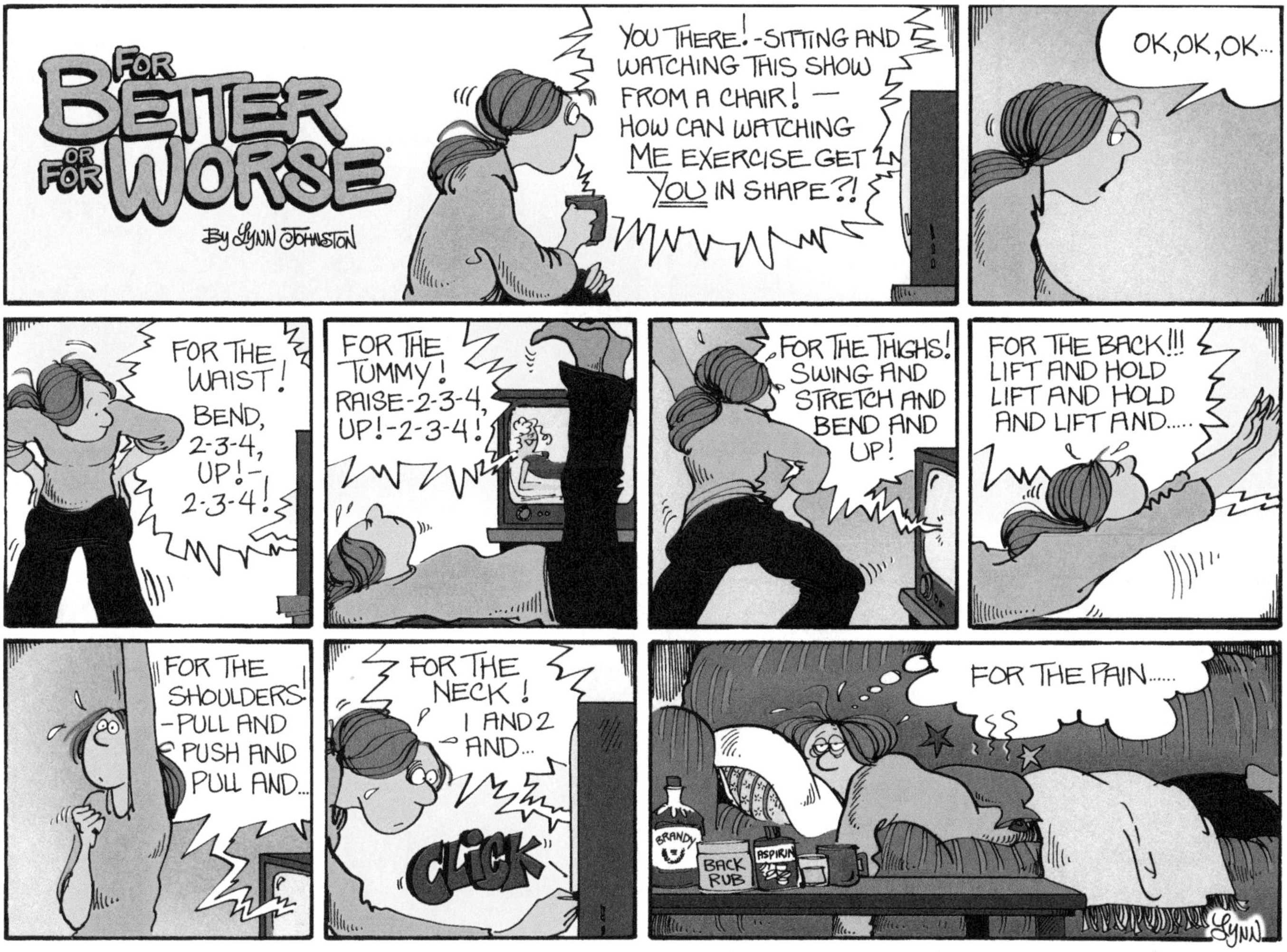
FOR BETTER OR FOR WORSE
BY LYNN JOHNSTON
YOU THERE! -SITTING AND WATCHING THIS SHOW FROM A CHAIR! — HOW CAN WATCHING ME EXERCISE GET YOU IN SHAPE?!
OK,OK,OK...
FOR THE WAIST! BEND, 2-3-4, UP!- 2-3-4!
FOR THE TUMMY! RAISE-2-3-4, UP!-2-3-4!
FOR THE THIGHS! SWING AND STRETCH AND BEND AND UP!
FOR THE BACK!!! LIFT AND HOLD LIFT AND HOLD AND LIFT AND.....
FOR THE SHOULDERS! -PULL AND PUSH AND PULL AND...
FOR THE NECK! 1 AND 2 AND...
CLICK
FOR THE PAIN......
BRANDY
BACK RUB
ASPIRIN
LYNN

Feeling soft and out of shape, a few of us decided to create an exercise group. We found a capable leader who, for a modest sum, agreed to make us sweat a couple of afternoons a week. She turned out to be a drill sergeant. After a few serious workouts, we were all stiff and sore. I remember lying on the couch in pain, feeling muscles I didn't know existed. I thought that running after, picking up, and carrying kids would have put us all ahead of the game.

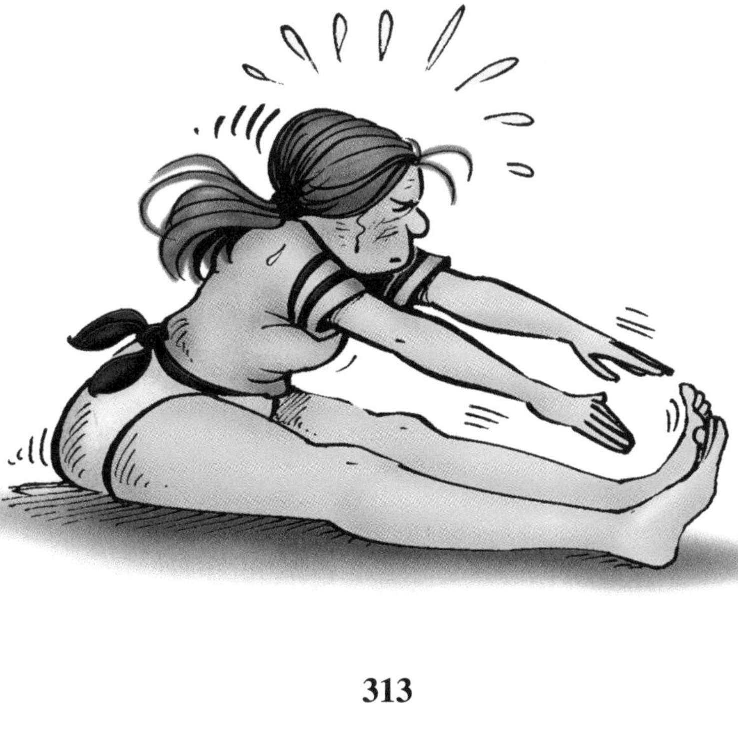

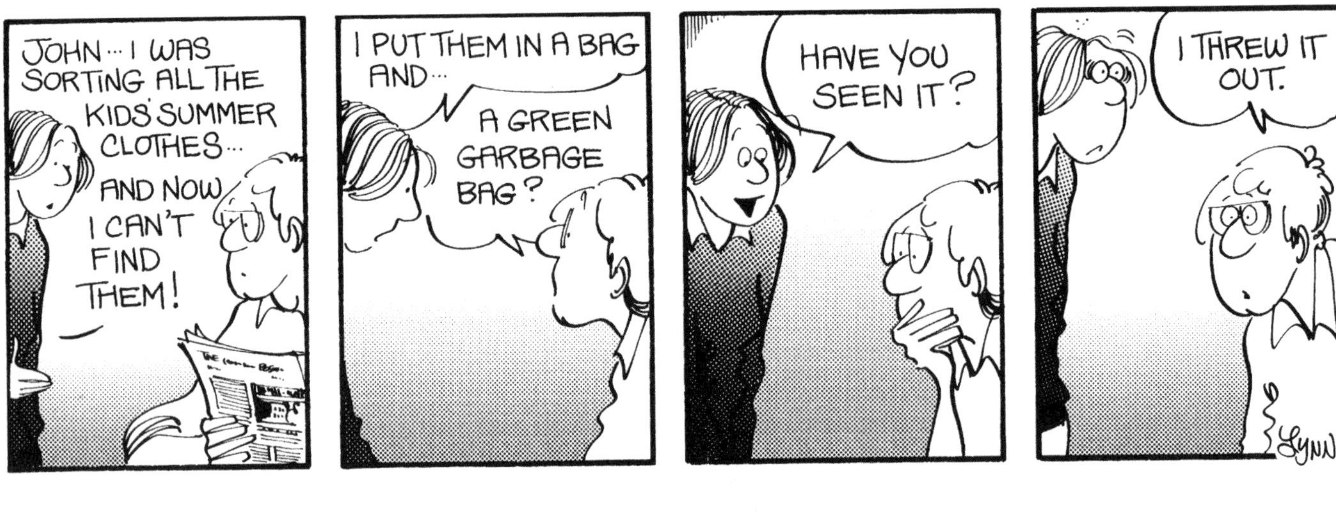
JOHN... I WAS SORTING ALL THE KIDS' SUMMER CLOTHES...
AND NOW I CAN'T FIND THEM!
I PUT THEM IN A BAG AND...
A GREEN GARBAGE BAG?
HAVE YOU SEEN IT?
I THREW IT OUT.
LYNN

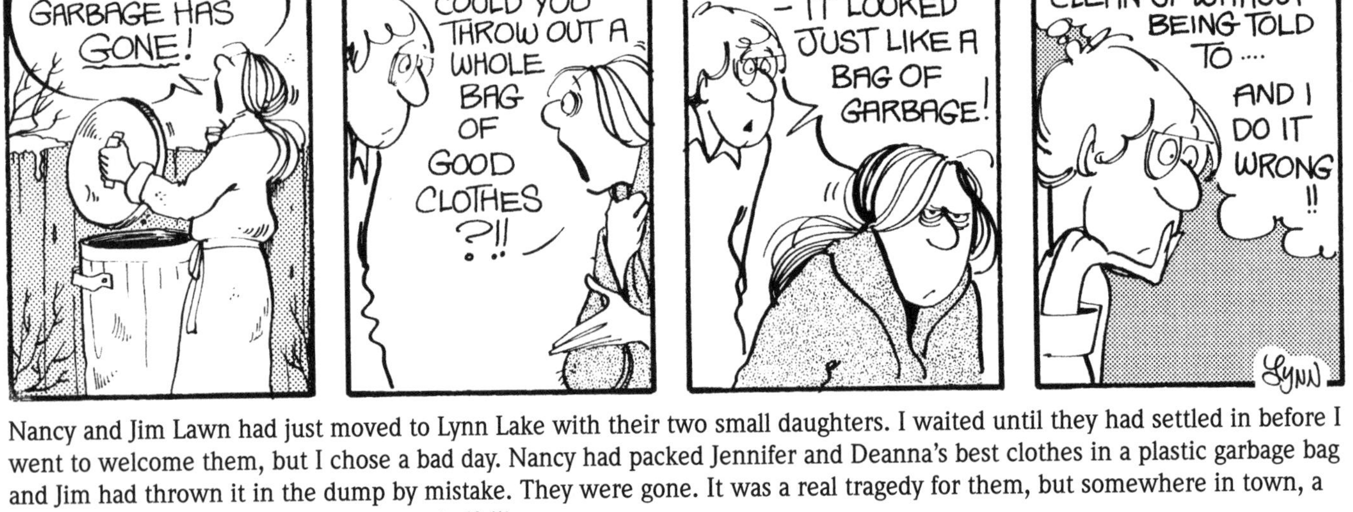
OH, NO! - THE GARBAGE HAS GONE!
JOHN - HOW COULD YOU THROW OUT A WHOLE BAG OF GOOD CLOTHES ?!!
?!!
HOW WAS I TO KNOW? - IT LOOKED JUST LIKE A BAG OF GARBAGE!
....THE ONE DAY I CLEAN UP WITHOUT BEING TOLD TO....
AND I DO IT WRONG !!
LYNN

Nancy and Jim Lawn had just moved to Lynn Lake with their two small daughters. I waited until they had settled in before I went to welcome them, but I chose a bad day. Nancy had packed Jennifer and Deanna's best clothes in a plastic garbage bag and Jim had thrown it in the dump by mistake. They were gone. It was a real tragedy for them, but somewhere in town, a very happy family was checking out a windfall!

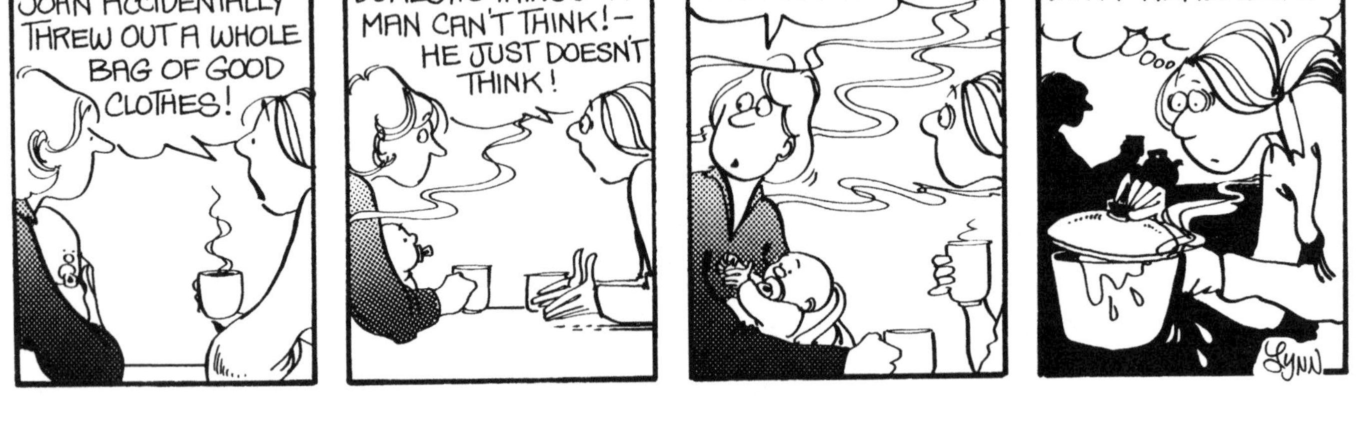
HONESTLY, ANNE - JOHN ACCIDENTALLY THREW OUT A WHOLE BAG OF GOOD CLOTHES!
WHEN IT COMES TO DOMESTIC THINGS - A MAN CAN'T THINK! - HE JUST DOESN'T THINK!
ELLY... UH... YOUR SOUP IS BURNING.
I THINK. - I JUST DON'T REMEMBER.
LYNN

HERE YOU ARE, GUYS ..... A GENUINE CULINARY TREAT!
FROM MOTHER'S KITCHEN COMES REAL, HONEST-TO-GOODNESS HOME MADE SOUP!
WHAT'S THE MATTER? THIS ISN'T OUT OF A CAN .... IT'S REAL!
I KNOW.
...WE LIKE THE STUFF IN THE CAN.
LYNN

MICHAEL, HAVE YOU FINISHED YOUR BREAKFAST?
NOPE.
HAVE YOU DONE YOUR TEETH?
UH, NO.
HAVE YOU GOT YOUR HOMEWORK READY TO TAKE TO SCHOOL?
UM.. NOT YET.
DON'T YOU REALIZE YOU'VE ONLY GOT A FEW MINUTES BEFORE YOU'RE REALLY LATE?!!
UH HUH.
WHY PANIC WHEN YOU HAVE SOMEONE ELSE TO PANIC FOR YOU?!
LYNN

This strip has a story behind it. I was travelling quite a bit for work and was often waiting to board a plane somewhere. I was enroute to New York and sitting in the lounge were all kinds of folks heading to meetings and events and so on. Our flight had been delayed. Some were late for connecting flights, some were unable to contact people who were meeting them. We were all getting frustrated and anxious. An hour went by with no information. Then another hour passed. Eventually we were all furious. The tension was awful ... but then a miracle occurred. A man went completely berserk — he stood up, cursing the airline, and the attendants at the gate. He threw down his briefcase and stomped on it, shouting and waving his arms. He threatened to sue. He screamed obscenities. At that point, the rest of us relaxed. We all watched as someone else acted out our frustrations perfectly. As he ranted, we said to ourselves, "Yeah, that's right. That's exactly how I feel."

By the time the authorities came, the lounge was a quiet place full of calm people. It was instant stress relief. It occurred to me that I performed this same service for my family; the more irate I became about something, the less concerned they were!

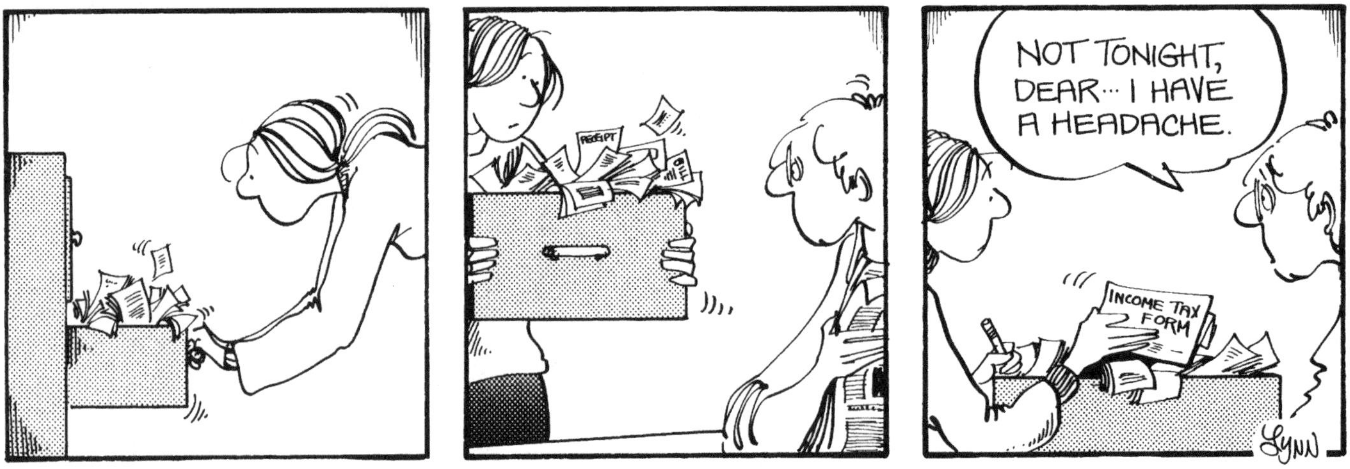
RECEIPT
NOT TONIGHT, DEAR... I HAVE A HEADACHE.
INCOME TAX FORM
Lynn

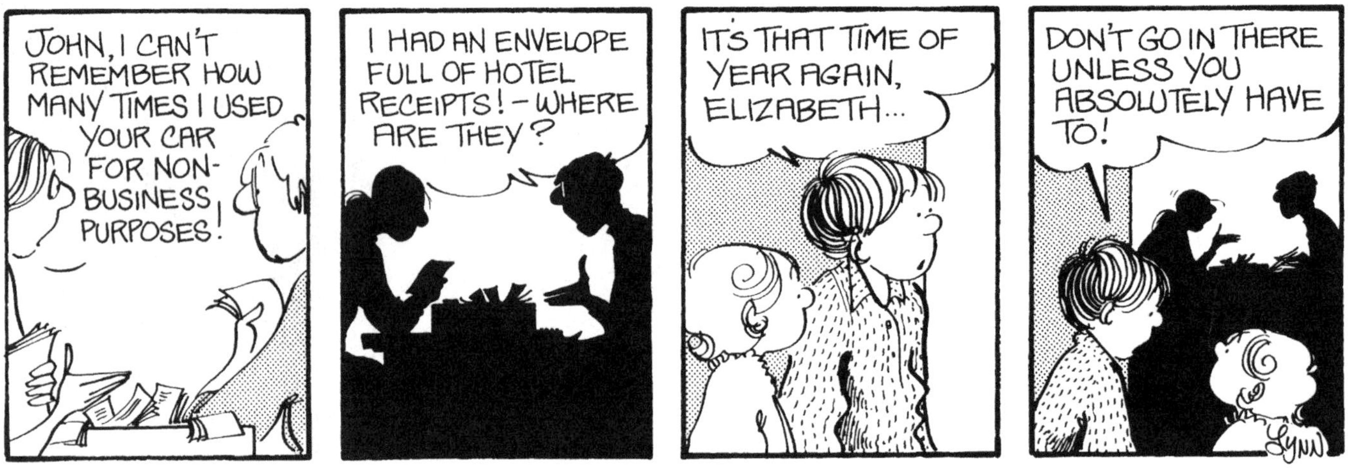
JOHN, I CAN'T REMEMBER HOW MANY TIMES I USED YOUR CAR FOR NON-BUSINESS PURPOSES!
I HAD AN ENVELOPE FULL OF HOTEL RECEIPTS! – WHERE ARE THEY?
IT'S THAT TIME OF YEAR AGAIN, ELIZABETH...
DON'T GO IN THERE UNLESS YOU ABSOLUTELY HAVE TO!
Lynn

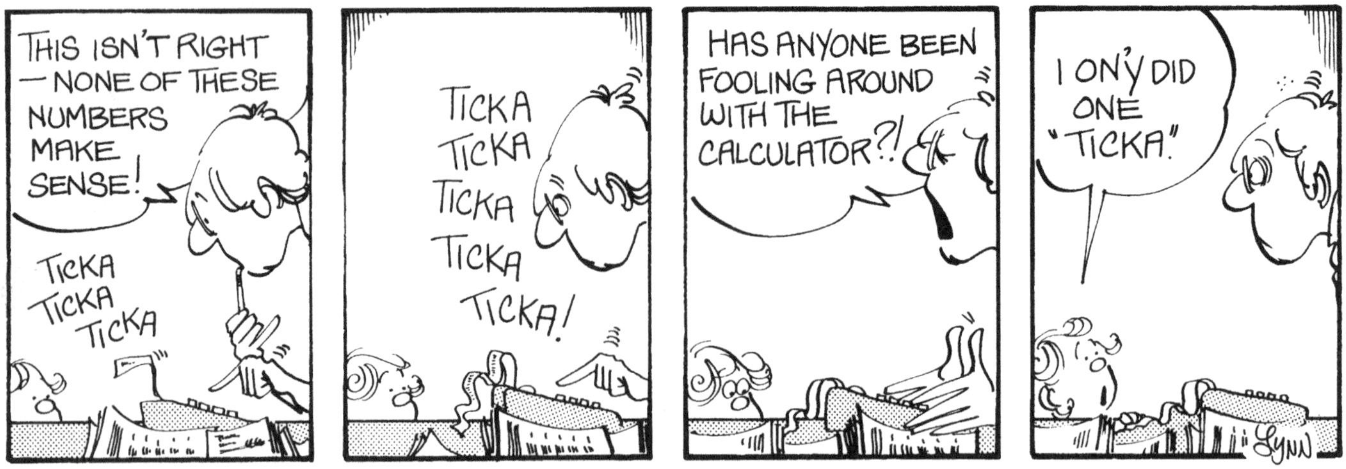
THIS ISN'T RIGHT — NONE OF THESE NUMBERS MAKE SENSE!
TICKA TICKA TICKA
TICKA TICKA TICKA TICKA TICKA!
HAS ANYONE BEEN FOOLING AROUND WITH THE CALCULATOR?!
I ON'Y DID ONE "TICKA."
Lynn

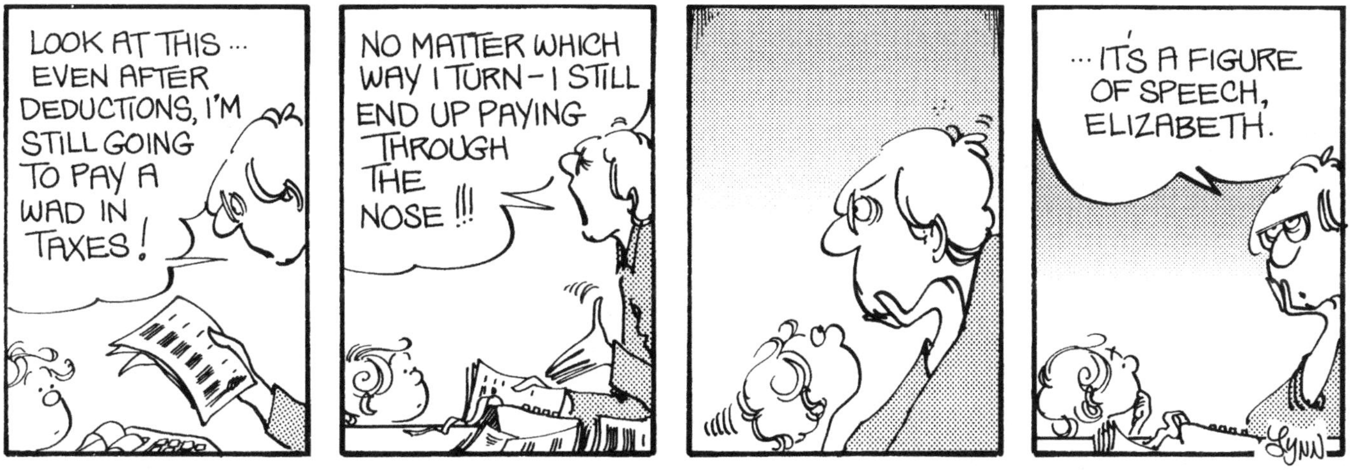
LOOK AT THIS ... EVEN AFTER DEDUCTIONS, I'M STILL GOING TO PAY A WAD IN TAXES!
NO MATTER WHICH WAY I TURN - I STILL END UP PAYING THROUGH THE NOSE !!!
... IT'S A FIGURE OF SPEECH, ELIZABETH.
LYNN

Strips like this one were always hard to translate. Apparently, "paying through the nose" only makes sense in English!

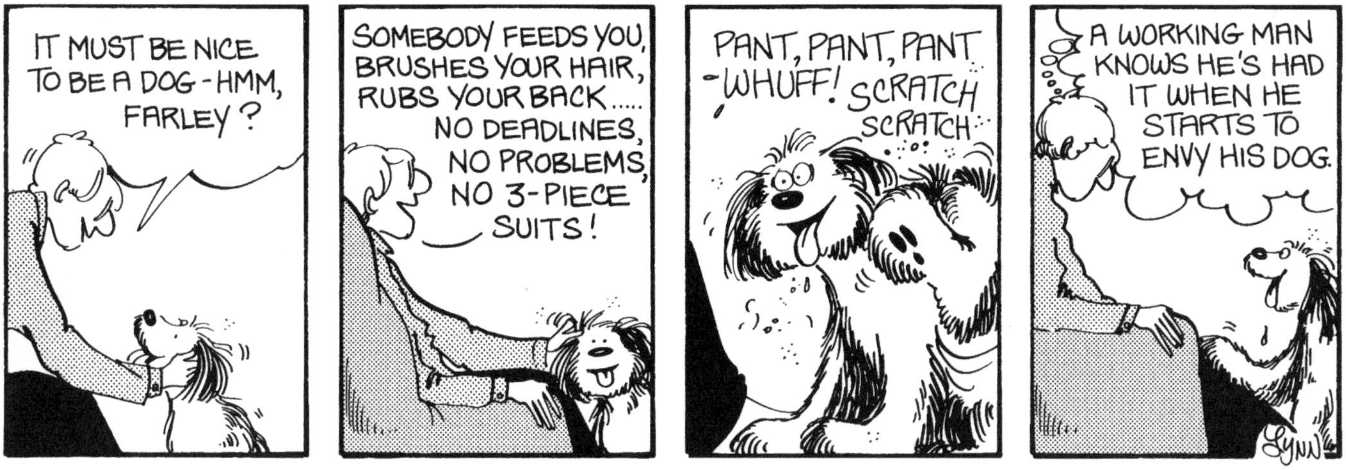
IT MUST BE NICE TO BE A DOG - HMM, FARLEY?
SOMEBODY FEEDS YOU, BRUSHES YOUR HAIR, RUBS YOUR BACK..... NO DEADLINES, NO PROBLEMS, NO 3-PIECE SUITS!
PANT, PANT, PANT
WHUFF!
SCRATCH
SCRATCH
A WORKING MAN KNOWS HE'S HAD IT WHEN HE STARTS TO ENVY HIS DOG.
LYNN

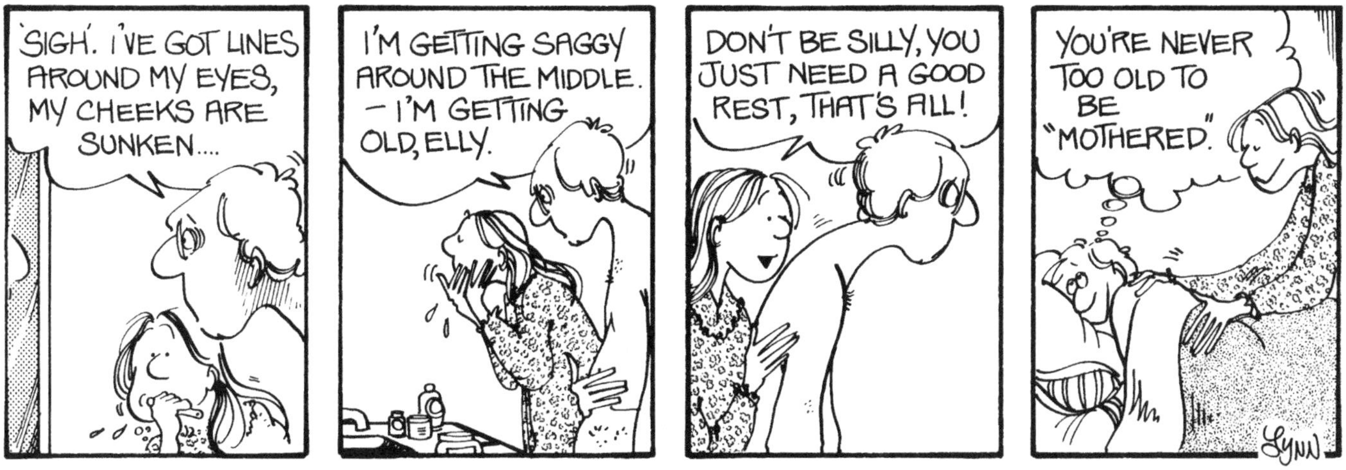
'SIGH'. I'VE GOT LINES AROUND MY EYES, MY CHEEKS ARE SUNKEN....
I'M GETTING SAGGY AROUND THE MIDDLE. - I'M GETTING OLD, ELLY.
DON'T BE SILLY, YOU JUST NEED A GOOD REST, THAT'S ALL!
YOU'RE NEVER TOO OLD TO BE "MOTHERED."
LYNN

FOR BETTER OR FOR WORSE
BY LYNN JOHNSTON
MOM, LAWRENCE GOT 3 DOLLARS - AN' I ONLY GOT...
ALL RIGHT - HERE.
THANK GOODNESS SOMEONE'S STILL HAPPY WITH THE CHANGE!
MOM, I'M GONNA GET THIS - OK?
YOU CAN'T AFFORD IT, MICHAEL - YOU ONLY HAVE 3 DOLLARS.
BUT THIS IS $2.99!
DON'T FORGET - YOU HAVE TO PAY TAX.
TAX? - WHAT'S TAX?!
DON'T YOU KNOW WHAT TAX IS MICHAEL?
THAT'S WHEN THE GOVERMINT MAKES YOU PAY MORE FOR SOMETHIN' THAN IT'S WORTH!!
LYNN

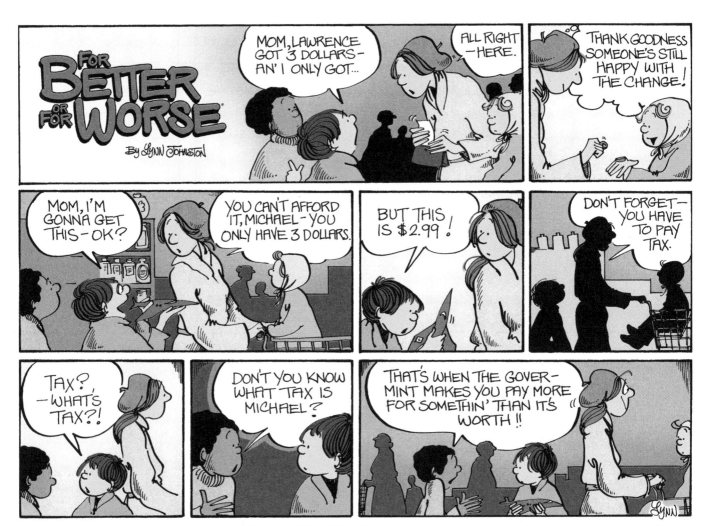

This was when three dollars bought a toy that would last! We tried to introduce the concept of earning and saving, and waiting until you could afford the things you want, but understanding money takes time.

Aaron had a weekly allowance, and what didn't go to Fergie's candy counter went to the toy department at "The Bay." The Lynn Lake Hudson's Bay store was a long cinder-block building that carried everything from groceries to long underwear. The toy department was smack dab in the middle of the store. We couldn't navigate the aisles without going past the toys, and Aaron knew the entire inventory. He liked Leggo, in particular, and wanted every kit.

We insisted that he buy these kits with his own money. Every week, he'd skip down to see if his box was still on "hold," put a dollar more down on his prize, and calculate how much more he had to pay. It was a great way to make a toy mean something! Aaron learned about what things cost. He learned about taxes, and he learned a lot about planning and patience … and in so doing, I learned a lot about him.

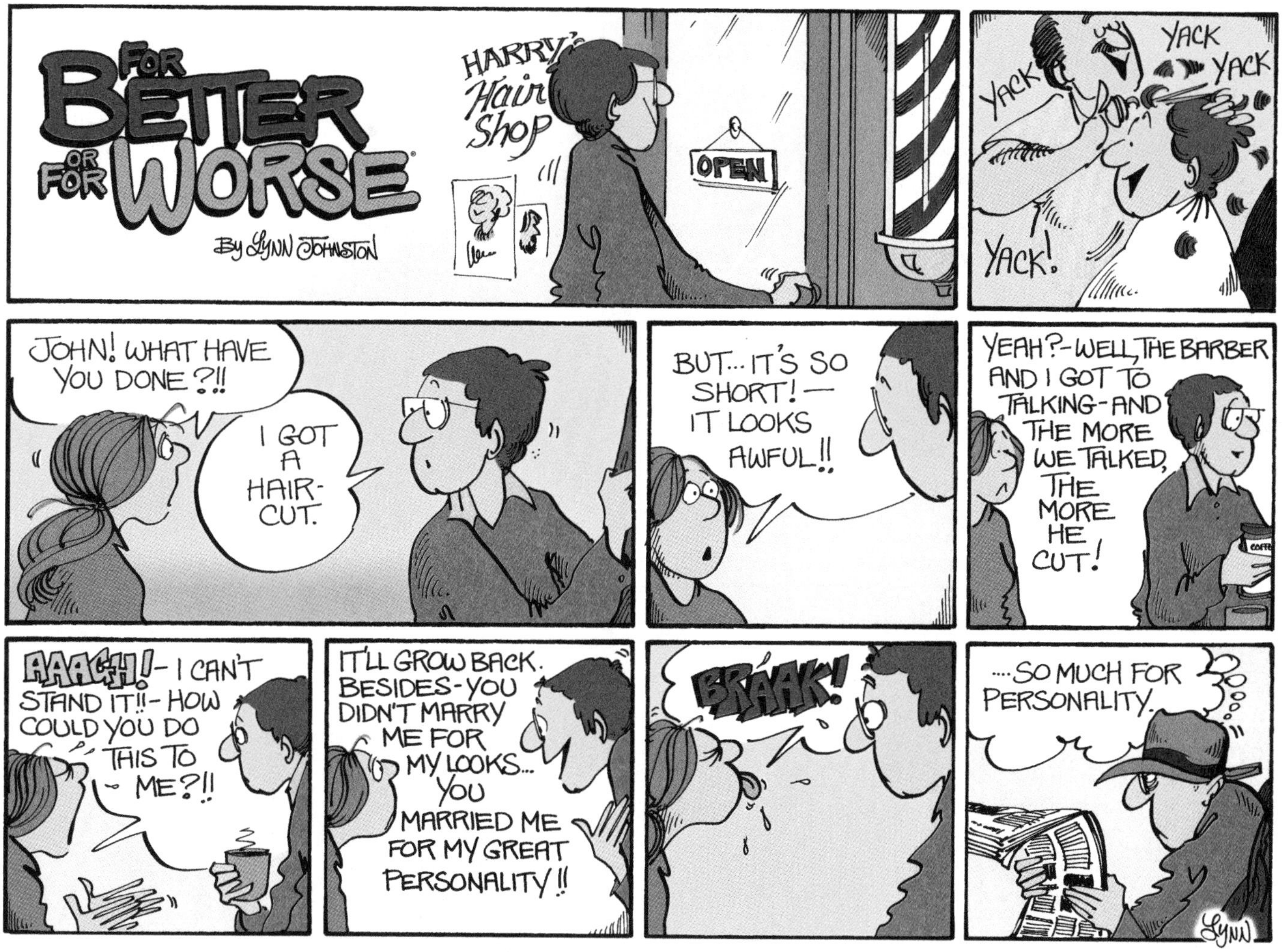
For Better or For Worse
By Lynn Johnston
HARRY'S Hair Shop
OPEN
YACK YACK YACK YACK! YACK
JOHN! WHAT HAVE YOU DONE?!!
I GOT A HAIR-CUT.
BUT... IT'S SO SHORT! — IT LOOKS AWFUL!!
YEAH?-WELL, THE BARBER AND I GOT TO TALKING-AND THE MORE WE TALKED, THE MORE HE CUT!
AAAGH!- I CAN'T STAND IT!!- HOW COULD YOU DO THIS TO ME?!!
IT'LL GROW BACK. BESIDES-YOU DIDN'T MARRY ME FOR MY LOOKS... YOU MARRIED ME FOR MY GREAT PERSONALITY!!
BRAAK!
....SO MUCH FOR PERSONALITY.
Lynn

Eddy King, our local barber, was a neighbour and friend. Our cabins on Berge Lake were side by side. Whenever Rod had a chance to talk to Eddie, it was usually a long conversation. When it came to giving a haircut, Eddie would cut for as long as the conversation lasted. Occasionally, Rod would come home with almost no hair left — I hated it! I kept hoping that next time he had his hair cut, they would have much less to say!

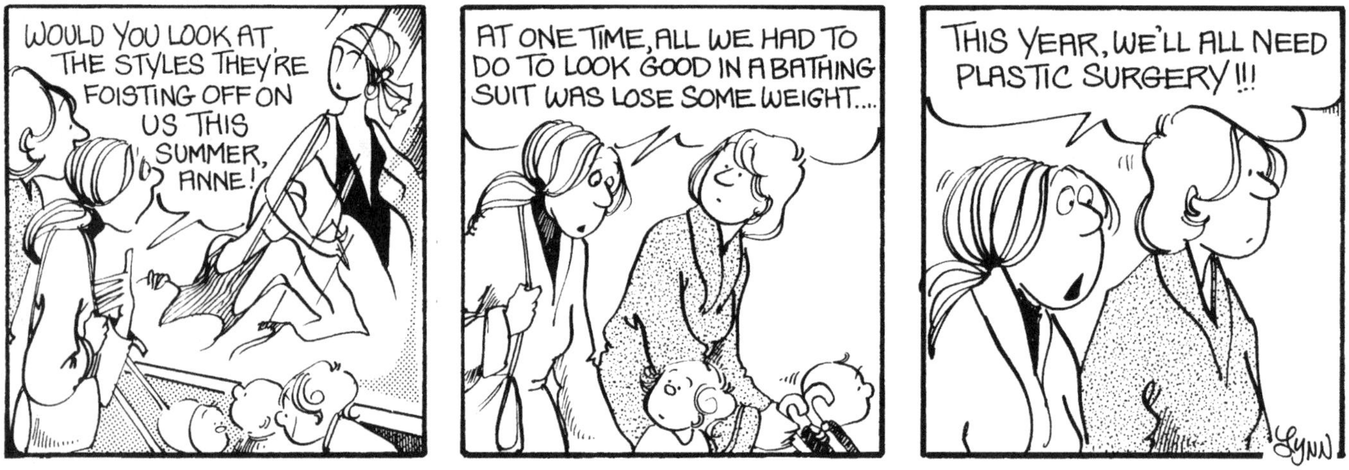
WOULD YOU LOOK AT, THE STYLES THEY'RE FOISTING OFF ON US THIS SUMMER, ANNE!
AT ONE TIME, ALL WE HAD TO DO TO LOOK GOOD IN A BATHING SUIT WAS LOSE SOME WEIGHT....
THIS YEAR, WE'LL ALL NEED PLASTIC SURGERY!!!
LYNN

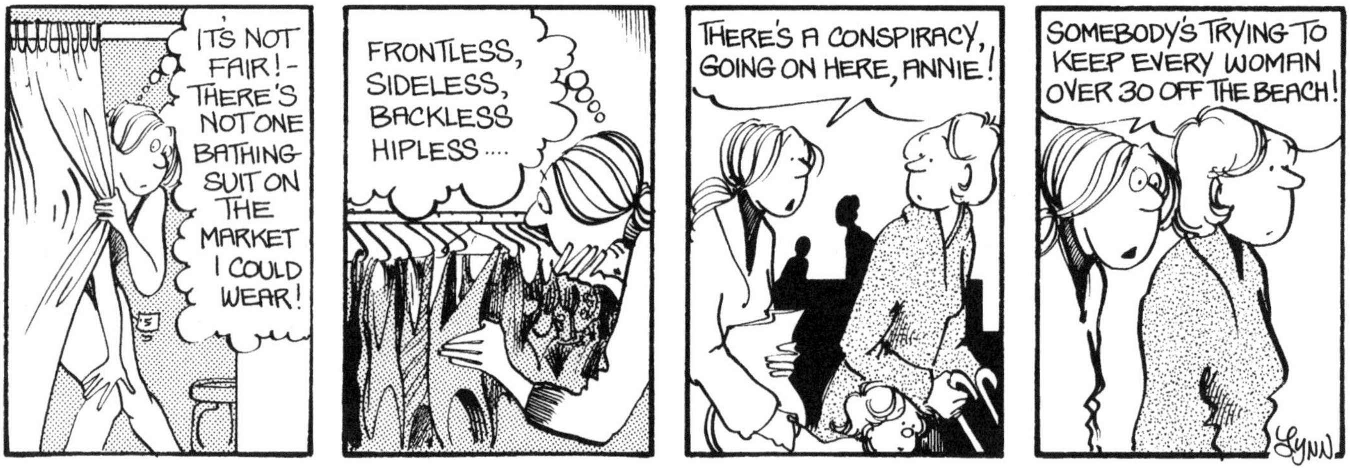
IT'S NOT FAIR! - THERE'S NOT ONE BATHING SUIT ON THE MARKET I COULD WEAR!
FRONTLESS, SIDELESS, BACKLESS HIPLESS....
THERE'S A CONSPIRACY, GOING ON HERE, ANNIE!
SOMEBODY'S TRYING TO KEEP EVERY WOMAN OVER 30 OFF THE BEACH!
LYNN

Every year, it's the same thing. Those of us who want to retain some dignity on the beach have a hard time finding the swimwear to do it in. When I would vent my frustration in the paper, I would always get mail from grateful women who shared my point of view.

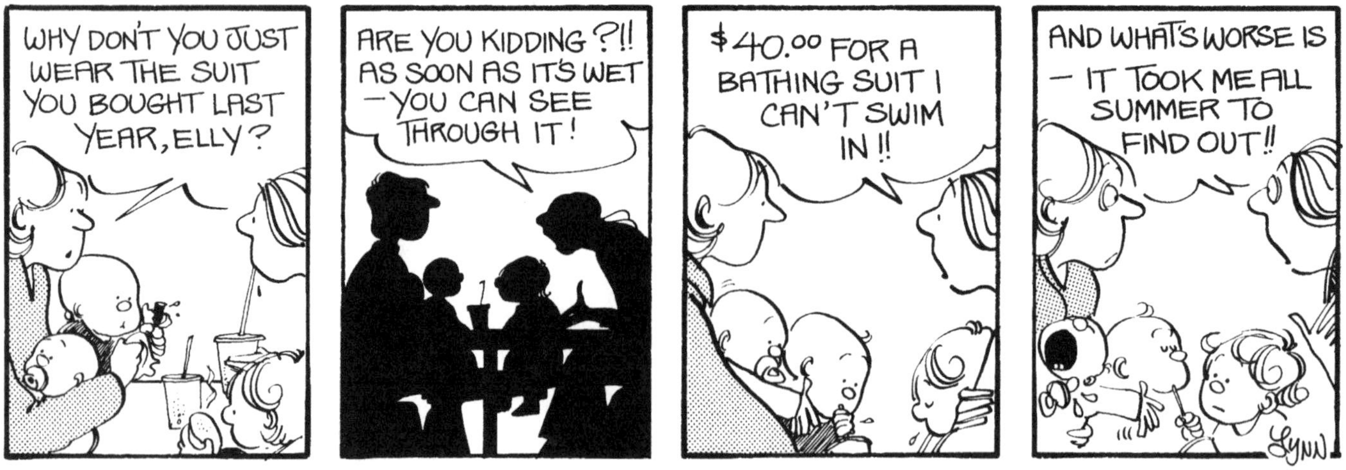
WHY DON'T YOU JUST WEAR THE SUIT YOU BOUGHT LAST YEAR, ELLY?
ARE YOU KIDDING?!! AS SOON AS IT'S WET — YOU CAN SEE THROUGH IT!
$40.00 FOR A BATHING SUIT I CAN'T SWIM IN!!
AND WHAT'S WORSE IS — IT TOOK ME ALL SUMMER TO FIND OUT!!
LYNN

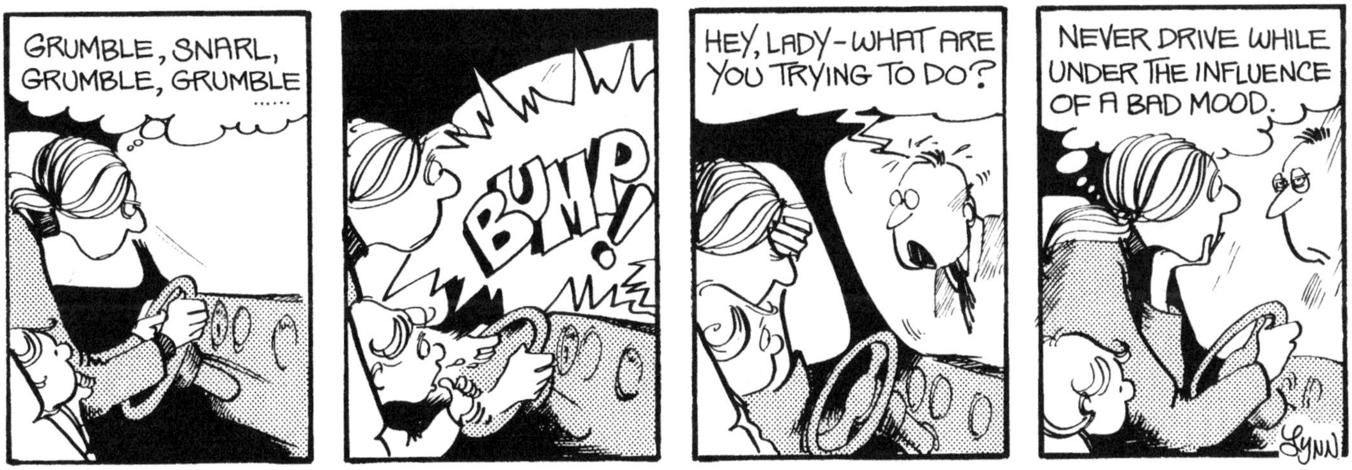
GRUMBLE, SNARL, GRUMBLE, GRUMBLE ......
BUMP!
HEY, LADY - WHAT ARE YOU TRYING TO DO?
NEVER DRIVE WHILE UNDER THE INFLUENCE OF A BAD MOOD.
LYNN

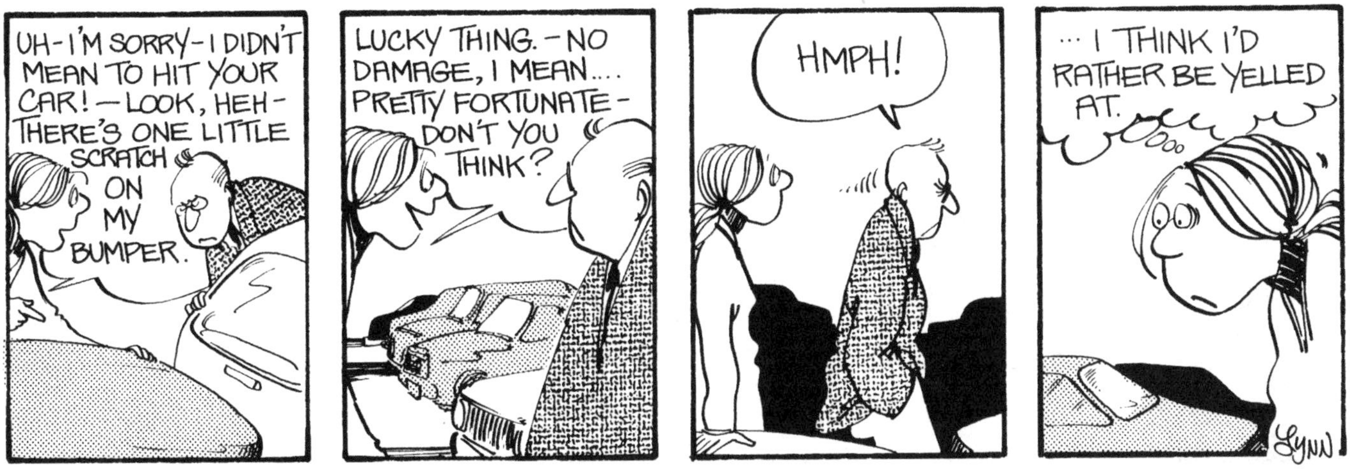
UH - I'M SORRY - I DIDN'T MEAN TO HIT YOUR CAR! — LOOK, HEH - THERE'S ONE LITTLE SCRATCH ON MY BUMPER.
LUCKY THING. - NO DAMAGE, I MEAN.... PRETTY FORTUNATE - DON'T YOU THINK?
HMPH!
... I THINK I'D RATHER BE YELLED AT.
LYNN

After a few months of navigating small-town streets, I soon forgot how to drive in the city. If I had to drive in Winnipeg, I would panic at the speed of the traffic and the variety of signs and lights. I did rear-end a man on Portage Avenue, and his admonishment in public made me blush for months afterwards.

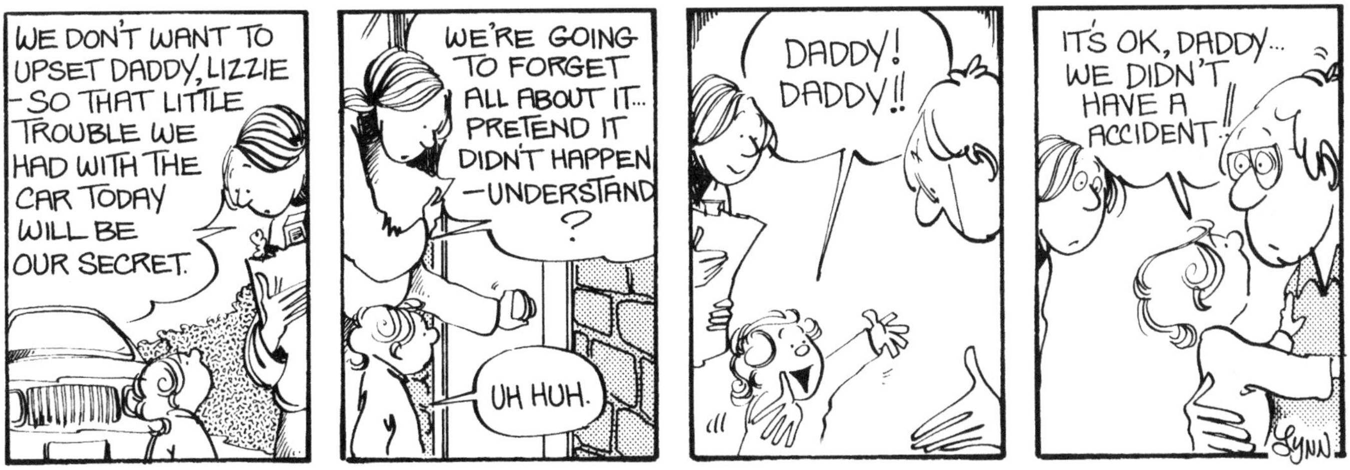
WE DON'T WANT TO UPSET DADDY, LIZZIE - SO THAT LITTLE TROUBLE WE HAD WITH THE CAR TODAY WILL BE OUR SECRET.
WE'RE GOING TO FORGET ALL ABOUT IT... PRETEND IT DIDN'T HAPPEN - UNDERSTAND?
UH HUH.
DADDY! DADDY!!
IT'S OK, DADDY... WE DIDN'T HAVE A ACCIDENT!!
LYNN

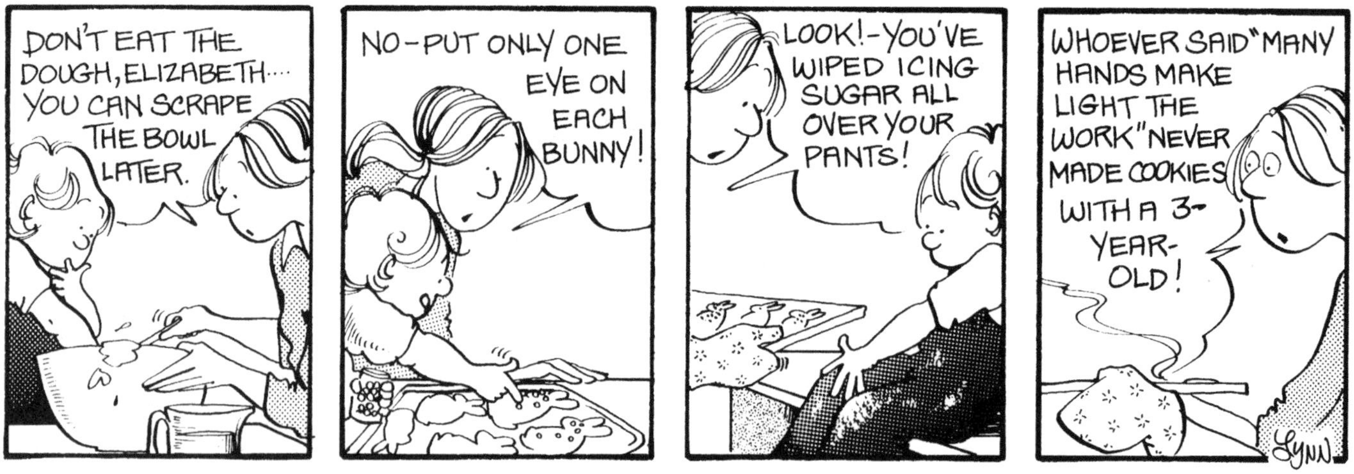
DON'T EAT THE DOUGH, ELIZABETH.... YOU CAN SCRAPE THE BOWL LATER.
NO-PUT ONLY ONE EYE ON EACH BUNNY!
LOOK!-YOU'VE WIPED ICING SUGAR ALL OVER YOUR PANTS!
WHOEVER SAID "MANY HANDS MAKE LIGHT THE WORK" NEVER MADE COOKIES WITH A 3-YEAR-OLD!
LYNN

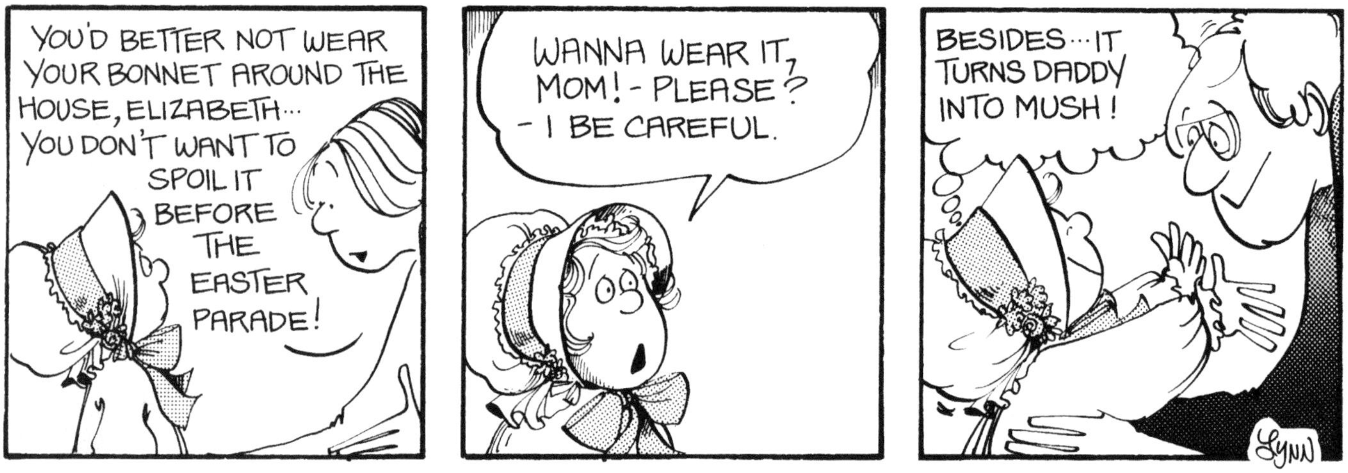
YOU'D BETTER NOT WEAR YOUR BONNET AROUND THE HOUSE, ELIZABETH... YOU DON'T WANT TO SPOIL IT BEFORE THE EASTER PARADE!
WANNA WEAR IT, MOM! - PLEASE? - I BE CAREFUL.
BESIDES... IT TURNS DADDY INTO MUSH!
LYNN

I still have this little outfit — carefully preserved in my closet upstairs. Some things you just shouldn't part with!

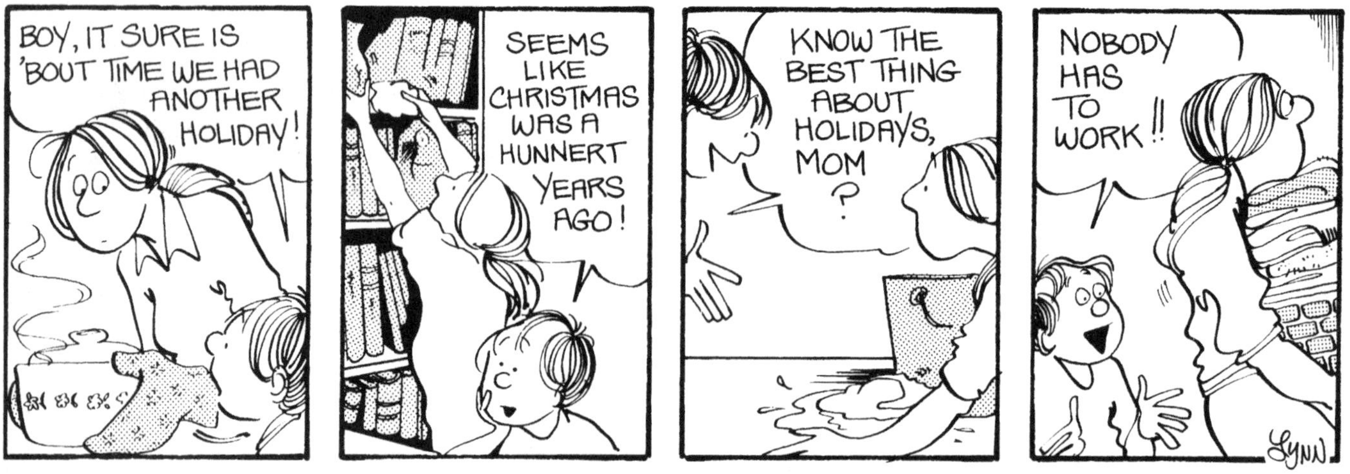
BOY, IT SURE IS 'BOUT TIME WE HAD ANOTHER HOLIDAY!
SEEMS LIKE CHRISTMAS WAS A HUNNERT YEARS AGO!
KNOW THE BEST THING ABOUT HOLIDAYS, MOM?
NOBODY HAS TO WORK!!
LYNN

WHAT??- YOU DON'T WANT TO GO IN THE EASTER PARADE?
BUT, LIZZIE!- IT TOOK ME HOURS TO MAKE THAT BONNET- I FIXED YOUR DRESS, I—
DON'T FORCE HER, MRS. PATTERSON.... AFTER ALL— ARE THESE LITTLE PAGEANTS FOR THE CHILDREN, OR FOR THE PARENTS?!
THERE'S ONE OF THOSE IN EVERY CROWD....
LYNN

Katie did not want to go to the Easter service. She didn't want to be in the parade, and she didn't want to wear the hat. What finally persuaded her to go was Aaron saying that he'd get all the chocolate, the cake, and the other goodies and she'd get none. Even though I was not pleased with his sentiments, I appreciated his help.

Katie dressed up for the Easter Parade.

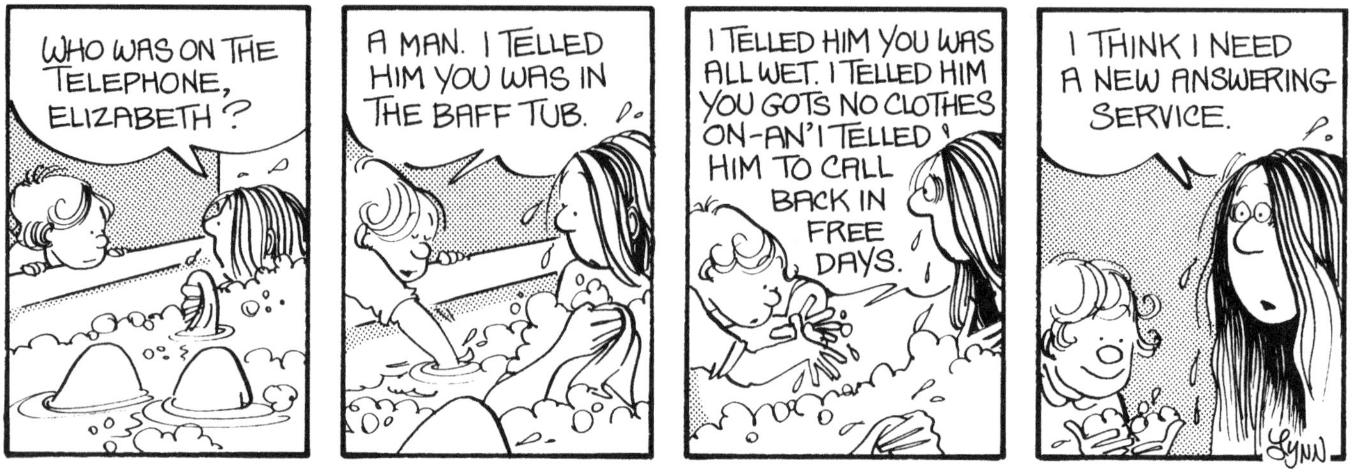
WHO WAS ON THE TELEPHONE, ELIZABETH?
A MAN. I TELLED HIM YOU WAS IN THE BAFF TUB.
I TELLED HIM YOU WAS ALL WET. I TELLED HIM YOU GOTS NO CLOTHES ON-AN' I TELLED HIM TO CALL BACK IN FREE DAYS.
I THINK I NEED A NEW ANSWERING SERVICE.
LYNN

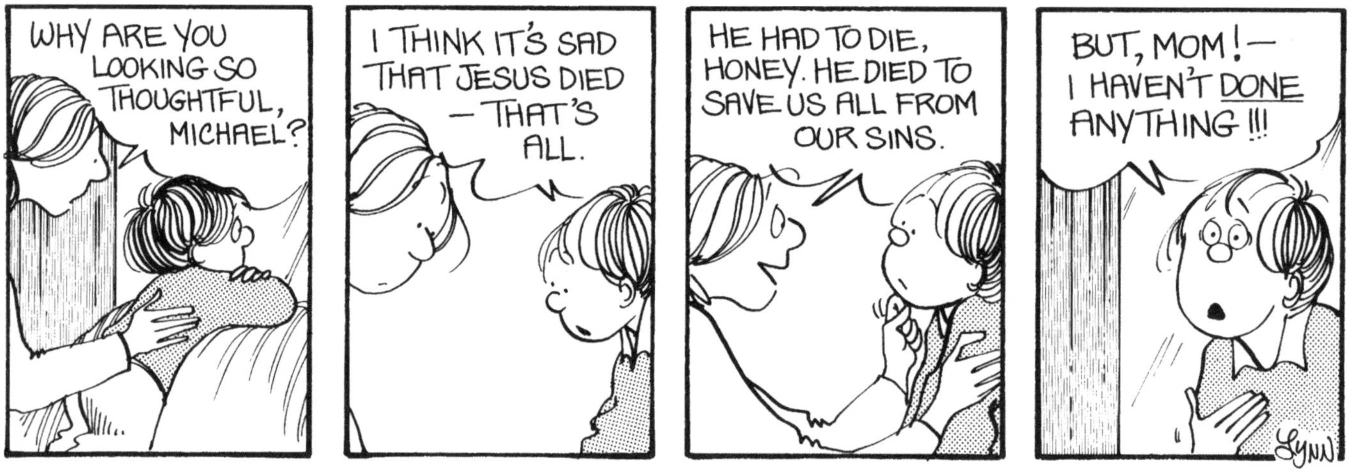
WHY ARE YOU LOOKING SO THOUGHTFUL, MICHAEL?
I THINK IT'S SAD THAT JESUS DIED —THAT'S ALL.
HE HAD TO DIE, HONEY. HE DIED TO SAVE US ALL FROM OUR SINS.
BUT, MOM!— I HAVEN'T DONE ANYTHING!!!
LYNN

The concept of being born a sinner confused me. As a kid, I was unable to process this — it just didn't make sense. I hoped in time I'd understand. I'm still waiting.

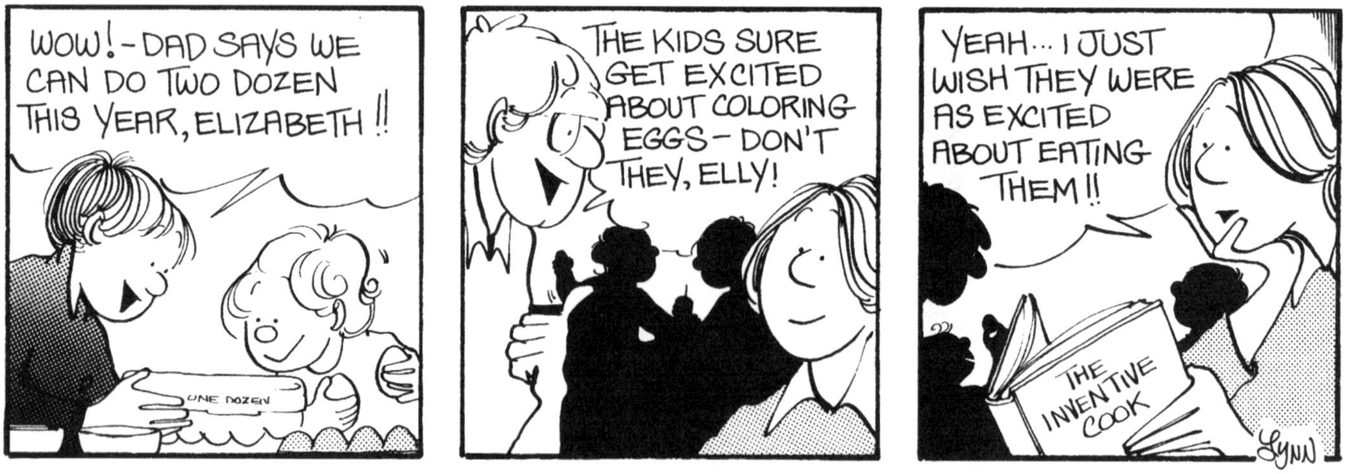
WOW!-DAD SAYS WE CAN DO TWO DOZEN THIS YEAR, ELIZABETH!!
ONE DOZEN
THE KIDS SURE GET EXCITED ABOUT COLORING EGGS- DON'T THEY, ELLY!
YEAH... I JUST WISH THEY WERE AS EXCITED ABOUT EATING THEM!!
THE INVENTIVE COOK
LYNN

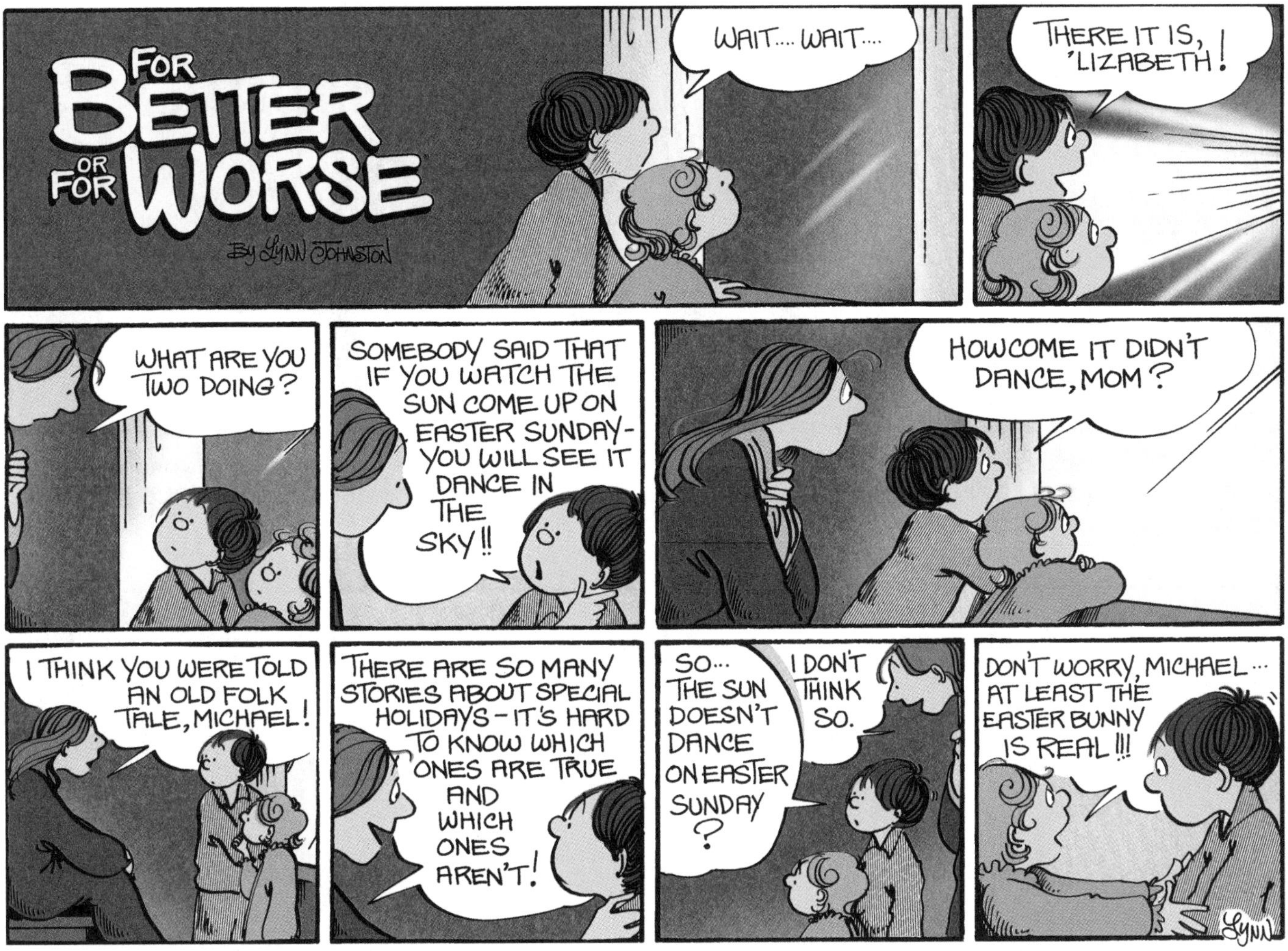
FOR BETTER OR FOR WORSE
By Lynn Johnston
WAIT.... WAIT....
THERE IT IS, 'LIZABETH!
WHAT ARE YOU TWO DOING?
SOMEBODY SAID THAT IF YOU WATCH THE SUN COME UP ON EASTER SUNDAY - YOU WILL SEE IT DANCE IN THE SKY!!
HOW COME IT DIDN'T DANCE, MOM?
I THINK YOU WERE TOLD AN OLD FOLK TALE, MICHAEL!
THERE ARE SO MANY STORIES ABOUT SPECIAL HOLIDAYS - IT'S HARD TO KNOW WHICH ONES ARE TRUE AND WHICH ONES AREN'T!
SO... THE SUN DOESN'T DANCE ON EASTER SUNDAY?
I DON'T THINK SO.
DON'T WORRY, MICHAEL... AT LEAST THE EASTER BUNNY IS REAL!!!
LYNN

This was a story my dad told us: "If you get up early on Easter Sunday morning, you will see the sun dance as it rises." Dutifully, Alan and I would get up to see if the story was true, but we never saw the sun dance on Easter morning. I think Dad had bet on two things: one, he never expected my brother and me to actually get out of a warm bed so early, and two, in Vancouver, it always seemed to rain on Easter. His explanation for why the sun hadn't danced was that we probably didn't BELIEVE enough! I guess we believed enough in the Easter bunny, though — because every year, he showed up without fail!

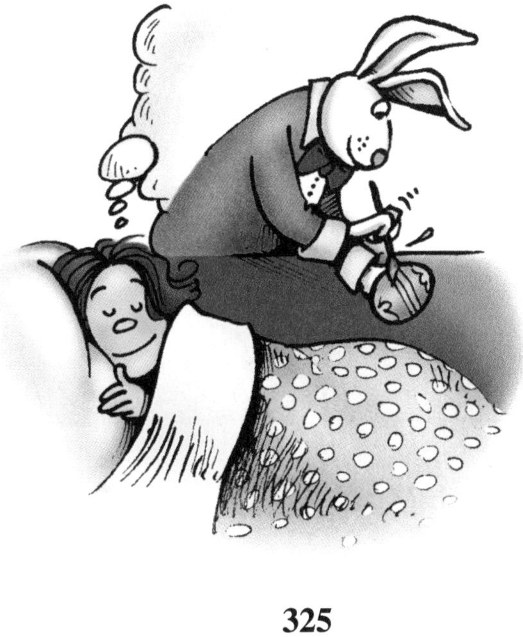

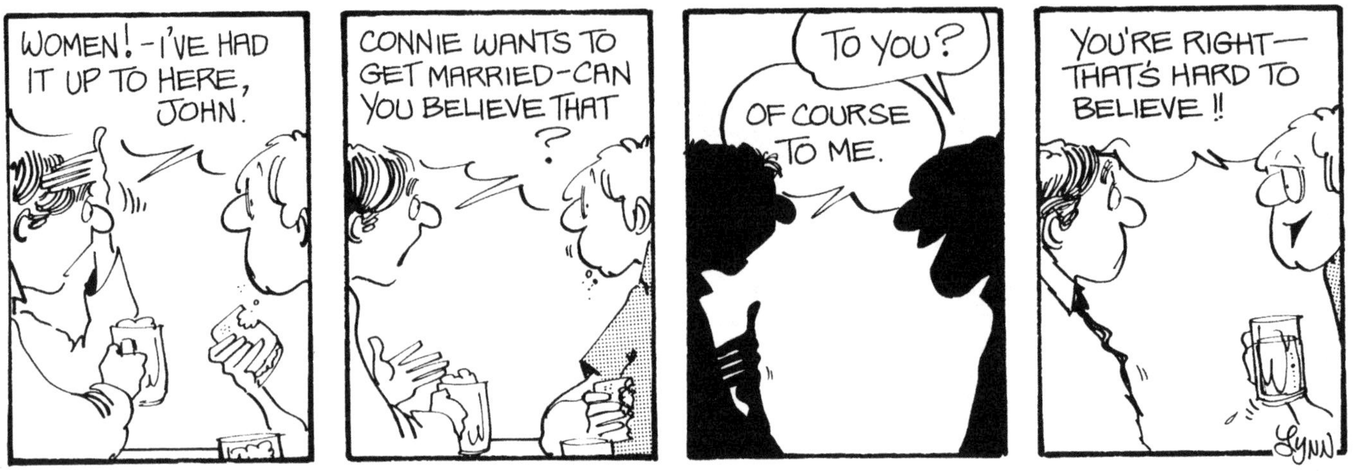
WOMEN! - I'VE HAD IT UP TO HERE, JOHN!
CONNIE WANTS TO GET MARRIED - CAN YOU BELIEVE THAT?
OF COURSE TO ME.
TO YOU?
YOU'RE RIGHT— THAT'S HARD TO BELIEVE !!

It's interesting to think about how almost "desperate" I was as a single mother. Not to "snag" a man; not to find a replacement for my ex. I just wanted to be wanted by someone who would treat me and my child with respect and affection. I was responsible for another life, but I needed someone in MY life, too.

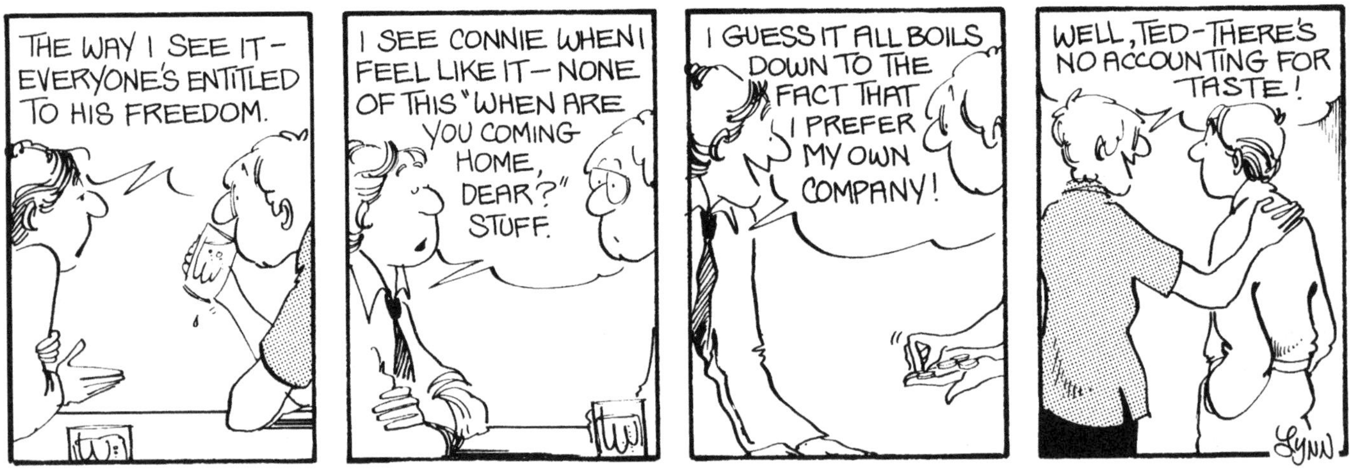
THE WAY I SEE IT - EVERYONE'S ENTITLED TO HIS FREEDOM.
I SEE CONNIE WHEN I FEEL LIKE IT — NONE OF THIS "WHEN ARE YOU COMING HOME, DEAR?" STUFF.
I GUESS IT ALL BOILS DOWN TO THE FACT THAT I PREFER MY OWN COMPANY!
WELL, TED - THERE'S NO ACCOUNTING FOR TASTE!

I wanted Ted to be desired by Connie, but thoroughly disliked by the readers, and it worked! People regularly told me to have her dump him, but a good story requires a "bad guy," and like all relationships, this one needed to work itself out.

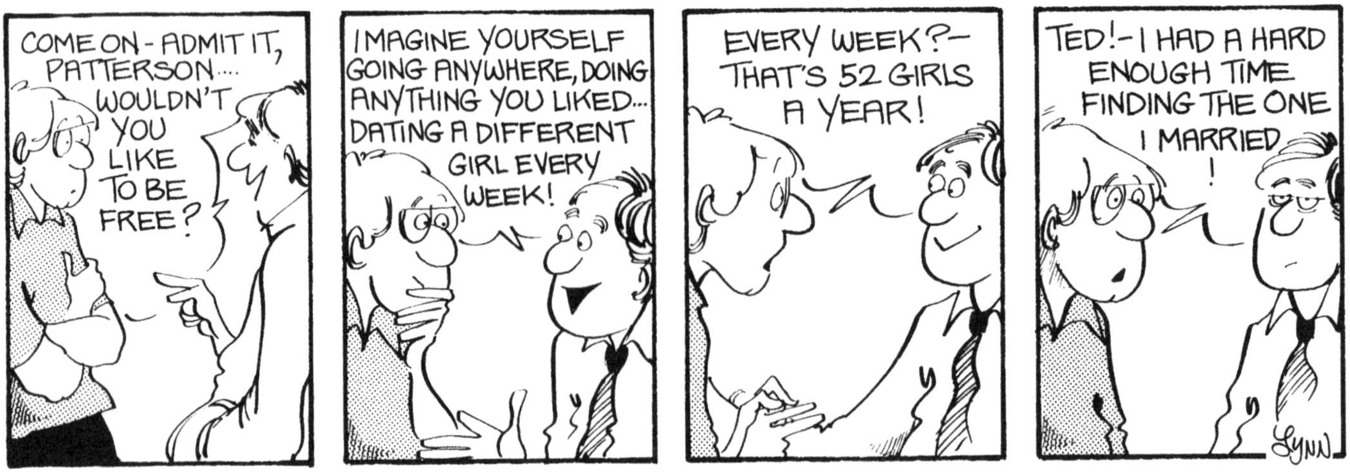
COME ON - ADMIT IT, PATTERSON.... WOULDN'T YOU LIKE TO BE FREE?
IMAGINE YOURSELF GOING ANYWHERE, DOING ANYTHING YOU LIKED... DATING A DIFFERENT GIRL EVERY WEEK!
EVERY WEEK? — THAT'S 52 GIRLS A YEAR!
TED! - I HAD A HARD ENOUGH TIME FINDING THE ONE I MARRIED!

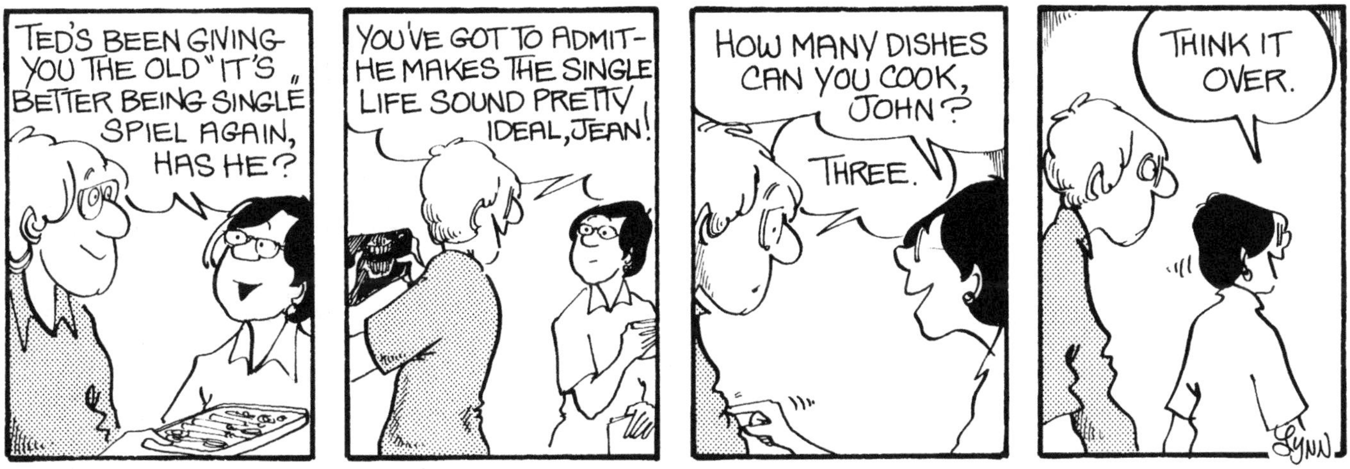
TED'S BEEN GIVING YOU THE OLD "IT'S BETTER BEING SINGLE" SPIEL AGAIN, HAS HE?
YOU'VE GOT TO ADMIT- HE MAKES THE SINGLE LIFE SOUND PRETTY IDEAL, JEAN!
HOW MANY DISHES CAN YOU COOK, JOHN?
THREE.
THINK IT OVER.

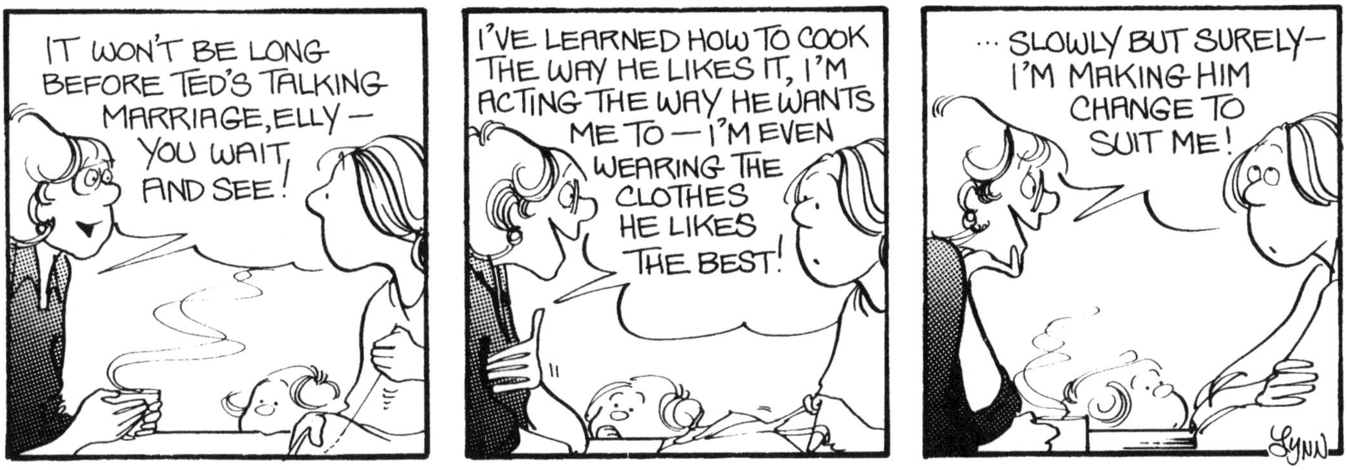
IT WON'T BE LONG BEFORE TED'S TALKING MARRIAGE, ELLY — YOU WAIT, AND SEE!
I'VE LEARNED HOW TO COOK THE WAY HE LIKES IT, I'M ACTING THE WAY HE WANTS ME TO — I'M EVEN WEARING THE CLOTHES HE LIKES THE BEST!
... SLOWLY BUT SURELY— I'M MAKING HIM CHANGE TO SUIT ME!

I expected my first spouse to change after I married him. I hoped that he would have more confidence and more self-control. In retrospect, I'd now advise people to accept their prospective partners the way they are. If their quirks irritate you before you marry, I guarantee they will drive you stark raving mad afterward!

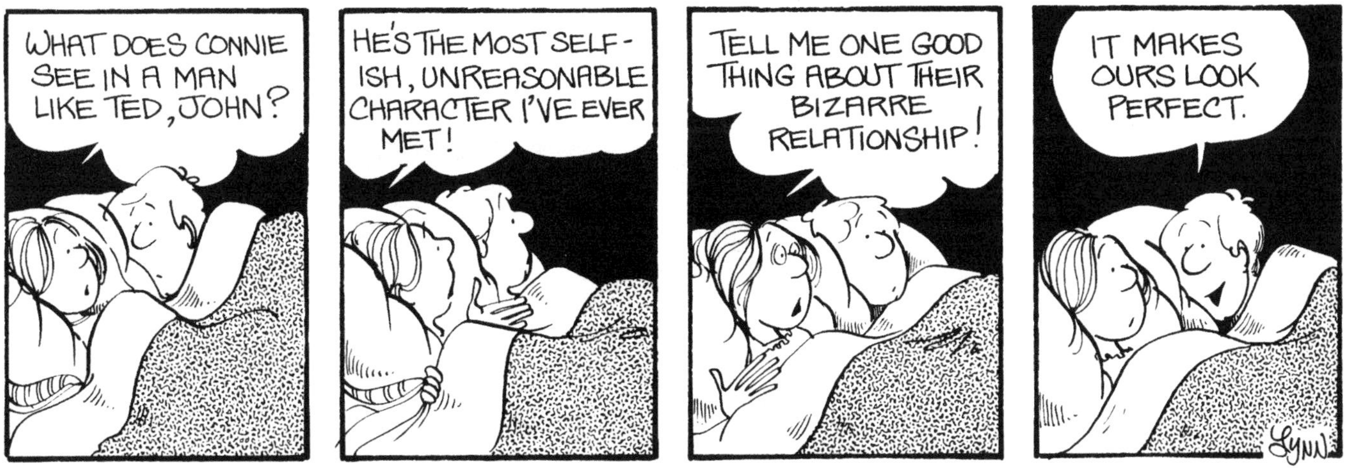
WHAT DOES CONNIE SEE IN A MAN LIKE TED, JOHN?
HE'S THE MOST SELF-ISH, UNREASONABLE CHARACTER I'VE EVER MET!
TELL ME ONE GOOD THING ABOUT THEIR BIZARRE RELATIONSHIP!
IT MAKES OURS LOOK PERFECT.

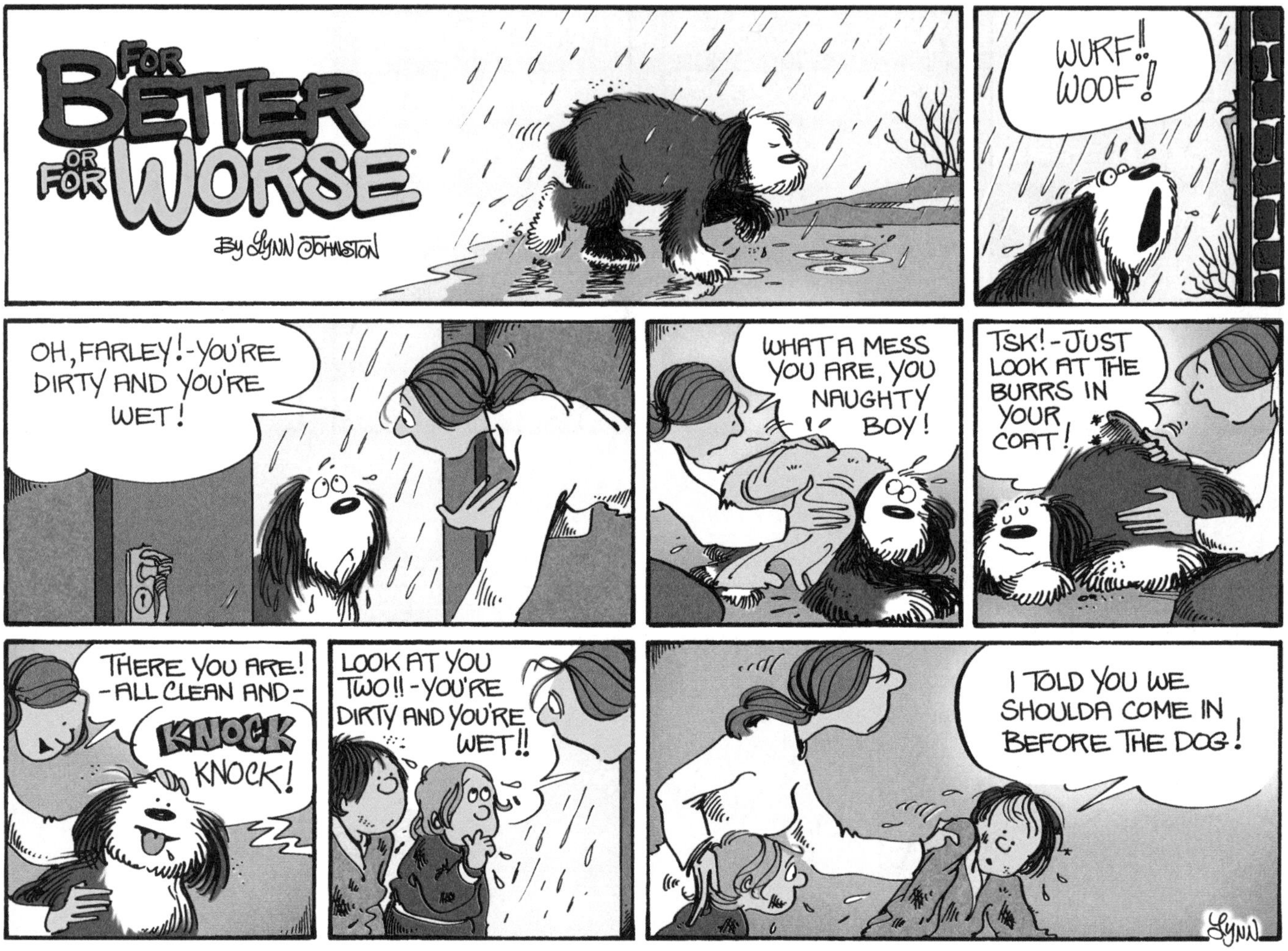
FOR BETTER OR FOR WORSE
BY LYNN JOHNSTON
WURF!! WOOF!
OH, FARLEY!-YOU'RE DIRTY AND YOU'RE WET!
WHAT A MESS YOU ARE, YOU NAUGHTY BOY!
TSK!-JUST LOOK AT THE BURRS IN YOUR COAT!
THERE YOU ARE! -ALL CLEAN AND-
KNOCK KNOCK!
LOOK AT YOU TWO!! -YOU'RE DIRTY AND YOU'RE WET!!
I TOLD YOU WE SHOULDA COME IN BEFORE THE DOG!
LYNN

Farley had great wide hairy feet, and every time he came indoors, I wiped them as best I could — knowing that dirt would come in anyway, and I'd just have to deal with it. When my kids came in carrying the same amount of flotsam, however, I bounced around, pointing at the inevitable grime and water, telling them in no uncertain terms that they had to be more careful and considerate and bla, bla, bla. …

Maybe we're so much more patient with dogs because they can't talk back!

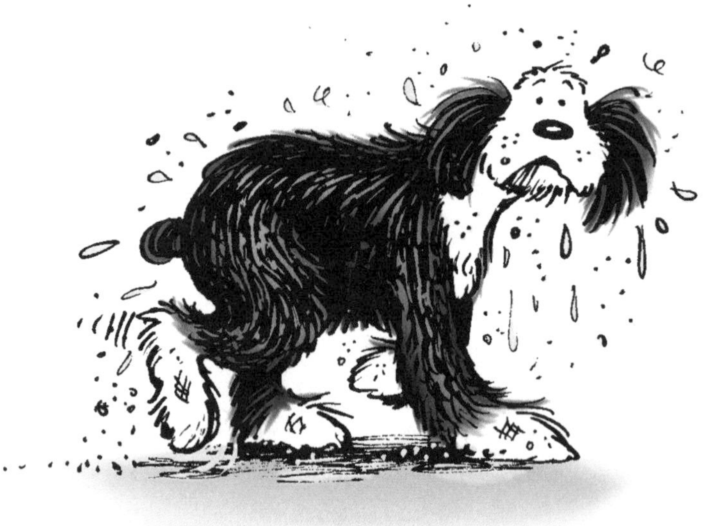

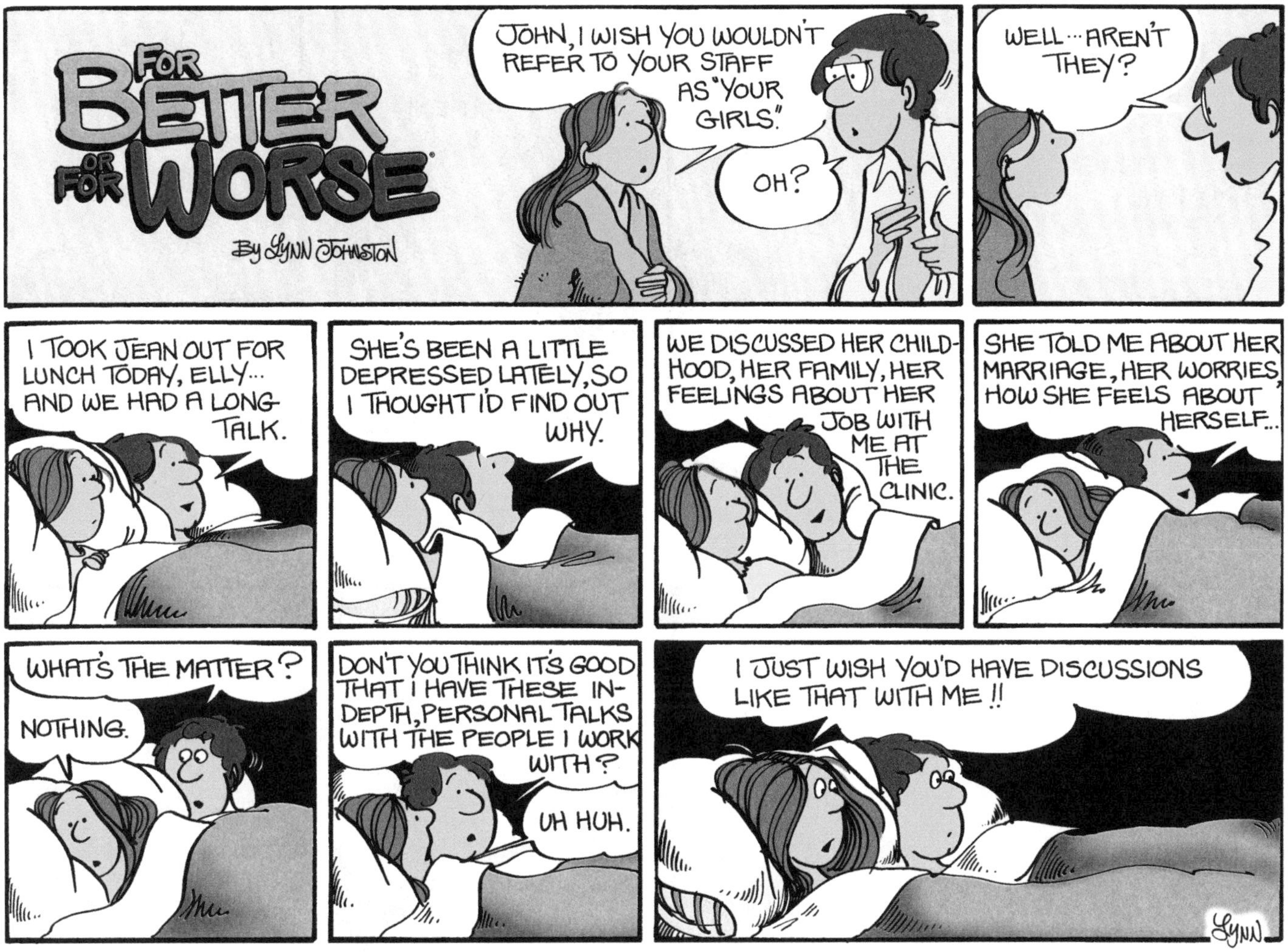
FOR BETTER OR FOR WORSE
BY LYNN JOHNSTON
JOHN, I WISH YOU WOULDN'T REFER TO YOUR STAFF AS "YOUR GIRLS."
OH?
WELL... AREN'T THEY?
I TOOK JEAN OUT FOR LUNCH TODAY, ELLY... AND WE HAD A LONG TALK.
SHE'S BEEN A LITTLE DEPRESSED LATELY, SO I THOUGHT I'D FIND OUT WHY.
WE DISCUSSED HER CHILDHOOD, HER FAMILY, HER FEELINGS ABOUT HER JOB WITH ME AT THE CLINIC.
SHE TOLD ME ABOUT HER MARRIAGE, HER WORRIES, HOW SHE FEELS ABOUT HERSELF...
WHAT'S THE MATTER?
NOTHING.
DON'T YOU THINK IT'S GOOD THAT I HAVE THESE IN-DEPTH, PERSONAL TALKS WITH THE PEOPLE I WORK WITH?
UH HUH.
I JUST WISH YOU'D HAVE DISCUSSIONS LIKE THAT WITH ME !!
LYNN

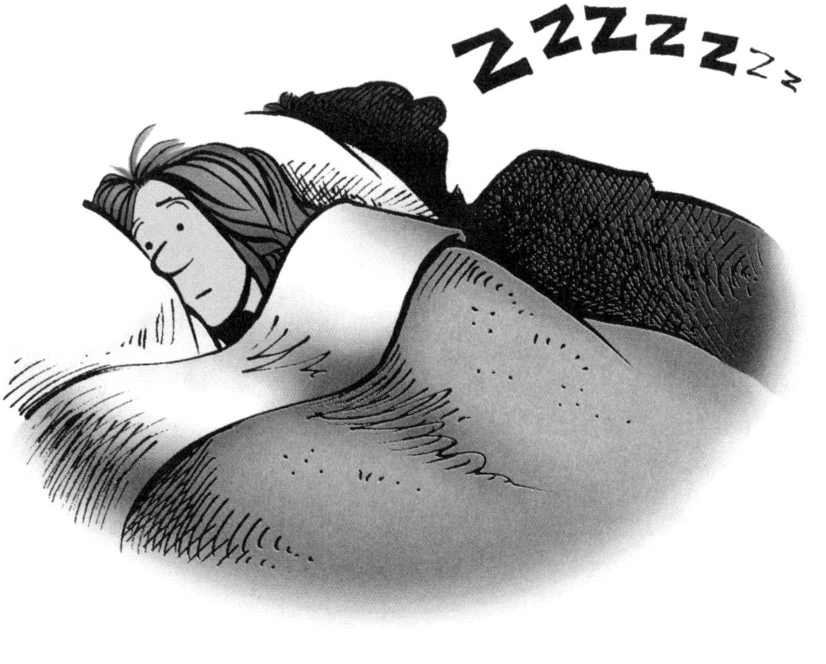
ZZZZZZzz

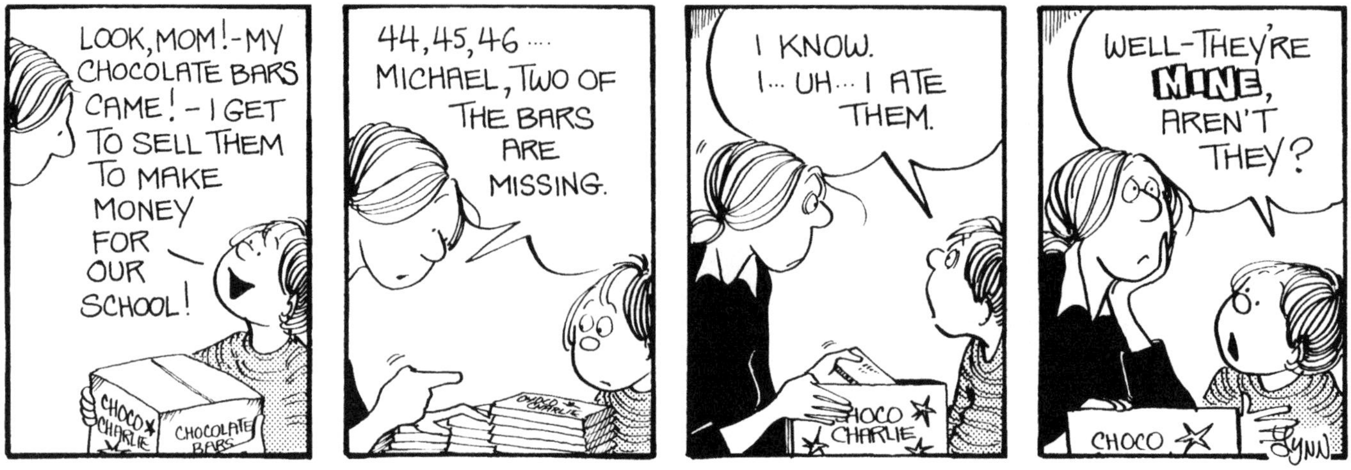
LOOK, MOM! - MY CHOCOLATE BARS CAME! - I GET TO SELL THEM TO MAKE MONEY FOR OUR SCHOOL!
CHOCO CHARLIE
CHOCOLATE BARS
44, 45, 46 ....
MICHAEL, TWO OF THE BARS ARE MISSING.
I KNOW. I... UH... I ATE THEM.
WELL - THEY'RE MINE, AREN'T THEY?
CHOCO
LYNN

Aaron did eat two bars and he then had to pay for them.

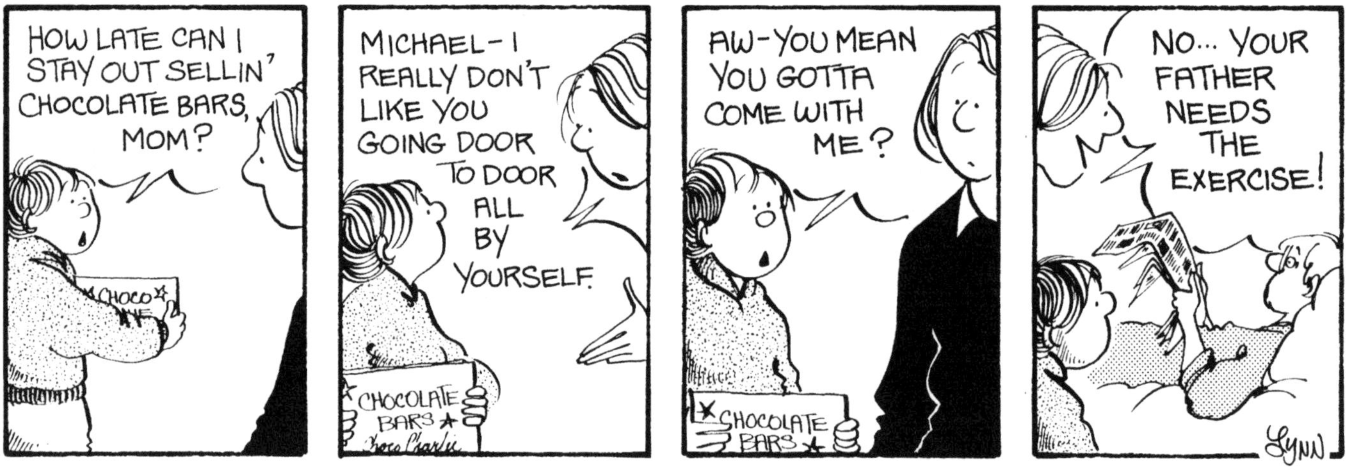
HOW LATE CAN I STAY OUT SELLIN' CHOCOLATE BARS, MOM?
CHOCO
MICHAEL - I REALLY DON'T LIKE YOU GOING DOOR TO DOOR ALL BY YOURSELF.
CHOCOLATE BARS
AW - YOU MEAN YOU GOTTA COME WITH ME?
CHOCOLATE BARS
NO... YOUR FATHER NEEDS THE EXERCISE!
LYNN

The number of times we were faced with the daunting task of selling chocolate bars door-to-door, was absurd. This subject brought in a lot of mail. Some folks sold them at work, but for us, a dental clinic was not the place to fundraise with candy!

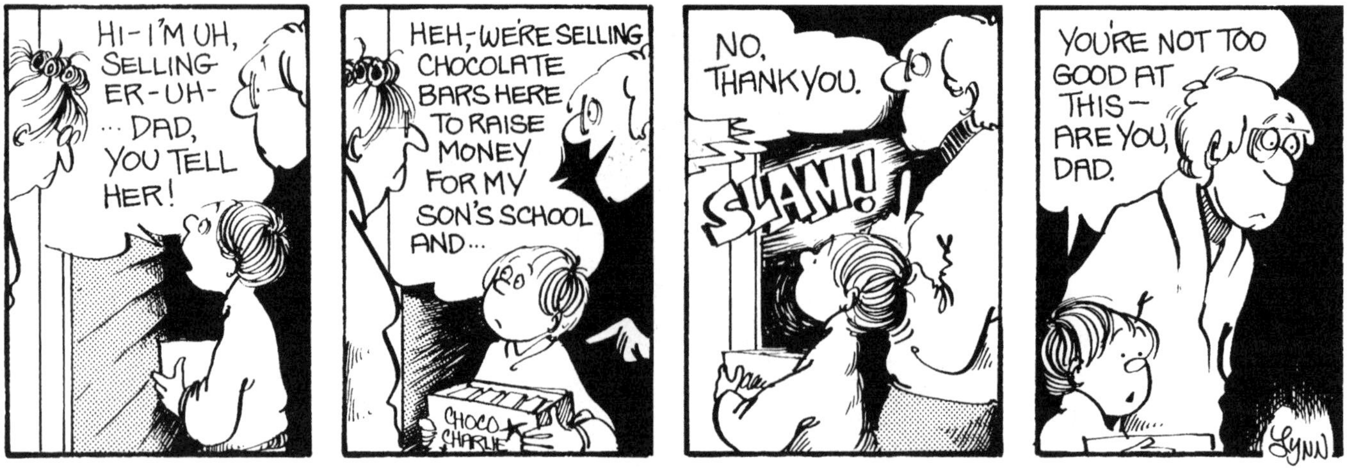
HI - I'M UH, SELLING ER - UH - ... DAD, YOU TELL HER!
HEH; WE'RE SELLING CHOCOLATE BARS HERE, TO RAISE MONEY FOR MY SON'S SCHOOL AND...
CHOCO CHARLIE
NO, THANK YOU.
SLAM!
YOU'RE NOT TOO GOOD AT THIS - ARE YOU, DAD.
LYNN

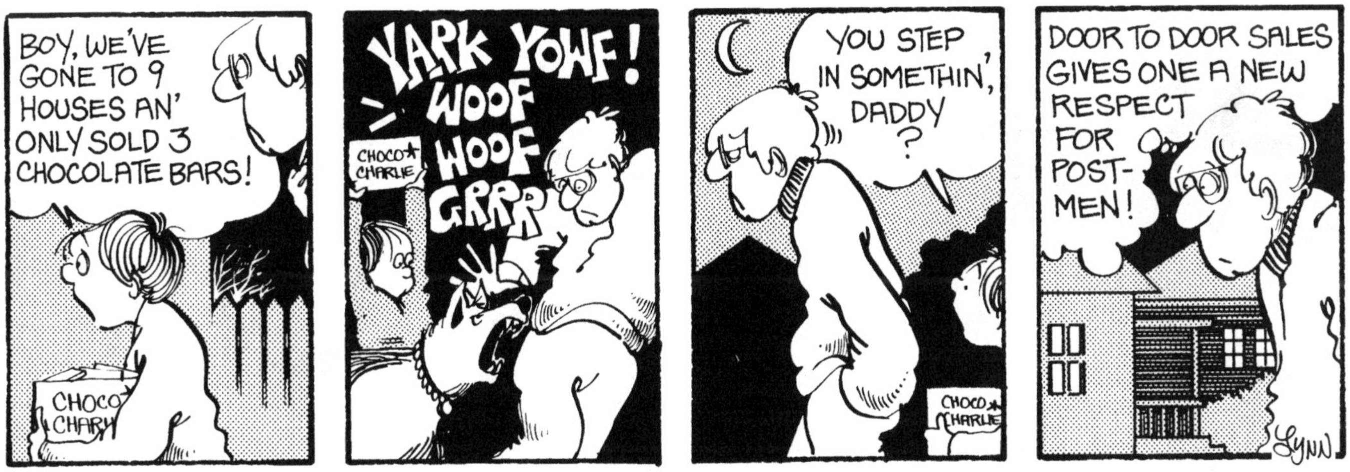
BOY, WE'VE GONE TO 9 HOUSES AN' ONLY SOLD 3 CHOCOLATE BARS!
YARK YOWF! WOOF WOOF GRRR
CHOCO CHARLIE
YOU STEP IN SOMETHIN', DADDY?
CHOCO CHARLIE
DOOR TO DOOR SALES GIVES ONE A NEW RESPECT FOR POST-MEN!
LYNN

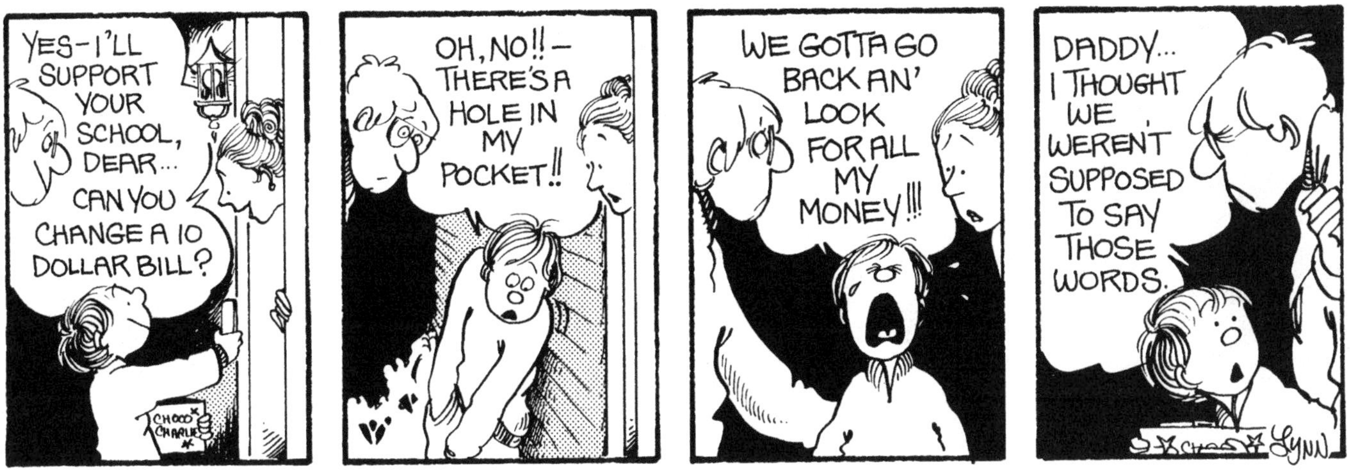
YES-I'LL SUPPORT YOUR SCHOOL, DEAR...
CAN YOU CHANGE A 10 DOLLAR BILL?
CHOCO CHARLIE
OH, NO!!– THERE'S A HOLE IN MY POCKET!!
WE GOTTA GO BACK AN' LOOK FOR ALL MY MONEY!!!
DADDY... I THOUGHT WE WEREN'T SUPPOSED TO SAY THOSE WORDS.
LYNN

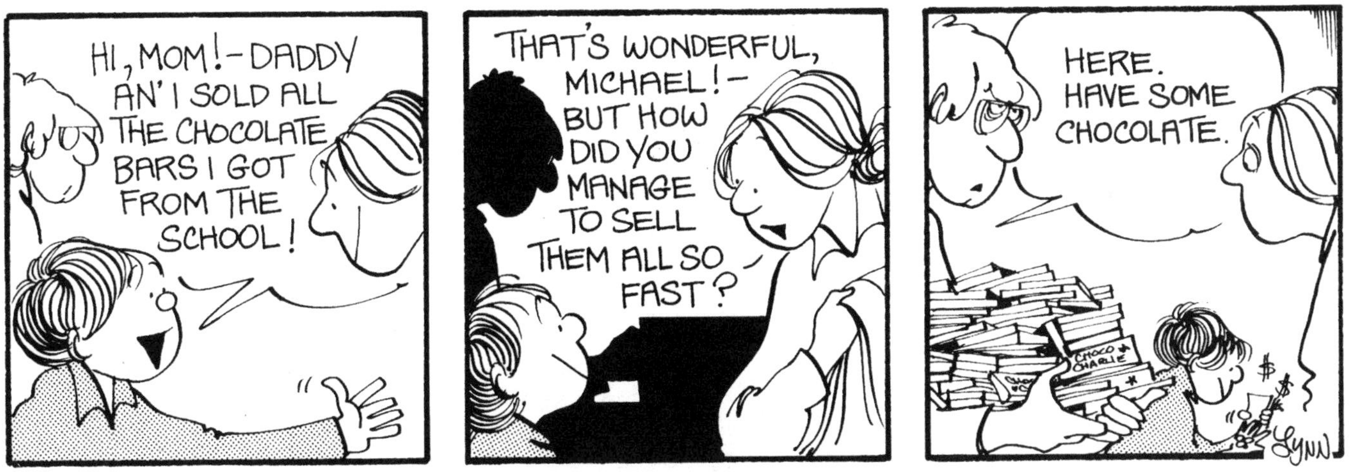
HI, MOM!–DADDY AN' I SOLD ALL THE CHOCOLATE BARS I GOT FROM THE SCHOOL!
THAT'S WONDERFUL, MICHAEL!– BUT HOW DID YOU MANAGE TO SELL THEM ALL SO FAST?
HERE. HAVE SOME CHOCOLATE.
CHOCO CHARLIE
LYNN

After Aaron was "taken" by big kids on the school bus who promised to pay him later, we ended up buying all of the chocolate bars. The next time there was a drive, we asked if we could just contribute directly to the school.

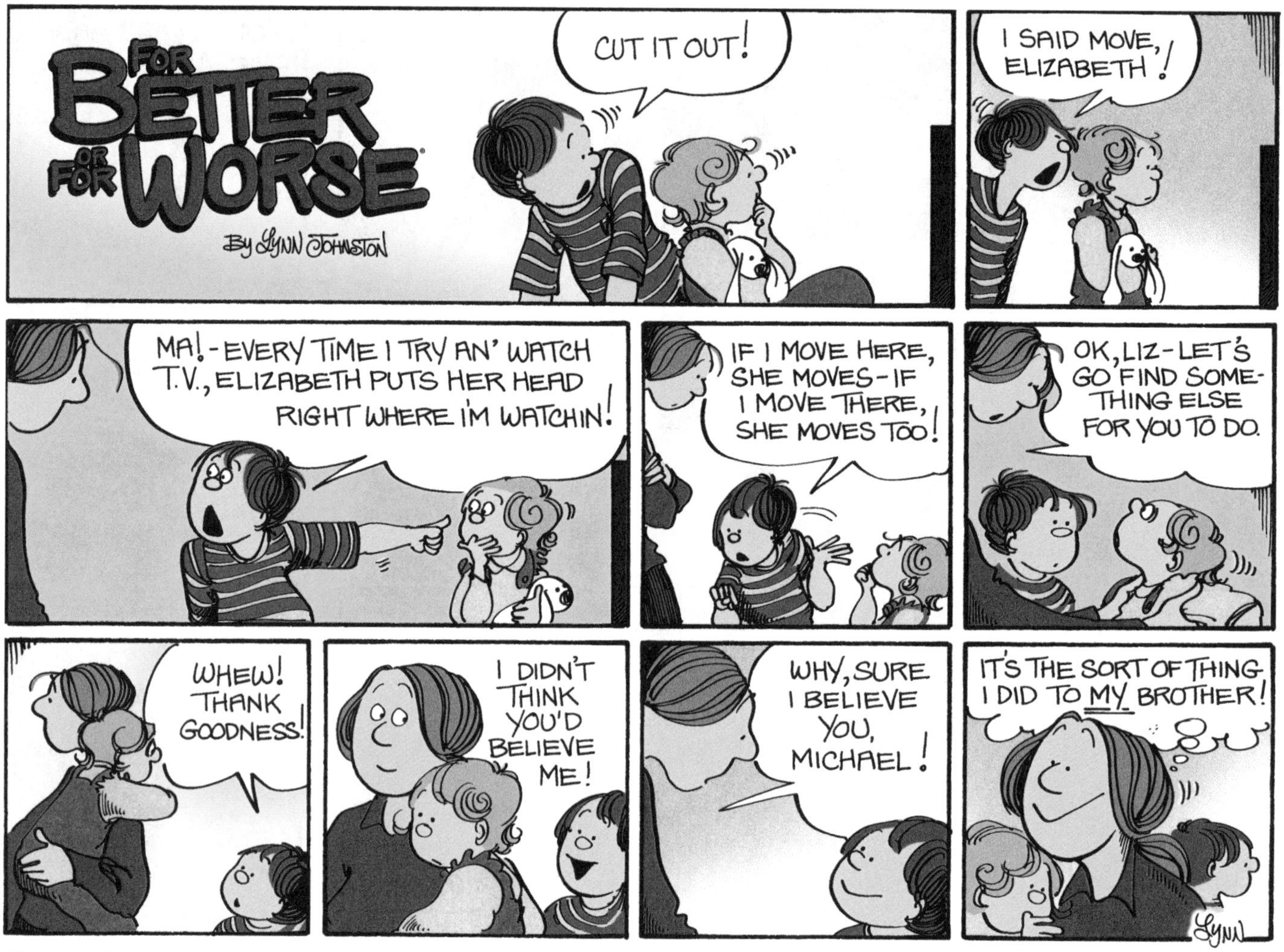
FOR BETTER OR FOR WORSE
By Lynn Johnston
CUT IT OUT!
I SAID MOVE, ELIZABETH!
MA! - EVERY TIME I TRY AN' WATCH T.V., ELIZABETH PUTS HER HEAD RIGHT WHERE I'M WATCHIN!
IF I MOVE HERE, SHE MOVES - IF I MOVE THERE, SHE MOVES TOO!
OK, LIZ - LET'S GO FIND SOMETHING ELSE FOR YOU TO DO.
WHEW! THANK GOODNESS!
I DIDN'T THINK YOU'D BELIEVE ME!
WHY, SURE I BELIEVE YOU, MICHAEL!
IT'S THE SORT OF THING I DID TO MY BROTHER!
Lynn

The punch line says it all!

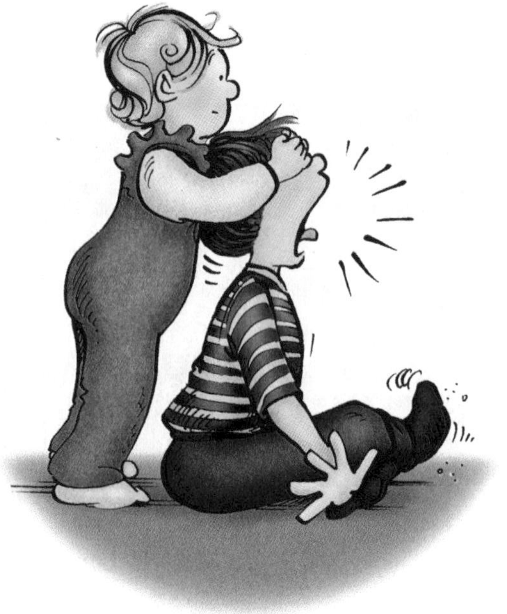

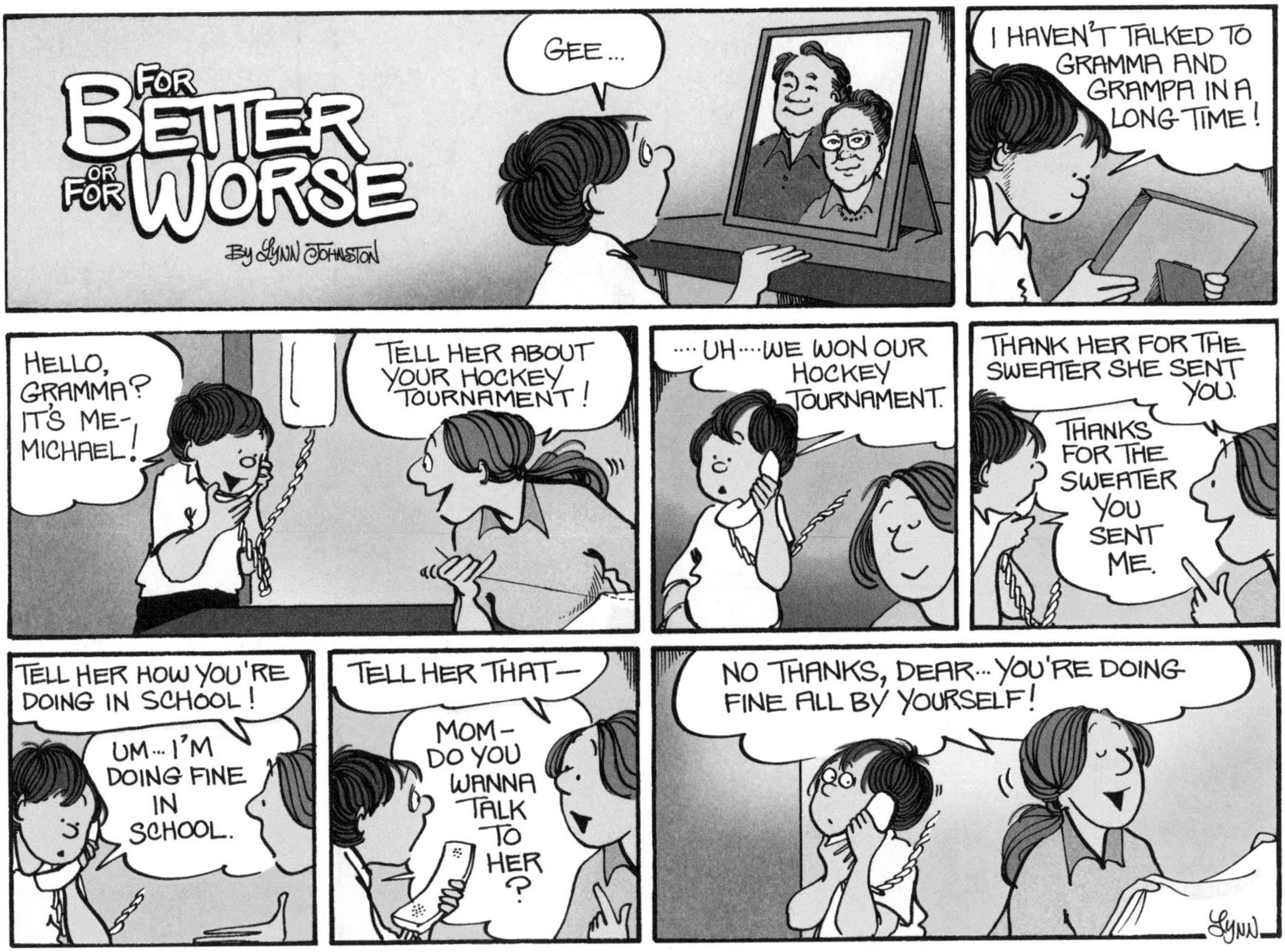
FOR BETTER OR FOR WORSE
BY LYNN JOHNSTON
GEE...
I HAVEN'T TALKED TO GRAMMA AND GRAMPA IN A LONG TIME!
HELLO, GRAMMA? IT'S ME- MICHAEL!
TELL HER ABOUT YOUR HOCKEY TOURNAMENT!
.... UH.... WE WON OUR HOCKEY TOURNAMENT.
THANK HER FOR THE SWEATER SHE SENT YOU.
THANKS FOR THE SWEATER YOU SENT ME.
TELL HER HOW YOU'RE DOING IN SCHOOL!
UM... I'M DOING FINE IN SCHOOL.
TELL HER THAT—
MOM- DO YOU WANNA TALK TO HER?
NO THANKS, DEAR... YOU'RE DOING FINE ALL BY YOURSELF!
LYNN

Because of the three-hour time difference between Ontario and Vancouver, we had a hard time making phone calls. Either my folks were having dinner (and hated to be disturbed) or we were. If I called during the day, the kids were out. In the afternoon, my folks were out. The odd time we had a conversation (at a good time for both parties) everyone wanted to talk at once!

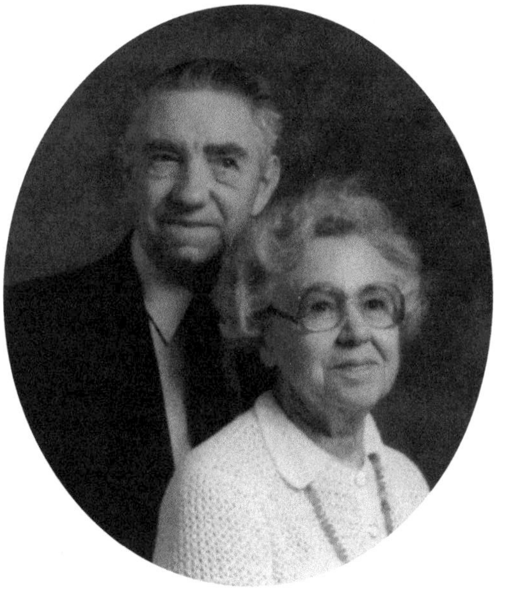

My dad and mom!

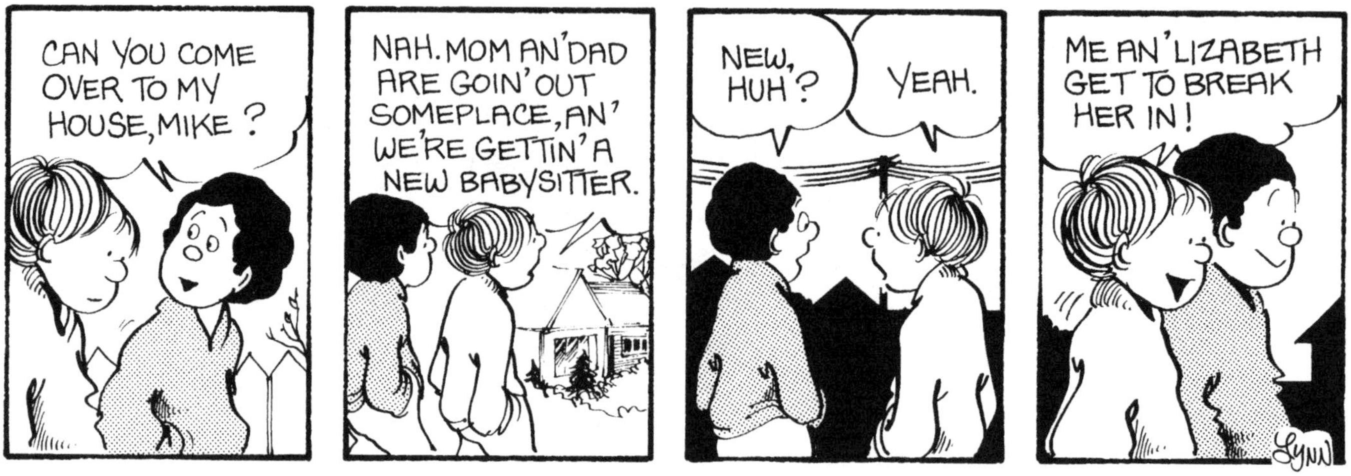
CAN YOU COME OVER TO MY HOUSE, MIKE ?
NAH. MOM AN'DAD ARE GOIN' OUT SOMEPLACE, AN' WE'RE GETTIN' A NEW BABYSITTER.
NEW, HUH ?
YEAH.
ME AN' LIZABETH GET TO BREAK HER IN !
LYNN

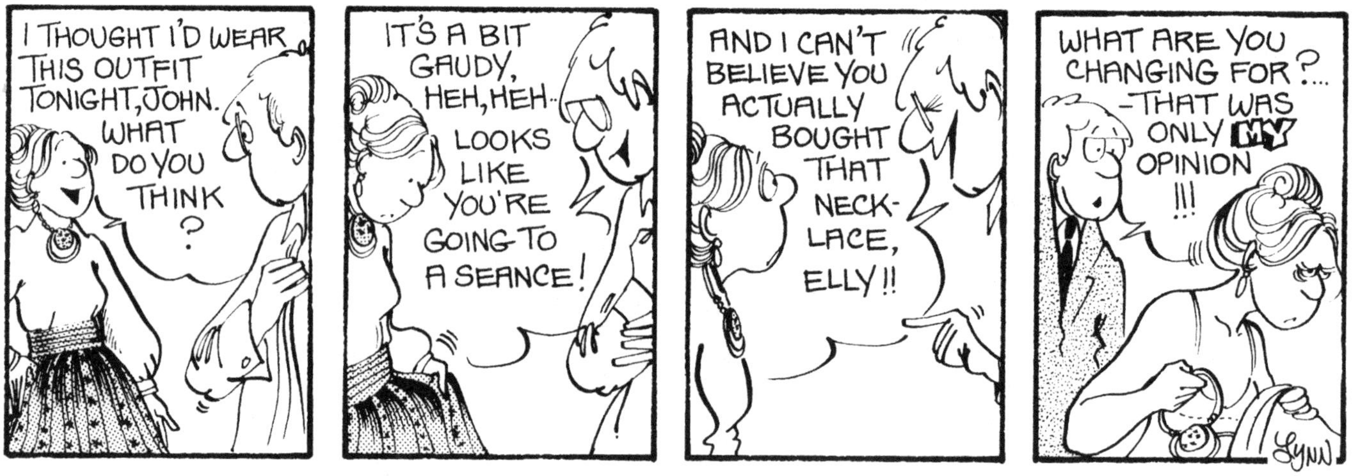
I THOUGHT I'D WEAR THIS OUTFIT TONIGHT, JOHN. WHAT DO YOU THINK ?
IT'S A BIT GAUDY, HEH, HEH.. LOOKS LIKE YOU'RE GOING TO A SEANCE !
AND I CAN'T BELIEVE YOU ACTUALLY BOUGHT THAT NECK-LACE, ELLY !!
WHAT ARE YOU CHANGING FOR ?... -THAT WAS ONLY MY OPINION !!!
LYNN

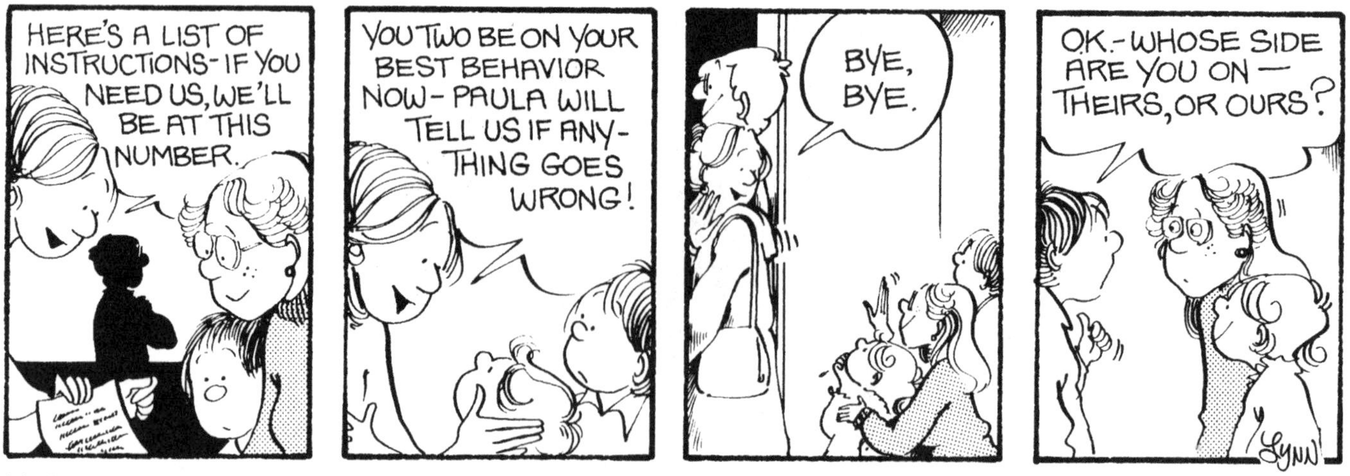
HERE'S A LIST OF INSTRUCTIONS- IF YOU NEED US, WE'LL BE AT THIS NUMBER.
YOU TWO BE ON YOUR BEST BEHAVIOR NOW- PAULA WILL TELL US IF ANY-THING GOES WRONG !
BYE, BYE.
O.K.- WHOSE SIDE ARE YOU ON — THEIRS, OR OURS ?
LYNN

My friend Loretta Clarke had four beautiful daughters who were wonderful babysitters. Lynn Lake was so small that we were always within walking distance from home. If there was an emergency, we could always return in a flash, but Loretta would often be called before we were and would solve the problem first!

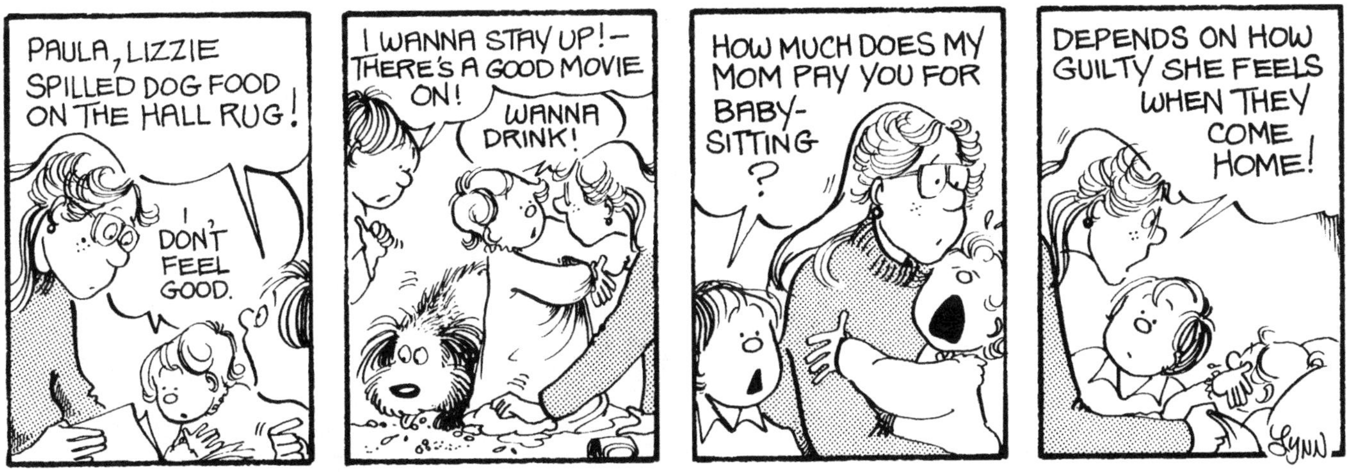
PAULA, LIZZIE SPILLED DOG FOOD ON THE HALL RUG!
I DON'T FEEL GOOD.
I WANNA STAY UP! – THERE'S A GOOD MOVIE ON!
WANNA DRINK!
HOW MUCH DOES MY MOM PAY YOU FOR BABY-SITTING?
DEPENDS ON HOW GUILTY SHE FEELS WHEN THEY COME HOME!
LYNN

This is from my own recollection as a teenage babysitter. I'd have to be a disciplinarian, but I was too young to be taken seriously, so I had to play two roles: the friendly big kid, and the tough cop who'd turn the kid in to the authorities if they didn't shape up. It wasn't an easy job sometimes — and I earned every cent I made.

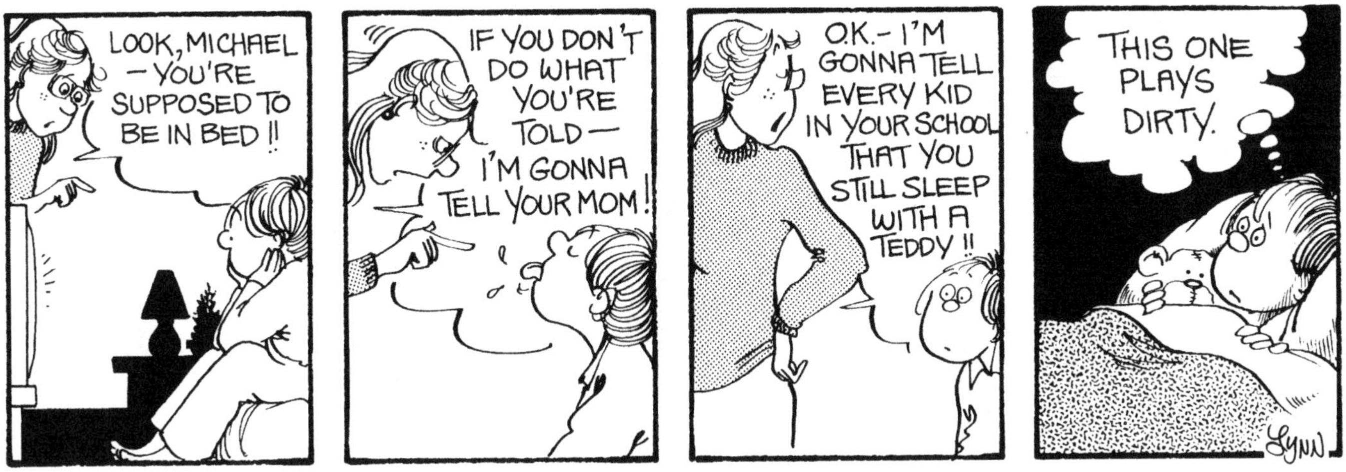
LOOK, MICHAEL – YOU'RE SUPPOSED TO BE IN BED!!
IF YOU DON'T DO WHAT YOU'RE TOLD – I'M GONNA TELL YOUR MOM!
O.K. – I'M GONNA TELL EVERY KID IN YOUR SCHOOL THAT YOU STILL SLEEP WITH A TEDDY!!
THIS ONE PLAYS DIRTY.
LYNN

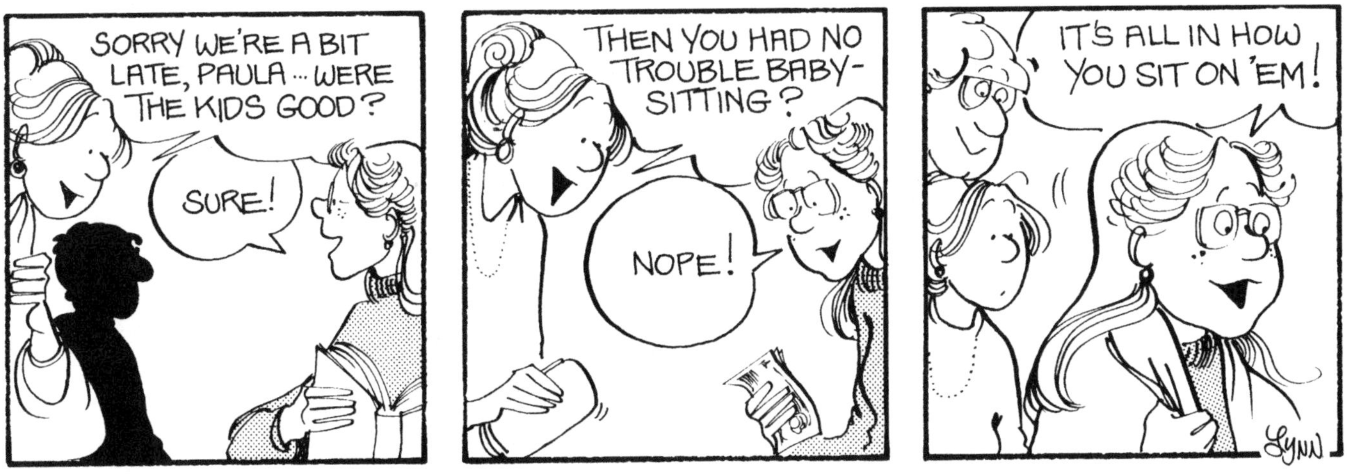
SORRY WE'RE A BIT LATE, PAULA ... WERE THE KIDS GOOD?
SURE!
THEN YOU HAD NO TROUBLE BABY-SITTING?
NOPE!
IT'S ALL IN HOW YOU SIT ON 'EM!
LYNN

I always thought the word "babysitter" was funny. As a teenager, I actually sat on one of my charges once in order to make a point ... and then bribed the little runt not to tell his parents!

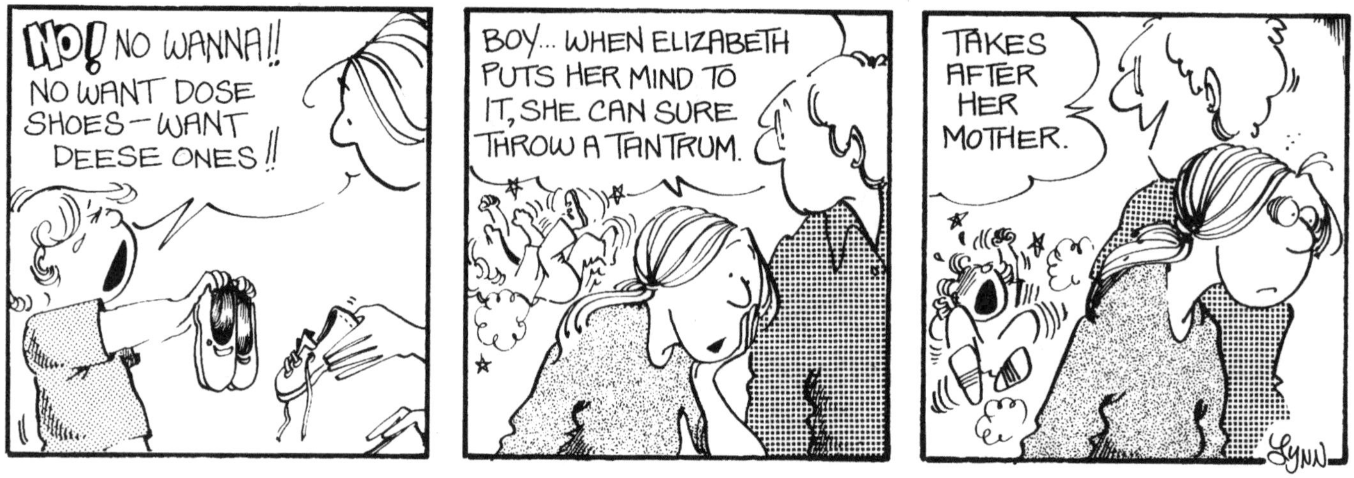
NO! NO WANNA!! NO WANT DOSE SHOES—WANT DEESE ONES!!
BOY... WHEN ELIZABETH PUTS HER MIND TO IT, SHE CAN SURE THROW A TANTRUM.
TAKES AFTER HER MOTHER.
LYNN

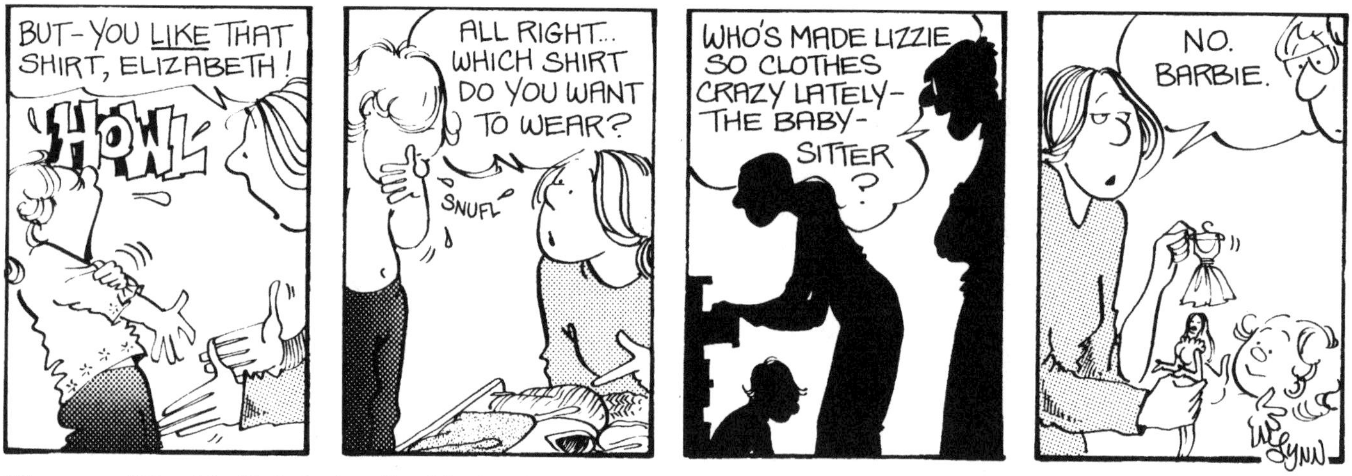
BUT-YOU LIKE THAT SHIRT, ELIZABETH!
HOWL
ALL RIGHT... WHICH SHIRT DO YOU WANT TO WEAR?
SNUFL
WHO'S MADE LIZZIE SO CLOTHES CRAZY LATELY-THE BABY-SITTER?
NO. BARBIE.
LYNN

Like many little girls, Katie had a pile of Barbie dolls, clothes, and paraphernalia. Her tantrums weren't about wearing pretty things, however, she just wanted to be comfortable. It was I who wanted her to look pretty!

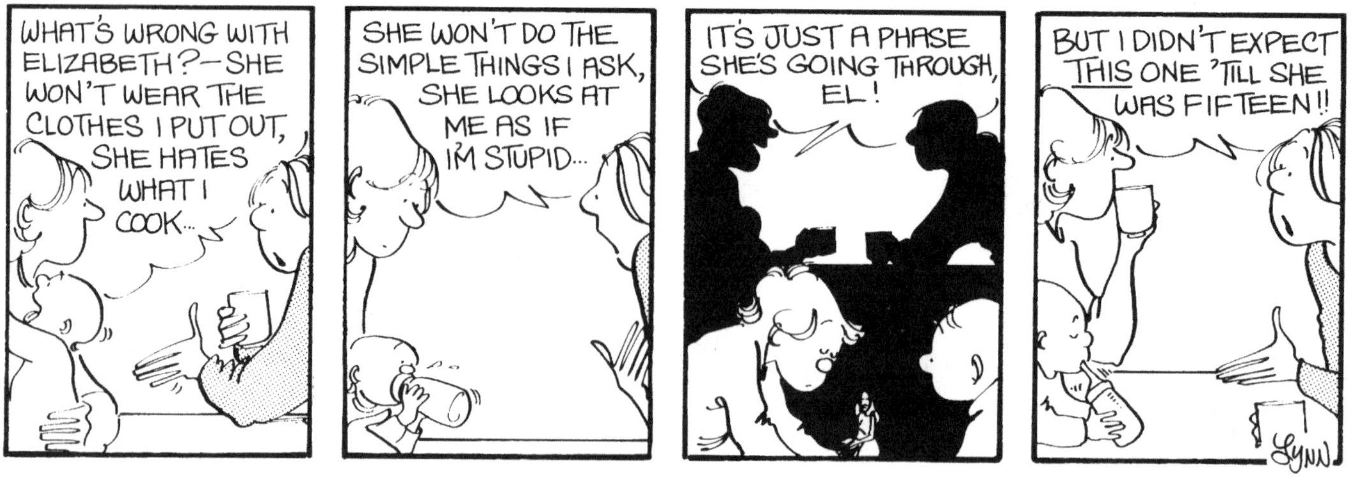
WHAT'S WRONG WITH ELIZABETH?—SHE WON'T WEAR THE CLOTHES I PUT OUT, SHE HATES WHAT I COOK...
SHE WON'T DO THE SIMPLE THINGS I ASK, SHE LOOKS AT ME AS IF I'M STUPID...
IT'S JUST A PHASE SHE'S GOING THROUGH, EL!
BUT I DIDN'T EXPECT THIS ONE 'TILL SHE WAS FIFTEEN!!
LYNN

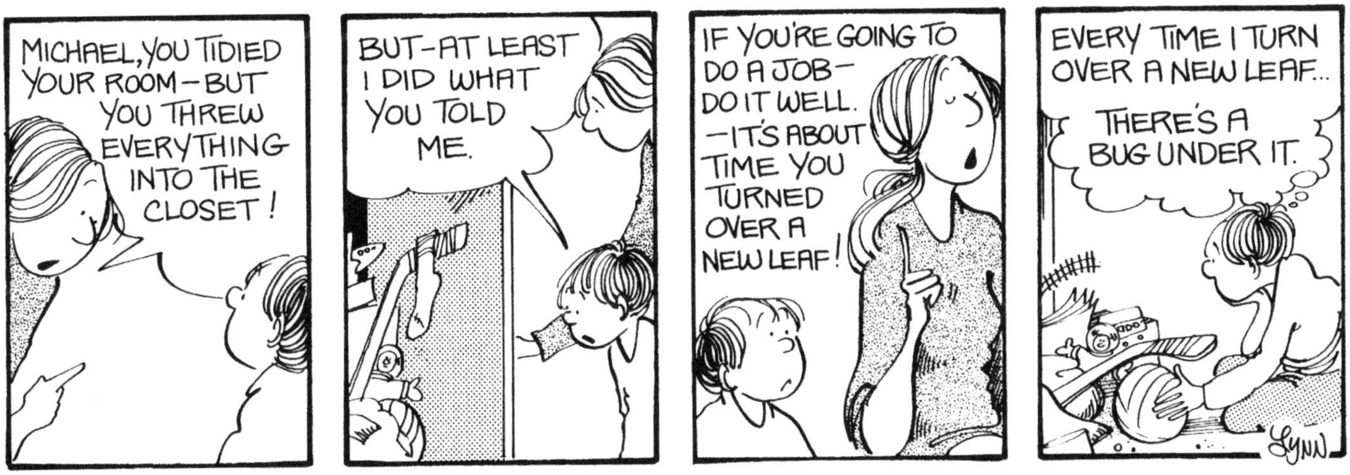
MICHAEL, YOU TIDIED YOUR ROOM – BUT YOU THREW EVERYTHING INTO THE CLOSET!
BUT – AT LEAST I DID WHAT YOU TOLD ME.
IF YOU'RE GOING TO DO A JOB – DO IT WELL. – IT'S ABOUT TIME YOU TURNED OVER A NEW LEAF!
EVERY TIME I TURN OVER A NEW LEAF...
THERE'S A BUG UNDER IT.
LYNN

I was happy with this punch line. In cartooning, a phrase like "turning over a new leaf" usually leads to a smart reply. You can also change the words: "A nerd in the hand is worth two in the bush." I always caution new cartoonists against using a familiar quote unless they are leading up to a zinger in the last panel.

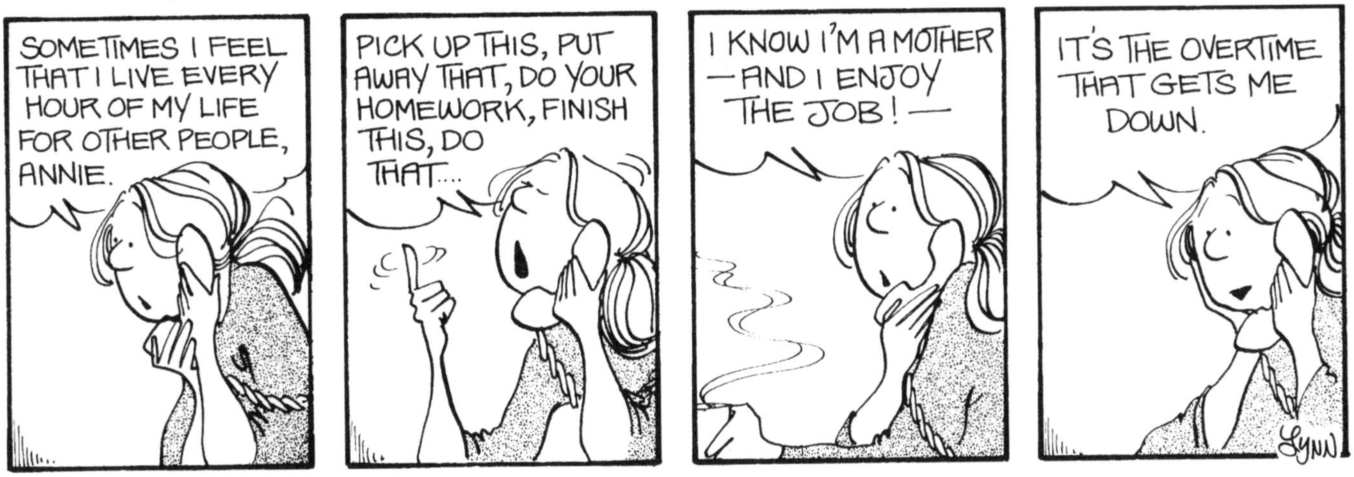
SOMETIMES I FEEL THAT I LIVE EVERY HOUR OF MY LIFE FOR OTHER PEOPLE, ANNIE.
PICK UP THIS, PUT AWAY THAT, DO YOUR HOMEWORK, FINISH THIS, DO THAT....
I KNOW I'M A MOTHER – AND I ENJOY THE JOB! –
IT'S THE OVERTIME THAT GETS ME DOWN.
LYNN

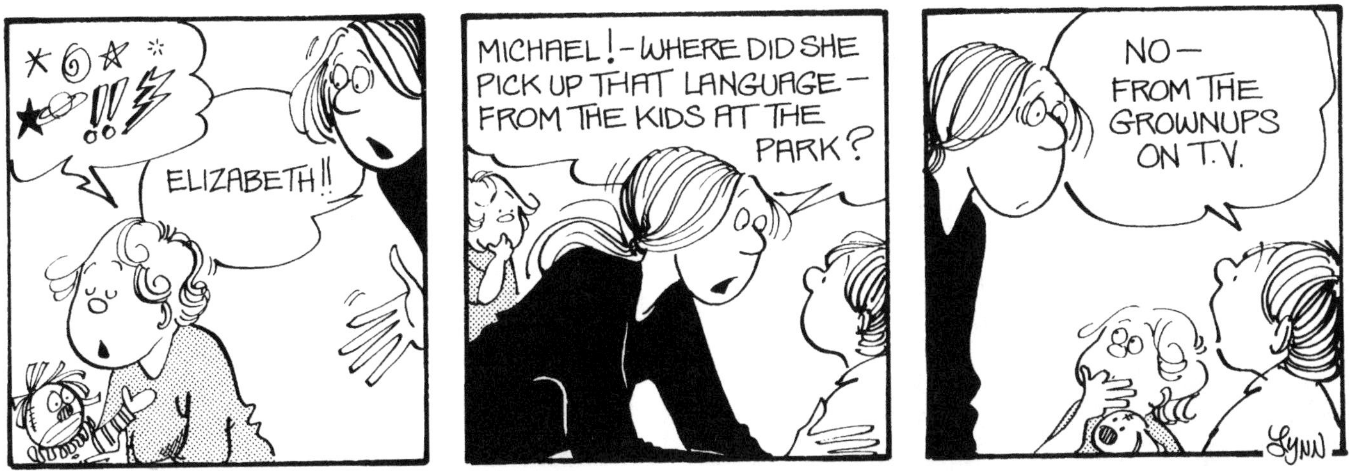
ELIZABETH!!
MICHAEL! – WHERE DID SHE PICK UP THAT LANGUAGE – FROM THE KIDS AT THE PARK?
NO – FROM THE GROWNUPS ON T.V.
LYNN

In my own small way, I took every opportunity to chastise the media for incorporating so much bad language into everything we see. Movies and television shows are filled with trashy material — this destroys our children's respect for our language, and for us, as well!

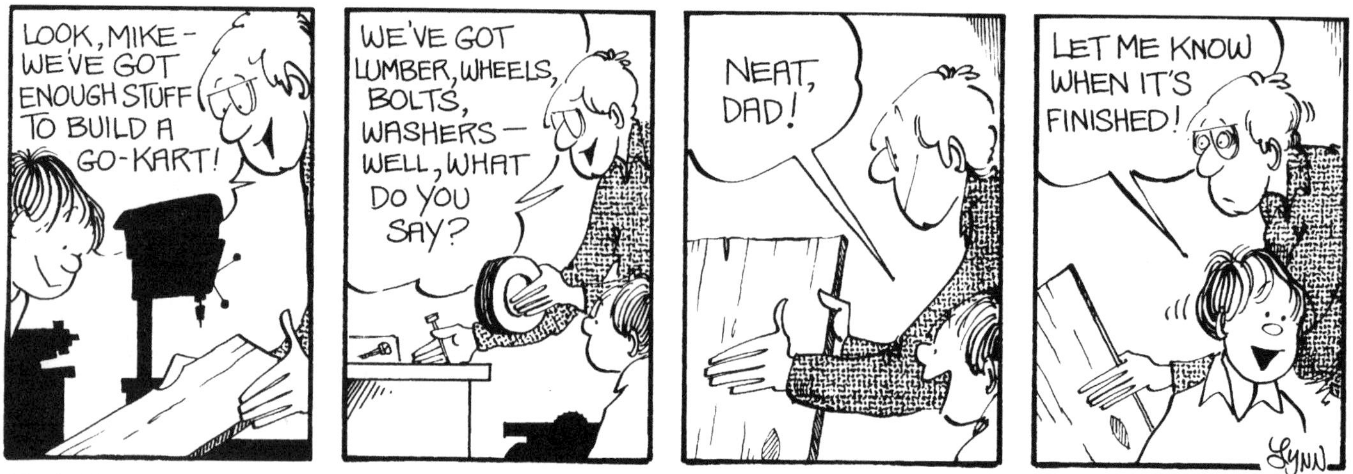
LOOK, MIKE- WE'VE GOT ENOUGH STUFF TO BUILD A GO-KART!
WE'VE GOT LUMBER, WHEELS, BOLTS, WASHERS- WELL, WHAT DO YOU SAY?
NEAT, DAD!
LET ME KNOW WHEN IT'S FINISHED!
LYNN

My dad built a go-kart for my brother and me out of roller skates, a long board, and a butter box. It was more like a scooter, but it went fast, and we were the envy of the neighbourhood.

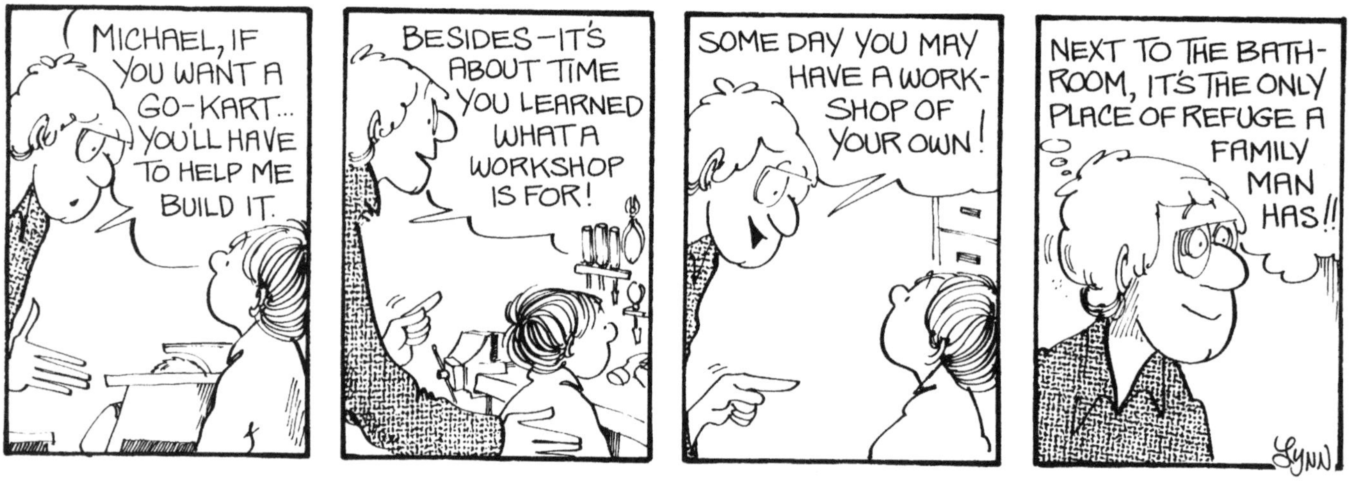
MICHAEL, IF YOU WANT A GO-KART... YOU'LL HAVE TO HELP ME BUILD IT.
BESIDES-IT'S ABOUT TIME YOU LEARNED WHAT A WORKSHOP IS FOR!
SOME DAY YOU MAY HAVE A WORK-SHOP OF YOUR OWN!
NEXT TO THE BATH-ROOM, IT'S THE ONLY PLACE OF REFUGE A FAMILY MAN HAS!!
LYNN

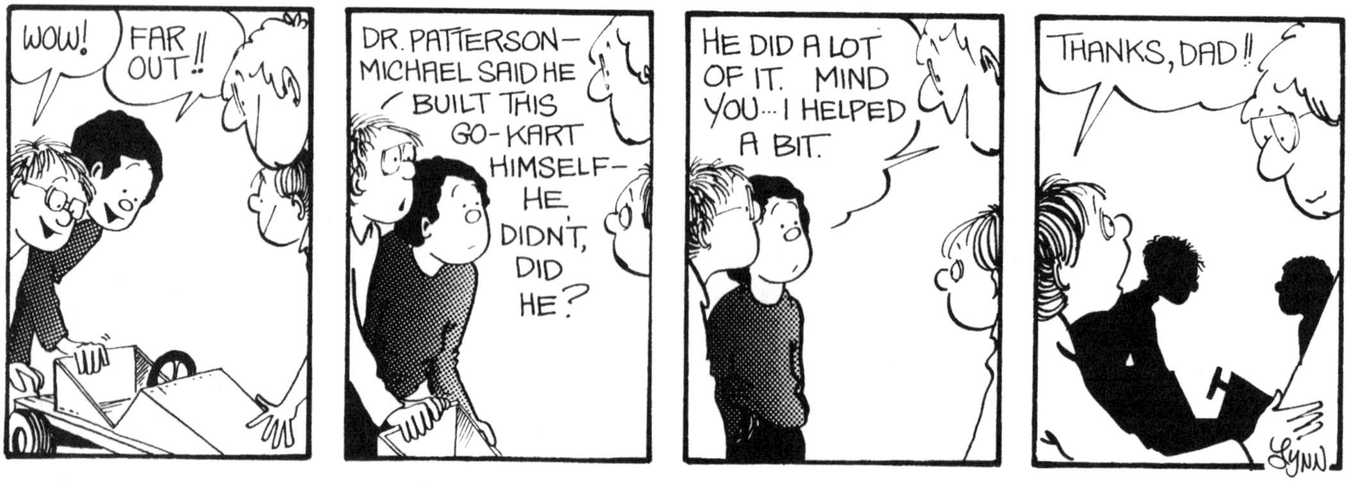
WOW!
FAR OUT!!
DR. PATTERSON- MICHAEL SAID HE BUILT THIS GO-KART HIMSELF- HE DIDN'T, DID HE?
HE DID A LOT OF IT. MIND YOU... I HELPED A BIT.
THANKS, DAD!!
LYNN

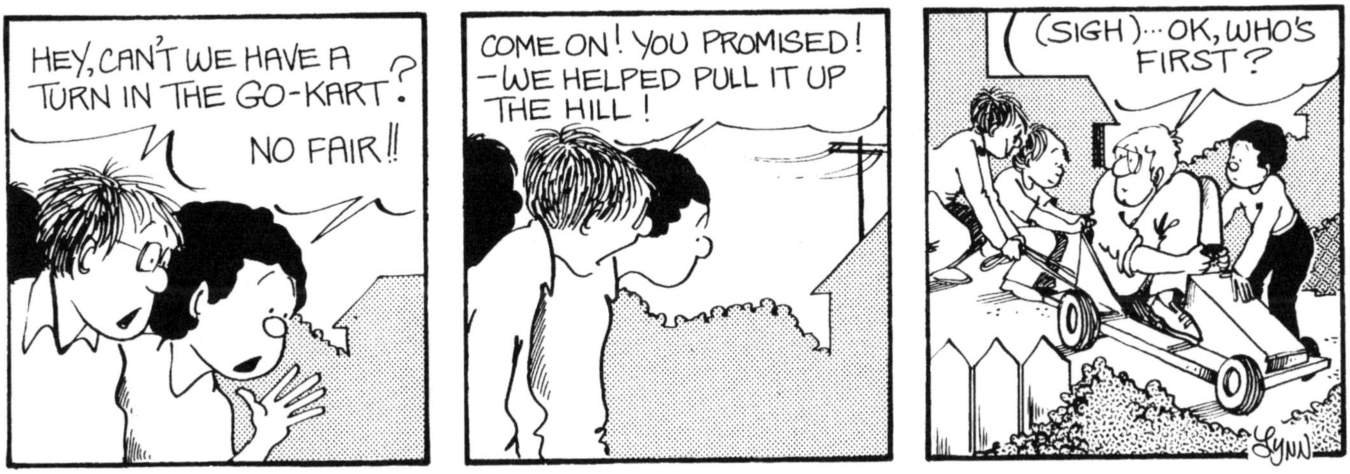
HEY, CAN'T WE HAVE A TURN IN THE GO-KART?
NO FAIR!!
COME ON! YOU PROMISED! –WE HELPED PULL IT UP THE HILL!
(SIGH)... OK, WHO'S FIRST?
LYNN

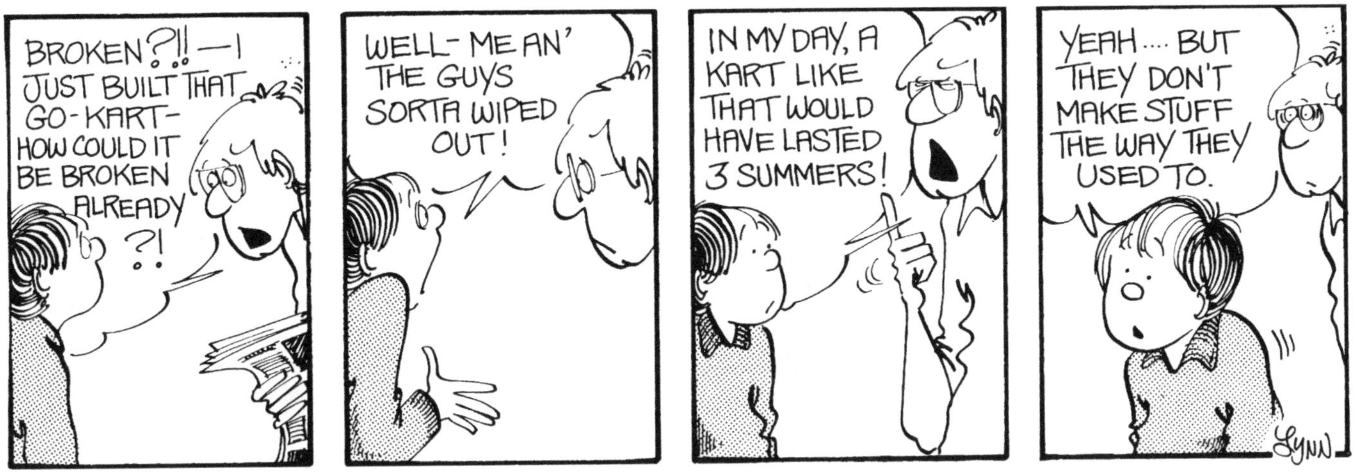
BROKEN?!! —I JUST BUILT THAT GO-KART– HOW COULD IT BE BROKEN ALREADY?!
WELL– ME AN' THE GUYS SORTA WIPED OUT!
IN MY DAY, A KART LIKE THAT WOULD HAVE LASTED 3 SUMMERS!
YEAH.... BUT THEY DON'T MAKE STUFF THE WAY THEY USED TO.
LYNN

Later, Alan decided to build a more conventional go-kart. He took apart our old baby carriage and used the wheels. This looked good, but the axles and the wheels were too flimsy to withstand our abuse. Mom was angered by the destruction of the carriage, so he removed the carriage wheels and took apart our wagon instead!

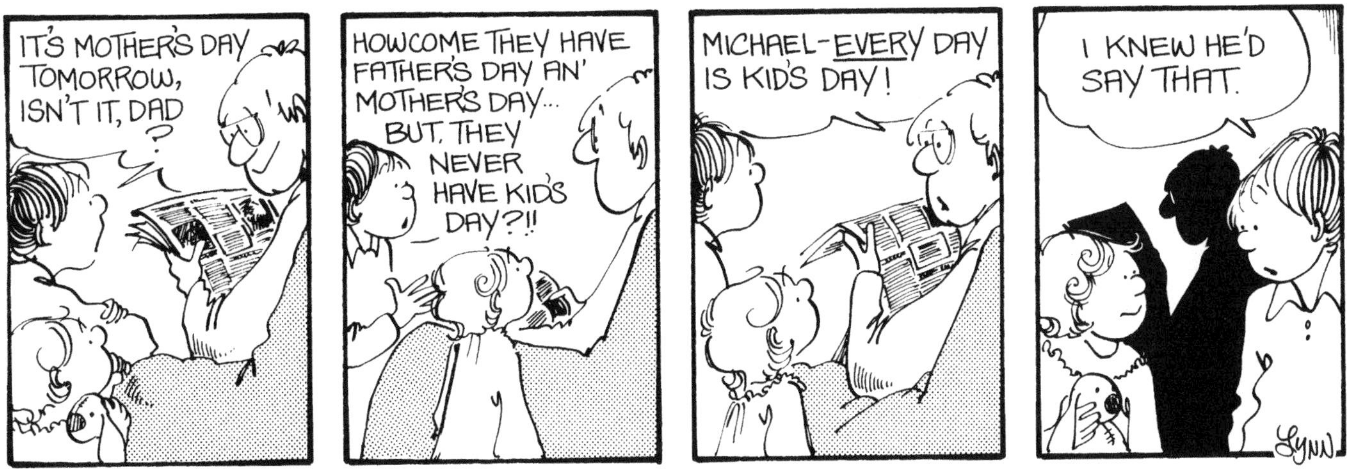
IT'S MOTHER'S DAY TOMORROW, ISN'T IT, DAD?
HOWCOME THEY HAVE FATHER'S DAY AN' MOTHER'S DAY... BUT, THEY NEVER HAVE KID'S DAY?!!
MICHAEL–EVERY DAY IS KID'S DAY!
I KNEW HE'D SAY THAT.
LYNN

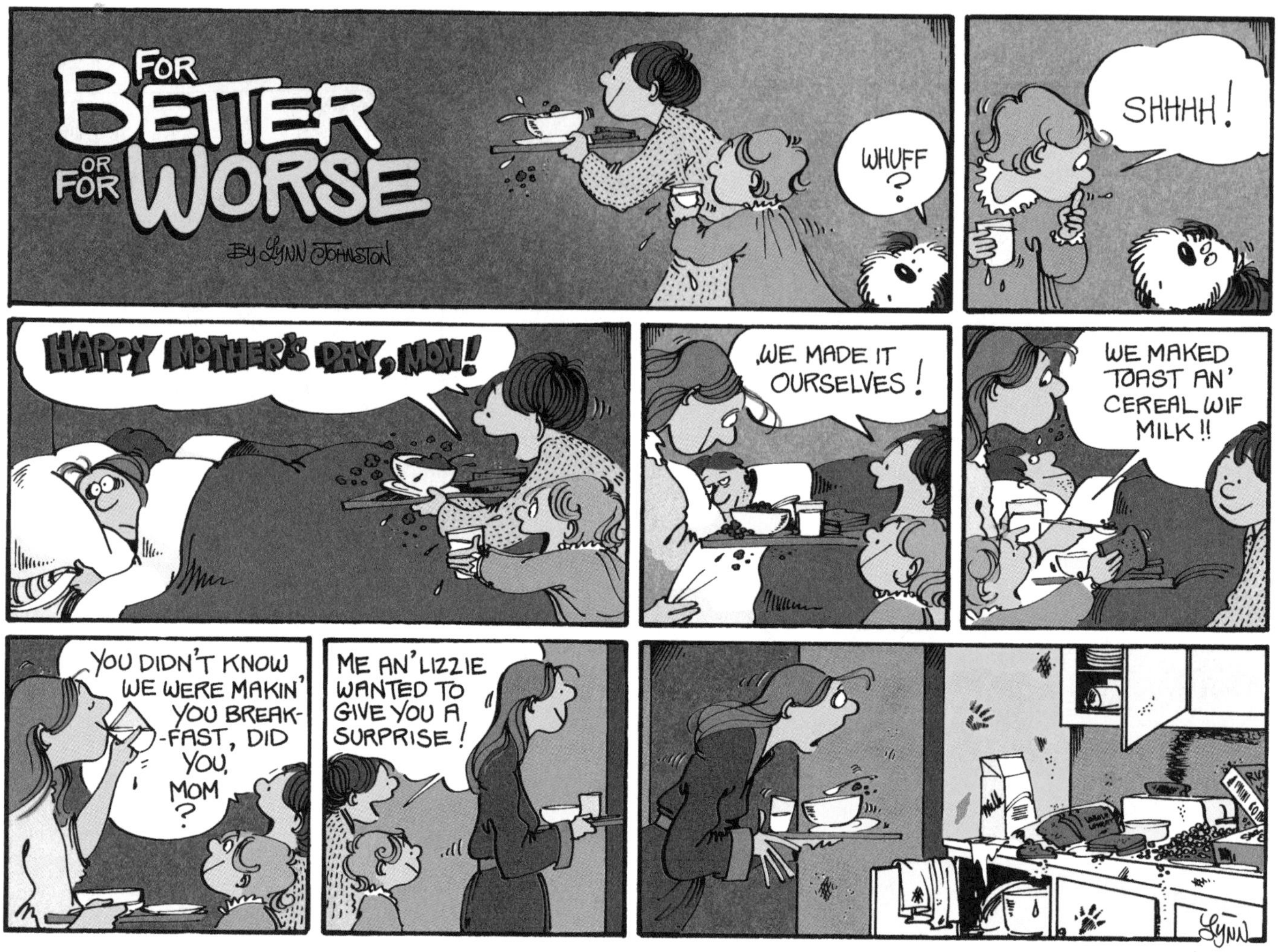
FOR BETTER OR FOR WORSE
BY LYNN JOHNSTON
WHUFF ?
SHHHH!
HAPPY MOTHER'S DAY, MOM!
WE MADE IT OURSELVES!
WE MAKED TOAST AN' CEREAL WIF MILK!!
YOU DIDN'T KNOW WE WERE MAKIN' YOU BREAK--FAST, DID YOU, MOM ?
ME AN' LIZZIE WANTED TO GIVE YOU A SURPRISE!
LYNN

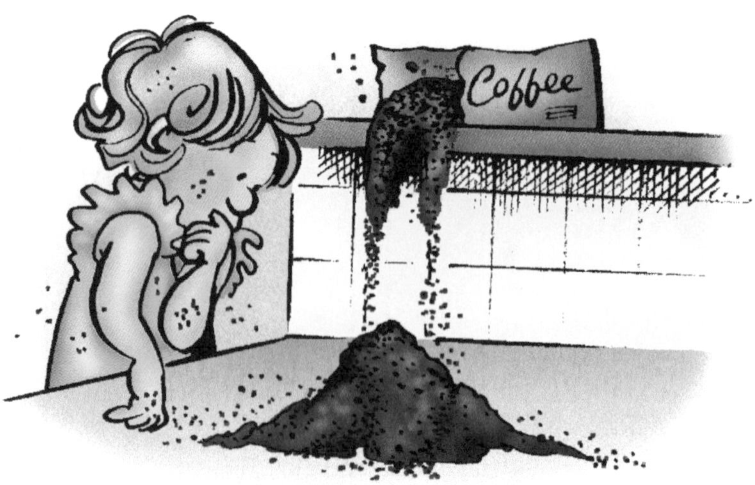
Coffee

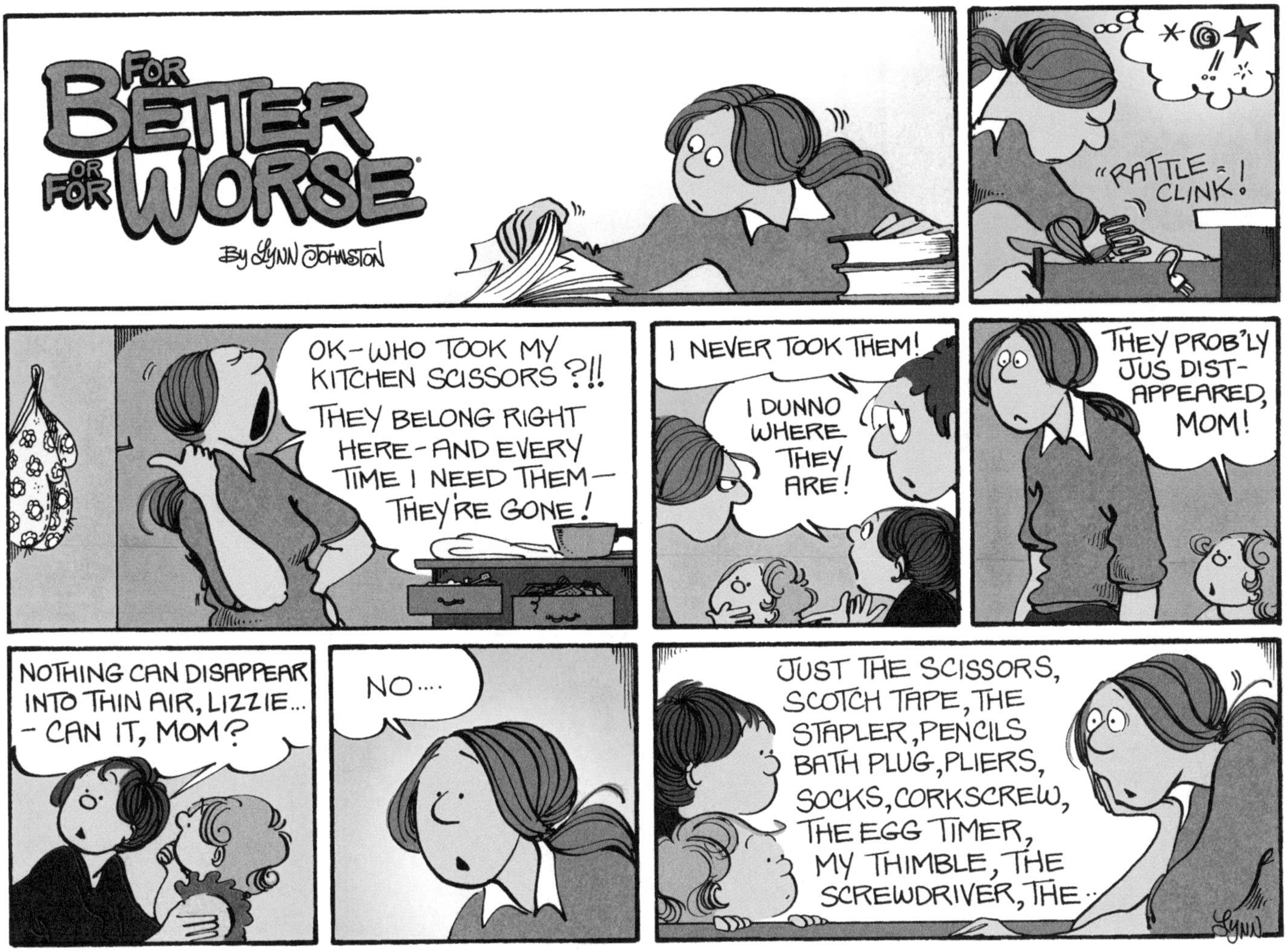
FOR BETTER OR FOR WORSE
BY LYNN JOHNSTON
"RATTLE = CLINK!
OK-WHO TOOK MY KITCHEN SCISSORS ?!!
THEY BELONG RIGHT HERE-AND EVERY TIME I NEED THEM- THEY'RE GONE!
I NEVER TOOK THEM!
I DUNNO WHERE THEY ARE!
THEY PROB'LY JUS DIST-APPEARED, MOM!
NOTHING CAN DISAPPEAR INTO THIN AIR, LIZZIE... - CAN IT, MOM?
NO....
JUST THE SCISSORS, SCOTCH TAPE, THE STAPLER, PENCILS BATH PLUG, PLIERS, SOCKS, CORKSCREW, THE EGG TIMER, MY THIMBLE, THE SCREWDRIVER, THE..
LYNN

I could never find my kitchen scissors. After looking high and low, I would buy a new pair, and eventually those would disappear, too. This scenario was typical of a time when Kate and Aaron were small and things ended up in the garden, at the neighbours', or in the workshop — never to be seen again.

When Katie was a teenager, I made a declaration one day: She was grounded until she cleaned her room. Begrudgingly, she did so. The result? No fewer than nine pairs of scissors were discovered among the debris. The moral of the story? … A string on the kitchen scissors might look silly, but you'll always know where to find them!

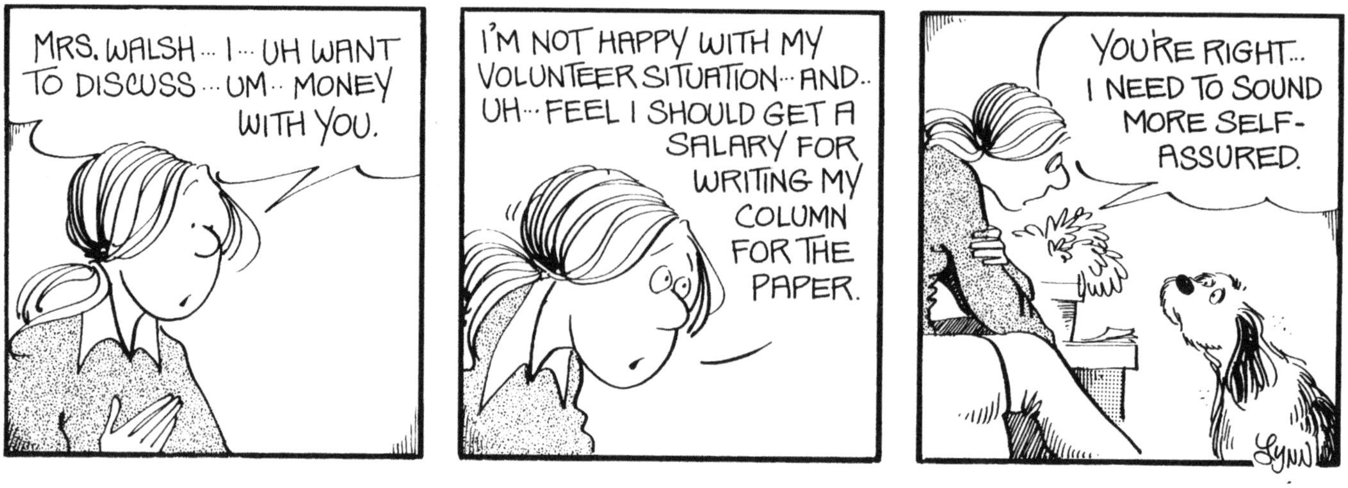
MRS. WALSH... I... UH WANT TO DISCUSS... UM.. MONEY WITH YOU.
I'M NOT HAPPY WITH MY VOLUNTEER SITUATION... AND.. UH... FEEL I SHOULD GET A SALARY FOR WRITING MY COLUMN FOR THE PAPER.
YOU'RE RIGHT... I NEED TO SOUND MORE SELF-ASSURED.
LYNN

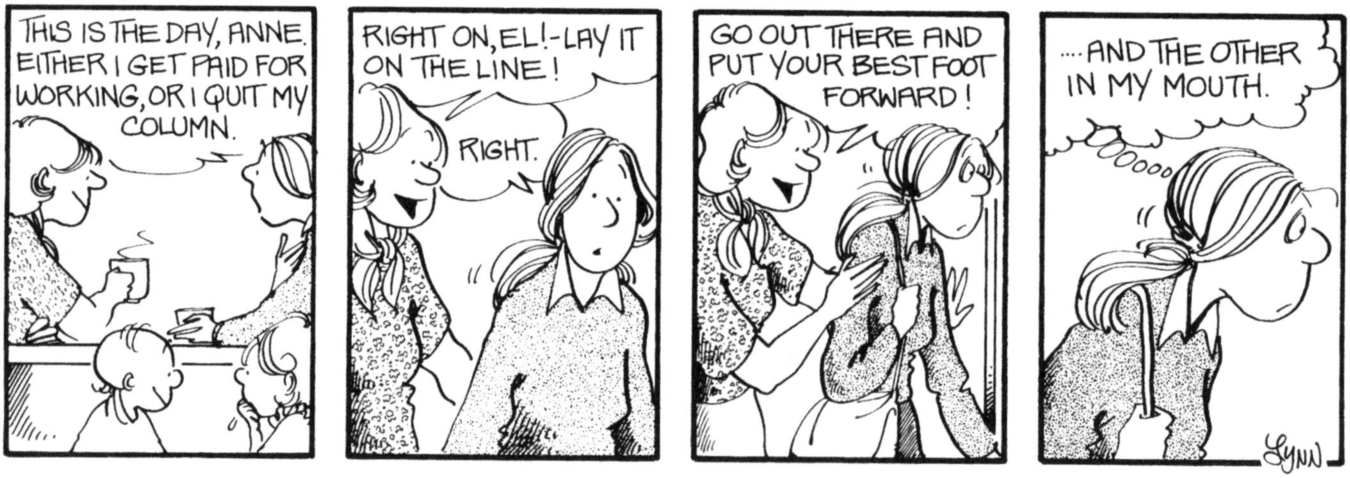
THIS IS THE DAY, ANNE. EITHER I GET PAID FOR WORKING, OR I QUIT MY COLUMN.
RIGHT ON, EL!-LAY IT ON THE LINE!
RIGHT.
GO OUT THERE AND PUT YOUR BEST FOOT FORWARD!
....AND THE OTHER IN MY MOUTH.
LYNN

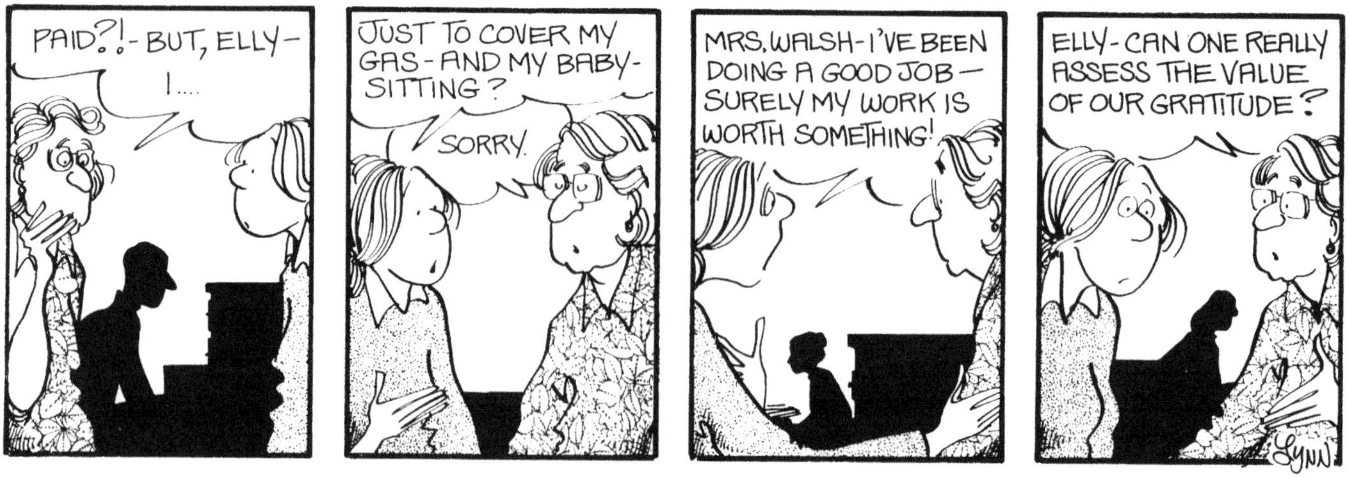
PAID?!- BUT, ELLY- I....
JUST TO COVER MY GAS - AND MY BABY-SITTING?
SORRY.
MRS. WALSH - I'VE BEEN DOING A GOOD JOB - SURELY MY WORK IS WORTH SOMETHING!
ELLY- CAN ONE REALLY ASSESS THE VALUE OF OUR GRATITUDE?
LYNN

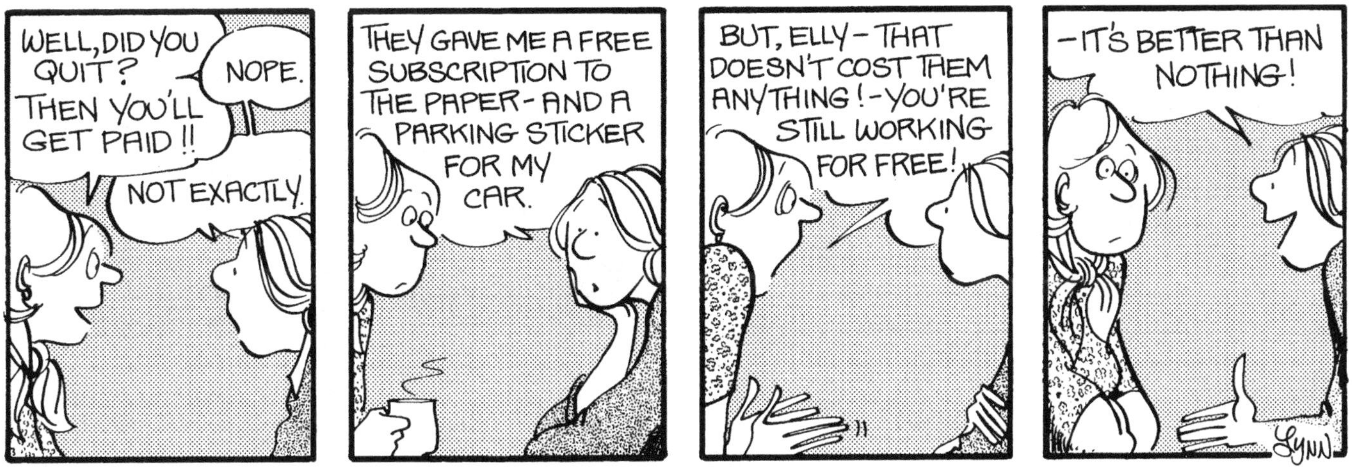
WELL, DID YOU QUIT? THEN YOU'LL GET PAID !!
NOPE.
NOT EXACTLY.
THEY GAVE ME A FREE SUBSCRIPTION TO THE PAPER - AND A PARKING STICKER FOR MY CAR.
BUT, ELLY - THAT DOESN'T COST THEM ANYTHING! - YOU'RE STILL WORKING FOR FREE!
- IT'S BETTER THAN NOTHING!
LYNN

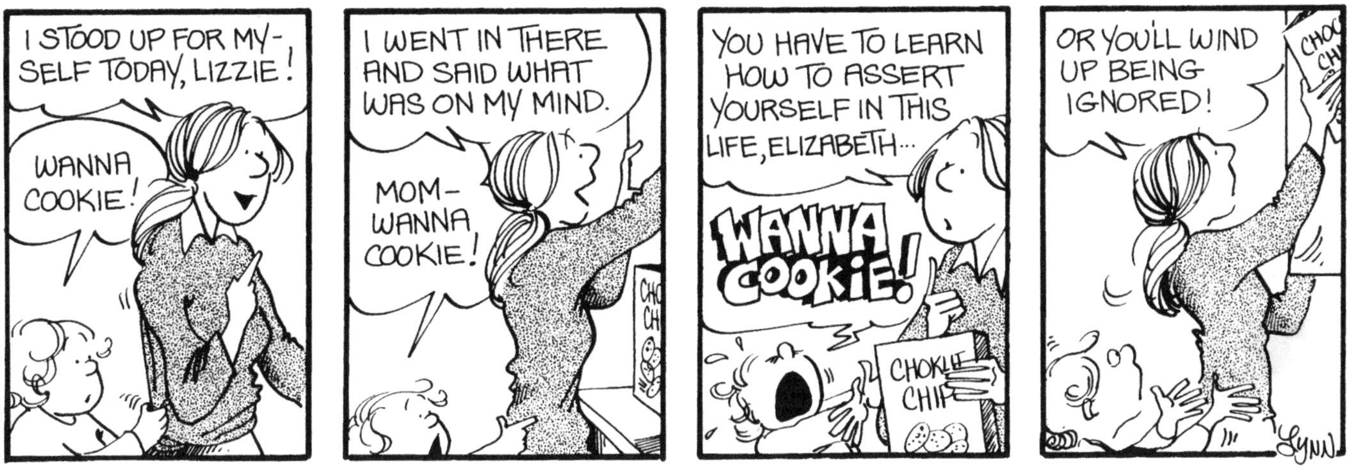
I STOOD UP FOR MY-SELF TODAY, LIZZIE!
WANNA COOKIE!
I WENT IN THERE AND SAID WHAT WAS ON MY MIND.
MOM-WANNA COOKIE!
YOU HAVE TO LEARN HOW TO ASSERT YOURSELF IN THIS LIFE, ELIZABETH...
WANNA COOKIE!
CHOKLIT CHIP
OR YOU'LL WIND UP BEING IGNORED!
LYNN

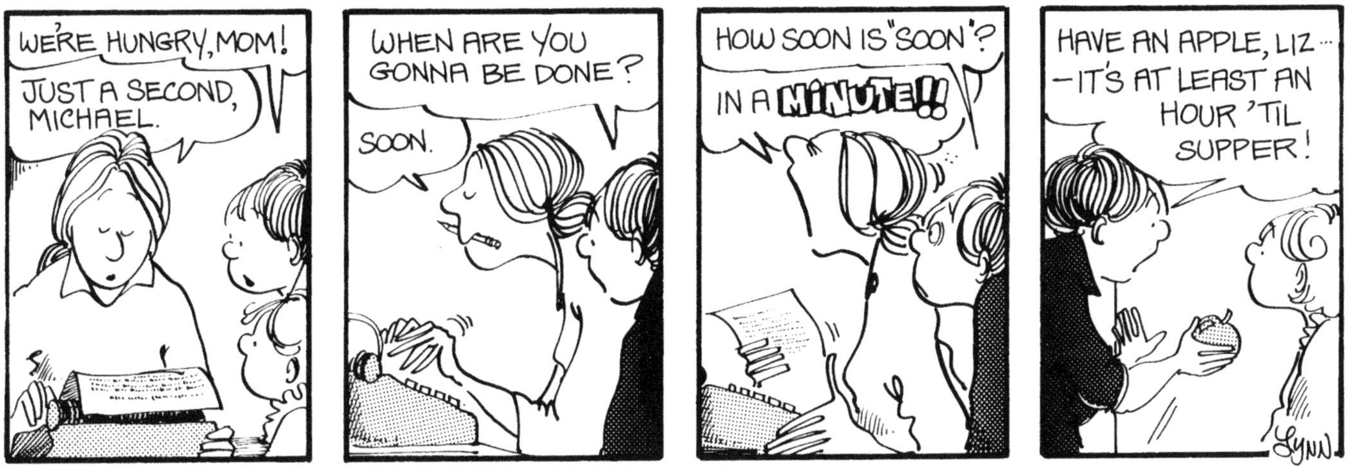
WE'RE HUNGRY, MOM!
JUST A SECOND, MICHAEL.
WHEN ARE YOU GONNA BE DONE?
SOON.
HOW SOON IS "SOON"?
IN A MINUTE!!
HAVE AN APPLE, LIZ... - IT'S AT LEAST AN HOUR 'TIL SUPPER!
LYNN

This is what life was like when I was focused on my work. Time disappeared when I went into the world of *For Better or For Worse.* Aaron and Kate were used to waiting for me to come back to Earth. In the meantime, they learned to be self-sufficient.

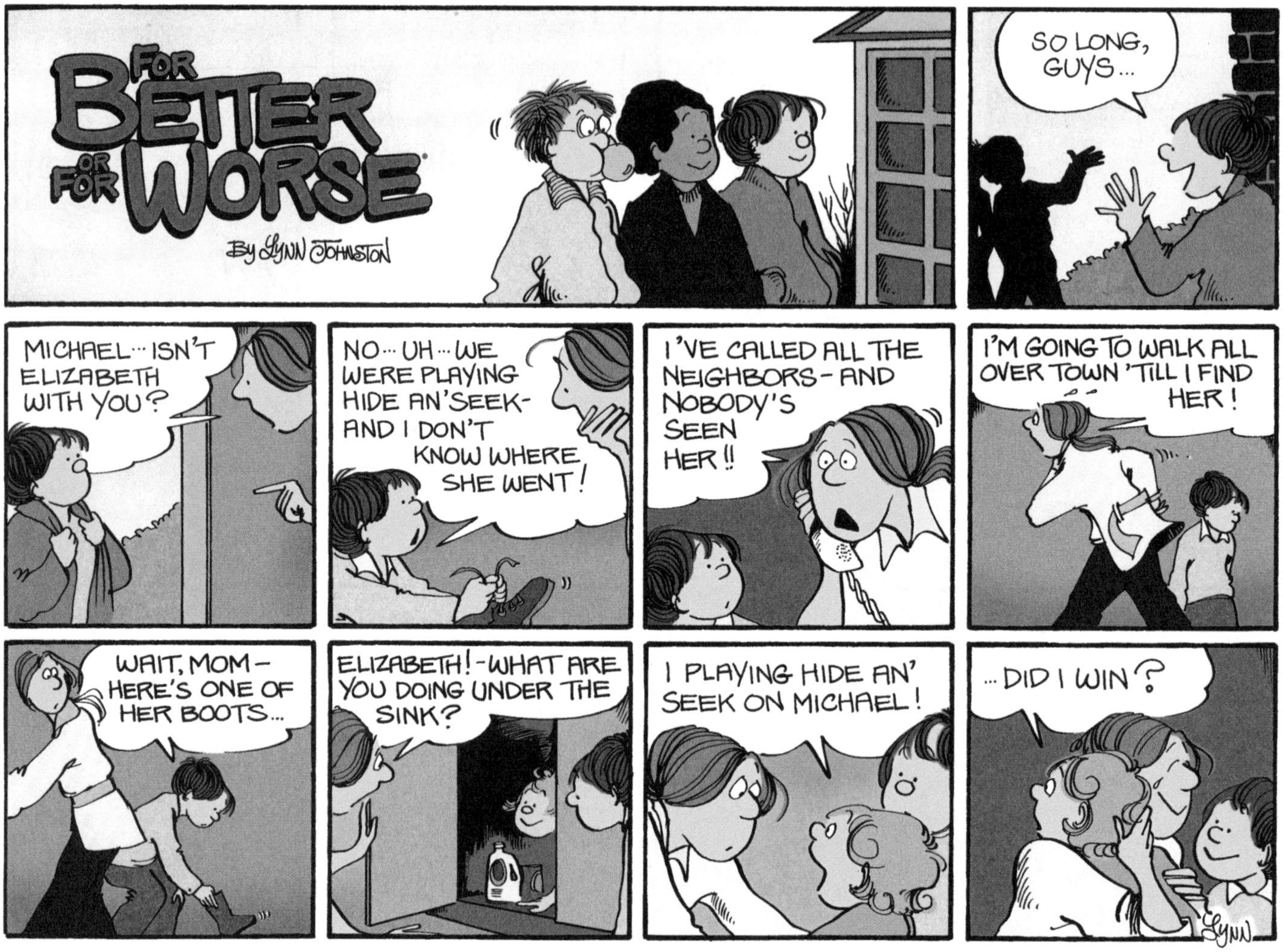
FOR BETTER OR FOR WORSE
BY LYNN JOHNSTON
SO LONG, GUYS...
MICHAEL... ISN'T ELIZABETH WITH YOU?
NO... UH... WE WERE PLAYING HIDE AN'SEEK- AND I DON'T KNOW WHERE SHE WENT!
I'VE CALLED ALL THE NEIGHBORS - AND NOBODY'S SEEN HER!!
I'M GOING TO WALK ALL OVER TOWN 'TILL I FIND HER!
WAIT, MOM - HERE'S ONE OF HER BOOTS...
ELIZABETH! - WHAT ARE YOU DOING UNDER THE SINK?
I PLAYING HIDE AN' SEEK ON MICHAEL!
...DID I WIN?
LYNN

Katie was able to crawl into the tiniest places, and we did "lose" her in our roomy house from time to time. One of her favourite spots was under the kitchen sink, which meant I had to put the soaps and cleaners in another place. Convenience always takes a backseat to safety!

As a kid, I loved hide-and-seek. I attended kindergarten in a private home across the street from ours. Our teacher, Miss Stewart, often had us play this game, but we had to stay within the classroom. How dull! I knew her house well, and when it was my turn to hide, I left the room and hid in her broom closet. Kids searched for me, and Miss Stewart hollered. One day I eventually got bored waiting for them to find me, so I decided to surprise them all by taking my clothes off. When Miss Stewart opened the door to the broom closet, there I was in my birthday suit. Immediately, she pulled a small rug off the floor, flung it in front of me, and told the class of giggling kids to go back to their chairs and wait. At once, I was shoved into my duds. Her sister watched the class as Miss Stewart marched me across the street to my house. Mom opened the door to a barrage of complaints, accepted me into the house, thanked Miss Stewart, and sent me to my room. That day, I was expelled from kindergarten. I guess this was the last straw!

FOR BETTER OR FOR WORSE
BY LYNN JOHNSTON
MICHAEL, WILL YOU PLEASE DO YOUR DROOLING SOME-WHERE ELSE!
MOM, THERE'S A CHERRY IN THIS CAKE, HERE ... CAN I PULL IT OUT?
NO. YOU'VE HAD 2 PIECES. YOU CANNOT PULL OUT THAT CHERRY!
BUT, IT'S JUST STICKING OUT HERE AND...
I SAID NO!!!
OOPS.
POIT!
IT SORT OF FELL OUT. - CAN I HAVE IT?
FOR THE LAST TIME - NO!
LYNN

One of my mom's tastiest recipes was for a cherry loaf cake. Unable to resist maraschino cherries, I would pull out the ones closest to the surface, leaving "mouse holes" in the cake as it sat on the counter to cool. I remember my mom being pretty irate by my inconsiderate attack on her baking, but I regarded it as a compliment, an honest display of appreciation. Her punishment one day was to make me bake the same cake on my own to see how much work it was. When it came out of the oven, it was beautiful. I was so proud of having made my favourite cake, I couldn't wait for my dad to see it. When he came in after work, I led him straight to the kitchen, and discovered that my mother had picked all the visible cherries out of it.

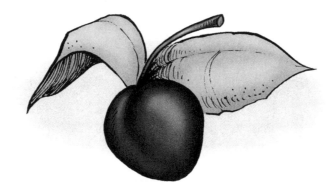

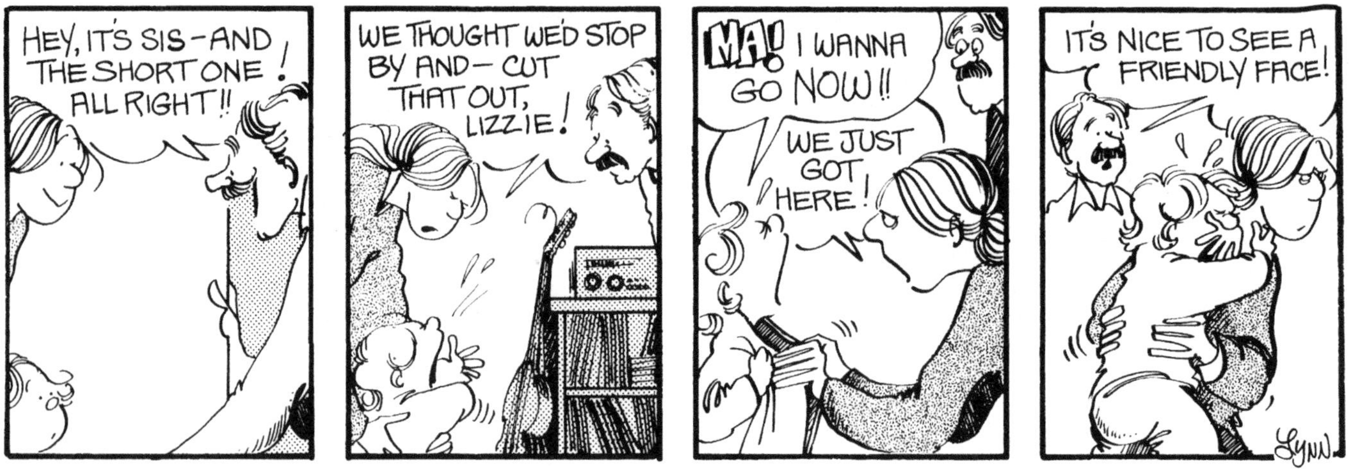
HEY, IT'S SIS - AND THE SHORT ONE! ALL RIGHT!!
WE THOUGHT WE'D STOP BY AND - CUT THAT OUT, LIZZIE!
MA! I WANNA GO NOW!!
WE JUST GOT HERE!
IT'S NICE TO SEE A FRIENDLY FACE!
Lynn

Alan would often call my kids "short one," which I thought was charming. One day on a business trip, I got into an elevator with a woman and her young son. I looked down at him and said, "Hiya, short one!" His mom immediately berated me for saying cruel things to a child who had an illness and was abnormally small for his age. AAAUGH!

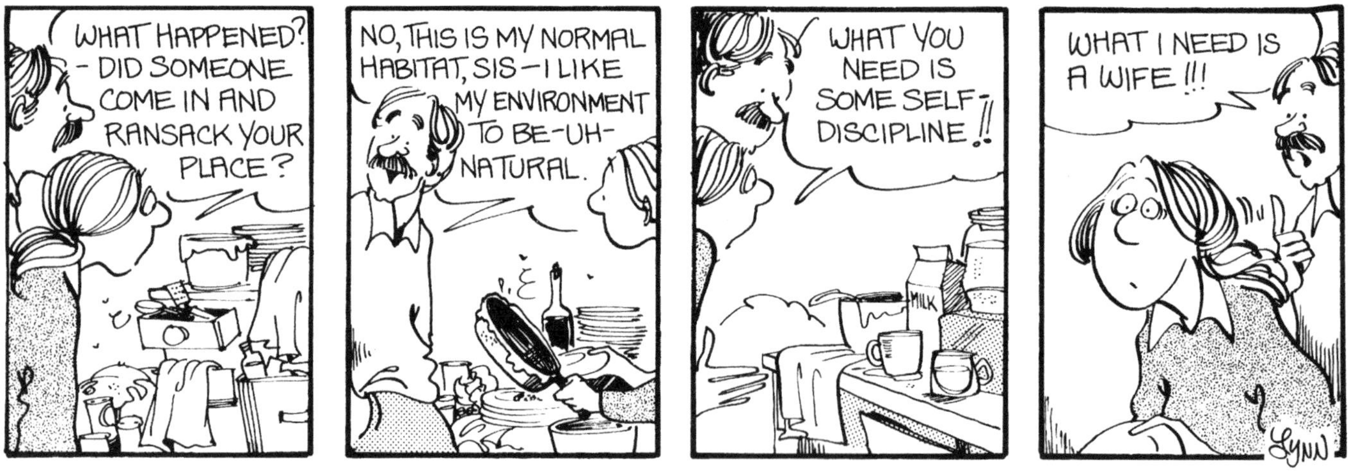
WHAT HAPPENED? - DID SOMEONE COME IN AND RANSACK YOUR PLACE?
NO, THIS IS MY NORMAL HABITAT, SIS - I LIKE MY ENVIRONMENT TO BE - UH - NATURAL.
MILK
WHAT YOU NEED IS SOME SELF-DISCIPLINE!!
WHAT I NEED IS A WIFE!!!
Lynn

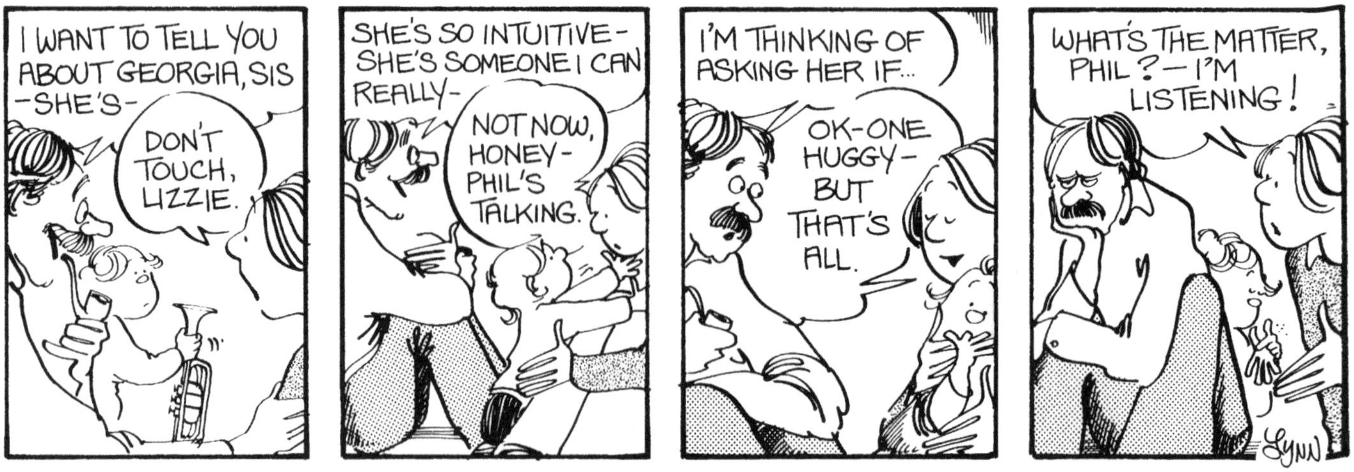
I WANT TO TELL YOU ABOUT GEORGIA, SIS - SHE'S -
DON'T TOUCH, LIZZIE.
SHE'S SO INTUITIVE - SHE'S SOMEONE I CAN REALLY -
NOT NOW, HONEY - PHIL'S TALKING.
I'M THINKING OF ASKING HER IF...
OK - ONE HUGGY - BUT THAT'S ALL.
WHAT'S THE MATTER, PHIL? - I'M LISTENING!
Lynn

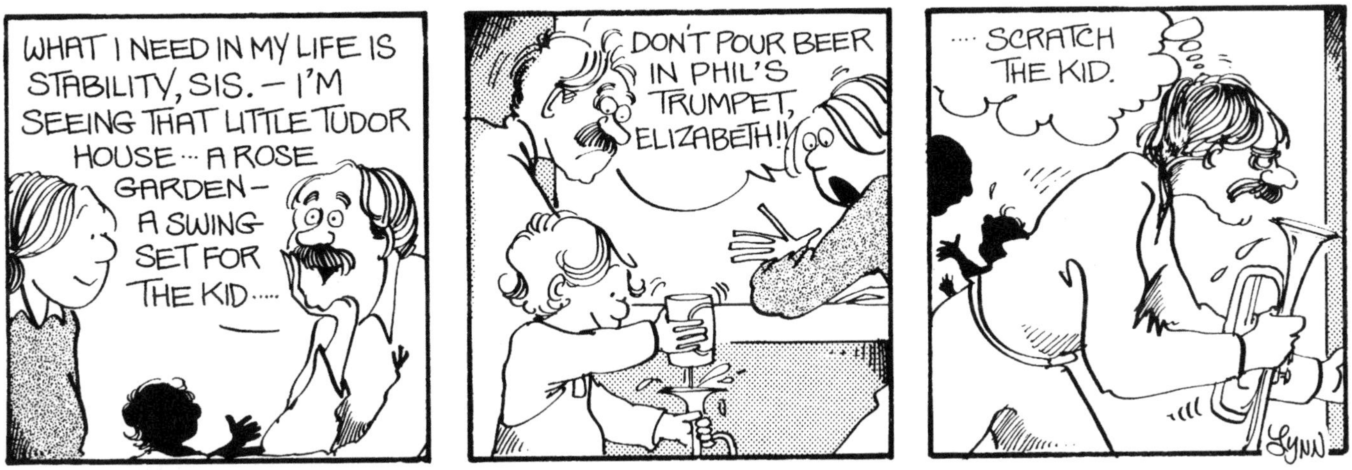
WHAT I NEED IN MY LIFE IS STABILITY, SIS. – I'M SEEING THAT LITTLE TUDOR HOUSE ... A ROSE GARDEN – A SWING SET FOR THE KID.....
DON'T POUR BEER IN PHIL'S TRUMPET, ELIZABETH!!
.... SCRATCH THE KID.
LYNN

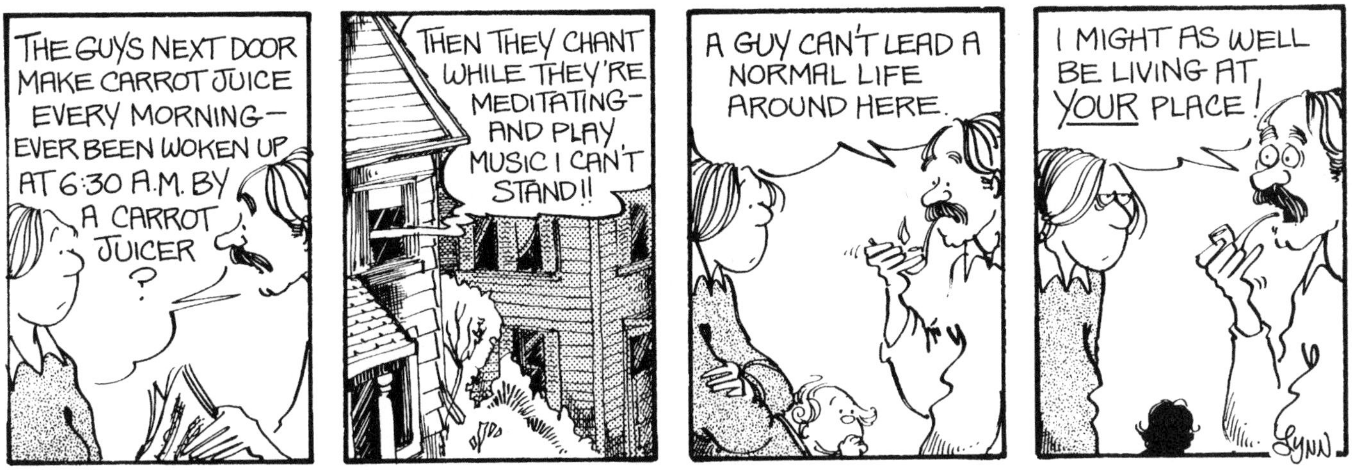
THE GUYS NEXT DOOR MAKE CARROT JUICE EVERY MORNING – EVER BEEN WOKEN UP AT 6:30 A.M. BY A CARROT JUICER ?
THEN THEY CHANT WHILE THEY'RE MEDITATING – AND PLAY MUSIC I CAN'T STAND!!
A GUY CAN'T LEAD A NORMAL LIFE AROUND HERE.
I MIGHT AS WELL BE LIVING AT YOUR PLACE!
LYNN

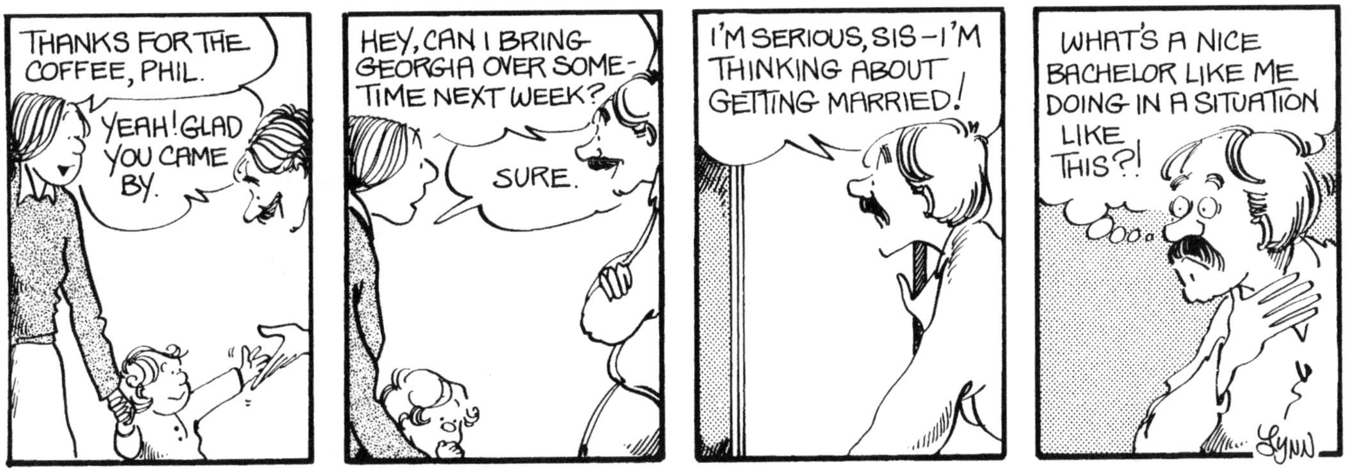
THANKS FOR THE COFFEE, PHIL.
YEAH! GLAD YOU CAME BY.
HEY, CAN I BRING GEORGIA OVER SOME-TIME NEXT WEEK?
SURE.
I'M SERIOUS, SIS – I'M THINKING ABOUT GETTING MARRIED!
WHAT'S A NICE BACHELOR LIKE ME DOING IN A SITUATION LIKE THIS?!
LYNN

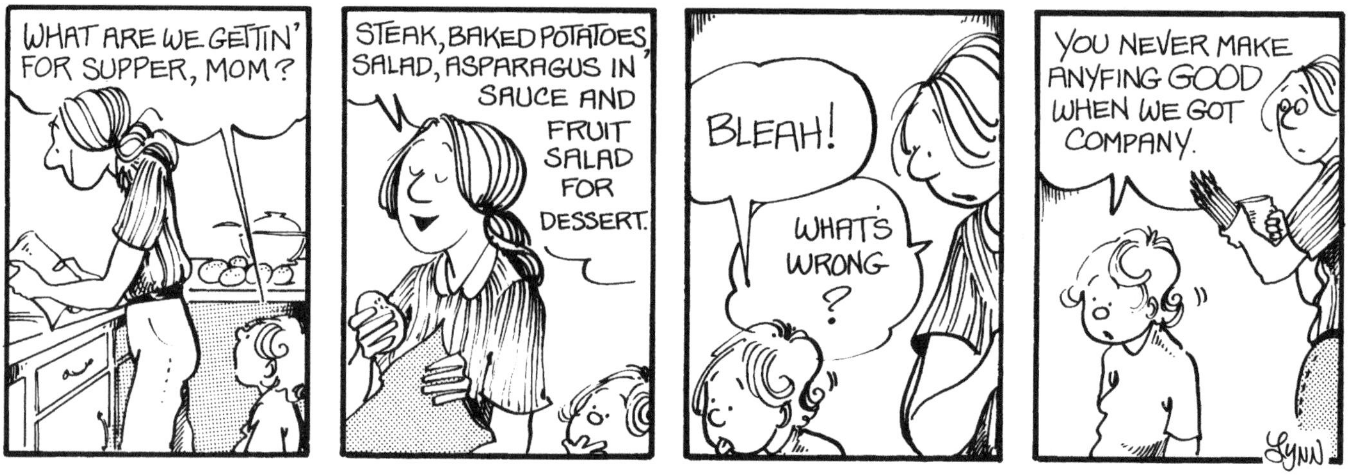
WHAT ARE WE GETTIN' FOR SUPPER, MOM?
STEAK, BAKED POTATOES, SALAD, ASPARAGUS IN SAUCE AND FRUIT SALAD FOR DESSERT.
BLEAH!
WHAT'S WRONG?
YOU NEVER MAKE ANYFING GOOD WHEN WE GOT COMPANY.
LYNN

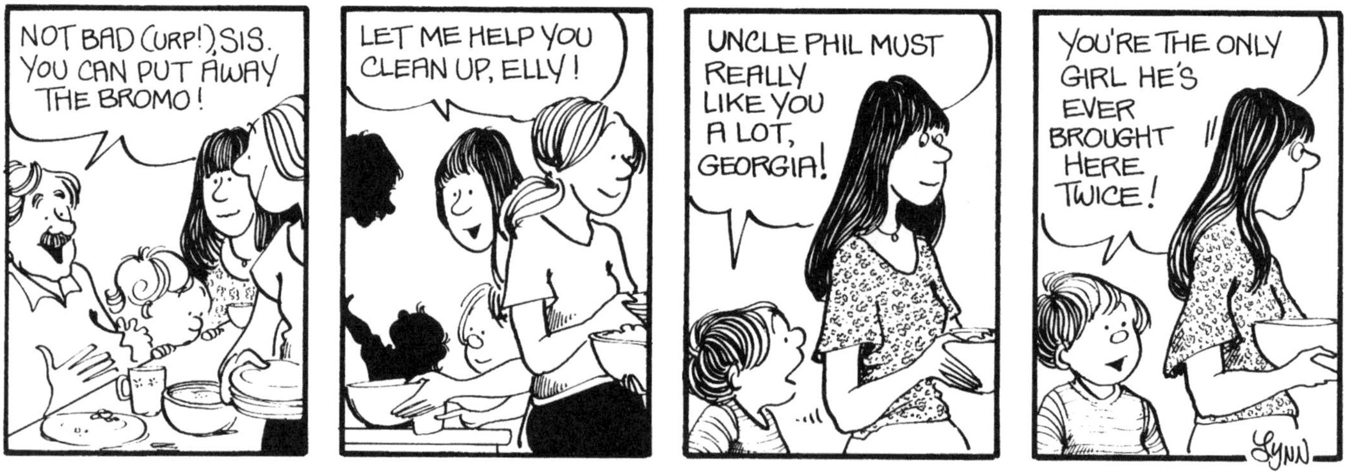
NOT BAD (URP!), SIS. YOU CAN PUT AWAY THE BROMO!
LET ME HELP YOU CLEAN UP, ELLY!
UNCLE PHIL MUST REALLY LIKE YOU A LOT, GEORGIA!
YOU'RE THE ONLY GIRL HE'S EVER BROUGHT HERE TWICE!
LYNN

As it turned out, Georgia and Alan's future wife, Joan, looked a lot alike. I had even decided to call Georgia "Geo" for short!

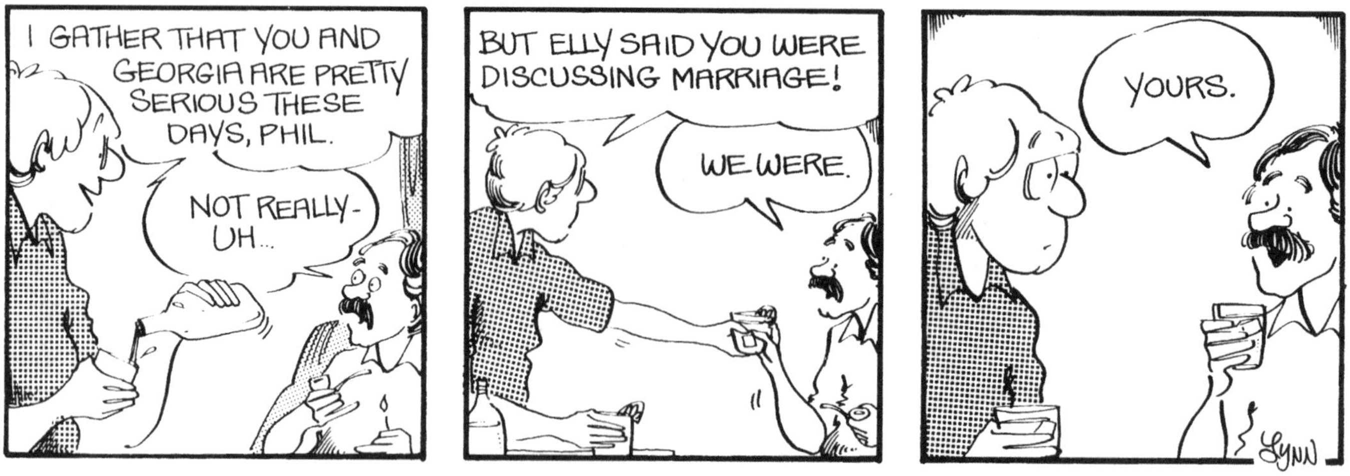
I GATHER THAT YOU AND GEORGIA ARE PRETTY SERIOUS THESE DAYS, PHIL.
NOT REALLY-UH...
BUT ELLY SAID YOU WERE DISCUSSING MARRIAGE!
WE WERE.
YOURS.
LYNN

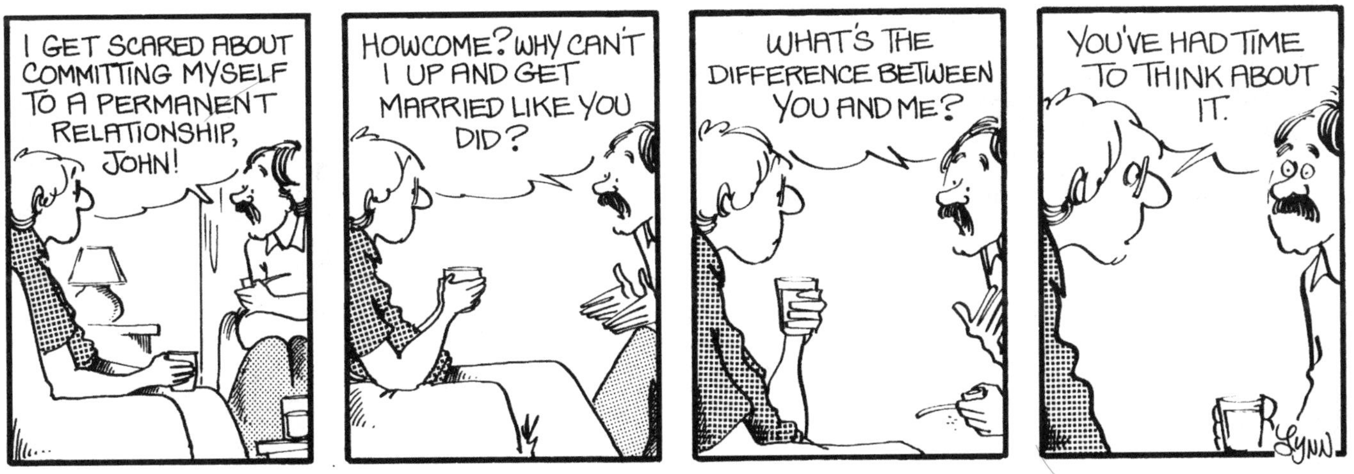
I GET SCARED ABOUT COMMITTING MYSELF TO A PERMANENT RELATIONSHIP, JOHN!
HOWCOME? WHY CAN'T I UP AND GET MARRIED LIKE YOU DID?
WHAT'S THE DIFFERENCE BETWEEN YOU AND ME?
YOU'VE HAD TIME TO THINK ABOUT IT.
Lynn

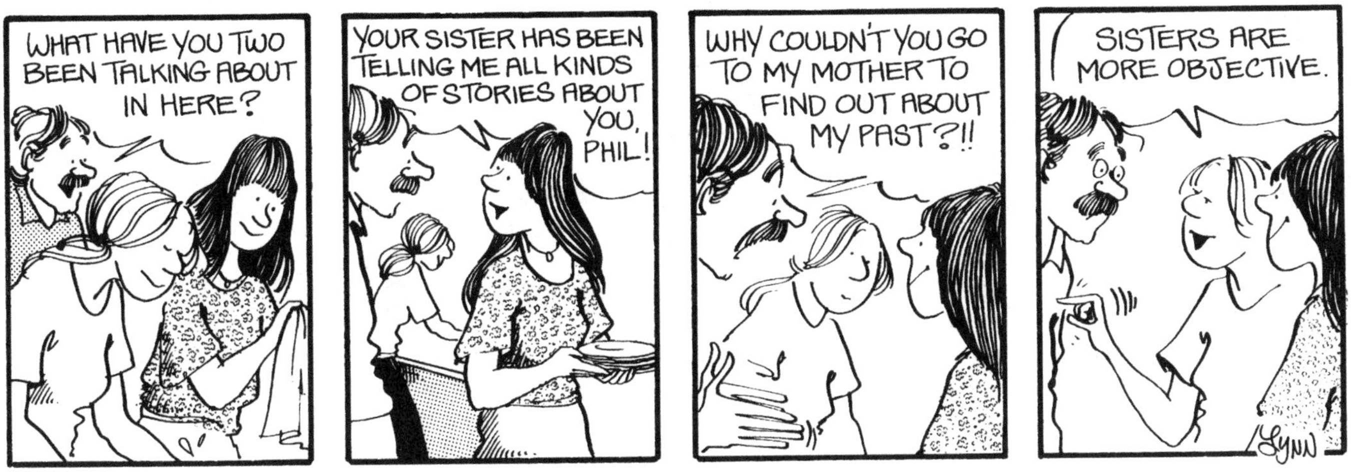
WHAT HAVE YOU TWO BEEN TALKING ABOUT IN HERE?
YOUR SISTER HAS BEEN TELLING ME ALL KINDS OF STORIES ABOUT YOU, PHIL!
WHY COULDN'T YOU GO TO MY MOTHER TO FIND OUT ABOUT MY PAST?!!
SISTERS ARE MORE OBJECTIVE.
Lynn

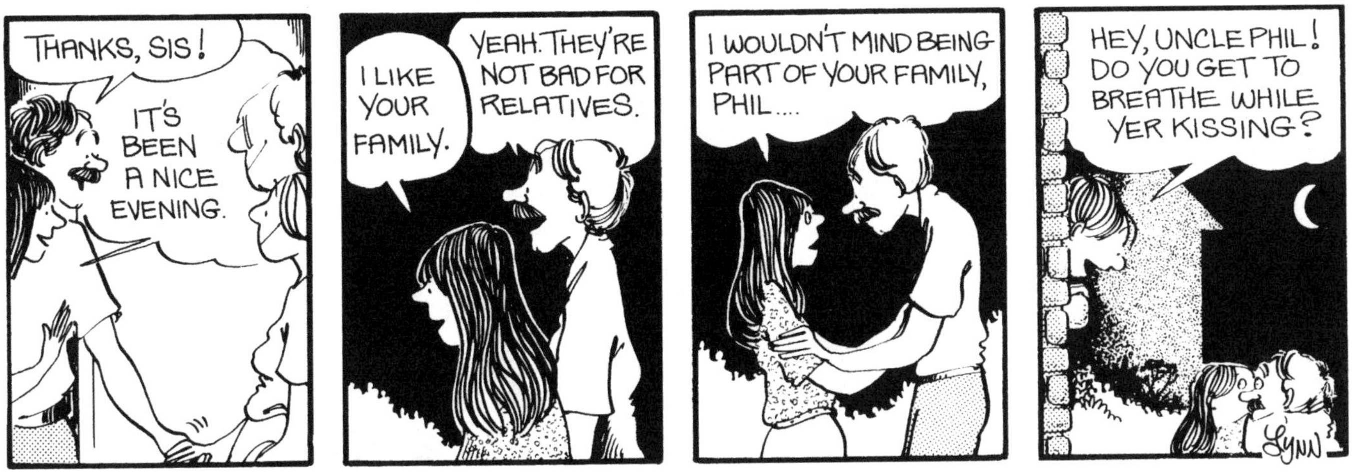
THANKS, SIS!
IT'S BEEN A NICE EVENING.
I LIKE YOUR FAMILY.
YEAH. THEY'RE NOT BAD FOR RELATIVES.
I WOULDN'T MIND BEING PART OF YOUR FAMILY, PHIL....
HEY, UNCLE PHIL! DO YOU GET TO BREATHE WHILE YER KISSING?
Lynn

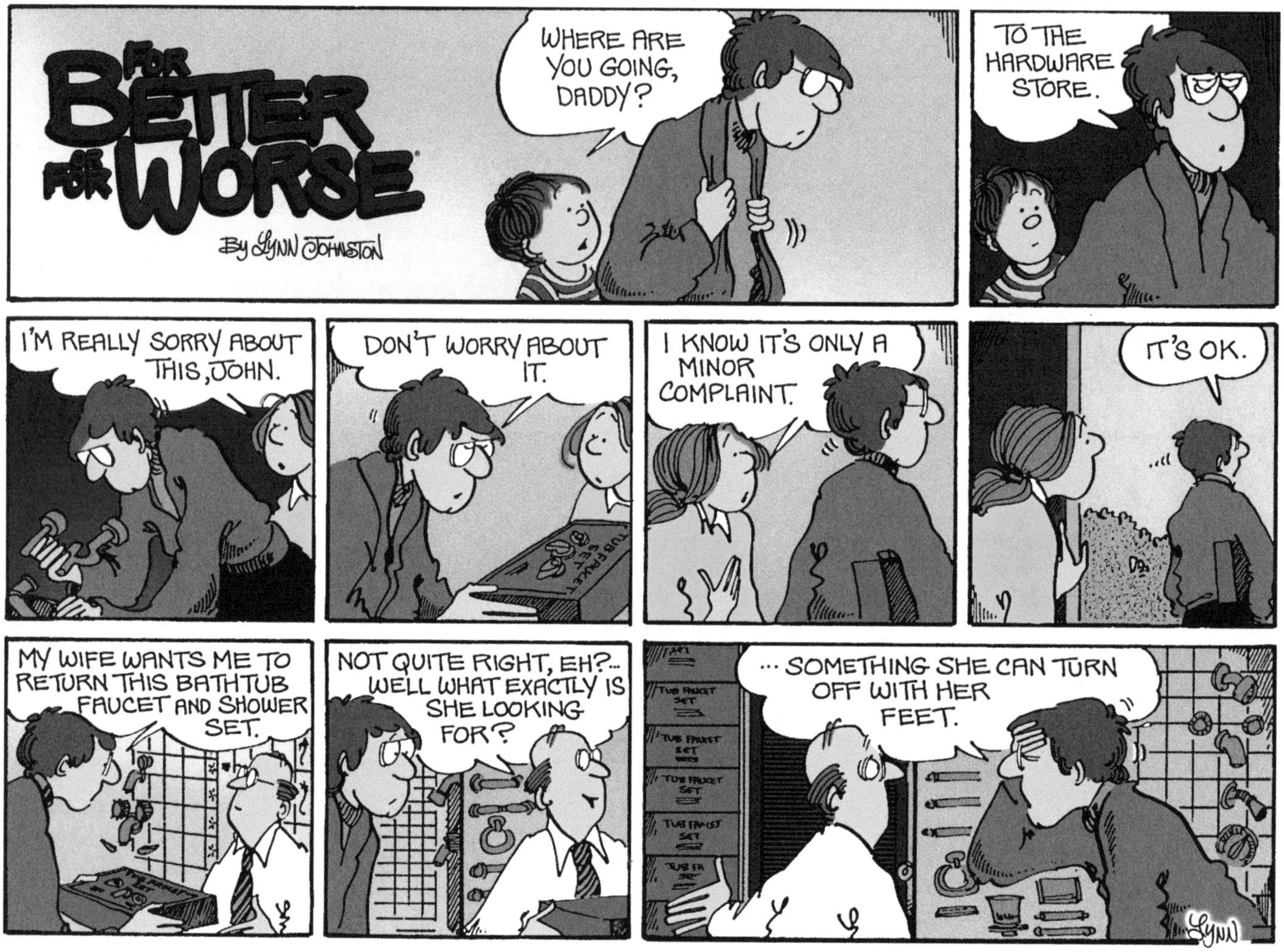
FOR BETTER OR FOR WORSE
BY LYNN JOHNSTON
WHERE ARE YOU GOING, DADDY?
TO THE HARDWARE STORE.
I'M REALLY SORRY ABOUT THIS, JOHN.
DON'T WORRY ABOUT IT.
I KNOW IT'S ONLY A MINOR COMPLAINT.
IT'S OK.
MY WIFE WANTS ME TO RETURN THIS BATHTUB FAUCET AND SHOWER SET.
NOT QUITE RIGHT, EH?... WELL WHAT EXACTLY IS SHE LOOKING FOR?
... SOMETHING SHE CAN TURN OFF WITH HER FEET.
LYNN

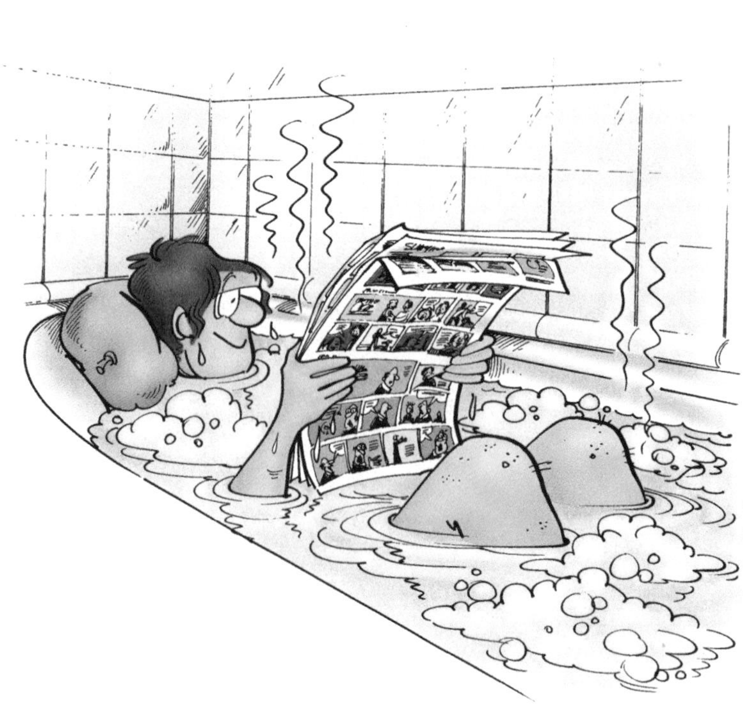

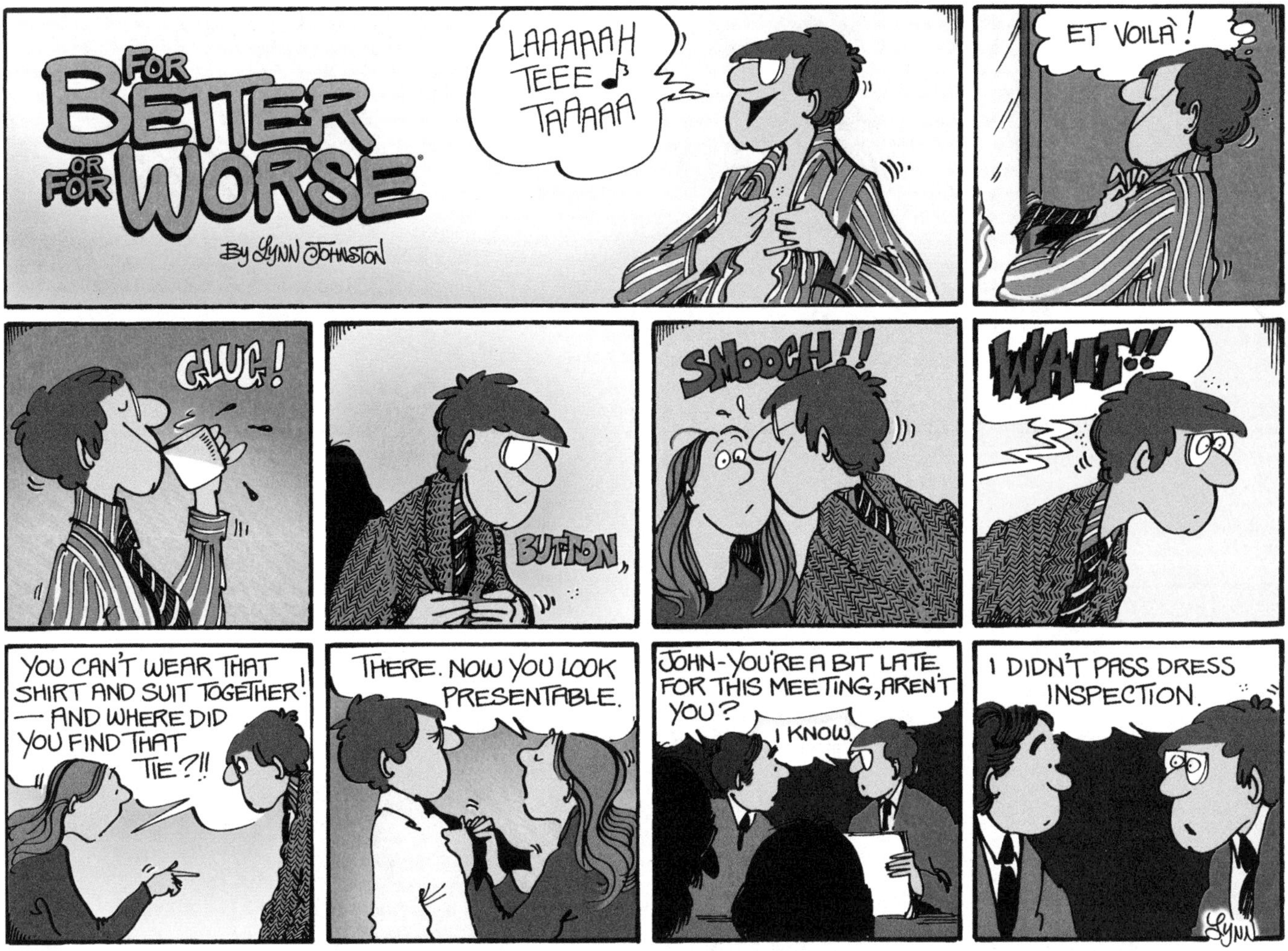
FOR BETTER OR FOR WORSE
By Lynn Johnston
LAAAAAH TEEE TAAAAA
ET VOILÀ!
GLUG!
BUTTON
SMOOCH!!
WAIT!!
YOU CAN'T WEAR THAT SHIRT AND SUIT TOGETHER! — AND WHERE DID YOU FIND THAT TIE?!!
THERE. NOW YOU LOOK PRESENTABLE.
JOHN-YOU'RE A BIT LATE FOR THIS MEETING, AREN'T YOU?
I KNOW.
I DIDN'T PASS DRESS INSPECTION.
Lynn

Letters from readers told me that I wasn't the only one who checked out their husband's wardrobe before letting him leave the house. Mine put comfort before fashion, which meant that anything well worn was kept to wear again and again and again. Whatever configuration the hangers presented was what he wore. If a checked shirt was hanging next to striped pants … bingo! An outfit. Throwing away a comfortable suit was hard to do — even if the styles had changed twice since its purchase. Getting him to buy a new one, or any new clothes for that matter, was nearly impossible! This drove me crazy.

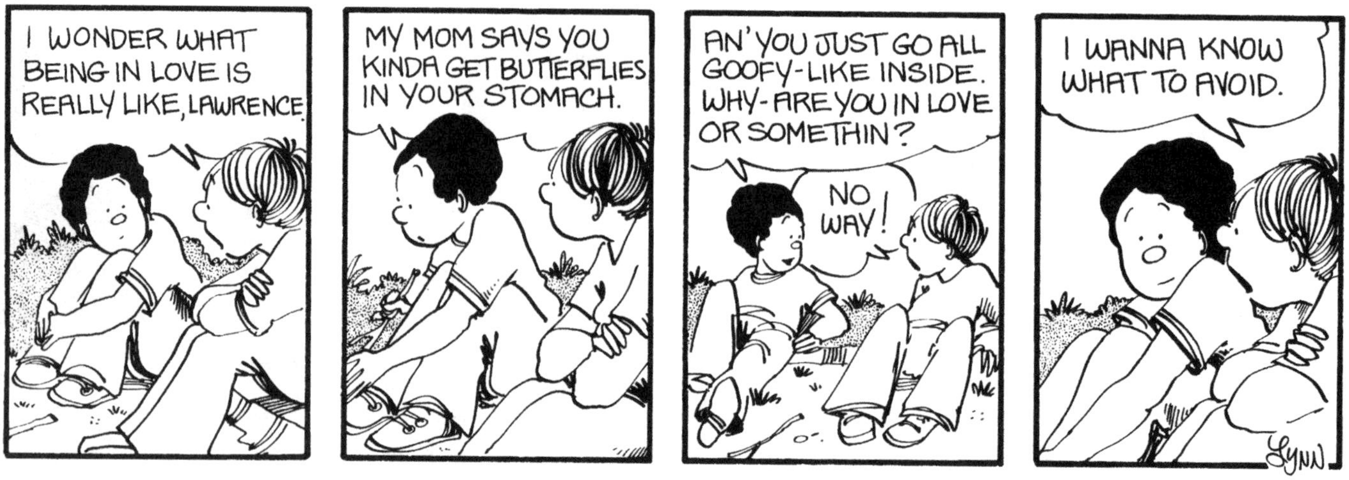
I WONDER WHAT BEING IN LOVE IS REALLY LIKE, LAWRENCE
MY MOM SAYS YOU KINDA GET BUTTERFLIES IN YOUR STOMACH.
AN' YOU JUST GO ALL GOOFY-LIKE INSIDE. WHY- ARE YOU IN LOVE OR SOMETHIN?
NO WAY!
I WANNA KNOW WHAT TO AVOID.
LYNN

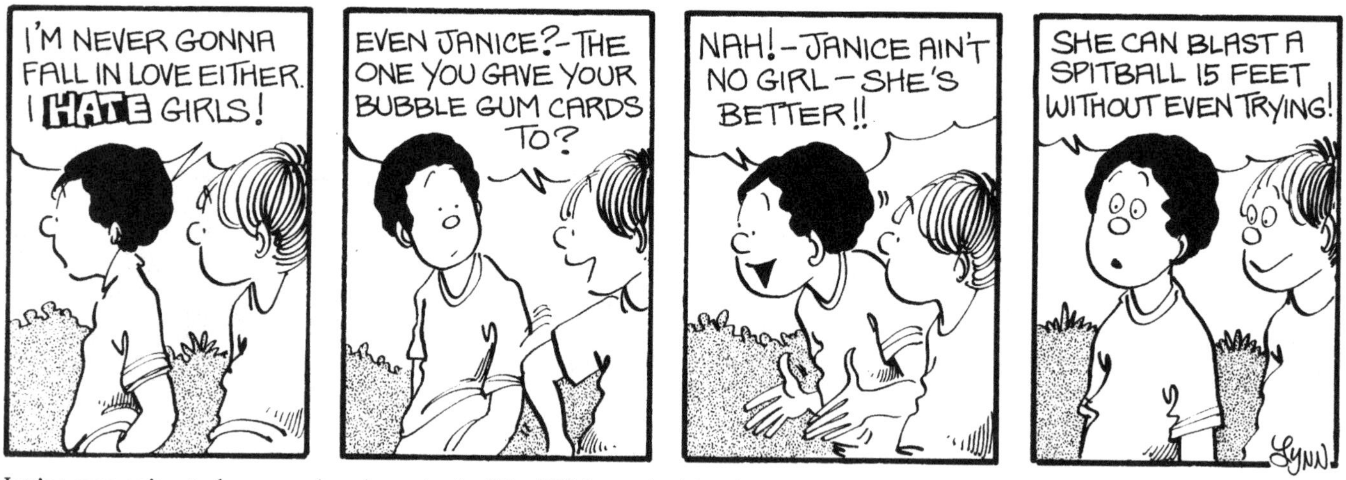
I'M NEVER GONNA FALL IN LOVE EITHER. I HATE GIRLS!
EVEN JANICE?-THE ONE YOU GAVE YOUR BUBBLE GUM CARDS TO?
NAH! - JANICE AIN'T NO GIRL - SHE'S BETTER!!
SHE CAN BLAST A SPITBALL 15 FEET WITHOUT EVEN TRYING!
LYNN

Janice was going to be a regular character in *FBorFW*. I was looking forward to having a rough-and-tumble girl down the block who would be an even match for the boys. She was named for a tough kid I knew growing up, and I hoped to explore some of my more daring exploits through her.

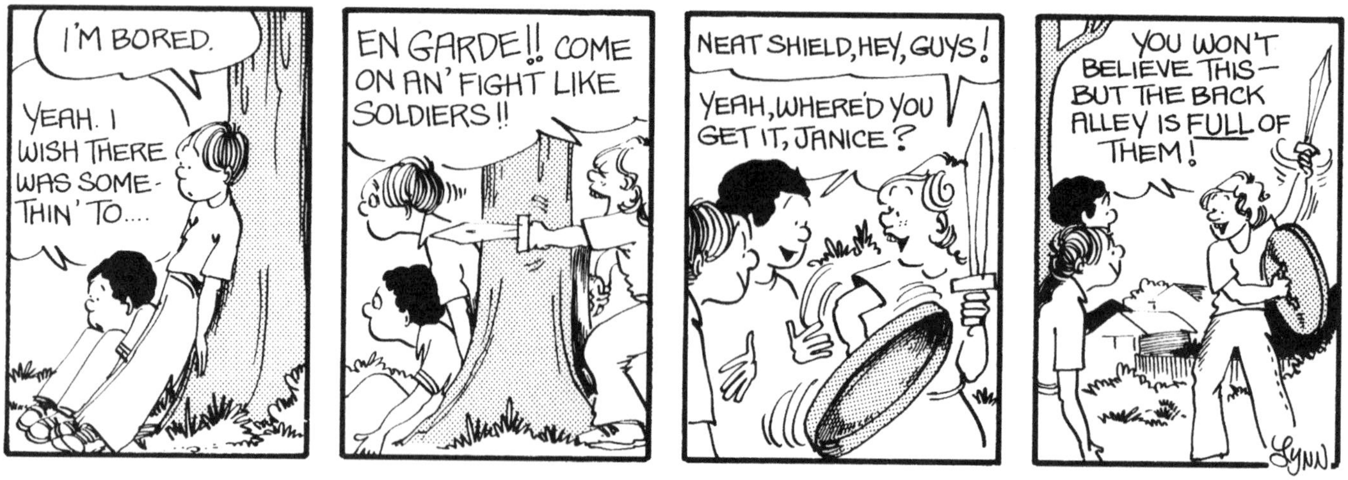
I'M BORED.
YEAH. I WISH THERE WAS SOME-THIN' TO....
EN GARDE!! COME ON AN' FIGHT LIKE SOLDIERS!!
NEAT SHIELD, HEY, GUYS!
YEAH, WHERE'D YOU GET IT, JANICE?
YOU WON'T BELIEVE THIS- BUT THE BACK ALLEY IS FULL OF THEM!
LYNN

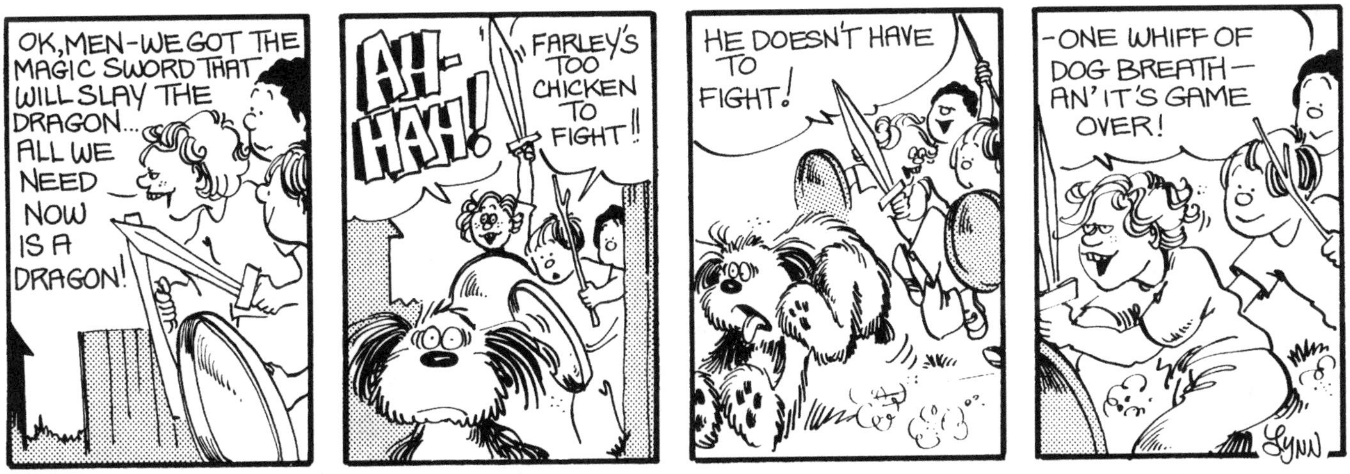
OK, MEN-WE GOT THE MAGIC SWORD THAT WILL SLAY THE DRAGON... ALL WE NEED NOW IS A DRAGON!
AH-HAH!
FARLEY'S TOO CHICKEN TO FIGHT!!
HE DOESN'T HAVE TO FIGHT!
-ONE WHIFF OF DOG BREATH- AN' IT'S GAME OVER!
LYNN

Sticks and trash can lids were feudal weapons in the lane behind our Lynn Lake house. I imagined Mike and Lawrence battling Janice and other "enemies" in an ongoing quest for neighbourhood supremacy. Sadly, Janice soon disappeared. Perhaps she came on too strong. Perhaps I bowed to reader criticism. Either way, I lost a neat character and some potentially good story lines.

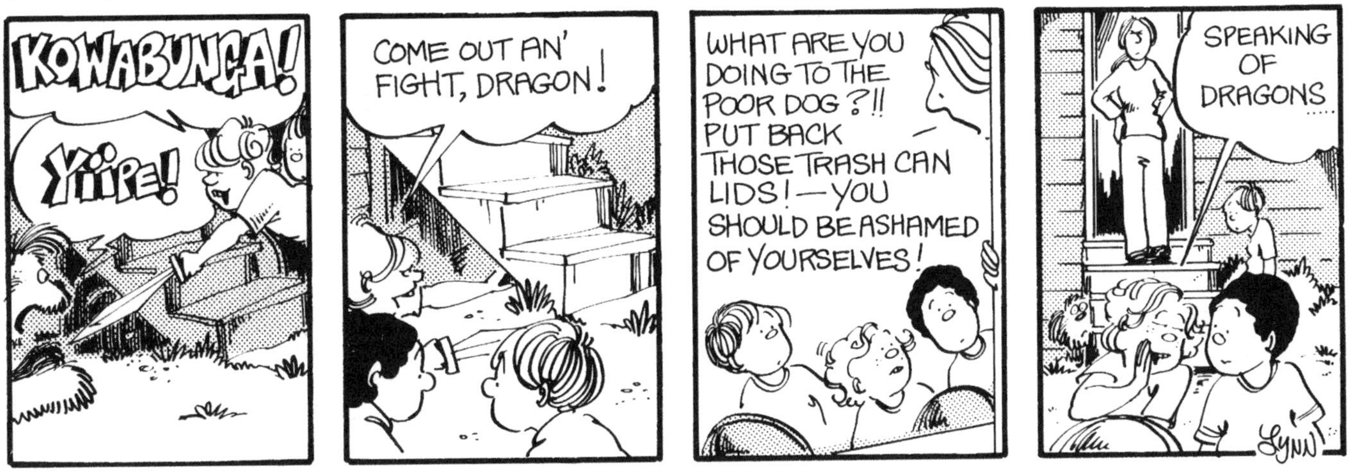
KOWABUNGA!
YIIPE!
COME OUT AN' FIGHT, DRAGON!
WHAT ARE YOU DOING TO THE POOR DOG?!! PUT BACK THOSE TRASH CAN LIDS!-YOU SHOULD BE ASHAMED OF YOURSELVES!
SPEAKING OF DRAGONS.....
LYNN

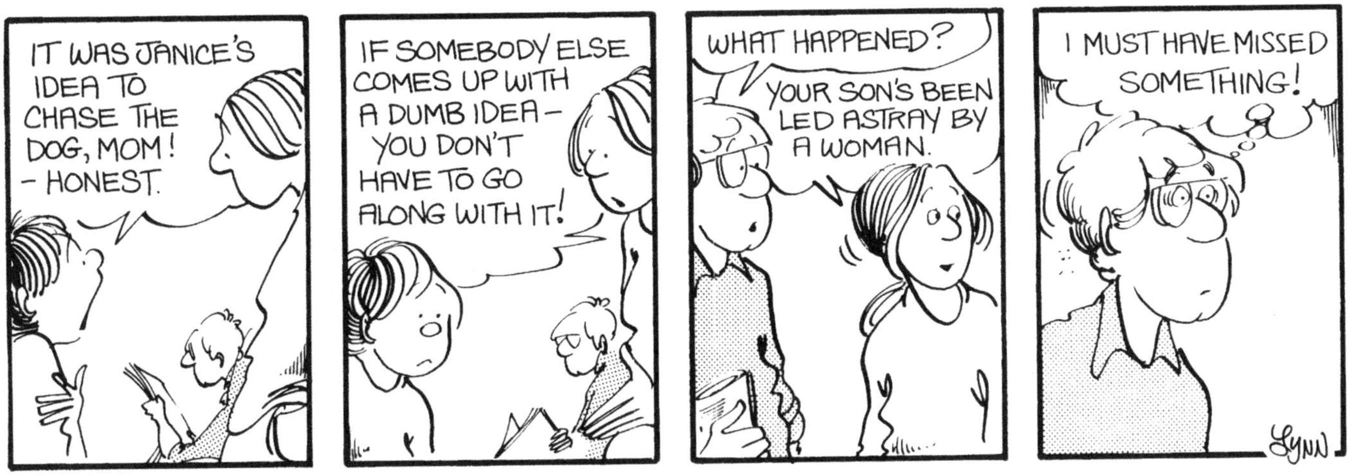
IT WAS JANICE'S IDEA TO CHASE THE DOG, MOM! - HONEST.
IF SOMEBODY ELSE COMES UP WITH A DUMB IDEA- YOU DON'T HAVE TO GO ALONG WITH IT!
WHAT HAPPENED?
YOUR SON'S BEEN LED ASTRAY BY A WOMAN.
I MUST HAVE MISSED SOMETHING!
LYNN

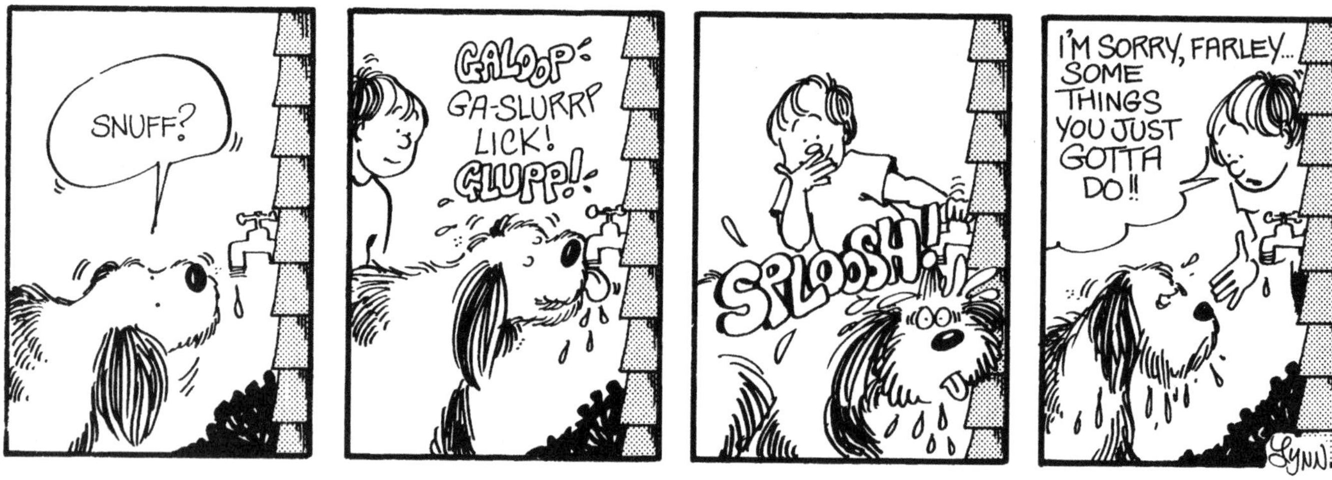
SNUFF?
GALOOP
GA-SLURRP
LICK!
GLUPP!
SPLOOSH!
I'M SORRY, FARLEY... SOME THINGS YOU JUST GOTTA DO!!
LYNN

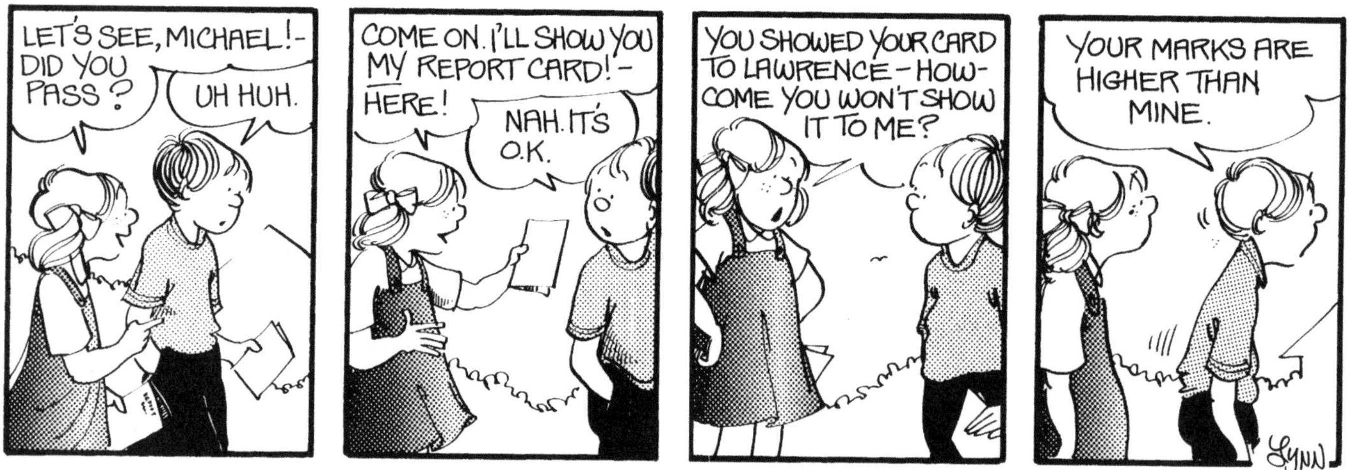
LET'S SEE, MICHAEL! - DID YOU PASS?
UH HUH.
COME ON. I'LL SHOW YOU MY REPORT CARD! - HERE!
NAH. IT'S O.K.
YOU SHOWED YOUR CARD TO LAWRENCE - HOW-COME YOU WON'T SHOW IT TO ME?
YOUR MARKS ARE HIGHER THAN MINE.
LYNN

The kids who were eager to show their report cards always had good ones — no F, D, or C appeared on their neatly prepared sheets. I always tried to avoid these too-good-to-be-true types. Instead, I gravitated toward the mixed-bag students who had A's in the stuff they liked and a "pass" in everything else!

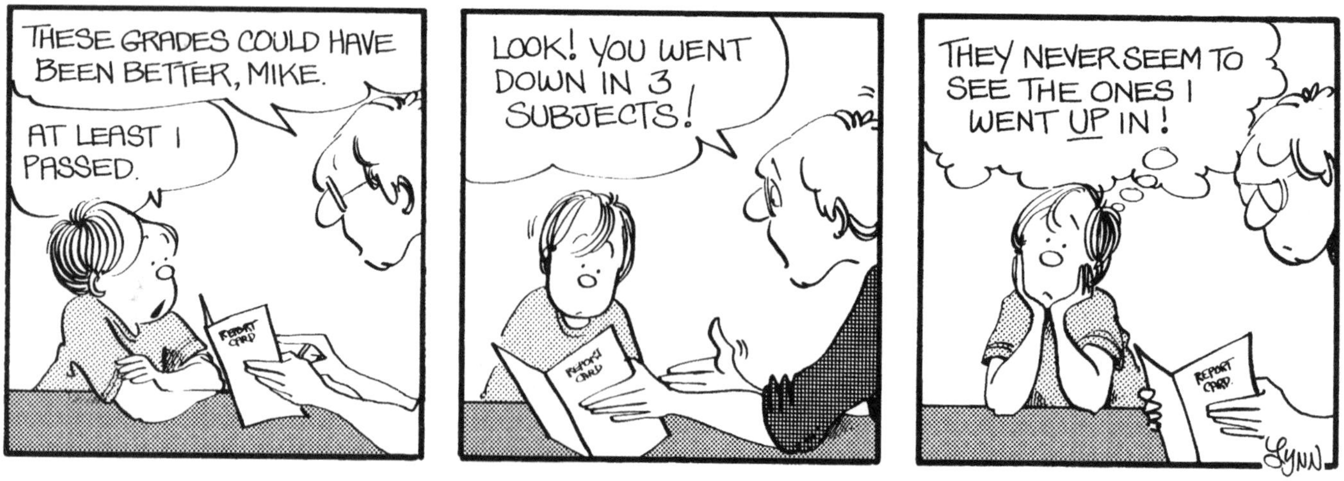
THESE GRADES COULD HAVE BEEN BETTER, MIKE.
AT LEAST I PASSED.
REPORT CARD
LOOK! YOU WENT DOWN IN 3 SUBJECTS!
REPORT CARD
THEY NEVER SEEM TO SEE THE ONES I WENT UP IN!
REPORT CARD
LYNN

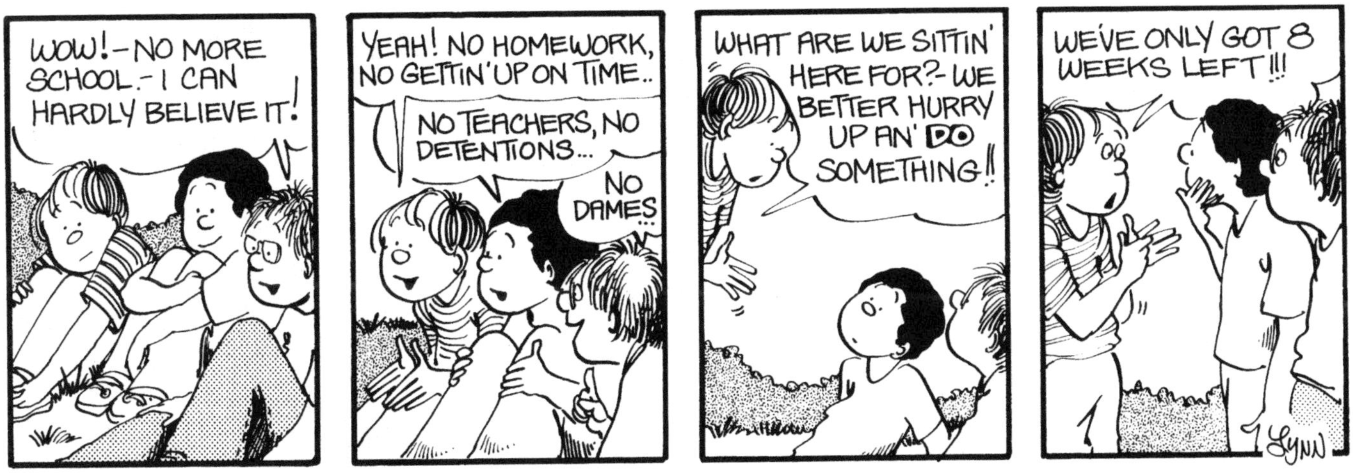
WOW!-NO MORE SCHOOL.-I CAN HARDLY BELIEVE IT!
YEAH! NO HOMEWORK, NO GETTIN' UP ON TIME..
NO TEACHERS, NO DETENTIONS...
NO DAMES...
WHAT ARE WE SITTIN' HERE FOR?-WE BETTER HURRY UP AN' DO SOMETHING!!
WE'VE ONLY GOT 8 WEEKS LEFT!!!
LYNN

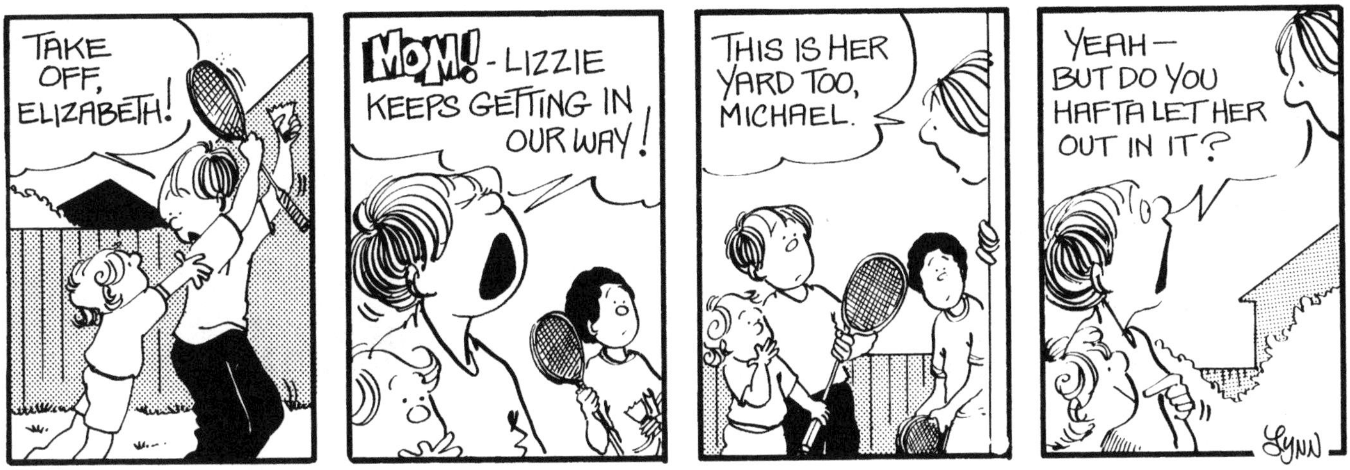
TAKE OFF, ELIZABETH!
MOM!-LIZZIE KEEPS GETTING IN OUR WAY!
THIS IS HER YARD TOO, MICHAEL.
YEAH-BUT DO YOU HAFTA LET HER OUT IN IT?
LYNN

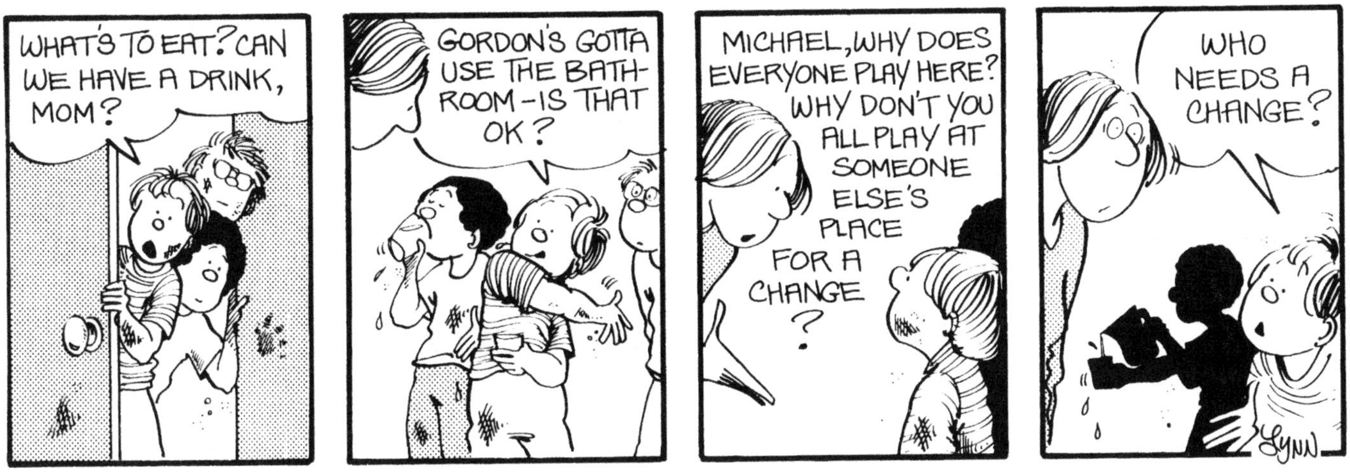
WHAT'S TO EAT? CAN WE HAVE A DRINK, MOM?
GORDON'S GOTTA USE THE BATH-ROOM-IS THAT OK?
MICHAEL, WHY DOES EVERYONE PLAY HERE? WHY DON'T YOU ALL PLAY AT SOMEONE ELSE'S PLACE FOR A CHANGE?
WHO NEEDS A CHANGE?
LYNN

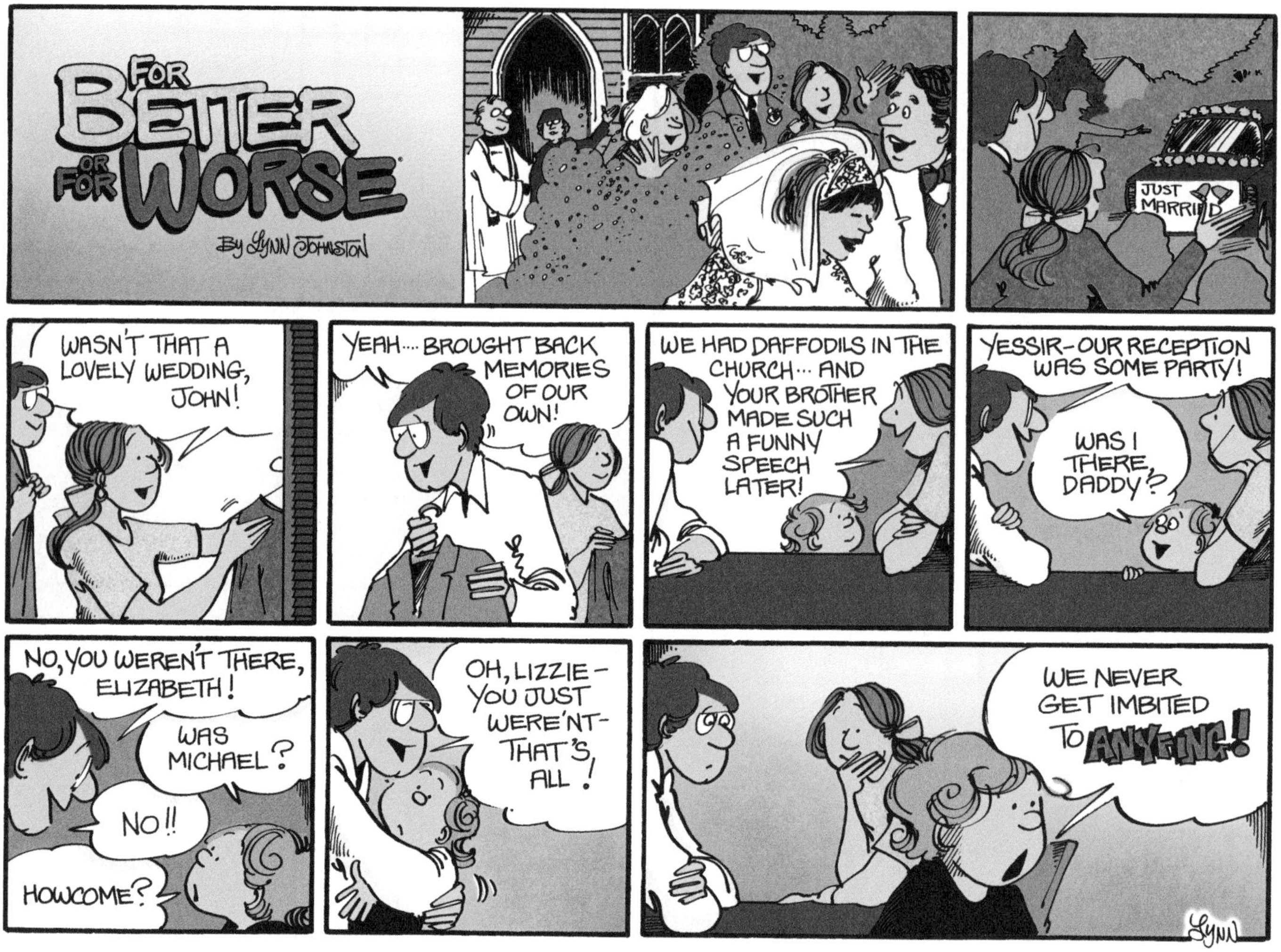
FOR BETTER OR FOR WORSE
BY LYNN JOHNSTON
JUST MARRIED
WASN'T THAT A LOVELY WEDDING, JOHN!
YEAH.... BROUGHT BACK MEMORIES OF OUR OWN!
WE HAD DAFFODILS IN THE CHURCH... AND YOUR BROTHER MADE SUCH A FUNNY SPEECH LATER!
YESSIR-OUR RECEPTION WAS SOME PARTY!
WAS I THERE, DADDY?
NO, YOU WEREN'T THERE, ELIZABETH!
WAS MICHAEL?
NO!!
HOWCOME?
OH, LIZZIE - YOU JUST WERE'NT - THAT'S ALL!
WE NEVER GET IMBITED TO ANYFING!
LYNN

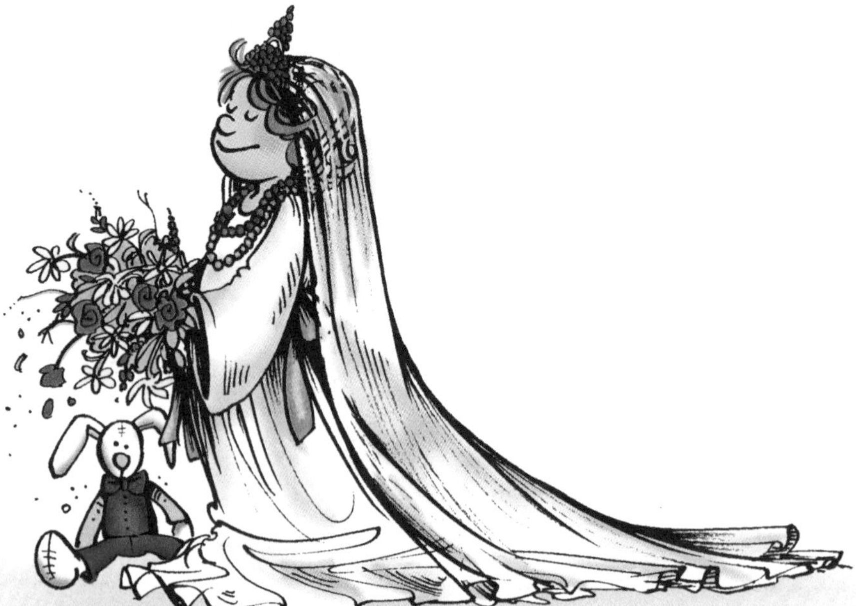

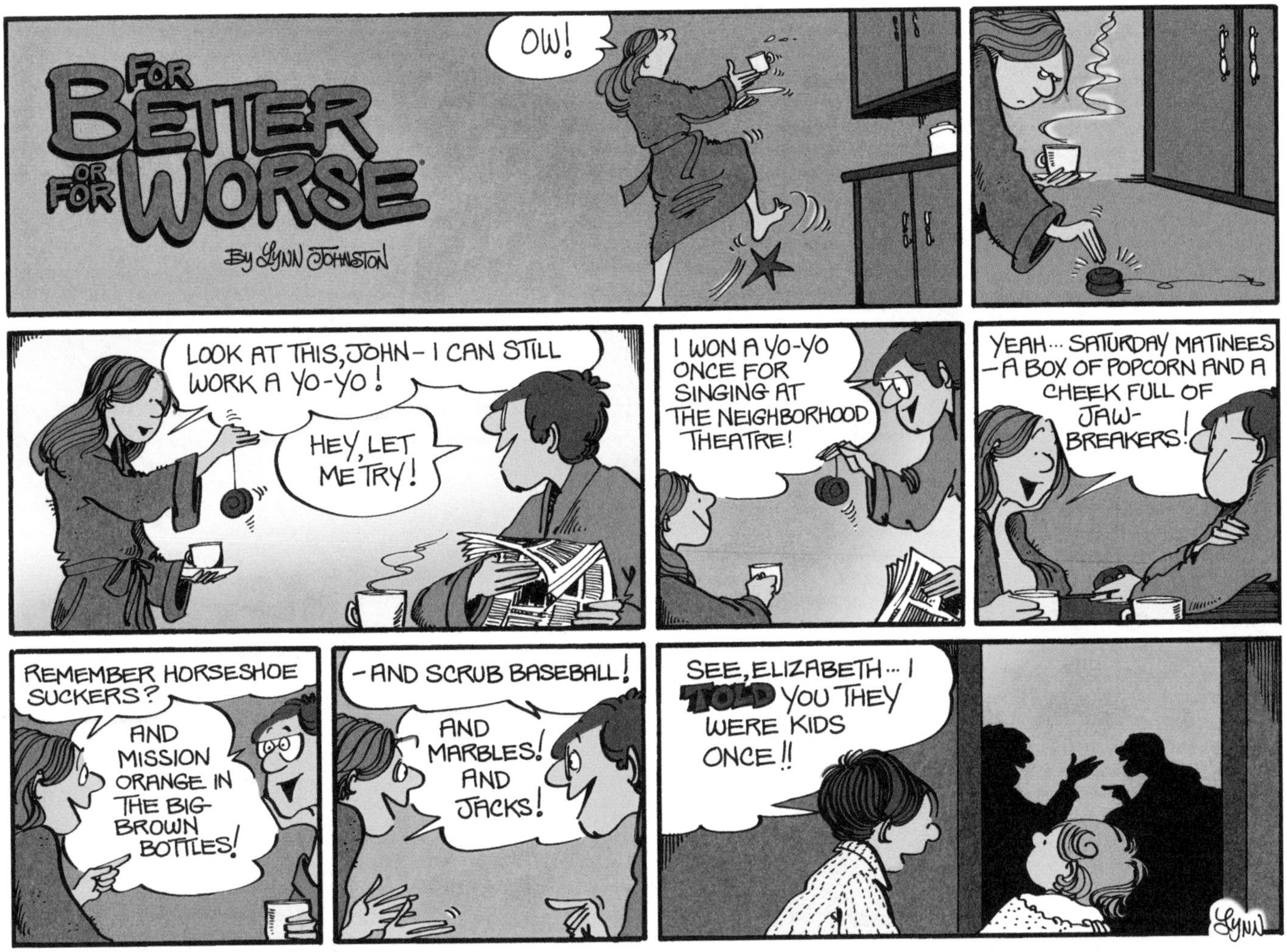
FOR BETTER OR FOR WORSE
BY LYNN JOHNSTON
OW!
LOOK AT THIS, JOHN - I CAN STILL WORK A YO-YO!
HEY, LET ME TRY!
I WON A YO-YO ONCE FOR SINGING AT THE NEIGHBORHOOD THEATRE!
YEAH... SATURDAY MATINEES - A BOX OF POPCORN AND A CHEEK FULL OF JAW-BREAKERS!
REMEMBER HORSESHOE SUCKERS?
AND MISSION ORANGE IN THE BIG BROWN BOTTLES!
- AND SCRUB BASEBALL!
AND MARBLES! AND JACKS!
SEE, ELIZABETH... I TOLD YOU THEY WERE KIDS ONCE!!
LYNN

It was hard to imagine my parents as children. To me, they had been born old and were just getting older. When they talked about days gone by, the photographs they turned to were black and white. Our world was in colour. What they talked about was hard to relate to. It was more like hearing a story than a real event.

Maybe it's because they had too much to do to enjoy the kind of childhood we had — they both grew up during the Depression, and had to work in order to help their families survive. Neither of my parents had the luxury of going to college or university. They learned from books and through experience, and were intellectuals in their own right.

I hoped that my kids would relate to my stories, but life changes so much between generations that Aaron and Katie probably listened with an attitude much like mine had been: "If you really were a kid at one time ... why don't you understand kids NOW?"

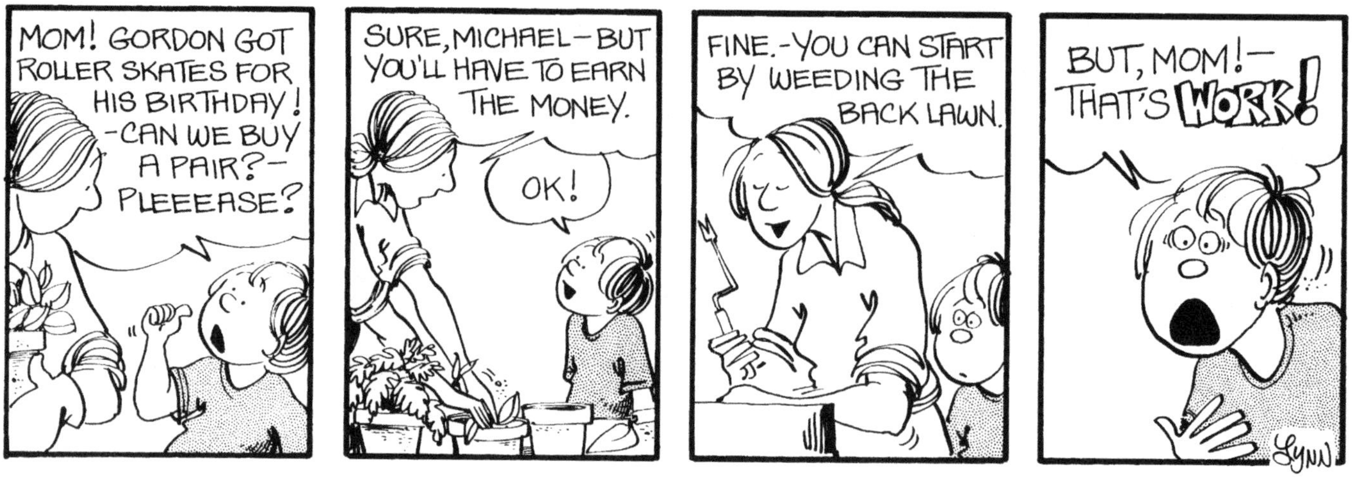
MOM! GORDON GOT ROLLER SKATES FOR HIS BIRTHDAY! -CAN WE BUY A PAIR?- PLEEEASE?
SURE, MICHAEL- BUT YOU'LL HAVE TO EARN THE MONEY.
OK!
FINE.-YOU CAN START BY WEEDING THE BACK LAWN.
BUT, MOM!- THAT'S WORK!
LYNN

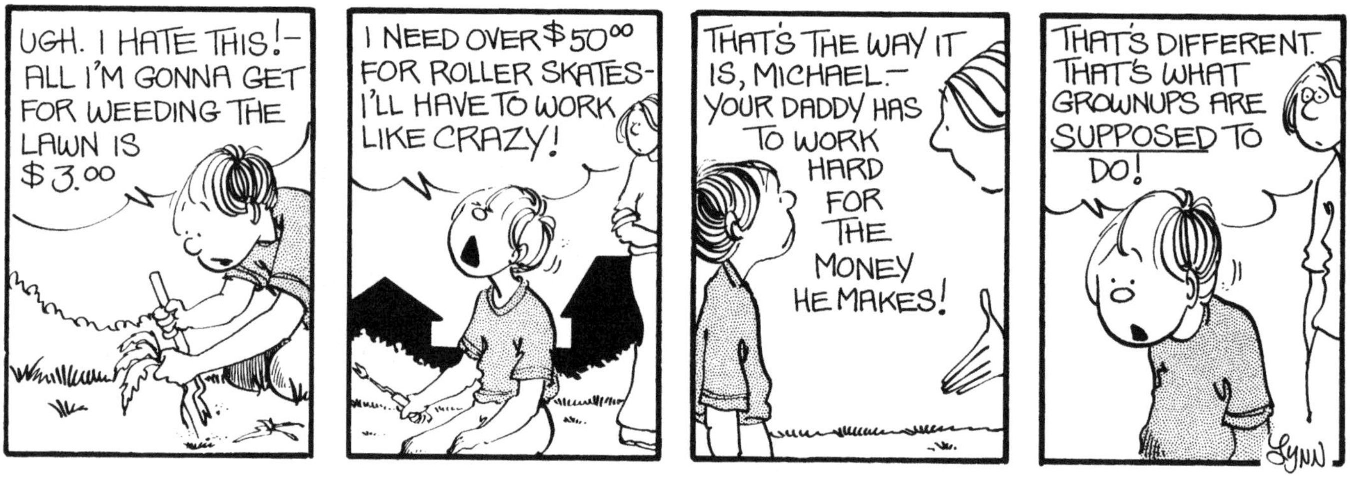
UGH. I HATE THIS!- ALL I'M GONNA GET FOR WEEDING THE LAWN IS $3.00
I NEED OVER $50.00 FOR ROLLER SKATES- I'LL HAVE TO WORK LIKE CRAZY!
THAT'S THE WAY IT IS, MICHAEL.- YOUR DADDY HAS TO WORK HARD FOR THE MONEY HE MAKES!
THAT'S DIFFERENT. THAT'S WHAT GROWNUPS ARE SUPPOSED TO DO!
LYNN

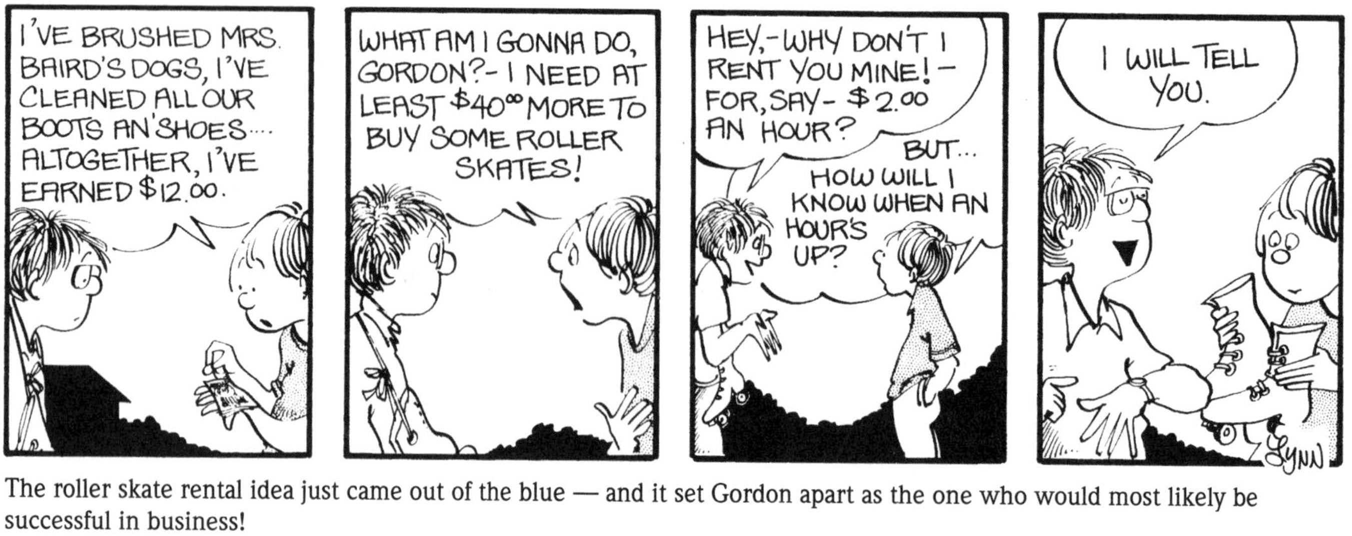
I'VE BRUSHED MRS. BAIRD'S DOGS, I'VE CLEANED ALL OUR BOOTS AN' SHOES.... ALTOGETHER, I'VE EARNED $12.00.
WHAT AM I GONNA DO, GORDON?- I NEED AT LEAST $40.00 MORE TO BUY SOME ROLLER SKATES!
HEY,-WHY DON'T I RENT YOU MINE!- FOR, SAY- $2.00 AN HOUR?
BUT... HOW WILL I KNOW WHEN AN HOUR'S UP?
I WILL TELL YOU.
LYNN

The roller skate rental idea just came out of the blue — and it set Gordon apart as the one who would most likely be successful in business!

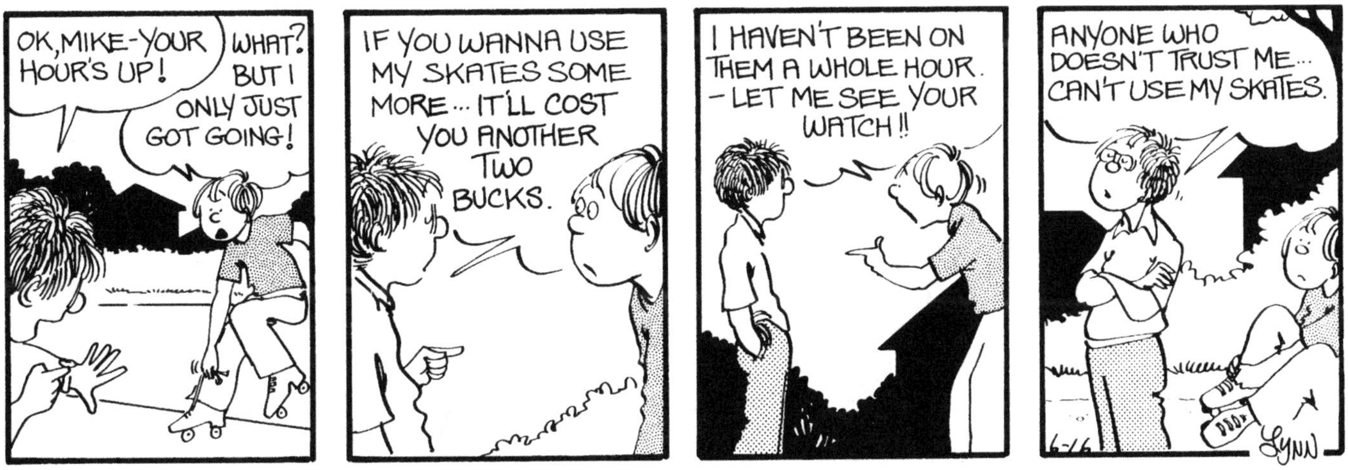

OK, MIKE-YOUR HOUR'S UP!
WHAT? BUT I ONLY JUST GOT GOING!
IF YOU WANNA USE MY SKATES SOME MORE... IT'LL COST YOU ANOTHER TWO BUCKS.
I HAVEN'T BEEN ON THEM A WHOLE HOUR. - LET ME SEE YOUR WATCH!!
ANYONE WHO DOESN'T TRUST ME... CAN'T USE MY SKATES.


Of course, he would have to learn how to keep his clients coming back!

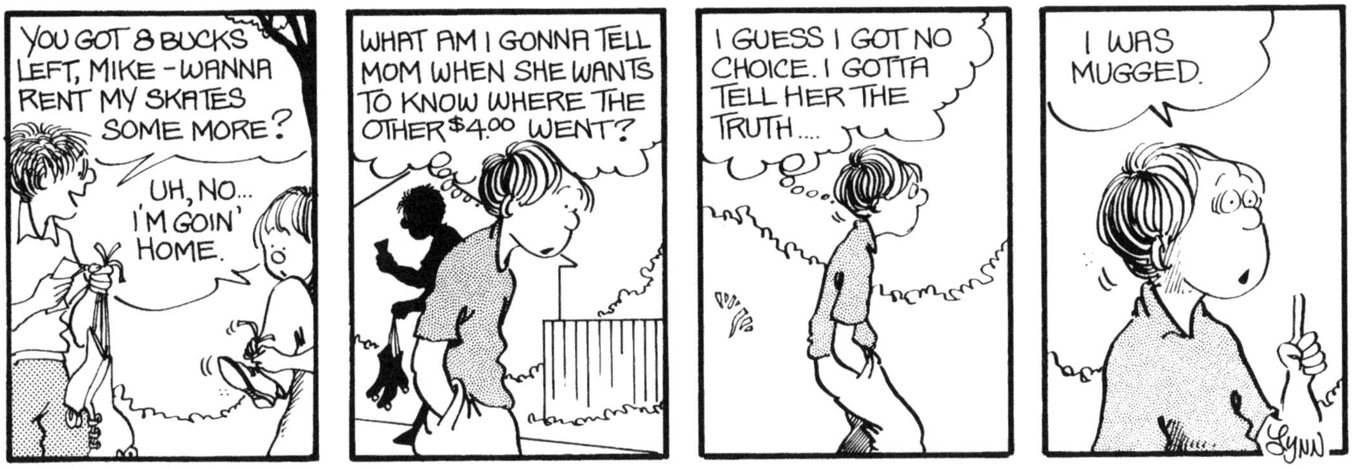

YOU GOT 8 BUCKS LEFT, MIKE - WANNA RENT MY SKATES SOME MORE?
UH, NO... I'M GOIN' HOME.
WHAT AM I GONNA TELL MOM WHEN SHE WANTS TO KNOW WHERE THE OTHER $4.00 WENT?
I GUESS I GOT NO CHOICE. I GOTTA TELL HER THE TRUTH....
I WAS MUGGED.


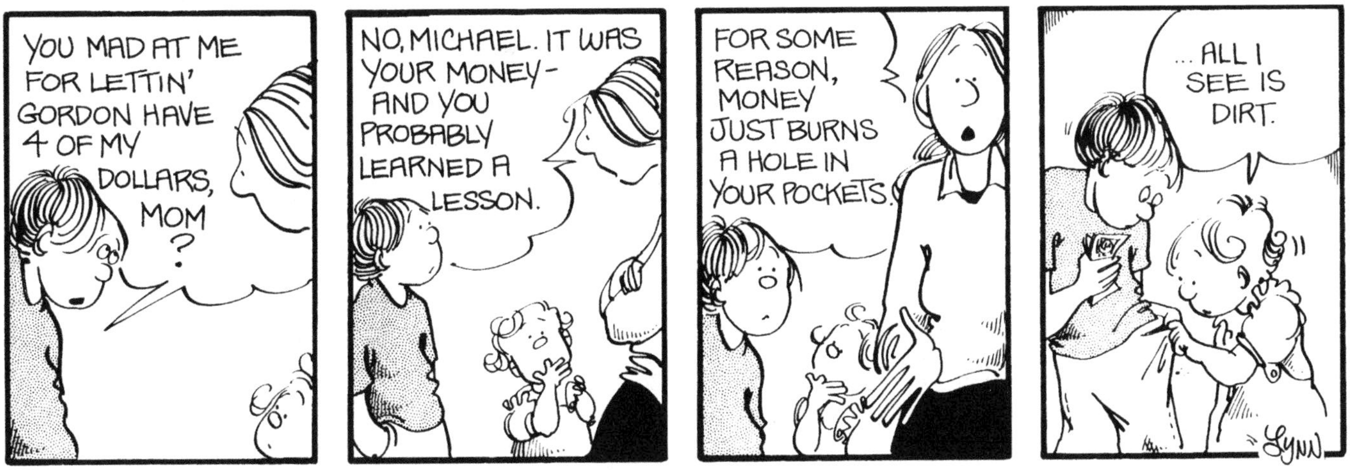

YOU MAD AT ME FOR LETTIN' GORDON HAVE 4 OF MY DOLLARS, MOM?
NO, MICHAEL. IT WAS YOUR MONEY - AND YOU PROBABLY LEARNED A LESSON.
FOR SOME REASON, MONEY JUST BURNS A HOLE IN YOUR POCKETS.
... ALL I SEE IS DIRT.

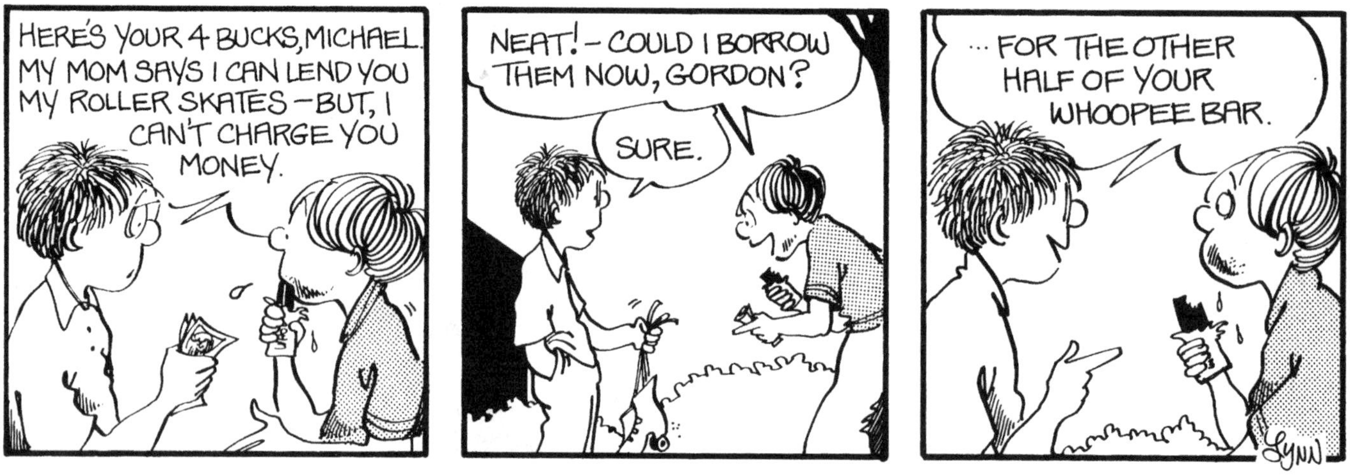
HERE'S YOUR 4 BUCKS, MICHAEL. MY MOM SAYS I CAN LEND YOU MY ROLLER SKATES — BUT, I CAN'T CHARGE YOU MONEY.
NEAT! — COULD I BORROW THEM NOW, GORDON?
SURE.
... FOR THE OTHER HALF OF YOUR WHOOPEE BAR.
LYNN

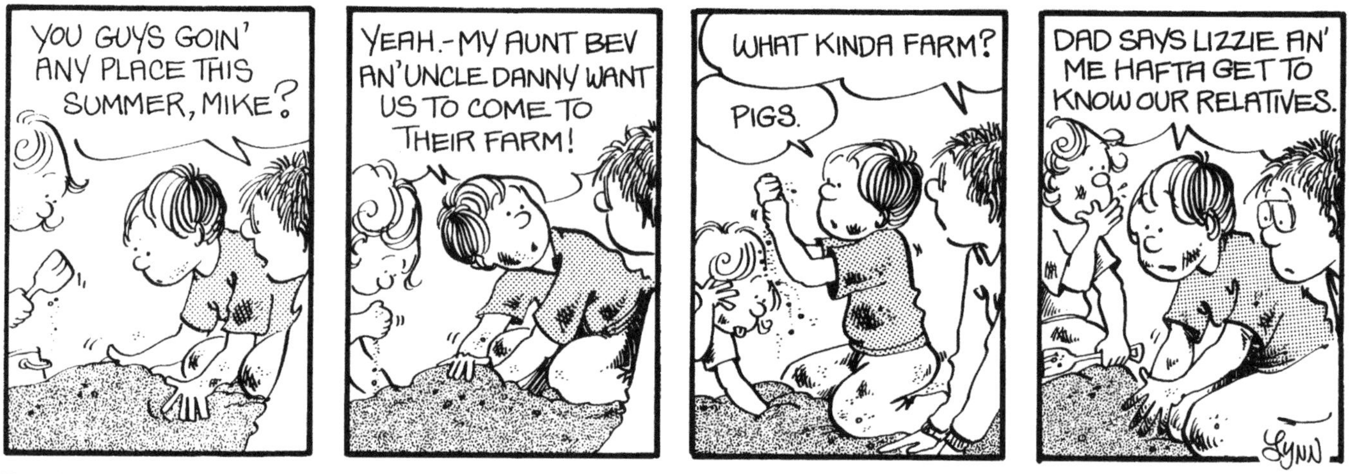
YOU GUYS GOIN' ANY PLACE THIS SUMMER, MIKE?
YEAH. — MY AUNT BEV AN' UNCLE DANNY WANT US TO COME TO THEIR FARM!
WHAT KINDA FARM?
PIGS.
DAD SAYS LIZZIE AN' ME HAFTA GET TO KNOW OUR RELATIVES.
LYNN

For three months one year, Rod and I worked on his sister and brother-in-law's farm. They grew grain and raised pigs, and I quickly went from being a city girl to driving the combine, chasing piglets, and building bins. It was an extraordinary experience, and the farm became one of my favourite places to take the Pattersons!

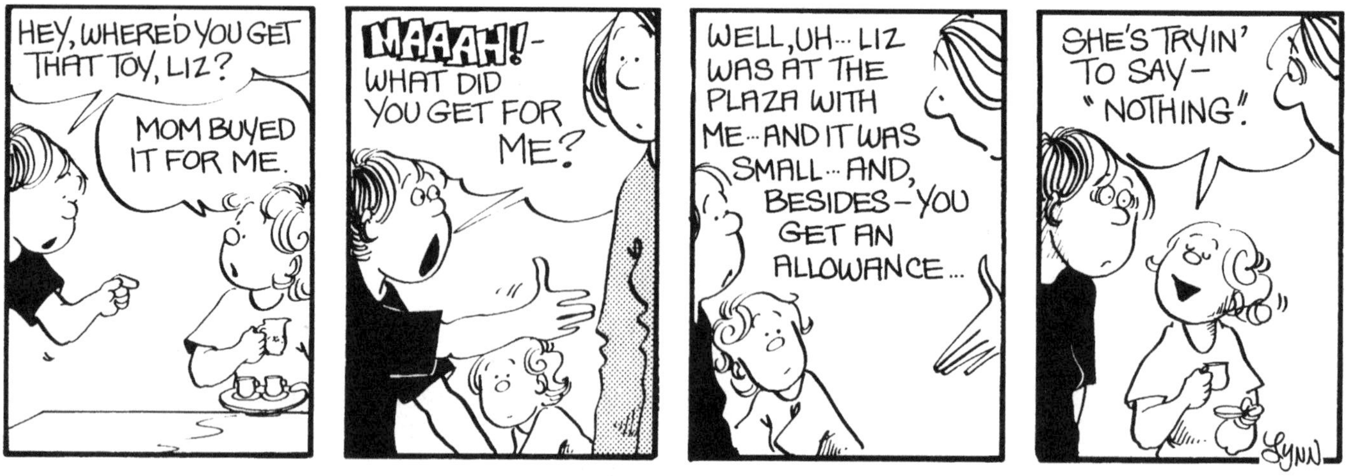
HEY, WHERE'D YOU GET THAT TOY, LIZ?
MOM BUYED IT FOR ME.
MAAAH! — WHAT DID YOU GET FOR ME?
WELL, UH... LIZ WAS AT THE PLAZA WITH ME... AND IT WAS SMALL... AND, BESIDES — YOU GET AN ALLOWANCE...
SHE'S TRYIN' TO SAY — "NOTHING."
LYNN

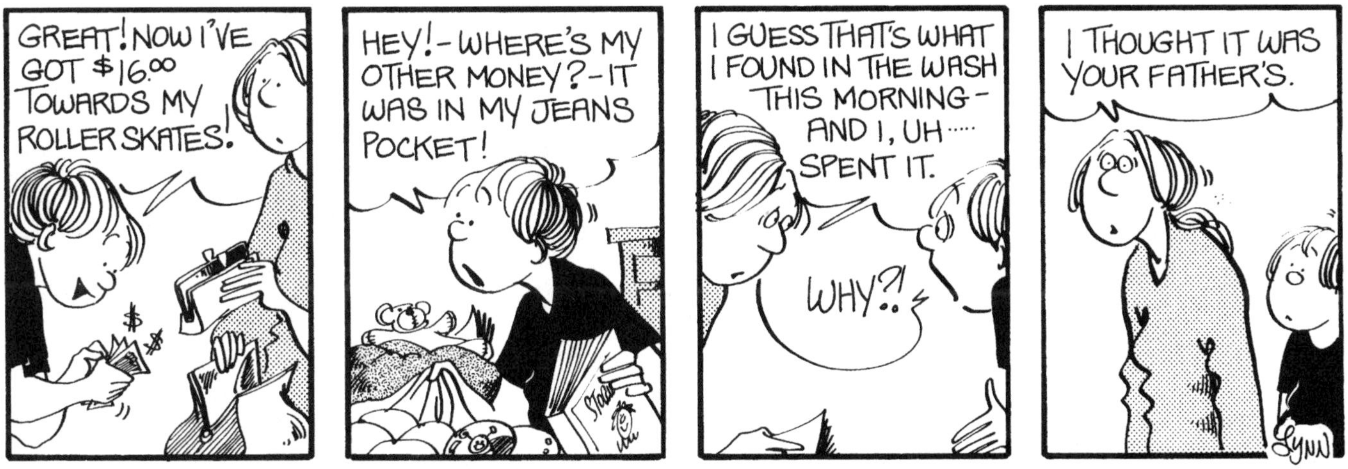
GREAT! NOW I'VE GOT $16.00 TOWARDS MY ROLLER SKATES!
HEY! - WHERE'S MY OTHER MONEY? - IT WAS IN MY JEANS POCKET!
I GUESS THAT'S WHAT I FOUND IN THE WASH THIS MORNING - AND I, UH..... SPENT IT.
WHY?!
I THOUGHT IT WAS YOUR FATHER'S.
LYNN

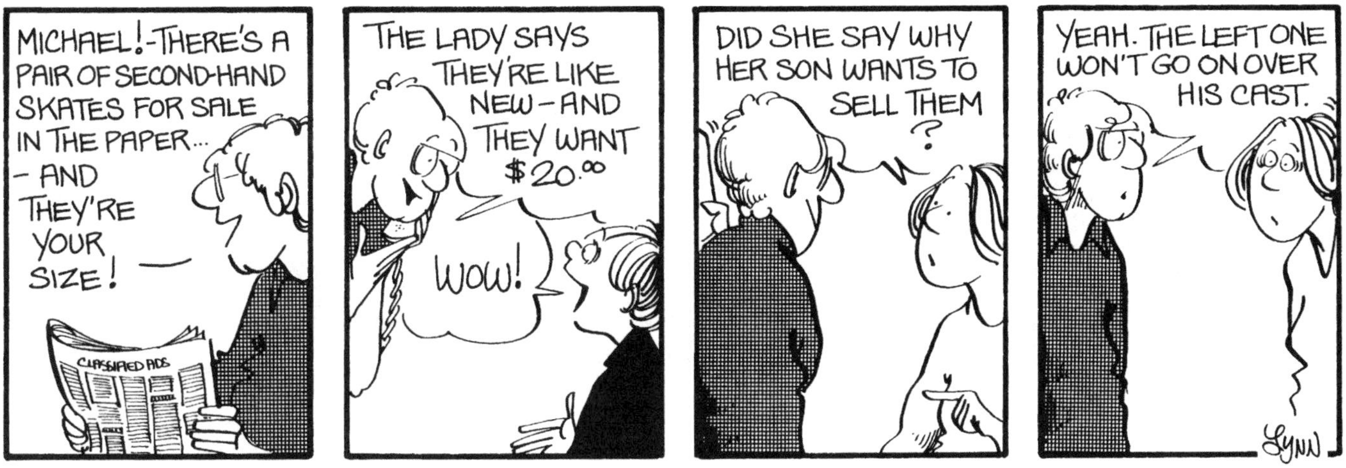
MICHAEL! - THERE'S A PAIR OF SECOND-HAND SKATES FOR SALE IN THE PAPER... - AND THEY'RE YOUR SIZE!
CLASSIFIED ADS
THE LADY SAYS THEY'RE LIKE NEW - AND THEY WANT $20.00
WOW!
DID SHE SAY WHY HER SON WANTS TO SELL THEM?
YEAH. THE LEFT ONE WON'T GO ON OVER HIS CAST.
LYNN

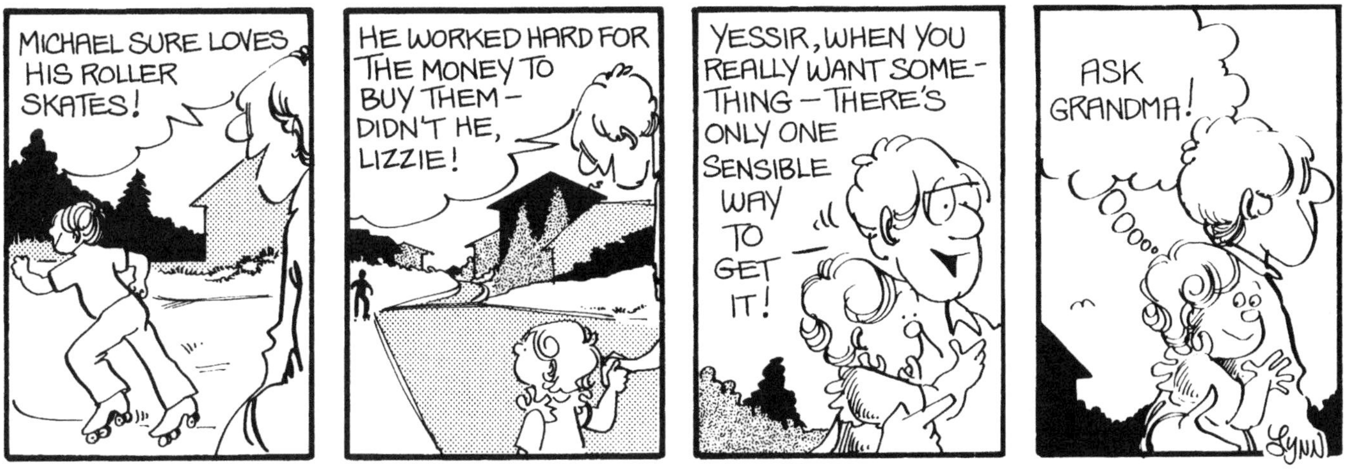
MICHAEL SURE LOVES HIS ROLLER SKATES!
HE WORKED HARD FOR THE MONEY TO BUY THEM - DIDN'T HE, LIZZIE!
YESSIR, WHEN YOU REALLY WANT SOME-THING - THERE'S ONLY ONE SENSIBLE WAY TO GET IT!
ASK GRANDMA!
LYNN

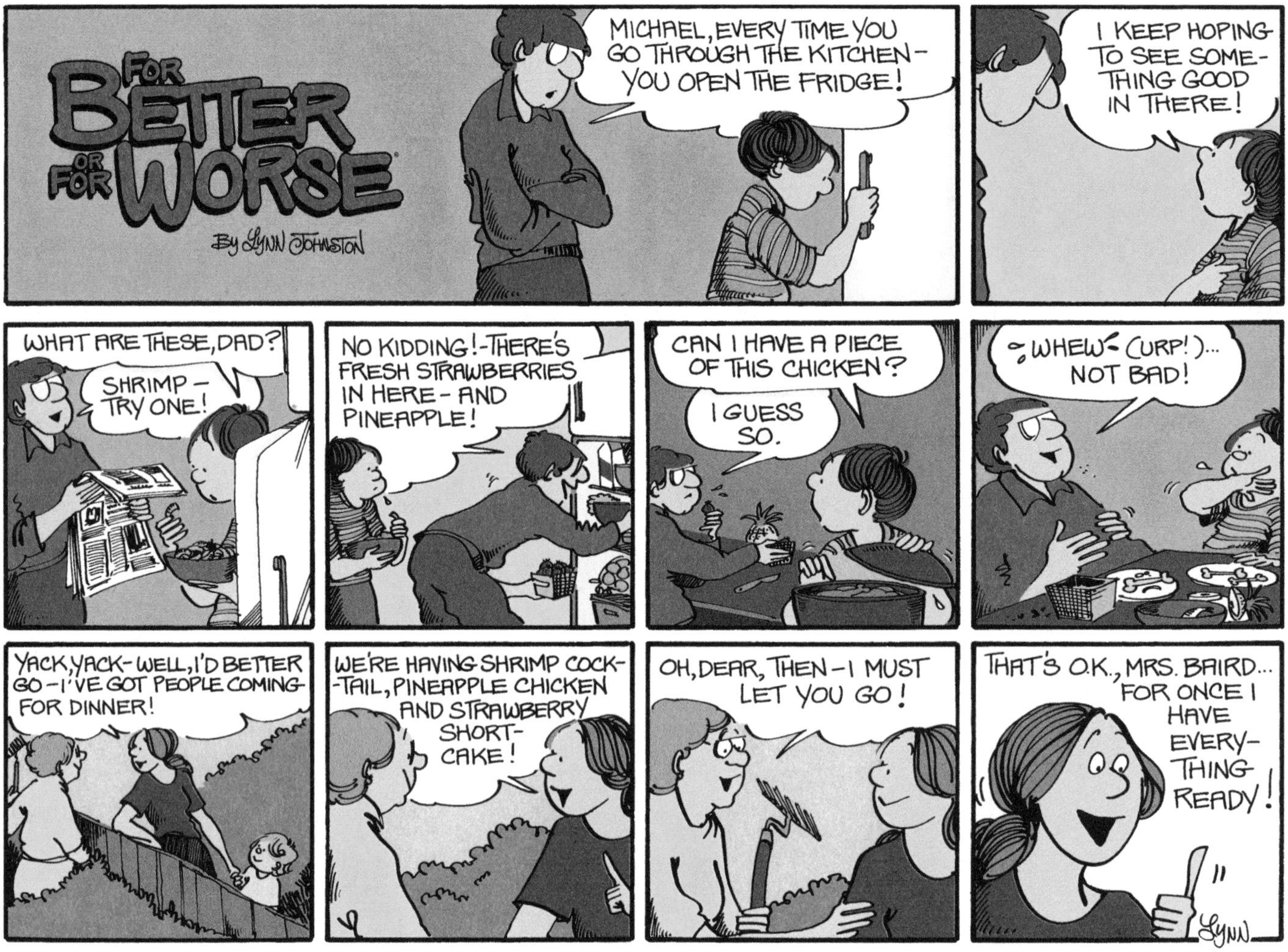
For Better or For Worse
By Lynn Johnston
MICHAEL, EVERY TIME YOU GO THROUGH THE KITCHEN - YOU OPEN THE FRIDGE!
I KEEP HOPING TO SEE SOMETHING GOOD IN THERE!
WHAT ARE THESE, DAD?
SHRIMP - TRY ONE!
NO KIDDING! - THERE'S FRESH STRAWBERRIES IN HERE - AND PINEAPPLE!
CAN I HAVE A PIECE OF THIS CHICKEN?
I GUESS SO.
WHEW (URP!)... NOT BAD!
YACK, YACK - WELL, I'D BETTER GO - I'VE GOT PEOPLE COMING FOR DINNER!
WE'RE HAVING SHRIMP COCKTAIL, PINEAPPLE CHICKEN AND STRAWBERRY SHORTCAKE!
OH, DEAR, THEN - I MUST LET YOU GO!
THAT'S O.K., MRS. BAIRD... FOR ONCE I HAVE EVERYTHING READY!
LYNN

Sometimes a friend would tell me something that was so perfect for a comic strip that I couldn't wait to go home and draw it up. My friend Loretta was a wonderful cook. She often had friends over for dinner, and was always well prepared ahead of time. In our small northern town, certain fruits and vegetables were hard to come by, so when a shipment of fresh food arrived, we all got into cooking mode. Loretta had filled her fridge in preparation for a neighbourhood get-together, but had forgotten to remind her family that the food was for company. By the time she discovered their scavenging, it was too late to replace the groceries. When she told me what had happened, I remember laughing so hard that I couldn't catch my breath. A few weeks later ... the same thing happened at MY place!

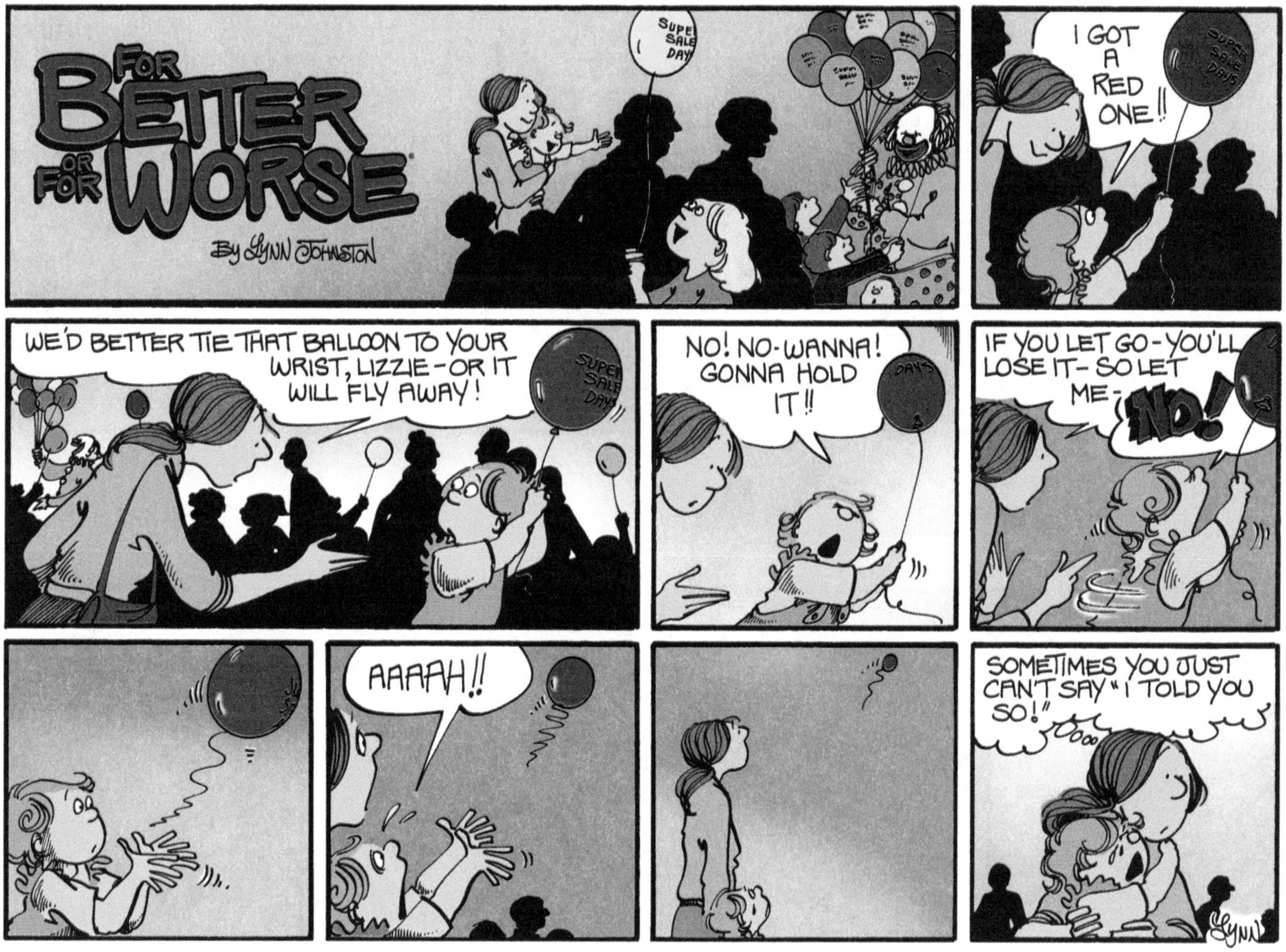
FOR BETTER OR FOR WORSE
BY LYNN JOHNSTON
SUPER SALE DAYS
I GOT A RED ONE!!
WE'D BETTER TIE THAT BALLOON TO YOUR WRIST, LIZZIE - OR IT WILL FLY AWAY!
NO! NO-WANNA! GONNA HOLD IT!!
IF YOU LET GO - YOU'LL LOSE IT - SO LET ME -
NO!
AAAAH!!
SOMETIMES YOU JUST CAN'T SAY "I TOLD YOU SO!"
LYNN

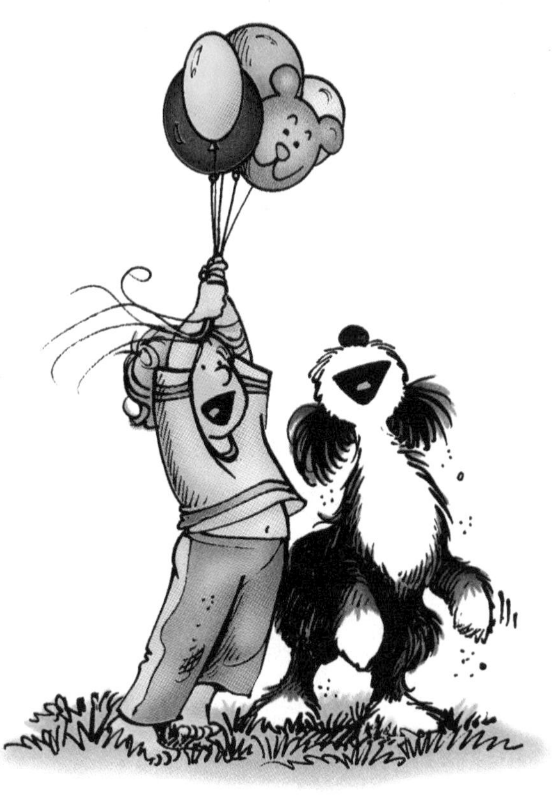

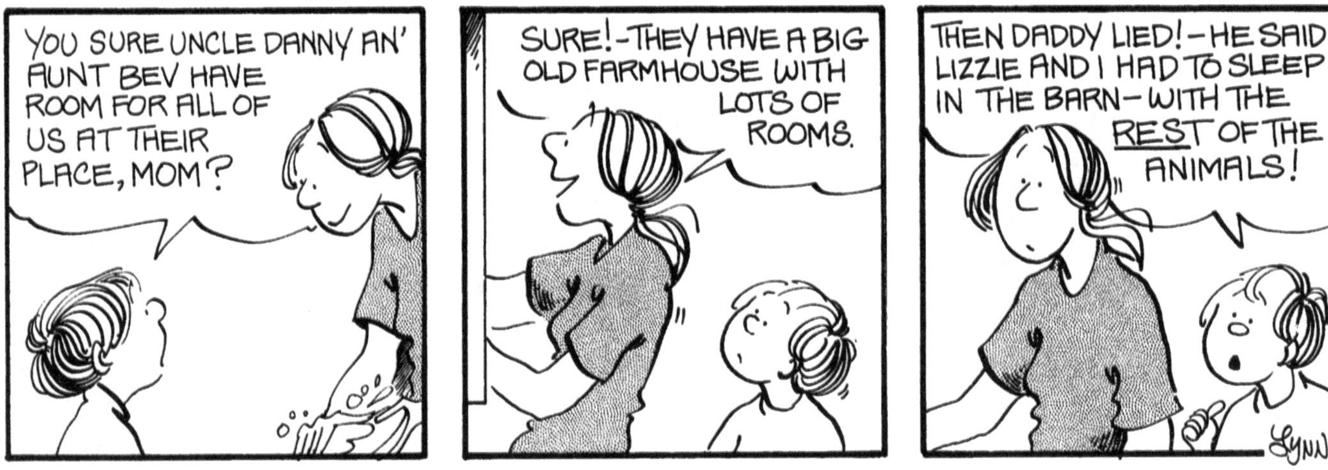
YOU SURE UNCLE DANNY AN' AUNT BEV HAVE ROOM FOR ALL OF US AT THEIR PLACE, MOM?
SURE! - THEY HAVE A BIG OLD FARMHOUSE WITH LOTS OF ROOMS.
THEN DADDY LIED! - HE SAID LIZZIE AND I HAD TO SLEEP IN THE BARN - WITH THE REST OF THE ANIMALS!
LYNN

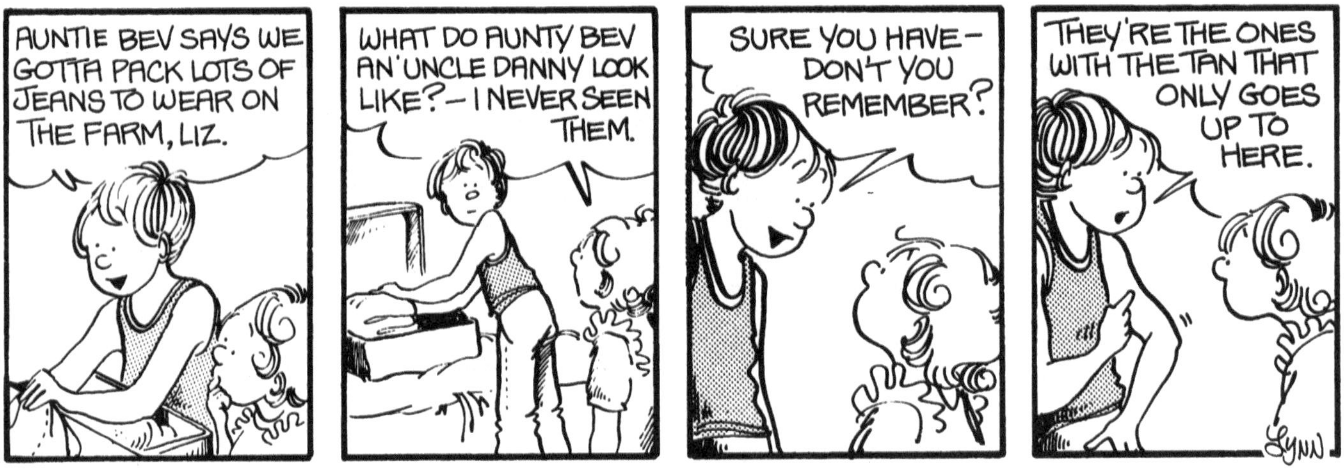
AUNTIE BEV SAYS WE GOTTA PACK LOTS OF JEANS TO WEAR ON THE FARM, LIZ.
WHAT DO AUNTY BEV AN' UNCLE DANNY LOOK LIKE? - I NEVER SEEN THEM.
SURE YOU HAVE - DON'T YOU REMEMBER?
THEY'RE THE ONES WITH THE TAN THAT ONLY GOES UP TO HERE.
LYNN

Auntie Bev and Uncle Danny were closely based on my sister and brother-in-law, Beth and Don Cruikshank, of Miami, Manitoba. They are both such wonderful characters, I hardly had to make anything up!

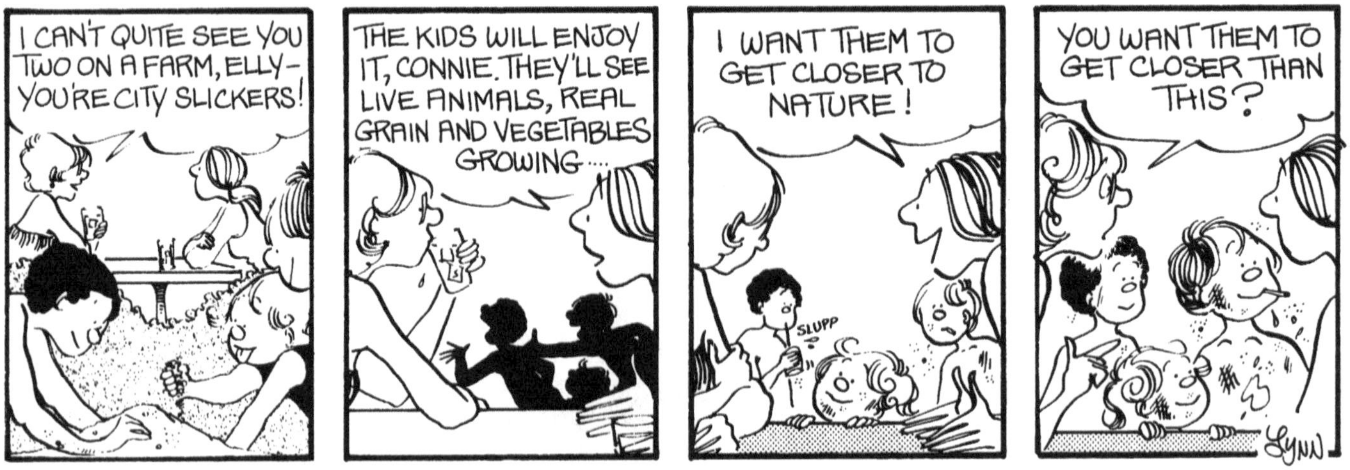
I CAN'T QUITE SEE YOU TWO ON A FARM, ELLY - YOU'RE CITY SLICKERS!
THE KIDS WILL ENJOY IT, CONNIE. THEY'LL SEE LIVE ANIMALS, REAL GRAIN AND VEGETABLES GROWING....
I WANT THEM TO GET CLOSER TO NATURE!
SLUPP
YOU WANT THEM TO GET CLOSER THAN THIS?
LYNN

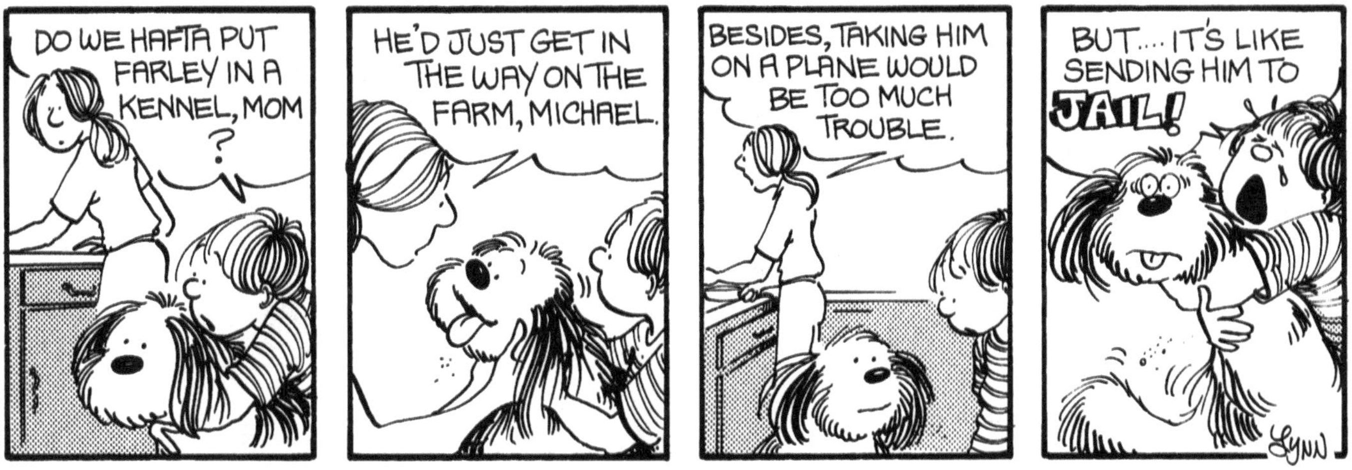
DO WE HAFTA PUT FARLEY IN A KENNEL, MOM ?
HE'D JUST GET IN THE WAY ON THE FARM, MICHAEL.
BESIDES, TAKING HIM ON A PLANE WOULD BE TOO MUCH TROUBLE.
BUT.... IT'S LIKE SENDING HIM TO JAIL!
LYNN

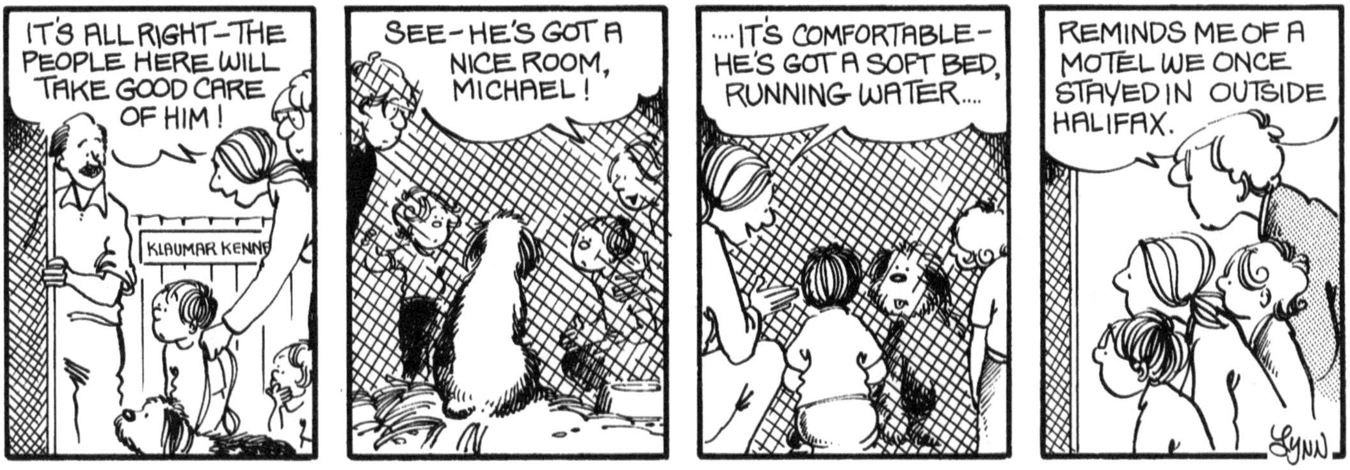
IT'S ALL RIGHT–THE PEOPLE HERE WILL TAKE GOOD CARE OF HIM!
KLAUMAR KENNE
SEE–HE'S GOT A NICE ROOM, MICHAEL!
....IT'S COMFORTABLE–HE'S GOT A SOFT BED, RUNNING WATER....
REMINDS ME OF A MOTEL WE ONCE STAYED IN OUTSIDE HALIFAX.
LYNN

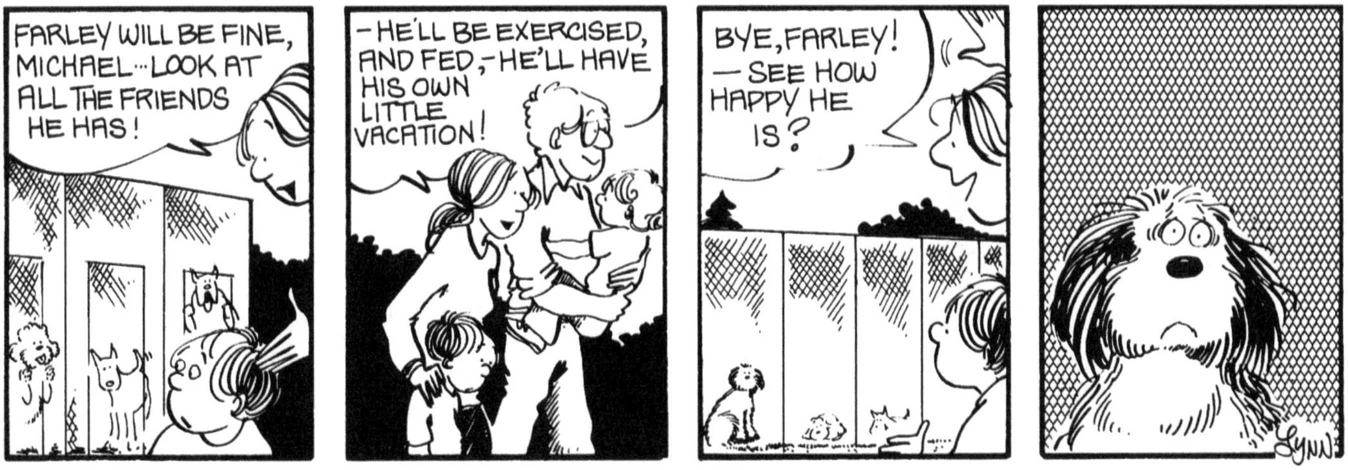
FARLEY WILL BE FINE, MICHAEL...LOOK AT ALL THE FRIENDS HE HAS!
–HE'LL BE EXERCISED, AND FED,–HE'LL HAVE HIS OWN LITTLE VACATION!
BYE, FARLEY! —SEE HOW HAPPY HE IS?
LYNN

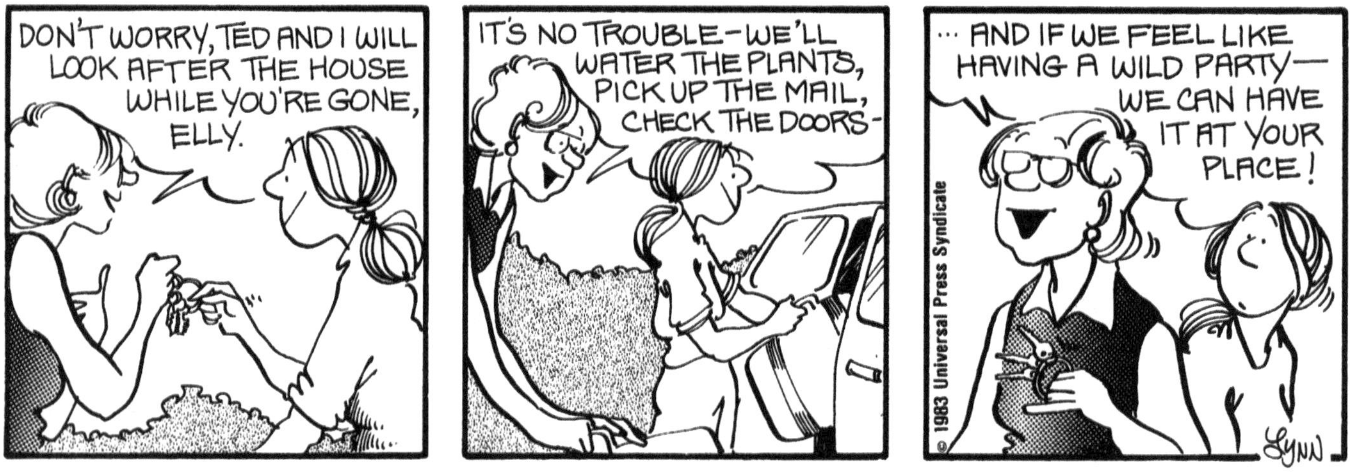
DON'T WORRY, TED AND I WILL LOOK AFTER THE HOUSE WHILE YOU'RE GONE, ELLY.
IT'S NO TROUBLE—WE'LL WATER THE PLANTS, PICK UP THE MAIL, CHECK THE DOORS-
... AND IF WE FEEL LIKE HAVING A WILD PARTY— WE CAN HAVE IT AT YOUR PLACE!
© 1983 Universal Press Syndicate
LYNN

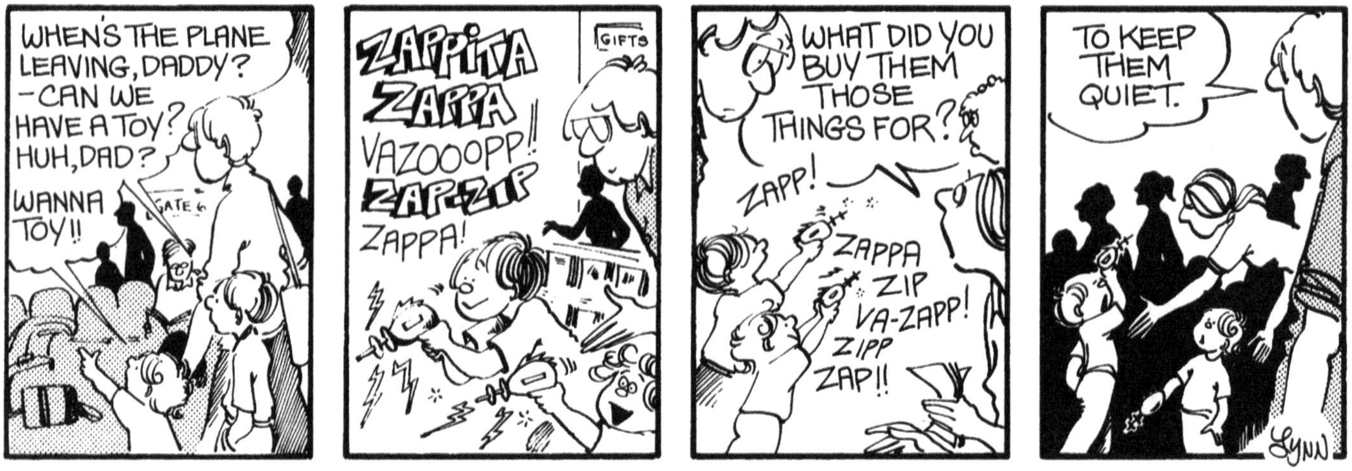
WHEN'S THE PLANE LEAVING, DADDY? —CAN WE HAVE A TOY? HUH, DAD?
WANNA TOY!!
GATE 6
GIFTS
ZAPPITA ZAPPA VAZOOOPP!! ZAP-ZIP ZAPPA!
WHAT DID YOU BUY THEM THOSE THINGS FOR?
ZAPP! ZAPPA ZIP VA-ZAPP! ZIPP ZAP!!
TO KEEP THEM QUIET.
LYNN

Aaron wanted to take his transparent plastic spacegun with him to Winnipeg, and did not want it to go out of his sight.

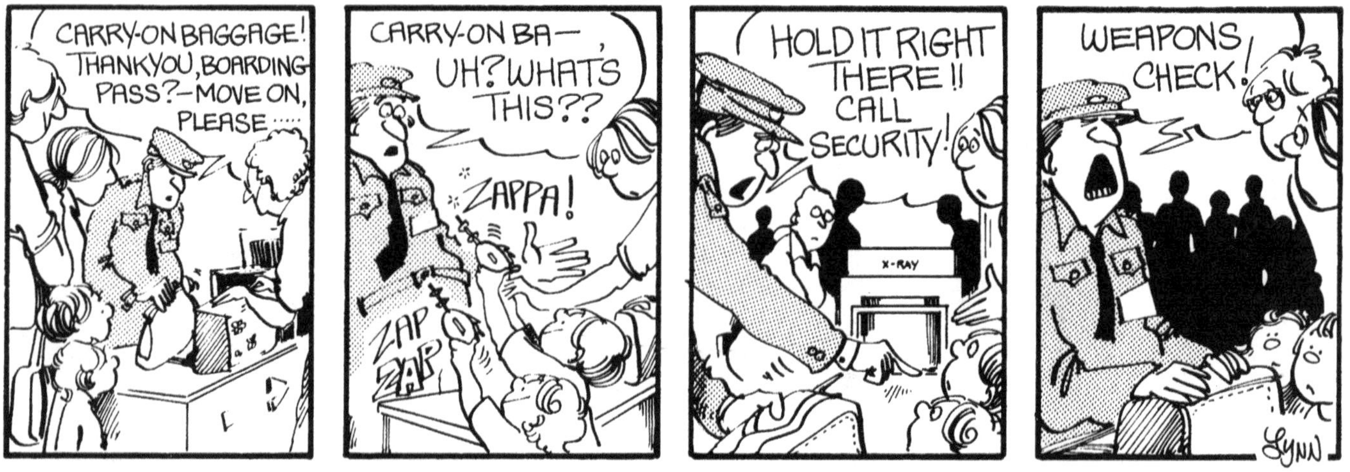
CARRY-ON BAGGAGE! THANKYOU, BOARDING PASS?—MOVE ON, PLEASE.....
CARRY-ON BA—, UH? WHAT'S THIS??
ZAPPA!
ZAP ZAP
HOLD IT RIGHT THERE!! CALL SECURITY!
X-RAY
WEAPONS CHECK!
LYNN

This was long before the strict security measures of today. In Toronto, however, he pointed it at a man in a uniform, and we were immediately stopped, searched, and reprimanded for trying to bring a weapon onto the plane. It was funny, but we should have known better!

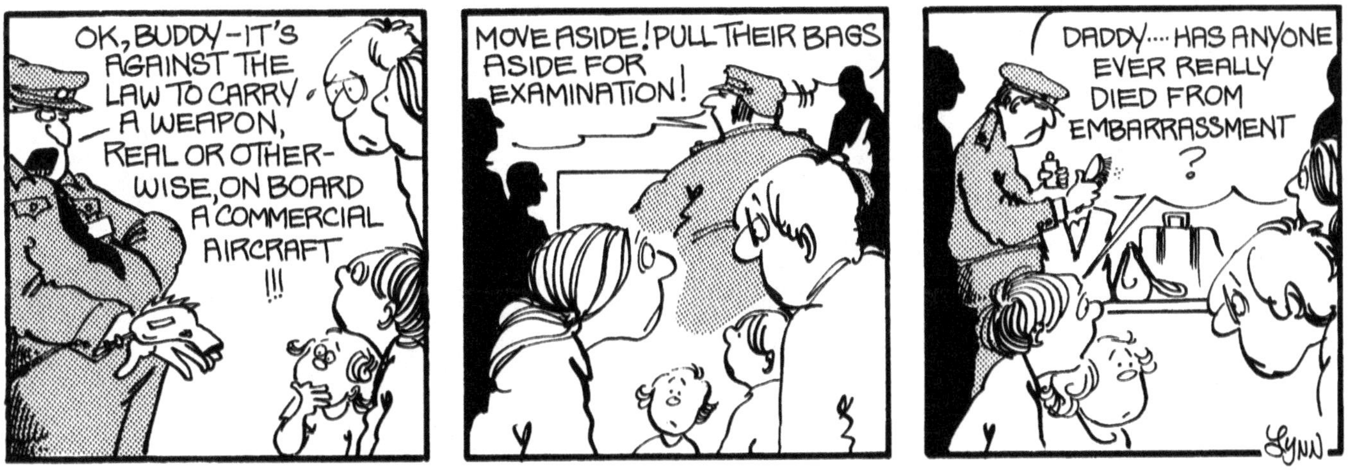
OK, BUDDY–IT'S AGAINST THE LAW TO CARRY A WEAPON, REAL OR OTHER-WISE, ON BOARD A COMMERCIAL AIRCRAFT !!!
MOVE ASIDE! PULL THEIR BAGS ASIDE FOR EXAMINATION!
DADDY.... HAS ANYONE EVER REALLY DIED FROM EMBARRASSMENT ?
LYNN

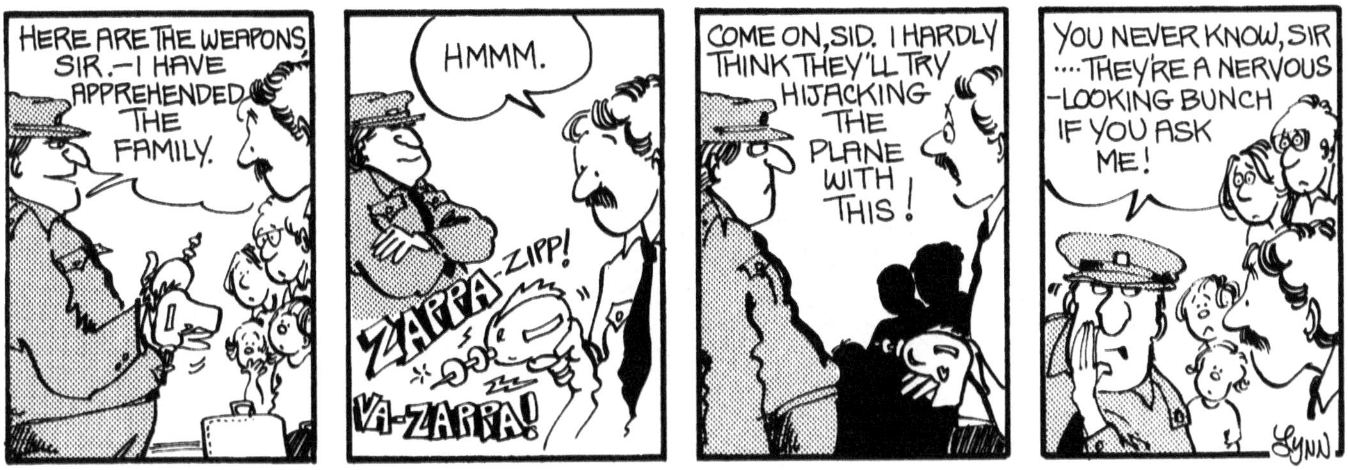
HERE ARE THE WEAPONS, SIR.–I HAVE APPREHENDED THE FAMILY.
HMMM.
ZAPPA-ZIPP!
VA-ZAPPA!
COME ON, SID. I HARDLY THINK THEY'LL TRY HIJACKING THE PLANE WITH THIS!
YOU NEVER KNOW, SIR .... THEY'RE A NERVOUS-LOOKING BUNCH IF YOU ASK ME!
LYNN

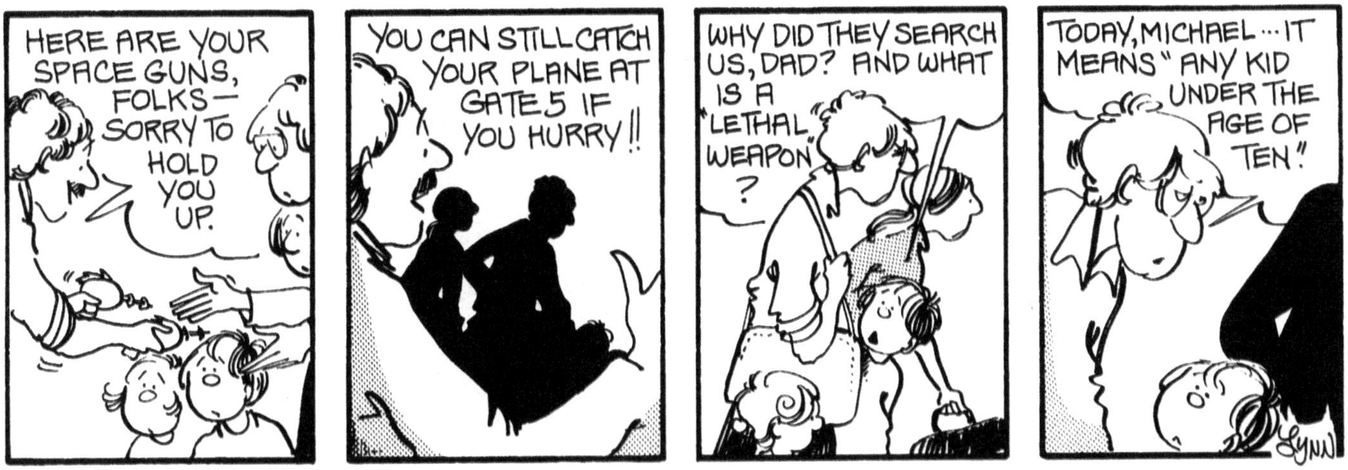
HERE ARE YOUR SPACE GUNS, FOLKS– SORRY TO HOLD YOU UP.
YOU CAN STILL CATCH YOUR PLANE AT GATE 5 IF YOU HURRY!!
WHY DID THEY SEARCH US, DAD? AND WHAT IS A "LETHAL WEAPON" ?
TODAY, MICHAEL ... IT MEANS "ANY KID UNDER THE AGE OF TEN."
LYNN

**HEY THERE, FOLKS! — IT'S BEEN A LONG TIME!**

**THIS COULDN'T BE MICHAEL, COULD IT? — AND WHO'S THIS BIG GIRL?**

**YEAH! LIZZIE AN' I HAVE GROWN A LOT SINCE YOU SAW US, UNCLE DANNY!**

**WHAT SORTA FERTILIZER YOU BEEN USING?**

I used photographs of Beth and Don in order to get a likeness and, although it's not easy for me to do caricatures, I managed to draw "Uncle Danny" so well, he was once recognized on the street in Winnipeg!

Beth and Don.

368

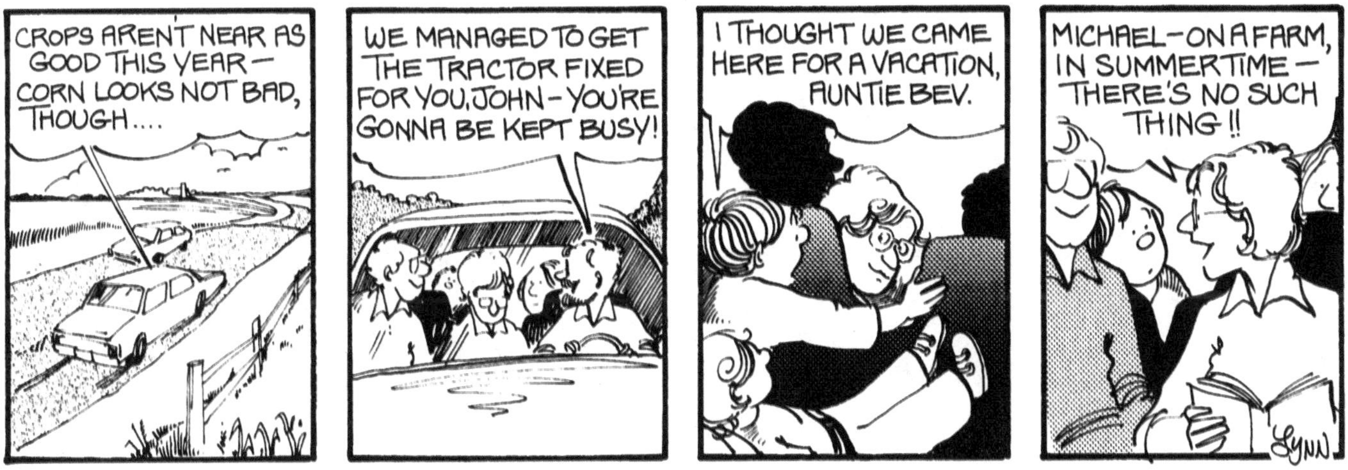
CROPS AREN'T NEAR AS GOOD THIS YEAR — CORN LOOKS NOT BAD, THOUGH....
WE MANAGED TO GET THE TRACTOR FIXED FOR YOU, JOHN - YOU'RE GONNA BE KEPT BUSY!
I THOUGHT WE CAME HERE FOR A VACATION, AUNTIE BEV.
MICHAEL—ON A FARM, IN SUMMERTIME — THERE'S NO SUCH THING !!
LYNN

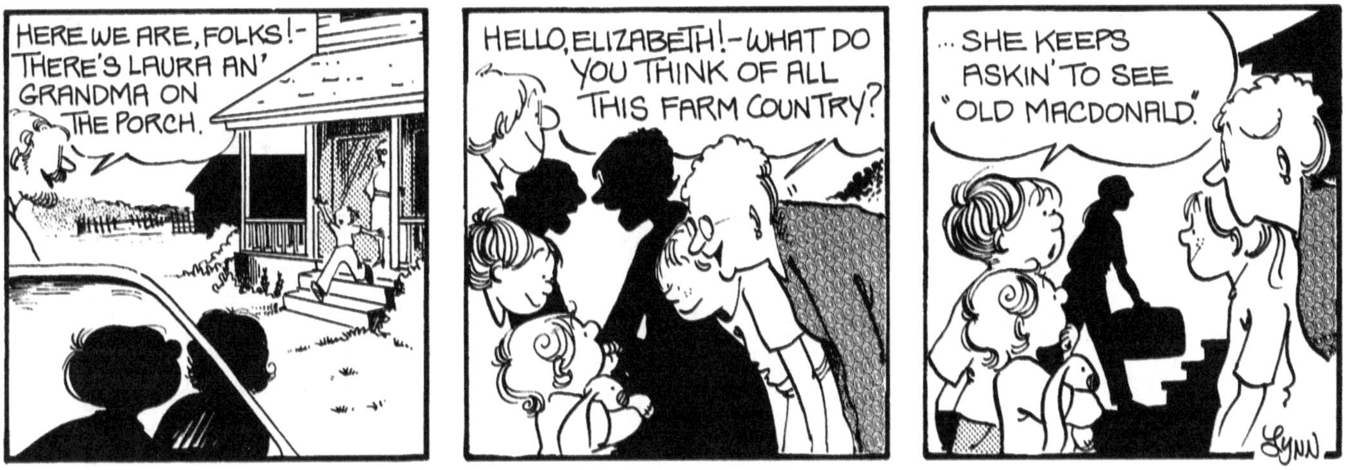
HERE WE ARE, FOLKS! - THERE'S LAURA AN' GRANDMA ON THE PORCH.
HELLO, ELIZABETH! - WHAT DO YOU THINK OF ALL THIS FARM COUNTRY?
... SHE KEEPS ASKIN' TO SEE "OLD MACDONALD."
LYNN

I used photos of Beth and Don's house as reference, too. The older lady here is Dan's mother — she made few appearances after this.

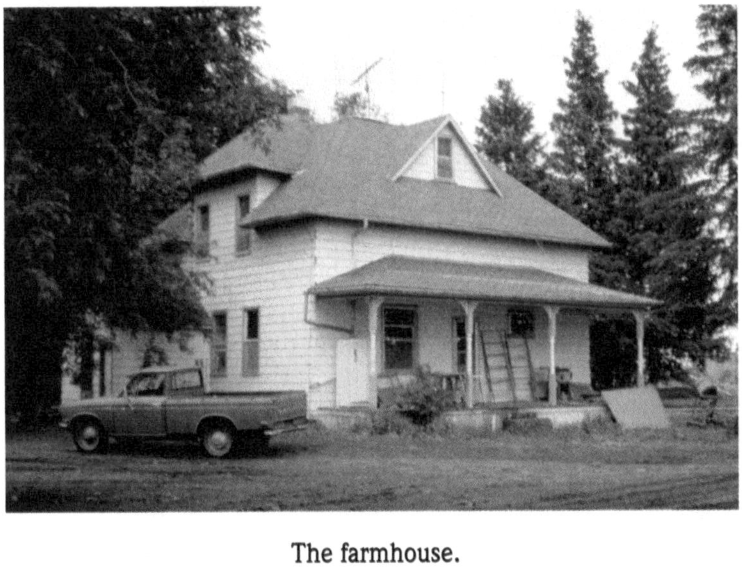

The farmhouse.

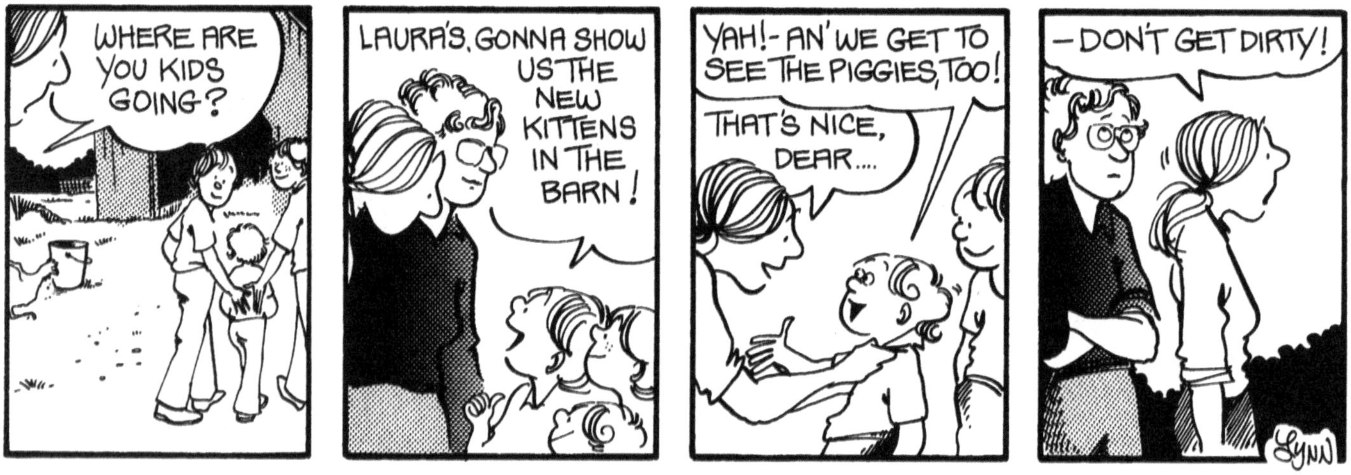
WHERE ARE YOU KIDS GOING?
LAURA'S, GONNA SHOW US THE NEW KITTENS IN THE BARN!
YAH!- AN' WE GET TO SEE THE PIGGIES, TOO!
THAT'S NICE, DEAR....
-DON'T GET DIRTY!
LYNN

Laura was a combination of Beth and Don's three daughters: Lauren, Chrissy, and Arli. It was much easier writing about one cousin in the strip than three!

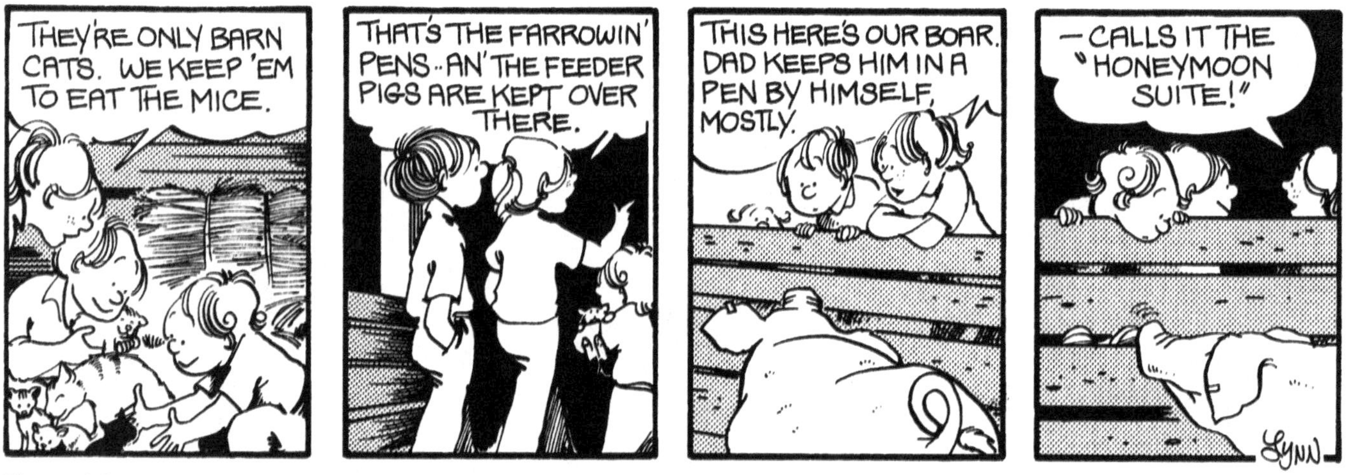
THEY'RE ONLY BARN CATS. WE KEEP 'EM TO EAT THE MICE.
THAT'S THE FARROWIN' PENS - AN' THE FEEDER PIGS ARE KEPT OVER THERE.
THIS HERE'S OUR BOAR. DAD KEEPS HIM IN A PEN BY HIMSELF, MOSTLY.
-CALLS IT THE "HONEYMOON SUITE!"
LYNN

The real farm story began before Katie was born. Rod and I were newly married, and Aaron was about three when we drove west from our home in Dundas, Ontario, and became farmhands for the summer at Don and Beth's place in Miami, Manitoba. *For Better or for Worse* wasn't even an idea at the time. Rod was still in dental school, and we needed the work!

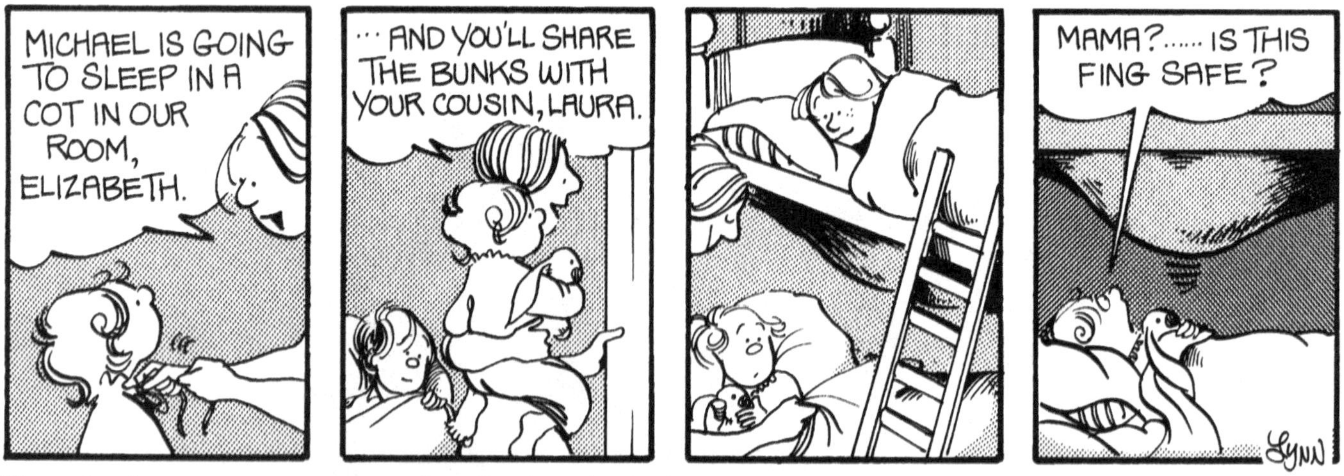
MICHAEL IS GOING TO SLEEP IN A COT IN OUR ROOM, ELIZABETH.
... AND YOU'LL SHARE THE BUNKS WITH YOUR COUSIN, LAURA.
MAMA?...... IS THIS FING SAFE?
LYNN

These sleeping arrangements were made up for the strip. As the hired hands, Rod, Aaron, and I shared a small white house across the road from the main farm. We had a lot to do, and eventually Rod's parents took pity on Aaron and took him back to Lynn Lake — a much safer environment for a curious small boy.

Working on a farm was something I had never imagined doing. My experience with farm machinery was having to draw pieces of equipment for a client who put out parts-and-supplies catalogues.

One of my catalogue illustrations.

The day we arrived in Beth and Don's yard, Beth appeared at the door wearing her veterinary overalls and carrying a medical kit. In my pink shorts, white blouse, and big hoop earrings, I bounced out of the car, and we both looked at each other, thinking, "Well, what have we got here?"

After a hasty introduction, I asked if there was anything I could do to help. Beth said, "I've got fifty piglets to castrate. You can give me a hand with that." We took Aaron to the house across the road, and Don's mom got him settled in his room. Rod went out into the fields to look for Donnie, and I changed. "What do you wear to a castration?" I wondered. In jeans and a T-shirt, I joined Beth in the pig barn and went to work. It wasn't a hard job, but it was dirty. I learned how to grab the fat piggies by the hind legs. Thin ones I could catch with one hand, just above the hips. Females I marked with blue chalk and released. The males I flipped over onto a bench and held, while Beth disinfected their groin areas, quickly removed their testicles, and injected them with an antibiotic. The barn cats watched with enthusiasm as Beth and I became a cohesive unit: grab, cut, release, grab, cut, release. I was amazed at how the piglets went right back to playing and eating as soon as I let them go.

When we had finished, we walked back to the main house in time to see Rod and Donnie coming in from the fields on the tractor. When I happily told them what I had done and how easy it had been ... both guys looked a little pale. My first day on the job, and already I had established myself as a woman to be reckoned with.

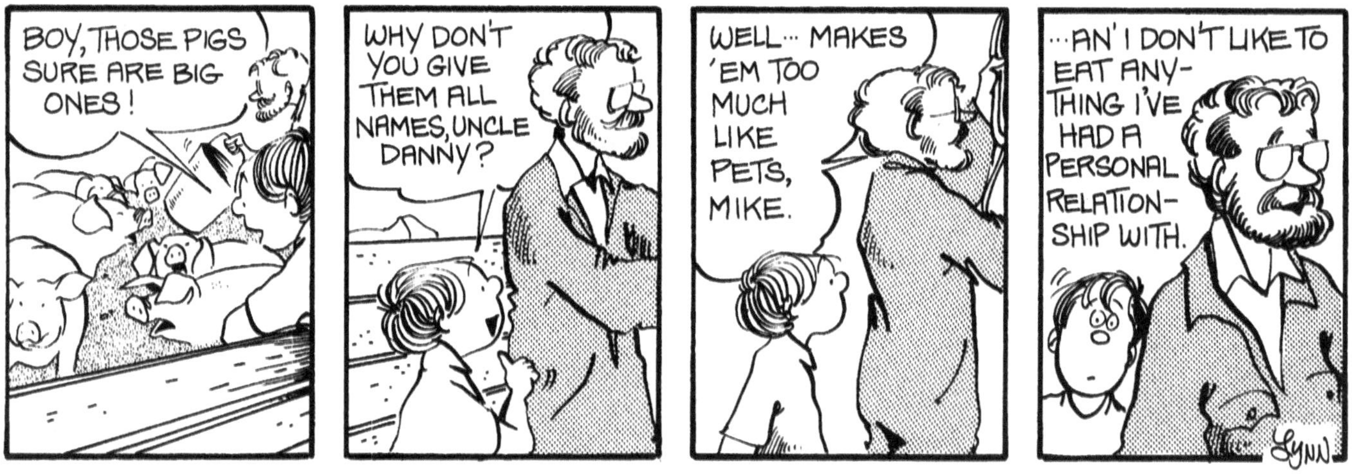
BOY, THOSE PIGS SURE ARE BIG ONES!
WHY DON'T YOU GIVE THEM ALL NAMES, UNCLE DANNY?
WELL... MAKES 'EM TOO MUCH LIKE PETS, MIKE.
...AN' I DON'T LIKE TO EAT ANYTHING I'VE HAD A PERSONAL RELATIONSHIP WITH.
LYNN

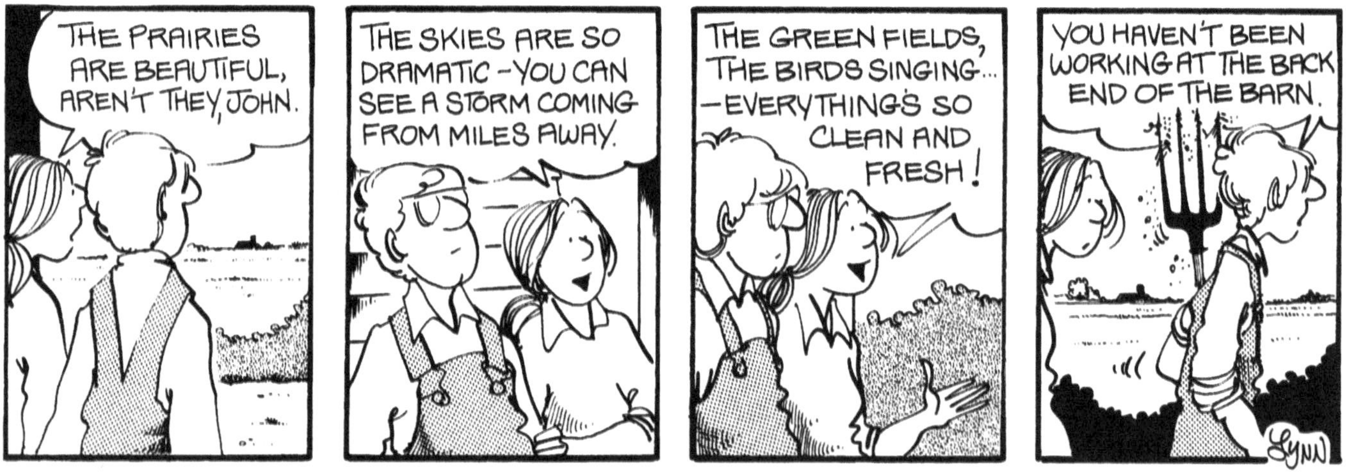
THE PRAIRIES ARE BEAUTIFUL, AREN'T THEY, JOHN.
THE SKIES ARE SO DRAMATIC - YOU CAN SEE A STORM COMING FROM MILES AWAY.
THE GREEN FIELDS, THE BIRDS SINGING... - EVERYTHING'S SO CLEAN AND FRESH!
YOU HAVEN'T BEEN WORKING AT THE BACK END OF THE BARN.
LYNN

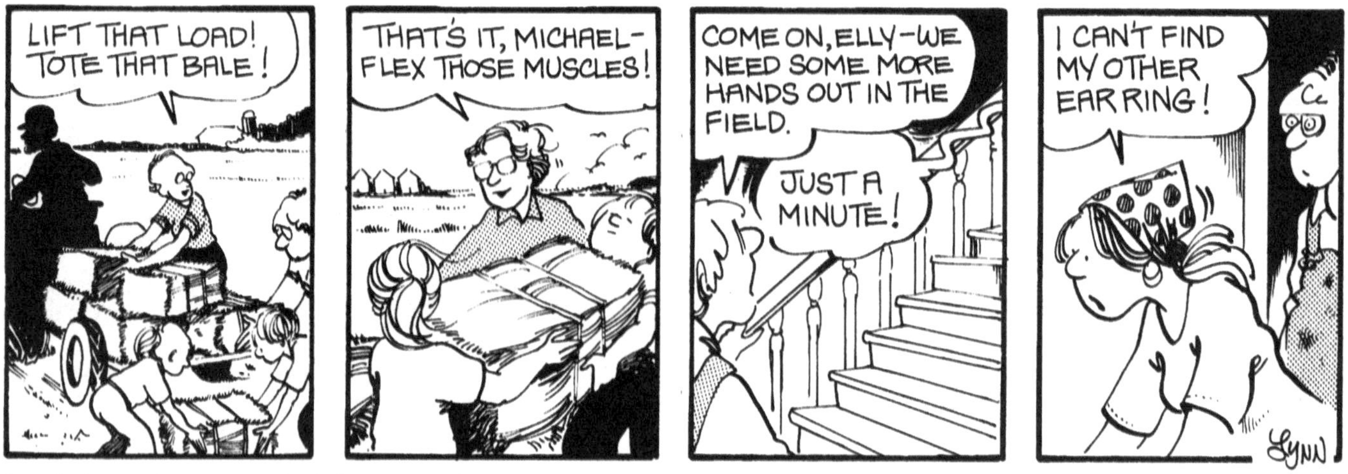
LIFT THAT LOAD! TOTE THAT BALE!
THAT'S IT, MICHAEL - FLEX THOSE MUSCLES!
COME ON, ELLY - WE NEED SOME MORE HANDS OUT IN THE FIELD.
JUST A MINUTE!
I CAN'T FIND MY OTHER EAR RING!
LYNN

People in rural areas watched this series closely — to see if I'd "get it right." I soon got letters telling me that the bailing twine was going the wrong way in this illustration! No matter what you THINK you know, it's best to check your references!

THERE'S A LOT TO LEARN ON A FARM, MICHAEL.
FOR EXAMPLE - THAT FEATHERY STUFF IS OATS, WHEAT HAS A TALL, GRASS-LIKE STALK.
THEY'RE GROWING WHEAT IN THAT FIELD, TOO.
THAT ONE? - BUT, IT'S MOSTLY WEEDS!
THEY'RE FARMIN' ORGANIC.
LYNN

Aaron on the tractor.

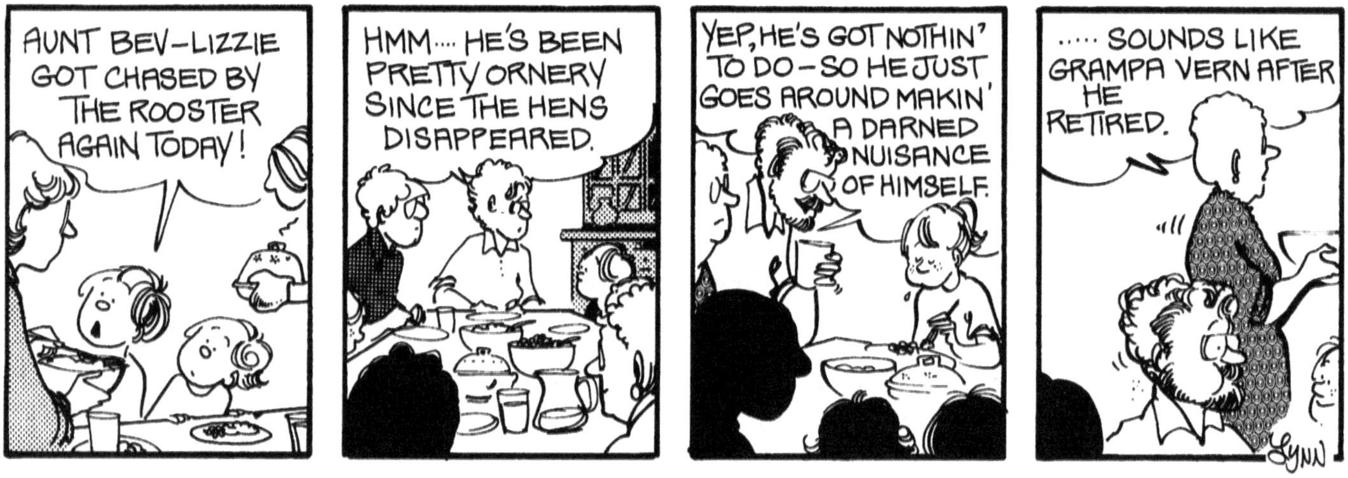
AUNT BEV-LIZZIE GOT CHASED BY THE ROOSTER AGAIN TODAY!
HMM.... HE'S BEEN PRETTY ORNERY SINCE THE HENS DISAPPEARED.
YEP, HE'S GOT NOTHIN' TO DO-SO HE JUST GOES AROUND MAKIN' A DARNED NUISANCE OF HIMSELF.
..... SOUNDS LIKE GRAMPA VERN AFTER HE RETIRED.
LYNN

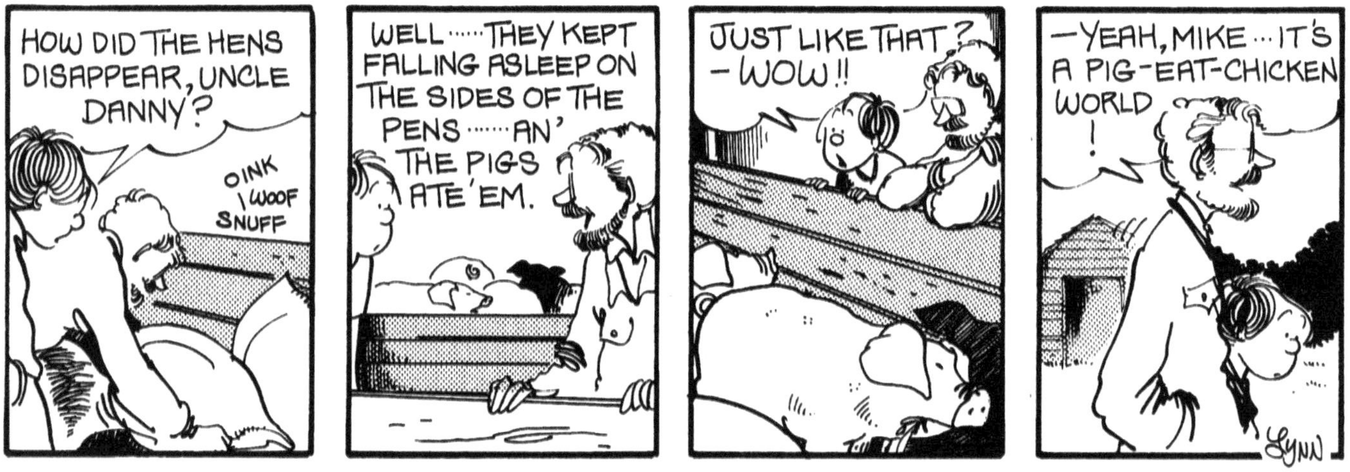
HOW DID THE HENS DISAPPEAR, UNCLE DANNY?
OINK
WOOF
SNUFF
WELL..... THEY KEPT FALLING ASLEEP ON THE SIDES OF THE PENS...... AN' THE PIGS ATE 'EM.
JUST LIKE THAT? -WOW!!
-YEAH, MIKE...IT'S A PIG-EAT-CHICKEN WORLD!
LYNN

The chickens really did disappear. They were free-range birds, locked up in the barn only at night. We didn't know if foxes or pigs had eaten them, but alone, the rooster was a miserable sucker. He would run at us and attack. For Aaron, this was terrifying because he was so small! Beth and I bought a hen, but she disappeared, too. So ... we made the rooster disappear.

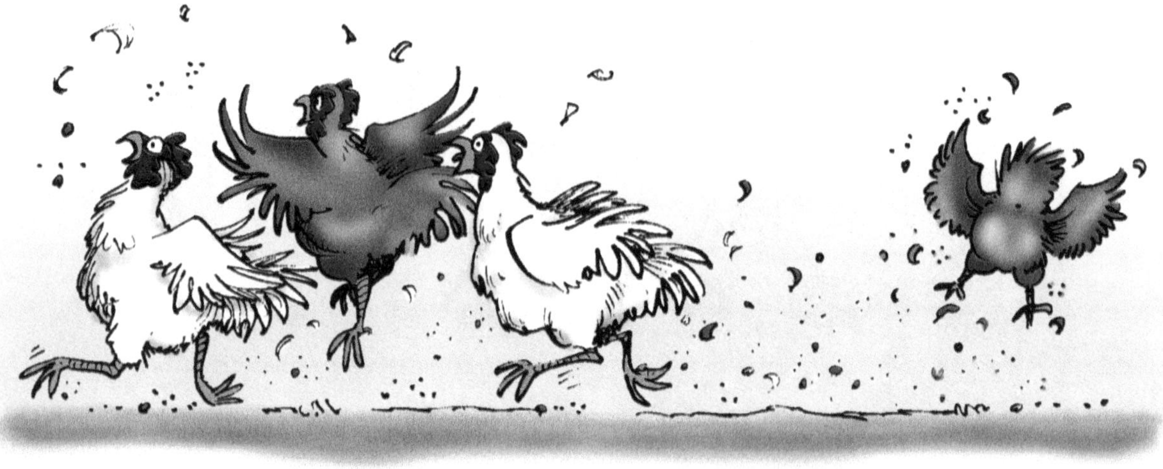

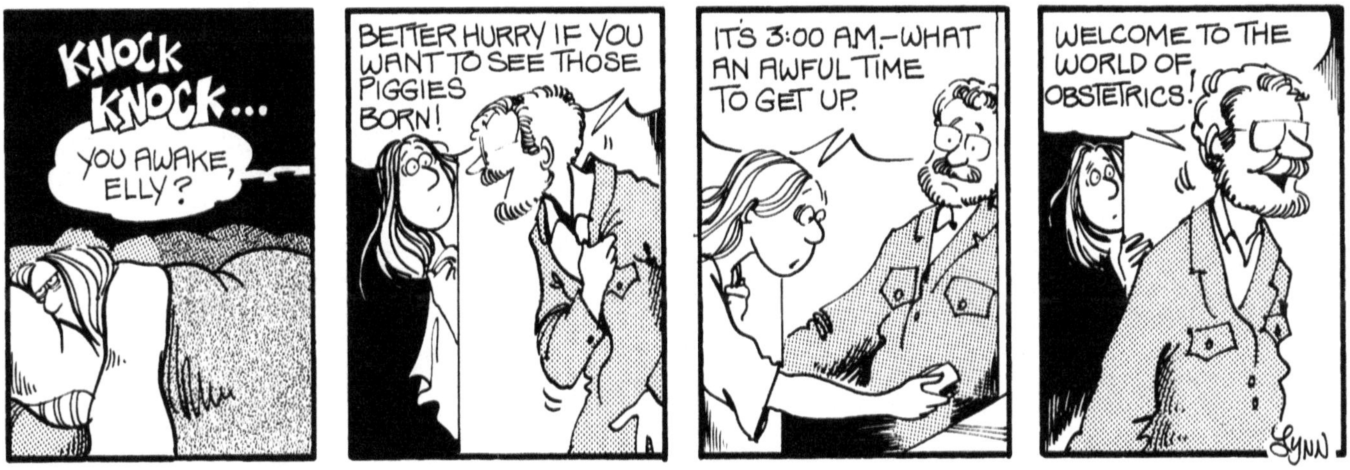
KNOCK KNOCK...
YOU AWAKE, ELLY?
BETTER HURRY IF YOU WANT TO SEE THOSE PIGGIES BORN!
IT'S 3:00 AM.—WHAT AN AWFUL TIME TO GET UP.
WELCOME TO THE WORLD OF OBSTETRICS!
LYNN

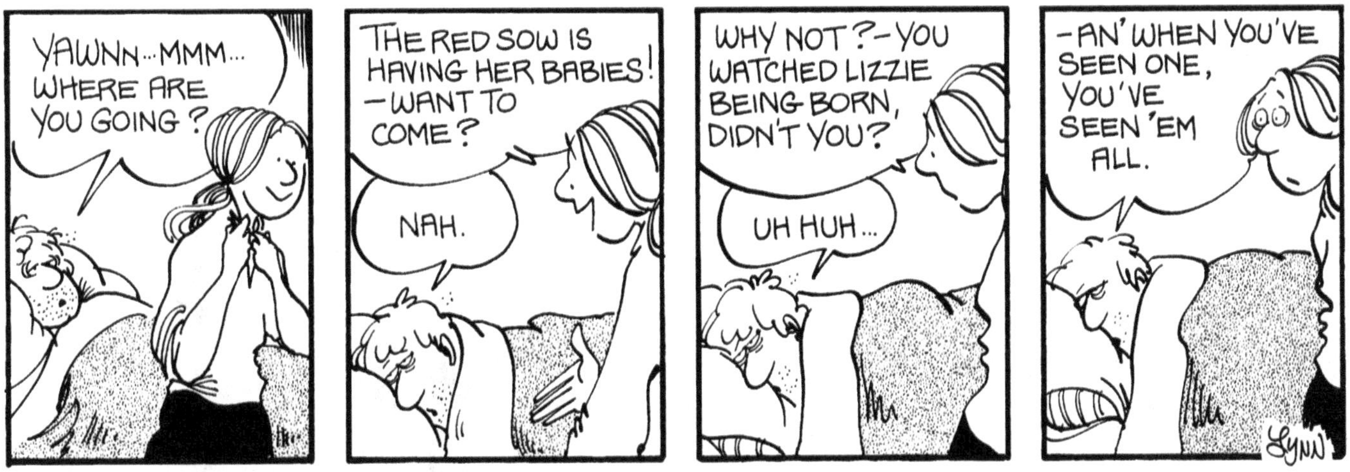
YAWNN...MMM... WHERE ARE YOU GOING?
THE RED SOW IS HAVING HER BABIES! —WANT TO COME?
NAH.
WHY NOT?—YOU WATCHED LIZZIE BEING BORN, DIDN'T YOU?
UH HUH...
—AN' WHEN YOU'VE SEEN ONE, YOU'VE SEEN 'EM ALL.
LYNN

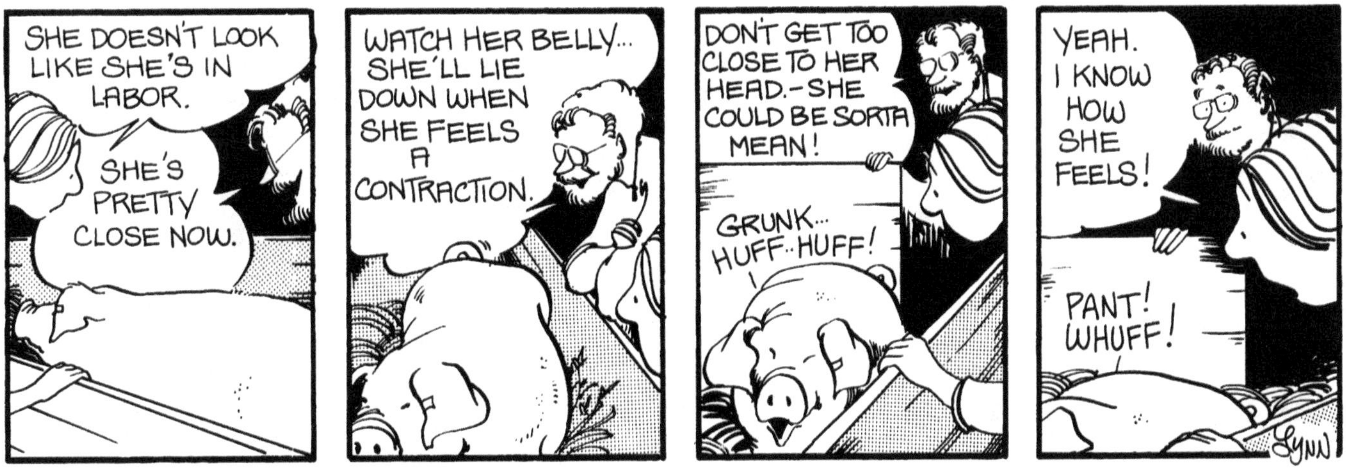
SHE DOESN'T LOOK LIKE SHE'S IN LABOR.
SHE'S PRETTY CLOSE NOW.
WATCH HER BELLY... SHE'LL LIE DOWN WHEN SHE FEELS A CONTRACTION.
DON'T GET TOO CLOSE TO HER HEAD.—SHE COULD BE SORTA MEAN!
GRUNK... HUFF..HUFF!
YEAH. I KNOW HOW SHE FEELS!
PANT! WHUFF!
LYNN

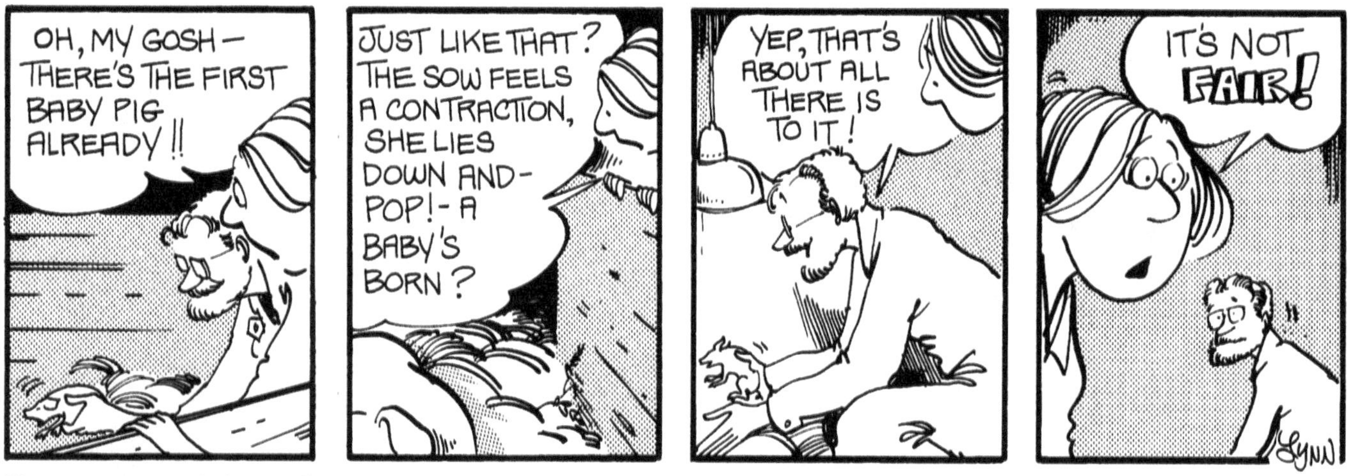
OH, MY GOSH — THERE'S THE FIRST BABY PIG ALREADY!!
JUST LIKE THAT? THE SOW FEELS A CONTRACTION, SHE LIES DOWN AND- POP!- A BABY'S BORN?
YEP, THAT'S ABOUT ALL THERE IS TO IT!
IT'S NOT FAIR!
LYNN

There were two pig barns. One was for farrowing and had the "honeymoon suite" at the back. This was where the boar was brought when his services were needed. The rest of the stalls were where the piglets were born. Like a maternity ward, this area was clean and well ventilated. The babies came at all hours of the night, and watching a sow give birth was interesting. Her tummy ripples, she lies down, and SQUIRT! Out pops a piggie. Don would wipe it off on the straw and put it aside so mom wouldn't step or roll on it, and the process would begin again. The thing that struck me was how fast these babies were born. I struggled and snorted away for hours to produce my offspring. This "pop 'em out" method just didn't seem fair!

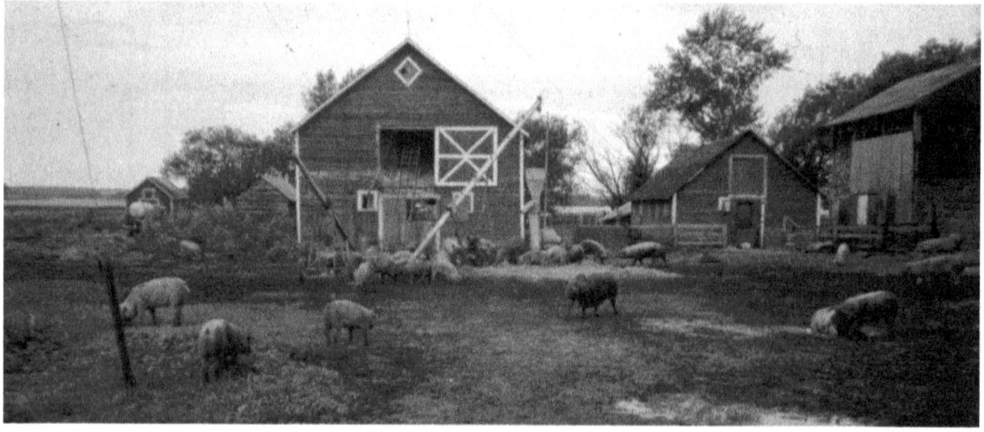

Beth and Don's pig barns.

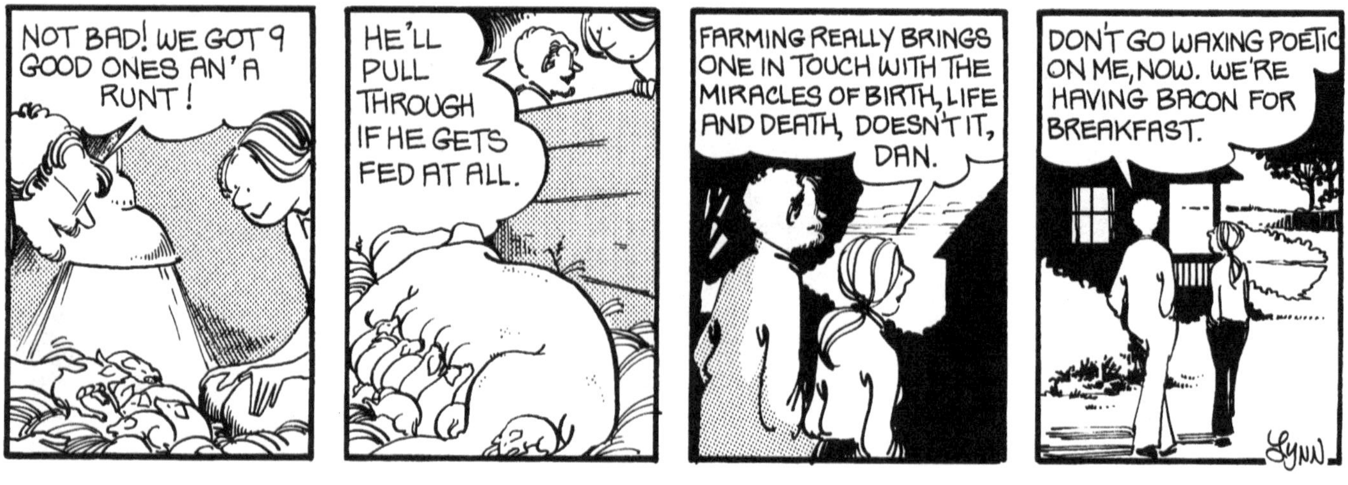
NOT BAD! WE GOT 9 GOOD ONES AN' A RUNT!
HE'LL PULL THROUGH IF HE GETS FED AT ALL.
FARMING REALLY BRINGS ONE IN TOUCH WITH THE MIRACLES OF BIRTH, LIFE AND DEATH, DOESN'T IT, DAN.
DON'T GO WAXING POETIC ON ME, NOW. WE'RE HAVING BACON FOR BREAKFAST.
LYNN

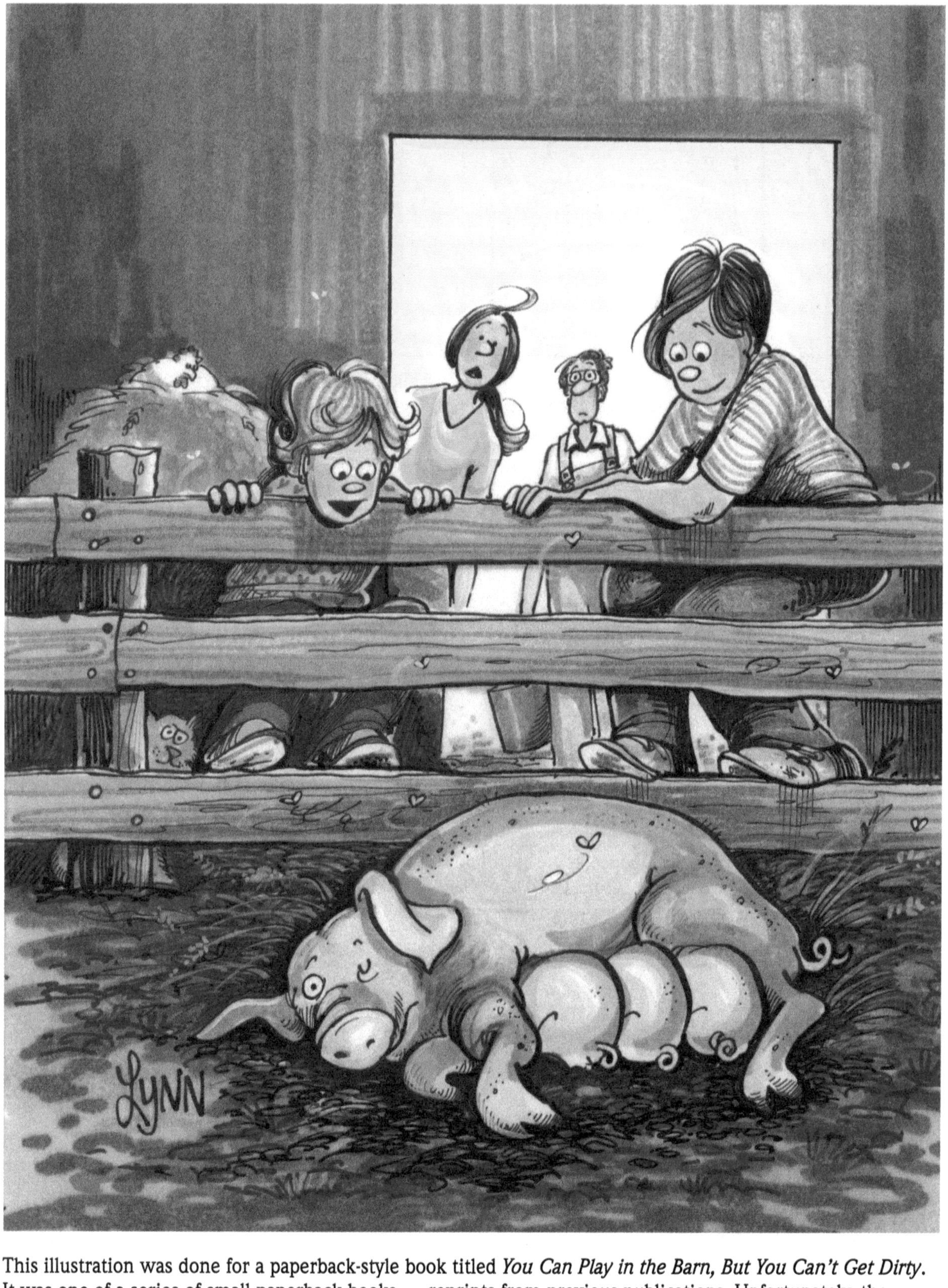
LYNN

This illustration was done for a paperback-style book titled *You Can Play in the Barn, But You Can't Get Dirty*. It was one of a series of small paperback books — reprints from previous publications. Unfortunately, the publisher put this cover on the wrong content — nothing in the book was farm-related. I didn't discover this until it was already on the shelves. I asked that the publication be recalled and, after some kafuffle, it was. The publisher then cancelled the contract, and that was fine with me. There might still be a few copies of this book kicking around out there — if you find one, let me know!

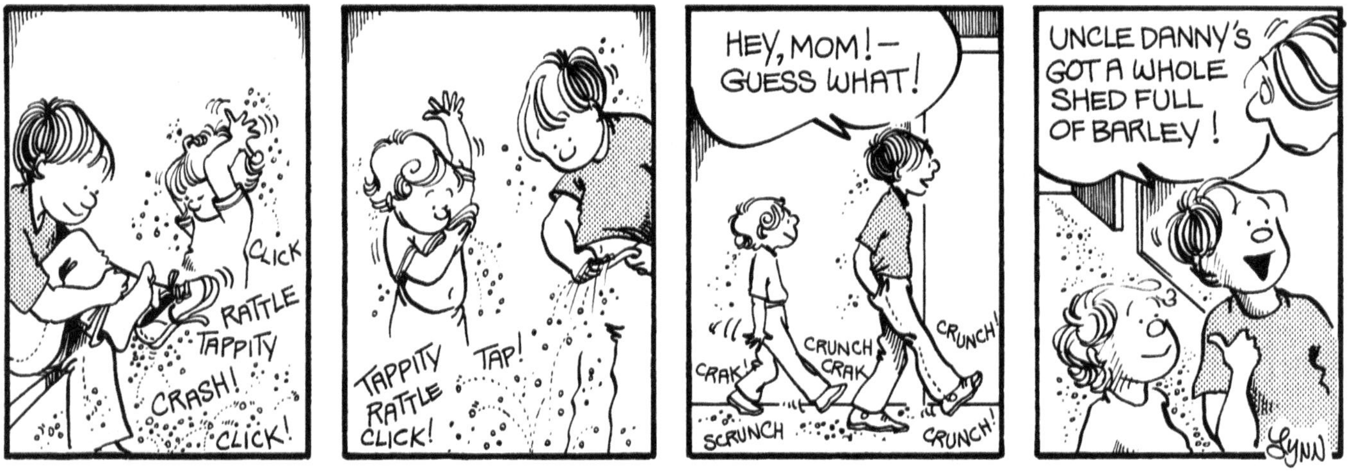
CLICK
RATTLE
TAPPITY
CRASH!
CLICK!
TAPPITY
RATTLE
CLICK!
TAP!
HEY, MOM! — GUESS WHAT!
CRAK!
CRUNCH
CRAK
CRUNCH!
SCRUNCH
CRUNCH!
UNCLE DANNY'S GOT A WHOLE SHED FULL OF BARLEY!
LYNN

The day Aaron was found playing in a grain bin the guys were preparing to empty was the day my in-laws took him home with them. If we hadn't spotted him in time, he could easily have drowned in the seed or been caught in the auger. I was unprepared for so many dangers. On a farm, you have to be vigilant and prepared for just about anything!

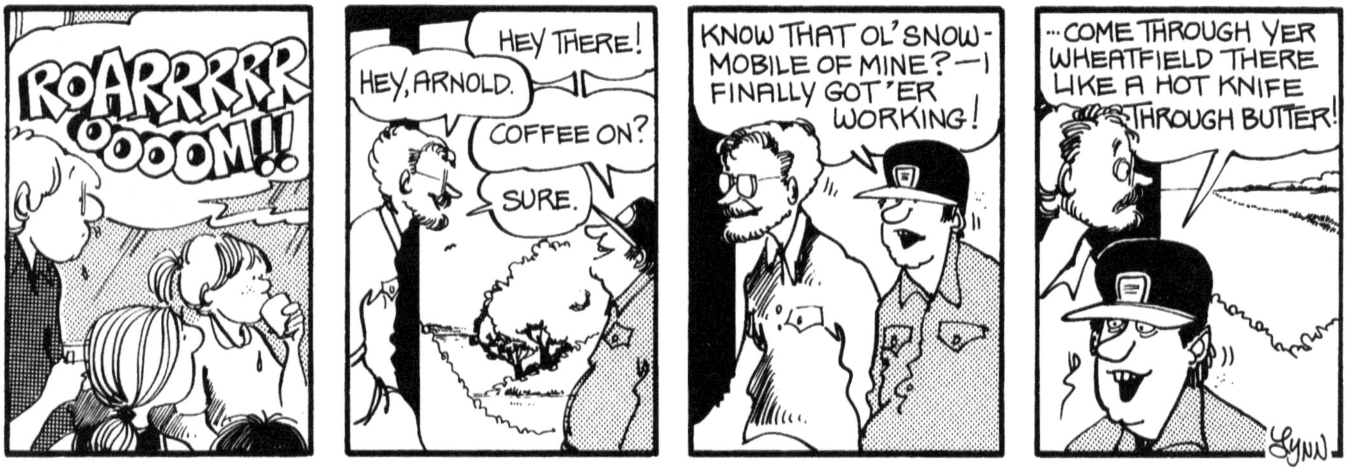
ROARRRRR OOOOOM!!
HEY THERE!
HEY, ARNOLD.
COFFEE ON?
SURE.
KNOW THAT OL' SNOW-MOBILE OF MINE? — I FINALLY GOT 'ER WORKING!
...COME THROUGH YER WHEATFIELD THERE LIKE A HOT KNIFE THROUGH BUTTER!
LYNN

One morning, I awoke to a strange noise. I looked out the window to see the wheat field parting like the Red Sea. In a cloud of dust, smoke, and flying chaff, Freddy Parkinson (Don's brother-in-law and neighbour) was driving toward the house on an old snowmobile. He roared into the yard and then calmly announced that he'd come for coffee.

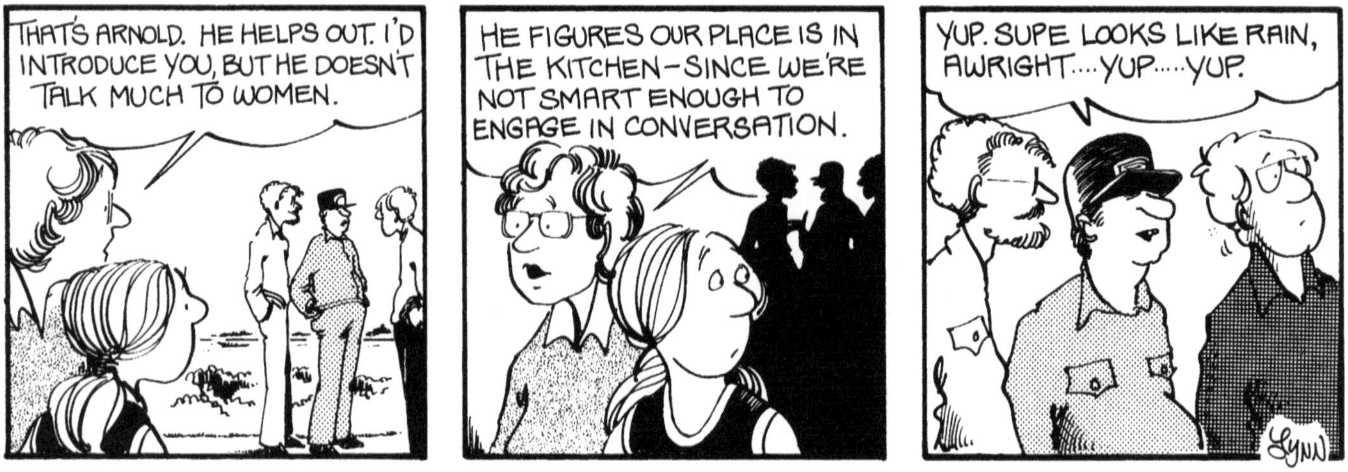
THAT'S ARNOLD. HE HELPS OUT. I'D INTRODUCE YOU, BUT HE DOESN'T TALK MUCH TO WOMEN.
HE FIGURES OUR PLACE IS IN THE KITCHEN — SINCE WE'RE NOT SMART ENOUGH TO ENGAGE IN CONVERSATION.
YUP. SURE LOOKS LIKE RAIN, AWRIGHT.... YUP..... YUP.
LYNN

Beth and Don had a hired man who rarely spoke — but when he did, it was about crops and weather ... and nothing else!

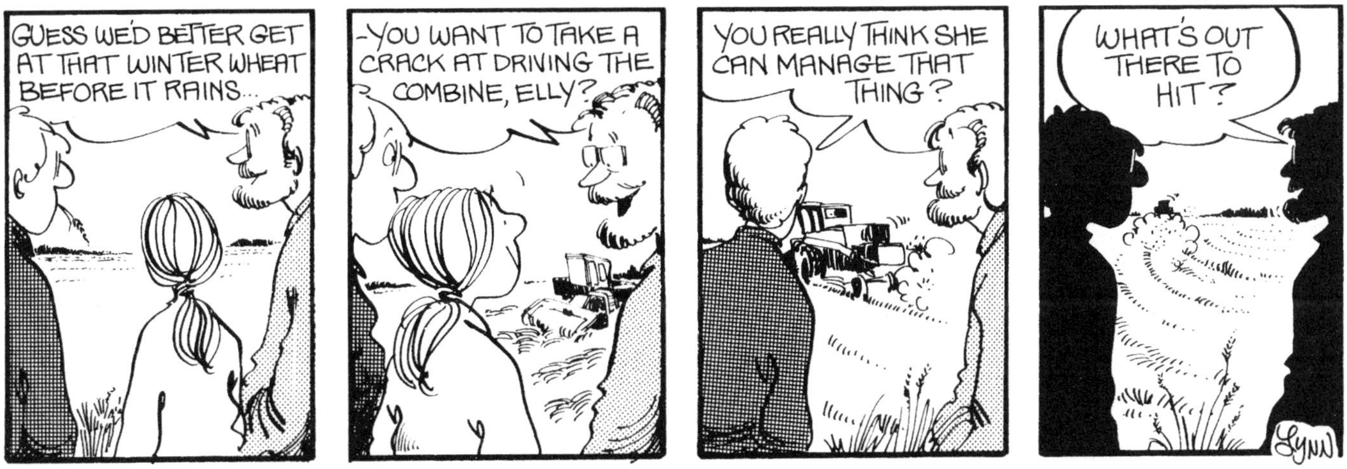
GUESS WE'D BETTER GET AT THAT WINTER WHEAT BEFORE IT RAINS...
-YOU WANT TO TAKE A CRACK AT DRIVING THE COMBINE, ELLY?
YOU REALLY THINK SHE CAN MANAGE THAT THING?
WHAT'S OUT THERE TO HIT?
LYNN

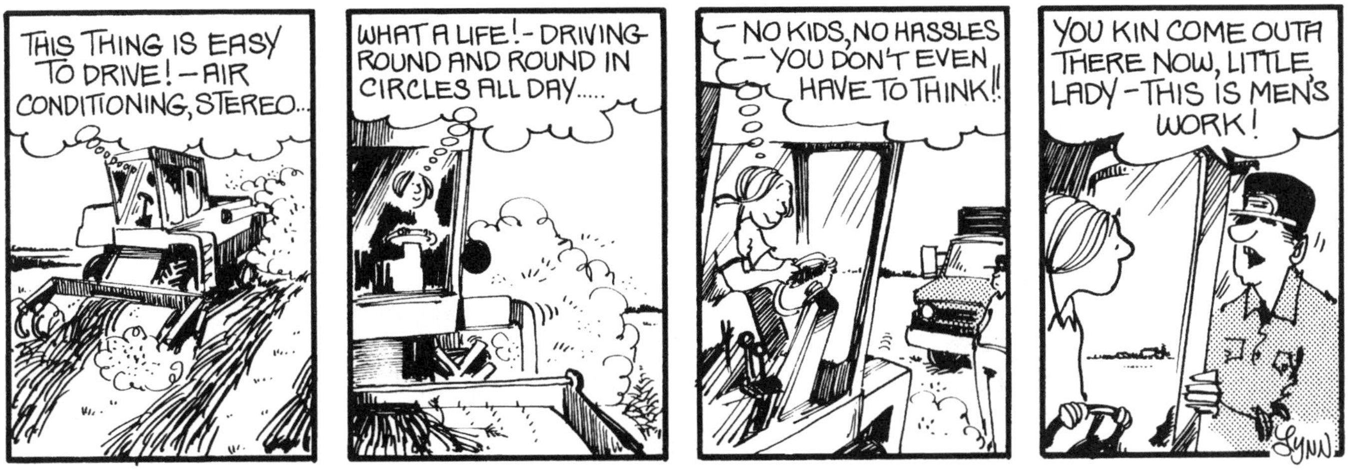
THIS THING IS EASY TO DRIVE! —AIR CONDITIONING, STEREO...
WHAT A LIFE! - DRIVING ROUND AND ROUND IN CIRCLES ALL DAY.....
— NO KIDS, NO HASSLES — YOU DON'T EVEN HAVE TO THINK!!
YOU KIN COME OUTA THERE NOW, LITTLE LADY - THIS IS MEN'S WORK!
LYNN

I discovered that driving the combine was preferable to cooking for the crew and dragging plates of food into the fields. Sitting in an air-conditioned cab and listening to country music beats a hot kitchen anytime!

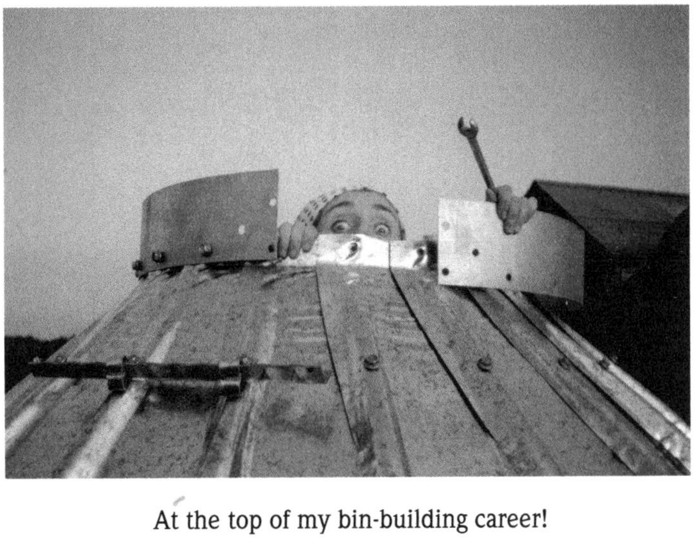

At the top of my bin-building career!

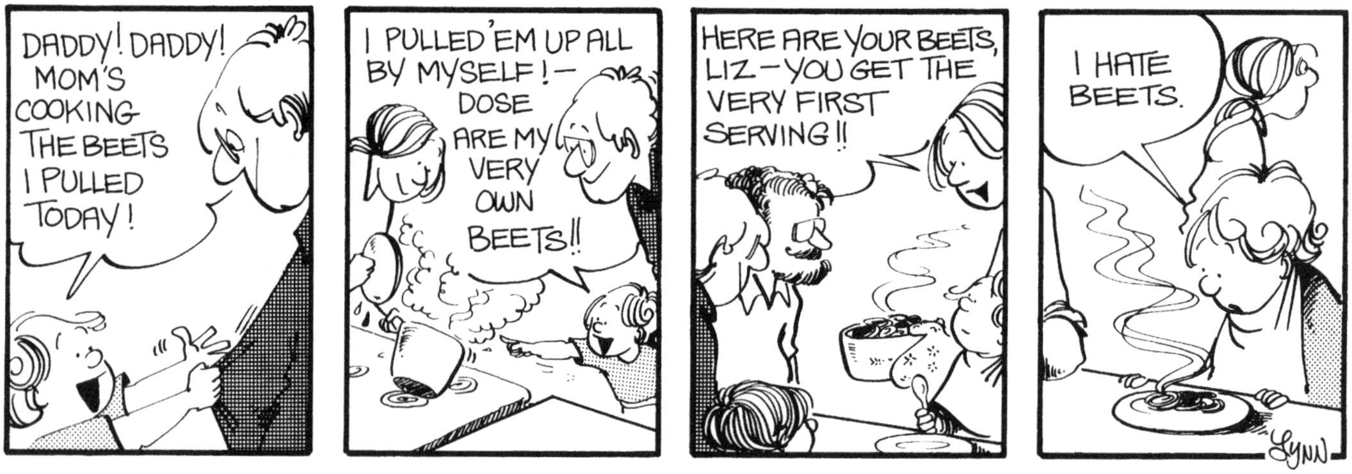
DADDY! DADDY! MOM'S COOKING THE BEETS I PULLED TODAY!
I PULLED 'EM UP ALL BY MYSELF! — DOSE ARE MY VERY OWN BEETS!!
HERE ARE YOUR BEETS, LIZ — YOU GET THE VERY FIRST SERVING!!
I HATE BEETS.

One of the pleasures of living on the farm was eating fresh garden veggies. We had fresh meat, too. We knew where it was raised and where it had been butchered. This was all new to someone used to buying groceries in cellophane packages.

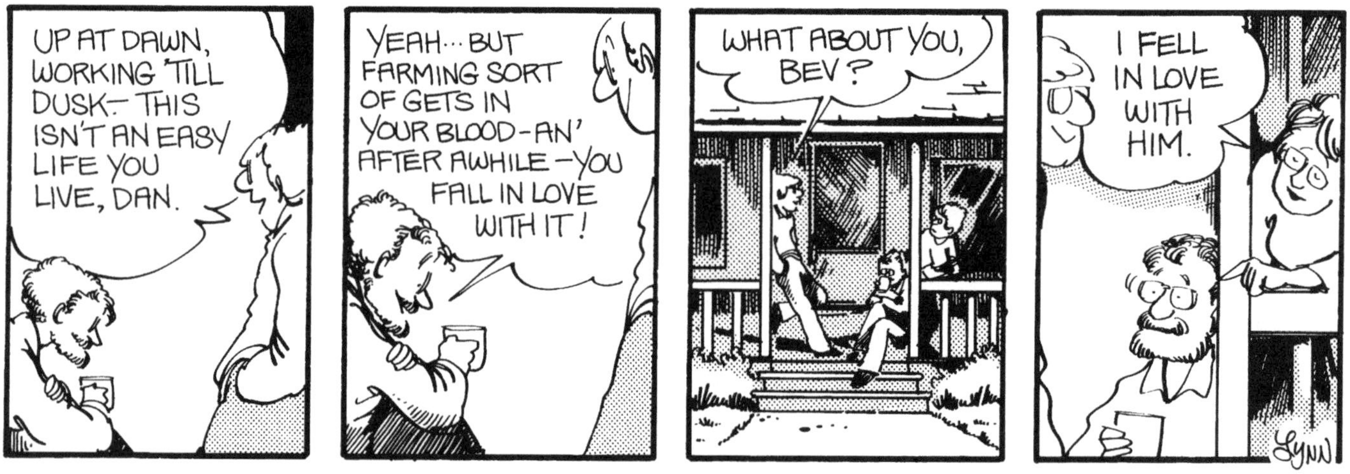
UP AT DAWN, WORKING 'TILL DUSK — THIS ISN'T AN EASY LIFE YOU LIVE, DAN.
YEAH... BUT FARMING SORT OF GETS IN YOUR BLOOD - AN' AFTER AWHILE — YOU FALL IN LOVE WITH IT!
WHAT ABOUT YOU, BEV?
I FELL IN LOVE WITH HIM.

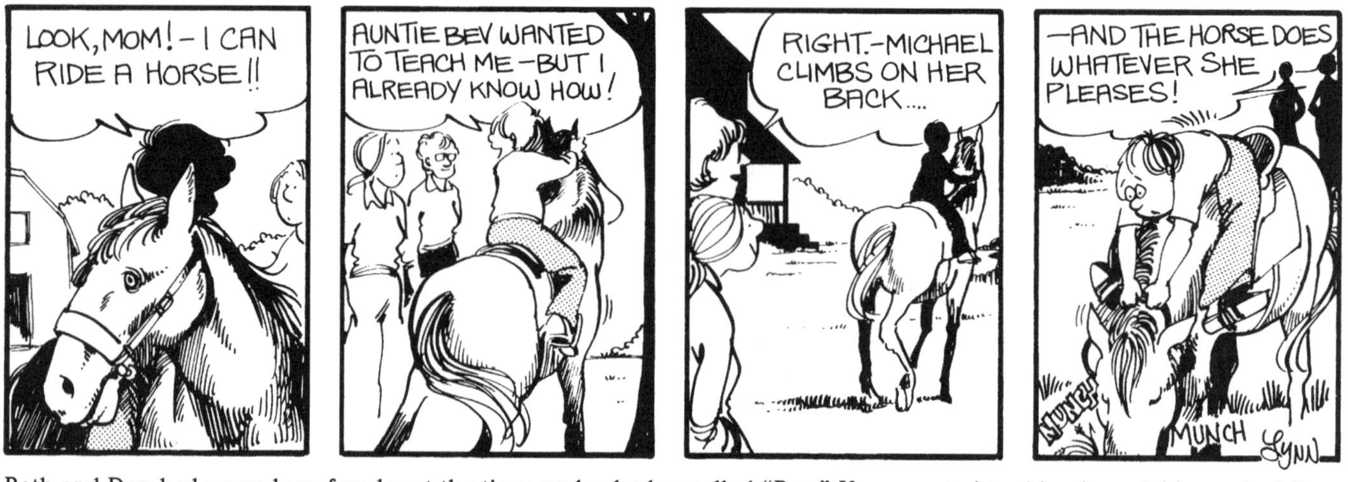
LOOK, MOM! — I CAN RIDE A HORSE!!
AUNTIE BEV WANTED TO TEACH ME — BUT I ALREADY KNOW HOW!
RIGHT. — MICHAEL CLIMBS ON HER BACK....
— AND THE HORSE DOES WHATEVER SHE PLEASES!
MUNCH
MUNCH

Beth and Don had a number of mules at the time, and a donkey called "Roy." If we wanted to ride, the neighbours had fine horses and all the tack. Although I was invited to do so, I never mounted one of their steeds. I did help Beth sew one up after an accident, though — but that's another story!

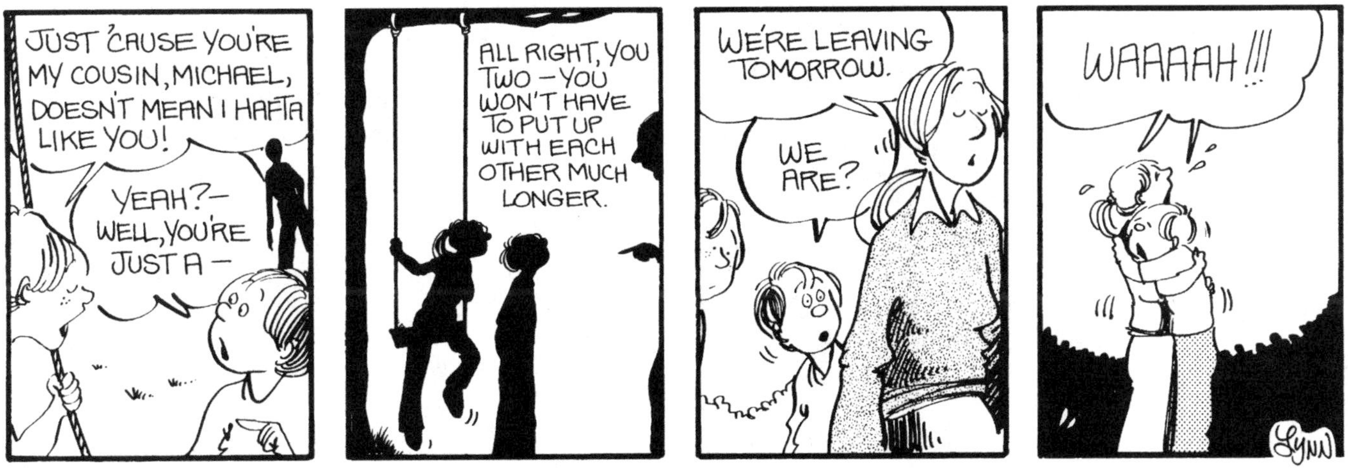
JUST 'CAUSE YOU'RE MY COUSIN, MICHAEL, DOESN'T MEAN I HAFTA LIKE YOU!
YEAH?— WELL, YOU'RE JUST A —
ALL RIGHT, YOU TWO — YOU WON'T HAVE TO PUT UP WITH EACH OTHER MUCH LONGER.
WE'RE LEAVING TOMORROW.
WE ARE?
WAAAAH!!!
LYNN

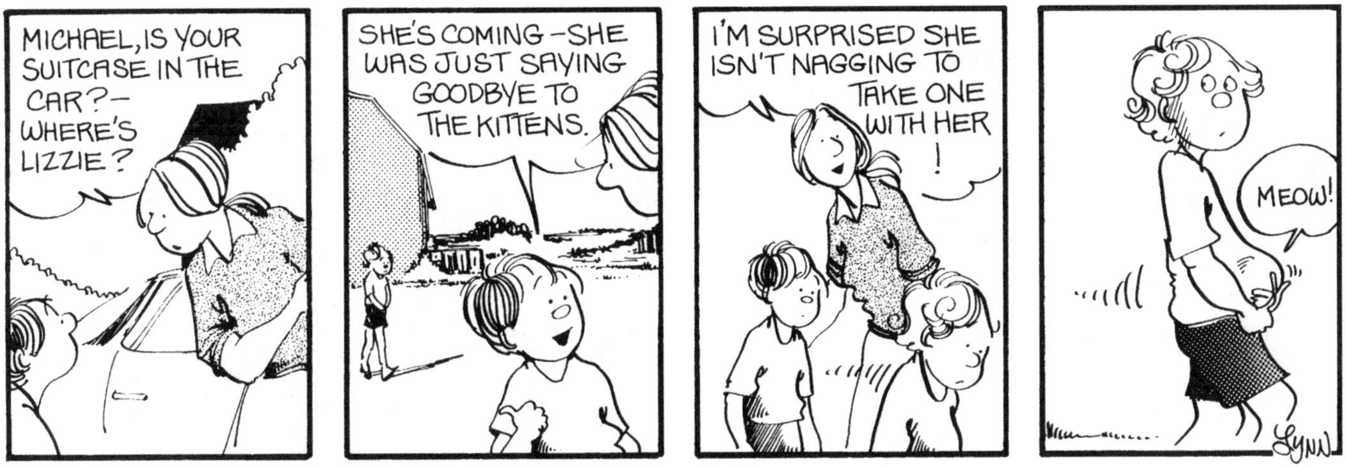
MICHAEL, IS YOUR SUITCASE IN THE CAR?— WHERE'S LIZZIE?
SHE'S COMING — SHE WAS JUST SAYING GOODBYE TO THE KITTENS.
I'M SURPRISED SHE ISN'T NAGGING TO TAKE ONE WITH HER!
MEOW!
LYNN

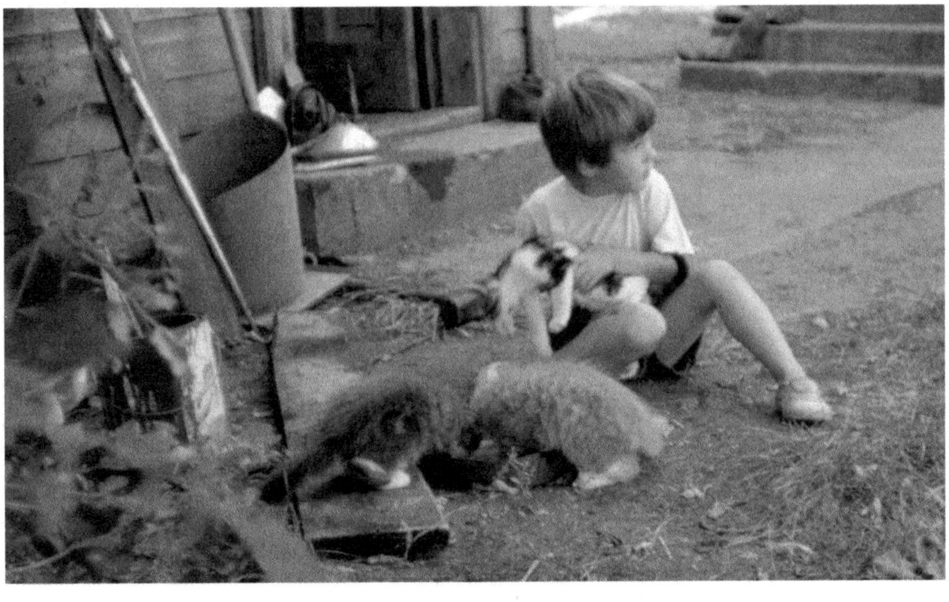

Aaron loved playing with the kittens.

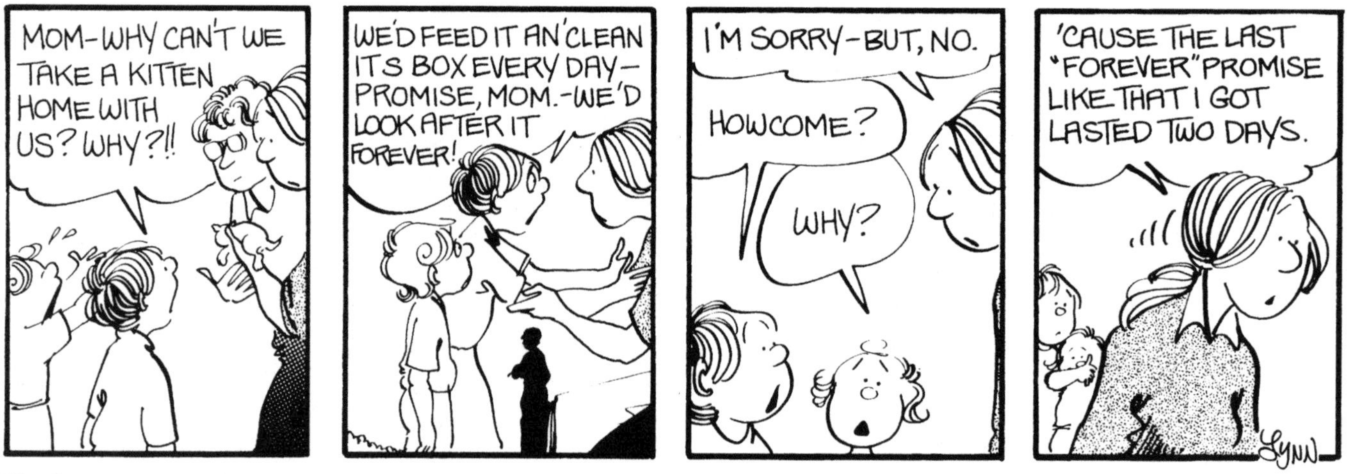
MOM-WHY CAN'T WE TAKE A KITTEN HOME WITH US? WHY?!!
WE'D FEED IT AN' CLEAN ITS BOX EVERY DAY— PROMISE, MOM.-WE'D LOOK AFTER IT FOREVER!
I'M SORRY-BUT, NO.
HOWCOME?
WHY?
'CAUSE THE LAST "FOREVER" PROMISE LIKE THAT I GOT LASTED TWO DAYS.
LYNN

The barn cats were feral, for the most part — but awfully cute. It was hard not to take one home with us.

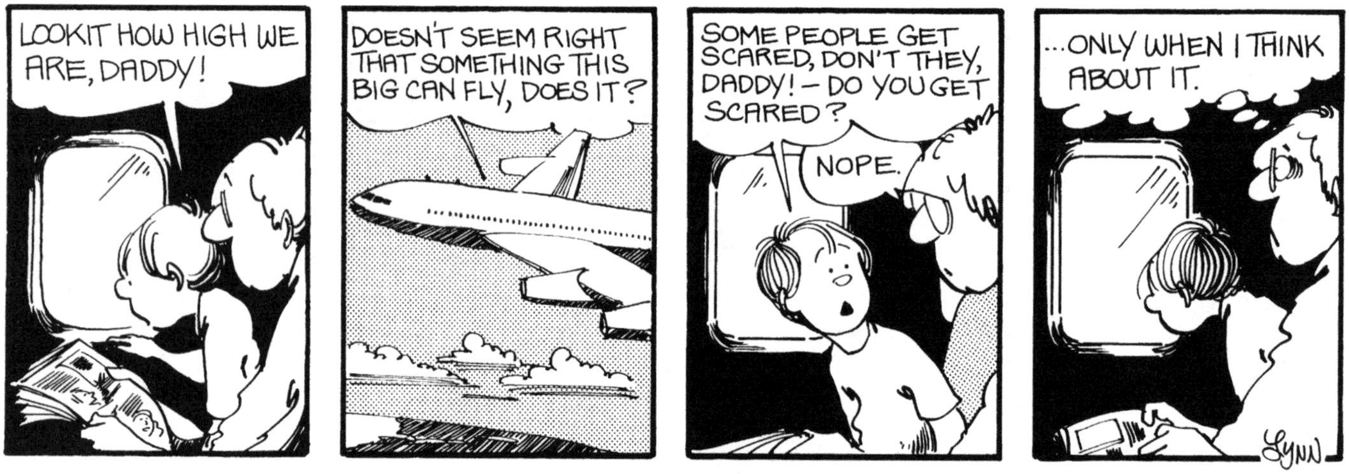
LOOKIT HOW HIGH WE ARE, DADDY!
DOESN'T SEEM RIGHT THAT SOMETHING THIS BIG CAN FLY, DOES IT?
SOME PEOPLE GET SCARED, DON'T THEY, DADDY! — DO YOU GET SCARED?
NOPE.
...ONLY WHEN I THINK ABOUT IT.
LYNN

The months I worked on Beth and Don's farm will stay with me forever. When our work was over, Ruth and Tom brought Aaron back down to Miami, Manitoba, from Lynn Lake, and we drove home to Dundas, Ontario, again. When we later moved up to Lynn Lake, ourselves, we were able to visit Beth and Don more often — and knowing the routines, we would always pitch in.

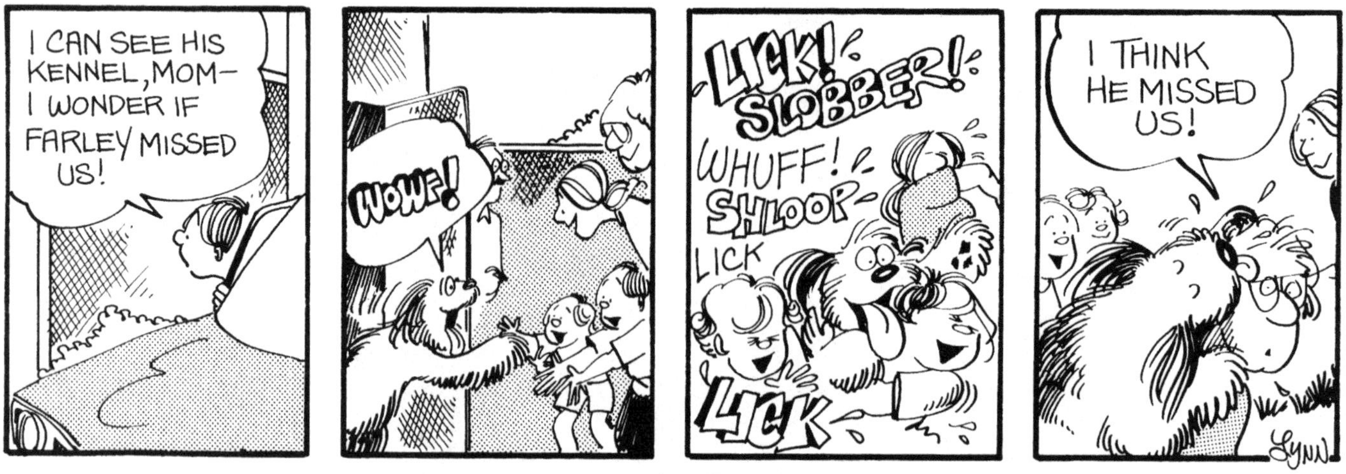
I CAN SEE HIS KENNEL, MOM— I WONDER IF FARLEY MISSED US!
WOWF!
LICK! SLOBBER!
WHUFF!
SHLOOP
LICK
LICK
I THINK HE MISSED US!
LYNN

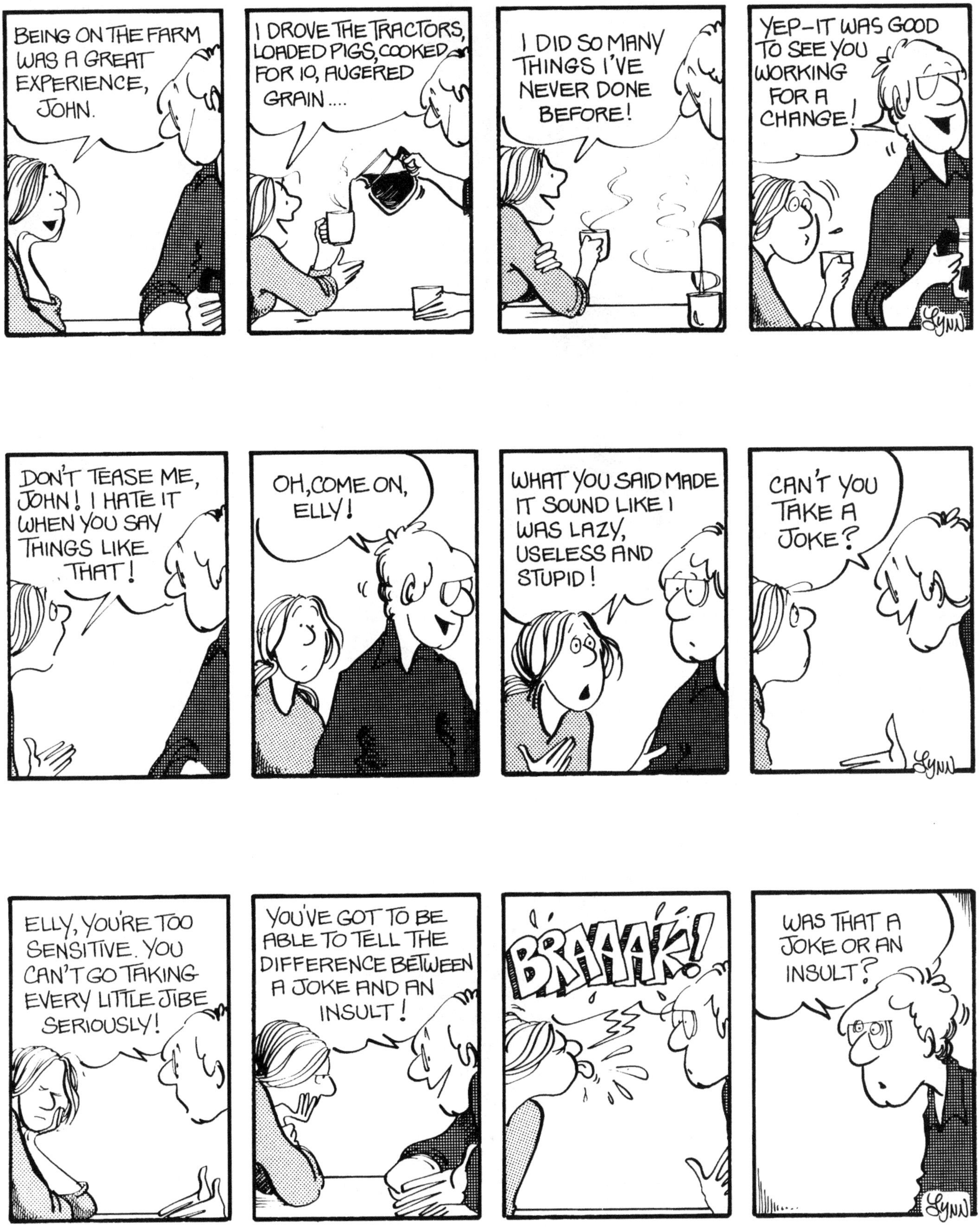
BEING ON THE FARM WAS A GREAT EXPERIENCE, JOHN.
I DROVE THE TRACTORS, LOADED PIGS, COOKED FOR 10, AUGERED GRAIN....
I DID SO MANY THINGS I'VE NEVER DONE BEFORE!
YEP-IT WAS GOOD TO SEE YOU WORKING FOR A CHANGE!
LYNN
DON'T TEASE ME, JOHN! I HATE IT WHEN YOU SAY THINGS LIKE THAT!
OH, COME ON, ELLY!
WHAT YOU SAID MADE IT SOUND LIKE I WAS LAZY, USELESS AND STUPID!
CAN'T YOU TAKE A JOKE?
LYNN
ELLY, YOU'RE TOO SENSITIVE. YOU CAN'T GO TAKING EVERY LITTLE JIBE SERIOUSLY!
YOU'VE GOT TO BE ABLE TO TELL THE DIFFERENCE BETWEEN A JOKE AND AN INSULT!
BRAAAK!
WAS THAT A JOKE OR AN INSULT?
LYNN

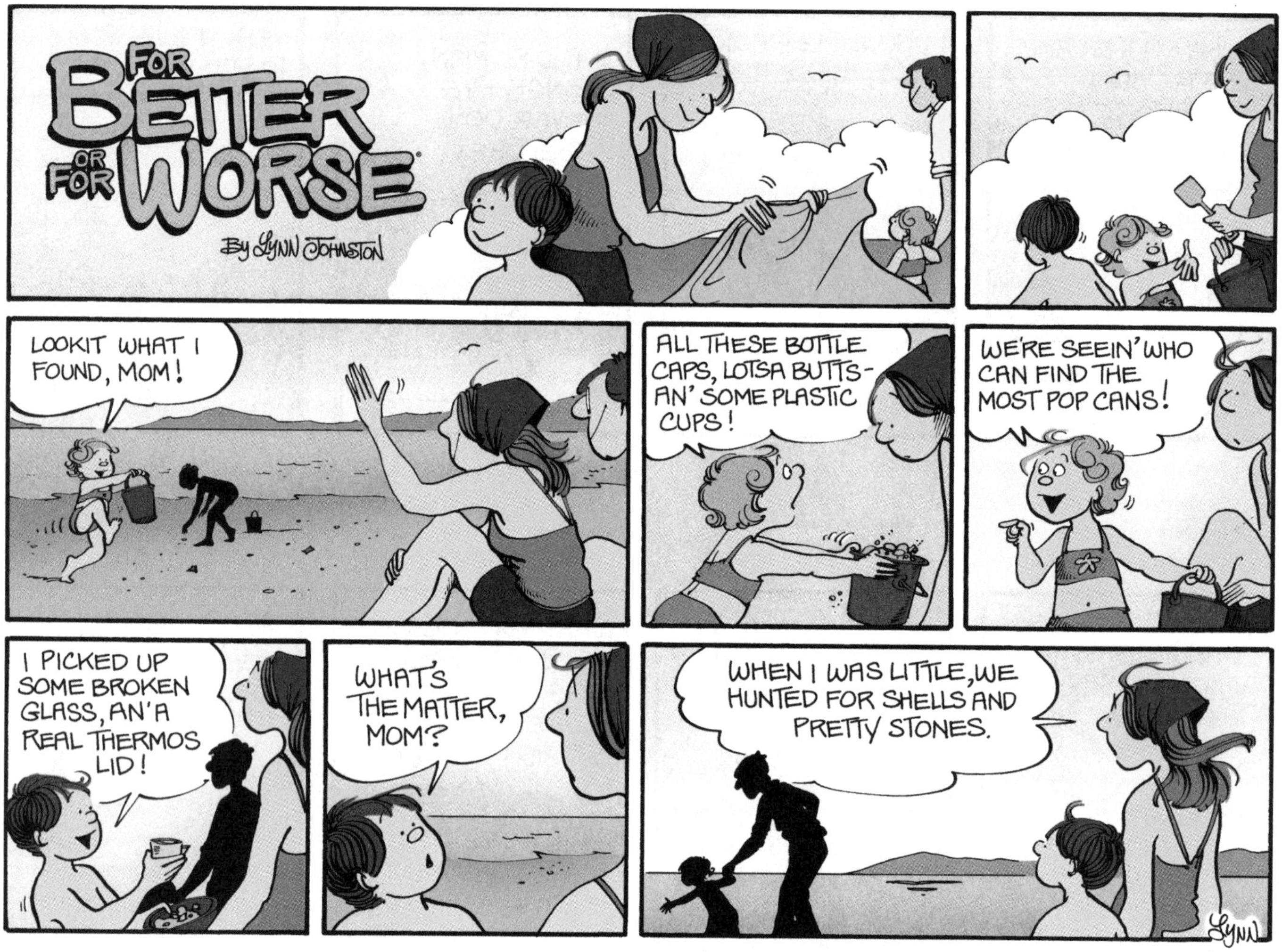
FOR BETTER OR FOR WORSE
BY LYNN JOHNSTON
LOOKIT WHAT I FOUND, MOM!
ALL THESE BOTTLE CAPS, LOTSA BUTTS-AN' SOME PLASTIC CUPS!
WE'RE SEEIN' WHO CAN FIND THE MOST POP CANS!
I PICKED UP SOME BROKEN GLASS, AN'A REAL THERMOS LID!
WHAT'S THE MATTER, MOM?
WHEN I WAS LITTLE, WE HUNTED FOR SHELLS AND PRETTY STONES.
LYNN

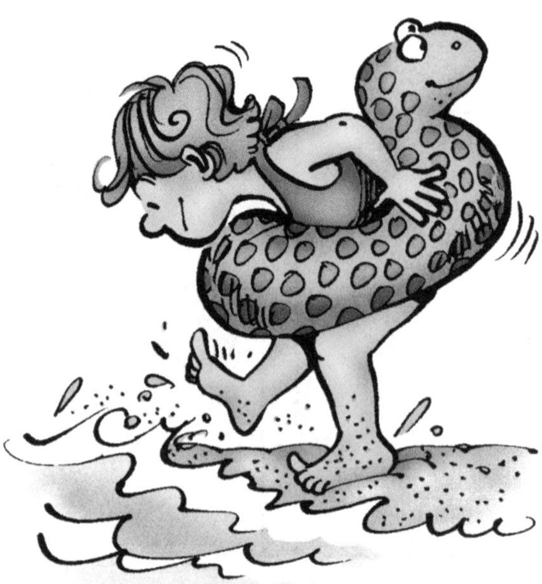

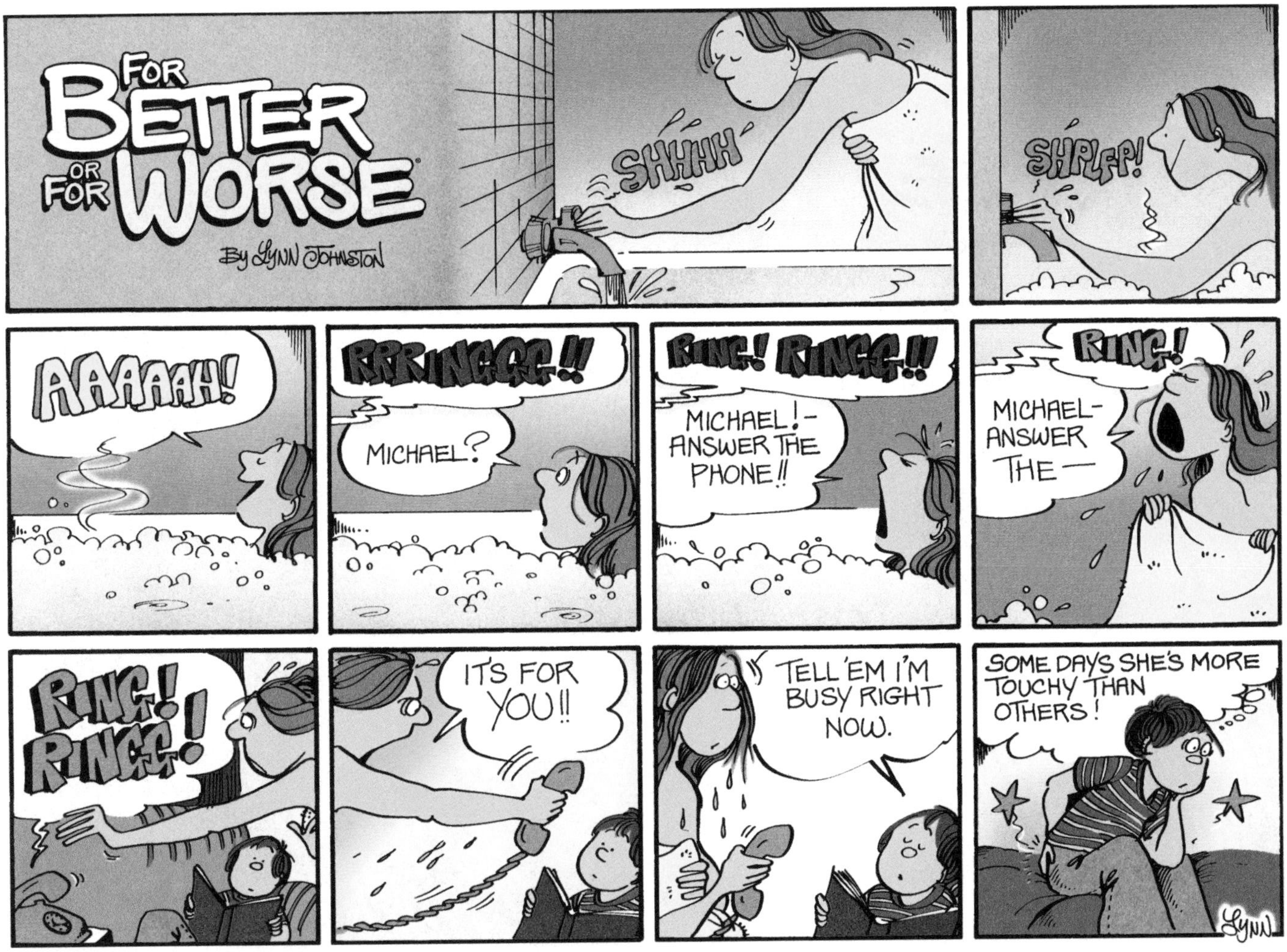
FOR BETTER OR FOR WORSE
BY LYNN JOHNSTON
SHHHH
SHPLFP!
AAAAAAH!
RRRINGGG!!
MICHAEL?
RING! RINGG!!
MICHAEL! - ANSWER THE PHONE!!
RING!
MICHAEL- ANSWER THE —
RING! RINGG!
IT'S FOR YOU!!
TELL 'EM I'M BUSY RIGHT NOW.
SOME DAYS SHE'S MORE TOUCHY THAN OTHERS!
LYNN

If I suggested that spanking was a disciplinary tactic in our home, I got mail. Rarely did things get so out of hand! There were times, however, when a swat happened and was more of a blow to the ego than a sting on the behind. Still, any "violent" image was seriously frowned upon by my readers — who in the crafted and edited world of cartoons, preferred clever commentary to a loss of control.

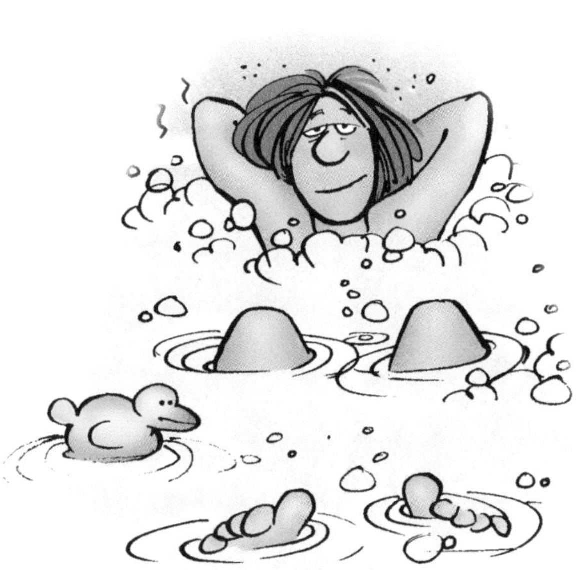

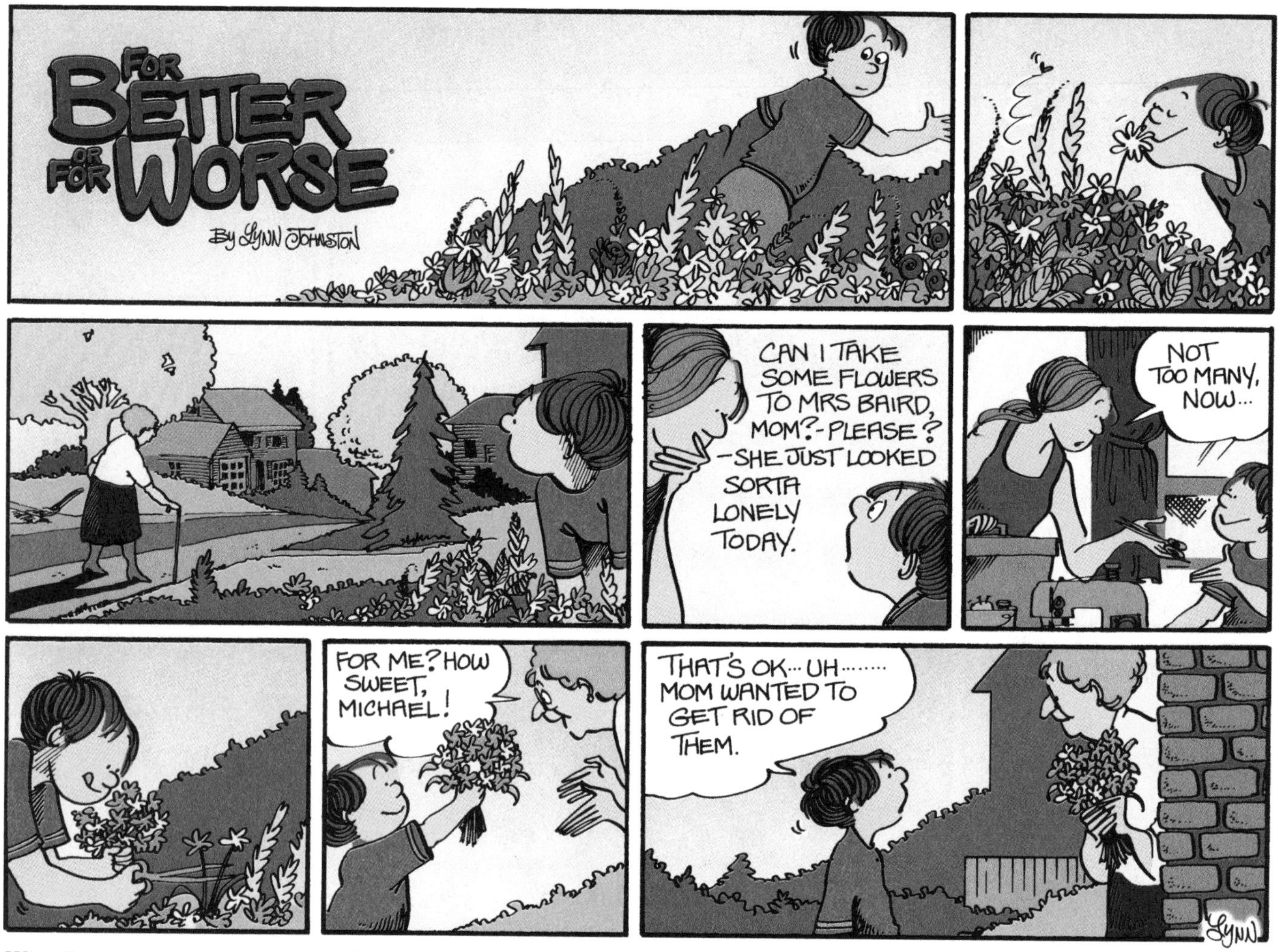
FOR BETTER OR FOR WORSE
BY LYNN JOHNSTON
CAN I TAKE SOME FLOWERS TO MRS BAIRD, MOM?-PLEASE? -SHE JUST LOOKED SORTA LONELY TODAY.
NOT TOO MANY, NOW...
FOR ME? HOW SWEET, MICHAEL!
THAT'S OK... UH....... MOM WANTED TO GET RID OF THEM.
LYNN

What I wanted to say here was — Michael had a kind heart. He wanted to cheer up an elderly neighbour, but was embarrassed by his own actions and played down the gift by saying the flowers were something his mother wanted to get rid of. I don't think the punch line worked too well, and this strip sort of missed the mark. Sometimes the hardest thing about describing a situation like this is ... well, describing a situation like this!!

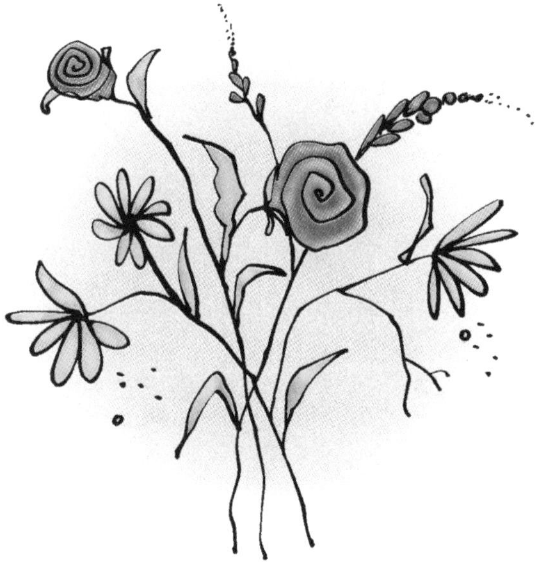

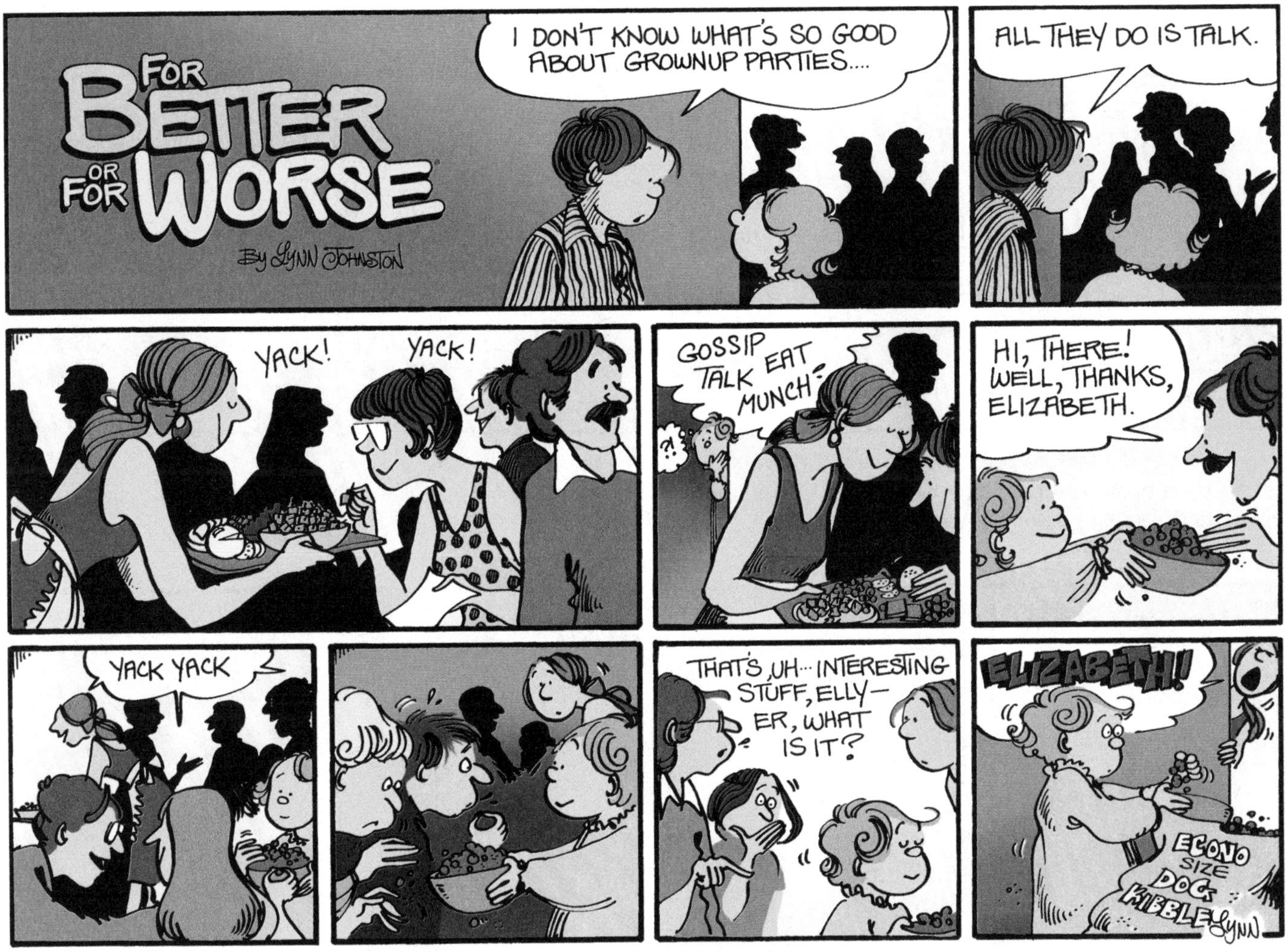
FOR BETTER OR FOR WORSE
BY LYNN JOHNSTON
I DON'T KNOW WHAT'S SO GOOD ABOUT GROWNUP PARTIES....
ALL THEY DO IS TALK.
YACK!
YACK!
GOSSIP TALK EAT MUNCH
HI, THERE! WELL, THANKS, ELIZABETH.
YACK YACK
THAT'S, UH... INTERESTING STUFF, ELLY— ER, WHAT IS IT?
ELIZABETH!
ECONO SIZE DOG KIBBLE
LYNN

Lynn Lake parties were always well attended. To celebrate summer one year, a soiree was given by one of the teachers. Guests all thought to bring plenty of libation for the event, but little actual sustenance. Sheena, our hostess, had prepared munchies and some packaged, hot hors d'oeuvres, but eventually folks, well into the sauce, wanted something substantial to eat, and were starting to gnaw their napkins. I wandered into Sheena's kitchen, hoping to find more food, and I noticed a giant, open bag of dog kibble in the corner. I took one of her fancy serving bowls, filled it with kibble, and joined her as she walked about the room offering munchies and dip. Deep in conversation, guests readily dug into the bowls, tossed the contents into their mouths, and went on talking. At least five people had eaten the kibble before Paul Bergan, the music teacher, piped up: "Hey!!! That tastes like dog food!" I was caught. I thought the prank would go down well, but food would have gone down better! Several of us ran home, emptied our fridges, and a grand potluck ensued. Folks still remember that party, but only Paul admits he ate kibble.

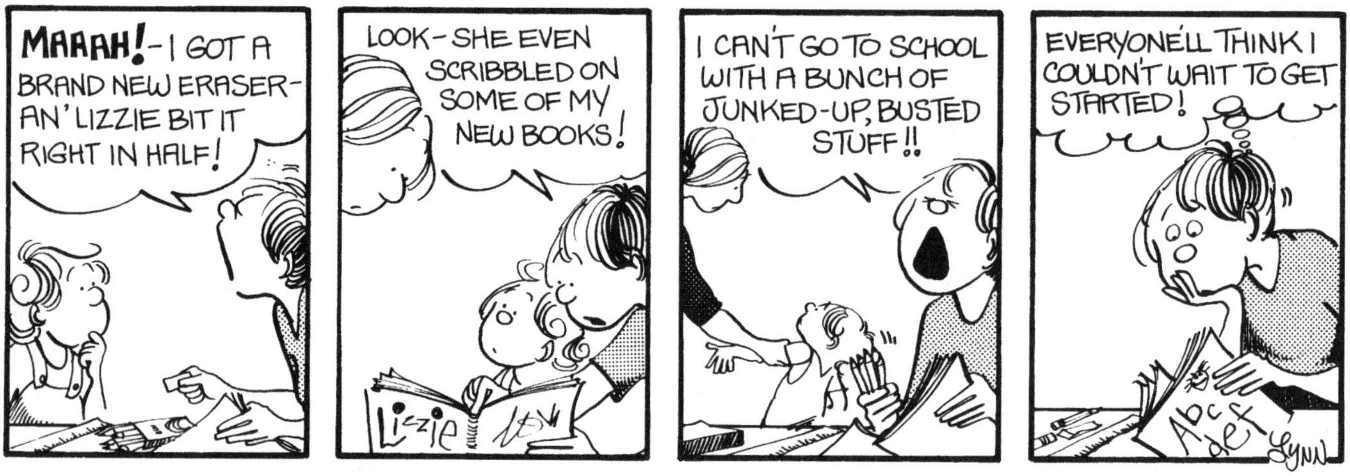
MAAAH!-I GOT A BRAND NEW ERASER-AN' LIZZIE BIT IT RIGHT IN HALF!
LOOK-SHE EVEN SCRIBBLED ON SOME OF MY NEW BOOKS!
Lizzie
I CAN'T GO TO SCHOOL WITH A BUNCH OF JUNKED-UP, BUSTED STUFF!!
EVERYONE'LL THINK I COULDN'T WAIT TO GET STARTED!
Abc def
LYNN

I can still feel the texture and taste the sweet, rubbery flavour of a brand-new eraser. I had no restraint when it came to chewing on them, and I did bite them in half. My mother would bark at me for destroying a brand-new eraser, but MY reasoning was that I now had two!

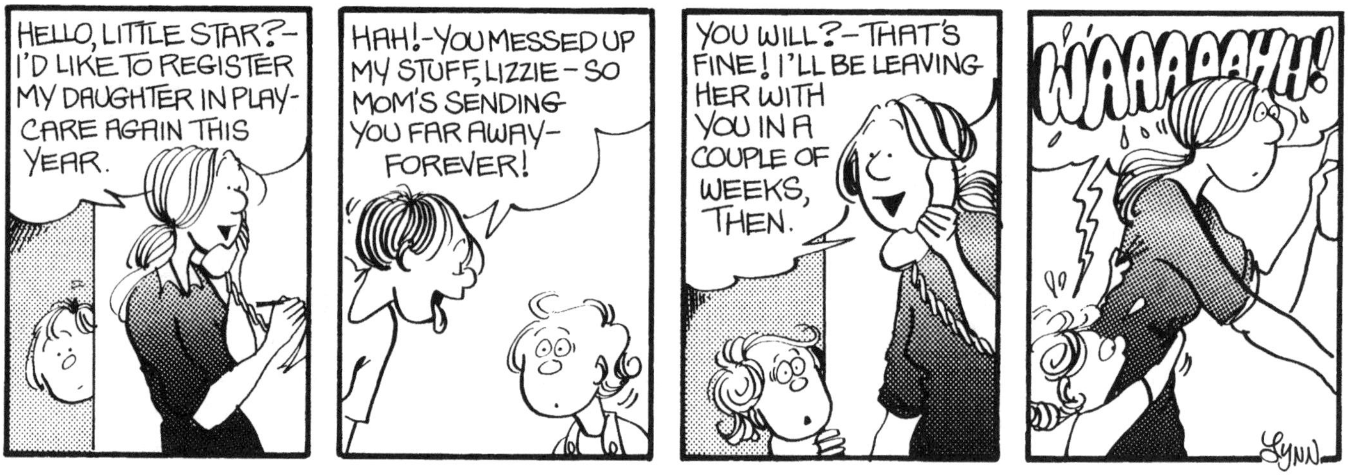
HELLO, LITTLE STAR?-I'D LIKE TO REGISTER MY DAUGHTER IN PLAY-CARE AGAIN THIS YEAR.
HAH!-YOU MESSED UP MY STUFF, LIZZIE-SO MOM'S SENDING YOU FAR AWAY-FOREVER!
YOU WILL?-THAT'S FINE! I'LL BE LEAVING HER WITH YOU IN A COUPLE OF WEEKS, THEN.
WAAAAAHH!
LYNN

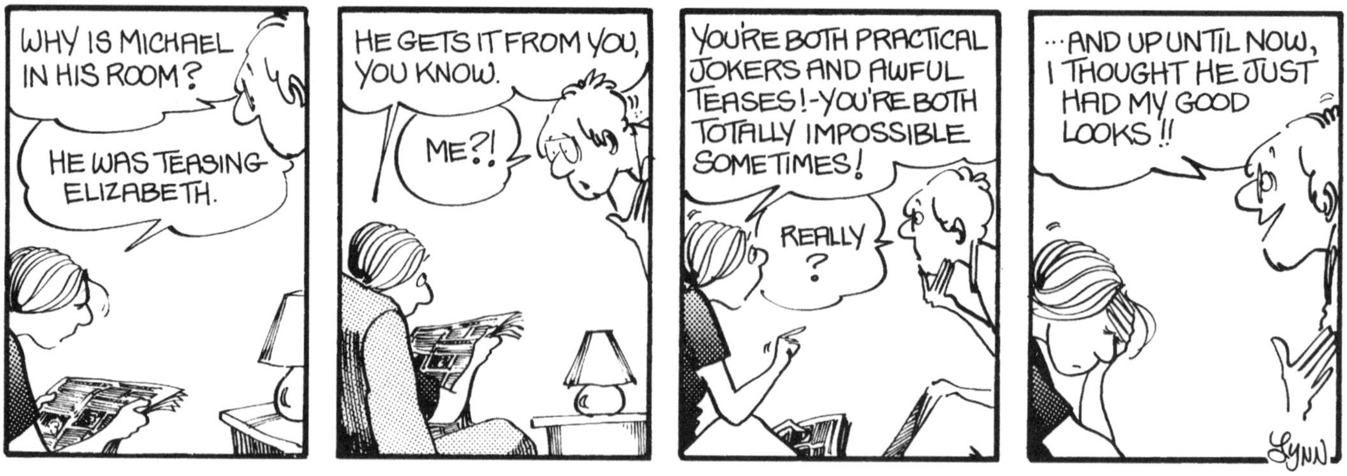
WHY IS MICHAEL IN HIS ROOM?
HE WAS TEASING ELIZABETH.
HE GETS IT FROM YOU, YOU KNOW.
ME?!
YOU'RE BOTH PRACTICAL JOKERS AND AWFUL TEASES!-YOU'RE BOTH TOTALLY IMPOSSIBLE SOMETIMES!
REALLY ?
...AND UP UNTIL NOW, I THOUGHT HE JUST HAD MY GOOD LOOKS!!
LYNN

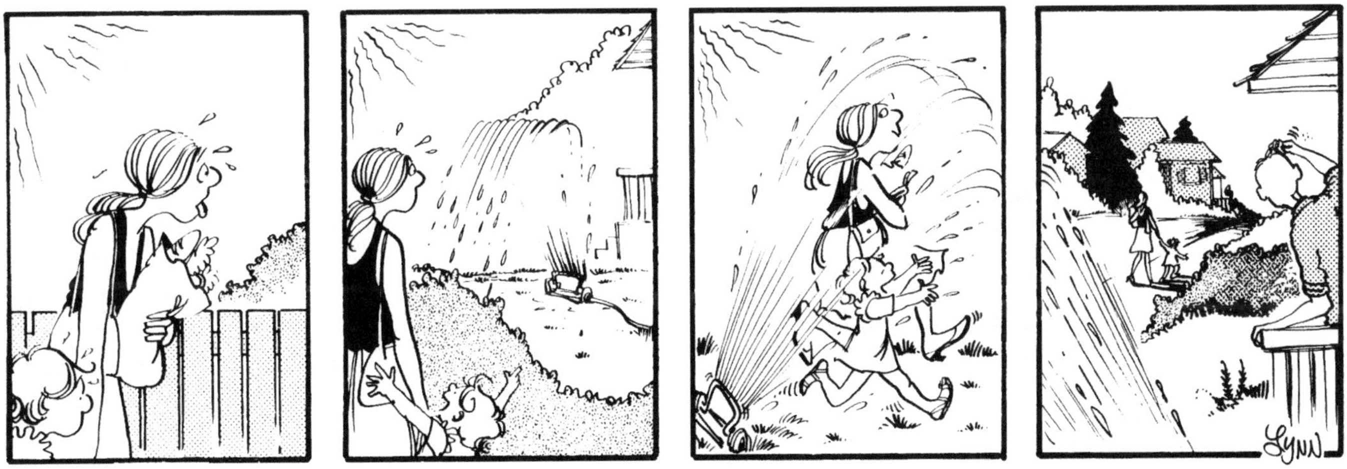

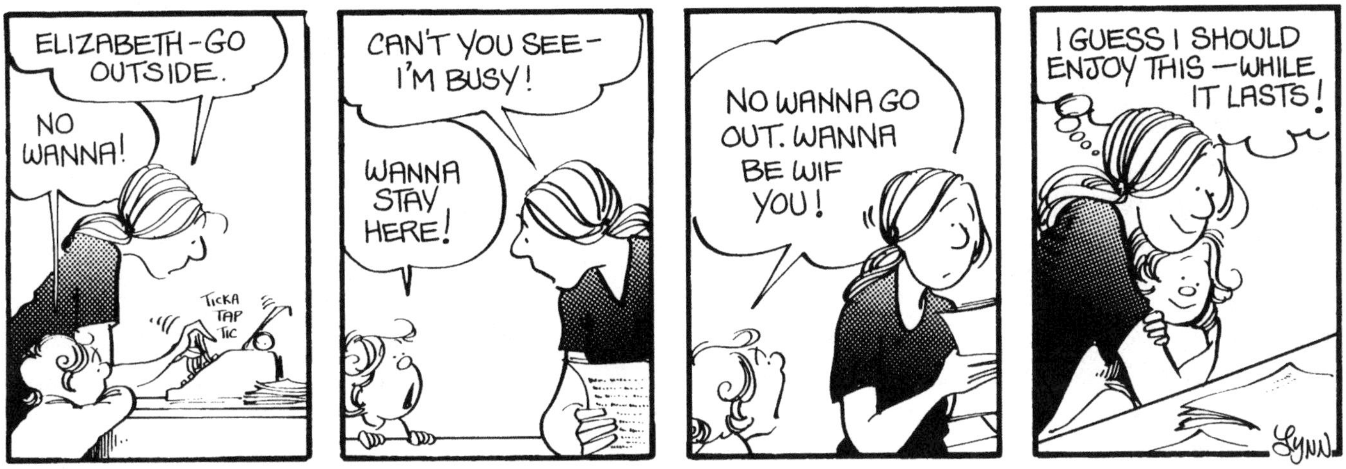

ELIZABETH-GO OUTSIDE.
NO WANNA!
TICKA TAP TIC
CAN'T YOU SEE-I'M BUSY!
WANNA STAY HERE!
NO WANNA GO OUT. WANNA BE WIF YOU!
I GUESS I SHOULD ENJOY THIS—WHILE IT LASTS!
LYNN


*For Better or For Worse* required a lot of time and focus. I did have to stop sometimes and wonder what was more important — Aaron and Katie or my deadlines. I'm glad now that I took the time to be with them and later worked until midnight!

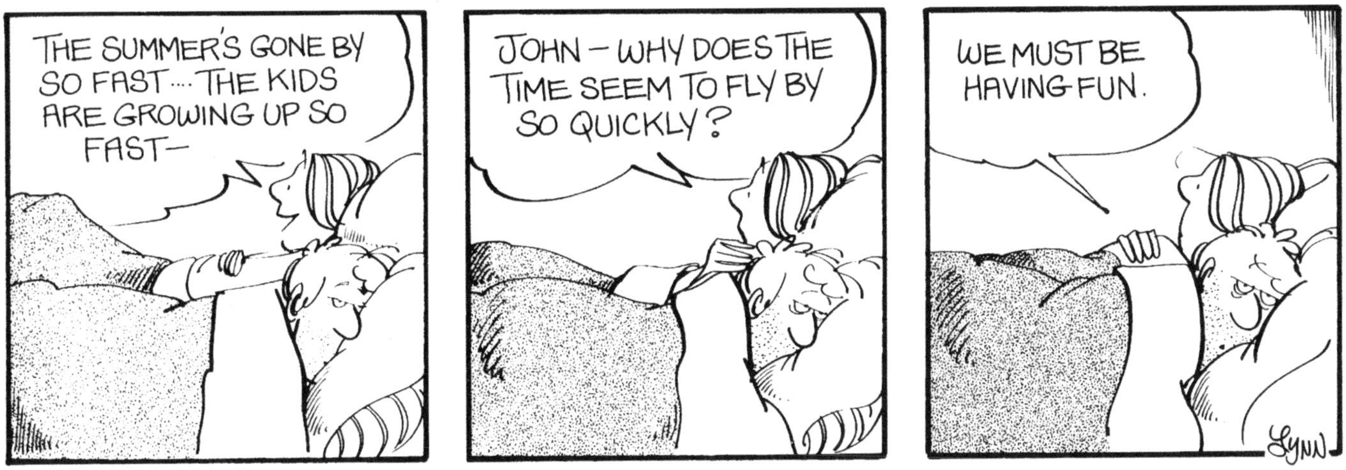

THE SUMMER'S GONE BY SO FAST.... THE KIDS ARE GROWING UP SO FAST-
JOHN - WHY DOES THE TIME SEEM TO FLY BY SO QUICKLY?
WE MUST BE HAVING FUN.
LYNN

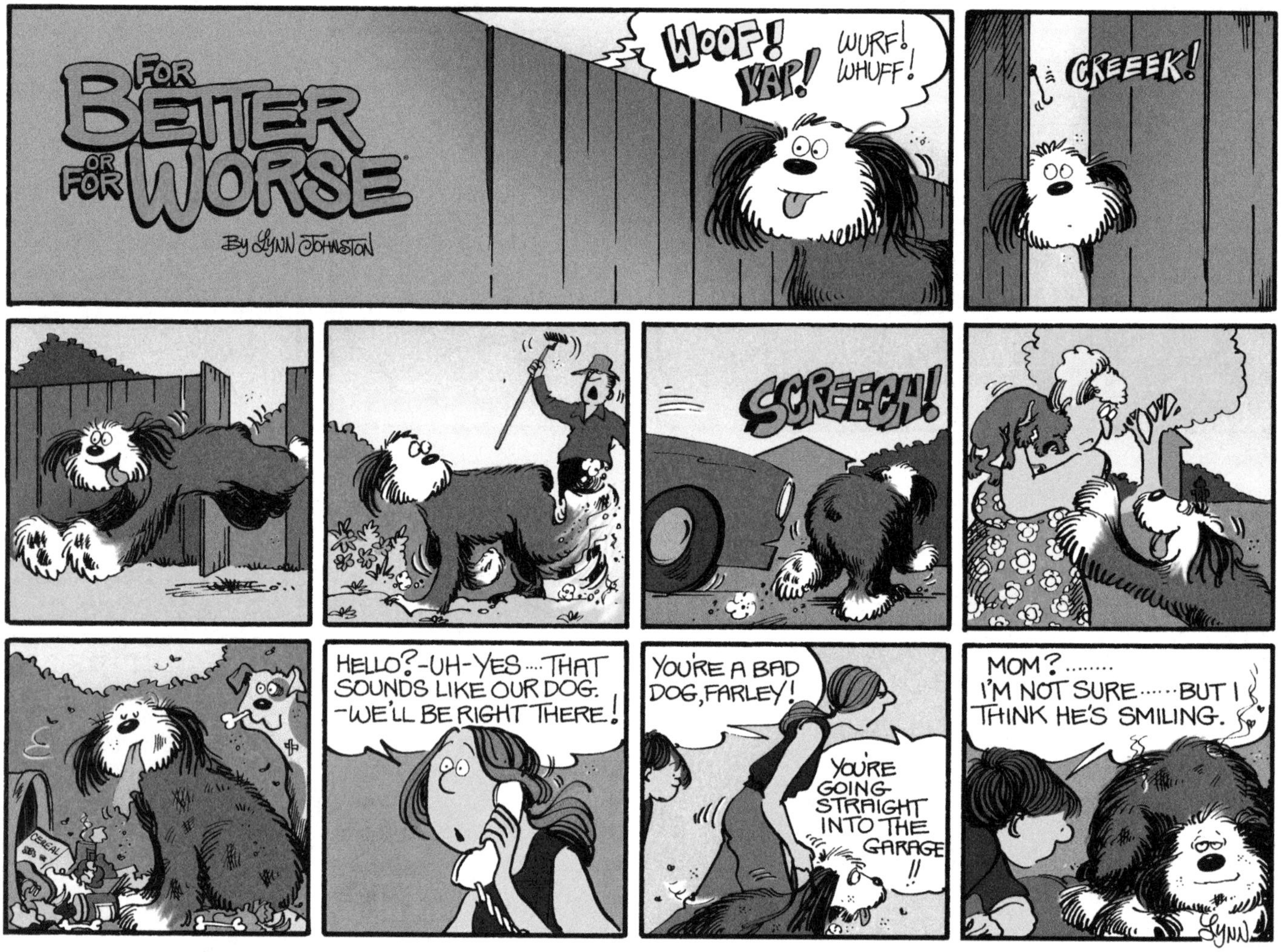
FOR BETTER OR FOR WORSE
BY LYNN JOHNSTON
WOOF! YAP!
WURF! WHUFF!
CREEEK!
SCREECH!
HELLO?-UH-YES.....THAT SOUNDS LIKE OUR DOG. -WE'LL BE RIGHT THERE!
YOU'RE A BAD DOG, FARLEY!
YOU'RE GOING STRAIGHT INTO THE GARAGE!!
MOM?........ I'M NOT SURE......BUT I THINK HE'S SMILING.
LYNN

Yes, this was another opportunity for readers to reprimand me for not being a responsible dog owner. Still, one has to wonder: Even with all of their good intentions, did these people never have something like this happen? "He who is without sin" and all that? I always wanted to say, "Folks, it's a cartoon dog!"

When you make a published statement every day, and you tell it like it is ... be prepared to be told off!

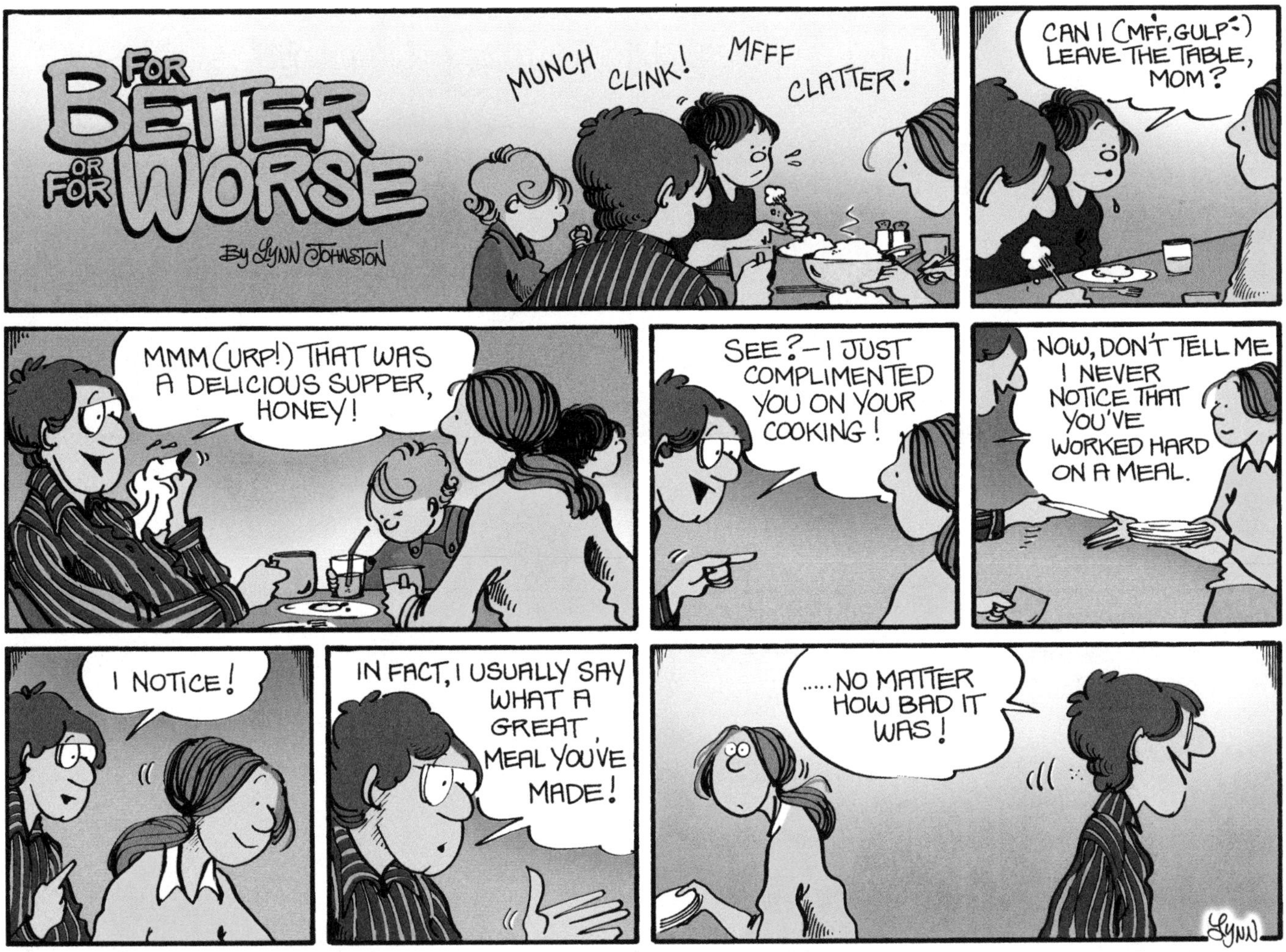
FOR BETTER OR FOR WORSE
BY LYNN JOHNSTON
MUNCH
CLINK!
MFFF
CLATTER!
CAN I (MFF, GULP) LEAVE THE TABLE, MOM?
MMM (URP!) THAT WAS A DELICIOUS SUPPER, HONEY!
SEE?—I JUST COMPLIMENTED YOU ON YOUR COOKING!
NOW, DON'T TELL ME I NEVER NOTICE THAT YOU'VE WORKED HARD ON A MEAL.
I NOTICE!
IN FACT, I USUALLY SAY WHAT A GREAT MEAL YOU'VE MADE!
.....NO MATTER HOW BAD IT WAS!
LYNN

I am actually a pretty good cook. (You don't have to serve gourmet fare to impress the gullets of an average clan.) What I made received few complaints or arguments. The strip, however, thrived on sarcasm and conflict — NOT complaining about Elly's cooking would have been dull.

It occurred to me that my family ate as if they were at a restaurant; food arrived, went down, and was taken for granted — along with the cook. I wished my family would compliment me sometimes, or at least discuss the menu. After all, a good meal is a sign of love, care, and affection, and should receive some praise! This strip was a personal cry for attention. My husband objected to the punch line — and rightly so!

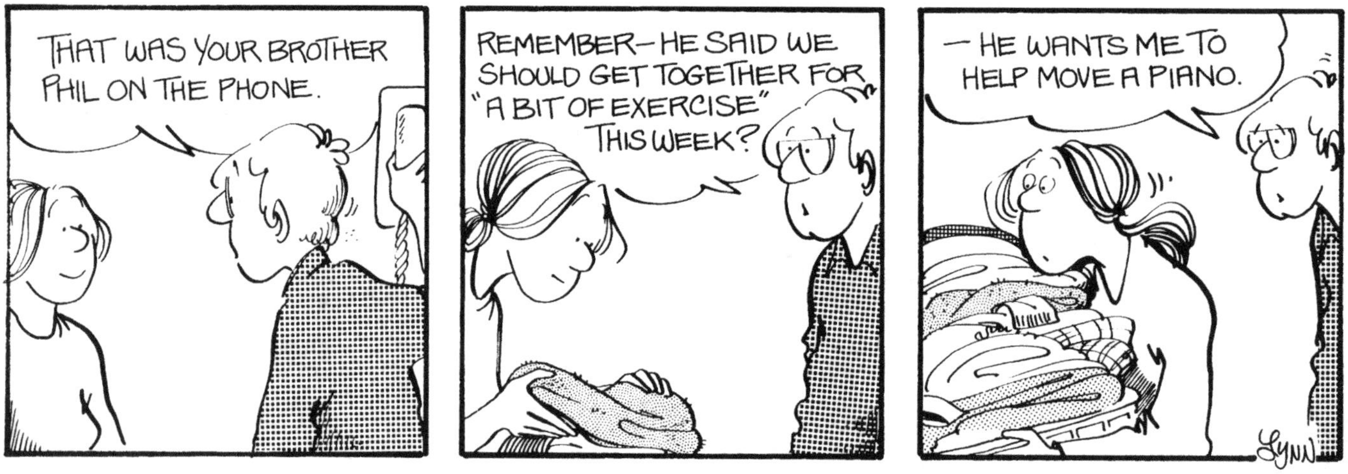
THAT WAS YOUR BROTHER PHIL ON THE PHONE.
REMEMBER—HE SAID WE SHOULD GET TOGETHER FOR "A BIT OF EXERCISE" THIS WEEK?
—HE WANTS ME TO HELP MOVE A PIANO.

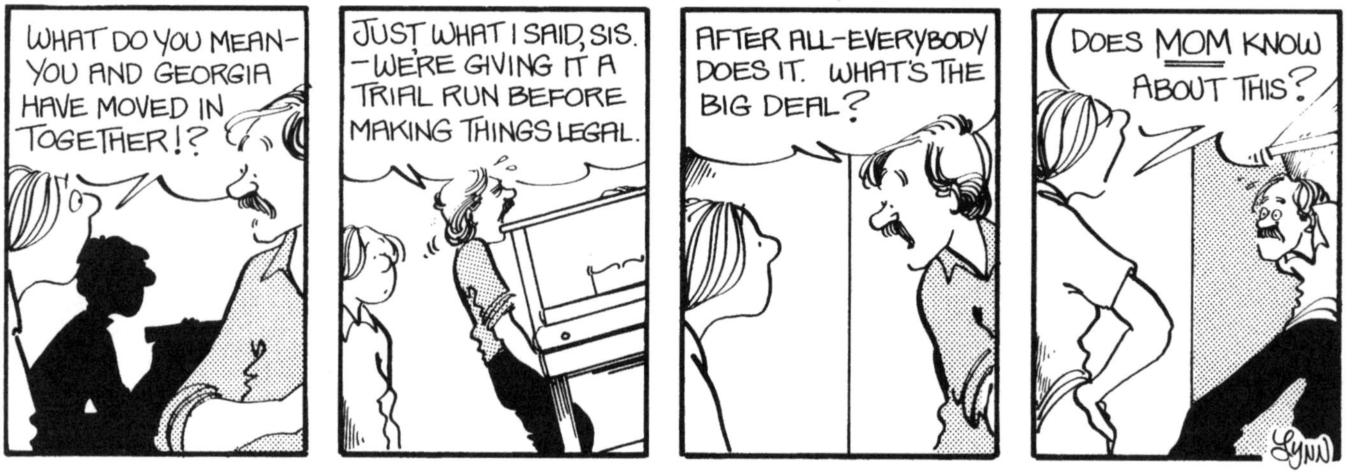
WHAT DO YOU MEAN—YOU AND GEORGIA HAVE MOVED IN TOGETHER!?
JUST WHAT I SAID, SIS. —WE'RE GIVING IT A TRIAL RUN BEFORE MAKING THINGS LEGAL.
AFTER ALL—EVERYBODY DOES IT. WHAT'S THE BIG DEAL?
DOES MOM KNOW ABOUT THIS?

As promised, I did not have Phil and Georgia share a space until my brother, Alan, and his wife, Joan, were married!

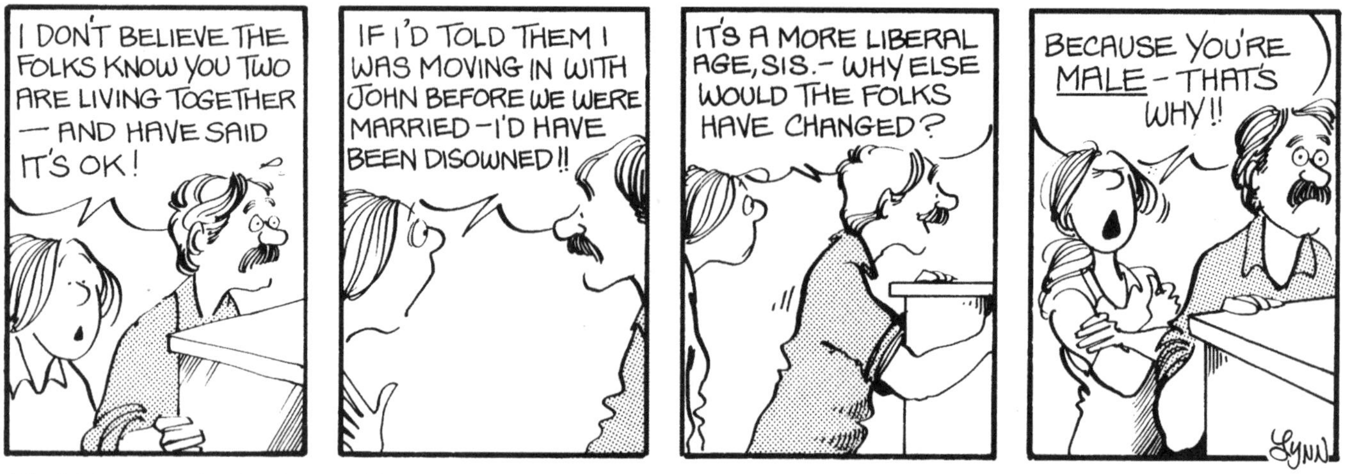
I DON'T BELIEVE THE FOLKS KNOW YOU TWO ARE LIVING TOGETHER —AND HAVE SAID IT'S OK!
IF I'D TOLD THEM I WAS MOVING IN WITH JOHN BEFORE WE WERE MARRIED—I'D HAVE BEEN DISOWNED!!
IT'S A MORE LIBERAL AGE, SIS.—WHY ELSE WOULD THE FOLKS HAVE CHANGED?
BECAUSE YOU'RE MALE—THAT'S WHY!!

All of this rant is absolutely true! My mom would have disinherited me if I had moved in with a boyfriend before marriage. She had a double standard when it came to Alan ... he was, after all, a boy!

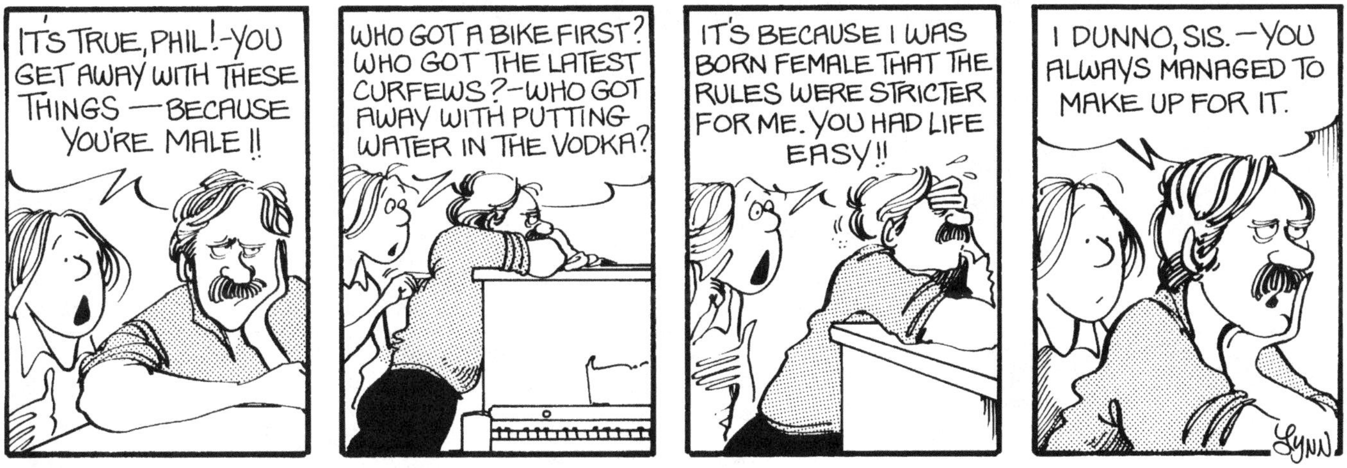
IT'S TRUE, PHIL! -YOU GET AWAY WITH THESE THINGS —BECAUSE YOU'RE MALE !!
WHO GOT A BIKE FIRST? WHO GOT THE LATEST CURFEWS?-WHO GOT AWAY WITH PUTTING WATER IN THE VODKA?
IT'S BECAUSE I WAS BORN FEMALE THAT THE RULES WERE STRICTER FOR ME. YOU HAD LIFE EASY!!
I DUNNO, SIS. —YOU ALWAYS MANAGED TO MAKE UP FOR IT.
LYNN

This dialogue between my brother and me really happened. My brother's wonderful wit often came out like a crafted punch line.

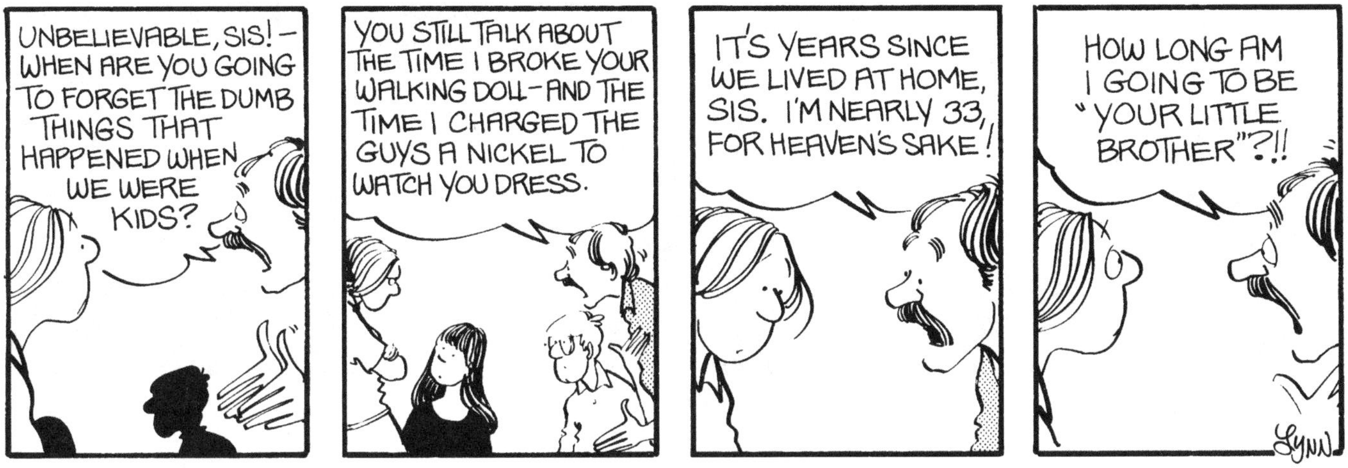
UNBELIEVABLE, SIS! -WHEN ARE YOU GOING TO FORGET THE DUMB THINGS THAT HAPPENED WHEN WE WERE KIDS?
YOU STILL TALK ABOUT THE TIME I BROKE YOUR WALKING DOLL-AND THE TIME I CHARGED THE GUYS A NICKEL TO WATCH YOU DRESS.
IT'S YEARS SINCE WE LIVED AT HOME, SIS. I'M NEARLY 33, FOR HEAVEN'S SAKE!
HOW LONG AM I GOING TO BE "YOUR LITTLE BROTHER"?!!
LYNN

Alan broke my walking doll by holding both legs and making her walk as fast as possible. She wasn't meant for BOYS to play with!

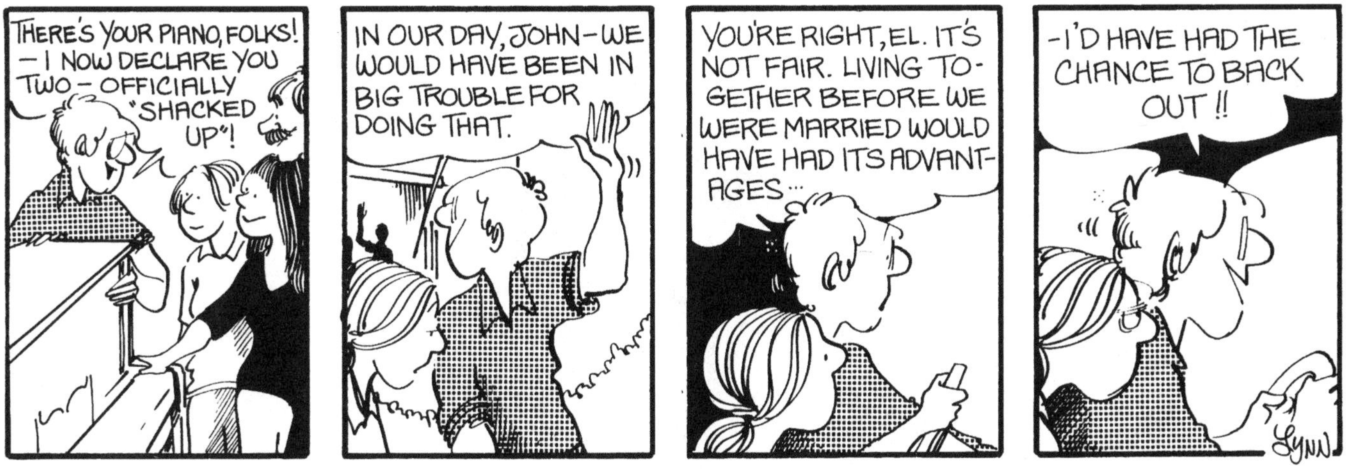
THERE'S YOUR PIANO, FOLKS! - I NOW DECLARE YOU TWO - OFFICIALLY "SHACKED UP"!
IN OUR DAY, JOHN-WE WOULD HAVE BEEN IN BIG TROUBLE FOR DOING THAT.
YOU'RE RIGHT, EL. IT'S NOT FAIR. LIVING TOGETHER BEFORE WE WERE MARRIED WOULD HAVE HAD ITS ADVANTAGES...
-I'D HAVE HAD THE CHANCE TO BACK OUT !!
LYNN

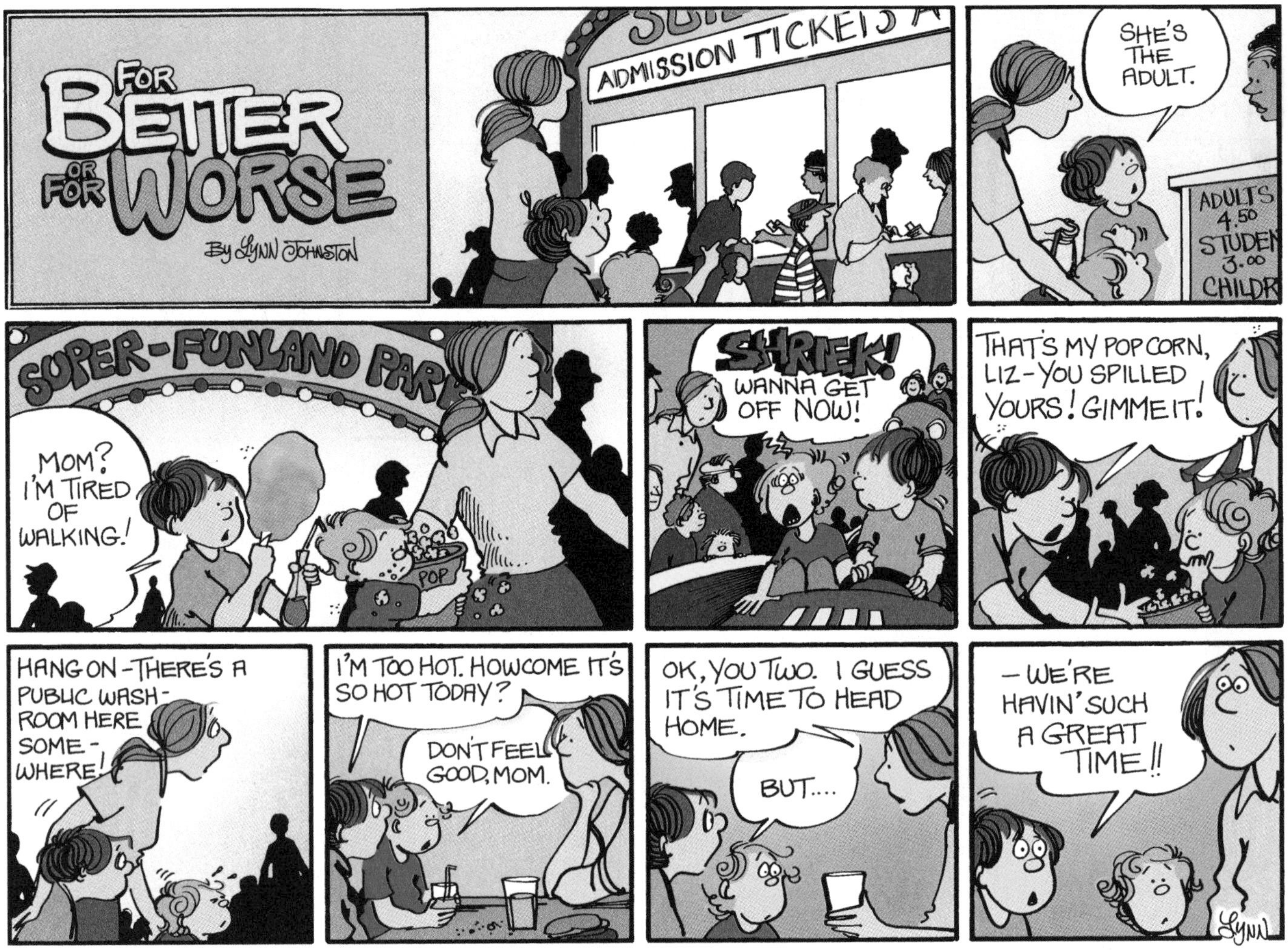
FOR BETTER OR FOR WORSE
BY LYNN JOHNSTON
ADMISSION TICKETS
SHE'S THE ADULT.
ADULTS 4.50
STUDEN 3.00
CHILDR
SUPER-FUNLAND PARK
MOM? I'M TIRED OF WALKING!
POP
SHRIEK! WANNA GET OFF NOW!
THAT'S MY POP CORN, LIZ-YOU SPILLED YOURS! GIMME IT!
HANG ON-THERE'S A PUBLIC WASH-ROOM HERE SOME-WHERE!
I'M TOO HOT. HOWCOME IT'S SO HOT TODAY?
DON'T FEEL GOOD, MOM.
OK, YOU TWO. I GUESS IT'S TIME TO HEAD HOME.
BUT....
-WE'RE HAVIN' SUCH A GREAT TIME!!
LYNN

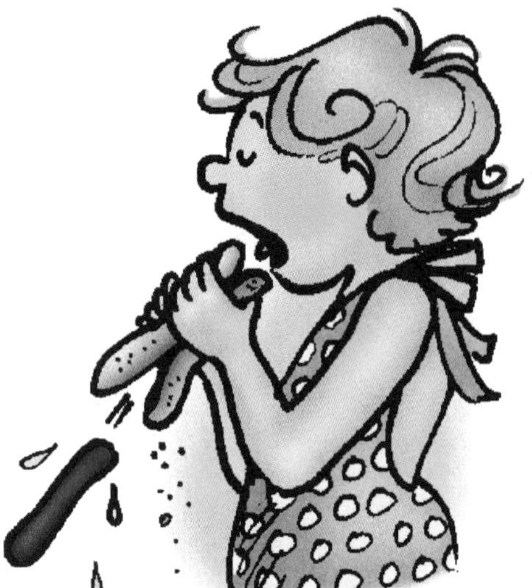

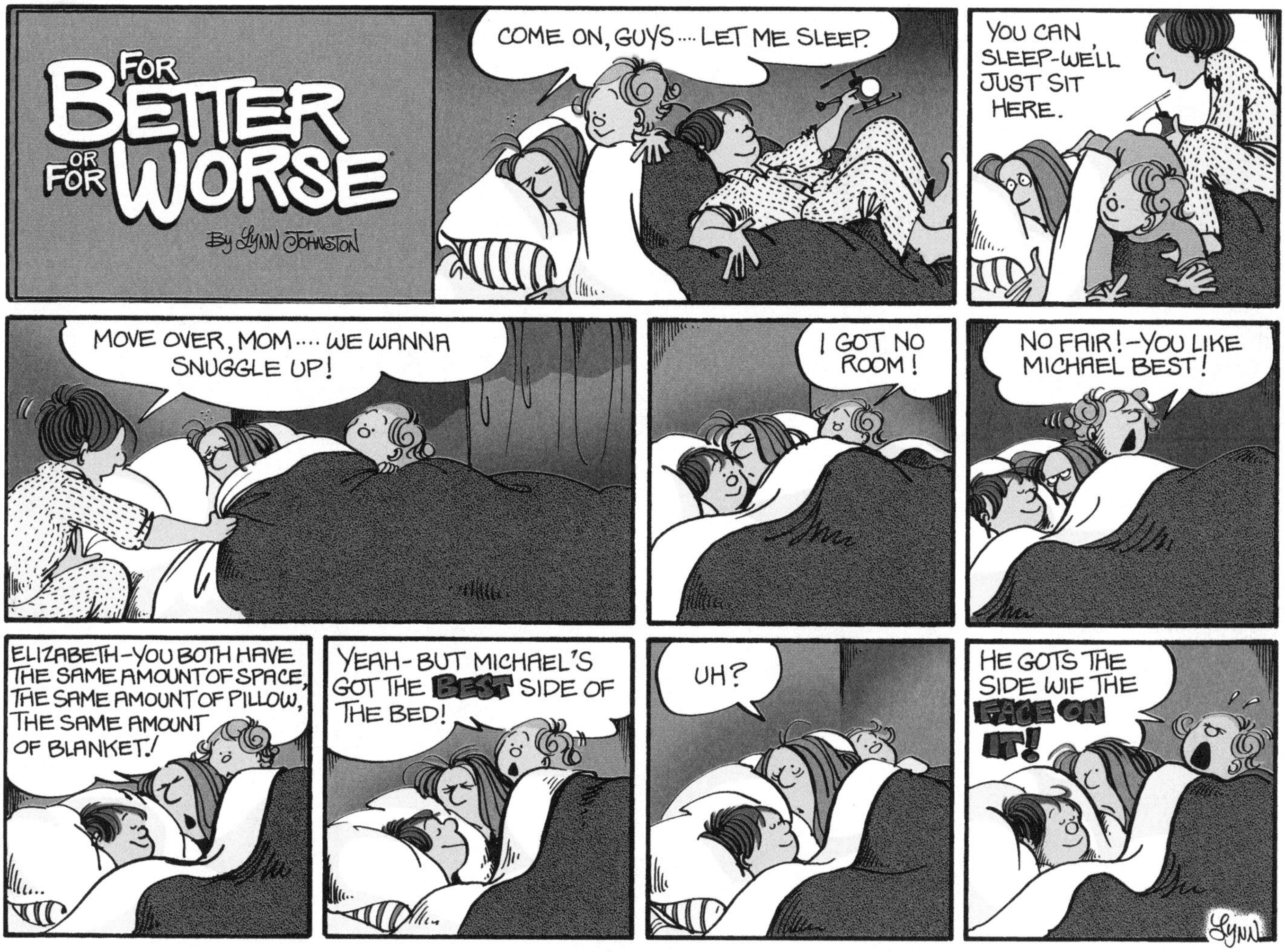
FOR BETTER OR FOR WORSE
By Lynn Johnston
COME ON, GUYS.... LET ME SLEEP.
YOU CAN SLEEP-WE'LL JUST SIT HERE.
MOVE OVER, MOM.... WE WANNA SNUGGLE UP!
I GOT NO ROOM!
NO FAIR!-YOU LIKE MICHAEL BEST!
ELIZABETH-YOU BOTH HAVE THE SAME AMOUNT OF SPACE, THE SAME AMOUNT OF PILLOW, THE SAME AMOUNT OF BLANKET!
YEAH-BUT MICHAEL'S GOT THE BEST SIDE OF THE BED!
UH?
HE GOTS THE SIDE WIF THE FACE ON IT!
Lynn

This is one of my favourite strips. On rare occasion, the kids would climb into bed with us — and Katie, despite morning breath, wanted the side with "the face on it!"

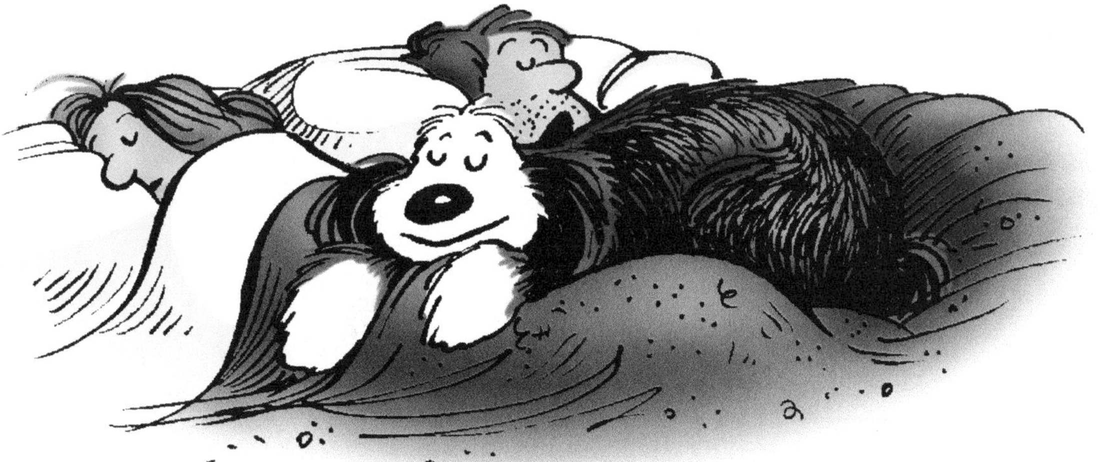

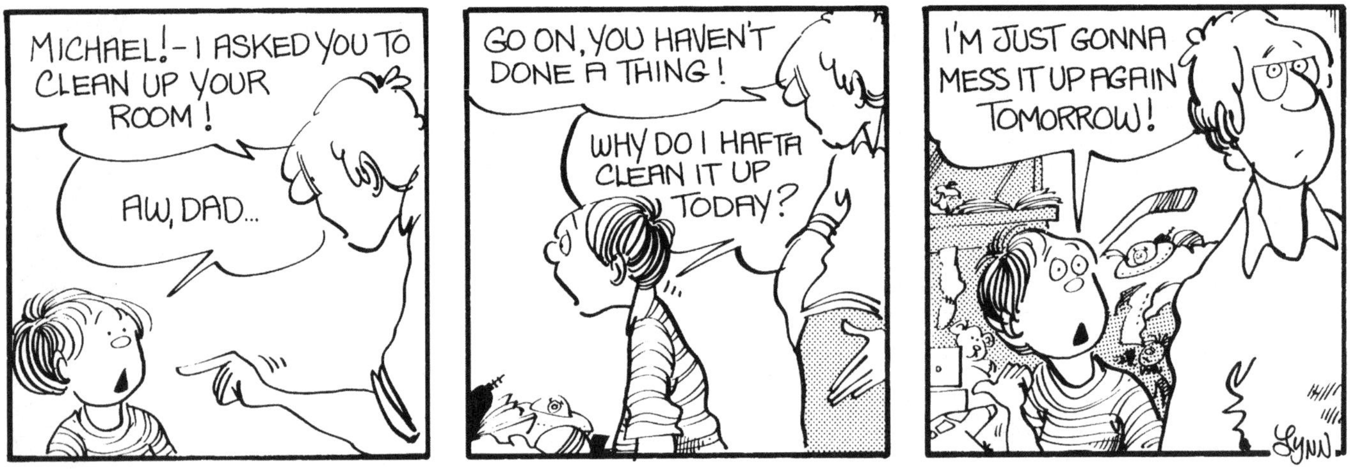
MICHAEL!-I ASKED YOU TO CLEAN UP YOUR ROOM!
AW, DAD...
GO ON, YOU HAVEN'T DONE A THING!
WHY DO I HAFTA CLEAN IT UP TODAY?
I'M JUST GONNA MESS IT UP AGAIN TOMORROW!
LYNN

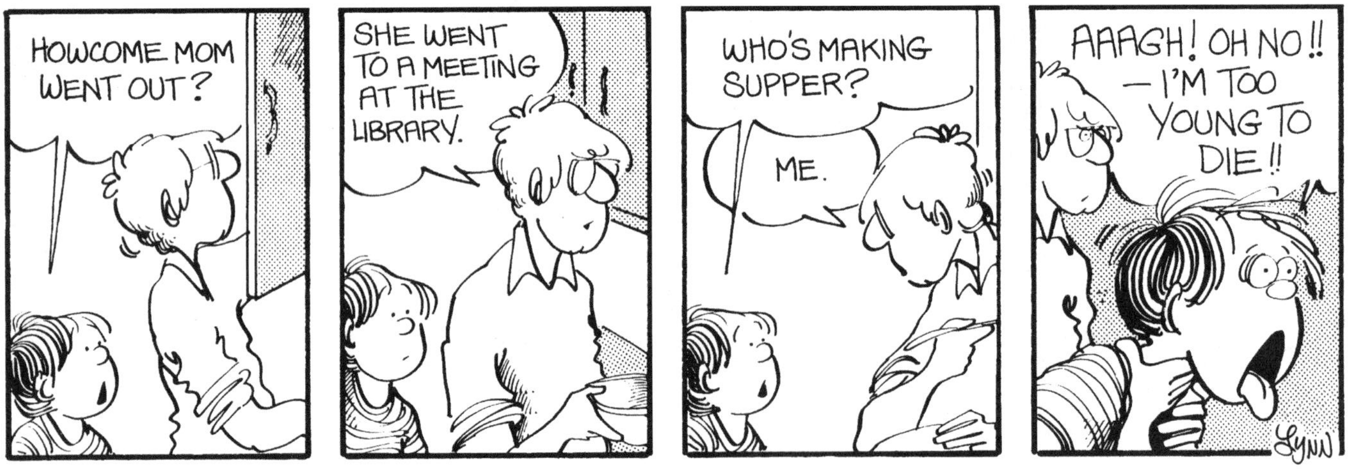
HOWCOME MOM WENT OUT?
SHE WENT TO A MEETING AT THE LIBRARY.
WHO'S MAKING SUPPER?
ME.
AAAGH! OH NO!! —I'M TOO YOUNG TO DIE!!
LYNN

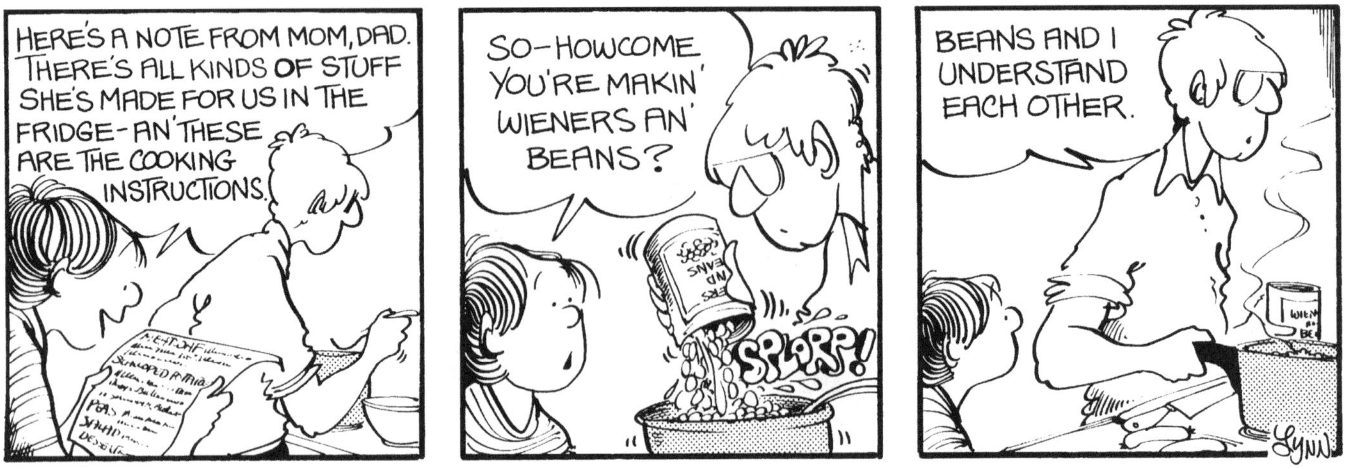
HERE'S A NOTE FROM MOM, DAD. THERE'S ALL KINDS OF STUFF SHE'S MADE FOR US IN THE FRIDGE-AN' THESE ARE THE COOKING INSTRUCTIONS.
SO-HOWCOME YOU'RE MAKIN' WIENERS AN' BEANS?
SPLORP!
BEANS AND I UNDERSTAND EACH OTHER.
LYNN

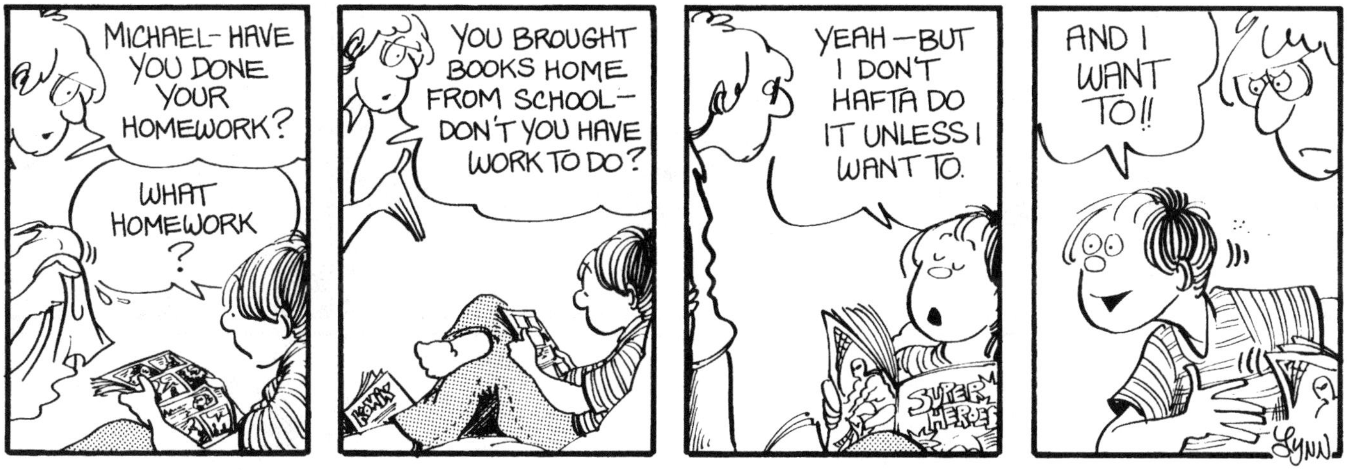
MICHAEL- HAVE YOU DONE YOUR HOMEWORK?
WHAT HOMEWORK ?
YOU BROUGHT BOOKS HOME FROM SCHOOL- DON'T YOU HAVE WORK TO DO?
YEAH — BUT I DON'T HAFTA DO IT UNLESS I WANT TO.
SUPER HERO
AND I WANT TO!!
LYNN

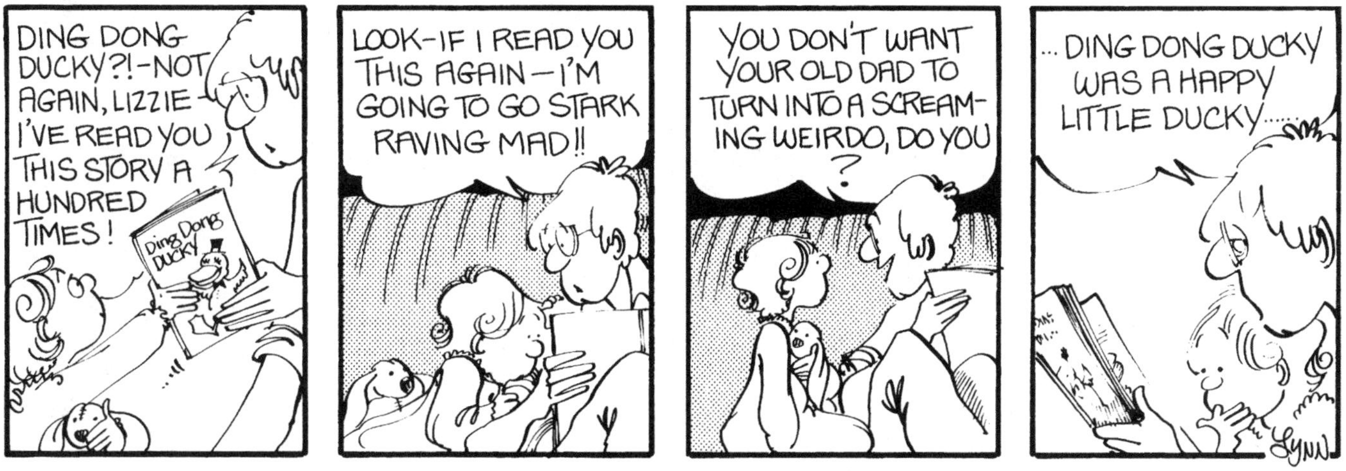
DING DONG DUCKY?!-NOT AGAIN, LIZZIE-I'VE READ YOU THIS STORY A HUNDRED TIMES!
Ding Dong DUCKY
LOOK-IF I READ YOU THIS AGAIN — I'M GOING TO GO STARK RAVING MAD!!
YOU DON'T WANT YOUR OLD DAD TO TURN INTO A SCREAMING WEIRDO, DO YOU ?
... DING DONG DUCKY WAS A HAPPY LITTLE DUCKY......
LYNN

I read the same books over and over again until the kids could "read" along with me. I don't remember resenting the repetition — it helped them to learn. Aaron, in particular, could pick out individual words long before he started school. He loved to look through the newspaper and circle all of the "ands"!

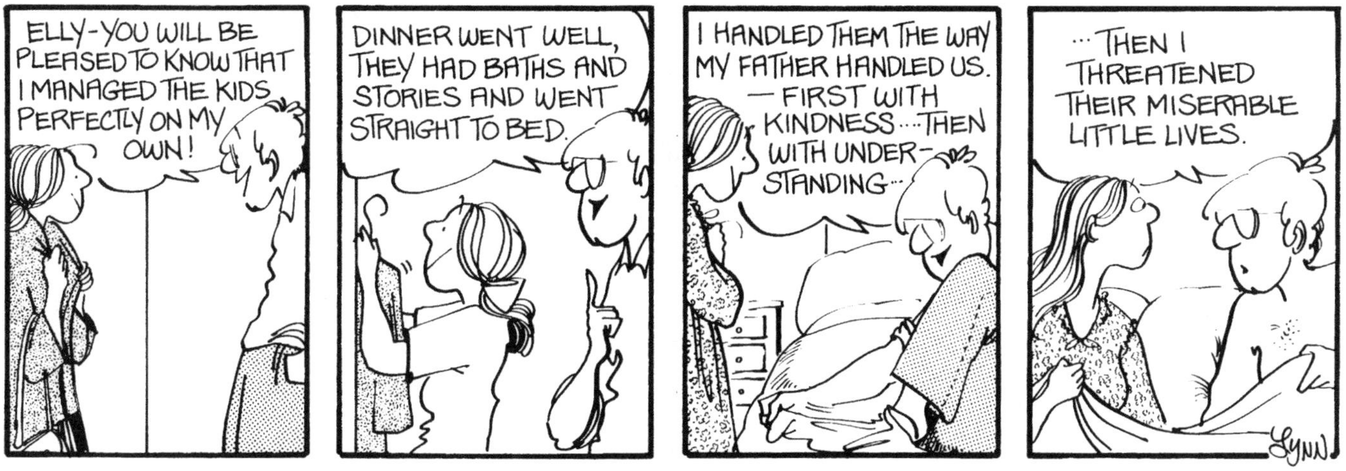
ELLY-YOU WILL BE PLEASED TO KNOW THAT I MANAGED THE KIDS PERFECTLY ON MY OWN!
DINNER WENT WELL, THEY HAD BATHS AND STORIES AND WENT STRAIGHT TO BED.
I HANDLED THEM THE WAY MY FATHER HANDLED US. — FIRST WITH KINDNESS ... THEN WITH UNDERSTANDING...
... THEN I THREATENED THEIR MISERABLE LITTLE LIVES.
LYNN

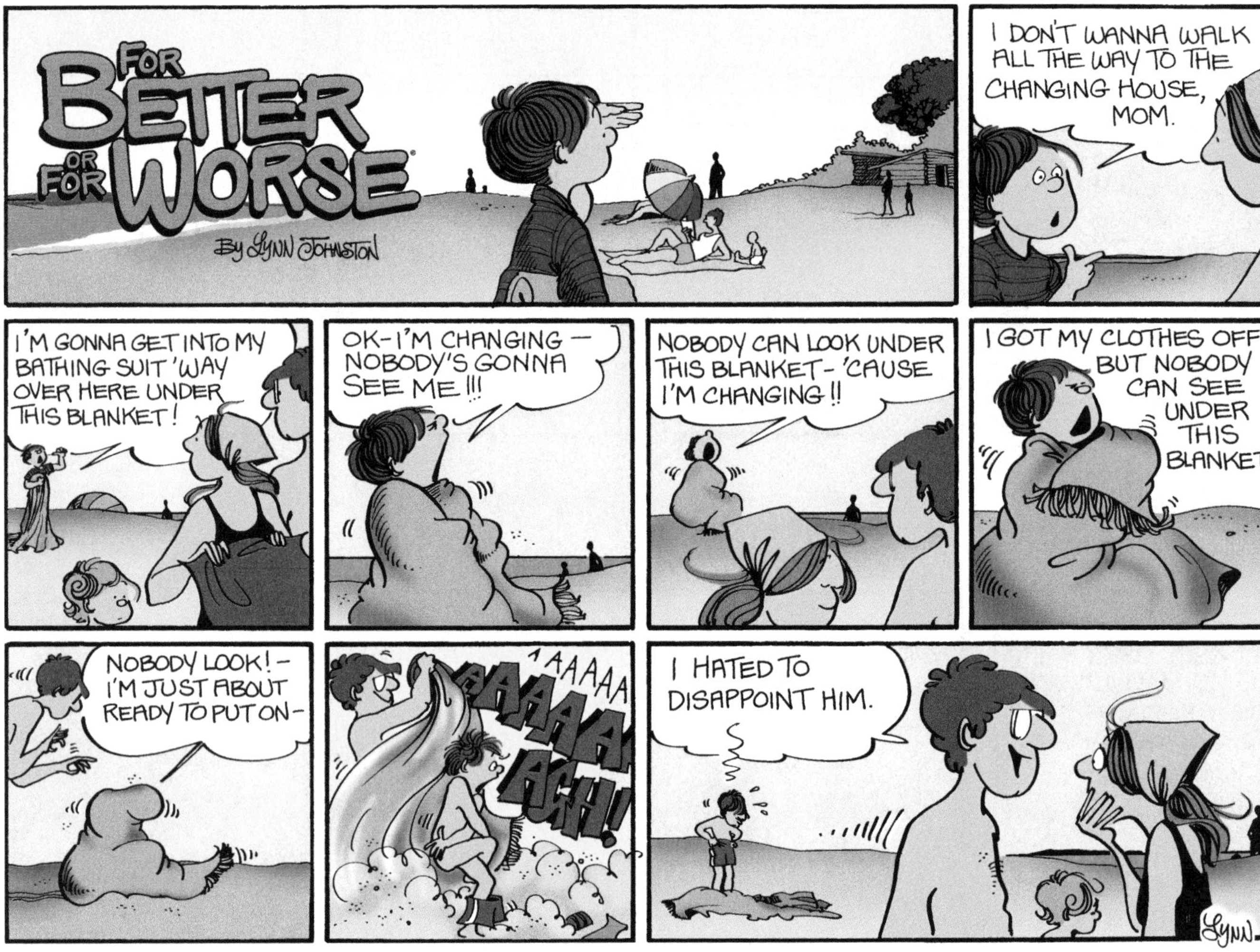
FOR BETTER OR FOR WORSE
BY LYNN JOHNSTON
I DON'T WANNA WALK ALL THE WAY TO THE CHANGING HOUSE, MOM.
I'M GONNA GET INTO MY BATHING SUIT 'WAY OVER HERE UNDER THIS BLANKET!
OK-I'M CHANGING - NOBODY'S GONNA SEE ME!!!
NOBODY CAN LOOK UNDER THIS BLANKET- 'CAUSE I'M CHANGING!!
I GOT MY CLOTHES OFF- BUT NOBODY CAN SEE UNDER THIS BLANKET!
NOBODY LOOK! - I'M JUST ABOUT READY TO PUT ON-
AAAAAAAAAAAAAAAAGH!
I HATED TO DISAPPOINT HIM.
LYNN

Here is another strip that got me into hot water. Removing Michael's towel while he was changing was a reportable offense! The problem with a static image is, the subtle elements, which would otherwise explain things, are not there. You can't show little things like eye movement, shrugs, knowing smiles, and reassuring gestures. The artist knows the situation is all in fun, but the audience does not. What should be funny is therefore sometimes misinterpreted.

As kids, we would change on the beach under our towels so fast that even the swiftest voyeur was unable to catch us in the buff. We'd yell out, "I'm changing!!" just to goad someone into pulling off our towels. That's what kids do! Anyway, this ran, and I knew as I saw it in print that I would soon be getting more mail. I learned another lesson … but then again, this job is all "towel and error"!

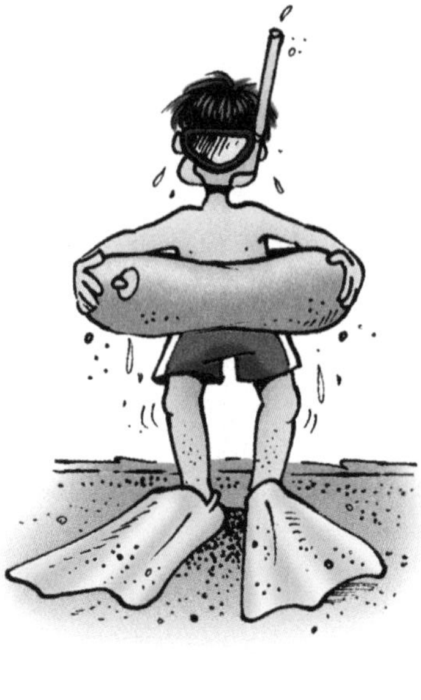

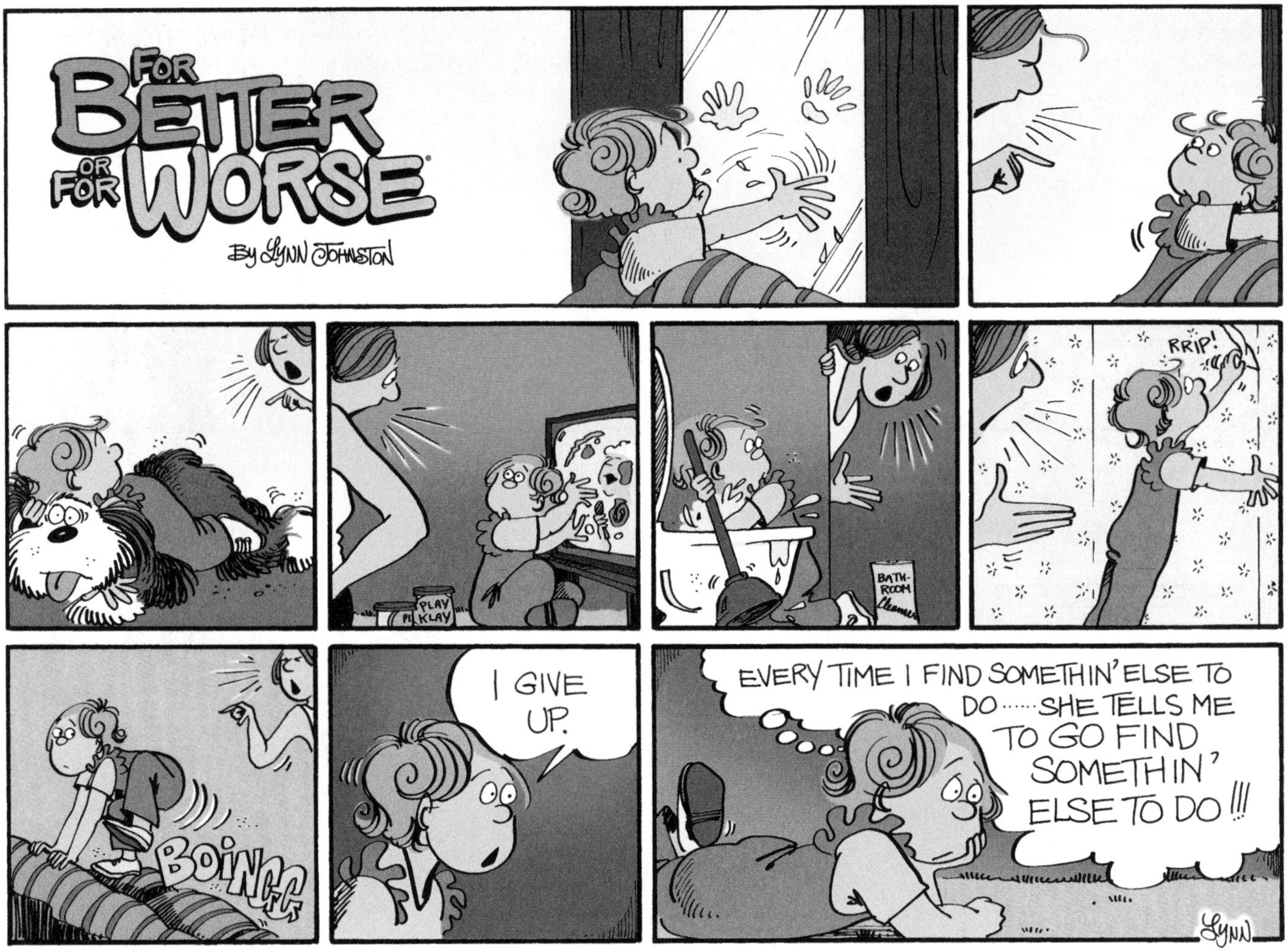
FOR BETTER OR FOR WORSE
BY LYNN JOHNSTON
RRIP!
PLAY KLAY
BATH-ROOM
BOINGG
I GIVE UP.
EVERY TIME I FIND SOMETHIN' ELSE TO DO...... SHE TELLS ME TO GO FIND SOMETHIN' ELSE TO DO!!!
LYNN

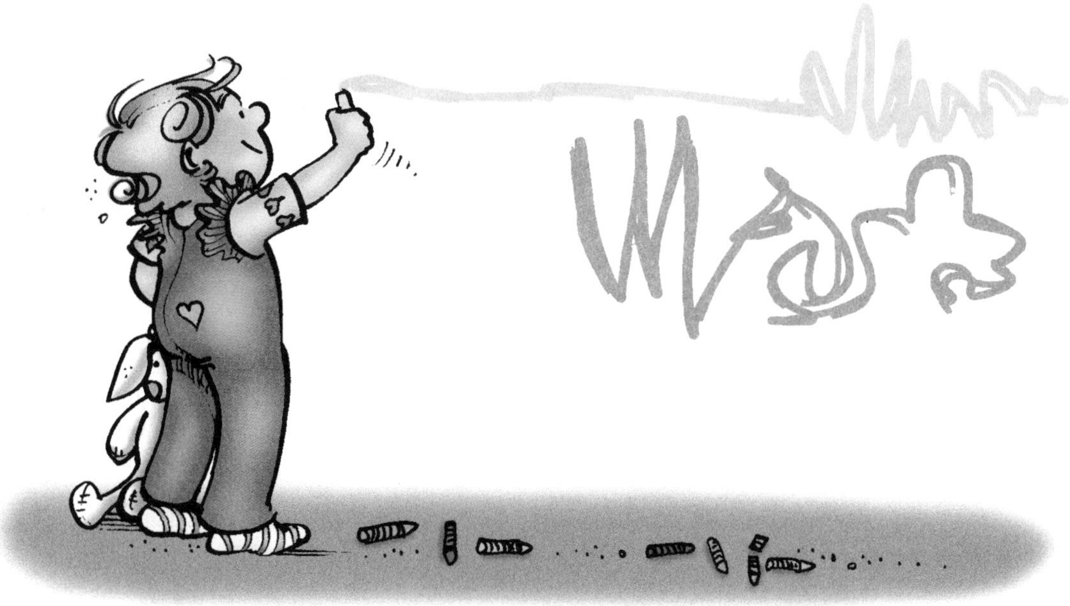

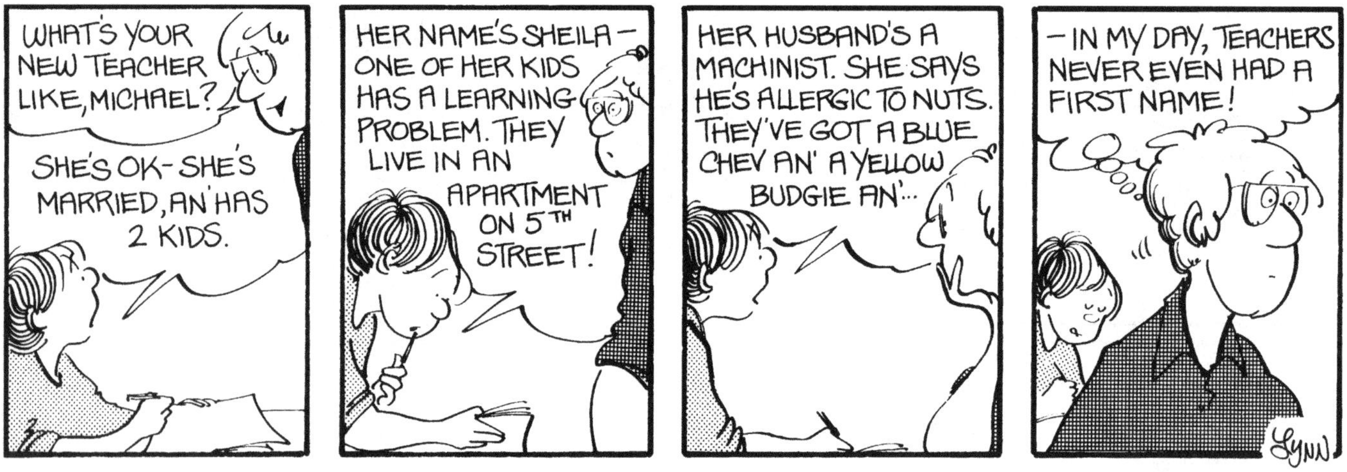
WHAT'S YOUR NEW TEACHER LIKE, MICHAEL?
SHE'S OK- SHE'S MARRIED, AN' HAS 2 KIDS.
HER NAME'S SHEILA - ONE OF HER KIDS HAS A LEARNING PROBLEM. THEY LIVE IN AN APARTMENT ON 5TH STREET!
HER HUSBAND'S A MACHINIST. SHE SAYS HE'S ALLERGIC TO NUTS. THEY'VE GOT A BLUE CHEV AN' A YELLOW BUDGIE AN'...
- IN MY DAY, TEACHERS NEVER EVEN HAD A FIRST NAME!
LYNN

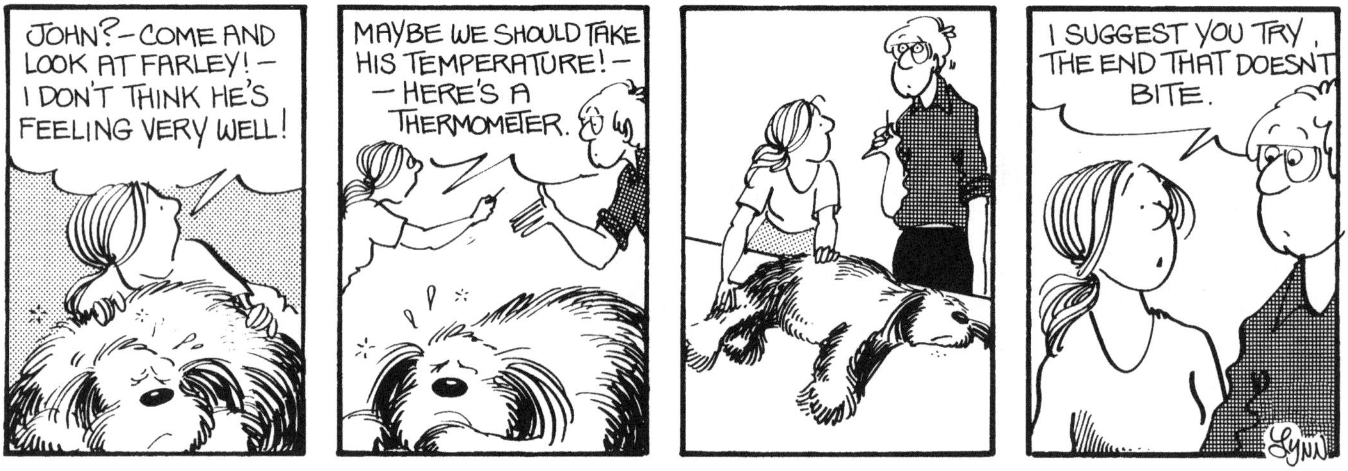
JOHN?- COME AND LOOK AT FARLEY! - I DON'T THINK HE'S FEELING VERY WELL!
MAYBE WE SHOULD TAKE HIS TEMPERATURE! - - HERE'S A THERMOMETER.
I SUGGEST YOU TRY THE END THAT DOESN'T BITE.
LYNN

People complained when they saw things in the strip they thought were bad for Farley, and poured out their concern.

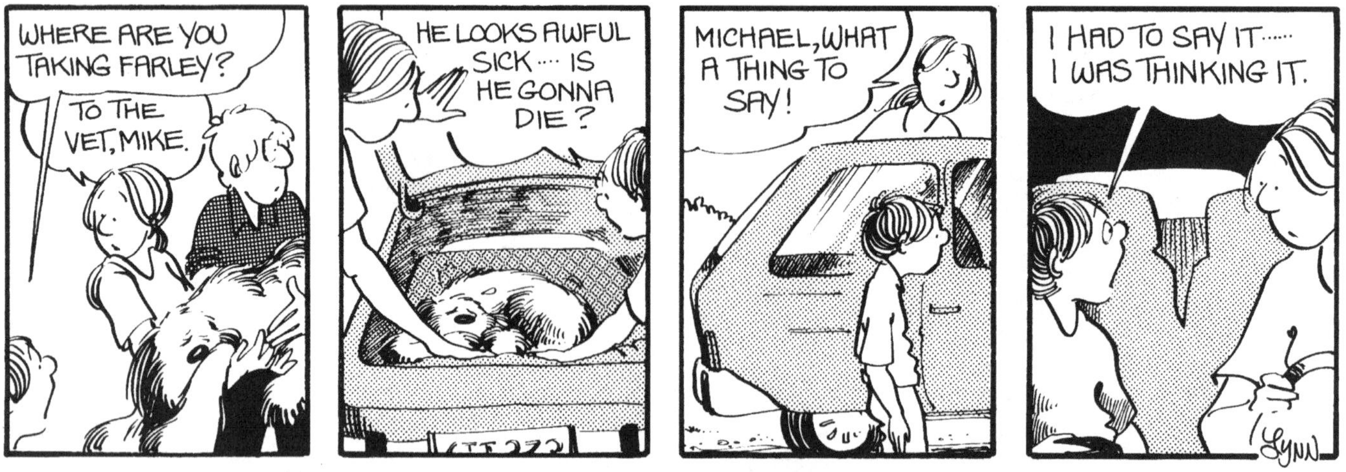
WHERE ARE YOU TAKING FARLEY?
TO THE VET, MIKE.
HE LOOKS AWFUL SICK.... IS HE GONNA DIE?
MICHAEL, WHAT A THING TO SAY!
I HAD TO SAY IT...... I WAS THINKING IT.
LYNN

This short vignette about Farley's illness made close followers of casual readers who thought they were going to witness his demise.

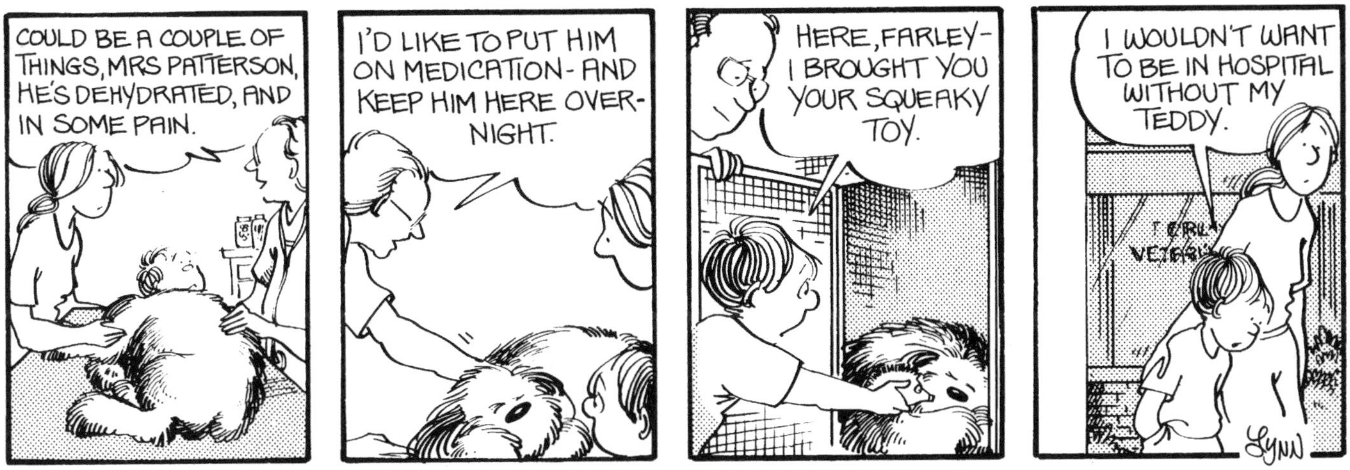
COULD BE A COUPLE OF THINGS, MRS PATTERSON, HE'S DEHYDRATED, AND IN SOME PAIN.
I'D LIKE TO PUT HIM ON MEDICATION - AND KEEP HIM HERE OVER-NIGHT.
HERE, FARLEY- I BROUGHT YOU YOUR SQUEAKY TOY.
I WOULDN'T WANT TO BE IN HOSPITAL WITHOUT MY TEDDY.
LYNN

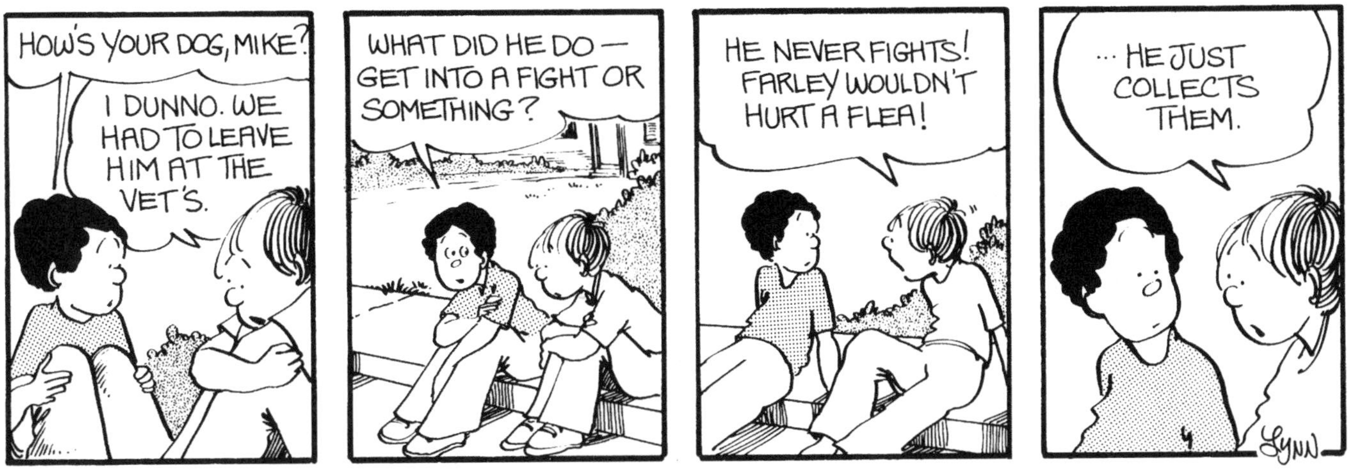
HOW'S YOUR DOG, MIKE?
I DUNNO. WE HAD TO LEAVE HIM AT THE VET'S.
WHAT DID HE DO — GET INTO A FIGHT OR SOMETHING?
HE NEVER FIGHTS! FARLEY WOULDN'T HURT A FLEA!
...HE JUST COLLECTS THEM.
LYNN

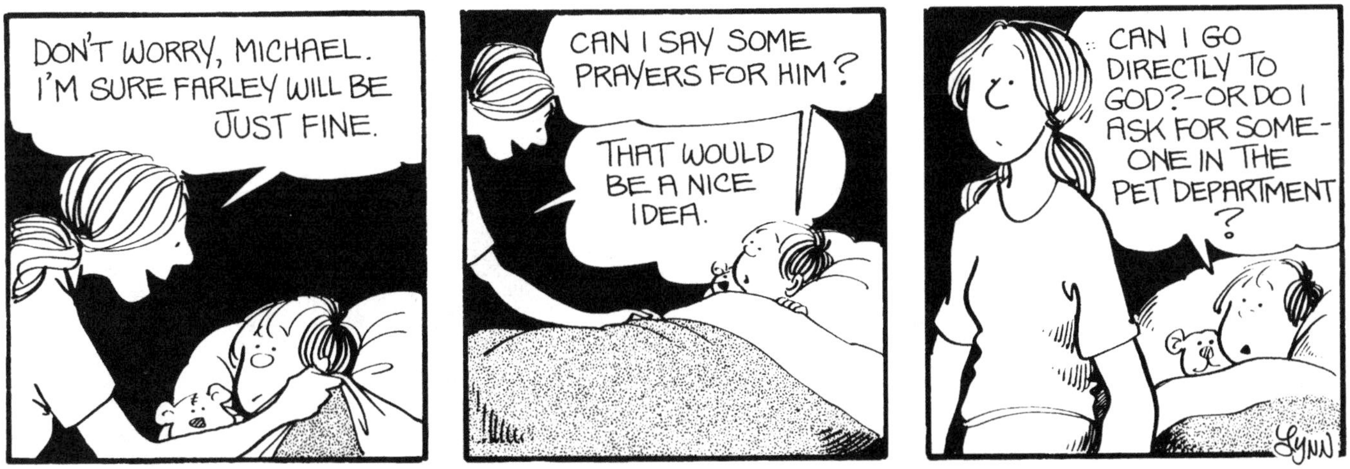
DON'T WORRY, MICHAEL. I'M SURE FARLEY WILL BE JUST FINE.
CAN I SAY SOME PRAYERS FOR HIM?
THAT WOULD BE A NICE IDEA.
CAN I GO DIRECTLY TO GOD?-OR DO I ASK FOR SOME-ONE IN THE PET DEPARTMENT?
LYNN

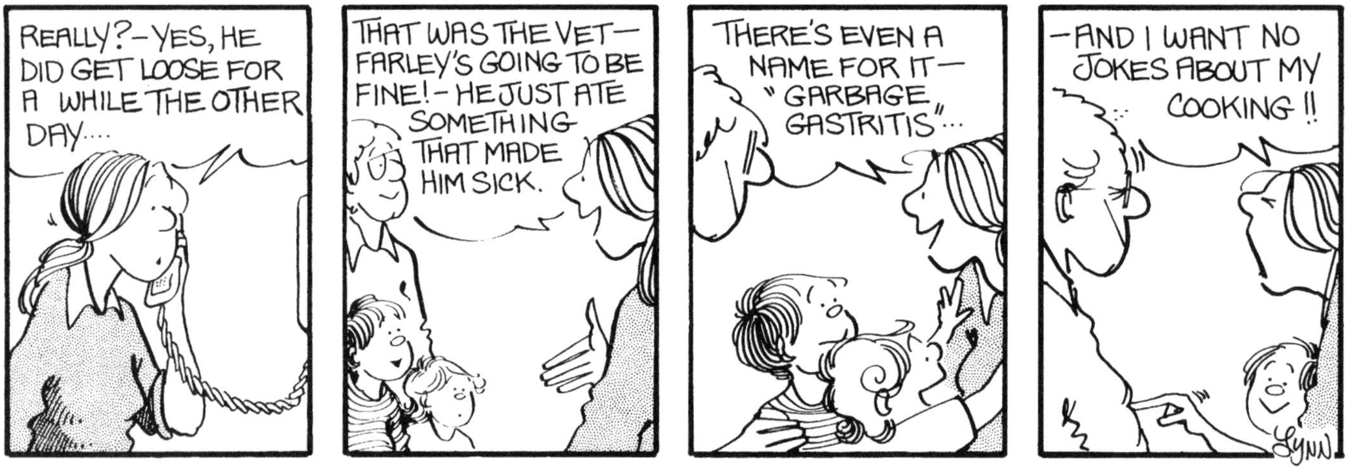
REALLY?–YES, HE DID GET LOOSE FOR A WHILE THE OTHER DAY....
THAT WAS THE VET– FARLEY'S GOING TO BE FINE!–HE JUST ATE SOMETHING THAT MADE HIM SICK.
THERE'S EVEN A NAME FOR IT– "GARBAGE GASTRITIS"...
–AND I WANT NO JOKES ABOUT MY COOKING!!
LYNN

I had consulted with my sister-in-law, the veterinarian, and asked her to describe a scenario in which Farley would have a common non-life-threatening illness, but serious enough to consult a vet. Beth suggested "garbage gastritis," which I thought was a wonderfully funny name for an illness — so that's what Farley had.

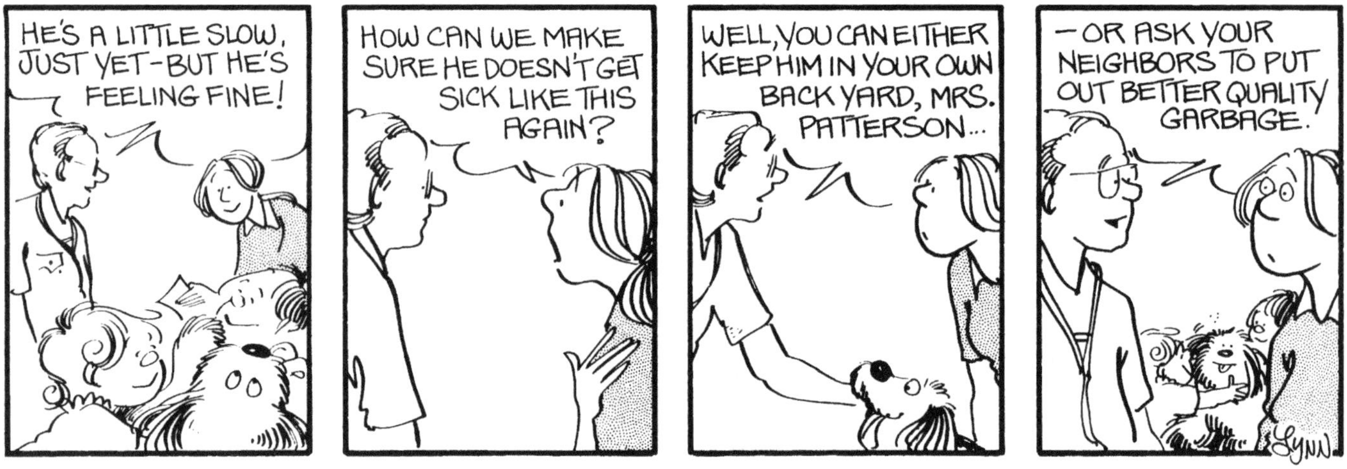
HE'S A LITTLE SLOW, JUST YET–BUT HE'S FEELING FINE!
HOW CAN WE MAKE SURE HE DOESN'T GET SICK LIKE THIS AGAIN?
WELL, YOU CAN EITHER KEEP HIM IN YOUR OWN BACK YARD, MRS. PATTERSON...
–OR ASK YOUR NEIGHBORS TO PUT OUT BETTER QUALITY GARBAGE.
LYNN

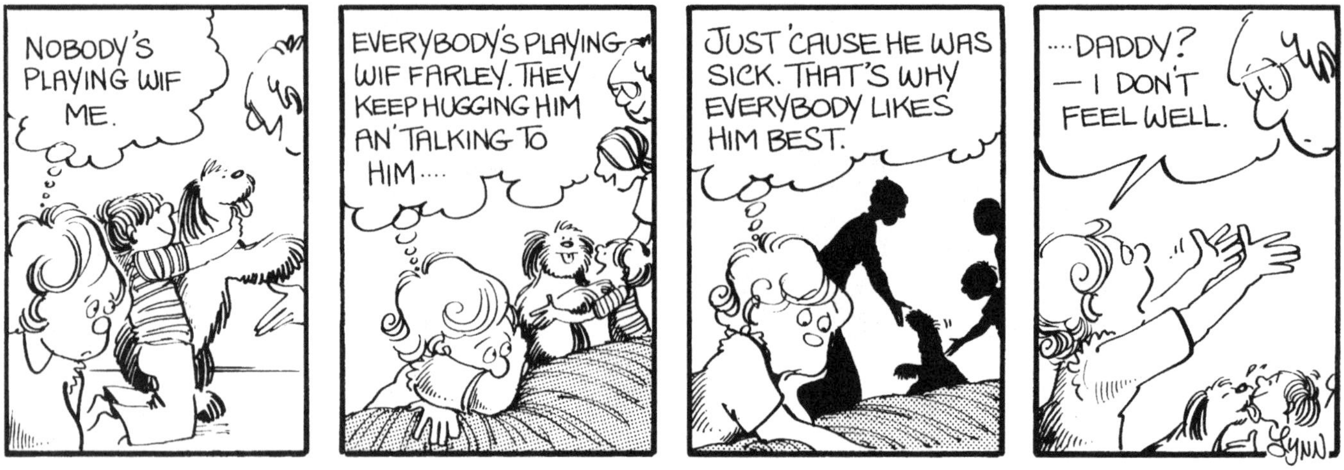
NOBODY'S PLAYING WIF ME.
EVERYBODY'S PLAYING WIF FARLEY. THEY KEEP HUGGING HIM AN' TALKING TO HIM....
JUST 'CAUSE HE WAS SICK. THAT'S WHY EVERYBODY LIKES HIM BEST.
....DADDY? –I DON'T FEEL WELL.
LYNN

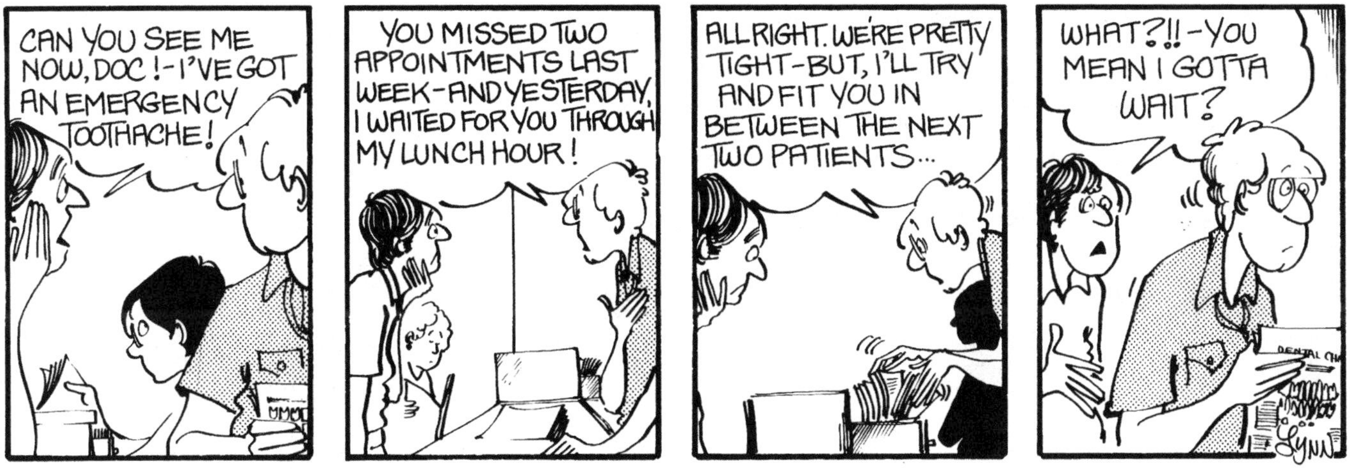
CAN YOU SEE ME NOW, DOC! - I'VE GOT AN EMERGENCY TOOTHACHE!
YOU MISSED TWO APPOINTMENTS LAST WEEK - AND YESTERDAY, I WAITED FOR YOU THROUGH MY LUNCH HOUR!
ALL RIGHT. WE'RE PRETTY TIGHT - BUT, I'LL TRY AND FIT YOU IN BETWEEN THE NEXT TWO PATIENTS...
WHAT?!! - YOU MEAN I GOTTA WAIT?
LYNN

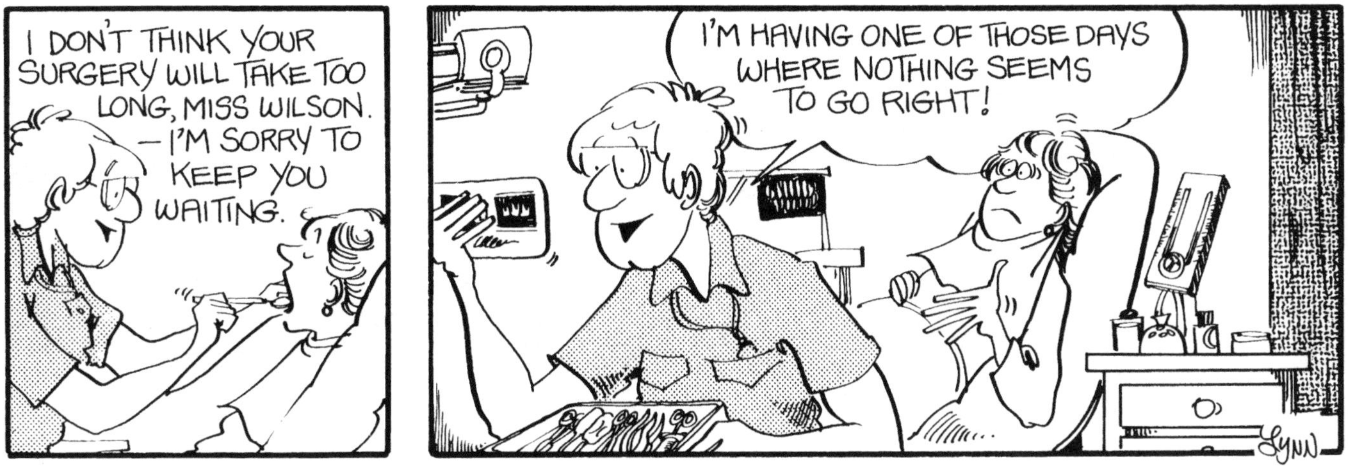
I DON'T THINK YOUR SURGERY WILL TAKE TOO LONG, MISS WILSON. - I'M SORRY TO KEEP YOU WAITING.
I'M HAVING ONE OF THOSE DAYS WHERE NOTHING SEEMS TO GO RIGHT!
LYNN

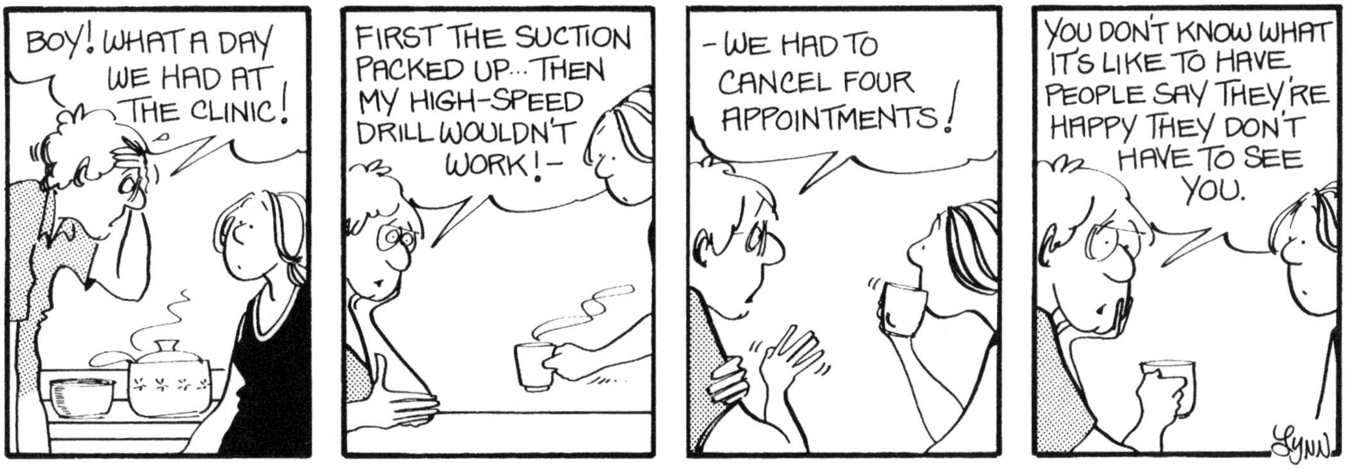
BOY! WHAT A DAY WE HAD AT THE CLINIC!
FIRST THE SUCTION PACKED UP... THEN MY HIGH-SPEED DRILL WOULDN'T WORK! -
- WE HAD TO CANCEL FOUR APPOINTMENTS!
YOU DON'T KNOW WHAT IT'S LIKE TO HAVE PEOPLE SAY THEY'RE HAPPY THEY DON'T HAVE TO SEE YOU.
LYNN

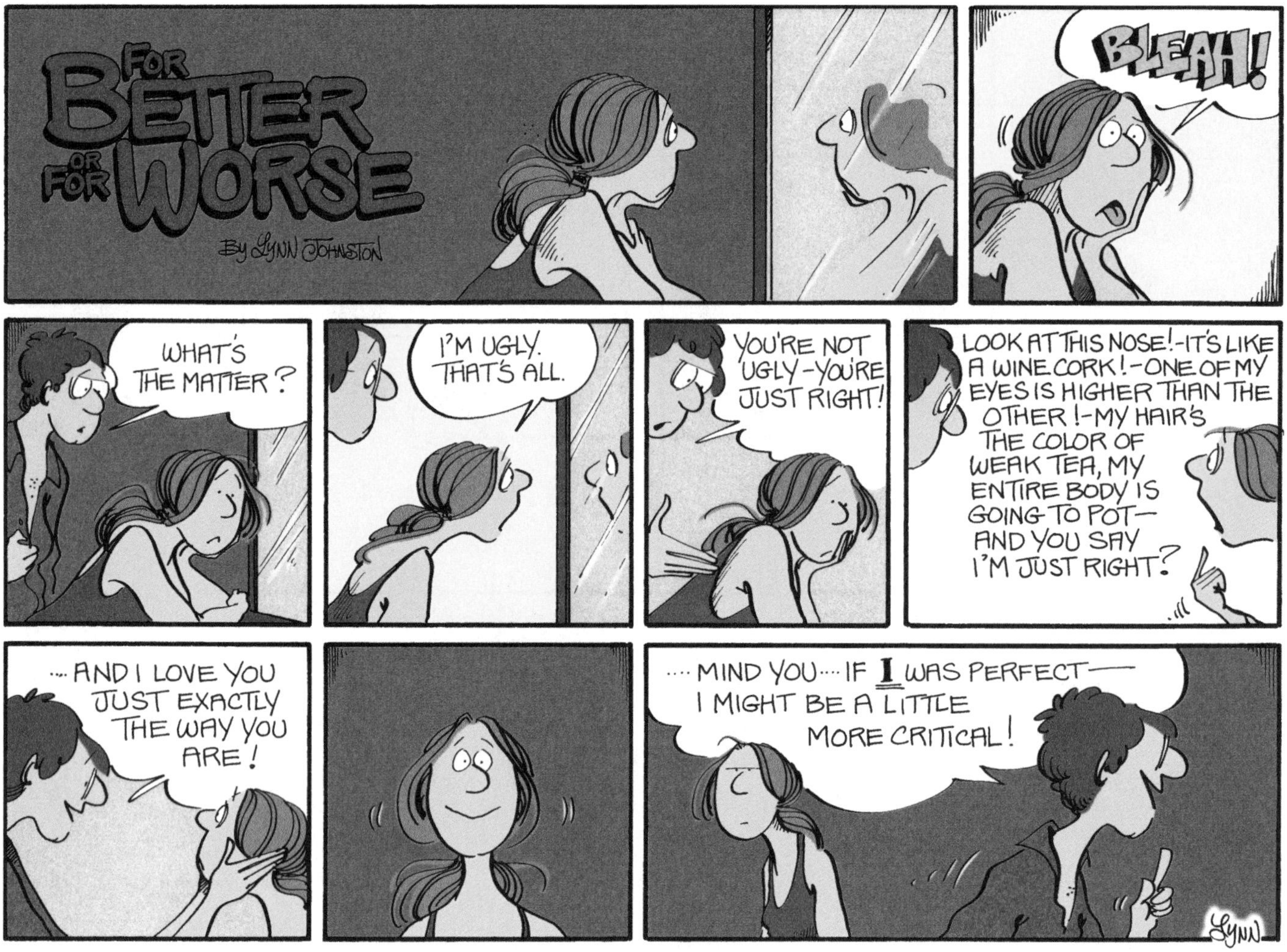
FOR BETTER OR FOR WORSE
BY LYNN JOHNSTON
BLEAH!
WHAT'S THE MATTER?
I'M UGLY. THAT'S ALL.
YOU'RE NOT UGLY - YOU'RE JUST RIGHT!
LOOK AT THIS NOSE! - IT'S LIKE A WINE CORK! - ONE OF MY EYES IS HIGHER THAN THE OTHER! - MY HAIR'S THE COLOR OF WEAK TEA, MY ENTIRE BODY IS GOING TO POT - AND YOU SAY I'M JUST RIGHT?
....AND I LOVE YOU JUST EXACTLY THE WAY YOU ARE!
....MIND YOU.... IF I WAS PERFECT — I MIGHT BE A LITTLE MORE CRITICAL!
LYNN

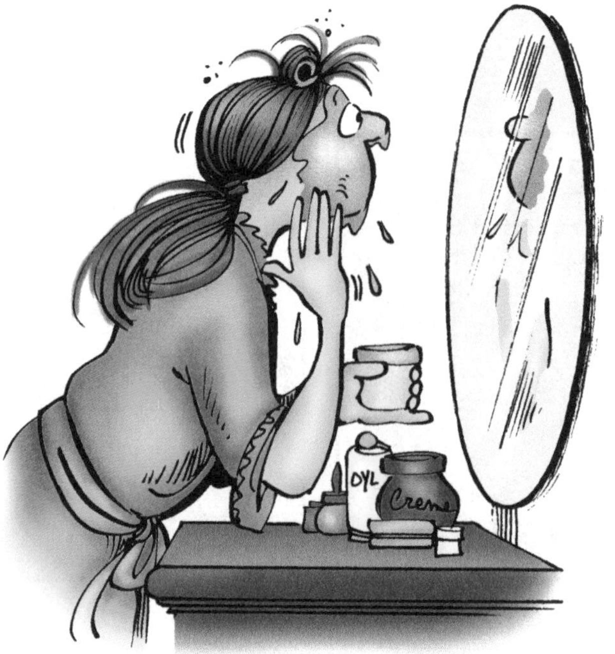
OYL
Creme

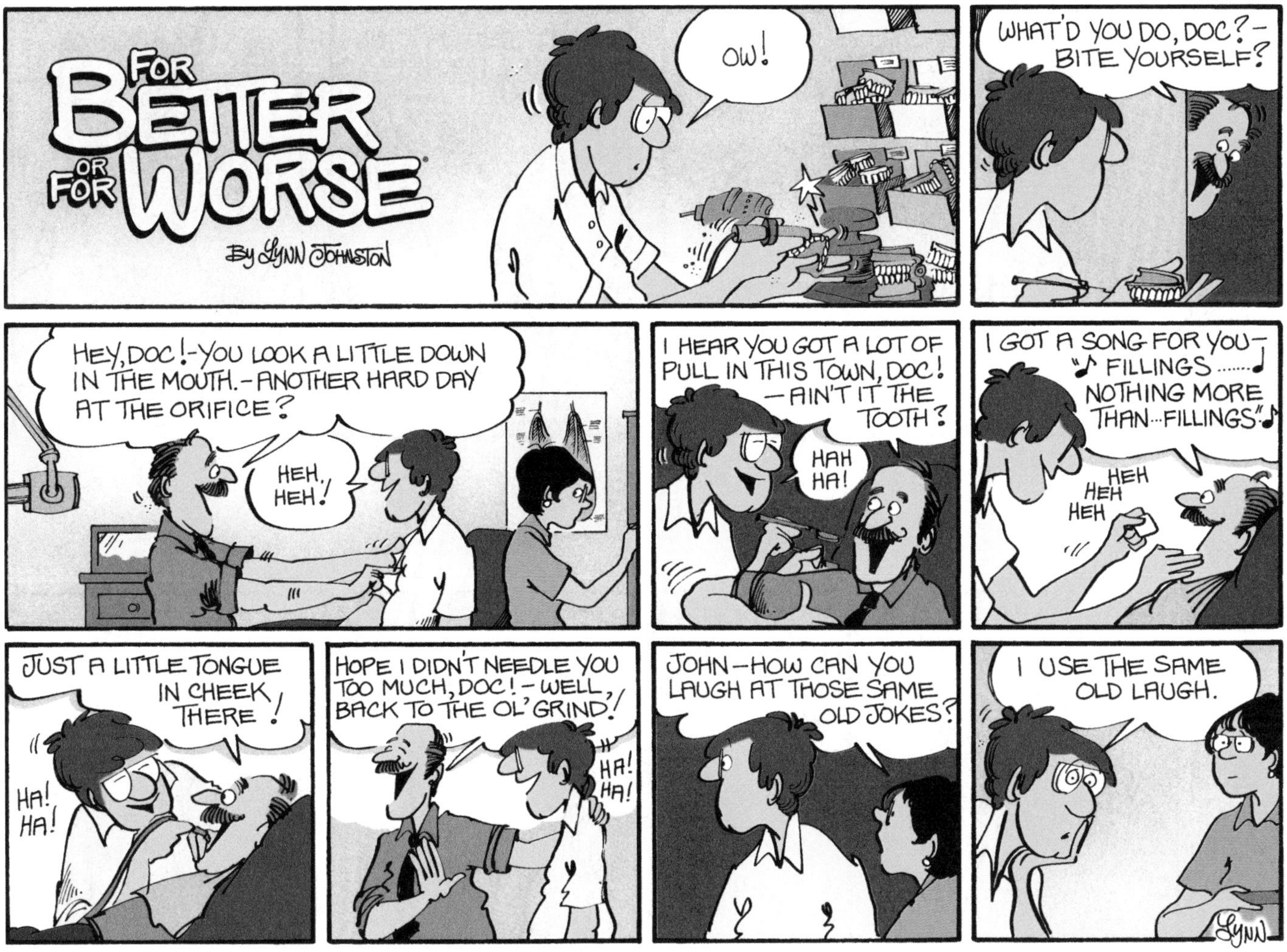
FOR BETTER OR FOR WORSE
BY LYNN JOHNSTON
OW!
WHAT'D YOU DO, DOC?-BITE YOURSELF?
HEY, DOC!-YOU LOOK A LITTLE DOWN IN THE MOUTH.-ANOTHER HARD DAY AT THE ORIFICE?
HEH, HEH!
I HEAR YOU GOT A LOT OF PULL IN THIS TOWN, DOC! -AIN'T IT THE TOOTH?
HAH HA!
I GOT A SONG FOR YOU- "FILLINGS ...... NOTHING MORE THAN...FILLINGS"
HEH HEH HEH
JUST A LITTLE TONGUE IN CHEEK THERE!
HA! HA!
HOPE I DIDN'T NEEDLE YOU TOO MUCH, DOC!-WELL, BACK TO THE OL' GRIND!
HA! HA!
JOHN-HOW CAN YOU LAUGH AT THOSE SAME OLD JOKES?
I USE THE SAME OLD LAUGH.
LYNN

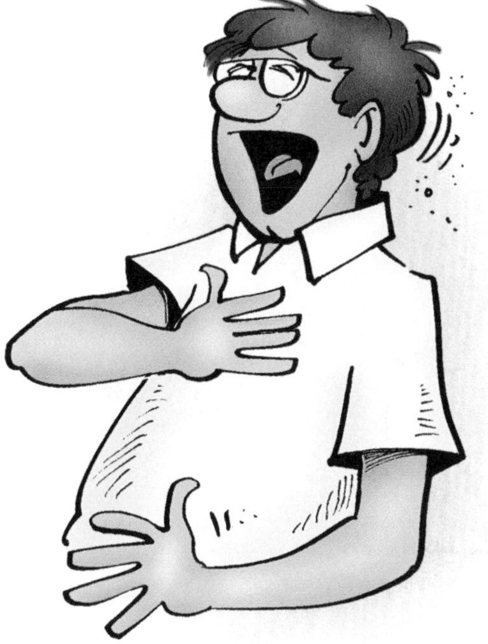

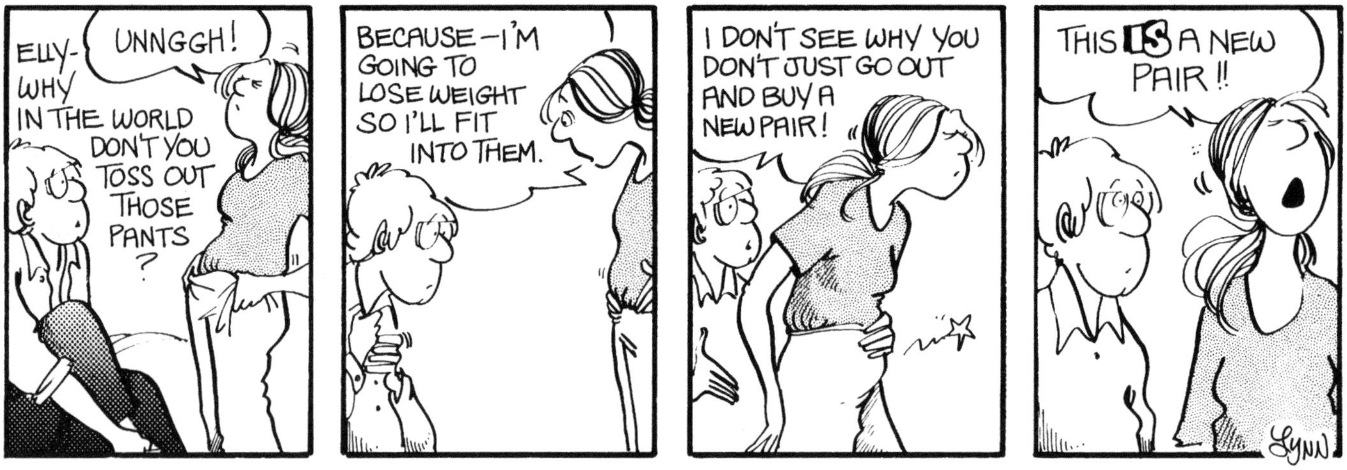
UNNGGH!
ELLY- WHY IN THE WORLD DON'T YOU TOSS OUT THOSE PANTS?
BECAUSE - I'M GOING TO LOSE WEIGHT SO I'LL FIT INTO THEM.
I DON'T SEE WHY YOU DON'T JUST GO OUT AND BUY A NEW PAIR!
THIS IS A NEW PAIR!!
LYNN

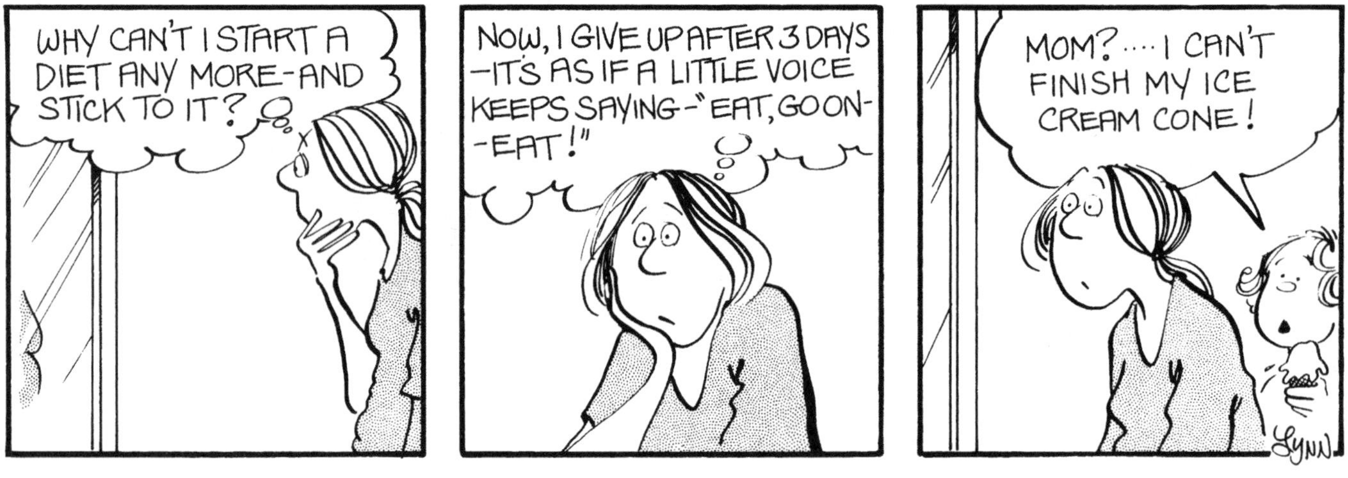
WHY CAN'T I START A DIET ANY MORE - AND STICK TO IT?
NOW, I GIVE UP AFTER 3 DAYS - IT'S AS IF A LITTLE VOICE KEEPS SAYING - "EAT, GO ON - EAT!"
MOM?.... I CAN'T FINISH MY ICE CREAM CONE!
LYNN

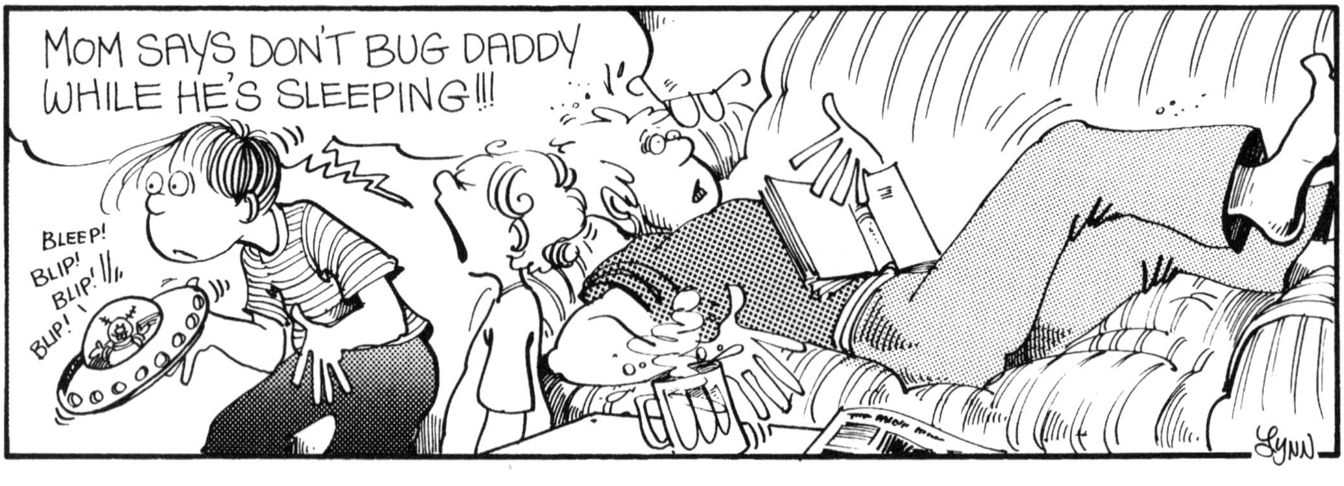
MOM SAYS DON'T BUG DADDY WHILE HE'S SLEEPING!!!
BLEEP! BLIP! BLIP! BLIP!
LYNN

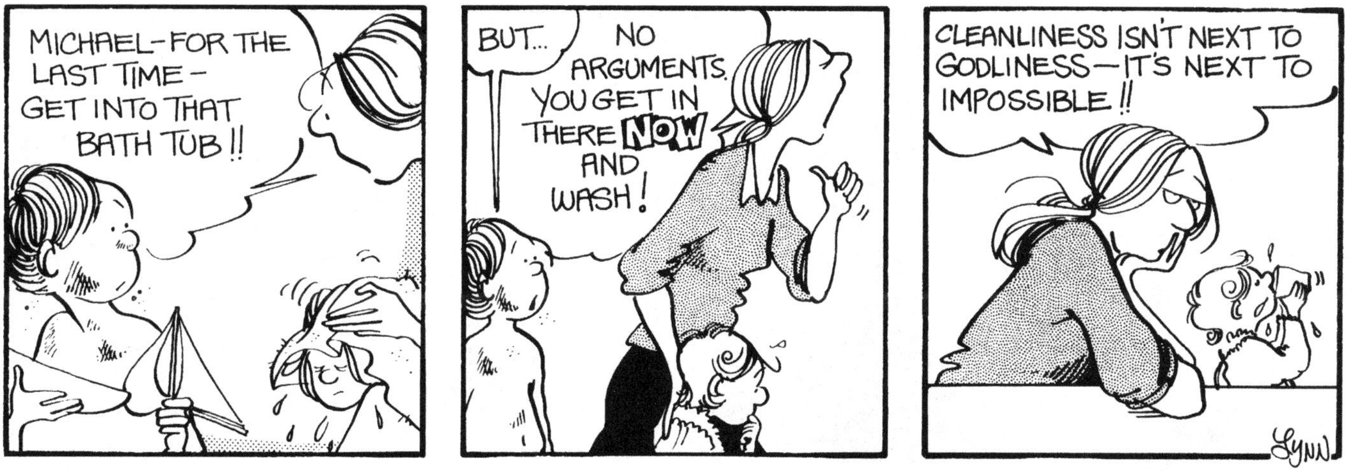
MICHAEL-FOR THE LAST TIME - GET INTO THAT BATH TUB !!
BUT...
NO ARGUMENTS. YOU GET IN THERE NOW AND WASH!
CLEANLINESS ISN'T NEXT TO GODLINESS—IT'S NEXT TO IMPOSSIBLE !!

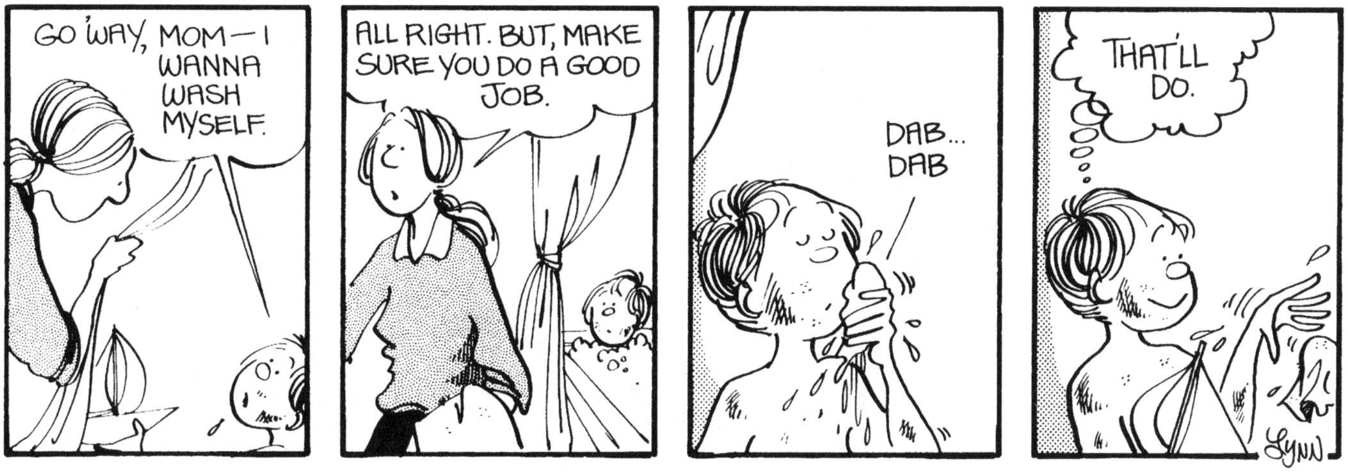
GO 'WAY, MOM—I WANNA WASH MYSELF.
ALL RIGHT. BUT, MAKE SURE YOU DO A GOOD JOB.
DAB... DAB
THAT'LL DO.

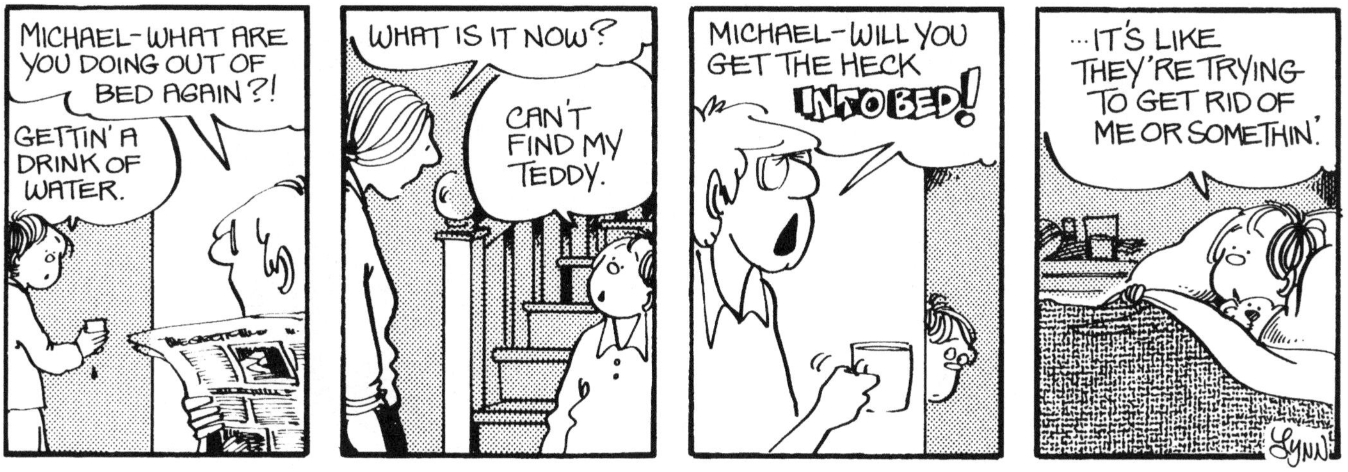
MICHAEL-WHAT ARE YOU DOING OUT OF BED AGAIN?!
GETTIN' A DRINK OF WATER.
WHAT IS IT NOW?
CAN'T FIND MY TEDDY.
MICHAEL-WILL YOU GET THE HECK INTO BED!
...IT'S LIKE THEY'RE TRYING TO GET RID OF ME OR SOMETHIN'.

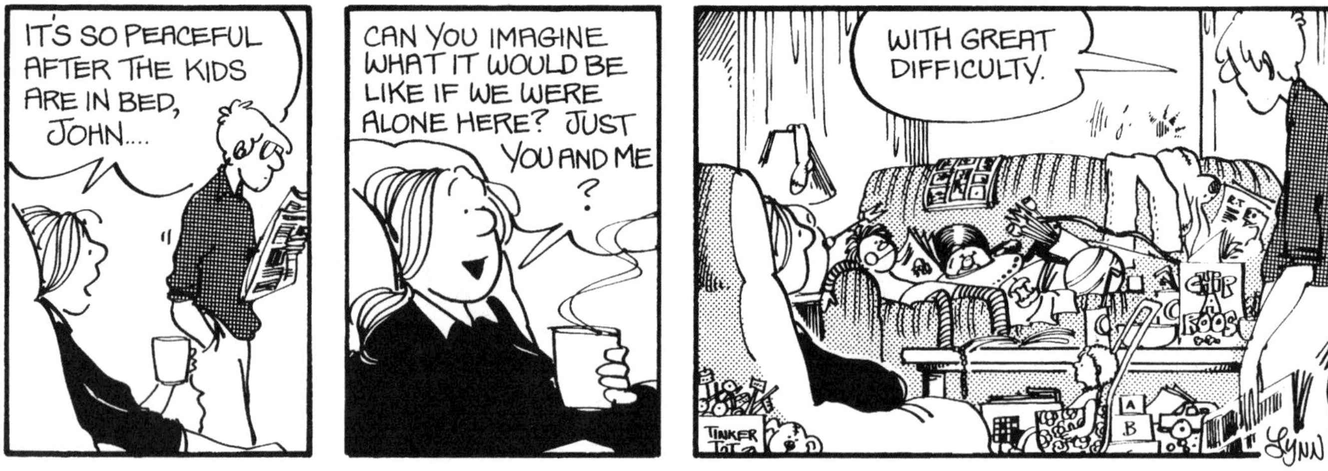
IT'S SO PEACEFUL AFTER THE KIDS ARE IN BED, JOHN....
CAN YOU IMAGINE WHAT IT WOULD BE LIKE IF WE WERE ALONE HERE? JUST YOU AND ME
?
WITH GREAT DIFFICULTY.
TINKER TOY
A
B
LYNN

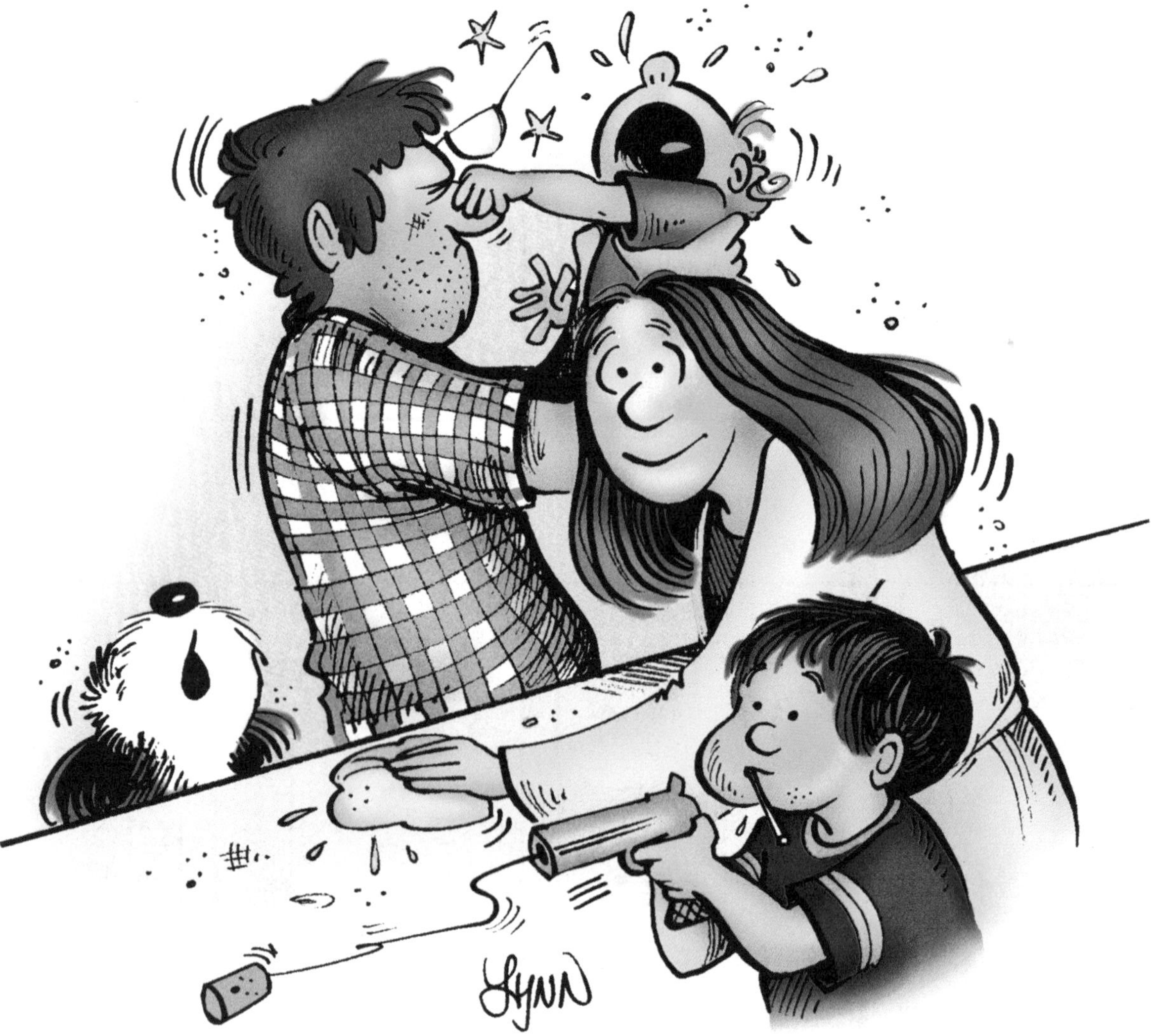
LYNN

Lynn Johnston was born in Collingwood, Ontario, and grew up in British Columbia. Today, she lives in Corbeil, Ontario. Johnston is the first woman to receive a Reuben Award for Cartoonist of the Year by the National Cartoonists Society, in 1985. She also has received the Order of Canada and claims a star on Canada's Walk of Fame.

*For Better or For Worse* has been syndicated since 1979, and was named Best Syndicated Comic Strip in 1992. *For Better or For Worse* appears in more than two thousand newspapers in twenty-three countries, and is translated into eight languages for a devoted readership of more than 220 million. The strip boasts a lively Web presence at www.fborfw.com.